OFFICIAL STRATEGY GUIDE

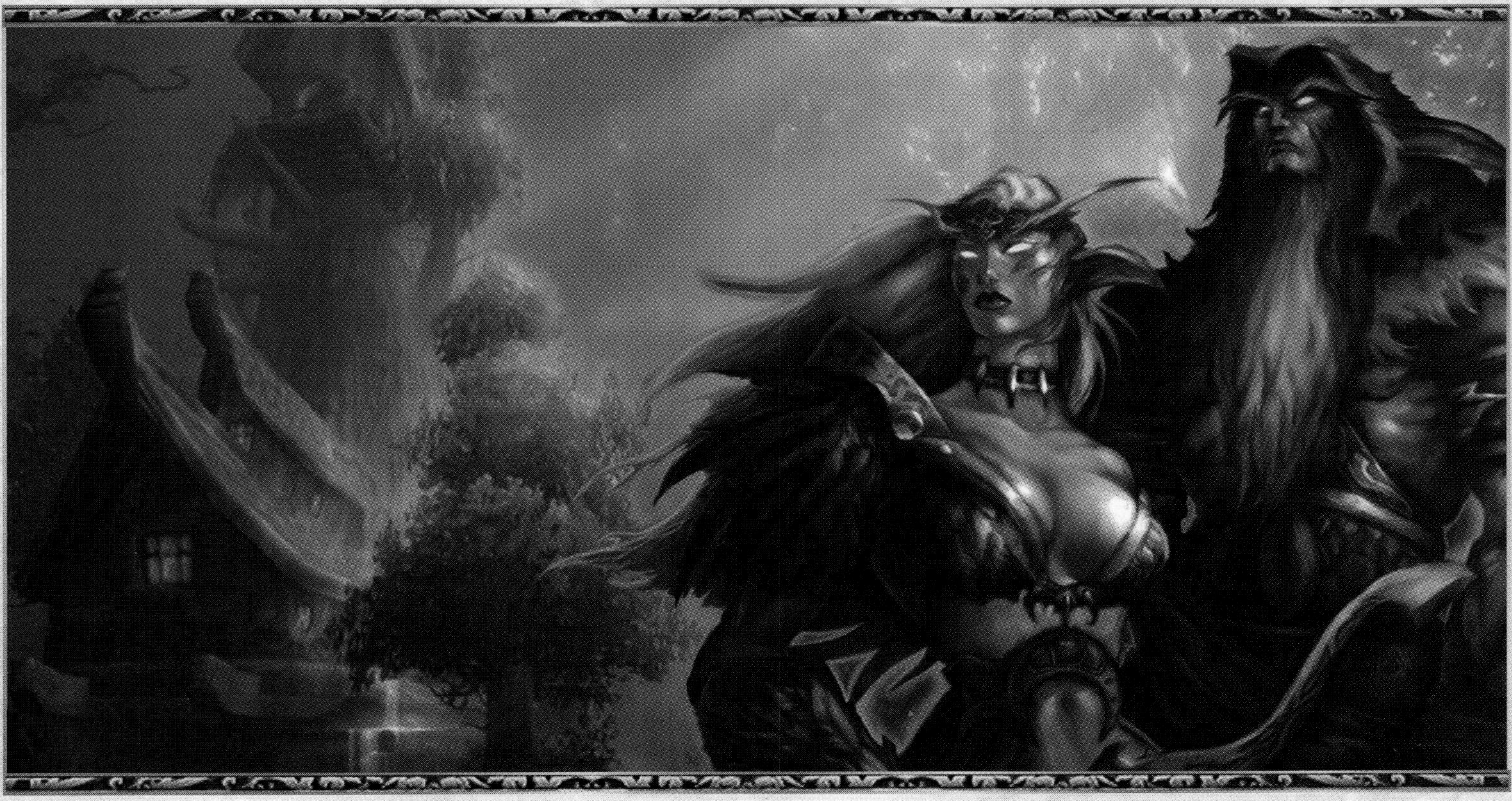

BY MICHAEL LUMMIS AND DANIELLE VANDERLIP

I - AN INTRODUCTION TO MMORPGS

II - LEARNING YOUR PLACE IN THE WORLD

III - YOUR FIRST DAY

IV - JOINING THE TROOPS

V - RISING IN THE RANKS

VI - THE FINEST TOOLS

VII - RAIDS

VIII - TO THE BATTLE

IX - CRAFTING & PROFESSIONS

X - Guilds

XI - The World of Azeroth

XII - Equipment Tables

XIII - Items

XIV - Bestiary

XV - Pet Shop

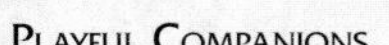

AN INTRODUCTION TO ONLINE GAMING

Welcome to the *World of Warcraft*. This massive online game takes you into a new time of friction between the Alliance of the Eastern Kingdoms and Thrall's Horde. In this time, where the Forsaken Undead fight along ranks of Trolls, Orcs, and Tauren, there are sure to be glorious battles against the Humans and their allies: the Dwarves, Night Elves and Gnomes. You're going to be part of it all, and we're here to lend our hands to the cause.

This strategy guide was designed to assist all levels of players. People who are new to *Warcraft*, online games, and this style of MORG (Multiplayer Online Role-playing Game) are going to have a gentle start. This guide explains the terms that appear in the community, the methods of creating and building a character, and how to handle yourself in various situations.

For those with greater MORG experience, the guide brings you up to speed with class explanations, tactics, long-term strategies for increasing your power and getting the most out of your Talent specializations. Those switching to *World of Warcraft* from other MORGs should find these chapters of tremendous value while looking at long-term options for play and mastery.

Even those lucky players that have been playing for months are going to be happy with this resource. Though the introductory chapters are familiar to you, half of this guide was made to be a long-term resource. You may have formed your own playstyle, taken a character to Level 60, and been through your share of Instance Dungeons, but it's going to be nice having tables for all the Classes, Professions, Monsters, and Items in the game at the turn of a page. Our guide has enhanced maps, multiple levels of Bestiary information, and even a few laughs hidden here and there as well.

And for the legions of Penny Arcade fans out there, the comics in this guide should look quite familiar in style. It's our honor to show these exclusive comics to you. Enjoy!

GLOSSARY OF TERMS

AC *Armor Class -x* The stat that determines the amount of damage an attack will be reduced by.

Add Refers to an additional mob attacking the group. Often group members say "add" in order to inform everyone that's focused on one target that another has joined in and will need to be dealt with.

AoE *Area of Effect*

AFK *Away from Keyboard* - Informs group mates or those around that someone is going to step away from their keyboard.

AFKFAF *Away From Keyboard for a Few* - Informs group mates or those around that a player is going to step away from their keyboard for an extended period of time.

Aggro *Aggressive* - Used in many ways. 1) If a mob is aggro, it attacks anyone that approaches. 2) In group combat with a mob, the term applies to whoever has "drawn aggro" away from the other players or is the player that the mob is focusing on.

Aggro Radius The distance from a mob that a PC needs to be in order to aggro a mob. This is defined by the level difference between the mob and the PC. A high level PC will not draw aggro from the same mob as a low PC would. The low level PC is more likely to draw aggro from a farther distance.

AGI *Agility* - Increases a) attack power with ranged weapons, b) armor, c) the chance for a critical hit with ranged weapons, and d) the chance to dodge attacks. Rogues gain a stronger bonus than other classes and both Hunters and Rogues increase their attack power with melee weapons based partially on Agility.

AH *Auction House* - Location where players can bid or place items on auction.

AI *Artificial Intelligence* - NPCs and mobs have a limited Artificial Intelligence that dictates the way they act and react to PCs, other NPCs and mobs.

AKA *Also Known As*

Alt This refers to someone's alternate character. "Let me log onto my alt." Their main character is the one they spend most time playing.

AoE *Area of Effect Spell* - Spells and abilites that will do damage to a range instead of a single target. For example, a bomb would inflict damage on anyone within its damage radius. (Also see *PBAoE*)

AP *Attack Power* - As this stat increases, your DPS increases correspondingly.

AR *Attack Rating* - The stat that partially determines whether you will hit a target. (Equal to 5X you Level plus any bonuses from talents and/or items.)

Avatar Your character or representation of yourself in the game.

Bait 1. *n.* Items used while fishing in *World of Warcraft*. 2. *v.* A term used to describe the actions of a player or group in PvP. A player (group) can bait other players in order to lure them into a trap or act as bait to lure other players into a trap.

BB *Booty Bay* - A town in Stranglethrone Vale.

BFD *Blackfathom Deeps* - An instance in Ashenvale.

Bind 1. To set your home point for your character by interacting with an innkeeper and asking to rest there. Players receive a Hearthstone in order to return to their bind point. (See *Hearthstone*) 2. To have equipment permanently bind to your character making it untradeable.

Bind Camping Waiting at a known bind point for players and killing them as they spawn.

BoA *Bind on Aquire* - Some equipment and items bind as soon as they are looted and are not tradeable thereafter, although they may still be sold to merchants (sometimes called BoP for Bind on Pickup).

BoE *Bind on Equip* - Some equipment or items within the game bind to a player when equipped, but remain tradeable if not worn. These items are sellable to vendors even after being equipped.

BRB *Be Right Back*

BRD *Blackrock Depths* - An instance in Blackrock Mountain.

BRS *Blackrock Spire* - An instance in Blackrock Mountain.

BRT *Be Right There*

Buff A beneficial spell type that is cast either on yourself or on another PC granting enhanced stats.

Bug A glitch in the game that was never intended as part of the game design.

Camp/Camping 1. Waiting for a specific event to occur or a monster to spawn. 2. Hunting an area. If a specific hunting spot already has a group of PCs, it's camped.

Carebear A term used to describe people that do not enjoy PvP combat. This term is also sometimes wrongly applied to those that Role-play or like to play the role of a merchant rather than a fighter or killer.

Cast To use a spell.

Caster Any character that uses spells as their primary attack and defense.

CC Crowd Control (See Mez)

Chain Casting To cast spell after spell in rapid succession.

Cheese To exploit an imbalance in the game.

Clan (See *Guild*)

Combat Pet An NPC that can be called up and controlled by a PC to fight with them.

Con Short for "Consider." 1. The method in which PCs can decide if a mob is within their range to kill or not. 2. Applies to Quests and Items and how they compare with a character's level.

Corpse Camping Tactic used to kill a player as they respawn from death.

CR *Corpse Run* - Running back to your corpse after you die.

CR/XR *The Crossroads* - The central hub for Horde to meet up in the Barrens on the continent of Kalimdor.

Creep Coined in Blizzard's RTS games (*Warcraft* and *StarCraft*) in reference to enemy creatures. (See *Mob*)

Creep Jacking A term from *Warcraft 3* where players attack other players while they're already engaged in combat with neutral monsters.

Critters Non-hostile mobs such as rabbits, chickens, squirrels, cows etc.

CSR *Customer Service Representative* - An employee of either the publishing company or creating company of an MMORPG that attends to customer needs and handles any service related issues.

CTD *Crash to Desktop* – This occurs when the game suddenly stops, closes, and sends you back to your computer desktop.

DD *Direct Damage* - A spell that's cast on a creature and does immediate damage.

Debuff A spell type that weakens a PC or mob by lowering their resistances or stats.

Defense The stat that partially determines whether an attack will hit. (Equal to 5X your Level plus any bonuses from talents and/or items.)

Dispel A spell that strips away the beneficial spells of a PC or MOB.

Designated Looter Someone chosen by a party or group to loot all mobs killed by the party.

DMG An abbreviation refering to Weapon Damage.

DnD *Do not Disturb*

DOT *Damage over Time* - A type of spell that does damage over time to the creature or target it is cast on.

DPS *Damage Per Second* - How much damage you can inflict on a player or mob per second.

Duping An exploit in which multiple objects such as armor, weapons, or gold are created in order to cheat the game.

DW Duskwood, a zone south of Elwynn Forest.

Emotes Animated or non-animated ways of expressing how you or your character feels at any given moment.

Exploit Misusing mechanics of the game to gain an advantage that is not allowed per the terms of use of the game.

Farming Killing mobs over and over again for loot. For example, instance farming, ogre farming, etc.

FFA *Free for All* - Generally in reference to looting rights on slain creatures.

FH *Full Health*

FL *Full Life*

FM *Full Mana*

Gank Killing someone quickly because they are taken by complete surprise, AFK, or considerably lower level.

GG *Good Game*

Ghosting The behavior of a mob, NPC or PC that seems to flicker in and out of your view and "jumps" between locations in relation to your character.

Gimp To create and develop a weak character by accident or because of inexperience.

Grief The act of disrupting someone else's enjoyment of the game by using dishonorable tactics such as: leap frogging, corpse camping, bind camping, ganking, or kill stealing.

Griefer Someone that purposely attempts to ruin the enjoyment of the game for others often by using exploits. (See *Grief*)

Grind/Grinding Killing mobs repeatedly in order to gain experience, foregoing quests.

GM *Game Master* - Someone employed by Blizzard Entertainment to assist and help players.

GS *Goldshire* - A town just outside of Stormwind.

GTG *Good to Go*

GUI *Graphical User Interface* - The visual interface used for accessing commands & menus and viewing game information.

Guild Group of players with like goals and attitudes that work together as a team. AKA Clan.

Hate AKA "aggro" in other games, this is the measure of how much a monster wants to kill you.

HB *Hillsbrad Foothills* - Area southeast of Silverpine forest in Azeroth.

HP *Hit Points* - AKA Health.

HOT *Heal Over Time* - Much like the DOT, spells of this variety offer a dose of healing each "tick."

Hybrid Character that uses both magic and melee in conjunction with each other, without specializing in either.

IC *In Character* - This usually prefaces a sentence to let other people know that you're speaking from the viewpoint of your character or role-playing.

IF *Ironforge* - Dwarven Capitol City in Azeroth.

IMO *In My Opinion*

IMHO *In My Humble Opinion*

INC *Incoming* - Used to alert other party members that a mob is incoming. Usually used to get your party ready for battle.

Instance AKA Instance Dungeon. A dungeon in which only your party interacts with the mobs and objects within. Each group or party enters their own Instance separate from other players.

INT *Intellect* - Increases a) the rate in which weapon skills are learned, b) mana points, and c) the chance to score critical hits with spells.

Kite Technique used for killing mobs by doing damage (by range) and then rooting or snaring them. It's usually used by casters and long range damage dealers to kill with minimum risk to their character.

KOS *Kill on Sight* - Status of aggro between NPCs and PCs when on opposite factions. Also the state of relations between Horde and Alliance. Generally all Horde are KOS to Alliance and vice versa.

KS *Kill Steal* - To tap a mob away from someone else. (See *Tap*)

KSer/Kill Stealer Someone that either purposely or accidently kills something you were fighting and steals the experience.

Lag Game play becomes slow and may cause adverse effects. Usually caused by either server side or connection issues.

Lag Spike A more drastic lag experience where game play may pause for an extended period of time or even crash your game.

Leap Frog A tactic sometimes used to dash past other parties while they fight mobs in order to beat them to a named NPC or resource object. This behavior is not deemed acceptable by most honorable players.

Leech Term used to describe the act of gaining experience or items from other players without helping or contributing to acquisition of experience or items. This can be a negative term depending on its use.

L337 Speak AKA Leet or Elite. A way of typing that uses alternate numbers, letters, and symbols in place of the traditional alphabet.

Leveling Act of gaining experience by killing mobs, crafting or questing to advance your character.

LFG *Looking for Group* - Used to convey that a Player is looking to join or create a group.

LFM *Looking for More* – Looking for more players for an instance.

Link Also known as "Linking an Item." Shift + Left clicking on an item to show it in the chat window for others to see.

Link Death This occurs when a character loses connection to the server. AKA LD.

LMAO *Laugh My Ass Off*

LOL *Laugh Out Loud* - A term used to show that something was funny enough that they were laughing out loud, even if it couldn't be heard.

LOM *Low on Mana*

Loot To take the treasure from a defeated mob or from a chest.

LOS *Line of Sight* - Determines wheather a spell/ranged attack can occur and whether a target can be "seen."

Lowbie Someone that is of a low level or in the early stages of character development.

LvL *Level*

LTNS *Long Time No See*

Lunchbox Crate or chest that, when looted, contains only food and drink.

Main This is in reference to someone's primary character that receives most of the player's attention. This is generally a high level character. "Let me log in my main."

Master Looter Someone chosen by a party or group to loot all mobs killed by the party.

Med/Medding - Healing/Drinking or just generally preparing for combat.

Melee To fight either weaponless or with weapons face to face.

Mez *Mesmerize* - Refers to spells, such as Polymorph, that temporarily incapacitate a target. Some of these abilites lock you in place in addition to rendering you helpess. Typically, any damage inflicted on the target will break the mez.

ML *Master Looter*

MMO *Massively Multiplayer Online*

MOG *Massively Online Game*

MORG *Massively Online Role-playing Game* - (See *MMORPG*)

MMORPG *Massively Multi-player Online Role-Playing Game* - A game type based on fictional characters and places in which many people connect to a server and interact with each other within the environment.

mob Short for "Mobile." Has become associated with NPCs and monsters/creatures that can be fought. (Created in the high-point of MUDDs).

MUDD Multi-user Dungeons and Dragons type of games. These are text-only Role-playing games that were the forebears of the graphical MMORPGs we know today.

MT *Mistell* - Used when soemone accidentally sends a message that is intended for another party to the wrong person/group.

NBG/Need Before Greed A looting choice used by groups. This offers players the chance to dictate from the start who is going to get which items. For example, casters often look for cloth armor drops and have no need for leather, mail or plate drops. So, they'd get cloth and the others would get any other armor drops. (See also *Random*)

Nerf A term used by players to describe the perception that aspects of the game by the developers have been weakened. Often these adjustments are done on character class types, spells etc. These adjustments are carried out by the developer to achieve a balance of game play.

Ninja Loot The act of looting (taking) items from a kill that do not belong to you.

Ninja Looter A person that loots a kill out of turn or during a battle to gain more than the rest of the group.

NM *Never Mind*

Noob/Newbie Someone that is new to the environment/game. This sometimes has negative connotations, though it is also used to explain why a player may need more help than others.

NPC *Non-Player Character* - A computer-controlled character within the game with whom PCs can interact. (e.g., Vendors and Trainers)

Nuke A spell that causes heavy damage. Can be AoE or single target.

Nuker A direct damage caster that can do heavy damage.

OMW *On My Way*

OOC *Out of Character* - This usually prefaces a sentence to let others know that you're speaking out of character or without role-playing.

OOM *Out of Mana*

Over Nuke Over nuking occurs when a caster casts too many high damage spells in a row only to draw the aggro of the mob away from the tank.

Own/Pwn Commonly used as a part of L337 speak. It means to defeat someone soundly. Often used as a taunt.

Paper Doll The representation of your character's body parts and the slots (places) that can be filled with armor or jewelry. (It's generally a 2D [flat] representation.)

PBAoE *Point Blank Area of Effect* - An AoE that is centered on the caster. Often used by casters standing in the middle of a group of defending tanks to damage the enemy while remaining relatively safe.

Party A group of people that band together to adventure.

PC *Player Character* - A character controlled by another player.

Pet An NPC that's given commands by a player to help them hunt or do battle. Hunters take beasts as pets and Warlocks summon theirs.

PK *Player Kill*

PKer *Player Killer*

PL *Powerlevel* - (See *Powerleveling*)

POP Abbreviation of "Repopulation," often used as a shortened term for the re-spawn of monsters.

Profession Crafting and gathering abilities that can be learned from trainers throughout Azeroth.

Port *Portal* – A player-created transport device to help people travel from place to place. Mages can open portals to other cities while Warlocks summon other players through their portals.

Pot Shortened term for Potion.

Powerleveling 1. Steadily and quickly using knowledge of the mechanics of the game to level up at a much faster and intensive pace than other players. 2. Having higher level characters assist lower characters in quests or grinding to speed up their leveling process.

Proc Items may have an added effect that has a chance of activating. The activation of these special abilities is referred to as "proc." E.g., A weapon with a special effect will "proc" every so often.

PST *Please Send Tell*

Puller Person who pulls monsters for the party.

Pulling One of the players in a party heads out and leads one or more of the monsters back to the party so that the party can attack them. The idea is to prevent too many monsters from attacking at once by drawing them to a "safe" zone.

PvE *Player vs. Environment* - Used to describe a type of game-play in which a player is pitted against the Environment in the game.

PvP *Player vs. Player* - Used to describe a type of game-play in which a player is pitted against other players.

PvM *Player vs. Monster* - Used to describe gameplay in which monster 'bashing' is the primary means of conflict.

Raid A raid is a large-scale attack on an area by a group of players.

Random A group often has more than one player wishing to have a certain item. In some cases, they agree to "Random for it." By typing "/random 100", the game system will randomly generate a number up to 100 for each player doing so. Typically, the highest roll wins.

Res *Resurrection* - A type of spell used to bring other players back to life after they have been killed by a mob or the environment. AKA Rez.

Res Sickness When a player is resurrected by a player or via a Soulstone, they receive reduced stats for a period of time.

Resistance The degree to which a character (or target) can withstand or resist a certain type of damage.

A higher resistance translates into less hit points being lost. Some powers or item effects increase resistance.

Re-Spawn A monster that has been killed and has spawned (been created) again.

Rest The state of the character. An indicator of how tired a character is, which affects how much experience is gained from killing monsters, illustrates the character's rest state. Well Rested characters receive more experience points than characters in their Rested or Normal states.

RF *Razorfen* - An area within the Barrens.

RFD *Razorfen Downs* – An instance dungeon in Barrens.

RFK *Razorfen Kraul* - Instanced dungeon located in the Barrens.

ROFL *Rolling on the Floor Laughing* - A term used to let others know that something was funny enough for them to literally roll on the floor laughing.

Root A spell used to lock a target in place. A number of roots can be broken when the rooted target receives damage—even from a DoT.

Round Robin A method of looting that allows each character to have a "turn."

RP *Role-Play* - The act of stepping into the role of your character. To speak or act as you believe your in-game character would speak or act.

RR *Redridge Mountains* - Area east of Elwynn Forest.

SF *Shadowfang Keep* - This is an instanced zone within Silverpine Forest.

SH/Strath *Stratholme* – An instance in Eastern Plaguelands.

SM *Scarlet Monastery* - This is an instanced zone within the Tirisfal Glades.

Small Pets An animal that follows the player around without actually interacting with the world. While they don't directly influence the player or monsters, some consider them cool to have around, especially rare ones.

Snare A spell or ability that reduces the movement speed of the affected target. Most often, snares are not removed when the target receives damage.

Socials (See *Emotes*)

Soulbound Equipment or items that are bound to a player and not tradeable to other players. These items are sellable to vendors however.

Spawns The location or process of monsters appearing when they're created in the world.

Spec *Specialization* - What your character designed to do based on talents. For example, a Shadow Priest is spec'd differently from a Holy Priest even though they're both priests.

Spell Stacking A skill used to stack multiple spells on a mob to maximize the damage that can be done. This often refers to debuffs or even using Dispell to remove beneficial buffs.

SPI *Spirit* - The stat that affects the rate at which mana and health is regenerated (in and out of combat)..

Spiking This occurs when internet connection and exchange of information fluctuates dramatically.

STA *Stamina* - The stat that affects the amount of hit points assigned to a character.

Stack A number of identical items placed in a single inventory slot, to conserve space. Only certain items can be stacked.

Stat *Statistic* - These are the numbers that help define your character. I.e. Strength, Stamina, Intellect etc.

Stone *Hearthstone* - Hearthstones are used to transport players back to the inn at which they're bound.

STR *Strength* - The stat that affects your attack power with melee weapons and increases the amount of damage that can be blocked with a shield.

Stun Short duration spells or abilities that fully incapacitate the target. No damage or abilities will break the stun.

STV *Stranglethorn Vale* - Located in southern-western Eastern Kingdoms.

SW *Stormwind* - Capitol city of the Humans in the Eastern Kingdoms.

TP *Talent Point* - Points earned as a player levels that can be used to purchase new talents.

Tank A melee character that can take heavy damage while keeping the aggro off the more fragile casters. (e.g., Warrior) Typically, a solid group will consist of two tanks: the main tank (MT) and secondary tank or offtank.

Tap When a player attacks a creature first, this is called tapping. When a creature is tapped, only the person or party that has engaged the creature will gain experience or loot from it.

Taunt Related to Aggro. An ability that allows a player to draw the attention of a monster off of another player and onto him/herself.

TB *Thunderbluff* - Capitol city of the Tauren on the continent of Kalimdor.

Tell This is a private message that can be sent directly to another player within the game. (See *Whisper*)

Temple/ST *Sunken Temple* - An instance in Swamp of Sorrows

Threat Related to Aggro. This is what a character "gives off" to generate or draw monster aggro. Certain abilities create higher threat (either because they're extremely effective or designed to do so).

Toon A term used in reference to your animated character in game.

Train A string of mobs or PCs that are chasing another PC or group of PCs. Often these are being led to guards to be killed.

Twink 1. *n.* A character that owns items that are normally above their capability of obtaining on their own. 2. *v.* The act of leveling a character faster and easier by killing mobs that are beyond their means of killing themselves.

Über German slang for "super," originally meaning "over." Has become a term used to describe anything possessing extreme power or ability.

UBRS *Upper Blackrock Spire* - A tough portion of Blackrock Spire where many good items drop.

UC *Undercity* - Undead capital city in the ruins of Lodaeron.

VC *Van Cleef* – Boss of Deadmines instance in Westfall. Sometimes used interchangeably with "Deadmines." (ie. LFG VC is the same as LFG Deadmines.)

WC *Wailing Caverns* - Instanced Dungeon in the Barrens

WF *Westfall* - Area in Azeroth just south of southwest of Elwynn Forest.

Whisper A private message AKA /tell.

WTB *Want to Buy* - This is used in place of spelling out the entire phrase to let people know they are looking to buy something particular. "WTB Wyrmslayer Rune."

WTS *Want to Sell* - This is used in place of spelling out the entire phrase to let people know that someone is selling an item. "WTS Kenaryn's Charm."

WTT *Want to Trade* - Tells other players that you're willing to trade an item for another.

XP *Experience*

Zerg A method of attack which involves many people rushing an objective all at once with no real strategy or method. This usually involves a high amount of deaths on the part of those zerging, though is often an effective if controversial method of conquest. (Phrase coined from the Blizzard game *StarCraft*. Zergs are an alien race that multiply quickly and cheaply to overrun opponents with overwhelming numbers.)

ZFK/Zul *Zul Farrak* - Instance in Northern Tanaris.

Zone Area of the map with a designated theme, mobs and scenery. These areas have borders much like a state or country, though invisible they define areas.

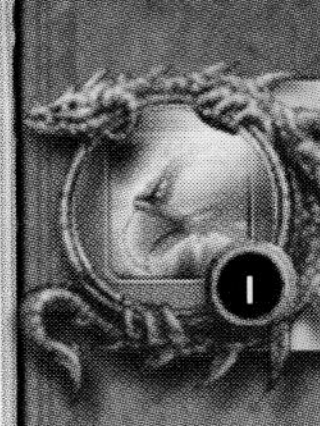

NAMING YOUR CHARACTER

What's in a name? Gamer names can encase a player's entire gaming career while some people change their name from game to game. In MMORPGs, your name can become famous or infamous and choosing the right one can take on a whole new level of importance.

The most significant thing you must consider are Blizzard's own naming policies. If you don't abide by them, you can expect a visit from your friendly neighborhood GM.

Naming Tips

***World of Warcraft* Name Generator:** *World of Warcraft* has a random name generator that you can use to pull up a variety of names. If you don't like the one it chooses, keep clicking until you the right one strikes you.

External Name Generators: There are many suitable fantasy name generators on the web that are worth looking into. These typically offer more names than you could ever imagine, but finding the perfect name may become a more difficult task than you'd imagine.

Keep it Simple: Differentiating yourself by creating an incredibly complex name may sound like a good idea—at first. The first time someone needs to send you a /tell or offer a long distance guild or party invite, you may reconsider that decision. You're not going to receive quick tells and may end up losing important contacts. Keep your name simple and unique. Players will still recognize you and will also be able to type your name quickly.

Combine Names: Try taking a couple names that you like and combining them or reordering them to make something new.

Avoid Well-Known Fiction Characters: Do what you can to avoid even getting close to these names. GMs will make you change the name if they catch you and it's generally looked upon as bad form. Some examples of names to avoid: Gandalf, Legolas, Gimli, Drizzt, Sephiroth, etc. An even more important rule is not to choose a name that already exists within the World of Warcraft mythology. Unless you have permission from Blizzard, you can't take on that character's role.

Avoid Real World Celebrities: This is another name type that the GMs will force you to change quickly should they catch you (or if another player brings it to their attention). No one wants to see Madonna the Night Elf Priestess running around the glades of Darnassus.

Avoid any Religious Figures: You may think it's a great idea to use a recognized religious name for role-play or may simply find it funny, but there is no doubt that someone will be offended. Once again, a GM will ask you to change your name should this occur.

Combine Words with Care: Names like Moonwind, Farstriker and others are great ways to give your character a descriptive name. It sets the tone for the kind of character they are without much explanation needed. Take care to keep the words appropriate to the fantasy setting. Names like Faxmonkey or anything along those lines aren't going to cut it no matter how hard you pretend that you really are an ape from Feralas in disguise looking for a few good fax machines.

Avoid Foreign Words or Insults: GMs aren't all multi-lingual experts and can't be expected to know if your name is anything other than a bad word or insult of some sort. Be ready to defend your name and have a good reason for it. Even if it's in Drow, don't expect them to know right off unless they were one in a former life.

Open a Book: Many great names can be found in books and literature, but be careful. Don't use any name that could potentially have a copyright or trademark attached to it. Take a look in books on mythology, fantasy novels, fables and any other source with creative names. There is bound to be one that strikes you as fitting your character just right.

ETIQUETTE IN THE WORLD OF WARCRAFT

Online games have their own systems of social rules; there are certainly more interactions in a game like *World of Warcraft* than with offline roleplaying games, where people are seldom able to compete or cooperate while playing. *World of Warcraft* creates an environment where both positive and negative interactions between players are intended to occur, but even the negative ones are set within certain guidelines. Behaviors that fall outside of normal etiquette can be considered rude, inappropriate, or even as griefing. To make friends and have a smooth experience in-game, it pays to learn the rules up front.

WHILE HUNTING

The environment is primarily cooperative in the open field, where players are aligned against the monsters that stalk Azeroth. Whether soloing or grouping to accomplish this, there are ways to keep from stepping on other people's toes. Beyond that, it's good to know when someone else is doing something that is genuinely disrespectful so that you can advise them (at first), avoid them if they continue, and ignore them if no change occurs.

YOU TOOK MY MOBS!!!

Mob ownership is often a point of contention during PvE hunting. Soloists and groups run into situations where other characters will come through and kill some of the same targets in the area where they were already hunting. The first point here is to use a cool head; everyone has a right to go after monsters. Even when a higher level person is attacking a beast, they may be after trade items that are useful, doing a backlog of old quests, or just farming something for their allies.

Instead of reacting with a negative attitude, see what can be done for both sides from the beginning. If you are on a kill quest, offer to bring the other person/people into your group—everyone benefits from this. By the same logic, if you're on a collection quest and someone else is going after the same targets for different reasons, it may still be faster to group together and hunt. Granted, soloing for collection quests is ideal, but it's better to get some items than none.

For whatever reason, an alliance may not be an option. This happens often enough as well. No problem. State what you're doing and see if the other players are willing to give you the space to continue. If they can't outright help, at least they can give you enough mobs to maintain the same kill rate and excitement. Fair enough for everyone concerned.

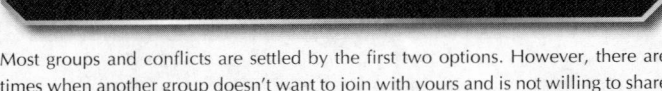

HOW TO HANDLE HUNTING CONFLICTS

- Try to work together with newcomers for mutual benefit
- Agree to leave each other enough targets and space
- Find a better hunting spot if nothing can be arranged
- Avoid aggressive players and report any griefing to a GM after you're certain that it's intentional

Most groups and conflicts are settled by the first two options. However, there are times when another group doesn't want to join with yours and is not willing to share anything in the region. That doesn't make them griefers—it's still within their rights to kill as much as they can within the area (that is your right as well).

If the other group refuses to have a comfortable attitude, you may try another camp of the same creature; there are often several camps of important monsters in a given region. This doesn't mean that you are backing down or acting like a coward. Rather, it shows that you're sensible enough to have a good time and keep from wasting your night, experience points, and energy fighting for meager kills on a single quest. You can always come back later.

Okay, so is there any griefing at all that occurs in regard to mob ownership? Well, yes. Even with the tapping system in place, there are ways for people to make life difficult for many other classes. Someone with a real chip on their shoulder can use fast abilities to tap a monster just before your anticipated pull. This negates the experience and treasure you receive from the kill, so it's a bad situation. If someone does this once, ignore it entirely (it was most likely an accident). However, a person who follows your party around and does this multiple times is absolutely trying to get in your way. Ask the person what they are doing, then report anything foul in their response to a GM. If they ignore you and keep doing it, find a new place to hunt and ditch the offenders. Even at this stage, they may simply be too young, inexperienced, or otherwise hindered to know what they are doing.

TREASURE DISTRIBUTION

When hunting in a group, especially when that group is composed of strangers, it is very wise to establish loot rules ahead of time. The dominant form of drop rules is to makes a pledge of Need Before Greed (NBG). This means that any character in the group who needs an item is placed in priority above someone who would just sell the item to a vendor or give it to an alternate character/guildie. This keeps parties together in a better atmosphere of cooperation. By agreeing on this before any powerful items drop, people save minutes of wasted hunting time trying to figure out who gets what.

When you join a group that prefers to go onto Round Robin and accept the whims of fate, make sure you're comfortable with that up front. If you think Round Robin is unfair, say so from the beginning. Your argument will have far more credibility when the group is forming compared to later, when there is a drop you want that someone else is standing over. When Round Robin is agreed to, at most ask the other person for a chance to have the item or trade something for it. When you agree to loot rules, accept that it won't always go your way. Being upset that Round Robin is fickle makes no sense if you already said you were fine with it in the past.

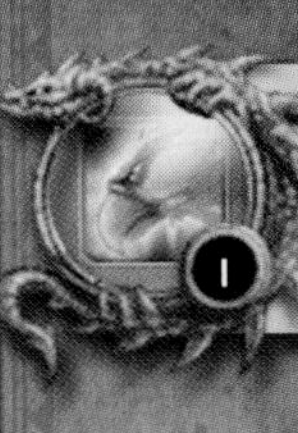

Multiple people may need an item that falls, especially when that item is particularly powerful. For these cases, Need Before Greed won't give the group an immediate answer. To quickly solve the issue, use **[/random 100]** and let the highest roller have the item (only people who need the item should be allowed to roll). Also, being able to use an item doesn't necessarily mean that you need it. A Warrior with an entire set of Superior Level 30 equipment shouldn't be rolling to snag Level 25 mail drops that a lower-level tank is direly in need of equipping.

The muddiest waters come when several people can use an item and it's an upgrade, but one class may need the upgrade far more than others. Consider a party with a Mage who uses swords, a Warrior (also specializing in blades), and a Rogue who likes having a sword as well. Who needs the Epic sword that those lovely elite trolls just dropped? Do all of them? Yes and no, of course.

The Warrior would use it a great deal. The Rogue would too. For the Mage, it would be an improvement, but that player wouldn't be using it nearly as often. A conundrum, for certain. In these cases, it's better if the Mage backs off, but it isn't required either. So, the "right" thing to do for the Mage is to let the primary melee characters roll for it while looking for lesser swords. The "right" thing for the Warrior and Rogue is to accept the Mage's request to roll if he does push forward. Either side has the ability to walk away looking respectable, even if they don't come away with a rare item!

Fast Drop Guidelines

- Set drop rules before leaving town
- Use [/random 100] to determine the looter in cases where multiple people need something
- Don't spend large amounts of time determining treasure distribution (more fighting = more treasure anyway!)
- If a player acts poorly, you don't have to group with them again, but making a scene hurts the rest of the group

When someone tries to slip things past the group by picking up items without reporting them or by pretending to need something they don't, it's best to follow a few steps. First, try to mention that the item is needed for someone else and see if that is enough to get things done. People do pick up items without noticing on occasion. An honest mistake is an honest mistake. However, a consistent pattern of doing this, or a few "accidents" with Bind on Pickup items can be quite telling. If a person has been doing this, tell them to stop. Even when the offending player is skilled and useful to the party, you may want to stop grouping with them in future runs if they're dragging morale down and causing group disputes.

Ninja Looting is the process of taking a powerful item (usually a Bind on Acquire item from an Instance) before others have a chance to decide who should receive the item. A common scenario is for the looter of a powerful enemy to look on the body, report a powerful drop, then stand back up (because it's BoA, they cannot loot it themselves without ruining everyone else's chance for the item). The body is free for anyone in the group to loot after that point. While the party is rolling for the item, a Ninja Looter could ignore the roll, rush the body, and grab the item. The finishing touch is to use their Hearthstone, return home, drop out of the group, and log off for the night. This sounds odd, but it does happen from time to time.

What do you do about Ninja Looters?

Put them on your Ignore List and don't group with them again. These players aren't likely to be considerate of your group's needs in the future, and it certainly brings down everyone's mood when the best items of a long Instance go up in smoke. Move on, keep finding your favorite allies, and don't worry about it. Instances are repeatable, and there are more evenings, more encounters, and plenty more treasure for you. As for the Ninja Looter, imagine how things are going to go for him when nobody wants to group with him for end-game content a couple months in the future. Having a bad reputation isn't much fun, and a few good items aren't worth the trouble.

DEALING WITH INCOMPETENT PLAYERS

Not everyone has the same level of skill in the *World of Warcraft*. Indeed, there's a huge gap between the most adept and experienced players and those who are new to MOGs, *World of Warcraft*, and cooperative play in general. As with many suggestions, the best default should be to allow for some mistakes and be patient with others. Yet, there are still times when a player is performing so badly that something must be done about it.

When someone in your group (most likely a person in a pickup group) is performing poorly and getting others killed, have the group leader take the first step. The group leader should stop for a short rest (area allowing) and explain how the party should be performing. If the new player is pulling extra monsters onto a party, advise them on how to **[/assist]** and where to stand. When they outright pull monsters that aren't desired, tell them that they aren't responsible for pulling and that a different player is already handling that.

Some young or inexperienced players take time to get used to this; having been engaged by single-player games, they expect to do everything themselves. Acting this way may not seem rude or ineffective to them, so do your best to be friendly while figuring out where the person's skill/intentions/experiences stand.

Unless the player is outright rude in their response to your party's suggestions, keep them around at least for the quest/expedition that you invited them to join. Good etiquette dictates that the group should stay together until the task is done, even if the weakest link in the party does not improve. Cutting a player for performing poorly is rude. That said, no one is obliged to take unskilled players out for every quest and every raid. If you aren't interested in helping that player improve their skills, don't group with them in the future. That is absolutely your choice.

SPAM INVITATIONS

It's best to look for groups with the tools available (general chat, searching in a zone for people who are using the /lfg tag, etc.). Walking around an area inviting everyone you see into a group is not polite. Ask first and you will find that it is much easier to collect a better grade of players!

The same is true for duels. Practicing with your character in 1 on 1 PvP is exciting, and many other players will be happy to join you in duels, especially near towns when they are not engaged with quests, other parties, etc. However, spamming a person with duel invites is absurdly rude and will land you on an Ignore List some of the time. The best duels take time to set up, with fun talk, mutual bows, and a brief discussion for any rules that are desired. Duels do not simulate true PvP anyway, and out-of-the-blue ones aren't worth the breach in manners.

ASKING FOR HELP

As long as you don't demand help from anyone, it is perfectly polite to ask for assistance when going after difficult fights, quests, and such. This can be done on the general chat channel or from people in the area. If you see people fighting their way toward a quest mob that you need to fight, there is nothing wrong with asking to join them. When you can't get close enough for **[/say]** to work, whisper to one of the members in the group. People rarely mind grabbing an extra person for a few kills, especially when it helps the soloer out.

A side issue of this is when your party is standing close to an important quest NPC, getting ready for the fight. Because some of these monsters are hard to find (because of wandering, spawn problems, etc.), it is polite to either yell or send a message over general to let people know that that enemy is not long for this world. By doing this you give others the chance to ask for an invite if they are close. Players don't just appreciate this; they love when parties are this considerate and will be more inclined to do the same themselves in the future.

REQUESTING BUFFS FROM STRANGERS

When soloing, you find that certain buffs make a huge difference to your performance. A Warrior out by his lonesome will be greatly improved by a Priest's Stamina buff (Power Word: Fortitude). Getting conjured food and water from Mages is another huge boost to soloers, because it's effectively free to both parties. However, no one is obligated to help a solo character with abilities that cost time or mana to cast. The best way to get what you want here is to approach characters that are out in the field and ask politely for the buffs or spells that you desire.

Don't be afraid to help the person in question polish off a few monsters; because of the tap system you receive 0 experience and they get their kills substantially faster. That is usually a good way to help out while waiting for a response. Also, if you have buffs that are useful, throw those on the stranger while they make up their mind (it won't hurt your request, certainly).

If a Mage conjures a large quantity of food/water for you, throw a modest tip in there even if the Mage doesn't ask for it; that person is going to have a short bit of downtime for what they gave you, and a nice tip will make them feel better about being generous. Besides, the cost of buying vendor food and water is so much higher that you save entire gold pieces at the moderate levels just by getting Mage assistance; encourage them!

From the buffer's perspective, it is nice to receive tips. However, a kind "thanks" is what you should expect and require for future assistance. When people don't thank you for your time and effort, it's not worth helping them time and time again. On the other side, if you do not demand a tip, don't expect one from every character you help (many may be too poor to make things sweet for you). Thus, if you aren't going to feel right about helping someone unless money is exchanged, tell the other players up front. Selling your services is perfectly acceptable. Pretending to donate them and getting upset when people don't realize your expectations is a bit unfair.

TRAINS

Running through a region often causes a number of monsters to collect in your path, following behind. Even if you are high enough level to survive this, there are sometimes grave consequences to these trains (so called because it looks a tad like a train, with you as the engine and the monsters as cars following behind). When these monsters break off from the chase, they have a chance to aggro on various players during the trip home. This can cause many deaths and problems to lower-level players in an area, and there is no fun or etiquette in that.

If you're running around with a train behind you, avoid other players by as wide a margin as possible. And, if your way is blocked by a party (at dungeon entrances or other such bottlenecks), be willing to stop and die with honor. It's far better to die to your train than to cause another party to wipeout. Besides, the party you just protected may have a rezzer, offer you a group for future protection, etc.

JUMPING IN

It is fairly common to see other players in trouble. A bad pull or just a poor turn of luck can place another character or entire party in a situation they cannot win. There is no hard and fast rule for what you are supposed to do at that point. If you believe your character would turn the tide of battle, feel free to jump in. When you know the other party needs help, take a fresh target and pull that away (you get the experience and treasure, but they have one fewer problem to deal with). However, if you think the other group might be fine and are uncertain, jump onto a tapped mob; there is almost no way to give offense by doing that because the other party still gets their loot and experience.

Perhaps the situation is entirely hopeless. When a dozen monsters get trained onto a small party in a dungeon it is unlikely that they will evacuate safely. Don't jump in when the battle is hopeless (just get out of the way and hope for your own survival). Adding on to a failing battle makes things even more chaotic and could even cause a fleeing party to stop and try to hold their ground.

If you're a rezzer or your group has such a character, send one of the characters a whisper and ask if their groups wants a rez (not everyone does if the map is small enough and the graveyard is somewhat close by). It's worth a short moment to resurrect the group if that is what they want. The good will is nice to have, and your party may need a rez one day too. You never know who will be around when that time comes.

STAYING IN A GROUP

Groups may form for a single quest, an hour of play, or even a single battle. Proper manners here vary, but the basic key is to be honest about how long you intend to group with a party and stick to your word. If you join someone for a quest, say that you are able to stay around for "X" amount of time and that is your limit. Work to get the quest done, then stay to make sure that it is done for everyone before leaving. In the event that you must leave unexpectedly, apologize, give at least some of the reason, and offer to make things up to people later.

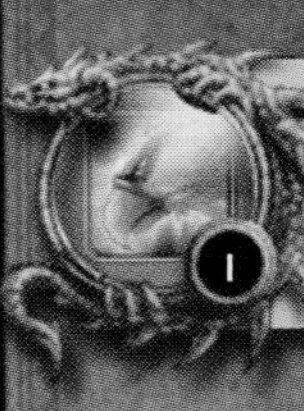

By the same token, don't assume that everyone who leaves suddenly is being a jerk and ditching the group. Phone calls, family, lightning, penguin outbreaks, and other problems simply occur. If you group with someone a couple times and they consistently ditch after finishing their part of the quest, don't group with them in the future (at least, if that type of thing upsets you).

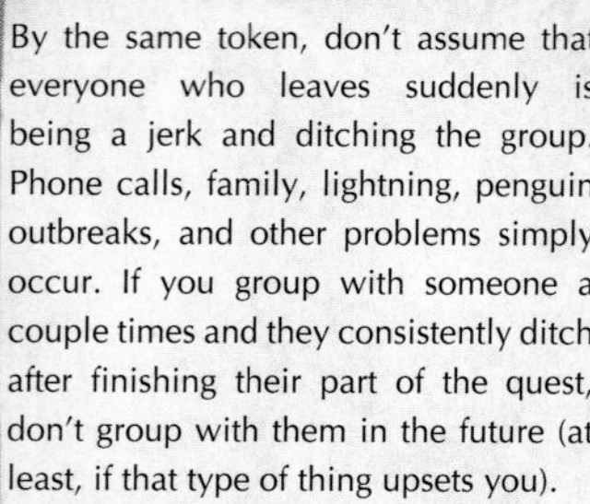

GRABBING RESOURCES

Resources that spawn at static points (e.g. metal and herbs) are available to everyone, and it is another case where "first come, first serve" is the rule. Yet, there are a few ways to keep from doing unfair things while collecting. Because many resource points have monsters nearby, parties and solo characters must fight to clear the area first, unless they are high enough level to simply sneak past and grab what they want. Regardless, if you see a person clearing the area near a resource point, do not rush past and steal that point. Whisper to the person or party and ask if they are going after the resource node; if they say yes, move on and look for another (you should get to the next point first since that person is still going after the last one).

If you badly need points for your skills, you may ask a person for a chance to access the resource point without taking anything. With Mining and Herbalism, the point is given for using the resource node, not for taking what is inside it. Thus, a whack on a vein of ore or a moment looking through the herb cluster gives you everything you need. There is no harm in asking for a chance to do this, and most harvesters won't have a problem letting you try, especially after they find that you are good to your word.

In groups, there may be several resource collectors of the same type (two Skinners, two Miners, etc.). As the party is moving into the area, discuss how you plan to tradeoff resources. For mines, it may be that everyone gets a hit for points, then the metal is split evenly. For Skinning it may be that just one person skins each monster, for time reasons, and the Skinners trade who is on duty.

BACK IN TOWN

Even in the somewhat relaxed state of standing in town, hawking wares and seeking various trainers, there are proper ways to conduct yourself. Knowing these helps when selling items, buying things from other players, and just in making your way around.

WHERE IS EVERYTHING?

Some of the NPCs in cities can be hard to find. A system is in place that allows players to ask the guards of major cities where to find various NPCs. Right-click on the guards to bring up a list of the NPCs and locations they are aware of, then choose the person you seek (a blip on the mini-map appears to help guide you there).

Sometimes, you in the General Chat Channel ask where different NPCs and stores are located. Try to provide an answer for difficult questions when possible. If the players are asking for answers to simple questions that they have access to, direct them to the source they should be using ("The Quest description tells you where those monsters are" or "Ask a city guard; they will put a marker on your map").

If you have questions, ask in General and see if people are willing and able to help. There is nothing wrong with asking every few minutes if you don't receive assistance and are still having trouble. This is an area where "Please" "Thank You" and general courtesy goes a long way. The more polite you are, the more often future questions will be answered. Also, players tend to provide more information when they feel connected to the person asking the question. "Does anyone know if the Mo'Grosh Crystal is a shared drop? :)" will get more attention than "Is Mo'Grosh Crystal shared?"

The best tendency is to try and find things you need on your own at first, because many items, stores, NPCs, and quest targets are quite accessible. Asking where to go and what to do the moment you receive a quest frustrates other players on chat, and they won't be as likely to help after several rounds of queries. Instead, wait until the tools available to you are exhausted. Look around, reread quests or pertinent text, ask your guild or party, and then go into General Chat. Also, feel free to whisper a personal "Thanks!" to anyone who helps you. Showing that you are genuinely appreciative of their help is a suitable payment for the time they spent typing an answer.

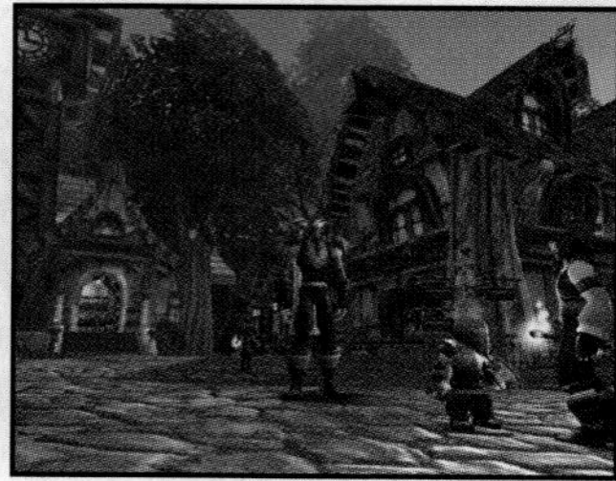

ON THE BATTLEFIELDS OF PVP

Many of the rules that govern play in PvE change when dealing with players of the opposite faction. This is a desired aspect of the game for many people, and it is best to choose a server that fits your view of etiquette from the beginning if you are worried about certain aspects of competitive play. PvP is one of the rare times when server is what dictates etiquette more than common sense, disposition, or morality.

WHEN TO ATTACK

Going after enemies of the opposite faction is a matter of duty on the FvF server, to a fair extent. Disrupting another player of your faction when they are fighting a monster would be griefing; doing the same thing to an opposing faction's player is acceptable (perhaps even desired depending on how bitter the rivalry is on the server).

Indeed, attacking other players in a PvP or FvF environment is anticipated and encouraged. Any civility that you want to put into such combat (waiting until enemies are fully healed, outside of combat, have seen you, etc.) is above and beyond what others expect from you. Much like in real life, indulging your enemies in this way is a risk that won't always be returned. Let roleplaying and your sense of enjoyment dictate these responses instead of standard etiquette. If you want to be a dirty, rotten, backstabbing fiend that leaps onto hapless foes at the worst of times, go ahead and do it!

Is it possible to grief members of the opposition? Yes, there could be griefing, but this would only be an issue if there was a bug that was exploited against members of one faction. Things that would normally be considered griefing are often allowable otherwise. Training monsters into enemies is not griefing; it's a viable strategy. Again, you may not choose to do it, but your enemies have every right and ability to do it against your party. Be prepared.

GANKING

Ganking is the process of going after characters of much lower level. If ganking doesn't do anything for you and it makes other people's lives difficult, is it wrong? No. Some people on both sides of the war see ganking as a practice of griefers. However, this is not an act of griefing because it is a game dynamic that is mutually agreed upon by the parties involved (the targeted players chose to come to a server where non-instanced PvP is a reality). Thus, they knew the risks and consented to the attack simply by joining the server.

That said in defense of gankers, it still is not an act that will earn you respect from the majority of players unless you accomplish your attacks in novel and exciting ways. Using stealth or invisibility to get into contested areas where relatively low-level enemies are questing and going after solo targets is fairly simple. Charging in with raiding parties, fighting out in the open, going after larger groups, etc. is the way to have more fun and truly challenge yourself.

Play as you wish. Those who want to avoid this style of gaming are absolutely free to join the servers where Faction-based combat is restricted to instances and opt-in combat (e.g. defending city NPCs that are being attacked).

CORPSE CAMPING

When an enemy dies, their corpse becomes a respawn point (once their spirit returns). Very few PvPers are going to take EXP penalties for their deaths, so it is almost inevitable that the person who died will return to their corpse. Corpse Camping is the act of patrolling the region where an enemy has died while waiting for the person to return (the followup is to attack the recently rezzed character and kill them a second time).

Again, this is not griefing. However, it is both obstructive to the other person's enjoyment (since they can't even get enough health to have a good fight with you), and it holds your party in place instead of getting you more experience, money, combat, etc. The camped person is free to log off and return at a later point when you are gone, and it's impossible to know if that is the case. So, it is often better to get your kills, move on, and know that the victim could be after you at any time (enjoy the rush).

As far as etiquette goes, people are far happier on both sides when corpse camping is minimal. Very few players enjoy being camped this way, and most classes simply don't have the ability to get away safely when five or six people are boxing them into a small area. The flipside of this is what happens when a ganker/corpse camper goes down. Suddenly, tons of people are ready to camp the offending party, and the hunter quickly becomes the hunted.

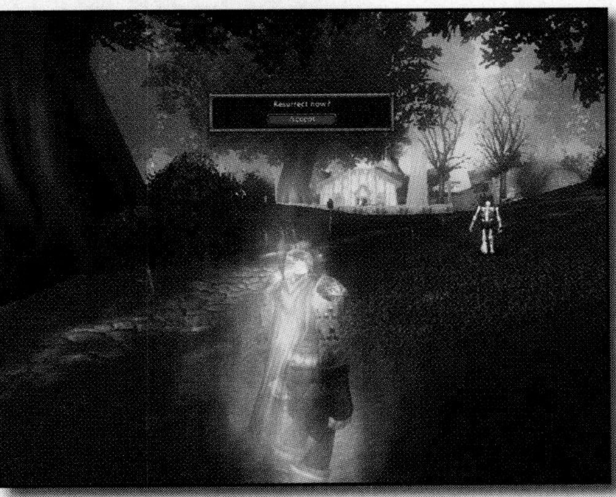

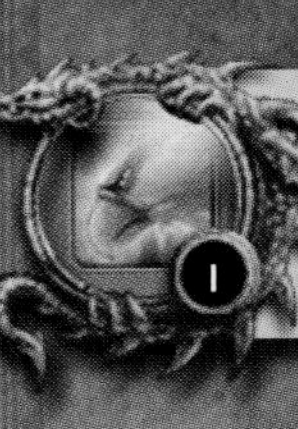

10 THINGS WORTH KNOWING

There are certain aspects of MORG play that are almost universal. Appropriately, these are present in the *World of Warcraft* and should be explained for people who are new to the game, genre, or even to Blizzard games from the past.

I PATIENCE IS THE KEY TO GLORY

It's invariably true that patience leads to greatness in many tasks. Most roleplaying games have a huge element of this, and MOGs are even more representative of the idea. It's impossible for players to sit down and see everything there is to the *World of Warcraft* in one day (or week, or month, ...). Thus, no matter how hard you try there is no way to rush through the game world and get to the "end." In fact, though there is an end-game portion of content where players are capped in level, there's never going to be a heavy hand on your shoulder saying "The game is over now, please go somewhere else."

Regardless of anyone else's view of how fast someone should play, level, and enjoy the game, there is no specific time to reach a quest or an area. Take a week hunting for Kodo Leather in Mulgore, or try exploring all of Kalimdor at level 20 if you are truly brave. Nothing that you enjoy in *World of Warcraft* is wasted time. The world is here for you to enjoy! Take it easy and play as you wish. Indeed, the levels are more exciting, the gameplay refreshing, and every group a bit better when you remember that fun is more important than getting the next skill, level, Wombat of Slaying, etc.

II LEARN WHAT YOU CAN HANDLE

It's exciting to push your character to the very limits of survivability. This is good to try on a limited basis for several reasons. First off, it provides a nice rush (even if you eventually lose and have to do a short corpse run). Beyond that, this type of testing brings you closer to your characters; understanding how to get every last bit of power out of a class will make every difference when it comes to complex challenges such as Player Vs. Player combat and Instances.

Though you naturally cover the limits of your character over time, simply by playing the game and dealing with the troublesome situations that arise from large pulls, trains from other groups, and ambushes out in the wild, testing still has its place. The issue here is that intentionally testing your class makes the process more analytic; you can prepare new strategies, test them out, and really see the effects. It's much harder to keep a keen eye out when you are surprised.

Try finding situations that push your character to the limit to see what things your race/class/style combo are best for countering. Try going against single targets of high level in solo encounters; engage entire groups of equal or slightly lower-level monsters; grab wide aggro from a huge range of enemies and try to flee successfully. These tests reveal a great deal about the strengths of a player and that person's chosen character.

III FIND A CLASS THAT SUITS YOUR MENTALITY

A character's class defines what they are capable of doing in so many ways. Though every class is quite impressive in *World of Warcraft*, even in solo encounters, there are styles of fighting that are more effective for certain classes. For instance, Warriors handle groups of enemies far better than most alternatives (they have high hit points, impressive armor, and a Rage bar that is easier to fill when there are more targets bringing aggro). Casters, on the other hand, are much faster at bringing down single foes, but have to be more careful in how they approach fights; success for casters involves damage at range, frustrating enemy advances, and using mana efficiently.

CLASS STYLE QUICKLIST

CLASS NAME	DOMINANT TRAITS
Druid	Shapeshifting; Style Flexibility; Can Act as Substitute Tank, Rogue, or Caster; Damage at All Ranged; Backup Healing
Hunter	Powerful, Consistent Pets; Notable Ranged Damage, Traps, Tracking of Beasts and Sentient Enemies, Moderate Armor
Mage	High Burst Damage; Long Range; Snare Enemies; Create Free Food/Water/ Mana Gems; Instant Damage; Combat Control; Very Fragile Hit Points and Armor
Paladin	Decent Damage; Backup Healing; Resurrection; Strong Armor; Survival Abilities; Great Vs. Undead; Alliance-Only Class
Priest	Powerful, Fast, and Efficient Healing; Stamina Buff; Protective Shield Buff; Anti-Undead Powers; Impressive Damage; Fragile Hit Points and Armor
Rogue	High, Sustained Damage; Stealth; Modest Armor; Light Hit Points, Lockpicking
Shaman	Totems for AoE Status Effects; Ranged Magic; Substantial Melee Damage; Moderate Armor; Resurrection; Horde-Only Class
Warlock	Multiple DOTs; Fear; Extensive Pet Summoning; Many Channeling Spells; Blurred Line Between Hit Points and Mana (Can Use One to Gain the Other); Complex Class
Warrior	Very High Survivability; Gather Aggro; Damage Mitigation; Versatile Melee

Choose a class that matches your mentality and play style, especially for the first character that you choose. Players who thrive on getting up close and personal will feel much more comfortable with Warriors and Rogues. Those who prefer fast kills and don't mind downtime can thrive with a Mage. Warlocks aren't fast killers, but they have very little downtime. So, look into each of the classes and make a logical choice based on the character that you want to play.

Don't be afraid to message players of specific classes and ask them about their experiences. Use forums for the same purpose and see how actual players feel about their play experience. This avoids the path of reaching Level 20 before realizing that a class is good but still not your style. Of course, it's good to try everything yourself in the long run, but that's a different issue.

IV CHOOSE A RACE THAT LOOKS AND FEELS RIGHT

Though class selection is dictated by logic, race is a decision based on aesthetics. Certainly, there are starting advantages to some race/class combinations (Tauren Warriors have quite high starting damage per second, Gnomes have more mana to throw around than other races, etc.). Still, these advantages dim over time as equipment choices, levels, and player skill dwarf (pun intended) the fairly minimal lead that even the most intuitive combinations create. A Dwarven Warrior has over 60 more hit points at level one compared to a Gnome Warrior (over twice the Gnome's hit points!). At level 30, however, this difference is trivial.

Instead, the choice of a character's race is a great time to go with your heart. That character will race across the world at the bottom of your screen for months to come. Pick a race that looks and feels right to you! This yields a starting location that suits your playstyle, since all of the starting areas are geared to the races that inhabit them. Also, it conveys an immediate sense of closeness between you and your character; the more you enjoy your character, the better each level seems.

VOICE EMOTES

Other fun things to try are various voice emotes for the sex/race combination of your character. Create a character and try the [/v flirt] and [/v silly] commands five or six times each. If the humor of the combination works for you, the style of that race's quests are likely going to synch as well.

Don't let stats or racial traits decide race for you unless that is truly important to you! If you are interested in playing any combination, no matter how odd at first, go for it and have no regrets. In *World of Warcraft*, player skill and a good reputation get you into high quality groups far more often than race, class, etc.

V INVEST IN FRIENDS AND SKILLED ALLIES

And speaking of good groups, there are a few tips to help with finding them. While you are playing, even at low levels, try to see which people are active in General Chat in a helpful way. Make note of polite, informed players and how they are dealing with each other. Out in the field, see who is eager to buff ungrouped characters, jump in to help other characters when a pull goes poorly, etc. Don't be afraid to "waste" some time getting to know the other players; the ones who stay involved with their characters into the higher levels may be your companions for months to come. And, the sooner you become friends with the more friendly and skilled players, the sooner pickup groups will be a thing of the past.

Ironically, to get away from pickup groups, people have to rush into many of them. The best times to do this are for kill quests, elite quests, and other activities where having more people around aids the process even when they are strangers. Try to keep track of all the people you enjoy grouping with. Had a good time with Player A—ask if you can put that person on your Friends list. They will most likely do the same for you. Continue this and there will be a cluster of a dozen or more people from other guilds that you know and like in no time (leading to faster groups with more familiarity, less down time, and more fun).

On the whole, the best players to choose for your list are the people who click with your personality and style of play. Even when some players are unskilled and make mistakes, they may be wonderful choices in the long run. You cannot train someone to be an exciting friend; skill in MORGs on the other hand is easily acquired over time by someone willing to learn. The vast majority of players who start off poorly but have the will to practice and learn end up being quite good by the time they reach high levels.

VI TRY EVERYTHING AT LEAST ONCE

There are many classes, races, and areas to explore. Even if one thing grabs you from the start, you become a better player by understanding where everyone else has been. Look into both factions even if you are sold on one of them. Playing a dedicated Alliance character, it is quite an eye-opener to see the Barrens as a soldier of the Horde. Learning how the other side works together, quests, and levels aids in countering those tactics with your original character. Also, there is a chance that somewhere you haven't been will completely capture your heart. A player that immediately chooses to play as an Orc may fall in love with Mulgore or even pine away for the beauty of Elwynn Forest.

For those with enough patience, try starting characters in each of the six initial regions to see if there is something special in one of them. Spending a couple hours on this your first day may pay off with a character you didn't even know you wanted to play.

VII IDENTIFY GOALS AND SUITABLE TARGETS

There are many goals for a player to seek in a given session. Sure, it is possible to play without more than an urge to beat monsters and have a good time (a goal unto itself, honestly). If that is all that you are looking for, recognize that and take a leisurely pace; fight the monsters you enjoy fighting even if there aren't any quests for that area. With a casual pace, it is entirely possible to group with a huge level range of friends and just do whatever you want!

When you have a more specific goal do what you can to identify the best targets for accomplishing that. Indeed, someone looking for the best experience on a given evening should queue the most quests for an area, find a group that is willing to stay together for at least a few hours, then plow through those quests with military efficiency. Or, when quests are dry for multiple areas, gather a high kill-rate party and grind epic mobs in an Instance. By choosing the right party and monster type to gain experience you achieve your goals.

Or, if you want money, go after enemies beneath your level in a very small party (or solo). Try to get into areas with huge numbers of targets that you can fight in tandem, looking for a maximal kill rate without any major concern for experience (it comes in decently, but not as well as when focusing on quests and epic battles). Taking down high quantities of targets yields more rare drops. This is a fine way to fill out guild equipment needs while accumulating extra coin.

The global point is to do what you like without worrying about experience per hour (unless experience per hour is your goal, of course). People love to explore, roleplay, dance around Ironforge with stray Gnomes, etc. Experiment, find your favorite activities, then indulge.

VIII THE RIGHT PLACE AT THE RIGHT TIME

While leveling, there are certainly better places to get the job done at any given point. Because questing is such a major aspect of *World of Warcraft*, it is quite useful to know where the most quests are throughout the game. One of the keys to progressing smoothly comes in traveling back and forth between equivalent regions; when quests are depleted in one area, try another for a time then return to see if new things are available.

In Alliance lands, a person may be hunting in Loch Modan from levels 12-14, then suddenly find a few of the remaining quests to be a bit challenging (or they will simply wish for a change). For a change of pace and some easy experience, move down into Westfall and do all of the quests there for the early levels. By the time Westfall becomes old news for your budding adventurer, Loch Modan's "tougher" quests should be just right. Or, there is always a trip out to Darkshore for yet another batch of level-appropriate quests. Horde characters often bounce between The Barrens and Silverpine Forest for the exact same reasons.

IX USE ALL RESOURCES

In-game, using your resources means that it is important to keep in touch with other players via the chat channels and the guild you choose. Be confident in yourself and try to find answers through exploring and testing, but don't be hesitant to ask others for help when things become muddled or frustrating. Buy quality items from other players as well, and be fast to sell the good things you find but can't use (this will make more coin than vendoring the items and substantially help others at the same time).

Outside of the game itself, there are web sites, guild pages, and forums waiting for you. Each of these offers a different aspect of assistance for mastering your character in the *World of Warcraft*. Guild pages offer social interaction, networking, and a feeling of playing a game outside the game. Open forums have tons of information on quests problems, upcoming game changes, and developments in the world (this is even more the case once there are many servers and each starts to have its own flavor). Obviously, strategy guides have a good place because they can go into the game with you; kept beside your computer, they offer fast information, data charts, etc. Also, guides can be taken around for perusal when a computer won't be available (commute by train, long trips, and such).

If you want to know everything there is to know about *World of Warcraft*, play long, play hard, and use as many sources as you see fit.

X TAKE BREAKS

Eating, sleeping, work, friends, and all of the other needs demand their own time, but there are also breaks in-game that can be useful to you. For one, it is nice to have a few characters to play unless you are madly driven to reach level cap in the least possible time. Having a few characters gives a player the breathing room to play according to a given mood instead of being forced into the same style each evening. It is nice to have a tank for slugging things out, a caster for ranged spellcasting, a crafting and farming character for making money and finding special gear, and whatever else calls to you.

By switching around the characters you play, the game stays more vibrant and has fewer demands on you. Instead, you get to go with your mood each time you play. The only serious downside of having multiple characters is that friends on the same server may out-level you. That is one of the many perks of having a guild; there is often a cluster of people in every region, so you won't be left out by leveling at a different pace than the "average" player. For that matter, it is pretty darn hard to find an average player when it comes to leveling, since there is a huge range in terms of speed and style of play.

20 THINGS I WISH SOMEONE HAD TOLD ME

1. You can't put a SPACE in your name.
2. WASD and the arrow keys are your movement keys.
3. SHIFT + B or SHIFT + Left Clicking on any bag opens all your bags.
4. T targets the closest enemy and TAB toggles between targets.
5. Monsters that come up as "Red" on your indicator are aggressive and will attack if you get too close!
6. Pull abilities/spells from your ability menu/spellbook to your Hotbar to access them quickly. (This is also true for the Throwing/Shooting/Fishing abilities.)
7. NumLock (or Clear for Mac users) is Auto Run.
8. Different icons on your pointer indicate what type of NPC/object you're targeting and whether you can interact with them.
9. M opens your map. You'll reveal more of your region map by exploring.
10. Most trainers reside in the capitol cities.
11. You don't have to equip your Skinning Knife, Blacksmith's Hammer, etc. to perform your craft. You simply have to have it in your inventory.
12. SHIFT + Left Clicking an item/quest during chat will link it to the chat window.
13. Murlocs are evil.
14. Not all races can speak to one another. Alliance and Horde members can't understand what the other side is saying.
15. The Right Mouse button controls the camera and can be a keyless substitute for strafing.
16. SHIFT + Right Clicking is the key to inventory management. While shopping, this allows you to purchase/sell more than one item at a time. You can choose the amount of money during a trade and split items in your own inventory.
17. When purchasing an item from another player, you'll need to pull coins from your backpack.
18. If your breath gauge expires while you're in water, so do you!
19. Different colored items have different quality. Gray items are inferior and white are standard. Green, blue, purple and other colored items are the "special" ones.
20. Stop reading and go play!

THE DO'S AND THE DO NOT'S

Throughout the Introduction we list many aspects of play, etiquette, strategies, and so forth. This list tries to condense as much advice as possible into a quick reference sheet that you can come back to while taking a bit of a breather.

DO!

- Play to have fun
- Make friends and skilled allies
- Look into gathering professions for high profit (e.g. Mining, Skinning, Herbalism)
- When grinding, focus on EXP per hour, not EXP per kill
- Use inns and capital cities to accumulate more rest time when logging out
- Use your Hearthstone to get home quickly (it replenishes every hour)
- Find high quality food and water for your level (downtime should be minimized)
- Fight creatures below your level for fast kills (good for money, solo EXP)
- Fight elite monsters in groups for better treasure, especially in special Instances
- Sell useful items to other players for better prices and a better community
- Ask questions if you become frustrated, lost, or confused
- Try to find things out on your own before asking for help
- Use chat channels to alert others when going after wandering quest targets (e.g. The Defias Messenger)
- Keep undead out of direct sunlight and try not to feed them between noon and dusk
- Stay in groups while others finish their quests
- Try to help others who run into trouble
- Agree on party goals, loot rules, and duration of play before setting out
- Apologize if you do something that gets people killed
- Listen to experienced players and share experiences that you gain with others
- Say "Good Group" at the end of the night and thank everyone who came along
- Try to type in coherent English so that everyone understands you
- Understand when others don't type perfectly with 16 Murlocs on their backs
- Use item enhancements even at early levels (learn about enchanting, armor patches, and blacksmithing upgrades even if you don't use those professions)
- Raise your reputation with neutral factions for added quests
- Avoid killing city-based NPCs unless you don't care about gaining a bad reputation
- Look through the Auction House to learn about normal prices; try to avoid impulse buying before you know what things are worth

DON'T

- Be forced into playing a certain way if it doesn't feel right
- Let stats or trends keep you from making the character you want
- Get locked into a single character (the classes are too enjoyable to try just one)
- Be afraid to ask for help, buffs, or directions
- Demand things from other players (such as help, buffs, or directions)
- Spam group, guild, or duel invites to anyone
- Steal boss mobs, chests, or resources from groups that are trying to fight over to those things
- Call Tauren cows, all-beef patties, burgers, or big game
- Be greedy about drops that other players can use when you cannot
- Forget to sleep at some point (you need to get bonus experience sometime)
- Get angry at the other faction; get even and enjoy it!
- Leave your group hanging (if you say five minutes, try to mean five minutes)

Do: Keep all your clothes on.

Don't: Take off all your clothes.
CENSORED

UNDERSTANDING EQUIPMENT, ENEMIES, AND LEVELS

Levels of NPCs, monsters, and equipment mean a great deal in just about every MOG on the market. Just because there are items of stunning power out there doesn't imply that you should be wielding them from the beginning. Indeed, the theory behind *World of Warcraft* is that you must build your character's skills and abilities to the point where they are able to wield the items of greatest power. The same is true for which enemies you are able to fight; the bitter and hard-fought skirmishes your friends have against Defias Pillagers in Westfall will seem like a fond memory in a few weeks when you begin engaging the Trolls of Stranglethorn Vale!

SHADES OF QUALITY: THE EQUIPMENT SYSTEM

For almost all forms of equipment, there are ways to quickly judge their approximate power and usefulness to you. The minimum level of an item reveals when you can use it, and the color of said item provides a rough idea of how powerful that piece is at that level.

The table below lists the different equipment tiers.

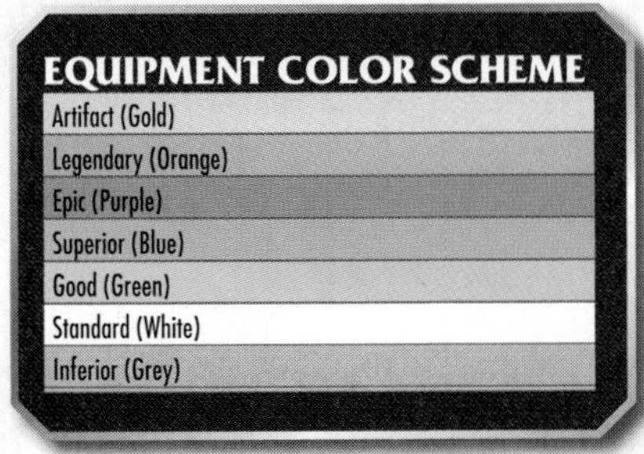

EQUIPMENT COLOR SCHEME
Artifact (Gold)
Legendary (Orange)
Epic (Purple)
Superior (Blue)
Good (Green)
Standard (White)
Inferior (Grey)

Items of Inferior quality are only useful when nothing else is available. This happens most often when you reach levels where new slots of equipment can be used (shoulderpads are the most common example beyond level one).

After Inferior and Standard items, there are the higher-quality tiers. Many of these are either set to Bind on Acquire or Bind on Equip. Bind on Acquire (BoA) is a state that will lock an item to the first person who picks it up or adds it into their inventory. For a crafter, this means that the item can only be produced for your own needs. For a person out in the field, it means that the character who loots a corpse with a BoA item receives that item and be unable to trade it. Thus, BoA items can only be sold to vendors. Almost all quest rewards are BoA.

Bind on Equip items (BoE) are far more versatile because they can be looted by anyone, traded for other items, sold to players, or to a vendor. As long as no one equips a BoE item, the piece is still tradable. Once equipped, a BoE item functions the same as any BoA.

WHAT EQUIPMENT CAN I EXPECT TO SEE AS I LEVEL?

Obviously, characters don't receive Legendary and Artifact items at the drop of a hat. Indeed, these items are rarely found by anyone. As the game evolves during its first couple years, it's likely that more of these items will be added. Early on, it's a fair guess to say that very few are going to be found.

Characters progress through their levels with a variety of items, covering many tiers of quality. Inferior equipment is primarily available for Level 1 characters; after that stage these poor goods exist as vendor bait (they sell decently to merchants and can supplement the cash gained from your normal hunting). The reason Inferior items are seldom used is that they have very high level requirements for the stats they convey. Thus, you are likely to find something much better before even having a chance to stumble on an Inferior item for a given level.

Standard Items are still a form of stopgap for most types of equipment. After you push your way out of the starting areas, there are many chances to equip better items than these. Standard equipment often has a slightly high level requirement, modest stats, and few or no bonuses at all. Mail-wearing classes are far more likely to grab these because basic armor is still a ton better than no armor. However, cloth and leather-wearing classes rely more on stat bonuses from their equipment, so Standard gear has even less call from them.

Good items are frequently BoE and are rewards for many quests or as drops from monsters in an area. These treats are often just right in terms of the level where they are found, and they have decent stats and modifiers. A character suited in items with Good quality and of appropriate level will perform quite well. Think of Good items as being par for a skilled adventurer; if you keep Good gear of equivalent level to your character, battles against reasonable foes become very safe. Try to stay within three to five levels of your character when it comes to this gear.

Everything after that point, dealing with superior and epic items, is going to be about luck and patience. If you are driven to assemble the perfect set of gear for each level, it takes considerable time going against slow-spawning mobs in the wilderness (rare monsters), bosses in Instances, and large numbers of general enemies. There is nothing wrong with this approach. Leveling for your character is slightly slower under this method, but your power at any given level is often better than those who are rushing forward. It's a tradeoff, and both methods have their virtues.

The higher-end items are gained through sheer luck by fighting for hour upon hour and keeping your fingers crossed. Or, for those with a more methodic approach, from taking on Instances. Instance areas have elite enemies with powerful skills and allies. It isn't easy to take down Instances of your level, and even the best players travel to these in groups of five (or more). Named Instance characters are reliable for superior item drops, but a number of runs through each Instance are needed to find all of the drops and to equip entire parties with such goodies.

NPCS, ALLIES, AND ENEMIES

Much like items, people you encounter in the *World of Warcraft* are "color-coded" as well. For both enemies and allies, there are color distinctions that are important to understand. This is what is commonly referred to as how they "Con."

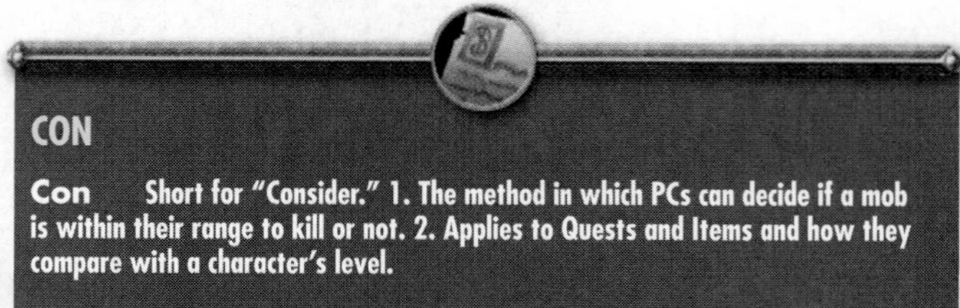

CON

Con **Short for "Consider." 1. The method in which PCs can decide if a mob is within their range to kill or not. 2. Applies to Quests and Items and how they compare with a character's level.**

Other characters of your faction and NPCs will be either blue or green in appearance when you highlight their avatar. A bar appears that lists that person's name, class/job, and level. The color of that bar declares whether that person is in a /PvP state. A blue bar means that the target is not currently set for PvP in that area. A green bar means that the person is a viable PvP target for enemies from the opposing faction. NPCs are always viable targets.

Enemies and Beasts have their colors as well. Creatures out in the wilderness may be yellow if they are passive. These neutral creatures do not attack anything on sight, regardless of proximity. You are free to walk up next to a Deer, Zhevra, or any other neutral creatures without fear of reprisal. If you attack these creatures, however, they will aggro on you and engage in battle just like any proper foe.

AGGROING NEUTRAL CREATURES

Even area-of-effect debuffs from your party can cause neutral creatures to aggro. To avoid this, use fire control and hold back on AoE activities when there are neutral creatures in the way.

Also note that many neutral creatures are shy and will retreat from the area if there is a battle taking place. This prevents some problems with accidental aggro.

More aggressive creatures, such as various predators, undead beings, demons, members of the opposing faction, etc. will appear with a red bar when they are highlighted. Red stands for an aggressive creature; these foes will aggro on you simply for stepping within a certain distance. That distance is determined by the difference between your level and the hostile creature.

AGGRO DISTANCE

Aggro distance, as stated, is computed by determining the different in level between you and the enemy. Being lower level than the creature increases the distance from which it chooses to attack. Thus, very low characters for a given region have predators and enemies alike racing across fair distances for a chance at some fresh meat.

On the flipside, characters who are much higher level than the hostile monsters in an area won't aggro them without walking right next to them.

Finally, some enemies have a higher aggro range than others. Wolves, Coyotes, certain casters, and various additional foes aggro at a greater distance than your level deviance dictates. It doesn't take long to learn which enemies do this for an area; you are then free to use greater caution when trying to avoid attacks from such targets.

The Reputation System allows for more variety in certain NPCs. Regions with complex NPCs are given a faction of their own. Goblin towns, rogue elements of the Alliance and Horde, and fully independent groups feature this. If you improve relations with these groups, their mood changes to a Friendly one with your character. However, attacking NPCs of these factions turns them against your character.

NPCs just beneath Neutral are Unfriendly. Though they won't attack you outright, they don't offer to speak with your character, sell, or give quests to you.

Beneath Unfriendly is the Hostile Ranking; this turns previously passive NPCs into aggressive ones. Unless steps are taken to raise your faction with them dramatically, expect to be fighting these enemies from there on out.

REPUTATION QUICKLIST

CONDITION	EFFECT
Exalted	The highest level of reputation a player can achieve with a faction
Revered	Special reputation level reserved for special heroes
Honored	10% discount on bought items from vendors
Friendly	Standard reputation level for factions on a player's team
Neutral	Standard reputation level for factions not on a player's team that are not KOS
Unfriendly	Cannot buy, sell, or interact
Hostile	KOS
Hated	Target tries to kill you on sight; enemy factions are set to this rank

NOT EVERYONE COMES ALONE

There are several ways for enemies to get help from other creatures in the region. First off, some aggressive creatures try to bring allies from the moment they are pulled. Humanoid mobs are the most notable for this, but there are beasts that do this as well. This makes camps of enemies harder to fight because even ranged attacks will bring several foes.

Another method that some humanoids and beasts have (especially with foes like Raptors) is to call for help. These calls can even bring creatures that are from different races; for example, a Druid may respond to the call of a wounded Raptor. There is little to be done about these calls for help because they occur instantly. The best thing to do is pull such foes back to areas where their calls won't grab anything that you aren't already interested in fighting.

Then, there is a third way for certain enemies to seek aid. When badly wounded, a number of intelligent foes run away (some of them at very high speed). If the monsters bump into any allies along the way, they will return with friends. Using snare and stun abilities can help quite a bit to prevent this from occurring. For classes without such tools, try to save damage for the end of the fight (by saving mana, instant abilities, etc.) so that the creatures can be struck down when they try to run.

WHAT ARE THOSE SPECIAL PICTURES BY CERTAIN MOBS?

Elite monsters have special icons that surround their pictures in the interface. Elite monsters have a gold dragon border around their portraits; these creatures have roughly triple the normal hit points for a similar mob of that level (they also have more powerful attacks and abilities in many cases). Be wary of these mobs, but know that they drop better treasure and are worth far more experience, so hunting them in parties is quite lucrative.

Often, the strategies for fighting Elite mobs is different from those used against normal creatures. The general changes are that long-term abilities are even more powerful when fighting Elites (DOTs, debuffs, and short-term buffs are wonderful in these slower fights). Instead of using the philosophy of "Bring it down quickly to stay alive," the characters are pushed more toward "Bring it down safely and with maximal control of the situation." Use snares to keep these monsters from rushing off to heal or get allies.

Now and then you also see creatures with grey dragon borders around their names. First off, these are specific creatures instead of a racial type. Each monster of this type has a name ("Murgos Pugnose" instead of a generic Defias), and will be involved with an important quest, a rare spawn, etc. The power level of named monsters varies tremendously. Some of these are just named and meant to be finished at the end of the quest, having no particularly special abilities or attributes. Others may have new attacks, abilities not normally given to their race, and deal far more damage than one might expect. This is all a matter of experience and cannot be predicted simply by looking at the creature.

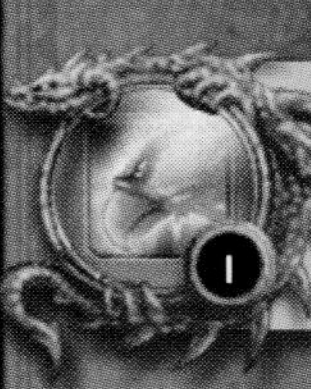

THE BASICS OF PARTY DYNAMICS

Grouping is such a central aspect of MORG play that it's discussed several times in this guide (each time with increased detail). Here in the Introduction, our examination of groups focuses primarily on the basic mechanics and reasons for getting into groups. Later on, we'll explain more about performing in high-level groups and in a wider variety of situations.

WHAT IS A PARTY?

Parties are formed when characters decide to work together. By sharing the duties in combat, far more monsters can be brought to defeat, and safety is dramatically improved. Normal groups can be as large as five characters.

To start a party, target another person and type [/invite], or invite a player from far away by using the character's full name [/invite Serene]. Using character portraits is another way to interact with people nearby (right-click on the person's portrait and choose invite from the list of options that appears).

People who are invited into a group have a query box that appears on their screen; it asks whether they wish to join the inviter's group. If they decline, the inviter is informed by both a sound and a text message. If they join, the new character's portrait is added in the upper-left side of the screen. You are able to see their hit points and mana/energy/rage bars (which update in real time).

So, a group at its core is a joining of characters that are going to attempt some challenges together. With two to five people, groups can attempt all of the quests or hunting activities that are normally available to characters. The quicklist below explains some of the differences when doing tasks in a group.

DIFFERENCES BETWEEN SOLOING AND GROUPING

- Parties share their experience from kills
- Looted money is divided evenly between participating group members
- Bodies Are lootable for items based on a system decided by the group leader (Master, Round Robin, Group Loot, Need Before Greed, or Free-For-All)
- Quests can be shared between members (so long as the prerequisites are completed by all members)
- Enables the Party chat channel (used by typing [/p "Text"])
- Character information is displayed for all group members

Ultimately, groups are able to accomplish more things than a solo player, especially in the later stages of the game. The quantity and type of loot you receive improves dramatically when going through Instances, Raids, and other group-related content.

LOOT SYSTEMS EXPLAINED

Party loot systems are very important to most players. Unless you only play with friends and guildmates, it's important to find a fair system that distributes loot in a way that keeps everyone content.

The Master Looter system allows the party leader to loot all of the monster bodies, then assign loot to the appropriate characters within the group. This takes more time for many parties because the looter has to manage quite a few more items and trades. Beyond that, Bind on Acquire items cannot be traded. This means that the looter has to "unlock" the body (by clicking on it then backing away), and that opens the body for looting by everyone in the group.

Round Robin is entirely fair in one sense, because it gives corpses to each person in turn, making sure that everyone gets their chance for some loot. Yet, chance has it that one character could get many good items on a given run while others receive very little. Also, Round Robin makes it likely that players receive items that their characters cannot use to their fullest ("My Mage got some new plate armor, woot."). Thus, players still end up trading a great deal and often implement Need Before Greed rules.

The fastest and most efficient system, yet the hardest one to use in pickup groups, is Free-for-All. The glory of FFA is that everyone in the group can grab bodies and loot without delay. The process is very fast, and whoever has the free time to loot can do it for the others in the group. When Bind on Acquire items fall, the best person for an item is decided and takes the item. For vendor bait (items of selling value but little power), everyone just tries to grab their share. In a party of friends, FFA is incredible. In a party of strangers, there is a fair chance of someone getting burned (doing all the fighting while some other player is scooping up everything that isn't nailed down).

Systems have been added to allow group leaders to set a Threshold for items and allow immediate rolling for items. Anything that drops of a certain quality level at or above the Threshold spawns a box for the group members (they can pass on the item or roll randomly for it). The player who rolls the highest immediately gets the item.

Need Before Greed mode expands on this by disallowing a roll for characters who cannot use the item in question.

Which system is the best to use? As you have probably guessed, it depends on the group, its leader, and the needs of the current mission.

LOOT SYSTEMS

NAME	BEST FOR	DESCRIPTION
Master	Careful Distribution	Group Leader Loots All Bodies and Redistributes
Round Robin	Speed With Some Equality	Each Characters Gets a Corpse to Loot (In Turns)
Group Loot	Avoiding Ninja Looters	Allows Everyone to Roll on Powerful Items
Need Before Greed	Raising the Fairness of Drops	Only Allows Characters Who Can Use an Item to Get It
Free-for-All	Pure Speed and Ease of Use	Everyone Can Loot Any Corpse

WHAT IS A RAIDING PARTY?

Raiding parties are basically groups of parties. For difficult Instances, large-scale PvP attacks, or actual raid areas, these large groups are welcome (or even needed).

The first stage of a raiding party is to gather several fully-independent groups. This isn't a situation where everyone just clumps together and it doesn't matter which person is in which group. Indeed, leadership and organization are either the beauty or bane of raid work. Without organization, it is extremely hard to succeed when there are so many people together in a tight area.

Thus, groups need to have an experienced leader at their head. The raid leader/organizer should often be the person with the most experience and skill in commanding for the given task. That means a talented PvPer should be at the head of a raiding party against another faction. A person who has been down Blackrock Spire 30+ times should lead two groups into the Instance.

Raiding parties are discussed at much greater length later in the guide, primarily in the Advanced Player vs. Environment chapter. Raids aren't needed or often done by characters at the lower or even mid-tier levels, so knowing what they are is more than enough for now. Learn more about raids in Chapter 7.

WHEN TO GROUP

Groups offer many things to both casual and hardcore players. But, that doesn't mean they are perfect for everything. It's good to know what you want before seeking a group; this makes it much easier to achieve your goals.

Groups are able to complete quests at a faster pace for Kill Quests, Escorts, and Exploration/Delivery Quests. However, groups are far slower when dealing with Collection Quests (especially if ground spawns are involved). If pure speed is an issue, it's wise to solo while collecting items, and group when attacking monsters, escorting, or exploring high-level areas.

When it comes to farming coin, the situation is quite complex. Solo characters get a fair bit of money if they go after the right targets in an area with many monsters. Yet, food/water expenses and downtime reduce income by a substantial margin. On the flipside, groups of five people have quite a few pockets. Duos (groups with only two characters) are actually pretty optimal for farming weaker monsters. If money is your goal, try soloing humanoid monsters or forming a duo with a complementary partner.

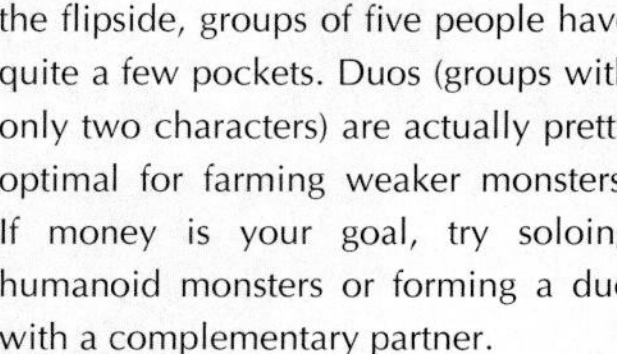

DUOS

Many duos work quite well, but certain combinations are even better for specific tasks. Remember that everyone has both strengths and weaknesses; if you choose a duo that accounts for the weaknesses, it makes life much easier. For example, Warriors hold aggro, making the fighting safer for low armor classes (Rogues, Mages, Priests).

Even beyond the class pairings, try to find someone willing to play to the duos strengths and minimize weaknesses. If a Priest and Mage group, it is obvious that tanking isn't a strongpoint of the pair. Instead, those two would succeed quickly by using their high DPS and leaning heavily on burst damage to keep enemies from engaging for long periods.

Fun is a fine goal, and groups are easily the best target for having a good time. Making friends with good players and nice people makes the game better no matter what you enjoy. Even for quests when groups aren't needed, having buddies around reduces (or even removes) any tedium from slaying entire bands of roving wolves and bears.

GOOD REASONS TO GROUP

- Trying to complete red or elite quests
- Dealing with kill/explore/escort quests
- Farming for money in small groups
- Taking on Instances in full groups
- Forming raids for high-end content
- Safety in PvP-intense areas (e.g. Hillsbrad)
- To play with friends!

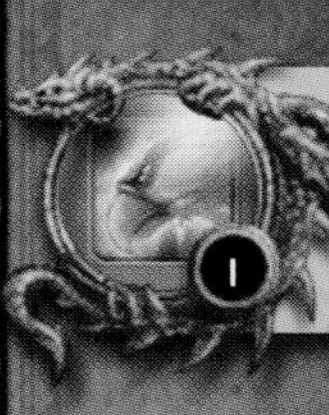

WHEN NOT TO GROUP

Okay, so you see the reasons to party and the times when it is desired/needed. Here is the other side of grouping; there are goals that make grouping a bad idea.

Gaining experience in a group can be slow at certain stages of the game. Unlike a number of MORGs, *World of Warcraft* is dedicated to making it easy to level even when you play as a solo character. Indeed, leveling during solo play is perfectly fast if you keep your skills, gear, and items up to par. Take a great deal of food/water out with you and slash down the beasts of the open field. This pulls in experience at a very impressive clip, dwarfing just about any group that can't get into motion quickly, find very target-rich areas, and stay focused the entire time.

During the low levels, quests are worth an even higher percentage of total experience gained. If you're trying to fly through the levels, jump into groups for the group-friendly quests (as listed above), but solo all of the collection quests. Grinding solo kills on the way to and from quests is also a major way to improve experience efficiency. These are efficient kills because you gain hit points and mana on the move, so your character is getting to fight without the same level of downtime.

This is an obvious point, but it's not useful to group when the players you meet are unfriendly, uncooperative, or just don't match your style of play. If a group isn't enjoyable, it's not worth your time. Gold, experience, and leveling means so much more when you're having a good time, and players who enjoy the game tend to have better characters. Even with a stat-specific view of things, happier players end up with more potent characters (these people play more because they are having a good time, and more hours equals more experience, treasure, and power).

WHAT COMPRISES A "GOOD" GROUP

This is certainly a subject for debate, but good groups are the ones that fulfill your goals without making game time stressful. You, as a player, get to decide what a good group is for your needs. If you want pure experience and money, simply look for the groups that are intense, dedicated to a high kill-count, and play consistently. If fun is your target, find players who relax a bit more, joke around, talk more, and explore.

There are so many players on each sever that there are always people who share your interests and goals. Don't try to push other players into your mold; it takes less time and is better for everyone is you seek like-minded players from the beginning. Let the PvPers fight, let the roleplayers get into their roles, etc.

WHAT IS A QUEST?

The *World of Warcraft* has a Quest system in place that not only helps you learn the history of the land, but also gives experience separate from killing creatures. Experience earned from these quests does not count against your rest state and automatically adjusts the experience needed until your state changes. There are many different types of quests players can take part in. This is designed to make leveling fun and interesting; the system also helps to guide players from one area to the next at appropriate times, making it easier to know where it's "safe" to continue adventuring.

TYPES OF QUESTS

There are many types of quests that are offered in the *World of Warcraft* from simple Kill Quests to the more involved Storyline Quests. They are designed to allow players to decide on the amount of time investment they want to make.

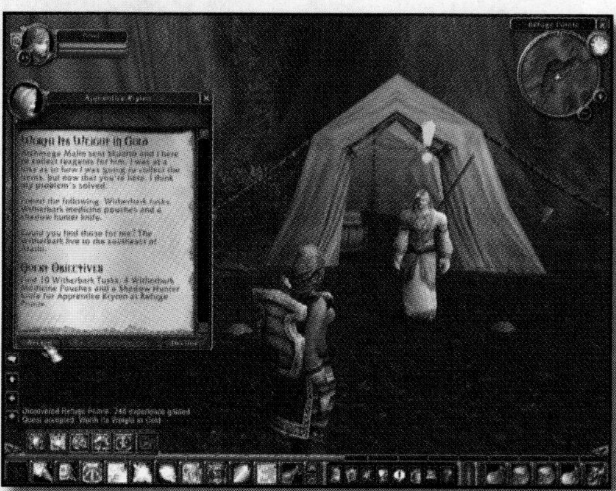

KILL QUEST

Kill Quests ask you to go out and either kill a number of creatures or a named NPC. These types of quests are often best to do in a group if time is an issue. While the experience of the kills is spread out among the group, everyone gets credit for the kills. Often when killing an NPC for a quest you are required to bring back proof of the kill. These quests allow all the group members to loot the item off of the corpse and do not have to be repeated in order for all members to get the item. The few exceptions ask that you complete the quest alone.

GATHER QUEST

Gather quests (also known as Collection Quests by many players) request that you go out get a specific number of items either from a location or from creatures. These can be done in groups to accomplish the quest safely; note that only one of the item at a time is lootable from any creature. Unlike the Kill Quests requiring you to bring back a head or an item, these are not shared quest items.

DELIVERY QUEST

These quests require that you deliver an item from one place to another. The risk isn't in facing any particular creature or killing anything on your way (generally speaking). The risk comes from traveling through hostile territory and making it through alive. As an additional challenge, some of these quests are timed. Packages must be delivered within that time in order to be successful.

ESCORT QUEST

Escort Quests ask you to keep an NPC safe as you travel through dangerous territory. These are often difficult to do solo and an entire group can benefit from completing it together. Often you must defeat creatures that attempt to kill the person/creature you are escorting and keep the escort safe until they reach a designated location.

QUEST MODIFIERS

Not all quests play by the same rules. Some quests are race/class specific, and others are only given by certain factions. These quest modifiers are explained below.

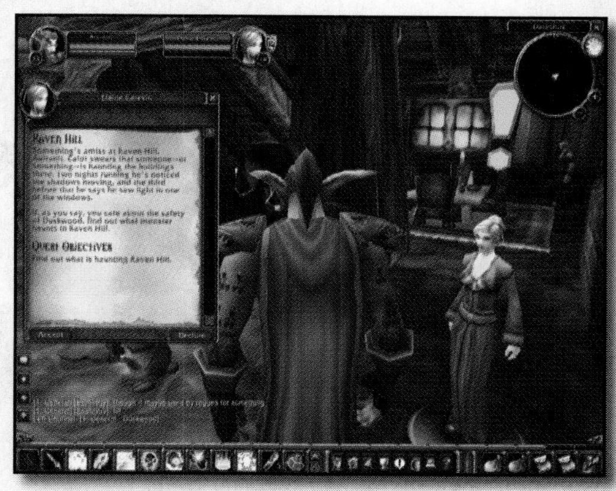

FACTION QUEST

Faction quests involve gaining faction with an NPC or group of NPCs in order to complete the quest. This can involve killing opposing NPCs or by doing some task that they would like done. Because the Reputation System can rise and fall based on your actions toward certain factions, these quests are often repeatable. Thus, you have a means of staying in good graces with a faction even if there are occasional problems (Sorry I killed your Auntie, but here is a Troll Necklace!).

CLASS QUEST

Class Quests are specific to one class. They grant new powers, knowledge, abilities, or special items to the character that completes them. These can be done solo or in a group depending on your own abilities, but the group gains little unless they are of the same class. Find other characters entering the Class Quest or try to help others going their own quests in return for assistance on yours.

SERIES QUESTS

Series Quests are quests that are a part of a larger and evolving storyline. As players accomplish each part of the quest, it gets more difficult as you complete each one. The last quest is often a final encounter against a boss monster and offers a fantastic reward.

ELITE QUESTS

Elite Quests pit you against NPCs that are indicated as being elite. These NPCs have more hit points than others of their level and are much tougher to kill. These are generally group-friendly quests and may take you and your group into Instances. Elite Quests often take the most time to complete.

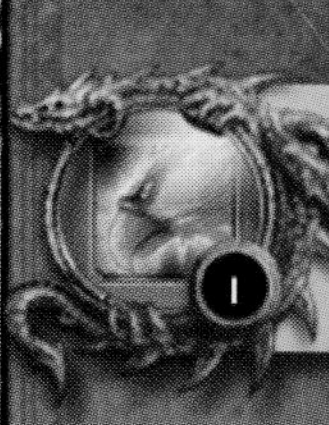

FINDING AND COMPLETING QUESTS

It's easy to find quests in many areas. Quest givers that have quests available in your level range have yellow exclamation points above their heads. NPCs that have a silver exclamation point above their head have a quest waiting for you when you reach a higher level.

Only a few quests within *World of Warcraft* are repeatable. Once a quest giver has given you all the quests they can, no more exclamation marks hover over their head.

After Right Clicking on a quest-giving NPC, a quest log appears to tell you what the quest is all about and what kind of reward you shall receive. Players have the option of either accepting the quest or turning down the request. Don't worry if you turn down a quest. It is possible to return to the NPC to get it once more. Just be careful about turning one down that may be a part of a series.

Quests are stored in your log file on your hotbar and can be brought up by using the default "L" hotkey. Twenty quests can be stored in your log at any time (any additional quests are ignore until some of these are cleared or abandoned).

Your log file automatically organizes your quests for you and puts them into categories based on where the quest was received. It also is color coded to indicate how difficult a quest is for you.

CLUSTERING QUESTS

To save a lot of running time, cluster your quests by doing several in one area at a time rather than running around from place to place. For that matter, complete several quests in a specific section of a map before returning to town (this is very efficient and leads to faster leveling).

Grey indicates the quest is easy and will only give a fraction of normal experience for having completed it at a lower level. Generally this is as little as 1/10th of the entire possible experience.

Green indicates a quest is easy with a minimal amount of danger. You will receive normal experience for it however; this may seem small compared to the level you are at.

Yellow indicates the quest is within equal range of your level and has significant risk however with proper preparedness can be accomplished either alone or with a minimal group. At this range experience is right on target for your level.

Orange indicates the quest is difficult and will most likely need a group. Experience should be better than normal.

Red indicates danger! With a solid group you may well pull it off, but it's likely a good idea not to solo. Death may be the only thing you get out of going up against a quest that difficult. Give it a level or two and watch to see when it changes to orange or yellow to make it more attainable.

QUEST COLORS

COLOR	DIFFICULTY	RESULT
Red	Requires Group	Very High Experience (Items of Considerable Power for Current Level)
Orange	May Require Group	High Quest Experience (Items of Higher Level)
Yellow	Standard	Full Quest Experience
Green	Easy	Almost Full Experience
Grey	Trivial	Substantial Reduction of Quest Experience

It is as easy to find the end of a quest as it is the start of one. Ending quest NPCs have a yellow question mark over their heads. In addition, these NPCs appear on your minimap, so guiding your character back to them is very easy.

BUT WAIT THERE'S MORE?

Make sure to double-check an NPC that you turn a quest into. They may have another yellow exclamation point over their head indicating they have another quest or a follow-up quest for you. (This often takes up to a minute as the character speaks about the previous quest.)

When finishing a quest you are often given an award in addition to the experience. Rewards are often in the form of cash and/or a choice of objects. Even if you are unable to use an item it is possible to sell it to a vendor. Quest items are soulbound and cannot be traded between players; sell unusable items to a vendor and enjoy the extra cash. Or, if you are an Enchanter, disenchant the item and use the ingredients for creating something more powerful.

QUEST SHARING

An exciting feature of *World of Warcraft* is the ability to share quests. If your character is the only person with a certain quest in a group, it is easy to "give" the quest to everyone else in the party who's in close proximity. In effect, you become the quest giver for the others, though they return to the normal NPC for their completion rewards.

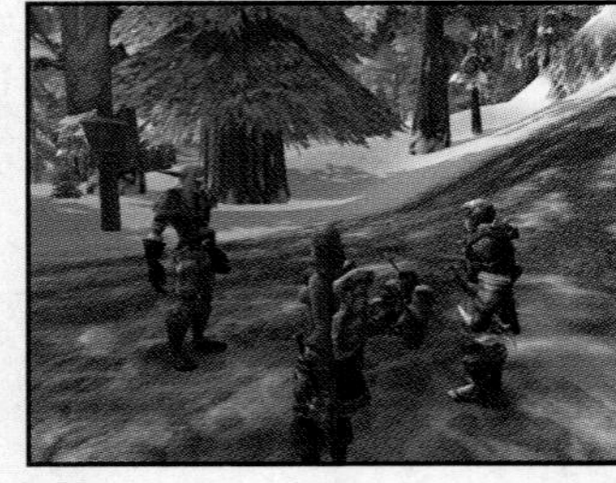

You cannot share quests if there are prerequisites that the rest of the party haven't accomplished, if the quest requires the delivery of an item, or if the quest is class/race related and they aren't of said class/race.

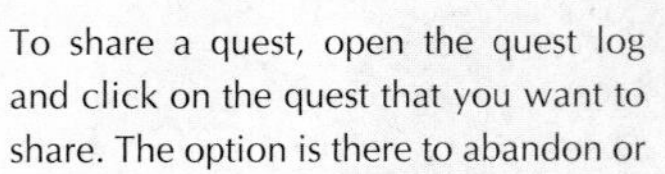

To share a quest, open the quest log and click on the quest that you want to share. The option is there to abandon or share the quest; choose "Share" and your entire party is queried with that quest (if they accept it, you are good to go).

ABANDONING QUESTS

At any time, you are free to abandon a quest. This clears the quest out of your log (making room for other quests). The original NPC that gave you the quest resets, thus enabling you to start the quest again at a later point. You can abandon quests for the quest log space, for convenience (if you know you won't do the quest again), or to make a second attempt at a quest you have failed. Timed Quests and Escort Quests are the most likely to fail; these should be abandoned and tried a second time.

DEATH AND REBIRTH

The lives of adventurers would be short indeed if death were a permanent fixture in MOGs. Either that or people would spend far more time inside inns, hoping that various abominations wouldn't burst through the door. To make the game world a bit more fun, and much more survivable, Blizzard has implemented a system without vicious death penalties. This section explains the various types of death that your character could face and how to respond to these situations.

WAYS TO DIE

Characters that are slain drop to the ground and are taken out of your control. It's impossible to move, cast spells, speak normally, or do anything of importance to yourself or your group. Private and guild messages are allowed, so you can message nearby folks to let them know if you need a "Rez" (Resurrection).

Your character enters this state when his or her hit points drop to zero. Falling from too high a distance, being struck by physical or mystical forces, or drowning can all cause you to die. There's no starvation in *World of Warcraft*, nor are their status effects that directly cause death. In other words, Poisons can delete your Hit Points until death overcomes your character, but there are no "instant death" abilities or similar dangers. Keep your hit points high and life goes on. (Of course, if you simply get hit with a single shot that does enough damage to wipe out your entire health bar, you will die.)

THE PATH TO BETTER HEALTH

There are several ways to respond after your character dies. Each method of revival has different consequences, so it's wise to learn all three methods before stepping onto the field of battle.

RETURNING TO YOUR BODY (RELEASE AND RETURN)

The most common method of revival comes from "Releasing" and returning to your corpse. Click on the Release button that appears once your character falls; this teleports you to the nearest graveyard for your faction. As a spirit, you can see the world around you, but other characters and monsters are hidden from view. Only other spirits of your faction and the nearby Spirit Healer are visible.

A blip on the minimap appears to lead you toward your body. (This could appear as an arrow on the circumference of the minimap indicating the correct direction.) Follow this and don't worry about random monsters. Take a direct path and only avoid a fast route if the land prevents a direct line to your body (impassable barriers often force you off track). Once you get near your body, the line between life and death blurs (this causes monsters to become visible to your spirit). Move closer to your corpse until an option appears to "Revive." Click on this in a spot where you are safe from the aggro of nearby monsters or PvPers.

Reviving in this manner has no penalty on your character's experience. Also, you are returned to your body with 50% of your maximum hit points and mana (these return normally after that point). There is no Resurrection Sickness, and you are free to adventure normally.

When returning to your body, make sure that all the spiders are gone.
Hey! Hey, I see you back there! There's like thirty of you guys!
I told you this wasn't going to work.
Just be cool!

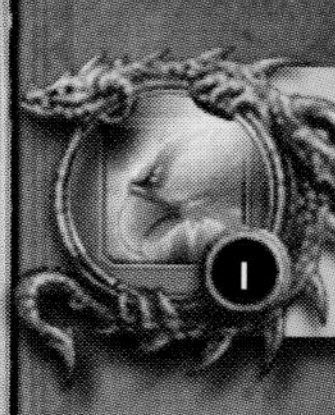

GLOSSARY OF TERMS
NAMING YOUR CHARACTER
ETIQUETTE
10 THINGS WORTH KNOWING
THE DO'S AND THE DO NOT'S
EQUIPMENT, ENEMIES, & LEVELS
PARTY DYNAMICS
WHAT IS A QUEST?
DEATH AND REBIRTH
MIGRATING PLAYERS
MACROS
KEYBOARD LAYOUTS
EXPRESSIONS

RESURRECTION (REZ)

If there's an allied person in the area where your body falls, Resurrection may be possible. Shaman, Paladins, Priests, and Warlocks have various powers to Resurrect player characters. In the first case, Shaman, Paladins, and Priests cast spells on corpses that bring a button onto the dead player's screen. If you wish to be Resurrected, click on the button that appears.

You appear almost instantly in the area, alive but not well. Depending on the spell used, your character may have as little as 1% of their hit points and mana. Beyond that, you are afflicted by Resurrected Sickness, a malady that dramatically reduces your attributes for a short period. There are stages of Rez Sickness, with each stage lasting between 1 and 2 minutes. The first two stages of Rez Sickness are by far the worst, and your character should be able to resume fighting once these are weathered.

Other than Resurrection Sickness, there are no penalties to accepting a Resurrection. Your character suffers no experience penalty or long-term attribute harm. Thus, the tradeoff with Resurrection over a Release and Return is a matter of time at low attributes vs. a possibly long walk.

In general, if the walk is greatly shorter than the first stage or two of Rez Sickness, it's better to Release and Return, even when a rezzer offers to help you.

Warlocks and Soulstones

Okay, there were four classes mentioned at the beginning of this subsection. Warlocks are able to Resurrect people as well, but it's a special Warlock ability that merits an explanation. Warlocks turn Soul Shards (collected from enemies as the creatures die) into various stones. One of these items is a Soulstone. Warlocks give these to other characters, and they have an ability to automatically Resurrect those who die.

If you have a Soulstone, it is activated 5 seconds after you die. Your character returns to life in the location where you fell, afflicted with Rez Sickness and having few hit points and little mana. The Soulstone is destroyed in the process.

This power is quite good for use in Instance Dungeons, where losing a character with Resurrect almost spells the end of a good expedition. Even a total party wipeout can be reversed with these items (always give the first Soulstone to the party's primary rezzer).

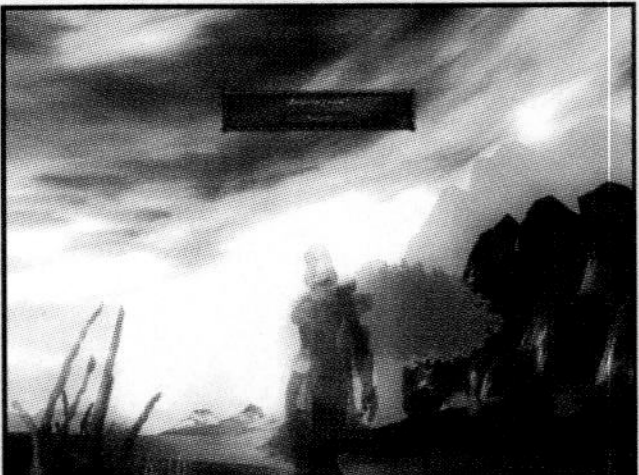

THE SPIRIT HEALER (REZ AT SH)

Okay, so there had to be a costly method somewhere. People who cannot retrieve their bodies, are too tired or frustrated to try, or who want a Very fast rez without any Sickness can choose to Resurrect at the Spirit Healer.

In every graveyard, a Spirit Healer patiently waits within the astral realm for those unfortunate adventurers whose spirits will soon join them. These floating figures of death and rebirth return people to life where their spirit stands (thus, you appear at the graveyard of the nearest allied faction). Even if you make the long run to a farther graveyard and use their Spirit Healer, your body appears at the yard closest to your corpse. The good news is that you appear with all stats intact, ready to fight immediately.

Does this mean that the Spirit Healer is a bad deal for most players? Yes, most of the time it does, but in no way is the Spirit Healer a bad thing to consider in special cases. If you are so far away from your corpse that a run would cost major time and frustration, it might be worth a rez at the SH. Or, if you die way out in the ocean somewhere, or at a place that is almost unreachable anyway, it's worth avoiding the trouble.

In odd cases, during a fight near your graveyard, you can use the SH to enter a battle almost immediately after dying (avoiding the PvP Resurrection Timer). This is a dramatic case where someone really cares more about winning than their long-term goals, but it's nice to have options.

DEATH IN INSTANCE DUNGEONS

Instances won't allow characters to return to their corpses from the outside the dungeon; this would make it too easy to regroup and continue fighting in the more challenging Instances. Though Resurrection spells and Soulstones work in the same manner inside and outside the Instance Dungeons, trying to Release and Return to your body fails. Instead, as soon as your spirit enters the Instance Dungeon, your body reincorporates at the beginning of the dungeon.

In terms of experience and safety, this is actually a great thing. You revive faster and are often in a location that is quite safe from aggro. The hidden penalty here is simply that parties aren't able to survive losing a character during an Instance run without using either Resurrection or a Warlock Ritual of Summoning (once the person has revived normally).

MIGRATING PLAYERS

Blizzard and their *Warcraft* series has been a solid gaming foundation for many years. *Warcraft* is considered one of the most successful RTS series' in gaming and now they have taken it a step further. What once was a point and click, a "zug zug" and a "my liege" is now a living breathing 3D world. When once you were a general, or even a god in some cases, you are now sucked down into the root of the game looking up as one of the players among many. This may be a bit of an adjustment for those that have never ventured into the MMORPG climate before. For those that have played MOGs before, it will still be a slight adjustment, though one easily made.

For those entering into the MMORPG genre for the first time, the *World of Warcraft* forces a slight adjustment to your thinking. There are codes of conduct and rules of interaction among those that have been in the MMORPG community that differ somewhat from those that circulate the RTS or FPS venues. Be patient as you learn. While you don't need to completely change your gaming style, you will have to blend it with those around you.

Where once you commanded your own armies and they listened without question, now you are one of the many and must work not only as a part of a team, but as one of the multitudes in a team. Most RTS players have experienced teamwork in the form of alliances vying against others and understand all too well how good teamwork can work in their favor. However, in this case you've been shrunk down and placed into the *World of Warcraft* as one of the peons until you work your way up in the ranks. Where before your underlings listened to your every whim and performed their duties exactly to your specifications, now you must deal with other players as singular as you are. Saying "jump" no longer makes others jump—at least not until you earn their respect.

Those that have played FPS' primarily understand the teamwork involved easily enough if you have ever participated in Capture the Flag or Team Deathmatch events. However, where everyone once had the same resources and character type, here everyone is different based on their class and race. Without knowledge of others capabilities, it is more difficult to work together as a team. Things work slower. There is more time for interaction with others beyond a simple macro.

Terms that you may have used regularly before have changed and new ones have been blended in. Those that have played the *Warcraft* series know creatures you have fought as "creeps" and you'll now hear them being referred to as "mobs." The same applies if you are transitioning from another MMORPG only the opposite. It's understandable to want to hold on to what you've always known, however times change and all transitioning players will need to learn the terms of the other players until it all shakes out.

The interface will be both familiar and alien. For those coming from *Warcraft*, you'll be used to seeing a slightly different layout for your stat bars and hotkeys. For Instance Party members will no longer sit in the middle bottom of your interface, but instead will show in the upper left side.

While the placement is not the same the elements are very similar and work similarly. Some things have to change for the mechanic for a 3D game vs. a 2D game, but the fundamental ideas are still very much intact.

In many cases those that have played the *Diablo* series will find the *World of Warcraft* interface a bit more familiar. Hotkeys run along the bottom bar and can be shifted between quickly and easily. Quest information and statistics can be pulled up with other hotkeys on the bar, a linked hotkey on your keyboard, or a simple mouse click.

If you have been used to using point and click to move about the world, don't worry; a version of point and click is in the game and for those that are used to wasd and keyboard movement that is available also. It's all based on your preference and getting used to the mechanics that are in place.

WHAT'S THE SAME? TRANSITIONING FROM WARCRAFT

Here is just a sampling of many of the things you will find to be the same. In many cases things you knew in game, such as Moon Wells, are not a useable resource. They are used as back-story and environmental atmosphere. Ancients wander the pathways of the Night Elf territory rather than sit rooted in place. Griffons and Zeppelins are not troops to be commanded, but instead are a public means of transportation for players to travel between continents or regions of the map.

The Storyline: Those that have played *Warcraft* will already be familiar with the storyline within the *World of Warcraft*. Things have picked up right after the end of *Warcraft III: The Frozen Throne* and are continuing; only now, the players are a part of it all.

The Geography: While some areas are yet to be available the names should be familiar: the destroyed city of Lordaeron, Stormwind, Ashenvale and Tidus Stair among many.

Potions and Scrolls: There are many types of potions and scrolls in the game. Players can even take alchemy in order to learn how to make their own potions.

Monsters: Many of the creatures within the game will be familiar. While some of the names may seem slightly different in other areas, you'll easily recognize them.

Playable Races: You'll be familiar with the races within the *World of Warcraft*. This is your chance at last to slip into their skin and play.

Magic and Melee: As you go up in level, so too can you learn new abilities much the same as you did in *Warcraft III*. However now you will need to visit a trainer and there are many options that open up to you.

Quests: NPCs that offer quests appear with yellow exclamation points over their heads much the same as you've experienced in *Warcraft III*.

There are many more similarities that a transitioning player will find exciting and the joy of discovering similarities and differences is infectious.

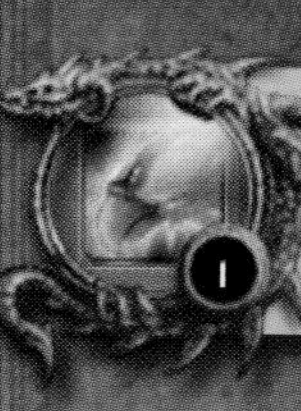

WHAT'S THE SAME? TRANSITIONING FROM OTHER MMORPGS

There are many elements within the *World of Warcraft* that transitioning MMORPG players will find comforting. There are too many to list however we have contained a sampling of things you can find.

Auction Houses: In *World of Warcraft,* players are able to place their items for sale in Auction Houses to sell at a set price or at a bidder's price. These help take out the need to hawk your wares in an trade channel. While Auction Houses may not be run the same as in other games, the similiarities of function are enough to help transitioning players feel right at home.

Guild Management Features: Guilds and Clans are a mainstay of MMORPGs and the ability to manage them well is important. There are ways of keeping tabs on players, putting notes on them, creating new ranks, placing a message of the day and even creating a guild tabard for guild members to wear.

Chat Management Features: Players can create their own chat channels and windows, change the font color and the things that appear in those chat boxes among other things. This is another feature that has become popular in MORGs over the years as they have progressed.

PvE: Those that come from PvE heavy games will understand the need to manage aggro and pathing issues that come with different areas. Experienced players will find it comforting to know that many of their tactics still work the same as before. Others, such as kiting, may require an adjustment in your hunting methods.

Grouping: Parties, creating parties and managing parties all have great useable features that experienced players will appreciate.

One of the greatest adjustments comes from using the interface if you are unfamiliar with the RTSs that Blizzard has produced, though the interface is customizable for tech savvy players.

NEW PLAYERS

There will inevitably be many new players that will find themselves drawn to the *World of Warcraft.* Some may have never wanted to play the RTS series and find themselves interested in its newest incarnation as an MMORPG. Some may have never played an MMORPG as well and are entering into the game as a whole new adventure.

The best advice is to read all the documentation you can and be patient both with yourself and others. *World of Warcraft* does not have as steep of a learning curve as many other games and Blizzard has created a world that is rich to explore along with in-game touches that help you to learn.

One such example of a place that helps players is within the Undead city of Undercity. Within the Mage quarter there is a demonstrator, or DEMONstrator (if we play with the pun involved), that helps give a general idea to budding Warlocks on the kinds of pets they can look forward to earning in the future as well as some of their strengths and weaknesses. For the starting player this can be a handy resource.

Death is relatively painless and offers the opportunity to try new things, experiment and learn. Whether you are a long time player or new to it all, there is plenty that will keep your interested. Don't be afraid to use other players as a resource as well. While occasionally you may run into some rude players (or those RPing rude characters), generally speaking, most people are willing to help.

MACROS

Macros allow users to create hotkeys that can perform custom commands based on the player's individual needs. They can utilize the many slash (/) commands in the game and have over 300 different icons from which to choose and assign to the individual macros.

While there are many things that macros allow you to do, there are some things that they won't. They will not allow you to create bots (automated characters) or automate long strings of tasks. Macros only allow 256 characters (including spaces); they must be short and to the point. They will, however, allow you to simplify many tasks.

CREATING MACROS

There are two ways to open the macro creation tool. Either type **/ macro** in the chat window or click on the dialogue balloon icon on the left side of your default chat window. This opens up a box of commands including the macro choice at the bottom.

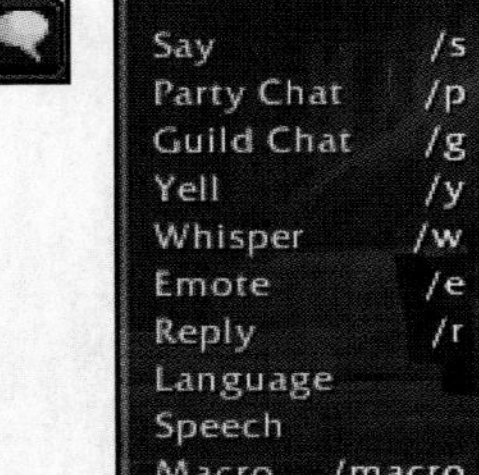

Once you have begun your macro creation, select the "new" option at the bottom of the box.

A new box appears to the right allowing you to name your macro and choose the icon that is assigned to it.

Name your macro, choose your new icon and then select "okay." That puts your new icon into the macro creation box for editing. In the box at the bottom, you can type in the command that you want to use. In this example we used a heal spell.

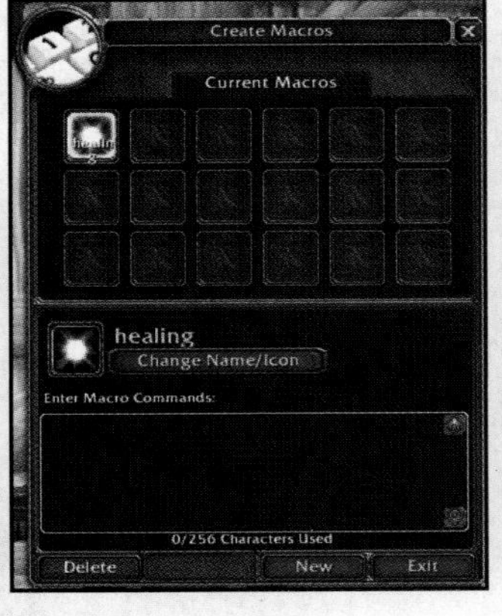

There are two different ways you can add a spell or ability to your macro. You can type it in **/cast Greater Heal(Rank 1)** or you can open your spell book and Shift + Click on the correct spell or ability. Once you've finished your macro, just click on the "X" in the upper right corner.

To edit your macro, open the macro creation interface and click on the icon of the macro you wish to edit. You'll be able to change the name, the icon and the function of the macro quickly and easily.

SLASH COMMANDS

Here are the "slash" commands (commands beginning with "/") available in the game. You can search through the commands in your chat dialogue box by typing in the first letter of the command you would like to search for (Example: /b), then use the Tab key to scroll through them.

EMOTES IN MACROS

Macros can easily incorporate emotes. Refer to the Expressions section of this guide to see the emotes available to you.

The macro sections follow this format:

MACRO NAME

Macro Description

Macro Example

GENERAL COMMANDS

/ASSIST

Your character assists the target.

/CAST

This command allows you to cast spells by name.

/cast Mana Burn (Rank 1)

/EM OR /ME

Creates an emote.

/em takes a bow while looking quite embarrassed.

/EXIT

Quits the game

/FOLLOW (/F)

Allows you to follow another player.

/follow Wilhelm

/INVITE (/INV)

Invites a player into your party/group.

/invite Wilhelm

/LOGOUT

Logs you out of the game.

/PLAYED

Shows the amount of time you have played your character.

/PVP

This command puts your character in pvp mode so that you can be attacked.

/RANDOM

Generates a number between two specified numbers. This can be useful in determining looting rights or other decisions.

/random 1 100

/SIT

Takes your character from a standing position to a sitting position. Players regenerate faster while sitting.

GENERAL COMMANDS

/ASSIST

Your character assists the target.

/CAST

This command allows you to cast spells by name.

/cast Mana Burn (Rank 1)

/EM OR /ME

Creates an emote.

/em takes a bow while looking quite embarrassed.

/EXIT

Quits the game

/FOLLOW (/F)

Allows you to follow another player.

/follow Wilhelm

/INVITE (/INV)

Invites a player into your party/group.

/invite Wilhelm

/LOGOUT

Logs you out of the game.

/PLAYED

Shows the amount of time you have played your character.

/PVP

This command puts your character in pvp mode so that you can be attacked.

/RANDOM

Generates a number between two specified numbers. This can be useful in determining looting rights or other decisions.

/random 100

/SIT

Takes your character from a standing position to a sitting position. Players regenerate faster while sitting.

/STAND

Takes your player from the sitting position to the standing position.

/WHO

Lists the players online.

CHAT COMMANDS

/# OR /C OR /CSAY

Send text to channel #

/2 Where can I find the rogue trainer?

/ANNOUNCEMENTS (/ANN)

Toggles the join and leave announcements on a channel.

/AFK

Sets an Away From Keyboard flag and message if you wish.

/afk having lunch

/BAN

Bans a player from a channel.

/CHATHELP (/CHAT)

List of chat commands.

/CHATLIST, /CHATWHO, OR /CHATINFO <CHANNEL>

List channels, or channel members.

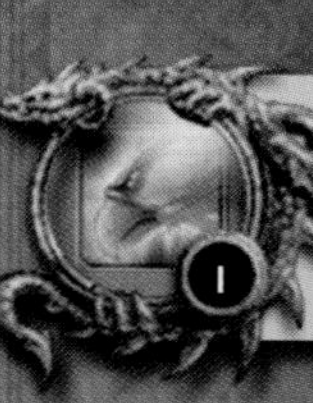

/CHATINVITE OR /CINVITE

Invite a player to a channel.

/DND

Sets a "Do Not Disturb" flag and a message—if you wish.

/dnd phonecall

/JOIN, /CHANNEL, OR /CHAN

Join a specific channel.

/join Raid

/KICK

Kick a player off a channel.

/LEAVE, /CHATLEAVE, OR /CHATEXIT

Leave a channel.

/leave general

/MODERATOR (/MOD)

Change a player's moderator status.

/MODERATE

Toggle moderation on a channel

/MUTE, /SQUELCH, /UNVOICE, /UNMUTE, /UNSQUELCH, OR /VOICE

Change a player's permission.

/PARTY (/P)

Sends a message to your party/group.

/PASSWORD

Change password.

/pass Raid blunderbuss

/REPLY (/R)

Sends a private message to the last person that whispered to you or sent a tell. Use the Tab key to scroll through those that last whispered as well.

/SAY (/S)

Sends a message to those that are nearby you in a public channel.

/TELL (/T) OR /WHISPER (/W)

This sends a private message to the person to whom you wish to speak.

/tell Wilhelm Meet me at the Zepplin.

/whisper Wilhelm Meet me at the Zepplin.

Use the Tab key to scroll through the people who last whispered to you.

/UNBAN

Unbans a player from a channel.

/UNMODERATOR (/UNMOD)

Changes the moderator status of a player.

/YELL (/Y)

Sends a message out to zone.

GUILD COMMANDS

/GINFO

Gives the start date, number of players and number of accounts in your guild.

/G

Sends a message to your guild channel.

/O

Sends a message to the officer channel of the guild.

/GDEMOTE

Demotes a player one rank within your guild

/GDISBAND

Allows a guild leader to disband the guild.

/GHELP

Lists all the available guild commands.

/GINVITE

Invites another player to join your guild

/GLEADER

Allows the current guild leader to transfer leadership to another online player.

/GMOTD

Sets the guild's message of the day

/GPROMOTE

Promotes a player one rank within your guild

/GQUIT

Quits you from your guild

/GREMOVE

Removes a player from your guild

/GROSTER

Gives an entire guild roster (This is an officer and guildmaster command only)

MACRO IDEAS

There are many times that you want to make it known who you are healing, who you are targeting or what you are bringing back. All these things are possible by using macros.

In addition to being able to use the slash commands in the game, you also have the ability to use **%T** in place of any target with which you wish to interact. This can be useful in allowing a macro to serve more than one function by allowing it to draw on the name of the target on an individual basis rather than needing to create a macro for every named creature or person that you would want to use it on.

SAY MACRO

/say Hello Necco vs /say Hello %T

By using the %T in place of a person's name, you can now use the command to put anyone's name in its place instead of tailoring the macro to just one person specifically. Another way you could use the macro function is to create one that tells your party who you're healing or what you're casting.

SPELL MACRO

/cast Greater Heal(rank 1)

/p healing %T

Now your macro is set up so that not only do you cast your spell on the person you have targeted, but you inform your party of the fact. This sort of macro can also be used for those that are pulling a mob to the party by letting them know the kind of mob to expect.

WARNING MACRO

/cast Mind Blast(rank 2)

/p incoming %T. Heads up!

With the above macro, your party knows that you're coming with a Big Mob versus just pulling a Tiny Mob or whatever other mobs might be in that area. There are many possibilities for creating useful and time-saving macros. Take the time to experiment with what works for you and in no time you'll wonder how you ever got along without them.

KEYBOARD LAYOUTS

PC KEYBOARD

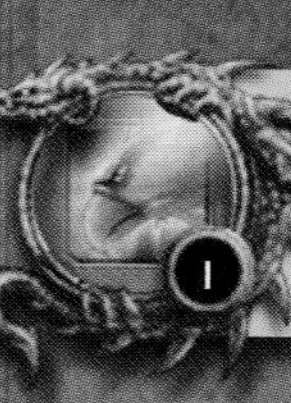

MOVEMENT

KEY	ACTION
clear (Mac)	Auto Run
Num Lock (PC)	Auto Run
W	Move Forward
A	Turn Left
S	Move Backward
D	Turn Right
Q	Strafe Left
E	Strafe Right
Space Bar	Jump
X	Toggle Sit/Stand
Z	Toggle Sheathe/ Unsheathe Weapon
NumPad /	Toggle Run/Walk

HOTBAR

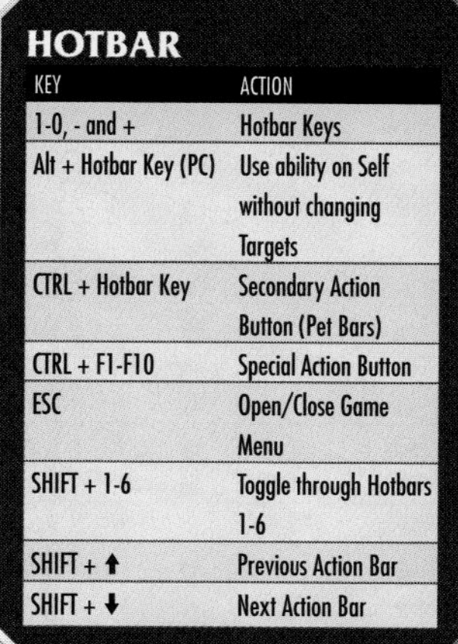

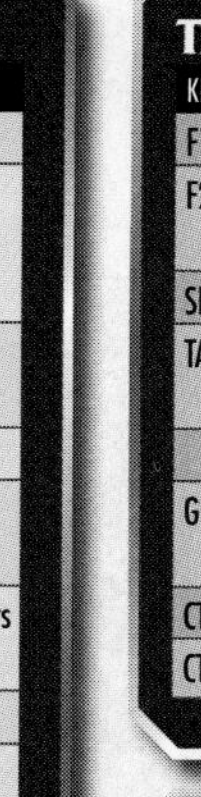

KEY	ACTION
1-0, - and +	Hotbar Keys
Alt + Hotbar Key (PC)	Use ability on Self without changing Targets
CTRL + Hotbar Key	Secondary Action Button (Pet Bars)
CTRL + F1-F10	Special Action Button
ESC	Open/Close Game Menu
SHIFT + 1-6	Toggle through Hotbars 1-6
SHIFT + ↑	Previous Action Bar
SHIFT + ↓	Next Action Bar

TARGETING

KEY	ACTION
F1	Target Self
F2 - F5	Target Party Members 2 - 5
SHIFT + F1 - F5	Target Party Pets 1 - 5
TAB	Select Front Hostile Target
	Toggle Hostile Targets
G	Select Last Hostile Target
CTRL + TAB	Target Nearest Friend
CTRL + SHIFT + TAB	Target Previous Friend

CHARACTER INFO

KEY	ACTION
C	Character Pane
SHIFT + C	Combat Log
I	Ability Pane
SHIFT + I	Pet Book
K	Skill Pane
L	Quest Log
N	Talent Pane
O	Social Pane
P	Spellbook
U	Reputation Pane

CAMERA

KEY	ACTION
Help (Mac)	Pitch Up
Insert (PC)	Pitch Up
Delete	Pitch Down
Home	Next Camera View
End	Previous Camera View
Y	Flip Camera
Keypad 2	Back
Keypad 4	Rotate Left
Keypad 8	Rotate Right
Right Mouse Button + A	Rotate Left
Right Mouse Button + D	Rotate Right

INVENTORY

KEY	ACTION
B	Open/Close Backpack
F8	Open/Close Bag 1
F9	Open/Close Bag 2
F10	Open/Close Bag 3
F11	Open/Close Bag 4
F12	Open/Close Bag 5
	Close All Bags
SHIFT + B	Open/Close All Bags

CHAT

KEY	ACTION
ENTER	Initiate Chat
/	Initiate Chat Command
R	Reply to a /whisper or /tell
/em	Initiate Emote
/v	Initiate Voice Command

ATTACKING

KEY	ACTION
T	Attack Target
SHIFT + T	Pet Attack Target
F	Assist Target

DISPLAY

KEY	ACTION
V	Show Name Plates
ALT + Z	Toggle HUD
F13 (Mac)	Capture Screenshot
Print Screen (PC)	Capture Screenshot
M	Opens Map

SOUND

KEY	ACTION
CTRL + M	Toggle Music
CTRL + S	Toggle Sound
CTRL + +	Master Volume Up
CTRL + -	Master Volume Down

MAC KEYBOARD

EXPRESSIONS

The *World of Warcraft* is an interactive world full of adventure, danger and even a bit of humor. While some of the available emotes have animations, some do not. There are even some special emotes that have sound. The possibilities for expressing the mood and personality of your character are seemingly endless. Not only are there many to choose from within the game, but you have the ability to create your own as well.

Basic Emotes

Type a "/" in front of the emote you wish to use.

/agree

/amaze

/apologize...

Created Emotes

Type "/em" in front of the text you wish to use.

/em traipses through the field picking herbs

Voice Emotes

Type /v in front of the command you wish to use.

/v oom

/v rasp

The most important thing to keep in mind is to have fun and experiment. You are only limited by your own imagination.

BASIC EMOTES

Here is the list of basic emotes. There may even be more than this, but it will be up to you to find them. Many emotes may change based on your race or your target. By not targeting anyone and typing "/laugh" your character would say, "Geriana laughs." Targeting someone and doing the same thing results in, "Geriana laughs at Barth."

BASIC EMOTES

EMOTE	ANIMATED?	TEXT
Agree	No	You agree.
Amaze	No	You are Amazed!
Angry	Yes	You raise your fist in anger.
Apologize	No	You apologize to everyone. Sorry!
Applaud	Yes	You applaud. Bravo!
Applause	Yes	You applaud. Bravo!
Beckon	No	You beckon everyone over to you.
Beg	Yes	You beg everyone around you. How pathetic.
Belch	No	You let out a loud belch.
Bite	No	You look around for someone to bite.
Bleed	No	Blood oozes from your wounds.
Blink	No	You blink your eyes.
Blood	No	Blood oozes from your wounds.
Blow	Yes	You blow a kiss into the wind.
Blush	Yes	You blush.
Boggle	Yes	You boggle at the situation.
Bonk	No	You bonk yourself on the noggin. Doh!
Bored	No	You are overcome with boredom. Oh the drudgery!
Bounce	No	You bounce up and down.
Bow	Yes	You bow down graciously.
BRB	No	You let everyone know you'll be right back.
Burp	No	You let out a belch.
Bye	Yes	You wave goodbye to everyone. Farewell!
Cackle	Yes	You cackle maniacally at the situation.
Calm	No	You remain calm.
Cat	No	You scratch yourself. Ah, much better!
Catty	No	You scratch yourself. Ah, much better!
Cheer	Yes	You cheer!
Chew	Yes	You begin to eat.
Chicken	No	With arms flapping, you strut around. Cluck, Cluck, Chicken!
Chuckle	Yes	You let out a hearty chuckle.
Clap	Yes	You clap excitedly.
Cold	No	You let everyone know that you are cold.
Comfort	No	You need to be comforted.
Commend	Yes	You commend everyone on a job well done.
Confused	Yes	You are hopelessly confused.
Congrats	Yes	You congratulate everyone around you.
Congratulate	Yes	You congratulate everyone around you.
Cough	No	You let out a hacking cough.
Cower	No	You cower in fear.
Crack	No	You crack your knuckles.
Cringe	No	You cringe in fear.
Cry	Yes	You cry.
Cuddle	No	You need to be cuddled.
Curious	Yes	You express your curiosity to those around you.
Curtsey	Yes	You curtsey.
Dance	Yes	You burst into dance.
Disappointed	No	You frown.
Doh	No	You bonk yourself on the noggin. Doh!
Doom	No	You threaten everyone with the wrath of doom.
Drink	Yes	You raise a drik in the air before chugging it down. Cheers!
Drool	No	A tendril of drool runs down your lip.
Duck	No	You duck for cover.
Eat	Yes	You begin to eat.
Eye	No	You cross you eyes.
Farewell	Yes	You wave goodbye to everyone. Farewell!
Fart	No	You fart loudly. Whew...what stinks?
Fear	No	You cower in fear.
Feast	Yes	You begin to eat.
Fidget	No	You fidget.
Flap	Yes	With arms flapping, you strut around. Cluck, Cluck, Chicken!
Flex	Yes	You flex your muscles. Oooooh so strong!
Food	No	You are hungy!
Frown	No	You frown.
Gasp	Yes	You gasp.
Gaze	No	You gaze off into the distance.
Giggle	Yes	You giggle.
Glad	No	You are filled with happiness!
Glare	No	You glare angrily.
Gloat	Yes	You gloat over everyone's misfortune.
Goodbye	Yes	You wave goodbye to everyone. Farewell!
Greet	Yes	You greet everyone warmly.
Greetings	Yes	You greet everyone warmly.
Grin	No	You grin wickedly.
Groan	No	You begin to groan.
Grovel	Yes	You grovel on the ground, wallowing in subservience.
Guffaw	Yes	You let out a boisterous guffaw!
Hail	Yes	You hail those around you.
Happy	No	You are filled with happiness!
Hello	Yes	You greet everyone with a hearty hello!
Hi	Yes	You greet everyone with a hearty hello!
Hug	No	You need a hug!
Hungry	No	You are hungry!
Impatient	No	You fidget.
Insult	Yes	You think everyone around you is a son of a motherless ogre.
Introduce	No	You introduce yourself to everyone.
JK	No	You were just kidding!
Kiss	Yes	You blow a kiss into the wind.
Kneel	Yes	You kneel down.
Knuckles	No	You crack your knuckles.
Lavish	No	You praise the Light.
Lay	Yes	You lie down.
Laydown	Yes	You lie down.
Lick	No	You lick your lips.
Lie	Yes	You lie down.
Liedown	Yes	You lie down.
Listen	No	You are listening!

Mad	Yes	You raise your fist in anger.
Massage	No	You need a massage!
Moan	No	You moan suggestively.
Mock	No	You mock life and all it stands for.
Moon	No	You drop your trousers and moon everyone.
Mourn	Yes	In quiet contemplation, you mourn the loss of the dead.
No	No	You clearly state, NO.
Nod	No	You nod.
Nosepick	No	With a finger deep in one nostril, you pass the time.
Panic	No	You run around in a frenzied state of panic.
Peer	No	You peer around, searchingly.
Peon	Yes	You grovelon the ground, wallowing in subservience.
Pest	No	You shoo the measly pests away.
Pick	No	With a finger deep in one nostril, you pass the time.
Plead	Yes	You drop to your knees and plead in desperation.
Point	Yes	You point over yonder.
Poke	No	You poke your belly and giggle.
Ponder	Yes	You ponder the situation.
Pounce	No	You pounce out from the shadows.
Praise	No	You praise the Light.
Pray	Yes	You pray to the Gods.
Purr	No	You purr like a kitten.
Puzzled	Yes	You are puzzled. What's going on here?
Question	Yes	You want to know the meaning of life.
Raise	No	You raise your hand in air.
Rdy	No	You let everyone know that you are ready!
Ready	No	You let everyone know that you are read!
Rear	No	You shake your rear.
Roar	Yes	You roar with bestial vigor. So fierce!
Rude	Yes	You make a rude gesture.
Salute	Yes	You stand at attention and salute.
Scratch	No	You scratch yourself. Ah, much better!
Sexy	No	You're too sexy for your tunic… so sexy it hurts.
Shake	No	You shake your rear.
Shimmy	No	You shimmy before the masses.
Shindig	Yes	You raise a drink in the air before chugging it down. Cheers!
Shiver	No	You shiver in your boots. Chilling!
Shoo	No	You shoo the measly pests away.
Shrug	Yes	You shrug. Who knows?
Shy	Yes	You are so shy!
Sigh	No	You let out a long, drawn-out sigh.
Sit	Yes	N/A
Slap	No	You slap yourself across the face. Ouch!
Sleep	Yes	You fall asleep. Zzzzzzz.
Smell	No	You smell the air around you. Wow, someone stinks!
Smirk	No	A sly smirk spreads across your face.
Snarl	No	You bare your teeth and snarl.
Snicker	No	You quietly snicker to yourself.
Sniff	No	You sniff the air around you.
Snub	No	You snub all the lowly peons around you.
Sob	Yes	You cry.
Soothe	No	You need to be soothed.
Sorry	No	You apologize to everyone. Sorry!
Spit	No	You spit on the ground.
Spoon	No	You need to be cuddled.
Stare	No	You stare off into the distance.
Stink	No	You smell the air around you. Wow, someone stinks!
Strong	Yes	You flex your muscles. Oooooh so strong!
Strut	Yes	With arms flapping, you strut around. Cluck, Cluck, Chicken!
Surprised	No	You are so surprised!
Surrender	Yes	You surrender to your opponents.
Talk	Yes	You talk to yourself since no one else seems interested.
TalkEx	Yes	You talk excitedly with everyone.
TalkQ	Yes	You want to know the meaning of life.
Tap	No	You tap your foot. Hurry up already!
Taunt	Yes	You taunt everyone around you. Bring it fools!
Tease	No	You are such a tease.
Thank	No	You thank everyone around you.
Thanks	No	You thank everyone around you.
Thirsty	No	You are so thirsty. Can anyone spare a drink?
Threat	No	You threaten everyone with the wrath of doom.
Tickle	No	You want to be tickled. Hee hee!
Threaten	No	You threaten everyone with the wrath of doom.
Tired	No	You let everyone know that you are tired.
TY	No	You thank everyone aroud you.
Veto	No	You veto the motion on the floor.
Victory	Yes	You bask in the glory of victory.
Volunteer	No	You raise your hand in the air.
Wave	Yes	You wave.
Weep	Yes	You cry.
Welcome	Yes	You welcome everyone.
Whine	No	You whine pathetically.
Whistle	No	You let forth a sharp whistle.
Wicked	No	You grin wickedly.
Wickedly	No	You grin wickedly.
Work	No	You begin work.
Wrath	No	You threaten everyone with the wrath of doom.
Yawn	No	You yawn sleepily.
Yay	No	You are filled with happiness.

VOICE EMOTES

Voice emotes can be used by typing in the command /v before the emote that you want to use. Often, they have more than one phrase associated with them. Different races and genders have some different emotes associated with them, so don't be afraid to experiment.

/v assist	/v help
/v charge	/v incoming
/v cheer	/v no
/v fire	/v oom
/v flee	/v rasp
/v flirt	/v silly
/v followme	/v thankyou
/v goodbye	/v wait
/v grats	/v welcome
/v heal	/v yes
/v hello	

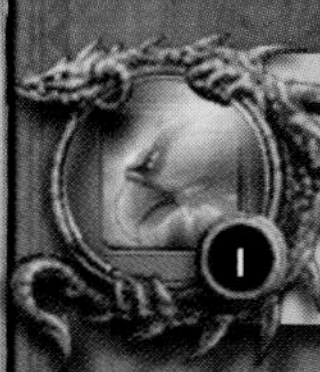

LEARNING YOUR PLACE IN THE WORLD

A GLIMPSE OF THE WORLD

Before entering the world of Azeroth, it's good to know how things fair in these interesting times. Though many lands have been entirely changed by wars between the Alliance and Horde and these battles against the Burning Legion, vitality and peace have fought their way back where possible.

This section describes the current conditions of Azeroth, its lands, and its inhabitants. Understanding these aspects is important for roleplayers and general gamers alike, because it greatly impacts quest stories, ongoing wars between the factions, and other complex matters.

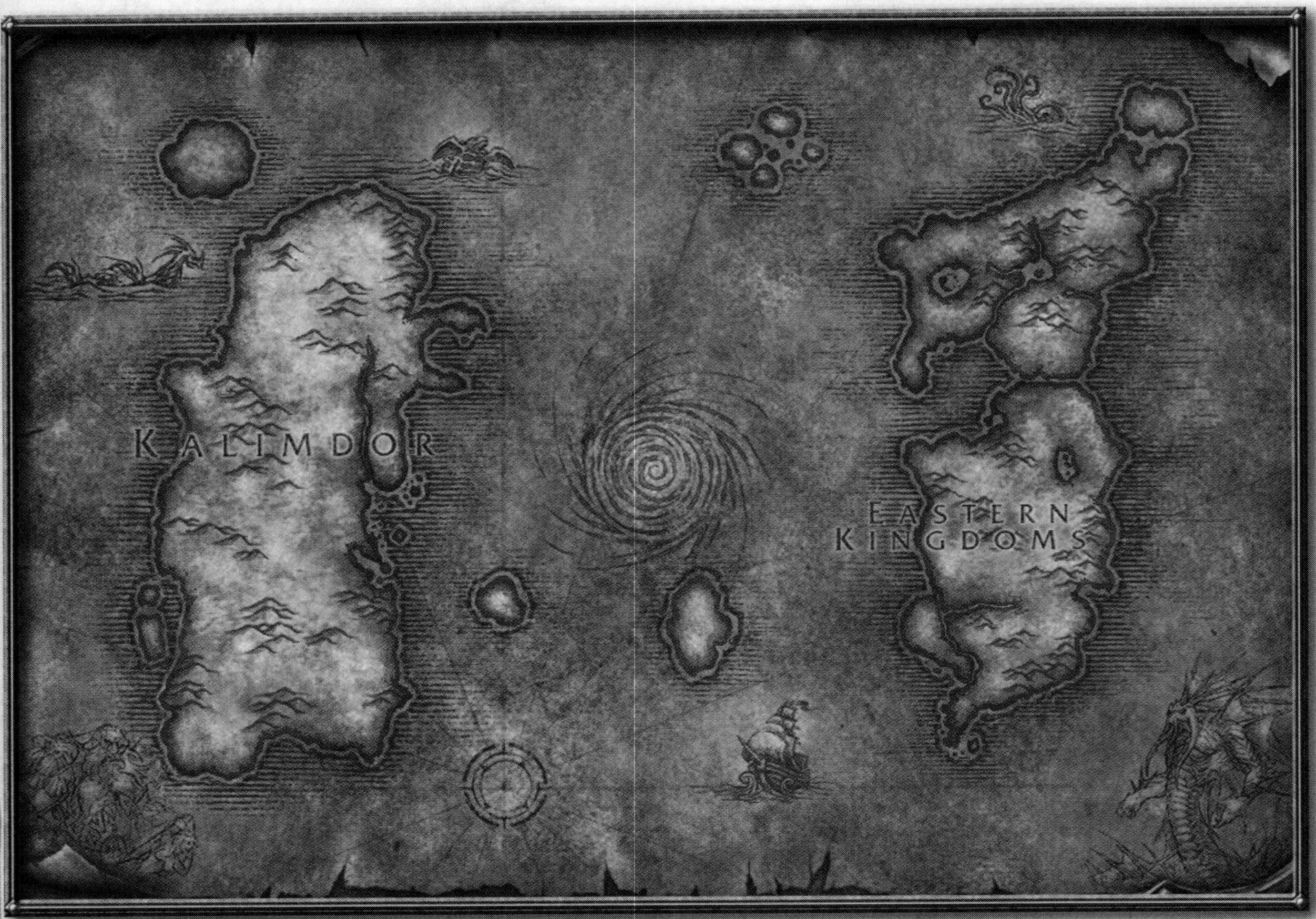

THE EASTERN KINGDOMS

The Eastern Kingdoms have been through tumultuous times since the days when Lordaeron stood proud and strong. The northern lands are now a place of plague, disruption, Undead, and religious zealotry. Wars cover the lands to the south, and the looming threat posed by the Dark Portal prevents complacency from any of the races that live there.

LORDAERON

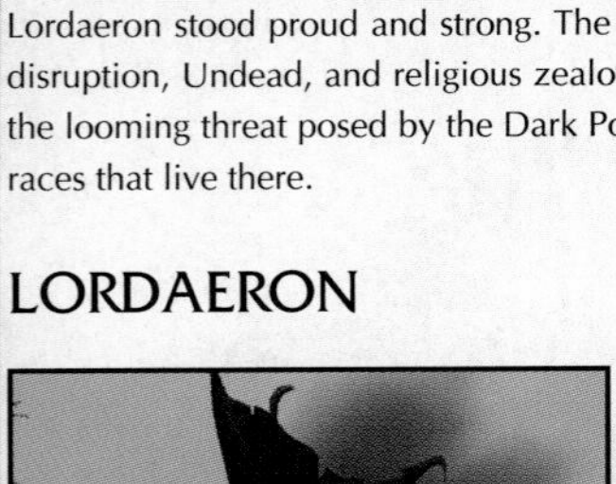

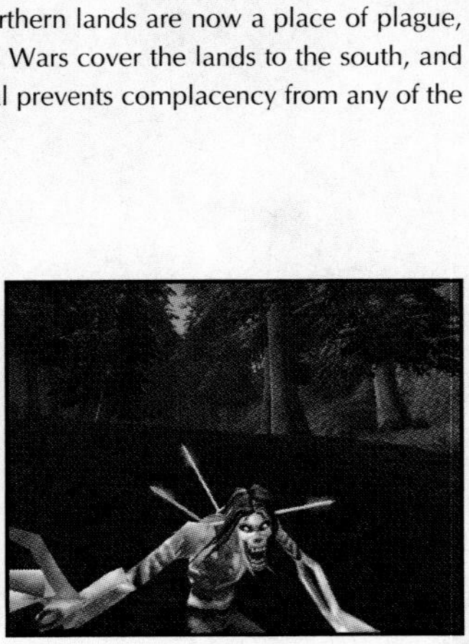

The Undead of Lordaeron fly the flag of the Horde now, no matter how loose the "friendship" is between the Orcs and the Forsaken. Because of Lordaeron's proximity to the lands of Dwarves and Humans, the Undead are always fighting; Hillsbrad is embroiled in raids and combat on a daily basis. Neither side has been able to gain a heavy foothold in the other's territory, so it's unknown how events will unfold in that region.

Little noticed by the Humans of Stormwind, Lordaeron faces enemies at home as well. The Forsaken are being attacked by Human Zealots even within their borders, but the worse fear is that a plague of mindlessness will overcome their senses. This Scourge is the driving force behind the Undead's allegiance to the Horde. Many of the new poisons and diseases being spread by the Forsaken are done to increase their "recruitment" of living beings into the ranks of the Undead.

Living on the doorstep of the Plaguelands, Undercity is in an almost constant war with poisoned beasts. Those who stray too far from the protected fields of Tirisfal Glades shall know the perils of such troubled times, whether they are living or dead already. South of home, in Silverpine Forest, the Undead must contend with Dalaran troops and the forces of Arugal (a mystic of great power and anger).

KHAZ MODAN

In Khaz Modan, the Dwarves of Ironforge face unrest and a most uncivil war against the Dark Iron Dwarves. It is unknown how many of the Dwarves in Ironforge are loyal to this rebellious faction, but rumors make the problem out to be far worse than the council lets on.

In Loch Modan, there are also many skirmishes against the feral Troggs and several clans of Ogres. Though the Dwarves are quite aggressive about patrolling their territory, many of their finest soldiers are spread too thin to prevent incursions by enemy forces. Word has reached the capital recently that even the outpost at Dun Algaz has been attacked; even to the point where its current status is unknown.

The Gnomes are faced with exile from Gnomeregan; many of their number have been turned mad by exposure to deadly concoctions, brewed during their fights against the Troggs. The Gnomes currently stay in the outer parts of Dun Morogh and in Ironforge itself, working on ideas to reclaim their homeland. To assist the Dwarves, they helped in the creation of a train that runs between Ironforge and Stormwind.

AZEROTH

Farther south, the Humans would perhaps be able to rally and aid their various allies if they had not problems of their own. The Defias, a gang of powerful brigands and thieves, has grown to such strength that people wonder why their leader has been so absent on the matter. With new attacks by Orc clans in Redridge Mountains and a most desperate state of affairs in Duskwood as well, even lands vital to Stormwind's safety are threatened.

Westfall, along the coast, has seen more than attacks from the Defias. Gnolls have formed a massive contingent in Westfall, lighting great fires to herald their army. Hundreds of these creatures now hold the mountains in the south-east and many areas along the coastline. The local militia is horribly outnumbered, but their cries to the capital have gone unanswered.

Elwynn Forest, hailed for its safe roads and pleasant farms, is no longer such a gentle place either. Not only are the Defias rampant, but Kobolds and Murlocs have higher numbers than ever before. Elwynn's mines are silent, and approaching the lakes and ponds of the area begs for trouble.

Even the people inside Stormwind have felt the shakings of coming times. So many Defias members were thrown into the Stockades of the city in such a short time that conditions became untenable. A riot has succeeded in pushing the guards out of the Stockades, and it is now entirely off limits to the general public. Several guardsmen didn't make it to the surface, and the Defias are holding their ground.

KALIMDOR

The western continent of Kalimdor is home to many of the Horde's races. Though weary from fighting and the destruction of their lands, these rugged folk have turned many defeats into victory overall. The current wave of trouble daunts not the Orcs, who continue to thrive under Thrall's strength and wisdom. Yet, peace is too much to ask.

CENTRAL KALIMDOR

Central Kalimdor is where the majority of the Horde's races are raised and trained. Durotar is the seat of the Horde; Orgrimmar is the greatest city of the east, and both Orcs and Trolls flock there to find safety, trade, and kinship. Trouble in this red, dusty land comes from the many Centaur who infest Central Kalimdor. Thrall has made push after push to throw the Centaur into exile, but their numbers remain. In addition, a number of cultists live in Durotar, and their numbers are growing. These demon worshippers are of the foulest sort, and the Horde does not tolerate their presence.

On the other side of Kalimdor, the Tauren live in moderate peace in Mulgore. Thrall aided the great Tauren in their battles against the Centaur, and this has firmly pulled the Tauren into the Horde's fold. Though Thousand Needles is mostly lost to the Tauren for now, the city of Thunderbluff is a sight that brings comfort to even an Undead Horde traveler. How many Humans would dare to attack the high and defended peaks of this isolated haven?

Between Mulgore and Durotar are the Barrens, where the small village of Crossroads has been growing. Though Centaur, Harpies, and many beasts live in this open land, the Horde has done well in keeping the northern Barrens clear of greater threats. Sadly, this cannot be said for the south; Dwarves mine and work openly near Dustwallow Marsh, and the Quillboars there have massive numbers and better equipment than their northern equivalents. Growing efforts by these factions in the south has made travel into Southern Kalimdor quite treacherous.

SOUTHERN KALIMDOR

Southern Kalimdor is a dangerous place, save for several outposts of Gnomes and Goblins. There are few actual towns in this remote corner of Azeroth, and fighting between the Horde and Alliance is not uncommon.

Thousand Needles is desolate, and the Centaur are still entrenched enough to prevent the Tauren from returning to the area. High in the peaks, a town continues to service the Horde members who come through, but Freewind Post is a small place with little more than the geography of the land to protect itself.

The Salt Flats, in the eastern edge of Thousand Needles lead down into Tanaris, a desert where Drakes and insectoid monsters thrive. Both the Horde and Alliance are able to find shelter in these areas by seeking the Gnomes and Goblins who create neutral communities in these arid climes. Gadgetzan is the largest of these towns, and crafters come from far and wide to meet the skilled Alchemists and Blacksmiths who work there.

Feralas is west of Thousand Needles, and is a jungle of great beauty. The Horde and Alliance both lay claim here and the Night Elves have positions at the eastern and western edges of the land (their main town is on a small island in the north-east). The Horde settled on the mainland, toward the center of the jungle. Many Ogres, Yeti, and unaligned Tauren have clans in Feralas, so the fighting there is rarely limited to the greater struggle between the great factions.

NORTHERN KALIMDOR

Northern Kalimdor is primarily the territory of the Night Elves. Though pushed from their former homes, the Night Elves retain some power in these regions and are working to heal the damage done by the Burning Legion.

Darkshore is on the far north-west of Kalimdor. Just across the sea from Teldrassil, the town of Auberdine is a focal point for crafters and those who protect the wilderness. The Naga that threaten much of the coast have retained some power here, primarily toward the ruins of Blackfathom Deeps. Elsewhere in Darkshore, the trouble is mostly centered around a disease that has gotten into both the Firbolg and beasts of the forest.

Ashenvale is the older home of the Night Elves, when they were immortal and at the heights of their civilization. Now, it is but a seed for their return to greatness. Twisted, crazed trees come down from the entrance into Felwood, while demonic leavings taint some of the waters and land throughout Ashenvale. The Golden Road into the Barrens is a dangerous path, as many Horde members come into Ashenvale from there. Some of these wanderers are looking to explore the forest; others have darker motives.

The north-east of Kalimdor is dangerous for all but the strongest of heroes to explore. Azshara, Winterspring, and Felwood are all laced with ancient magics and creatures of overwhelming power.

TELDRASSIL

Things are somewhat calmer for the Night Elves of Teldrassil than for many members of the Alliance. After fighting against the Burning Legion, the Night Elves sustained such losses that they have moved to Darnassus as their new capital. This city, located on a large island north of Kalimdor, is but a glimmer of the Night Elves' true glory, but is has some measure of peace. Yet, the land still suffers, and the Druids of Teldrassil fight every day to stop the taint that runs through so much of Kalimdor's woods.

Though loose members of the Alliance, the Night Elves aren't engaged in attacks with the Horde. Being separated by water, it is somewhat difficult for the Horde to attack Teldrassil, and it is harder for the Horde's members to focus their anger on the Night Elves, who have consistently tried to remain neutral in their dealings. Indeed, it is the Humans, Dwarves, and Gnomes who have interfered so many times in the dealings of Orc and Troll that Night Elves are often seen only as guilty by association.

THE HISTORY OF AZEROTH

Before Warcraft

-10000

The Night Elves awaken in the world and found a great society in the heart of Kalimdor. They tinker with primitive magic and inadvertently set it loose throughout the world of Azeroth.

The demonic Burning Legion, lured by the resultant energies, launches a massive invasion in order to drain the world of its innate magic. The Night Elves, unable to defeat the raging Demons, and are forced to ally themselves with the ancient Dragons in order to banish the Legion from the world. The ensuing conflict is so apocalyptic, that the greater land-mass of Kalimdor is broken apart and smashed beneath the sea.

The Night Elves vow to never use magic again, for fear that the Legion would return.

-6000

Unwilling to give up its precious magics, a small band of Night Elves is exiled from Kalimdor. Travelling to the newly formed eastern lands, they found the kingdom of Quel'Thalas and begin to refer to themselves as High Elves. The High Elves are continually besieged by the native Troll warbands.

-2900

The Human Empire of Arathor is founded in Lordaeron. It later expanded to also encompass Azeroth.

-2700

The High Elves, on the verge of losing their continuing war against the Trolls, seek the aid of the Humans of Arathor. In exchange for their help against the Trolls, the High Elves agree to teach men in the ways of magic. The combined army of Elves and Humans succeeds in wiping out the majority of Trolls in Lordaeron.

-2600

The Humans' reckless use of magic allows agents of the Burning Legion to find their way back into the world. The Order of Tirisfal is founded. The powerful Guardians of Tirisfal are charged with fighting a secret war against the agents of the Legion, unbeknownst to the general populace.

-200

Internal struggles and the pressures of over-expansion cause the fragmentation of the Human Empire of Arathor into seven autonomous nations. Azeroth and Lordaeron are two.

-45

The Guardian, Aegwynn, defeats Sargeras, the Lord of the Burning Legion in single combat. Sargeras' malevolent spirit bonds with the soul of Aegwynn's unborn child.

-40

Though banished from Azeroth, the Burning Legion corrupts the Orcish clans on the world of Draenor. The once noble, shamanistic Orc clans unite and become a rampaging Horde under the rule of the malevolent Shadow Council. By enlisting the aid of demonic magiks, the Orcs were able to decimate all Draenei with little loss. However the victory had its cost, and the now corrupted Orcs could only think of war and bloodlust, and without an enemy to fight, battled among themselves.

-37

Aegwynn gives birth to her son, Medivh, who is destined to become the Last Guardian.

-1

Medivh, driven mad by the spirit of Sargeras, opens the Dark Portal. He contacts Gul'dan, leader of the Shadow Council, and makes a dark deal. In exchange for the destruction of Azeroth, Medivh agrees to hand over the location to the tomb of Sageras. Both are pawns to the Burning Legion. The Orcish Horde begins its invasion of Azeroth.

Warcraft: Orcs and Humans

0

Medivh is killed by his best friend, Lord Lothar, and his own apprentice, Khadgar. The Orc Warlock, Gul'dan was in Medivh's mind at the moment of his death, and consequently suffered a vicious backlash that left him unconscious for weeks. After five grueling years of attrition, the Horde finally conquers the nations of Azeroth and Khaz Modan and claims Blackrock Spire as its base of operations.

Blackhand, the Horde's current warchief was slain and succeeded by Orgrim Doomhammer. Doomhammer disbanded into groups of Raiders who were thought to be loyal to Blackhand. By torturing Gul'dan's spy, Garona, Doomhammer located and slaughtered the Horde Walocks. Gul'dan was forced to bow to his new superior. To gain Doomhammmer's trust, he slaughtered his own Necrolytes, and used their spirits to create Death Knights.

Lord Lothar leads an exodus of refugees to the northern nation of Lordaeron. Once there, he convinces the leaders of the seven Human nations to unite in arms against the Horde. The separate nations of the Arathorian empire are reunited as the Alliance of Lordaeron. Through the chaos, Thrall was born. This young Orc was found and captured by humans, and raised as a slave and gladiator.

Warcraft II: Tides of Darkness

6

Orgrim Doomhammer, the Warchief of the Horde, launches his mighty fleets to invade the shores of Lordaeron. The unstoppable Horde pushes its way into the heartland of Lordaeron and succeeds in destroying the High Elves' ancient kingdom of Quel'Thalas. Gul'dan attempts to free Sargeras. Orgrim Doomhammer discovers the plan and kills Gul'dan.

The Alliance forces push back, but Lord Lothar is killed during the siege of Blackrock Spire. Spurred by the death of their beloved leader, the Alliance armies crush Blackrock Spire and push the Horde back to the threshold of the Dark Portal. The Dark Portal is destroyed by Khadgar and the Horde is defeated. The renegade orcs are rounded up and placed into internment camps by the Alliance.

Warcraft II Expansion: Beyond the Dark Portal

8

The ancient Orc Shaman, Ner'zhul, rallies the few clans still left on Draenor and reopens the Dark Portal. He orders his clans to steal a number of artifacts from Azeroth that will allow him to open multiple Portals in Draenor. The Alliance sends its armies, led by the wizard Khadgar, through the Dark Portal in order to stop Ner'zhul's schemes. The two armies clash throughout the hellish world of Draenor for months.

Empowered by the stolen artifacts, Ner'zhul opens a number of Portals in Draenor. Yet, before he can lead his clans through them, their energies spiral out of control and begin to destroy the very fabric of that world. The Alliance heroes, knowing that they would be trapped forever, are forced to destroy the Dark Portal so that Azeroth is not consumed by the raging energies.

The blasted world of Draenor tears itself apart. The Alliance grows uneasy as the Orcish internment camps are reopened. Only a few, scattered Orc clans evade the Alliance's wrath and eke out a living in the harsh wilderness.

Thrall's Tale: Lord of the Clans

18

Thrall, a young Orc raised as a Human slave and gladiator, escapes from bondage and sets off on a quest to discover his stolen heritage. Thrall succeeds in reuniting a number of renegade Orc clans and leads them in revolt against the Alliance Regional Wardens. With the threat of a new Horde looming over them, the Alliance nations begin to bicker and quarrel. Tensions run high amongst the Human leaders.

Thrall becomes the new Warchief of the Horde and helps to reintroduce his people to their abandoned shamanistic culture. The reinvigorated Horde finally begins to lose the last traces of the Legion's demonic corruption. Civil strife rages through the nations of the Alliance as threat of a new, unseen foe draws near - The Burning Legion returned

Warcraft 3: Reign of Chaos

20

Without the Guardians of Tirisfal, Human forces begin to crumble. The Night Elves at Kalimdor sense the disturbance and feel that they are somehow responsible. [Warcraft 3 Begins.] Ner'zhul returns as a Lich King, who has long transformed his loyal followers into minions of the living dead. Named by others as the Scourge, Ner'zhul takes hold of frozen continent of Northrend. From here he seeks to rule a world of the dead.

Prince Arthas rides forth to battle the Scourge and instead falls prey to the cursed Blade Frostmourne. He becomes one of the most powerful Deathknights and rides out to bring a plague to his own people of Lordaeron. After killing his own father Arthas is lead on a series of tasks until at last the Alliance is formed at the promptings of the prophet Medivh and the Burning Legion's connection to the Well of Eternity is cut off forever.

Warcraft 3: The Frozen Throne

21

After 10000 years of being imprisoned, Illidan is set free. At the behest of Kil'jaeden, he sets off to destroy the Frozen Throne in order to destroy the Lich King. He is thwarted in his plans by his former jailor Maiev and fails in his mission. After being recaptured and then set free again, Illidan sets out to destroy the Lich King once more. The Lich King, sensing his danger as he is imprisoned in his frozen throne, calls Arthas forth.

Arthas manages to outmaneuver Illidan and uses Frostmourne to shatter the icy throne freeing the helm and breastplate of the Lich King. Donning the armor, Arthas merges with the old Lich and becomes the new Lich King. An uneasy truce between the Horde and the Alliance is reached as both sides move on to lick their wounds and rebuild.

The Orcs leave for Kalimdor to resettle in a new land. Jaina Proudmoore resettles on the Coast of Southern Kalimdor. Grand Admiral Daelin arrives with a large Armada looking for survivors. His hatred for the Horde is great and he sets against them once more only for his own daughter, Jaina Proudmoore to set herself and her forces against him. The Orc allow Jaina Proudmoore to resettle in peace, but tensions are still there.

25

World of Warcraft Begins...

WORLD FACTIONS AND REPUTATION

Within the world of Azeroth there are many different factions that will affect how you are able to interact with the world you now live in. Gaining and losing favor is a simple enough process that can be achieved through doing quests or killing NPCs and mobs.

Each player is able to monitor the state of their reputation with all of the factions they interact with by opening the Reputation tab on their character sheet in game. You can do this quickly by using the "U" hotkey.

The Horde and Alliance comprise factional teams all their own. If you are on the opposing side, all of your faction for the other team will always be locked at the "War" status, which is the lowest possible faction. While you cannot change your status with the opposing team, don't become too comfortable with the thought that it guarantees you a cushy ride on your own team. Faction can be raised or lowered depending on the choices you make for each racial faction.

Each race begins with a bonus among their own race. The Forsaken (Undead) begin with a lower reputation among their allies, the Trolls, Tauren and Orcs. The Trolls, Tauren and Orcs start with a lower reputation with the Forsaken as well. After all, they are mostly in an alliance of convenience.

While you cannot declare war on your own faction, you can certainly fall very much out of favor with them by your actions. Your reputation affects how you interact with NPCs throughout the game so choose your actions carefully.

REPUTATION LEVELS

Reputation has seven different levels of like or dislike that are color coded. To put it simply, the best reputations are green, neutral is yellow and red is hostile.

Exalted: The highest level of reputation a player can achieve with a faction

Revered: Special reputation level reserved for special heroes

Honored: 10% discount on bought items from vendors

Friendly: Standard reputation level for factions on a player's team

Neutral: Standard reputation level for factions not on a player's team that are not KOS

Unfriendly: Cannot buy, sell, or interact

Hostile: KOS (Kill on Sight)

Hated: KOS; all opposing team factions are set permanently to the lowest level here

Gaining negative reputation with your own faction is possible though not the best choice when you need to rely on banking and purchasing goods along with a safehaven from which to operate.

WORLD FACTIONS

There are many factions in the world though every character starts their time with showing the factions of the Horde and Alliance at their default start point. Exploring the world and interacting with new factions adds them to your reputation sheet showing whether you have done so either positively or negatively. We have included a list of factions. In time, expect to discover even more than these.

Here is a list of Factions.

ALLIANCE

Darnassus
Gnomeregan Exiles
Ironforge
Stormwind

HORDE

Darkspear Trolls
Orgrimmar
Thunder Bluff
Undercity

STEAMWHEEDLE CARTEL

Booty Bay
Everlook
GadgetzanRatchett

OTHER

Argent Dawn
Bloodsail Buccaneers
Gelkis Clan Centaurs
Magram Clan Centaurs
Ravenholdt
Syndicate

THE CITIES OF AZEROTH

A HISTORY

Many of Azeroth's cities have risen and fallen through the many wars that have plagued the land. There are a few that still stand strong even after the ravages of the Burning Legion and Scourge have torn through.

DARNASSUS

High atop the boughs of the great tree Teldrassil lies the wondrous city of Darnassus, the new refuge of the reclusive Night Elves. Druids, Hunters, and Warriors alike make their homes among the rows of wood crafted lodges and delicately tended groves. The Temple of the Moon rises like a shining beacon above the trees, flanked by the colonnaded Hall of Justice, where the vigilant Sentinels gather to safeguard the land. Ruled by the high Priestess, Tyrande Whisperwind, Darnassus stands as a tranquil testament to all that the Night Elves hold sacred. A city in tune with the rush and flow of nature, Darnassus was built along the shores of a large lake, with elegant bridges spanning its crystalline waters. Elsewhere, the falling leaves of the forest carpet the soft pathways of the city.

At first glance Darnassus seems a tranquil refuge for the Night Elves and fitting replacement for their lost home in Ashenvale. However, Darnassus was created without nature's blessing and the creatures around this fair city suffer greatly for it. The great tree was planted for the most selfish of reasons, to regain their lost immortality by creating a tree that would bind their souls to the eternal world.

"Opulent" is the first word that may spring to mind when gazing around this grand city. It's a city alive and breathing with brightly colored foliage and softly glowing lights. Wisps float serenely along the pathways and large Ancient Protectors cast their gaze about them looking for any sign of danger.

The Tradesman's Terrace is in the southwestern section of the city. Buildings of pagoda inspired architecture line the pathways with their signs prominently announcing the weapons and armor they are selling. On the west end of the city, the Temple of the Moon sits with a large welcoming walkway leading into the moonlit and mystical alcove within. A large alabaster statue stands proudly in the center of a pool of water. Trainers surround the lower ring around the pool and, at the top of the ramps, the Lady Tyrande Whisperwind herself stands.

To the east of the Temple, and in the center of the city surrounded by water, stands a large tree in the shape of a bear. Inside lies no heart, but the treasures of its citizens are kept here in the bank. Just slightly to the northwest of the bank sits the rune-surrounded portal to Rut'theran Village on the sea. In the northern region of the city, smaller Protectors make their rounds, their woody creaking blends in with the sounds of the smaller creatures as they make their patrols through the Cenarion Enclave.

The eastern portion of the city contains the Craftsman's Terrace. Herein the various craftsmen sell their wares and train the next to carry on their traditions. It is a visually beautiful city and one worth making the trip to if you don't happen to be on the wrong side of the war.

IRONFORGE

While many Dwarven strongholds fell during the Second War, the mighty city of Ironforge—nestled in the wintry peaks of Dun Morogh—was never breached by the invading Horde. A testament to the Dwarves' expertise of shaping rock and stone, Ironforge was constructed in the heart of the mountain itself: an expansive underground city of craftsmen, explorers, miners and Warriors. Although the Alliance has been weakened by recent events, the Dwarves of Ironforge, led by King Magni Bronzebeard, are forging a new future in the world.

The first Dwarves came up from the depths of the earth and founded Khaz Modan after the Titan shaper Khaz'goroth. Constructing an altar for their Titan father, the Dwarves crafted a mighty forge within the heart of the mountain. Thus, the city that grew around the forge would be called "Ironforge" ever after.

With the loss of their beloved Gnomeregan to invaders, what was left of the Gnomish people took residence within the safe halls of their friends and neighbors. The entrance to Ironforge can be imposing to any newcomer. It's large, stony façade and heavy metal portcullis look ready to shut out even the most powerful of the Titans.

Within the city, the sounds of hammers falling rings out through the hustle and bustle. Large openings run through the center of the pathways. Gazing beneath your feet may reveal the source of the heat. Grated catwalks sit above hot molten metal guarding any from a clumsy and costly mistake of falling in.

Following the outer ring of the great city leads past the Military Quarter and toward Tinkertown. This is the Gnomish region of the city made quite evident by the technological marvels even intertwined within their architecture. Overlarge gears rotate around the hallways as you pass underneath. The King of Gnomes, Tinker Mekkatorque, stands watch over his people and watches as everyone comes and goes from the latest in innovations, the Tram to and from Stormwind.

The library of Ironforge sits in the outer ring of Ironforge in the northeastern section of the city. The Explorer's League keeps watche over the many volumes of research and history they have managed to gather. Even with their love of the Forge, the Dwarves have switched their focus to searching for their very own origins and embracing archaeology.

Perhaps the darkest of the areas are the Forlorn Caverns. Strangely enough, there seems to be some decent fishing for those looking for a break from the usual monotony of work. The northwestern area of the city houses the Mystic Ward. The vibrancy of the architecture is a striking contrast after emerging from the Forlorn Caverns. Within the very heart of the city is the Great Forge itself. Oversized anvils are worked on diligently by craftsman that barely break a sweat although the heat is nearly unbearable. It is worth taking the time to walk through and get to know. There are always new surprises around every corner and it is a fitting home.

STORMWIND

The city of Stormwind stands as the last bastion of Human power in Azeroth. Rebuilt after the Second War, Stormwind is a marvel of Human design and engineering. Stormwind's guards keep the peace within the city's walls, while the young king, Anduin Wrynn, rules from his mighty keep. The Bazaar District bustles with trade from across the continent and beyond, while adventurers of every sort can be found wandering the streets of Old Town. Unaffected by the ravages of the Scourge in the north, Stormwind still faces its own threats, both from without and from within.

Stormwind is the last of the great human cities to have been reclaimed and rebuilt as a human stronghold after the Burning Legion brought it to ruins. With Lordaeron in the hands of the Forsaken and many of the cities that once housed the great kingdoms of humanity in ruins, Stormwind remains a hub of commerce and safety.

The entrance to Stormwind itself is a testament to the legacy of the heroes lost in time to the horrors of war. Each one bears a plaque with the name of the honoree. It is rightly called the Valley of Heroes and all that enter it can't but help feel their chest swell in pride at the legacy of the Alliance.

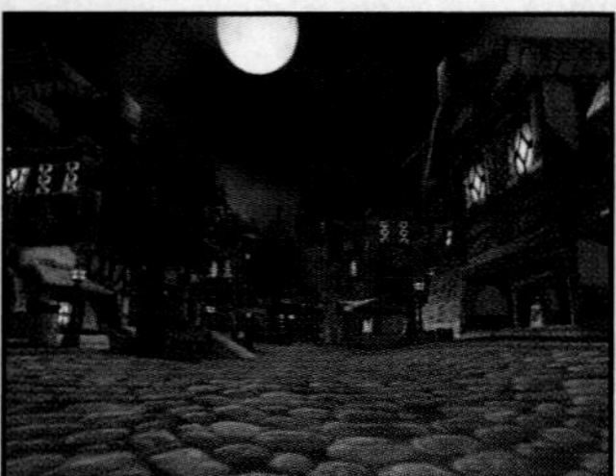

Once passing through the Valley of Heroes, you enter the Trade District. Shops crowd against the cobblestone walkways and citizens bustle about from place to place hocking their wares and children scamper between the legs of passerby's. Word has it that Stormwind may just have the best cheese in all of Azeroth. There is plenty of shopping to be found throughout the city.

To the right of the Trade District is Old Town. As you move in that direction, you'll notice the large canals that run through the city and more small shops line the waterways. Old Town is a smaller, more compact version of the Trade District. It has a cozy charm to it. North of Old Town lies the Dwarven District. It's a haze-covered area of the city as the pollution of the many fires settles over it. Large beast-like machines sit around the region of the city as if waiting to snatch up some imaginary creature for a snack.

Stormwind Keep lies between the Old Town and the Dwarven District. The boy king Anduin Wrynn stands at court with his advisers by his side. Few stop by to pay their respects. At the northernmost area of the city lies Cathedral Square. The tall spires of the Cathedral of Light itself loom protectively over this portion of the city. Its beauty is unmatched and even children are brought by to tour and view where the great Paladins and Priests train.

The west is the Park where Druids go to find their center and train. The Night Elves have managed to bring a piece of Darnassus here with them by placing up their own small touches on this green oasis among the clean white stones of Stormwind. Even what appears to be a moonwell sits in the center of the park.

To the south is the Mage Quarter, but just to the east sit the Stockades. This is a dangerous place for any citizen to go and should be approached with care. Soldiers are lined up on the outer edges receiving medical care from the wounds they received from riots that broke out among the Defias prisoners.

Within the Mage Quarter, a tall tower stands with a spiraling ramp twisting about it. It is truly one of the grandest of wizard towers any could possibly hope to see. At the top lies a strange portal that swirls in luminescent green as if to peer out into the cosmos itself. Passing through it leads deeper into the Wizard's Sanctum. There is plenty to explore throughout this great city and should you gain a thirst from doing so, stop by the Blue Recluse. They advertise a free drink and you can send out a postcard at the mailbox as well.

ORGRIMMAR

Named in honor of the legendary Orgrim Doomhammer, Orgrimmar was founded to be the capital city of the Orcs' new homeland. Built within a huge, winding canyon in the harsh land of Durotar, Orgrimmar stands as one of the mightiest cities in the world. Behind Orgrimmar's immense walls, elderly Shaman patiently share their knowledge with the Horde's newest generation of leaders, while Warriors spar in the gladiatorial arena, honing their skills in preparation for the trials that await them in this dangerous land.

After freeing his people from captivity among the humans, Thrall set out to brave the sea and bring his people to a new land to start a new society for the Orcs. They named the land itself "Durotar" after his deceased father, the former clan leader of the Frostwolves. It is in Orgrimmar that the new seat of power resides for all of the Orcs that survive to this day. No longer are the clans fractured and now they stand united as one nation.

The entrance to Orgrimmar yawns widely as the Orc guards stand by. To the east of it stands the Zeppelin Tower. The architecture is crude and yet speaks volumes of the craftsmen that built this city. Although different from conventionally accepted cities, none can say that there isn't a complex and harsh beauty invoked by the sight of the city. Bonfires burn high atop the rocks and throughout the city, leaving a faint smoky haze.

The distinctive tile roofs of the city intermingle with the red rock of the terrain; wooden carvings, shaped like horns, give off a menacing air as tanned hides are stretched over rooftops and across the rocks to filter out the relentless desert sun. After entering the city, the first region is the Valley of Strength. It serves as a central hub for banking and the buying and selling of all sorts of goods and services.

Just up the tower and across the rope bridge to the west lies the Valley of Spirits and the passageway to the western exit of the city. North of the Valley of Strength is the shadier end of town: the Cleft of Shadow. From the area emanates a purple glow and within are the Warlocks and Rogues among some few vendors that serve their purpose.

Wrapping around the Cleft of Shadow is the Drag; it's filled with shops and trainers. This area is well-shaded from the ravages of the desert sun and a good place to cool off. The desert breeze can be heard blowing through the rocks. To the northeast, through the Drag, is the Valley of Honor where the Orcs work their ways with metal and train their warriors. There is even a small pond for a little fishing after a hard workout.

Out through the Drag once more, and following the curve of the path to the north, you''l find the Valley of Wisdom and the seat of power for Warchief Thrall. Even more impressive than Grommash Hold, however is the monolithic demon plates out front. It is the demon armor of Monnoroth himself set there to remind the Orcs of the grand sacrifice made to defeat the beast and begin the path of reclaiming their honor. Even as crude as the city seems, it is a marvel of Orc ingenuity and determination to live off a harsh land and thrive despite all odds.

THUNDER BLUFF

The great city of Thunder Bluff lies atop a series of mesas that overlook the verdant grasslands of Mulgore. The once nomadic Tauren recently established the city as a center for trade caravans, traveling craftsmen and artisans of every kind. The proud city also stands as a refuge for the brave adventurers who stalk their dangerous prey through the plains of Mulgore and its surrounding areas. Long bridges of rope and wood span the chasms between the mesas, topped with tents, longhouses, colorfully painted totems, and spirit lodges. The mighty chief, Cairne Bloodhoof, watches over the bustling city, ensuring that the united Tauren tribes live in peace and security. Thunder Bluff sits high above the plains of Mulgore. The only means of arrival are by using the lifts from the plains below or flying in on one of the Wyverns that serve the area.

Brightly painted totems and tents made with stretched animal skins and wood struts lashed together sit atop the mesas giving the true feeling of being a part of a tribal community. The strong Tauren do much of their trade and banking on the main mesa. The winds are strong high atop the mesas and the Tauren capture this energy with brightly colored windmills atop the buildings. A series of rope bridges and towers interlink the varying levels and mesas into one continuous city.

Cairn Bloodhoof, leader of the Tauren sits at the top level. All Tauren seeking his favor and the way of the hunter that is so precious to their very culture carry out his will.

The southeastern most mesa houses the Hunter's Rise where aspiring Hunters go to train within the Hunter's Hall. Standing at the edge of the mesa here will give way to an amazing vista to the southeast. Watch your step however. There are no guardrails to keep you from falling to your death. The Tauren are more surefooted than that to care for such things. On the northern most mesa, the Elder Rise can be found where the wisest of Tauren reside. Druids can seek their wise council and learn more about their path in the Hall of the Elders. The Spirit Rise lies to the west. The large head of a Kodo is fastened to the side of the Shaman trainers as if in silent watch and granting its power to those that train there.

Down along the side of the mesa is a path leading down into a cavern that resounds of dripping pools of water and quietly spoken conversation. Large yellow mushrooms surround the edges of the water. The Priest and Mage trainers sit and patiently give their knowledge to those that seek their counsel. The mists of the pools rise ever so silently giving the already eerily glowing cavern a more surreal appearance.

Despite the simple nature of their city, the Tauren have all that is necessary for their people. They put their efforts into their accomplishments and leave their city simple and functional.

UNDERCITY

Far beneath the ruined capital city of Lordaeron, the royal crypts have been turned into a bastion of evil and undeath. Originally intended by Prince Arthas to be the Scourge's seat of power, the budding "Undercity" was abandoned when Arthas was recalled to aid the Lich King in distant Northrend. In Arthas' absence, the Dark Lady, Sylvanas Windrunner, led the rebel Forsaken to the Undercity, and claimed it for her own. Since taking up residence, the Forsaken have worked to complete the Undercity's construction by dredging the twisted maze of catacombs, tombs, and dungeons that Arthas began.

Once the seat of power for the Humans, Lordaeron fell to the plague released by the Cult of the Damned. The new Lich King Arthas sought to make it his new home but found his conquest had been taken over by Sylvanas Windrunner. She has finished carving out what Arthas began building and claimed it for the Forsaken. While much of humanity has given up ever reclaiming Tirisfal Glades from the Scourge and Forsaken, a small band of Scarlet Crusaders still attempt to wrest back the cursed land from them. To the naked eye, the Ruins of Lordaeron look empty and uninhabitable. A Warlock will tell you otherwise. With a quick cast they can aid you in seeing the ghostly inhabitants that wander what appears to be an empty ruin.

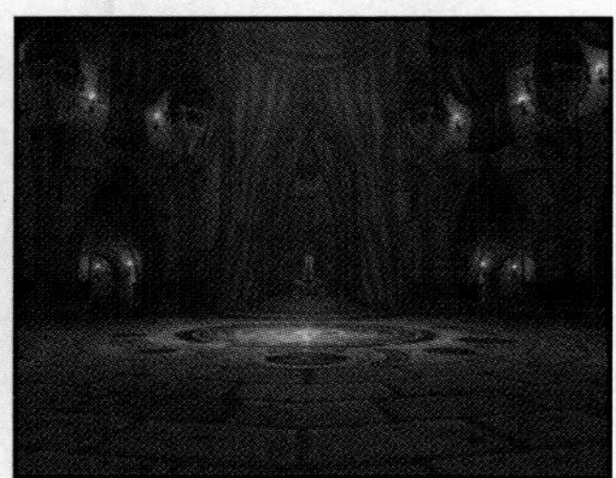

Deeper in the throne room sits bare and empty. The throne of a king destroyed by his own son is but a hollow shell of the greatness it once possessed. Pathways take you down past the Undercity Guardians. Their large hulking forms past decay and oozing the remnants of the plague. The Trade Quarter is in the heart of this city. Shops surround it on all levels and the bank sits prominently in the center. The grim décor of skulls and horns reflects the tastes of the denizens, all backlit by a constant green pool of slime.

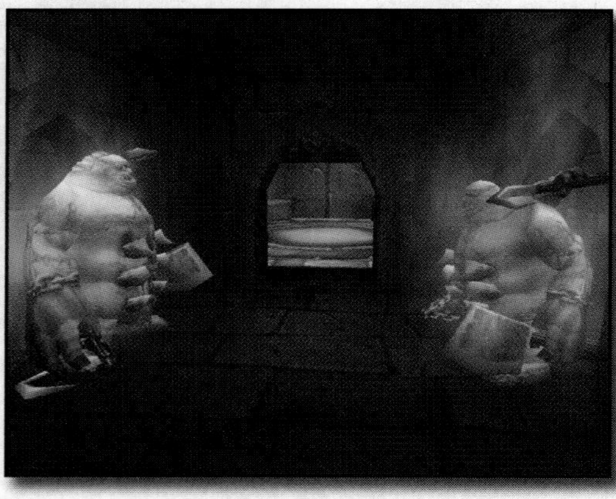

Taking the stairs down past the bank leads to an outer circle of merchants and canals. Each section of this part of the city is divided into quarters with an inner and outer ring and a bridge between the two. Colorful banners of decaying fabric is draped around the entrances in a mockery of festivity while skulls on signs point the way to the different areas. The inner circle of this region houses merchants and profession trainers among many other things. The Undead have thought of everything possible to help them in their pursuits.

The northeastern quarter (outermost ring) of the city houses the Magic Quarter where Warlocks and Mages can train in their arts. A 'demon'stration of Warlock pets is ongoing next to the building and can be quite informative. In the inner circle robes and implements befitting a mage can be purchased here. Moving clockwise takes you to the rogue quarter. Trainers wait here to improve the stealthy lives of all rogues that come to them with greed and murder in their hearts. Within the inner circle poisons and daggers can be purchased.

In the southwestern region of the city, the Apothecarium and the Royal Quarter are found. The Royal Apothecary Society does many of their experiments with the plague in this region. Their laboratory is something in and of itself to see with bits and pieces of various creatures strewn about and experiments being carried on in an adjoining room on some unlucky Humans. The crackling static of their experiments will set any visitor's hair on end.

Deep within the Royal Quarter the demon Varimathras stands at the side of the Dark Lady herself. His imposing figure is enough to make any be respectful of her every wish. To the northwest region is the Warrior Quarter. Warriors train and strain against target dummies while the Priests stand along the building and gaze down at the occurrences. Nearby the sewers lead out into the grounds of Tirisfal Glades near the Scarlet Crusade's southern Tower. The bats of Undercity use this as a means to gain access in and out of the city. If there was a pulse among the Undead, Undercity would resonate with it, but instead it's cold and clammy countenance casts a pallor among its visitors in what many would find unwelcoming. The Undead that reside here however seem quite at ease at what their Dark Lady has carved out for them even with the remnants of the Scourge and the overzealous Scarlet Crusade breathing down their necks.

A GLIMPSE
HISTORY
CITIES
RACES
CLASSES

THE RACES OF AZEROTH

World of Warcraft is a world built on war and conflict. The races of Azeroth have found themselves choosing sides and allying in order to stay safe from their many enemies and the creatures that roam it. Two factions have come of this; the Horde and the Alliance. Choosing a faction means choosing a side in the war so consider carefully.

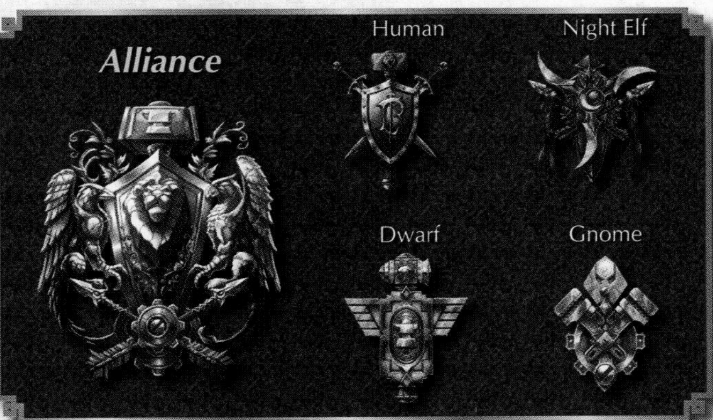

DWARVES

STARTING STATISTICS

CLASS	STRENGTH	AGILITY	STAMINA	INTELLECT	SPIRIT
Warrior	25	16	25	19	19
Paladin	24	16	25	19	20
Hunter	22	19	24	19	20
Rogue	23	19	24	19	19
Priest	22	16	23	21	22

Racial Traits

Stoneform: Activate to gain immunity to poison, disease, and bleed. Gain 5% AC bonus. Lasts 20 sec. 3 min. cooldown.

Treasure Finding: Activate to see treasure chests on mini map. Lasts until canceled. No cooldown.

Frost Resistance: +10 Cold Resistance.

Gun Specialization: +5 Gun Skill

Languages: Dwarvish, Common

The stoic Dwarves of Ironforge spent countless generations mining treasures from deep within the earth. Hidden within their impregnable stronghold of Ironforge Mountain, they rarely ventured beyond the wintry peaks of Dun Morogh. Recently, however, the Dwarves unearthed a series of ruins that held secrets to their ancient heritage. Driven to discover the truth about his people's fabled origins the great King Magni Bronzebeard ordered that the Dwarves shift their industry from mining to archaeology. As part of the Grand Alliance, the stalwart Dwarven armies have been called away to battle the merciless Horde in far away lands. In these perilous times, the defense of the mountain kingdom falls to brave Dwarves like you. The spirits of the ancient kings watch over you and the very mountains are your strength. The future of your people is in your hands.

It is said that the Dwarves were once called "Earthen." As the children of the Titans they were to shape and guard the earth from deep within. With the implosion of the Well of Eternity, the Earthen sealed themselves away until some unknown event mysteriously woke them from their slumber. In time they made their way to the surface though kept to what they knew and found homes within the mountains, founding their home of Ironforge.

Three clans rose among them and they lived in a relative peace amongst one another until High King Anvilmar passed away leaving no heir. War broke out among the three factions until Madoran Bronzebeard at last managed to gain leverage and cast out the other clans. The Bronzebeards rule the Ironforge Dwarves to this day.

Role-play Tips

Playing a Dwarf can be a fun undertaking. They are generally fearless, stout fighters and are usually up for some good ale after a long hard day. The Dwarves in Azeroth have another mission as well in finding the archeology that will unlock the answers to their past. Be creative with their personality. While it's easy to have them be an ale swilling, gun-toting braggart, they can't all be. Perhaps your Dwarf finds the thrill of exploring and archaeology to be right up their alley.

GNOMES

STARTING STATISTICS

CLASS	STRENGTH	AGILITY	STAMINA	INTELLECT	SPIRIT
Warrior	18	23	21	23	20
Rogue	16	26	20	23	20
Mage	15	23	19	26	22
Warlock	15	23	20	25	22

Racial Traits

Escape Artist: Activate to break out of a Root or Snare effect. 1.5 sec cast time. 1 min. cooldown.

Expansive Mind: Increase Intellect 5%.

Arcane Resistance: +10 Arcane Resistance.

Technologist: +15 skill bonus to Engineering.

Languages: Common, Gnomish

The eccentric, often-brilliant Gnomes are held as one of the most peculiar races of the world. With their obsession for developing radical new technologies and constructing marvels of mind-bending engineering, it's a wonder that any Gnomes have survived to proliferate. Over the years the Gnomes have contributed ingenious weapons to aid the Grand Alliance in its fierce battles against the Horde. Thriving within the wondrous techno city of Gnomeregan, the Gnomes shared the resources of the forest of Dun Morogh peaks with their Dwarven cousins. Yet recently a barbaric menace rose up from the bowels of the earth and invaded Gnomeregan. Aided by their Dwarven allies, the Gnomes fought a valiant battle to save their beloved city. Nevertheless Gnomeregan was irrevocably lost. The surviving Gnomes fled to the safety of the Dwarven stronghold of Ironforge. There they remain devising strategies to retake their city. As a Gnome of proud standing, it falls to you to answer the challenge and lead your curious people to a brighter future.

It is their passion and it shows in their choice of environs when visiting their small section of the city. With the energy they exhibit and their affinity for their inventions, you begin to wonder if you should see a wind-up key on their backs.

The Gnomes work hard to this day within the well fortified halls of Ironforge to create bigger and better inventions.

Role-play Tips

Gnomes are excitable with an innate curiosity for anything mechanical. They are gadget hounds and good at it too. They can be role-played in many different ways from the reclusive inventor to the bouncy hyper rogue. They can be fun and funny creatures and may have a curious sort of humor that many will find infectious. Of course, they can also be a bit much to take and many will find they have the urge to strangle them. If you fall into the latter category, then you may just be playing your Gnome perfectly.

HUMANS

STARTING STATISTICS

CLASS	STRENGTH	AGILITY	STAMINA	INTELLECT	SPIRIT
Warrior	23	20	22	20	20
Paladin	22	20	25	20	21
Rogue	21	23	21	20	20
Priest	20	20	20	22	23
Mage	20	20	20	23	22
Warlock	20	20	21	24	22

The noble Humans of Stormwind are a proud, tenacious race. Though the recent invasion of the demonic Burning Legion decimated their sister kingdom of Lordaeron, the defenders of Stormwind stand vigilant against any who would threaten the sanctity of their lands. Nestled in the foothills of Elwynn Forest, Stormwind city is one of the last bastions of Human power in the world. Ruled by the child king Anduin Wrynn, the people of Stormwind remain steadfast in their commitment to the Grand Alliance. Backed by their stalwart allies, the armies of Stormwind have been called away to fight the savage Horde on distant battlefields. With the armies gone, the defense of Stormwind now falls to its proud citizens. You must defend the kingdom against the foul mongrels that encroach upon it and hunt down the subversive traitors who seek to destroy it from within. Now is the time for heroes; now Humanity's greatest chapter can be told.

Humans once lived a nomadic life in tribes wandering from place to place as the seasons changed or hunting became lean. It wasn't until the rise of the Arathi that they began to form within one nation. They founded the fortified city of Strom and as they grew, so did they gain the attention of the High Elves who, like them, were suffering brutal attacks from the Trolls. As allies, they beat back the Trolls and the High Elves began to teach their newfound friends the ways of magic. As they grew, the Humans came in touch with the Dwarves and while the Dwarves were unsure of these strange new people, they developed a strong bond between them.

Racial Traits

Perception: Activate to increase stealth detection radius by 10 yards. Lasts 20 sec. 3 min. cooldown.

Human Spirit: Increase Spirit 5%.

Diplomacy: 10% bonus to faction point gain.

Sword Specialization: +5 to Sword skill.

Languages: Common

NIGHT ELVES

STARTING STATISTICS

CLASS	STRENGTH	AGILITY	STAMINA	INTELLECT	SPIRIT
Warrior	20	25	21	20	20
Hunter	17	28	20	20	21
Rogue	18	28	20	20	20
Priest	17	25	19	22	23
Druid	18	25	19	22	22

Racial Traits

Shadowmeld: Activate while immobile and out of combat to enter stealth mode. Lasts until canceled. No cooldown.

Quickness: Dodge chance increased 2%.

Wisp Spirit: Become a wisp when dead with movement speed increase of 50%. (Other ghosts receive 25% boost.)

Nature Resistance: +10 Nature Resistance.

Languages: Darnassian, Common

For ten thousand years the immortal Night Elves cultivated a druidic society within the shadowed recesses of Ashenvale forest. Yet recently the catastrophic invasion of the Burning Legion shattered the tranquility of their ancient civilization. Led by the Arch Druid Malfurion Stormrage and the Priestess Tyrande Whisperwind, the mighty Night Elves rose to challenge the demonic onslaught. Though victorious, the Night Elves were forced to sacrifice their cherished immortality and watch their beloved forests burn. Seeking to regain their immortality, a number of wayward Druids conspired to plant a special tree that would link their spirits to the eternal world. Despite Malfurion's warnings that nature would never bless such a selfish act, the Druids planted the great tree Teldrassil off the stormy coasts of northern Kalimdor. Within the twilight boughs of the colossal tree, the wondrous city of Darnassus took root. However, the great tree was not consecrated with nature's blessing and soon fell prey to the corruption of the Burning Legion. Now the wildlife and even the limbs of the great tree itself are tainted by a growing darkness. As one of the few Night Elves left in the world, it is your sworn duty to defend Darnassus and the wild children of nature against the Legion's encroaching corruption.

Night Elves were once known as the Kaldorei and have lived on Kalimdor for thousands upon thousands of years. It was through much of their delving into the magic of the Well of Eternity that called attention to Sargeras and the Burning Legion. It was Malfurion Stormrage's own Brother Illidan that caused the creation of the moon wells after his betrayal of his people so enamored of magic was he. It was through his betrayal and the luring power of the arcane that tapped them into a source of evil that corrupted their very souls. It is why to this day, that the Night Elves continue their vigil to restore the natural state to what it once was.

Role-play Tips

Night Elves are one of the oldest races on Azeroth. They can feel the corruption of the earth on which they live down to their very bones and so have an affinity for it. Night Elves can be played in a variety of ways from the haughty to the benevolent. What is most important is staying true to the core values of the Night Elves. It is the restoration of nature back to its proper state that drives them and going against that should be thought out carefully. While exceptions can be made to the unwritten rules, it is best to go along with the flow of the main story and enhance it rather than cheapen it.

In time, the region of Lordaeron grew so large that it fractured into smaller kingdoms, each with its own beliefs, government and lifestyle. The Humans began to outstrip their teachers in their use of magic, which alarmed their High Elf friends. The same corruption that had filled the world before was becoming evident. To combat this problem, the Council of the Silvermoon joined with the Magocrat Lords of Arathor in a pact. They formed a secret order called the Guardians of Tirisfal. The Guardians sought to protect the world from the onslaught of the demons of the Burning Legion should they return. To this end, it was the last Guardian who made a terrible misjudgment in her power and slew the Demon Lord Sargeras a bit too easily. She then took his body and secreted it away where none would find it. However, Sargeras was too clever and instead implanted his spirit into that of her unborn child who would one day be the inheritor of her powers.

Role-play Tips

The Humans are a proud hardworking people and are perhaps one of the most versatile races to role-play. Like any society, it takes all kinds and they certainly have them; from the noblest Paladin, to the Warlock dabbling with demons, to the Rogue with their hands in everyone's pockets. Their versatility makes them one of the easier races to play. They can be anything to anyone and the only specific role that you may find yourself needing to adhere to is the lack of real interaction with the Horde. You can't even speak to them even if you wanted to.

ORCS

STARTING STATISTICS

CLASS	STRENGTH	AGILITY	STAMINA	INTELLECT	SPIRIT
Warrior	26	17	24	17	23
Hunter	20	23	20	17	24
Rogue	24	20	23	17	23
Shaman	24	17	23	28	25
Warlock	23	17	23	19	25

Racial Traits

Blood Fury: Activate to increase Strength by 25% and receive 5% health loss every 3 sec. Lasts 20 sec. 2 min. cooldown.

Hardiness: 25% resistance to stun and knockout effects.

Command: Pet melee damage increased by 5%.

Axe Specialization: +5 to Axe skill.

Languages: Orcish

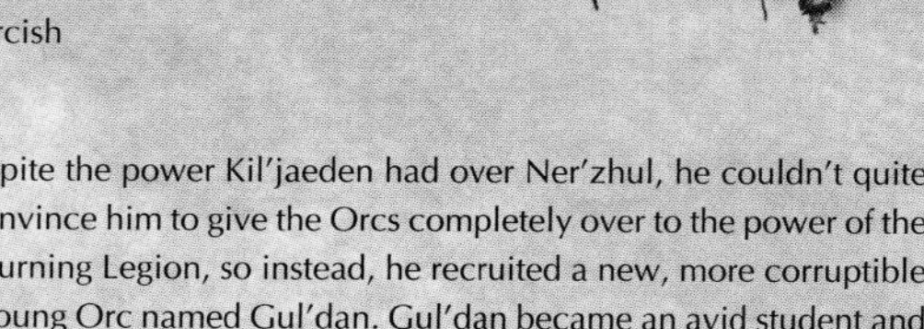

Long ago the Orcish Horde was corrupted by the Burning Legion and lured to the world of Azeroth. For generations the Orcs made war upon the Human kingdoms of Stormwind and Lordaeron. Though the Horde was ultimately defeated, a visionary young war chief named Thrall rose to lead his people in their darkest hour. Under Thrall's rule, the Orcs freed themselves from the chains of demonic corruption and embraced their Shamanistic heritage. After years of wandering the Orcs founded their own kingdom in the harsh wastelands of Durotar. Based in the warrior city of Orgrimmar they stand ready to destroy all who would challenge their supremacy. As a proud defender of Durotar, it is your duty to crush your enemies both seen and unseen, for the nefarious agents of the Burning Legion still wander the land.

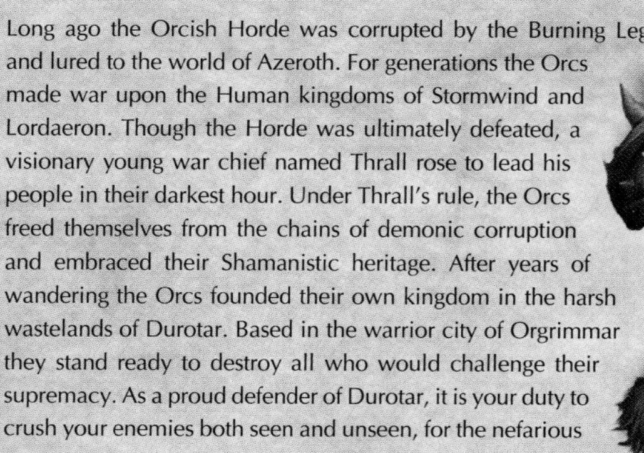

It was Sargeras' second-in-command, Kil'jaeden, who discovered Draenor and the races that lived there. Finding the Orcs to be a race worth molding into a driving force of bloodlust, he began to corrupt them, turning them from their Shamanistic ways toward the power of Warlockry. The powerful Shaman Ner'Zhul was seduced by the power of Kil'jaeden and all the demon offered and it was not long before he led his people against the peaceful Draenei utterly destroying them.

Despite the power Kil'jaeden had over Ner'zhul, he couldn't quite convince him to give the Orcs completely over to the power of the Burning Legion, so instead, he recruited a new, more corruptible young Orc named Gul'dan. Gul'dan became an avid student and a powerful warlock among his people.

In time, Gul'dan, under the manipulation of Kil'jaeden, maneuvered all of the Orc clans into partaking in a ritual that would make them indebted slaves to the Burning Legion and give them a blood lust they could not quench. He opened a portal into Azeroth where they began to work the will of the Burning Legion once more upon the denizens of the land.

The power of the Alliance overcame them; however, with Sargeras' spirit locked away in the nether once more, the Orcs were brought low. It was a new young Orc called Thrall that lifted the Orcs up once more by freeing his brethren and restoring them to the spiritual Shamanic roots that would quench the taint of the demons that once ruled them.

Role-play Tips

The Orcs are probably one of the most scarred of races. They have been through more than most and continue to try to recover from their ill use by the Burning Legion. These are a hardened people carving out their place among the harsher and more barren climates of Kalimdor. Orcs aren't generally perceived as the brightest of Azeroth's races, however in ways of war they can be quite unmatched in their cunning and ferocity. Play up to both their strengths and weaknesses.

TAUREN

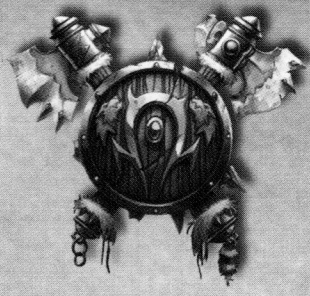

STARTING STATISTICS

CLASS	STRENGTH	AGILITY	STAMINA	INTELLECT	SPIRIT
Warrior	28	15	24	15	22
Hunter	25	18	23	15	23
Druid	26	15	23	16	24
Shaman	26	15	22	17	24

Racial Traits

War Stomp: Activate to stun opponents within 5 yards. Lasts 2 sec. 2 min. cooldown.

Endurance: Max health increased by 5%.

Cultivation: 15 skill bonus to Herbalism.

Nature Resistance: +10 Nature Resistance.

Languages: Orcish, Taurahe

Once a nomadic people, the Tauren roamed the endless plains of the Barrens hunting the mighty Kodo. Scattered across the land, the wandering tribes were united only by their common hatred for their sworn enemy, the marauding Centaur. Seeking aid against the Centaur, the great chieftain Cairne Bloodhoof befriended the savage Orcs who had recently journeyed to Kalimdor. With the Orcs' help, Cairne and his tribe were able to drive back the Centaur and claim the grasslands of Mulgore for their own. Upon the windswept mesa of Thunderbluff, Bloodhoof built a refuge for his people. Over time, the scattered tribes united under a single banner. Though the noble Tauren are peaceful in nature the rights of the great hunt are venerated as the heart of their spiritual culture. As a tribesman of Mulgore, you must test your skills in the wild and prove yourself in the great hunt.

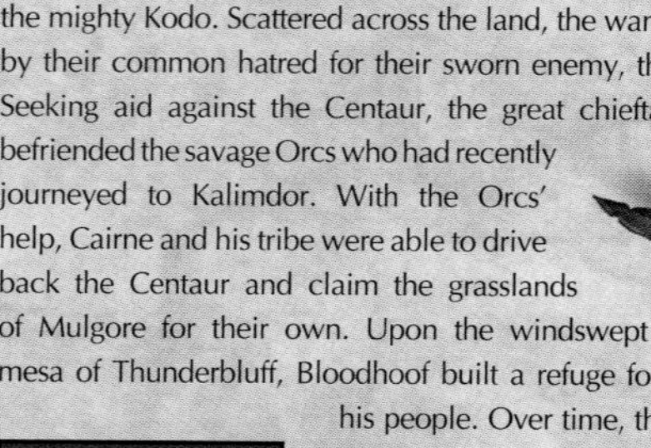

The Tauren found mutual benefits in befriending the Orcs and Trolls. While the Orcs and Trolls helped the Tauren to drive back the Centaur and keeping their lands safe, the Tauren have aided (and continue to aid) them in continuing a spiritual path as a Shamanistic society.

Role-play Tips

The Tauren revere the hunt and respect the bounty of the land greatly. While they may have some among them that are more the "bull in a china shop" type, they are generally level-headed and dependable. They are a deeply spiritual people and call upon the power of the great spirits of their past as well as use Shamanistic powers. When role-playing a Tauren, avoid the trap of playing them as a big dumb cow. They are neither dumb, nor cows, they are simply Tauren. They are noble, patient, and resourceful.

TROLLS

STARTING STATISTICS

CLASS	STRENGTH	AGILITY	STAMINA	INTELLECT	SPIRIT
Warrior	24	22	23	16	21
Hunter	21	25	22	16	22
Rogue	22	25	22	16	21
Priest	21	22	21	18	24
Shaman	22	22	22	17	23
Mage	21	22	21	19	23

Racial Traits

Berserking: Activate when "wounded" to increase melee and spellcasting speed by 25%. Lasts 20 sec. 2 min. cooldown.

Regeneration: 10% health regen bonus. 10% active in combat.

Beast Slaying: 5% damage bonus to Beasts.

Throwing Weapon Specialization: +5 to Throwing Weapon skill.

Languages: Orcish, Troll

The vicious Trolls that populate the numerous jungle isles of the South Seas are renowned for their cruelty and dark mysticism. Barbarous and superstitious, they carry a seething hatred for all other races. Long since exiled from its ancestral homeland in Stranglethorn Vale, the Darkspear tribe was nearly destroyed by rampaging Murlocs. Rescued by the young Warchief Thrall and his Orcish warriors, the Darkspear tribe swore allegiance to the Horde. Led by the cunning Shadow Hunter, Vol'jin, the Darkspears now make their home in Durotar along with their Orcish allies. As one of the only surviving Darkspears, it falls to you to regain the glory of your tribe.

The Trolls have a long history of war with the Humans. Even before the Burning Legion came into the land, they had waged war against the Humans and Elves with hit and run raiding parties. They hate the Humans above all other races; however, after nearly being completely wiped from the face of Azeroth. They relish in protecting their new homes in Durotar and look for any reason to convince the remaining Horde of the complete treachery of the Humans. It was Grand Admiral Proudmoore's attack on the Horde that enraged them even more and the fires of hate burn even hotter within the breasts of the Trolls. For now, they cooperate with the remaining members of the Horde to maintain their homes and to retain their alliances that let their people continue to rebuild.

Role-play Tips

The remaining members of the Darkspear Tribe are loyal to their friends: the Orcs. They work to rebuild themselves and make their tribe strong once more. They are fierce and capable fighters who seethe with a burning hatred of the Humans. Use this to your advantage in creating your character. You can expand the hatred to include the rest of the Alliance as well, after all they are allied with the Humans. Though being a Troll, you probably don't need too much reason to hate anyone not of your tribe.

UNDEAD

STARTING STATISTICS

CLASS	STRENGTH	AGILITY	STAMINA	INTELLECT	SPIRIT
Warrior	22	18	23	18	25
Rogue	20	21	22	18	25
Priest	19	18	21	20	28
Mage	19	18	21	21	27
Warlock	18	18	22	20	27

Racial Traits

Will of the Forsaken: Activate to become immune to fear, sleep, and charm effects. Lasts 20 sec. 3 min. cooldown.

Cannibalize: Increase health regen by 200% while consuming a corpse. Lasts 15 sec. 3 min. cooldown.

Underwater Breathing: Underwater breath increased by 4x.

Shadow Resistance: +10 Shadow Resistance.

Languages: Gutterspeak, Orcish

Bound to the iron will of the tyrant Lich King, the vast Undead armies of the Scourge seek to eradicate all life on Azeroth. Led by the Banshee Sylvanus Windrunner, a group of renegades broke away from the Scourge and freed themselves of the Lich King's domination. Known by some as the Forsaken, this group fights a constant battle not only to retain its freedom from the Scourge, but also to slaughter those who would hunt them as monsters. With Sylvanus as their Banshee Queen, the Forsaken have built a dark stronghold beneath the ruins of Lordaeron's former capital city. This hidden Undercity forms a sprawling labyrinth that stretches beneath the haunted woods of the Tirisfal Glades. Though the very land is cursed, the zealous Humans of the Scarlet Crusade still cling to their scattered holdings, obsessed with the eradication of the Undead and retaking their homeland. Convinced that the primitive races of the Horde can help them achieve victory over their enemies the forsaken have entered an alliance of convenience. Harboring no true loyalty for their new allies, they go to any lengths to ensure their dark plans come to fruition. As one of the Forsaken, you must massacre any who pose a threat to the new order, Human, Undead, or otherwise.

With undeath comes new capabilities and immunities no other race is afforded. The Undead do not need to draw breath to fill their lungs nor have any need for mortal hang-ups. Theirs is an unlife of working for not only their own survival, but of revenge and power. Their dark lands are plagued by the remnants of the Scourge and the vile Scarlet Crusade, but they remain vigilant in their pursuit to rid themselves of both menaces and establish themselves as a force not to be reckoned with.

Role-play Tips

The Undead are a versatile race to role-play. They were once normal Human beings until the plague swept through their villages and turned them into the creatures they are today. They are hunted by the Alliance as abominations to be dealt with the same as the Scourge. In turn, the Undead are fighting a battle on two fronts, one with the Scourge and one with the Alliance, only keeping the others of the Horde as allies because they cannot afford any more enemies. They are a nucleic society bound together by a hideous chance of fate and work to make the most of their lack of life. Play up their role in creating a new plague to sweep through the rest of Azeroth. Remember, the Undead do not breathe as well, they do not feel like others, they do not do a lot of things that others do. In that lie their strengths and weaknesses. Use them, expand on them and be creative. They have many possibilities.

This section offers a glimpse of the role that each class plays within Azeroth. All of the classes have played a part in the history of the world, and this shapes how they are viewed by other lands and within the great cities of the realms. Choosing a class is an opportunity to immerse yourself in the past events of Azeroth and work within its framework to decide the events of the future, as your group progresses within its chosen aims.

DRUID

The keepers of nature, the Druids care for the natural world, its creatures, and the balance of existence. Many of them have watched over the world through the Emerald Dream, an ethereal realm that exists separate from Azeroth but is intimately interwoven with it. This spirit world allows the regulation of the ebb and flow of nature and the evolutionary path of the world itself, and is the realm of one of the great Dragons: Ysera the Dreamer.

To help guide the course of the natural world, the Druids entered into the Emerald Dream, agreeing to exist apart from their friends and loved ones in an extended state of hibernation. However, because of the threat posed by Archimonde and the Burning Legion, the Druids awoke and used their power to fight against the demonic forces. Currently, some of the Druids have reentered the Emerald Dream, while others have stayed in Azeroth, working to repair the great damage that has been done to nature.

The Druids exist apart from political boundaries of empires and clans. What does it matter if one is Horde or Alliance in the great expanse of nature? The Night Elves and Tauren, united in their love of the land, have set aside their differences to work together, safeguarding Azeroth and helping to mend areas contaminated by pain and war. Therefore, the Druids offer hope of what all of Azeroth could accomplish if all the races worked for the betterment of the world together.

HUNTER

The lands of Azeroth are home to a great many beasts, everything from wolves and cats to bears and large birds, to name but a few. These species care nothing for the war between Horde and Alliance; their lives are filled with their own struggle to find food and live from day to day. By the same token, there have always been those individuals who exist outside of the boundaries of civilized society. These free spirits have found a connection to nature and a way of living with it. These wilderness people have taken the chance to explore the various lands of Azeroth and formed bonds linking themselves with the beasts of the world.

A Hunter is never without their weapon and their partner, the beast that they formed a relationship with. The two of them work together and learn from each other. This allows the Hunter to embrace the natural world and their pets to be free from some of the more pressing aspects of their existence, such as finding prey and having a safe place to rest.

Some of the races have taken easily to this way of life. The Tauren and Night Elves have a great respect for nature as a whole, and working as partners with it is an extension of that. The Trolls, as well, have never moved far away from the rhythms of the natural world. For these peoples, becoming a Hunter allows them the chance to bond with nature and the beasts within it.

For others, it appeals to their independent spirit. The Dwarves and Orcs are strong individuals, and some of them have grown tired of the political bickering of the cities and accepted the wilderness as their homes. These are Hunters who seek to find their own ways in the world.

MAGE

The call of magic is a powerful one. Some have decided to dedicate their lives to it, studying it, practicing it, and spreading it throughout the world. In the history of Azeroth, no other kingdom fully embraced the force of magic as strongly as that of Dalaran, where the entire culture was guided by mages. As a political entity, Dalaran was a source of great knowledge not jaded by certain moral concerns, seeking only to understand and harness the nature of magical power.

The kingdom of Dalaran no longer exists. Destroyed by the Burning Legion, its remnants have fled throughout the lands of Azeroth, and the practitioners of magic have taken new apprentices and students. This has led to knowledge of magic being spread throughout all of Azeroth.

In the Alliance lands, Humans and Gnomes have had a great thirst for knowledge. They have always been characterized by their curiosity and willingness to learn. Within the Horde, the Trolls also seek to understand the world and their place in it. The Undead, as well, have lost none of their curiosity in the passage into unlife, and some of them take easily to the pursuit of power.

PALADIN

The Paladins are the champions of Light and the Defenders of the Alliance. Within the Alliance, the Paladins are dedicated fighters, safeguarding the populace from the various threats against them. These men and women uphold honor and bravery, and their cause is to protect the people, honor the will of the nation, and bring Light against the Darkness.

Lordaeron used to be a center for the Paladins, a bright shining city that was a bastion of civilization. The defending Paladins were a great force of order and respect for their nation. However, there were dark forces at work, and a great sickness took hold of the land, spreading the curse of the Undead throughout the country. Lordaeron was destroyed and some of its Paladins corrupted, leaving the rest of the knightly order to fight against the Undead and their former comrades.

The Paladins' ranks are formed from the Humans and Dwarves of the Eastern Kingdoms. These people are stout defenders and work within the boundaries of their political organizations. Beyond all else, though, the Paladins are dedicated to ideals of honor and bravery, and they believe in the cause of Light.

PRIEST

Holy and Shadow are elemental forces of the gods, separate from those of the world itself. There are those individuals that seek to use them within the world, dedicating themselves to the worship of greater forces. For these people, the use of these elemental forces is a gift of the gods, requiring great study and great reverence.

The pursuit of Holy magic is the love of life and healing, replenishing and protecting the caster and those for whom they care. Shadow is the opposite, a force of raw destructive power that damages the target and wounds the spirit. Both forces are powerful and require skill to use properly.

Those dedicated to healing of the mind and soul often become priests, because of the appeal of Holy magic to salve the wounded. However, because of the strength that Shadow promises, darker individuals move to its worship. Within the races, Humans, Dwarves, Night Elves, Undead, and Trolls all have the religious structure and reverent nature that being a Priest requires.

ROGUE

All that it takes to be a Rogue is an individual nature drawn to working behind the scenes and a willingness to let certain laws and strictures slide. The Rogue is a person that prefers to move in the shadows, striking where least expected and taking advantage of opportunities where they present themselves.

Of course this appeals to thieves, spies, and assassins. Any nation with strong political and national organization has a share of people who don't believe that they should be governed. Because this is a group defined by individual spirit, it crosses racial and political boundaries, with people of strong independence working for their own beliefs.

There are those among the Humans, Dwarves, Gnomes, Night Elves, Orcs, Undead, and Trolls who seek to find their own paths. Only the Tauren avoid these activities, believing them to be dishonorable.

SHAMAN

The Shaman are the spiritual leaders of their clans and tribes, guiding the peoples of the Horde to their destinies. Gifted with great insight, the Shaman seek to provide the best lives for their people within Azeroth, forming a network between several disparate races.

The races of the Horde have always had strong beliefs and a willingness to defend them. In addition, most have a clan/tribal political structure, with loyalty to their tribe being strongly values. The Shaman help to meld these tribal forces together, so that all the various tribes and peoples can accomplish a unified goal that benefits all of them.

It was the Shaman of the Orcs that lead them into Kalimdor, where they formed bonds with the Tauren and Trolls that lived there. Only the Undead have no Shaman, and even within the Horde, this is viewed as disquieting. The Tauren, Orcs, and Trolls have a common set of beliefs, while the goals of the Undead remain somewhat mysterious.

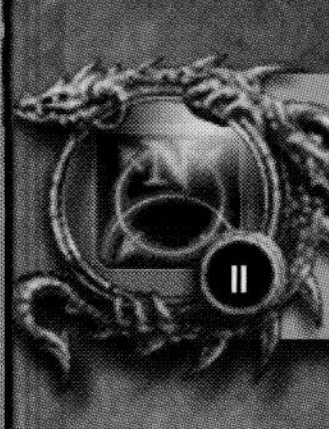

WARLOCK

For some mages, the lure of dark power and knowledge proved too great for mere study. They found a new wellspring of chaotic magic, allowing them to reach into the strength of the demons. Gifted with the ability to manipulate these demonic forces, the Warlocks are powerful sorcerers, and the pacts that they form with demons are a sign of their devotion to dark arts.

Demons are never far from a Warlock's call, and the Warlock is a master at controlling them. These sinister creatures follow the Warlock's orders, attacking enemies and protecting their master. A Warlock's servant fights for them, and often the Warlock thinks nothing of sacrificing their demonic pet if the situation calls for it; a new summoning spell is all that it takes to drag the demon back to the world of Azeroth.

Because of their devotion to dark arts, Warlocks are feared and distrusted by most of the races. Within the lands of the Alliance, Warlocks are shunned and their places of teaching are outside of major cities. The Orcs also have a great deal of suspicion toward Warlocks; most want nothing to do with demons ever again, and Orc history is replete with pain and anguish caused by their involvement with the demons. Only the Undead fully accept Warlocks as part of their civilization, giving them freedom and respect. However, despite the mistrust engendered by these practices, there will always be people who pursue dark but powerful knowledge.

WARRIOR

The roar of battle, the thrill of combat, the joy of victory: all of these things appeal to certain individuals. With the heart pumping and adrenaline rushing, they truly feel alive! Anyone interested in tactics and the feel of melee battle can find satisfaction and happiness in being a Warrior.

For some, this means that they can protect their friends and allies. They can guide the course of battles so that the entire group is whole and healthy. For others, it gives them a chance to rush full tilt into the fray, reveling in the pleasure of physical combat. Still others take a more mercenary approach, doing it for the feeling of accomplishment that can be gained by doing a good job for good money.

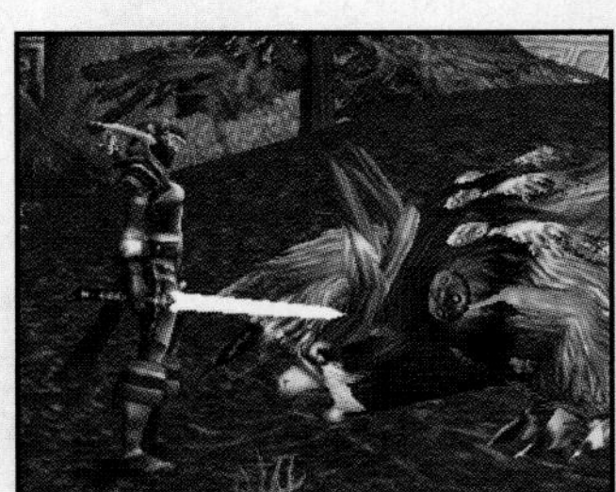

In the Alliance, warriors can be found from all the races. Humans, Night Elves, Dwarves, and Gnomes all value their defenders, and with the threats that the nations have had to face, all are valued. In the Horde, Tauren, Trolls, and Undead all have their share of warriors, and each of them plays a strong role. Only the Orcs are left without, for the ranks of Orc warriors were depleted during the fierce wars they have had to fight.

DUN MOROGH

Dwarves and Gnomes have been part of the Alliance for quite some time. These industrious folk have also supported each other, and that shows in the way both races live in close proximity without savaging each other every few years. Yet, there are clear differences between these two cultures. The Dwarves are strong, courageous, and proud. They produce blades, guns, armor, and great buildings of stone. Gnomes are more inquisitive, building gadgets that are not always of immediate use or even known purpose. Together, the two races make Dun Morogh a land of many trades.

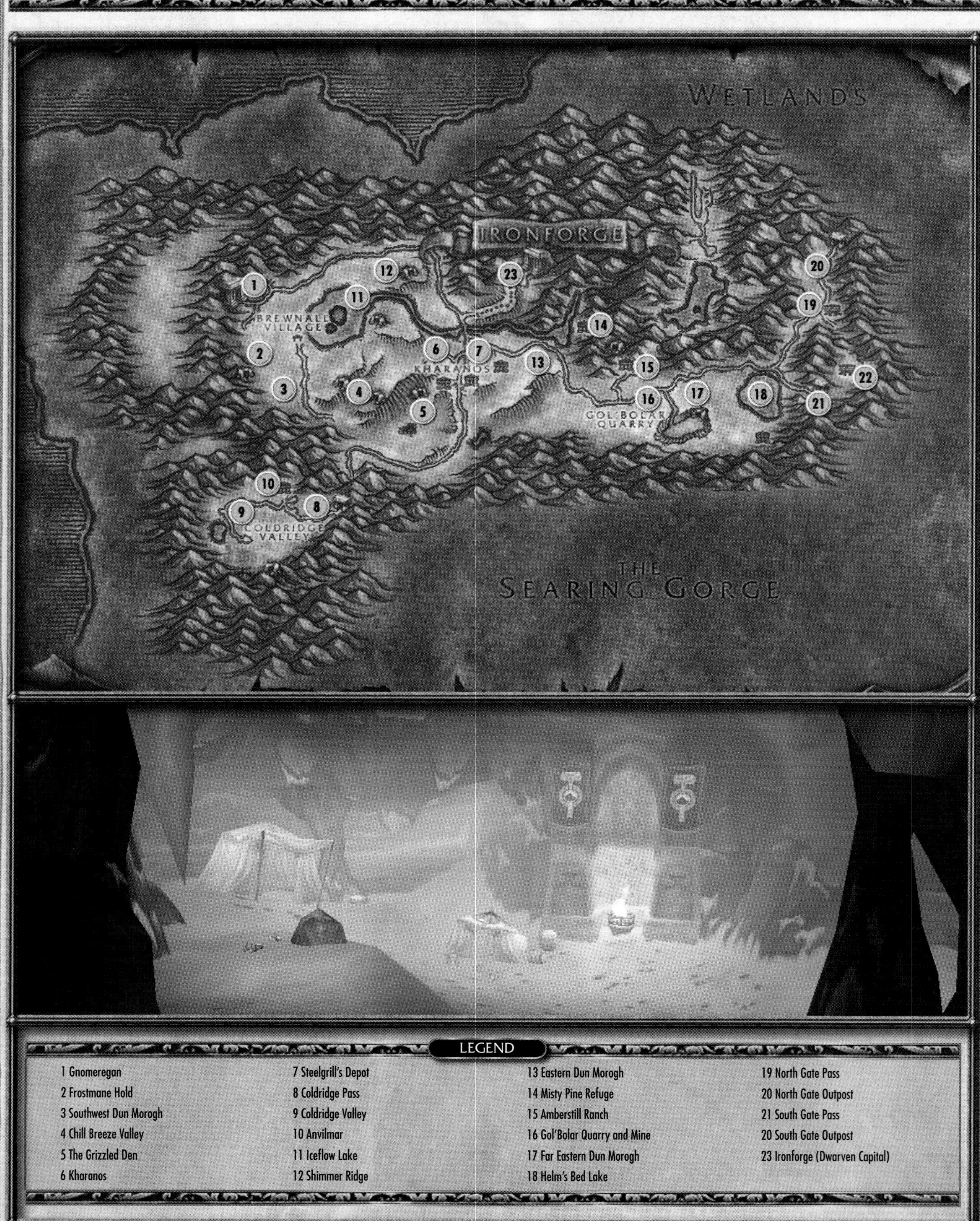

LEGEND

1 Gnomeregan	7 Steelgrill's Depot	13 Eastern Dun Morogh	19 North Gate Pass
2 Frostmane Hold	8 Coldridge Pass	14 Misty Pine Refuge	20 North Gate Outpost
3 Southwest Dun Morogh	9 Coldridge Valley	15 Amberstill Ranch	21 South Gate Pass
4 Chill Breeze Valley	10 Anvilmar	16 Gol'Bolar Quarry and Mine	20 South Gate Outpost
5 The Grizzled Den	11 Iceflow Lake	17 Far Eastern Dun Morogh	23 Ironforge (Dwarven Capital)
6 Kharanos	12 Shimmer Ridge	18 Helm's Bed Lake	

Anyone who suddenly appears inside Ironforge or any number of Dwarven strongholds might think that the land outside was blasted with heat and steam. Yet, Dun Morogh is a cold land, high in the mountains where a biting wind becomes one's frequent companion. Between rocky crags and icy lakes, the Yetis, Trolls, and beasts find their niche, but there are rewards in this isolated land. Potent herbs find a way to poke through the snows, desperate for light, and metal seems to pour up through the earth as well. For the wary eye, Dun Morogh is a place of great riches!

ANVILMAR

Anvilmar is a place of rest in southern Dun Morogh. Mainly a Dwarven site, the merchants, trainers, and travelers who come through are often on their way to more comfortable climes. Luckily, your first steps out here are quite safe. There is very little danger from the weaker Troggs and Wolves that dominate the hunting grounds nearby, and people are friendly in Anvilmar, offering many quests and services to those who are willing to work.

One of the first people to approach is Balir Frosthammer. This local toughman is angry at the Troggs for their recent attacks; instead of ignoring the dull "buggers," he wants to bring them to heel. He asks that you slay 5 Rockjaw Troggs and 5 Burly Rockjaw Troggs. (**A New Threat**) Both are found in the local fields, though more of the Burly Troggs are seen in camps west of Anvilmar.

Before leaving the merchants, also accept **Dwarven Outfitters** from Sten Stoutarm (he's also near the area where you start off). He wishes to receive some Tough Wolf Meat, 12 pieces in total. The Wolves in the local fields are neutral, very easy to kill, and are so close to the Troggs that it takes almost no time to get this tiny quest completed. Another quick quest for those in the area comes from Felix Whindlebolt, who needs his box (**A Refugee's Quandary**) returned to him (it's in the snow south of Anvilmar).

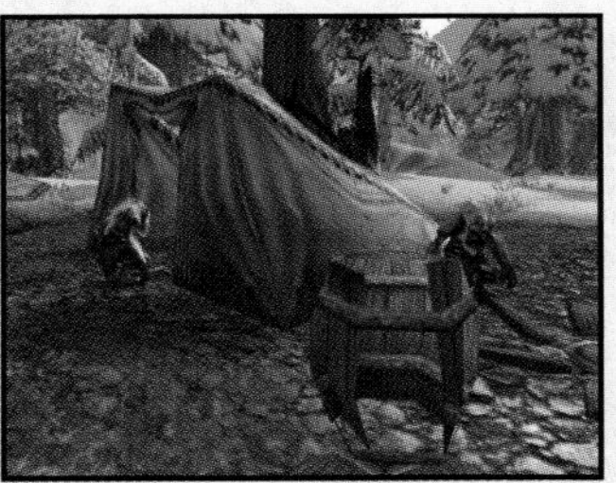

Run down into the fields and start hacking or casting away. The Troggs and Wolves won't group together, so none of these fights should challenge even a novice player. If your health starts to get low after a series of encounters, rest and chew on any food for health or take a drink for mana.

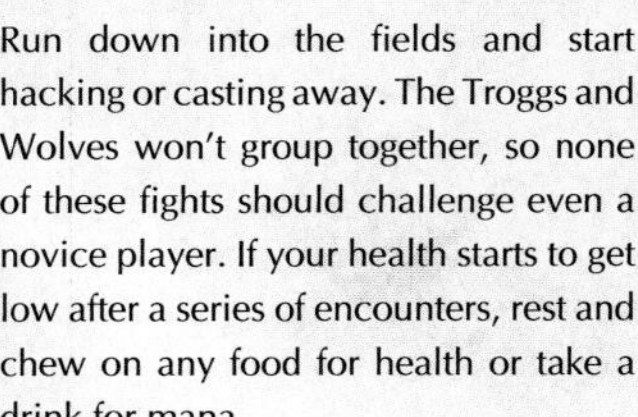

When the Troggs are slain and the Tough Wolf Meat is collected, return to the merchants and trade those in for a couple pieces of equipment. Sell spare items that were found during the fighting (unless you can use them), then go inside Anvilmar; the entrance is north and just a tad west from the merchants. There are trainers inside for all of the starting Dun Morogh classes, and your early abilities are all quite important to take before looking into tougher quests.

While training, take the Mug of Scalding Mornbrew from Adlin Pridedrift to Durnan Furcutter (**Scalding Mornbrew Delivery**), inside of Anvilmar, and return the mug to Adlin. This is a short dropoff that doesn't require any substantial effort.

More imposing and enjoyable are some of the quests outside of the small settlement. To the west are several small camps where more wilderness-oriented folk live. Take the **Coldridge Valley Mail Delivery** quest from Sten Stoutarm and seek Talin Keeneye (just west down the path from Anvilmar). Talin is worried about the boom in the Small Crag Boar population and wants you to help with thinning the ranks. (**The Boar Hunter**) Deliver your letter to him and accept this short hunting quest. Slay the boars and return before continuing on the mail route, now moving south into the lower part of the valley.

Grelin Whitebeard takes his package from you without trouble, but he does have a few chores for those who are feeling brave. He doesn't like the fact that aggressive Trolls are living in the area in and around the cave to the south, but he also doesn't want to bother the army with such a trifling matter. Instead, he offers to reward you quite fairly for slaying 15 Frostmane Troll Whelps. (**The Troll Cave**) The Trolls have enough to their numbers that you're free to kill the ones outside until the quest is done; adventuring into cave itself occurs soon enough.

If you see other players in the area while killing Whelps, feel free to ask them if they want to group. Because this quest is a kill task, it is extremely fast when you have a partner or two. Even better, the next stage of the quest is given when Grelin rewards you for the Whelps and asks that their leader be slain as well. Grik'nir the Cold lives at the back of the Troll cave and has stolen Grelin's **Stolen Journal**. With a partner to help, this is a very easy quest, and it can be soloed instead if you're careful about fighting monsters while avoiding additional aggro.

Grelin is fairly generous with his rewards, and returning the journal is certainly a good step for you. Return to Anvilmar to sell (and possibly train, depending on the level you have reached); when you're done, take the eastern road out toward Coldridge Pass. Drop off the final letter to the Dwarves at the top of the hill, just before the pass, and grab **Supplies to Tannock** from Hands Springsprocket.

Fight the Troggs inside and move forward until you leave the sheltered valley behind and head into Dun Morogh proper. The road leads to the fine town of Kharanos, where more quests and adventure wait. If you're interested in getting more experience and goodies on the way, stay close to the road and fight the slightly stronger enemies there (at least, they're stronger compared with the timid beasts of Anvilmar).

KHARANOS AND STEELGRILL'S DEPOT

The first point of order in this new region is to go inside the inn (on the right side of town) and talk to the innkeeper there. Tannock Frosthammer is the keeper of the inn; he'll reward you for delivering the supplies from Hands (back in Anvilmar). Also, speak with Tannock and set your home point here in Kharanos, which is a fine central location.

Ragnar Thunderbrew provides a suitable task; to learn the recipe for **Beer Basted Boar Ribs**, you need 6 Crag Boar Ribs and a Rhapsody Malt (purchased inside the inn). Because you are hunting boars anyway, it's a perfect quest to grab. This can be done very early on without any trouble at all. Collect this, but don't head out yet.

Tharek Blackstone has forged some tools for Beldin Steelgrill. This short delivery quest is a fine act to get out of the way because it provides fast experience and knowledge of where Steelgrill's Depot is stationed. (**Tools for Steelgrill**) Since there are several quests out of the Depot, it's good to find it early. Take the quest and run northeast from Kharanos (the Depot is just over the hill). Drop off the tools and talk to the fine Dwarves who work there before leaving.

Pilot Bellowfiz has a good quest, **Stocking Jetsteam**, that is best done while running around for other tasks. Because he wants Chunks of Boar Meat and Thick Bear Fur, the beasts of the area become fine targets of opportunity while working on other quests (doing this at the same time as Beer Basted Boar Ribs saves you some effort). Take **Evershine** from Bellowfiz as well; killing creatures in your way out to the distant location of Brewnall Village should nearly complete the quest.

Pilot Stonegear has another quest worth grabbing (**The Grizzled Den**) while you're still at Steelgrill's Depot. To add that cozy feeling to his engine, Stonegear wants some Wendigo Manes, 8 in all. These are taken from the Wendigos who live southwest of Kharanos, in and around a large cave there. Get this quest now, but do it after either getting a partner or finishing several easier quests first; the Wendigos are not difficult, but their lair is more profitable when fully explored. Thus, it's better to go there when you have another couple levels or a nice group.

BREWNALL VILLAGE

With a number of quests collected, it's time to start getting things done. Move north a tad and west from the road out of Kharanos and start fighting on the way toward Brewnall Village (just west of the Iceflow Lake). There should be a number of boars and bears along the way, so there are at least two quests being worked on just by fighting here and there!

The Evershine quest has a single-handed axe or a decent staff reward, but you can't collect these simply by making the run. Indeed, when you get to Brewnall and speak with Rejold Barleybrew; he gives you the Cask of Evershine that you need after a tidy kill quest is completed. (**A Favor for Evershine**) Go out into the wild and bring down 6 Ice Claw Bears and 8 each of Elder Crag Boars and Snow Leopards. This helps polish off anything outstanding for your earlier quest!

The other quest to get is Bitter Rivals from Marleth Barleybrew. Because you have several quest dropoffs at Kharanos and Steelgrill's Depot to hit soon, take care of Bitter Rivals on the way. Take that now, then complete it while running errands back at home. Bitter Rivals is fairly easy to accomplish; buy some Thunderbrew Ale at the inn and use that to distract the Dwarf who is guarding the Thunder Lager in the basement. Wait until the Dwarf is gone, and then switch the Barrel of Lager for one of Barleybrew Scalder. Done and done.

Before returning to Brewnall, train and sell items, then take care of the two southern quests. First is The Grizzled Den, which you received back at Steelgrill's Depot. Now is a fine time to kill the Wendigos and collect the substantial supply of metal, leather, and cloth that are available inside the cave.

WENDIGOS HAVE IT ALL

Wendigos can be skinned for their leather. In addition, they frequently drop coin and cloth. Add to that the supply of copper in their dungeon and you have an area that is *perfect* for crafters, even in groups. Low-level sorts interested in raising their new trades often find that the Wendigos offer much while demanding little.

After collecting the Wendigo Manes, move west and through one of the small mountain passes to the north. On your map, there's a pair of caves; both of these involve a single quest that can be quickly completed. The left cave is reached by climbing the mountains east of its location; there are some wooden platforms there, hinting that something important is above. Climb over the ridge and talk to Tundra MacGrann. (**Stolen Stash**) He is having major problems because his Dried Meats have been stolen by an elite Wendigo. MacGrann isn't strong enough to fight the monster on his own, and you aren't likely to win against it either. What to do?

There are several ways to complete Tundra MacGrann's Stolen Stash quest. Climb down the mountains and look at the eastern cave. Old Icebeard lives there, and the lockbox of meat is inside his den. Patient folks who are solo can simply wait for Icebeard to wander away from his cave (he does this from time to time). Rush in, grab the meat, and tear back to MacGrann for a set of mail bracers. Groups can simply fight the beast, which is perfectly fine too. Or, a pair of two adventurers can trade aggro with Icebeard, having one person grab the box and then return to distract the Wendigo for their partner. Fast and simple too.

Turn in the southern quests and talk to Senir Whitebeard about Frostmane Hold. A rarity, this Dwarf doesn't like to get his hands dirty and finish work on his own. He gives another western quest that you should do on your next run out to Brewnall, as discussed shortly.

In addition, visit the Gnomes who live in the northern part of Kharanos, in a house on the west side. They offer **Operation Recombobulation**, an exciting quest that takes you to the edge of Gnomeregan. Finish this quest by killing the Leper Gnomes out there for two sets of parts, Restabilization Cogs and Gyromechanic Gears. This is great timing because the Gnomes aren't that far from Brewnall, and another trip is needed to finish Bitter Rivals and grab several additional quests.

BREWNALL REVISITED, TROLLS, AND GNOMEREGAN

The Leper Gnomes are spread out enough in the west that even a solo character can handle them without many problems (just be wary of wandering Gnomes and the dangers associated with them adding). It rarely takes more than 15-20 kills to get everything done there and then return to Brewnall. Instead of making a full trip back to Kharanos, it's better to finish events at Frostmane Hold here and now, when you're close to the Troll's stronghold.

Move south from Gnomeregan and look for the cave on the map that hugs the western walls of the area. That is Frostmane. If your level is still a tad low, ask for a companion while entering the place (forming a group now is wise anyway, since the next couple quests are quite challenging). Killing the five Headhunters is pretty much mandatory to get into the cave and explore it, so don't worry about that aspect of the quest. Simply fight in toward the back of the cave and wait until it says that you have completed the goal of exploring Frostmane Hold.

Stop back in Brewnall on the way northeast and talk to Rejold Barleybrew. Rejold is trying to brew The Perfect Stout, and he needs Shimmerweed to accomplish this lofty goal. Take heed; the Trolls up on Shimmer Ridge are some of the deadliest enemies near Brewnall, and they work well together. Are you brave enough to stick your neck out for a better drink?

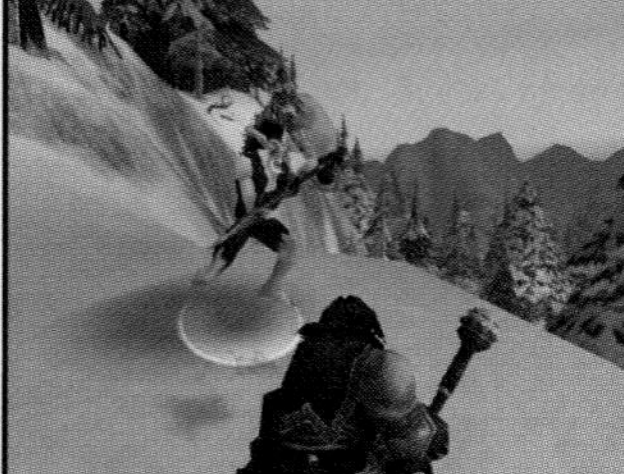

DECISIONS, DECISIONS

Though you have quests to turn in back in Kharanos now, it saves major travel time to get this quest done before leaving the area (this time, you won't be coming back east, so the trip would be "wasted" if you returned now). That said, The Perfect Stout is *very* hard to solo, and having a partner or an extra level could make the difference. So, decide whether to do The Perfect Stout now or after a short run for dropoffs/training instead.

The path up to Shimmer Ridge is northeast of Brewnall, at the northern end of the mountains by the ice lake. Fighting the Trolls along the path up is easy, but look out for patrollers. Shimmerweed does not drop often off of these Trolls, but it does fall from time to time. For a slow victory, keep camping the easy Trolls along the paths and just wait for the Shimmerweed. It's not fast or particularly fun compared with other quests in the area, but it gets the job done.

Or, for a better (more dangerous) time, take a couple buddies and storm the campsites that are both west and east along crude paths on the ridge. All of the Trolls are skilled at ranged combat, with thrown spears and magic. This makes groups of the Trolls quite capable of killing adventurers. If there are multiple casters in a cluster ahead, consider having the party divide and kill both at a slightly slower pace (using interrupts to their fullest to minimize caster DPS).

Baskets of Shimmerweed are found in the camps, and this dramatically aids in the completion of the quest when you are lucky enough to find them. These ground spawns can be opened in the same way as chests, and they take just as long to respawn.

With the full supply that Rejold requested, descend back into Brewnall and give the brewer his prize. The experiment appears to be a great success, and Rejold has a final request: take a barrel of the new Shimmer Stout to Mountaineer Barleybrew. There is a guard area at the very edge of Dun Morogh, before the tunnel into Loch Modan. Mountaineer Barleybrew is on the eastern side of the cleared area. Hold onto the barrel while finishing your tasks in Dun Morogh and Ironforge, then complete this later on, when heading out of the region.

IRONFORGE AND THE ROAD TO LOCH MODAN

With Frostmane Hold done, Senir Whitebeard gives you The Reports and bids you take them to Senator Barin Redstone of Ironforge. It's about time that you get to see the great city, and with the troubles of the land settling (thanks to your good deeds), a short break should be pleasant. Walk along the north road out of Kharanos, but take it all the way up to Ironforge, the capital. There are many things to do here, especially for crafters (seek the many city trainers to collect any trades that you wish to pursue). The Senator is found in the King's chamber (in the High Seat), so include a stop there during your circuit through Ironforge.

IRONFORGE POINTS OF INTEREST

LOCATION	USEFUL STORES/NPCS
Main Gate	Inn, Bank, Visitor's Center, General Goods, Auction House
Mystic Ward	Mage/Portal Trainer, Paladin Trainer, Priest Trainer
Forlorn Cavern	Rogue Trainer, Lockpicking Trainer, Fishing Trainer, Warlock/Demon Trainer
Hall of Explorers	Quest Recipients
Tinker Town	Gnomeregan Quests, Engineering Trainer, Alchemy Trainer, Stormwind/Ironforge Tram
Military Ward	Inn, Warrior Trainer, Hunter Trainer, Survival Trainer
Great Forge	Griffon Master, Herbalism Trainer, First Aid Trainer, Enchanting Trainer, Mining Trainer, Blacksmith Trainer, Tailoring Trainer, Leatherworking Trainer, Skinning Trainer, High Seat

With the capital explored and many fine quests completed, it's appropriate for you to seek Loch Modan, the beautiful land east of Dun Morogh. There are still some exciting places to see before you leave your homeland, so start making your way east and look for some of the following hotspots.

There is a ranch just a minute or so east of Ironforge. Rudra Amberstill is a Ram breeder there, yet he is beset with troubles caused by a monster named Vagash. He asks that you help him by **Protecting the Herd**. Vagash is found on the other side of the mountain, just north of the ranch. Climb west and around the bulk of the mountains and bring a friend or two unless you are greatly prepared for an ugly fight! Vagash is Level 11 and is an elite Wendigo, so take that into consideration before the fight starts. Offer the Fang of Vagash as proof to Rudra that the attacks will stop (he has either a leather chestpiece or a two-handed mace to give as rewards).

Two glorious quests are given by the Dwarves at the Gol'Bolar Quarry. Stop there as you continue east and talk to Senator Mehr Stonehallow, **The Public Servant**, in the camp just above the quarry. He is frustrated by the Troggs' attack on the mine and its miners. Without much of a choice, he demands that the Troggs be put down. Kill 10 Rockjaw Bonesnappers to turn the tide against the assaulting forces. Foreman Stonebrow, standing nearby, also wants to see **Those Blasted Troggs** punished for their violence against the worksite. For his part, 6 Skullthumpers must be put to rest.

With a group, these two quests are frighteningly easy and fast. If alone, take the quarry very slowly and fight near the walls to avoid as many patrol issues as possible. Be careful of Troggs that stand behind ice pillars and such near the dungeon entrance, and be sure to stay well rested in case sudden adds demand more from your hit points and mana.

A CRAFTER'S DREAM

The Wendigo Cave was good, but the Quarry is an even better location for crafters of all sorts. There is a wealth of copper inside the mine itself, but there are also veins outside of it (in the general Quarry). Beyond that, the Troggs are a fine source of Linen and drop money as well. Herbalists will also be pleased because of the high concentration of Earthroot near the Quarry and both Silverleaf and Peacebloom within a short run west.

In the far northeast is a short quest that you can finish to ease the mind of a troubled Dwarf. Pilot Hammerfoot is guarding some engines in that area, but he won't leave the region until he's convinced that his friend Mori is either alive and well or dead and lost. (**The Lost Pilot**) Mori charged off into the hills some time back, and you can help out be discovering his fate. Move farther north along the road, then break west when you can. Deeper in, the body of Mori is found.

Though slain, Mori was able to account for his fate before his death. In his journal, the Dwarf wrote of a powerful Ice Claw Bear named **Mangeclaw**. Vengeance was the pilot's final wish, and it would further aid his companions to know that this was done. Look slightly south and scour the area for the bear, then slay the beast. Tell Pilot Hammerfoot when the mission of vengeance is complete.

The road east leads directly through a guardpost where Mountaineer Barleybrew works; give him his brother's barrel of Shimmer Stout. The Dwarf also wants one of his friends to try the mixture, and he passes the brew along with a request that it be sent to Mountaineer Kadrell of Loch Modan (one of the Thelsamar guards). Because you were on your way into Loch Modan already, this offers no expense of time or energy.

Congratulations on your successes in Dun Morogh. Rams are breeding happily, the Dwarfs have raised a fine toast in your name, and even the snow seems to have receded a bit because of such fine efforts. New challenges wait in Loch Modan and in lands such as Westfall to the south and Darkshore across the ocean, but those are adventures for another time.

ELWYNN FOREST

This walkthrough explains your first day with a character in Elwynn Forest; we take you from Level 1 and Northshire Abbey to Goldshire, then on to the more distant farms and the Eastvale Logging Camp, and eventually to the city of Stormwind and the roads beyond! The goal of the walkthrough is to safely and comfortably guide new players through their first ten to twelve levels and describe the quests, actions, and secrets of Elwynn.

LEGEND

1 Westbrook Garrison	6 The Maclure Vineyards	11 Echo Ridge Mine	16 Tower of Azora
2 Forest's Edge	7 Jerod's Landing	12 Northshire Vineyards	17 Stone Cairn Lake and Hero's Vigil
3 Mirror Lake Orchard	8 Goldshire	13 Jasperlode Mine	18 Eastvale Logging Camp
4 Fargodeep Mine	9 Crystal Lake	14 Southern Elwynn Forest	19 Ridgepoint Tower
5 The Stonefield Farm	10 Northshire Valley	15 Brackwell Pumpkin Patch	20 Stormwind (Human Capital)

Elwynn Forest is the pleasant home of Stormwind City and the basket of Human civilization in the east. Surrounded by settled farms, lumber mills, and mines, everything is within arm's reach in Elwynn. Humans who take up the call of adventure start here, where life is mostly safe and settled. Better to get your feet wet in Elwynn than to plunge headfirst into the troubles of more distant lands.

NORTHSHIRE

Northshire Abbey is tucked into a protected valley on the northern side of Elwynn Forest. Few enemies of import have ever seen the gentle streams of Northshire or sieged this humble land. Adventurers who begin here start close to the Abbey itself. Note the merchants standing outside, near their wagons and wares (they are fine folk to sell items to after your upcoming hunting).

Standing on a small hill outside of the abbey is Deputy Willem, a brave man of Northshire (he has a Yellow Quest Indicator over his head). Willem has several tasks for you, but he first wishes that you go inside and speak with Marshal McBride. (**A Threat Within**) Step into the quiet halls of the Abbey and do as Willem requests. Marshal McBride is standing by the front of the building and cannot be missed. Talk to the Marshal and find out what troubles have come upon Northshire recently. McBride wants to have some of the Kobolds outside cleared out; they are not major threats, but it's inappropriate to have them here, making trouble. (**Kobold Camp Cleanup**)

Accept this task and leave the building. Turn right and look around the side of the abbey to find Eagan Peltskinner. He wants to see some of the Timberwolves brought into line as well, and have Wolf Meat brought back to him. (**Wolves Across the Border**) Because the Wolves are near the Kobolds, it's wise to accept this chore also and do them both at the same time.

The Wolves and Kobold Vermin are just north of the abbey entrance. Fight the Wolves as you make your approach to the Kobold camps and stock the meat away for Eagan. When you have enough, tear into the Kobold Vermin. There are slightly more powerful Kobold Workers mixed in with the Vermin, but they too are neutral to you, being horribly trained and inexperienced in real combat. If there are many targets and few others hunting, dive into the Vermin and avoid the Workers. If you must wait for Vermin targets, fight some of the Workers to pass the time to see the difference between levels of monsters.

When enough Vermin have been eradicated, return to the abbey and collect your reward for both Eagan's quest and the Marshal's. The Marshal isn't terribly pleased with what he's hearing about the Kobold presence; he wants more investigation done (**Investigate Echo Ridge**). Return to the camps and fight 10 Kobold Workers; many of these are near the actual entrance to the Echo Ridge Mine, set into the northern hillside, but enough are in the camps to support multiple hunters. As a kill task, this duty goes faster in groups, but the difficulty is so minimal here that doing so is entirely a matter of taste.

With 10 Workers down, seek out Marshal McBride once again. Fully convinced of the problem now, he asks that you fight inside the mine and kill both Workers and Laborers. This time he's offering rewards that are a bit more generous (for Leather or Mail wearers certainly), so the quest is a bit more pleasing to complete. (**Skirmish at Echo Ridge**)

Fighting inside the mines is safe enough; Kobold Laborers are still passive brutes, so you dictate who to fight and when to do so. Rest between battles if your Health or Mana become depleted (feel free to use the modest Food or Water available to you, as these are worth very little and can decrease downtime).

McBride needs no reminder to pay you once you bring him the final tally of the fallen Kobolds. Don the new armor, if possible, and talk to Deputy Willem again; he now has other duties for you (more challenging than the battle for the Echo Ridge Mine). Indeed, a foul gang known as the Defias has taken control of the nearby Vineyards. They have substantial numbers and an aggressive disposition, and there is no choice but to go in fighting! The Deputy has chosen you for this task. (**Brotherhood of Thieves**)

Before leaving, talk to Eagan Peltskinner; he'll mention that a friend of his is in a bit of trouble. This Milly Osworth is nearby, standing just east of the abbey. Talk to her about her lost harvest. **Milly's Harvest** is a quest to get Harvest Buckets from the Vineyards across the water. Collect 8 of these before returning, and do this while fighting the Defias to get multiple quests done at the same time. Return to Milly when you are done then take her manifest to Brother Neals, in the bell tower of the Abbey.

The Vineyards are to the east, across a small stream. If you cross at the bridge, be wary of the two Defias on the other side (these aggressive enemies will attack you once they are aware of your approach). Either look for lone Defias to avoid larger fights and being outnumbered, or grab fellow adventurers in the region for a Defias hunting party! Groups do well in the fields, where there are many more targets. Individuals have better luck a bit farther north, where the Defias are more spread out.

Beyond killing the Defias, Willem wants Garrick Padfoot brought down for his cruel and unforgivable crimes. (**Bounty on Garrick Padfoot**) This Defias scoundrel is almost due east, at a shack along the mountains. Be sure to gather his head to complete your sweep through Northshire! A single Defias stands at the cabin with Garrick, so you are likely to have a fight with both of them at once. Concentrate on Garrick first to ensure the quest's completion, and then worry about bringing down the spare Defias.

Speak to Marshal McBride one more time to see if he needs any final help. There are some documents that need to be delivered to Goldshire, and this is going to be your next stop anyway (what fortune!), so there is no harm in doing this for the Marshal.

Collect all of the final rewards for the quests you've done and bid farewell to these comfortable haunts; you have already graduated to a greater field of battle! Your character is likely to be around Level 5 with all of the quests done, and you have a few items to equip from both the quests and from random drops (if fate has been kind). Remember to put any 6 Slot Bags you find into their own slots for added storage, and talk to Falkhaan Isenstrider on the way out of the valley (he gives you a quest to seek the Lion's Pride Inn in Goldshire).

GOLDSHIRE

The road leading away from Northshire heads directly into Goldshire, to the south, so it's not a difficult trip. Out in central Elwynn Forest, there are many more aggressive monsters. Notice the hostile Wolves and Defias that lurk near the edge of the road; fight these if you wish for more money and experience, but be wary of other hostiles who might join the fray and cause trouble during the encounters.

It takes just over a minute to make the trip to Goldshire. The small town opens into a central square, flanked by the town's Inn, Forge, and local vendors.

HEARTHSTONES

Speak with the Innkeeper and ask for a place to rest. This binds you to this particular inn. Though the stones have a one hour cooldown, use them frequently to cut down on travel time back from more distant quests (like those out to the Eastvale Logging Camp).

Marshal Dughan is always standing outside of the inn, watching for trouble from those who wander through town. Hand him the documents from Northshire and see what is next in your journeys. The Kobolds are a problem down south as well, and the Fargodeep Mine is having far worse problems that the one at Echo Ridge. You are needed to explore the mine and find out how bad the infestation has become. (**The Fargodeep Mine**)

Don't rush off to do this quite yet. There are several tasks in Goldshire that involve Kobolds, and it's always a boon to be working on several quests at the same time. Grab the quests from Remy (outside, by the vendors) and William Pestle (just inside the inn, on the left). Now you have two types of items to collect from the Kobolds and a quest to search the mines to the south, where there are tons of Kobolds! Win-win, eh? (**Kobold Candles** and **Gold Dust Exchange**)

Odds are that you don't feel quite ready for the Fargodeep Mine by yourself (the creatures are higher level than early Goldshire arrivals, group together, and are in decent numbers at several points in the mine). So, there are two options at this point. One route is to band together with three or four fellow adventurers and take on the mines without hesitation (a large group will have to clear Fargodeep several times to get all of the Gold Dust and Candles they need, but the safety level is much higher).

Or, if you feel like a more solitary path, try walking south and diverting to the west slightly when you see the large hill for the mine. Just west of that area is the Stonefield Farm. There are quests here that you can start on without searching for partners.

Look around the farm and speak with everyone there. "Auntie" Bernice Stonefield has lost her necklace, and she is pretty darn sure where it snuck off to: a boy from the nearby Maclure Vineyards that has been causing trouble pretty much since he was born. (**The Lost Necklace**) Bernice wants you to find the lad and get the necklace back from him.

Fight some of the creatures in and around the farms while running east to the Maclure Vineyards, and certainly take out Kobold targets of opportunity outside of the mines (where they are unlikely to receive assistance), and poke your head around the eastern farm (just on the other side of the mine). Billy did steal that necklace, sure enough, but he isn't telling where it is. If you really want the answer, without resorting to horrible violence, the boy demands 4 chunks of Boar Meat. (**Pie for Billy**) Beyond that, he wants you to have those made into a pie for him by Bernice Stonefield (yes, the kid has plenty of nerve).

Talk to Maybell Maclure before leaving to fight the boars. She has a romantic problem and wishes to avoid an Elizabethan ending to it; her family hates the Stonefields, but she is in love with Tommy Joe, a young man who hails from there. Her family wouldn't accept it under any circumstance, so she needs help to run away and find a new life with him. (**Young Lovers**) This involves a bit of running around, but you're going to be doing that anyway (getting Boar Meat, making a pie, and so forth).

Kill enough Boars to get the meat, and do all this while moving back and forth, hitting more Kobolds and gaining general experience. By the time you bring Billy his pie, you should be up around Level 6 (where another quest opens). Ma Stonefield is a wee jealous of a prize-winning boar that the Brackwell's have. Princess, as she is known, is a big girl, and you get the lovely job of ending her reign of girth. That quest can wait, but it's good to have. (**Princess Must Die!**)

After getting the pie to Billy and finding out that a Kobold actually has the necklace, it's really time to look at Fargodeep, which has up to four quests to complete if you haven't gotten a chance to go inside yet. (**Goldtooth**) Start looking for a group that is already working the mine or planning to, and continue about your business with other quests until a slot opens in a nifty group, or until you are high enough to do the mine on your own (at around Level 8).

Continuing on Maybell's quests will pass the time productively, if you're waiting. Talk to Tommy Joe at the south-western part of his family's farm. He tells you that his grandmother can be trusted to help and that she's smart enough to come up with an answer. (**Speak with Gramma**) She sends you into Goldshire with a note for William Pestle, inside the inn. He can make a potion to help the young lovers run off together, but he needs several Crystal Kelp Fronds. (**Collecting Kelp**) Just east of town is Crystal Lake, where many Murlocs frolic in the clear water. Isolated Murlocs patrol the outer edge of the lake, and these are perfect targets for your quest.

Return to the two farms and clear up the Lovers' quests (**The Escape**), once you have the potion, and plow through the Fargodeep/Kobold quests that remain. This brings home plenty of experience and puts your character into a better position for wandering around the rest of Elwynn; many of the wandering monsters aren't quite as scary now.

GOLDTOOTH

Because there are casters and such near Goldtooth, it's important to see what abilities your class has to disrupt caster activities. Make sure you know how to stun, interrupt casting, or otherwise cripple these potent ranged foes.

Back in Goldshire, Marshal Dughan sends you off to the final mine of the region. (**The Jasperlode Mine**) He wants the Jasperlode Mine explored as well. That mine is in the center of Elwynn, but east of the Northshire road. The Kobolds that were seen around that mine are tougher, and some talk of Spiders has reached town too. If you still have a group from the previous quests, try to keep them together for dealing with both the Jasperlode Mine and Princess. It won't take very long to get both of these done in a party, and it's so much easier.

Exploring the Jasperlode Mine doesn't take long once you arrive, because the quest is considered completed once you make it a short distance into the mine. Quest-hungry players often leave at that point. Those eager for skill points and early tradeskills should stay and fight the Spiders and Kobolds for a time.

Princess and two tough Boars wander around the Pumpkin Patch, south of the road and somewhat far east from the Maclure Vineyards. Princess is a hefty girl, and she can deal substantial damage to people. Have tanks engage her before ranged folks get in on the act (this prevents her from charging). Attack Princess first and have any allies bring her down; even if party members fall during the fight, they should be able to return to loot Princess before her body disappears.

THE EASTVALE LOGGING CAMP

The Marshal has more than enough troubles for one time, and the situation in the east has him worried in a more pressing way than even the Kobold insurgence. Murloc attacks in the east have caused people in the Eastvale Logging Camp to get a bit nervous, and they already have to deal with Defias brigands and rumors of war in Redridge. To rectify the situation, report to Guard Thomas; he's by the bridge just shy of the Logging Camp. (**Further Concerns**)

EQUIPMENT IMPROVEMENTS

With a spare bit of cash players can fill out their equipment a bit by this point in the game. Sure, those silver are hard fought, but the sum of 5 to 10 silver won't mean much in the long run, and getting a better weapon or armor piece at a critical period can make all the difference. So, if you've been unlucky in rewards and drops, stop by Stormwind and see what's available in the Trade Channels. An inexpensive flight or train ride up to Ironforge is always available as well (if you want to see the Auction House).

Take the road east and fight some of the woodland creatures along the way if you're interested in more experience and the chance for some loot. It isn't a terribly long journey, and Guard Thomas does have an interesting quest or two for dealing with the Murloc threat. **Find the Lost Guards** is the first quest; it requires you to see what happened to two soldiers who disappeared recently. Look of the west bank of the river when it meets Stone Cairn Lake to find the first guard, then cross the river and clear the first Murloc camp to find the other. Many characters need help clearing the Murloc camp, but there are often people in the area who are willing to do this (lone characters can try to break the camp by pulling a couple Murlocs at a time, but it's a dangerous proposition for new recruits).

With the plight of the guards discovered, Guard Thomas can assign a **Bounty on Murlocs** who started the bloody affair. Take the fight to the Murlocs and receive a probably weapon upgrade for your troubles (dagger, mace, or sword). Thomas also offers a reward for a kill quest against the Prowlers and Bears in the area; this is another perfect group quest because it can easily be finished by a few people. (**Protect the Frontier**)

Supervisor Raelen has a quest from inside the Logging Camp. Talk to this worker and find out about the Wood Piles that are scattered around near the camp. Gathering these is easy to do while you hunt for Prowlers and Bears, so this is a fast and simple quest unless many other players are picking up the wood already. (**A Bundle of Trouble**)

Before leaving the Logging Camp, talk to Sara Timberlain (SW in camp) and get the collection quest against the Defias. (**Red Linen Goods**) Any of the Defias in Elwynn will do for this, so it's a fine target of opportunity quest while other tasks are being done. Most people come back to the camp several times anyway.

Guard Thomas sends you back to Goldshire with your duties done, and Marshal Dughan hands you a marker for some armor. Indeed, this has to be taken back to Sara Timberlain, so wait until you have the Defias Bandanas and do them both at the same time.

STORMWIND CITY

With a bit of spare fighting and good fortune, you are probably going to hit Level 10 soon. That's a great time to visit Stormwind, if you haven't already. Take the Candles from William Pestle to his brother Morgan, at a shop close to the front entrance of Stormwind. (**Delivery to Stormwind**)

HELPFUL GUARDS

The guards in Stormwind know where a fair number of NPCs are located. Talking to a City Guard allows you to ask where various trainers and stores can be found (these are then marked on your minimap after the conversation has concluded). Don't feel shy about pestering guards for such information—they just like to help out.

While in town, do any training that wasn't finished back in Goldshire, and learn any trades that just aren't available in the earlier towns.

STORMWIND BY DISTRICTS

DISTRICT	QUICK POINTS OF INTEREST
Trade	Griffons, Inn, Trade Supplies, Guild Functions, Bank
Old Town	Cooking, Leatherworking, Skinning, Warrior/Rogue Barracks
Mage's Quarter	Alchemy, Enchanting, Herbalism, Tailoring, Mage's Tower
Cathedral	Quests, Priest/Paladin Training, First Aid
Park	Hunter Training
Dwarven District	Blacksmithing, Engineering, Mining, Forge, Anvil
Canal District	Fishing Trainer

Many characters have a class quest around Level 10 that is based off of a Stormwind mission. Talk with your trainers in the city to find out where to start and what to do for these special tasks. Most involve granting special aspects of your class that are essential to future operations (Defensive Stance for Warriors, Resurrection for Paladins, etc.).

CLEANING UP THE SCRAPS

The final bits of victory to be found in Elwynn are based around the Westbrook Garrison. The tower and barracks over there are close to the Westfall border, and a heavy Gnoll population has taken control of the southern portion along the river. Talk to Deputy Rainer outside of the barracks to start **Riverpaw Gnoll Bounty**. Also, peek around the front of the tower; there is a Wanted Poster attached to a placard there. Read this to gain a second Gnoll quest (to kill Hogger, one of the nastiest Gnolls to dare tread into Elwynn Forest). (**Wanted: Hogger**) Make sure you have both quests and dig in.

Try to collect other players while running this collection quest, and hold back on attacking Hogger until another person or two has joined. Hogger is likely to present your first encounter with an elite monster; that by itself is a worthy reward for your duties. Yet, Marshal Dughan of Goldshire rewards you wonderfully if you bring Hogger's Huge Gnoll Claw back to town.

ELITE FOES

Hogger presents a more dangerous target because he is elite. This Gnoll has about three times as many hit points of a normal Gnoll of his level. A Level 10 character can often beat a Level 11 monster without any problems, but Hogger lasts much longer, does fair damage, and can defeat solo players with fair regularity.

Be sure to wait until Hogger is alone before pulling him (it's always easier that way). Use long-term abilities during the fight to ensure that Hogger stays as debuffed as possible, and buff yourself before going in, unless you have formed a party.

You may find a Gold Pickup Schedule on the Gnolls, especially if you come across Gruff Swiftbite (at the southern side of the camp). This special item begins a quest to find **The Collector**. Take the schedule to Marshall Dughan, who asks that you bring The Collector's Ring back to him (to prove that justice has been meted out). Travel to the Brackwell Pumpkin Patch and search for Morgan the Collector. Kill any Defias who get in your way and eventually Morgan is found (he can appear at several places around the patch). With the ruffian slain, loot him for the ring and return to the Marshal for your reward.

TELDRASSIL

Teldrassil is the new home of the brave Night Elves, a people who have taken arms and magic to battle against demons and restore the balance of their spirits. With the former capital of Elven power nearly destroyed by the fighting against the demons, this refuge has grown greatly in prominence. Those ancient and animated trees that remain to protect the forest have gathered here to stop any final advance from the evil remnants. Now the Night Elves are shaking off their suffering and readying themselves for the next chapter in their history.

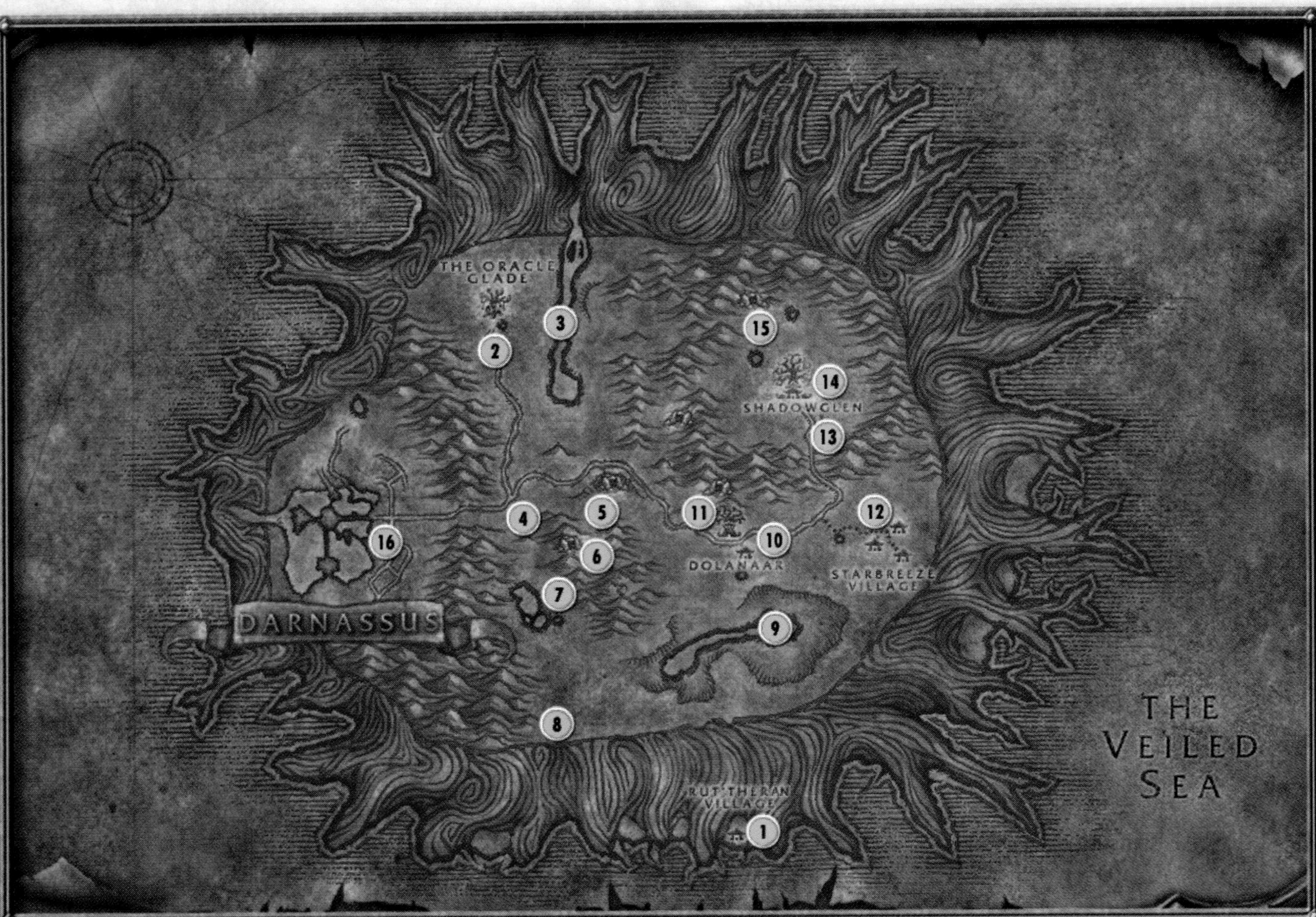

LEGEND

1 Rut'theran Village
2 The Oracle Glade
3 Wellspring River
4 Road to Darnassus
5 Ban'ethil Hollow
6 Ban'ethil Barrow Den
7 Pools of Arlithrien
8 Gnarlpine Hold
9 Lake Al'Ameth
10 Dolanaar
11 Fel Rock
12 Starbreeze Village
13 Shadowglen
14 Aldrassil
15 Shadowthread Cave
16 Darnassus (Night Elven Capital)

Teldrassil is a large island off the coast of Kalimdor. Isolated from the effects of many recent troubles, the land itself is free from some of the greater taint that plagues many of Kalimdor's forests. Yet even here, there are the stirrings of disease and corruption.

The greatest problems that exist in Teldrassil involve the tainting of natural creatures and beasts by a force of evil in the forest. Your duties often involve seeking this taint in an attempt to isolate it, eliminating the corruption, or to destroying the creatures who are beyond salvation.

ALDRASSIL

Aldrassil is the starting town, in the north-east of Teldrassil, where your character begins the journey into greatness. As with all lowbie fields, the majority of the creatures are neutral and won't attack unless engaged directly. A single large building at the center of this forested valley houses trainers, vendors, and the leaders of Aldrassil.

NIGHT ELVES HAVE METTLE, NOT METAL!

If you want to be a miner, be warned that Teldrassil is starved for metal. No one out here will train you in the hearty art of mining, and the problems don't end there. Copper is so rare out here that you won't find any of it. If mining is of tremendous importance to you, create the Night Elf you want and head to the mainland (this is doable even at low levels).

On the flipside, Peacebloom and Silverleaf are in great abundance, so harvesters who prefer Herbalism are often quite happy here. Skinners, too, have abundant resources from which to gather as many beasts in the area are skinnable.

Speak to a nearby Night Elf after watching the introduction to Teldrassil. Pan about until you spot Melithar Staghelm. Talk to him and find out about the Dryad who protects the local wood. (**The Woodland Protector**) Her name is Tarindrella, and she is close by. Melithar encourages you to seek her! Tarindrella wanders south of the town building; speak with her to find out about the Grells and the problems they are causing. These minor foes collect the Fel Moss that is a corrupting force in the region (having driven out the peaceful Firbolgs already). Agree to slay the Grells while collecting Fel Moss from them!

Speak also with Conservator Ilthalaine before going after the Grells. The Conservator is worried about the populations of both Young Nightsabers and Young Thistle Boars. These need to be thinned out, and fighting them while going after Grells and during your return trip is a fine way to gain extra coin and experience here. (**The Balance of Nature**)

Hunt the three targets mentioned above, then return to Aldrassil and turn in your quests. After selling any spare loot and equipping 6-slot bags (if you found some of them), look around for your class trainer. Most of the trainers are inside the main section of the building, but the more nature-loving folks (such as the Druid trainer) are in the higher branches of the building. Get your character any new skills, then speak with Ilthalaine a second time.

To complete the ongoing balance of beast populations, he wishes that four Mangy Nightsabers and just as many Thistle Boars be culled. Both targets are on the northern side of Aldrassil in fair numbers. On the west side of the building, standing outside, is Gilshalan Windwalker, and he has a northern quest also so talk to him while heading out. (**Webwood Venom**) Collecting Webwood Venom Sacs for him is simple, as these spiders are in high numbers near a cave to the north-west. Go after both quests simultaneously for a more efficient run!

POISON

All of the major breeds of spiders in Teldrassil are venomous. This makes fighting them a slow process due to increased downtime (especially when you factor Night Elves' limited hit points at low levels). Though needed for quests, the spiders are better avoided when hunting for money or basic experience.

While making the various runs back and forth from the spider cave, there is a longer quest to grab. To save a life, talk to Dirania Silvershine (outside, and east of the main building) and ask her about her Friend in Need. She is worried that a Night Elf man named Iverron hasn't been around to see her lately. Look to the west of the Webwood Spider Cave, in a small valley. A wounded Night Elf male named Iverron is there. He was bitten by the largest of the foul spiders and will soon perish.

To save him, get his quest and return to town (best to do this at the same time you are making your first go at the spiders). Speak with Dirania Silvershine again; luckily, she knows how to make the antidote. Fight the Grells for 7 Hyacinth Mushrooms while collecting ground spawns of them to supplement your numbers, and looks around the northern pond to snag all 4 Moonpetal Lilies. The Webwood Ichor is easily obtained from the spiders you are already fighting, so that is a simple chore.

Have Dirania make the antidote and rush it to Iverron while making your move to grab the **Webwood Egg** (the next step for things inside the cave). This is a very efficient way to grab extra experience in the starting area.

Turn in the quests to their respective NPCs and accept when Gilshalan sends you back into the cave for a genuine Webwood Egg. There are said to be hundreds of these inside the north-west cavern, so the only worry comes from fighting past all of the poisonous beasts. Run out to the cave and seek the upper levels of the tunnel complex (the paths wind upward on the left side of the cavern). Only one of the spiders is as high as fifth level, so even a solo character can move through the place safely (just don't try to fight more than a single target simultaneously). Grab a Webwood Egg from up top and return triumphantly to town.

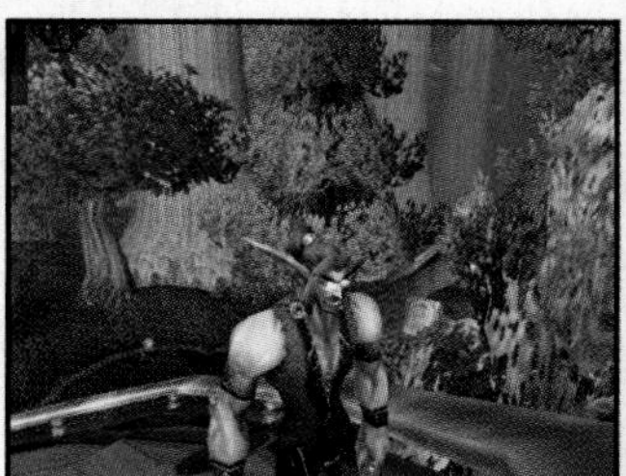

Gilshalan sends you upstairs for a minor chore after the Webwood quests are completed. He asks you to **Speak with Tenaron**. This accomplished Night Elf won't take much of your time, and he merely asks that you fill a Phial with the waters from the Moonwell just north of town. (**Crown of the Earth**) This only takes a minute, and you won't even have to fight there unless you want a few more Thistle Boars under your belt.

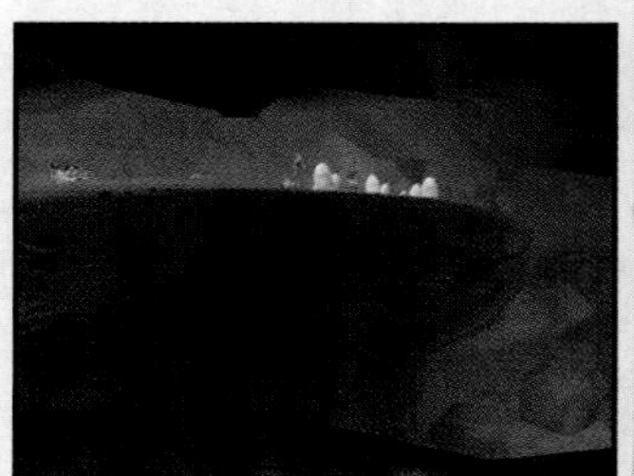

FILLING THE PHIAL

Just click on the Moonwell when you get the pointer with the gear on it. This indicates that you can interact with the object at which you're pointing.

JUMPING OFF!

It's very fast to jump off of the high branches after speaking with Tenaron. To survive, leap down onto the lower tiers of the branches and ramp. It's fun and saves a surprising amount of run time while rushing after the Moonwell.

With all of your tasks in Aldrassil completed, Tenaron hands you a vessel with the Moonwell water and requests that you take it to Dolanaar, a large town near the center of Teldrassil. It's about time to head in that direction anyway, so that's a fitting conclusion to your time in Aldrassil.

ENTERING DOLANAAR

Following Tenaron's bidding, it's time to seek the greater town of Dolanaar. Finish selling extra items to the vendors below, and make sure to train with the masters that specialize in your class. With that done, take the southern road away from Aldrassil and into the greater wilds of this majestic land.

Stick to the road, and fight creatures nearby when you wish, then speak to the lone Satyr, Zenn Foulhoof, on the right side of the path, by a tree. He seems almost friendly, and is willing to award you a simple quest. (**Zenn's Bidding**) Return items from the Nightsabers, Strigid Owls, and Webwood Spiders that cover the local area. It takes a number of kills to collect everything, so this is best accomplished while you are busy with other quests!

Press on to Dolanaar and talk to everyone in town. The north building has Athridas Bearmantle, who wants you to enter the Firbolg village to the east; there is another Night Elf there who he is worried about. This is one of the first quests to you can quickly complete, so grab that. (**A Troubling Breeze**) Walk upstairs in the same building and ask Tallonkai Swiftroot about the **Emerald Dreamcatcher**. It's located in a small building at the southern end of Starbreeze and won't take long to grab when you make it out there.

Zarrin is a cook who works well with odd dishes. Seek this teacher of fine things for a quest to learn the **Recipe of the Kaldorei** (a fine piece of spider-cooking cuisine). Zarrin asks that you bring 10 Small Spider Legs back from your hunt before learning this.

Another trade quest from this area comes from Syral Bladeleaf, a herb seller of Dolanaar. Syral wants you to bring six Elixirs of Lion's Strength and two Elixirs of Minor Defense. (**Elixirs for the Bladeleafs**) She promises to open free trade with you when you're done with this task.

Before leaving, speak to Corithras Moonrage at the southern end of town. He receives Tenaron's phial and asks you to fill another from the Moonwell to the east (this is just outside Starbreeze Village). This action continues the Crown of the Earth quest.

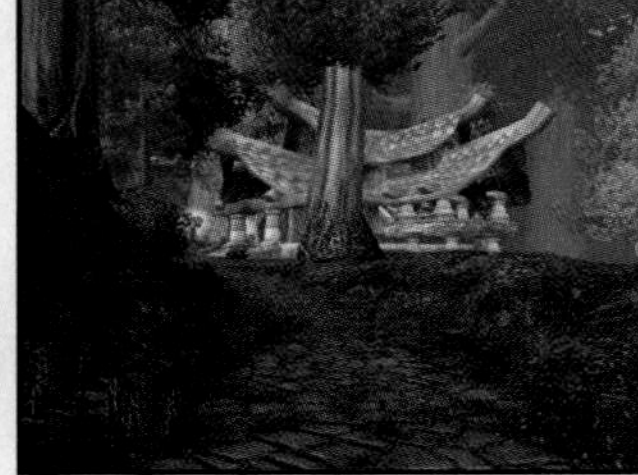

DOLANAAR, A GOOD HOME

Talk to Innkeeper Keldamyr in Dolanaar to set your home point. With all the running back and forth that needs to be done, especially for some of the later Teldrassil quests, it's nice to have the option of getting back there quickly.

Run east, mostly following the road until you see the outskirts of Starbreeze Village and the Moonwell. Jump into the Moonwell and right-click on the Phial to fill it with the special water. That is one quest that won't give anyone trouble!

Next, push slowly into the village and beware of the Firbolgs (they have become quite feral and attack almost anything they see). The first large building on the right has two floors, and Gaerolas Talvethren is on the top floor. Fight the few Firbolg in the way and head upstairs. Gaerolas isn't in great shape, but he tells you what has happened and asks you to send word of it back to Athridas in Dolanaar. Before leaving, curve around to the south-eastern cottage of Starbreeze and search the dresser.

Return to Dolanaar, fighting the beasts for Zenn along the way, then turn in the quests you have completed. The next stage of the **Emerald Dreamcatcher** is more challenging and involves slaying a Firbolg leader and a number of casters (all north of Starbreeze Village). Take a companion or two if you are uncertain of victory, then run out to complete that while polishing off Zenn's quest. Make the turn in to Zenn himself and to Tallonkai Swiftroot.

RECOVER AND CLEAR THE LAKE

By now, it's probably time to train again and sell a few things. Talk to any of the craft trainers in town as well if you want to learn Cooking, Alchemy, or Herbalism (they are all on the south side; look to the north to find the First Aid trainer). There are a fair number of quests to grab now, and it's time to round them up. Talk to everyone and focus on getting Seek Redemption from Syral Bladeleaf. To make things right with her, leave town and walk south until you reach Lake Al'Ameth. There are Fel Cones near the trees there, so Seek Redemption can be completed while walking around the lake. First, speak to Denalan, on the eastern edge of the lake.

Denalan has two quests that are done while looking for Fel Cones. He is a darn fine person, and he too wants to find out what is harming the land. Accept the tasks of collecting Timberling Sprouts and Tiberling Seeds. The Sprouts are found all around the lake (and other bodies of water in Teldrassil). Right-click on these growing plants to collect them while moving around. Fight the aggressive Timberlings you come across to gain their seeds. If your eyes are sharp and can spot the steaming Fel Cones, all three quests can be done in a single pass around the lake!

Turn in everything to Denalan and receive his shipment to Rellian Greenspyre. Rellian is in Darnassus, the capital, and can be found on the either the east side of town, just outside the Warrior's Terrace, or north of the bridges (before reaching the Druid's Grove). Do not head out to Darnassus just yet.

Again, it is a good time to seek a small group. Tallonkai Swiftroot wants to see the head of Melenas, minus the body. Melenas is a dark Satyr who lives in a cave called Fel Rock, just north of Dolanaar. (**Twisted Hatred**) There are many aggressive Grells in the cave, and that is why having a few buddies can make a huge difference. Search the cave while killing the nasty monsters and look for the wandering Melenas; though he stops in the north-western corner atop a ledge, he also patrols from time to time. Target Melenas first when jumping the brute, and bring him down to make sure the quest is a success. Even if you die afterward, return to the body and loot it for a fine victory.

With that done, there are several quests west of town that can be done in a loop. If you still have a group it is even easier, since one of the small dungeons is on the list and can be quite challenging solo.

WEST OF TOWN: HOME OF THE DRUIDS

Athridas Bearmantle also has a quest to gather The Relics of Wakening. With a small group in tow, grab that quest, The Road to Darnassus (from a Sentinel just west of town), and the next step of Crown of the Earth. Move west, toward the mountains ahead, and look for the Gnarlpine Ambushers that lurk south of the road. The quest for these is very fast, as you only need to kill six. Follow the hill that rises to the south, beyond the Ambushers, and notice the slightly stronger Firbolgs beyond.

AVENGERS ARE EVIL!

Avengers are a troublesome class of enemies. The Firbolgs are one of the races that have Avengers, and there are a number of them out in the forests of Teldrassil. When you slay another Firbolg near an Avenger, the Avenger bursts into a Rage and starts to attack very quickly with devastating results. Try to slay Avengers first.

If there are casters around, they need to be brought down quickly as well. To solve this conundrum, have one person attack a caster to interrupt their spells while the other party members beat on the Avenger. This way, both enemies are limited in their ability to let loose! It's not optimal, but fighting both casters and Avengers at the same time never is.

At the top of the hill is a dungeon (Ban'ethil Barrow Den). Below are the relics that you are seeking, but dozens of Firbolg patrol the corridors and make life difficult for anyone who tries to enter. Move slowly with your group, taking on only one or two Firbolg at a time, and search the rooms of the dungeon for the four artifacts. This is not your only goal in the dungeon. A restless spirit resides in a room on the second tier of the dungeon. Oben Rageclaw has been slain, yet the Firbolg use his body to attack intruders. Oben's spirit wants this to end. Slay Shamans for Oben until you find the Shaman Voodoo Charm. (**The Sleeping Druid**) Return this to Oben, then agree to slay his body. Seek the animated corpse at the lowest level of the dungeon, fight it, then use the Charm to give this druid final rest.

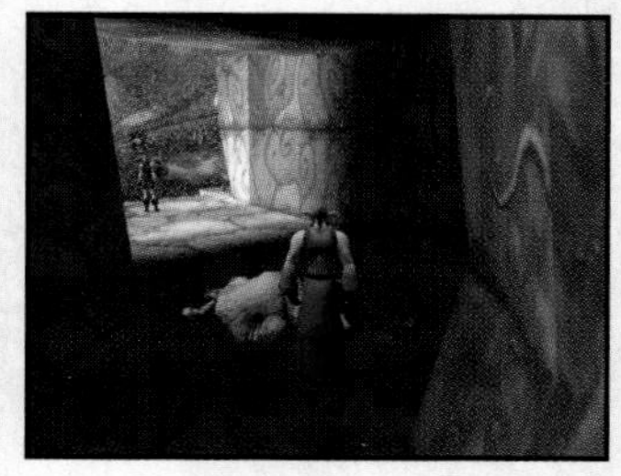

Return the artifacts to town after speaking with Oben again. Athridas is ready to have you go after **Ursal the Mauler**, the very Firbolg who began this war against the Druids of Teldrassil. Move into the south-west, in the area by the very base of Teldrassil (Gnarlpine Hold). While getting into position, fill your Phial at the next Moonwell (completing another part of **Crown of the Earth**), and steal a piece of fruit from the glowing tree south of the Moonwell. (**Glowing Fruit**) The fruit can be taken to Denalan for some extra experience.

Ursal is somewhat easy to kill, yet the many Firbolgs around him offer moderate resistance. Hopefully you can carry the group from the last dungeon onward and plow through Ursal's allies without trouble. Be wary of the Avengers and casters, since these enemies carry a wicked punch.

DARNASSUS AND THE NORTHERN QUESTS

Return to town and rejoice. All of the substantially challenging quests are done in Teldrassil, and the remaining ones are much easier with the skills you are already beginning to master. The next part for **Crown of the Earth** takes you up to the Oracle Glade, in the north-eastern section of Teldrassil. Sell, train, and grab that final quest before moving out.

The house on the side of the road as you head toward Darnassus has a Skinner and Leatherworking Trainer. Stop there for a second if you are interested, then pass all the way to the capital. Before striking out to the Oracle Glade, complete Denalan's dropoff to Rellian; better late than never, eh? Rellian wants you to collect Tumors from the larger Timberlings that live along the Wellspring River, east of Oracle Glade. Accept that quest, and hit the temple of the south side of town for Tears of the Moon. Priestess A'moora gives you that quest, and she is on the upper tier of the temple.

DARNASSUS POINTS OF INTEREST

LOCATION	USEFUL STORES/NPCS
North Side	Druid, Hunter, and Rogue Trainers; Arch Druid Fandral Staghelm, Night Elf Mount Vendor
East Side	Warrior Trainer, Craft Trainers, Inn (North-East)
Central	Bank
West Side	Teleporter to Docks
South Side	Priest Trainer, Darnassus Temple, Chief Archaeologist Greywhisker, Priestess A'moora

Now that you are loaded up with quests for the northern area, head out from town and walk to the Wellspring River. Fight the Timberlings as you plod north along the banks, and keep your eyes peeled for a dark-colored Timberling named **Blackmoss the Fetid**. Kill that one if you see him (his heart can be turned in to Denalan for additional experience, and you soon shall see Denalan for other rewards, so it's win-win).

Once the tumors are happily yours, walk along the north side of the area and search for the spider, Lady Sathrah. This magnificent spider has been tainted, like so many things in the land, and you need to slay her. Take the Spinnerets from her body after the deed is done. Also, continue just west of her usual location to find a second glowing tree (another piece of fruit can be picked there). As always, Denalan is happy to receive these. (**The Shimmering Frond**)

Steer toward the center of the region and talk to the Night Elves who live there (and fill up your Phial from the Moonwell there). Recently, a messenger to Darnassus was murdered by the Harpies that fly to the west. (**The Enchanted Glade**) Sentinel Arynia Cloudsbreak needs to see their numbers beaten back, and she asks you to take up the challenge. Agree to this, then fight west and slightly north into a tiny cubby between the western wall and the trees where the Harpies are congregating. Not only do these kills help to rake in the Bloodfeather Belts that you need but there is also a trapped tiger named Mist. Talk to the wounded beast and escort it back to the Glade in safety. Turn in the belts and receive the reward for that and saving Mist. Return to Darnassus after that to receive rewards from the temple and from Rellian.

With Teldrassil almost done, it's time to wrap up a few loose ends. Talk to Denalan and give him the final few goodies that you found in the north. With the tumors to examine, he'll ask that you destroy the Timberling with the most Gargantuan Tumor that he has seen. This is certainly one that has the power to damage the land further because it has been so badly tainted. **Oakenscowl** is the Timberling's name, and he is undoubtedly the most powerful monster in all of starting land. Bring several allies to attack Oakenscowl, who lives south-west of the lake, just inside a small cave.

Bid Denalan farewell after receiving your reward, sell and train in Dolanaar, then wave to all of the friends you have made there. Darnassus beckons, and the mists of Darkshore are coming soon after. To reach the foreign coast, look for a glowing pagoda on the western end of Darnassus; this teleports people out to Rut'theran Village, where a Hippogriff Master sends novice and veteran alike over the seas.

Elune be praised!

DUROTAR

Durotar is the new homeland of the Orcs and Trolls on the continent of Kalimdor. It was Thrall who led the Orcs to this new desolate land and began to rebuild what his people had long lost to the Burning Legion and then to the Alliance as a result of their folly. Thrall rescued the Trolls as well and what are left of their tribe has also taken up residence in Durotar. There are still troubles within Durotar however. Quillboars, Kolkar Raiders and the last vestiges of Proudmoore's fleet still harry the new residents.

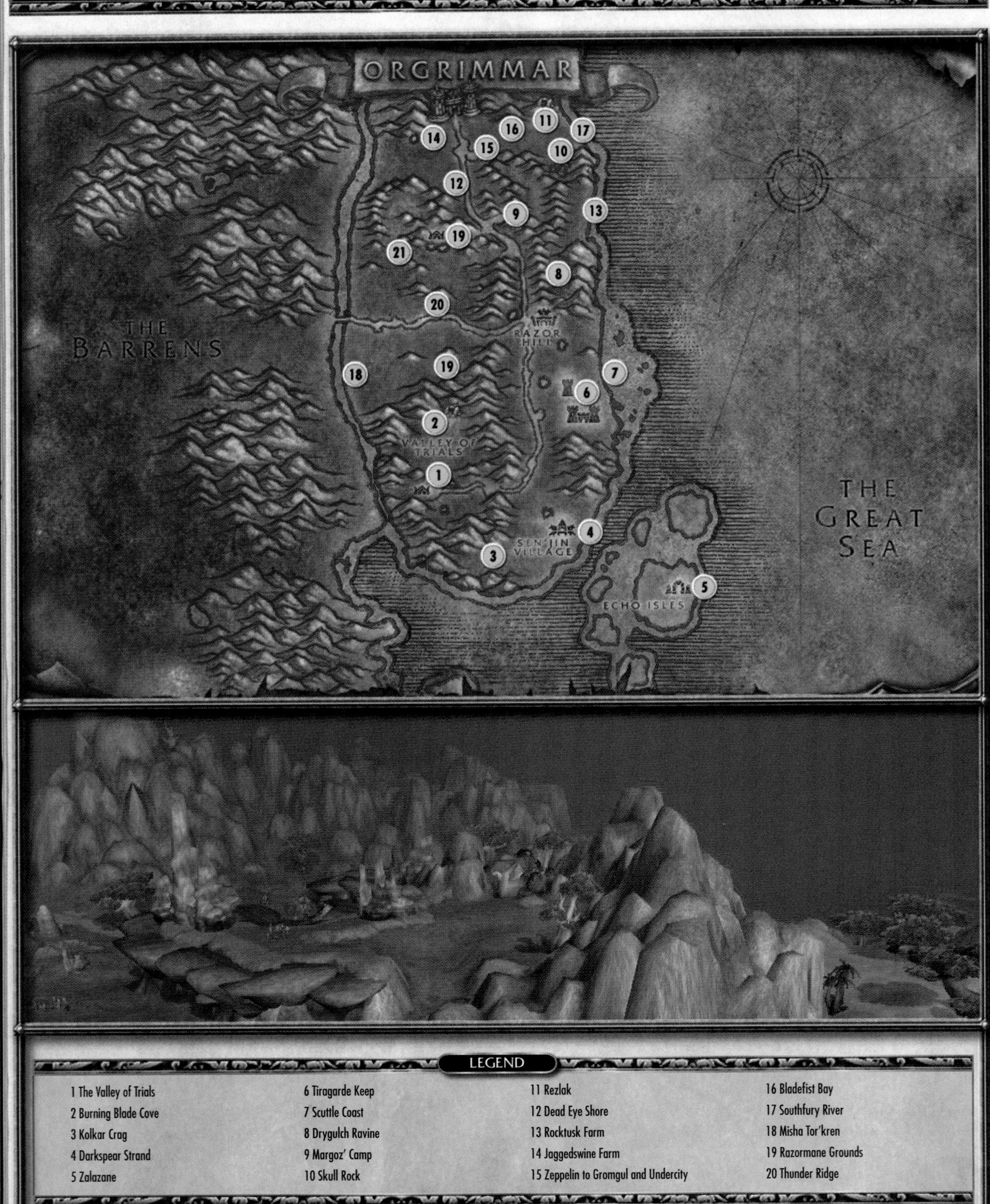

LEGEND

1 The Valley of Trials
2 Burning Blade Cove
3 Kolkar Crag
4 Darkspear Strand
5 Zalazane
6 Tiragarde Keep
7 Scuttle Coast
8 Drygulch Ravine
9 Margoz' Camp
10 Skull Rock
11 Rezlak
12 Dead Eye Shore
13 Rocktusk Farm
14 Jaggedswine Farm
15 Zeppelin to Gromgul and Undercity
16 Bladefist Bay
17 Southfury River
18 Misha Tor'kren
19 Razormane Grounds
20 Thunder Ridge

Durotar is mostly a desert region with the capital city of Orgrimmar to the North, the river to the west and the ocean to the east. Caverns wend their way through the land creating valleys that enemies have taken refuge in and islands pepper the southeastern coast.

THE VALLEY OF TRIALS

The Valley of Trials is the starting point for all new orcs and trolls. It sits nestled within a valley in the southwestern region of Durotar. The beginning trainers and a small few vendors are located here.

CLASS QUESTS

All starting players have a missive in their packs upon starting. When right-clicking this message will give you a quest to seek out your class trainer. You're awarded 40 experience points upon completion of the quest.

At level 10, classes that have class specific quests are able to get the quest from their trainer should one be available.

The Valley of Trials is a great starting place for Orcs and Trolls. There are minimal amounts of running involved at this point and the quests all revolves around the same contained area.

When you first come into the world, you'll find yourself face to face with Eitrigg. He's your introduction into the **New Horde** and directs you to seek out Gornak to begin your journey. Gornak wants to help you to gain strength, albeit a bit reluctantly. He tasks you with killing 10 Mottled Boars. (**Cutting Teeth**)

Galgar is nearby and has another quest for you as well. He wants you to collect 10 cactus apples for him so he can make his **Cactus Apple Surprise**. He claims that Cactus Apple Surprise can do wonders and cool you down. Both of these quests are a fairly easy way to start your time as an Orc or Troll.

Right in the beginning part of the Valley of Trials you'll see plenty of Mottled Boars roaming around. They're not aggressive. Also sprinkled around the area are cactus and cactus apples. You'll know them by the rosy blooms on the cacti. Right-click on them to gather the apples; they respawn relatively quickly.

Once you've killed all of the boars and gathered the apples, return to The Valley of Trials and complete the quests by speaking to the appropriate NPCs. Gornak will want you to prove your prowess further by killing Scorpids and collecting 8 of their tails. It seems anti-venom is created from an extraction of venom from their stingers. Fortunately, Scorpids are not aggressive here. **(Sting of the Scorpid)**

You'll now be able to speak to Zureetha Fargaze and get the latest quest from her. She tells you of the coven called the Burning Blade that has taken up residence nearby. She would like you to slay their **Vile Familiars**.

Head back out into the Valley of Trials to the north again where you just gathered Cactus Apples and killed Mottled Boars. As you travel north toward the Scorpids you'll notice a tree with an injured troll beneath it. Hana'zua will tell you have a Scorpid that is named **Sarkoth** that has injured him with his stinger. He managed to slice off one of the claws however, he would like revenge and for you to bring him the other to show that Sarkoth has been slain.

Move through the area nearby and kill the Scorpids and collect their tails. A bit more northeast you'll come across **Vile Familiars** that you need to kill. Be careful here. It's better to fight them up close since they have a ranged fireball.

Once all of the Vile Familiars and Scorpids have been killed, head to the southeast of where you found Hana'zua. There is a slight ramp up to a new area in which you will find **Sarkoth**. Sarkoth is larger than any other Scorpid and has orange bands across it. He's very easy to identify and is also aggressive - unlike the other Scorpids.

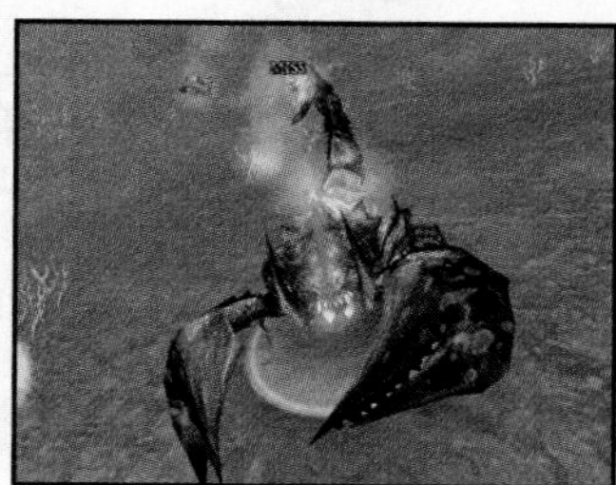

Once you kill him, loot his claw and return to Hana'zua. He's very grateful to see that you've triumphed and is now resolute that he won't just lie down and die. He asks you to help by letting Gornek know back in The Valley of Trials that he needs assistance.

Return to The Valley of Trials, turn in the Scorpid quest **(Sting of the Scorpid)** and **Sarkoth** quest to Gornek then see Zureetha Fargaze. She now has a new more dangerous mission for you. She would like you to venture into the cave of the Burning Blade and retrieve a medallion off of an agent of the Burning Blade within. **(Burning Blade Medallion)**

You need to carefully maneuver into the cave clearing the way as you go. Vile Fiends and Felstalkers await inside. As you follow the path deeper into the cave, you arrive at a spot where the cave opens a bit. Take the right path and follow it as it curves back to the left again and then straight. At the end of the path, you come across Yarog Baneshadow. Kill him and collect the medallion.

Carefully make your way back out of the dungeon and check back in with Zureetha Fargaze. Your time within the Valley of Trials is at an end. Now you must make your way to **Report to Sen'jin Village** and let Gadrin know of the Burning Blade. As you exit the Valley of Trials, you'll notice a peon waiting at the a crossroads. He needs your help in delivering some food to the innkeeper in Razor Hill. **(A Peon's Burden)** It seems he's too much of a coward to do it himself. Go north along the road to Razor Hill and check-in at the Inn.

Don't worry about picking up the Razor Hill Quests as of yet. Run south to Sen'jin Village instead to begin those.

SEN'JIN VILLAGE

Sen'jin Village lies to the southeast of The Valley of Trials. Trolls populate it. To its east are the Echo Isles and some of their most dangerous foes. On the way into Sen'jin Village notice Lar Prowltusk. He tells you of the Kolkar Aggression quest in which he asks you to infiltrate their stronghold and destroy their attack plans against the Orcs and Trolls.

Continue farther into the village and find Master Gadrin near a small puddle of water. He has three quests for you. For **Mishina's Skull**, he tells you of his brother's spirit being trapped by a Warlock in the Echo Isles. He wants you to find the skull within a circle of power and return it to him.

He also tells you of a witch doctor named Zalazane that is hexing Trolls and placing them under his spell. He has used other Darkspear Trolls to continue kidnapping so that he can place them under his sway. He wants you to kill 8 Voodoo Trolls and 8 Hexed Trolls and to bring him Zalazane's head. Lastly, he requests that you report your findings of the Burning Blade to Orgnil in Razor Hill as well as tell Orgnil of the troubles the Darkspear Trolls are experiencing themselves. **(Report to Orgnil)**

Master Vornal is nearby and also has a quest ready for you called **A Solvent Spirit**. He asks you to collect some Makrura eyes and some Crawler Mucus to help him in his alchemical studies. There is one more quest giver named Vel'rin Fang who asks you to help him keep up on the supply of hides. He asks you to bring 4 Durotar Tiger Hides. **(Practical Prey)**

Head southeast to the beach and Darkspear Strand to start killing Crawlers and the occasional Makruras. Be careful of nearby Scorpids as well. While Crawlers are not hostile, Makruras and Scorpids are. Follow the coastline as you hunt. Return to Master Vornal once you have collected everything you need. Turning in the quest should see you around Level 6.

Use your Hearthstone to make a quick trip back up to Razor Hill. Report to Orgnil and complete the quest. He has another quest for you, but don't take it now. Come back to it. Instead, speak with cook Torka. He wants you to **Break a Few Eggs** by going into the Echo Isles and taking Bloodtalon Lasher eggs and bringing them back to him. Accept the quest and head south to Sen'jin once more.

TRAINING

Don't forget to train every chance you get. Generally, classes receive spells or new abilities every 2 levels.

It's time for a swim out to the islands to gather eggs and pelts. Swim to the second largest island to the south along the island chain. Here you'll find plenty of Raptors and Durotar Tigers.

There are two Raptor locations that have eggs. They're both on the west side of the island and usually have a single raptor guarding both locations; a group of purple eggs at the bottom of a tree is your target. Right-click to collect them.

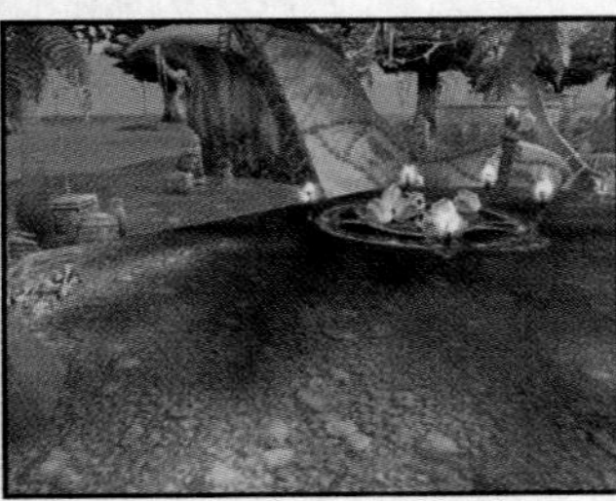

Once you have gotten all 4 hides and 2 eggs, move to the main island. You can get the third egg here and make your way over to the Trolls. Move to the south end of the island carefully. Kill any Tailashers or Tigers that get in your way. There's an odd looking flattened short hill with a Hexed Troll standing guard. **Mishina's Skull** is at the top of the hill.

Scale the backside of the hill to reach to the skull pile. Watch out for **Zalazane** who makes a circuit up the hill and back down from time to time. He's Level 10 and a bit out of your solo range—for now. Swim back to Sen'jin village and turn in the quests you have finished: **Mishina's Skull** and **Practical Prey**. Go ahead and use your Hearthstone to make a quick stop back in Razor Hill to turn in the raptor eggs.

It's time to visit the Kolkar Raiders and put an end to their scheming. Make your way into the Kolkar Crag and start clearing your way to the first tent on the left. The Attack Plan for the Valley of Trials is lying on the floor inside the tent. Right-click them to destroy them. **(Thwarting Kolkar Aggression)**

The next plan is farther in and to the right. Clear the Kolkar Raiders and make your way to the next plan on the ground. Destroy the Attack plan for Razor Hill then make your way back further into the area. Clear the Kolkar Raiders and make your way to the last plan. It should be the Attack plan for Orgrimmar. Once those are complete head back to Lar Prowltusk and complete the quest. A little more swimming and the quests of Sen'jin Village will be complete.

VOODOO AND HEXED TROLLS

Voodoo and Hexed Trolls for the most part are nicely spaced out along the outer perimeter of the camp. Voodoo Trolls however can cast a fire dot and are better off being fought in close proximity.

It's time to deal with Zalazane. Swim back to the large island where you got **Mishina's Skull**. Kill the Hexed and Voodoo Trolls you need to. Once you have managed to kill the ones you need, take the back side of the hill where you got Mishina's skull again and wait for Zalazane. This is the safest possible spot to fight him without having to wade into the center of the camp to get him. Once you have managed to kill him, return to camp and check back in with Master Gadrin. When finished it's time to move up to Razor Hill.

RAZOR HILL AND DUROTAR

Razor Hill sits solidly in the center of Durotar. This is a primarily Orc location and houses the Inn and many trainers. Pick up all of the available quests in Razor Hill. Orgnil wants you to venture into Thunder Ridge to kill Fizzle Darkstorm, a Burning Blade Warlock. **(Dark Storms)**

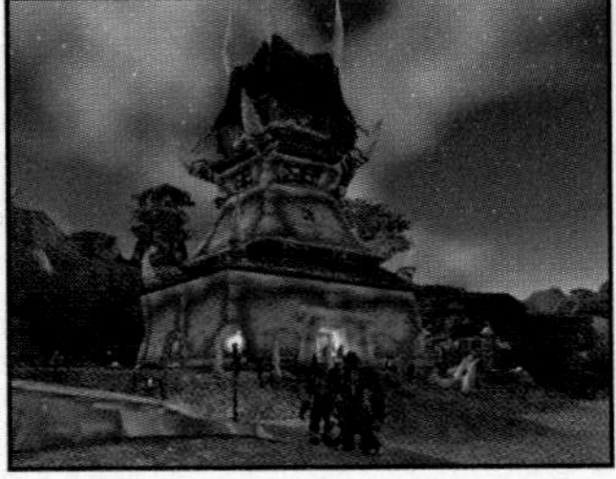

Gar'Thok is waiting for you at the top of the tower nearby. He has two quests for you. For **Vanquish the Betrayers**, he wants you to venture into the remains of Tiragarde Keep to kill 10 Kul Tiras Sailors, 8 Kul Tiras Marines and Lieutenant Benedict. As Admiral Proudmoore's reserves, they have moved back into the region and need to be shown the door.

He also speaks of the **Encroachment** of the Razormane Quillboars that are to the west. Their presence is no longer to be tolerated and they need to be driven from Durotar. You must kill 4 Quillboars, 4 Scouts, 4 Dustrunners and 4 Battleguards. Begin by making your way southeast toward Tiragarde Keep. Kill sailors and marines as you make your way toward the main keep on the interior.

As you enter the keep, you can only turn to the right. Once you turn to the right it will force you again to the left. Take the first left again and head around the corner toward the stairs. Once up the stairs, take the ramp to the left. This leads to a main room where the Lieutenant waits.

Kill all of the Lieutenant's minions and then him. Loot the Silver Key that he has and go back to the stairs that you passed when you made the left into the room. Go up the stairs out on to the landing. Kill any sailors or marines that are in the way and open the box at the end of the walk. There's an Aged Envelope inside. It starts a quest if you right-click it. **(Admiral Proudmoore's Orders)**

Stop by Gar'Thok and turn in both quests. He tells you to rush to Orgrimmar to let Thrall's right hand man Nazgrel know about what you have found. He also wants you to swim out into the Scuttle Coast to get some tools from the wreckage of the ships and bring them to him so he can better learn of the abilities of the enemy. The only things that you need to keep in mind as you swim out to get the tools are that the Makruras will attack you and that you need to resurface to get air from time to time. There are tools in small chests in the ship wreckage. **(From the Wreckage)**

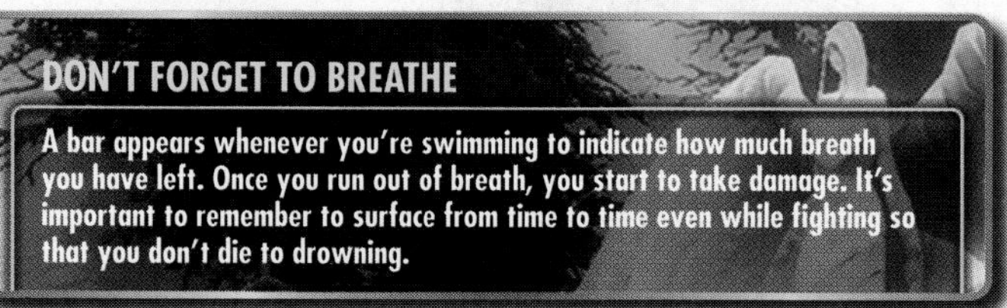

DON'T FORGET TO BREATHE

A bar appears whenever you're swimming to indicate how much breath you have left. Once you run out of breath, you start to take damage. It's important to remember to surface from time to time even while fighting so that you don't die to drowning.

It's time to see Orgrimmar. The rest of the quests you have are still a bit challenging so take the time to run to Orgrimmar now and complete the **Admiral Proudmoore's Orders** quest. There's a Goblin named Rezlak off to the left as you near Orgrimmar. Stop by and pick up the quest he has waiting for you. He would like you to recover some supplies that were waylaid by the Dustwind Harpies in nearby Razorwind Canyon. Accept his quest and continue on to Orgrimmar. **(Securing the Lines)**

Travel the north road in Orgrimmar and then take the first right turn toward the Valley of Wisdom. Run straight through the Drag into the Valley of Wisdom and into Thrall's Fortress. Nazgrel is waiting all the way in the back of the building near Thrall himself. Nazgrel thanks you and tells you that he advises Thrall of what he has learned.

With that there is nothing more left in Orgrimmar save to exit and travel down to Razorwind Canyon. There are two ways to enter the canyon. One is from the north and one is from the west. The entrance to the west is less populated by Harpies and perhaps the easiest path to take. Look for small tan sacks on the ground. These are the items you need to collect. Just right-click to pick them up. Return to Rezlak when you're done and he will have the next part of the quest for you.

Rezlak would like your help in **Securing the Lines**. He feels that if you kill enough of the Harpies it makes it safe for other supply cargos to come through. He would like you to kill 12 Dustwind Furies and 8 Dustwind Witches. The Dustwind Furies aren't too difficult, however the Dustwind Witches can be a bit more of a challenge. It's important to try to take them on one at a time.

To get to them, you need to go back into Razorwind Canyon and (if entering from the west) take the right turn and pass through the small tunnel. Take your time and work your way through the Harpies. They tend to respawn relatively quickly so be wary of what is around you at all times. Once you have completed this, return to Rezlak for your reward.

Return to Razor Hill and head over to the Razormane Grounds. The camp to the left has the Quillboars and Scouts that you must kill. Stay on the outer edges and pick off the ones you need. In the opposite camp are the Dustrunners and Battleguards. The Dustrunners are casters, so get in close to fight them.

Once you have completed that, make your way down into Thunder Ridge. You will need to kill Thunder Lizards as you go to get to the encampment for Fizzle. Picking up at least one other person to join your group will make this quest go much faster and much easier. (**Dark Storms**)

Carefully lure the outer guards to you and kill them. Then follow the ledge to the right to get behind the camps. Clear each camp from the backside working your way around the camp counterclockwise until you only have Fizzle and his pet left in the center. You will need to work quickly since the mobs you have killed earlier should be respawning soon. Kill him and collect the claw from him.

Return to Orgnil and turn in the claw. He will want you to see Margoz further north toward Orgrimmar to see if he has more on the Burning Blade for you. Check in with Gar'Thok and complete the **Encroachment** quest.

Run north toward Orgrimmar and over to Margoz' encampment. He wants you to venture into **Skull Rock** to gather the collars that the Burning Blade wears. It seems to give them powers that he would like to examine further. By grouping with others you're able to make your way all the way in to Gazz'uz at the end of the dungeon. He has a Burning Eye of Shadow on him that initiates another quest. **(Burning Shadows)** You need to take the Burning Eye to Neeru Fireblade in the Cleft of Shadow in Orgrimmar.

Return the collars to Margoz and he creates a sample collar to take to Neeru as well. He's unable to fathom the magic himself, but is confident that Neeru will be able to. In Orgrimmar you'll find Neeru Fireblade down in the bottom area of the Cleft of Shadow. He has a continuing quest for you that takes you out into the Barrens.

Travel back out of Orgrimmar to a small house just southwest of Orgrimmar where you will find Misha Tor'kren. It seems she and her son had an argument and he stormed out of the house. She is very worried about him and would like some sign of his fate. **(Lost but not Forgotten)**

Head west and follow the river south in search of Kron's Amulet. While the quest says to kill every crocolisk you come across, it's easy to spot the one you want. He's an ancient crocolisk with bright green scales. Kill him and collect the amulet. Misha, while saddened by the knowledge of the fate of her son, will be thankful to have some peace of mind. With this last quest complete, it is now time to move out of Durotar. You should have a couple quests that take you out into the Barrens. Good Luck!

MULGORE

The Tauren, once a nomadic people, have taken up residence within the plains and mesas of Mulgore. They walk the paths of the ancient Shaman, the nature empowered Druids and the ways of the Warrior and Hunter. The hunt is a right of passage for all Tauren. It is through hunting the beasts of the land that they gain strength and learn the lessons of the world. While the Tauren may have found a new home, it is not a wholly safe and peaceful one. Centaur, Harpies, Dwarves and Bristleback Quillboars (along with the indigenous beasts of the land) are something to take task with.

LEGEND

L Lift
1 Camp Narache
2 Well
3 Seer Graytongue
4 Chief Sharptusk Thornmantle
5 Antur Fallow
6 Stonebull Lake
7 Palemane Camps
8 The Rolling Plains
9 Palemane Rock
10 Bloodhoof Village
11 Winterhoof Waterwell
12 Windfury Harpies
13 The Venture Co. Mine
14 Ravaged Caravan
15 Thunderhorn Water Well
16 Bael'Dun Digsite
17 Seer Wiserunner
18 Wildmane Water Well
19 The Golden Plains
20 Spirit Rise
21 Windfury Ridge
22 Red Rocks- Sacred Burial Ground
23 Elder Rise
24 Hunter's Rise
25 Venture Co Buildings

YOUR FIRST DAY

Mulgore's located near the center of Kalimdor just west of the Barrens. After being displaced from their homeland by the Kolkar Centaurs, the nomadic Tauren took up residence in Mulgore and became one tribe. The Tauren are very much in tune with the land around them and hunt the creatures of the land to not only prove their place within their own society, but to provide for each other. Dwarves have taken up excavation on their land disturbs the very fabric of nature.

CAMP NARACHE

Camp Narache is your starting point as a fresh Tauren ready to prove yourself worthy to become a citizen of Thunder Bluff. It's a tiny village nestled in the crook of a mountain range. The area it is in is called Red Cloud Mesa. Creatures that reside here are Plainstriders, Mountain Cougars, Battleboars and Bristleback Quillboars. Plainstriders and Cougars are not aggressive.

Your first encounter is with Grull Hawkwind. Once you have finished watching the opening movie, you will find yourself face to face with him making finding your first quest giver extremely convenient. He asks you to help provide for the village by collecting plainstrider feathers and meat. (**The Hunt Begins**)

Before you head off to complete this task, there are two more quests to pick up. One involves opening your inventory and reading the tablet within. By right-clicking on it, you can accept a task to report to your class trainer within the village. Pick up some easy experience and acquaint yourself with where their location for future training.

Next, visit the Chief of the village (Chief Hawkwind) and pick up a quest from him. (**A Humble Task**) It seems his mother has gone off to collect some water but hasn't come back as of yet. The well is nearby and just slightly southeast of the village. You can kill Plainstriders and take care of this quest very easily within the area around the well. The well is within sight from nearby the village by cresting a small hill. Talk to the mother and collect the water needed to complete the quest. Once you have all of the Plainstrider Feathers, Meat and the water from the well, head back to the village to turn in those quests.

The chief will be very pleased that you took it upon yourself to aid his mother. He gives you the **Rites of the Earthmother** task and asks you to seek out Seer Graytongue to the west of the village. Grull Hawkwind would like you to prove yourself even further by collecting 5 Cougar Pelts. (**The Hunt Continues**) It seems these are highly valued by the village and will make some nice pieces of clothing for the children and mend the tents of the village.

Brave Windfeather is nearby waiting to speak with you as well. He has heard of you and would like you to put you to task. Where others have failed before, he hopes that you can succeed. It seems the Bristleback Quillboars plague the Tauren and he would like you to venture into the Brambleback Ravine to the east. Within, there's a makeshift village and their chief. Collect his head and Windfeather will reward you well. (**Break Sharptusk**)

Once you've collected all of these quests, head toward the west of the village. You should see a small tent up on the hill and a bonfire burning. Seer Graytongue is waiting for you there. On the way, start killing the Mountain Cougars. They're not aggressive.

Seer Graytongue sets you on the path to the **Rite of Strength**. You need to battle the enemies of the tribe, the Bristleback Quillboars to the east in the ravine; collect 5 of their belts and return to Chief Hawkwind.

Before you venture as far as the ravine however, finish collecting the Cougar Pelts and turn those in to Grull Hawkwind. He has a new task for you. (**The Battleboars**) It seems the Battleboars of Brambleblade Ravine are encroaching on the Tauren's hunting grounds. They're trained to be aggressive by the Bristleback Quillboars. He asks you to slay them and bring back some snouts and flanks so that they can make stew for the young of the tribe. Head to the east after doing some training.

Outside the Ravine you'll find the Battleboars. They're aggressive, so carefully make your way to the cave that enters into the Ravine proper. The Bristleboars are spaced out enough that you should be able to pick and choose your battles relatively careful. There are also Battleboars inside the ravine with the Quillboars from who you can collect the snouts, flanks and belts as you make your way toward the chief.

The first path on the right takes you toward your destination. It then splits; take the left curve in the road. It curves back to the right. There's a larger opening that has a building standing larger than the rest in the area. This is the chief's. Inside he has two other Quillboars with him. Carefully clear the area outside the building and then attempt to draw the others to you. If done well, you only need to fight one NPC inside and can draw him to you with a careful aggro pull.

Once you have the chief's head, start making your way carefully out of the ravine. If you still need more belts, snouts or flanks, there are plenty of opportunities on the way out.

Turn in all of the quests that you have just completed. By the time you're done, you should have reached Level 4. Chief Hawkwind has one more quest for you before you venture out of the Redcloud Mesa area. He wants you to continue in the **Rites of the Earthmother** and asks you to deliver a totem to Baine Bloodhoof in the Bloodhoof Village. Baine is the chief of Bloodhoof village and the son of Cairne Bloodhoof, chief of Thunder Bluff. It's his hope that by completing the rites you'll impress the Elders enough to gain acceptance with them.

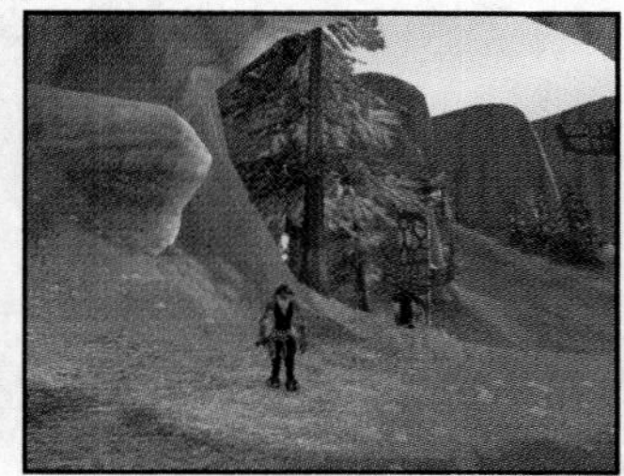

On your way along the path and just before you leave Red Cloud Mesa, you'll come upon Antur Fallow. She asks you to deliver some furs to her father at the Inn in Bloodhoof Village so she can complete her own Rite of Strength task. (**A Task Unfinished**)

BLOODHOOF VILLAGE

Bloodhoof Village is located to the north and a bit east on the road from Red Cloud Mesa. It sits on the banks of Stonebull Lake. It is only a slightly larger village than Camp Narache, but has all of the class trainers available to Tauren.

Make your way to the Innkeeper first before you visit anyone else. He rewards you and you can bind there. There are several NPCs that have quests waiting for you, provided you have managed to reach Level 5. Harken Windtotem, Mull Thunderhorn, Baine Bloodhoof, Maur Raincaller and Ruul Eagletalon each have quests. Check in with Baine to complete the Rites of the Earthmother quest and pick up **Sharing the Land** and the **Rite of Vision** from him.

Sharing the Land consists of killing Palemane Gnolls. They have taken up residence to the south and the west (Palemane Rock) of Bloodhoof Village and are killing creatures indiscriminately. They're unwilling to come to any agreements with the Tauren. He feels the only thing they now understand is force. Kill 10 Palemane Tanners, 8 Palemane Skinners and 5 Palemane Poachers.

For the **Rite of the Vision** it seems you need to visit Zarlman Two-Moons to continue. Luckily, he's nearby in the village. This is yet another quest in the long line of the **Rites of the Earthmother** you need to complete. Harken Windtotem wants you to kill Swoops and collect 8 Trophy Feathers to prove your cunning as a hunter. These feathers are used to reward hunters within the village for their cleverness and as a badge of honor. (**Swoop Hunting**)

Ruul Eagletalon would like you to collect Windfury Harpy Talons for him as a test of your strength. By doing so, you'll better prepare yourself for the trials beyond the Tauren lands. (**Dangers of the Windfury**) Mull Thunderhorn is concerned over the cleansing of the sacred water wells. It seems Venture Co. Goblins have been poisoning them. Collect Prairie Wolf Paws and Plainstrider Talons so that he can create a cleansing totem. (**Poison Water**)

Maur Raincaller has had a run-in with a strider called **Mazzranache** who has a venomous bite. He needs some hard-to-find animal parts in order to clean out the infection that he has gotten as a result. While you don't need to kill Mazzranache, he's not easy to miss with his bright flamingo pink color.

COLLECTING ANIMAL PARTS

While a large queue of quests requiring animal parts will seem daunting, it's actually much easier than you think to get these quests done. By collecting all of these quests at once, you'll be able to kill as you move along the plains and collect as many of the parts as you need at once rather than killing the same creatures repetitively.

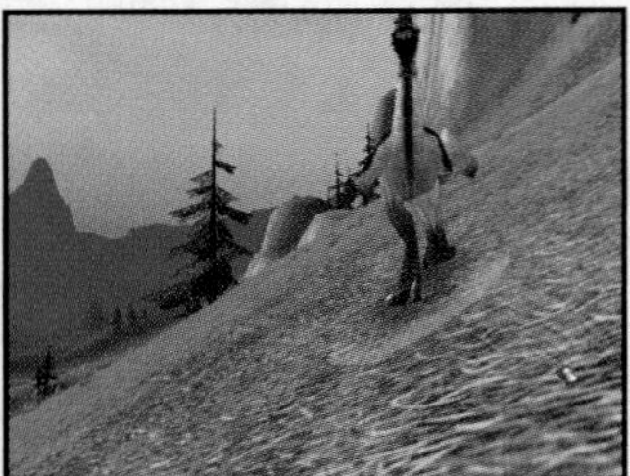

For the **Rite of Vision**, Zarlman Two-Moons asks you to collect 2 Well Stones and 2 Ambercorn in order to create a special potion that will help you along on your vision quest.

Once you have gathered all of those quests, begin collecting all the necessary requested items. Winterhoof Well is just to the southeast of Bloodhoof Village. You won't need to clear out the entire well in order to get at the well stones, but instead can clear an area on one side of it to get them. Ambercorn are easy to find and look like giant pinecones sitting beneath the trees here and there.

After you've accomplished gathering the Well Stones and Ambercorn, head slightly northeast toward the crossroads and find Morin Cloudstalker. He asks you to go to **The Ravaged Caravan** to take a look inside of one of the containers there. As you're wandering the plains, kill the needed animals and collect the parts requested. Swoops can be a bit of a challenge when they attack at the same time you're fighting other creatures. Take the time to kill them as quickly and efficiently as possible to collect their quills before killing any other animals around them.

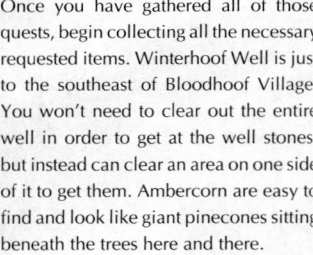

Return to Bloodhoof Mull Thunderhorn and turn in the well stones and ambercorn to receive the next part of the quest. (**Winterhoof Cleansing**) Return to the well and complete the cleansing process. Clear an area near the well so that you can safely stand near it and right-click on the cleansing totem. The well will begin to glow and have a bit of a light surround it to show that it has been cleansed.

Return to the village and turn in the Swoops' Trophy Quills to Harken Windtotem and check in with Mull Thunderhorn again. He has the next quest ready for you to cleanse the Thunderhorn Well. (**Thunderhorn Totem**) You can pick up the items he asks for as you go from here.

Baine Bloodhoof has another quest in the village at Level 6. (**Dwarven Digging**) He wants you to collect 5 Prospector Picks and break them on an anvil. He suggests you can do it within their camp or to go to Thunder Bluff. There is a third place that better suits your needs if you're a bit patient.

Turn in the animal parts to Maur Raincaller to complete the **Mazzranache** quest. Return to Zarlman Two-Moons to continue the **Vision Quest**. He creates the Water of the Seers for you to drink near the tribal fire. Go ahead and drink it now to continue the quest. A ghostly wolf appears to lead you to your destination. It leads you to a cave to the Northwest where you can speak to Seer Wiserunner. He gives you the next part of the quest called the **Rite of Wisdom**.

Travel south from the cave and skip past the Windfuries for now. You will see the Bael'Dun Digsite to your right as you continue on. Carefully make your way to the outer fringes of it and start killing Dwarves. There's no need to go into the site; carefully pull one Dwarf at a time from the edges rather than risk dying to multiple Dwarves.

BAEL'DUN FORGE

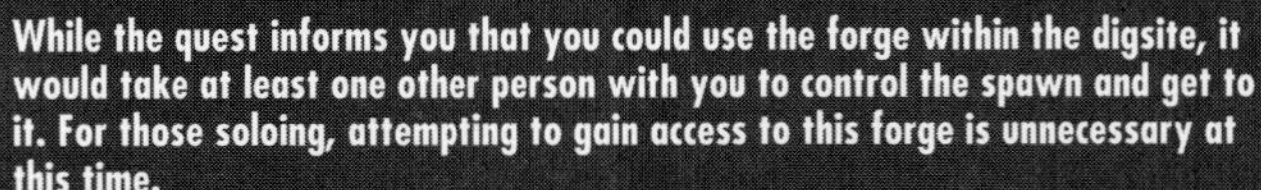

While the quest informs you that you could use the forge within the digsite, it would take at least one other person with you to control the spawn and get to it. For those soloing, attempting to gain access to this forge is unnecessary at this time.

Travel farther south to Palemane Rock to finish up the **Sharing the Land** Quest. It won't take long if you take your time to clear the camp and then venture into the small dungeon itself and back out.

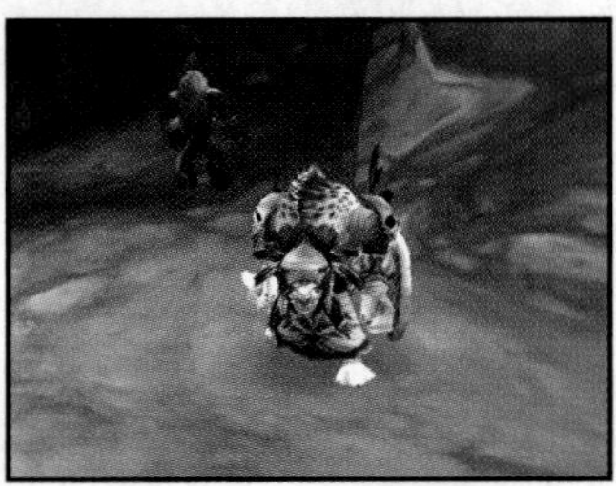

Straight east from the Bael'Dun Digsite is **the Ravaged Caravan**. It's easier to get to the crate from the north of the caravan. Take your time to clear a path to the center of the caravan where you need to right-click on the crate to examine the contents. Once you do, you can return to Morin Cloudstalker. Before you do, however, stop in at the village once more.

In the village see Baine Bloodhoof again and turn in the **Sharing the Land** Quest, then stop by Mull Thunderhorn to turn in the components for the continuation of the **Thunderhorn Totem**. Check back in with Morin Cloudstalker to turn in the next part of the Ravaged Caravan Quest. He now wants you to kill 14 Venture Co. Workers and 6 Supervisors. He also wants you to venture farther into Venture Co. territory and get Supervisor **Fitzsprocket's Clipboard**.

Before you venture up to deal with the Venture Co., head southeast to the Harpies and kill them for their claws. (**Dangers of the Windfury**) You should easily be able to handle them and survive without needing to gain more levels or find a group.

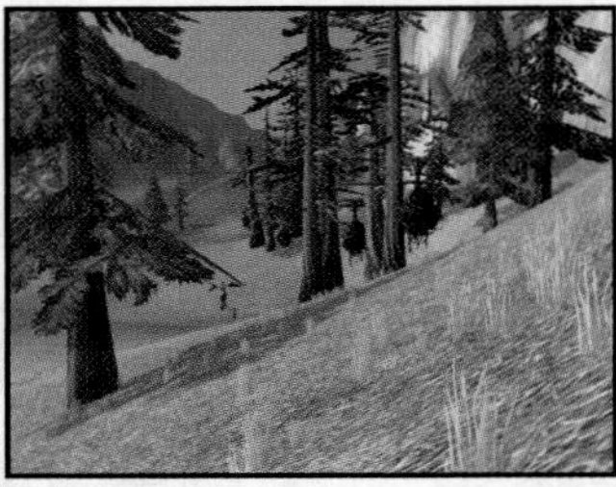

WINDFURY WITCHES

When killing windfury's keep in mind that the Windfury Witches are casters of lightning. It's best to get close to them when possible to kill them more quickly and minimize the damage they do.

Take the road back north toward **The Ravaged Caravan** and head east to the Venture Co. Mine. Below the mine itself is a small village of workers. You may need at least one other person to make your way to Supervisor Fitzsprocket, but at this point the most important thing is to clear a path up to the mine entrance. Just left of the mine is a forge. You can finally break those Dwarven tools you've been hanging on to all this time in relative safety.

As you go along through the mine, you should meet your kill quota for Workers and Supervisors. If you have successfully killed Supervisor Fitzsprocket for his clipboard and not taken out enough of the underlings, take some time to raid the village below by picking off the ones you need that linger along the edges.

Return to Morin Cloudstalker to turn in the clipboard and turn in the Venture Co. quest. It's time to return to the village again and speak with Mull Thunderhorn. Turn in the animal parts you have gathered for him and get the **Thunderhorn Cleansing** totem. The Thunderhorn Water Well is just north of Bloodhoof Village. Turn in the **Dwarven Digging** quest to Baine Bloodhoof. He no longer has any new quests for you. Also turn in the **Dangers of the Windfury** quest to Ruul Eagletalon.

Skorn Whitecloud will be waiting nearby to give you a new quest. In order to prove you are truly ready to be a hunter, he asks you to gather 4 Flatland Prowler Claws and turn them in to Melor Stonehoof in Thunder Bluff. (**The Hunter's Way**) It seems that once you prove yourself to Melor, your path may be assured in the ways of the Hunter.

Also, stop by and speak with Lorekeeper Raintotem. He charges you with clearing out an ancient burial ground and killing 8 Bristleback Interlopers. (**A Sacred Burial**) Go north to the Thunderhorn Water Well so that it can be cleansed. Clear a path through the surrounding Goblins and use the totem. A beam of light appears to show that the well has been cleansed. Return to Bloodhoof Village and get the Wildmane Water Well quest. Mull Thunderhorn needs Alpha Wolf teeth in order to create the last cleansing totem. (**Wildmane Totem**) These Wolves can be found to the southeast of Bloodhoof Village nearby or far to the north beneath Thunder Bluff. Head to the southeast to take care of the ones that are nearby.

KOLKAR RAIDERS

When hunting Alpha Wolves in the southeast region of Mulgore, beware the Kolkar raiders that wander in the area in pairs. It's best to stay relatively near the road rather than risk drawing agro from the swoops, prairie wolves and Kolkar as well as the Alpha Wolves.

Move toward the north as you go along to discover Red Rocks. Up on the hill there is the ancient burial ground. Kill your way through the Razormanes Interlopers as a means to complete **A Sacred Burial** until you can speak to the Ancient Spirit within. It's easier to approach from the northwest side and slip in against the wall.

The Ancient Spirit congratulates you on completing the **Rite of Wisdom** and whether you are ready or not to accept it, they have given over the duty of protecting Thunder Bluff to you. Your last step will be to enter into Thunder Bluff to stand face to face with the Tauren leader Cairne Bloodhoof at last.

THUNDER BLUFF

Return to Bloodhoof Village to turn in the first part of the Wildmane Water Well quest and get the Wildmane Cleansing Totem. The Wildmane Water Well is located to the north of Thunder Bluff. (**Wildmane Cleansing**) Take the west road from Bloodhoof Village to Thunder Bluff. It's time to enter the city at last. At the base of Thunder Bluff is a lift that will take you up to the city proper. Wait for the lift to come down to you and step lively to get on before it goes back up without you. You will arrive in the main complex of Thunder Bluff.

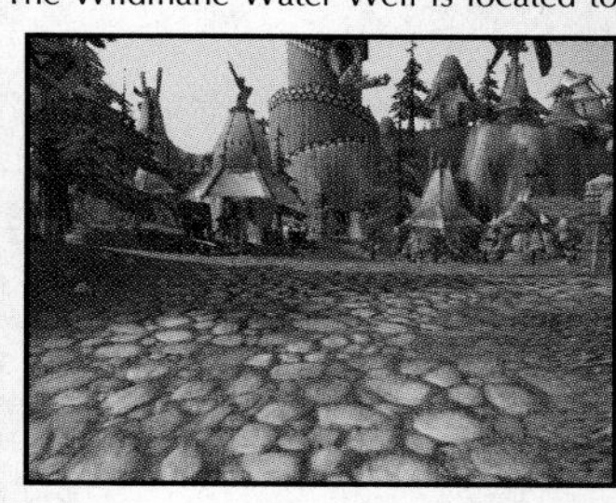

WATCH YOUR STEP!

Be careful when navigating the lifts of Thunder Bluff as well as navigating around the city itself. It's very easy to fall from the mesa tops and die. There are few that can survive such a fall without careful preparation.

Here you meet up with Eyahn Eagletalon. (**Preparation for Ceremony**) It seems he's running very short on time and is trying to prepare a headdress for his brother and needs to ask you a favor. He needs 6 Azure Feathers and 6 Bronze Feathers from the Harpies that are to the north and northwest of Thunder Bluff.

From here, follow the signs to Hunter's rise. It should be to the south of the main area of Thunder Bluff. Deliver the 4 Flatland Prowler Claws to Melor Stonehoof. Melor has faith in the judgment of Skorn Whitecloud and sets you on the path to becoming a true Tauren Hunter. He tells you to continue the path you need to speak to **Segra Darkthorn** at the Crossroads in the Barrens. She can guide you.

Take the wooden bridge to Melor Stonehoof's right to see Cairne Bloodhoof at last. He stands in the doorway of a large tented building on the east side of the mesa. Cairne confirms that you have at last completed the **Rites of the Earthmother** and earned your place among the other citizens of Thunder Bluff however, you must continue to prove yourself to remain worthy. He charges you to kill the Kodo called **Arra'chea**. The Kodo proves a difficult beast to track and is best left until the last of your other quests are complete.

Take the eastern lift down to the main prairie and head up to the Furies to the north. Kill and collect the feathers that are needed for Eyahn Eagletalon. Make your way to the east and start south a bit to the Wildmane Water Well. It's located near a small area with Goblin buildings. Work your way carefully in and cleanse the water well. (**Wildmane Cleansing**)

Now is a good time to look for others to join with you to find and kill **Arra'chea**. It can be an elusive kodo and by having many eyes watch for it, you will all be able to find it more easily and all get credit for the kill. **Arra'chea** has a tendency to wander slightly southeast of Thunder Bluff and takes a clockwise pattern in the Golden Plains. There is no doubt a kodo is nearby when you feel the ground shake around you or hear the thunderous fall of their feet on the ground.

Once **Arra'chea** has been killed, head back to Bloodhoof Village one last time to turn in the **Wildmane Cleansing** quest. All the wells are now untainted and Mull Thunderhorn will be pleased. Continue north along the road once more and turn in the harpy feathers to Eyahn Eagletalon and continue on to Cairne Bloodhoof. All of the quests available for now have been completed at this point and the last thing to do is to venture out to the Barrens to the east and find new adventures.

TIRISFAL GLADES

With the spread of the plague throughout Lordaeron and the transformation of the once proud High Elf Sylvanas Windrunner into a Banshee, a new breed of Undead was born. Rebelling against the Scourge and the Lich King that had created her new life, Sylvanas gathered together the willful Undead and fought against the mindless ones under his control. With victory in their hands, they claimed Lordaeron and Tirisfal Glades as their new seat of power. These new Undead known as the Forsaken now fight against the Lich Kings forces while fighting off the Alliance who wishes the destruction of all Undead touched by the taint of the Scourge.

LEGEND

1 Deathknell
2 Night Web's Hollow
3 Solliden Farmstead
4 Nightmare Vale
5 Stillwater Pond
6 Agamand Mills
7 Cold Hearth Manor
8 Brill
9 Garren's Haunt
10 Ruins of Lordaeron
11 Undercity
12 Brightwater Lake
13 Balnir Farmstead
14 The Bulwark
15 Crusader Outpost
16 Venomweb Vale
17 Faol's Rest
18 Whispering Gardens-Scarlet Monastery
19 Scarlet Watch Post
20 Zepplin to Orgrimmar and Grom'Gol-Outpost
21 The North Coast
22 Gunther's Retreat

You have awoken from the crypt as one of the Forsaken. You are not alone however. Not only are there many that the plague has transformed, but the Horde stands with you in an alliance born of need rather than trust.

DEATHKNELL

Once you ascend the stairs, you gaze upon Deathknell. Right-click the scroll in your pack to see your first task. Each class is given their own quest that takes them to their trainer. The Warlock, Mage and Priest trainers are all located within the church. The Rogue and Warrior trainers are in the second building across from the church.

Stop to speak with Undertaker Mordo as you leave the Crypt. He has a yellow exclamation point hanging over his head to indicate he has a quest for you.

Accept the **Rude Awakening** quest. Continue on down the road and stop off in the church on the left to see Shadow Priest Sarvis. Shadow Priest Sarvis gives you the **Mindless Ones** quest and Novice Elreth gives you **The Damned** quest.

WARLOCK DEMON QUEST

Warlocks receive their first demon pet quest at Level 1 along with the normal quests everyone else gets. Do this quest before any others; return to the trainer and get the Summon Imp spell from the start. The imp helps kill quickly and effectively. By completing this quest, you'll also be Level 2 and able to take the Night Web's Hollow quest from Executor Arren.

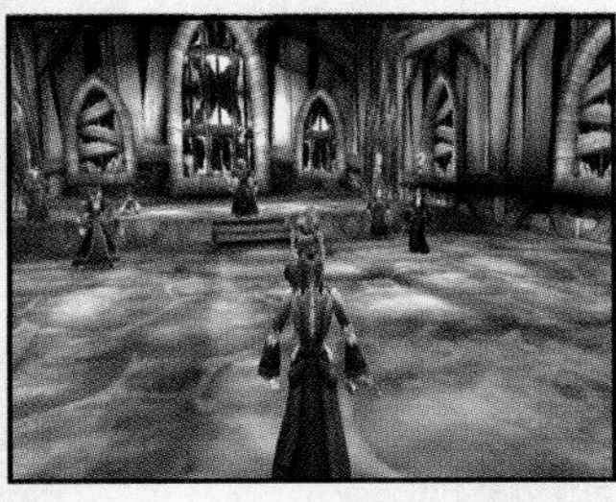

Bats and Wolves are behind the graveyard and just a bit farther are the Mindless and Wretched Zombies. **The Mindless Ones** is a kill quest and only requires that you kill 5 Mindless Zombies and 3 Wretched Zombies. **The Damned Quest** is a collection quest. You will need to loot 4 Scavenger Paws and 4 Duskbat Wings to turn in.

Priest Sarvis has a new quest for you called **Rattling the Rattlecages;** you need to kill 12 Rattlecage Skeletons. They can be found farther down the road behind the buildings to the right. Stop by Deathguard Saltain and pick up his new quest. (**Scavenging Deathknell**) You can find the piles of boxes he's looking for in the buildings with the Rattlecages. Stop by Executor Arren also before you move on. You'll receive the **Night Web's Hollow** quest, which take you a bit deeper into Deathknell.

Before heading to Night Web's Hollow, do **Rattling the Rattlecages** and **Scavenging Deathknell**. It's easier to make a sweep toward the cave to the north since you'll already be headed that way. Night Web's Hollow is located farther down the road and off to the west. The young Night Web Spiders hide in the grass among other places outside the cave proper. Within the cave itself you will find the full-grown Night Web spiders. Kill 8 Young Night Web Spiders and 6 Night Web Spiders then return to Priest Sarvis, Deathguard Saltain and Executor Arran for your rewards.

Executor Arran has more in store for you. He needs you to kill members of the Scarlet Crusade and bring back 8 Armbands. (**The Scarlet Crusade)** Their camp is east of Deathknell. Return to Executor Arran once you have the 8 Armbands.

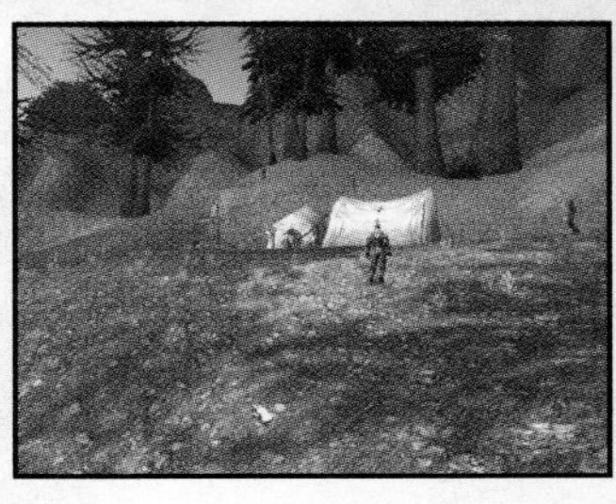

The Red Messenger pits you against Meven Korgal in the camp nearby. He is in the center of the camp from which you just collected armbands. This is a quest in which everyone with the quest can loot the item, so while you may miss out on a little extra experience, you still obtain the item.

When you return to Executor Arran, he sends you on to report to Executor Zygand in Brill. (**Vital Intelligence)** Deathknell is finished for you. As you leave, meet up with David Trias. He has **A Rogue's Deal** in which he asks you to deliver a letter to Innkeeper Renee in Brill.

BRILL

Down the road toward Brill you encounter Deathguard Simmer who tells you of the **Fields of Grief**. He asks you to gather 10 Pumpkins from Solliden Farmstead and turn them into Apothecary Johaan. Tempting as it may be, don't do it just yet. Tirisfal Glades is a dangerous place. Stick to the road. If Decrepit Darkhounds attack, you should be able to handle them with a bit of effort, but beware should more come.

On the way to Brill, keep an eye out for an Abomination named Gordo. He walks the road from Brill and wanders near the woods. **Gordo's Task** asks you to pick some weeds that his master sent him for. The weeds are easy to pick out and are typically near the road. Don't venture too far into the woods. Once you have the weeds, continue toward Brill once more.

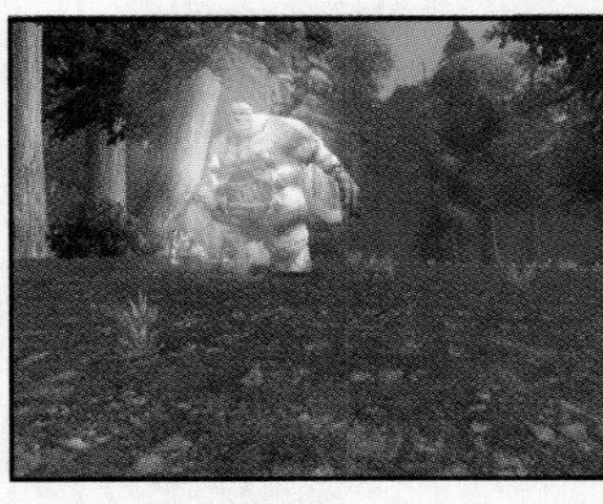

Stop by quickly and see Junior Apothecary Holland to turn in the Gloomweed you picked up. He will be upset at Gordo's incompetence in telling you to get the wrong plant and assigns you to instead collect **Doom Weed** to the north. Check in at the Inn and turn in **A Rogue's Task** to the Innkeeper. She gives you a little something for your trouble and waves you along. Speak with the Innkeeper to make this your new resting place.

Check in with Executor Zygand. Turn in the papers and listen to what he says about your next task. **At War with the Scarlet Crusade** is not quite over. He wants you to kill 10 Scarlet Warriors. This must be your lucky day because they guard a tower next to the Solliden Farmstead. Don't go there just yet though. There's another quest that Deathguard Dillinger would like you to help him with. He has **A Putrid Task** for you. He wants you to collect 7 Putrid Claws from Rotting Dead and Ravaged Corpses. The Rotting Dead and Ravaged Corpses are just to the west a bit of the Brill graveyard. They're a bit tougher than the Mindless and Wretched Zombies you were killing earlier.

Turn in the quest and head inside the town hall. Magistrate Sevren has another task for you that is also nearby. Magistrate Sevren is a bit concerned. Rot Hide Gnolls are using corpses to bolster the army of the Scourge. He asks you to kill 8 Rot Hide Gnolls, 5 Rot Hide Mongrels and to collect 8 Embalming Ichor. **The Graverobbers** can be found just north of Brill at Garren's Haunt. There are many Gnolls guarding the way. Work on the Doom Weed quest while killing the Rot Hide Gnolls; the weed is found in abundance in this area.

The dig sight for the Graverobbers is at the end of the road that splits off to the left before you reach the farm. Kill them, collect ichor and work your way east toward the farm to kill Mongrels. Be cautious in how you deal with them.

Once you've completed killing the Gnolls and collecting the Embalming Ichor, head back to see Junior Apothecary Holland and Magistrate Sevren. He has two more quests for you: **The Prodigal Lich** and **Forsaken Duties**.

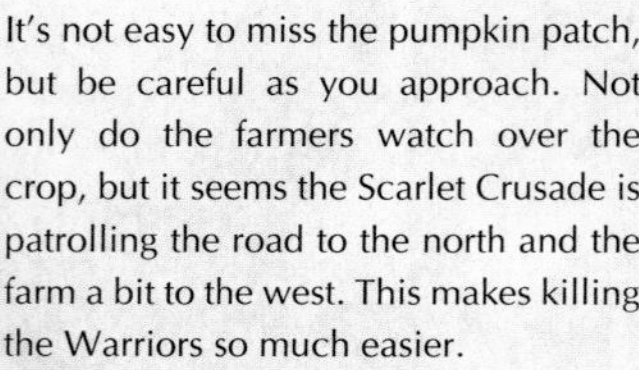

Stop by the Town Hall and right-click on the wanted poster. (**Wanted: Maggot Eye**!) On the way out, Deathguard Dillinger should have another quest available for you. He informs you that the Scourge are setting up a base at the Agamand Mills and the **Mills are Overrun**. Accept his quest before moving on.

It's time to go see about some Pumpkins. The first part of **At War with the Scarlet Crusade** in Tirisfal Glades and the **Fields of Grief** can be done at the same time.

It's not easy to miss the pumpkin patch, but be careful as you approach. Not only do the farmers watch over the crop, but it seems the Scarlet Crusade is patrolling the road to the north and the farm a bit to the west. This makes killing the Warriors so much easier.

Patrol from east to west and pick Pumpkins while killing a few Warriors. You'll be done fairly quickly. Kill 10 Scarlet Crusade Warriors and pick 10 Pumpkins before returning to Brill.

It's time to travel to Agamand Mills. They can be found in the Northwest region of Tirisfal Glades. The farther north you go, the higher level the Darkeye Bonecasters and Rattlecage Soldiers become. Bonecasters provide the skulls you need and Soldiers provide the ribs. It may take some time, but if you start either at the first tower or the southernmost region of the Mills, you should be able to pick your way through them safely. Watch out for those Darkhounds.

If you're lucky, you'll find a **Letter to Yvette**. Accept the quest to deliver **A Letter Undelivered** before you leave. She's in the Inn in Brill. Stop at Deathgaurd Dillinger and turn in the skulls and ribs and collect your reward.

Take your Pumpkins to the Apothecary Johaan. There's a Scarlet Crusader being held hostage in the basement of the Inn. Take him the formula-laced Pumpkin for part two of the **Fields of Grief**. Apothecary Johaan has another task for you as well. He would like you to collect Darkhound Blood as a part of **A New Plague**.

Check in with Executor Zygand in front of the town hall. Not surprisingly, he has another quest for you to kill more of the Scarlet Crusaders. (**At War with the Scarlet Crusade**) You will need to kill Captain Perrine this time as well to try to knock out the command structure behind the Scarlet Crusaders. As you head toward the Inn to visit the prisoner you'll notice Deathguard Burgess has a new quest for you. He wants you to bring him rings off of the Scarlet Crusaders as **Proof of Demise**.

Inside the Inn, Coleman Farthing is waiting with a little bit of revenge on his mind. (**The Haunted Mills**) He asks you to kill Devlin Agamand. Accept the quest and head down to the basement to see the Scarlet Crusader captive and give him the potion-laced pumpkin.

If you have the **Letter to Yvette**, she's in the corner of the Inn. Upstairs, Gretchen Dedmar needs your help. **The Chill of Death** seeps in her bones and in order to continue her work she wants you to pick up some Bat Pelts and Course Thread so she can sew herself something a little warmer.

THE BALNIR FARMSTEAD

It's time to venture to Undercity and the ruins of Lordaeron. As you go, stop off quickly to the east at the split in the road to visit the tents set up nearby. It's time to take care of **Forsaken Duties** and speak with Deathguard LInnea. She tells you that the **Rear Patrol** has somehow been compromised and word is that the Scourge has snuck up from behind the Bulwarks. She asks you to kill Bleeding Horrors and Wandering Spirits at the Balnir Farmstead. (**Return to the Magistrate**)

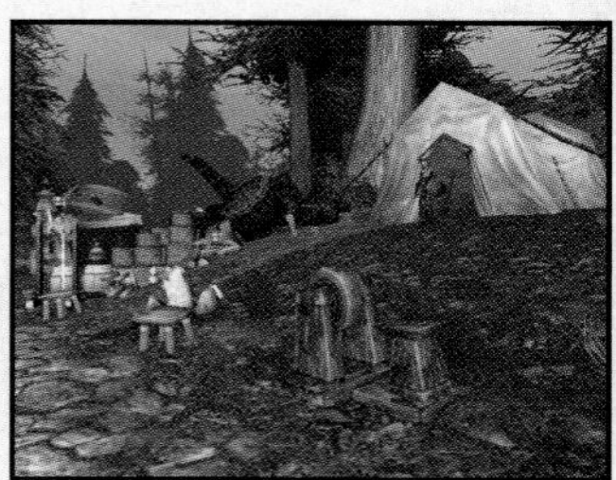

Continue back down to the Southwest toward the Crusader tower. Be careful at the tower. The humans are prone to help each other should they run for help. There are Missionaries and Zealots at the back of the tower and it's no problem finding more Crusaders to kill. The Captain is inside the tower (usually with two comrades). Don't forget to collect rings as you are killing. If you do not get all the rings now, don't worry. There's another opportunity to get all the rings you need, though the sooner you get it done the better.

Once you've finished all three quests (four if you got all of your rings) return to Brill. Stop at the general trade vendor and purchase some Coarse Thread. You should now have everything Gretchen requested. Go inside the inn and upstairs to give it to her.

Turn in the ring quest to Deathguard Burgess. Return to Executor Zygand and turn in the quest to get the third part of **At War with the Scarlet Crusade**. Return to the Magistrate in the city hall and turn in the report to him from Deathgaurd Linnea. Take the Darkhound Blood to Apothecary Johaan and turn it in. He has a new quest for **A New Plague** that takes you back toward Garren's Haunt and the North Shore.

Continue past the farm for now and head right to the shoreline. Don't get too close to the shore. Murlocs like to wait under the water and you can never tell just how many of them may be hiding. Collect the 5 Vile Fins from the Murlocs. Once you complete that, work on getting a reward for Maggot Eye. You will find him in a house at the northern end of the farm at Garren's Haunt. He has a lot of other Gnolls around him. Maggot Eye is Level 11 and a tough nut to crack.

Once both quests are complete, run back to Brill. Turn the Vile Fins in to Apothecary Johaan and receive two more quests. One new quest is **A Delivery to Silverpine** (don't worry about right now) and the other is the last part of **A New Plague**.

There are three more quests to do, all in the same region. Start with the **Rear Guard Patrol** at Balnir's Farmstead. It lies to the southeast of Brill along the road. Be careful not to go too far. There are some powerful creatures patrolling the Bulwark.

As you approach the Farmstead, Bleeding Horrors are easy to make out in the distance. The Wandering Spirits however, take a bit of concentration as their ghostly forms float smoothly over the field. Kill 8 Bleeding Horrors and 8 Wandering Spirits.

Once you've finished with the Bleeding Horrors and Wandering Spirits, pay a visit to the Scarlet Crusader Outpost just a bit northeast of the farm. While you could attempt to approach it from the front and climb the steep hill; it's better to come from the rear. There's an easier grade just to the west of the tower and plenty of Crusaders to kill as you make your way to the tower. Kill 5 Friars and Captain Vachon. Group for this quest. Captain Vachon is well protected. The Crusaders here range from Level 8 to 11. If you haven't finished the **Proof of Demise** quest, you should be able to finish it up here. Even if you finish this part of **At War with the Scarlet Crusade,** continue killing until you have all of your rings to turn in (if you haven't already).

There's an opening onto a new field to the east of the tower. Venomweb Vale hides the spiders for Apothecary Johaan's newest experiment with the plague.

When you have completed this quest, return to Brill. Pick your way carefully through and you won't have any problems. It's time to go back to the tents and check in with Deathguard Linnea for the **Rear Guard Patrol**. Once through there, it's on to Brill.

Check in with Executor Zygand and receive the next **At War with the Crusade** quest. Turn in the spider venom to Apothecary Johaan and he tasks you with one more experiment. (**A New Plague**) Take the concoction to the Dwarf who comments on finally getting a drink. Visit your trainer for some new goodies.

UNDERCITY

Go to Undercity to speak with Bethor Iceshard and start The **Prodigal Lich Quest**. It's easy to get confused at first as to where you need to go, but it gets easier if you remember that the Undead have created the Undercity beneath the ruins of Lordaeron. Be careful not to fall into the green ooze. Sure you don't have to worry about breathing, but it does have a tendency to do some damage to your flesh.

Take the elevator down to the heart of Undercity then follow the stairs all the way down to the bottom beneath the bank. Head down through the Trade Quarter and into the outer rings. Bethor Iceshard is located in the Mages Quarter in the outer ring in the northeast corner of the city at the Temple of the Damned.

You'll find him up the stairs and toward the front of the building. He knows he's one of the freed forsaken, however, the lich does not realized that he is not the only forsaken that is of his own free will. In the meantime, all of his minions attack any who venture near. Bethor would like to find out who this lich is and needs proof of the **Lich's Identity**. He wants the Lich's book.

Venture up and out of Undercity and head toward the lake. Bethor and his book are on the larger island. Approach the island from the left side, which is closest to the book. Kill the minions from the shore to the area near Bethor and take the book. Once you have the book, jog back to Undercity and check in with Bethor Iceshard.

Bethor is pleased that it is in an old friend of his. (**The Prodigal Lich Returns**) Make your way back to the island, fight through the Lich's pets and give him the gem. He asks you to **Prove Your Allegiance** by summoning and killing Lilith Nefara by placing a candle from his box on the altar on the small island.

The small island has two creatures wandering on it. You must kill them before you summon Lilith. Kill her and return to Gunther Arcanus.

Gunther is pleased that you have dispatched Lilith. He gives you a nether Gem to take back to Bethor Iceshard. (**The Prodigal Lich Returns**) Return to Bethor in the Undercity and get your reward. Now pay Devlin Agamand a visit. **The Haunted Mills** asks you to bring back the remains of Devlin Agamand to Coleman Farthing in the Inn.

Run to Agamand Mills, but take it slow as you approach near the tower. Devlin should be near the road on the left side. Kill him and return to the Inn.

Coleman Farthing is more satisfied now, but not completely. He asks you to return once more to bring him the other three remains of the Agamand family: Nissa, Gregor and Thurmond Agamand. (**Deaths in the Family**)

Nissa is the easiest to find at the Mills. At the end of the road in the very first house she waits in Banshee form. You need to kill all of the Darkeye Bonecasters and Rattlecage Soldiers nearby and then kill her to get the remains. Follow the road a bit farther, taking the left split to the first windmill on the right. Gregor wanders behind it and down the road a bit and back normally, and can be spotted by his hunched and bulbous form. Thurmond is all the way down at the end of the road. He looks similar to Bleeding Horrors, so you'll recognize him easily. When you have gotten all three of the remains, return to Coleman Farthing in Brill.

There's just one more quest that takes you to Agamand Mills. Speak with Magistrate Sevren to get **The Family Crypt**. He wants you to slay the Scourge's local Military leader Captain Dargol as well as slay Wailing and Rotting Ancestors as you go along. Wailing Ancestors are easy to pick out. These are the Banshees floating about and are casters. Rotting Ancestors are the brute force and resemble Bleeding Horrors. The crypt can be found by going off following the road back to the split and taking the one to the right.

Kill as you work your way down carefully. As you go you'll easily meet the kill requirement for the quest. The final stairs down in the center lead to the Captain and several Wailing and Rotting Ancestors. Once the captain is dead and you have retrieved his skull, stone to Brill.

Once in Brill turn in the skull to Magistrate Sevren. There is just one last task to do and if possible, now is the time to ask for a group to do it. **At War with the Scarlet Crusade** needs you to go to one last place and kill three more people.

The Crusader Outpost is way to the north with the tower built onto the Cliffside and looming over the sea below. Be wary as you travel. There are easily four people within the tower at this point. If it's possible, try to pull the front bodyguard by either pulling from an outside edge or getting just close enough to aggro the front NPCs as a pull.

Once both bodyguards are dead and Melrache is also, head back in victory. You have successfully completed all of the quests up to this level as well as put a dent in the power of the Scourge and Scarlet Crusade in Tirisfal Glades. Hearthstone back to Brill. Check in with Executor Zygand one last time and turn in your quest. You're ready to go beyond the boundaries of Tirisfal Glades. Don't you have a certain letter you have in your inventory?

JOINING THE TROOPS

Before getting involved with specific class abilities, data tables, and so forth, it's important to evaluate play strategies that are used by all characters in *World of Warcraft*. This chapter explains various methods to improve your ability to gather money, rise in level, move around Azeroth, engage in combat, and find special areas.

COMMON TACTICS

It takes considerable time to teach someone about *World of Warcraft*. This game has enough complexity to keep players reeling for many days, even while learning the basics. This section is organized to give you the tips and ideas to cut down on lost opportunities during that learning phase. There's always money and experience to be made, and there is no harm in starting from the beginning!

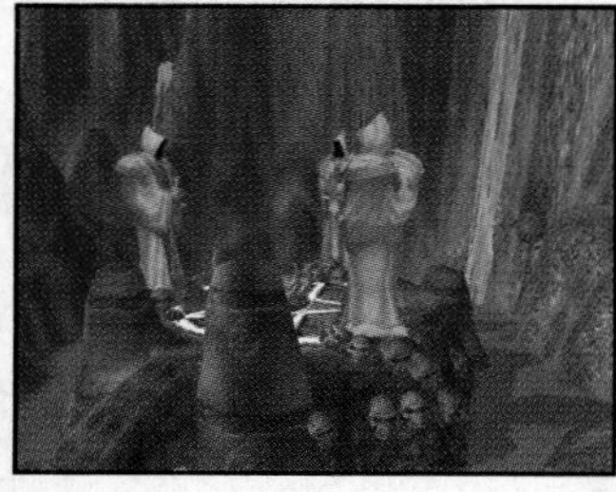

GAINING EXPERIENCE

Experience points get you closer to your next level. Characters currently progress from Levels 1 to 60 and each advancement brings better attributes, higher hit points/mana, and the potential for greater deeds. Whether you focus on pulling in XP is one thing, but everyone gains levels if they enjoy the game and keep heading out into the wilds.

KILLING MONSTERS

The most basic way to gain experience is to walk into an area with monsters and start fighting them. Every victory against a monster of (or around) an equivalent level gets you experience. These points add up nicely if you try to kill monsters as quickly as possible. Trying to gain levels solely through monster killing is called "grinding" by many players. Some people find this method dull because it offers less variety of action compared to questing, going exploring, and so forth. Others feel relaxed by bringing down a stable flow of money, experience, and nasty monsters. There is nothing wrong with this method if it's what you enjoy. There are plenty of areas where non-stop hunting can keep players busy for weeks!

WHAT MAKES AN EQUIVALENT MOB

Monsters are worth experience if they are close to your character's level. A 20% difference in levels between your character and the monster OR a difference of five levels is allowed; whichever is greater will be used.

Anything beneath this threshold gives zero experience, because the challenge is trivial. However, such creatures still drop treasure.

QUICK EQUIVALENCE CHART

CHARACTER LEVEL	ALLOWED LEVELS OF DIFFERENCE
25	5
30	6
40	8
50	10
60	12

Grinding itself can be a very fast method for leveling. Or, it can be slower than other available techniques; this entirely depends on the current level of your character, your equipment, local quest options, and more subtle aspects of play. Indeed, some grinders are able to gain levels with extreme speed by choosing a class and character concept that is geared for soloing and finding areas where tandem fighting (going after one mob, then another right afterward, then another, etc.) is easy to do.

CHECKLIST FOR A GOOD GRINDING AREA

- Many Monsters Available
- Enough Space between Monsters that They Can Be Fought Individually
- Creatures in Area Lack Powerful Special Abilities that Harm your Class/Race
- Monster Levels are Just Low Enough to Keep the Kills Fast and Downtime Short (A Couple Levels under Your Character's Level)
- Little to No Competition for Kills
- A Vendor is Somewhat Accessible for Periodically Dropping off Loot
- Preferably, a Graveyard is Close Enough to Shorten Downtime if an Accident Happens; This Isn't as Important as the Other Factors

QUESTING FOR EXPERIENCE

During the lower levels (certainly through Levels 1 to 30), characters gain quite a bit of experience through questing. It isn't hard to gather multiple quests from towns in this period, and completing several at a time is both easy and exciting. The awards for turning in these quests catapults characters through their levels. And, when played correctly, the best elements of grinding and questing can be combined once players understand the locations in which they're adventuring.

First off, it's useful to grind while approaching quest sites and while leaving them! If you have a quest in the northwest of The Barrens, asking you to kill Harpies, it is helpful to kill Centaur, Raptors, and other enemies on the way. Walking to the edge of a zone may take five or six minutes (more in a number of cases). That time is somewhat wasted if you simply run because your characters are full on hit points/mana and have nothing to use it on.

Instead, blast monsters along your way to gain experience and keep the time interesting. This slows your questing somewhat, but it dramatically improves experience gained per hour of play. Those who grind and quest do very well for themselves, especially in the early game.

Pick and Choose

A subset of questing is to avoid getting all quests in a region while doing only those that fit your character's needs. This becomes quite common at the later levels, when people prefer to fight in certain regions, Instances, and such.

To Pick and Choose means to look through all available quests and decide which ones have rewards that you need or which ones have targets that you want to kill anyway. This is a solid, mercenary approach. If your character likes to grind against Trolls in the Hinterlands, there is no reason on Azeroth not to help the local Dwarves (who have a few problems with said Trolls). Grinding is all well and good, but dropping off a quest each time you head back to sell loot nets practically free experience when you play in this manner.

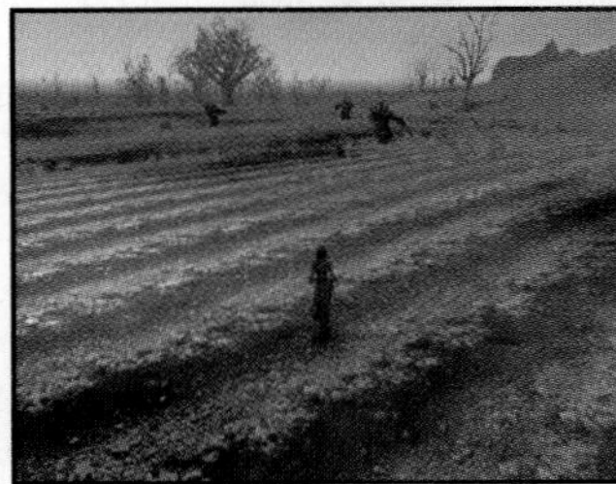

UNDERSTANDING ATTRIBUTES

At the most basic level of play, higher attributes equal a better character. However, you're often forced to decide which attributes are the most important to your style of play and character concept. It's crucial to understand what the attributes do, how they affect your class, and which systems can be influenced by your choices.

ATTRIBUTES

ATTRIBUTE	PURPOSE
Strength	Improve Damage (DPS), Raise % Chance to Block w/ a Shield
Agility	Higher % Chance to Dodge, Higher Critical Hit Rate, Increases Damage for Some Characters (e.g. Rogues)
Spirit	Improves Rate of Hit Point/Mana Gain While Out of Combat
Stamina	Raises Hit Points (10 Hit Points/Point of Stamina)
Intellect	Raises Mana (10 Mana/Point of Intellect)

Strength improves your character's DPS and helps to block incoming attacks. Warriors always need a fair bit of Strength, but all melee characters are interested in getting more when they can.

Agility affects Dodge and Critical Hit percentages for all characters. This makes Agility a secondary damage attribute for tanks (Warriors, Paladins, etc.) and a primary damage attribute for Rogues and Hunters. The reason for this is that ranged damage is influenced by Agility. Also, Rogues receive half of their damage bonuses from Strength and half from Agility!

Spirit determines how many hit points/mana you regain with each tick of the game's clock. All characters gain at a full rate outside of battle and have a lesser rate of mana regeneration in battle (it requires special Talents to regenerate health while taking damage). A person's class affects the amount of regeneration that goes toward either hit points or mana, but Spirit raises the rate for both types. Having a very high Spirit reduces downtime by a fair margin.

Stamina gives characters ten hit points for every point of Stamina they gain. This is a flat sum and does not suffer from diminishing returns and other complexities of the earlier attributes.

Intellect is similar to Stamina, though it gives mana to characters instead of health. Characters with higher Intellect are able to learn skills faster than those who are at or below par for this attribute.

It's easy to understand how the latter attributes influence your character, since they're linear, but the other attributes are subtle enough to require further explanation.

STAYING ON PAR

For each level of your character, there is a hidden par value for your attributes. This value is meant to reflect the improvements that are available to your character during advancement. If you stay at par, your percentages won't change in a major way; Critical Hit rates, Dodging, and such are meant to be fluid yet stay within certain bounds.

If your character falls below par by having low-level equipment, not spending talent points, or otherwise focusing on different elements, your percentage in different tasks may drop! Look at your character now and compare the numbers for Block, Critical Hit, and Dodge to what you had five levels ago; there is no guarantee of improvement in these things.

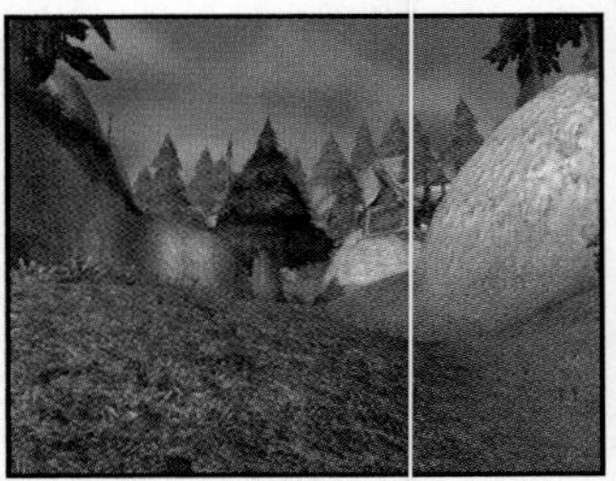

HOW DO I LOOK AT MY PERCENTAGES?

To see your chance to Block, Dodge, and Critically Hit Opponents, open your Abilities Menu (the hotkey is "I") and highlight these given aspects. They should be listed on the first page.

For even more interesting data, remove various pieces of equipment and notice the immediate and profound changes to said percentages. Equipment choices matter!

Read the new entry to learn about specializing your character. This gives you control over which parts of your class are dominant in battle.

SPECIALIZING A CHARACTER

Nobody in Azeroth is meant to be exactly the same. There are many ways to configure your character for different forms of combat, and this goes well beyond a person's class. Use of talents, style, equipment, and profession(s) all make a difference in the end result.

The big question for each player is, "What do they want to accomplish in battle?" Are you a healer, a damage dealer, a support character? Do you want to be good for short bursts or for sustained effort? Is disruption of enemy forces more important to you than getting kills and glory?

Before jumping into the "how" end of things, it's best to investigate "why!"

PERKS OF CHARACTER SPECIALIZATION

Customizing your character is an enjoyable experience because you're making an avatar into your own reflection of a class. You're leaving the simple distinction of Warrior/Rogue/Mage, etc. behind; what appears in its place is your representation of that class. Making a name for yourself, exploring new ideas and style choices, and seeking new modes of victory are all waiting down this path. The rewards are considerable.

If you stay along a general line, your character ends up with few weaknesses (only those given by your race/class). However, you're rarely able to play to your strengths unless you develop them. Specializing your character makes it much easier to win in battles where you are able to use your advantages.

Does this mean that you lose more often when you cannot focus on your strengths if you heavily customize? Yes, it does. In a well-balanced game, there have to be penalties to your choices as well as perks, and *World of Warcraft* makes great efforts to balance your options.

The reason this isn't as much of a problem as it sounds is that a skilled player can often take advantage of the edges given to them. Against many mobs and even some players, the ability to drive forward with your best abilities precludes the weaknesses of your deficits. That is why specializing and customizing is useful, doable, and a great deal of fun.

USING YOUR TALENT POINTS

The most obvious form of customization is provided directly by the class system. At Level 10, you start gaining talents. The abilities gained from this system are very powerful, especially when people devote their characters into specific lines; the deeper stages of specific talent lines are quite impressive and rewarding.

Before spending these points, take a long look at the lines available to your character. Because of the extended hours involved in reaching the higher levels, it's nice to know what you're getting into. Instead of taking any talent that looks nice now, come up with a path that nets as many permanent, useful talents as possible.

On the whole, there are several varieties of talent specializations. These are not identified directly, but an astute player can see where specific talents are the most useful. Anything that reduces downtime and raises efficiency in battle is good for extended fighting against weaker targets; this is a style more for soloers than group members. On the other hand, abilities that are expensive, but raise burst damage and effectiveness, are critical in Instances and PvP fighting.

Decide what variety of character you are interested in playing. There's always the chance that your needs and interests will change, but many people know somewhat what they enjoy doing from the very beginning. Try to create a talent path that advances the areas of the game you enjoy.

GENERAL ABILITY TRADEOFFS

ABILITY TYPE	POWERFUL FOR	WEAKEST IN
Burst Damage/Healing	PvP	Group Settings
Efficient Damage/Healing	Soloing	PvP
Increased Potential Damage/Healing	Grouping/Instances	Soloing
Higher Survivability	Grouping/Tanks	Large Scale PvP
Disable Enemies	Specific Hunting	General Combat

PvP builds are often about doing the greatest amount of activity in a short period. Instant abilities, helpful passive talents, and other reactive perks are the focus here. Player vs. Player combat is often much shorter in duration than fighting against monsters in the field or in Instances. Thus, efficiency is almost worthless compared to immediate power and survival. Specialize in burst healing or damage to be able to respond to the unpredictability of facing live, intelligent players in PvP combat.

Soloers need to be independent; they don't have backup healing, easy damage, or safety. This necessitates a build where the character is fully functional in multiple aspects of play. Efficiency is stressed because there are no allies to fall back on, and long downtime is a very bad thing if you don't have anyone to talk to or to keep the experience rolling. If you are a soloist, seek talents that make your favorite actions more effective, then use those abilities to their fullest.

Group-friendly builds are some of the most specialized characters of all. These builds are intended to extend the weaker areas of many classes while honing specific strengths that are useful to allies. Seek increased potential in areas that are hailed by groups (better defense for a tank, more potent and dependable heals for a healer, and safe/constant damage from DPS classes). The group is present to negate the weaknesses of each member while extending the strengths of each member's build.

Remember that a soloist can group, a PvPer can and will farm Instances, and so forth. Everyone should be capable of filling a variety of roles, but it's going to be harder going against your element. Choose the line that makes your favorite roll more enjoyable, because that is what you spend the most time doing.

HONING EQUIPMENT

Talents are by no means the end of character customization. Equipment choices account for a great deal of a person's effectiveness. This doesn't boil down to a simple numbers game (i.e. go for higher level gear all the time and don't stop). Rather, a focus on the type of equipment that completes your build is needed.

The most basic example is for casters who are rising in level. These characters need both Spirit and Intellect (Spirit for regaining mana and Intellect for having a large pool of mana to draw from). A soloist wants to have quite a high Spirit to maintain their mana and minimize downtime, since they are the ones casting in each battle. PvPers, at the other end, need to survive their current encounter no matter what the mana cost; they use Intellect for having the highest possible DPS for a given encounter. Even if recovery is slow as nails, they are free to drink water and cheer their victory.

Again, ask yourself what type of character you want to play! Look at your attributes and choose a primary attribute and a secondary one. When selecting armor pieces, weapons, and other equipment, try to find pieces that add heavily to your primary attribute while supporting your secondary choice. Or, if you self full self-sufficiency, try to raise three attributes as well as possible. The key is to find out what you need for your style.

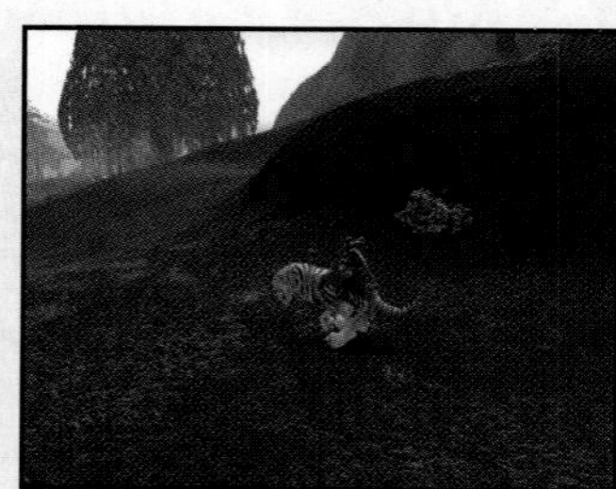

ATTRIBUTE PREFERENCE EXAMPLES

CLASS/STYLE	PRIMARY ATTRIBUTE	SECONDARY ATTRIBUTE
Defensive Tank	Stamina (Hit Points)	Agility (Critical Hits/Dodge)
Offensive Warrior	Strength (Damage)	Agility (Critical Hits)
Group Rogue	Agility (Critical Hit/Damage)	Strength (Even More Damage)
Solo Rogue	Agility (Critical Hit/Damage)	Stamina (Needed Survivability)
PvP Mage	Intellect (Maximum Mana/Magical Criticals)	Stamina (Extra Hit Points)
Group Mage	Intellect/Spirit Balance	Stamina
Solo Mage	Spirit (Mana Regen)	Intellect

These examples are neither exhaustive nor perfect. There are major exceptions created when people see a niche that needs to be filled. Imagine a PvP Mage who enjoys going into large-scale battles that last for several minutes of direct fighting. Such a character might shun the pure Intellect model and grab more Spirit and use more efficient spells than a standard nuking Mage.

The goal is not to memorize a specific table to select what you need. Instead, view the process that others use to create their customized equipment sets and see how it relates to your character.

Weapon Speed

Weapons have an added stat that bears consideration. Though the damage you do over time is presented freely by DPS, weapon speed has a bearing on many special abilities. Before going too far, it's useful to understand what DPS means. DPS absolutely reveals how well a weapon can perform under minimal circumstances. Higher DPS equates to higher damage regardless of weapon speed (thus, the whole use of the term *Damage Per Second,* as this accounts for the variance between slow and fast weaponry).

Yet, so few battles are fought in a vacuum; there are many peripheral factors that bring weapon speed back into play. Anything that adds direct, damage bonuses to spells or weapons is a great boon for fast attacks. If you use a Sharpening Stone that adds +6 damage to all attacks, a dagger benefits from this more than a slow, two-handed sword. The reason is that the bonus is flat; that +6 is better if it occurs every 1.5 seconds instead of every 4.0 seconds.

Faster weapons and spells are thus better for characters that focus on equipment that adds directly to damage.

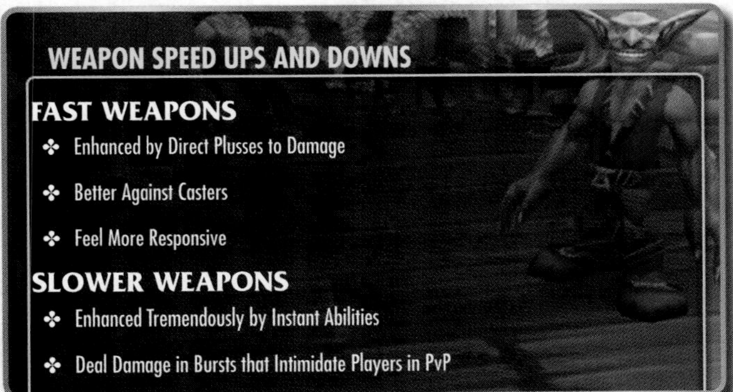

WEAPON SPEED UPS AND DOWNS
FAST WEAPONS
Enhanced by Direct Plusses to Damage
Better Against Casters
Feel More Responsive
SLOWER WEAPONS
Enhanced Tremendously by Instant Abilities
Deal Damage in Bursts that Intimidate Players in PvP

On the flipside, slower weapons can be desirable as well. You may suffer from lost strike opportunities while wielding slow weapons, since there is a long lead-up time, but watch what happens when instant abilities are brought into the equation. Some attacks are made outside of the normal combat flow; these often cost Energy or Rage and are commonly made by Rogues and Warriors. In these cases, an attack that does full weapon damage is much more daunting when used with a slow weapon. DPS has NO EFFECT on the damage done by instant, special attacks. Instead, it's the fully computed damage of the weapon that is applied.

If a Gnome Warrior has a dagger that does 30 to 50 damage a swing and a two-handed sword that does 60 to 100 over twice the time, it seems that neither is much better a weapon. Yet, an instant attack from the sword does double damage at the same cost.

Without worrying about special abilities, fast weapons do have a nice perk against casters; that is the ability to disrupt spells sooner and more often. This assists in stopping Channeling spells and slowing regular ones. Slow weapons don't fill this role nearly as well, forcing their users to rely on sheer kill power to stop casters from having their way.

A more subjective element of weapon speed is that faster weapons are more active and provide a higher element of frantic play to combat. Some players enjoy fast weapons for the chaotic aspect of back-and-forth hacking they provide. Others like the slower weapons because they are a bit more methodic.

Both sides are personal, subjective, and have only a slight impact on character effectiveness. Primarily, it is easier to avoid attacks from a slow-weapon wielder by running behind them and using terrain to your advantage. However, experienced players compensate for this enough to make it a small matter.

REFINING YOUR PLAYSTYLE

Once you have the talents, equipment, and knowledge to support your interests, victory comes from refining the techniques you use in battle. Which attacks aren't as useful in light of your new talents; which moves are now essential, and need to be used earlier in the fight? Try to work on pounding your technique into a trim and effective weapon of its own. If you want to get really scientific about it, time your battles against monsters of the same type and level and see if you can reduce the period it takes to defeat them. The same method can be used to reduce damage taken (kill time and limiting damage taken are often linked to some extent anyway).

Look at the abilities you use in battle. Which of these make the most difference over the course of the battle? If you have status buffs and debuffs, see if there are better times to cast them. Some of these can be done before battle is engaged, so work on mastering a lead in to fights that frees your character to use direct combat abilities as soon as possible.

Perhaps a reorganization of the quickbar is in order at this stage. One thing that slows players down a great deal is the inefficient use of the game's interface. Many players who take the time to customize their quickbars are impressed at the difference in their character's performance. Keep abilities that aren't used often on entirely different bars and streamline the buttons that are used in each and every combat. Try to use an ascending order that fits the progression of battle, such that your fingers know where to go without you losing time looking down at the keyboard.

Even these issues are part of customization. If something doesn't feel right, work hard to change it. Look through the key bindings and make sure everything is where you need it to be; Stance/Form shifting can be bound to keys. You may want to put those beneath your most active fingers to smooth the transitions.

MAKING MONEY AND FINDING GEAR

Being an adept player is great, but money still makes the world go around. Buying from vendors and players is only one sink for money and you're going to need plenty of cash just for those folks! Trainers take their fair share as well, and by the end of the day very few people have more gold than they need. So, how do you plan to stay in the black?

UNDERSTAND LOOT TABLES

Being out in the wild is interesting when looking for treasure. Unlike the rewards for quests or defeating specific, named enemies, there are many random pieces of treasure that drop from normal creatures. This is entirely random within the bounds of loot tables.

This means that people hunting for higher-level loot may push the bar a bit and shoot for enemies on the next loot table; this is a sound way to seek better gear for characters entering the new threshold. Of course, the downside is that creature difficulty experiences a bit of a jump every ten levels as well. Still, the leap in difficulty at these levels is trivial compared to the increase in item value!

SELLING TO VENDORS

Just as the most simple way to gather experience comes from grinding against monsters, you can gather a great deal of money from selling loot to vendors. Almost all of the creatures in the wild have something worth selling (whether they are living, dead, beast, or construct). Fight against creatures at a fast rate and harvest their goodies for future sale to players and vendors.

Sell anything that cons grey to your character and then take a look into the uses for the various crafting items and other goodies that fall. If there is a market for the remainder of your inventory, hold onto that until you can make an Auction House run.

It's a very big mistake to be picky about the items you pick up from monsters. Sure, some creatures are terrible about dropping good stuff (darn Slimes), but even these enemies occasionally have a rare gem or magical item to snag. Beyond that, if you have tons of space in your bags, there is no reason not to grab everything in sight! It takes almost no time to sell items, and every single sale adds up. Indeed, it sounds foolish not to loot a corpse with a mere silver piece on it. Why then, would anyone stop collecting vendor trash that could add up to many gold pieces in the long run?

For faster looting, hold down shift while right-clicking on bodies; this loots everything at once and is slightly faster for getting you on your way again. BoA items won't bind to you by doing this; a query bar pops up instead, and you have the choice to take the item or leave it on the body.

GATHERING MATERIALS

There are plenty of craftsfolk out there who need a constant supply of leather, cloth, metal, herbs, and magical powders. If you aren't interested in creating items, try out the gathering professions. In any event, selling the ingredients for crafted items to their creators is profitable throughout the levels. Use the Auction House to accomplish this unless you have friends or guild sources that need first crack at these items.

Knowing where to gather your items can make the difference between slim pickings and a lucrative trade. People don't usually go to Teldrassil for making it rich as a Miner, eh. Indeed, talk to other people and learn where some of the best spots are for getting the items you seek. Open fields have more beasts for leather, humanoid caves often have both metal deposits and cloth to harvest, and herbs are specifically located because of their inability to grow in inhospitable regions.

Don't let your inventory control you either. You may harvest enough material to fill your bank vault and your packs, but understand what your merchandise is worth. Stay current on the going rates for your items and only slide a bit under that quantity when selling. A few silvers can attract a buyer almost as quickly as entire gold pieces worth of discounts. It's similar to running away from a bear when you have a Gnome in your party; you don't have to outrun the bear, you just have to outrun the Gnome. [Editor's note: No, Gnome's don't run slower than other races.] When competing against other sellers, there is no need to cut the market.

FARMING FOR LOOT

There may be specific places that bring in money at a fast pace for your character. Perhaps you have a group that brings down groups quickly with AoEs. Or, you may have a favorite cave where there is metal, and the creatures drop cloth and vendor loot that sells half-decently. In any event, farming for money is a tradition with a long and glorious past.

Much like grinding with experience in mind, you can grind with loot in mind. Find an area with as many of the target monsters as possible and hop to it. Though this is often a good solo practice, groups sometimes form with different needs. Perhaps you are trying to get an uncommon elemental drop (Breath of Wind or some equivalent piece), and another character wishes to hunt for experience in the same area. Joining together can help both individuals; agree to divide loot in a way that lets you farm for your items while the grinder gets what they need as well.

Small teams with different professions work nicely in this field as well. Having a person to skin, another to mine, a cloth gatherer, and so forth keeps the peace perfectly. Everyone can get what they want while journeying around the world without having to roll for items for split things evenly. Associations of crafters don't have to be unified by a guild tabard.

BECOME ONE WITH THE AUCTION HOUSE

The Auction House is a blessing in every way. Having a major center of trade opens the window for players to cooperate with everyone in their faction (and beyond, in the case of the neutral Auction House of Gadgetzan). Setting your Hearthstone to a capital city with an Auction House is rarely a bad choice, considering how often people return here to talk, trade, and find new items.

Sell useful items through the Auction House instead of vendoring them. Players who do this make far more money in the long run. There is a deposit every time you puts items into the AH, and this increases proportionally as you set the timer for an auction for a longer duration.

The best bet for keeping your money flowing freely is to sell only your higher quality items (the ones that move quickly through the AH). People are rarely interested in equipment of low quality, so the profits for such items are higher through vendoring. Watch the AH by the searching for the very items you wish to sell and see what prices they are going for (and if people are really bidding on them). If the products aren't moving well, try a lower buyout that the other sellers.

If moving inventory is more important to you than the raw price, try very low starting bids. This really encourages impulse buying for anything useful; as long as the price is still low, players may push back and forth trying to keep their bid on the item. This sometimes leads to prices above what the players would have paid originally, but they become somewhat attached to the auction itself. You can't count on this, but it does happen.

TESTER TIP

Managing the Auction House

by Christopher Burton

Tradeskills are part and parcel of the merchant lifestyle. Even if you never put needle to thread, or don't have the strength to beat iron into swords, you have to understand enough about crafts (and crafters) to figure out what they need. Finding out what's in demand and getting it to buyers (for a price) is the heart of the merchant lifestyle. When it comes to the specifics of how to go about making a profit buying and selling items, there are only three general rules that you need to remember.

- Buy Low, Sell High
- Know Your Target Buyers
- Have Patience

There are several different approaches that can be taken to making money. The first way to make cash is by auctioning raw materials. The second lies in auctioning items to adventurers, and the third is buying items and re-selling them for a higher price. These are not mutually exclusive, though focusing on one at first is a good way to get established and learn how the goods are flowing.

The first approach, supplying raw materials, is a good one for the adventurer who wants to make some money when they return from their quests. Most of the raw materials (metals, herbs, leather, and cloth) can be gathered from fallen foes or gathered while moving around. If you want to make money selling raw materials, you'll need to pick up one of the gathering professions. It's usually beneficial to stick to one gathering profession, as that leaves a slot open for a future crafting profession. Once you have the skill, use it! Use it at every possible opportunity. Skin everything you can, even if it won't raise the skill. Mine every resource pile, and pick every flower you see. This gives you a large stockpile of resources, which you can take back the Auction House.

In this approach, the target buyers are the crafters. They are the ones who are going to be interested in what you have. Start off by using the browse feature of the Auction House to find out the current prices for your types of resources, as well as how many lots are currently for sale. Take Light Leather as an example. You see that there are 20 lots for sale, most of them starting with an opening bid of 10 silver. If all of them have bids, there is likely still a demand for what you have.

Because there is a demand, let your opening bid be slightly higher than current market price. Try to get a feel for what the closing bids are likely to be by looking at the prices of items that have only a short time left to go. However, why stop at what everyone else is making? Be ruthless! Crafters are often impatient and don't want to wait for the auctions to end, so offer them a buyout price (at twice the final expected bid) to get the item immediately. Then, set the auction length to the maximum, which encourages the impatient ones to use the buyout price. Thusly, if it looks like 10 silver tends to be the final bid, let your opening bid be about 8 silver, and set your buyout price at about 18. Timing is crucial in this. If you start your auction right before peak playing times (late afternoon for your time zone, usually), the auction has all night for people to look over it.

However, don't forget rule number three: always be patient. If leather isn't selling (e.g. no one is bidding on it), don't try and put yours up for sale at a reduced price. If you have no choice, accept that you're likely to make little money on the deals.

The second approach is to supply items to adventurers. First off, decide if you're going to auction items that you find, or if these are going to be items that you create. If you're going to take the crafter route, it helps to have the requisite gathering skill, so that you can supply your own materials. This helps you avoid the people who use the approach we just mentioned! Adventurers have a wide range of items from which to choose. Usually they are looking for something specific, a certain type of axe, for instance. In order to make money, you need to be flexible. If you have a variety of items, try and browse for each to get an idea of how much to price them. Always include a buyout price, as every adventurer will be tempted by the option to get it immediately. If you have no idea of how much your specific item is worth, take a look at other items of that type and level. So, if you have a one-handed axe with a minimum level of 9 you want to sell, see what other one-handed, Level 9 axes tend to cost. If they tend to start at 8 silver, try an opening bid of 6 silver.

This gets the attention of the buyer. Set the auction at 24 hours and offer a 15 silver buyout price; they'll often take it rather than risk someone coming along and bidding them out. What makes this all the more fun is that by starting with a lower bid than the competition, you're more likely to get multiple bids, which encourages buyouts. If you're making the items, consider sticking to green (Good Quality) items, as enchanters will always want green items to break down for parts. If you don't have Good or Superior items, try re-selling the same goods a bit cheaper later that day. Adding additional features, like applying an armor kit before selling, can also be effective. However, there may come a time when something just doesn't sell. In this case, vendor it and remember that item as one that doesn't sell well! Be patient, stay cool, and try again.

Finally, you can try and make money by buying items and re-selling them. Obviously, this is an approach that requires that you have some seed cash on hand. This is best used in conjunction with one of the other approaches, as you are likely to come across good deals while browsing around trying to establish prices. For this approach, Enchanting is a good skill to have, because you can break down the magical items you acquire cheaply into magical reagents that have a higher resale value. Go through each category in the Auction House and bid on every green item you can, especially the cheap lower level items. Having a huge number of bids at

once is vital, since you should only expect to win about half (at best). However, the ones that come to you can be quickly disenchanted and the components sold for a high price (as always, offer a high buyout!). It's a good market to look into because there is usually a demand, supply is often low (few people like sacrificing magical items), and stacks of various enchanting components always fetch a good price.

Timing is a bit strange on this approach, as the peak buying times for enchanting components seems to be the weekend. However, always keep an eye on the auctions, and jump on chances. This is because you can sometimes come across major bargains that can be taken advantage of. For instance, you are browsing and see that there are only a few glimmering shards for sale. Each one seems to sell for about 50 silver, though there is a stack of nine that has 50 silver as its buyout price. This is an opportunity. Grab the stack immediately for 50 silver, then turn right around and auction each shard in the stack with an opening bid of 50 and a buyout of 75. This doesn't happen often, but it has the potential to make you some serious cash, and even if only one or two sell you have completely recouped your investment. Some may come back to you, to be auctioned again another day. Keep them safe and wait for your chance while you attend to the other parts of your budding mercantile empire.

GOODS AND SERVICES

Your characters can also make money by selling services to other players. Because everyone can master two professions (at most), it's common for players to need the services of other people from time to time. Blacksmiths attach Shield Spikes, Riding Spurs (for mounts), and other such goodies for weapons and armor. Enchanters prepare special concoctions to boost the power of items. Rogues can learn Lockpicking and open lockboxes for a decent tip.

When advertising your own skills, use the Trade channel and prepare a text macro that quickly states your available skills and associated costs. Try to keep this to two lines to prevent your message from filling up everyone's message windows. Use your macro periodically, but not more often than every few minutes. While doing this, participate in the channel and help others; it helps to have a clientele that already knows who you are and respects your attitude.

To receive services, ask in Trade if anyone has the skill level you seek in a profession. Be up front about what you want, and they often are just as forthcoming about the price they require for their time. Don't by shy about saying "How much do you want?" if they don't list a specific sum. Under the friendliest conditions, the other character may not answer firmly. Be sure to tip such people if you can afford to; it keeps the goodwill flowing and won't hurt you on any return visits.

SPENDING YOUR WEALTH

There are more ways to spend money than to make it; that is the usual way of things. Carefully choosing when and where to spend your hard-earned cash is very important, especially at low levels (where it's very hard to make substantial amounts).

LEARN CLASS ABILITIES FIRST

Before looking for new items or having fun with your money, make sure that your character's abilities are current. Every even level, talk to your class trainers and see which new abilities are available. If you use said abilities or would like to, buy these before any purchases of equipment, services, or whatever else you enjoy. Having abilities trained to their fullest is extremely important, and the cost is minimal if you're willing to do some hunting on the side from time to time.

To avoid taking a more substantial hit to the wallet every two levels, it's possible to ignore some abilities (for some classes). If you're a Warrior who never uses Berserk Stance, don't train in Slam or Cleave. A sword-wielding Rogue could forgo Backstab and Ambush for quite some time too. Almost all classes have abilities that they may not use, depending on playstyle. Save money in the short term by holding off on their purchase. It's always possible to return later and train these skills when the cost is lower (compared to your total earnings).

KEEP EQUIPMENT UP TO DATE

Many, many gold pieces go toward keeping your character's equipment up to date. At first, quests and general loot are able to keep many characters up to speed. Decent items drop somewhat easily over the first 20 levels, and there are substantial numbers of quests with useful rewards.

In the mid and later levels, however, characters start to need rarer equipment. This necessitates going to crafters more often and buying Good or Superior items from the Auction House. When doing this on a budget, look for the items you need over several days and only jump at bids that are priced below the norm. This saves you considerable money (at the cost of your time and patience). If you instead need an item as soon as possible, pay the premium and start buying out everything that looks nice; the sellers will love you.

THE BANK

Using the bank saves characters from losing bag space. It's unfortunate to lose vendorable items because you have your bags loaded with ammunition, food, potions, skins, and whatever else has crept in there. Anything that isn't needed for a specific outing should be left in the bank vault and taken out at your convenience (especially trade goods).

For a one-time investment of cash, you can purchase extra bag slots in your bank vault. Notice how quickly the prices rise for additional slots; it is far more effective to use high-end bags than to purchase many bank slots. Each new tier of space costs ten times what the previous slot cost, so people need a frightening sum to unlock the later ones.

Though bags are a bit costly early on, crafters can save you tremendous time and frustration by creating some of the larger bags at a decent price. Ask your guild or friends if they know a good Tailor, then see if those folks are able to set you up with four larger bags at a fair cost. It's only worth buying bags from stores when you are entirely wealthy and only need a spare 6-Slot for an alternate character; otherwise, crafters are able to make bags at much lower prices.

As a side note, bags start at 6-slot containers and move up toward 16-slot backpacks. Though crafters are wonderful for making all of the lower-level items, you need to hunt on the 50+ Loot Table to find the 16-slotters. The way the tables work, expect to have a new bag size on each new loot table.

BAG SIZE BY LOOT TABLES

MONSTER LEVEL	POSSIBLE BAG DROP
1 to 10	6-Slot Bag (Linen Equivalent)
11+	8-Slot Bag (Wool Equivalent)
21+	10-Slot Bag (Silk Equivalent)
31+	12-Slot Bag (Mageweave Equivalent)
41+	14-Slot Bag (Runecloth Equivalent)
51+	16-Slot Bag (Mooncloth Equivalent)

SPEND WISELY

The simple way to decide what to spend money on is to look at future earning potential. What items/skills are going to help you make money faster? Is it going to help you more to master a ranged weapon or get a new chest piece? Look at what your character does well and what they do poorly; spend money at both ends of that spectrum first, then deal with the in-between later. Mages deal tons of damage but die quickly (spend money on doing even more damage or on saving your rump). Don't fret over raising less important attribute, peripheral abilities, and other such concerns until you know that your best equipment is on par and your central abilities are fully trained.

Beyond that, do a bit of research to avoid spending money at the wrong time. If there are important class quests coming up, you often have some nice items in your future; it's better to buy equipment for slots that aren't going to receive quest upgrades anytime soon.

EXPLORING

Moving around the world and seeing the impressive variety of locations is a source of lasting joy. The zones in Azeroth are well differentiated, so it's a shame not to fully explore Kalimdor and the Eastern Kingdoms. This is a task that has subtle but worthwhile benefits for future play, since you also learn more about camp locations, monster variety, and other such matters while exploring.

FILLING IN YOUR MAPS

Region maps start off without many locations uncovered. It is your responsibility to fill out the map over time by visiting the major points of interest. Each location you discover opens a new section of the map and awards you an exploration bonus (a slight gift of experience). Though this process isn't profitable by itself, given that hunting earns far more experience than wandering, it feels very good to have your maps uncovered for all major regions.

Instead of racing off to fully explore each map when you enter a new region, take the time to explore naturally, following the direction of quests and hunting to guide you. This way, you are never just exploring. You're finishing quests, making money, gaining experience from multiple sources, and having a good time. If you choose to grind your way through an entire zone, fighting everything you see, the map uncovers just as nicely as it you spent all the time looking about and avoiding those fun skirmishes.

If you have trouble getting a specific section to come clear, try to walk closer to the major buildings, caves, and general landmarks inside that area. Just because a new text name appears in your map header doesn't mean that the area is uncovered (that doesn't happen until you receive the "You Have Discovered XXX" message and get the experience bonus. Walk deeper into each new area to find such bonuses.

GOING INTO SMALLER DUNGEONS (MICRODUNGEONS)

Dungeons are a useful point of interest because they often have heavy fighting, metal deposits, and quests to complete. Try to find where all of the dungeons are located when you're exploring even if you don't have quests for them at the time; it's common for quests to send people all around the world for various goals, and knowing where you are going can cut down on lost time.

Microdungeons are found in most regions. These areas are part of the normal terrain (in other words, you face no loading screen and can freely walk into the dungeons and back out without delay). There are often many monsters in microdungeons, but they won't usually be much tougher than the beasts and enemies walking out in the fields nearby.

Microdungeons are some of the best places to camp for metal in Azeroth. Though you can get more metal by running around entire areas, taking everything you see (once you know the spawn points for the deposits), there are several benefits to camping a cave. For one, the creatures there are worth plenty of experience if you are at the right level for fighting in the dungeon (which is often the case if you stay current on your Mining). Getting metal, experience, and loot at the same time is a major boon. Beyond that, the flow of metal out of a dungeon is reliable compared to searching external sources that people can mine casually.

TAKING ON WORLD DUNGEONS

World Dungeons are very different from microdungeons. As you might guess, these dungeons are much larger than their cousins. However, this is one of the superficial differences between the two. In fact, there are far more daunting challenges in World Dungeons.

TRAITS OF WORLD DUNGEONS

- These Dungeons are Instanced (Every Group Goes into Their Own Version of the Dungeon)
- There is a Loading Screen to Mark the Separation between the Shared Game World and the Instance
- Many Creatures in World Dungeons are Elite
- Battles inside World Dungeons are Often Harder, Involve Scripted Bosses (in Some Cases), and Have Greater Rewards
- Horde and Alliance Members can do All World Dungeons (Even Those in Enemy Territory)

If you've missed the term Instance before, it means that an area is not part of the shared world. If twenty groups go there, twenty versions (Instances) of the dungeon are created. So, only your group is going to head into the fire; expect no surprise assistance or enemy intervention.

At the suggested levels, parties without five people and very impressive gear may have trouble. Unlike fighting out in the field, World Dungeons are meant to challenge, frustrate, and even defeat parties that aren't experienced enough to survive the complex battles within.

This is not a measure of a party's worth, since the vast majority of groups have to contend with full wipeouts and other such setbacks the first few times they try to overcome new World Dungeons.

To make your attempts safer, be sure to mold the group before it heads into a World Dungeon. Find people who you know and trust to play their characters with high skill. Beyond that, make sure everyone is willing to dedicate several hours to completing the task (most of the World Dungeons are somewhat long, and having people leave in the middle can be disastrous for the group). Practice techniques against many of the creatures early in the dungeon and get a feel for the style of the place. In general, a group that has trouble early on needs a couple more levels or some better gear before they can complete that Instance.

So, how do you power up (besides simply leveling)? One aspect is to complete as much of a World Dungeon as possible. There are often potent items that drop off of named enemies throughout these areas; some of said items are going to help gear-up the group. Beyond that, the experience in the Instance is going to cut down on the time and difficulty of future efforts, since extra adds, rough strategies, and other problems are less common once everyone has been in the dungeon several times.

Choose a very good leader for every Instance run. It is so important to have skilled and trusted leadership that a well-run group can function better than one with members of higher level, carrying better equipment. If you want to be a leader, run the Instance multiple times, look for key ways to avoid extra aggro, reduce fight times, and finish the boss battles without losing people left and right. Exchange strategies with other party leaders and test out new methods frequently to keep your groups trim. With a good leader, Instances can be run sooner and without resorting to specific class combinations.

WORLD DUNGEON

DUNGEON NAME	EXPECTED LEVELS	REGION
Ragefire Chasm	13 to 15	Orgrimmar
Deadmines	15 to 20	Westfall (SW Moonbrook)
Wailing Caverns	15 to 21	The Barrens (Cave SW of Crossroads)
The Stockades	23 to 26	Stormwind (Jail on West Side)
Gnomeregan	24 to 33	Dun Morogh (NW of Map)
Razorfen Kraul	25 to 31	The Barrens (Southern End, West of Road)
Blackfathom Deeps	20 to 27	Darkshore (Ruins Near Tower of Althalaxx)
Shadowfang Keep	18 to 25	Silverpine Forest (Above Pyrewood Village)
The Scarlet Monastery	30 to 40	Tirisfal Glades (NE Encampment of Humans)
Uldaman	35 to 45	The Badlands (East Just After Loch Modan Entrance)
Razorfen Downs	35 to 40	The Barrens (Southern End, East of Road)
Zul'Farrak	43 to 47	Tanaris Desert (NW Side of Map)
The Sunken Temple	44 to 50	Swamp of Sorrows (Center of Lake)
Blackrock Depths	48 to 56	Burning Steppes (West Side of Map)
Blackrock Spire	53 to 60	Burning Steppes (West Side of Map)
Strathome	55 to 60	Eastern Plaguelands (Just Above Darrowmere Lake)
Scholomance	57-60	Western Plaguelands

GROUP ROLES

This section takes the general knowledge and tactics of this chapter and expands it to cover group roles and functionality. Being able to control your character, rise in level and power, and find the right items is enough to bring you up in the ranks. However, a group with five soloers is not as effective a group with five players who are skilled at grouping! There are tricks that work quite well when you have others on your side that would be worthless when tried solo. Learning these creates a synergy within well-played groups; that edge is what leads to victory in World Dungeons, Raids, and mass PvP combat.

ROLES: IN SHORT

Going past the terminology, players benefit from understanding that the true components of a group are capable of providing. Look at the following list and consider the way battles are won in a mathematic sense. By reducing incoming damage, shortening encounters, and extending survival time, characters of different roles are able to assist the greater needs of a group in separate ways. When facing various and unknown opponents, it is essential to have multiple answers to each problem.

GROUP ROLES AND FUNCTIONS

ROLE	IMPORTANCE IN BATTLE
Tank	Gathers Aggro, Reduces Total Group Damage Taken
DPS	Deals Damage, Reduces Duration of Battle by Killing Enemies
Healer	Allows Group Members to Survive Lethal Damage and Continue Fighting, Reduces Downtime

These are the three primary components of a battle in this game. A tank reduces incoming damage, a DPS class reduces battle time, and a healer reduces downtime and extends survivability. It's for this reason that many form a core group out of a Warrior/Mage/Priest combination. Yet, there are five slots in a group, and careful mixing of roles can lead to mastery in these three areas without using any of the above classes (though it takes more effort to do this).

THE TANK

Suggested Classes: Warrior, Paladin, Druid

Protectors come in many forms, but their role is never trivialized. Tanks are meant to consolidate enemies (bringing them together onto a single target); they excel at doing this by being able to attack multiple enemies and use abilities that are instant/fast to use. Warriors are the primary tanks of Azeroth. This is ensured by the ability to automatically damage, debuff, and Taunt enemies who enter a battle.

Yet, gathering aggro is only half of a tank's purpose. If a tank takes as much damage as a weaker party member, the issue of healing and aggro control becomes grim. A party that cannot heal wounded Mages and Priests quickly enough won't be able to save a Warrior without shield, armor, abilities, or talents. Indeed, the reason tanks are chosen to draw aggro upon themselves is that they take *less* damage from enemies than those who wear lighter armor and specialize in other roles.

Turn a round of battle into some simple math. If a party has 600 points of damage incoming (before armor is taken into consideration), how much is actually dealt by the end of the round? If only cloth-wearers are struck, the majority of that damage is inflicted upon the party. We'll say 500 points land, and the healers now need to use their resources to make up for that.

It those 600 points are directed entirely toward tanks, the enhanced armor and abilities of that group can reduce the damage down to a far smaller quantity (perhaps 200-300 points by avoiding attacks, negating them, armor absorption, etc.). In this better case, the healers of the party only need to make up for about half of the damage, even though the incoming damage was exactly the same.

That is the glory of a tank. You're able to make damage disappear from the battle equation. Keep targets focused on your heavy armor and thick shield to save healer mana, reduce aggro on other characters, and give DPS characters a chance to attack faster and with greater efficiency.

DAMAGE DEALERS (DPS CHARACTERS)

Suggested Classes: Mage, Rogue

Almost every class can deal damage if configured properly. Yet, the classes that come into damage in a natural way are the ones with light armor and few hit points. This person's duty is to knock down enemies quickly and prevent them from harming the party. Every foe that falls is unable to deal damage for the rest of the fight, meaning that DPS characters are able to protect the party by negating enemy activity.

The most effective way for DPS characters to operate is to deal targeted damage to enemies who are most likely to die quickly (or to target the enemies who deal the most damage). To wound all enemies is not good enough for most situations; it is the slaying of targets that offers the true benefit of damage! Thus, damage done by DPS characters needs to be concentrated so that each target dies as quickly as possible. A leader should be chosen among the damage dealers, and this person picks each target with a mind for kill rate vs. threat of target. The faster the kill, the better the target. The more dangerous the target, the more important the kill. Quickly rate all of the enemies in a battle along these lines to decide what needs to be destroyed, then start opening the metaphoric can of beatdowns on your list.

FACTORS IN CREATING YOUR OWN HATE LIST

The advice here has been fairly complex. Creating a Hate List (just like the AI does against your party) is not easy for people who are new to the role. Yet, it becomes much easier with time, so that is some comfort.

To decide which targets come first, look at how past battles have gone. Which enemies deal the most damage to your party? Casters, creatures with major debuffs/combat control, and other such aggressive foes are usually high risk. Luckily, they are also softer kills. This ranks highly for both criteria you use.

Take down high damage or combat control targets as soon as possible, then move on to foes with less opportunity. Often, the most enduring targets are the weakest, so they can be dispatched at the end of combat. Bosses are the big exception to this; removing any substantial allies a boss has may not be possible because of a boss' immense DPS (in other words, you may have to ignore fast kills to make a mad scramble against a superior target).

HEALER

Suggested Classes: Priest, Shaman, Druid

Healers extend the length of time a group can survive in a battle; they also decrease downtime between battles to raise experience and money-gained efficiently. This is done by using mana to negate damage done against a group. With careful casting and high Spirit, these characters can dramatically lengthen the survival time of a group.

Also, there is a targeted advantage to the boost healers provide. Though tanks are able to reduce damage coming in against a party, they have only a few chances to turn the tide of battle if aggro is cemented and they fall close to death. If the tank goes down because of this, all of the potential that protector brought to the group disappears in an instant. Healers smooth out damage so that individual members of the group do not die before their time. Proper healing ensures that tanks last as long as possible, use all of their abilities and items, then only start to die off when the group has nothing left to give. Preventing premature deaths is as much a part of a healer's service as ensuring total group survivability.

Backup healers (such as Paladins, Druids or Shaman who haven't focused on healing) lack some of the healing efficiency and potential of a solid and true healer. This does not remove their functionality, but it means that they contribute only a fraction of a healer's role. As such, it's important to have two secondary healers if the role of a primary healer is not filled.

As for the abilities themselves, healing magic is often a subject for complex tactics. Using less efficient healing spells or using the right spells at the wrong times can waste hundreds of mana in a given fight. This is just as bad as having a tank take unneeded damage. Healers should use the minimal and fastest heals to keep their groups up to speed (always shoot for a spell that you take your target close to their maximum hit points without overshooting). In predictable fights, that translates to waiting and letting tanks take damage until their health is at the right place for an efficient heal.

During more frantic combat, it's hard to maintain composure. When multiple characters are taking damage and monsters are flying back and forth, it's essential that the healers focus on saving lives. Keep trickling the spells to the entire group while the tanks hold all the aggro they can. Only unleash the massive, aggro-drawing flurry of heals (or group heal) when it's make or break time. Once that happens, hope that you can do enough to allow a secondary rezzer to survive and bring you back, because considerable aggro is coming your way.

HYBRID CLASSES

Can Include: Druid, Battle/Berserk Warrior, Paladin, Shaman

Depending on build and style, a number of classes can fill several roles in the group. Once the three necessities are filled (damage mitigation, DPS, and healing), try to spread around the rest of the duties so that everyone has a backup. It dramatically improves a healer's survivability to have a backup; this way someone can heal the healer! The same is true for the efficiency of DPS characters and safety of tanks. Because characters with several roles are versatile by nature, two such members can backup all three characters of the primary group!

For example, take a very standard party configuration (Warrior, Mage, Priest), then add a second Warrior and a Paladin. If the second Warrior uses a two-handed weapon and is specced for damage, it is easy to deal substantial damage (aiding our DPS Mage), while doing limited tanking against adds that are too much for the real tank to snag. The Paladin supports the Priest perfectly by both healing, offering Resurrection potential if the Priest falls, and by pulling aggro off of the Priest when the Tanks have a problem.

WILD CARDS

Suggested Classes: Hunter, Warlock

Pet classes often have support abilities that don't evenly fall into the three main categories, but that doesn't lessen their usefulness. Hunters and Warlocks each have abilities that raise a group's potential to survive and thwart enemies. Hunter tracking is good on the offense, and having a pet to throw away during tight pulls is never a bad thing (hurray for disposable allies, sorry Mr. Raptor).

Warlocks are able to pull group members from distant locations, create Soulstones to negate party wipeouts, and do enough damage/DOTing/debuffing to supplement other casters in the group.

EXPAND THE ENVELOPE

Everyone has an idea of the "perfect" group. However, there isn't one, per se. The perfect group is actually formed when everyone involved a) accomplishes their goals (whether it's grinding, hunting for loot, questing, etc.), b) enjoys one another's company, and c) has fun. Extremely successful groups have been formed with non-standard configurations.

Try grouping with different classes and even the same class line-up with each character having different specs (e.g. DPS Warrior vs. Defense Warrior) to discover what works best for you. Don't immediately turn down a Shadow-specced Priest because you want a Holy-specced Priest for healing. Consider the Shadow Priest a support addition and find a healer to fill their role. Having preconceived notions about how classes should be played leads to repetitive play and an unyielding mindset. Keep an open mind when recruiting for your group and see what happens.

ROLE-PLAYING

World of Warcraft is an MMORPG and within that is the very important RP for Role-Playing. It's important to keep this in mind when diving into the game. The world of Azeroth is a rich and vibrant world full of history from the *Warcraft* series and deserves some attention. From the moment you enter into the game, a tale of the race you have chosen unwinds before your very eyes as you soar over the land and settle into your new home.

Despite the rich history of paper gaming and the advent of MUDDs, Role-playing is still a very misunderstood aspect of MMORPGs. Those that partake in it are often mislabeled as uninterested in more than just talking to others and pretending to be something they are not. Along with this misunderstanding comes the belief that all role-players use Shakespearean or speak in Old English. These beliefs are archaic and misinformed at the least.

STEPPING INTO CHARACTER

There are many levels to which you can take your role-playing. The most basic is creating a character. Some may wonder how this is role-playing at all. It's the most basic principal of role-play. It's the suspension of disbelief and becoming something that you are not in everyday life. For instance, in real life you may be a clerk at a video store. In the *World of Warcraft* you're a two-handed axe-wielding Orc with a penchant for killing everything in your path. Not one word would need to be uttered and everyone that you encountered would see you as an Orc. There isn't much more to it than that.

From the very start, your name will be the most telling thing about your character. It's important to choose one that fully reflects the kind of character you want to be known as.

The next levels of role-play involve actually developing a persona for your character. Some players take the time outside of the game to sit and write a history of their character. For those new to this method, you don't even need to write an entire story. Develop questions that help flesh out your character's background. Where were they born? Do they have any phobias? Interests? Are they geared to specifically hate another race? Or do they find themselves liking a supposed enemy? (Tauren and Night Elves are a great example. Both races have an affinity for nature and could feasibly see that as something in common.)

Don't be afraid to expand your imagination and write about anything you want when it comes to your character. No one ever has to read any of it, but the most important thing is that you know and understand how you would like to play your character to get the most enjoyment out of it. For those that want to dig into their character and their development even further, take time to read through the history of *Warcraft* and learn all you can about fitting in to your new world.

SPEECH IN GAME

There are many players that immerse themselves into their character so much that they never speak out of character unless absolutely necessary. These are the types of players that use speech as a medium to convey the essence of their character to others. There's a sense of full immersion that comes into play by shutting out the real world and becoming a very real citizen of Azeroth.

What is usually misunderstood, however, is the kind of speech necessary. The assumption is that role-players use Shakespearean or Old English as a means of good role-play. This isn't true and doesn't necessarily fit into this particular world. Not only does it not fit into the style of Azeroth, but also communication is often key to getting things done unless you just happen to be hanging out at the local inn or tavern. The last thing other players want to encounter is a Shakespearean spewing Night Elf that has to take the time to say "Healing thee sir Ironknot with mine most eminent Flash Heal." In this case, it's best to leave that to a nicely worded macro anyway.

Another pitfall of speech when in reference to Shakespearean is that it is probably the most abused of speech patterns you could come across. Unless someone is a classically trained Shakespearean actor, they are going to hit the pitfalls of proper usage of words such as thee, thine, thou and any other possessives.

Some players like to add a little something to their characters by giving them a Scottish bent by using words such as Lad, Laddy, Lass etc., or even by making them into a basically grunting peon. It's important to keep in mind whether that works well with your racial type. While there are often exceptions to the rules, too many exceptions just make a quirk common.

CARRYING ON TO THE BOARDS

Once you have the hang of your character, you may want to relay the tales of their great victories, encounters and exploits on the boards for others to read. This can be a fun way of feeling connected to other players and their experiences as well as developing ongoing storylines between yourself, your guild and/or others.

Some simple guidelines to stick with are as follows:

Spell Check I know this sounds a bit uptight, but if you want people to read and enjoy your story, go over it carefully and confirm that you've corrected any spelling errors.

Paragraphs It's easy to get excited and carried away with what you're talking about. Take the time to break the thoughts and ideas into smaller segments. People are more likely to read the entire thing.

Beware Length As much as it would be great to post a novella on the boards, it may not actually get read. People cruising the boards are often looking for something they can scan and leave. It needs to be short enough to make them want to read it and interesting enough to entice them to read the whole thing.

Don't Abuse Other Characters If it's not your character, don't involve them in the story. If you'd like to incorporate someone else's character, ask permission from the creator before doing so. This can be a major gaffe in role-play. It's important to understand that unless you actually killed another player in game, you cannot kill them out of game even on the boards unless you plan to make it into some bizarre dream sequence.

Expect Feedback You may not always get feedback, but expect feedback (whether good or bad) if you post on a public board. Try to take any suggestions in stride and don't take what people say personally.

FOSTERING ROLE-PLAY IN OTHERS

The number one killer of new role-players isn't players that don't role-play, but those that do. There can often be an elitist attitude of what is and isn't possible within the realm of imagination in a setting such as Azeroth. This can be a real turn-off to those that have never previously tried role-play.

To help others feel more comfortable about trying something new, it's important to be careful about the kind of advice you offer. Never tell someone they "can't." It's a sure way of making them rebel. Explain a different option to them, offering constructive advice instead of slamming their decisions.

Go with the flow when others role-play. Even if you disagree with how they're doing it, you can't change them. The most you can do is adjust and meld your RP to what they offer and, if all else fails, role-play that they're a lunatic. Wasting your energy on telling someone how to do it the way you want or what you perceive as the "right way" detracts from everyone's experience.

Don't give up on non-role-players. Even the most stalwart of anti-RPers find themselves going along with things as long as nothing is expected of them. Role-play is what everyone makes of it and doesn't have any set rules. It's a creative process and, much like art, is often subjective.

EXCEPTIONS TO THE RULES

While it's true there are no hard and fast rules to what exactly is allowable within the bounds of role-play, there are issues that should be taken to heart.

Stick to the availability of possibilities within the *World of Warcraft*. There are so many great things possible such as exploding sheep, Dwarves carrying guns and more, that there is little reason to go beyond the possible.

Be careful about making exceptions of racial attributes. Each race has their own quirks and characteristics based on their history and the kind of race they are as a whole. While sometimes it's fun to make an exception to the racial type, it's important to be careful about how many exceptions are made. If everyone made an exception it wouldn't be unique anymore and part of role-playing effectively is finding a way to be unique in an almost ordinary way.

If you're going to create a story that's out of this world, do your research and make it work. There's nothing that bothers others more than not only being told a far-fetched tale, but also being told one that has no foundation. Give your character a leg to stand on even if it's based on insanity.

The most important thing is to let your character be who they are. Often enough, if you've done your job in developing their foundation and given them a name of worth, they'll take on a life of their own. From there it's just about having fun.

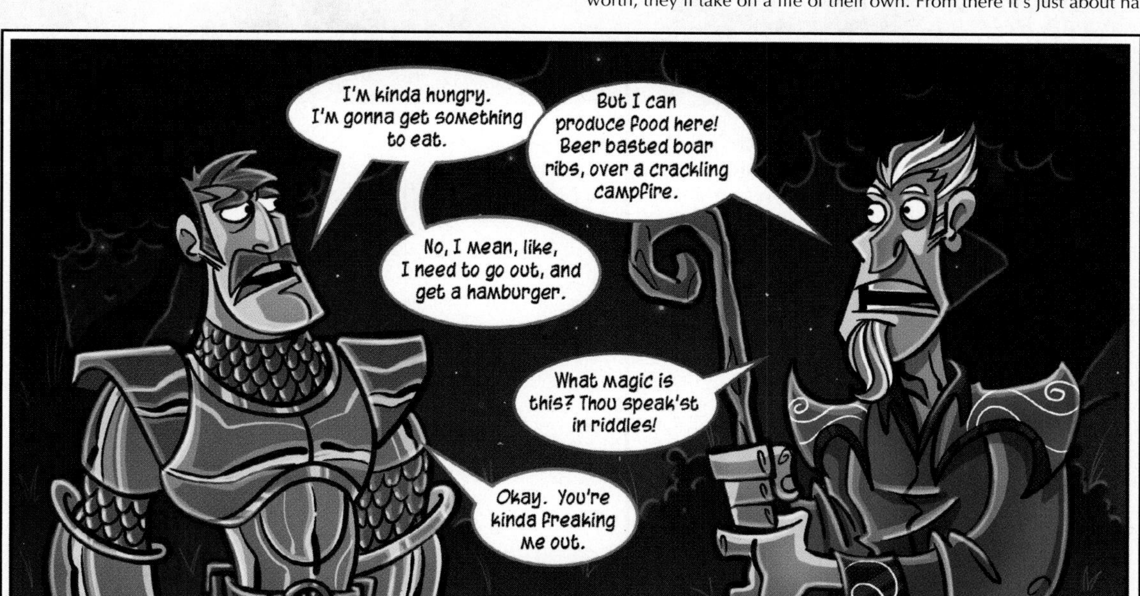

PROFESSIONS 101

There's an entire section devoted to Professions later in the guide, yet several aspects of the crafting system are worth developing here for incoming players. This section uncovers the basics of choosing your Professions, the terminology of the system, and how to know what you're looking for in-game.

WHAT ARE PROFESSIONS?

Professions cover the resource gathering, item creation, and service oriented systems in *World of Warcraft*. Each character is allowed to learn and maintain two of these trades, and doing so can be used for profit, improved equipment and usable items, or simply for the enjoyment of supporting friends/your guild.

Professions have trainers (just like classes) found in small towns and large cities alike. There are higher concentrations of trainers in the capitals, and so much trade happens there that people often seek those specific trainers to do most of their work.

Trainers are needed to initially grab a Profession, but they're also needed to gain new tiers of skills, and to pick up extra recipes for various items. All of these projects cost money, so it is often a question of much how time and money you wish to invest in a Profession. In the later stages, many Professions are worth sizable fortunes (especially the ones that gather resources for other Professions). As long as you are willing to throw the extra energy into these skills, they're quite lucrative in the long run.

LIST OF PROFESSIONS

PROFESSION	PURPOSE	BENEFITS
Alchemy	Create Potions/Transmute Metals	Attribute Enhancement, Create High-End Metals
Blacksmithing	Forge Weapons, Chain/Plate Armor, and Peripheral Equipment	Increase Weapon Damage and Speed (for 2H), Improve Shields, Increase Mount Speed
Enchanting	Improve Equipment	Sell Enchantments for Profit, Raise Attributes on Gear
Engineering	Construct Bombs, Rifles, and Accessories	Battle Pets, AoE Explosives, Ammunition
Herbalism	Gather Herbs	Ingredients for Alchemy, Sell for Profit
Leatherworking	Make Leather Armor, Ammo Bags, and Armor Patches	Add Bonuses to Ranged Combat, Increase Armor Rating
Mining	Mine Metal	Ingredients for Blacksmithing and Engineering, Sell for Profit
Skinning	Skin Beast Corpses for Leather	Ingredients for Leatherworking, Sell for Profit
Tailoring	Sew Cloth Armor and Items, Make Bags	Sell Bags to Other Characters

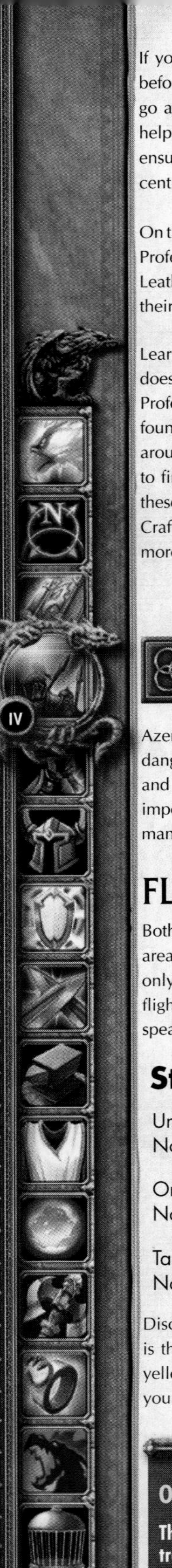

If you're part of a large guild, it is often wise to ask what Professions are needed before venturing into this territory. It's possible that starting these trades could go against the interests of the guild and end up wasting your investment. It really helps guilds focus their efforts on one or two characters for each Profession, thus ensuring that the materials discovered by the guild members are being sent to a central source.

On the other hand, if you want to be independent, it's wise to take two complementary Professions. Take Mining and Blacksmithing as an example (Skinning and Leatherworking, Herbalism and Alchemy, etc.). This enables a character to gather their own ingredients and create items out of these.

Learning how to create various items does not stop at the trainer for most Professions. Hidden recipes can be found on monsters and special vendors around the world. Talk to other crafters to find out more about the locations of these items (and read the tables in our Crafting and Professions Chapter for more info as well).

WHAT ARE SECONDARY SKILLS?

SECONDARY SKILLS

SKILL	PURPOSE	BENEFITS
Cooking	Create Food/Fires	Reduce Downtime w/Food and Spirit Buffs
First Aid	Stitch Bandages	Allow for Fast Healing of Moderate Damage
Fishing	Collect Items from Water	Ingredients for Cooking, Spare Equipment, Find Recipes for Other Trades

Secondary Skills aren't limited by anything except time and money. Each character can take these skills whether they are interested in Professions or not. In fact, many soloers take all three skills to reduce downtime and increase their self-sufficiency without losing constant money on store-bought food and such.

TRANSPORTATION IN AZEROTH

Azeroth is a world that's been torn apart by war and dark magic. There are many dangerous places to explore. Learning the various ways to do so can save both time and frustration when walking is just too slow and swimming to another continent impossible. Thankfully, through the ingenuity of the races of Azeroth, there are many means of travel, most of which are quite affordable.

FLIGHT PATHS

Both Alliance and Horde players have the means to use Flight Paths to travel from area to area within the continent they're currently on. These flights are for individuals only, so there's no need to argue over who gets the window seat. In order to use flight paths, you must first discover them. To do so, travel to each one by foot and speak with the appropriate master. Home city flight points are active from the start.

Starting Flight Paths

Undead
None

Orc/Troll
None

Tauren
None

Humans
Stormwind to Ironforge

Night Elves
Teldrassil to Darkshore

Dwarves/Gnomes
Ironforge to Stormwind

Discovering a new node is as simple as discovering a new quest. The only difference is that the Flight Master has a green exclamation point over their head instead of yellow. There are four different types of air transportation available depending on your faction.

ORIGINATION FEES

The cost of traveling to a home city is based on the origination of the flight. For traveling from a home city to a home city, the fee is a standard 50 copper.

Alliance

Gryphons The Gryphons of Aerie Peak have a history of serving with the Alliance through times of war. To this day they still transport messages between Ironforge and Stormwind as well as transport travelers for a small fee to the various Alliance controlled regions.

Hippogryphs These magical creatures once served the Alliance by carrying Sentinel Archers into battle and to this day still patrol Northern Kalimdor for threats. Passengers that pay their fee can be taken with them along their patrol routes.

ALLIANCE FLIGHT PATHS

KALIMDOR

DESTINATION	REGION	COST
Astranaar	Ashenvale	3 30
Auberdine	Dark Shore	Origination Fee
Everlook	Winterspring	10 20
Feathermoon Fortress	Feralas	7 30
Gadgetzan	Tanaris	7 30
Nighthaven Village	Moonglade	8 30
Nijel's Point	Desolace	5 30
Ruth'Theran Village	Teldrassil	Free
Stonetalon Peak	Stonetalon Mountains	3 30
Thalanaar	Thousand Needles	4 30
Theramore	Dustwallow Marsh	4 30
Theramore	Dustwallow Marsh	6 30

EASTERN KINGDOMS		
DESTINATION	REGION	COST
Aerie Peak	The Hinterlands	7 30
Booty Bay	Stranglethorn	6 30
Darkshire	Duskwood	3 30
Ironforge	Dun Morogh	Origination Fee
Lakeshire	Redridge	2 10
Menethil Harbor	Wetlands	3 30
Nethergarde Keep	Blasted Lands	8 30
Refuge Point	Arathi	5 30
Sentinel Hill	Westfall	1 10
Southshore	Hillsbrad	3 30
Stormwind	Elwynn Forest	Origination Fee
Thelsamar	Loch Modan	1 10

Horde

Wyvern Wyverns are sentient creatures willingly allied with the Orcs of Kalimdor. They carry payers throughout the lands surrounding Orgrimmar and Thunder Bluff. They have a distinctive look with the body and head of a lion, bat like wings and the tail of a scorpion. They are said to share an ancestry with Dragons and Gryphons.

Vampire Bats These creatures are a perfect fit with the Forsaken. Hailing from Zul Aman they, much like their Kalimdor counterparts, savor the thrill of battle and carry those that pay their fee throughout the regions surrounding Lordaeron. It is said they also serve as messengers for the Dark Lady.

HORDE FLIGHT PATHS

KALIMDOR		
DESTINATION	REGION	COST
Camp Mojache	Feralas	7 30
Crossroads	Barrens	1 10
Everlook	Winterspring	10 20
Free Wind Post	Thousand Needles	4 30
Gadgetzan	Tanaris	7 30
Malaka'jin	Stonetalon Mountains	2 10
Orgrimmar	Durotar	Origination fee
Shadowsprey Village	Desolace	5 30
Thunder Bluff	Mulgore	Origination fee
Valormak	Azshara	8 30

EASTERN KINGDOMS		
DESTINATION	REGION	COST
Booty Bay	Stranglethorn Vale	6 30
Grom'gol	Stranglethorn Vale	6 30
Hammerfall	Arathi Highlands	5 30
Kargath	Badlands	6 30
Stonard	Swamp of Sorrows	6 30
Tarren Mill	Hillsbrad Foothills	3 30
The Sepulcher	Silverpine Forest	1 10
Undercity	Tirisfal Glades	Origination fee

BOATS, ZEPPELINS AND THE TRAM

There are three other methods of travel that fall within the "mass transit" category. There are no fees for using them, but they're on a set schedule and have limited routes.

Boats are a part of the mass transit system crossing between continents, though only one boat is easily accessible to both factions. The Zeppelin traverses the ocean as well and is available to the Horde.

The Deeprun Tram is a technological marvel connecting Stormwind and Ironforge. It was built as a faster means of travel and support between the cities. In Stormwind, it's located in the Dwarven quarter and in Ironforge, it's located in Tinkertown. The entryways into the Tram are instance portals, but don't worry too much about whether you are walking into danger. The Tram is quite safe and the scenery is quite pleasant.

PLEASE KEEP YOUR HANDS AND FEET IN

As tempting as it may be to take a leap of faith, it's better to keep all of your fingers and toes accounted for. (Only the Undead are excused from having to account for them all.) Resist the temptation to jump off any of these modes of transportation when traveling. It may result in injury or even death and a very long and tedious recovery time to get your body again.

NEUTRAL BOATS

There's a boat that travels between Booty Bay and Ratchet that can be used by both the Alliance and Horde. For those that are on a PvP server, this could be a rather exciting trip. Boats are not safe territory and if you look closely enough, you can see bloodstains intermingled with the salt stains in the wooden planks.

ALLIANCE BOATS

There are two different boats located in Darkshore. One is the boat that takes passengers to Rut'theran in Teldrassil. The other takes passengers to Menethil Harbor in the Eastern Kingdoms.

There is a third boat located in Menethil Harbor that carries passengers to Theramore Isle in Kalimdor. Theramore Isle is a part of Dustwallow Marsh granting easy access to the Barrens and beyond.

Each boat travels in a circuitous route that should take a total of 5 minutes with an additional minute pause between each port. Should you miss your boat, another will be along shortly. If you crash out of the game, your character will return to the previous port from which they left.

BOAT NEUTRALITY VS. FACTIONAL

There really isn't any difference between a boat that is neutral or the Alliance boats other than the ease of accessibility. Booty Bay is neutral territory (contested on PvP servers) and the others are all located in Alliance territory thus difficult to get to for Horde characters.

ZEPPELINS

The Goblins have always been masters of engineering feats only second to (though they'd never admit it) Gnome engineering. They have created great Zeppelins that can travel between three major points within the world of Azeroth and transport members of the Horde en masse. Even better, it's free! Undercity, Orgrimmar and Grom'gol are all on the Zeppelin's route.

MOUNTS

Players that have reached the ripe level of 40 have the luxury of being able to purchase a mount to speed them on their way. There are six general types of mounts available for purchase, however, you must have a good enough reputation with the racial faction from who you're trying to buy one. Faction is usually good with your home race; extreme circumstances could put you in danger of losing this ranking however. In addition to the price of a mount, players need to pay a 20 gold training fee to a riding instructor.

NO FIGHTING ALLOWED

While on a mount, players are not able to engage in combat however can be hit by mobs or other players.

NO GOLD NECESSARY

Warlocks and Paladins are able to quest for a mount at 40 instead of needing to purchase one. Warlocks can gain a Felsteed and Paladins a Charger.

ALLIANCE RACIAL MOUNTS

RACE	MOUNT	LEVEL	TRAINER LOCATION	COST
Dwarf	Gray Ram	40	Amberstill Ranch, Dun Morogh	80
Dwarf	White Ram	40	Amberstill Ranch, Dun Morogh	80
Dwarf	Brown Ram	40	Amberstill Ranch, Dun Morogh	80
Dwarf	Black Ram	60	Amberstill Ranch, Dun Morogh	1000
Dwarf	Frost Ram	60	Amberstill Ranch, Dun Morogh	1000
Gnome	Red Mechanostrider	40	Steelgrill's Outpost, Dun Morogh	80
Gnome	Blue Mechanostrider	40	Steelgrill's Outpost, Dun Morogh	80
Gnome	Green Mechanostrider	40	Steelgrill's Outpost, Dun Morogh	80
Gnome	Unpainted Mechanostrider	40	Steelgrill's Outpost, Dun Morogh	80
Gnome	White Mechanostrider	60	Steelgrill's Outpost, Dun Morogh	1000
Gnome	Icy Blue Mechanostrider	60	Steelgrill's Outpost, Dun Morogh	1000
Human	Pinto	40	Eastvale Logging Camp	80
Human	Brown Horse	40	Eastvale Logging Camp	80
Human	Chestnut Mare	40	Eastvale Logging Camp	80
Human	Palomino	60	Eastvale Logging Camp	1000
Human	White Stallion	60	Eastvale Logging Camp	1000
Night Elf	Striped Frostsaber	40	Cenarion Enclave, Darnassus	80
Night Elf	Spotted Frostsaber	40	Cenarion Enclave, Darnassus	80
Night Elf	Striped Nightsaber	40	Cenarion Enclave, Darnassus	80
Night Elf	Frostsaber	60	Cenarion Enclave, Darnassus	1000
Night Elf	Nightsaber	60	Cenarion Enclave, Darnassus	1000

HORDE RACIAL MOUNTS

RACE	MOUNT	LEVEL	TRAINER LOCATION	COST
Troll	Emerald Raptor	40	Sen'jin Village, Durotar	80
Troll	Violet Raptor	40	Sen'jin Village, Durotar	80
Troll	Turquoise Raptor	40	Sen'jin Village, Durotar	80
Troll	Ivory Raptor	60	Sen'jin Village, Durotar	1000
Troll	Mottled Red Raptor	60	Sen'jin Village, Durotar	1000
Orc	Timber Wolf	40	Valley of Honor, Orgrimmar	80
Orc	Dire Wolf	40	Valley of Honor, Orgrimmar	80
Orc	Brown Wolf	40	Valley of Honor, Orgrimmar	80
Orc	Red Wolf	60	Valley of Honor, Orgrimmar	1000
Orc	Arctic Wolf	60	Valley of Honor, Orgrimmar	1000
Undead	Brown Skeletal Horse	40	Brill, Tirisfal Glades	80
Undead	Blue Skeletal Horse	40	Brill, Tirisfal Glades	80
Undead	Red Skeletal Horse	40	Brill, Tirisfal Glades	80
Undead	Green Skeletal Horse	60	Brill, Tirisfal Glades	1000

MAGE AND WARLOCK

Mages and Warlocks have their own means of transportation they can use to help others.

Warlocks have the ability to summon group members at level 20 with the aid of two other people. This can become a quick and efficient way to add players to a dungeon without having to backtrack to the beginning or hope the new addition can make a mad dash in. It's also an important means of calling in backup for PvP encounters.

Mages have portals for their three main factional cities. Members of their party are then able to use these.

Alliance	**Alliance**
Stormwind (Level 40)	Stormwind (Level 20)
Ironforge (Level 40)	Ironforge (Level 20)
Darnassus (Level 50)	Darnassus (Level 30)
Horde	**Horde**
Orgrimmar (Level 40)	Orgrimmar (Level 20)
Undercity (Level 40)	Undercity (Level 20)
Thunderbluff (Level 50)	Thunderbluff (Level 30)

Mages also have self-only teleport spells.

At level 30, Shaman can gain Astral Recall, which acts similarly to a Hearthstone. However, it has a 15 minute cool down in comparison to a Hearthstone's 1 hour long wait.

OTHER FORMS OF TRANSPORTATION

Shaman and Druids have travel forms that they can use instead of needing to purchase a mount. At level 20 Shaman gain Ghost Wolf, which increases their speed to 50% above normal run speed. At level 30, Druids can transform as well with the same speed boost that the Shaman enjoys with Ghost Wolf. Druids can also take on the Aquatic form of a seal at level 16 that allows them to breathe underwater and swim at a normal speed rather than having to take a 50% speed penalty like other classes.

Hearthstones can be used as another means of transportation though with a high cool down value of one hour, it should be used only when necessary. Keeping your bind point in a central activity area for you will help speed up any questing or grouping you do as well by allowing you to return quickly to join others.

USING THE MAIL SYSTEM

World of Warcraft allows you to mail items and currency to other players rather than having to travel across the world to trade in person. You can also send mail to your other characters (bye bye mules). However, the two restrictions are: 1) you can't send mail to members of the opposite faction and 2) a character can't send mail to his/herself. Mailboxes are found outside of inns across the world of Azeroth and, like many mailboxes, often take on different appearances depending on the location.

You can pick your mail up at any mailbox anywhere in Azeroth. You don't have to go to a particular one in order to get it. To access a mailbox, simply Right Click on it to open the interface. A new window will pop up showing any mail that's waiting for you.

ONE AT A TIME

You are only able to send one item or one stack of items at a time in the mail. Money doesn't count toward this limit, so you can send money and an item or stack of items all at once.

READING YOUR MAIL

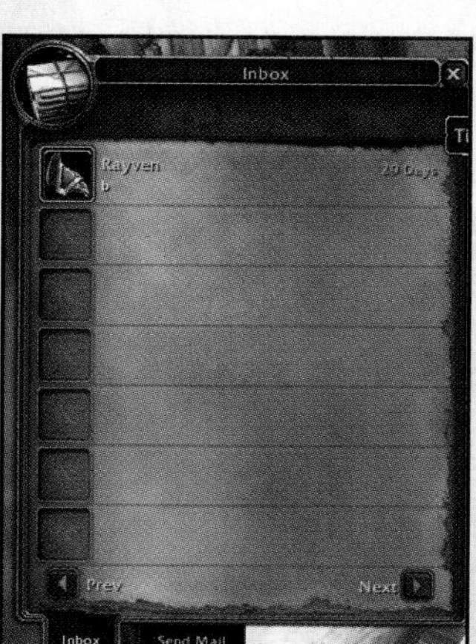

To read your mail, Left Click on the item you wish to read. A new window opens with the message, item and/or coin showing. Click on the item to take it. To the right of the message there's a note on how many days you can leave the mail in the mailbox before it's returned to the sender.

SENDING MAIL

To send mail, click on the send tab. A different interface opens in the window prompting you to type in the name of the person you wish to send the mail to and the subject. You'll need to type both the player name and the subject in order to send the mail.

MAIL ISN'T FREE

To send mail, it costs 30cp coins per mailing. It's a minimal amount to pay, however, and if you're worried about getting back the postage, you could always send it COD.

Don't forget to add in the item you want! You can click and drag an item from your inventory to the mailbox slot for items. Include any COD charges or money you want by typing in the amount of coins you wish to send. COD can be a great way to handle sales that bypass the auction houses. When you're sure you have everything in your mail message that you want, click the send button.

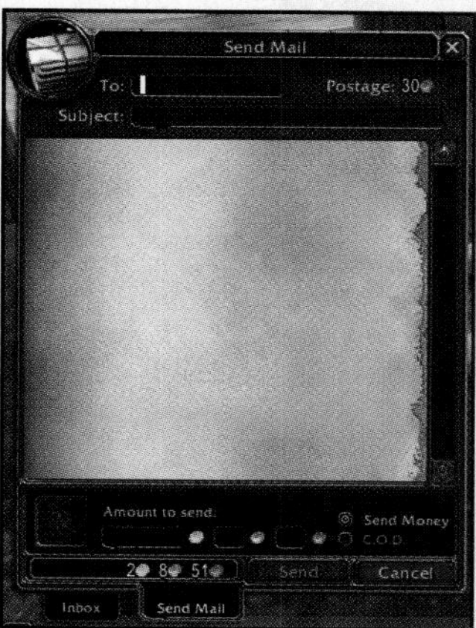

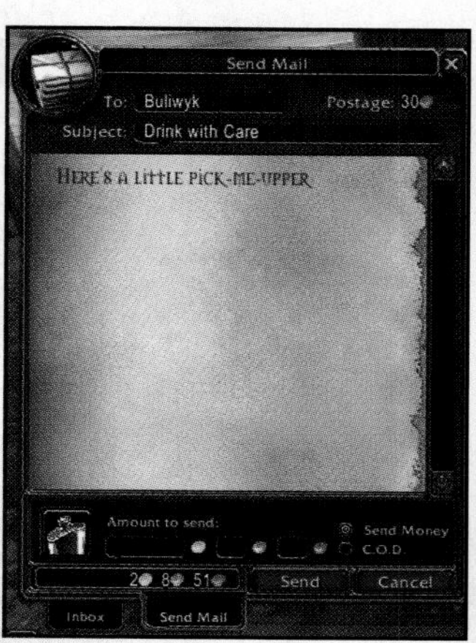

SEND A GIFT

You can surprise a friend by sending a gift-wrapped item in the mail. Gift paper can be bought at general vendors and used by clicking the paper and then the item you wish to send. You cannot wrap stackable items however. If you were thinking of sending out a few mail bombs or an exploding sheep, the sad truth is that you can't wrap it.

DRUID

Druids are the keepers of nature and the world itself. Using their force of will and spirit, these protectors wander the Emerald Dream, focusing the power of the land. As a Druid, you have the power to shapeshift and use different forms of spells to rejuvenate yourself and allies while dealing damage to enemies. Outside, where nature seems so close at hand, your roots are able to hold enemies in place, plaguing melee opponents with frustration. Ultimately, the Druids are jacks of all trades and masters of none; they can fill almost any role well, and round out groups splendidly.

A DRUID'S TALE

We met above the Wailing Caverns and meditated for a short time to see if the stories were true. Indeed, I could feel that the place had become lost to our order, and that some of the finest Druids of the region were now against us. It was a sad thought, but we pushed it out of our minds and rose together. We were to go into the caves below in several groups.

The Raptors below were different; the diseases of mind and body had affected them, turning them into something unnatural. Several of them had been hiding in adjacent caverns and came out when we passed deeper into the Wailing Caverns. I held a moment to bring my focus together, then raised my arms to call nature's strength into the room. My companions changed into their altered selves to defend us, as Calimos took the form of a great bear, and Mariyn became a cat to slip behind our attackers. Together, we lashed into the beasts until peace was granted them. And we continued.

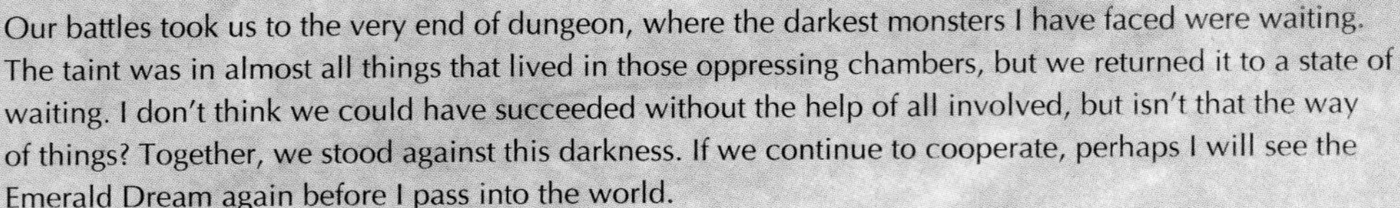

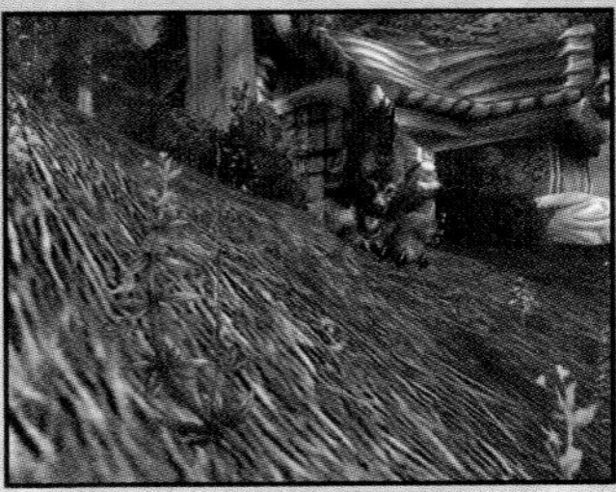

Our battles took us to the very end of dungeon, where the darkest monsters I have faced were waiting. The taint was in almost all things that lived in those oppressing chambers, but we returned it to a state of waiting. I don't think we could have succeeded without the help of all involved, but isn't that the way of things? Together, we stood against this darkness. If we continue to cooperate, perhaps I will see the Emerald Dream again before I pass into the world.

INTRODUCTION TO PLAYING THE DRUID

If you like the idea of being able to play a different set of classes with the same character, Druids are the perfect thing for you! These casters are able to heal, nuke, root, and engage in modest melee skirmishes, but they can Shapeshift and become powerful beasts. Through these forms, Druids can mimic the abilities of Warriors and Rogues! This means that a Druid can act as a group's backup Tank, a DPS class, or a spare Healer. It's hard to go wrong with options like that, and the Talent choices of a Druid make a huge difference in terms of customization.

Groups don't often grab a Druid as their first choice because of the uncertainty for what each Druid can do well, but there are certainly ways to make a Druid appealing as a soloer, a group member, or as a PvPer. With a focus on healing abilities, Druids are able to respond extremely well to backup and even some primary healer duties. Specced for soloing, a Druid can rip through targets as a DPS attacker and switch from cat form to their caster (natural) form to heal after battles; it offers a low-downtime, exciting way to work through the game's outside areas.

Also, people look to Druids for their stackable buffs; other classes are able to raise specific attributes (Intellect and Stamina being obvious targets for Mages and Priests). The Druid buffs add a damage shield and a spell that raises all attributes, increases armor, and improves resists! Mark of the Wild isn't a good buff—it's an incredible buff.

RACES AND STARTING ATTRIBUTES

RACE	STRENGTH	STAMINA	AGILITY	INTELLECT	SPIRIT
Night Elf	22	21	22	23	21
Tauren	25	23	19	20	22

ATTRIBUTES APPLIED

Strength	Increases Damage
Stamina	Higher Hit Points
Agility	Raises Chance to Get a Critical Hit and Dodge
Intellect	More Mana, Faster Rate for Gaining Weapon Skills
Spirit	Improves Hit Point/Mana Recovery in All Forms

ITEMS AND EQUIPMENT

Druids are able to wear up to leather armor, and they wield Staves naturally. Beyond that, they are able to train in Spears, Two-Handed Maces, and Unarmed Fighting. Both Spears and Two-Handed Maces are popular for their damage output, while Staves are desired for their bonuses to caster attributes. The best choice for your Druid is one that enhances your preferred style of fighting (more damage if you prefer the melee aspects of Druids, or choose higher Intellect and Spirit to follow the caster line).

Keeping armor up to date doesn't sound as important for a caster, since you are going to get chewed up no matter what, but that just isn't the case (especially with Druids). This class' ability to switch forms and fighting styles necessitates the best armor possible, even if leather is your cap. Druids that transform into bears to providing tank support to a party should remain on the lookout for any boost to their armor value.

Attributes are rough to deal with as a Druid (you need practically everything). Intellect is very nice to supplement the weaker mana pool of the Druid. Spirit helps all of the animal forms to a decent extent, so that is a decent secondary choice. Beyond that, look for gear that improves your favorite form: Strength and Stamina for the bear, Agility and more Agility for the cat. Unlike most classes, it's often wise to go for equipment that has more total bonuses than any single bonus (e.g. better to have +15 to Agility and Spirit than +25 to Agility).

CHOOSING YOUR PROFESSION

There are a number of good choices in this area, so it's debatable which path to take. Druids benefit highly from Alchemy/Herbalism (for various potions, all of which can aid the Druid at one time or another). Yet, Leatherworking and Skinning helps a great deal with armor. Caster Druids are probably a bit better off with Alchemy, while Shapeshifting Druids gain more from Leatherworking.

If you know that your character is going to have a pile of money (by being twinked, supported by your guild, etc.), perhaps it's fine to take Leatherworking and Alchemy, and simply purchase/snag the supplies for them from others.

Secondary Skills aren't as vital to Druids as they are to non-magical classes that melee. First Aid and Cooking are downtime reducers that benefit everyone, but these have diminishing returns for a class that can move between melee and magic without delay.

CLASS ABILITIES

Druid Abilities are divided by the form needed to cast them. For ranged magic, the natural form of the Druid is used. As a bear the Druid can take far more damage and use Warrior abilities. As a cat the Druid is stealthy and able to deal much higher damage.

Notice that the form of a Druid also dictates which secondary bar they have (Mana for the caster, Rage for the bear, and Energy for the cat).

ABILITY	RANK	LEVEL	TYPE
Mark of the Wild	1	1	Restoration
Moonfire	1	4	Balance
Rejuvenation	1	4	Restoration
Thorns	1	6	Balance
Wrath	2	6	Balance
Entangling Roots	1	8	Balance
Healing Touch	2	8	Restoration
Bear Form (Shapeshift)	N/A	10	Feral Combat
Demoralizing Roar	1	10	Feral Combat
Growl	1	10	Feral Combat
Mark of the Wild	2	10	Restoration
Maul	1	10	Feral Combat
Moonfire	2	10	Balance
Rejuvenation	2	10	Restoration
Enrage	N/A	12	Feral Combat
Regrowth	1	12	Restoration
Bash	1	14	Feral Combat
Cure Poison	N/A	14	Restoration
Healing Touch	3	14	Restoration
Thorns	2	14	Balance
Wrath	3	14	Balance
Aquatic Form (Shapeshift)	N/A	16	Feral Combat
Moonfire	3	16	Balance
Rejuvenation	3	16	Restoration
Swipe	1	16	Feral Combat
Entangling Roots	2	18	Balance
Faerie Fire	1	18	Balance
Maul	2	18	Feral Combat
Nature's Grasp	2	18	Balance
Regrowth	2	18	Restoration
Cat Form (Shapeshift)	N/A	20	Feral Combat
Claw	1	20	Feral Combat
Demoralizing Roar	2	20	Feral Combat
Growl	2	20	Feral Combat
Healing Touch	4	20	Restoration
Mark of the Wild	3	20	Restoration
Prowl	1	20	Feral Combat
Rip	1	20	Feral Combat
Starfire	1	20	Balance
Moonfire	4	22	Balance
Rejuvenation	4	22	Restoration
Remove Curse	N/A	22	Restoration
Shred	1	22	Feral Combat
Soothe Animal	1	22	Balance
Wrath	4	22	Balance
Rake	1	24	Feral Combat
Regrowth	3	24	Restoration
Swipe	2	24	Feral Combat
Thorns	3	24	Balance
Tiger's Fury	1	24	Feral Combat
Abolish Poison	N/A	26	Restoration
Dash	1	26	Feral Combat
Healing Touch	5	26	Restoration
Maul	3	26	Feral Combat
Starfire	2	26	Balance
Challenging Roar	1	28	Feral Combat
Claw	2	28	Feral Combat
Cower	1	28	Feral Combat
Entangling Roots	3	28	Balance
Moonfire	5	28	Balance
Nature's Grasp	3	28	Balance
Rejuvenation	5	28	Restoration
Rip	2	28	Feral Combat
Bash	2	30	Feral Combat
Faerie Fire	2	30	Balance
Faerie Fire (Bear)	2	30	Balance
Faerie Fire (Cat)	2	30	Balance
Growl	3	30	Feral Combat
Mark of the Wild	4	30	Restoration
Regrowth	4	30	Restoration
Shred	2	30	Feral Combat
Tranquility	1	30	Restoration
Travel Form (Shapeshift)	N/A	30	Feral Combat
Wrath	5	30	Balance
Demoralizing Roar	3	32	Feral Combat
Healing Touch	6	32	Restoration
Ravage	1	32	Feral Combat
Track Humanoid	N/A	32	Feral Combat
Maul	4	34	Feral Combat
Moonfire	6	34	Balance
Rake	2	34	Feral Combat
Rejuvenation	6	34	Restoration
Starfire	3	34	Balance
Swipe	3	34	Feral Combat
Thorns	4	34	Balance
Entangling Roots	4	36	Balance
Pounce	1	36	Feral Combat
Regrowth	5	36	Restoration
Rip	3	36	Feral Combat
Tiger's Fury	2	36	Feral Combat
Claw	3	38	Feral Combat
Healing Touch	7	38	Restoration
Nature's Grasp	4	38	Balance
Shred	3	38	Feral Combat
Soothe Animal	2	38	Balance
Wrath	6	38	Balance
Cower	2	40	Feral Combat
Dire Bear Form (Shapeshift)	N/A	40	Feral Combat
Growl	4	40	Feral Combat
Mark of the Wild	5	40	Restoration
Moonfire	7	40	Balance
Prowl	2	40	Feral Combat
Rejuvenation	7	40	Restoration
Tranquility	2	40	Restoration
Demoralizing Roar	4	42	Feral Combat
Faerie Fire	3	42	Balance
Faerie Fire (Bear)	3	42	Balance
Faerie Fire (Cat)	3	42	Balance
Maul	5	42	Feral Combat
Ravage	2	42	Feral Combat
Regrowth	6	42	Restoration
Starfire	4	42	Balance
Healing Touch	8	44	Restoration
Rake	3	44	Feral Combat
Rip	4	44	Feral Combat
Swipe	4	44	Feral Combat
Thorns	5	44	Balance
Bash	3	46	Feral Combat
Dash	2	46	Feral Combat
Moonfire	8	46	Balance
Pounce	2	46	Feral Combat
Rejuvenation	8	46	Restoration
Shred	4	46	Feral Combat
Wrath	7	46	Balance
Claw	4	48	Feral Combat
Entangling Roots	5	48	Balance
Nature's Grasp	5	48	Balance
Regrowth	7	48	Restoration
Tiger's Fury	3	48	Feral Combat
Growl	5	50	Feral Combat
Healing Touch	9	50	Restoration
Hurricane	2	50	Balance
Mark of the Wild	6	50	Restoration
Maul	6	50	Feral Combat
Ravage	3	50	Feral Combat
Starfire	5	50	Balance
Tranquility	3	50	Restoration
Cower	3	52	Feral Combat
Demoralizing Roar	5	52	Feral Combat
Moonfire	9	52	Balance
Rejuvenation	9	52	Restoration
Rip	5	52	Feral Combat
Faerie Fire	4	54	Balance
Faerie Fire (Bear)	4	54	Balance
Faerie Fire (Cat)	4	54	Balance
Rake	4	54	Feral Combat
Regrowth	8	54	Restoration
Shred	5	54	Feral Combat
Soothe Animal	3	54	Balance
Swipe	5	54	Feral Combat
Thorns	6	54	Balance
Wrath	8	54	Balance
Healing Touch	10	56	Restoration
Pounce	3	56	Feral Combat
Claw	5	58	Feral Combat
Entangling Roots	6	58	Balance
Maul	7	58	Feral Combat
Moonfire	10	58	Balance
Nature's Grasp	6	58	Balance
Ravage	4	58	Feral Combat
Rejuvenation	10	58	Restoration
Starfire	6	58	Balance
Growl	6	60	Feral Combat
Hurricane	3	60	Balance
Mark of the Wild	7	60	Restoration
Prowl	3	60	Feral Combat
Regrowth	9	60	Restoration
Rip	6	60	Feral Combat
Tiger's Fury	4	60	Feral Combat
Tranquility	4	60	Restoration

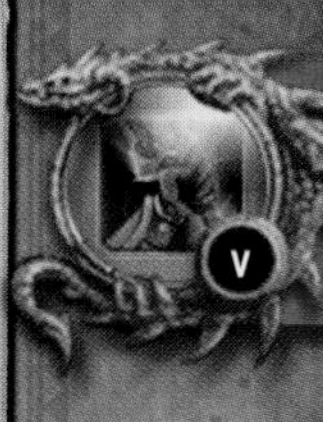

BALANCE

The forces of Balance lend the Druid powers of ranged damage, natural fury, and the ability to bind their foes to the ground (when outdoors).

ENTANGLING ROOTS

RANK	LEVEL	MANA	RANGE	CASTING TIME	COOLDOWN	COST TO TRAIN	EFFECT
1	8	50	30yd	1.5	-	2	Roots the target in place and causes 20 nature damage over 12 sec. Only useable outdoors.
2	18	65	30yd	1.5	-	22	Roots the target in place and causes 50 nature damage over 15 sec. Only useable outdoors.
3	28	80	30yd	1.5	-	54	Roots the target in place and causes 90 nature damage over 18 sec. Only useable outdoors.
4	36	95	30yd	1.5	-	1 40	Roots the target in place and causes 140 nature damage over 21 sec. Only useable outdoors.
5	48	110	30yd	1.5	-	3 10	Roots the target in place and causes 200 nature damage over 24 sec. Only useable outdoors.
6	58	125	30yd	1.5	-	3 50	Roots the target in place and causes 270 nature damage over 27 sec. Only useable outdoors.

FAERIE FIRE

RANK	LEVEL	MANA	RANGE	CASTING TIME	COOLDOWN	COST TO TRAIN	EFFECT
1	18	55	30yd	IC	-	22	Decrease the armor of the target by 175 for 40 sec. While affected, the target cannot stealth or turn invisible.
2	30	75	30yd	IC	-	55	Decrease the armor of the target by 285 for 40 sec. While affected, the target cannot stealth or turn invisible.
3	42	95	30yd	IC	-	1 80	Decrease the armor of the target by 395 for 40 sec. While affected, the target cannot stealth or turn invisible.
4	54	115	30yd	IC	-	2 90	Decrease the armor of the target by 505 for 40 sec. While affected, the target cannot stealth or turn invisible.

FAERIE FIRE (BEAR)

RANK	LEVEL	MANA	RANGE	CASTING TIME	COOLDOWN	COST TO TRAIN	EFFECT
2	30	5 Rage	30yd	IC	-	10	Decrease the armor of the target by 285 for 40 sec. While affected, the target cannot stealth or turn invisible.
3	42	5 Rage	30yd	IC	-	50	Decrease the armor of the target by 395 for 40 sec. While affected, the target cannot stealth or turn invisible.
4	54	5 Rage	30yd	IC	-	70	Decrease the armor of the target by 505 for 40 sec. While affected, the target cannot stealth or turn invisible.

FAERIE FIRE (CAT)

RANK	LEVEL	MANA	RANGE	CASTING TIME	COOLDOWN	COST TO TRAIN	EFFECT
2	30	15 Energy	30yd	IC	-	10	Decrease the armor of the target by 285 for 40 sec. While affected, the target cannot stealth or turn invisible.
3	42	15 Energy	30yd	IC	-	50	Decrease the armor of the target by 395 for 40 sec. While affected, the target cannot stealth or turn invisible.
4	54	15 Energy	30yd	IC	-	70	Decrease the armor of the target by 505 for 40 sec. While affected, the target cannot stealth or turn invisible.

HURRICANE

RANK	LEVEL	MANA	RANGE	CASTING TIME	COOLDOWN	COST TO TRAIN	EFFECT
2	50	884	-	IC	1 min	60	Creates a violent storm in the area surrounding the caster, causing 75 Nature damage to all nearby enemies every 1 sec, and reducing the attack speed of all nearby enemies by 20%. Lasts 10 sec.
3	60	1125	-	IC	1 min	1	Creates a violent storm in the area surrounding the caster, causing 101 Nature damage to all nearby enemies every 1 sec, and reducing the attack speed of all nearby enemies by 20%. Lasts 10 sec.

MOONFIRE

RANK	LEVEL	MANA	RANGE	CASTING TIME	COOLDOWN	COST TO TRAIN	EFFECT
1	4	25	30yd	IC	-	80	Burns the enemy for 7 to 9 Arcane damage and then an additional 12 Arcane damage over 9 sec.
2	10	50	30yd	IC	-	3	Burns the enemy for 13 to 17 Arcane damage and then an additional 32 Arcane damage over 12 sec.
3	16	75	30yd	IC	-	18	Burns the enemy for 25 to 31 Arcane damage and then an additional 52 Arcane damage over 12 sec.
4	22	105	30yd	IC	-	34	Burns the enemy for 40 to 48 Arcane damage and then an additional 80 Arcane damage over 12 sec.
5	28	150	30yd	IC	-	54	Burns the enemy for 61 to 73 Arcane damage and then an additional 124 Arcane damage over 12 sec.
6	34	190	30yd	IC	-	90	Burns the enemy for 81 to 97 Arcane damage and then an additional 164 Arcane damage over 12 sec.
7	40	235	30yd	IC	-	1 30	Burns the enemy for 105 to 125 Arcane damage and then an additional 212 Arcane damage over 12 sec.
8	46	280	30yd	IC	-	1 90	Burns the enemy for 130 to 154 Arcane damage and then an additional 264 Arcane damage over 12 sec.
9	52	325	30yd	IC	-	4	Burns the enemy for 157 to 185 Arcane damage and then an additional 320 Arcane damage over 12 sec.
10	58	375	30yd	IC	-	3 50	Burns the enemy for 189 to 221 Arcane damage and then an additional 384 Arcane damage over 12 sec.

NATURE'S GRASP

RANK	LEVEL	MANA	RANGE	CASTING TIME	COOLDOWN	COST TO TRAIN	EFFECT
2	18	65	-	IC	15 sec	5 50	While active, any time an enemy strikes the caster they have a 35% chance to become afflicted by Entangling Roots (Rank 2). Only useable outdoors. 1 charge. Lasts 45 sec.
3	28	80	-	IC	15 sec	13	While active, any time an enemy strikes the caster they have a 35% chance to become afflicted by Entangling Roots (Rank 3). Only useable outdoors. 1 charge. Lasts 45 sec.
4	38	95	-	IC	15 sec	40	While active, any time an enemy strikes the caster they have a 35% chance to become afflicted by Entangling Roots (Rank 4). Only useable outdoors. 1 charge. Lasts 45 sec.
5	48	110	-	IC	15 sec	80	While active, any time an enemy strikes the caster they have a 35% chance to become afflicted by Entangling Roots (Rank 5). Only useable outdoors. 1 charge. Lasts 45 sec.
6	58	125	-	IC	30sec	90	While active, any time an enemy strikes the caster they have a 35% chance to become afflicted by Entangling Roots (Rank 6). Only useable outdoors. 1 charge. Lasts 45 sec.

SOOTHE ANIMAL

RANK	LEVEL	MANA	RANGE	CASTING TIME	COOLDOWN	COST TO TRAIN	EFFECT
1	22	50	40yd	IC	-	34s	Soothes the target beast, reducing the range at which it will attack you by 10 yards. Only affects targets level 40 or lower. Lasts 15 sec.
2	38	75	40yd	IC	-	1g 40s	Soothes the target beast, reducing the range at which it will attack you by 10 yards. Only affects targets level 55 or lower. Lasts 15 sec.
3	54	100	40yd	IC	-	2g 90s	Soothes the target beast, reducing the range at which it will attack you by 10 yards. Only affects targets level 70 or lower. Lasts 15 sec.

STARFIRE

RANK	LEVEL	MANA	RANGE	CASTING TIME	COOLDOWN	COST TO TRAIN	EFFECT
1	20	95	30yd	3.5	-	19s	Causes 89 to 109 Arcane damage to the target.
2	26	135	30yd	3.5	-	67s	Causes 137 to 167 Arcane damage to the target
3	34	180	30yd	3.5	-	90s	Causes 201 to 241 Arcane damage to the target.
4	42	230	30yd	3.5	-	1g 80s	Causes 280 to 334 Arcane damage to the target.
5	50	275	30yd	3.5	-	2g 40s	Causes 362 to 428 Arcane damage to the target.
6	58	315	30yd	3.5	-	3g 50s	Causes 445 to 525 Arcane damage to the target.

THORNS

RANK	LEVEL	MANA	RANGE	CASTING TIME	COOLDOWN	COST TO TRAIN	EFFECT
1	6	35	30yd	IC	-	1s	Thorns sprout from the friendly target causing 3 Nature damage to attackers when hit. Lasts 10 min.
2	14	60	30yd	IC	-	9s	Thorns sprout from the friendly target causing 6 Nature damage to attackers when hit. Lasts 10 min.
3	24	105	30yd	IC	-	53s	Thorns sprout from the friendly target causing 9 Nature damage to attackers when hit. Lasts 10 min.
4	34	170	30yd	IC	-	90s	Thorns sprout from the friendly target causing 12 Nature damage to attackers when hit. Lasts 10 min.
5	44	240	30yd	IC	-	2g 60s	Thorns sprout from the friendly target causing 15 Nature damage to attackers when hit. Lasts 10 min.
6	54	320	30yd	IC	-	2g 90s	Thorns sprout from the friendly target causing 18 Nature damage to attackers when hit. Lasts 10 min.

WRATH

RANK	LEVEL	MANA	RANGE	CASTING TIME	COOLDOWN	COST TO TRAIN	EFFECT
2	6	35	30yd	1.7	-	1s	Causes 25 to 29 nature damage to the target
3	14	55	30yd	2	-	9s	Causes 44 to 52 nature damage to the target
4	22	70	30yd	2	-	34s	Causes 63 to 73 nature damage to the target.
5	30	100	30yd	2	-	55s	Causes 101 to 115 nature damage to the target.
6	38	125	30yd	2	-	1g 40s	Causes 139 to 157 nature damage to the target.
7	46	155	30yd	2	-	1g 90s	Causes 188 to 210 nature damage to the target.
8	54	180	30yd	2	-	4g 60s	Causes 236 to 264 nature damage to the target.

FERAL COMBAT

Shapeshifting is the core of Druid versatility. This allows all Druids to reach speedier forms of travel (under water and above ground) or to become either a tank or DPS class. Bear Form is gained at Level 10, Aquatic Form at 16, Cat Form is 20, Travel Form at 30, and Dire Bear at Level 40.

AQUATIC FORM (SHAPESHIFT)

RANK	LEVEL	MANA	RANGE	CASTING TIME	COOLDOWN	COST TO TRAIN	EFFECT
N/A	16	23	-	IC	1.5 sec	10c	Shapeshift into aquatic form, increasing swim speed by 50% and allowing the druid to breathe underwater.

BASH

RANK	LEVEL	RAGE	RANGE	CASTING TIME	COOLDOWN	COST TO TRAIN	EFFECT
1	14	10	10yd	IC	1min	9s	Bashes the target, stunning him for 2 sec
2	30	10	10yd	IC	1 min	55s	Bashes the target, stunning him for 3 sec
3	46	10	10yd	IC	1 min	1g 90s	Bashes the target, stunning him for 4 sec.

BEAR FORM (SHAPESHIFT)

RANK	LEVEL	MANA	RANGE	CASTING TIME	COOLDOWN	COST TO TRAIN	EFFECT
N/A	10	65	-	IC	1.5 sec	10c	Shapeshift into a bear, increasing attack power by 30, armor contribution from items by 65%, health by 25, and health gained per point of stamina by 2. Also allows the use of various bear abilities.

CAT FORM (SHAPESHIFT)

RANK	LEVEL	MANA	RANGE	CASTING TIME	COOLDOWN	COST TO TRAIN	EFFECT
N/A	20	65	-	IC	1.5sec	10c	Shapeshift into cat form, increasing attack power by 40 and allowing the use of various cat abilities.

CHALLENGING ROAR

RANK	LEVEL	RAGE	RANGE	CASTING TIME	COOLDOWN	COST TO TRAIN	EFFECT
1	28	15	-	IC	10min	54s	Taunts all nearby enemies for 6 sec.

CLAW

RANK	LEVEL	ENERGY	RANGE	CASTING TIME	COOLDOWN	COST TO TRAIN	EFFECT
1	20	45	10yd	IC	-	10c	Claw the enemy, causing 27 additional damage. Awards 1 combo point.
2	28	45	10yd	IC	-	54s	Claw the enemy, causing 39 additional damage. Awards 1 combo point.
3	38	45	10yd	IC	-	1g 40s	Claw the enemy, causing 57 additional damage. Awards 1 combo point.
4	48	45	10yd	IC	-	3g 50s	Claw the enemy, causing 88 additional damage. Awards 1 combo point.
5	58	45	10yd	IC	-	3g 50s	Claw the enemy, causing 115 additional damage. Awards 1 combo point.

COWER

RANK	LEVEL	ENERGY	RANGE	CASTING TIME	COOLDOWN	COST TO TRAIN	EFFECT
1	28	20	10yd	IC	-	54	Cower, causing no damage but lowering your threat a small amount, making the enemy less likely to attack you.
2	40	20	10yd	IC	-	1 30	Cower, causing no damage but lowering your threat a medium amount, making the enemy less likely to attack you.
3	52	20	10yd	IC	-	4	Cower, causing no damage but lowering your threat a large amount, making the enemy less likely to attack you.

DASH

RANK	LEVEL	MANA	RANGE	CASTING TIME	COOLDOWN	COST TO TRAIN	EFFECT
1	26	-	-	IC	5min	67	Increases movement speed by 50% for 15 sec.
2	46	-	-	IC	5min	1 90	Increases movement speed by 60% for 15 sec.

DEMORALIZING ROAR

RANK	LEVEL	RAGE	RANGE	CASTING TIME	COOLDOWN	COST TO TRAIN	EFFECT
1	10	10	-	IC	-	3	The druid roars, decreasing nearby enemies' attack power by 30. Lasts 30 sec.
2	20	10	-	IC	-	19	The druid roars, decreasing nearby enemies' attack power by 50. Lasts 30 sec.
3	32	10	-	IC	-	1 10	The druid roars, decreasing nearby enemies' attack power by 65. Lasts 30 sec.
4	42	10	-	IC	-	1 80	The druid roars, decreasing nearby enemies' attack power by 100. Lasts 30 sec.
5	52	10	-	IC	-	4	The druid roars, decreasing nearby enemies' attack power by 130. Lasts 30 sec.

DIRE BEAR FORM (SHAPESHIFT)

RANK	LEVEL	MANA	RANGE	CASTING TIME	COOLDOWN	COST TO TRAIN	EFFECT
N/A	40	65	-	IC	1.5sec	1 30	Shapeshift into a dire bear, increasing attack power by 120, armor contribution from items by 125%, health by 525, and health gained per point of stamina by 2. Also allows the use of various bear abilities.

ENRAGE

RANK	LEVEL	MANA	RANGE	CASTING TIME	COOLDOWN	COST TO TRAIN	EFFECT
N/A	12	-	30yd	IC	20sec	8	Generates 20 rage over 10 sec, but significantly reduces armor. The druid is considered in combat for the duration.

GROWL

RANK	LEVEL	RAGE	RANGE	CASTING TIME	COOLDOWN	COST TO TRAIN	EFFECT
1	10	5	10yd	IC	-	3	Adds a small amount of threat to the target.
2	20	5	10yd	IC	-	19	Adds a medium amount of threat to the target.
3	30	5	10yd	IC	-	55	Adds a high amount of threat to the target.
4	40	5	10yd	IC	-	1 30	Adds a very high amount of threat to the target.
5	50	5	10yd	IC	-	2 40	Adds a very high amount of threat to the target.
6	60	5	10yd	IC	-	3 90	Adds a very high amount of threat to the target.

MAUL

RANK	LEVEL	RAGE	RANGE	CASTING TIME	COOLDOWN	COST TO TRAIN	EFFECT
1	10	15	-	Next Melee	-	10	Increases the druid's next attack by 18 damage.
2	18	15	-	Next Melee	-	22	Increases the druid's next attack by 27 damage.
3	26	15	-	Next Melee	-	67	Increases the druid's next attack by 37 damage.
4	34	15	-	Next Melee	-	90	Increases the druid's next attack by 49 damage.
5	42	15	-	Next Melee	-	1 80	Increases the druid's next attack by 71 damage.
6	50	15	-	Next Melee	-	2 40	Increases the druid's next attack by 101 damage.
7	58	15	-	Next Melee	-	3 50	Increases the druid's next attack by 128 damage.

POUNCE

RANK	LEVEL	ENERGY	RANGE	CASTING TIME	COOLDOWN	COST TO TRAIN	EFFECT
1	36	50	10yd	IC	-	1 50	Pounce, stunning the target for 2 sec and causing 90 damage over 18 sec. Must be prowling and behind the target. Awards 1 combo point.
2	46	50	10yd	IC	-	1 90	Pounce, stunning the target for 2 sec and causing 120 damage over 18 sec. Must be prowling and behind the target. Awards 1 combo point.
3	56	50	10yd	IC	-	6 40	Pounce, stunning the target for 2 sec and causing 150 damage over 18 sec. Must be prowling and behind the target. Awards 1 combo point.

PROWL

RANK	LEVEL	MANA	RANGE	CASTING TIME	COOLDOWN	COST TO TRAIN	EFFECT
1	20	-	-	IC	10sec	19	Allows the Druid to prowl around, but reduces your speed to 60% of normal. Lasts until cancelled.
2	40	-	-	IC	10sec	1 30	Allows the Druid to prowl around, but reduces your speed to 65% of normal. Lasts until cancelled.
3	60	-	-	IC	10sec	3 90	Allows the Druid to prowl around, but reduces your speed to 70% of normal. Lasts until cancelled.

RAKE

RANK	LEVEL	ENERGY	RANGE	CASTING TIME	COOLDOWN	COST TO TRAIN	EFFECT
1	24	40	10yd	IC	-	53	Rake the target for 15 damage and an additional 30 damage over 9 sec. Awards 1 combo point.
2	34	40	10yd	IC	-	90	Rake the target for 22 damage and an additional 45 damage over 9 sec. Awards 1 combo point.
3	44	40	10yd	IC	-	2 50	Rake the target for 34 damage and an additional 60 damage over 9 sec. Awards 1 combo point.
4	55	40	10yd	IC	-	2 90	Rake the target for 46 damage and an additional 75 damage over 9 sec. Awards 1 combo point.

RAVAGE

RANK	LEVEL	ENERGY	RANGE	CASTING TIME	COOLDOWN	COST TO TRAIN	EFFECT
1	32	60	10yd	IC	-	1● 10●	Ravage the target, causing 350% damage plus 147 to the target. Must be prowling and behind the target. Awards 1 combo point.
2	42	60	10yd	IC	-	1● 80●	Ravage the target, causing 350% damage plus 273 to the target. Must be prowling and behind the target. Awards 1 combo point.
3	50	60	10yd	IC	-	2● 40●	Ravage the target, causing 350% damage plus 217 to the target. Must be prowling and behind the target. Awards 1 combo point.
4	58	60	10yd	IC	-	3● 50●	Ravage the target, causing 350% damage plus 343 to the target. Must be prowling and behind the target. Awards 1 combo point.

RIP

RANK	LEVEL	ENERGY	RANGE	CASTING TIME	COOLDOWN	COST TO TRAIN	EFFECT
1	20	30	10yd	IC	-	19●	Finishing move that causes damage over time. Damage increases per combo point: 1 point: 42 damage over 12 sec. 2 points: 66 damage over 12 sec. 3 points: 90 damage over 12 sec. 4 points: 114 damage over 12 sec. 5 points: 138 damage over 12 sec.
2	28	30	10yd	IC	-	54●	Finishing move that causes damage over time. Damage increases per combo point: 1 point: 60 damage over 12 sec. 2 points: 96 damage over 12 sec. 3 points: 132 damage over 12 sec. 4 points: 168 damage over 12 sec. 5 points: 204 damage over 12 sec.
3	36	30	10yd	IC	-	54●	Finishing move that causes damage over time. Damage increases per combo point: 1 point : 84 damage over 12 sec. 2 points: 132 damage over 12 sec. 3 points: 180 damage over 12 sec. 4 points: 228 damage over 12 sec. 5 points: 276 damage over 12 sec.
4	44	30	10yd	IC	-	1● 50●	Finishing move that causes damage over time. Damage increases per combo point: 1 point : 120 damage over 12 sec. 2 points: 186 damage over 12 sec. 3 points: 228 damage over 12 sec. 4 points: 318 damage over 12 sec. 5 points: 384 damage over 12 sec.
5	52	30	10yd	IC	-	2● 50●	Finishing move that causes damage over time. Damage increases per combo point: 1 point: 162 damage over 12 sec. 2 points: 252 damage over 12 sec. 3 points:342 damage over 12 sec. 4 points: 432 damage over 12 sec. 5 points: 522 damage over 12 sec.
6	60	30	10yd	IC	-	3● 90●	Finishing move that causes damage over time. Damage increases per combo point: 1 point : 228 damage over 12 sec. 2 points: 354 damage over 12 sec. 3 points: 480 damage over 12 sec. 4 points: 606 damage over 12 sec. 5 points: 732 damage over 12 sec.

SHRED

RANK	LEVEL	ENERGY	RANGE	CASTING TIME	COOLDOWN	COST TO TRAIN	EFFECT
1	22	60	10yd	IC	-	34●	Shred the target, causing 225% damage plus 54 to the target. Must be behind the target. Awards 1 combo point.
2	30	60	10yd	IC	-	55●	Shred the target, causing 225% damage plus 72 to the target. Must be behind the target. Awards 1 combo point.
3	38	60	10yd	IC	-	1● 90●	Shred the target, causing 225% damage plus 99 to the target. Must be behind the target. Awards 1 combo point.
4	46	60	10yd	IC	-	1● 90●	Shred the target, causing 225% damage plus 144 to the target. Must be behind the target. Awards 1 combo point.
5	54	60	10yd	IC	-	2● 90●	Shred the target, causing 225% damage plus 180 to the target. Must be behind the target. Awards 1 combo point.

SWIPE

RANK	LEVEL	RAGE	RANGE	CASTING TIME	COOLDOWN	COST TO TRAIN	EFFECT
1	16	20	10yd	IC	4sec	18●	Swipe 3 nearby enemies, inflicting 18 damage.
2	24	20	10yd	IC	4sec	53●	Swipe 3 nearby enemies, inflicting 25 damage.
3	34	20	10yd	IC	4sec	90●	Swipe 3 nearby enemies, inflicting 36 damage.
4	44	20	10yd	IC	4sec	2● 60●	Swipe 3 nearby enemies, inflicting 60 damage.
5	54	20	10yd	IC	4sec	2● 90●	Swipe 3 nearby enemies, inflicting 83 damage.

TIGER'S FURY

RANK	LEVEL	ENERGY	RANGE	CASTING TIME	COOLDOWN	COST TO TRAIN	EFFECT
1	24	30	-	IC	-	53●	Increases damage done by 10 for 4 sec.
2	36	30	-	IC	-	1● 50●	Increases damage done by 20 for 4 sec.
3	48	30	-	IC	-	3● 10●	Increases damage done by 30 for 4 sec.
4	60	30	-	IC	-	3● 90●	Increases damage done by 40 for 4 sec.

TRACK HUMANOID

RANK	LEVEL	MANA	RANGE	CASTING TIME	COOLDOWN	COST TO TRAIN	EFFECT
N/A	32	-	-	IC	-	1● 10●	Shows the loacation of all nearby humanoids on the minimap. Only one type of thing can be tracked at a time.

TRAVEL FORM (SHAPESHIFT)

RANK	LEVEL	MANA	RANGE	CASTING TIME	COOLDOWN	COST TO TRAIN	EFFECT
N/A	30	23	-	IC	1.5sec	10●	Transforms the druid into a travel form, increasing movement speed by 40%.

RESTORATION

Through Restoration, Druids are able to heal themselves and their allies. Though left without the ability to raise others from the dead, Druids make a huge difference as secondary healers in groups.

ABOLISH POISON

RANK	LEVEL	MANA	RANGE	CASTING TIME	COOLDOWN	COST TO TRAIN	EFFECT
N/A	26	100	30yd	IC	-	67●	Attempts to cure 1 poison effect on the target, and 1 more poison effect every 2 seconds for 8 sec.

CURE POISON

RANK	LEVEL	MANA	RANGE	CASTING TIME	COOLDOWN	COST TO TRAIN	EFFECT
N/A	14	40	30yd	IC	-	9	Cures 1 poison effect on the target.

HEALING TOUCH

RANK	LEVEL	MANA	RANGE	CASTING TIME	COOLDOWN	COST TO TRAIN	EFFECT
2	8	60	40yd	2sec	-	2	Heals a friendly target for 88 to 112.
3	14	120	40yd	2.5sec	-	9	Heals a friendly target for 195 to 243.
4	20	205	40yd	3	-	19	Heals a friendly target for 363 to 445.
5	26	300	40yd	3.5	-	67	Heals a friendly target for 572 to 694.
6	32	370	40yd	3.5	-	1 10	Heals a friendly target for 742 to 894.
7	38	445	40yd	3.5	-	1 40	Heals a friendly target for 936 to 1120.
8	44	545	40yd	3.5	-	2 60	Heals a friendly target for 1199 to 1427.
9	50	660	40yd	3.5	-	2 40	Heals a friendly target for 1516 to 1796.
10	56	790	40yd	3.5	-	6 40	Heals a friendly target for 1890 to 2230.

MARK OF THE WILD

RANK	LEVEL	MANA	RANGE	CASTING TIME	COOLDOWN	COST TO TRAIN	EFFECT
1	1	20	30yd	IC	-	10	Increases the friendly target's armor by 25 for 30 min.
2	10	50	30yd	IC	-	3	Increases the friendly target's armor by 65 and all attributes by 2 for 30 min.
3	20	100	30yd	IC	-	19	Increases the friendly target's armor by 142 and all attributes by 5 for 30 min.
4	30	160	30yd	IC	-	55	Increases the friendly target's armor by 150, all attributes by 6 and all resistances by 15 for 30 min.
5	40	240	30yd	IC	-	1 30	Increases the friendly target's armor by 195, all attributes by 8 and all resistances by 20 for 30 min.
6	50	340	30yd	IC	-	2 40	Increases the friendly target's armor by 240, all attributes by 10 and all resistances by 25 for 30 min.
7	60	445	30yd	IC	-	3 90	Increases the friendly target's armor by 285, all attributes by 12 and all resistances by 30 for 30 min.

REGROWTH

RANK	LEVEL	MANA	RANGE	CASTING TIME	COOLDOWN	COST TO TRAIN	EFFECT
1	12	120	40yd	2sec	-	8	Heals a friendly target for 84 to 98 and another 98 over 21 sec.
2	18	205	40yd	2sec	-	22	Heals a friendly target for 164 to 188 and another 175 over 21 sec.
3	24	280	40yd	2sec	-	53	Heals a friendly target for 240 to 274 and another 259 over 21 sec.
4	30	350	40yd	2sec	-	55	Heals a friendly target for 318 to 360 and another 343 over 21 sec
5	36	420	40yd	2sec	-	1 50	Heals a friendly target for 405 to 457 and another 427 over 21 sec.
6	42	510	40yd	2sec	-	1 80	Heals a friendly target for 511 to 575 and another 546 over 21 sec.
7	48	615	40yd	2sec	-	3 10	Heals a friendly target for 646 to 724 and another 686 over 21 sec.
8	54	740	40yd	2sec	-	2 90	Heals a friendly target for 809 to 905 and another 861 over 21 sec.
9	60	880	40yd	2sec	-	3 90	Heals a friendly target for 1003 to 1119 and another 1064 over 21 sec.

REJUVINATION

RANK	LEVEL	MANA	RANGE	CASTING TIME	COOLDOWN	COST TO TRAIN	EFFECT
1	4	25	40yd	IC	-	80	Heals the target for 32 over 12 sec.
2	10	40	40yd	IC	-	3	Heals the target for 56 over 12 sec.
3	16	75	40yd	IC	-	18	Heals the target for 116 over 12 sec.
4	22	105	40yd	IC	-	34	Heals the target for 180 over 12 sec.
5	28	135	40yd	IC	-	54	Heals the target for 244 over 12 sec.
6	34	160	40yd	IC	-	90	Heals the target for 304 over 12 sec.
7	40	195	40yd	IC	-	1 30	Heals the target for 388 over 12 sec.
8	46	235	40yd	IC	-	1 90	Heals the target for 488 over 12 sec.
9	52	280	40yd	IC	-	4	Heals the target for 608 over 12 sec.
10	58	335	40yd	IC	-	3 50	Heals the target for 756 over 12 sec.

REMOVE CURSE

RANK	LEVEL	MANA	RANGE	CASTING TIME	COOLDOWN	COST TO TRAIN	EFFECT
N/A	22	60	30yd	IC	-	34	Dispels 1 curse from the target.

TRANQUILITY

RANK	LEVEL	MANA	RANGE	CASTING TIME	COOLDOWN	COST TO TRAIN	EFFECT
1	30	500	-	IC	10min	55	Regenerates all nearby group members for 94 every 2 seconds for 10 sec. Druids must channel to maintain the spell.
2	40	675	-	IC	10min	1 30	Regenerates all nearby group members for 138 every 2 seconds for 10 sec. Druids must channel to maintain the spell.
3	50	925	-	IC	10min	2 40	Regenerates all nearby group members for 205 every 2 seconds for 10 sec. Druids must channel to maintain the spell.
4	60	1235	-	IC	10min	3 90	Regenerates all nearby group members for 294 every 2 seconds for 10 sec. Druids must channel to maintain the spell.

TALENTS

Druid Talents take the class far and wide, enabling the character to become a deft caster, a master of their Shifting forms, or a quality healer. The Balanced line offers many of the mystic improvements, raising the attack damage, efficiency, and critical potential of Druid combat spells. Feral Combat brings the Druid's Cat and Bear forms closer in-line with Rogues and Warriors, respectively, making the class far more effective at DPS work and Tanking. Finally, the Restoration line aids healing spells with decreased Threat, improved efficiency, and some interruption avoidance. Restoration also has some supplementary additions to the Druid's Shifting Forms.

BALANCED

TALENT NAME	RANKS	PREREQUISITES	EFFECTS
Improved Wrath	5	None	Reduces the cast time of your Wrath spell by .1 seconds (Per Rank)
Nature's Grasp	1	None	Adds an Instant ability the Gives You a 35% Chance to Root Melee Attackers
Improved Nature's Grasp	4	1 Point in Nature's Grasp	Increases Chance for Nature's Grasp to Root Attackers by 15% - Progression: 15%/30%/45%/65%
Improved Entangling Roots	3	5 Points in Balance	Gives you a 40% chance to avoid interruption (by damage) when casting Entangling Roots - Progression: 40%/70%/100%
Improved Moonfire	5	5 Points in Balance	Increases damage and chance to critical w/ Moonfire by 3% (Per Rank)
Nature's Reach	2	5 Points in Balance	Increases the range of Wrath, Entangling Roots, Faerie Fire, Moonfire, and Starfire by 10% (Per Rank)
Swiftshifting	3	5 Points in Balance	Reduces the cooldown on non-Shapeshifting spells by .5 seconds (Per Rank) after returning to caster form
Improved Starfire	5	10 Points in Balance	Adds a 3% chance (Per Rank) for a 3 second stun to Starfire
Omen of Clarity	1	10 Points in Balance	Adds an Instant ability to buff your weapon (each hit you land gives a chance to gain Clearcasting)
Improved Thorns	5	15 Points in Balance	Adds a 5% chance (Per Rank) to Thorns to causes an additional 100% damage
Moonglow	5	5 Points in Improved Moonfire, 15 Points in Balance	Reduces the Mana cost of Moonfire and Starfire by 2% (Per Rank)
Moonfury	5	20 Points in Balance	Increases the damage done by Starfire and Moonfire by 2% (Per Rank)
Nature's Grace	1	20 Points in Balance	Critical strikes w/ Wrath, Starfire, and Moonfire add buff that reduces Regrowth/Healing Touch casting time by one second (lasts one spell)
Weapon Balance	5	1 Point in Omen of Clarity, 20 Points in Balance	Increases the damage done with melee weapons by 2% (Per Rank)
Vengeance	5	25 Points in Balance	Increases critical damage of Starfire, Moonfire, and Wrath by 20% (Per Rank)
Hurricane	1	30 Points in Balance	Adds an Instant ability to summon a storm that deals 53 Nature Damage each second (for ten seconds) and slows enemy attacks by 20%

FERAL COMBAT

TALENT NAME	RANKS	PREREQUISITES	EFFECTS
Ferocity	5	None	Reduces the cost of Maul, Swipe, Claw, and Rake by one Rage/Energy (Per Rank)
Improved Demoralizing Roar	5	None	Increases the Attack Power debuff of Demoralizing Roar by 5% (Per Rank)
Improved Bash	2	5 Points in Feral Combat	Increases the stun duration of Bash by .5 seconds (Per Rank)
Sharpened Claws	5	5 Points in Feral Combat	Increases for critical strike chance by 1% (Per Rank) (Bear and Cat Form Only)
Improved Prowl	5	10 Points in Feral Combat	Increases prowling speed by 3% (Per Rank)
Feral Charge	1	10 Points in Feral Combat	Adds an Instant ability to charge and stun enemies for one second, interrupting spells for five seconds
Blood Frenzy	5	5 Points in Sharpened Claws, 10 Points in Feral Combat	Cat Form critical strikes that add combo points by a 20% chance (Per Rank) to add a free combo point
Primal Fury	5	5 Points in Sharpened Claws, 10 Points in Feral Combat	Give 20% chance (Per Rank) to gain five Rage during Crit Strike (Bear Form)
Improved Shred	2	15 Points in Feral Combat	Reduces the Energy cost of Shred by 5 (Per Rank)
Predatory Strikes	5	15 Points in Feral Combat	Increases the Attack Power boost from Cat Form ability by 4% (Per Rank)
Faerie Fire (Bear)	1	15 Points in Balance	Adds the ability to cast Faerie Fire in Bear Form
Faerie Fire (Cat)	1	15 Points in Balance	Adds the ability to cast Faerie Fire in Cat Form
Thick Hide	5	20 Points in Feral Combat	Increases Armor (gained by items) by 2% (Per Rank) in Bear Form
Feline Swiftness	1	20 Points in Feral Combat	Improves outdoor movement speed by 30% in Cat Form
Strength of the Wild	4	5 Points in Predatory Strikes, 25 Points in Feral Combat	Increases your Strength in Bear and Cat Form by 3% (Per Rank)
Improved Ravage	2	25 Points in Feral Combat	Increase chance for Ravage to critically strike by 5% (Per Rank)
Primal Instinct	1	30 Points in Feral Combat	Reduces the Mana cost of Shapeshifting abilities by 25%
Improved Pounce	2	30 Points in Feral Combat	Adds a 50% chance (Per Rank) for Pounce to add a free combo point

RESTORATION

TALENT NAME	RANKS	PREREQUISITES	EFFECTS
Improved Mark of the Wild	5	None	Increases the Effects of Mark of the Wild by 7% (Per Rank)
Furor	5	None	Gives you a 20% chance (Per Rank) to gain 10 Rage when Shifting into Bear Form
Nature's Focus	5	5 Points in Restoration	Adds a 20% chance (Per Rank) to avoid interruption (by damage) when casting Healing Touch/Regrowth
Improved Healing Touch	5	5 Points in Restoration	Reduces the Mana cost of Healing Touch by 4% (Per Rank)
Improved Enrage	2	5 Points in Furor, 5 Points in Restoration	Reduces the Armor penalty and required time for Enrage to generate Rage (Reduced by 2 seconds Per Rank)
Combat Endurance	5	10 Points in Restoration	Allows 2% (Per Rank) of Health regeneration to work during combat
Gift of Nature	1	10 Points in Restoration	Improves the effect of Healing Touch, Rejuvenation, Regrowth, and Tranquility by 5%
Intensity	5	10 Points in Restoration	Adds a 20% chance (Per Rank) to gain 20 Energy when Shifting into Cat Form
Reflection	5	15 Points in Restoration	Increases Mana regeneration by 2% (Per Rank)
Improved Rejuvenation	5	15 Points in Restoration	Increases the effect of your Rejuvenation spells by 3% (Per Rank)
Nature's Swiftness	1	5 Points in Nature's Focus, 20 Points in Restoration	Adds an Instant ability that makes your next Nature spell cast Instantly
Subtlety	5	1 Point in Gift of Nature, 20 Points in Restoration	Reduces threat accrued while Healing by 4% (Per Rank)
Improved Tranquility	2	20 Points in Restoration	Adds a 40% chance (Per Rank) to avoid interruption (by damage) while casting Tranquility
Improved Regrowth	5	25 Points in Restoration	Increases the chance to critical with Regrowth by 10% (Per Rank)
Innervate	1	5 Points in Reflection, 30 Points in Restoration	Adds an Instant ability with a six minute cooldown that allows 100% of mana regeneration during casting for 20 seconds

Playing a Druid varies greatly from area to area, group to group, and even from moment to moment. Because so much can be done to change the dynamic of a Druid in battle, it takes considerable practice to master all facets of this class. Once done, a Druid can seamlessly switch between the major roles of group members, taking over for anyone who falls short during a fight.

First off, be sure to have your keys bound so that Shapeshifting between forms is fast and easy. Using Control + the Function Keys is somewhat standard, but placing the keys beneath the numbers or anywhere close to your hand's natural placement is sensible.

COMBAT IN CASTER FORM

A simple fight for a Druid comes down to throwing some damage at range (Starfire or Wrath), then hitting the target with Moonfire and Faerie Fire during their approach. Crush enemies in melee combat while regenerating mana and head off to the next kill when everything is done. This is a Balanced Druid's approach to fighting, and it's perfectly effective against a wide range of monsters.

Starfire is a great spell for maintaining efficient damage, and its maximum damage dealt is solid for a given level (compared to Wrath). What Wrath offers is the ability to dump a fair amount of mana into a target over a short period, because of its brief casting time, a Druid can spam Wrath into one or even multiple targets.

As for Healing, notice that HoTs are more expensive in terms of mana per hit points restored, though Regrowth has a fairly short casting time. Rejuvenation heals far less, but is an instant cast and has a trivial cost; because this spell only causes a short break in mana regeneration, it's quite useful to slap on while entering melee.

Healing Touch is the spell to spam when your group needs consistent and efficient healing. This spell is effective at bringing back decent amounts of life in large battles. If things start to get so bad that a primary healer is losing the fight against multiple wounds, use Tranquility to help everyone get back on their feet (and prepare to deal with some aggro). This group heal is best during the later stages of a difficult fight, when everyone has grabbed their share of aggro; finish off any target that is on you and get in the clear so your Channeling won't be interrupted.

If Balance is your primary Talent line, having Hurricane can be a huge good to Caster Form tactics. If multiple enemies are inbound against your group, it's powerful to be able to deal damage against them and reduce their attack speed.

When outdoors and in need of extra mana, it's possible to use Entangling Roots against enemies and move out of their attack range. While you begin regaining mana, they continue to take damage. This is a good way to handle adds; slap them with Entangling Roots and back away until they cannot contribute to the fight with any melee or ranged attacks. Handled correctly, this becomes a very substantial method of outdoor crowd control.

Before going into your alternate Forms, using any spells, potions, or items that are needed in future combat (these things aren't usable once in an Animal Form, but the effects transfer when you Shift). So, drink potions for Strength, Armor, etc. before going down on all fours.

CAT FORM

Use Cat Form as a way to solo or add DPS to a group. Druids deal very high damage in Cat Form, especially is specced in Feral Combat. The best trick with this is to lean on the DPS for several kills, until health begins to get low, then switch to your Caster Form for some healing magic. Restore any buffs, Shapeshift back into a Cat, then repeat the process.

In groups, the Cat offers high damage by harping on back attacks (Shred). When there is a high-level or generally skilled tank holding aggro, this is a good choice for assisting the group's kill rate. It's easy to do more damage over time as a Cat than you can in Caster Form, and all of that mana you build up is perfect for going into a healing frenzy (between battles or when the group is in a pinch). It's hard not to fall in love with the Cat for this reason; Druids are constantly adding to the group without sacrificing healing potential or damage.

At Level 32, Druids in Cat Form can use their Track Humanoid ability. This is a rare ability that's not available to other classes. As such, Druids have a few perks in PvE and PvP combat. When trying to avoid or hunt down PvP opponents, this ability dramatically improves your group's chance at gaining the initiative. Attacking when enemies are already engaged, distracted, or just looking the wrong way can be enough to overwhelm superior numbers and levels.

BEAR FORM

The Bear Form isn't needed as often as the Cat because there are so many Warriors out in the world. Yet, the group you choose may have Battle Stance Warriors or only Paladins for doing the tank work, and they may need a bit of help. Bear Form is decent for Taunting, solid for surviving damage, and can certainly make it worth a group's time to include you in their exploits. As with the Cat Form, save mana for important times and switch back to Caster for bursts of activity.

If Bear Form is often needed in the groups you enjoy, invest in as high an Armor Rating as you can reach. Take Talents such as Thick Hide, use Defense Potions, and emulate as much of a Warrior's mentality as you can.

Read through the class description for Warriors to gain better ideas for Taunting, selecting the right targets to gather aggro, and so forth.

HUNTER

Hunters view nature as a force with which to ally. They spend much of their time with an animal companion. The bond that forms between the two is rather strong. To attack either is to bring down the wrath of both. With powerful attacks in melee and at range, and a friend willing to put its life on the line at your command, the Hunter makes a potent addition to any group.

A HUNTER PROWLS

There were too many in the camp for us to charge. The Scarlet Crusade wasn't stupid either; none would venture out of the camp alone. We decided to try and get a smaller group to come to us. Denegar, our Dwarven Warrior, volunteered to "ask if they had a cup and sugar and run back." Denegar had the heaviest armor of all of us, and we were still unsure if even he could survive the trip back with enemies at his back. I decided that I would do it.

I strung my bow and moved a bit closer. I took aim and waited until I had a good shot. I hit the fanatic in the shoulder. As any halfwit would do, the man called to his friends before running toward me. I made a quick retreat back to the others. As the enemy made their charge, I shot my target in the leg. Now there were only two in the initial attack. Denegar made his intentions clear by swinging his two-handed axe above his head and bringing it down against the enemy's shield. It wasn't a hit, but the message was clear. Denegar was not to be ignored. As the Warriors closed in on Denegar, I pulled back and began peppering them with arrows. Their armor was as good as Denegar's. This wasn't to be a fast fight.

After several minutes, the group had brought the first of the two enemies down and switched to the second. I was taking aim when something moved on the edge of my vision. I dodged aside as a sword cut through the air I had occupied only a moment before. There was a Scarlet Warrior with two arrows in him and a very unhappy look on his face standing between me and the rest of the group. I had a bow in one hand, and an arrow in the other. The fanatic let a smile form on his face as he began advancing. That was long enough. Talon, my wolf companion and best friend, sank his teeth into the man's arm and nearly drug him to the ground. With his attention on Talon, I dropped my bow and arrow and unslung my two axes. With both of us attacking, the man couldn't fight effectively against either of us. After a few moments both Talon and I were sporting several wounds and our target was still standing. A look of horror crossed his face as a ball of fire slammed into his chest. This was followed by a scream of Dwarven rage and the arrival of the rest of the group. The Priest made quick work to restore the vigor Talon and I had lost through the fight. It had gone from two against one to six against one! The odds weren't in the Scarlet Crusader's favor.

INTRODUCTION TO PLAYING THE HUNTER

Hunters have a certain mystique about them. The idea of fighting along side a life-long friend can be very appealing. The Hunter's strength is derived from combining the abilities of the Hunter with those of a pet. While this gives Hunters more choices than many classes, it takes practice and experimenting to find what works best in each situation.

At range, the Hunter is hard to beat. With high-damage attacks, movement-hindering abilities, and a pet to bite at the heels of attackers, fighting a Hunter at range is dangerous at best and foolhardy at worst. The movement hindering abilities allow the Hunter to bring targets to a group in a more organized and less stressful fashion.

Starting with Leather armor and progressing to Mail at Level 40, Hunters aren't fragile. Combine this with dual-wield or a two-handed weapon, and a pet, and they're almost as dangerous in melee as they are at range.

Hunters gain enough hit points to survive the attention of monsters for a short time. However, a long, drawn-out fight is something to be avoided as Hunters can't take nearly the hits Warriors can. Here is where the bond between Hunter and pet becomes so clear. Your companion is willing to do anything you ask. This includes keeping the attention of an enemy while you stay at long range and calmly fire away or sit on its back hacking away.

Keeping you and your party safe is something your pet is happy to do. Keeping your pet safe is what Hunters do in return for the boundless loyalty you receive.

RACES AND STARTING ATTRIBUTES

RACE	STRENGTH	STAMINA	AGILITY	INTELLECT	SPIRIT
Dwarf	22	19	24	19	20
Night Elf	17	28	20	20	21
Orc	23	20	23	17	24
Tauren	23	18	23	15	23
Troll	21	25	22	16	22

ATTRIBUTES APPLIED

Strength	Partially Increases Damage Done in Melee
Stamina	Higher Hit Points
Agility	Raises Chance to Get a Critical Hit, Dodge and Increases Damage Done at Range and in Melee
Intellect	Faster Rate for Gaining Weapon Skills and Higher Mana
Spirit	Improves Hit Point and Mana Recovery

ITEMS AND EQUIPMENT

Properly equipped, a Hunter can function both in melee and at range. This flexibility gives you the choice where to fight. Many Hunters choose to fight at range when possible as many of their abilities are dependant upon using our Bow (or Gun).

A Bow (or Gun) is your primary form of damage at range. As such, it must be kept up-to-date. This includes ammunition. Different types of arrows and shot give different DPS bonuses. Always use the highest level ammunition available. Finding a weapon that does high DPS and has Agility bonuses is even better as Agility affects ranged damage.

Food is fairly important to a Hunter—it's for your pet! Keeping pets fed and happy is as important as almost any equipment you could possibly buy. Hunters should restock their food supply before heading out of town. Be sure to know which foods you create likes as well, since each race has different needs.

Bags and ammunition containers are fairly important. Quivers and Ammo Pouches give bonuses to firing speed. They can only hold Arrows or Shot and take a bag slot. This means that where most classes have one backpack and four bags, you have one backpack, three bags, and an ammunition container. Keep in mind that Hunters carry more food than many others (you're feeding two after all). So, Hunters have far less room than many characters, and even less if Skinning is one of your professions.

Any non-armor equipment should be used to increase stats. The foremost is Agility. Agility heightens your critical hit chance, which is useful in both melee and ranged combat. It also increases damage in ranged combat and increases your dodge rate and some damage in melee.

KEEPING A PET

Since a pet is the second half of your character, having a fully trained and leveled pet is very important. Find a pet you enjoy having that is the same level as you. Having a friend to help can make this less dangerous as taming cannot be interrupted and can fail. Your partner should do nothing besides distract the creature unless the taming fails, at which time you'll need help killing the unfriendly beast.

Once the pet has agreed to become your friend, help the bond flourish by feeding it. Feeding raises a pet's happiness level. This level affects how much damage a pet does in combat, so it shouldn't be overlooked.

PETS NEVER STOP EATING

Your pet needs to be fed constantly. Watch its happiness icon. Feed it whenever its Happiness Level falls. This ensures maximum damage!

Happiness level affects your pets loyalty level, which in turn affects how many training points your pet has.

PET HAPPINESS

PET HAPPINESS LEVEL	EFFECT
Happy	125% of normal damage; gaining loyalty
Content	100% of normal damage; gaining loyalty
Unhappy	75% of normal damage; losing loyalty

LIONS, TIGERS, AND BEARS

There are many beasts in the world. Finding the one that is right for you might take a while and may even change several times. It takes quite some time for pets to really bond to their master, so avoid changing pets too often.

Not every beast can use all the abilities you teach. Some body-types are inadequate for performing certain attacks. Trying to teach a Crab to Bite is a noble effort, but it doesn't have the mouth to do any damage.

Different beasts also have different diets. Bears and Nightsabres have no qualms about eating almost any meat you give them. Striders and Owls are a bit pickier about their food. Your pet's diet is listed in the Pet Details screen.

EXCHANGING SKILLS

Training has two facets. Hunters teach pets abilities and learn abilities from their pets. Many pets naturally have abilities. Learn these by watching your pet perform. This usually takes a short while before you gain the ability in the Beast Training menu. Once you know the ability, it's possible to teach the ability to any pet you acquire (with the aforementioned restrictions).

It's essential to tame pets beyond your primary beast for gaining extra abilities. To keep up with abilities, you have to constantly tame higher-level beasts, learn their abilities, and teach them to your pet. A creature without abilities is like a Hunter without a pet.

CHOOSING YOUR PROFESSION

Crafting your own armor is a solid choice. Skinning and Leatherworking keep you from being out of date with armor as you can keep low-level items replaced with higher-level items. If you skin everything you can, you'll also have leather left over for friends or to sell at the Auction House.

For a Gun Hunter, Engineering is another choice (also paired with Mining). Being able to craft your own gun helps keep your second most important item (your pet being most important) up-to-date. Engineering also allows you to craft your own bullets. This can save you a great deal of money throughout your career. Having Bombs and some of the gadgets that Engineering gives you offers even more options during combat.

The secondary trades of Fishing and Cooking should not be taken for granted. With as much food as pets eat (they eat far more than Hunters), having a cost-effective supply can be invaluable. A side benefit is that you also gain higher-quality food, for when it is needed.

CLASS ABILITIES

Hunters, like casters, use Mana for their special attacks. These abilities either do extra Damage, hinder the enemy's abilities, protect the Hunter, or help the Hunter's Pet. Mana can be raised by items and recovers fastest when you are out of combat.

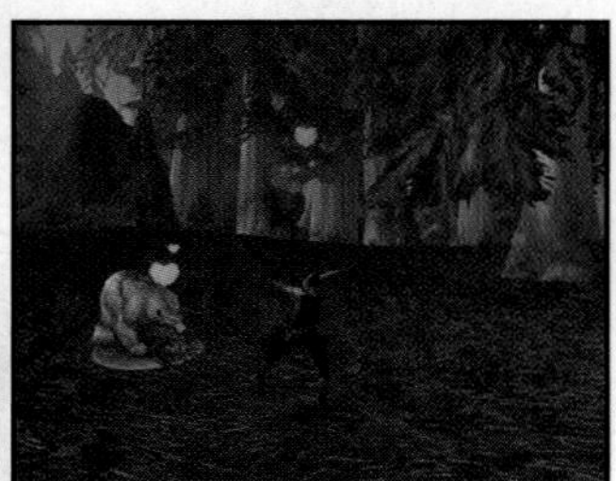

Hunters and their pets both get abilities. The tables below reflect both types of abilities.

ABILITY	RANK	LEVEL	TYPE
Autoshot	N/A	1	Ranged Combat
Raptor Strike	1	1	Outdoorsmanship
Aspect of the Monkey	N/A	4	Beast Mastery
Serpent Sting	1	4	Ranged Combat
Arcane Shot	1	6	Ranged Combat
Hunter's Mark	1	6	Ranged Combat
Concussive Shot	1	8	Ranged Combat
Parry	N/A	8	Outdoorsmanship
Raptor Strike	2	8	Outdoorsmanship
Aspect of the Hawk	1	10	Beast Mastery
Beast Training	N/A	10	Beast Mastery
Feed Pet	N/A	10	Beast Mastery
Revive Pet	N/A	10	Beast Mastery
Serpent Sting	2	10	Ranged Combat
Tame Beast	N/A	10	Beast Mastery
Arcane Shot	2	12	Ranged Combat
Mend Pet	1	12	Beast Mastery
Wing Clip	1	12	Outdoorsmanship
Eagle Eye	N/A	14	Beast Mastery
Eyes of the Beast	N/A	14	Beast Mastery
Scare Beast	1	14	Beast Mastery
Immolation Trap	1	16	Outdoorsmanship
Raptor Strike	3	16	Outdoorsmanship
Aspect of the Hawk	2	18	Beast Mastery
Mongoose Bite	1	18	Outdoorsmanship
Multi-Shot	1	18	Ranged Combat
Serpent Sting	3	18	Ranged Combat
Arcane Shot	3	20	Ranged Combat
Aspect of the Cheetah	N/A	20	Beast Mastery
Concussive Shot	2	20	Ranged Combat
Disengage	1	20	Outdoorsmanship
Dual Wield	N/A	20	Outdoorsmanship
Freezing Trap	1	20	Outdoorsmanship
Mend Pet	2	20	Beast Mastery
Hunter's Mark	2	22	Ranged Combat
Scorpid Sting	1	22	Ranged Combat
Beast Lore	N/A	24	Beast Mastery
Glimpse of Instincts	N/A	24	Beast Mastery
Raptor Strike	4	24	Outdoorsmanship
Immolation Trap	2	26	Outdoorsmanship
Rapid Fire	N/A	26	Ranged Combat
Serpent Sting	4	26	Ranged Combat
Arcane Shot	4	28	Ranged Combat
Aspect of the Hawk	3	28	Beast Mastery
Frost Trap	N/A	28	Outdoorsmanship
Mend Pet	3	28	Beast Mastery
Aspect of the Beast	N/A	30	Beast Mastery
Concussive Shot	3	30	Ranged Combat
Feign Death	N/A	30	Outdoorsmanship
Mongoose Bite	2	30	Outdoorsmanship
Multi-Shot	2	30	Ranged Combat
Scare Beast	2	30	Beast Mastery
Flare		32	Ranged Combat

ABILITY	RANK	LEVEL	TYPE
Raptor Strike	5	32	Outdoorsmanship
Scorpid Sting	2	32	Ranged Combat
Disengage	1	34	Outdoorsmanship
Explosive Trap	1	34	Outdoorsmanship
Serpent Sting	5	34	Ranged Combat
Arcane Shot	5	36	Ranged Combat
Immolation Trap	3	36	Outdoorsmanship
Mend Pet	3	36	Beast Mastery
Viper Sting	1	36	Ranged Combat
Aspect of the Hawk	4	38	Beast Mastery
Wing Clip	2	38	Outdoorsmanship
Aspect of the Pack	N/A	40	Beast Mastery
Concussive Shot	4	40	Ranged Combat
Freezing Trap	2	40	Outdoorsmanship
Hunter's Mark	3	40	Ranged Combat
Mail	N/A	40	Outdoorsmanship
Raptor Strike	6	40	Outdoorsmanship
Volley	1	40	Ranged Combat
Multi-Shot	3	42	Ranged Combat
Scorpid Sting	3	42	Ranged Combat
Serpent Sting	6	42	Ranged Combat
Arcane Shot	6	44	Ranged Combat
Explosive Trap	2	44	Outdoorsmanship
Mend Pet	4	44	Beast Mastery
Mongoose Bite	3	44	Outdoorsmanship
Immolation Trap	4	46	Outdoorsmanship
Scare Beast	3	46	Beast Mastery
Viper Sting	2	46	Ranged Combat
Aspect of the Hawk	5	48	Beast Mastery
Disengage	3	48	Outdoorsmanship
Raptor Strike	7	48	Outdoorsmanship
Concussive Shot	5	50	Ranged Combat
Serpent Sting	7	50	Ranged Combat
Volley	2	50	Ranged Combat
Arcane Shot	7	52	Ranged Combat
Mend Pet	6	52	Beast Mastery
Scorpid Sting	4	52	Ranged Combat
Explosive Trap	3	54	Outdoorsmanship
Multi-Shot	4	54	Ranged Combat
Immolation Trap	5	56	Outdoorsmanship
Raptor Strike	8	56	Outdoorsmanship
Viper Sting	3	56	Ranged Combat
Aspect of the Hawk	6	58	Beast Mastery
Hunter's Mark	4	58	Ranged Combat
Mongoose Bite	4	58	Outdoorsmanship
Serpent Sting	8	58	Ranged Combat
Volley	3	58	Ranged Combat
Arcane Shot	8	60	Ranged Combat
Concussive Shot	6	60	Ranged Combat
Freezing Trap	3	60	Outdoorsmanship
Mend Pet	7	60	Beast Mastery
Wing Clip	3	60	Outdoorsmanship

KEEPING YOUR ABILITIES ORGANIZED

The Hunter gets a great number of abilities; they have abilities in ranged combat, melee combat, and pet abilities. Organizing these abilities in the quickbars makes it easier to change between ranged combat and melee combat.

Pets have their own quickbar and ranged abilities should be on another quickbar. Melee abilities should be on yet a separate quickbar with Aspects. Having abilities that affect your pet (Feeding, Taming, etc.) on another quickbar keeps everything organized and easy to find.

Setting up your quickbars as you level in this way keeps them relatively static for the rest of your career keeps you from having to relearn which hotkeys are for which abilities.

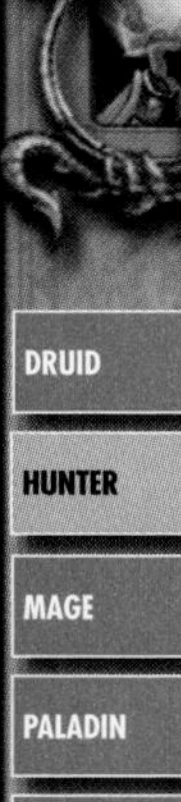

BEAST MASTERY

This line controls your abilities that modify you, your group, and your pets. Aspects control the various attribute bonuses that you receive, and only one of these can be active at the same time. Other abilities in this line serve to gather pets, control the behavior of beasts, and protect them while under your care.

ASPECT OF THE BEAST

RANK	LEVEL	MANA	RANGE	CASTING TIME	COOLDOWN	COST TO TRAIN	EFFECT
N/A	30	50		IC		80	The hunter takes on the aspects of a beast, sharing any detection abilities with her pet, becoming untrackable and able to track beasts.

ASPECT OF THE CHEETAH

RANK	LEVEL	MANA	RANGE	CASTING TIME	COOLDOWN	COST TO TRAIN	EFFECT
N/A	20	40		IC		29	The hunter takes on the aspects of the cheetah, increasing movement speed by 20%. If the hunter takes damage, he will be dazed for 4 sec. Only one Aspect can be active at a time.

ASPECT OF THE HAWK

RANK	LEVEL	MANA	RANGE	CASTING TIME	COOLDOWN	COST TO TRAIN	EFFECT
1	10	20		IC		3	The hunter takes on the aspects of the hawk, increasing Ranged Attack Power by 20. Only one Aspect can be active at a time.
2	18	35		IC		29	The hunter takes on the aspects of a hawk, increasing Ranged Attack Power by 35. Only one Aspect can be active at a time.
3	28	50		IC		81	The hunter takes on the aspects of the hawk, increasing Ranged Attack Power by 50. Only one Aspect can be active at a time.
4	38	70		IC		2 30	The hunter takes on the aspects of a hawk, increasing Ranged Attack Power by 70. Only one Aspect can be active at a time.
5	48	90		IC		4 20	The hunter takes on the aspects of a hawk, increasing Ranged Attack Power by 90. Only one aspect can be active at a time.
6	58	110		IC		5 30	The hunter takes on the aspects of a hawk, increasing Ranged Attack powers by 110. Only one Aspect can be active at a time.

ASPECT OF THE MONKEY

RANK	LEVEL	MANA	RANGE	CASTING TIME	COOLDOWN	COST TO TRAIN	EFFECT
N/A	4	20		IC		50	The hunter takes on the aspects of a monkey, increasing chance to dodge by 8%. Only one aspect can be active at a time.

ASPECT OF THE PACK

RANK	LEVEL	MANA	RANGE	CASTING TIME	COOLDOWN	COST TO TRAIN	EFFECT
N/A	40	100		IC		1 60	The hunter and her group take on the aspects of a pack of cheetahs, increasing movement speed by 20%. If a pack member takes damage, they will be dazed for 4 sec. Only one Aspect can be active at a time.

BEAST LORE

RANK	LEVEL	MANA	RANGE	CASTING TIME	COOLDOWN	COST TO TRAIN	EFFECT
N/A	24	40	40 yd	IC		71	Gather information about the target beast. The tooltip will display damage, health, armor, any special resistances and diet.

BEAST TRAINING

RANK	LEVEL	MANA	RANGE	CASTING TIME	COOLDOWN	COST TO TRAIN	EFFECT
N/A	10					10	Lets the Hunter train his pet with various abilities that he has learned.

EAGLE EYE

RANK	LEVEL	MANA	RANGE	CASTING TIME	COOLDOWN	COST TO TRAIN	EFFECT
N/A	14	25	50000 yd	IC		12	Zooms in the Hunter's vision.

EYES OF THE BEAST

RANK	LEVEL	MANA	RANGE	CASTING TIME	COOLDOWN	COST TO TRAIN	EFFECT
N/A	14	20	40 yd	3 sec		12	Take direct control of your pet and see through its eyes for 1 min.

FEED PET

RANK	LEVEL	MANA	RANGE	CASTING TIME	COOLDOWN	COST TO TRAIN	EFFECT
N/A	10		10 yd	IC		3	Feed your pet the selected item. Feeding your pet increases happiness. Using food close to the Pet's level will have a better result.

GLIMPSE OF INSTINCTS

RANK	LEVEL	MANA	RANGE	CASTING TIME	COOLDOWN	COST TO TRAIN	EFFECT
N/A	24	50		IC		71	Share your pet's senses, gaining any detection or tracking abilities for 30 sec.

MEND PET

RANK	LEVEL	MANA	RANGE	CASTING TIME	COOLDOWN	COST TO TRAIN	EFFECT
1	12	50	20 yd	IC		8	Heals your pet 20 health every second while you focus. Lasts 5 sec.
2	20	90	20 yd	IC		29	Heals your pet 38 health every second while you focus. Lasts 5 sec.
3	28	155	20 yd	IC		81	Heals your pet 68 health every second while you focus. Lasts 5 sec.
3	36	225	20 yd	IC		1 50	Heals your pet 103 health every second while you focus. Lasts 5 sec.
4	44	300	20 yd	IC		2 50	Heals your pet 142 health every second while you focus. Lasts 5 sec.
6	52	385	20 yd	IC		5 30	Heals your pet 189 health every second while you focus. Lasts 5 sec.
7	60	480	20 yd	IC		4 70	Heals your pet 245 health every second while you focus. Lasts 5 sec.

REVIVE PET

RANK	LEVEL	MANA	RANGE	CASTING TIME	COOLDOWN	COST TO TRAIN	EFFECT
N/A	10	499		10 sec		3	Revive your pet, returning it to life with 15% of its health.

SCARE BEAST

RANK	LEVEL	MANA	RANGE	CASTING TIME	COOLDOWN	COST TO TRAIN	EFFECT
1	14	35	10 yd	1.5 sec	30 sec	12	Scares a beast, causing it to run in fear for up to 10 sec. Damage caused may interrupt the effect. Only one beast can be feared at a time.
2	30	50	10 yd	1.5 sec	30 sec	80	Scares a beast, causing it to run in fear for up to 15 sec. Damage caused may interrupt the effect. Only one beast can be feared at a time.
3	46	75	10 yd	1.5 sec	30 sec	3 70	Scares a beast, causing it to run in fear for up to 20 sec. Damage caused may interrupt the effect. Only one beast can be feared at a time.

TAME BEAST

RANK	LEVEL	MANA	RANGE	CASTING TIME	COOLDOWN	COST TO TRAIN	EFFECT
N/A	10	299	30 yd	IC		3	Begins taming a beast to be your companion. Your armor is greatly reduced while you focus on taming the beast for 20sec. If you lose the beast's attention for any reason, the taming process will fail. Once tamed, the beast will be very unhappy and disloyal. Try feeding the pet immediately to make it happy.

OUTDOORSMANSHIP

Outdoorsmanship covers the traps and other tricks that Hunters use to disable and thwart enemies.

DISENGAGE

RANK	LEVEL	MANA	RANGE	CASTING TIME	COOLDOWN	COST TO TRAIN	EFFECT
1	20	50	10 yd	IC		29 ●	Attempts to disengage from the target, reducing threat. Cancels combat.
2	34	100	10 yd	IC		1 ● 80 ●	Attempts to disengage from the target, reducing threat. Cancels combat. More effective than Disengage (Rank 1).
3	48	150	10 yd	IC		4 ● 20 ●	Attempts to disengage from the target, reducing threat. Cancels combat. More effective than Disengage (Rank 2).

DUAL WIELD

RANK	LEVEL	MANA	RANGE	CASTING TIME	COOLDOWN	COST TO TRAIN	EFFECT
N/A	20					23 ●	Allows one-hand and off-hand weapons to be equipped in the off-hand.

EXPLOSIVE TRAP

RANK	LEVEL	MANA	RANGE	CASTING TIME	COOLDOWN	COST TO TRAIN	EFFECT
1	34	275		IC	15 sec	1 ● 80 ●	Place a fire trap that explodes when an enemy approaches, causing 100 to 130 fire damage and burning all enemies for 150 additional Fire damage over 20 sec to all within 10 yards. Trap will exist for 1 min. Traps can only be placed when out of combat. Only one trap can be active at a time.
2	44	395		IC	15 sec	2 ● 50 ●	Place a fire trap that explodes when an enemy approaches causing 139 to 187 Fire damage and burning all enemies for 240 additional Fire damage over 20 sec to all within 10 yards. Trap will exist for 1 min. Traps can only be placed when out of combat. Only one trap can be active at a time.
3	54	520		IC	15 sec	5 ● 80 ●	Place a fire trap that explodes when an enemy approaches causing 201 to 257 Fire damage and burning all enemies for 330 additional Fire damage over 20 sec to all within 10 yards. Trap will exist for 1 min. Traps can only be placed when out of combat. Only one trap can be active at a time.

FEIGN DEATH

RANK	LEVEL	MANA	RANGE	CASTING TIME	COOLDOWN	COST TO TRAIN	EFFECT
N/A	30	80		IC	10 min	80 ●	Feign death which may trick enemies into ignoring you. Lasts up to 5 min, but resurrection penalties are applied when the effect ends.

FREEZING TRAP

RANK	LEVEL	MANA	RANGE	CASTING TIME	COOLDOWN	COST TO TRAIN	EFFECT
1	20	50		IC	15 sec	29 ●	Place a frost trap that freezes the first enemy that approaches, preventing all action for up to 10 sec. Any damage caused will break the ice. Trap will exist for 1 min. Traps can only be placed when out of combat. Only one trap can be active at a time.
2	40	75		IC	15 sec	1 ● 60 ●	Place a frost trap that freezes the first enemy to approach, preventing all action for up to over 15 sec. Any damage caused will break the ice. Trap will exist for 1 min. Traps can only be placed when out of combat. Only one trap can be active at a time.
3	60	100		IC	15 sec	4 ● 70 ●	Place a frost trap that freezes the first enemy to approach, preventing all action for up to over 20 sec. Any damage caused will break the ice. Trap will exist for 1 min. Traps can only be placed when out of combat. Only one trap can be active at a time.

FROST TRAP

RANK	LEVEL	MANA	RANGE	CASTING TIME	COOLDOWN	COST TO TRAIN	EFFECT
N/A	28	60		IC	15 sec	81 ●	Place a frost trap that creates an ice slick around itself when the first enemy approaches it. All enemies within 10 yards will be slowed to 40% of their normal movement speed. Trap will exist for 1 min. Traps can only be placed when out of combat. Only one trap can be active at a time.

IMMOLATION TRAP

RANK	LEVEL	MANA	RANGE	CASTING TIME	COOLDOWN	COST TO TRAIN	EFFECT
1	16	50		IC	15 sec	18 ●	Place a fire trap that will burn the first enemy to approach for 105 fire damage over 15 sec. Trap will exist for 1 min. Traps can only be placed when out of combat. Only one trap can be active at a time.
2	26	90		IC	15 sec	90 ●	Place a fire trap that will burn the first enemy to approach for 215 fire damage over 15 sec. Trap will exist for 1 min. Traps can only be placed when out of combat. Only one trap can be active at a time.
3	36	135		IC	15 sec	1 ● 50 ●	Place a fire trap that will burn the first enemy to approach for 340 Fire damage over 15 sec. Trap will exist for 1 min. Traps can only be placed when out of combat. Only one trap can be active at a time.
4	46	190		IC	15 sec	3 ● 70 ●	Place a fire trap that will burn the first enemy to approach for 510 Fire damage over 15 sec. Trap will exist for 1 min. Traps can only be placed when out of combat. Only one trap can be active at a time.
5	56	245		IC	15 sec	6 ● 40 ●	Place a fire trap that will burn the first enemy to approach for 690 Fire damage over 15 sec. Trap will exist for 1 min. Traps can only be placed when out of combat. Only one trap can be active at a time.

MAIL

RANK	LEVEL	MANA	RANGE	CASTING TIME	COOLDOWN	COST TO TRAIN	EFFECT
N/A	40					1 ● 30 ●	--

MONGOOSE BITE

RANK	LEVEL	MANA	RANGE	CASTING TIME	COOLDOWN	COST TO TRAIN	EFFECT
1	18	25	10 yd	IC	5 sec	18 ●	Counterattack the enemy for 20 damage. Can only be performed after you dodge.
2	30	35	10 yd	IC	5 sec	80 ●	Counterattack the enemy for 40 damage. Can only be performed after you dodge.
3	44	45	10 yd	IC	5 sec	2 ● 50 ●	Counterattack the enemy for 65 damage. Can only be performed after you dodge.
4	58	60	10 yd	IC	5 sec	5 ● 30 ●	Counterattack the enemy for 95 damage. Can only be performed after you dodge.

PARRY

RANK	LEVEL	MANA	RANGE	CASTING TIME	COOLDOWN	COST TO TRAIN	EFFECT
N/A	8					2	Gives a chance to parry enemy melee attacks.

RAPTOR STRIKE

RANK	LEVEL	MANA	RANGE	CASTING TIME	COOLDOWN	COST TO TRAIN	EFFECT
1	1	15	5 yd	IC	6 sec		A strong attack that increases melee damage by 5.
2	8	25	5 yd	IC	6 sec	2	A strong attack that increases melee damage by 11.
3	16	35	5 yd	IC	6 sec	18	A strong attack that increases melee damage by 21.
4	24	45	5 yd	IC	6 sec	71	A strong attack that increases melee damage by 34.
5	32	55	5 yd	IC	6 sec	1 50	A strong attack that increases melee damage by 50.
6	40	70	5 yd	IC	6 sec	1 60	A strong attack that increases melee damage by 80.
7	48	85	5 yd	IC	6 sec	4 20	A strong attack that increases melee damage by 110.
8	56	100	5 yd	IC	6 sec	6 40	A strong attack that increases melee damage by 140.

WING CLIP

RANK	LEVEL	MANA	RANGE	CASTING TIME	COOLDOWN	COST TO TRAIN	EFFECT
1	12	40	10 yd	IC		8	Inflicts 5 damage and reduces the enemy target's movement speed to 50% of normal for 10 sec.
2	38	60	10 yd	IC		2 30	Inflicts 25 damage and reduces the enemy target's movement speed to 50% of normal for 10 sec.
3	60	80	10 yd	IC		4 70	Inflicts 50 damage and reduces the enemy target's movement speed to 50% of normal for 10 sec.

RANGED COMBAT

Ranged Combat is the primary field for a Hunter's DPS. These abilities allow Hunters to hit at range with greater strength and abilities.

ARCANE SHOT

RANK	LEVEL	MANA	RANGE	CASTING TIME	COOLDOWN	COST TO TRAIN	EFFECT
1	6	25	8-35 yd	IC	6 sec	1	An Instant shot that causes 13 Arcane Damage
2	12	35	8-35 yd	IC	6 sec	8	An Instant shot that causes 21 Arcane Damage
3	20	50	8-35 yd	IC	6 sec	29	An instant shot that causes 33 Arcane damage.
4	28	80	8-35 yd	IC	6 sec	81	An instant shot that causes 59 Arcane damage.
5	36	105	8-35 yd	IC	6 sec	1 50	An instant shot that causes 83 Arcane damage.
6	44	135	8-35 yd	IC	6 sec	2 50	An instant shot that causes 115 Arcane damage.
7	52	160	8-35 yd	IC	6 sec	5 30	An instant shot that causes 145 Arcane damage.
8	60	190	8-35 yd	IC	6 sec	4 70	An instant shot that causes 183 Arcane damage.

AUTOSHOT

RANK	LEVEL	MANA	RANGE	CASTING TIME	COOLDOWN	COST TO TRAIN	EFFECT
N/A	1	0	35	4 sec		No Cost	Automatically shoots the target until cancelled. Requires Ranged Weapon.

CONCUSSIVE SHOT

RANK	LEVEL	MANA	RANGE	CASTING TIME	COOLDOWN	COST TO TRAIN	EFFECT
1	8	25	8-35 yd	IC	10 sec	2	Dazes the target, slowing movement speed to 50% of normal for 3 sec and causes additional threat.
2	20	40	8-35 yd	IC	11 sec	20	Dazes the target, slowing movement speed to 50% of normal for 3 sec and causes additional threat. More effective then Concussive Shot (Rank 1)
3	30	60	8-35 yd	IC	12 sec	80	Dazes the target, slowing movement speed to 50% of normal for 3 sec and causes additional threat. More effective then Concussive Shot (Rank 2)
4	40	80	8-35 yd	IC	10 sec	1 60	Dazes the target, slowing movement speed to 50% of normal for 3 sec and causes additional threat. More effective then Concussive Shot (Rank 3)
5	50	105	8-35 yd	IC	10 sec	3 50	Dazes the target, slowing movement speed to 50% of normal for 3 sec and causes additional threat. More effective then Concussive Shot (Rank 4)
6	60	130	8-35 yd	IC	10 sec	4 70	Dazes the target, slowing movement speed to 50% of normal for 3 sec and causes additional threat. More effective then Concussive Shot (Rank 5)

FLARE

RANK	LEVEL	MANA	RANGE	CASTING TIME	COOLDOWN	COST TO TRAIN	EFFECT
N/A	32	50	30 yd	IC	15 sec	1 50	Exposes all hidden and invisible enemies within 30 yards of the targeted area for 30 sec.

HUNTER'S MARK

RANK	LEVEL	MANA	RANGE	CASTING TIME	COOLDOWN	COST TO TRAIN	EFFECT
1	6	15	100 yd	IC		1	Places the Hunter's Mark on the target, increasing the Ranged Attack Power of all attackers against that target by 20. In addition, the target of this ability can always be seen by the hunter whether it stealths or turns invisible. The target also appears on the mini-map. Lasts for 10 mins.
2	22	30	100 yd	IC		56	Places the Hunter's Mark on the target, increasing the Ranged Attack Power of all attackers against that target by 45. In addition, the target of this ability can always be seen by the hunter whether it stealths or turns invisible. The target also appears on the mini-map. Lasts for 10 mins.
3	40	45	100 yd	IC		1 60	Places the Hunter's Mark on the target, increasing the Ranged Attack Power of all attackers against that target by 75. In addition, the target of this ability can always be seen by the hunter whether it stealths or turns invisible. The target so appears on the mini-map. Lasts for 10 mins.
4	58	60	100 yd	IC		5 30	Places the Hunter's Mark on the target, increasing the Ranged Attack Power of all attackers against that target by 110. In addition, the target of this ability can always be seen by the hunter whether it stealths or turns invisible. The target so appears on the mini-map. Lasts for 10 mins.

MULTI-SHOT

RANK	LEVEL	MANA	RANGE	CASTING TIME	COOLDOWN	COST TO TRAIN	EFFECT
1	18	100	8-35 yd	IC	10 sec	29	Fires several missiles, hitting 3 targets.
2	30	140	8-35 yd	IC	10 sec	80	Fires several missiles, hitting 3 targets for an additional 40 damage.
3	42	175	8-35 yd	IC	10 sec	3	Fires several missiles, hitting 3 targets for an additional 80 damage.
4	54	210	8-35 yd	IC	10 sec	5 80	Fires several missiles, hitting 3 targets for an additional 120 damage.

RAPID FIRE

RANK	LEVEL	MANA	RANGE	CASTING TIME	COOLDOWN	COST TO TRAIN	EFFECT
N/A	26	100		IC	5 min.	90	Decreases shot time by 40% for 15 sec.

SCORPID STING

RANK	LEVEL	MANA	RANGE	CASTING TIME	COOLDOWN	COST TO TRAIN	EFFECT
1	22	70	8-35 yd	IC		56	Stings the target, reducing Strength and Agility by 20 for 20 sec. Only one Sting per Hunter can be active on any one target.
2	32	90	8-35 yd	IC		1 50	Stings the target, reducing Strength and Agility by 29 for 20 sec. Only one Sting per Hunter can be active on any one target.
3	42	125	8-35 yd	IC		3	Stings the target, reducing Strength and Agility by 45 for 20 sec. Only one Sting per Hunter can be active on any one target.
4	52	165	8-35 yd	IC		5 30	Stings the target, reducing Strength and Agility by 68 for 20 sec. Only one Sting per Hunter can be active on any one target.

SERPENT STING

RANK	LEVEL	MANA	RANGE	CASTING TIME	COOLDOWN	COST TO TRAIN	EFFECT
1	4	15	8-35 yd	IC		50	Stings the target, causing 20 Nature damage over 15 sec. Only one Sting per Hunter can be active on any one target.
2	10	30	8-35 yd	IC		3	Stings the target, causing 40 Nature damage over 15 sec. Only one Sting per Hunter can be active on any one target.
3	18	50	8-35 yd	IC		29	Stings the target, causing 80 Nature damage over 15 sec. Only one Sting per Hunter can be active on any one target.
4	26	80	8-35 yd	IC		90	Stings the target, causing 140 Nature damage over 15 sec. Only one Sting per Hunter can be active on any one target.
5	34	115	8-35 yd	IC		1 80	Stings the target, causing 210 Nature damage over 15 sec. Only one Sting per Hunter can be active on any one target.
6	42	150	8-35 yd	IC		3	Stings the target, causing 290 Nature damage over 15 sec. Only one Sting per Hunter can be active on any one target.
7	50	190	8-35 yd	IC		3 50	Stings the target, causing 385 Nature damage over 15 sec. Only one Sting per Hunter can be active on any one target.
8	58	230	8-35 yd	IC		5 30	Stings the target, causing 490 Nature damage over 15 sec. Only one Sting per Hunter can be active on any one target.

VIPER STING

RANKRANKLEVEL		MANA	RANGE	CASTING TIME	COOLDOWN	COST TO TRAIN	EFFECT
1	36	135	8-35 yd	IC		1 50	Stings the target, draining 616 mana over 8 sec. Only one Sting per Hunter can be active on any one target.
2	46	175	8-35 yd	IC		3 70	Stings the target, draining 848 mana over 8 sec. Only one Sting per Hunter can be active on any one target.
3	56	215	8-35 yd	IC		6 40	Stings the target, draining 1108 mana over 8 sec. Only one Sting per Hunter can be active on any one target.

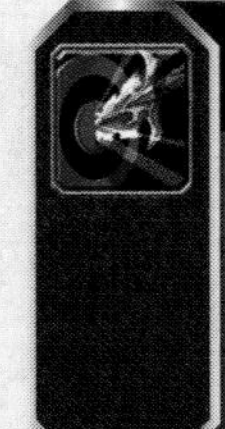

VOLLEY

RANK	LEVEL	MANA	RANGE	CASTING TIME	COOLDOWN	COST TO TRAIN	EFFECT
1	40	350	8-35 yd	IC	1 min.	1 60	Continuously fires a volley of ammo at the target area, causing 40 Arcane damage to enemy targets within 8 yards every second for 6 sec.
2	50	420	8-35 yd	IC	1 min.	3 50	Continuously fires a volley of ammo at the target area, causing 50 Arcane damage to enemy targets within 8 yards every second for 6 sec.
3	58	490	8-35 yd	IC		5 30	Continuously fires a volley of ammo at the target area, causing 60 Arcane damage to enemy targets within 8 yards every second for 6 sec.

MARKSMANSHIP

TALENT NAME	RANKS	PREREQUISITES	EFFECTS
Improved Concussive Shot	5	None	Gives your Concussive Shot a 4% (Per Rank) chance to stun the target for 3 sec.
Efficiency	5	None	Reduces the mana cost of your Shots and Stings by 2% (Per Rank).
Improved Hunter's Mark	5	5 Points in Marksmanship	Increases the Ranged Attack Power bonus of your Hunter's Mark spell by 3% (Per Rank)
Lethal Shots	5	5 Points in Marksmanship	Increases your critical strike chance with ranged weapons by 1% (Per Rank)
Aimed Shot	1	10 Points in Marksmanship	An aimed shot that increases ranged damage by 70.
Improved Arcane Shot	5	10 Points in Marksmanship	Reduces the cooldown of your Arcane Shot by 0.2 sec (Per Rank)
Barrage	2	10 Points in Marksmanship	Increases the damage done by your Multi-Shot and Volley spells by 5% (Per Rank)
Mortal Shots	5	15 Points in Marksmanship	Increases the damage done by your Serpent Sting by 2% (Per Rank)
Improved Serpent Sting	5	5 Points in Lethal Shots, 15 Points in Marksmanship	Increases your ranged weapon critical strike damage bonus by10% (Per Rank)
Scatter Shot	1	20 Points in Marksmanship	A short-range shot that deals 50% weapon damage and confuses the target for 4 sec. Any damage caused will remove the effect.
Hawk Eye	3	20 Points in Marksmanship	Increases the range of your ranged weapons by 2 yards (Per Rank)
Improved Scorpid Sting	3	20 Points in Marksmanship	Reduces the Stamina of targets affected by your Scorpid Sting by 10% of the amount of Strength Reduced (Per Rank)
Ranged Weapon Specialization	5	25 Points in Marksmanship	Increases the damage you deal with ranged weapons by 1% (Per Rank)
Trueshot Aura	1	3 Points in Hawk Eye, 30 Points in Marksmanship	Increases the Ranged and Melee Attack Power of party members within 30 yards by 30.

BEAST MASTERY

TALENT NAME	RANKS	PREREQUISITES	EFFECTS
Improved Aspect of the Hawk	5	None	Increases the Ranged Attack Power bonus of your Aspect of the Hawk by 4% (Per Rank)
Endurance Training	5	None	Increases the Health of your pets by 2% (Per Rank)
Bestial Discipline	2	5 Points in Beast Mastery	Increases the duration of your Eyes of the Beast by 30 sec. (Per Rank)
Improved Aspect of the Monkey	3	5 Points in Beast Mastery	Increases the Dodge bonus of your Aspect of the Monkey by 1% (Per Rank)
Improved Eyes of the Beast	5	5 Points in Beast Mastery	Increases the maximum Focus of your pets by 4% (Per Rank)
Improved Revive Pet	2	10 Points in Beast Mastery	Reduces the casting time of your Revive Pet spell by 2 sec. (Per Rank)
Bestial Swiftness	1	10 Points in Beast Mastery	Increases the outdoor movement speed of your pets by 30%
Unleashed Fury	5	10 Points in Beast Mastery	Increases the damage done by your pets by 2% (Per Rank)
Pathfinding	5	10 Points in Beast Mastery	Increases the speed bonus of your Aspect of the Cheetah and Aspect of the Pack by 1% (Per Rank)
Thick Hide	5	15 Points in Beast Mastery	Increases the Armor rating of your pets by 2% (Per Rank)
Improved Mend Pet	2	15 Points in Beast Mastery	Increases the amount healed by your Mend Pet spell by 5% (Per Rank)
Ferocity	5	15 Points in Beast Mastery	Increases the critical strike chance of your pets by 3% (Per Rank)
Intimidation	1	20 Points in Beast Mastery	Increases the threat caused by your pet by 50% for 10 sec.
Frenzy	5	5 Points in Ferocity, 25 Points in Beast Mastery	Gives your pet a 20% chance (Per Rank) to gain a 30% attack spead increase for 8 sec. After dealing a critical strike.
Spirit Bound	1	2 Points in Improved Mend Pet, 30 Points in Beast Mastery	Every time your pet strikes an enemy, you gain 20 health

SURVIVAL

TALENT NAME	RANKS	PREREQUISITES	EFFECTS
Precision	5	None	Increases your chance to hit with melee weapons by 1% (Per Rank)
Improved Raptor Strike	5	None	Reduces the cooldown of your Raptor Strike by 0.2 sec. (Per Rank)
Entrapment	5	5 Points in Survival	Gives your Immolation Trap, Frost Trap and Explosive Trap an increased chance to entrap the target, preventing them from moving for 5 sec. - Progression 5%/10%/15%/25%/30%
Lightning Reflexes	3	5 Points in Survival	Increases your Dodge chance by 1% (Per Rank)
Improved Wing Clip	5	5 Points in Survival	Gives your Wing Clip ability a 4% chance (Per Rank) to immobilize the target for 5 sec.
Improved Immolation Trap	5	10 Points in Survival	Increases the damage done by your Immolation Trap by 3% (Per Rank)
Improved Mongoose Bite	5	3 Points in Lightning Reflexes, 10 Points in Survival	Increases the damage done by your Mongoose Bite ability by 4% (Per Rank)
Deterrence	1	10 Points in Survival	When activated, increases your Dodge and Parry chance by 25% for 10 sec.
Improved Freezing Trap	3	15 Points in Survival	Increases the duration of your Freezing Trap by 2 sec. (Per Rank)
Improved Disengage	2	15 Points in Survival	Increases the amount of Threat reduced by your Disengage ability by 10% (Per Rank)
Deflection	5	1 Point in Deterrence, 15 Points in Survival	Increases your Parry chance by 1% (Per Rank)
Improved Frost Trap	2	20 Points in Survival	Increases the duration of your Frost Trap's movement slowing effect by 1.5 sec. (Per Rank)
Savage Strikes	5	20 Points in Survival	Increases your critical strike chance with melee weapons by 1% (Per Rank)
Counterattack	1	1 Point in Deterrence, 20 Points in Survival	A strike that becomes active after parrying an opponent's attack. This attack deals 40 damage and immobilizes the target for 5 sec. Counterattack cannot be blocked, dodged, or parried.
Improved Explosive Trap	2	25 Points in Survival	Increases the initial damage done by your Explosive Trap by 30% (Per Rank)
Melee Specialization	5	25 Points in Survival	Increases the damage you deal with melee weapons by 1% (Per Rank)
Lacerate	1	1 Point in Savage Strikes, 30 Points in Survival	Wounds the target causing them to bleed for 77 damage over 21 sec.

DRUID
HUNTER
MAGE
PALADIN
PRIEST
ROGUE
SHAMAN
WARLOCK
WARRIOR

STRATEGIES

Hunter strategies involve keeping the target where you want it. Wing Clip a target to slow its movement, back off and unload into it until your foe gets into melee again (then finish it off with some short, melee work). Or, have your pet attack first and Growl a couple times and unload into the target with reckless abandon (healing your pet if it needs help).

GENERAL TIPS

Bringing the enemy down as quickly as possible is what the Hunter is made for. Cast Aspect of the Hawk and use Hunter's Mark on the target. This doesn't draw aggro, but increases all ranged damage dealt to your target. Send your pet in to attack since it takes a moment to get there. Begin the fight by using Serpent Sting so the DoT will run its full course. With your pet attacking and holding the enemy's attention, keep shooting until the enemy is dead.

If the battle is to be a long one, use Serpent Sting early. It's a free attack that causes damage over time. Have your pet using Growl whenever it has enough health and you have aggro. This helps keep the enemy at range.

Change to Aspect of the Monkey when the enemy closes to melee. This increases your dodge rate and gives you more opportunities to use Mongoose Bite. When the enemy runs, just wait for it to run a few steps and hit it with Arcane Shot.

Get comfortable moving from melee to range and back again. Knowing when to move into and out of melee combat helps you keep your health and mana high while still doing damage.

Mana only regenerates when you haven't cast for a short while. Keeping this in mind, cast your battle spells in bunches to allow regeneration between and during fights. Casting Arcane Shot every time it recharges increases your damage, but leaves you low on mana at the end of the fight. Only unload your mana supply if a fight is dangerous and threatening you (or your pet's) life.

PULLING LIKE A PRO

The Hunter has many tools that aid in pulling. Using Hunter's Mark lets everyone know which enemy you intend to shoot. This helps a great deal when coordinating attacks with other party members.

Set a trap before you pull. Freeze Traps Root a single enemy giving you and your party more time to act. Hitting another with Wing Clip before running back to the party slows it and removes a second enemy from the initial charge. If only one enemy is coming, consider using the Immolation Trap. Once aggro is consolidated, just drag the enemy over the trap for added damage.

Bringing one enemy to the party at a time makes managing aggro easier and keeps everyone on the same target. This can turn even the most stressful areas into organized fighting.

Part of pulling is avoiding unintended pulls. Many enemies run for help when they get low on health. You or your party may not be prepared for a second wave if the first has not been dealt with. Have Wing Clip ready to slow fleeing enemies and Arcane Shot to bring them down before they make things worse.

A FRIEND IN NEED IS A FRIEND INDEED

Your pet is quite useful in many circumstances. If you're engaged in melee and low on health, have your pet Growl until the enemy turns to your pet. Back off and open fire. Helping you decide how to fight an enemy is a strong ability of your pet.

Having your pet hold unexpected adds is a useful as well. This keeps the casters of the party safe without putting undo pressure on the tank or healer. Your pet can't hold them forever and will need help before long, but it buys the group time. Party members can't see your pet's health bar without stopping what they are doing and clicking on your pet. You are your pet's voice. Warn the party if your pet needs help or a heal.

Cower and Mend Pet can save your pet's life. When your pet is taking too much damage and you need to take aggro, have the pet use Cower while you use Mend Pet. This lowers your pet's Threat, heals your pet, and generates Threat for you, pulling the monster away. Mend Pet is a HoT, so don't wait until the last minute to use it.

The ultimate sacrifice is one your pet is willing to make. If things go horribly wrong when soloing or in a group, your pet can make a difference. Use Growl until your pet has aggro, then run away. Your pet will hold the enemy until you get far enough away to make it out. You can use Revive Pet to see your friend again and it's faster and less frustrating then running back to your corpse. True, your beloved pet may not be as happy when you resummon him, but who would be after such an event.

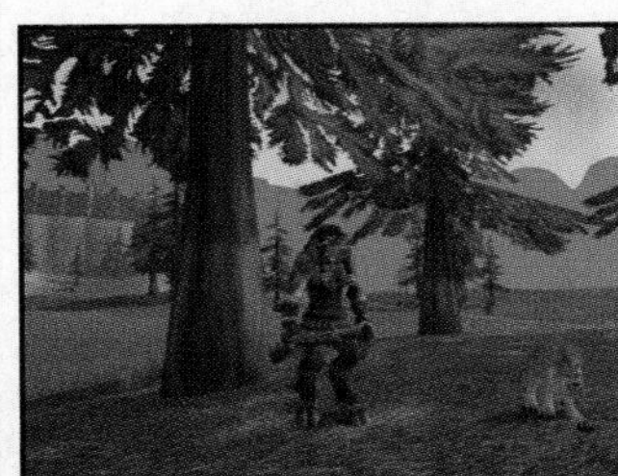

PETS NEED BUFFS

If you're grouping, make sure to request a Stamina buff for your pet as well. The extra hit points go a long way during battles and pets are often overlooked during the pre-hunt buffing session.

TIMED ABILITIES

Timed abilities are useful when everything starts going wrong or simply to save frustration. Rapid Fire allows you to reduce your firing time by a significant amount for 15 seconds. If something needs to die quickly, use this to increase your DPS substantially.

Feign Death is most useful when soloing. Because it only saves you and you can't Resurrect other party members, it doesn't save much time. Use Feign Death when your pet is dead and you are losing the fight. The enemy may think it killed you and return home feeling victorious. Wait until the enemy has left, get up and rest. You mimic the effect of death so closely that upon waking, Resurrection Sickness affects you. Take the time to recover, Revive your pet, and continue.

When the party gets multiple targets and the leader calls for "AOEs," Volley is your friend. Volley fires continuous shots into the targeted area for six seconds. These damage all enemies in the area. This should be used cautiously as any enemies that haven't been taunted or damaged will focus on you.

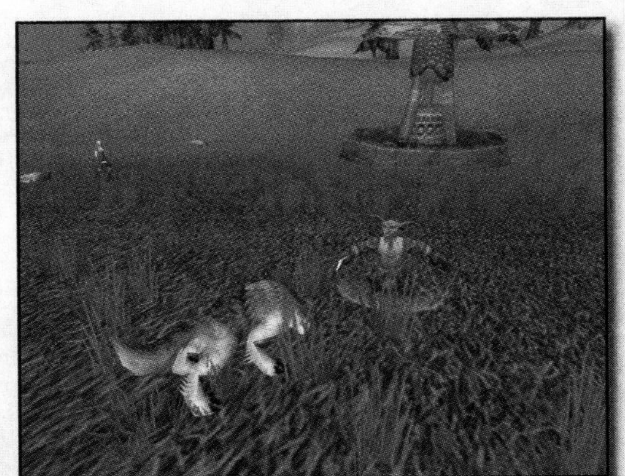

MAGE

Mages are the ranged, damage-dealers in *World of Warcraft*. These masters of elemental fire and cold have studies the arcane arts for years, dedicating themselves to the destruction of their enemies. Though fragile in melee combat and have poor health, Mages are able to make themselves known on the field of battle. No class fully rivals the range of a Mage, and the number of AoE spells available to this class is daunting by itself. Join the ranks of the mystic elite if you want to dish out the damage (and run like mad if it's not enough).

THE TRUE THREAT

The cries of battle carried over the forest like a melody. I felt so many precious souls being brought again into the world: new, fresh, dedicated to a different cause. The right concoction of plague, violence, and temporary unpleasantness was always a good way to make people see things in a new light.

Waiting for our Warriors to bring the ranks of Human invaders together, I poked my head up (ever so slightly) and saw that the time was approaching. The Humans and several of their Alliance vermin were closing in for the kill; that is how they saw it at least. Visibly, our Warriors below were in a bad place. As they feigned disorder and went into a rout, I readied the true attack. Looking over at Ishnaron, my Warlock ally, I nodded. He knew what to do.

We were over the hill in an instant. As we rolled into position, clacking across the cold ground, a Void Walker came through the shadows and laid into the Humans, distracting them. Our Warriors turned and began to ffight with renewed vigor, and I summoned the power of frost to begin a mighty blizzard. The Humans called out to one another, lost in the sudden storm. Perhaps they were praying for warmth and life to return to them. Ishnaron answered one such prayer.

Running into the center of the Human party, he threw forth his arms and opened a gateway into a foul and horrible place (even by my perception); flames and fury came through the gateway, spilling around the Warlock in a storm of destruction. Though Ishnaron was injured by the heat, his potions and equipment were tailored to protect him. The same could not be said for the Humans, who fell like chaff in the wind.

I laughed for the victory at hand. The Humans had again underestimated the Forsaken; perhaps they would learn. Perhaps.

INTRODUCTION TO PLAYING THE MAGE

Mages love to bring damage to the table, whether to individual targets or entire groups. Using a massive amount of mana, this is a class with burst damage galore. Though you may think of yourself as a bit of a glass cannon (all damage and no defense), the truth is that Mages can survive quite well as long as they temper their casting. Using spells at the right time can make all the difference between unsurvivable aggro and staying in the clear.

The first defense of a Mage comes through range. Mage spells are cast at long range and can be very deadly. Beyond the range itself, there is some use to the delay between a successful cast and the spell's impact for bolts. Most long-range Mage spells are bolts, so there is time to start casting a second spell before your first bolt impacts (against monsters this is a great boon, though players rarely let you have such free rein). Cast at maximum range for almost everything you do and allow as much reaction time as possible when seeing if there are adds.

Speaking of adds, Mages have an ability that they love while soloing and while playing in groups: Polymorph, for combat control. Turning enemies into sheep prevents them from doing any damage to you or your friends for a considerable duration. Though it takes a short cast and fair mana to accomplish this, using combat control makes all the difference in big fights (allowing tanks more time to grab aggro, healers more room to use mana-efficient spells, etc.).

What else do Mages get besides long-range bolts and combat control? They get a powerful Intellect buff (for themselves and allies, meaning that all casters are quickly your friends). Mages can summon free food and drink so that everyone in the party recovers quickly during downtime. Later on, Mages summon Mana Gems (for fast mana recovery during combat), and there are the AoE spells mentioned earlier.

Using AoE magic, Mages are able to do horrendous damage to large groups without delay. This gives a major place to Mages in large-scale PvP and when fighting in groups tailored for besting monsters with AoE tactics.

RACES AND STARTING ATTRIBUTES

RACE	STRENGTH	STAMINA	AGILITY	INTELLECT	SPIRIT
Gnome	20	21	22	24	22
Human	21	22	21	23	22
Troll	21	22	20	22	24
Undead	20	23	19	23	24

ATTRIBUTES APPLIED

Strength	Modest Improvements to Melee Damage
Stamina	Higher Hit Points
Agility	Minorly Increases Chance to Dodge
Intellecwt	More Mana, Raise Critical Hit with Spells
Spirit	Improves Hit Point/Mana Regeneration

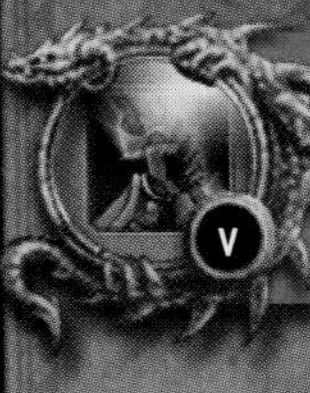

ITEMS AND EQUIPMENT

Equipment doesn't make the same difference for Mages that it does for Warriors; after all, you are wearing cloth garments, not mithril plates! However, the attributes on various armor pieces allow for customization of great importance, so Mages do care about their equipment very much (just for different reasons than a heavy tank).

Instead of looking for DPS, weapon speed, improved Armor Rating, and similar values, Mages try to collect items that improve Intellect, Spirit, and sometimes Stamina. This is done to keep the casters casting as much as possible. Spirit equipment won't help your total casting or critical hits, but it improves mana regeneration. Intellect is a heavy attribute because critical hits and maximum mana come from that stat. This creates a difficult choice for many casters. "Would I rather cast a little and fight often or cast a ton and have longer downtime?"

Mixed equipment choices are very good if you aren't sure which type of fighting you plan on doing from day to day. Spirit and Intellect mix well together, and you lose little from either side from getting the most of these. Intellect-heavy gear raises your potential damage (because of the criticals) and helps to keep you chain-casting in longer fights. Intellect-heavy builds are very good for Instances and PvP fights. Spirit builds aren't as common, but they are very efficient for fighting lighter enemies out in the field (reducing downtime incredibly). Use high Spirit to keep things rolling while farming experience and money.

Equipment that gives bonuses to damage change in popularity over time, as they are subject to a number of rebalances. Ultimately, this form of equipment is going to raise a character's maximum damage while sacrificing the ability to cast for as long or regain mana as effectively. For very short PvP battles, gear that improved damage may be a fine choice. However, in PvE field fighting and Instances, it seems that Spirit and Intellect offer greater rewards.

One thing that is nice to have for adding some damage while regaining mana is a quality wand. Use these during rest periods in a fight to keep doing some damage without breaking the flow of mana regen.

CHOOSING YOUR PROFESSION

Mages have a number of solid Profession choices. Taking Tailoring is useful for creating modest gear earlier on in your career (to help with staying up to date before tackling tougher enemies). Because Tailoring doesn't have a Gathering Profession, you are free to take Enchanting with it. Between the two, you are able to make and enchant your own items.

Herbalism and Alchemy allow Mages to create a number of potions to boost their spell damage and resistance against enemy spells. Combined with Fishing (to gain certain rare ingredients), this is a solid combo, especially for Mages who plan on farming their own high-level gear from Instances.

Cooking isn't the most useful skill to grab on the side; Mages have such immediate access to food and drink that making additional sustenance isn't as impressive. First Aid may help a group, but it isn't as useful in the all-or-nothing battles that Mages often face alone, and it competes with Tailoring for cloth drops. As usual, your character may benefit from taking whatever you wish, but Mages certainly don't need to rely heavily on peripheral skills.

ABILITY	RANK	LEVEL	TYPE
Arcane Intellect	1	1	Arcane Spells
Fireball	1	1	Fire Spells
Frost Armor	1	1	Frost Spells
Conjure Water	1	4	Arcane Spells
Frostbolt	1	4	Frost Spells
Conjure Food	1	6	Arcane Spells
Fire Blast	1	6	Fire Spells
Fireball	2	6	Fire Spells
Arcane Missiles	1	8	Arcane Spells
Frostbolt	2	8	Frost Spells
Polymorph	1	8	Arcane Spells
Conjure Water	2	10	Arcane Spells
Frost Armor	2	10	Frost Spells
Frost Nova	1	10	Frost Spells
Conjure Food	2	12	Arcane Spells
Dampen Magic	1	12	Arcane Spells
Fireball	3	12	Fire Spells
Slow Fall	N/A	12	Arcane Spells
Arcane Explosion	1	14	Arcane Spells
Arcane Intellect	2	14	Arcane Spells
Fire Blast	2	14	Fire Spells
Frostbolt	3	14	Frost Spells
Arcane Missiles	2	16	Arcane Spells
Detect Magic	N/A	16	Arcane Spells
Flamestrike	1	16	Fire Spells
Amplify Magic	1	18	Arcane Spells
Fireball	2	18	Fire Spells
Remove Curse	1	18	Arcane Spells
Blink	1	20	Arcane Spells
Blizzard	1	20	Frost Spells
Conjure Water	3	20	Arcane Spells
Fire Ward	1	20	Fire Spells
Frost Armor	3	20	Frost Spells
Frostbolt	4	20	Frost Spells
Mana Shield	1	20	Arcane Spells
Polymorph	2	20	Arcane Spells
Teleport: Ironforge	N/A	20	Portal Magic
Teleport: Orgrimmar	N/A	20	Portal Magic
Teleport: Stormwind	N/A	20	Portal Magic
Teleport: Undericty	N/A	20	Portal Magic
Arcane Explosion	2	22	Arcane Spells
Conjure Food	3	22	Arcane Spells
Fire Blast	3	22	Fire Spells
Frost Ward	1	22	Frost Spells
Scorch	1	22	Fire Spells
Arcane Missiles	3	24	Arcane Spells
Counterspell	1	24	Arcane Spells
Dampen Magic	2	24	Arcane Spells
Fireball	5	24	Fire Spells
Flamestrike	2	24	Fire Spells
Cone of Cold	1	26	Frost Spells
Frost Nova	2	26	Frost Spells
Frostbolt	5	26	Frost Spells
Arcane Intellect	3	28	Arcane Spells
Blizzard	2	28	Frost Spells
Conjure Mana Agate	N/A	28	Arcane Spells
Mana Shield	2	28	Arcane Spells
Scorch	2	28	Fire Spells
Amplify Magic	2	30	Arcane Spells
Arcane Explosion	3	30	Arcane Spells
Conjure Water	4	30	Arcane Spells
Fire Blast	4	30	Fire Spells
Fire Ward	2	30	Fire Spells
Fireball	6	30	Fire Spells
Ice Armor	1	30	Frost Spells
Pyroblast	2	30	Fire Spells
Teleport Thunder Bluff	N/A	30	Portal Magic
Teleport: Darnassus	N/A	30	Portal Magic
Arcane Missiles	4	32	Arcane Spells
Conjure Food	4	32	Arcane Spells
Flamestrike	3	32	Fire Spells
Frost Ward	2	32	Frost Spells
Frostbolt	6	32	Frost Spells
Cone of Cold	2	34	Frost Spells
Scorch	3	34	Fire Spells
Arcane Intellect	4	36	Arcane Spells
Blast Wave	2	36	Fire Spells
Blizzard	3	36	Frost Spells
Dampen Magic	3	36	Arcane Spells
Fireball	7	36	Fire Spells
Mana Shield	3	36	Arcane Spells
Pyroblast	3	36	Fire Spells
Arcane Explosion	4	38	Arcane Spells
Conjure Mana Jade	N/A	38	Arcane Spells
Fire Blast	5	38	Fire Spells
Frostbolt	7	38	Frost Spells
Arcane Missiles	5	40	Arcane Spells
Conjure Water	5	40	Arcane Spells
Fire Ward	3	40	Fire Spells
Flamestrike	4	40	Fire Spells
Frost Nova	3	40	Frost Spells
Ice Armor	2	40	Frost Spells
Polymorph	3	40	Arcane Spells
Portal: Ironforge	N/A	40	Portal Magic
Portal: Orgrimmar	N/A	40	Portal Magic
Portal: Stormwind	N/A	40	Portal Magic
Portal: Undercity	N/A	40	Portal Magic
Scorch	4	40	Fire Spells
Amplify Magic	3	42	Arcane Spells
Cone of Cold	3	42	Frost Spells
Conjure Food	5	42	Arcane Spells
Fireball	8	42	Fire Spells
Frost Ward	3	42	Frost Spells
Pyroblast	4	42	Fire Spells
Blast Wave	3	44	Fire Spells
Blizzard	4	44	Frost Spells
Frostbolt	8	44	Frost Spells
Mana Shield	4	44	Arcane Spells
Arcane Explosion	5	46	Arcane Spells
Fire Blast	6	46	Fire Spells
Ice Barrier	2	46	Frost Spells
Scorch	5	46	Fire Spells
Arcane Missiles	6	48	Arcane Spells
Conjure Mana Citrine	N/A	48	Arcane Spells
Dampen Magic	4	48	Arcane Spells
Fireball	9	48	Fire Spells
Flamestrike	5	48	Fire Spells
Ice Barrier	3	48	Frost Spells
Pyroblast	5	48	Fire Spells
Cone of Cold	4	50	Frost Spells
Conjure Water	6	50	Arcane Spells
Fire Ward	4	50	Fire Spells
Frostbolt	9	50	Frost Spells
Ice Armor	3	50	Frost Spells
Portal: Darnassus	N/A	50	Portal Magic
Portal: Thunder Bluff	N/A	50	Portal Magic
Blast Wave	4	52	Fire Spells
Blizzard	5	52	Frost Spells
Conjure Food	6	52	Arcane Spells
Frost Ward	4	52	Frost Spells
Ice Barrier	4	52	Frost Spells
Mana Shield	5	52	Arcane Spells
Scorch	6	52	Fire Spells
Amplify Magic	4	54	Arcane Spells
Arcane Explosion	6	54	Arcane Spells
Fire Blast	7	54	Fire Spells
Fireball	10	54	Fire Spells
Frost Nova	4	54	Frost Spells
Ice Barrier	5	54	Frost Spells
Pyroblast	6	54	Fire Spells
Arcane Intellect	5	56	Arcane Spells
Arcane Missiles	7	56	Arcane Spells
Flamestrike	6	56	Fire Spells
Frostbolt	10	56	Frost Spells
Cone of Cold	5	58	Frost Spells
Conjure Mana Ruby	N/A	58	Arcane Spells
Ice Barrier	6	58	Frost Spells
Scorch	7	58	Fire Spells
Blast Wave	5	60	Fire Spells
Blast Wave	6	60	Fire Spells
Blizzard	6	60	Frost Spells
Dampen Magic	5	60	Arcane Spells
Fire Ward	5	60	Fire Spells
Fireball	11	60	Fire Spells
Ice Armor	4	60	Frost Spells
Ice Barrier	7	60	Frost Spells
Mana Shield	6	60	Arcane Spells
Polymorph	4	60	Arcane Spells
Pyroblast	7	60	Fire Spells
Pyroblast	8	60	Fire Spells

The three types of magic available to this class are Arcane, Fire, and Frost. Arcane spells offer many Instant abilities, useful burst damage, and quite a bit of aggro generation. The Arcane line is also the shortest in range, with some important spells being almost point-blank.

Fire magic has the best range and uses bolts to pulverize enemies. Damage is high from Fire magic, and the costs are often quite high as well.

Frost magic is fairly efficient at lower levels and it has many status effects to frustrate enemies. Snares and Roots are available to Mages who rely heavily on the Frost Line and back it up with Talents.

ARCANE SPELLS

One of your few direct defenses is found in the Arcane Line. Once Mages get Mana Shield, it's possible to use this spell to survive direct onslaughts for a short period. Make sure to get out of harm's way quickly, since these don't last forever.

Polymorph is in this spell line (for combat control), and beyond that there are many fast or Instant-cast spells with fair damage but only moderate efficiency.

Never forget to use Arcane Intellect, as this is a class-defining buff (raising Intellect for you or allied targets).

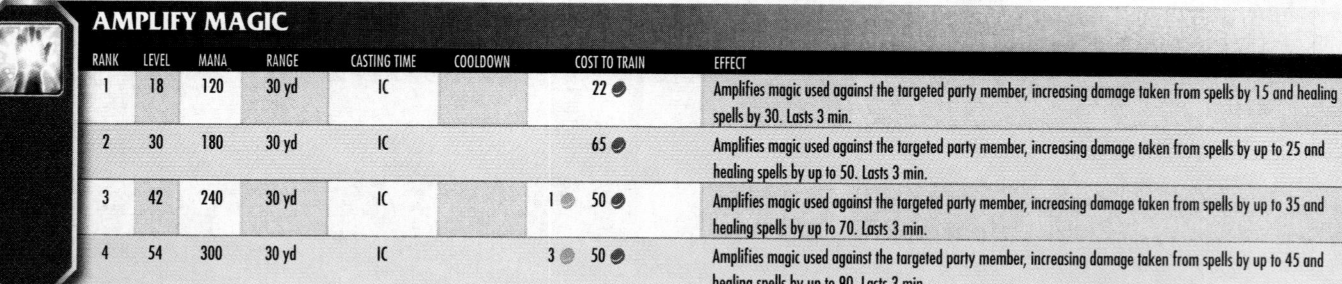

AMPLIFY MAGIC

RANK	LEVEL	MANA	RANGE	CASTING TIME	COOLDOWN	COST TO TRAIN	EFFECT
1	18	120	30 yd	IC		22	Amplifies magic used against the targeted party member, increasing damage taken from spells by 15 and healing spells by 30. Lasts 3 min.
2	30	180	30 yd	IC		65	Amplifies magic used against the targeted party member, increasing damage taken from spells by up to 25 and healing spells by up to 50. Lasts 3 min.
3	42	240	30 yd	IC		1 50	Amplifies magic used against the targeted party member, increasing damage taken from spells by up to 35 and healing spells by up to 70. Lasts 3 min.
4	54	300	30 yd	IC		3 50	Amplifies magic used against the targeted party member, increasing damage taken from spells by up to 45 and healing spells by up to 90. Lasts 3 min.

ARCANE EXPLOSION

RANK	LEVEL	MANA	RANGE	CASTING TIME	COOLDOWN	COST TO TRAIN	EFFECT
1	14	75	01.5 sec			9	Causes an explosion of arcane magic around the caster, causing 36 to 41 Arcane damage to all targets within 10 yards.
2	22	120	01.5 sec			42	Causes an explosion of arcane magic around the caster, causing 62 to 68 Arcane damage to all targets within 10 yards.
3	30	185	01.5 sec			65	Causes an explosion of arcane magic around the caster, causing 97 to 105 Arcane damage to all targets within 10 yards.
4	38	250	01.5 sec			1 20	Causes an explosion of arcane magic around the caster, causing 139 to 151 Arcane damage to all targets within 10 yards.
5	46	315	01.5 sec			3 70	Causes an explosion of arcane magic around the caster, causing 195 to 212 Arcane damage to all targets within 10 yards.
6	54	390	01.5 sec			3 50	Causes an explosion of arcane magic around the caster, causing 255 to 276 Arcane damage to all targets within 10 yards.

ARCANE INTELLECT

RANK	LEVEL	MANA	RANGE	CASTING TIME	COOLDOWN	COST TO TRAIN	EFFECT
1	1	60	30 yd	IC		10	Increase the target's Intellect by 2 for 30 min.
2	14	185	30 yd	IC		9	Increases the target's Intellect by 7 for 30 min.
3	28	520	30 yd	IC		81	Increases the target's Intellect by 15 for 30 min.
4	36	945	30 yd	IC		1 50	Increases the target's Intellect by 22 for 30 min.
5	56	1510	30 yd	IC		4 80	Increases the target's Intellect by 31 for 30 min.

ARCANE MISSILES

RANK	LEVEL	MANA	RANGE	CASTING TIME	COOLDOWN	COST TO TRAIN	EFFECT
1	8	85	30 yd	IC		2	Launches Arcane Missiles at the enemy, causing 24 Arcane damage each second for 3 sec.
2	16	140	30 yd	IC		18	Launches Arcane Missiles at the enemy, causing 36 Arcane damage each second for 4 sec.
3	24	235	30 yd	IC		53	Launches Arcane Missiles at the enemy, causing 56 Arcane damage each second for 5 sec.
4	32	320	30 yd	IC		1 10	Launches Arcane Missiles at the enemy, causing 83 Arcane damage each second for 5 sec.
5	40	410	30 yd	IC		1 10	Launches Arcane Missiles at the enemy, causing 115 Arcane damage each second for 5 sec.
6	48	500	30 yd	IC		3 10	Launches Arcane Missiles at the enemy, causing 159 Arcane damage each second for 5 sec.
7	56	595	30 yd	IC		4 80	Launches Arcane Missiles at the enemy, causing 202 Arcane damage each second for 5 sec.

BLINK

RANK	LEVEL	MANA	RANGE	CASTING TIME	COOLDOWN	COST TO TRAIN	EFFECT
1	20	75	Self	IC	1 min	19	Teleports the caster 20 yards forward, unless something is in the way. Also frees the caster from any bonds.

CONJURE FOOD

RANK	LEVEL	MANA	RANGE	CASTING TIME	COOLDOWN	COST TO TRAIN	EFFECT
1	6	60	Inventory	3 sec		1	Conjures 2 muffins, providing the mage and his allies with something to eat. Conjured items disappear if logged out for more than 15 minutes.
2	12	105	Inventory	3 sec		6	Conjures 2 loaves of bread, providing the mage and his allies with something to eat. Conjured items disappear if logged out for more than 15 minutes.
3	22	180	Inventory	3 sec		42	Conjures 2 loaves of rye, providing the mage and his allies with something to eat. Conjured items disappear if logged out for more than 15 minutes.
4	32	285	Inventory	3 sec		1 10	Conjures 2 loaves of pumpernickel, providing the mage and his allies with something to eat. Conjured items disappear if logged out for more than 15 minutes.
5	42	420	Inventory	3 sec		1 50	Conjures 2 loaves of sourdough, providing the mage and his allies with something to eat. Conjured items disappear if logged out for more than 15 minutes.
6	52	585	Inventory	3 sec		4	Conjures 2 sweet rolls, providing the mage and his allies with something to eat. Conjured items disappear if logged out for more than 15 minutes.

CONJURE MANA AGATE

RANK	LEVEL	MANA	RANGE	CASTING TIME	COOLDOWN	COST TO TRAIN	EFFECT
N/A	28	530	Inventory	3 sec		81	Conjures a Mana Agate that can be used to instantly restore 375 to 425 mana. Conjured items disappear if logged out for more than 15 minutes.

CONJURE MANA CITRINE

RANK	LEVEL	MANA	RANGE	CASTING TIME	COOLDOWN	COST TO TRAIN	EFFECT
N/A	48	1130	Inventory	3 sec		3 10	Conjures a Mana Citrine that can be used to instantly restore 775 to 925 mana. Conjured items disappear if logged out for more than 15 minutes.

CONJURE MANA JADE

RANK	LEVEL	MANA	RANGE	CASTING TIME	COOLDOWN	COST TO TRAIN	EFFECT
N/A	38	800	Inventory	3 sec		1 20	Conjures a Mana Jade that can be used to instantly restore 550 to 650 mana. Conjured items disappear if logged out for more than 15 minutes.

CONJURE MANA RUBY

RANK	LEVEL	MANA	RANGE	CASTING TIME	COOLDOWN	COST TO TRAIN	EFFECT
N/A	58	1470	Inventory	3 sec		5 30	Conjures a Mana Ruby that can be used to instantly restore 1000 to 1200 mana. Conjured items disappear if logged out for more than 15 minutes.

CONJURE WATER

RANK	LEVEL	MANA	RANGE	CASTING TIME	COOLDOWN	COST TO TRAIN	EFFECT
1	4	60	Inventory	3 sec		50	Conjures 2 (+2 every level) bottles of water, providing the mage and his allies with something to drink. Conjured items disappear if logged out for more than 15 minutes.
2	10	105	Inventory	3 sec		4	Conjures 2 bottles of fresh water, providing the mage and his allies with something to drink. Conjured items disappear if logged out for more than 15 minutes.
3	20	190	Inventory	3 sec		19	Conjures 2 bottles of purified water, providing the mage and his allies with something to drink. Conjured items disappear if logged out for more than 15 minutes.
4	30	285	Inventory	3 sec		65	Conjures 2 bottles of spring water, providing the mage and his allies with something to drink. Conjured items disappear if logged out for more than 15 minutes.
5	40	420	Inventory	3 sec		1 10	Conjures 2 bottles of mineral water, providing the mage and his allies with something to drink. Conjured items disappear if logged out for more than 15 minutes.
6	50	585	Inventory	3 sec		2 80	Conjures 2 bottles of sparkling water, providing the mage and his allies with something to drink. Conjured items disappear if logged out for more than 15 minutes.

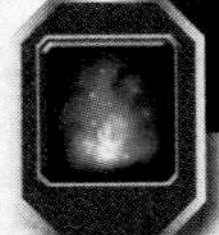

COUNTERSPELL

RANK	LEVEL	MANA	RANGE	CASTING TIME	COOLDOWN	COST TO TRAIN	EFFECT
1	24	100	30 yd	IC	30 sec	53	Counters the enemy's spell, preventing him from casting that spell again for 15 sec. Generates a high amount of threat.

DAMPEN MAGIC

RANK	LEVEL	MANA	RANGE	CASTING TIME	COOLDOWN	COST TO TRAIN	EFFECT
1	12	80	30 yd	IC		6	Dampens magic used against the targeted party member, decreasing damage taken from spells by 10 and healing spells by 20. Lasts 3 min.
2	24	140	30 yd	IC		53	Dampens magic used against the targeted party member, decreasing damage taken from spells by up to 20 and healing spells by up to 40. Lasts 3 min.
3	36	200	30 yd	IC		1 50	Dampens magic used against the targeted party member, decreasing damage taken from spells by up to 30 and healing spells by up to 60. Lasts 3 min.
4	48	260	30 yd	IC		3 10	Dampens magic used against the targeted party member, decreasing damage taken from spells by up to 40 and healing spells by up to 80. Lasts 3 min.
5	60	320	30 yd	IC		3 90	Dampens magic used against the targeted party member, decreasing damage taken from spells by up to 50 and healing spells by up to 100. Lasts 3 min.

DETECT MAGIC

RANK	LEVEL	MANA	RANGE	CASTING TIME	COOLDOWN	COST TO TRAIN	EFFECT
N/A	16	35	40 yd	IC		18	Detects beneficial magic effects on the target for 2 min.

MANA SHIELD

RANK	LEVEL	MANA	RANGE	CASTING TIME	COOLDOWN	COST TO TRAIN	EFFECT
1	20	40	Self	IC		19	Absorbs 120 physical damage, draining mana instead. Drains 2.0 mana per damage absorbed. Lasts 1 min.
2	28	60	Self	IC		81	Absorbs 210 physical damage, draining mana instead. Drains 2.0 mana per damage absorbed. Lasts 1 min.
3	36	80	Self	IC		1 50	Absorbs 300 physical damage, draining mana instead. Drains 2.0 mana per damage absorbed. Lasts 1 min.
4	44	100	Self	IC		3 30	Absorbs 390 physical damage, draining mana instead. Drains 2.0 mana per damage absorbed. Lasts 1 min.
5	52	120	Self	IC		4	Absorbs 480 physical damage, draining mana instead. Drains 2.0 mana per damage absorbed. Lasts 1 min.
6	60	140	Self	IC		3 90	Absorbs 570 physical damage, draining mana instead. Drains 2.0 mana per damage absorbed. Lasts 1 min.

POLYMORPH

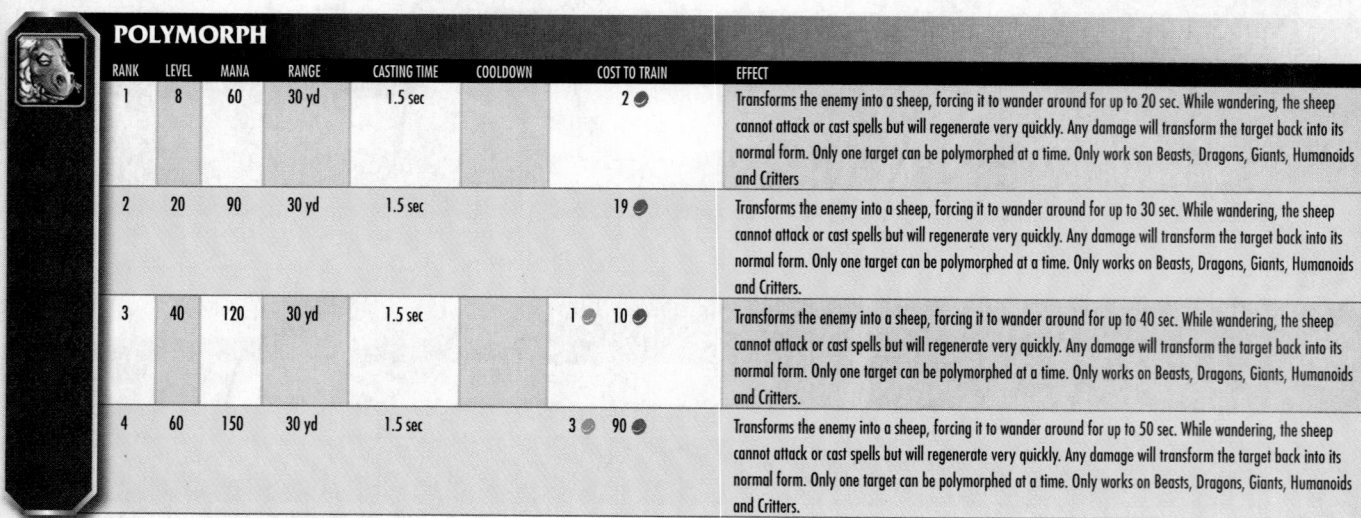

RANK	LEVEL	MANA	RANGE	CASTING TIME	COOLDOWN	COST TO TRAIN	EFFECT
1	8	60	30 yd	1.5 sec		2	Transforms the enemy into a sheep, forcing it to wander around for up to 20 sec. While wandering, the sheep cannot attack or cast spells but will regenerate very quickly. Any damage will transform the target back into its normal form. Only one target can be polymorphed at a time. Only work son Beasts, Dragons, Giants, Humanoids and Critters
2	20	90	30 yd	1.5 sec		19	Transforms the enemy into a sheep, forcing it to wander around for up to 30 sec. While wandering, the sheep cannot attack or cast spells but will regenerate very quickly. Any damage will transform the target back into its normal form. Only one target can be polymorphed at a time. Only works on Beasts, Dragons, Giants, Humanoids and Critters.
3	40	120	30 yd	1.5 sec		1 10	Transforms the enemy into a sheep, forcing it to wander around for up to 40 sec. While wandering, the sheep cannot attack or cast spells but will regenerate very quickly. Any damage will transform the target back into its normal form. Only one target can be polymorphed at a time. Only works on Beasts, Dragons, Giants, Humanoids and Critters.
4	60	150	30 yd	1.5 sec		3 90	Transforms the enemy into a sheep, forcing it to wander around for up to 50 sec. While wandering, the sheep cannot attack or cast spells but will regenerate very quickly. Any damage will transform the target back into its normal form. Only one target can be polymorphed at a time. Only works on Beasts, Dragons, Giants, Humanoids and Critters.

SLOW FALL

RANK	LEVEL	MANA	RANGE	CASTING TIME	COOLDOWN	COST TO TRAIN	EFFECT
N/A	12	40	Self	IC		6	Slows falling speed for 30 sec.

FIRE SPELLS

Fire magic has the Fireball spell for long-range bolting, Scorch for fast casting, and Flamestrike for hitting everything in an area. Scorch can be aided considerably by gear that raises Fire damage per spell, but this equipment is hard to come by and lacks high attribute bonuses.

BLAST WAVE

RANK	LEVEL	MANA	RANGE	CASTING TIME	COOLDOWN	COST TO TRAIN	EFFECT
2	36	270	0	IC	45 sec	40	A wave of flame radiates outward from the caster, damaging all enemies caught within the blast for 216 to 259 fire damage, and dazing them for 6 sec.
3	44	355	0	IC	45 sec	80	A wave of flame radiates outward from the caster, damaging all enemies caught within the blast for 296 to 352 fire damage, and dazing them for 6 sec.
4	52	450	0	IC	45 sec	1 10	A wave of flame radiates outward from the caster, damaging all enemies caught within the blast for 389 to 461 fire damage, and dazing them for 6 sec.
5	60	460	0	IC	45 sec	1	A wave of flame radiates outward from the caster, damaging all enemies caught within the blast for 508 to 590 fire damage, and dazing them for 6 sec.
6	60	545	0	IC	45 sec	3 90	A wave of flame radiates outward from the caster, damaging all enemies caught within the blast for 480 to 566 fire damage, and dazing them for 6 sec.

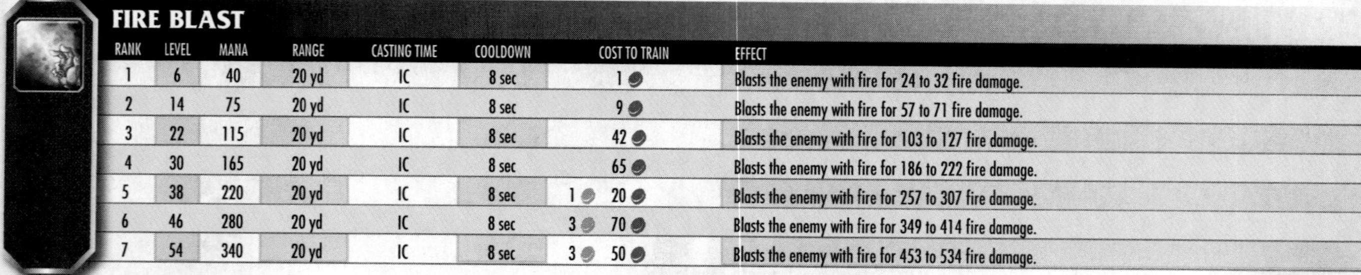

FIRE BLAST

RANK	LEVEL	MANA	RANGE	CASTING TIME	COOLDOWN	COST TO TRAIN	EFFECT
1	6	40	20 yd	IC	8 sec	1	Blasts the enemy with fire for 24 to 32 fire damage.
2	14	75	20 yd	IC	8 sec	9	Blasts the enemy with fire for 57 to 71 fire damage.
3	22	115	20 yd	IC	8 sec	42	Blasts the enemy with fire for 103 to 127 fire damage.
4	30	165	20 yd	IC	8 sec	65	Blasts the enemy with fire for 186 to 222 fire damage.
5	38	220	20 yd	IC	8 sec	1 20	Blasts the enemy with fire for 257 to 307 fire damage.
6	46	280	20 yd	IC	8 sec	3 70	Blasts the enemy with fire for 349 to 414 fire damage.
7	54	340	20 yd	IC	8 sec	3 50	Blasts the enemy with fire for 453 to 534 fire damage.

FIRE WARD

RANK	LEVEL	MANA	RANGE	CASTING TIME	COOLDOWN	COST TO TRAIN	EFFECT
1	20	85	Self	IC	30 sec	42	Absorbs 105 fire damage. Lasts 30 sec.
2	30	135	Self	IC	30 sec	65	Absorbs 185 fire damage. Lasts 30 sec.
3	40	195	Self	IC	30 sec	1 10	Absorbs 300 fire damage. Lasts 30 sec.
4	50	255	Self	IC	30 sec	2 80	Absorbs 430 fire damage. Lasts 30 sec.
5	60	320	Self	IC	30 sec	3 90	Absorbs 585 fire damage. Lasts 30 sec.

FIREBALL

RANK	LEVEL	MANA	RANGE	CASTING TIME	COOLDOWN	COST TO TRAIN	EFFECT
1	1	30	30 yd	1.5 sec		No Cost	Hurls a fiery ball that causes 14 to 22 fire damage and an additional 2 damage over 4 sec.
2	6	45	35 yd	2 sec		1	Hurls a fiery ball that causes 31 to 45 fire damage and an additional 3 damage over 4 sec.
3	12	65	35 yd	2 sec		6	Hurls a fiery ball that causes 55 to 75 fire damage and an additional 6 damage over 6 sec.
2	18	95	35 yd	2.5 sec		22	Hurls a fiery ball that causes 84 to 116 fire damage and an additional 12 damage over 8 sec.
5	24	140	35 yd	3 sec		53	Hurls a fiery ball that causes 139 to 187 fire damage and an additional 20 damage over 8 sec.
6	30	185	35 yd	3 sec		65	Hurls a fiery ball that causes 199 to 265 fire damage and an additional 28 damage over 8 sec.
7	36	220	35 yd	3 sec		1 50	Hurls a fiery ball that causes 255 to 335 fire damage and an additional 32 damage over 8 sec.
8	42	260	35 yd	3 sec		1 50	Hurls a fiery ball that causes 334 to 435 fire damage and an additional 40 damage over 8 sec.
9	48	305	35 yd	3 sec		3 10	Hurls a fiery ball that causes 412 to 531 fire damage and an additional 56 damage over 8 sec.
10	54	350	35 yd	3 sec		3 50	Hurls a fiery ball that causes 499 to 639 fire damage and an additional 64 damage over 8 sec.
11	60	395	35 yd	3 sec		3 90	Hurls a fiery ball that causes 589 to 751 fire damage and an additional 76 damage over 8 sec.

FLAMESTRIKE

RANK	LEVEL	MANA	RANGE	CASTING TIME	COOLDOWN	COST TO TRAIN	EFFECT
1	16	195	30 yd	3 sec		18	Calls down a pillar of fire, burning all enemies within the area for 52 to 68 fire damage and an additional 48 damage over 8 sec.
2	24	330	30 yd	3 sec		53	Calls down a pillar of fire, burning all enemies within the area for 96 to 123 fire damage and an additional 88 damage over 8 sec.
3	32	490	30 yd	3 sec		1 10	Calls down a pillar of fire, burning all enemies within the area for 154 to 192 fire damage and an additional 140 damage over 8 sec.
	4	40	650	30 yd	3 sec	1 10	Calls down a pillar of fire, burning all enemies within the area for 233 to 289 fire damage and an additional 204 damage over 8 sec.
5	48	815	30 yd	3 sec		3 10	Calls down a pillar of fire, burning all enemies within the area for 306 to 377 fire damage and an additional 276 damage over 8 sec.
6	56	990	30 yd	3 sec		4 80	Calls down a pillar of fire, burning all enemies within the area for 394 to 482 fire damage and an additional 356 damage over 8 sec.

PYROBLAST

RANK	LEVEL	MANA	RANGE	CASTING TIME	COOLDOWN	COST TO TRAIN	EFFECT
2	30	195	35 yd	6 sec	1 min	20	Hurls an immense fiery boulder that causes 284 to 360 fire damage and an additional 100 damage over 12 sec.
3	36	240	35 yd	6 sec	1 min	40	Hurls an immense fiery boulder that causes 364 to 459 fire damage and an additional 132 damage over 12 sec.
4	42	285	35 yd	6 sec	1 min	40	Hurls an immense fiery boulder that causes 427 to 541 fire damage and an additional 164 damage over 12 sec.
5	48	335	35 yd	6 sec	1 min	80	Hurls an immense fiery boulder that causes 528 to 663 fire damage and an additional 196 damage over 12 sec.
6	54	385	35 yd	6 sec	1 min	90	Hurls an immense fiery boulder that causes 630 to 787 fire damage and an additional 240 damage over 12 sec.
7	60	440	35 yd	6 sec	1 min	1	Hurls an immense fiery boulder that causes 752 to 934 fire damage and an additional 280 damage over 12 sec.
8	60	440	35 yd	6 sec	1 min	3 90	Hurls an immense fiery boulder that causes 715 to 891 fire damage and an additional 268 damage over 12 sec.

SCORCH

RANK	LEVEL	MANA	RANGE	CASTING TIME	COOLDOWN	COST TO TRAIN	EFFECT
1	22	50	30 yd	1.5 sec		42	Scorch the enemy for 53 to 65 fire damage.
2	28	65	30 yd	1.5 sec		81	Scorch the enemy for 77 to 93 fire damage.
3	34	80	30 yd	1.5 sec		1 80	Scorch the enemy for 101 to 122 fire damage.
4	40	100	30 yd	1.5 sec		1 10	Scorch the enemy for 143 to 170 fire damage.
5	46	115	30 yd	1.5 sec		3 70	Scorch the enemy for 170 to 202 fire damage.
6	52	135	30 yd	1.5 sec		4	Scorch the enemy for 210 to 251 fire damage.
7	58	150	30 yd	1.5 sec		5 30	Scorch the enemy for 245 to 289 fire damage.

FROST SPELLS

Frost magic stays high in efficiency, with a good bolt! When area of effect spells are needed, Cone of Cold does immediate damage with Chill effects, and Blizzard offers more damage with the added bonus of being an Instant. Using Ice Armor prevents enemies from having an easy chase after a fleeing Mage (making it an essential buff).

BLIZZARD

RANK	LEVEL	MANA	RANGE	CASTING TIME	COOLDOWN	COST TO TRAIN	EFFECT
1	20	320	30 yd	IC		19	Ice shards pelt the target area doing 204 damage over 8 sec.
2	28	520	30 yd	IC		81	Ice shards pelt the target area doing 356 damage over 8 sec.
3	36	720	30 yd	IC		1 50	Ice shards pelt the target area doing 524 damage over 8 sec.
4	44	935	30 yd	IC		3 30	Ice shards pelt the target area doing 756 damage over 8 sec.
5	52	1160	30 yd	IC		4	Ice shards pelt the target area doing 988 damage over 8 sec.
6	60	1400	30 yd	IC		3 90	Ice shards pelt the target area doing 1256 damage over 8 sec.

CONE OF COLD

RANK	LEVEL	MANA	RANGE	CASTING TIME	COOLDOWN	COST TO TRAIN	EFFECT
1	26	210	0	IC	10 sec	67	Targets in a cone in front of the caster take 98 to 108 frost damage and are slowed to 50% of normal speed for 8 sec.
2	34	290	0	IC	10 sec	1 80	Targets in a cone in front of the caster take 146 to 160 frost damage and are slowed to 50% of normal speed for 8 sec.
3	42	380	0	IC	10 sec	1 50	Targets in a cone in front of the caster take 213 to 234 frost damage and are slowed to 50% of normal speed for 8 sec.
4	50	465	0	IC	10 sec	2 80	Targets in a cone in front of the caster take 277 to 304 frost damage and are slowed to 50% of normal speed for 8 sec.
5	58	555	0	IC	10 sec	5 30	Targets in a cone in front of the caster take 352 to 383 frost damage and are slowed to 50% of normal speed for 8 sec.

FROST ARMOR

RANK	LEVEL	MANA	RANGE	CASTING TIME	COOLDOWN	COST TO TRAIN	EFFECT
1	1	60	Self	IC		No Cost	Increase armor by 30. If an enemy strikes the caster, they may have their movement slowed by 70% and attacks slowed by 20%. Lasts 30 min.
2	10	125	Self	IC		4	Increases armor by 110. If an enemy strikes the caster, they may have their movement slowed to 70% and attacks slowed by 20%. Lasts 30 min.
3	20	270	Self	IC		19	Increases armor by 200. If an enemy strikes the caster, they may have their movement slowed to 70% and attacks slowed by 20%. Lasts 30 min.

FROST NOVA

RANK	LEVEL	MANA	RANGE	CASTING TIME	COOLDOWN	COST TO TRAIN	EFFECT
1	10	55	0	IC	25 sec	4	Blasts enemies near the caster for 19 to 22 cold damage and freezes them in place for up to 8 sec.
2	26	85	0	IC	25 sec	67	Blasts enemies near the caster for 33 to 37 cold damage and freezes them in place for up to 8 sec.
3	40	115	0	IC	25 sec	1 10	Blasts enemies near the caster for 56 to 62 cold damage and freezes them in place for up to 8 sec.
4	54	145	0	IC	25 sec	3 50	Blasts enemies near the caster for 75 to 83 cold damage and freezes them in place for up to 8 sec.

FROST WARD

RANK	LEVEL	MANA	RANGE	CASTING TIME	COOLDOWN	COST TO TRAIN	EFFECT
1	22	85	Self	IC	30 sec	40	Absorbs 105 frost damage. Lasts 30 sec.
2	32	135	Self	IC	30 sec	1 10	Absorbs 185 frost damage. Lasts 30 sec.
3	42	195	Self	IC	30 sec	1 50	Absorbs 300 frost damage. Lasts 30 sec.
4	52	255	Self	IC	30 sec	4	Absorbs 430 frost damage. Lasts 30 sec.

FROSTBOLT

RANK	LEVEL	MANA	RANGE	CASTING TIME	COOLDOWN	COST TO TRAIN	EFFECT
1	4	25	30 yd	1.5 sec		50	Launches a bolt of frost at the enemy, causing 18 to 20 frost damage and slowing movement speed for 5 sec.
2	8	35	30 yd	1.8 sec		2	Launches a bolt of frost at the enemy, causing 18 to 20 frost damage and slowing movement speed for 5 sec.
3	14	50	30 yd	2.2 sec		9	Launches a bolt of frost at the enemy, causing 51 to 57 frost damage and slowing movement speed for 6 sec.
4	20	65	30 yd	2.6 sec		19	Launches a bolt of frost at the enemy, causing 74 to 82 frost damage and slowing movement speed for 7 sec.
5	26	100	30 yd	3 sec		67	Launches a bolt of frost at the enemy, causing 126 to 138 frost damage and slowing movement speed for 7 sec.
6	32	130	30 yd	3 sec		1 10	Launches a bolt of frost at the enemy, causing 180 to 197 frost damage and slowing movement speed for 8 sec.
7	38	160	30 yd	3 sec		1 20	Launches a bolt of frost at the enemy, causing 227 to 247 frost damage and slowing movement speed for 8 sec.
8	44	195	30 yd	3 sec		3 30	Launches a bolt of frost at the enemy, causing 307 to 332 frost damage and slowing movement speed for 9 sec.
9	50	225	30 yd	3 sec		2 80	Launches a bolt of frost at the enemy, causing 371 to 402 frost damage and slowing movement speed for 9 sec.
10	56	260	30 yd	3 sec		4 80	Launches a bolt of frost at the enemy, causing 450 to 486 frost damage and slowing movement speed for 9 sec.

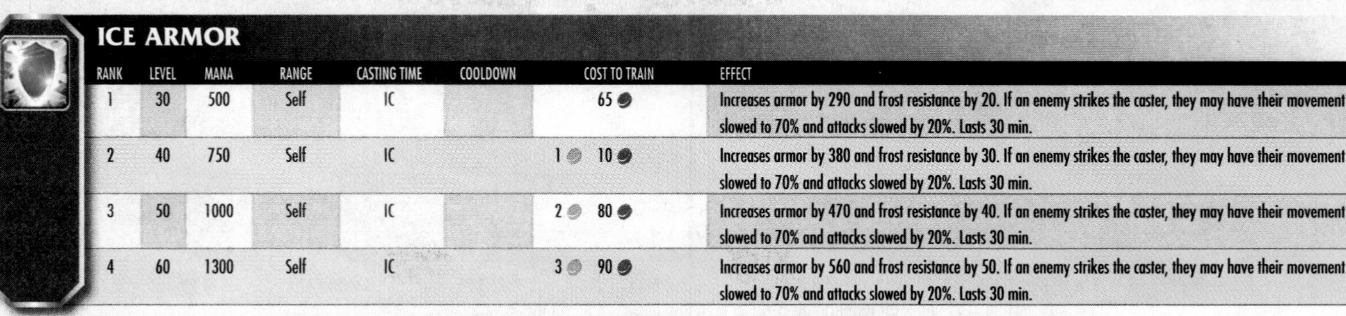

ICE ARMOR

RANK	LEVEL	MANA	RANGE	CASTING TIME	COOLDOWN	COST TO TRAIN	EFFECT
1	30	500	Self	IC		65s	Increases armor by 290 and frost resistance by 20. If an enemy strikes the caster, they may have their movement slowed to 70% and attacks slowed by 20%. Lasts 30 min.
2	40	750	Self	IC		1g 10s	Increases armor by 380 and frost resistance by 30. If an enemy strikes the caster, they may have their movement slowed to 70% and attacks slowed by 20%. Lasts 30 min.
3	50	1000	Self	IC		2g 80s	Increases armor by 470 and frost resistance by 40. If an enemy strikes the caster, they may have their movement slowed to 70% and attacks slowed by 20%. Lasts 30 min.
4	60	1300	Self	IC		3g 90s	Increases armor by 560 and frost resistance by 50. If an enemy strikes the caster, they may have their movement slowed to 70% and attacks slowed by 20%. Lasts 30 min.

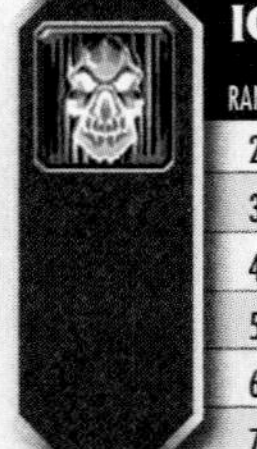

ICE BARRIER

RANK	LEVEL	MANA	RANGE	CASTING TIME	COOLDOWN	COST TO TRAIN	EFFECT
2	46	360	Self	IC	2 min	90s	Instantly shields you, absorbing 568 damage. Lasts 1 min. While the shield holds, spells will not be interrupted.
3	48	370	Self	IC		1g 10s	Instantly shields you, absorbing 571 damage. Lasts 1 min. While the shield holds, spells will not be interrupted.
4	52	420	Self	IC		1g 30s	Instantly shields you, absorbing 700 damage. Lasts 1 min. While the shield holds, spells will not be interrupted.
5	54	435	Self	IC	2 min	3g 10s	Instantly shields you, absorbing 707 damage. Lasts 1 min. While the shield holds, spells will not be interrupted.
6	58	480	Self	IC	2 min	3g 50s	Instantly shields you, absorbing 826 damage. Lasts 1 min. While the shield holds, spells will not be interrupted.
7	60	425	Self	IC	2 min	3g 90s	Instantly shields you, absorbing 848 damage. Lasts 1 min. While the shield holds, spells will not be interrupted.

PORTAL MAGIC

A time-saving feature of the Mages is that they are able to Teleport themselves (and later their group as well) to major cities across Azeroth. This power is gained at Level 20, and it limited to the two central cities of your faction at that time. Later, at Level 30, the more distant capital is added. It's after that that group Teleportation becomes possible.

PORTAL

LOCATION	RANK	LEVEL	MANA	RANGE	CASTING TIME	COOLDOWN	COST TO TRAIN	EFFECT
Darnassus	N/A	50	850	10 yd	10 sec		2g 80s	Creates a portal, teleporting group members that run through it to Darnassus.
Ironforge	N/A	40	850	10 yd	10 sec		1g 10s	Creates a portal, teleporting group members that run through it to Ironforge.
Orgrimmar	N/A	40	850	10 yd	10 sec		1g 10s	Creates a portal, teleporting group members that run through it to Orgrimmar.
Stormwind	N/A	40	850	10 yd	10 sec		1g 10s	Creates a portal, teleporting group members that run through it to Stormwind.
Thunder Bluff	N/A	50	850	10 yd	10 sec		2g 80s	Creates a portal, teleporting group members that run through it to Thunder Bluff.
Undercity	N/A	40	850	10 yd	10 sec		1g 10s	Creates a portal, teleporting group members that run through it to Undercity.

TELEPORT

LOCATION	RANK	LEVEL	MANA	RANGE	CASTING TIME	COOLDOWN	COST TO TRAIN	EFFECT
Darnassus	N/A	30	120	Self	10 sec		80s	Teleports the caster to Darnassus.
Ironforge	N/A	20	120	Self	10 sec		30s	Teleports the caster to Ironforge.
Orgrimmar	N/A	20	120	Self	10 sec		30s	Teleports the caster to Orgrimmar.
Stormwind	N/A	20	120	Self	10 sec		30s	Teleports the caster to Stormwind.
Thunder Bluff	N/A	30	120	Self	10 sec		80s	Teleports the caster to Thunder Bluff.
Undercity	N/A	20	120	Self	10 sec		30s	Teleports the caster to Undercity.

TALENTS

Mages drive into a single Talent line even sooner than most other classes. It's wise to choose your primary line first and focus on that quite heavily until it is completed, then to switch into a secondary Talent line.

Arcane Talents are wonderful for raising Mana efficiency, Damage, and base functionality for the class. With an improved Intellect buff, Presence of Mind (for essentially a massive, Instant cast), and Evocation to renew lost mana, this line has much to offer.

Fire Talents make Mages into even more powerful casters at range (with longer bolts, a chance for Stun, and major damage up front and over time). Chosen often as either a primary or a secondary Talent line, the Fire Talents are extremely functional. Added abilities improve the Fire line's power to bring AoE's into a battle (Blast Wave) or deal huge damage from surprise attacks (Pyroblast).

Frost Talents are there to frustrate and halt enemy advances. Though lacking in the power to immediately bring down enemy troops in the same way, this specialization improves the Chill Effects of almost all Frost magic. Also, Root effects are added to some spells, making it even harder for melee enemies to advance on groups that have Frost Mages at the ready. Groups with heavy ranged capabilities gain the most from having this line maxed.

ARCANE LINE

TALENT NAME	RANKS	PREREQUISITES	EFFECTS
Arcane Subtlety	3	None	Reduces Threat of Arcane spells by 20% - Progression: 20%/30%/40%
Arcane Focus	5	None	Reduces Resist rate of Arcane spells by 2% (Per Rank)
Improved Arcane Missiles	5	None	Adds a 20% chance (Per Rank) to avoid interruption (by damage) while Channeling Arcane Missiles
Wand Specialization	5	5 Points in Arcane	Increase Wand damage by 5% (Per Rank)
Arcane Concentration	5	5 Points in Arcane	Adds a 2% chance (Per Rank) to gain Clearcast when your spell hits a target
Improved Dampen Magic	2	10 Points in Arcane	Increase the effect of Dampen Magic by 25% (Per Rank)
Improved Arcane Explosion	5	10 Points in Arcane	Reduces the casting time of Arcane Explosion by .3 seconds (Per Rank)
Evocation	1	10 Points in Arcane	Adds an Instant ability to Channel Mana at a 1500% rate for 8 seconds
Improved Mana Shield	2	15 Points in Arcane	Increase the damage absorbed by Mana Shield by 50% - Progression: 50%/75%
Improved Counterspell	2	15 Points in Arcane	Adds a 50% chance (Per Rank) to add a 4 second Silence to your target
Arcane Meditation	5	1 Point in Evocation, 15 Points in Arcane	Allows 2% (Per Rank) of your mana regeneration to continue while casting
Presence of Mind	1	20 Points in Arcane	Adds in Instant ability to make the next spell Instant (must have under a 10 second casting time)
Arcane Mind	4	1 Point in Evocation, 20 Points in Arcane	Increases maximum Mana by 2% (Per Rank)
Arcane Instability	3	1 Point in Presence of Mind, 20 Points in Arcane	Increases spell damage and critical strike chance by 1% (Per Rank)
Arcane Power	1	3 Points in Arcane Instability, 30 Points in Arcane	Adds an Instant ability for 15 seconds that raises spell damage by 35% (costs are also raised 35%)

FIRE LINE

TALENT NAME	RANKS	PREREQUISITES	EFFECTS
Improved Fireball	5	None	Reduces the casting time of Fireball by .1 seconds (Per Rank)
Impact	5	None	Adds a 2% chance (Per Rank) for Fireball to stun for 2 seconds
Ignite	5	5 Points in Fire	Critical Strikes by Fire spells cause targets to burn for 8% of the spell's damage (Per Rank) over 4 seconds
Improved Fire Blast	5	5 Points in Fire	Reduces the cooldown of Fire Blast by .5 seconds - Progression: .5/.8/1/1.3/1.5
Flame Throwing	2	5 Points in Fire	Increases the range of Fire spells by 3 yards (Per Rank)
Incinerate	2	10 Points in Fire	Increases your chance for Fire Blast and Scorch to critical by 2% (Per Rank)
Pyroblast	1	5 Points in Improved Fireball, 10 Points in Fire	Adds a slow-casting bolt that deals extremely high damage to targets
Improved Flamestrike	3	10 Points in Fire	Increases the chance to critical with Flamestrike by 5% (Per Rank)
Burning Soul	3	10 Points in Fire	Gives Fire spells a 25% chance to avoid delays when you are damaged - Progression: 25%/50%/65%
Improved Scorch	5	15 Points in Fire	Burns the target for an additional 5% damage (Per Rank) over 4 seconds
Improved Fire Ward	2	15 Points in Fire	Allows Fire Ward to reflect 20% of damage back at the caster of the spell - Progression: 20%/35%
Critical Mass	3	20 Points in Fire	Increases the critical chance for fire spells to critical by 2% (Per Rank)
Blast Wave	1	3 Points in Improved Flamestrike, 20 Points in Fire	Adds a forward AoE that deals damage and Dazes enemies for 6 seconds
Fire Power	5	3 Points in Critical Mass, 25 Points in Fire	Increases Fire spell damage by 2% (Per Rank)
Combustion	1	5 Points in Fire Power, 30 Points in Fire	Adds an Instant ability that guarantees a critical with your next Fire spell

FROST LINE

TALENT NAME	RANKS	PREREQUISITES	EFFECTS
Improved Frostbolt	5	None	Reduces the casting time of Frostbolt by .1 seconds (Per Rank)
Permafrost	5	None	Increases the duration of Chill effects by 1 second - Progression 1/1.5/2/2.5/3
Ice Shards	5	5 Points in Frost	Increase critical strike damage of Frost spells by 20% (Per Rank)
Winter's Chill	3	5 Points in Frost	Increases the power of Chill effects by 4% - Progression: 4%/7%/10%
Improved Frost Nova	3	5 Points in Frost	Reduces the cooldown of Frost Nova by 1 second (Per Rank)
Piercing Ice	3	10 Points in Frost	Increases the damage done by Frost spells by 2% (Per Rank)
Cold Snap	1	10 Points in Frost	Adds an Instant ability that completes the cooldown of all Frost Spells
Improved Blizzard	3	10 Points in Frost	Adds a Chill effect to the spell Blizzard; Movement is slowed by 63% -Progression: 63%/43%/28%
Arctic Reach	2	15 Points in Frost	Increase the range of Frostbolt and the radius of Frost Nova/Cone of Cold by 10% (Per Rank)
Frost Channeling	3	1 Point in Cold Snap, 15 Points in Frost	Reduces the Mana cost of Frost spells by 5% (Per Rank)
Shatter	5	3 Points in Improved Frost Nova, 15 Points in Frost	Increases the chance to critically strike against Frozen targets by 10% (Per Rank)
Improved Frost Ward	1	15 Points in Frost	50% of damage absorbed by Frost Ward is added to your Mana
Ice Block	1	20 Points in Frost	Adds in Instant ability that protects you from spells and melee for 10 seconds (you cannot move, attack, or cast during this time)
Improved Cone of Cold	3	20 Points in Frost	Increases damage dealt by Cone of Cold by 15% - Progression: 15%/25%/35%
Frostbite	5	25 Points in Frost	Adds a 3% chance (Per Rank) for Chill effects to Freeze a target for 5 seconds
Ice Barrier	1	1 Point in Ice Block, 30 Points in Frost	Adds an Instant ability to Shield the caster (damage does not interrupt casting while the Shield holds)

STRATEGIES

Mages are all about keen strategy and tactics. This is one of those classes that dies easily if you aren't fast on your feet and good with your keys, because your Armor Rating isn't going to stay close to decent. In fact, Mages and damage mitigation only go together in the sentence, Mages have no damage mitigation. So, avoid the damage entirely and stay mobile.

The key is to find ways to maximize the spell line(s) you enjoy the most. On the whole, Mages use a primary spell line with elements from the other two, and this is more than a Talent issue. Indeed, the spell lines have entirely different purposes, and your strategy should reflect the spells you prefer using (or vice versa).

ARCANE TRICKS

The Arcane line has lots of fun to offer at close and long range. One of the first things that you get out of this is the ability to create food and drink. Use this to reduce the downtime of your character and any allies you group with. Beyond that, giving away extra supplies of this sort is useful for making friends in a region, even if they aren't grouped with you. If you have a side goal of meeting new people, scouting for the right guild, and such, try offering to make people extra food/drink in General Chat.

As early as Level 8, you receive the Polymorph spell. To practice its use, save up your full supply of mana and intentionally take on two monsters at the same time. Normally, this is a very bad situation, because Mages cannot mitigate damage in any positive way. So, use your best Fireball to bolt one target and "Sheep" the other opponent to prevent them from adding into combat. Use kiting tricks to blow down the initial target then choose whether to proceed with the second foe (who will soon come out of Polymorph) or run away.

Master Polymorph and learn which targets are best to hit with it. During group battles, later in your career, it's a huge boost to Sheep an incoming caster to prevent them from flanking your group. Be aware that Polymorph allows enemies to heal quickly, so it's always useful to hit fresh targets with Polymorph instead of wounded ones.

Arcane Missiles can dish out the damage quickly, so learning how to avoid interruption is key for its use. Use Frost and kiting techniques to have the range for safe casting when soloing, or wait in groups to unload Arcane Missiles until one of your allies has consolidated aggro. Either way, Arcane Missiles are bread and butter for burst DPS against a single mob.

If you are even stopped during a kiting run (by nets, rooting, etc.) use Blink to hop out of harm's way as soon as possible. Trading blows is a bad idea no matter how you cut it, and Blink is your best hope for getting out of tight places.

Arcane Explosion is the ultimate in fast AoE potential. With the right Talents, this spell eventually offers Instant damage with a decent radius that doesn't cost much Mana. Parties with a single tank may not benefit as much from this, since they commonly kill one foe at a time in each battle. However, groups with a backup tank can consolidate more aggro and allow Mages to spam Arcane Explosion against several foes. This is a solid technique to bring down foes all at once (especially if combined with a Berserk Stance Warrior as the secondary tank).

FUN WITH FIRE

Arcane spells sounded like so much fun, but Fire is just as insane. Damaging single targets with Fireball is solid, especially when backed with Fire-enhancing potions/gear. The range (and possible Stun) from this bolt makes it a deadly option for solo use and group play. Practice getting the most out of Fireball range by chaining these spells together at max range (see how much you can get in before a monster arrives). Bolt, bolt, then slam some Instant damage home before taking a single hit. Fireball, Fireball, Fire Blast is certainly effective for waking someone up. Frost Nova during final enemy approach, then skirt away for more good times.

Flamestrike does moderate AoE damage at range, and can certainly help you contribute to a party that wants to bring down multiple enemies at the same time. Yet, Fire-Talented Mages are going to appreciate the Instant use of Blast Wave and its potential to Daze opponents. Using this at a "wave" of incoming targets can give you maneuvering room while allies get their position against the opponents.

Pyroblast is a slow spell; you only get this with Fire Talents, and there is much to consider before relying on it. Pyroblast takes more time to cast than many equivalent spells. The best time to use Pyroblast is in a situation where your enemy isn't prepared for the incoming attack (neutral mobs, aggressive foes out of range, or unaware PvP targets). Using Combustion and Pyroblast together is certainly an option, and this is a fine way to start important battles.

LEAVING ENEMIES OUT IN THE COLD

Before your specialization is complete, Frost is a great complement to either of the other two lines. Using a fast Frostbolt snares your enemies and prevents them from reaching allies in time to deal as much damage. It's hard to say no to that. Later on, as Mages move away from Frost into other lines or fully become Frost casters, there are more tricks to this selection of spells.

Frost Nova is a spell from heaven for getting out of melee trouble. In both PvE and PvP, Frost Nova offers one of the most reliable means to stop melee attackers and give you flight time. The moderate root caused by Frost Nova is more than enough to get you out to range; use the remaining time to hurl new Frostbolts at your target to renew that good-old Chill effect!

At higher levels, Cone of Cold and Blizzard are good to tradeoff during AoE combat. Blizzard (when improved with Talents) is just incredible for doing damage while halting enemies. Adding Chill to this AoE negates the needs to use less-damaging spells while slowing enemies.

Ice Barrier (also gained through Talents), gives you a chance to act like a Priest on defense. Shield yourself with this spell and launch a couple of short spells to Chill and wound your opponents. Combining the previous spells is useful; so, raise Ice Barrier then use Blizzard to smash enemies as safely as possible.

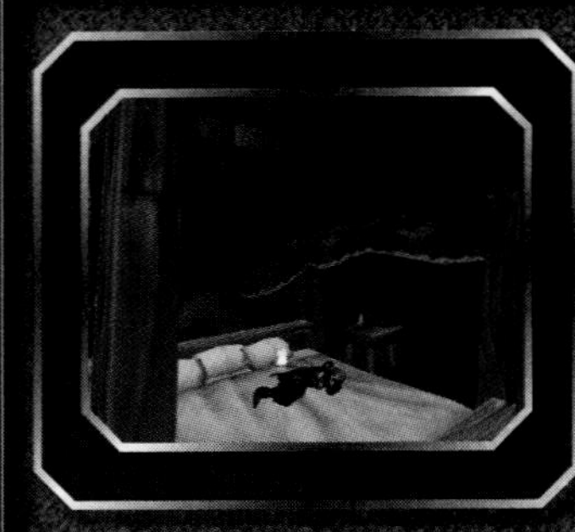

PALADIN

Paladins are the high-survivability melee fighters of the Eastern Kingdoms. With their heavy armor and robust physique, they have the ability to absorb an enemy's attacks, making them strong tanks. It's in difficult situations, though, that Paladins truly shine, and their use of Holy magic allows them some of a healer's powers, including the ability to heal themselves and others and to Resurrect the fallen. Because of their mixture of healing and damage-dealing potential, a Paladin makes a wonderfully self-sufficient soloer as well as an asset in any good group.

THE LIGHT STANDS STRONG

Duskwood used to be a forest of brightly lit glades and shining leaves. Now, the sunlight doesn't even penetrate to the woodland floor, and everything is colored with a bluish haze of fog. The townsfolk of Darkshire even whisper that their allies have forsaken them, as the Undead infest the graveyards and wander the land, attacking any unwary traveler. But the Light never leaves any place or anyone's heart fully, and I had come to give what aid I could in defense of the people.

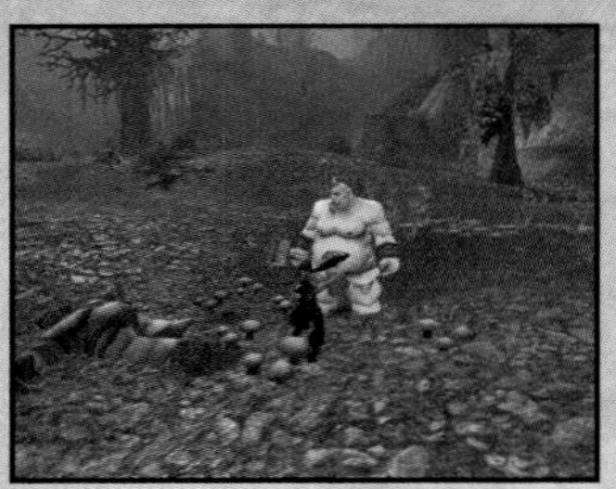

That morning, death came to the streets of Darkshire as an abomination stalked through the town itself. I heard the calls of the town crier as the Night Watch, the citizen's militia, rallied. Other brave defenders of the Alliance came to the cry as well: a strong Warrior, a dedicated Priest, and a slim Night Elf Rogue. Standing beside them, basking in an Aura of Defense, I knew that we could outlast whatever the darkness brought.

We smelled the creature before we saw it, but as it came out of the fog it was obvious that this was no natural beast. Cobbled together of sickly pale flesh and putrescent organs, it immediately set upon us. My ffirst attempt to exorcize the creature damaged, but did not destroy, it, so I slammed my mace hard into its midsection, whispering a prayer under my breath as I did so.

We fought well and hard that day. Using the strength of the crusader, the Priest and I attacked with Holy magic and strikes. The Warrior and Rogue did their parts as well, and I healed them as the monster's blows pummeled down. But this creature was strong, very strong. At one point, I was forced to call upon the Light to protect me from the creature's attacks, and its fist rained down without effect upon a shield of Light itself. This gave the Priest the time needed to save our group, and as I watched, the Warrior ffinally landed the strikes needed to fell the abomination.

The Rogue had fallen during the course of the battle, but I was able to call the Night Elf back. Together, we had all stood against one of the worst horrors ever to walk Azeroth. One day, we will reclaim Duskwood, and all its citizens will roam in tranquil gardens and bright glades again. Until that day, may the Light protect and guide you, and give you the strength you need to stand against the darkness!

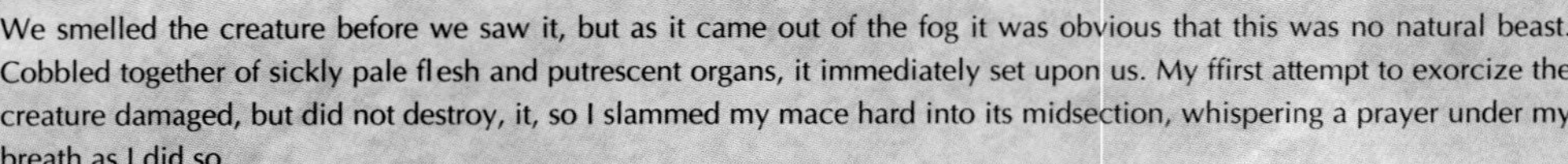

INTRODUCTION TO PLAYING THE PALADIN

Like Warriors, Paladins are strong melee fighters with the ability to take large amounts of damage. They have high hit points, and the use of heavy armor (chain early on, plate after Level 40) lets them really take the hits. This means that Paladins outlast their opponents in battles, pounding away at their enemies with attacks while absorbing any damage that their foe sends their way.

Paladins are not the class for those that want to hack and slash and wade through their enemies. Rather, Paladins are steady and consistent damage dealers, with regular attacks that slice away at their target's hit points. Although a Paladin's attacks are not weak by any means, it's best to say that this fighter is in it for the long haul.

What Paladins excel at is surviving things that would bring down any other class. Not only do they have the heavy armor and hit points, but they have some very nice Holy abilities that allow them to heal themselves (or others) during battle. These basic healing spells are augmented by two very powerful abilities: Lay on Hands and Divine Favor. Lay on Hands instantly restores all hit points at the cost of all the Paladin's mana, and Divine Favor gives the Paladin limited invulnerability. Combined, this results in an opponent having to fight through a Paladin two or three times over as the Paladin restores their hit points during the fight.

One of the things that Paladins find difficult is dealing with multiple opponents, particularly in group situations. To really get a monster centered on only them, a Paladin has to use their Holy Strike (a powerful Holy-based melee attack) against the creature. However, this is on a timer, and if there are multiple enemies, one of them at least is going to start looking for more vulnerable members of the group. Paladins also have a harder time against casters, because of taking more damage from magical attacks and lacking abilities that interrupt spells. Instead, Paladins have to rely on what they do best: taking the damage and repeatedly hitting their enemy.

When it comes down to it, Paladins are less active a class than some of the others. (If you want an active melee class, try Warrior or Rogue.) Paladin combat abilities are somewhat limited, and their combat style is predictable. They do not dance in battle but, instead, participate in a down and dirty slugfest.

Because of their healing abilities and staying power, Paladins are very good soloers, and they are very self-sufficient. In a group, though, Paladins can add some interesting options, including Auras and Seals. Auras provide different effects for the entire party, such as raising Defense or Attack Power. Seals are temporary magical buffs that do a variety of things, such as increase (or decrease) the amount of threat directed toward the person with the Seal, or adding damage against Undead. Only one Seal and Aura can be active at a time per Paladin in the group.

If you are looking for a class that can take care of itself and you enjoy melee combat, then the Paladin is a wonderful choice. Your healing abilities have the potential to save lives, especially in long fights, and you can rest assured that you will outlive your opponents. Being a Paladin means being patient and dedicated, and those that are looking for a solid fight, or who want to do a lot of tanking and a *little* healing, will enjoy this class.

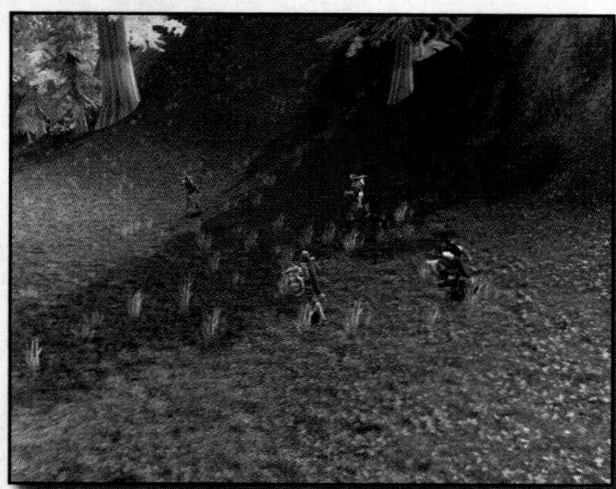

RACES AND STARTING ATTRIBUTES

RACE	STRENGTH	STAMINA	AGILITY	INTELLECT	SPIRIT
Dwarf	24	23	19	20	23
Human	23	22	21	21	22

ATTRIBUTES APPLIED

Strength	Increases Damage and Chance to Block
Stamina	Raises Hit Points
Agility	Improves Chance to Get a Critical Hit and Dodge
Intellect	Raises Mana Pool
Spirit	Improves Hit Point and Magic Point Recovery

ITEMS AND EQUIPMENT

Paladins are very equipment dependent. To do their best in the field and the dungeon, they need to have up to date armor and weapons, the best that they can afford or acquire. To keep taking those hits, Paladins need strong armor; remember, they are always going to be in the middle of the fray. Also, to keep aggro and do damage, you want as powerful a weapon as you can get, and that means investing time and money into your equipment.

What should you put the most time and money into first? Having a good set of chest and leg armor is one of the best investments that you can make. This allows you to absorb the most damage and keeps you in the fight the longest. Having that good set of armor allows you to conserve your mana to use in damage-dealing Holy Strikes instead of costly healing spells; and, in addition, it means that if you do need those healing spells, you have the mana available to cast them. So having that good armor is a life saver.

If you really want to be the ultimate in defensive survivability, use a shield and one-handed weapon. A shield can add large amounts to your Paladin's Armor Rating. Put a Shield Spike on it to add some offensive power and you have a character that uses the Paladin's best assets. Keep your eyes open for quests that give shield rewards or look in the Auction House for one that suits you.

Try to keep that Armor Rating as high as you can. Don't be worried about being spendy with armor, because it makes up for it a dozen times over. For an extra boost, try to get very good pieces enchanted or patched to give it that special something.

In terms of what attributes to look for, Stamina is always appreciated. There is never anything wrong with more hit points. If you find that you are soloing often, concentrate a bit more on Strength to raise your damage and shorten the length of fights. On the other hand, if you group more, lean a bit more on Spirit and Intelligence. This gives you the ability to do more healing work and regenerate the mana you lose to that during a fight.

Getting a weapon that is up to your level is more important than what type of weapon that you pick. However, one-handed maces do not do as much damage as some of the other weapons (swords are often a bit higher on DPS).

Your weapon should do as much damage as possible. Some of the slower weapons are very nice for that because your regular attacks do more damage per hit and your big attack ability, Holy Strike, is on a timer (so you aren't missing out on doing anything fancy during the course of the fight).

ONE-HANDED VS. TWO-HANDED WEAPONS

As always, your weapon is a matter of personal choice. Paladins are very flexible in terms of moving between one-handed and two-handed weapons because they have healing abilities. What a Paladin loses in terms of armor by not having a shield they can always make up for by healing themselves during battle. However, you may want to put a bit more into Spirit equipment to restore that mana quickly during fights if you decide on going for a two-handed weapon.

CHOOSING YOUR PROFESSION

Knowing how to make your own equipment is a wonderful thing for Paladins. If you want to invest in crafted armor, move into Mining and Blacksmithing. Paladins are very good at self-sufficiency, and making your own armor/weapons follows that perfectly. In addition, it's rather enjoyable to be out gathering usable materials while exploring the world at the same time.

For a PvP Paladin, or one interested in doing a great deal of soloing, Engineering is a wonderful thing to pick up. Paladins only get one interrupt against spell casters: the Hammer of Justice—a stun ability. This is on a fairly long timer; by and large you only use it once a fight (at best). Using Bombs to interrupt an enemy's spell can be very helpful, sometimes making all the difference in difficult fights where magic is being tossed at you.

A Paladin's biggest downtime problem is running out of mana. Alchemy and Herbalism can keep that in check by allowing a Paladin to make replenishing Mana Potions, which can help in a fix. As long as a Paladin has the mana, they are ready to fight, and more fighting means more experience. Because of that, secondary trades like Cooking and First Aid aren't as crucial for a Paladin; they can take care of their own healing work and regenerate mana during the fight.

CLASS ABILITIES

There are several types of class abilities that a Paladin can use: Melee Combat, Auras & Seals, and Holy Magic.

All of a Paladin's Melee Combat abilities use a certain amount of mana and are on timers, which vary depending on the ability. Auras are buffs that affect the Paladin and everyone in their group (up to a certain range). As Paladins progress in level, they gain different Auras and more powerful ones. Seals are temporary buffs that can only be placed on one person each. Many of the Seals are only active for a very short period, but they have a variety of different effects and can help control the course of a battle. Holy magic includes healing spells, Divine Favor (temporary invulnerability), and offensive spells against the Undead.

ABILITY	RANK	LEVEL	TYPE
Devotion Aura	1	1	Protection
Holy Light	1	1	Holy Magic
Holy Strike	1	1	Combat Abilities
Divine Protection	1	4	Protection
Healing Aura	1	4	Holy Magic
Holy Light	2	6	Holy Magic
Purify	N/A	6	Holy Magic
Holy Strike	2	8	Combat Abilities
Parry	N/A	8	Combat Abilities
Seal of Protection	1	8	Protection
Crusader Strike	1	10	Combat Abilities
Devotion Aura	2	10	Protection
Hammer of Justice	1	10	Combat Abilities
Lay on Hands	1	10	Holy Magic
Healing Aura	2	12	Protection
Dominance Aura	1	14	Combat Abilities
Holy Light	3	14	Holy Magic
Seal of Fury	N/A	14	Combat Abilities
Holy Strike	3	16	Combat Abilities
Seal of Righteousness	1	16	Combat Abilities
Divine Protection	2	18	Protection
Retribution Aura	1	18	Combat Abilities
Devotion Aura	3	20	Protection
Exorcism	1	20	Holy Magic
Seal of Protection	2	20	Protection
Sense Undead	N/A	20	Holy Magic
Crusader Strike	2	22	Combat Abilities
Healing Aura	3	22	Protection
Holy Light	4	22	Holy Magic
Seal of Salvation	N/A	22	Protection
Dominance Aura	2	24	Combat Abilities
Holy Strike	4	24	Combat Abilities
Turn Undead	1	24	Holy Magic
Hammer of Justice	2	26	Combat Abilities
Seal of Righteousness	2	26	Combat Abilities
Wisdom Aura	1	26	Protection
Exorcism	2	28	Holy Magic
Resistance Aura	1	28	Protection
Retribution Aura	2	28	Combat Abilities
Cleanse	N/A	30	Holy Magic
Devotion Aura	4	30	Protection
Holy Light	5	30	Holy Magic
Lay on Hands	2	30	Holy Magic
Seal of Protection	3	30	Protection
Seal of Reckoning	1	30	Combat Abilities
Healing Aura	4	32	Protection
Holy Strike	5	32	Combat Abilities
Crusader Strike	3	34	Combat Abilities
Divine Shield	1	34	Protection
Dominance Aura	3	34	Combat Abilities
Exorcism	3	36	Holy Magic
Seal of Righteousness	3	36	Combat Abilities
Seal of Sacrifice	N/A	36	Protection
Wisdom Aura	2	36	Protection
Holy Light	6	38	Holy Magic
Retribution Aura	3	38	Combat Abilities
Turn Undead	2	38	Holy Magic
Devotion Aura	5	40	Protection
Hammer of Justice	3	40	Combat Abilities
Holy Strike	6	40	Combat Abilities
Judgement	1	40	Holy Magic
Redemption	N/A	40	Holy Magic
Seal of Reckoning	2	40	Combat Abilities
Healing Aura	5	42	Protection
Resistance Aura	2	42	Protection
Dominance Aura	4	44	Combat Abilities
Exorcism	4	44	Holy Magic
Crusader Strike	4	46	Combat Abilities
Holy Light	7	46	Holy Magic
Seal of Righteousness	4	46	Combat Abilities
Wisdom Aura	3	46	Protection
Holy Strike	7	48	Combat Abilities
Retribution Aura	4	48	Combat Abilities
Devotion Aura	6	50	Protection
Divine Shield	2	50	Protection
Judgement	2	50	Holy Magic
Lay on Hands	3	50	Holy Magic
Seal of Reckoning	3	50	Combat Abilities
Exorcism	5	52	Holy Magic
Healing Aura	6	52	Protection
Turn Undead	3	52	Holy Magic
Dominance Aura	5	54	Combat Abilities
Hammer of Justice	4	54	Combat Abilities
Holy Light	8	54	Holy Magic
Holy Strike	8	56	Combat Abilities
Seal of Righteousness	5	56	Combat Abilities
Wisdom Aura	4	56	Protection
Crusader Strike	5	58	Combat Abilities
Resistance Aura	3	58	Protection
Retribution Aura	5	58	Combat Abilities
Devotion Aura	7	60	Protection
Exorcism	6	60	Holy Magic
Judgement	3	60	Holy Magic
Seal of Reckoning	4	60	Combat Abilities

COMBAT ABILITIES

These Melee Combat Abilities are the sum of a Paladin's damage-dealing potential. They can be used at any time at any position in the fight provided that their timer is active and the Paladin has the requisite amount of mana.

CRUSADER STRIKE

RANK	LEVEL	MANA	RANGE	CASTING TIME	COOLDOWN	COST TO TRAIN	EFFECT
1	10	25	7 yd	IC	1 hour	3	A strike that causes 12 damage and increases the holy damage taken by the target by 6 per Crusader Strike. Can be applied up to 5 times. Lasts 30 sec.
2	22	40	7 yd	IC		42	A strike that causes 27 damage and increases the holy damage taken by the target by 10 per Crusader Strike. Can be applied up to 5 times. Lasts 30 sec.
3	34	55	7 yd	IC		1 80	A strike that causes 46 damage and increases the holy damage taken by the target by 15 per Crusader Strike. Can be applied up to 5 times. Lasts 30 sec.
4	46	70	7 yd	IC		2 80	A strike that causes 69 damage and increases the holy damage taken by the target by 22 per Crusader Strike. Can be applied up to 5 times. Lasts 30 sec.
5	58	90	7 yd	IC		7 10	A strike that causes 103 damage and increases the holy damage taken by the target by 30 per Crusader Strike. Can be applied up to 5 times. Lasts 30 sec.

DOMINANCE AURA

RANK	LEVEL	MANA	RANGE	CASTING TIME	COOLDOWN	COST TO TRAIN	EFFECT
1	14	None	Party	IC		12	Increases attack power of all party members within 30 yards by 25. Players may only have one Aura on them per Paladin at any one time.
2	24	None	Party	IC		71	Increases attack power of all party members within 30 yards by 45. Players may only have one Aura on them per Paladin at any one time.
3	34	None	Party	IC		1 80	Increases attack power of all party members within 30 yards by 65. Players may only have one Aura on them per Paladin at any one time.
4	44	None	Party	IC		3 30	Increases attack power of all party members within 30 yards by 95. Players may only have one Aura on them per Paladin at any one time.
5	54	None	Party	IC		5 80	Increases attack power of all party members within 30 yards by 130. Players may only have one Aura on them per Paladin at any one time.

HAMMER OF JUSTICE

RANK	LEVEL	MANA	RANGE	CASTING TIME	COOLDOWN	COST TO TRAIN	EFFECT
1	10	30	10 yd	IC	1 min	3	Stuns the target for 3 sec.
2	26	50	10 yd	IC	1 min	90	Stuns the target for 4 sec.
3	40	75	10 yd	IC	1 min	1 60	Stuns the target for 5 sec.
4	54	100	10 yd	IC	1 min	5 80	Stuns the target for 6 sec.

HOLY STRIKE

RANK	LEVEL	MANA	RANGE	CASTING TIME	COOLDOWN	COST TO TRAIN	EFFECT
1	1	20	0	Next melee	10 sec	No Cost	Consecrates your weapon, inflicting 10 to 12 additional damage on your next attack. All damage caused is considered holy damage.
2	8	40	0	Next melee	10 sec	2	Consecrates your weapon, inflicting 20 to 24 additional damage on your next attack. All damage caused is considered holy damage.
3	16	60	0	Next melee	10 sec	18	Consecrates your weapon, inflicting 36 to 42 additional damage on your next attack. All damage caused is considered holy damage.
4	24	85	0	Next melee	10 sec	71	Consecrates your weapon, inflicting 58 to 66 additional damage on your next attack. All damage caused is considered holy damage.
5	32	120	0	Next melee	10 sec	1 50	Consecrates your weapon, inflicting 90 to 112 additional damage on your next attack. All damage caused is considered holy damage.
6	40	150	0	Next melee	10 sec	1 60	Consecrates your weapon, inflicting 121 to 137 additional damage on your next attack. All damage caused is considered holy damage.
7	48	180	0	Next melee	10 sec	4 20	Consecrates your weapon, inflicting 157 to 177 additional damage on your next attack. All damage caused is considered holy damage.
8	56	215	0	Next melee	10 sec	6 40	Consecrates your weapon, inflicting 201 to 225 additional damage on your next attack. All damage caused is considered holy damage.

PARRY

RANK	LEVEL	MANA	RANGE	CASTING TIME	COOLDOWN	COST TO TRAIN	EFFECT
N/A	8	None				2	Gives a chance to parry enemy melee attacks.

RETRIBUTION AURA

RANK	LEVEL	MANA	RANGE	CASTING TIME	COOLDOWN	COST TO TRAIN	EFFECT
1	18	None	Party	IC		29	Causes 4 Holy damage to any creature that strikes a nearby party member. Players may only have one Aura on them per Paladin at any one time.
2	28	None	Party	IC		1 10	Causes 8 Holy damage to any creature that strikes a nearby party member. Players may only have one Aura on them per Paladin at any one time.
3	38	None	Party	IC		2 30	Causes 12 Holy damage to any creature that strikes a nearby party member. Players may only have one Aura on them per Paladin at any one time.
4	48	None	Party	IC		4 20	Causes 16 Holy damage to any creature that strikes a nearby party member. Players may only have one Aura on them per Paladin at any one time.
5	58	None	Party	IC		7 10	Causes 20 Holy damage to any creature that strikes a nearby party member. Players may only have one Aura on them per Paladin at any one time.

SEAL OF FURY

RANK	LEVEL	MANA	RANGE	CASTING TIME	COOLDOWN	COST TO TRAIN	EFFECT
N/A	14	115	30 yd	IC		12	Places a Seal on the party member, increasing threat caused by 50% for 20 sec. Players may only have one Seal on them per Paladin at any one time.

SEAL OF RECKONING

RANK	LEVEL	MANA	RANGE	CASTING TIME	COOLDOWN	COST TO TRAIN	EFFECT
1	30	95	30 yd	IC		78	Places a Seal on a friendly target that lasts 30 sec. Every time the Sealed character strikes an enemy, the Sealed character gains 16 health. Players may only have one Seal on them per Paladin at any one time.
2	40	135	30 yd	IC		1 60	Places a Seal on a friendly target that lasts 30 sec. Every time the Sealed character strikes an enemy, the Sealed character gains 24 health. Players may only have one Seal on them per Paladin at any one time.
3	50	185	30 yd	IC		3 50	Places a Seal on a friendly target that lasts 30 sec. Every time the Sealed character strikes an enemy, the Sealed character gains 35 health. Players may only have one Seal on them per Paladin at any one time.
4	60	250	30 yd	IC		5 90	Places a Seal on a friendly target that lasts 30 sec. Every time the Sealed character strikes an enemy, the Sealed character gains 50 health. Players may only have one Seal on them per Paladin at any one time.

SEAL OF RIGHTEOUSNESS

RANK	LEVEL	MANA	RANGE	CASTING TIME	COOLDOWN	COST TO TRAIN	EFFECT
1	16	20	30 yd	IC	20 sec	18	Places a Seal on the friendly target. Increasing attack power by 60 against undead enemies. Lasts 25 sec. Players may only have one Seal on them per Paladin at any one time.
2	26	35	30 yd	IC	20 sec	90	Places a Seal on the friendly target. Increasing attack power by 115 against undead enemies. Lasts 25 sec. Player may only have one Seal on them per Paladin at any one time.
3	36	55	30 yd	IC	20 sec	1 50	Places a Seal on the friendly target. Increasing attack power by 180 against undead enemies. Lasts 25 sec. Players may only have one Seal on them per Paladin at any one time.
4	46	80	30 yd	IC	20 sec	2 80	Places a Seal on the friendly target. Increasing attack power by 265 against undead enemies. Lasts 25 sec. Players may only have one Seal on them per Paladin at any one time.
5	56	110	30 yd	IC	20 sec	6 40	Places a Seal on the friendly target. Increasing attack power by 370 against undead enemies. Lasts 25 sec. Players may only have one Seal on them per Paladin at any one time.

HOLY MAGIC

This includes a Paladin's ability to heal themselves and others, the use of limited invulnerability (self only), and Undead-specific attack abilities. Historically, in Azeroth, Paladins have had an antagonistic relationship to the Undead, and using all the power that the Light has to remove these unclean creatures is a special gift given to Paladins.

CLEANSE

RANK	LEVEL	MANA	RANGE	CASTING TIME	COOLDOWN	COST TO TRAIN	EFFECT
N/A	30	40	30 yd	IC		78	Cleanses a friendly target, removing 1 poison effect, 1 disease effect, and 1 magic effect.

EXORCISM

RANK	LEVEL	MANA	RANGE	CASTING TIME	COOLDOWN	COST TO TRAIN	EFFECT
1	20	85	30 yd	IC	15 sec	29	Causes 84 to 96 Holy damage to an undead target.
2	28	135	30 yd	IC	15 sec	1 10	Causes 152 to 172 Holy damage to an undead target.
3	36	180	30 yd	IC	15 sec	1 50	Causes 217 to 245 Holy damage to an undead target.
4	44	235	30 yd	IC	15 sec	3 30	Causes 304 to 342 Holy damage to an undead target.
5	52	285	30 yd	IC	15 sec	5 30	Causes 393 to 439 Holy damage to an undead target.
6	60	345	30 yd	IC	15 sec	5 90	Causes 505 to 563 Holy damage to an undead target.

HEALING AURA

RANK	LEVEL	MANA	RANGE	CASTING TIME	COOLDOWN	COST TO TRAIN	EFFECT
1	4	None	Party	IC		50	Increases the health regeneration of the Paladin and nearby group members by 10 every 5 seconds. Only works out of combat. Players may only have one Aura on them per Paladin at any one time.

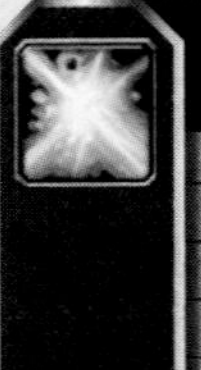

HOLY LIGHT

RANK	LEVEL	MANA	RANGE	CASTING TIME	COOLDOWN	COST TO TRAIN	EFFECT
1	1	35	40 yd	2.5 sec		No Cost	Heals a friendly target for 39 to 47.
2	6	60	40 yd	2.5 sec		1	Heals a friendly target for 76 to 90.
3	14	120	40 yd	2.5 sec		12	Heals a friendly target for 176 to 204.
4	22	195	40 yd	2.5 sec		42	Heals a friendly target for 322 to 368.
5	30	260	40 yd	2.5 sec		78	Heals a friendly target for 470 to 532.
6	38	330	40 yd	2.5 sec		2 30	Heals a friendly target for 639 to 721.
7	46	430	40 yd	2.5 sec		2 80	Heals a friendly target for 889 to 997.
8	54	550	40 yd	2.5 sec		5 80	Heals a friendly target for 1207 to 1349.

JUDGEMENT

RANK	LEVEL	MANA	RANGE	CASTING TIME	COOLDOWN	COST TO TRAIN	EFFECT
1	40	495	0	2 sec	1 min	1 60	Sends bolts of holy power in all directions, causing 253 to 303 Holy damage to all undead near the Paladin.
2	50	645	0	2 sec	1 min	3 50	Sends bolts of holy power in all directions, causing 362 to 428 Holy damage to all undead near the Paladin.
3	60	805	0	2 sec	1 min	5 90	Sends bolts of holy power in all directions, causing 490 to 576 Holy damage to all undead near the Paladin.

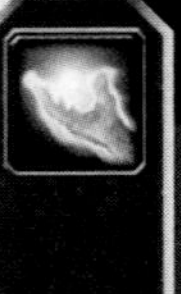

LAY ON HANDS

RANK	LEVEL	MANA	RANGE	CASTING TIME	COOLDOWN	COST TO TRAIN	EFFECT
1	10	None	20 yd	IC		3	Heals a friendly target for an amount equal to the Paladin's maximum health. Drains all of the Paladin's remaining mana when used.
2	30	None	20 yd	IC	1 hour	78	Heals a friendly target for an amount equal to the Paladin's maximum health and restores 250 of their mana. Drains all of the Paladin's remaining mana when used.
3	50	None	20 yd	IC	1 hour	3 50	Heals a friendly target for an amount equal to the Paladin's maximum health and restores 550 of their mana. Drains all of the Paladin's remaining mana when used.

PURIFY

RANK	LEVEL	MANA	RANGE	CASTING TIME	COOLDOWN	COST TO TRAIN	EFFECT
N/A	6	25	30 yd	IC		1	Purifies the friendly target, removing 1 disease effect and 1 poison effect.

REDEMPTION

RANK	LEVEL	MANA	RANGE	CASTING TIME	COOLDOWN	COST TO TRAIN	EFFECT
N/A	40	150	40 yd	10 sec	1 hour	1 60	Brings a dead player back to life with 100% of their health and mana.

SENSE UNDEAD

RANK	LEVEL	MANA	RANGE	CASTING TIME	COOLDOWN	COST TO TRAIN	EFFECT
N/A	20	None	Self	IC		29	Shows the location of all nearby undead on the minimap until cancelled. Only one type of tracking can be used at a time.

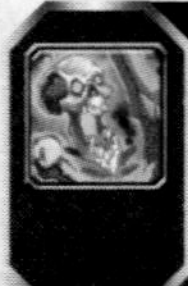

TURN UNDEAD

RANK	LEVEL	MANA	RANGE	CASTING TIME	COOLDOWN	COST TO TRAIN	EFFECT
1	24	35	20 yd	1.5 sec	30 sec	71	The targeted undead enemy will be compelled to flee for up to 10 sec. Only one target can be turned at a time.
2	38	50	20 yd	1.5 sec	30 sec	2 30	The targeted undead enemy will be compelled to flee for up to 15 sec. Only one target can be turned at a time.
3	52	75	20 yd	1.5 sec	30 sec	5 30	The targeted undead enemy will be compelled to flee for up to 20 sec. Only one target can be turned at a time.

PROTECTION

Seals are short-term buffs that Paladins use on themselves and group members. Only one of these can be active on a person at the same time (per Paladins). An Aura affects all members of a group at the same time, and only one such Aura can be active per Paladin.

DEVOTION AURA

RANK	LEVEL	MANA	RANGE	CASTING TIME	COOLDOWN	COST TO TRAIN	EFFECT
1	1	None	Party	IC		10	Gives 55 additional armor to party members within 30 yards. Players may only have one Aura on them per Paladin at any one time.
2	10	None	Party	IC		3	Gives 160 additional armor to party members within 30 yards. Players may only have one Aura on them per Paladin at any one time.
3	20	None	Party	IC		29	Gives 275 additional armor to party members within 30 yards. Players may only have one Aura on them per Paladin at any one time.
4	30	None	Party	IC		78	Gives 390 additional armor to party members within 30 yards. Players may only have one Aura on them per Paladin at any one time.
5	40	None	Party	IC		1 60	Gives 505 additional armor to party members within 30 yards. Players may only have one Aura on them per Paladin at any one time.
6	50	None	Party	IC		3 50	Gives 620 additional armor to party members within 30 yards. Players may only have one Aura on them per Paladin at any one time.
7	60	None	Party	IC		5 90	Gives 735 additional armor to party members within 30 yards. Players may only have one Aura on them per Paladin at any one time.

DIVINE PROTECTION

RANK	LEVEL	MANA	RANGE	CASTING TIME	COOLDOWN	COST TO TRAIN	EFFECT
1	4	15	Self	IC	5 min	50	You are protected from all physical attacks and spells for 6 sec, but during that time you cannot attack or use physical abilities yourself.
2	18	35	Self	IC	5 min	29	You are protected from all physical attacks and spells for 8 sec, but during that time you cannot attack or use physical abilities yourself.

DIVINE SHIELD

RANK	LEVEL	MANA	RANGE	CASTING TIME	COOLDOWN	COST TO TRAIN	EFFECT
1	34	75	Self	IC	5 min	1 80	Protects the paladin from all damage and spells for 10 sec, but reduces attack speed by 50%.
2	50	110	Self	IC	5 min	3 50	Protects the paladin from all damage and spells for 12 sec, but reduces attack speed by 50%.

HEALING AURA

RANK	LEVEL	MANA	RANGE	CASTING TIME	COOLDOWN	COST TO TRAIN	EFFECT
2	12	None	Party	IC		8	Increases the health regeneration of the Paladin and nearby group members by 25 every 5 seconds. Only works out of combat. Players may only have one Aura on them per Paladin at any one time.
3	22	None	Party	IC		42	Increases the health regeneration of the Paladin and nearby group members by 40 every 5 seconds. Only works out of combat. Players may only have one Aura on them per Paladin at any one time.
4	32	None	Party	IC		1 50	Increases the health regeneration of the Paladin and nearby group members by 60 every 5 seconds. Only works out of combat. Players may only have one Aura on them per Paladin at any one time.
5	42	None	Party	IC		3	Increases the health regeneration of the Paladin and nearby group members by 90 every 5 seconds. Only works out of combat. Players may only have one Aura on them per Paladin at any one time.
6	52	None	Party	IC		5 30	Increases the health regeneration of the Paladin and nearby group members by 125 every 5 seconds. Only works out of combat. Players may only have one Aura on them per Paladin at any one time.

PLATE MAIL

RANK	LEVEL	MANA	RANGE	CASTING TIME	COOLDOWN	COST TO TRAIN	EFFECT
	N/A	40		N/A		1 60	Allows the Warrior to Equip Plate Armor.

RESISTANCE AURA

RANK	LEVEL	MANA	RANGE	CASTING TIME	COOLDOWN	COST TO TRAIN	EFFECT
1	28	None	Party	IC		1 10	Increases nearby group member's resistance to all magic by 25. Players may only have one Aura on them per Paladin at any one time.
2	42	None	Party	IC		3	Increases nearby group member's resistance to all magic by 40. Players may only have one Aura on them per Paladin at any one time.
3	58	None	Party	IC		7 10	Increases nearby group member's resistance to all magic by 55. Players may only have one Aura on them per Paladin at any one time.

SEAL OF PROTECTION

RANK	LEVEL	MANA	RANGE	CASTING TIME	COOLDOWN	COST TO TRAIN	EFFECT
1	8	20	30 yd	IC	5 min	2	A targeted party member is protected from all physical attacks for 6 sec, but during that time they cannot attack or use physical abilities. Players may only have one Seal on them per Paladin at any one time.
2	20	30	30 yd	IC	5 min	29	A targeted party member is protected from all physical attacks for 8 sec, but during that time they cannot attack or use physical abilities. Players may only have one Seal on them per Paladin at any one time.
3	30	40	30 yd	IC	5 min	78	A targeted party member is protected from all physical attacks for 10 sec, but during that time they cannot attack or use physical abilities. Players may only have one Seal on them per Paladin at any one time.

SEAL OF SACRIFICE

RANK	LEVEL	MANA	RANGE	CASTING TIME	COOLDOWN	COST TO TRAIN	EFFECT
N/A	36	60	30 yd	IC		1 50	Places a Seal on the party member, splitting 50% of all damage taken with the caster. Lasts 30 sec. Players may wonly have one Seal on them per Paladin at any one time.

SEAL OF SALVATION

RANK	LEVEL	MANA	RANGE	CASTING TIME	COOLDOWN	COST TO TRAIN	EFFECT
N/A	22	10	30 yd	IC	15 sec	42	Places a Seal on the party member, reducing the amount of all threat generated by 50% for 30 sec. Players may only have one Seal on them per Paladin at any one time.

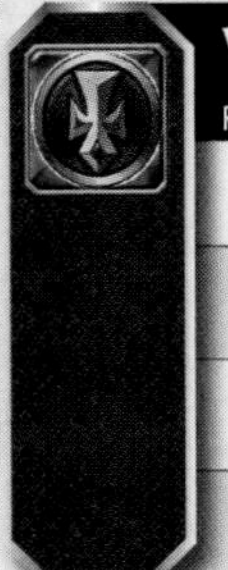

WISDOM AURA

RANK	LEVEL	MANA	RANGE	CASTING TIME	COOLDOWN	COST TO TRAIN	EFFECT
1	26	None	Party	IC		90	Increases the mana regeneration of party members within 30 yards by 6 every 5 seconds. Players may only have one Aura on them per Paladin at any one time.
2	36	None	Party	IC		1 50	Increases the mana regeneration of party members within 30 yards by 8 every 5 seconds. Players may only have one Aura on them per Paladin at any one time.
3	46	None	Party	IC		2 80	Increases the mana regeneration of party members within 30 yards by 10 every 5 seconds. Players may only have one Aura on them per Paladin at any one time.
4	56	None	Party	IC		6 40	Increases the mana regeneration of party members within 30 yards by 13 every 5 seconds. Players may only have one Aura on them per Paladin at any one time.

TALENTS

HOLY

TALENT NAME	RANKS	PREREQUISITES	EFFECTS
Improved Lay on Hands	2	None	Gives the target of your Lay on Hands spell a 15% bonus (Per Rank) to their armor value from items for 1 min.
Spiritual Focus	5	None	Gives your Flash of Light and Holy Light spells a 14% chance (Per Rank) to not lose casting time when you take damage
Improved Holy Light	3	None	Increases the amount healed by your Holy Light spell by 4% (Per Rank)
Revelation	2	5 Points in Holy	Reduces the cooldown of your Lay on Hands and Divine Intervention spells by 10 min (Per Rank)
Illumination	5	5 Points in Holy	After getting a critical effect from your Flash of Light or Holy Light spell, gives you a 20% chance (Per Rank) to gain mana equal to the base cost of the spell
Improved Blessing of Wisdom	5	5 Points in Holy	Increases the effect of your Blessing of Wisdom by 4% (Per Rank)
Divine Favor	1	10 Points in Holy	When activated, gives your next Flash of Light or Holy Light spell a 100% critical effect chance
Improved Seal of Righteousness	5	10 Points in Holy	Increases the damage done by your Seal of Righteousness by 3% (Per Rank)
Improved Flash of Light	3	10 Points in Holy	Reduces the mana cost of your Flash of Light spell by 4% (Per Rank)
Improved Concentration Aura	3	15 Points in Holy	Increases the effect of your Concentration Aura by an additional 5% (Per Rank)
Divine Wisdom	5	5 Points in Improved Blessing of Wisdom, 15 Points in Holy	Increases your total mana by 2% (Per Rank)
Sanctity Aura	1	5 Points in Improved Seal of Righteousness, 20 Points in Holy	Increases Holy damage done by party members within 30 yards by 10%. Players may only have one Aura on them per Paladin at any one time.
Improved Seal of Light	5	20 Points in Holy	Increases the amount healed by your Seal of Light by 3% (Per Rank) and the duration of your Judgement by 6 sec.
Divine Strength	5	25 Points in Holy	Increases your Strength by 2% (Per Rank)
Holy Shock	1	1 Point in Sanctity Aura, 30 Points in Holy	Blasts the target with Holy energy, causing 205-219 Holy damage.

PROTECTION

TALENT NAME	RANKS	PREREQUISITES	EFFECTS
Improved Devotion Aura	5	None	Increases the armor bonus of your Devotion Aura by 5%
Redoubt	5	None	Increases your chance to block attacks with your shield by 6% (Per Rank) for 10 sec after being the victim of a critical strike
Improved Blessing of Protection	2	5 Points in Protection	Reduces the cooldown of your Blessing of Protection by 60 sec. (Per Rank)
Toughness	5	5 Points in Protection	Increases your armor value from items by 2% (Per Rank)
Blessing of Sanctuary	1	10 Points in Protection	Places a Blessing on the friendly target, reducing damage dealt frm all sources by 7 for 5 min. Players may only have one Blessing on them per Paladin at any one time.
Improved Seal of Fury	5	10 Points in Protection	Increases the amount of threat generated by your Seal of Fury and Judgement of Fury by 3% (Per Rank)
Shield Specialization	5	10 Points in Protection	Increases the amount of damage absorbed by your shield by 5% (Per Rank)
Improved Blessing of Freedom	5	10 Points in Protection	Increases the duration of your Blessing of Freedom by 1 sec. (Per Rank)
Improved Seal of Justice	5	15 Points in Protection	Increases the frequency that your Seal of Justice stuns the opponent by 1 per minute (Per Rank)
Reckoning	5	20 Points in Protection	Gives you a 20% chance (Per Rank) to gain an extra attack after being the victim of a critical strike
Holy Shield	1	5 Points in Shield Specialization, 20 Points in Protection	Increases chance to block by 30% for 10 sec, and deals 40 Holy damage for each attack blocked while active. Each block expends a charge. 4 charges
Improved Blessing of Salvation	2	20 Points in Protection	Increases the duration of your Blessing of Salvation by 5 min. (Per Rank)
One-Handed Weapon Specialization	5	25 Points in Protection	Increases the damage you deal with one-handed melee weapons by 1% (Per Rank)
Repentance	1	5 Points in Improved Seal of Justice, 30 Points in Protection	Puts the enemy target in a state of meditation for up to 6 sec. Any damage caused will awaken the target. Only works against Humanoids.

RETRIBUTION

TALENT NAME	RANKS	PREREQUISITES	EFFECTS
Improved Blessing of Might	5	None	Increases the Attack Power bonus of your Blessing of Might by 4%
Benediction	5	None	Reduces the mana cost of your Retribution spells by 3% (Per Rank)
Two-Handed Weapon Specialization	5	5 Points in Retribution	Increases the damage you deal with two-handed melee weapons by 1% (Per Rank)
Improved Seal of the Crusader	5	5 Points in Retribution	Increases the Attack Power bonus of your Seal of the Crusader and the Holy damage increase of your Judgement of the Crusader by 3% (Per Rank)
Deflection	5	10 Points in Retribution	Increases your Parry chance by 1% (Per Rank)
Vengeance	5	10 Points in Retribution	Gives you a 3% bonus (Per Rank) to Physical and Holy damage you deal for 8 sec. after dealing a critical strike
Seal of Command	1	10 Points in Retribution	Fills the Paladin with the spirit of command for 30 sec. giving the Paladin a chance to deal additional Holy damage equal to the damage of the Paladin's weapon. Only one Seal can be active on the Paladin at any one time. Unleashing this Seal's energy will judge an enemy for 30 sec. causing 24 Holy damage any time the enemy becomes stunned. Only one judgement per Paladin can be active at any one time.
Anticipation	5	10 Points in Retribution	Increases your Defense skill by 2 (Per Rank)
Improved Retribution Aura	5	1 Point in Seal of Command, 15 Points in Retribution	Increases the damage done by your Retribution Aura by 5% (Per Rank)
Precision	3	5 Points in Deflection, 20 Points in Retribution	Increases your chance to hit with melee weapons by 1% (Per Rank)
Consecration	1	20 Points in Retribution	Consecrates the land beneath the Paladin, doing 120 Holy damage over 8 sec. to enemies who enter the area
Conviction	5	5 Points in Vengeance, 25 Points in Retribution	Increases your chance to get a critical strike with melee weapons by 1% (Per Rank)
Blessing of Kings	1	30 Points in Retribution	Places a Blessing on the friendly target, increasing total stats by 10% for 5 min. Players may only have on Blessing on them per Paladin at any one time.

STRATEGIES

The core strategy for being a Paladin is doing whatever you need to keep yourself (and others) alive while harping on your timed combat abilities as much as possible. Every time you have the opportunity to use Holy Strike is your chance to do massive damage; every time you can stun the enemy with Hammer of Justice they lose the opportunity to attack. In the meanwhile, use regular attacks and healing as needed, knowing that you have the hit points to outlast the onslaught.

GENERAL TIPS

The basic strategy for being a Paladin is fairly easy and infinitely repeatable. They have a limited range of combat abilities, so you get to use nearly all the ones you have early in your career.

First, choose the Aura that fits your role the best. If you aren't sure which one works for a given situation, default to Devotion Aura. There is never anything wrong with having more armor, and it works well for anything you are likely to come into contact with.

Start off most fights with Holy Strike. This is your most powerful attack, and you want to use it as often as you can in the course of battle. As soon as the timer becomes active, hit it and slam into the creature. The only time that you may want to hold onto it is during the very end of a fight where the creature may try to run away. When they get close to the end of their hit points, use Holy Strike to knock them all the way down before they can high-tail it away from you. Of course, you shouldn't be saving Holy Strike throughout the entire battle; the timer is fairly quick, and you should be able to get in at least two of them before you have to wait for the end.

Hammer of Justice is also very good for keeping enemies from running. Unlike Warriors and Mages, Paladins don't have anything to slow down a fleeing enemy. That means that Paladins have to follow running opponents as quickly as possible before they get away. Stunning the creature as it runs in fear keeps the mob from getting away (and possibly bringing friends against you).

If you aren't fighting a running enemy, use Hammer of Justice early in the fight. If the fight lasts for a while (lucky for you?) you may get to use the stun twice. This ability is also a Paladin's only interrupt. Before you go toe-to-toe with any caster, you should have this ability available. Magic users deal nasty damage, and avoiding even one spell is worthwhile.

If at all possible, hold off on the healing spells until the end of battle. That way, you can regenerate your mana over the course of a fight and limit your downtime. In addition, using drinks like sweet nectar can be expensive, and you want to save your money for even better things, like new armor. Paladins are excellent at moving from fight to fight with few meal breaks, but mana breaks can be a different matter in the higher levels. To increase your number of kills and slice downtime, find enemies that are tough but deal modest damage over time (perfect for a slow pounder).

If you need to heal yourself during the fight, there are a couple of options. Casting Healing Light is a long process, so you don't want to wait until you are at death's door. If the enemy attacks slowly, you can absorb the hits and take the damage, knowing that your healing can handle the abuse. If, however, you are dealing with fast attackers, stun them with Hammer of Justice and heal while they are stunned. For multiple attackers, use your Divine Favor for its limited invulnerability and heal yourself while you are uninterrupted by attacks.

LIFE ON YOUR OWN

Paladins make wonderful, reliable soloers. They have the ability to take damage and the survivability to outlive most engagements. Their healing abilities also let them avoid most downtime.

One big concern with being a soloer is that you must choose your targets with care. There are some creatures that Paladins have an easier time fighting than others. First off, Paladins are not the class to break camps. Pally pulling, which involves moving on the outside of a camp just enough to grab one or two enemies, requires skill and practice. Bad luck can result in a Paladin or group being overwhelmed by the entire enemy camp. So you want to limit yourself to grabbing enemies on the outskirts of camps or single targets.

What are good targets for soloers? Well, the *best* target that any Paladin can have is Undead. Holy magic does extra damage to these creatures, and all of a Paladin's combat abilities are centered on that. In addition, Paladins get a wonderful offensive Undead-specific spell to aid them in a fight: Exorcism. This spell is mana-intensive, but it does very nice damage against your enemies. Paladins also get a Seal that raises their damage against Undead, and a spell called Turn Undead that makes them run in fear. If you find yourself swarmed by too many Undead, you can always force a few of them to flee (giving you time to ditch or heal yourself).

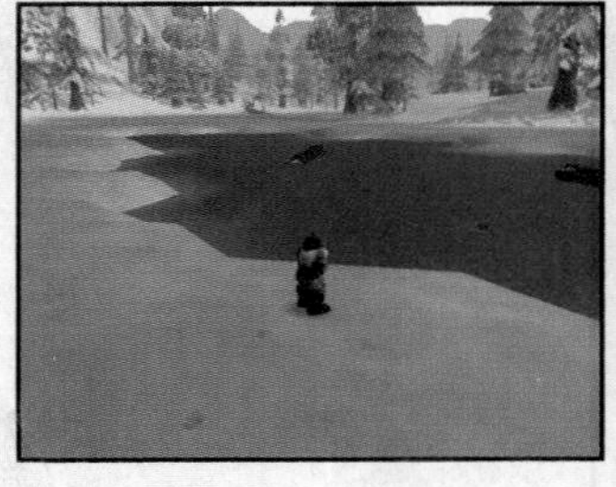

Other good targets include most beasts. These creatures don't run away frequently, which means that you don't have to worry about chasing after them. It also doesn't really matter too much to a Paladin how fast or much they attack for, because healing is always an option. Even the special attacks that some beasts have, like Poison or Disease, don't slow down a Paladin very much, because they have Holy Magic that can remove these effects (Purify and Cleanse). Diseases like Rabies, which keep hit points and mana from regenerating, can be easily removed by a Paladin after a battle instead of the 10-minute waiting time that another class would spend crippled.

JOINING A PARTY

Most groups love having Paladins because they can serve as a tank and a limited healer. So when you go into a group, expect most of them to ask you to concentrate on healing others over dealing raw melee damage.

The Paladin should always be the first person to do the healing, even (and especially) if there is a primary healer in the party. First, remember that you have all the hit points that you need for a long battle. Priests and Druids don't have the same survivability. Healing spells raise threat levels, and if a Paladin is healing, they have a better chance of getting the mob's attention. Finally, when the Paladin runs out of mana, the healer can take over, giving the Paladin a chance to regenerate. Using a Paladin as a healer this way decreases the amount of time that the party has to spend sitting and regenerating hit points and mana.

Having a Priest and Paladin combination in the group gives special benefits. In this case, a Paladin can help the Priest not only through healing but also through adding to damage. In this case, instead of using Holy Strike first, use Crusader Strike. This ability raises the damage done by Holy Magic, including any Holy Strikes done by the Paladin and Holy Smites done by the Priest.

Crusader Strike is also good in very long fights, specifically, fights against Elite mobs. These enemies have high hit points, so any boost to a Paladin's damage is nice. A good technique is to use Crusader Strike, then Holy Strike, and repeat. You get the most damage for the time that you spend attacking and your party gets all the healing that it needs to keep fighting.

GETTING OUT OF TROUBLE

You have two major get-out-of-trouble abilities: Divine Favor and Lay on Hands. Divine Favor is your limited immunity; you can do it once every 5 minutes, it doesn't have a mana cost, but you can't attack or cast offensive spells while it is active. Lay on Hands restores all a target's hit points at the cost of all a Paladin's mana.

The most important thing to note before you use either of them is how much mana you have. If you have a good supply of mana, but few hit points, use Divine Favor. While you are invulnerable, heal yourself. In the higher levels, your Divine Favor lasts long enough that you can get two good Holy Light healing spells through.

However, Holy Light is mana expensive and not mana efficient. There are situations where you are reaching the low limits of everything, hit points and mana, and your potions have already been used. You may be outnumbered and unable to flee. Or, you can't heal someone in your party enough and the enemy is not leaving them be. What do you do? Lay on Hands. True, you won't have any mana for a time, but it makes all the difference in life or death situations. Just remember that LoH has a one hour cooldown, so you can't use it often.

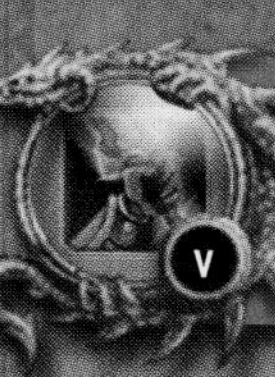

PRIEST

Priests are the primary healers in *World of Warcraft*. Without the healing spells of a Priest, many a Warrior would be unable to survive grabbing five enemies or a Mage able to live through their spell casting. It is these healing spells that make a Priest extremely valuable to groups, and few parties turn down a skilled Healer. However, a Priest's usefulness is not limited to only healing spells. They are also offensive casters, doing damage using both Holy and Shadow magic. Left to their own devices, Priests are no fading flowers resigned to depending on the good graces of others; instead, they are fully capable of defending themselves, performing damage-dealing spells and avoiding some of the worst aspects of an enemy's attacks.

PRIESTLY RECKONING

What started as a tiny battle was quickly becoming a widespread conflict. It seemed as though the entire area was embroiled with Orcs, and there were magical bolts and the sounds of combat all around in a chaotic fray.

We had come to the Redridge Mountains, to Stonewatch Keep, to defend Lakeshire and its citizens from the Horde. In particular, we were searching for Tharil'zun, an Orc known for his cleverness and aggression, the leader of a group of Orc skirmishers. Lakeshire would never be safe as long as this creature held command, and we could not rest without hard proof of his demise. We would leave Stonewatch Keep only with Tharil'zun's head.

But an Orc and his head are not easily parted, and Tharil'zun was far from alone. All it took was one of his retinue scurrying away like a coward to warn the others. Suddenly, we found ourselves overwhelmed by Orcs of enormous ferocity, strength, and the ability to use dark magic.

At first, I added what damage I could by smiting the enemy with the Holy magic that springs forth when called upon. But our group was quickly taking damage, and I rushed to their assistance. The Warrior Tielyn nodded at me in response to the new energy that flooded into her and continued her grim task of slicing into the enemy. Suddenly, I heard Anat, a Mage, cry out. Standing over her, sword raised high, was a thick-bodied Orc fighter. In another second, that sword would swing down and cut the Mage's life; I summoned great force of will and shaped the power of the Light into an elegant shield. The Orc's sword crashed down onto the barrier, but Anat remained unharmed. The Orc even looked surprised as Anat rallied, focusing her magic into a bolt that blasted into the Orc's face.

Tharil'zun himself came into the battle. Knowing that I would have to ensure that our little group survived his onslaught, I used only a small amount of offensive Shadow magic against him: enough to ensure a steady decrease of his power through a simple word—Pain. After that, my attention was completely enwrapped by healing our group, keeping Tielyn, Anat, and the others as safe and healthy as possible. Finally, with a last strangled gasp, Tharil'zun fell forward, dead.

We saved many good people of Lakeshire, I know. And, more importantly, none of my friends were lost in the battle. To help your friends and stop your enemies is the truest thing that anyone can accomplish, and we did a great deed that day.

INTRODUCTION TO PLAYING THE PRIEST

There are several classes with healing potential, but none of them outheals a Priest. This is a class with a wide range of different healing abilities, and Priests have the most powerful and efficient healing spells of any other character in the game.

It's this healing ability that ensures that Priests always have a valuable place in any group. There are always spots available for someone who is willing to keep the rest of the group dealing damage and killing enemies.

However, Priests are not relegated to only healing duties, and they are capable of doing damage against monsters on their own. The proper placement of an offensive spell can do as much to save a party member as a well-timed heal. If a monster is dead, then it can't very well attack your party member, can it? In addition, this means that Priests are perfectly capable of dispatching their own enemies, and they do not need to be constantly shepherded by escorts.

Keep in mind, though, that being a Priest is a matter of temperament. If you find that you enjoy casting large amounts of offensive spells and hate healing, then a Mage may be more your cup of tea. Similarly, if you only want to heal occasionally and want to do more melee damage, a Paladin has some similar abilities to Priests and more survivability.

Exactly what Priests don't have is the heavy armor to withstand a determined assault. Faced with multiple opponents or high-damage enemies, a Priest's cloth armor is no barrier. The use of Power Word: Shield, a temporary spell that absorbs damage and keeps a Priest from being interrupted, can only go so far. It's best for a Priest to keep fights short, sweet, and at range as much as possible.

If you enjoy saving other people and want to throw in a bit of offensive damage on your own, being a Priest is a great choice. You can really have a wonderful time with some of the more social aspects of *World of Warcraft* as well as be a competent soloer if you find that is what you want. Being a Priest means that you are a flexible and versatile healer first and a caster second.

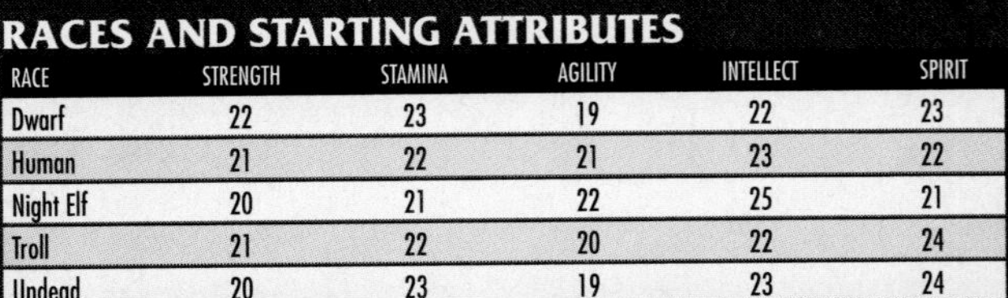

RACES AND STARTING ATTRIBUTES

RACE	STRENGTH	STAMINA	AGILITY	INTELLECT	SPIRIT
Dwarf	22	23	19	22	23
Human	21	22	21	23	22
Night Elf	20	21	22	25	21
Troll	21	22	20	22	24
Undead	20	23	19	23	24

ATTRIBUTES APPLIED

Strength	Higher Melee Damage
Stamina	Higher Hit Points
Agility	Higher Chance to Dodge, More Melee Criticals
Intellect	Higher Mana Pool and Greater Chance for Critical Heals
Spirit	Greater Mana and Hit Point Regeneration

ITEMS AND EQUIPMENT

What you're equipped with is not as important as what bonuses your equipment has. There are three major attributes that your character should concentrate on: Intellect, Spirit, and Stamina.

The choice between Intellect and Spirit is a most interesting one. Intellect increases the amount of mana that a Priest has available to them. More mana means that they can cast greater amounts of spells before resting (both more healing and damage spells). In addition, Priests with high Intellect have a higher chance of landing critical hits with those spells, and there is very good damage to be done with a critical offensive spell.

On the other hand, both healing and damage spells are magic intensive. It's very easy for a Priest to cast away all of their mana, leaving them to rely on their melee damage or magical wands. This is not a good situation for a Priest to be in, and Priests with little mana are very vulnerable. If you have a high Spirit, you can cast your spells more freely, knowing that you can regenerate your magic points while doing some fighting. It can also decrease your amount of downtime, and that's very useful for a Priest, who can spend a lot of time trying to keep their magic points high.

Choosing between Spirit and Intellect is a very personal decision, and there are benefits to each. Try and experiment so that you can find the set of armor that works best for what you want to do. If you find that you run out of magic points frequently and cannot cast the number of spells that you want to, concentrate more on Intellect equipment. If your casting is high but you can't regenerate magic as well (say, in a group where the few heals that you have to make are very expensive), invest more in Spirit gear. If you think that you are going to be in many different types of situations, look for balanced equipment. There is no need to make an either/or choice in the matter: go for both.

The only other attribute to look for in equipment is Stamina. Stamina is tied to how many hit points a Priest has available to them. Because Priests don't have heavy armor (or even modest armor), even little improvements in Stamina are useful. If at all possible, increase your amount of health or armor by supplementing your equipment with enchantments or patches.

HOLY AND SHADOW ATTRIBUTES

There are certain pieces of equipment that increase the power of your Holy or Shadow spells. Depending on the type of Priest that you make, these items can be very useful to you. If you are a Shadow-based Priest or Holy-based Priest, by all means go for the rare off-hand item that raises the power of your spells.

Investing in a weapon is also a personal decision. Keep an eye out for ones that raise the attributes that you want. Maces, Daggers, and Staves are all valid choices, and some of them give very nice bonuses to Spirit and Intellect (Staves in particular). Staves are often focused more toward caster attributes, so they are a sound investment for many Priests.

Wands are important to purchase for doing damage when your mana is depleted. These ranged weapons cost nothing to activate (a huge plus), and allow your character to plug away at targets, not accruing very much aggro, while regenerating mana. It is very nice to have a melee weapon that gives you the bonuses you need while relying on wands for simple damage.

WHAT TO SPEND MONEY ON

More than anything else, make sure that your Priest is fully trained. Without the spells of your level, Priests lose vital abilities. Training can be expensive, especially at the higher levels, but the amount you spend is far worth it.

CHOOSING YOUR PROFESSION

A very good set of Professions to take as a Priest is Herbalism and Alchemy. While you're wandering through Azeroth, you can harvest the herbs that you find. During some crafting breaks, you can make these into useful potions. These potions have a variety of effects, but they complement a Priest's abilities well. For instance, being able to manufacture your own Healing Potions and Mana Potions for emergency situations can be a lifesaver. Using a Healing Potion doesn't cost any magic points and can give your Priest the hit points they need to outlast an encounter. Mana Potions can make the difference between a group member living and dying when your magic points are gone.

Enchanting is also an interesting Profession to explore as a Priest. In this Profession, you break apart equipment pieces into usable components. These components are your ingredients for enchanting armor and weapons. Enchanting gives bonuses to attributes or damage, and these can be either temporary or permanently associate with the piece of equipment. Because a Priest's equipment is so intimately associated with attribute bonuses, being able to control and boost attributes on equipment is very useful.

As a cloth wearer, Tailoring allows a Priest to create their own armor. The early Tailoring recipes create equipment that doesn't have any major bonuses to attributes, but later products are quite powerful. As a Tailor, Priests use the cloth materials that drop from humanoid mobs, so gathering the majority of the crafting ingredients is simply a matter of fighting enemies.

For secondary skills, First Aid is a nice one to pick up. This allows a Priest to create bandages that heal themselves or group members when not in combat. This can significantly reduce the amount of downtime that a Priest spends trying to regain their magic points. Time spent fighting equals time spent gaining experience—and then levels.

CLASS ABILITIES

There are three major lines of Class Abilities for Priests: Holy, Shadow, and Discipline. The use of these abilities always has an associated cost in magic points. There are both defensive and offensive effects for Holy and Shadow, and the proper mixture of them is important for a Priest.

Below are the tables listing these Class Abilities with their associated information.

ABILITY	RANK	LEVEL	TYPE
Holy Smite	1	1	Holy Magic
Power Word: Fortitude	1	1	Discipline
Lesser Heal	1	1	Holy Magic
Lesser Heal	2	4	Holy Magic
Shadow Word: Pain	1	4	Shadow Magic
Smite	2	6	Holy Magic
Power Word: Shield	1	6	Discipline
Fade	1	8	Shadow Magic
Renew	1	8	Holy Magic
Lesser Heal	3	10	Holy Magic
Mind Blast	1	10	Shadow Magic
Resurrection	1	10	Holy Magic
Shadow Word: Pain	2	10	Shadow Magic
Power Word Fortitude	2	12	Discipline
Power Word Shield	2	12	Discipline
Inner Fire	1	12	Discipline
Cure Disease	N/A	14	Holy Magic
Holy Smite	3	14	Holy Magic
Psychic Scream	1	14	Shadow Magic
Renew	2	14	Holy Magic
Heal	1	16	Holy Magic
Mind Blast	2	16	Shadow Magic
Dispel Magic	1	18	Discipline
Power Word: shield	3	18	Discipline
Shadow Word: Pain	3	18	Shadow Magic
Fade	2	20	Shadow Magic
Flash Heal	1	20	Holy Magic
Inner Fire	2	20	Discipline
Mind Soothe	1	20	Shadow Magic
Renew	3	20	Holy Magic
Shackle Undead	1	20	Discipline
Heal	2	22	Holy Magic
Smite	4	22	Holy Magic
Mind Blast	3	22	Shadow Magic

ABILITY	RANK	LEVEL	TYPE
Mind Vision	1	22	Shadow Magic
Power Word: Fortitude	3	24	Discipline
Power Word: Shield	4	24	Discipline
Mana Burn	1	24	Discipline
Flash Heal	2	26	Holy Magic
Renew	4	26	Holy Magic
Resurrection	2	26	Holy Magic
Shadow Word: Pain	4	26	Shadow Magic
Heal	3	28	Holy Magic
Mind Blast	4	28	Shadow Magic
Psychic Scream	2	28	Shadow Magic
Fade	3	30	Shadow Magic
Holy Fire	2	30	Holy Magic
Smite	5	30	Holy Magic
Power Word: Shield	5	30	Discipline
Inner Fire	3	30	Discipline
Mind Control	1	30	Shadow Magic
Prayer of Healing	1	30	Holy Magic
Shadow Protection	1	30	Shadow Magic
Abolish Disease	1	32	Holy Magic
Flash Heal	3	32	Holy Magic
Mana Burn	2	32	Discipline
Renew	5	32	Holy Magic
Heal	4	34	Holy Magic
Levitate	N/A	34	Discipline
Mind Blast	5	34	Shadow Magic
Shadow Word: Pain	5	34	Shadow Magic
Dispel Magic	2	36	Discipline
Holy Fire	3	36	Holy Magic
Power Word: Fortitude	4	36	Discipline
Power Word: Shield	6	36	Discipline
Mind Flay	2	36	Shadow Magic
Mind Soothe	2	36	Shadow Magic

ABILITY	RANK	LEVEL	TYPE
Flash Heal	4	38	Holy Magic
Smite	6	38	Holy Magic
Renew	6	38	Holy Magic
Fade	4	40	Shadow Magic
Greater Heal	1	40	Holy Magic
Inner Fire	4	40	Discipline
Mana Burn	3	40	Discipline
Mind Blast	6	40	Shadow Magic
Prayer of Healing	2	40	Holy Magic
Shackle Undead	2	40	Discipline
Divine Spirit	2	42	Discipline
Holy Fire	4	42	Holy Magic
Power Word: Shield	7	42	Discipline
Psychic Scream	3	42	Shadow Magic
Resurrection	3	42	Holy Magic
Shadow Protection	2	42	Shadow Magic
Shadow Word: Pain	6	42	Shadow Magic
Flash Heal	5	44	Holy Magic
Mind Control	2	44	Shadow Magic
Mind Flay	3	44	Shadow Magic
Mind Vision	2	44	Shadow Magic
Renew	7	44	Holy Magic
Greater Heal	2	46	Holy Magic
Holy Smite	7	46	Holy Magic
Mind Blast	7	46	Shadow Magic
Holy Fire	5	48	Holy Magic
Power Word: Fortitude	5	48	Discipline
Power Word: Shield	8	48	Discipline
Mana Burn	4	48	Discipline
Divine Spirit	3	50	Discipline
Fade	5	50	Shadow Magic
Flash Heal	6	50	Holy Magic
Holy Nova	2	50	Holy Magic
Inner Fire	5	50	Discipline

ABILITY	RANK	LEVEL	TYPE
Prayer of Healing	3	50	Holy Magic
Renew	8	50	Holy Magic
Shadow Word: Pain	7	50	Shadow Magic
Greater Heal	3	52	Holy Magic
Mind Blast	8	52	Shadow Magic
Mind Flay	4	52	Shadow Magic
Mind Soothe	3	52	Shadow Magic
Holy Fire	6	54	Holy Magic
Smite	8	54	Holy Magic
Power Word: Shield	9	54	Discipline
Flash Heal	7	56	Holy Magic
Mana Burn	5	56	Discipline
Psychic Scream	4	56	Shadow Magic
Renew	9	56	Holy Magic
Shadow Protection	3	56	Shadow Magic
Greater Heal	4	58	Holy Magic
Holy Nova	3	58	Holy Magic
Mind Blast	9	58	Shadow Magic
Mind Control	3	58	Shadow Magic
Resurrection	4	58	Holy Magic
Shadow Word: Pain	8	58	Shadow Magic
Fade	6	60	Shadow Magic
Holy Fire	7	60	Holy Magic
Power Word: Fortitude	6	60	Discipline
Power Word: Shield	10	60	Discipline
Inner Fire	6	60	Discipline
Mind Flay	5	60	Shadow Magic
Prayer of Healing	4	60	Holy Magic
Shackle Undead	3	60	Discipline

DISCIPLINE

Discipline includes many of your defensive abilities. Mainly this is your buff line, but there is also one very important spell here (Power Word: Shield). This spell absorbs a certain amount of damage and prevents the target from being interrupted during spell casting.

Priests also have an Undead-specific targeted spell. Shackle Undead keeps the enemy from moving, casting spells, or attacking, but any damage done to the enemy frees it from the shackles. This form of combat control is vital in PvP against the Horde and is also quite useful against elite monsters that are Undead.

DISPEL MAGIC

RANK	LEVEL	MANA	RANGE	CASTING TIME	COOLDOWN	COST TO TRAIN	EFFECT
1	18	75	30 yd	IC		29	Dispels magic on the target, removing 1 harmful spell from a friend or 1 beneficial spell from an enemy.
2	36	125	30 yd	IC		1 50	Dispels magic on the target, removing 2 harmful spell from a friend or 2 beneficial spell from an enemy.

DIVINE SPIRIT

RANK	LEVEL	MANA	RANGE	CASTING TIME	COOLDOWN	COST TO TRAIN	EFFECT
2	42	610	30 yd	IC		70	Holy power infuses the target, increasing their Spirit by 29 for 30 min.
3	50	860	30 yd	IC		1 60	Holy power infuses the target, increasing their Spirit by 35 for 30 min.

POWER WORD: FORTITUDE

RANK	LEVEL	MANA	RANGE	CASTING TIME	COOLDOWN	COST TO TRAIN	EFFECT
1	1	60	30 yd	IC		10	Holy Power Infuses the target increasing their Stamina by 3 for 30min.
2	12	155	30 yd	IC		8	Holy power infuses the target increasing their Stamina by 8 for 30 min.
3	24	400	30 yd	IC		71	Holy power infuses the target increasing their Stamina by 18 for 30 min.
4	36	745	30 yd	IC		1 50	Holy power infuses the target increasing their Stamina by 42 for 30 min.
5	48	1170	30 yd	IC		4 20	Holy power infuses the target increasing their Stamina by 56 for 30 min.
6	60	1695	30 yd	IC		4 70	Holy power infuses the target increasing their Stamina by 70 for 30 min.

POWER WORD: SHIELD

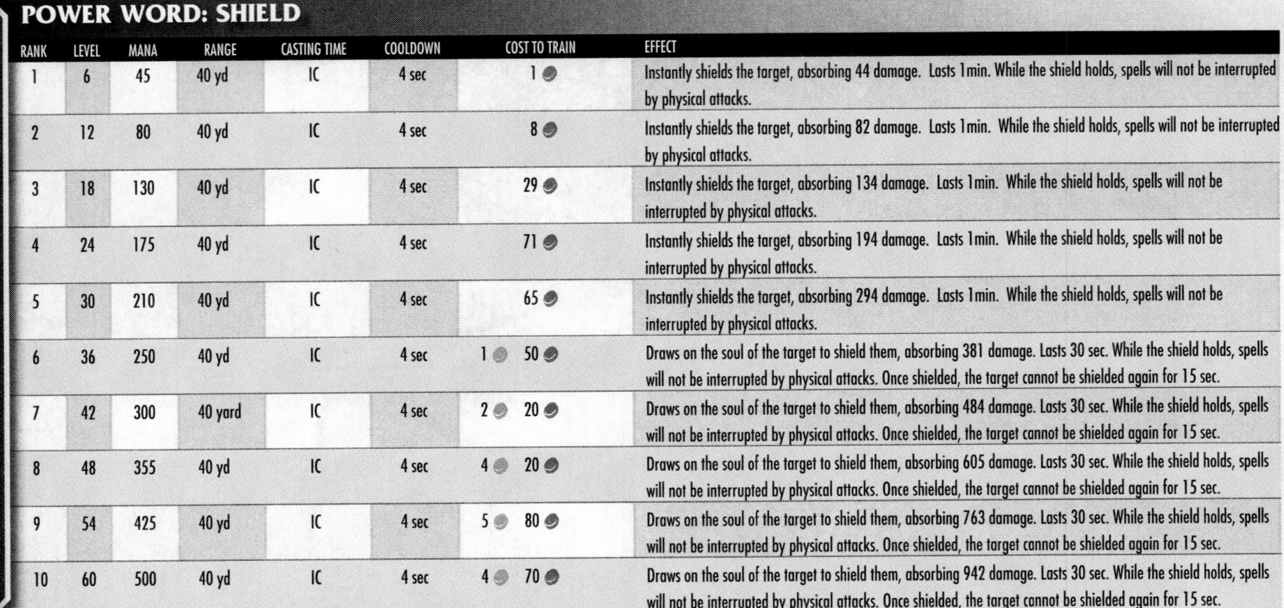

RANK	LEVEL	MANA	RANGE	CASTING TIME	COOLDOWN	COST TO TRAIN	EFFECT
1	6	45	40 yd	IC	4 sec	1	Instantly shields the target, absorbing 44 damage. Lasts 1min. While the shield holds, spells will not be interrupted by physical attacks.
2	12	80	40 yd	IC	4 sec	8	Instantly shields the target, absorbing 82 damage. Lasts 1min. While the shield holds, spells will not be interrupted by physical attacks.
3	18	130	40 yd	IC	4 sec	29	Instantly shields the target, absorbing 134 damage. Lasts 1min. While the shield holds, spells will not be interrupted by physical attacks.
4	24	175	40 yd	IC	4 sec	71	Instantly shields the target, absorbing 194 damage. Lasts 1min. While the shield holds, spells will not be interrupted by physical attacks.
5	30	210	40 yd	IC	4 sec	65	Instantly shields the target, absorbing 294 damage. Lasts 1min. While the shield holds, spells will not be interrupted by physical attacks.
6	36	250	40 yd	IC	4 sec	1 50	Draws on the soul of the target to shield them, absorbing 381 damage. Lasts 30 sec. While the shield holds, spells will not be interrupted by physical attacks. Once shielded, the target cannot be shielded again for 15 sec.
7	42	300	40 yard	IC	4 sec	2 20	Draws on the soul of the target to shield them, absorbing 484 damage. Lasts 30 sec. While the shield holds, spells will not be interrupted by physical attacks. Once shielded, the target cannot be shielded again for 15 sec.
8	48	355	40 yd	IC	4 sec	4 20	Draws on the soul of the target to shield them, absorbing 605 damage. Lasts 30 sec. While the shield holds, spells will not be interrupted by physical attacks. Once shielded, the target cannot be shielded again for 15 sec.
9	54	425	40 yd	IC	4 sec	5 80	Draws on the soul of the target to shield them, absorbing 763 damage. Lasts 30 sec. While the shield holds, spells will not be interrupted by physical attacks. Once shielded, the target cannot be shielded again for 15 sec.
10	60	500	40 yd	IC	4 sec	4 70	Draws on the soul of the target to shield them, absorbing 942 damage. Lasts 30 sec. While the shield holds, spells will not be interrupted by physical attacks. Once shielded, the target cannot be shielded again for 15 sec.

INNER FIRE

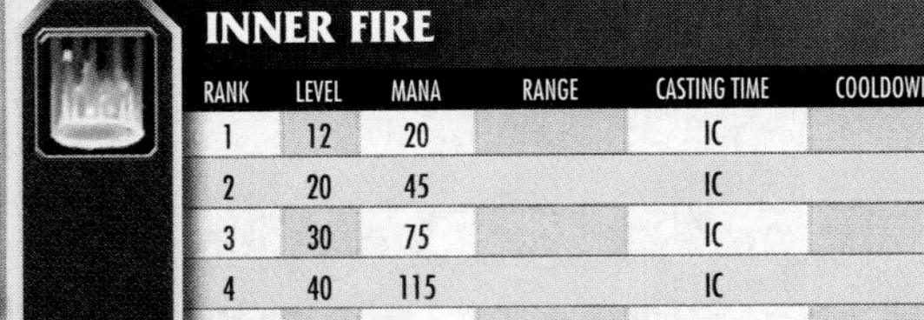

RANK	LEVEL	MANA	RANGE	CASTING TIME	COOLDOWN	COST TO TRAIN	EFFECT
1	12	20		IC		8	A burst of Holy energy fills the caster, increasing her attack power by 20 and armor by 60 for 3 min.
2	20	45		IC		23	A burst of Holy energy fills the caster, increasing her attack power by 35 and armor by 100 for 3 min.
3	30	75		IC		65	A burst of Holy energy fills the caster, increasing her attack power by 50 and armor by 140 for 3 min.
4	40	115		IC		1 30	A burst of Holy energy fills the caster, increasing his attack power by 70 and armor by 630 for 3 min.
5	50	165		IC		2 80	A burst of Holy energy fills the caster, increasing his attack power by 90 and armor by 780 for 3 min.
6	60	225		IC		4 70	A burst of Holy energy fills the caster, increasing his attack power by 110 and armor by 930 for 3 min.

LEVITATE

RANK	LEVEL	MANA	RANGE	CASTING TIME	COOLDOWN	COST TO TRAIN	EFFECT
N/A	34	80		IC		1 10	Allows the caster to levitate, floating a few feet above the ground. While levitating, you will fall at a reduced speed and travel over water-like surfaces. Lasts 1 min.

MANA BURN

RANK	LEVEL	MANA	RANGE	CASTING TIME	COOLDOWN	COST TO TRAIN	EFFECT
1	24	95	30 yd	3 sec		71	Drains 191 to 203 mana from a target. For each mana drained in this way, the target takes 0.5 damage.
2	32	140	30 yd	3 sec		1 10	Drains 309 to 329 mana from a target. For each mana drained in this way the target takes 0.5 damage.
3	40	185	30 yd	3 sec		1 30	Drains 442 to 468 mana from a target. For each mana drained in this way, the target takes 0.5 damage.
4	48	225	30 yd	3 sec		4 20	Drains 576 to 610 mana from a target. For each mana drained in this way, the target takes 0.5 damage.
5	56	270	30 yd	3 sec		4 80	Drains 738 to 780 mana from a target. For each mana drained in this way, the target takes 0.5 damage.

SHACKLE UNDEAD

RANK	LEVEL	MANA	RANGE	CASTING TIME	COOLDOWN	COST TO TRAIN	EFFECT
1	20	90	30 yd	1.5 sec		23	Shackles the target undead enemy for up to 30 sec. The shackled unit is unable to move, attack or cast spells. Any damage caused will release the target. Only one target can be shackled at a time.
2	40	120	30 yd	1.5 sec		1 30	Shackles the target undead enemy for up to 40 sec. The shackled unit is unable to move, attack or cast spells. Any damage caused will release the target. Only one target can be shackled at a time.
3	60	150	30 yd	1.5 sec		4 70	Shackles the target undead enemy for up to 50 sec. The shackled unit is unable to move, attack or cast spells. Any damage caused will release the target. Only one target can be shackled at a time.

HOLY

Holy abilities include your healing spells. Because of the wide variety in healing spells, you can ensure that you are able to choose just the right one for a given situation. There are spells to counter poison and disease. Renew heals over time. Flash Heal has a short casting time with fair Hit Point healing. Greater Heal has a long casting time but heals high amounts of hit points.

There is also an offensive spell, Holy Smite, which does Holy damage against a target. Just because you are interested in healing doesn't mean that you can't dish out a bit of damage.

ABOLISH DISEASE

RANK	LEVEL	MANA	RANGE	CASTING TIME	COOLDOWN	COST TO TRAIN	EFFECT
1	32	100	30 yd	IC		1 10	Attempts to cure 1 disease effect every 5 seconds for 20 sec.

CURE DISEASE

RANK	LEVEL	MANA	RANGE	CASTING TIME	COOLDOWN	COST TO TRAIN	EFFECT
N/A	14	60	30 yd	IC		9	Removes 1 disease from the friendly target.

FLASH HEAL

RANK	LEVEL	MANA	RANGE	CASTING TIME	COOLDOWN	COST TO TRAIN	EFFECT
1	20	125	40 yd	1.5 sec		23	Heals a friendly target for 170 to 208.
2	26	155	40 yd	1.5 sec		67	Heals a friendly target for 226 to 274.
3	32	185	40 yd	1.5 sec		1 10	Heals a friendly target for 327 to 393.
4	38	215	40 yd	1.5 sec		2 30	Heals a friendly target for 400 to 478.
5	44	265	40 yd	1.5 sec		2 50	Heals a friendly target for 518 to 616.
6	50	315	40 yd	1.5 sec		2 80	Heals a friendly target for 644 to 764.
7	56	380	40 yd	1.5 sec		4 80	Heals a friendly target for 812 to 958.

GREATER HEAL

RANK	LEVEL	MANA	RANGE	CASTING TIME	COOLDOWN	COST TO TRAIN	EFFECT
1	40	545	40 yd	4 sec		1 30	A slow casting spell that heals a single target for 1201 to 1353.
2	46	665	40 yd	4 sec		3 70	A slow casting spell that heals a single target for 1531 to 1717.
3	52	800	40 yd	4 sec		5 30	A slow casting spell that heals a single target for 1919 to 2147.
4	58	960	40 yd	4 sec		5 30	A slow casting spell that heals a single target for 2396 to 2674.

HEAL

RANK	LEVEL	MANA	RANGE	CASTING TIME	COOLDOWN	COST TO TRAIN	EFFECT
1	16	170	40 yd	3 sec		18	Heal your target for 247 to 285.
2	22	265	40 yd	3.5 sec		42	Heal your target for 421 to 481.
3	28	375	40 yd	4 sec		81	Heal your target for 670 to 762.
4	34	450	40 yd	4 sec		1 30	Heal your target for 948 to 1072.

HOLY FIRE

RANK	LEVEL	MANA	RANGE	CASTING TIME	COOLDOWN	COST TO TRAIN	EFFECT
2	30	170	30 yd	5 sec	1 min	20	Consumes the enemy in flames that causes 164 to 208 Fire damage and an additional 48 Fire damage over 8 sec.
3	36	205	30 yd	5 sec	1 min	40	Consumes the enemy in flames that causes 211 to 265 Fire damage and an additional 60 Fire damage over 8 sec.
4	42	245	30 yd	5 sec	1 min	60	Consumes the enemy in flames that causes 267 to 333 Fire damage and an additional 76 Fire damage over 8 sec.
5	48	280	30 yd	5 sec	1 min	1 10	Consumes the enemy in flames that causes 320 to 398 Fire damage and an additional 92 Fire damage over 8 sec.
6	54	325	30 yd	5 sec	1 min	1 50	Consumes the enemy in flames that causes 391 to 483 Fire damage and an additional 112 Fire damage over 8 sec.
7	60	365	30 yd	5 sec	1 min	1 60	Consumes the enemy in flames that causes 464 to 570 Fire damage and an additional 128 Fire damage over 8 sec.

HOLY NOVA

RANK	LEVEL	MANA	RANGE	CASTING TIME	COOLDOWN	COST TO TRAIN	EFFECT
2	50	265		IC	5 sec	70	Causes an explosion of holy light around the caster, causing 113 to 123 Holy damage to all targets within 10 yards. The effect also temporarily reduces your threat level against nearby targets for 5 sec.
3	58	315		IC	5 sec	1 30	Causes an explosion of holy light around the caster, causing 143 to 157 Holy damage to all targets within 10 yards. The effect also temporarily reduces your threat level against nearby targets for 5 sec.

SMITE

RANK	LEVEL	MANA	RANGE	CASTING TIME	COOLDOWN	COST TO TRAIN	EFFECT
1	1	25	30 yd	1.5 sec		No Cost	Smite an enemy for 13 to 17 holy damage
2	6	35	30 yd	2 sec		1	Smite an enemy for 24 to 28 holy damage.
3	14	65	30 yd	2.5 sec		9	Smite an enemy for 54 to 62 holy damage.
4	22	100	30 yd	2.5 sec		42	Smite an enemy for 96 to 110 holy damage.
5	30	150	30 yd	2.5 sec		65	Smite an enemy for 160 to 182 holy damage.
6	38	195	30 yd	2.5 sec		2 30	Smite an enemy for 212 to 240 holy damage.
7	46	245	30 yd	2.5 sec		3 70	Smite an enemy for 287 to 323 holy damage.
8	54	295	30 yd	2.5 sec		5 80	Smite an enemy for 371 to 415 holy damage.

LESSER HEAL

RANK	LEVEL	MANA	RANGE	CASTING TIME	COOLDOWN	COST TO TRAIN	EFFECT
1	1	35	40 yd	1.5 sec		No Cost	Heal your target for 43-53
2	4	50	40 yd	2 sec		50	Heal your target for 66-80.
3	10	85	40 yd	2.5 sec		3	Heal your target for 142 to 166.

PRAYER OF HEALING

RANK	LEVEL	MANA	RANGE	CASTING TIME	COOLDOWN	COST TO TRAIN	EFFECT
1	30	410		3 sec		65	A powerful prayer heals nearby party members for 293 to 313.
2	40	560		3 sec		1 30	A powerful prayer heals nearby party members for 444 to 472.
3	50	770		3 sec		2 80	A powerful prayer heals nearby party members for 657 to 696.
4	60	1030		3 sec		4 70	A powerful prayer heals nearby party members for 939 to 991.

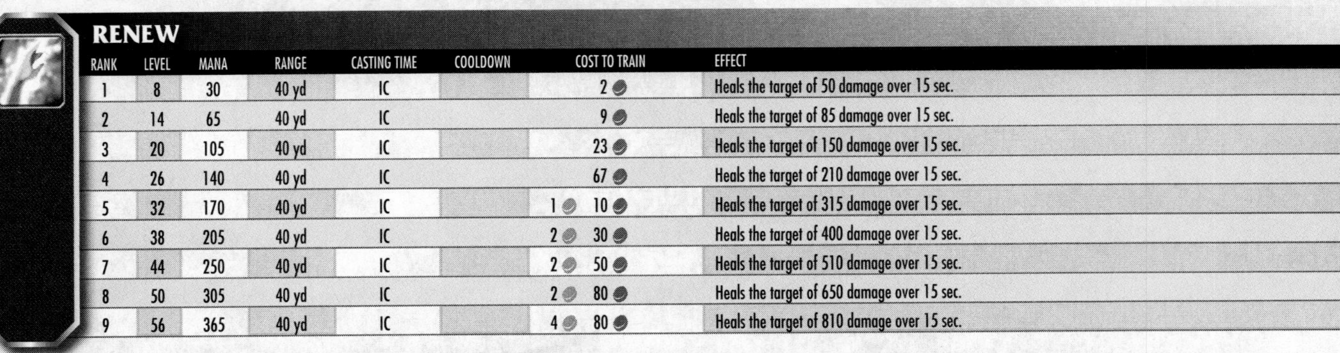

RENEW

RANK	LEVEL	MANA	RANGE	CASTING TIME	COOLDOWN	COST TO TRAIN	EFFECT
1	8	30	40 yd	IC		2s	Heals the target of 50 damage over 15 sec.
2	14	65	40 yd	IC		9s	Heals the target of 85 damage over 15 sec.
3	20	105	40 yd	IC		23s	Heals the target of 150 damage over 15 sec.
4	26	140	40 yd	IC		67s	Heals the target of 210 damage over 15 sec.
5	32	170	40 yd	IC		1g 10s	Heals the target of 315 damage over 15 sec.
6	38	205	40 yd	IC		2g 30s	Heals the target of 400 damage over 15 sec.
7	44	250	40 yd	IC		2g 50s	Heals the target of 510 damage over 15 sec.
8	50	305	40 yd	IC		2g 80s	Heals the target of 650 damage over 15 sec.
9	56	365	40 yd	IC		4g 80s	Heals the target of 810 damage over 15 sec.

RESURRECTION

RANK	LEVEL	MANA	RANGE	CASTING TIME	COOLDOWN	COST TO TRAIN	EFFECT
1	10	150	40 yd	10 sec		3s	Brings a dead player back to life with 15% of their health and mana.
2	26	250	40 yd	10 sec		2g 20s	Brings a dead player back to life with 30% of their health and mana.
3	42	400	40 yd	10 sec		2g 20s	Brings a dead player back to life with 40% of their health and mana.
4	58	500	40 yd	10 sec		5g 30s	Brings a dead player back to life with 50% of their health and mana.

SHADOW

Shadow abilities are, in general, centered onto offensive and combat control spells. In this area, you find your strongest offensive spell, Mind Blast, as well as a powerful damage over time spell, Shadow Word: Pain. In later levels, Priests also acquire some combat control spells. This includes the ability to make your enemies run away from you or allow you to control them temporarily.

FADE

RANK	LEVEL	MANA	RANGE	CASTING TIME	COOLDOWN	COST TO TRAIN	EFFECT
1	8	40		IC	30 sec	2s	Fade out, reducing the caster's threat level on all enemies by a small amount for 10sec.
2	20	75		IC	30 sec	23s	Fade out, reducing the caster's threat level on all enemies by a medium amount for 10sec.
3	30	125		IC		65s	Fade out, reducing the caster's threat level on all enemies by a high amount for 10sec.
4	40	175		IC	30 sec	1g 30s	Fade out, discouraging enemies from attacking you for 10 sec. More effective than Fade (rank 3).
5	50	225		IC	30 sec	2g 80s	Fade out, discouraging enemies from attacking you for 10 sec. More effective than Fade (rank 4).
6	60	275		IC	30 sec	4g 70s	Fade out, discouraging enemies from attacking you for 10 sec. More effective than Fade (rank 5).

MIND BLAST

RANK	LEVEL	MANA	RANGE	CASTING TIME	COOLDOWN	COST TO TRAIN	EFFECT
1	10	50	30 yd	1.5 sec	8 sec	3s	Blasts the target for 39 to 43 shadow damage, but causes a high amount of threat.
2	16	80	30 yd	1.5 sec	8 sec	18s	Blasts the target for 72 to 78 shadow damage, but causes a high amount of threat.
3	22	110	30 yd	1.5 sec	8 sec	42s	Blasts the target for 112 to 120 shadow damage, but causes a high amount of threat.
4	28	150	30 yd	1.5 sec	8 sec	81s	Blasts the target for 167 to 177 shadow damage, but causes a high amount of threat.
5	34	185	30 yd	1.5 sec	8 sec	1g 30s	Blasts the target for 217 to 231 shadow damage, but causes a high amount of threat.
6	40	225	30 yd	1.5 sec	8 sec	1g 30s	Blasts the target for 279 to 297 shadow damage, but causes a high amount of threat.
7	46	265	30 yd	1.5 sec	8 sec	3g 70s	Blasts the target for 346 to 366 shadow damage, but causes a high amount of threat.
8	52	310	30 yd	1.5 sec	8 sec	5g 30s	Blasts the target for 425 to 449 shadow damage, but causes a high amount of threat.
9	58	350	30 yd	1.5 sec	8 sec	5g 30s	Blasts the target for 503 to 531 shadow damage, but causes a high amount of threat.

MIND CONTROL

RANK	LEVEL	MANA	RANGE	CASTING TIME	COOLDOWN	COST TO TRAIN	EFFECT
1	30	350	20 yd	2 sec		65s	Controls a humanoid mind up to level 32, but slows it's attack speed by 20%. Lasts 1min, but the target gets a chance to break free every 5 seconds.
2	44	550	20 yd	3 sec		2g 50s	Controls a humanoid mind up to level 47, but slows it's attack speed by 20%. Lasts 1 min, but the target gets a chance to break free every 5 seconds.
3	58	750	20 yd	3 sec		5g 30s	Controls a humanoid mind up to level 62, but slows it's attack speed by 20%. Lasts 1 min, but the target gets a chance to break free every 5 seconds.

MIND FLAY

RANK	RANK	LEVEL	MANA	RANGE	CASTING TIME	COOLDOWN	COST TO TRAIN	EFFECT
2	36	100	20 yd	IC		40s	Assault the target's mind with Shadow energy, causing 186 damage over 3 sec and slowing the target to 50% of their movement speed.	
3	44	135	20 yd	IC		60s	Assault the target's mind with Shadow energy, causing 261 damage over 3 sec and slowing the target to 50% of their movement speed.	
4	52	165	20 yd	IC		1g 30s	Assault the target's mind with Shadow energy, causing 330 damage over 3 sec and slowing the target to 50% of their movement speed.	
5	60	205	20 yd	IC		1g 60s	Assault the target's mind with Shadow energy, causing 426 damage over 3 sec and slowing the target to 50% of their movement speed.	

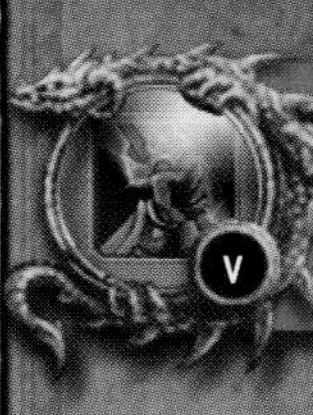

MIND SOOTHE

RANK	LEVEL	MANA	RANGE	CASTING TIME	COOLDOWN	COST TO TRAIN	EFFECT
1	20	50	40 yd	IC		23	Soothes the target, reducing the range at which it will attack you. Only affects targets level 40 or lower. Lasts 15 sec.
2	36	70	40 yd	IC		50	Soothes the target, reducing the range at which it will attack you. Only affects targets level 55 or lower. Lasts 15 sec.
3	52	90	40 yd	IC		5 30	Soothes the target, reducing the range at which it will attack you. Only affects targets level 55 or lower. Lasts 15 sec.

MIND VISION

RANK	LEVEL	MANA	RANGE	CASTING TIME	COOLDOWN	COST TO TRAIN	EFFECT
1	22	65	100 yd	IC		42	Allows the caster to see through the target's eyes for 1 min.
2	44	150	100 yd	IC		2 50	Allows the caster to see through the target's eyes for 1 min. Will not work if the target is in another Instance or on another continent.

PSYCHIC SCREAM

RANK	LEVEL	MANA	RANGE	CASTING TIME	COOLDOWN	COST TO TRAIN	EFFECT
1	14	100		IC	30 sec	9	The caster lets out a psychic scream, causing 2 nearby enemies to flee for 8 sec.
2	28	140		IC	30 sec	81	The caster lets out a psychic scream, causing 3 nearby enemies to flee for 8 sec.
3	42	180		IC	30 sec	2 20	The Caster lets out a psychic scream, causing 4 nearby enemies to flee for 8 sec.
4	56	210		IC	30 sec	4 80	The Caster lets out a psychic scream, causing 5 nearby enemies to flee for 8 sec.

SHADOW PROTECTION

RANK	LEVEL	MANA	RANGE	CASTING TIME	COOLDOWN	COST TO TRAIN	EFFECT
1	30	250	30 yd	IC		65	Increases the target's resistance to Shadow spells by 50 for 10 min.
2	42	450	30 yd	IC		2 20	Increases the target's resistance to Shadow spells by 75 for 10 min.
3	56	650	30 yd	IC		4 80	Increases the target's resistance to Shadow spells by 100 for 10 min.

SHADOW WORD: PAIN

RANK	LEVEL	MANA	RANGE	CASTING TIME	COOLDOWN	COST TO TRAIN	EFFECT
1	4	25	30 yd	IC		50	A word of darkness that causes 30 damage over 18 sec.
2	10	50	30 yd	IC		3	A word of darkness that causes 66 damage over 18 sec.
3	18	95	30 yd	IC		29	A word of darkness that causes 132 damage over 18 sec.
4	26	155	30 yd	IC		67	A word of darkness that causes 234 damage over 18 sec.
5	34	230	30 yd	IC		1 30	A word of darkness that causes 488 damage over 24 sec.
6	42	305	30 yd	IC		2 20	A word of darkness that causes 680 damage over 24 sec.
7	50	385	30 yd	IC		2 80	A word of darkness that causes 896 damage over 24 sec.
8	58	470	30 yd	IC		5 30	A word of darkness that causes 1136 damage over 24 sec.

TALENTS

The Priest Talent lines help to focus their class abilities, making them more powerful or more efficient. That being said, even a heavily Shadow-based Priest can heal or Holy-based Priest do damage over time. Rather than limiting the range of a Priest, Talents allow them to become more effective at a given line of spells.

In general, which Talents you decide to take depend on the role that you enjoy as a Priest. If you enjoy healing and playing in a group, consider focusing in Holy Talents. If you like the aggressive, offensive damage found in Shadow or enjoy soloing, then Shadow Talents are useful for you. Discipline, on the other hand, is a very balanced set of Talents, and raising the strength of buffs and defensive abilities can be valuable.

DISCIPLINE

TALENT NAME	RANKS	PREREQUISITES	EFFECTS
Unbreakable Will	5	None	Increases chance to resist Stun, Fear, and Silence by 3%
Silent Resolve	5	None	Reduces the Threat generated by your damage spells by 4%
Wand Specialization	5	5 Points in Discipline	Increases damage from wands by 5%
Improved Power Word: Shield	3	5 Points in Discipline	Reduces the duration of Weakened Soul by 5 seconds
Improved Power Word: Fortitude	2	5 Points in Discipline	Increases the effect of Power Word: Fortitude by 15%
Mental Agility	5	10 Points in Discipline	Reduces the cost of your Instant spells by 2%
Improved Shackle Undead	2	10 Points in Discipline	Decreases the chance for enemies to resist Shackle Undead by 5%
Martyrdom	2	10 Points in Discipline	Adds a 50% chance to gain Focused Casting for six seconds after your are critically hit
Inner Focus	1	5 Points in Mental Agility, 15 Points in Discipline	Adds an Instant ability to make your next spell free of cost and increase its chance to critical by 25%
Meditation	5	15 Points in Discipline	Increases your Mana Regeneration by 2%
Improved Inner Fire	3	15 Points in Discipline	Increases the effect of Inner Fire by 15%
Focused Casting	1	2 Points in Martyrdom, 20 Points in Discipline	Adds an Instant ability that lasts eight seconds and negates delays in casting from taking damage
Improved Mana Burn	2	25 Points in Discipline	Reduces the casting time of Mana Burn by .5 seconds
Divine Spirit	1	5 Points in Meditation, 30 Points in Discipline	Adds an spell that buffs a target's Spirit by 23 for 30 Minutes

HOLY

TALENT NAME	RANKS	PREREQUISITES	EFFECTS
Improved Holy Smite	3	None	Increases the critical strike damage of Holy Smite by 40%
Holy Specialization	5	None	Increases the chance to land a critical hit with Holy spells by 1%
Subtlety	5	None	Reduces Threat generated by healing spells by 4%
Spiritual Healing	5	5 Points in Holy Specialization, 5 Points in Holy	Increases Mana Regeneration by 50% after getting a critical with a healing spell (10% rate if you continue casting)
Inspiration	5	5 Points in Holy	Increases your target's armor by 5% after landing a critical heal
Improved Renew	5	10 Points in Holy	Increases the amount healed by Renew by 4%
Improved Resurrection	2	10 Points in Holy	Reduces the penalty of Resurrection Sickness by 10%
Holy Fire	1	3 Points in Improved Holy Smite, 15 Points in Holy	Adds a 5 second spell that deals immediate Fire damage and adds a Fire DOT
Improved Healing	5	15 Points in Holy	Reduces the Mana cost of Lesser Heal, Heal, and Greater Heal by 2%
Improved Flash Heal	2	1 Point in Inspiration, 15 Points in Holy	Gives a 35% chance to avoid interruption (by damage) while casting Flash Heal
Improved Shadow Protection	2	20 Points in Holy	Increases the amount gained by Shadow Resistance by 15%
Improved Prayer of Healing	2	20 Points in Holy	Reduces the Mana cost of Prayer of Healing by 10%
Combat Resurrection	1	2 Points in Improved Resurrection, 20 Points in Holy	Adds a 2 second spell that brings a dead player back to life with 50% Health/Mana and NO Resurrection Sickness
Master Healer	5	5 Points in Improved Healing, 25 Points in Holy	Increases the effectiveness of all healing spells by 2%
Holy Nova	1	30 Points in Holy	Adds an Instant ability to unleash an AoE Holy attack (deals damage and temporarily reduces Threat against nearby targets for 5 seconds)

SHADOW

TALENT NAME	RANKS	PREREQUISITES	EFFECTS
Spirit Tap	5	None	Adds a 20% chance to gain a 100% bonus to Spirit after killing a target that lasts 15 seconds (effect halves during continued casting)
Blackout	5	None	Gives all Shadow damage spells a 2% chance for a 3 second Stun
Shadow Affinity	5	5 Points in Shadow	Reduces the Threat of your Shadow spells by 5%
Improved Shadow Word: Pain	2	5 Points in Shadow	Increase the duration of Shadow Word: Pain by 3 seconds
Shadow Focus	5	5 Points in Shadow	Reduces your target's chance to resist Shadow spells by 2%
Improved Fade	2	5 Points in Shadow Affinity, 10 Points in Shadow	Increases the duration of Fade by 5 seconds
Improved Mind Blast	5	10 Points in Shadow	Reduces the cooldown of Mind Blast by .5 seconds
Improved Psychic Scream	2	15 Points in Shadow	Reduces the cooldown of Psychic Scream by 2 seconds
Shadow Weaving	5	15 Points in Shadow	Adds a 20% chance for Shadow spells to inflict a Shadow Vulnerability on your target (4% increased damage for 15 seconds)
Mind Flay	1	5 Points in Shadow Focus, 15 Points in Shadow	Adds a Channeling ability to deal heavy damage over three seconds and slow your target to 50% of their movement rate
Shadow Reach	3	15 Points in Shadow	Increases the range of Shadow damage spells by 6%
Vampiric Embrace	1	20 Points in Shadow	Adds a debuff to your target such that 20% of Shadow damage dealt to that target causes all of your party members to be healed (lasts one minute)
Silence	1	2 Points in Improved Psychic Scream, 25 Points in Shadow	Adds an Instant ability to Silence your target for 5 seconds (preventing casting)
Darkness	5	5 Points in Shadow Weaving, 25 Points in Shadow	Increases damage from your Shadow spells by 2%
Shadowform	1	30 Points in Shadow	Adds an Instant ability to assume a Shadowform, dealing 20% more Shadow damage and taking 20% less physical damage (you cannot cast Holy spells in this state)

STRATEGIES

The core Priest strategy involves the proper mixture of offensive and defensive spells that allows you to keep high amounts of magic points. Much of this depends on whether or not you are in a group: that is, whether your primary role is healing or doing damage. In a group, concentrate on doing modest damage with melee attacks or your wand until the primary tank is significantly wounded, then drop down a high hit point heal (such as Greater Heal). If any of the lower hit point group members get attacked, Power Word: Shield them and/or give them a Flash Heal.

On your own, use Shadow spells early. Start with Mind Blast, give the enemy some Shadow Word: Pain, and then hit them until your Mind Blast in available again. To keep yourself from being interrupted in the fight as you cast, Power Word: Shield yourself before you start. If at all possible, wait to heal yourself until after the fight; casting time is better spent doing damage against your target.

GENERAL TIPS

Keep your Stamina buff up at all times. Having those extra hit points makes a big difference for anyone, and the first thing you should do before moving out into the world should be to buff yourself. By the same token, as you add members to your group, give them each a Stamina buff. This makes a significant difference for other casters, who need all the hit points they can get. Your tanks won't complain about getting it either.

As you gain in different spells and abilities, keep an eye on which ones are most mana efficient. If Flash Heal takes less mana to cast, has a shorter casting time, and heals for only 100 hit points less than your normal Heal spell, concentrate on using Flash Heal. Or, if you are Holy-based Priest, using Holy Smite as your primary damage-dealing spell makes more sense than using Mind Blast, because your Holy talents decrease the amount of mana that you spend with Holy spells.

Power Word: Shield is a very powerful ability, but it is very mana intensive. In a group, only use it in emergency situations. First, it can eat through your mana reserves. Second, it generates threat against you, and if a monster is hitting you than you can't cast effectively. An excellent time to Shield is when a caster is jumped by multiple enemies. A bad time to Shield is right before a Warrior charges into a group of enemies (Warriors don't worry about being interrupted and have the hit points to handle the aggro). If the timing is off, you can end up being first on the enemy group's list, and the Warrior has to fight everything off of you.

If you are soloing, then Power Word: Shield is good to use right before you start off the fight. This keeps you from being interrupted or having to cast healing spells instead of offensive spells. This works especially well if the enemies you fight are fast-attacking ones, like Wolves or Cats.

When you are fighting longer battles, make sure to hit the mob with a Shadow Word: Pain. The damage over time that this spell gives is a steady drain on an enemy's hit points and brings them one step closer to defeat. Also, Shadow Word: Pain is not an expensive spell to cast, so you are not hampering your further casting at all. Instead, this can make a big difference against enemies with high hit points (like Elites) or high resistances to physical damage (like Turtles).

ALL BY YOUR LONESOME?

In *World of Warcraft*, it's completely possible for every class to solo up to maximum level, and this includes cloth-wearing primary healers. Instead of being dependent on a group, Priests on their own are very powerful, independent entities.

The primary goal as a solo Priest is to minimize the time that you spend regenerating mana. First off, if you're sitting, you aren't getting experience. Second, drinks are monetarily expensive, and there are better ways to spend your money (e.g. Training).

Strongly consider specializing in Shadow Magic for soloing because that line dramatically improves a Priest's kill rate. Start fights with a Mind Blast and Shadow Word: Pain to get your timer started and some damage going it at your enemy. Raise a Power Word: Shield as the foe arrives to reduce your need for future healing, then use melee/wand damage until the creature is badly harmed. Use a second Mind Blast if needed, or switch into Mind Flay if you need to deal damage and slow an opponent's retreat!

Of course if you don't mind downtime at all, just concentrate on offensive spell use. Start with the Shield to keep from being interrupted during casting and then switch between Mind Blast and Holy Smite. When the creature is dead, heal yourself as needed. It uses up magic points pretty quickly to play like this, but you can often kill two or three creatures before you have to fully regain your magic. Having a Mage buddy to supply you with free water from time to time helps a great deal with this method (even if you guys aren't grouped, a trip to buff the Mage and collect some drinks is suitable).

GROUP DYNAMICS

Your primary role as Priest in a party is that of healer. Your job is to keep people alive and fighting. If the fight is well in hand, you can toss in a few offensive spells (just don't Mind Blast to start off the fight), but by and large you let other characters do damage while you allow them to keep taking the hits. It's a tradeoff: you don't get injured, the monster gets hurt, and people who ordinarily couldn't handle concentrated aggro get to do heavy damage.

Every time that you heal, you generate a certain amount of threat. This really begins to come into play when your group is fighting multiple targets. If you heal too soon, you become the center of aggression, and that really puts a crimp in further healing (or living through the battle). So before you heal, keep an eye on who the enemies are fighting and how the fight is progressing. Try to give Tanks enough time to Taunt/damage all of the enemies who are incoming before starting your spell work. Warriors/Paladins don't need to be at full health all the time anyway; it makes them angry not to be at least a little injured.

There is also a definite order as to who should be healed first. Casters are the most fragile and need healing quickly if they are struck; use Flash Heal to get them what they need. Losing their damage output could easily turn the tide in favor of the enemy. Leather wearers like Rogues, Druids, and Hunters can take a bit more damage, and Lesser or standard Heals work very well for them. Paladins and Warriors can withstand large amounts of damage and have high hit points: Greater Heals when they reach below half health do wonders for them.

If everyone in your party is looking injured, don't hesitate to use group heals with Prayer of Healing. And while it's true that these spells do cause threat, like any other heal spell, they do not automatically cause you to be the sole focus of monster aggression. Instead, they are a very good and useful way of keeping an entire party active and fighting in a nasty situation.

There are also several things that a Priest can do to avoid enemy attention. Fade discourages enemies from attacking you, so use this if you are jumped by a monster. Psychic Scream causes enemies to flee from you, which can get multiple monsters away from you (they do come back, though). If you find yourself getting hit by monsters anyway, the last thing you should do is run around and away from your group. Stay calm, let everyone know, and give them a chance to get the enemy off of you. If you are leaping about frantically, you make targeting much more difficult and can end up bolting into other enemies.

In terms of combat control at higher levels, Priests do gain the ability to temporarily (for one minute) control enemies. This spell is called Mind Control and it only works on humanoid targets. The enemies get a chance to break free every five seconds. The first move by this enemy is to attack the Priest. So, Mind Control is not without its dangers, but it can be a very useful tool in defending the party especially against monsters that add on in the middle of a fight. Having two Priests in the party is a great strategy for Mind Control users. Have one Priest focus on the healing and the other on controlling adds.

CHANGING YOUR ROLE

It's extremely difficult to switch mentalities from solo to group to solo, etc. A soloing Priest needs a completely different ability set on their hotbar and is constantly using abilities and in combat. The role of a party's main healer is much different. Staying out of combat is the main idea and, though your spells would definitely add to the damage being done to a target, avoiding aggro is also a priority. Learn to curb your solo-style gameplay when grouping. Having to fend off opponents and constantly yelling, "On me!" is almost a threat to the party itself.

ROGUE

Rogues are a very interesting and complex melee class in *World of Warcraft*. These stealthers are able to stay out of sight (with a bit of luck and planning), and their surprise attacks are able to bring down soft targets at an impressive rate. Though challenged and wary of enemies in heavy armor, Rogues grin and strike fear into the hearts of anyone who isn't hidden under a veil of steel and mithril.

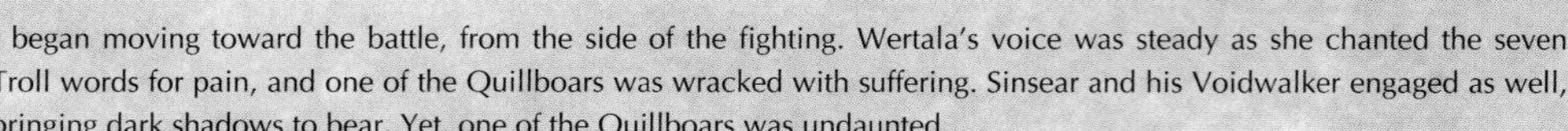

ATTACKING FROM THE SHADOWS

The night was dark and good, and I was glad for it. As the wind swept over the Barrens, I could hear the Quillboars walking all around me, but they are foolish creatures, and I am Saslen; they could see nothing. All they heard was the grunting of their fellows.

I turned back toward a far hill and used my dagger to reflect moonlight toward my companions. They could see it well enough to understand my message, "Four Quillboars." Gothara, Wertala, and Sinsear were ready to go. Moving with speed, Gothara rushed the camp of Quillboars, all shield and metal lashing forth. As the creatures turned to face the Tauren Warrior, she roared and put wariness into their hearts. Those who engaged her struck like children.

I began moving toward the battle, from the side of the fighting. Wertala's voice was steady as she chanted the seven Troll words for pain, and one of the Quillboars was wracked with suffering. Sinsear and his Voidwalker engaged as well, bringing dark shadows to bear. Yet, one of the Quillboars was undaunted.

Standing in the back, this creature started to bring the power of elemental flame out of the land. Already heavily engaged, the others wouldn't be able to bring their full force against this foe. But I had my own plan.

With a final step I placed myself an inch behind the caster. It still knew nothing of my presence, consumed by its spell. I woke it out of its reverie by cutting deeply into its back, four times in quick succession. These sinister blows nearly fell the caster, who turned to look at me with fear-filled eyes. Mumbling, trying to finish the spell, the Quillboar stumbled over the words, slurring them. The poison was already in full effect.

There were other enemies yet to fell, so I had no time to tarry. A final cut offered rest to the Quillboar. The creature's companions called for assistance; there wasn't anyone left to heed their cry.

INTRODUCTION TO PLAYING

RACES AND STARTING ATTRIBUTES

RACE	STRENGTH	STAMINA	AGILITY	INTELLECT	SPIRIT
Dwarf	22	23	22	20	23
Gnome	20	21	25	22	22
Human	21	22	24	21	22
Night Elf	20	21	25	23	21
Orc	22	22	23	20	23
Troll	21	22	23	20	24
Undead	20	23	22	21	24

ATTRIBUTES APPLIED

Strength	Slightly Increased Melee Damage
Stamina	Higher Hit Points
Agility	Substantial Increase in Critical Hit Rate, Improved Melee Damage, Higher Chance to Dodge
Intellect	Faster Rate for Gaining Weapon Skills
Spirit	Improves Hit Point Recovery

ITEMS AND EQUIPMENT

Rogues love their weapons, as do many melee classes. Whether a Rogue is going to go for daggers, swords, or maces depends heavily on their concept with Talents playing the biggest part. There are a number of issues here, including the fact that some abilities are impossible with heavier weapons. Ambush and Backstab, two hard-hitting attacks in the Rogue's lineup, are only possible with daggers.

Slower weapons are used more often with Sinister Strike, dealing immediate damage without the worry of position or Stealth. If you prefer the combat aspects of a Rogue, the Sinister Strike model is good for you. If Stealth and massive, sudden damage are your goal, a very slow dagger is absolutely divine.

Slow weapons, regardless of the type, are always the best choice for a Rogue (so long as they are current). The issue here is that Rogues have many immediate-use abilities. Without having to wait for the attack, the issue of weapon speed is avoided. Indeed, heavier weapons hit for more with instant attacks because they have higher total damage. Daggers that are almost up to two-second speeds are good for Stealthy Rogues, while the heaviest one-handed blades/maces suit the Sinister Strike Rogue well.

As for armor, look for Agility and Stamina aplenty. These attributes are needed for just about all Rogue builds. If you plan to do more group work, add more Strength to the mix and lose a bit of the Stamina (since you won't receive as much direct damage with a good tank around). If soloing, keep as much Stamina as possible; it makes a huge difference in what you can survive.

Ranged weapons are key for pulling if you don't want to rely on Sap. Get something you're comfortable using and rely on that for getting creatures out of thick spots. Because these aren't your primary sources of damage, it isn't as important to keep ranged weapons fully up-to-date.

Poisons offer a massive boost to your DPS. Rogues are able to use these after reaching Level 20. Invest in quality poisons and use them frequently when fighting anything of importance. Instant Poison is good for short fights against low-level monsters. Deadly Poison stacks well, a solid choice against Elites and other long-fight targets. Mind-Numbing Poison is a gem for disrupting the activity of casters.

CHOOSING YOUR PROFESSION

Rogues have a fair number of choices when it comes to their professions. Skinning and Leatherworking are perfectly fine for getting you into some adequate armor; being able to make pouches for ammo isn't a horrible thing either. At higher levels, your Skinning can also help to offset the cost of constant weapon searching and poison purchases.

For more damage, the combo of Mining and Engineering is suitable for all classes. Rogues benefit even more from having Bombs because they are in direct combat so often. Coupled with the innate power of this class to stun enemies all the time, Bombs are even better!

Secondary skills are very important to Rogues. Without heavy armor or the ability to heal magically, Rogues usually fall in love with Cooking and First Aid. Rogues kill quickly, but take a lot of damage as well, so reducing downtime greatly improves their experience efficiency.

CLASS ABILITIES

Rogues have several lines of abilities. Assassination covers a number of Stealth attacks and finishing moves. These abilities often do very high damage and are critical for starting and ending fights. The Combat line is what a Rogue brings to melee when they are engaged without Stealth. Poisons offer weapon enhancements to DPS or can give debuffs to enemy casting times/movement speed. Finally, the line of Subtlety controls Stealth itself, Vanishing from encounters, combat control (Sap), and trap disabling.

ABILITY	RANK	LEVEL	TYPE
Eviscerate	1	1	Assassination
Sinister Strike	1	1	Combat
Stealth	1	1	Subtlety
Backstab	1	4	Combat
Pick Pocket	1	4	Subtlety
Gouge	1	6	Combat
Sinister Strike	2	6	Combat
Evasion	N/A	8	Combat
Eviscerate	2	8	Assassination
Dual Wield	N/A	10	Combat
Sap	1	10	Subtlety
Slice and Dice	1	10	Assassination
Sprint	1	10	Combat
Backstab	2	12	Combat
Kick	1	12	Combat
Expose Armor	1	14	Assassination
Garrote	1	14	Assassination
Sinister Strike	3	14	Combat
Eviscerate	3	16	Assassination
Feint	1	16	Combat
Ambush	1	18	Assassination
Gouge	2	18	Combat
Parry	N/A	18	Combat
Backstab	3	20	Combat
Crippling Poison	1	20	Poisons
Rupture	1	20	Assassination
Stealth	2	20	Subtlety
Distract	N/A	22	Subtlety
Garrote	2	22	Assassination
Sinister Strike	4	22	Combat
Vanish	1	22	Subtlety
Detect Traps	N/A	24	Subtlety
Eviscerate	4	24	Assassination
Mind-numbing Poison	1	24	Poisons
Ambush	2	26	Assassination
Cheap Shot	N/A	26	Assassination
Expose Armor	2	26	Assassination
Kick	2	26	Combat
Backstab	4	28	Combat
Feint	2	28	Combat
Instant Poison	2	28	Poisons
Rupture	2	28	Assassination
Sap	2	28	Subtlety
Deadly Poison	1	30	Poisons
Disarm Trap	N/A	30	Subtlety
Garrote	3	30	Assassination
Kidney Shot	1	30	Assassination
Sinister Strike	5	30	Combat
Eviscerate	5	32	Assassination
Gouge	3	32	Combat
Ambush	3	34	Assassination

ABILITY	RANK	LEVEL	TYPE
Blinding Powder	1	34	Poisons
Blind	1	34	Subtlety
Sprint	2	34	Combat
Backstab	5	36	Combat
Expose Armor	3	36	Assassination
Instant Poison	3	36	Poisons
Rupture	3	36	Assassination
Deadly Poison	2	38	Poisons
Garrote	4	38	Assassination
Mind-numbing Poison	2	38	Poisons
Sinister Strike	6	38	Combat
Eviscerate	6	40	Assassination
Feint	3	40	Combat
Stealth	3	40	Subtlety
Ambush	4	42	Assassination
Kick	3	42	Combat
Slice and Dice	2	42	Assassination
Vanish	2	42	Subtlety
Backstab	6	44	Combat
Instant Poison	4	44	Poisons
Rupture	4	44	Assassination
Deadly Poison	3	46	Poisons
Expose Armor	4	46	Assassination
Garrote	5	46	Assassination
Gouge	4	46	Combat
Hemorrhage	2	46	Subtlety
Sinister Strike	7	46	Combat
Eviscerate	7	48	Assassination
Sap	3	48	Subtlety
Ambush	5	50	Assassination
Crippling Poison	2	50	Poisons
Kidney Shot	2	50	Assassination
Backstab	7	52	Combat
Feint	4	52	Combat
Instant Poison	5	52	Poisons
Mind-numbing Poison	3	52	Poisons
Rupture	5	52	Assassination
Deadly Poison	4	54	Poisons
Garrote	6	54	Assassination
Sinister Strike	8	54	Combat
Eviscerate	8	56	Assassination
Expose Armor	4	56	Assassination
Ambush	6	58	Assassination
Hemorrhage	3	58	Subtlety
Kick	4	58	Combat
Sprint	3	58	Combat
Backstab	8	60	Combat
Gouge	5	60	Combat
Instant Poison	6	60	Poisons
Rupture	6	60	Assassination
Stealth	4	60	Subtlety

ASSASSINATION

This is the line for dealing damage out of Stealth or for stunning opponents. Look to Eviscerate for brutal damage after building combo points, Cheap Shot for a stunning opener, or Ambush for the best damage coming out of Stealth.

AMBUSH

RANK	LEVEL	ENERGY	RANGE	CASTING TIME	COOLDOWN	COST TO TRAIN	EFFECT
1	18	60	7 yd	IC		29s	Ambush the target, causing 250% weapon damage plus 70 to the target. Must be Stealthed and behind the target. Requires a dagger in the main hand. Awards 1 combo point.
2	26	60	7 yd	IC		67s	Ambush the target, causing 250% weapon damage plus 100 to the target. Must be Stealthed and behind the target. Requires a dagger in the main hand. Awards 1 combo point.
3	34	60	7 yd	IC		1g 80s	Ambush the target, causing 250% weapon damage plus 125 to the target. Must be Stealthed and behind the target. Requires a dagger in the main hand. Awards 1 combo point.
4	42	60	7 yd	IC		2g 20s	Ambush the target, causing 250% weapon damage plus 185 to the target. Must be Stealthed and behind the target. Requires a dagger in the main hand. Awards 1 combo point.
5	50	60	7 yd	IC		4g 70s	Ambush the target, causing 250% weapon damage plus 230 to the target. Must be Stealthed and behind the target. Requires a dagger in the main hand. Awards 1 combo point.
6	58	60	7 yd	IC		7g 10s	Ambush the target, causing 250% weapon damage plus 290 to the target. Must be Stealthed and behind the target. Requires a dagger in the main hand. Awards 1 combo point.

CHEAP SHOT

RANK	LEVEL	ENERGY	RANGE	CASTING TIME	COOLDOWN	COST TO TRAIN	EFFECT
N/A	26	60	7 yd	IC		67s	Stuns the target for 4 sec. Must be Stealthed. Awards 2 combo points.

EVISCERATE

RANK	LEVEL	ENERGY	RANGE	CASTING TIME	COOLDOWN	COST TO TRAIN	EFFECT
1	1	35	7 yd	IC		No Cost	Finishing move that causes damage per combo point: 1 point: 7-11 damage, 2 points: 13-17 damage, 3 points: 19-23 damage, 4 points: 25-29 damage, 5 points: 31-35 damage
2	8	35	7 yd	IC		2s	Finishing move that causes damage per combo point: 1 point: 16-24 damage, 2 points: 29-37 damage, 3 points: 42-50 damage, 4 points: 55-63 damage, 5 points: 68-76 damage
3	16	35	7 yd	IC		18s	Finishing move that causes damage per combo point: 1 point: 29-43 damage, 2 points: 52-66 damage, 3 points: 75-89 damage, 4 points: 98-112 damage, 5 points: 121-135 damage
4	24	35	7 yd	IC		70s	Finishing move that causes damage per combo point: 1 point: 47-67 damage, 2 points: 84-104 damage, 3 points: 121-141 damage, 4 points: 158-178 damage, 5 points: 195-215 damage
5	32	35	7 yd	IC		1g 50s	Finishing move that causes damage per combo point: 1 point: 69-99 damage, 2 points: 123-153 damage, 3 points: 177-207 damage, 4 points: 232-261 damage, 5 points: 285-315 damage
6	40	35	7 yd	IC		2g	Finishing move that causes damage per combo point: 1 point: 104-148 damage, 2 points: 186-230 damage, 3 points: 268-312 damage, 4 points: 350-394 damage, 5 points: 432-476 damage
7	48	25	7 yd	IC		4g 20s	Finishing move that causes damage per combo point: 1 point: 158-226 damage, 2 points: 282-350 damage, 3 points: 406-474 damage, 4 points: 530-598 damage, 5 points: 654-722 damage
8	56	35	7 yd	IC		6g 40s	Finishing move that causes damage per combo point: 1 point: 216-312 damage, 2 points: 384-480 damage, 3 points: 552-648 damage, 4 points: 720-816 damage, 5 points: 888-984 damage

EXPOSE ARMOR

RANK	LEVEL	ENERGY	RANGE	CASTING TIME	COOLDOWN	COST TO TRAIN	EFFECT
1	14	25	7 yd	IC		12s	Finishing move that exposes the target for 30 sec, reducing armor per combo point: 1 point: 80 armor, 2 points: 160 armor, 3 points: 240 armor, 4 points: 320 armor, 5 points: 400 armor
2	26	25	7 yd	IC		67s	Finishing move that exposes the target for 30 sec, reducing armor per combo point: 1 point: 145 armor, 2 points: 290 armor, 3 points: 435 armor, 4 points: 580 armor, 5 points: 725 armor
3	36	25	7 yd	IC		1g 50s	Finishing move that exposes the target for 30 sec, reducing armor per combo point: 1 point: 210 armor, 2 points: 420 armor, 3 points: 630 armor, 4 points: 840 armor, 5 points: 1050 armor
4	46	25	7 yd	IC		2g 80s	Finishing move that exposes the target for 30 sec, reducing armor per combo point: 1 point: 275 armor, 2 points: 550 armor, 3 points: 825 armor, 4 points: 1100 armor, 5 points: 1375 armor
4	56	25	7 yd	IC		6g 40s	Finishing move that exposes the target for 30 sec, reducing armor per combo point: 1 point: 340 armor, 2 points: 680 armor, 3 points: 1020 armor, 4 points: 1360 armor, 5 points: 1700 armor

GARROTE

RANK	LEVEL	ENERGY	RANGE	CASTING TIME	COOLDOWN	COST TO TRAIN	EFFECT
1	14	50	7 yd	IC		12s	Garrote the enemy, causing 108 damage over 18 sec. Must be Stealthed and behind the target. Awards 1 combo point.
2	22	50	7 yd	IC		40s	Garrote the enemy, causing 162 damage over 18 sec. Must be Stealthed and behind the target. Awards 1 combo point
3	30	50	7 yd	IC		1g	Garrote the enemy, causing 222 damage over 18 sec. Must be Stealthed and behind the target. Awards 1 combo point
4	38	50	7 yd	IC		1g 80s	Garrote the enemy, causing 282 damage over 18 sec. Must be Stealthed and behind the target. Awards 1 combo point
5	46	50	7 yd	IC		2g 80s	Garrote the enemy, causing 348 damage over 18 sec. Must be Stealthed and behind the target. Awards 1 combo point
6	54	50	7 yd	IC		5g 80s	Garrote the enemy, causing 438 damage over 18 sec. Must be Stealthed and behind the target. Awards 1 combo point

KIDNEY SHOT

RANK	LEVEL	ENERGY	RANGE	CASTING TIME	COOLDOWN	COST TO TRAIN	EFFECT
1	30	25	7 yd	IC	20 sec	1	Finishing move that stuns the target. Lasts longer per combo point: 1 point: 1 second, 2 points: 2 seconds, 3 points: 3 seconds, 4 points: 4 seconds, 5 points: 5 seconds
2	50	25	7 yd	IC	20 sec	4 70	Finishing move that stuns the target. Lasts longer per combo point: 1 point: 2 second, 2 points: 3 seconds, 3 points: 4 seconds, 4 points: 5 seconds, 5 points: 6 seconds

RUPTURE

RANK	LEVEL	ENERGY	RANGE	CASTING TIME	COOLDOWN	COST TO TRAIN	EFFECT
1	20	25	7 yd	IC		23	Finishing move that causes damage over time. Lasts longer per combo point: 1 point: 45 damage over 6 secs, 2 points: 75 damage over 10 secs, 3 points: 105 damage over 14 secs, 4 points: 135 damage over 18 secs, 5 points: 165 damage over 22 secs
2	28	25	7 yd	IC		81	Finishing move that causes damage over time. Lasts longer per combo point: 1 point: 69 damage over 6 secs, 2 points: 115 damage over 10 secs, 3 points: 161 damage over 14 secs, 4 points: 207 damage over 18 secs, 5 points: 253 damage over 22 secs
3	36	25	7 yd	IC		1 50	Finishing move that causes damage over time. Lasts longer per combo point: 1 point: 96 damage over 6 secs, 2 points: 160 damage over 10 secs, 3 points: 224 damage over 14 secs, 4 points: 288 damage over 18 secs, 5 points: 352 damage over 22 secs
4	44	25	7 yd	IC		3 30	Finishing move that causes damage over time. Lasts longer per combo point: 1 point: 135 damage over 6 secs, 2 points: 225 damage over 10 secs, 3 points: 315 damage over 14 secs, 4 points: 405 damage over 18 secs, 5 points: 495 damage over 22 secs
5	52	25	7 yd	IC		4	Finishing move that causes damage over time. Lasts longer per combo point: 1 point: 186 damage over 6 secs, 2 points: 310 damage over 10 secs, 3 points: 434 damage over 14 secs, 4 points: 558 damage over 18 secs, 5 points: 682 damage over 22 secs
6	60	25	7 yd	IC		5 90	Finishing move that causes damage over time. Lasts longer per combo point: 1 point: 225 damage over 6 secs, 2 points: 425 damage over 10 secs, 3 points: 595 damage over 14 secs, 4 points: 765 damage over 18 secs, 5 points: 935 damage over 22 secs

SLICE AND DICE

RANK	LEVEL	ENERGY	RANGE	CASTING TIME	COOLDOWN	COST TO TRAIN	EFFECT
1	10	25		IC		3	Finishing move that increases melee attack speed by 20%. Lasts longer per combo point: 1 point: 9 seconds, 2 points: 12 seconds, 3 points: 15 seconds, 4 points: 18 seconds, 5 points: 21 seconds
2	42	25		IC		2 20	Finishing move that increases melee attack speed by 30%. Lasts longer per combo point: 1 point: 9 seconds, 2 points: 12 seconds, 3 points: 15 seconds, 4 points: 18 seconds, 5 points: 21 seconds

COMBAT

The Combat line keeps damage rolling after engagement. From the front, Sinister Strike adds damage and combo points, Kick is your interrupt, while Feint lowers threat. From behind, Backstab deals impressive damage. Use Gouge to disrupt opponents before fleeing or as a secondary interrupt for casters.

BACKSTAB

RANK	LEVEL	ENERGY	RANGE	CASTING TIME	COOLDOWN	COST TO TRAIN	EFFECT
1	4	60	7 yd	IC		50	Backstab the target, causing 150% weapon damage plus 15 to the target. Must be behind the target. Requires a dagger in the main hand. Awards 1 combo point.
2	12	60	7 yd	IC		8	Backstab the target, causing 150% weapon damage plus 30 to the target. Must be behind the target. Requires a dagger in the main hand. Awards 1 combo point.
3	20	60	7 yd	IC		23	Backstab the target, causing 150% weapon damage plus 48 to the target. Must be behind the target. Requires a dagger in the main hand. Awards 1 combo point.
4	28	60	7 yd	IC		81	Backstab the target, causing 150% weapon damage plus 69 to the target. Must be behind the target. Requires a dagger in the main hand. Awards 1 combo point.
5	36	60	7 yd	IC		1 50	Backstab the target, causing 150% weapon damage plus 90 to the target. Must be behind the target. Requires a dagger in the main hand. Awards 1 combo point.
6	44	60	7 yd	IC		3 30	Backstab the target, causing 150% weapon damage plus 135 to the target. Must be behind the target. Requires a dagger in the main hand. Awards 1 combo point.
7	52	60	7 yd	IC		4	Backstab the target, causing 150% weapon damage plus 165 to the target. Must be behind the target. Requires a dagger in the main hand. Awards 1 combo point.
8	60	60	7 yd	IC		5 90	Backstab the target, causing 150% weapon damage plus 210 to the target. Must be behind the target. Requires a dagger in the main hand. Awards 1 combo point.

KIDNEY SHOT

RANK	LEVEL	ENERGY	RANGE	CASTING TIME	COOLDOWN	COST TO TRAIN	EFFECT
N/A	10					3	Allows one-hand and off-hand weapons to be equipped in the off-hand.

EVASION

RANK	LEVEL	ENERGY	RANGE	CASTING TIME	COOLDOWN	COST TO TRAIN	EFFECT
N/A	8			IC	5 min	2	The rogue's dodge chance will increase by 50% for 15 sec.

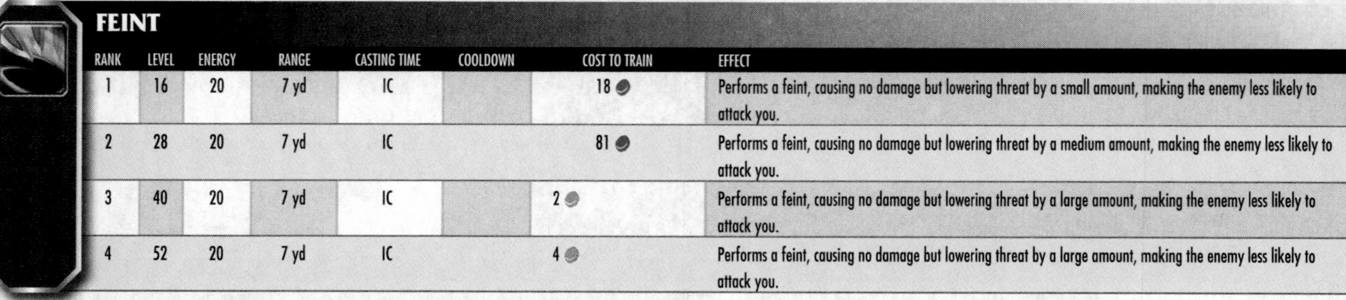

FEINT

RANK	LEVEL	ENERGY	RANGE	CASTING TIME	COOLDOWN	COST TO TRAIN	EFFECT
1	16	20	7 yd	IC		18c	Performs a feint, causing no damage but lowering threat by a small amount, making the enemy less likely to attack you.
2	28	20	7 yd	IC		81c	Performs a feint, causing no damage but lowering threat by a medium amount, making the enemy less likely to attack you.
3	40	20	7 yd	IC		2s	Performs a feint, causing no damage but lowering threat by a large amount, making the enemy less likely to attack you.
4	52	20	7 yd	IC		4s	Performs a feint, causing no damage but lowering threat by a large amount, making the enemy less likely to attack you.

GOUGE

RANK	LEVEL	ENERGY	RANGE	CASTING TIME	COOLDOWN	COST TO TRAIN	EFFECT
1	6	45	7 yd	IC	10 sec	1c	Causes 10 damage, disorients the opponent for 4 sec. and turns off your attack. Target must be facing you. Any damage caused will revive the target. Awards 1 combo point.
2	18	45	7 yd		10 sec	29c	Causes 20 damage, disorients the opponent for 4 sec. and turns off your attack. Target must be facing you. Any damage caused will revive the target. Awards 1 combo point.
3	32	45	7 yd	IC	10 sec	1s 50c	Causes 32 damage, disorients the opponent for 4 sec. and turns off your attack. Target must be facing you. Any damage caused will revive the target. Awards 1 combo point.
4	46	45	7 yd	IC	10 sec	2s 80c	Causes 55 damage, disorients the opponent for 4 sec. and turns off your attack. Target must be facing you. Any damage caused will revive the target. Awards 1 combo point.
5	60	45	7 yd	IC	10 sec	5s 90c	Causes 75 damage, disorients the opponent for 4 sec. and turns off your attack. Target must be facing you. Any damage caused will revive the target. Awards 1 combo point.

KICK

RANK	LEVEL	ENERGY	RANGE	CASTING TIME	COOLDOWN	COST TO TRAIN	EFFECT
1	12	25	7 yd	IC	10 sec	8c	A quick kick that injures a single foe for 15 damage and interrupts the spell being cast for 5 sec.
2	26	25	7 yd	IC	10 sec	67c	A quick kick that injures a single foe for 30 damage and interrupts the spell being cast for 5 sec.
3	42	25	7 yd	IC	10 sec	2s 20c	A quick kick that injures a single foe for 45 damage and interrupts the spell being cast for 5 sec.
4	58	25	7 yd	IC	10 sec	7s 10c	A quick kick that injures a single foe for 80 damage and interrupts the spell being cast for 5 sec.

PARRY

RANK	LEVEL	ENERGY	RANGE	CASTING TIME	COOLDOWN	COST TO TRAIN	EFFECT
N/A	18					29c	Gives a chance to parry enemy melee attacks.

SINISTER STRIKE

RANK	LEVEL	ENERGY	RANGE	CASTING TIME	COOLDOWN	COST TO TRAIN	EFFECT
1	1	45	7 yd	IC		No Cost	An instant strike that causes 3 damage in addiction to your normal weapon damage. Awards 1 combo point
2	6	45	7 yd	IC		1c	An instant strike that causes 6 damage in addiction to your normal weapon damage. Awards 1 combo point
3	14	45	7 yd	IC		12c	An instant strike that causes 10 damage in addiction to your normal weapon damage. Awards 1 combo point
4	22	45	7 yd	IC		40c	An instant strike that causes 15 damage in addiction to your normal weapon damage. Awards 1 combo point
5	30	45	7 yd	IC		1s	An instant strike that causes 22 damage in addiction to your normal weapon damage. Awards 1 combo point
6	38	45	7 yd	IC		1s 80c	An instant strike that causes 33 damage in addiction to your normal weapon damage. Awards 1 combo point
7	46	45	7 yd	IC		2s 80c	An instant strike that causes 52 damage in addiction to your normal weapon damage. Awards 1 combo point
8	54	45	7 yd	IC		5s 80c	An instant strike that causes 68 damage in addiction to your normal weapon damage. Awards 1 combo point

SPRINT

RANK	LEVEL	ENERGY	RANGE	CASTING TIME	COOLDOWN	COST TO TRAIN	EFFECT
1	10			IC	5 min	3c	Increases the rogue's movement speed by 50% for 15 sec. Does not break Stealth.
2	34			IC	5 min	1s 80c	Increases the rogue's movement speed by 60% for 15 sec. Does not break Stealth.
3	58			IC	5 min	7s 10c	Increases the rogue's movement speed by 70% for 15 sec. Does not break Stealth.

POISONS

Carry around several poisons to use for varying situations. Crippling Poison is only useful if you don't have a class nearby to help Snare enemies. Mind-Numbing Poison really helps against casters (and is only surpassed if you have a Warlock in your party to sit on them instead). Instant Poison knocks down targets in short fights. Deadly Poison is the king of longer fights with its higher chance to activate and stacking (very nice to keep on an offhand weapon).

BLINDING POWDER

RANK	LEVEL	SKILL	COST TO TRAIN	EFFECT
1	34	150	1s 20c	Create the reagent for the Blind ability.

CRIPPLING POISON

RANK	LEVEL	SKILL	COST TO TRAIN	EFFECT
1	20	1	23c	Coats a weapon with poison that lasts for 30 minutes. Each strike has a 30% chance of poisoning the enemy, slowing their movement speed to 50% of normal for 12 sec.
2	50	230	4s 70c	Coats a weapon with poison that lasts for 30 minutes. Each strike has a 30% chance of poisoning the enemy, slowing their movement speed to 30% of normal for 12 sec.

DEADLY POISON

RANK	LEVEL	SKILL	COST TO TRAIN	EFFECT
1	30	130	1	Coats a weapon with poison that lasts for 30 minutes. Each strike has a 30% chance of poisoning the enemy for 36 Nature damage over 12 sec. Stacks up to 5 times on a single target. 60 charges.
2	38	170	1 80	Coats a weapon with poison that lasts for 30 minutes. Each strike has a 30% chance of poisoning the enemy for 52 Nature damage over 12 sec. Stacks up to 5 times on a single target. 75 charges.
3	46	210	2 80	Coats a weapon with poison that lasts for 30 minutes. Each strike has a 30% chance of poisoning the enemy for 80 Nature damage over 12 sec. Stacks up to 5 times on a single target. 90 charges.
4	54	250	5 80	Coats a weapon with poison that lasts for 30 minutes. Each strike has a 30% chance of poisoning the enemy for 108 Nature damage over 12 sec. Stacks up to 5 times on a single target. 105 charges.

INSTANT POISON

RANK	LEVEL	SKILL	COST TO TRAIN	EFFECT
2	28	120	81	Coats a weapon with poison that lasts for 30 minutes. Each strike has a 20% chance of poisoning the enemy which instantly inflicts 30 to 38 Nature damage. 55 charges
3	36	160	1 50	Coats a weapon with poison that lasts for 30 minutes. Each strike has a 30% chance of poisoning the enemy which instantly inflicts 44 to 56 Nature damage. 70 charges.
4	44	200	3 30	Coats a weapon with poison that lasts for 30 minutes. Each strike has a 20% chance of poisoning the enemy which instantly inflicts 67 to 85 Nature damage. 85 charges
5	52	240	4	Coats a weapon with poison that lasts for 30 minutes. Each strike has a 20% chance of poisoning the enemy which instantly inflicts 92 to 118 Nature damage. 100 charges
6	60	280	5 90	Coats a weapon with poison that lasts for 30 minutes. Each strike has a 20% chance of poisoning the enemy which instantly inflicts 112 to 148 Nature damage. 115 charges

MIND-NUMBING POISON

RANK	LEVEL	SKILL	COST TO TRAIN	EFFECT
1	24	100	70	Coats a weapon with poison that lasts for 30 minutes. Each strike has a 20% chance of poisoning the enemy, increasing their casting time by 40% for 10 sec. 50 charges
2	38	170	1 80	Coats a weapon with poison that lasts for 30 minutes. Each strike has a 20% chance of poisoning the enemy, increasing their casting time by 50% for 12 sec. 75 charges
3	52	240	4	Coats a weapon with poison that lasts for 30 minutes. Each strike has a 20% chance of poisoning the enemy, increasing their casting time by 60% for 14 sec. 100 charges.

SUBTLETY

As you rise in this line, Stealth speed improves, Sap gains a longer duration, and eventually you receive a few battle additions. Vanish gets you into a state of Stealth even while engaged (vital for nailing a target with a second Ambush or for beginning an escape). Hemorrhage is a fine way to keep aggro lower in groups while aiding the total, party damage; it also aids in grabbing fast combo points!

BLIND

RANK	LEVEL	ENERGY	RANGE	CASTING TIME	COOLDOWN	COST TO TRAIN	EFFECT
1	34	30	10 yd	IC	5 min	1 80	Blinds the target, causing it to wander at 40% of move speed confused for up to 10 sec.

DETECT TRAPS

RANK	LEVEL	ENERGY	RANGE	CASTING TIME	COOLDOWN	COST TO TRAIN	EFFECT
N/A	24			IC		70	Hidden traps will become visible for 3 min.

DISARM TRAP

RANK	LEVEL	ENERGY	RANGE	CASTING TIME	COOLDOWN	COST TO TRAIN	EFFECT
N/A	30		5 yd	5 sec		1	Sneak up on the trap in order to disarm it. Don't get too close or the trap will go off.

DISTRACT

RANK	LEVEL	ENERGY	RANGE	CASTING TIME	COOLDOWN	COST TO TRAIN	EFFECT
N/A	22	30	30 yd	IC	30 sec	40	Throws a distraction, attracting the attention of all nearby monsters for 10 seconds. Does not break Stealth.

HEMORRHAGE

RANK	LEVEL	ENERGY	RANGE	CASTING TIME	COOLDOWN	COST TO TRAIN	EFFECT
2	46	35	7 yd	IC		70	An instant strike that damages the opponent and causes the target to hemorrhage, increasing any damage dealt to the target by 5. Lasts 30 charges or 15 secs. Awards 1 combo point.
3	58	35	7 yd	IC		1 80	An instant strike that damages the opponent and causes the target to hemorrhage, increasing any damage dealt to the target by 7. Lasts 30 charges or 15 secs. Awards 1 combo point.

PICK POCKET

RANK	LEVEL	ENERGY	RANGE	CASTING TIME	COOLDOWN	COST TO TRAIN	EFFECT
1	4		7 yd	IC		50	Pick the target's pocket.

SAP

RANK	LEVEL	ENERGY	RANGE	CASTING TIME	COOLDOWN	COST TO TRAIN	EFFECT
1	10	65	7 yd	IC		3	Disorients the target for 25 sec. Must be Stealthed. Only works on Humanoids that are not in combat. Any damage caused will revive the target. Only 1 target may be sapped at a time.
2	28	65	7 yd	IC		81	Disorients the target for 35 sec. Must be Stealthed. Only works on Humanoids that are not in combat. Any damage caused will revive the target. Only 1 target may be sapped at a time.
3	48	65	7 yd	IC		4 20	Disorients the target for 45 sec. Must be Stealthed. Only works on Humanoids that are not in combat. Any damage caused will revive the target. Only 1 target may be sapped at a time.

STEALTH

RANK	LEVEL	ENERGY	RANGE	CASTING TIME	COOLDOWN	COST TO TRAIN	EFFECT
1	1			IC	10 sec	10	Allows the rogue to sneak around, but reduces your speed to 50% of normal. Lasts until cancelled.
2	20			IC	10 sec	23	Allows the rogue to sneak around, but reduces your speed to 60% of normal. Lasts until cancelled.
3	40			IC	10 sec	2	Allows the rogue to sneak around, but reduces your speed to 65% of normal. Lasts until cancelled.
4	60			IC	10 sec	5 90	Allows the rogue to sneak around, but reduces your speed to 70% of normal. Lasts until cancelled.

VANISH

RANK	LEVEL	ENERGY	RANGE	CASTING TIME	COOLDOWN	COST TO TRAIN	EFFECT
1	22			IC	5 min	40	Allows the rogue to vanish from sight, entering an improved Stealth mode for 10 sec.
2	42			IC	5 min	2 20	Allows the rogue to vanish from sight, entering an improved Stealth mode for 10 sec.

TALENTS

Rogue Talent lines are all about damage and setting yourself up to do more damage. The pivotal point between these lines is to figure out when you want to deal said damage. Assassination brings better poison possibilities and hits very hard coming out of Stealth. Look here to have the best burst DPS early in a fight (including a move to start a fight with a critical Ambush at enhanced damage).

Combat Mastery puts its damage into a steady stream. Ignoring the short burst, the Combat line focuses on dealing its best damage over longer fights. Better weapon abilities, improvements to Dual-Wielding, and more efficient special attacks are here.

Subtlety is indeed a modest line for raw damage, but it reveals its strength through improvements to Stealth movement, anti-detection, reduced costs to several attacks, and better combat control. This is not a soloer's line; rather, Subtlety is for Rogues who want to engage in large amounts of scouting, PvP, and infiltration.

ASSASSINATION

TALENT NAME	RANKS	PREREQUISITES	EFFECTS
Improved Eviscerate	3	None	Increases the damage done by your Eviscerate ability by 5% (Per Rank)
Remorseless Attacks	5	None	Gives you a 20% damage bonus (Per Rank) on your next attack after killing an opponent
Malice	5	None	Increases your critical strike chance by 1% (Per Rank)
Ruthlessness	3	5 Points in Assassination	Gives your finishing moves a 20% chance (Per Rank) to add a combo point to your targget
Murder	2	5 Points in Assassination	Increases your chance to hit while using your Sap, Ambush, Garrote, or Cheap Shot abilities by 3% - Progression: 3%/5%
Improved Slice and Dice	3	5 Points in Assassination	Increases the duration of your Slice and Dice ability by 15% (Per Rank)
Relentless Strikes	1	3 Points in Ruthlessness, 10 Points in Assassination	Your finishing moves have a 20% chance per combo point to restore 25 energy.
Improved Expose Armor	3	10 Points in Assassination	Increases the armor reduced by your Expose Armor ability by 15% (Per Rank)
Lethality	5	5 Points in Malice, 10 Points in Assassination	Increases the damage done by your critical strikes by 10% (Per Rank) when using the Sinister Strike, Gouge, Backstab, Ambush or Eviscerate ability.
Vile Poisons	5	15 Points in Assassination	Increases the damage dealt by your poisons by 3% (Per Rank)
Improved Instant Poison	5	15 Points in Assassination	Adds a 2% chance (Per Rank) to apply Instant Poison to a target
Improved Kidney Shot	3	20 Points in Assassination	Reduces the cooldown of your Kidney Shot ability by 2 seconds - Progression: 2/4/5
Cold Blood	1	20 Points in Assassination	Instant cast-3 min cooldown- When activated, your next Sinister Strike, Backstab, Ambush or Eviscerate is guaranteed a critical strike.
Improved Deadly Poison	5	20 Points in Assassination	Adds a 3% chance (Per Rank) to apply Deadly Poison to your target
Seal Fate	5	1 Point in Cold Blood, 25 Points in Assassination	You have a 20% chance (Per Rank) to add an extra combo point when you critical with abilities that add combo points
Vigor	1	30 Points in Assassination	Increases your maximum Energy by 10

COMBAT MASTERY

TALENT NAME	RANKS	PREREQUISITES	EFFECTS
Improved Gouge	3	None	Increases the effect duration of your Gouge ability by 0.5 secs (Per Rank)
Improved Sinister Strike	2	None	Reduces the Energy cost of your Sinister Strike ability by 3 - Progression: 3/5
Lightning Reflexes	5	None	Increases your Dodge chance by 1% (Per Rank)
Improved Backstab	3	5 Points in Dagger Specialization, 3 Points in Improved Gouge, 5 Points in Combat	Increases the critical strike chance of your Backstab ability by 10% (Per Rank)
Deflection	5	5 Points in Combat	Increases your Parry chance by 1% (Per Rank)
Precision	5	5 Points in Combat	Increases your chance to hit with melee weapons by 1% (Per Rank)
Improved Evasion	2	10 Points in Combat	Increases the effect duration of your Evasion ability by 2 secs (Per Rank)
Riposte	1	5 Points in Deflection, 10 Points in Combat	This Instant ability is usable after a Parry; it deals 150% weapon damage and disarms the enemy for six seconds
Improved Sprint	3	10 Points in Combat	Reduces the cooldown of your Sprint ability by 30 sec (Per Rank)
Improved Kick	2	15 Points in Combat	Adds a 50% chance (Per Rank) that your target also becomes Silenced for 2 seconds after being kicked
Dagger Specialization	5	15 Points in Combat	Increases your chance to get a critical strike with Daggers by 1% (Per Rank)
Dual Wield Specialization	5	5 Points in Precision, 15 Points in Combat	Increases the damage done by your offhand weapon by 10% (Per Rank)
Mace Specialization	5	20 Points in Combat	Gives you a 1% chance to stun your target with a mace- Progression: 1%/2%/3%/4%/6%
Blade Flurry	1	20 Points in Combat	25 Energy, Instant cast, 5 min Cooldown, Req melee weapon- Increases your attack speed by 20%. In addition your normal melee weapon swings strike an additional nearby opponent. Lasts 15 sec.
Sword Specialization	5	20 Points in Combat	Increases your chance to get an extra swing with Swords by 1% - Progression: 1%/2%/3%/4%/6%
Fist Weapon Specialization	5	20 Points in Combat	Increases your chance to get a critical strike with Fist Weapons by 1% (Per Rank)
Throwing Weapon Specialization	2	25 Points in Combat	Increases the damage of thrown weapons by 10% (Per Rank)
Aggression	3	25 Points in Combat	Increases the damage of Sinister Strike and Ambush by 2% (Per Rank)
Adrenaline Rush	1	30 Points in Combat	Instant cast 6 min cooldown; doubles your Energy regeneration rate for 15 seconds

SUBTLETY

TALENT NAME	RANKS	PREREQUISITES	EFFECTS
Rapid Concealment	5	None	Reduces the cooldown of your Stealth ability by 1 sec (Per Rank)
Master of Deception	5	None	Improves your ability to avoid detection with each Rank
Camouflage	5	None	Increases your speed while Stealthed by 3% (Per Rank)
Elusiveness	5	5 Points in Subtlety	Reduces the cooldown of your Evasion, Vanish, and Blind abilities by 15 sec (Per Rank)
Opportunity	5	5 Points in Subtlety	Increases the damage dealt when striking from behind with your Backstab, Garrote or Ambush abilities by 4% (Per Rank)
Initiative	3	10 Points in Subtlety	Gives you a 15% chance (Per Rank) to add an additional combo point to your target when using your Ambush, Garrote or Cheap Shot ability.
Ghostly Strike	1	10 Points in Subtlety	50 Energy Instant Cast 20 sec cooldown 7yd range- A strike that deals 125% weapon damage and increases your chance to dodge by 15% for 5 sec. Awards 1 combo point.
Improved Garrote	2	5 Points in Opportunity, 10 Points in Subtlety	Increases the duration of Garrote by 3 Seconds (Per Rank) at a cost of 5% damage (Per Rank)
Improved Ambush	3	5 Points of Opportunity, 10 Points in Subtlety	Increases the critical strike chance of your Ambush ability by 15% - ProgressionL 15%/30%/40%
Improved Vanish	3	15 Points in Subtlety	Increases your movement speed while vanished by 10% (Per Rank)
Improved Rupture	3	15 Points in Subtlety	Increases the damage dealt by Rupture by 10% (Per Rank)
Improved Sap	3	15 Points in Subtlety	Gives you a 30% chance (Per Rank) to return to Stealth mode after using your Sap ability.
Preparation	1	20 Points in Subtlety	Instant cast- 10 min cooldown When activated, this ability immediately finishes the cooldown on your other Rogue abilities.
Improved Cheapshot	2	20 Points in Subtlety	Reduces the Energy cost of your Cheap Shot ability by 10 (Per Rank)
Improved Distract	2	20 Points in Subtlety	Increases the radius of your Distract ability by 3 yds. - Progression: 3/5
Setup	3	1 Point in Ghostly Strike, 25 Points in Subtlety	Gives you a 15% chance (Per Rank) to add a combo bubble to your target after dodging their attack.
Hemorrhage	1	25 Points in Subtlety	Engages an Instant strike that that adds a combo point and a debuff that increases melee damage to that target for 30 hits or 15 seconds
Premeditation	1	30 Points in Subtlety, Stealth	10 Energy, 1 sec cast, 2 min cooldown, 7 yd range- When used, adds 2 combo points to your target.

STRATEGIES

Rogue strategies rely heavily on the Talent line that they favor, but there are some tricks that are universal to the class. Many of these can be mastered early in a Rogue's career and become even more devastating as you gain experience.

MONEY!

Rogues have to spend piles of money on weapons, slightly better armor, enchantments, poison, and potions. Add this to food needs and the lost income of keeping cloth (for First Aid) instead of selling it, and Rogues seem very poor. Luckily, there are skills to counter this!

Skinning, if taken, offers one route to greater cash. After even a short time, Skinning shines as a way to make considerable funds, especially when materials are sold through the Auction House instead of vendored.

Pick Pocketing Humanoid monsters is a good way to find extra items that vendor well. Beyond that, there are sometimes higher-quality items on these creatures, so this is a skill worthy of using often. Humanoid monsters are already a fairly good source of income, since they drop money in the first place; combining this with Pick Pocketing is a pleasant boost. Grind against this mobs to make up for money shortfalls.

Lockpicking for other people can pull in a bit of cash for you as well. This skill opens Lockboxes that are found out in the wild (especially on Elite monsters). Offer to help other groups out by opening these boxes. Ask for a tip if you need money and be friendly about it. If the people can't afford to pay you, it's probably wise (and certainly kind) to open their boxes anyway. Making an honest request for a tip and not demanding one is a wonderful way to make some money and plenty of friends. Of course, if you prefer one or the other, vary the strategy to meet your needs or character concept.

SLAPPING ON COMBO POINTS

Many Rogue builds, regardless of Talents, use combo points heavily. These are required for all finishing moves, whether you are trying to score damage, reduce enemy armor, or keep those fiends out of commission as long as possible.

Using Ambush and Backstab isn't going to bring in the points quickly (these abilities use too much Energy). Instead, moves like Sinister Strike, Feint, and Hemorrhage are faster. If these moves fit your style of play already, use them heavily to accrue combo points. Sinister Strike can be used well with swords to deal high damage while working toward potent Eviscerates. Feint can get a monster off of you in the group situation while you prepare for a Stun or deadly finishing move. To stay low in profile, Hemorrhage raises group damage against a foe on the whole while giving you a cheap point!

STEALTH

Stealth is both offensive and defensive in nature, depending on who is creeping out in the bushes. Defensively, Stealth takes you away from harm by keeping your Rogue hidden from monsters and dangerous players. At longer range, things simply won't be able to see you; this exact distance of this varies tremendously, so it's wise to test often to get a feel for your "safe" range.

What Controls Stealth Detection Ranges?

- **Subtlety Rating of the Rogue**
- **Level Differences Between the Rogue and the Viewer**
- **Line of Sight (Creatures Don't "See" Behind Themselves)**
- **Current Generation of the Game (Stealth Detection Range is Likely to Take Time to Balance)**

Be wary of approaching targets that are higher-level than you without getting well behind them first. If you stand in a target's line-of-sight, it takes much higher Subtlety to stay hidden. Once revealed, you are a sitting duck (free to spells, abilities, ranged weapons, and general monster aggro).

The last item in this group sounds out of place, but it is wise to get a feel for these ranges each time there is a balance in the game. Stealth is such a challenging ability to balance that a perfect state is hard to reach. As this range changes over time, adjust your tactics to stay current.

THE BEST TARGETS

The best targets are found in enemies who die quickly. This is true for almost everyone, but Rogues have the ability to take many foes down quickly if the enemy has light armor. Using high DPS to its fullest, the Rogue can do so much damage that few enemies can ramp up to their full capabilities.

Part of this rests in going after lower-level targets when you are grinding for experience. Anything of higher level is going to keep you missing a moderate amount of the time, and this is a very bad thing for a Rogue (you can't afford to whiff on those early attacks). Stick to enemies two or three levels beneath you and go through them quickly.

Anything that isn't wearing heavy armor is a good target, but casters are the best. Right off the bat, you have the ability to Kick and disrupt casting. Add Garrote to that for a secondary interrupt, and things are sounding better. To make matters worse for casters, include Mind Numbing Poison to give yourself more leeway. Wait a moment before interrupting slow spells; get in an extra slice or two before using your abilities (this effectively "wastes" the caster's time with a spell that is going to fail either way).

Adds are very bad for Rogues because of the low damage tolerance this class displays. Avoid adds by using ranged weapons to pull, being aware of your grinding area, and starting a fight with Sap if two enemies are guaranteed to be involved.

SHAMAN

The heart and soul of the Horde centers around its naturalistic Shaman. These mystic people are able to fight for the Horde, cast elemental spells, heal the wounded, and drop totems of great power to wound and confuse enemies and buff allies. Shaman are able to fill many roles and may seem similar to Druids at first; yet, the differences between these classes grow with each level as the Druid becomes better able to focus on any single role at a time and the Shaman becomes more of a blend. Later on, the Shaman wears heavier armor (Chain), casts well at range, and gains substantial heals. All this takes a ton of training, practice, and careful planning, but it's worth the trouble many times over.

A SHAMAN'S RETRIBUTION

I asked the Earthmother for strength as I looked over the bodies of fallen Tauren, Dwarves, and Goblins. A tremendous battle between the fair people of Blood Hoof Village and the defilers of Venture Company had taken place near some of the eastern mines. I was returning to Thunder Bluff at the time, but I heard of the battle from several young Warriors who were resting, hoping to make another run at the remaining Venture Company workers.

I had gone to the mines alone, seething with anger, and now the dead were my companions. Begging the grace of the spirits of the world, I brought the Tauren back to themselves and bid them leave. "Return later and cleanse the place of any foulness that remains," I spoke. They must have seen something in my eyes, for it is rarely the place of our people to walk away when the land is ravaged, but they obeyed my order (still shaken from the return to their bodies).

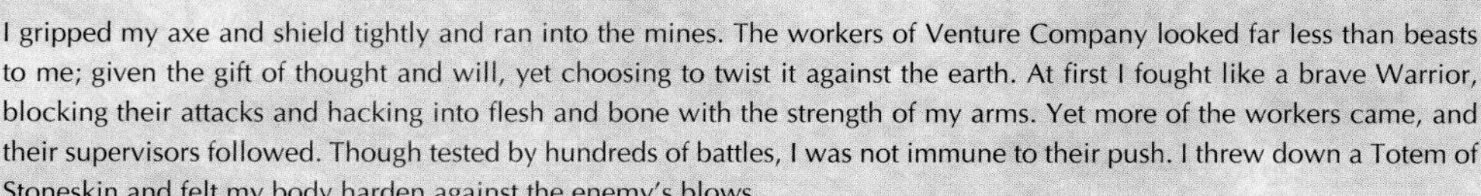

I gripped my axe and shield tightly and ran into the mines. The workers of Venture Company looked far less than beasts to me; given the gift of thought and will, yet choosing to twist it against the earth. At first I fought like a brave Warrior, blocking their attacks and hacking into flesh and bone with the strength of my arms. Yet more of the workers came, and their supervisors followed. Though tested by hundreds of battles, I was not immune to their push. I threw down a Totem of Stoneskin and felt my body harden against the enemy's blows.

Their push failed, and I had a moment's respite. I used this to heal my wounds and charge my weapon with the power of Rock! The next Goblin who came forward was bitten foully by my axe's swing and fell to the ground. Still more followed, and I felt that my anger had gotten me into a place from which I could no longer retreat. If this was my death, so be it, but the mine would be cleared of its darkness.

Then, as I saw at least six more of the enemies come out from the final room of the mines, I heard steps behind me and knew that I would be lost if they were Venture Company reinforcements. Yet, it was my people. They had ignored my words after all; bellowing like a storm, they crashed into the room and devoured the Goblins with fast and ferocious swings. When all was done, the mine was clear. The younger Tauren searched the bodies of the Goblins and found whatever they sought. They seemed happy to be alive, and honored to have saved a small corner of our land from harm.

I too was warmed by our victory. There is a greater joy in serving the world; it was too bad the people of Venture Company had turned their eyes from such beauty.

INTRODUCTION TO PLAYING

RACES AND STARTING ATTRIBUTES

RACE	STRENGTH	STAMINA	AGILITY	INTELLECT	SPIRIT
Orc	22	22	20	22	23
Tauren	23	23	19	22	22
Troll	21	22	20	22	24

ATTRIBUTES APPLIED

Strength	Increases Melee Damage and Chance to Block
Stamina	Higher Hit Points
Agility	Raises Chance to Get a Melee Critical Hit and Dodge
Intellect	Improved Mana Pool, Higher Chance for a Spell Critical, Faster Rate for Gaining Weapon Skills
Spirit	Improves Hit Point and Mana Recovery, Raises Chance for Weapon Procs to Enact

ITEMS AND EQUIPMENT

Shaman have plenty of needs when it comes to equipment. Because Shaman are so versatile, they need gear that holds up to many tests. High armor, a good shield, substantial DPS from a relatively fast weapon, and multiple attribute bonuses are desirable. Simply put, equipment is going to take most of your time and money to keep up-to-date, but saves you from almost any problem if maintained.

For melee, a good shield and solid armor pieces make a huge difference. Because Shaman are limited to Leather armor during the lower levels, it's hard to survive major aggro (this improves later on by learning how to wear Chain at Level 40). The good news and bad news is that it isn't hard to find attributes you need; the bad news is that you need almost everything.

Strength and Agility are useful, but they are secondary to Intellect, Stamina, and Spirit. Work on getting the best bonuses in your three primary stats while leveling and try not to focus too much on which of the three you are getting from a given item (just look for the best total bonuses to the three and let that guide you in item selection). Later on, you have more leeway to decide which direction to focus on. Stamina is incredibly useful for melee-centered and soloing Shaman. Intellect saves group on a daily basis, and Spirit builds are fun for grinding and evading downtime.

CHOOSING YOUR PROFESSION

Alchemy and Herbalism are very good professions for a Shaman. Having constant access to various attribute buffs, extra defense, and a supply of Health/Mana Potions can turn the time of many battles.

If you already have friends who are heavily into Alchemy, Enchanting is a great profession for a Shaman to master. Being able to customize your equipment without the massive expense of going to other players can help direct your finances toward higher-end gear.

Secondary skills don't come into play as often with Shaman as they do with non-magic classes. Having the ability to heal makes First Aid and Cooking a bit less impressive, but Fishing has a few useful ingredients for some potions. If you find yourself soloing, take Cooking and decide whether the others are good for you.

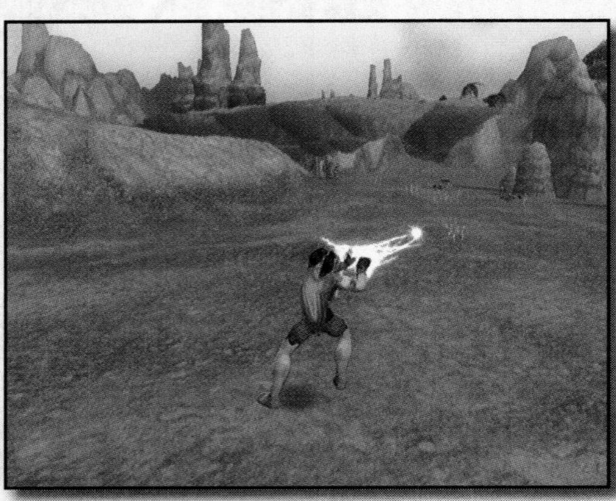

CLASS ABILITIES

Shaman have three central lines of spells that they use to flow into combat. Elemental Combat is a straight-forward damage line that has an interrupt, a variety of means to damage targets, and some damage-centered totems. Enhancement is better for aiding grouping because it has totems for resisting various damage forms. That line also aids a Shaman's ability to melee effectively. Restoration is the final line, covering various cast-time healing spells, the ability to Resurrect dead allies, and cure poison/disease.

ABILITY	RANK	LEVEL	TYPE
Rockbiter Weapon	1	1	Enhancement
Earth Shock	1	4	Elemental Combat
Earthbind Totem	1	6	Elemental Combat
Healing Wave	2	6	Restoration
Earth Shock	2	8	Elemental Combat
Lightning Bolt	2	8	Elemental Combat
Lightning Shield	1	8	Enhancement
Rockbiter Weapon	2	8	Enhancement
Stoneclaw Totem	1	8	Elemental Combat
Flame Shock	1	10	Elemental Combat
Flametongue Weapon	1	10	Enhancement
Strength of Earth Totem	1	10	Enhancement
Fire Nova Totem	1	12	Elemental Combat
Healing Wave	3	12	Restoration
Purge	1	12	Elemental Combat
Rebirth	1	12	Restoration
Earth Shock	3	14	Elemental Combat
Lightning Bolt	3	14	Elemental Combat
Stoneskin Totem	2	14	Enhancement
Cure Poison	1	16	Restoration
Lightning Shield	2	16	Enhancement
Rockbiter Weapon	3	16	Enhancement
Flame Shock	2	18	Elemental Combat
Flametongue Weapon	2	18	Enhancement
Healing Wave	4	18	Restoration
Stoneclaw Totem	2	18	Elemental Combat
Tremor Totem	N/A	18	Restoration
Frost Shock	1	20	Elemental Combat
Frostbrand Weapon	1	20	Enhancement
Ghost Wolf	1	20	Enhancement
Lesser Healing Wave	1	20	Restoration
Lightning Bolt	4	20	Elemental Combat
Searing Totem	2	20	Elemental Combat
Cure Disease	1	22	Restoration
Fire Nova Totem	2	22	Elemental Combat
Poison Cleansing Totem	N/A	22	Restoration
Water Breathing	N/A	22	Enhancement
Earth Shock	4	24	Elemental Combat
Frost Resistance Totem	1	24	Enhancement
Healing Wave	5	24	Restoration
Lightning Shield	3	24	Enhancement
Rockbiter Weapon	4	24	Enhancement
Stoneskin Totem	3	24	Enhancement
Strength of Earth Totem	2	24	Enhancement
Far Sight	N/A	26	Enhancement
Flametongue Weapon	3	26	Enhancement
Lightning Bolt	5	26	Elemental Combat
Magma Totem	1	26	Elemental Combat
Mana Spring Totem	1	26	Restoration
Fire Resistance Totem	1	28	Enhancement
Flame Shock	3	28	Elemental Combat
Flametongue Totem	1	28	Enhancement
Frostbrand Weapon	2	28	Enhancement
Lesser Healing Wave	2	28	Restoration
Stoneclaw Totem	3	28	Elemental Combat
Water Walking	N/A	28	Enhancement
Astral Recall	N/A	30	Enhancement
Grounding Totem	N/A	30	Enhancement
Healing Stream Totem	2	30	Restoration
Nature Resistance Totem	1	30	Enhancement
Searing Totem	3	30	Elemental Combat
Windfury Weapon	1	30	Enhancement
Chain Lightning	1	32	Elemental Combat
Fire Nova Totem	3	32	Elemental Combat
Healing Wave	6	32	Restoration
Lightning Bolt	6	32	Elemental Combat
Lightning Shield	4	32	Enhancement
Purge	2	32	Elemental Combat
Windfury Totem	1	32	Enhancement
Frost Shock	2	34	Elemental Combat
Rockbiter Weapon	5	34	Enhancement
Sentry Totem	N/A	34	Enhancement
Stoneskin Totem	4	34	Enhancement
Earth Shock	5	36	Elemental Combat
Flametongue Weapon	4	36	Enhancement
Lesser Healing Wave	3	36	Restoration
Magma Totem	2	36	Elemental Combat
Mana Spring Totem	2	36	Restoration
Windwall Totem	1	36	Enhancement
Disease Cleansing Totem	N/A	38	Restoration
Flametongue Totem	2	38	Enhancement
Frost Resistance Totem	2	38	Enhancement
Frostbrand Weapon	3	38	Enhancement
Lightning Bolt	7	38	Elemental Combat
Stoneclaw Totem	4	38	Elemental Combat
Strength of Earth Totem	3	38	Enhancement
Chain Heal	1	40	Restoration
Chain Lightning	2	40	Elemental Combat
Flame Shock	4	40	Elemental Combat
Healing Stream Totem	3	40	Restoration
Healing Wave	7	40	Restoration
Lightning Shield	5	40	Enhancement
Mail	N/A	40	Enhancement
Searing Totem	4	40	Elemental Combat
Windfury Weapon	2	40	Enhancement
Fire Nova Totem	4	42	Elemental Combat
Fire Resistance Totem	2	42	Enhancement
Grace of Air Totem	1	42	Enhancement
Windfury Totem	2	42	Enhancement
Lesser Healing Wave	4	44	Restoration
Lightning Bolt	8	44	Elemental Combat
Nature Resistance Totem	2	44	Enhancement
Rockbiter Weapon	6	44	Enhancement
Stoneskin Totem	5	44	Enhancement
Chain Heal	2	46	Restoration
Flametongue Weapon	5	46	Enhancement
Frost Shock	3	46	Elemental Combat
Magma Totem	3	46	Elemental Combat
Mana Spring Totem	3	46	Restoration
Mana Tide Totem	2	46	Restoration
Windwall Totem	2	46	Enhancement
Chain Lightning	3	48	Elemental Combat
Earth Shock	6	48	Elemental Combat
Flametongue Totem	3	48	Enhancement
Frostbrand Weapon	4	48	Enhancement
Healing Wave	8	48	Restoration
Lightning Shield	6	48	Enhancement
Stoneclaw Totem	5	48	Elemental Combat
Healing Stream Totem	4	50	Restoration
Lightning Bolt	9	50	Elemental Combat
Searing Totem	5	50	Elemental Combat
Windfury Weapon	3	50	Enhancement
Fire Nova Totem	5	52	Elemental Combat
Flame Shock	5	52	Elemental Combat
Lesser Healing Wave	5	52	Restoration
Strength of Earth Totem	4	52	Enhancement
Windfury Totem	3	52	Enhancement
Chain Heal	3	54	Restoration
Frost Resistance Totem	3	54	Enhancement
Rockbiter Weapon	7	54	Enhancement
Stoneskin Totem	6	54	Enhancement
Chain Lightning	4	56	Elemental Combat
Flametongue Weapon	6	56	Enhancement
Grace of Air Totem	2	56	Enhancement
Healing Wave	9	56	Restoration
Lightning Bolt	10	56	Elemental Combat
Lightning Shield	7	56	Enhancement
Magma Totem	4	56	Elemental Combat
Mana Spring Totem	4	56	Restoration
Mana Tide Totem	3	56	Restoration
Windwall Totem	3	56	Enhancement
Fire Resistance Totem	3	58	Enhancement
Flametongue Totem	4	58	Enhancement
Frost Shock	4	58	Elemental Combat
Frostbrand Weapon	5	58	Enhancement
Stoneclaw Totem	6	58	Elemental Combat
Earth Shock	7	60	Elemental Combat
Healing Stream Totem	5	60	Restoration
Lesser Healing Wave	6	60	Restoration
Nature Resistance Totem	3	60	Enhancement
Searing Totem	6	60	Elemental Combat
Windfury Weapon	4	60	Enhancement

ELEMENTAL COMBAT

Elemental Combat offers the teeth in a Shaman's spell line. These abilities deal direct damage through nukes, DOTs, and AoE totems. The Shaman's primary interrupt is here (Earth Shock) to instantly damage and interrupt casters. Chain Lightning offers the ability to slam several enemies at once, and Stoneclaw Totems can be dropped to Taunt enemies away from you or allies.

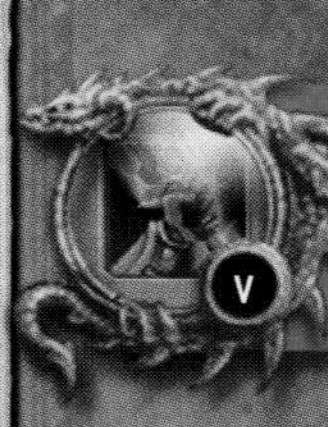

CHAIN LIGHTNING

RANK	LEVEL	MANA	RANGE	CASTING TIME	COOLDOWN	COST TO TRAIN	EFFECT
1	32	280	30 yd	2.5sec	-	1g	Hurls a lightning bolt at the enemy, dealing 191 to 217 nature damage and then jumping to additional nearby enemies. Each jump reduces the damage by 30%. Affects 3 total targets.
2	40	380	30 yd	2.5sec	6sec	1g 50s	Hurls a lightning bolt at the enemy, dealing 277 to 311 nature damage and then jumping to additional nearby enemies. Each jump reduces the damage by 30%. Affects 3 total targets.
3	48	490	30 yd	2.5sec	6sec	2g 50s	Hurls a lightning bolt at the enemy, dealing 378 to 424 nature damage and then jumping to additional nearby enemies. Each jump reduces the damage by 30%. Affects 3 total targets.
4	56	605	30 yd	2.5sec	6sec	3g 20s	Hurls a lightning bolt at the enemy, dealing 493 to 551 nature damage and then jumping to additional nearby enemies. Each jump reduces the damage by 30%. Affects 3 total targets.

EARTH SHOCK

RANK	LEVEL	MANA	RANGE	CASTING TIME	COOLDOWN	COST TO TRAIN	EFFECT
1	4	30	20 yd	IC	6sec	1s	Instantly shocks the target with concussive force, causing 17 to 19 Nature damage and disrupts the spell being cast for 2 sec.
2	8	50	20 yd	IC	6sec	2s	Instantly shocks the target with concussive force, causing 32 to 34 Nature damage and disrupts the spell being cast for 2 sec.
3	14	85	20 yd	IC	6sec	9s	Instantly shocks the target with concussive force, causing 60 to 64 Nature damage and disrupts the spell being cast for 2 sec.
4	24	145	20 yd	IC	6sec	42s	Instantly shocks the target with concussive force, causing 119 to 127 Nature damage and disrupts the spell being cast for 2 sec.
5	36	240	20 yd	IC	6sec	1g 30s	Instantly shocks the target with concussive force, causing 225 to 239 Nature damage and disrupts the spell being cast for 2 sec.
6	48	345	20 yd	IC	6sec	2g 50s	Instantly shocks the target with concussive force, causing 359 to 381 Nature damage and disrupts the spell being cast for 2 sec.
7	60	405	20 yd	IC	6sec	3g 90s	Instantly shocks the target with concussive force, causing 543 to 572 Nature damage and disrupts the spell being cast for 2 sec.

EARTHBIND TOTEM

RANK	LEVEL	MANA	RANGE	CASTING TIME	COOLDOWN	COST TO TRAIN	EFFECT
1	6	40	-	IC	-	1s	Summons an Earthbind Totem with 5 health at the feet of the caster for 45 sec that slows the movement speed of enemies within 10 yards.

FIRE NOVA TOTEM

RANK	LEVEL	MANA	RANGE	CASTING TIME	COOLDOWN	COST TO TRAIN	EFFECT
1	12	115	-	IC	15sec	8s	Summons a Fire Nova Totem with 5 health at the caster's feet that will cause 48 to 56 fire damage to attackers within 10 yards 4 seconds after the totem is created. Lasts 5 sec.
2	22	210	-	IC	15sec	36s	Summons a Fire Nova Totem with 5 health at the caster's feet that will cause 102 to 116 fire damage to attackers within 10 yards 4 seconds after the totem is created. Lasts 5 sec.
3	32	345	-	IC	15sec	1g	Summons a Fire Nova Totem with 5 health at the caster's feet that will cause 184 to 208 fire damage to attackers within 10 yards 4 seconds after the totem is created. Lasts 5 sec.
4	42	490	-	IC	15sec	1g 50s	Summons a Fire Nova Totem with 5 health at the caster's feet that will cause 281 to 317 fire damage to attackers within 10 yards 4 seconds after the totem is created. Lasts 5 sec.
5	52	640	-	IC	15sec	3g 20s	Summons a Fire Nova Totem with 5 health at the caster's feet that will cause 396 to 442 fire damage to attackers within 10 yards 4 seconds after the totem is created. Lasts 5 sec.

FLAME SHOCK

RANK	LEVEL	MANA	RANGE	CASTING TIME	COOLDOWN	COST TO TRAIN	EFFECT
1	10	55	20 yd	IC	6sec	4s	Instantly sears the target with fire, causing 21 damage immediately and 24 damage over 12 sec.
2	18	95	20 yd	IC	6sec	22s	Instantly sears the target with fire, causing 45 damage immediately and 44 damage over 12 sec.
3	28	165	20 yd	IC	6sec	72s	Instantly sears the target with fire, causing 86 damage immediately and 88 damage over 12 sec.
4	40	260	20 yd	IC	6sec	1g 50s	Instantly sears the target with fire, causing 152 damage immediately and 152 damage over 12 sec.
5	52	360	20 yd	IC	6sec	3g 20s	Instantly sears the target with fire, causing 230 damage immediately and 232 damage over 12 sec.

FROST SHOCK

RANK	LEVEL	MANA	RANGE	CASTING TIME	COOLDOWN	COST TO TRAIN	EFFECT
1	20	115	20 yd	IC	6sec	23s	Instantly shocks the target with frost, causing 89 to 95 damage and slowing movement speed to 50% of normal. Lasts 8 sec.
2	34	225	20 yd	IC	6sec	1g 20s	Instantly shocks the target with frost, causing 206 to 220 damage and slowing movement speed to 50% of normal. Lasts 8 sec.
3	46	325	20 yd	IC	6sec	2g 50s	Instantly shocks the target with frost, causing 333 to 353 damage and slowing movement speed to 50% of normal. Lasts 8 sec.
4	58	430	20 yd	IC	6sec	4g 30s	Instantly shocks the target with frost, causing 486 to 514 damage and slowing movement speed to 50% of normal. Lasts 8 sec.

LIGHTNING BOLT

RANK	LEVEL	MANA	RANGE	CASTING TIME	COOLDOWN	COST TO TRAIN	EFFECT
2	8	35	30 yd	2sec	-	2c	Casts a bolt of lightning at the target for 26 to 30 damage.
3	14	55	30 yd	2.5sec	-	9c	Casts a bolt of lightning at the target for 45 to 53 damage.
4	20	90	30 yd	3sec	3sec	23c	Casts a bolt of lightning at the target for 83 to 95 damage.
5	26	125	30 yd	3sec	-	67c	Casts a bolt of lightning at the target for 125 to 143 damage.
6	32	160	30 yd	3sec	-	1s	Casts a bolt of lightning at the target for 172 to 194 damage.
7	38	200	30 yd	3sec	-	1s 40c	Casts a bolt of lightning at the target for 227 to 255 damage.
8	44	235	30 yd	3sec	-	2s 50c	Casts a bolt of lightning at the target for 282 to 316 damage.
9	50	275	30 yd	3sec	-	2s 50c	Casts a bolt of lightning at the target for 347 to 389 damage.
10	56	315	30 yd	3sec	-	3s 20c	Casts a bolt of lightning at the target for 419 to 467 damage.

MAGMA TOTEM

RANK	LEVEL	MANA	RANGE	CASTING TIME	COOLDOWN	COST TO TRAIN	EFFECT
1	26	285	-	IC	-	67c	Summons a Magma Totem with 5 health at the feet of the caster for 20 sec that causes 22 fire damage to creatures within 8 yards every 2 seconds.
2	36	445	-	IC	-	1s 30c	Summons a Magma Totem with 5 health at the feet of the caster for 20 sec that causes 37 fire damage to creatures within 8 yards every 2 seconds.
3	46	615	-	IC	-	2s 50c	Summons a Magma Totem with 5 health at the feet of the caster for 20 sec that causes 54 fire damage to creatures within 8 yards every 2 seconds.
4	56	805	-	IC	-	3s 20c	Summons a Magma Totem with 5 health at the feet of the caster for 20 sec that causes 75 fire damage to creatures within 8 yards every 2 seconds.

PURGE

RANK	LEVEL	MANA	RANGE	CASTING TIME	COOLDOWN	COST TO TRAIN	EFFECT
1	12	45	30 yd	IC	-	9c	Purges the enemy target, removing 1 magic effect.
2	32	75	30 yd	IC	-	1s 20c	Purges the enemy target, removing 2 beneficial magic effects.

SEARING TOTEM

RANK	LEVEL	MANA	RANGE	CASTING TIME	COOLDOWN	COST TO TRAIN	EFFECT
2	20	65	-	IC	-	23c	Summons a Searing Totem with 5 health at your feet for 35 sec that attacks an enemy within 20.0 yards for 10 to 14 damage every 2 seconds.
3	30	110	-	IC	-	90c	Summons a Searing Totem with 5 health at your feet for 40 sec that attacks an enemy within 20.0 yards for 14 to 20 damage every 2 seconds.
4	40	160	-	IC	-	1s 50c	Summons a Searing Totem with 5 health at your feet for 45 sec that attacks an enemy within 20.0 yards for 20 to 28 damage every 2 seconds.
5	50	210	-	IC	-	2s 50c	Summons a Searing Totem with 5 health at your feet for 50 sec that attacks an enemy within 20.0 yards for 25 to 37 damage every 2 seconds.
6	60	265	-	IC	-	3s 90c	Summons a Searing Totem with 5 health at your feet for 55 sec that attacks an enemy within 20.0 yards for 32 to 46 damage every 2 seconds.

STONECLAW TOTEM

RANK	LEVEL	MANA	RANGE	CASTING TIME	COOLDOWN	COST TO TRAIN	EFFECT
1	8	20	-	IC	30sec	2c	Summons a Stoneclaw Totem with 50 health at the feet of the caster for 15 sec that taunts creatures within 8 yards to attack it.
2	18	40	-	IC	30sec	22c	Summons a Stoneclaw Totem with 150 health at the feet of the caster for 15 sec that taunts creatures within 8 yards to attack it.
3	28	65	-	IC	30sec	72c	Summons a Stoneclaw Totem with 220 health at the feet of the caster for 15 sec that taunts creatures within 8 yards to attack it.
4	38	95	-	IC	30sec	1s 40c	Summons a Stoneclaw Totem with 280 health at the feet of the caster for 15 sec that taunts creatures within 8 yards to attack it.
5	48	130	-	IC	30sec	2s 50c	Summons a Stoneclaw Totem with 390 health at the feet of the caster for 15 sec that taunts creatures within 8 yards to attack it.
6	58	170	-	IC	30sec	4s 30c	Summons a Stoneclaw Totem with 480 health at the feet of the caster for 15 sec that taunts creatures within 8 yards to attack it.

ENHANCEMENT

The Enhancement line builds on a Shaman's ability to deal damage indirectly while resisting the attacks of their foes. Weapon procs are found here (a number of them); damage shields can be summoned instantly and with high mana-efficiency; totems add resistance to melee, ranged, and magical damage; and there are additional totems that adds to the party's attributes.

ASTRAL RECALL

RANK	LEVEL	MANA	RANGE	CASTING TIME	COOLDOWN	COST TO TRAIN	EFFECT
N/A	30	150	-	10sec	15min	90c	Yanks the caster through the twisting nether back to his home location.

FAR SIGHT

RANK	LEVEL	MANA	RANGE	CASTING TIME	COOLDOWN	COST TO TRAIN	EFFECT
N/A	26	80	50000	2sec	-	67c	Changes the caster's viewpoint to the targeted location. Lasts 1 min. Only usable outdoors.

FIRE RESISTANCE TOTEM

RANK	LEVEL	MANA	RANGE	CASTING TIME	COOLDOWN	COST TO TRAIN	EFFECT
1	28	90	-	IC	-	72	Summons a Fire Resistance Totem with 5 health at the feet of the caster for 1 min that increases the fire resistance of party members within 20 yards by 50.
2	42	150	-	IC	-	1 50	Summons a Fire Resistance Totem with 5 health at the feet of the caster for 1 min that increases the fire resistance of party members within 20 yards by 75.
3	58	225	-	IC	-	4 30	Summons a Fire Resistance Totem with 5 health at the feet of the caster for 1 min that increases the fire resistance of party members within 20 yards by 100.

FLAMETONGUE TOTEM

RANK	LEVEL	MANA	RANGE	CASTING TIME	COOLDOWN	COST TO TRAIN	EFFECT
1	28	110	-	IC	-	72	Summons a Flametongue Totem with 5 health at the feet of the caster. The totem enchants all party members' weapons with fire if they are within 20 yards. Each hit causes 6.4 to 19.6 additional fire damage, based on the speed of the weapon. Slower weapons cause more fire damage per swing. Lasts 1.50 min.
2	38	170	-	IC	-	1 40	Summons a Flametongue Totem with 5 health at the feet of the caster. The totem enchants all party members' weapons with fire if they are within 20 yards. Each hit causes 9 to 27.9 additional fire damage, based on the speed of the weapon. Slower weapons cause more fire damage per swing. Lasts 1.50 min.
3	48	250	-	IC	-	2 50	Summons a Flametongue Totem with 5 health at the feet of the caster. The totem enchants all party members' weapons with fire if they are within 20 yards. Each hit causes 12.3 to 37.9 additional fire damage, based on the speed of the weapon. Slower weapons cause more fire damage per swing. Lasts 1.50 min.
4	58	340	-	IC	-	4 30	Summons a Flametongue Totem with 5 health at the feet of the caster. The totem enchants all party members' weapons with fire if they are within 20 yards. Each hit causes 15.8 to 48.7 additional fire damage, based on the speed of the weapon. Slower weapons cause more fire damage per swing. Lasts 1.50 min.

FLAMETONGUE WEAPON

RANK	LEVEL	MANA	RANGE	CASTING TIME	COOLDOWN	COST TO TRAIN	EFFECT
1	10	60	-	IC	-	4	Imbue the Shaman's weapon with fire. Each hit causes 3.8 to 11.8 additional fire damage, based on the speed of the weapon. Slower weapons cause more fire damage per swing. Lasts for 5 minutes.
2	18	110	-	IC	-	22	Imbue the Shaman's weapon with fire. Each hit causes 5.6 to 17.4 additional fire damage, based on the speed of the weapon. Slower weapons cause more fire damage per swing. Lasts for 5 minutes.
3	26	155	-	IC	-	67	Imbue the Shaman's weapon with fire. Each hit causes 8.5 to 26 additional fire damage, based on the speed of the weapon. Slower weapons cause more fire damage per swing. Lasts for 5 minutes.
4	36	240	-	IC	-	1 20	Imbue the Shaman's weapon with fire. Each hit causes 13.5 to 41.6 additional fire damage, based on the speed of the weapon. Slower weapons cause more fire damage per swing. Lasts for 5 minutes.
5	46	345	-	IC	-	2 50	Imbue the Shaman's weapon with fire. Each hit causes 22.1 to 68.2 additional fire damage, based on the speed of the weapon. Slower weapons cause more fire damage per swing. Lasts for 5 minutes.
6	56	475	-	IC	-	3 20	Imbue the Shaman's weapon with fire. Each hit causes 29.5 to 90.8 additional fire damage, based on the speed of the weapon. Slower weapons cause more fire damage per swing. Lasts for 5 minutes.

FROST RESISTANCE TOTEM

RANK	LEVEL	MANA	RANGE	CASTING TIME	COOLDOWN	COST TO TRAIN	EFFECT
1	24	90	-	IC	-	42	Summons a Frost Resistance Totem with 5 health at the feet of the caster for 1 min. The totem increases party members' frost resistance by 50, if within 20 yards.
2	38	150	-	IC	-	1 40	Summons a Frost Resistance Totem with 5 health at the feet of the caster for 1 min. The totem increases party members' frost resistance by 75, if within 20 yards.
3	54	225	-	IC	-	4 40	Summons a Frost Resistance Totem with 5 health at the feet of the caster for 1 min. The totem increases party members' frost resistance by 100, if within 20 yards.

FROSTBRAND WEAPON

RANK	LEVEL	MANA	RANGE	CASTING TIME	COOLDOWN	COST TO TRAIN	EFFECT
1	20	120	-	IC	-	23	Imbue the Shaman's weapon with frost. Each hit has a chance of causing 32 additional frost damage and slowing the target's movement speed to 75% for 8 sec. Lasts for 5 minutes.
2	28	170	-	IC	-	72	Imbue the Shaman's weapon with frost. Each hit has a chance of causing 48 additional frost damage and slowing the target's movement speed to 75% for 8 sec. Lasts for 5 minutes.
3	38	255	-	IC	-	1 40	Imbue the Shaman's weapon with frost. Each hit has a chance of causing 76 additional frost damage and slowing the target's movement speed to 75% for 8 sec. Lasts for 5 minutes.
4	48	370	-	IC	-	2 50	Imbue the Shaman's weapon with frost. Each hit has a chance of causing 122 additional frost damage and slowing the target's movement speed to 75% for 8 sec. Lasts for 5 minutes.
5	58	500	-	IC	-	4 30	Imbue the Shaman's weapon with frost. Each hit has a chance of causing 159 additional frost damage and slowing the target's movement speed to 75% for 8 sec. Lasts for 5 minutes.

GHOST WOLF

RANK	LEVEL	MANA	RANGE	CASTING TIME	COOLDOWN	COST TO TRAIN	EFFECT
1	20	100	-	3sec	3sec	23	Turns the Shaman into a Ghost Wolf, increasing speed by 40%.

GRACE OF AIR TOTEM

RANK	LEVEL	MANA	RANGE	CASTING TIME	COOLDOWN	COST TO TRAIN	EFFECT
1	42	190	-	IC	-	1 50	Summons a Grace of Air Totem with 5 health at the feet of the caster. The totem increases the agility of party members within 20 yards by 43. Lasts 1.25 min.
2	56	310	-	IC	-	3 20	Summons a Grace of Air Totem with 5 health at the feet of the caster. The totem increases the agility of party members within 20 yards by 67. Lasts 1.50 min.

GROUNDING TOTEM

RANK	LEVEL	MANA	RANGE	CASTING TIME	COOLDOWN	COST TO TRAIN	EFFECT
N/A	30	80	-	IC	15sec	90	Summons a Grounding Totem with 5 health at the feet of the caster that absorbs one harmful spell every 10 seconds for each nearby party member. Lasts 45 sec.

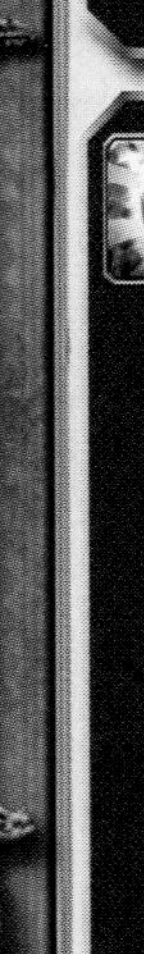

LIGHTNING SHIELD

RANK	LEVEL	MANA	RANGE	CASTING TIME	COOLDOWN	COST TO TRAIN	EFFECT
1	8	45	-	IC	-	2	The caster is surrounded by 3 balls of lightning. When a melee or ranged attacker hits the caster, the attacker will be struck for 13 Nature damage. This expends one lightning ball. Only one ball will fire every few seconds. Lasts 10 min.
2	16	80	-	IC	-	13	The caster is surrounded by 3 balls of lightning. When a melee or ranged attacker hits the caster, the attacker will be struck for 29 Nature damage. This expends one lightning ball. Only one ball will fire every few seconds. Lasts 10 min.
3	24	125	-	IC	-	42	The caster is surrounded by 3 balls of lightning. When a melee or ranged attacker hits the caster, the attacker will be struck for 51 Nature damage. This expends one lightning ball. Only one ball will fire every few seconds. Lasts 10 min.
4	32	180	-	IC	-	1	The caster is surrounded by 3 balls of lightning. When a melee or ranged attacker hits the caster, the attacker will be struck for 80 Nature damage. This expends one lightning ball. Only one ball will fire every few seconds. Lasts 10 min.
5	40	240	-	IC	-	1 50	The caster is surrounded by 3 balls of lightning. When a melee or ranged attacker hits the caster, the attacker will be struck for 114 Nature damage. This expends one lightning ball. Only one ball will fire every few seconds. Lasts 10 min.
6	48	305	-	IC	-	2 50	The caster is surrounded by 3 balls of lightning. When a melee or ranged attacker hits the caster, the attacker will be struck for 154 Nature damage. This expends one lightning ball. Only one ball will fire every few seconds. Lasts 10 min.
7	56	370	-	IC	-	3 20	The caster is surrounded by 3 balls of lightning. When a melee or ranged attacker hits the caster, the attacker will be struck for 198 Nature damage. This expends one lightning ball. Only one ball will fire every few seconds. Lasts 10 min.

RANK	LEVEL	MANA	RANGE	CASTING TIME	COOLDOWN	COST TO TRAIN	EFFECT
N/A	40		-	-	-	1 30	Armor Proficiency

NATURE RESISTANCE TOTEM

RANK	LEVEL	MANA	RANGE	CASTING TIME	COOLDOWN	COST TO TRAIN	EFFECT
1	30	90	-	IC	-	90	Summons a Nature Resistance Totem with 5 health at the feet of the caster for 1 min that increases the nature resistance of party members within 20 yards by 50.
2	44	150	-	IC	-	2 50	Summons a Nature Resistance Totem with 5 health at the feet of the caster for 1 min that increases the nature resistance of party members within 20 yards by 75.
3	60	225	-	IC	-	3 90	Summons a Nature Resistance Totem with 5 health at the feet of the caster for 1 min that increases the nature resistance of party members within 20 yards by 100.

ROCKBITER WEAPON

RANK	LEVEL	MANA	RANGE	CASTING TIME	COOLDOWN	COST TO TRAIN	EFFECT
1	1	30	-	IC	-	10	Imbue the Shaman's weapon, increasing attack power by 30 when using that weapon. Lasts for 5 minutes.
2	8	55	-	IC	-	2	Imbue the Shaman's weapon, increasing attack power by 53 when using that weapon. Lasts for 5 minutes.
3	16	100	-	IC	-	13	Imbue the Shaman's weapon, increasing attack power by 80 when using that weapon. Lasts for 5 minutes.
4	24	145	-	IC	-	42	Imbue the Shaman's weapon, increasing attack power by 117 when using that weapon. Lasts for 5 minutes.
5	34	220	-	IC	-	1 20	Imbue the Shaman's weapon, increasing attack power by 192 when using that weapon. Lasts for 5 minutes.
6	44	325	-	IC	-	2 50	Imbue the Shaman's weapon, increasing attack power by 357 when using that weapon. Lasts for 5 minutes.
7	54	445	-	IC	-	3 20	Imbue the Shaman's weapon, increasing attack power by 504 when using that weapon. Lasts for 5 minutes.

SENTRY TOTEM

RANK	LEVEL	MANA	RANGE	CASTING TIME	COOLDOWN	COST TO TRAIN	EFFECT
N/A	34	80	-	IC	-	1 20	Summons an immobile Sentry Totem with 100 health at your feet for 5 min that allows vision of nearby area and warns of enemies that attack it. Right-click on buff to switch back and forth between totem sight and Shaman sight.

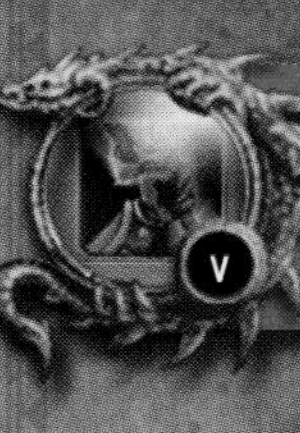

STONESKIN TOTEM

RANK	LEVEL	MANA	RANGE	CASTING TIME	COOLDOWN	COST TO TRAIN	EFFECT
2	14	75	-	IC	-	9 ●	Summons a Stoneskin Totem with 5 health at the feet of the caster. The totem protects party members within 20 yards, reducing melee damage taken by 6. Lasts 1 min.
3	24	110	-	IC	-	42 ●	Summons a Stoneskin Totem with 5 health at the feet of the caster. The totem protects party members within 20 yards, reducing melee damage taken by 10. Lasts 1 min.
4	34	140	-	IC	-	1 ● 20 ●	Summons a Stoneskin Totem with 5 health at the feet of the caster. The totem protects party members within 20 yards, reducing melee damage taken by 14. Lasts 1 min.
5	44	195	-	IC	-	2 ● 50 ●	Summons a Stoneskin Totem with 5 health at the feet of the caster. The totem protects party members within 20 yards, reducing melee damage taken by 20. Lasts 1 min.
6	54	260	-	IC	-	4 ● 40 ●	Summons a Stoneskin Totem with 5 health at the feet of the caster. The totem protects party members within 20 yards, reducing melee damage taken by 27. Lasts 1 min.

STRENGTH OF EARTH TOTEM

RANK	LEVEL	MANA	RANGE	CASTING TIME	COOLDOWN	COST TO TRAIN	EFFECT
1	10	30	-	IC	-	4 ●	Summons a Strength of Earth Totem with 5 health at the feet of the caster. The totem increases the strength of party members within 20 yards by 10. Lasts 45 sec.
2	24	80	-	IC	-	42 ●	Summons a Strength of Earth Totem with 5 health at the feet of the caster. The totem increases the strength of party members within 20 yards by 20. Lasts 1 min.
3	38	155	-	IC	-	1 ● 40 ●	Summons a Strength of Earth Totem with 5 health at the feet of the caster. The totem increases the strength of party members within 20 yards by 36. Lasts 1.25 min.
4	52	275	-	IC	-	3 ● 20 ●	Summons a Strength of Earth Totem with 5 health at the feet of the caster. The totem increases the strength of party members within 20 yards by 61. Lasts 1.50 min.

WATER BREATHING

RANK	LEVEL	MANA	RANGE	CASTING TIME	COOLDOWN	COST TO TRAIN	EFFECT
N/A	22	50	30	IC	-	36 ●	Allows the target to breathe underwater for 10 min.

WATER WALKING

RANK	LEVEL	MANA	RANGE	CASTING TIME	COOLDOWN	COST TO TRAIN	EFFECT
N/A	28	95	30	IC	-	72 ●	Allows the friendly target to walk across water and other water-like surfaces for 10 min.

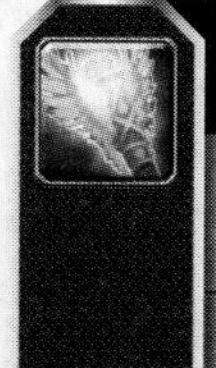

WINDFURY TOTEM

RANK	LEVEL	MANA	RANGE	CASTING TIME	COOLDOWN	COST TO TRAIN	EFFECT
1	32	115	-	IC	-	1 ●	Summons a Windfury Totem with 5 health at the feet of the caster. The totem enchants all party members weapons with wind, if they are within 20 yards. Each hit has a 20% chance of granting the attacker 1 extra attack with 315 extra attack power. Lasts 1.50 min.
2	42	175	-	IC	-	1 ● 50 ●	Summons a Windfury Totem with 5 health at the feet of the caster. The totem enchants all party members weapons with wind, if they are within 20 yards. Each hit has a 20% chance of granting the attacker 1 extra attack with 229 extra attack power. Lasts 1.50 min.
3	52	250	-	IC	-	3 ● 20 ●	Summons a Windfury Totem with 5 health at the feet of the caster. The totem enchants all party members weapons with wind, if they are within 20 yards. Each hit has a 20% chance of granting the attacker 1 extra attack with 122 extra attack power. Lasts 1.50 min.

WINDFURY WEAPON

RANK	LEVEL	MANA	RANGE	CASTING TIME	COOLDOWN	COST TO TRAIN	EFFECT
1	30	185	-	IC	-	90 ●	Imbue the Shaman's weapon with wind. Each hit has a 20% chance of granting you 2 extra attacks with 91 extra attack power. Lasts for 5 minutes.
2	40	280	-	IC	-	1 ● 50 ●	Imbue the Shaman's weapon with wind. Each hit has a 20% chance of granting you 2 extra attacks with 238 extra attack power. Lasts for 5 minutes.
3	50	395	-	IC	-	2 ● 50 ●	Imbue the Shaman's weapon with wind. Each hit has a 20% chance of granting you 2 extra attacks with 497 extra attack power. Lasts for 5 minutes.
4	60	530	-	IC	-	3 ● 90 ●	Imbue the Shaman's weapon with wind. Each hit has a 20% chance of granting you 2 extra attacks with 665 extra attack power. Lasts for 5 minutes.

WINDWALL TOTEM

RANK	LEVEL	MANA	RANGE	CASTING TIME	COOLDOWN	COST TO TRAIN	EFFECT
1	36	140	-	IC	-	1 ● 30 ●	Summons a Windwall Totem with 5 health at the feet of the caster. The totem protects party members within 20 yards, reducing ranged damage taken by 16. Lasts 1 min.
2	46	210	-	IC	-	2 ● 50 ●	Summons a Windwall Totem with 5 health at the feet of the caster. The totem protects party members within 20 yards, reducing ranged damage taken by 25. Lasts 1 min.
3	56	280	-	IC	-	3 ● 20 ●	Summons a Windwall Totem with 5 health at the feet of the caster. The totem protects party members within 20 yards, reducing ranged damage taken by 32. Lasts 1 min.

RESTORATION

The Restoration line of spells is what Shaman use to keep their allies, and themselves, alive during harsh battles. These spells turn the Shaman into a powerful secondary Healer, ready to draw aggro away from Priests and save Warriors from going down. In the worst events, the Shaman are ready to Resurrect the fallen and keep the group going even after near-wipeouts.

CHAIN HEAL

RANK	LEVEL	MANA	RANGE	CASTING TIME	COOLDOWN	COST TO TRAIN	EFFECT
1	40	260	40 yd	2.5sec	-	1 50	Heals the friendly target for 320 to 368, then jumps to heal additional nearby targets. Each jump reduces the effectiveness of the heal by 50%. Heals 3 total targets.
2	46	315	40 yd	2.5sec	-	2 50	Heals the friendly target for 405 to 465, then jumps to heal additional nearby targets. Each jump reduces the effectiveness of the heal by 50%. Heals 3 total targets.
3	54	405	40 yd	2.5sec	-	4 40	Heals the friendly target for 551 to 629, then jumps to heal additional nearby targets. Each jump reduces the effectiveness of the heal by 50%. Heals 3 total targets.

CURE DISEASE

RANK	LEVEL	MANA	RANGE	CASTING TIME	COOLDOWN	COST TO TRAIN	EFFECT
1	22	40	30 yd	IC	-	36	Cures 1 disease on the target.

CURE POISON

RANK	LEVEL	MANA	RANGE	CASTING TIME	COOLDOWN	COST TO TRAIN	EFFECT
1	16	40	30 yd	IC	-	13	Cures 1 poison effect on the target.

DISEASE CLEANSING TOTEM

RANK	LEVEL	MANA	RANGE	CASTING TIME	COOLDOWN	COST TO TRAIN	EFFECT
N/A	38	75	-	IC	-	1 40	Summons a Disease Cleansing Totem with 5 health at the feet of the caster that attempts to remove 1 disease effect from party members within 20 yards every 5 seconds. Lasts 1.50 min.

HEALING STREAM TOTEM

RANK	LEVEL	MANA	RANGE	CASTING TIME	COOLDOWN	COST TO TRAIN	EFFECT
2	30	80	-	IC	-	90	Summons a Healing Stream Totem with 5 health at the feet of the caster for 1 min that heals group members within 20 yards for 20 every 5 seconds.
3	40	95	-	IC	-	1 50	Summons a Healing Stream Totem with 5 health at the feet of the caster for 1 min that heals group members within 20 yards for 25 every 5 seconds.
4	50	110	-	IC	-	2 50	Summons a Healing Stream Totem with 5 health at the feet of the caster for 1 min that heals group members within 20 yards for 30 every 5 seconds.
5	60	125	-	IC	-	3 90	Summons a Healing Stream Totem with 5 health at the feet of the caster for 1 min that heals group members within 20 yards for 35 every 5 seconds.

HEALING WAVE

RANK	LEVEL	MANA	RANGE	CASTING TIME	COOLDOWN	COST TO TRAIN	EFFECT
2	6	50	40 yd	2sec	-	1	Heals a friendly target for 64 to 78.
3	12	90	40 yd	2.5sec	-	8	Heals a friendly target for 129 to 155.
4	18	170	40 yd	3sec	-	22	Heals a friendly target for 268 to 316.
5	24	220	40 yd	3sec	-	42	Heals a friendly target for 376 to 440.
6	32	290	40 yd	3sec	-	1	Heals a friendly target for 536 to 622.
7	40	375	40 yd	3sec	-	1 50	Heals a friendly target for 740 to 854.
8	48	485	40 yd	3sec	-	2 50	Heals a friendly target for 1017 to 1167.
9	56	615	40 yd	3sec	-	3 20	Heals a friendly target for 1367 to 1561.

LESSER HEALING WAVE

RANK	LEVEL	MANA	RANGE	CASTING TIME	COOLDOWN	COST TO TRAIN	EFFECT
1	20	105	40 yd	1.5sec	1.5sec	23	Heals a friendly target for 162 to 186.
2	28	145	40 yd	1.5sec	-	72	Heals a friendly target for 247 to 281.
3	36	185	40 yd	1.5sec	-	1 30	Heals a friendly target for 337 to 381.
4	44	235	40 yd	1.5sec	-	2 50	Heals a friendly target for 458 to 514.
5	52	305	40 yd	1.5sec	-	3 20	Heals a friendly target for 631 to 705.
6	60	357	40 yd	1.5sec	-	3 90	Heals a friendly target for 832 to 928.

MANA SPRING TOTEM

RANK	LEVEL	MANA	RANGE	CASTING TIME	COOLDOWN	COST TO TRAIN	EFFECT
1	26	120	-	IC	-	67	Summons a Mana Spring Totem with 5 health at the feet of the caster for 1 min that restores 12 mana every 5 seconds to group members within 20 yards.
2	36	150	-	IC	-	1 30	Summons a Mana Spring Totem with 5 health at the feet of the caster for 1 min that restores 16 mana every 5 seconds to group members within 20 yards.
3	46	180	-	IC	-	2 50	Summons a Mana Spring Totem with 5 health at the feet of the caster for 1 min that restores 20 mana every 5 seconds to group members within 20 yards.
4	56	205	-	IC	-	3 20	Summons a Mana Spring Totem with 5 health at the feet of the caster for 1 min that restores 24 mana every 5 seconds to group members within 20 yards.

MANA TIDE TOTEM

RANK	LEVEL	MANA	RANGE	CASTING TIME	COOLDOWN	COST TO TRAIN	EFFECT
2	46	40	-	IC	5min	50	Summons a Mana Tide Totem with 5 health at the feet of the caster for 12 sec that restores 150 mana every 3 seconds to group members within 20 yards.
3	56	60	-	IC	5min	70	Summons a Mana Tide Totem with 5 health at the feet of the caster for 12 sec that restores 240 mana every 3 seconds to group members within 20 yards.

POISON CLEANSING TOTEM

RANK	LEVEL	MANA	RANGE	CASTING TIME	COOLDOWN	COST TO TRAIN	EFFECT
N/A	22	75	-	IC	-	36	Summons a Poison Cleansing Totem with 5 health at the feet of the caster that attempts to remove 1 poison effect from party members within 20 yards every 5 seconds. Lasts 1.50 min.

REBIRTH

RANK	LEVEL	MANA	RANGE	CASTING TIME	COOLDOWN	COST TO TRAIN	EFFECT
1	12	140	40	10sec	-	8	Returns the spirit to the body, restoring a dead target to life with 1% of their health and mana.

TREMOR TOTEM

RANK	LEVEL	MANA	RANGE	CASTING TIME	COOLDOWN	COST TO TRAIN	EFFECT
N/A	18	75	-	IC	-	22	Summons a Tremor Totem with 5 health at the feet of the caster that shakes the ground around it, waking party members within 20 yards from harmful status effects. Lasts 1.50 min.

TALENTS

The Shaman Talent system closely follows the spell lines of this class. Elemental Combat takes a Shaman closer toward the ranged-damage (DPS) end of their abilities. Enhancement improves a Shaman's melee damage and survivability; it also improves on several of the group-enhancing totems that Shaman are loved for using! Restoration improves the efficiency of your totem spells, dramatically raises the ability of a Shaman to be a group healer, and even adds a totem that restores group mana.

ELEMENTAL COMBAT

TALENT NAME	RANKS	PREREQUISITES	EFFECTS
Improved Lightning Bolt	5	None	Reduces the Mana cost of your Lightning Bolt spell by 3% (Per Rank)
Concussion	5	None	Increases the damage done by your Shock spells by 1% (Per Rank)
Improved Stoneclaw Totem	5	5 Points in Elemental Combat	Increases the Health of your Stoneclaw Totem by 5% (Per Rank)
Call of Flame	5	5 Points in Elemental Combat	Increases the damage done by your Fire Totems by 2% (Per Rank)
Convection	5	5 Points in Concussion, 5 Points in Elemental Combat	Reduces the Mana cost of your Shock spells by 2% (Per Rank)
Improved Searing Totem	2	5 Points in Elemental Combat	Increases the duration of your Searing Totem by 10% (Per Rank)
Elemental Focus	1	10 Points in Elemental Combat	Gives you a 10% chance to enter a Clearcasting state after casting any Fire, Frost, or Nature damage spell. The Clearcasting state reduces the mana cost of your next damage spell by 100%
Call of Thunder	5	10 Points in Elemental Combat	Increases the critical strike chance of your Lightning spells by 1% - Progression 1/2/3/4/6
Reverberation	5	5 Points in Convection, 10 Points in Elemental Combat	Reduces the cooldown of your Shock spells by 0.2sec (Per Rank)
Improved Fire Nova Totem	2	15 Points in Elemental Combat	Reduces the delay before your Fire Nova Totem activates by 1 sec (Per Rank)
Elemental Fury	1	5 Points in Call of Thunder, 20 Points in Elemental Combat	Increases the critical strike damage done by your Fire, Frost, and Nature spells by 100%
Improved Magma Totem	2	20 Points in Elemental Combat	Reduces the Mana cost of your Magma Totem by 10% (Per Rank)
Lightning Mastery	5	25 Points in Elemental Combat	Reduces the cast time of your Lightning Bolt and Chain Lightning spells by 0.2 sec (Per Rank)
Improved Chain Lightning	2	25 Points in Elemental Combat	Increases the damage dealt by your Chain Lightning spell by 5% (Per Rank)
Elemental Mastery	1	1 Point in Elemental Fury, 30 Points in Elemental Combat	Instant Cast, 5 min cooldown When activated, this spell gives your next Fire, Frost, or Nature damage spell a 100% critical strike chance

ENHANCEMENT

TALENT NAME	RANKS	PREREQUISITES	EFFECTS
Ancestral Knowledge	5	None	Increases your maximum Mana by 1% (Per Rank)
Shield Specialization	5	None	Increases you chance to block attacks with a shield by 1% (Per Rank)
Improved Stoneskin Totem	3	5 Points in Enhancement	Increases the amount of damage absorbed by your Stoneskin Totem by 7% - Progression: 7%/14%/20%
Thundering Strikes	5	5 Points in Enhancement	Improves your chance to get a critical strike with your weapon attacks by 1% (Per Rank)
Improved Ghost Wolf	2	5 Points in Enhancement	Reduces the cast time of your Ghost Wolf spell by 1 sec (Per Rank)
Improved Lightning Shield	3	5 Points in Enhancement	Increases the damage done by your Lightning Shield orbs by 5% (Per Rank)
Improved Strength of Earth Totem	3	10 Points in Enhancement	Increases the amount of Strength raised by your Strength of Earth Totem by 5% (Per Rank)
Two-Handed Axes and Maces	1	10 Points in Enhancement	Allows you to use Two-Handed Axes and Two-Handed Maces.
Anticipation	5	10 Points in Enhancement	Increases your defense skill by 2 (Per Rank)
Flurry	5	5 Points in Thundering Strikes, 15 Points in Enhancement	Increases your attack speed by 10% for your next 3 swings after dealing a critical strike. - Progression: 10%/15%/20%/25%/30%
Improved Rockbiter Weapon	2	15 Points in Enhancement	Increases the Attack Power bonus of your Rockbiter Weapon by 5% (Per Rank)
Improved Flametongue Weapon	2	20 Points in Enhancement	Increases the damage done by your Flametongue Weapon effect by 5% (Per Rank)
Parry	1	20 Points in Enhancement	Gives a chance to parry enemy melee attacks.
Improved Frostbrand Weapon	2	20 Points in Enhancement	Increases the damage done by your Frostbrand Weapon Effect by 5% (Per Rank)
Improved Windfury Weapon	2	20 Points in Enhancement	Increases the chance to activate the Windfury Weapon effect by 2% (Per Rank)
Toughness	5	1 Point in Parry, 25 Points in Enhancement	Increases your armor value from items by 2% (Per Rank)
Improved Grounding Totem	2	25 Points in Enhancement	Increases the frequency that your Grounding Totem will absorb a spell by 2 sec (Per Rank)
Stormstrike	1	30 Points in Enhancement	440 Mana, Instant cast, 25 sec cooldown, 7yd range Gives you an extra attack. In addition, the next 2 sources of Nature damage dealt to the target are increased by 20%. Lasts 12 secs.
Improved Grace of Air Totem	3	30 Points in Enhancement	Increases the amount of Agility raised by your Grace of Air Totem by 5% (Per Rank)

RESTORATION

TALENT NAME	RANKS	PREREQUISITES	EFFECTS
Improved Healing Wave	5	None	Reduces the casting time of your Healing Wave spell by 0.1 sec (Per Rank)
Tidal Focus	5	None	Reduces the Mana cost of your healing spells by 1% (Per Rank)
Improved Rebirth	2	5 Points in Restoration	Reduces the casting time of your Rebirth spell by 2 sec (Per Rank)
Ancestral Healing	5	5 Points in Restoration	Increases your target's armor value from items by 5% (Per Rank) for 15 sec after getting a critical effect from one of your healing spells.
Totemic Focus	5	5 Points in Restoration	Reduces the Mana cost of your totems by 2% (Per Rank)
Eventide	5	10 Points in Restoration	Increases the duration of your Healing Stream and Mana Spring totems by 3% (Per Rank)
Combat Endurance	1	10 Points in Restoration	Allows 10% of your Health regeneration to work while in combat
Improved Lesser Healing Wave	5	10 Points in Restoration	Gives you a 15% chance (Per Rank) to avoid interruption caused by damage while casting Lesser Healing Wave.
Improved Healing Stream Totem	5	5 Points in Eventide, 15 Points in Restoration	Increases the effect of your Healing Stream totem by 4% (Per Rank)
Tidal Mastery	5	15 Points in Restoration	Increases the critical effect chance of your healing and Nature damage spells by 1% (Per Rank)
Improved Mana Spring Totem	5	5 Points in Eventide, 20 Points in Restoration	Increases the effect of your Mana Spring Totem by 5% (Per Rank)
Nature's Swiftness	1	5 Points in Tidal Mastery, 20 Points in Restoration	Instant Cast 3 min cooldown, When activated your next Nature spell with a casting time less than 10sec. Becomes an instant cast spell
Purification	5	25 Points in Restoration	Increases the effectiveness of your healing spells by 2% (Per Rank)
Mana Tide Totem	1	5 Points in Improved Mana Spring Totem, 30 Points in Restoration	20 Mana, Instant Cast, 5 min cooldown, Summons a Mana Tide Totem with 5 health at the feet of the caster for 12 sec that restores 120 mana every 3 seconds to group members within 20 yards

The primary factor in determining Shaman strategy rests on the duration of an upcoming fight. In longer fights, Shaman bring more and more interesting things to a group (and even to some extent gain this complexity when soloing). Shaman are most efficient and exiting when pressured into using many of their special AoE totems, which are pivotal in distinguishing this class from its rivals.

SURVIVAL

When you and your group are threatened, the class has many tricks to come out on top. In battles where there is risk to the party and a powerful monster (or a number of lesser foes), it's amazing to see what the totems can accomplish over time. Drop your Stoneskin totem and reduce incoming damage right off the bat! The effect of this totem belies the modest numbers on its description.

Reducing each enemy attack by six points (for example), adds up to hundreds of saved mana in healing when a group goes through 15 to 20 rounds of attacks against multiple foes. Considering that this totem lasts for an entire minute, those numbers are entirely legitimate. Add that this totem costs less than equivalent healing for that Shaman's level and it becomes even more beneficial!

The same math applies to the Healing Stream Totems. Though each tick seems like a trivial sum of health to restore, these powerhouses of HOT efficiency costs very little to drop, take no time to prepare, and account for about an entire Lesser Healing Wave worth of health to *each* member of the party who is damage during the next minute. You just can't beat efficiency like that, even if only one or two party members are taking damage.

BACKUP HEALING

Shaman have the ability to fight up close and do magical damage, so there are times when it doesn't seem like it is a Shaman's "duty" to heal. This is a complex issue, and a great deal of personal decisions enter into it, but there are a few important points to make.

Shaman have the ability to save lives, as do all healing classes. Dealing damage saves lives when the damage brings down a target that is threatening the group. Healing saves a life when it restores a person who would have fallen before the attacking enemies were slain. If you are in a group that is about to lose a member due to an attack, it is your responsibility to drop into healing duties for a time. Even in a selfish sense, everyone benefits from keeping each member alive during a fight because losing a person leads to major downtime (for a corpse run), or a substantial loss in capabilities for the next few minutes (if Resurrected and sick).

And, from a mana perspective, it costs much more to bring someone back from the dead than it does to give them a bit of healing.

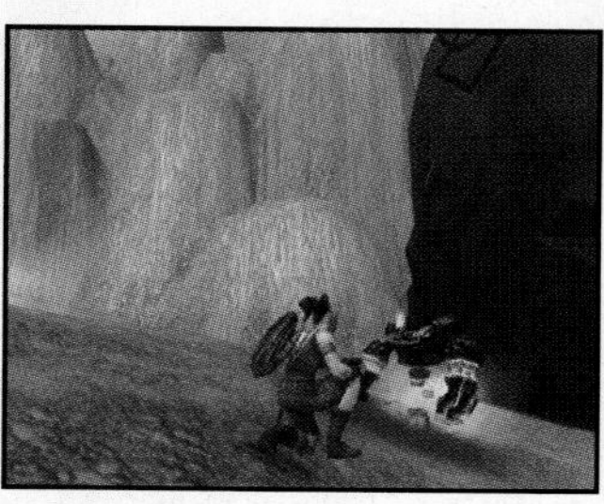

Looked at from a different angle, there is a great deal of good to be done by a secondary healer. Shaman have much better armor than Priests, especially in the later game. Healing a wounded character saves the primary healer from getting aggro; this is doubly important when the person being healed is the primary healer.

Shaman specced in the Restoration Talent line actually become quite skilled in healing. Combining this and an Intellect equipment build, a person can support entire groups as if playing a traditional Priest.

WORKING WITH OTHER SHAMAN

Shaman can only drop one totem from a given element at a time. Having other Shaman around is nice from the beginning because you can divvy totem duties (to stack various long-term positive effects for the tougher battles). Consider having one perhaps handle the buff totems while the other is responsible for bread and butter selections. This way, groups can have Tremor and Stoneskin at the same time, for example.

As for additional duties, they can be divided as well. If healing is in good shape with just one of the Shaman staying on backup duty, the other can switch over to a more aggressive posture and get the enemies knocked down faster with more Earth Shocks and Chain Lightning. Use Lightning Shield and deal even more damage, efficiently, in the event that your casting draws brief aggro. This militant style of casting is better later on, when Shaman have better armor, but it works well enough in the early days as well, so long as you don't overdo it on any single creature.

WARLOCK

Warlocks are a class of mystery and challenges that must be hidden, by necessity, from the normal villagers who populate the Horde and Alliance. While others shun the power of demon summoning and control, a rare few understand that power is merely a tool to be used as one sees fit. Without taking advantage of power, so we are sure to be the victims of it.

These casters are different than Mages, though damage can still be a focus for them. Warlocks use a mix of direct, magical assault and demonic pets to accomplish various tasks. Synergistically, these forces allow Warlocks to kill very efficiently over time. One great joy is that these summoners are able to choose from different types of pets as they level (starting with a Mage-like Imp, but leading toward pets that act as Warrior, Rogue, Priest, Mount, and so forth).

Warlocks start with the mystic staples: bolts from range, some direct damage, and so forth. From there, however, the variety expands again, as Warlocks master multiple forms of damage over time and debuffs to weaken their opponent. To top of the pile of tricks, these casters can create stones to instantly heal themselves (or allies if given away) and other stones that bring back the dead! Warlocks can even summon grouped allies from other parts of the world, instantly joining them with the bulk of the party before heading into danger.

Warlocks may sound challenging, or even a little daunting; they are! And, it's worth your time and practice to learn about these clever casters. If you want power at range and thrive on complex tricks and techniques, don't listen to those Mages who pretend to understand true power. Keep reading to learn the truth.

HIDDEN KNOWLEDGE

The door swung shut, but a cold wind had blown into the tavern. Several of the locals looked up at me, but they didn't stare long. Mages came through Goldshire all the time, and to them I seemed about as common as any caster with a mind for flame and glory. I purchased some basic supplies and made myself a fixture of the room for a time, waiting until nobody knew or cared what I was doing, then I slipped into the back room and down the staircase.

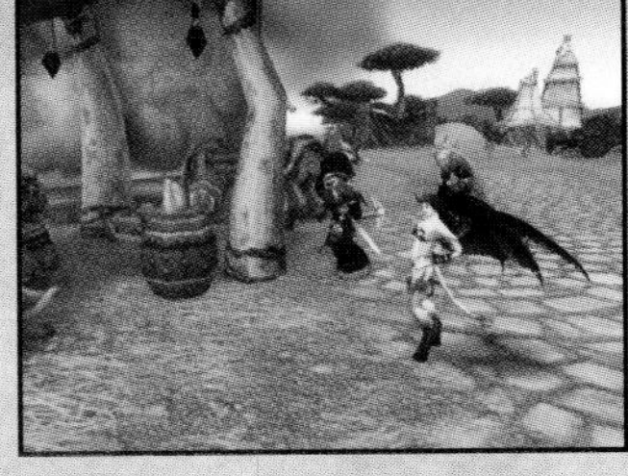

Though I had never been here, I had heard from others where to seek my trainer. There, in the dark storage room under the tavern, I found barrels of aging whisky and ale. The place smelled dry and a bit stale, but there was something else hovering in the air; an almost imperceptible hint of excitement and energy.

"Who are you?" a voice queried from the darkness.

I concentrated for a few moments instead of responding, bringing a powerful energy to bear in the room and a light shone where before there was nothing. Out of that stepped one of my Imps, snarling for a moment in its petulant manner.

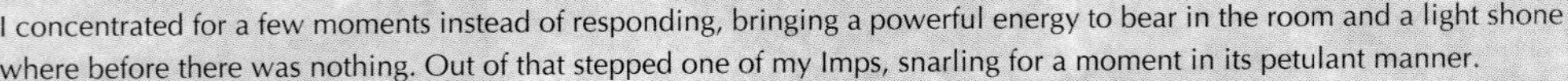

"I come as a man who wishes to learn," I said to the shadowy figure near the wall. "I have already begun my journey, but there is much still that I do not understand. Others have said that you are a person who can help me."

"We must all help ourselves," the other said while stepping slightly forward. "Yet," he added, "I can guide you toward greater things."

The stairs above us creaked for a moment, sounding as if someone was about to descend. Both of our hands reached into the folds of our robes, bringing out wands that cracked with a dark aura. Nothing approached; it was merely some buffoon upstairs who had wandered too heavily on the floor.

I smiled as I put my wand away. "I am ready."

INTRODUCTION TO PLAYING THE CLASS

RACES AND STARTING ATTRIBUTES

RACE	STRENGTH	STAMINA	AGILITY	INTELLECT	SPIRIT
Gnome	20	21	22	24	22
Human	21	22	21	23	22
Orc	22	22	20	22	23
Undead	20	23	19	23	24

ATTRIBUTES APPLIED

Attribute	Effect
Strength	Almost Nothing
Stamina	Higher Hit Points
Agility	Improved Dodge Rate
Intellect	Improved Mana Pool, Higher Chance for a Spell Critical
Spirit	Improved Hit Point and Mana Recovery

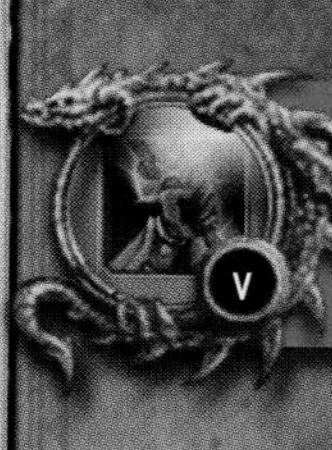

ITEMS AND EQUIPMENT

Warlocks aren't as dependent on equipment as a number of their rivals and comrades. Indeed, having a good wand and high bonuses to Spirit and intellect are enough by themselves to place Warlocks in a fairly good spot. These casters have many facets of play that revolve around the timing of their ability use, so stats are reduced slightly in importance (not to the point of being on the sidelines, of course).

The primary focus for a Warlock is to collect a heavy supply of Intellect and Spirit gear. With proper pet use, Warlocks can have some very effective and long fights against difficult opponents. A high Spirit stat gives you the chance to regenerate enough to come back into the fight after some wand use. Intellect is always there for having a good mana pool. With Warlocks, it's hard to focus on one over the other, since both play such a critical role.

Wands have already been mentioned; these ranged weapons are perfect for adding to solo or group damage when your mana is depleted (or when you wish to start regenerating mana as a monster dies of your DOTs). Stay current with these weapons as often as possible and practice their use and timing to make sure you get the maximum amount of damage out of their use.

CHOOSING YOUR PROFESSION

Warlocks can be happy with several choices in tradeskills. Tailoring and Enchanting both have allure because of their wide use in creating and improving moderate to high quality items for casters. This is a very good route for the solo Warlock.

Warlocks in large guilds may prefer Herbalism and Alchemy, for the potion potential. Yet, Warlocks don't use potions quite as often as some of the other casters because of their ability to shift mana into health and health into mana (though different abilities).

Because Warlocks get dinged up from time to time and like to use their health for various projects, it's very nice to have Cooking and First Aid to improve the efficiency of these powers. Quickly increasing your mana supply on the move and using First Aid to shore up any health problems can keep a Warlock in top form.

CLASS ABILITIES

Warlock abilities are able to cause massive trouble to enemies through DOTs, debuffs, and some direct damage. In addition, a Warlock's choice of pet modifies which buffs are cast on allies and how militant the Warlock is against enemies (Imps for damage at range, Succubus for melee damage, Voidwalker for defense, etc.).

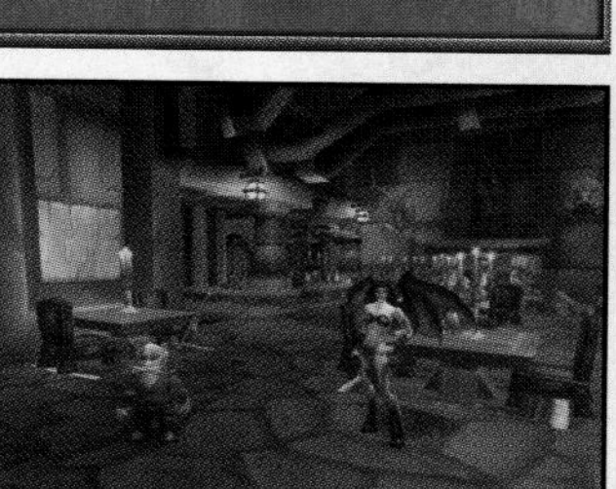

ABILITY	RANK	LEVEL	TYPE
Immolate	1	1	Destruction
Corruption	1	4	Affliction
Curse of Weakness	1	4	Affliction
Life Tap	1	6	Affliction
Shadow Bolt	2	6	Destruction
Curse of Agony	1	8	Affliction
Fear	1	8	Affliction
Create Minor Healthstone	N/A	10	Demonology
Demon Skin	2	10	Demonology
Drain Soul	1	10	Affliction
Immolate	2	10	Destruction
Curse of Weakness	2	12	Affliction
Health Funnel	1	12	Demonology
Shadow Bolt	3	12	Destruction
Corruption	2	14	Affliction
Curse of Recklessness	1	14	Affliction
Drain Life	1	14	Affliction
Life Tap	2	16	Affliction
Unending Breath	N/A	16	Demonology
Create Soulstone	N/A	18	Demonology
Curse of Agony	2	18	Affliction
Searing Pain	1	18	Destruction
Demon Armor	1	20	Demonology
Health Funnel	2	20	Demonology
Immolate	3	20	Destruction
Rain of Fire	1	20	Destruction
Ritual of Summoning	N/A	20	Demonology
Shadow Bolt	4	20	Destruction
Create Lesser Healthstone	N/A	22	Demonology
Curse of Weakness	3	22	Affliction
Drain Life	2	22	Affliction
Eye of Kilrogg (Summon)	N/A	22	Demonology
Corruption	3	24	Affliction
Drain Mana	1	24	Affliction
Drain Soul	2	24	Affliction
Sense Demons	1	24	Demonology
Curse of Tongues	1	26	Affliction
Detect Lesser Invisibility	N/A	26	Demonology
Life Tap	3	26	Affliction
Searing Pain	2	26	Destruction
Banish	N/A	28	Affliction
Create Lesser Firestone	N/A	28	Demonology
Curse of Agony	3	28	Affliction
Curse of Recklessness	2	28	Affliction
Health Funnel	3	28	Demonology
Shadow Bolt	5	28	Destruction
Demon Armor	2	30	Demonology
Drain Life	3	30	Affliction
Enslave Demon	1	30	Demonology
Hellfire	1	30	Destruction
Immolate	4	30	Destruction
Curse of the Elements	1	32	Affliction
Curse of Weakness	4	32	Affliction
Fear	2	32	Affliction
Shadow Ward	1	32	Demonology
Corruption	4	34	Affliction
Create Healthstone	N/A	34	Demonology
Drain Mana	2	34	Affliction
Rain of Fire	2	34	Destruction
Searing Pain	3	34	Destruction
Create Firestone	N/A	36	Demonology
Create Spellstone	N/A	36	Demonology
Health Funnel	4	36	Demonology
Life Tap	4	36	Affliction
Shadow Bolt	6	36	Destruction
Curse of Agony	4	38	Affliction
Detect Invisibility	N/A	38	Demonology
Drain Life	4	38	Affliction
Drain Soul	3	38	Affliction
Demon Armor	3	40	Demonology
Howl of Terror	1	40	Affliction
Immolate	5	40	Destruction
Curse of Recklessness	3	42	Affliction
Curse of Weakness	5	42	Affliction
Death Coil	1	42	Affliction
Hellfire	2	42	Destruction
Searing Pain	4	42	Destruction
Shadow Ward	2	42	Demonology
Corruption	5	44	Affliction
Curse of Shadow	1	44	Affliction
Drain Mana	3	44	Affliction
Enslave Demon	2	44	Demonology
Health Funnel	5	44	Demonology
Shadow Bolt	7	44	Destruction
Create Greater Firestone	N/A	46	Demonology
Create Greater Healthstone	N/A	46	Demonology
Curse of the Elements	2	46	Affliction
Drain Life	5	46	Affliction
Life Tap	5	46	Affliction
Rain of Fire	3	46	Destruction
Create Greater Spellstone	N/A	48	Demonology
Curse of Agony	5	48	Affliction
Soul Fire	1	48	Destruction
Curse of Tongues	2	50	Affliction
Death Coil	2	50	Affliction
Demon Armor	4	50	Demonology
Detect Greater Invisibility	N/A	50	Demonology
Immolate	6	50	Destruction
Searing Pain	5	50	Destruction
Curse of Weakness	6	52	Affliction
Drain Soul	4	52	Affliction
Health Funnel	6	52	Demonology
Shadow Bolt	8	52	Destruction
Shadow Ward	3	52	Demonology
Corruption	6	54	Affliction
Drain Life	6	54	Affliction
Drain Mana	4	54	Affliction
Hellfire	3	54	Destruction
Howl of Terror	2	54	Affliction
Create Major Firestone	N/A	56	Demonology
Curse of Recklessness	4	56	Affliction
Curse of Shadow	2	56	Affliction
Fear	3	56	Affliction
Life Tap	6	56	Affliction
Soul Fire	2	56	Destruction
Create Major Healthstone	N/A	58	Demonology
Curse of Agony	6	58	Affliction
Death Coil	3	58	Affliction
Enslave Demon	3	58	Demonology
Rain of Fire	4	58	Destruction
Searing Pain	6	58	Destruction
Create Major Spellstone	N/A	60	Demonology
Curse of the Elements	3	60	Affliction
Demon Armor	5	60	Demonology
Health Funnel	7	60	Demonology
Immolate	7	60	Destruction
Shadow Bolt	9	60	Destruction

AFFLICTION

Affliction is the line for debuffs, DOTs, and various foul tricks. Warlocks are able to place long-term damage on targets with Corruption and Curse of Agony. Life Tap is able to convert health into mana, which is always a fine way to limit downtime (especially when food or First Aid can be used). Against enemies who are focused on your pet or various allies, Drain Life restores some of your health at the expense of your target, while Drain Soul is the key to stealing the souls of your foes.

BANISH

RANK	LEVEL	MANA	RANGE	CASTING TIME	COOLDOWN	COST TO TRAIN	EFFECT
N/A	28	100	30 yd	1 sec	20min	50c	Banishes the enemy target, preventing all action but making it invulnerable for up to 30 sec. Only one target can be banished at a time.

CORRUPTION

RANK	LEVEL	MANA	RANGE	CASTING TIME	COOLDOWN	COST TO TRAIN	EFFECT
1	4	35	30 yd	2 sec	-	1c	Corrupts the target, causing 42 damage over 18 sec.
2	14	55	30 yd	2 sec	-	9c	Corrupts the target, causing 91 damage over 21 sec.
3	24	100	30 yd	2 sec	-	50c	Corrupts the target, causing 184 damage over 24 sec.
4	34	160	30 yd	2 sec	-	1s 10c	Corrupts the target, causing 324 damage over 27 sec.
5	44	225	30 yd	2 sec	-	1s 70c	Corrupts the target, causing 486 damage over 27 sec.
6	54	290	30 yd	2 sec	-	4s 40c	Corrupts the target, causing 666 damage over 27 sec.

CURSE OF AGONY

RANK	LEVEL	MANA	RANGE	CASTING TIME	COOLDOWN	COST TO TRAIN	EFFECT
1	8	25	30 yd	IC	-	2c	Curses the target with agony, causing 60 damage over 30 sec. Only one Curse per Warlock can be active on any one target.
2	18	50	30 yd	IC	-	29c	Curses the target with agony, causing 140 damage over 30 sec. Only one Curse per Warlock can be active on any one target.
3	28	90	30 yd	IC	-	50c	Curses the target with agony, causing 280 damage over 30 sec. Only one Curse per Warlock can be active on any one target.
4	38	130	30 yd	IC	-	1s 40c	Curses the target with agony, causing 450 damage over 30 sec. Only one Curse per Warlock can be active on any one target.
5	48	170	30 yd	IC	-	2s 50c	Curses the target with agony, causing 640 damage over 30 sec. Only one Curse per Warlock can be active on any one target.
6	58	215	30 yd	IC	-	4s 30c	Curses the target with agony, causing 870 damage over 30 sec. Only one Curse per Warlock can be active on any one target.

CURSE OF RECKLESSNESS

RANK	LEVEL	MANA	RANGE	CASTING TIME	COOLDOWN	COST TO TRAIN	EFFECT
1	14	40	30 yd	IC	-	9c	Curses the target with recklessness, increasing attack power by 20 but reducing armor by 140 for 2 min. Cursed enemies will not flee and will ignore fear effects. Only one Curse per Warlock can be active on any one target.
2	28	70	30 yd	IC	-	50c	Curses the target with recklessness, increasing attack power by 45 but reducing armor by 290 for 2 min. Cursed enemies will not flee and will ignore fear effects. Only one Curse per Warlock can be active on any one target.
3	42	100	30 yd	IC	-	2s 20c	Curses the target with recklessness, increasing attack power by 65 but reducing armor by 465 for 2 min. Cursed enemies will not flee and will ignore fear effects. Only one Curse per Warlock can be active on any one target.
4	56	130	30 yd	IC	-	6s 40c	Curses the target with recklessness, increasing attack power by 90 but reducing armor by 640 for 2 min. Cursed enemies will not flee and will ignore fear effects. Only one Curse per Warlock can be active on any one target.

CURSE OF SHADOW

RANK	LEVEL	MANA	RANGE	CASTING TIME	COOLDOWN	COST TO TRAIN	EFFECT
1	44	150	30 yd	IC	-	1s 70c	Curses the target, reducing Shadow and Arcane resistances by 60 for 2 min. Only one Curse per Warlock can be active on any one target.
2	56	200	30 yd	IC	-	3s 90c	Curses the target, reducing Shadow and Arcane resistances by 75 for 2 min. Only one Curse per Warlock can be active on any one target.

CURSE OF THE ELEMENTS

RANK	LEVEL	MANA	RANGE	CASTING TIME	COOLDOWN	COST TO TRAIN	EFFECT
1	32	100	30 yd	IC	-	1s 10c	Curses the target, reducing Fire and Frost resistances by 45 for 2 min. Only one Curse per Warlock can be active on any one target.
2	46	150	30 yd	IC	-	2s 20c	Curses the target, reducing Fire and Frost resistances by 60 for 2 min. Only one Curse per Warlock can be active on any one target.
3	60	200	30 yd	IC	-	2s 90c	Curses the target, reducing Fire and Frost resistances by 75 for 2 min. Only one Curse per Warlock can be active on any one target.

CURSE OF TONGUES

RANK	LEVEL	MANA	RANGE	CASTING TIME	COOLDOWN	COST TO TRAIN	EFFECT
1	26	80	30 yd	IC	-	70c	Forces the target to speak in Demonic, slowing the casting time of all spells by 50%. Only one Curse per Warlock can be active on any one target. Lasts 30 sec.
2	50	110	30 yd	IC	-	2s 80c	Forces the target to speak in Demonic, slowing the casting time of all spells by 60%. Only one Curse per Warlock can be active on any one target. Lasts 30 sec.

CURSE OF WEAKNESS

RANK	LEVEL	MANA	RANGE	CASTING TIME	COOLDOWN	COST TO TRAIN	EFFECT
1	4	35	30 yd	IC	-	1 ●	Damage caused by the target is reduced by 3 for 2 min. Only one Curse per Warlock can be active on any one target.
2	12	65	30 yd	IC	-	6 ●	Damage caused by the target is reduced by 6 for 2 min. Only one Curse per Warlock can be active on any one target.
3	22	105	30 yd	IC	-	40 ●	Damage caused by the target is reduced by 10 for 2 min. Only one Curse per Warlock can be active on any one target.
4	32	155	30 yd	IC	-	1 ● 10 ●	Damage caused by the target is reduced by 15 for 2 min. Only one Curse per Warlock can be active on any one target.
5	42	225	-	IC	-	2 ● 20 ●	Damage caused by the target is reduced by 22 for 2 min. Only one Curse per Warlock can be active on any one target.
6	52	310	30 yd	IC	-	3 ● 20 ●	Damage caused by the target is reduced by 31 for 2 min. Only one Curse per Warlock can be active on any one target.

DEATH COIL

RANK	LEVEL	MANA	RANGE	CASTING TIME	COOLDOWN	COST TO TRAIN	EFFECT
1	42	230	30 yd	IC	10min	1 ● 50 ●	Drains 287 of the enemy target's health, returning 100% to the caster.
2	50	290	30 yd	IC	10min	2 ● 80 ●	Drains 375 of the enemy target's health, returning 100% to the caster.
3	58	350	30 yd	IC	10min	2 ● 70 ●	Drains 470 of the enemy target's health, returning 100% to the caster.

DRAIN LIFE

RANK	LEVEL	MANA	RANGE	CASTING TIME	COOLDOWN	COST TO TRAIN	EFFECT
1	14	55	20 yd	IC	-	9 ●	Transfers 10 health every second from the target to the caster. Lasts 5 sec.
2	22	85	20 yd	IC	-	40 ●	Transfers 17 health every second from the target to the caster. Lasts 5 sec.
3	30	135	20 yd	IC	-	60 ●	Transfers 29 health every second from the target to the caster. Lasts 5 sec.
4	38	185	20 yd	IC	-	1 ● 40 ●	Transfers 41 health every second from the target to the caster. Lasts 5 sec
5	46	240	20 yd	IC	-	2 ● 20 ●	Transfers 55 health every second from the target to the caster. Lasts 5 sec.
6	54	300	20 yd	IC	-	4 ● 40 ●	Transfers 71 health every second from the target to the caster. Lasts 5 sec.

DRAIN MANA

RANK	LEVEL	MANA	RANGE	CASTING TIME	COOLDOWN	COST TO TRAIN	EFFECT
1	24	95	20 yd	IC	-	50 ●	Transfers 42 mana every 1 sec from the target to the caster. Lasts 5 sec.
2	34	155	20 yd	IC	-	1 ● 10 ●	Transfers 68 mana every 1 sec from the target to the caster. Lasts 5 sec.
3	44	225	20 yd	IC	-	1 ● 70 ●	Transfers 99 mana every 1 sec from the target to the caster. Lasts 5 sec.
4	54	310	20 yd	IC	-	4 ● 40 ●	Transfers 136 mana every 1 sec from the target to the caster. Lasts 5 sec.

DRAIN SOUL

RANK	LEVEL	MANA	RANGE	CASTING TIME	COOLDOWN	COST TO TRAIN	EFFECT
1	10	55	30 yd	IC	-	3 ●	Drains the soul of the target, causing 55 damage over 15 sec. If the target dies while being drained, and yields experience, the caster gains a Soul Shard. Soul Shards are required for other spells.
2	24	125	30 yd	IC	-	50 ●	Drains the soul of the target, causing 155 damage over 15 sec. If the target dies while being drained, and yields experience, the caster gains a Soul Shard. Soul Shards are required for other spells.
3	38	210	30 yd	IC	-	1 ● 40 ●	Drains the soul of the target, causing 295 damage over 15 sec. If the target dies while being drained, and yields experience, the caster gains a Soul Shard. Soul Shards are required for other spells.
4	52	290	30 yd	IC	-	3 ● 20 ●	Drains the soul of the target, causing 455 damage over 15 sec. If the target dies while being drained, and yields experience, the caster gains a Soul Shard. Soul Shards are required for other spells.

FEAR

RANK	LEVEL	MANA	RANGE	CASTING TIME	COOLDOWN	COST TO TRAIN	EFFECT
1	8	35	20 yd	1.5	-	2 ●	Strikes fear in the enemy, causing it to run in fear for up to 10 sec. Only 1 target can be feared at a time.
2	32	55	20 yd	1.5 sec	-	1 ● 10 ●	Strikes fear in the enemy, causing it to run in fear for up to 15 sec. Only 1 target can be feared at a time.
3	56	80	20 yd	1.5 sec	-	4 ● 40 ●	Strikes fear in the enemy, causing it to run in fear for up to 20 sec. Only 1 target can be feared at a time.

HOWL OF TERROR

RANK	LEVEL	MANA	RANGE	CASTING TIME	COOLDOWN	COST TO TRAIN	EFFECT
1	40	150	-	2 sec	40 sec	2 ●	Howl, causing all enemies within 10 yds to flee in terror for 10 sec.
2	54	200	-	2 sec	40 sec	3 ● 50 ●	Howl, causing all enemies within 10 yds to flee in terror for 15 sec.

LIFE TAP

RANK	LEVEL	HP	RANGE	CASTING TIME	COOLDOWN	COST TO TRAIN	EFFECT
1	6	14	-	IC	-	1 ●	Converts 14 health into 20 mana.
2	16	57	-	IC	-	18 ●	Converts 57 health into 65 mana.
3	26	112	-	IC	-	70 ●	Converts 112 health into 130 mana.
4	36	182	-	IC	-	1 ●	Converts 182 health into 210 mana.
5	46	294	-	IC	-	2 ● 20 ●	Converts 294 health into 300 mana.
6	56	404	-	IC	-	6 ● 40 ●	Converts 404 health into 420 mana.

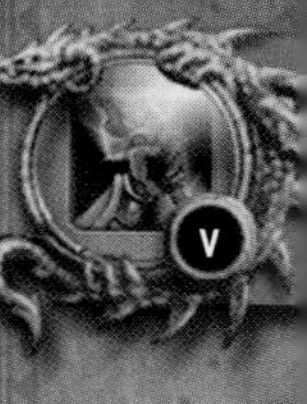
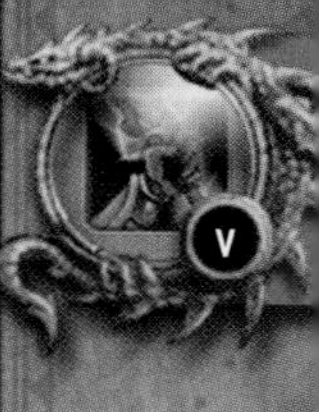

DEMONOLOGY

Many of a Warlocks buffs and special abilities are found in the Demonology line. Demon Skin/Armor is used to improve armor and health regeneration (and should always be active). Using Soul Shards, you can create Healthstones (instant health items that can be traded to allies). Various other stones are used to protect against magical damage (Spellstones), or assist in dealing elemental weapons damage (Firestones).

CREATE FIRESTONE

ABILITY	RANK	LEVEL	MANA	RANGE	CASTING TIME	COOLDOWN	COST TO TRAIN	EFFECT
Create Lesser Firestone	N/A	28	500	-	3 sec	-	50	Creates a Lesser Firestone which can be equipped in the off hand. When equipped, enchants the main hand weapon with fire, granting each attack a chance to deal 25 to 35 additional fire damage.
Create Firestone	N/A	36	700	-	3 sec	-	1	Creates a Firestone which can be equipped in the off hand. When equipped, enchants the main hand weapon with fire, granting each attack a chance to deal 40 to 60 additional fire damage.
Create Greater Firestone	N/A	46	900	-	3 sec	-	1 90	Creates a Greater Firestone which can be equipped in the off hand. When equipped, enchants the main hand weapon with fire, granting each attack a chance to deal 60 to 90 additional fire damage.
Create Major Firestone	N/A	56	1100	-	3 sec	-	3 90	When equipped, enchants the main hand weapon with fire, granting each attack a chance to deal 80 to 120 additional fire damage.

CREATE HEALTHSTONE

ABILITY	RANK	LEVEL	MANA	RANGE	CASTING TIME	COOLDOWN	COST TO TRAIN	EFFECT
Create Minor Healthstone	N/A	10	95	-	3 sec	-	3	Creates a Minor Healthstone that can be used to instantly restore 100 health.
Create Lesser Healthstone	N/A	22	240	-	3 sec	-	40	Creates a Lesser Healthstone that can be used to instantly restore 250 health.
Create Healthstone	N/A	34	475	-	3 sec	-	1 10	Creates a Healthstone that can be used to instantly restore 500 health.
Create Greater Healthstone	N/A	46	750	-	3 sec	-	2 20	Creates a Greater Healthstone that can be used to instantly restore 800 health.
Create Major Healthstone	N/A	58	1120	-	3 sec	-	4 30	Creates a Major Healthstone that can be used to instantly restore 1200 health.

CREATE SPELLSTONE

ABILITY	RANK	LEVEL	MANA	RANGE	CASTING TIME	COOLDOWN	COST TO TRAIN	EFFECT
Create Spellstone	N/A	36	500	-	5 sec	-	1	Creates a Spellstone for the caster. When equipped and used, the Spellstone removes all magic effects from the caster and will absorb 400 magic damage for 1 min.
Create Greater Spellstone	N/A	48	750	-	5 sec	-	2 50	Creates a Greater Spellstone for the caster. When equipped and used, the Greater Spellstone removes all magic effects from the caster and will absorb 650 magic damage for 1 min.
Create Major Spellstone	N/A	60	1000	-	5 sec	-	2 90	Creates a Major Spellstone for the caster. When equipped and used, the Major Spellstone removes all magic effects from the caster and will absorb 900 magic damage for 1 min.

CREATE SOULSTONE

RANK	LEVEL	MANA	RANGE	CASTING TIME	COOLDOWN	COST TO TRAIN	EFFECT
N/A	18	141	-	10 sec	-	29	Creates a Soulstone that can be used after death to restore its owner to life.

DEMON ARMOR

RANK	LEVEL	MANA	RANGE	CASTING TIME	COOLDOWN	COST TO TRAIN	EFFECT
1	20	275	-	IC	-	20	Protects the caster, increasing armor by 210, shadow resistance by 10 and health regeneration for 30 min.
2	30	520	-	IC	-	60	Protects the caster, increasing armor by 300, shadow resistance by 20 and health regeneration for 30 min.
3	40	800	-	IC	-	2 60	Protects the caster, increasing armor by 390, shadow resistance by 30 and health regeneration for 30 min.
4	50	1150	-	IC	-	2 80	Protects the caster, increasing armor by 480, shadow resistance by 40 and health regeneration for 30 min.
5	60	1580	-	IC	-	2 90	Protects the caster, increasing armor by 570, shadow resistance by 50 and health regeneration for 30 min.

DEMON SKIN

RANK	LEVEL	MANA	RANGE	CASTING TIME	COOLDOWN	COST TO TRAIN	EFFECT
2	10	120	-	IC	-	3	Protects the caster, increasing armor by 120 and health regeneration for 30 min

DETECT INVISIBILITY

ABILITY	RANK	LEVEL	MANA	RANGE	CASTING TIME	COOLDOWN	COST TO TRAIN	EFFECT
Detect Lesser Invisibility	N/A	26	50	30 yd	IC	-	70	Allows the friendly target to detect lesser invisibility for 10 min.
Detect Invisibility	N/A	38	90	30 yd	IC	-	1 40	Allows the friendly target to detect invisibility for 10 min.
Detect Greater Invisibility	N/A	50	140	30 yd	IC	-	2 80	Allows the friendly target to detect greater invisibility for 10 min.

ENSLAVE DEMON

RANK	LEVEL	MANA	RANGE	CASTING TIME	COOLDOWN	COST TO TRAIN	EFFECT
1	30	300	30 yd	3 sec	-	60	Enslaves the target demon, up to level 32, forcing it to do your bidding. While enslaved, the demon's attack speed is slowed by 30% and its casting speed is slowed by 30%. Lasts 5 min, but the target gets a chance to break free every 5 seconds.
2	44	500	30 yd	3 sec	-	1 70	Enslaves the target demon, up to level 47, forcing it to do your bidding. While enslaved, the demon's attack speed is slowed by 30% and its casting speed is slowed by 30%. Lasts 5 min, but the target gets a chance to break free every 5 seconds.
3	58	700	30 yd	3 sec	-	4 30	Enslaves the target demon, up to level 62, forcing it to do your bidding. While enslaved, the demon's attack speed is slowed by 30% and its casting speed is slowed by 30%. Lasts 5 min, but the target gets a chance to break free every 5 seconds.

EYE OF KILROGG (SUMMON)

RANK	LEVEL	MANA	RANGE	CASTING TIME	COOLDOWN	COST TO TRAIN	EFFECT
N/A	22	100	50000 yd	5 sec	-	40	Summons an Eye of Kilrogg and binds your vision to it. The eye is stealthy and quick, but very fragile.

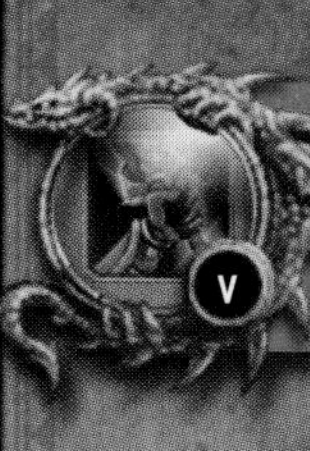

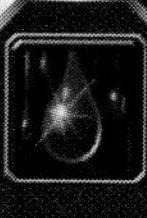

HEALTH FUNNEL

RANK	LEVEL	HP	RANGE	CASTING TIME	COOLDOWN	COST TO TRAIN	EFFECT
1	12	11 + 5/ sec	20 yd	IC	-	6	Gives 12 health to the caster's pet every second for 10 sec as long as the caster channels.
2	20	15 + 10/ sec	20 yd	IC	-	20	Gives 24 health to the caster's pet every second for 10 sec as long as the caster channels.
3	28	24 + 17/ sec	20 yd	IC	-	50	Gives 43 health to the caster's pet every second for 10 sec as long as the caster channels.
4	36	39 + 24/ sec	20 yd	IC	-	1	Gives 64 health to the caster's pet every second for 10 sec as long as the caster channels.
5	44	45 + 33/ sec	20 yd	IC	-	1 70	Gives 89 health to the caster's pet every second for 10 sec as long as the caster channels.
6	52	62 + 42/ sec	20 yd	IC	-	3 20	Gives 119 health to the caster's pet every second for 10 sec as long as the caster channels.
7	60	79 + 52/ sec	20 yd	IC	-	2 90	Gives 153 health to the caster's pet every second for 10 sec as long as the caster channels.

RITUAL OF SUMMONING

RANK	LEVEL	MANA	RANGE	CASTING TIME	COOLDOWN	COST TO TRAIN	EFFECT
N/A	20	300	30 yd	5 sec	-	20	Begins a ritual that summons the targeted group member. Requires the caster and 2 additional people to complete the ritual. In order to participate, all players must right-click the portal and not move until the ritual is complete.

SENSE DEMONS

RANK	LEVEL	MANA	RANGE	CASTING TIME	COOLDOWN	COST TO TRAIN	EFFECT
1	24	-	-	-	-	50	Shows the location of all nearby demons on the minimap until cancelled. Only one type of tracking can be used at a time.

SHADOW WARD

RANK	LEVEL	MANA	RANGE	CASTING TIME	COOLDOWN	COST TO TRAIN	EFFECT
1	32	135	-	IC	30 sec	1 10	Absorbs 185 shadow damage. Lasts 30 sec.
2	42	195	-	IC	30 sec	2 20	Absorbs 300 shadow damage. Lasts 30 sec.
3	52	255	-	IC	30 sec	3 20	Absorbs 430 shadow damage. Lasts 30 sec.

UNENDING BREATH

RANK	LEVEL	MANA	RANGE	CASTING TIME	COOLDOWN	COST TO TRAIN	EFFECT
N/A	16	50	30 yd	IC	-	18	Allows the target to breathe underwater for 10 min.

HELLFIRE

RANK	LEVEL	MANA	RANGE	CASTING TIME	COOLDOWN	COST TO TRAIN	EFFECT
1	30	645	-	IC	-	60	Ignites the area surrounding the caster, causing 83 fire damage to himself and 83 fire damage to all nearby enemies every 1 sec. Lasts 15 sec.
2	42	955	-	IC	-	2 60	Ignites the area surrounding the caster, causing 139 fire damage to himself and 145 fire damage to all nearby enemies every 1 sec. Lasts 15 sec.
3	54	1274	-	IC	-	4 40	Ignites the area surrounding the caster, causing 208 fire damage to himself and 216 fire damage to all nearby enemies every 1 sec. Lasts 15 sec.

DESTRUCTION

The Destruction line should be most familiar to players who like playing Mages; these spells include your primary bolt (Shadow Bolt), another DOT (Immolate), and other direct damage attacks, such as Searing Pain. Warlocks are able to use AoE attacks through the Destruction line, with Rain of Fire being one of the safer spells to use; Hellfire is gained later on and deals massive AoE damage at tremendous risk to the Warlock (don't forget to use Spellstones and other forms of protection to reduce damage taken during this time).

IMMOLATE

RANK	LEVEL	MANA	RANGE	CASTING TIME	COOLDOWN	COST TO TRAIN	EFFECT
1	1	25	30 yd	2 sec	-	10	Burns the enemy for 8 damage and then an additional 20 damage over 15 sec.
2	10	45	30 yd	2 sec	-	3	Burns the enemy for 19 damage and then an additional 40 damage over 15 sec.
3	20	90	30 yd	2 sec	-	20	Burns the enemy for 45 damage and then an additional 90 damage over 15 sec.
4	30	155	30 yd	2 sec	-	60	Burns the enemy for 90 damage and then an additional 165 damage over 15 sec.
5	40	216	30 yd	1.8 sec	-	2 60	Burns the enemy for 173 damage and then an additional 330 damage over 15 sec.
6	50	295	30 yd	1.5 sec	-	2 80	Burns the enemy for 255 damage and then an additional 485 damage over 15 sec.
7	60	370	30 yd	1.5 sec	-	2 90	Burns the enemy for 343 damage and then an additional 645 damage over 15 sec.

RAIN OF FIRE

RANK	LEVEL	MANA	RANGE	CASTING TIME	COOLDOWN	COST TO TRAIN	EFFECT
1	20	310	30 yd	IC	-	20	Calls down a fiery rain to burn enemies in the area of effect for 174 damage over 9 sec.
2	34	640	30 yd	IC	-	1 10	Calls down a fiery rain to burn enemies in the area of effect for 408 damage over 9 sec.
3	46	916	30 yd	IC	-	2 20	Calls down a fiery rain to burn enemies in the area of effect for 654 damage over 9 sec.
4	58	1255	30 yd	IC	-	4 30	Calls down a fiery rain to burn enemies in the area of effect for 954 damage over 9 sec.

SEARING PAIN

RANK	LEVEL	MANA	RANGE	CASTING TIME	COOLDOWN	COST TO TRAIN	EFFECT
1	18	50	30 yd	1.5 sec	-	22	Inflict searing pain on the enemy target, causing 41 to 51 Fire damage. Causes a high amount of threat.
2	26	75	30 yd	1.5 sec	-	40	Inflict searing pain on the enemy target, causing 59 to 71 Fire damage. Causes a high amount of threat.
3	34	100	30 yd	1.5 sec	-	90	Inflict searing pain on the enemy target, causing 86 to 104 Fire damage. Causes a high amount of threat.
4	42	127	30 yd	1.5 sec	-	1 50	Inflict searing pain on the enemy target, causing 127 to 152 Fire damage. Causes a high amount of threat.
5	50	152	30 yd	1.5 sec	-	2 80	Inflict searing pain on the enemy target, causing 164 to 196 Fire damage. Causes a high amount of threat.
6	58	185	30 yd	1.5 sec	-	2 70	Inflict searing pain on the enemy target, causing 220 to 259 Fire damage. Causes a high amount of threat.

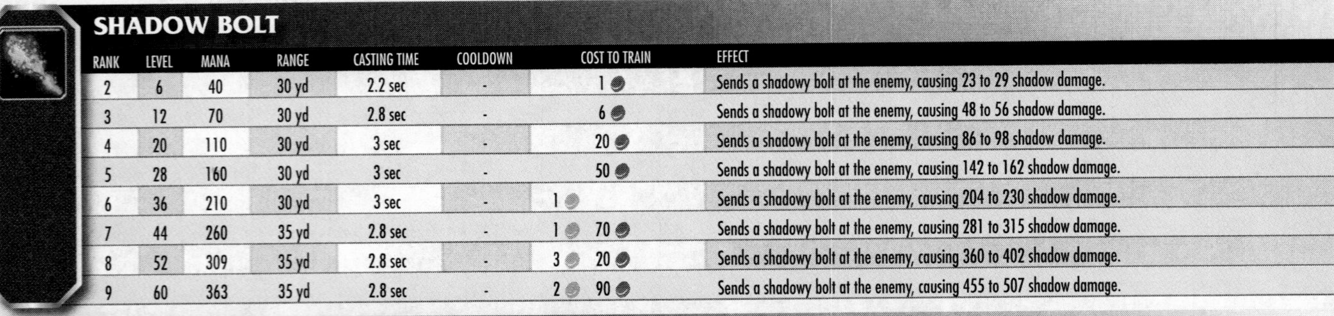

SHADOW BOLT

RANK	LEVEL	MANA	RANGE	CASTING TIME	COOLDOWN	COST TO TRAIN	EFFECT
2	6	40	30 yd	2.2 sec	-	1s	Sends a shadowy bolt at the enemy, causing 23 to 29 shadow damage.
3	12	70	30 yd	2.8 sec	-	6s	Sends a shadowy bolt at the enemy, causing 48 to 56 shadow damage.
4	20	110	30 yd	3 sec	-	20s	Sends a shadowy bolt at the enemy, causing 86 to 98 shadow damage.
5	28	160	30 yd	3 sec	-	50s	Sends a shadowy bolt at the enemy, causing 142 to 162 shadow damage.
6	36	210	30 yd	3 sec	-	1g	Sends a shadowy bolt at the enemy, causing 204 to 230 shadow damage.
7	44	260	35 yd	2.8 sec	-	1g 70s	Sends a shadowy bolt at the enemy, causing 281 to 315 shadow damage.
8	52	309	35 yd	2.8 sec	-	3g 20s	Sends a shadowy bolt at the enemy, causing 360 to 402 shadow damage.
9	60	363	35 yd	2.8 sec	-	2g 90s	Sends a shadowy bolt at the enemy, causing 455 to 507 shadow damage.

SOUL FIRE

RANK	LEVEL	MANA	RANGE	CASTING TIME	COOLDOWN	COST TO TRAIN	EFFECT
1	48	495	30 yd	6 sec	1min	2g 50s	Burn the enemy's soul, causing 671 to 843 Fire damage.
2	56	545	30 yd	6 sec	1min	3g 90s	Burn the enemy's soul, causing 764 to 956 Fire damage.

PET ABILITIES

Each of the Warlock's pets offers a different line of abilities. Take advantage of the variety and try to find the pet/ability combo that works best for you in each situation.

ABILITY	RANK	LEVEL	PET
Blood Pact	1	4	Imp
Firebolt	2	8	Imp
Blood Pact	2	14	Imp
Fire Shield	1	14	Imp
Sacrifice	N/A	16	Voidwalker
Consume Shadows	1	18	Voidwalker
Firebolt	3	18	Imp
Torment	2	20	Voidwalker
Soothing Kiss	1	22	Succubus
Fire Shield	2	24	Imp
Suffering	1	24	Voidwalker
Blood Pact	3	26	Imp
Consume Shadows	2	26	Voidwalker
Seduction	N/A	26	Succubus
Firebolt	4	28	Imp
Lash of Pain	2	28	Succubus
Torment	3	30	Voidwalker
Lesser Invisibility	N/A	32	Succubus
Consume Shadows	3	34	Voidwalker
Fire Shield	3	34	Imp
Soothing Kiss	2	34	Succubus
Lash of Pain	3	36	Succubus

ABILITY	RANK	LEVEL	PET
Suffering	2	36	Voidwalker
Blood Pact	4	38	Imp
Firebolt	5	38	Imp
Torment	4	40	Voidwalker
Consume Shadows	4	42	Voidwalker
Fire Shield	4	44	Imp
Lash of Pain	4	44	Succubus
Soothing Kiss	3	46	Succubus
Firebolt	6	48	Imp
Suffering	3	48	Voidwalker
Blood Pact	N/A	50	Imp
Consume Shadows	5	50	Voidwalker
Torment	5	50	Voidwalker
Lash of Pain	5	52	Succubus
Fire Shield	5	54	Imp
Consume Shadows	6	58	Voidwalker
Firebolt	1	58	Imp
Soothing Kiss	4	58	Succubus
Lash of Pain	6	60	Succubus
Suffering	4	60	Voidwalker
Torment	6	60	Voidwalker

IMP ABILITIES

Warlocks are able to do more damage at range through the Imp pet. This little creature won't stand up to direct punishment and acts much like a Mage, so don't bring him out when soloing; groups that want to blow down targets quickly and aren't worried about the Imp's volatile reputation will enjoy the Stamina buff and damage shield gained by having the little guy around.

BLOOD PACT

RANK	LEVEL	MANA	RANGE	CASTING TIME	COOLDOWN	COST TO TRAIN	EFFECT
1	4	-	20 yd	Instant	-	1s	Increases party members' Stamina by 2.
2	14	-	20 yd	Instant	-	9s	Increases party members' Stamina by 7.
3	26	-	20 yd	Instant	-	70s	Increases party members' Stamina by 16.
4	38	-	20 yd	Instant	-	1g 40s	Increases party members' Stamina by 27.
5	50	-	20 yd		-	2g 80s	Increases party members' Stamina by 38.

FIRE SHIELD

RANK	LEVEL	MANA	RANGE	CASTING TIME	COOLDOWN	COST TO TRAIN	EFFECT
1	14	60	30 yd	Instant	-	9s	Surrounds the target in a shield of fire. Every strike against the target causes 5 Fire damage to the attacker. The caster cannot cast Fire Shield on himself.
2	24	90	30 yd	Instant	-	50s	Surrounds the target in a shield of fire. Every strike against the target causes 7 Fire damage to the attacker. The caster cannot cast Fire Shield on himself.
3	34	115	30 yd	Instant	-	1g 10s	Surrounds the target in a shield of fire. Every strike against the target causes 9 Fire damage to the attacker. The caster cannot cast Fire Shield on himself.
4	44	140	30 yd	Instant	-	1g 70s	Surrounds the target in a shield of fire. Every strike against the target causes 11 Fire damage to the attacker. The caster cannot cast Fire Shield on himself.
5	54	165	30 yd	Instant	-	4g 40s	Surrounds the target in a shield of fire. Every strike against the target causes 13 Fire damage to the attacker. The caster cannot cast Fire Shield on himself.

FIREBOLT

RANK	LEVEL	MANA	RANGE	CASTING TIME	COOLDOWN	COST TO TRAIN	EFFECT
2	8	20	30 yd	2 sec	-	2s	Deals 12 to 14 damage to a target.
3	18	35	30 yd	2 sec	-	29s	Deals 22 to 26 damage to a target.
4	28	50	30 yd	2 sec	-	50s	Deals 33 to 37 damage to a target.
5	38	70	30 yd	2 sec	-	1g 40s	Deals 48 to 54 damage to a target.
6	48	95	30 yd	2 sec	-	4g 20s	Deals 67 to 75 damage to a target.
7	58	115	30 yd	2 sec	-	4g 30s	Deals 83 to 93 damage to a target.

SUCCUBUS ABILITIES

Acting like a Rogue, the Succubus is a high-DPS pet that gets into melee and smacks creatures around. In parties with a good Tank, the Succubus is very effective (getting behind targets and using Lash of Pain for decent shadow damage).

LASH OF PAIN

RANK	LEVEL	MANA	RANGE	CASTING TIME	COOLDOWN	COST TO TRAIN	EFFECT
2	28	80	7 yd	Instant	12 sec	70	Lashes the target, causing 44 Shadow damage. The Succubus must be behind the target.
3	36	105	7 yd	Instant	12 sec	1 50	Lashes the target, causing 60 Shadow damage. The Succubus must be behind the target.
4	44	125	7 yd	Instant	12 sec	1 70	Lashes the target, causing 73 Shadow damage. The Succubus must be behind the target.
5	52	145	7 yd	Instant	12 sec	3 20	Lashes the target, causing 87 Shadow damage. The Succubus must be behind the target.
6	60	160	8 yd	Instant	12 sec	3 90	Lashes the target, causing 99 Shadow damage. The Succubus must be behind the target.

LESSER INVISIBILITY

RANK	LEVEL	MANA	RANGE	CASTING TIME	COOLDOWN	COST TO TRAIN	EFFECT
N/A	32	100	-	Instant	-	1 10	Gives the Succubus Lesser Invisibility for up to 5 min.

SEDUCTION

RANK	LEVEL	MANA	RANGE	CASTING TIME	COOLDOWN	COST TO TRAIN	EFFECT
N/A	26	142	30 yd	Instant	30 sec	55	Seduces the target, preventing all actions for up to 15 sec. Any damage caused will remove the effect.

SOOTHING KISS

RANK	LEVEL	MANA	RANGE	CASTING TIME	COOLDOWN	COST TO TRAIN	EFFECT
1	22	30	7 yd	Instant	4 sec	30	Soothes the target, increasing the chance that it will attack something else.
2	34	50	10 yd	Instant	4 sec	1 10	Soothes the target, increasing the chance that it will attack something else.
3	46	75	10 yd	Instant	4 sec	2 20	Soothes the target, increasing the chance that it will attack something else.
4	58	100	10 yd	Instant	4 sec	4 30	Soothes the target, increasing the chance that it will attack something else.

VOIDWALKER ABILITIES

Your Voidwalker is a friend beyond doubt. This demon can Taunt and hold enemies away from you. Indeed, this is the soloers best bet for avoiding aggro and keeping pets alive during dangerous fights. It's even possible to Sacrifice the Voidwalker for temporary invulnerability (good for escapes when too many enemies join an encounter). Voidwalkers can heal themselves between fights, have impressive health, and are just plain tanky in disposition.

CONSUME SHADOWS

RANK	LEVEL	MANA	RANGE	CASTING TIME	COOLDOWN	COST TO TRAIN	EFFECT
1	18	85	7 yd	Instant	-	22	The Voidwalker consumes nearby shadows to bolster its form, recovering 325 health over 10 sec. Cannot be used while in combat.
2	26	150	7 yd	Instant	-	40	The Voidwalker consumes nearby shadows to bolster its form, recovering 575 health over 10 sec. Cannot be used while in combat.
3	34	215	7 yd	Instant	-	90	The Voidwalker consumes nearby shadows to bolster its form, recovering 840 health over 10 sec. Cannot be used while in combat.
4	42	285	7 yd	Instant	-	1 50	The Voidwalker consumes nearby shadows to bolster its form, recovering 1130 health over 10 sec. Cannot be used while in combat.
5	50	380	7 yd	Instant	-	1 80	The Voidwalker consumes nearby shadows to bolster its form, recovering 1505 health over 10 sec. Cannot be used while in combat.
6	58	481	7 yd	Instant	-	2 70	The Voidwalker consumes nearby shadows to bolster its form, recovering 1930 health over 10 sec. Cannot be used while in combat.

SACRIFICE

RANK	LEVEL	MANA	RANGE	CASTING TIME	COOLDOWN	COST TO TRAIN	EFFECT
N/A	16	-	50000 yd	Instant	-	15	Sacrifices the Voidwalker, making its owner invulnerable for 10 sec.

SUFFERING

RANK	LEVEL	MANA	RANGE	CASTING TIME	COOLDOWN	COST TO TRAIN	EFFECT
1	24	150	7 yd	Instant	2min	40	Taunts all nearby enemies, increasing the chance that they will attack the Voidwalker.
2	36	300	7 yd	Instant	2min	1	Taunts all nearby enemies, increasing the chance that they will attack the Voidwalker. More effective than Suffering (Rank 1).
3	48	450	7 yd	Instant	2min	2 50	Taunts all nearby enemies, increasing the chance that they will attack the Voidwalker. More effective than Suffering (Rank 2).
4	60	600	7 yd	Instant	2min	2 90	Taunts all nearby enemies, increasing the chance that they will attack the Voidwalker. More effective than Suffering (Rank 3).

TORMENT

RANK	LEVEL	MANA	RANGE	CASTING TIME	COOLDOWN	COST TO TRAIN	EFFECT
2	20	40	7 yd	Instant	5 sec	25	Taunts the creature, increasing the chance that it will attack the Voidwalker.
3	30	65	7 yd	Instant	5 sec	60	Taunts the creature, increasing the chance that it will attack the Voidwalker. More effective than Torment (Rank 2).
4	40	90	7 yd	Instant	5 sec	2 60	Taunts the creature, increasing the chance that it will attack the Voidwalker. More effective than Torment (Rank 3).
5	50	115	7 yd	Instant	5 sec	2 80	Taunts the creature, increasing the chance that it will attack the Voidwalker. More effective than Torment (Rank 4).
6	60	145	7 yd	Instant	5 sec	3 90	Taunts the creature, increasing the chance that it will attack the Voidwalker. More effective than Torment (Rank 5).

TALENTS

Warlock Talents are able to hone this class toward one of several ends. The Affliction line makes Warlocks even more effective with long-term satisfaction (better damage over time, higher efficiency with debuffs and DOTs, chances for instant casting from time-to-time, etc.).

Destruction goes toward the direct end of Warlock attacks, greatly improving the output of a Warlock's fire and bolt spells. Later in the line, there are Talents to improve the chance and power of critical spells.

AFFLICTION

TALENT NAME	RANKS	PREREQUISITES	EFFECTS
Suppression	5	None	Reduces the chance for enemies to resist your Affliction spells by 2% (Per Rank)
Improved Corruption	5	None	Reduces the casting time of your Corruption spell by 0.4 sec (Per Rank)
Improved Curse of Weakness	3	5 Points in Affliction	Increases the effect of your Curse of Weakness by 6%. - Progression: 6%/13%/20%
Improved Drain Soul	2	5 Points in Affliction	Gives you a 50% chance (Per Rank) to increase mana regen by 100% if your target dies while you are casting Drain Soul
Improved Life Tap	2	5 Points in Affliction	Increases the amount of Mana awarded by your Life Tap spell by 10% (Per Rank)
Improved Drain Life	5	5 Points in Affliction	Increases the Health drained by your Drain Life spell by 2% (Per Rank)
Improved Curse of Agony	3	10 Points in Affliction	Increases the damage done by Curse of Agony by 2% (Per Rank)
Fel Concentration	5	10 Points in Affliction	Gives you a 14% chance (Per Rank) to avoid interruption caused by damage while channeling the Drain Life, Drain Mana, or Drain Soul spell.
Amplify Curse	1	10 Points in Affliction	Instant Cast 5 min cooldown Increases the effect of your next Curse of Weakness, Curse of Agony, or Curse of Exhaustion by 50%.
Grim Reach	2	15 Points in Affliction	Increases the range of your Affliction spells by 10% (Per Rank)
Nightfall	2	15 Points in Affliction	Gives your Corruption and Drain Life spells a 2% chance to cause you to enter a Shadow Trance state after damaging the opponent. The Shadow Trance state reduces the casting time of your next Shadow Bolt spell by 100%. - Progression 2%/3%
Improved Drain Mana	2	15 Points in Affliction	Causes 15% of mana drained by this spell (Per Rank) to damage your target
Siphon Life	1	20 Points in Affliction	150 Mana 1.5 sec cast 30yd range Transfers 15 health from the target to the caster every 3 sec. Lasts 30sec.
Curse of Exhaustion	1	1 Point in Amplify Curse, 20 Points in Affliction	17 Mana Instant Cast 30 yd range Reduces the target's speed to 90% of normal for 15 sec. Only one Curse per Warlock can be active on any one target.
Improved Curse of Exhaustion	4	1 Point in Curse of Exhaustion, 20 Points in Affliction	Increases the speed reduction of your Curse of Exhaustion by 5% (Per Rank)
Shadow Mastery	5	1 Point in Siphon Life, 25 Points in Affliction	Increases the damage dealt by your Shadow spells by 2% (Per Rank)
Dark Pact	1	30 Points in Affliction	Instant Cast 20 yrd range Drains 250 of your pet's Mana returning 100% to you.

DEMONOLOGY

TALENT NAME	RANKS	PREREQUISITES	EFFECTS
Improved Healthstone	2	None	Increases the amount of health returned by a Healthstone by 10% (Per Rank)
Improved Imp	3	None	Increases the effect of an Imp's Firebolt, Fire Shield, and Bloodpact by 10% (Per Rank)
Demonic Embrace	5	None	Increases your total Stamina by 3% (Per Rank) at a loss of 1% of your Stamina (Also Per Rank)
Improved Health Funnel	2	5 Points in Demonology	Increases the amount of health returned by Health Funnel by 10% (Per Rank)
Improved Voidwalker	3	5 Points in Demonology	Increases the effects of your Voidwalker's Torment, Consume Shadows, and Suffering by 8% - Progression: 8%/16%/25%
Fel Intellect	5	5 Points in Demonology	Increases the maximum mana of your pets by 3% (Per Rank)
Improved Succubus	3	10 Points in Demonology	Increases the effect of your Succubus' Lash of Pain, Soothing Kiss, and Lesser Invisibility by 8% - Progression: 8%/16%/25%
Fel Domination	1	10 Points in Demonology	Adds an Instant ability that reduces pet summoning time by 5.5 seconds, and lowers mana cost by 50%
Fel Stamina	5	5 Points in Fel Intellect, 10 Points in Demonology	Increases the maximum health of your pets by 2% (Per Rank)
Master Summoner	2	1 Point in Fel Domination, 15 Points in Demonology	Reduces the summoning time of your pets by 2 seconds (Per Rank)
Master Conjuror	2	15 Points in Demonology	Reduces the mana cost and casting time of all stone-creation spells by 20% (Per Rank)
Improved Enslave Demon	5	20 Points in Demonology	Reduces the attack speed/casting speed penalty of your controlled demons by 2% (Per Rank)
Demonic Sacrifice	1	20 Points in Demonology	Sacrifices your pet for a 30 minute buff - Progression: Imp (Increases Fire Damage by 15%), Voidwalker (Increases health by 15%), Succubus (Increases Shadow Damage by 15%), Felhunter (Increases mana by 20%)
Improved Firestone	2	20 Points in Demonology	Increases the damage done by your Firestones by 15% (Per Rank)
Unholy Power	5	5 Points in Fel Stamina, 25 Points in Demonology	Increases melee damage done by your pets by 3% (Per Rank)
Soul Link	1	1 Point in Demonic Sacrifice, 30 Points in Demonology	Adds an Instant ability that splits damage taken between you and your pet for 30 seconds
Improved Spellstone	2	30 Points in Demonology	Increases the amount of damage absorbed by your Spellstones by 15% (Per Rank)

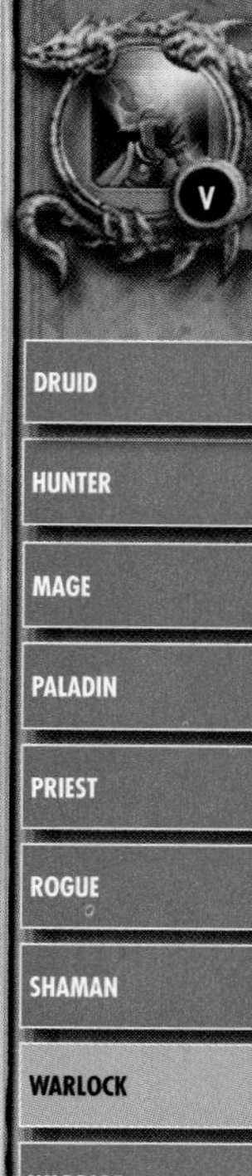

DESTRUCTION

TALENT NAME	RANKS	PREREQUISITES	EFFECTS
Improved Shadow Bolt	5	None	Your Shadow Bolt critical strikes increase the next 4 sources of Shadow damage dealt to the target by 4% (Per Rank)
Cataclysm	5	None	Reduces the Mana cost of your Destruction spells by 1% (Per Rank)
Bane	5	5 Points in Destruction	Reduces the casting time of your Shadow Bolt and Immolate spells by 0.1 sec (Per Rank)
Aftermath	5	5 Points in Destruction	Gives your Destruction spells a 2% chance (Per Rank) to daze the target for 5 sec.
Improved Firebolt	2	10 Points in Destruction	Reduces the casting time of your Imp's Firebolt spell by 0.5 sec (Per Rank)
Improved Lash of Pain	2	10 Points in Destruction	Reduces the cooldown of your Succubus' Lash of Pain spell by 3 sec (Per Rank)
Devastation	5	10 Points in Destruction	Increases the critical strike chance of your Destruction spells by 1% (Per Rank)
Shadowburn	1	10 Points in Destruction	130 mana, Instant cast 15 sec cooldown 20yd range Reagents: Soul Shard- Instantly blasts the target with 125 to 150 Shadow damage. This spell generates less threat than would normally be caused. Requires 1 Soul Shard. Awards 1 Soul Shard if the target dies from Shadowburn.
Intensity	2	15 Points in Destruction	Gives you a 35% chance (Per Rank) to resist interruption caused by damage while channeling the Rain of Fire or Hellfire spell.
Destructive Reach	2	15 Points in Destruction	Increases the range of your Destruction spells by 10% (Per Rank)
Improved Searing Pain	5	15 Points in Destruction	Increases the critical strike chance of your Searing Pain spell by 2% (Per Rank)
Pyroclasm	2	2 Points in Intensity, 20 Points in Destruction	Gives your Rain of Fire and Hellfire spells a 12% chance to stun the target for 3 sec. - Progression: 12%/25%
Improved Immolate	5	20 Points in Destruction	Increases the initial damage of your immolate spell by 5% (Per Rank)
Holocaust	1	5 Points in Devastation, 20 Points in Destruction	Increases the damage done by your critical strikes by 100%.
Inferno	5	25 Points in Destruction	Increases the damage done by your Fire spells by 2% (Per Rank)
Conflagrate	1	5 Points in Improved Immolate, 30 Points in Destruction	220 Mana 1.5 sec cast 10 sec cooldown 20yd range Ignites a target that is already afflicted by Immolate, dealing 214 to 256 damage and consuming the Immolate spell.

STRATEGIES

Okay, it's time to head out into the field and bring down enemies. There are great ways to do this as a Warlock, especially if you're patient. After Level 10, when you have the choice of Imp or Voidwalker as pets, the game gets quite interesting. Soloing is quite solid when you have the Voidwalker, so a great deal of strategy revolves around using the dark guy when you're alone.

SOME GENERAL TIPS

Your Curses make a huge difference in the outcome of a battle, whether you are alone or in a group. Curse of Tongues is the best way to say hello to casters, Curse of Weakness helps in groups to reduce incoming damage by a fraction, Curse of the Elements is vicious in groups with multiple casters or for times when you plan on unleashing many fire spells.

Fire resistance is very important to Warlocks who enjoy using Hellfire. In general, Warlocks just like to hurt themselves, so it's good to find ways to reduce the effect of such damage. Using fire resistance to counter Hellfire's negative aspects is such a case.

Always keep a heavy supply of Soul Shards around. These items are needed for so much of a Warlock's utility that it's very dangerous to run out of them. Summoning allies, grabbing more important pets, and even some of the special class spells later down the road cost shards. Don't be shy about having an entire bag dedicated to keeping extra shards, and replace these as soon as possible when the supply starts to drop.

Remember that only enemies that are worth experience to your Warlock can drop Soul Shards. Killing rabbits and cows is not going to get you what you need.

Give various stones to your allies in a group as soon as possible, since they can be useful at any point. Be sure to give Life/Soul Stones to group Healers first, since they are the ones that are most important to protect from a party wipeout.

STANDING ALONE

As stated, the Voidwalker is critical to powerful soloing. This tank is able to keep enemies attention fairly well. For you to do your part, stick with DOTs and watch the creatures fall into death without realizing that you are the one to blame. Slap Corruption, Curse of Agony, and an Immolate on targets once the Voidwalker has them in melee and switch to wand action as the DOTs do their dirty work.

For adds that your Voidwalker can handle, slap DOTs on them as well (to get them started while the first enemy is failing), just at a slower pace. However, a dangerous add can be Feared to give yourself time to bring down the first target. If it looks like Fear is going to backfire (by drawing more monsters), slam the initial target with a spam burst of Searing Pain. Kill that creature and get out of the area before a train of enemies comes back to haunt you. If necessary, Sacrifice your Voidwalker for extra time when the enemies are too plentiful or fast to avoid.

Against targets that attack quickly but do light damage to make life easier on your Voidwalker. Throwing a Curse of Weakness on these enemies instead of an extra DOT stops the foe from doing nearly as much to your Voidwalker.

Another type of solo work altogether (and not for the faint of heart or light of skill) is to ping-pong enemies. If you are confident of your abilities, bring out the Imp or Succubus and trade off aggro between yourself and the demon. Use higher-damage spells (bolts and fire magic), then kite the enemy while your ally smacks on its back. Once aggro exchanges, turn and repeat the onslaught.

IN A GROUP

Bring out the beloved Succubus or Imp in a group and watch the DPS of your extended character improve. Though the Imp is a dangerous creature if it stays in active mode, you can keep from pulling as many accidental enemies by setting the beast to passive mode and controlling him carefully. With the Imp's bolts and damage shield, he adds quite a percentage to a group's overall performance.

The Succubus is only at her best when a skilled tank is at the lead of a group. Work with the tank so that they know to keep the Succubus at the enemy's back at all times (for the best damage and good, old Lash of Pain).

Searing Pain draws way too much aggro for early use in a fight, but this spell is a good finisher for enemies who are about to drop.

Against enemies who love to run away and get you into wicked amounts of trouble, Curse of Recklessness can help. Put this on the target to reduce its armor and prevent flight; the modest attack bonus this provides your enemy is offset by the armor decrease. This isn't normally needed against light targets, but elites in tightly-packed areas are dangerous to have running around (sometimes even with Hamstring or other abilities slowing their movement).

WARRIOR

Warriors are the protectors in the *World of Warcraft*. These brave souls fight for both the Horde and Alliance, and neither side would survive for long without their perseverance. Focusing primarily on melee combat, Warriors use their heavy armor and damage mitigation to endure the attention of monsters; their role in a group is to gather as much of that aggression as possible. By doing this, weaker classes are left free to use their healing, higher DPS, and other such abilities without fear of reprisal and death. Both in the field and in dungeons, Warriors always have a place in a skilled group.

A WARRIOR'S STORY

The smell was worse than anything you could imagine, my friends. We approached the ancient homeland of the spiteful Gnomes, and a stench filled the air we breathed. It was more than the smoke that surrounded us; it was the very Gnomes that burst from the earth around our party. They were fouled with disease and hatred, a fate worse than many would have wished even for the wasteful beasts.

I heard Illiathu, our Shaman, cry out. Three of the demonic things had charged toward her, and I knew even her strength would fail before long against such an onslaught. Crying with all the strength the Earthmother grants me, I ran over and leapt onto the first. I stood still for a moment, paralyzed with fear even as my axe struck home. The others would have continued their attacks on Illiathu, intent on her falling Totems, but I was on them as well.

Swinging left and right, mocking their horrid faces and torturous heritage, I got their attention every way I knew how. They turned to me and struck helplessly against the finest steel our crafters can forge. The earth's bounty protected me, and in so doing I saved Illiathu. She used her time well, and even our blasted Mage (Undead scoundrel that he is) came forward to show great power.

I slew none of the plagued Gnomes that time, though I wounded them all during the fray. Yet, as we walked deeper into the realm of Gnomeregan, the others thanked me. I protected them as I protect Mulgore, tradition, and the honor of the Horde.

INTRODUCTION TO PLAYING A WARRIOR

Warriors are a common and beloved class, but there is something to put on the table from the first moment you consider playing this fine class; we are not the highest damage dealers in the game. Even specced for high damage and using Battle Stance to its fullest, we are hard pressed to rival a Mage or Rogue for bringing foes down. That isn't to say we are weak in direct combat, but it is our ability to sustain damage and maintain the attack that puts us at the head of a column.

Warriors gain enough hit points to take a few more hits than the other classes. Combine this with our heavy armor (chain armor early on, plate after gaining level 40) and many of the strongest enemies in the game won't have an easy time knocking us out of a fight. That is why so many groups want to have a Warrior in front; having a Warrior in a party makes every healer's mana efficiency improve. A blow that would do 100 hit points to a Priest may strike for a quarter of that to a well-equipped Warrior. In the long run, that saves mana and lives.

Paladins are tough as nails too, you say? It's true, they sure are. In fact, Paladins can survive a few things that would fell even a seasoned Warrior. What makes us better for a good fight? It's the ability to grab and hold aggro from monsters.

Not only do Warriors have a high survivability rate in combat, we are much better and ensuring the safety of others through Taunt, Mocking Blow, and other such powers. Paladins are pretty darn good at grabbing a single target, but they fail to approach the combat versatility of a Warrior. We can grab and hold multiple targets with far more dependability. Add special abilities that slow enemies down, stop their healing, and so forth, and Warriors sound even better!

If being a group leader, saving lives, and ripping monsters off of your friends sounds like a great deal, keep reading and go forward with pride. On the other hand, if getting into a melee class for raw, close-up damage is your goal, read through the Rogue class. Rogues are the kings of melee damage, despite a Warrior's large muscles and shining weaponry. Or, if survival is more important to you than saving allies, Paladins are similar in style, but have a tad more staying power at the expense of their group-saving tricks.

RACES AND STARTING ATTRIBUTES

RACE	STRENGTH	STAMINA	AGILITY	INTELLECT	SPIRIT
Dwarf	24	23	19	20	23
Gnome	22	21	22	22	22
Human	23	22	21	21	22
Night Elf	22	21	22	23	21
Orc	24	22	20	20	23
Tauren	25	23	19	20	22
Troll	23	22	20	20	24
Undead	22	23	19	21	24

ATTRIBUTES APPLIED

Strength	Increases Damage and Chance to Block
Stamina	Higher Hit Points
Agility	Raises Chance to Get a Critical Hit and Dodge
Intellect	Faster Rate for Gaining Weapon Skills
Spirit	Improves Hit Point Recovery

ITEMS AND EQUIPMENT

Warriors are more dependent on equipment than just about any other class. We need our weapons to be as high as possible when it comes to DPS (for the damage and for holding onto aggro). We also need armor that is extremely up-to-date, and peripheral items that raise Stamina and Strength as much as possible. Add bandages, food, and even some explosives to the mix, and Warriors are often laden with goodies.

Okay, so what are your priorities? As a Warrior, whether you solo or join a group, a massive investment in armor is paramount. Unless you're going with a two-handed weapon, a shield is one of your best items. Keep searching for quests with shield rewards and look for Instances where high-quality shields drop. Be sure to combine a Shield Spike to your shield for a bit of extra damage (it makes a difference).

Keep your Armor Rating as high as possible while being somewhat picky about which pieces you grab. When available, armor pieces with similar stats should be distinguished by the attributes they raise. A Warrior who goes for survivability wants to have as much Stamina as possible on their equipment. Enchant your items and always be on the lookout to replace gear that isn't quite right for your stats with better pieces.

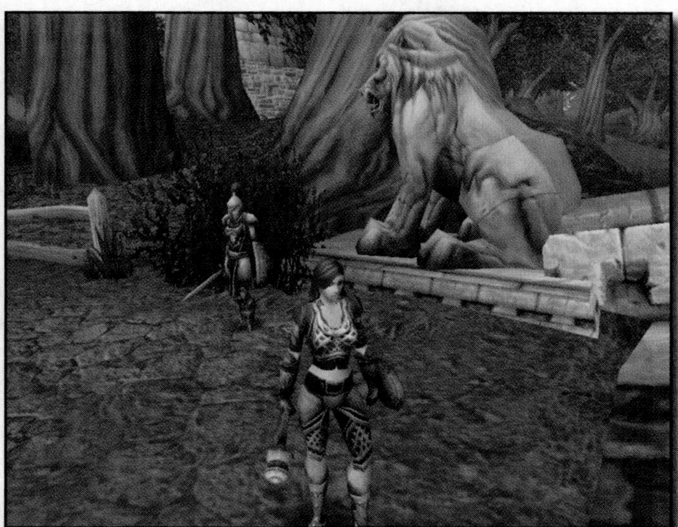

ATTRIBUTE LOVE

When deciding what attributes are most important to you (in terms of equipment bonuses), consider that many DPS Warriors need critical hits to do their best damage. This means Agility can actually surpass Strength in terms of usefulness. Having more critical hits can lead to incredible amounts of Rage.

Choosing a weapon is an important matter, being that Warriors are a melee class. Look into the Talent lines ahead of time and decide whether you're going to specialize in a specific weapon variety. This only happens if you are free to spend 25 points in the Arms Line, so there is a decent chance you won't need to worry about which weapon to use if you're defensively oriented.

Whatever the case, be aware that swords and axes do a tad more damage than maces. One-handed weapons are critical for a defensive Warrior (combined with a shield), while two-handed weapons deal more damage over time and are deadly when paired with the Arms Line. If you want to make a DPS (high damage) Warrior, look into dual wielding or a very slow two-handed weapon. In the later levels, two-handed weapons are devastating in the hands of a good Warrior.

CHOOSING YOUR PROFESSION

Creating your own arms and armor is rarely a bad thing. If that sounds fair to you, choose Blacksmithing and Mining as your professions. These complement each other perfectly, and you only need to grab items outside of these lines on rare occasions (for odd potions, leather pieces, or some Alchemy metalwork now and then). In terms of self-sufficiency, these are truly wise choices.

For a PvP Warrior, Engineering is a solid choice (also paired with Mining). Having bombs and some of the gadgets that Engineering provides is effective for turning the tide of nasty battles, especially if you're a very active fighter. Charge ahead of your group, use bombs to disrupt the incoming enemy lines, and continue forward for the softer targets. A short stun and some extra damage is more than enough to push initiative in your group's favor, and a frontline character has a greater chance to make these things happen.

Even more useful to a Warrior in action, however, are the secondary trades. Cooking and First Aid are very powerful for reducing downtime and limiting your need to buy expensive food from local vendors. Keep both of these trades at a fair level and use them heavily to improve your kill rate. Even in groups this does very good things (reducing the burden on your healers can greatly shorten quest and Instance times).

CLASS ABILITIES

Warriors have many abilities that are meant to be used in melee. These are not used through mana or energy, but instead with a system that is unique to this class. Rage is on a scale from 0 to 100, and unlike other classes, it stays at zero most of the time. When a Warrior strikes enemies or is hit by them, the Rage meter goes up. Using points from this bar engages various abilities to defend the Warrior, do extra damage, help the group, or otherwise aid in combat.

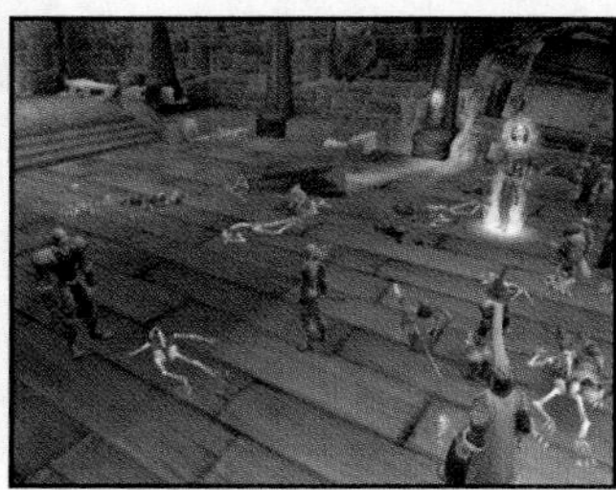

Below are the tables for these abilities, broken down by their limitations. Combat Abilities can be used at any time, regardless of a Warrior's current stance. The other three sections list the abilities that are tied to a specific stance.

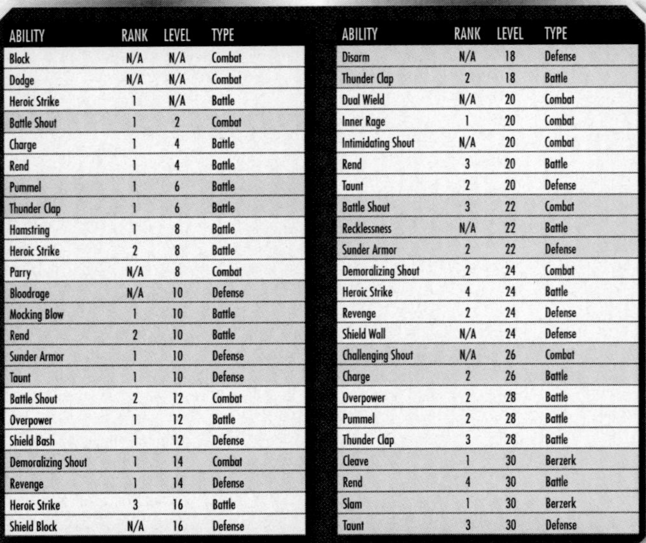

ABILITY	RANK	LEVEL	TYPE
Block	N/A	N/A	Combat
Dodge	N/A	N/A	Combat
Heroic Strike	1	N/A	Battle
Battle Shout	1	2	Combat
Charge	1	4	Battle
Rend	1	4	Battle
Pummel	1	6	Battle
Thunder Clap	1	6	Battle
Hamstring	1	8	Battle
Heroic Strike	2	8	Battle
Parry	N/A	8	Combat
Bloodrage	N/A	10	Defense
Mocking Blow	1	10	Battle
Rend	2	10	Battle
Sunder Armor	1	10	Defense
Taunt	1	10	Defense
Battle Shout	2	12	Combat
Overpower	1	12	Battle
Shield Bash	1	12	Defense
Demoralizing Shout	1	14	Combat
Revenge	1	14	Defense
Heroic Strike	3	16	Battle
Shield Block	N/A	16	Defense

ABILITY	RANK	LEVEL	TYPE
Disarm	N/A	18	Defense
Thunder Clap	2	18	Battle
Dual Wield	N/A	20	Combat
Inner Rage	1	20	Combat
Intimidating Shout	N/A	20	Combat
Rend	3	20	Battle
Taunt	2	20	Defense
Battle Shout	3	22	Combat
Recklessness	N/A	22	Battle
Sunder Armor	2	22	Defense
Demoralizing Shout	2	24	Combat
Heroic Strike	4	24	Battle
Revenge	2	24	Defense
Shield Wall	N/A	24	Defense
Challenging Shout	N/A	26	Combat
Charge	2	26	Battle
Overpower	2	28	Battle
Pummel	2	28	Battle
Thunder Clap	3	28	Battle
Cleave	1	30	Berzerk
Rend	4	30	Battle
Slam	1	30	Berzerk
Taunt	3	30	Defense

ABILITY	RANK	LEVEL	TYPE
Battle Shout	4	32	Combat
Hamstring	2	32	Battle
Heroic Strike	5	32	Battle
Shield Bash	2	32	Defense
Demoralizing Shout	3	34	Combat
Revenge	3	34	Defense
Sunder Armor	3	34	Defense
Mocking Blow	2	36	Battle
Slam	2	38	Berzerk
Thunder Clap	4	38	Battle
Cleave	2	40	Berzerk
Heroic Strike	6	40	Battle
Inner Rage	2	40	Combat
Plate Mail	N/A	40	Combat
Polearms	N/A	40	Combat
Rend	5	40	Battle
Taunt	4	40	Defense
Battle Shout	5	42	Combat
Demoralizing Shout	4	44	Combat
Overpower	3	44	Battle
Revenge	4	44	Defense
Charge	3	46	Battle
Slam	3	46	Berzerk

ABILITY	RANK	LEVEL	TYPE
Sunder Armor	4	46	Defense
Heroic Strike	7	48	Battle
Thunder Clap	5	48	Battle
Cleave	3	50	Berzerk
Pummel	3	50	Battle
Rend	6	50	Battle
Taunt	5	50	Defense
Battle Shout	6	52	Combat
Shield Bash	3	52	Defense
Demoralizing Shout	5	54	Combat
Hamstring	3	54	Battle
Revenge	5	54	Defense
Slam	4	54	Berzerk
Heroic Strike	8	56	Battle
Mocking Blow	3	58	Battle
Sunder Armor	5	58	Defense
Thunder Clap	6	58	Battle
Cleave	4	60	Berzerk
Inner Rage	3	60	Combat
Overpower	4	60	Battle
Rend	7	60	Battle
Taunt	6	60	Defense

BATTLE STANCE

Battle Stance is the first stance that your Warrior uses. Starting from first level, this is your tried-and-true selection of abilities. Though there are no modifiers to your Attack or Defense from being in Battle Stance, this is still considered to be a very aggressive style of play. Warriors engage sooner (through Charge), gain more Rage by sustaining their damage, and deal quite a bit more harm to enemies in their path.

CHARGE

RANK	LEVEL	RAGE	COST TO TRAIN	EFFECT
1	4	9	50	Charge an enemy, generate 9 Rage, and stun it for 1 sec. Cannot be used in combat.
2	26	12	90	Charge an enemy, generate 12 Rage, and stun it for 1 sec. Cannot be used in combat.
3	46	15	3 70	Charge an enemy, generate 15 Rage, and stun it for 1 sec. Cannot be used in combat.

HAMSTRING

RANK	LEVEL	RAGE	COST TO TRAIN	EFFECT
1	8	-10	2	Maims the enemy, causing 5 damage and slowing the enemy's movement to 40% of normal speed for 15 sec.
2	32	-10	1 10	Maims the enemy, causing 18 damage and slowing the enemy's movement to 40% of normal speed for 15 sec.
3	54	-10	4 40	Maims the enemy, causing 45 damage and slowing the enemy's movement to 40% of normal speed for 15 sec.

HEROIC STRIKE

RANK	LEVEL	RAGE	COST TO TRAIN	EFFECT
1	N/A	-15	No Cost	A strong attack that increases melee damage by 10.
2	8	-15	2	A strong attack that increases melee damage by 18.
3	16	-15	18	A strong attack that increases melee damage by 27.
4	24	-15	53	A strong attack that increases melee damage by 37.
5	32	-15	1 10	A strong attack that increases melee damage by 49.
6	40	-15	1 30	A strong attack that increases melee damage by 71.
7	48	-15	4 20	A strong attack that increases melee damage by 101.
8	56	-15	9 60	A strong attack that increases melee damage by 128.

MOCKING BLOW

RANK	LEVEL	RAGE	COST TO TRAIN	EFFECT
1	10	-10	3	A mocking attack that causes 7 damage and forces the target to focus attacks on you for 6 sec.
2	36	-10	2	A mocking attack that causes 21 damage and forces the target to focus attacks on you for 6 sec.
3	58	-10	7 10	A mocking attack that causes 60 damage and forces the target to focus attacks on you for 6 sec.

OVERPOWER

RANK	LEVEL	RAGE	COST TO TRAIN	EFFECT
1	12	-5	8	Instantly overpower the enemy, causing weapon damage plus 5. Only useable after the target dodges. The Overpower cannot be blocked, dodged or parried.
2	28	-5	1 10	Instantly overpower the enemy, causing weapon damage plus 15. Only useable after the target dodges. The Overpower cannot be blocked, dodged or parried.
3	44	-5	3 30	Instantly overpower the enemy, causing weapon damage plus 25. Only useable after the target dodges. The Overpower cannot be blocked, dodged or parried.
4	60	-5	5 90	Instantly overpower the enemy, causing weapon damage plus 35. Only useable after the target dodges. The Overpower cannot be blocked, dodged or parried.

PUMMEL

RANK	LEVEL	RAGE	COST TO TRAIN	EFFECT
1	6	-10	1	Pummel the target for 4 damage and interrupt the spell being cast for 4 sec.
2	28	-10	1 10	Pummel the target for 15 damage and interrupt the spell being cast for 4 sec.
3	50	-10	3 50	Pummel the target for 42 damage and interrupt the spell being cast for 4 sec.

RECKLESSNESS

RANK	LEVEL	RAGE	COST TO TRAIN	EFFECT
N/A	22	0	56	The warrior causes critical damage with every attack and is immune to fear effects for the next 15 sec, but armor is decreased.

REND

RANK	LEVEL	RAGE	COST TO TRAIN	EFFECT
1	4	-10	50c	Wounds the target causing them to bleed for 15 damage over 9 sec.
2	10	-10	3c	Wounds the target causing them to bleed for 28 damage over 12 sec.
3	20	-10	29c	Wounds the target causing them to bleed for 45 damage over 15 sec.
4	30	-10	1s 30c	Wounds the target causing them to bleed for 66 damage over 18 sec.
5	40	-10	1s 30c	Wounds the target causing them to bleed for 91 damage over 21 sec.
6	50	-10	3s 50c	Wounds the target causing them to bleed for 119 damage over 21 sec.
7	60	-10	5s 90c	Wounds the target causing them to bleed for 196 damage over 21 sec.

THUNDER CLAP

RANK	LEVEL	RAGE	COST TO TRAIN	EFFECT
1	6	-20	1c	Blasts nearby enemies with thunder slowing their attack speed by 10% for 10 sec and doing 7 Nature damage to them. Affects up to 4 targets.
2	18	-20	29c	Blasts nearby enemies with thunder slowing their attack speed by 10% for 10 sec and doing 13 Nature damage to them. Affects up to 4 targets.
3	28	-20	1s 10c	Blasts nearby enemies with thunder slowing their attack speed by 10% for 10 sec and doing 23 Nature damage to them. Affects up to 4 targets.
4	38	-20	2s 30c	Blasts nearby enemies with thunder slowing their attack speed by 10% for 10 sec and doing 33 Nature damage to them. Affects up to 4 targets.
5	48	-20	4s 20c	Blasts nearby enemies with thunder slowing their attack speed by 10% for 10 sec and doing 47 Nature damage to them. Affects up to 4 targets.
6	58	-20	7s 10c	Blasts nearby enemies with thunder slowing their attack speed by 10% for 10 sec and doing 56 Nature damage to them. Affects up to 4 targets.

BERSERK STANCE

Berserk Stance is extremely aggressive. Characters in this stance receive more damage from enemy attacks (20% more damage taken) and deal more damage through increased attack speed (a 10% improvement). Warriors in Berserk Stance have options to attack more often (through Slam) and to hit multiple opponents without delay (Cleave). These, by themselves, create a stance where damage is done with fair speed.

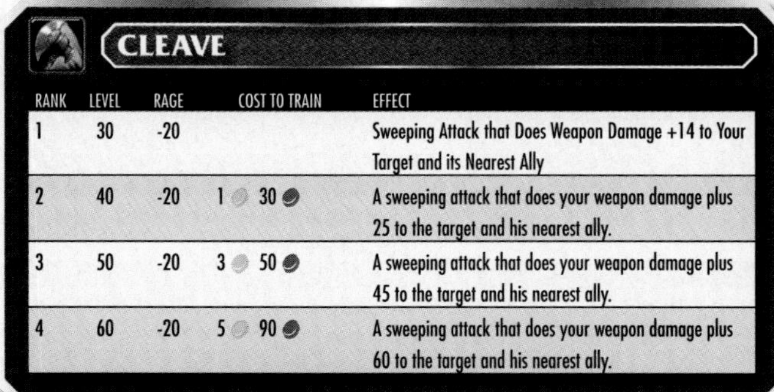

CLEAVE

RANK	LEVEL	RAGE	COST TO TRAIN	EFFECT
1	30	-20		Sweeping Attack that Does Weapon Damage +14 to Your Target and its Nearest Ally
2	40	-20	1s 30c	A sweeping attack that does your weapon damage plus 25 to the target and his nearest ally.
3	50	-20	3s 50c	A sweeping attack that does your weapon damage plus 45 to the target and his nearest ally.
4	60	-20	5s 90c	A sweeping attack that does your weapon damage plus 60 to the target and his nearest ally.

SLAM

RANK	LEVEL	RAGE	COST TO TRAIN	EFFECT
1	30	-15	1s 30c	Slams the opponent, causing weapon damage plus 37.
2	38	-15	2s 30c	Slams the opponent, causing weapon damage plus 54.
3	46	-15	3s 70c	Slams the opponent, causing weapon damage plus 85.
4	54	-15	4s 40c	Slams the opponent, causing weapon damage plus 112.

COMBAT ABILITIES

General Combat Abilities are used by Warriors in all three stances. These shouts and special moves are able to complement almost all forms of attack and defense, so they are especially important to master early on in your career.

BATTLE SHOUT

RANK	LEVEL	RAGE	COST TO TRAIN	EFFECT
1	2	-20	10c	The warrior shouts, increasing the party's attack power by 15. Lasts 2 min.
2	12	-20	8c	The warrior shouts, increasing the party's attack power by 35. Lasts 2 min.
3	22	-20	56c	The warrior shouts, increasing the party's attack power by 55. Lasts 2 min.
4	32	-20	1s 10c	The warrior shouts, increasing the party's attack power by 85. Lasts 2 min.
5	42	-20	4s 40c	The warrior shouts, increasing the party's attack power by 130. Lasts 2 min.
6	52	-20	5s 30c	The warrior shouts, increasing the party's attack power by 185. Lasts 2 min.

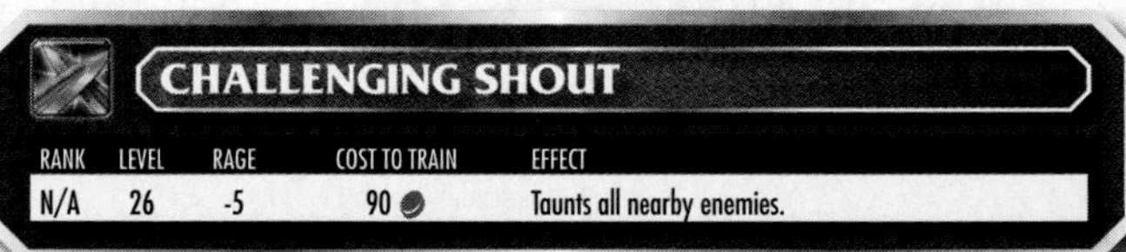

CHALLENGING SHOUT

RANK	LEVEL	RAGE	COST TO TRAIN	EFFECT
N/A	26	-5	90c	Taunts all nearby enemies.

DEMORALIZING SHOUT

RANK	LEVEL	RAGE	COST TO TRAIN	EFFECT
1	14	-10	12c	Reduces nearby enemies' attack power by 35 for 30 sec.
2	24	-10	53c	Reduces nearby enemies' attack power by 55 for 30 sec.
3	34	-10	1s 30c	Reduces nearby enemies' attack power by 70 for 30 sec.
4	44	-10	3s 30c	Reduces nearby enemies' attack power by 105 for 30 sec.
5	54	-10	4s 40c	Reduces nearby enemies' attack power by 175 for 30 sec.

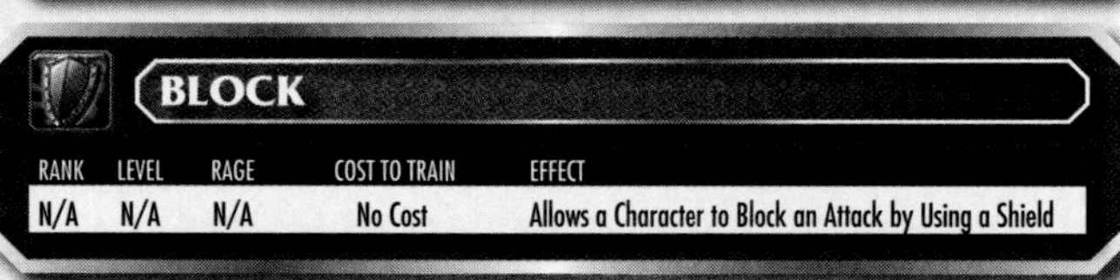

BLOCK

RANK	LEVEL	RAGE	COST TO TRAIN	EFFECT
N/A	N/A	N/A	No Cost	Allows a Character to Block an Attack by Using a Shield

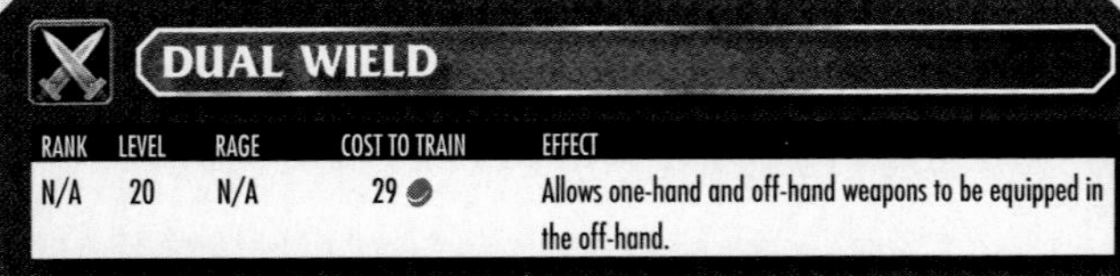

DUAL WIELD

RANK	LEVEL	RAGE	COST TO TRAIN	EFFECT
N/A	20	N/A	29 ●	Allows one-hand and off-hand weapons to be equipped in the off-hand.

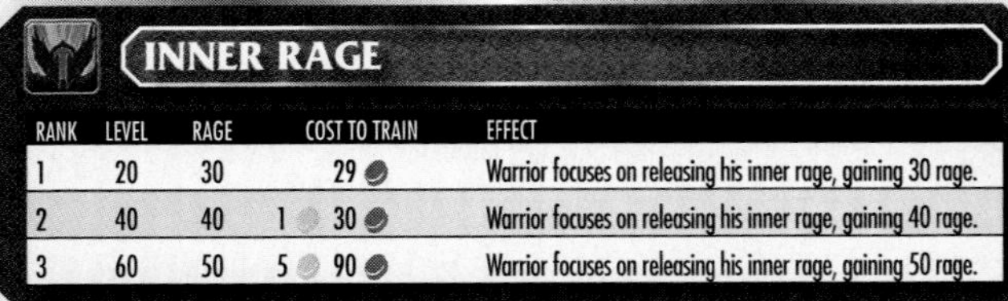

INNER RAGE

RANK	LEVEL	RAGE	COST TO TRAIN	EFFECT
1	20	30	29 ●	Warrior focuses on releasing his inner rage, gaining 30 rage.
2	40	40	1 ● 30 ●	Warrior focuses on releasing his inner rage, gaining 40 rage.
3	60	50	5 ● 90 ●	Warrior focuses on releasing his inner rage, gaining 50 rage.

INTIMIDATING SHOUT

RANK	LEVEL	RAGE	COST TO TRAIN	EFFECT
N/A	20	-25	29 ●	The warrior shouts, causing the targeted enemy to cower in terror. In addition, all other nearby enemies will flee in fear. Lasts 8 sec.

DEFENSIVE STANCE

Defensive Stance offers abilities that reduce damage to you and your party. When in this stance you increase by ten points in your Defense (effectively acting two levels higher in that stat), but your damage drops considerably because of losing many of the powerful Battle Stance and Berserk Stance abilities. Defensive Stance is almost unusable without having a shield, and many abilities directly require one.

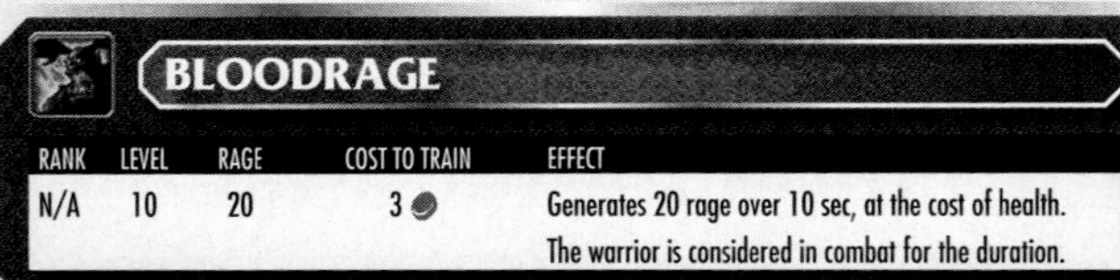

BLOODRAGE

RANK	LEVEL	RAGE	COST TO TRAIN	EFFECT
N/A	10	20	3 ●	Generates 20 rage over 10 sec, at the cost of health. The warrior is considered in combat for the duration.

DISARM

RANK	LEVEL	RAGE	COST TO TRAIN	EFFECT
N/A	18	-20	29 ●	Disarm the enemy's weapon for 10 sec.

REVENGE

RANK	LEVEL	RAGE	COST TO TRAIN	EFFECT
1	14	-5	12 ●	Instantly counterattack an enemy for 12 to 14 damage. Revenge must follow a block, dodge or parry.
2	24	-5	53 ●	Instantly counterattack an enemy for 18 to 22 damage. Revenge must follow a block, dodge or parry.
3	34	-5	1 ● 30 ●	Instantly counterattack an enemy for 25 to 31 damage. Revenge must follow a block, dodge or parry.
4	44	-5	3 ● 30 ●	Instantly counterattack an enemy for 43 to 53 damage. Revenge must follow a block, dodge or parry.
5	54	-5	4 ● 40 ●	Instantly counterattack an enemy for 64 to 78 damage. Revenge must follow a block, dodge or parry.

SHIELD BASH

RANK	LEVEL	RAGE	COST TO TRAIN	EFFECT
1	12	-10	8 ●	Bashes the target with your shield for 6 damage and interrupting the spell being cast for 8 sec.
2	32	-10	1 ● 10 ●	Bashes the target with your shield for 18 damage and interrupting the spell being cast for 6 sec.
3	52	-10	5 ● 30 ●	Bashes the target with your shield for 45 damage and interrupting the spell being cast for 6 sec.

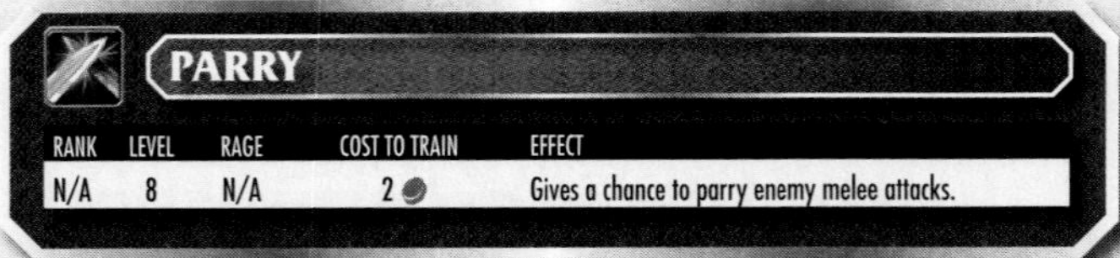

PARRY

RANK	LEVEL	RAGE	COST TO TRAIN	EFFECT
N/A	8	N/A	2 ●	Gives a chance to parry enemy melee attacks.

PLATE MAIL

RANK	LEVEL	RAGE	COST TO TRAIN	EFFECT
N/A	40	N/A	1 ● 60 ●	Allows the Warrior to Equip Plate Armor.

POLEARMS

RANK	LEVEL	RAGE	COST TO TRAIN	EFFECT
N/A	40	N/A	5 ●	Allows the Warrior to Equip Polearms.

SHIELD BLOCK

RANK	LEVEL	RAGE	COST TO TRAIN	EFFECT
N/A	16	-10	18 ●	Increases chance to block by 75% for 5 sec, but will only block 1 attack.

SHIELD WALL

RANK	LEVEL	RAGE	COST TO TRAIN	EFFECT
N/A	24	N/A	53 ●	Reduces the damage taken from melee attacks, ranged attacks and spells by 75% for 10 sec.

SUNDER ARMOR

RANK	LEVEL	RAGE	COST TO TRAIN	EFFECT
1	10	-15		Instant Attack that Lowers Enemy Armor by 90 (Can Stack up to 5 Times). Lasts 30 sec.
2	22	-15	56 ●	Sunders the target's armor, reducing it by 180 per Sunder Armor. Can be applied up to 5 times. Lasts 30 sec.
3	34	-15	1 ● 30 ●	Sunders the target's armor, reducing it by 270 per Sunder Armor. Can be applied up to 5 times. Lasts 30 sec.
4	46	-15	3 ● 70 ●	Sunders the target's armor, reducing it by 360 per Sunder Armor. Can be applied up to 5 times. Lasts 30 sec.
5	58	-15	7 ● 10 ●	Sunders the target's armor, reducing it by 450 per Sunder Armor. Can be applied up to 5 times. Lasts 30 sec.

TAUNT

RANK	LEVEL	RAGE	COST TO TRAIN	EFFECT
1	10	-5	3 ●	Taunts the target to attack you, causing a small amount of threat.
2	20	-5	29 ●	Taunts the target to attack you, causing a medium amount of threat.
3	30	-5	1 ● 30 ●	Taunts the target to attack you, causing a high amount of threat. More effective than Taunt (Rank 1).
4	40	-5	1 ● 30 ●	Taunts the target to attack you, causing a high amount of threat. More effective than Taunt (Rank 2).
5	50	-5	3 ● 50 ●	Taunts the target to attack you, causing a high amount of threat. More effective than Taunt (Rank 3).
6	60	-5	5 ● 90 ●	Taunts the target to attack you, causing a high amount of threat. More effective than Taunt (Rank 4).

TALENTS

Warriors Talents really help to push your characters toward either the defensive or aggressive ends of the spectrum. It's hard to walk the middle ground with a Warrior, and weapon choice plays into this quite distinctly. The Protection line encourages one-handed weapons, a shield, and the use of Defensive Stance. Arms works in conjunction with the Arms line, and it becomes stunning at high levels with two-handed weapons (because of its instant attacks and major damage improvements). Fury is a good place to boost shouts, Berserk Stance, and raise damage (especially against multiple targets).

ARMS

TALENT NAME	RANKS	PREREQUISITES	EFFECTS
Improved Heroic Strike	3	None	Reduce Cost of Heroic Strike by 1 Rage (Per Rank)
Deflection	5	None	Increases Chance to Parry by 1% (Per Rank)
Improved Rend	3	None	Increases Rend Damage by 15% - Progression: 15%/25%/35%
Improved Charge	2	5 Points in Arms	Increases Rage from Charge by 3 (Per Rank)
Tactical Mastery	5	5 Points in Arms	You Retain up to 5 Rage (Per Rank) When Changing Stances
Improved Thunder Clap	3	5 Points in Arms	Increases Damage of Thunder Clap by 15% - Progression: 15%/30%/40%
Improved Overpower	2	10 Points in Arms	Increases Chance for Overpower to Critically Strike by 25% (Per Rank)
Anger Management	1	5 Points in Tactical Mastery, 10 Points in Arms	Reduced Rage Decay by 30%
Deep Wounds	3	3 Points in Improved Rend, 10 Points in Arms	Critical Strikes add a 20% DOT (Per Rank) Over 12 Seconds
Two-Handed Weapon Specialization	5	15 Points in Arms	Increases Two-Handed Weapon Damage by 1% (Per Rank)
Impale	2	3 Points in Deep Wounds, 15 Points in Arms	Increases Critical Strike Damage from Abilities by 10% (Per Rank) in All Stances
Axe Specialization	5	20 Points in Arms	Increase Chance to Critically Hit With Axes by 1% (Per Rank)
Sword Specialization	5	20 Points in Arms	Adds a 1% Chance (Per Rank) to Land a Free, Second Hit
Mace Specialization	5	20 Points in Arms	Adds a 1% Chance (Per Rank) to Stun Your Target Each Hit - Progression: 1%/2%/3%/4%/6%
Sweeping Strikes	1	20 Points in Arms	Your Next 5 Attacks in Melee Can Hit an Added Target (Most Abilities Are Included)
Spear and Polearm Specialization	5	25 Points in Arms	Increases Chance to Critically Hit with Spears and Polearms by 1% (Per Rank)
Improved Hamstring	2	25 Points in Arms	Increases the Snare Effect of Hamstring by 10% (Per Rank)
Mortal Strike	1	30 Points in Arms	Adds a 20 Rage New Ability in Battle Stance (Deals an Instant 220% Attack that Debuffs Healing on the Target: 6 Second Cooldown)

FURY

TALENT NAME	RANKS	PREREQUISITES	EFFECTS
Improved Battle Shout	5	None	Increases the Duration of Battle Shout by 30 Seconds (Per Rank)
Cruelty	5	None	Increase Chance to Critically Hit by 1% (Per Rank)
Booming Voice	5	5 Points in Fury	Decreases Target's Chance to Resist Shouts by 2% (Per Rank)
Improved Demoralizing Shout	5	5 Points in Fury	Increases the Attack Debuff of Dem Shout by 5% (Per Rank)
Unbridled Wrath	5	5 Points on Fury	Adds an 8% Chance (Per Rank) to Gain 1 Free Rage With Every Attack
Piercing Howl	1	5 Points in Improved Demoralizing Shout, 15 Points in Fury	Adds a 10 Rage Ability that Instantly Causes Nearby Enemies to be Dazed for 6 Seconds
Enrage	5	10 Points in Fury	Adds an 8% Damage Bonus (Per Rank) for 4 Attacks After You Are Critically Struck
Improved Intimidating Shout	3	15 Points in Fury	Adds a 75% Chance for You to Cause Another Target (Per Rank) to Cower
Improved Inner Rage	5	15 Points in Fury	Reduced the Cooldown of Inner Rage by 40 Seconds (Per Rank)
Improved Slam	2	20 Points in Fury	Reduces the Casting Time of Slam by .5 Seconds (Per Rank)
Death Wish	1	20 Points in Fury	Adds a 10 Rage Ability That Increases Melee Damage by 20%, Makes You Immune to Fear, but Lowers Defense Against All Damage by 20% (Berserk Stance Only)
Blood Craze	3	5 Points in Enrage, 20 Points in Fury	Allows 6% of Your Health Regeneration During Combat for 5 Seconds After Being Critically Struck - Progression: 6%/13%/20%
Improved Cleave	2	20 Points in Fury	Adds a Target (Per Rank) to Your Cleave Attacks
Improved Challenging Shout	2	25 Points in Fury	Reduced the Cooldown of Challenging Shout by 2 Minutes - Progression: 2/3
Flurry	5	25 Points in Fury	Increases Attack Speed by 10% for 3 Swings After Scoring a Critical Hit - Progression: 10%/15%/20%/25%/30%
Bloodthirst	1	1 Point in Death Wish, 30 Points in Fury	Your Next melee attack AFTER a Killing Blow does 100% damage

PROTECTION

TALENT NAME	RANKS	PREREQUISITES	EFFECTS
Anticipation	5	None	Increases Your Defense by 2 (Per Rank)
Shield Specialization	5	None	Increases Your Chance to Block by 1% (Per Rank)
Improved Bloodrage	3	5 Points in Protection	Reduces the Delay of Rage Gained by Bloodrage by 2 Seconds - Progression: 2/4/5
Toughness	5	5 Points in Protection	Increase Your Armor Value from Items by 2% (Per Rank)
Iron Will	5	5 Points in Protection	Increases Your Chance to Resist Charm/Stun by 3% (Per Rank)
Last Stand	1	3 Points in Improved Bloodrage, 10 Points in Protection, 3 Points in Improved Bloodrage	Adds 30% of Your Maximum Hit Points to Your Current Total (These Hit Points Fade in 20 Seconds--Beware)
Improved Revenge	3	10 Points of Protection	Adds a 20% Chance for a 3 Second Stun to Your Revenge Attacks - Progression: 20%/30%/40%
Improved Taunt	2	10 Points in Protection	Increases the Effectiveness of Taunt by 10% (Per Rank)
Improved Sunder Armor	3	15 Points in Protection	Increases the Armor Debuff of Sunder Armor by 10% (Per Rank)
Improved Shield Block	3	5 Points in Shield Specialization, 15 Points of Protection	Adds .5 Seconds to Shield Block and Allows a Second Attack to be Blocked - Progression: .5/1/2
Defiance	5	2 Points in Improved Taunt, 10 Points in Protection	Increases the Threat Generated in Defensive Stance by 3% (Per Rank)
Improved Shield Bash	2	20 Points in Protection	Adds a 50% chance (Per Rank) to Silence the target for 3 seconds
Concussion Blow	1	3 Points in Improved Revenge, 20 Points in Protection	Adds a 15 Rage Ability With a 1 Second Casting Time that Stuns a Target for 5 Seconds
Improved Shield Wall	2	3 Points in Improved Shield Block, 20 Points in Protection	Increases the Duration of Shield Wall by 3 Seconds - Progression: 3/5
Improved Disarm	3	25 Points in Protection	Adds 2 Seconds (Per Rank) to the Duration of Disarm
One-Handed Weapon Specialization	5	25 Points in Protection	Increases One-Handed Weapon Damage by 1% (Per Rank)
Combat Endurance	1	30 Points in Protection	Allows 10% of Health Regeneration During Combat

STRATEGIES

The core Warrior strategies revolve around keeping enemies from doing their proper damage. Charge into battle for the free Rage, using Hamstring to snare opponents, then nail the targets in the back while higher DPS classes draw aggro but aren't attacked because they are standing at range. Or, try soloing and use Charge, Demoralizing Shout, Rend, and Heroic Strikes for the long haul (battles that are certain to last 12 seconds or longer).

GENERAL TIPS

Strategy comes down to using your abilities in the right order to keep enemies debuffed as much as possible while dealing maximum damage for the Rage. Use early Rage to get a Demoralizing Shout off, substantially reducing enemy damage for a low cost. This is pretty much free during a Charge, because of the initial Rage boost, so Charge and Demoralizing Shout even if you are a Defensive Warrior (you can always switch stances after using the free Rage).

Then, get Battle Shout going. This is a several minute ability that affects the entire party, so it's critical to have it up all the time. If you're having trouble getting extra Rage because of missed strikes and such, drop into Defensive Stance and use Bloodlust to snag more Rage and pull off that extra Battle Shout (it's a large boost to you and an even greater one to Rogues and Paladins grouped with you).

Make use of your abilities in the best possible way in each battle. Heroic Strike is wonderful, certainly, but the best uses of things like Hamstring, Sunder Armor, and Mocking Blow can turn the tide of battle far more than a dose of extra damage. Learn when to use these.

You have interrupts in both Battle and Defensive Stance (Pummel and Shield Bash respectively). These abilities are able to stop a target that is casting a spell or using a channeling ability; in the case where your target has a consistent casting time, use these interrupts at the latter stage of the casting to waste as much of your enemy's time as possible.

ON THE OFFENSE

Hamstring is your key snare; this makes sure that enemies can't run away from you, go after other targets quickly, or do anything effective in melee without paying some major time in moving around. Being an instant, Hamstring is stunningly powerful; save this for the end of battle against enemies who run to ensure a long session of back attacks and easy hits. Use it early in PvP against enemies who need to remain mobile (all casters, Rogues, etc.).

Rend is always an ability with some controversy surrounding its use. For a very low cost, Rend provides an immediate DOT against your opponent. In terms of damage per point of Rage, this is a very sound investment (the damage is not mitigated by armor, so comparing Rend to Heroic Strike in that light further improves Rend's efficiency). The rub is that you need to have the target survive for the entire duration of Rend for all that efficiency to get through. At higher levels, that can mean 21 seconds of fighting. Thus, Rend is a good tool for soloing Warriors or those who are going against elites or creatures with high armor. In groups where the kills are fast, use Heroic Strike for general damage instead.

Thunder Clap is not a damage dealer, nor does its debuff last long enough to warrant throwing 20 Rage down the pipe. Instead, use Thunder Clap as a way to grab new enemies' attention quickly. Use Thunder Clap and a Demoralizing Shout to secure light aggro and reduce the damage being done by a new swarm of enemies (this gives the group a bit more time to fight the targets before your healers start casting and drawing anything off of you).

Keep a ranged weapon and at least a single stack of ammunition around at all times, even if you don't like to pull with these items. In PvP and against some monsters, you're likely to be rooted from time to time. Standing around doing nothing while the rest of your group takes damage can be grueling. At least give yourself the option to shoot back, wound/disrupt casters, and so forth. If you need room on your quickbar for other things, put the ranged icons on a spare bar that can quickly be readied.

PROTECTING YOURSELF AND A PARTY

Taunt is the best (and sometimes the worst) aspect of Defensive Stance. This ability is quite powerful, have no doubt, but it is a consuming master. In a large group, fighting in challenging Instances, a Defensive Warrior is going to be using Taunt quite heavily. Each target requires at least a couple taps of the button, and the Rage from that adds up very quickly. Indeed, large fights prevent Warriors from having much Rage to spare for anything else. Taunt saves lives and leaves a group long in your favor, but be ready to tap the key often.

One fine way to act as a defensive tank without needing to spam Taunt as often is to wait several levels past the normal spot for hitting various Instances. If most people are heading into Deadmines a bit after 20, you may have a much better time holding back until passing into your mid 20s, or even a bit beyond. The delayed gratification of getting better gear may invalidate this suggestion, depending on your needs, but having Warriors who are higher level than the rest of the group makes those Warriors much more effective without needing to Taunt as often. Fewer Taunts means more Rage (which means more damage, and more damage leads to more aggro without using Taunt, etc.).

Sunder Armor is a common use of Rage when Taunt isn't being spammed. It reduces your target's armor (thus their ability to sustain damage falls substantially). This helps the most against targets that are specifically strong toward melee attacks, such as certain golems, turtles, and Instance bosses. Though your Warrior still isn't the one doing the most damage from this, Sunder Armor opens the way for Paladins and Rogues to be even more deadly in the battle. Use Sunder Armor more often in group settings where there are more melee folks in the party.

TIMED ABILITIES

Your timed abilities are quite good, and they come into play often. Inner Rage offers free Rage every five minutes (and that timer can be lowered dramatically through your Fury line). Because this instant ability costs nothing, it's vital during battles where your Rage is depleted and much remains to be done; longer fights where adds come in just as you are finishing major foes are perfect examples of Inner Rage usefulness.

Intimidating Shout is a blessing most of the time, but it must be used correctly. This AoE shout forces enemies to run in fear, but the creature you're targeting cowers instead. Feared enemies have a chance of breaking their fear if they start to take damage, so this is more an ability to buy time when healing, running, or other such factors are needed. Because running enemies have a tendency to bring friends, save Intimidating Shout for times when only a single target can be forced to stop fighting for the eight-second duration, or for conditions where there aren't nearby targets to join in the fray. Bandaging during this bonus time is often a sound idea.

Challenging Shout has a long cooldown, but at least it doesn't cost much to activate. Use this AoE Taunt to grab extra aggro during a phase where you don't have the Rage to manually Taunt a number of incoming creatures. Hit Demoralizing Shout and Challenging Shout after the brief cooldown for a good way to have the enemies jump on you and deal less damage. Be aware that this is not a strong Taunt, and it isn't dependable for maintaining aggro in the long term (do damage quickly and start Taunting before the enemies realize that a Mage is going nuts with Arcane Explosion on their backsides).

CLASS QUESTS

Warriors have many useful quests that are class-linked. Starting at Level 10, your trainers point you in the right direction to find extra weapons, your two special stances, and some additional armor. This is all quality equipment if you do the quests early on, so gather a group of fellow Warriors or a cluster of friends to help out with these chores.

LEARN DEFENSIVE STANCE

Level 10 is a major point for a budding Warrior. Your first Class Quest is to learn Defensive Stance. Talk to the Warrior Trainer in the secondary town of your starting region (e.g. the trainer in Brill, Goldshire, etc.). These folks send you up to the capital to find another NPC; get the main quest from these characters and fill the requirements to learn your new stance.

GET A LEVEL 10 WEAPON FOR YOUR CHARACTER

After mastering Defensive Stance, you are sent to other NPC to get a second quest. This Class Quest gets you a weapon that is quite reasonable for a Level 10 Warrior, and there are a number of options when it comes to your reward. Each of these quests is quite different, but they are short and easy to follow, fortunately.

A SHIELD FOR THE WARY SOLDIER

Another short Class Quest comes as you approach Level 20. If you are a defensive Warrior, return to your capital city and talk to the NPCs in your training area to find out where to go for this. Because the reward is a shield, and the quest is not required for future Class Quests, there is no driving need to complete this if you aren't interested in the reward.

However, the quest is short enough that the experience and sell value of the shield may be enough to warrant your time.

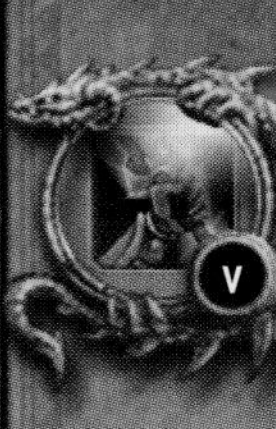

LEVEL 20: TIME TO GET ARMOR

This is where Warrior Class Quests start to converge for all of the races. Your armor quests also mark the point where things start getting much longer and more challenging. If you want to get your armor pieces early, it's going to take some help from higher-level people.

For both the Horde and Alliance, Warriors need to collect items from the far continent (Alliance Warriors head to Stonetalon, in Kalimdor, for most of their pieces and Horde Warriors need to do some fighting in Hillsbrad). For both sides, the first quest culminates in a journey to The Barrens; an Instance in the southern part of the zone called Razorfen Kraul has the enemy with the final piece. Bring a group in their higher 20s to defeat the elite enemies (Levels 25-28+) in that dungeon.

By completing the quest for the chest piece, the way is unlocked to go after several additional pieces. These quests involve a lot of traveling, but they are faster and much easier than the first stage. Taking groups of your level should be more than adequate for these.

BERSERK STANCE, HERE AT LAST

Talk to your trainers against at Level 30; they send you out to the water near Ratchet, in The Barrens. Walk south down the coast from Ratchet until the nearest island is almost directly east of your position. Swim out to the island and talk to the people there. This club for fighting against other Warriors offers a simple challenge to go against a series of foes around your level. Use bandages between fights to maintain health (and watch your back while playing on the PvP Servers), and the Islander teaches you Berserk Stance as your reward.

A LONG QUEST: YOUR LEVEL 30 WEAPON

An old weapon master in the Alterac Mountains is willing to aid both Alliance and Horde Warriors who help him summon and defeat a powerful spirit of wind. There are many pieces needed to complete the ritual, and these are quite challenging to retrieve for a Level 30 Warrior. The reward at the end of the journey is a truly fine two-handed weapon for your level, so it's all worth the effort if you get moving sooner rather than later.

Gather eight pieces of Liferoot (or buy them from an Herbalist) to get one of the three ingredients. Arathi is a good place to get Liferoot in small quantities, and the northern section of Stranglethorn Vale is a great choice two. Fortunately, those are the areas for the other two ingredients.

Stranglethorn Vale (SV) has a tribe of Trolls known as the Bloodscalps; search for these in the ruins in north-western SV. Fight until you have all 30 Tusks from these Trolls, and continue a tad longer if you also have the Collection Quests from Booty Bay and Grom'Gol to fight against these menaces.

The final stage, and by far the worst collection of the lot, is to get Essence of the Exile from Arathi. This mixture is made from the Charms of the Cresting, Burning, Thundering Exiles of the Arathi Highlands. These enemies are in their high 30s, and they pack a pretty mean punch even for people around that level. It also takes quite some time for the necessary Charms to drop, so look for a party that is willing to help.

Bring said party when you go to turn in the quest items as well. The Cyclonian is a powerful monster (and is elite), and being able to face a Level 40+ creature isn't something you are likely to survive yet.

THE FINEST TOOLS

It's said that clothes make the man (or woman); while not 100% true in *World of Warcraft*, it can make a difference in how your character performs. Finding and using the best equipment can give you the edge you've been looking for as well as allow you to further customize the kind of character you would like to play.

Many items have level requirements. It's essential to understand how the system works in order to know what equipment you can use, what its value is and how it can best benefit you. Items that are either too high in level or aren't usable by your class appear red. Once you meet their requirements, you'll be able to use them.

Items have a color-coded system to identify those that are of more value or rarer in nature than others. (See *Understanding Equipment, Enemies, and Quests* in the *Introduction to Online Gaming* section.) In general, gray items are sold directly to merchants rather than attempting to sell them at auction. Those lucky enough to acquire a blue item or, even better yet, a purple item usually end up either using the item themselves or auctioning it off if it's not a BoA item.

EQUIPMENT STATISTICS

It's important to understand what the stats on your equipment can do for you. Understanding how your equipment works and what stats best increase your abilities for your class can help you balance out ability with viability.

Strength It adds to your attack power and, correspondingly, your DPS. Strength does not affect Critical Hit chances at all. It won't improve your chance to block, but rather the amount that is blocked when you succeed. This amount is determined in part by Strength and in part by your shield.

Agility Your chance to land a Critical Hit with melee/ranged attacks is ruled by your Agility rating. The awarded bonus is higher for Rogues and Hunters than other classes. Agility also affects dodge. Once again, Rogues and Hunters receive a better Dodge bonus per point of Agility than other classes. Lastly, Agility adds directly to the Armor statistic.

Stamina Your health points are determined by your Stamina (in conjunction with the class you've chosen).

Intellect It affects three things. The obvious one is that your mana pool is increased as your Intellect increases. However, Intelllect also determines your chance to inflict a Critical Hit with magic spells. Finally, it grants a higher chance to increase melee skills, though it does not affect your ability to rank up your chosen professions.

Spirit This increases health and mana regeneration in and out of combat.

Attack Rating This is based upon your weapon skill and your level. Your stats won't affect this.

Attack Power Attack Power is affected by Strength (for every one point it equals two points of Attack Power) for all classes. However, for Rogues and Hunters, Agility adds one point extra per point of Agility.

Damage Weapon damage is affected by the damage of the weapon and Strength for all classes except Rogues and Hunters. Their weapon damage is affected by the weapon and an even combination of Strength and Agility.

Defense Only equipment that has a bonus to Defense itself will modify this stat.

Armor Physical damage reduction is affected by the Armor Rating on each piece of armor and, if you carry one, a shield. It only affects physical damage reduction and not magic damage reduction.

Magic Resistances There are various items that give resistances to the five magic damage lines: Arcane, Fire, Frost, Nature, and Shadow.

Other statistics on weapons and items are also worth noting such as the damage rate, speed and DPS. There are often other more specific modifiers on equipment (e.g. Block bonus for shield users).

CUSTOMIZING YOUR CHARACTER WITH EQUIPMENT

Once you understand how stats work with your equipment, you'll understand better what kind of equipment you need to enhance your character, provided you understand what your character needs to use most.

Hunters and Rogues both need Agility as their primary statistic. The secondary statistic can either be Stamina or Strength depending on whether you want to take or inflict damage.

Mages, Priests and Warlocks focus on items with boosts to their Intellect and Spirit. An increased mana pool and a chance to inflict a Critical Hit (Critical Heal in the Priest's case) usually outweighs the mana and health replenishment.

Warriors boost their Stamina and Strength. Durability and damage are the two defining characteristics of this class.

Druids need Intellect, but Strength and Stamina can't be overlooked. The main choices for this class depend entirely on how the player plans to spec the character.

Shaman require almost everything. Agility is the only attribute that is generally overlooked, but can also be useful. Again, determining the play style of the character helps decide which attributes to apply.

Paladins are similar in nature to Warriors. They focus on Stamina and Strength. However, Paladins have a mana pool and will want to keep a bit of extra Intellect to push up their ability to Lay On Hands and heal when needed.

JUGGLING ARMOR

Your armor is your first defense against attacks. If your shield goes down or you can't dodge the next blow, it's going to fall on your armor. This is why AR is important to help defray the damage dealt out by melee weapons.

After you consider the Armor Rating on your pieces, look into the statistics that go with it. Tailor your armor to achieve your desired stat breakdown. Focus less on what each item gives you, unless it's undeniably beastly, and more on the overall stat table. If an item gives you a few extra Strength and a nice boost to your Armor Rating, it may outweigh the item that only gives a bit more Strength.

At times, keeping a second set of armor on hand to help in specific situations may be the smart move. Maybe you're going up against a certain set of mobs or a dungeon that is filled with casters. Agility, for an increased dodge rate, may be an option. If you are in a group that doesn't require you to deal out as much damage, you may want to swap a Strength item for some Stamina or Intellect. Some armor may have resists that apply directly to the task at hand.

Knowing when to use which armor pieces and when to apply the "juggling" method is something that comes with experience. Veteran guild members or friends may offer advice on the application of this theory; soak up all the information and begin to develop your own playstyle and armory.

ARMOR TYPES

There are many different armor types and pieces available. What kind of armor you can wear is dictated by your class. Wearing armor has a hierarchy: Cloth up to Plate. Availability of armor always includes any armor that is below your wearing level. For instance, Rogues can wear leather, but they can also wear cloth pieces if they choose. Warriors and Paladins can wear all armor types and have the most variety from which to choose.

Cloth Mages, Warlocks and Priests all wear cloth armor. It generally doesn't have a high Armor Rating, but usually has more statistical advantages for the caster.

Leather Druids, Shaman, Hunters and Rogues wear leather armor to start off.

Mail Warriors and Paladins can start off by wearing mail. Shaman and Hunters can train at later levels to wear mail.

Plate Plate is the heaviest of armors and can only be worn by Paladins and Warriors who have trained it up.

CHOOSE YOUR WEAPON

Choosing your weapons depends on a few factors: character type, play style and availability. For character type, take into account whether you'll find yourself in melee range often or if you'll remain farther from the action. (Of course, when soloing, the answer is almost always that you'll be in melee range.) Do you need a fast weapon that deals out less damage, but can hit more often or do you need a slower weapon that hits for a ton each time it connects? Shield? Two Daggers? One Dagger and one Sword?

One-handed weapons are faster weapons that deal less damage than two-handed weapons. Your style dictates which you'll want to use along with whether or not you're playing a class that can dual wield. Even classes that can't dual wield can still use an off-hand item to enhance their stats. Weapons that fall into this category are: daggers, maces, swords, axes and fist weapons. Warriors that are more focused on defense often use what is called the "Sword and Board" or sword and shield combination for runs in dungeons where they need to focus more on drawing aggro than being a damage dealing monolith.

Two-handed weapons are slower, higher damage dealing weapons. Staves are often the choice of casters; not so much because of their speed or damage, but because of the stats that many inherently have. There is much debate over whether or not it's better to use a one-handed weapon with an item in the off-hand or to use the staff instead. It's more a matter of preference and about the items available to you. Should a great combination of one hand and off-hand item be made available, take it up. Warriors like to use two-handed axes or swords for putting out heavy damage. Two-handed weapons include: swords, maces, axes, polearms and staves.

Ranged Weapons go in an alternate slot and have nothing to do with one- or two-handed capabilities. Ranged weapons include throwing weapons, crossbows, bows, wands and guns. The addition of a quiver or ammo pouch can offer bonuses as well. Ranged weapons are great for all classes. They offer options where none were previously available. A rooted warrior can now be a threat at distance and casters can limit their mana use by employing the use of a wand.

Off-hand items, while not actual weapons, fall within this category as well. The bonus stats can sometimes make it worth giving up a two-handed slow weapon. In this case, a shield can fall in the category by giving extra armor and blocking capabilities. Casters, in particular, find these off-hand items useful for their stat boosting abilities as well.

TESTER TIP

TESTER TIP

Rogue Weapon Tips

by Rayven

A Rogue is built around daggers. Two skills that need a main hand dagger are Backstab and Ambush, not the ultimate Rogue skills, but something you'll miss if you use anything else in your main hand. But there are many viable tactics available to Rogues.

Dagger: Daggers with both speed and damage are the Rogue's best friend. The high speed on daggers lends itself perfectly to poison. Poisons are what sets us apart from many classes. They can DoT, nuke, snare, and even reduce a caster's casting time; combine those abilities with the fact that they stack on top of the damage itself and we've got a devastating ability set. Every time a weapon swings, there's a 5% chance to poison the enemy. So, a faster weapon translates into more chances to poison. By using all our abilities and the speed of the weapons, daggers are the main choice for Rogues.

Fist Weapons: These are the fastest weapons out there. They work even better with poison then daggers. I actually use a dagger in my main hand and a fist weapon in my off-hand. Granted, you do less damage in your off-hand, but poison is consistent.

Maces: Maces can be awesome in the hand of a Rogue. We have a skill that, when fully trained (3 talent points), gives us a 6% chance to stun the target. Stuns are awesome in any battle regardeless of whether it's PvP or PvE. On top of this, maces have some of the highest damage outputs in the game. They're slow, but inflict great damage. Equipping this in your main hand makes Sinister Strike, a skill you use 90% of the time, much more deadly than a when using a dagger. You can do some nasty damage and stuns with a mace, but you do give up Backstab and Ambush in the trade off.

Swords: Swords typically do more damage than daggers, but are slower. They're also great for Sinister Strike. However, they have no other bonuses. You'll typically see Rogues using swords when they acquire a weapon that does a ton more damage than their current one. If you're using a 15 DPS dagger and you find a 25 DPS sword, well, it's a no brainer. That's too much damage to pass up. Keep in mind that you'll lose the Backstab and Ambush abilities. However, there are some off-hand swords. Using them in your off-hand doesn't take anything away from using a dagger in your main hand. They're rare, but they exist. Swords are fantastic secondary weapons if you want to focus on physical damage over poison damage.

TESTER TIP

Shaman Weapon Choices

by Zavein Stormrider

I've got a melee-based Shaman. Demios focuses on Strength and Stamina, and her DPS is great for her level. I've played with a 1H axe, 1H maces, a 2h axe (all comparable level) and none of them stack above my current dagger. They never have and I doubt they ever will in PvE.

As a Shaman oriented on melee, I inevitably miss a percentage of the time, some damage is mitigated by the armor or I proc a percentage of the time. People argue that the damage is the same no matter what since a percentage is a percentage. Yet time and time again I find that I can take monsters down faster with a dagger and a proc, than I could with the other weapons, and that's usually because of the speed of the attack.

More attacks offer a greater chance of crits; a higher chance of crits gives more opportunities to use Flurry (a Shaman talent which gives a 30% speed increase for 3 hits). All this assumes that you're fighting monsters around your level.

For monsters below your level, I highly favor a slower weapon since on lower level monsters you land crits more frequently and a large weapon inflicts the first hit at the same speed as a faster weapon; getting a critical hit on the first hit with a high DPS weapon is a huge crit. On a monster much lower than you, it can mean most - or all - of its life on that single strike. Playing with a 2H axe at 39, I can one- to three-shot monsters up to about level 27.

In PvP I believe that I'll probably favor a 2H weapon since you end up dancing with the player more often than not and getting a nice, scary hit from time to time is better than nickel and diming them, I have yet to try it out to prove my theory.

As far as Shaman weapon procs go, I either go with Windfury or Firebrand. I use Windfury when I'm going against weaker armored monsters, since it increases the frequency of hits offering Flurry chances more often. Firebrand is best for high-armor monsters, since it adds flat damage above the melee damage. So, unless the monster is highly fire resistant, it's guaranteed damage.

Here are some other important things to understand about your equipment:

Shields have blocking values. Blocked attacks avoid an amount of damage based on your shield and your character's Strength.

Wands can be interrupted when the user takes damage. All classes that possess the Wand Proficiency skill can use them; fire, frost and shadow skills are not necessary unless it's a requirement on the weapon itself. Resistance in the appropriate school reduces wand damage accordingly. One good thing for casters is that wand use is not prevented when silenced. However, they're prevented in all the same situations in which melee combat is prevented.

Items that increase the critical hit percentage do not stack.

Items with procs are using time-based procs. Their proc frequencies are entered as the number of desired procs per minute, and their actual per-swing proc chances are calculated from that using the weapon's speed.

All quested items are soulbound to your character and cannot be traded or sold to other players. Vendors are the only option if you no longer wish to keep the item.

It's important to pay attention to items that are Bind on Acquire (BoA) or Bind on Equip (BoE). BoE items can still be traded or sold to others, provided you didn't try it on to see what it looked like.

When shopping at a vendor, mousing over an item shows both the stats for the item you're looking at and what you currently have equipped in the same slot. This allows you to compare what you have with what you're looking at.

TESTER TIP

Mage Choices

by Zophar

As a Mage, I prefer a dagger and an off-hand item. There are a few reasons why.

There are daggers that have excellent bonuses for Mages (Intellect bonuses aren't uncommon) and off-hand items that increase spell damage or offer additional abilities like healing, increased damage, mana restoration, increased run speed, etc. I find the utility of these items is better than working with a staff.

Other Mages might prefer the staff because of the larger Intellect and Spirit bonuses, giving them a larger mana pool and faster regeneration. This is a strong argument and simply comes down to play style.

Other Mages might prefer using a sword if they like to get up in an enemy's face and do some melee damage. Obviously, swords have a high DPS and many swords have nice "on hit" or "chance to" effects like doing extra fire damage or something similar. These are especially nice for Mages who wear equipment that increase their fire or spell damage, since that bonus also applies to the effect on the sword.

FINDING THE BEST LOOT

Once you know what kind of equipment works for you, it's time to start looking for it. There are several different ways to get your new gear; you can buy it, have it created by someone in a Profession, loot it, quest for it or, if you're lucky enough, get it from a friend or a guild who wants you to be all you can be. Here's more of a breakdown on getting the loot you need.

General Loot As you go through the world of Azeroth you will no doubt find a bit of blood on your weapons. Looting mobs often nets you some good weapons and gear. As you attain a higher level and begin battling more difficult mobs, it's more likely that you'll end up with some great drops. You may end up having to roll for them, however, so be sure to warm up those dice (or the /random command).

Questing Questing can be a great way to get that exact weapon, armor piece or hand held item for which you're looking—or at least to get you to the next level or two before looking for better. Most classes also have specific quests restricted to them that offer the right kind of items to help you advance.

Crafted Find someone working on a Profession that creates items you need. Often, they'll bargain with you for the needed materials and a reduced cost rather than having to pay a larger fee or having to outbid someone at auction for an item.

Vendors Vendors generally carry adequate equipment for purchase should you find you just need something to hold you over. Some vendors have rarer items, but are found in more remote locales than just a jump to your main city.

Auction If you can't find it some other way, try going to the auction houses. If you only have a certain amount of money to spend, try looking for buyout prices rather than trying to outbid someone. Just be careful not to pay too much for an item just because you feel you must have it *now*. Patience while watching the auctions may give you a better chance of getting what you want at a lower cost.

Friends/Guild Having friends or a guild that can help you get the gear you need or that can give you their hand-me-downs can make a big difference in your wallet. Being generous to others often comes back around to you.

RAID CONTENT UPDATE

Blizzard has plans (oh so many plans) for the high-end content for *World of Warcraft* and we picked the Jeffrey Kaplan's [JK] brain to help define for you what a raid is, how it works, and what's in store. Jeffrey is the lead raid content designer for the game. This interview often references his posting on the *World of Warcraft* website regarding raids. (www.worldofwarcraft.com/pvp/raid-article.shtml)

BRADY: Can you briefly explain what a "raid" will consist of in its most basic form?

JK: I would define a raid, in its most basic form, as any encounter that requires more than one standard group to complete.

BRADY: You mentioned that there will be all sorts of raids including instanced raids and those in the general area, short excursions and more grueling trials. What prompted the decision to offer such a variety?

JK: Players spend a great deal of time at the highest levels. Since they are no longer gaining experience and leveling up to meet new encounters in new zones, it's important to give them variety in the encounters that they do have access to. The last thing we want to do is kick out a bunch of cookie-cutter encounters. What's fun and challenging is learning the strategy for each new raid. If every raid follows the same guidelines then there won't be much variety or challenge in conquering them.

BRADY: Will the raid content be storyline driven as much of the quests are?

JK: Yes. *Warcraft's* Lore, as dictated by our VP of Creative Development, Chris Metzen, is what drives *WoW*. All of the high-end raid encounters play directly into Chris' storyline.

BRADY: Is there any plan to include some lower-level raid content so that people can be "trained" to work in big groups, or will they first get to experience this level of interaction near the level cap?

JK: Our normal instanced group dungeons already serve this purpose. Oftentimes, lower level players will form raid groups to *conquer* a higher level dungeon.

BRADY: Let's take a step back for a minute. Could you please explain the mechanics behind managing a raid group? This isn't just something that anyone can jump into and expect everything to go smoothly, is it?

JK: Well, if you're talking strictly about the mechanics of managing a raid group, I think our interface makes it extremely easy to do. Classes are color-coded and players' names can be dragged-and-dropped into the proper slots. Gone are the days of scribbling groups down on paper or forcing group leaders to invite certain people. With *WoW's* raid interface, the raid leader simply invites everyone and moves them to the proper spot.

BRADY: You mentioned the words "Onyxia" and "full-fledged dragon" in your journal. Care to offer any more nuggets of goodness to your fans reading this?

JK: Hopefully, Onyxia will prove to be a very fun encounter. By full-fledged dragon I meant that Onyxia would require a full raid force to conquer. Players in WoW get introduced to Dragonkin at a very young age. However, to kill an actual dragon is a different story. When people brag about killing Drakes and Whelps and Dragonspawn, they should take a step back and realize that killing an actual, full-fledged dragon is a much more challenging endeavor.

BRADY: Are there going to be any faction-specific raid zones that will be defended by one faction while the other faction attempts to gain access? In essence, is there any plan to combine PvP and raids?

JK: We've discussed this concept at great length. At this time, we're not prepared to reveal anything, however.

BRADY: You mentioned that there's a "top-heavy" plan being developed in your dev journal. The raids sound like a great way for hardcore fans to extend their gameplay. Is that level of playability going to be available to the casual gamer?

JK: By top heavy, I was also referring to our outdoor 55+ zones as well. In *WoW*, the casual gamer has access to higher level content. A lot of "casual" gamers manage to hit the level cap in our game. I think that's something that really sets us apart. In game, as well as through live updates, there are going to be quite a number of high level zones that will appeal to both casual and hardcore gamer alike.

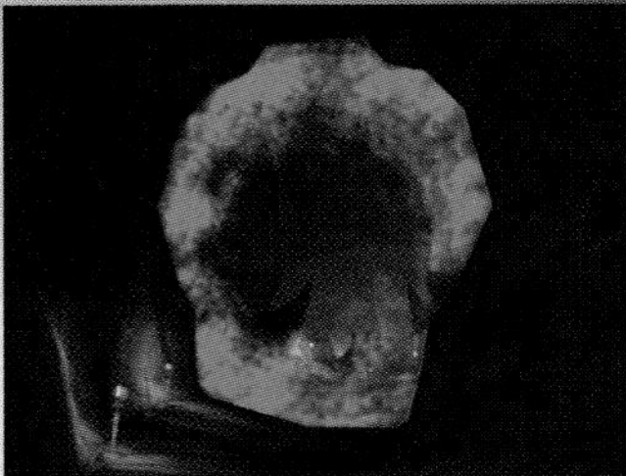

BRADY: So, you got to dig through Chris Metzen's lore to find the big beasties. How many are you holding in reserve just to blow fans away down the road?

JK: That's a secret ;)

BRADY: I'm sure that the development of the high level gameplay will continue, but can you give us an idea about how much will be ready when the game launches? How about a few months down the road?

JK: There will be some singular raid encounters (such as Onyxia) available as well as a full-fledged raid zone (The Molten Core). Also, many of our early live updates are scheduled to include raid zones.

TO THE BATTLE

PVP GENERAL INFORMATION

The land of Azeroth is a land in turmoil. Sides have been chosen and a tentative and uneasy peace between the Horde and Alliance is as fragile as newly blown glass. Each watches the other waiting to catch them in any wrong doing, all the while trying to avoid another war that might make them weak against the taint of the Scourge or another invasion by the Burning Legion.

World of Warcraft is divided into two factions, the Horde and the Alliance. The Horde consists of the Tauren, Forsaken Undead, Orcs and Trolls. The Alliance consists of the Night Elves, Humans, Gnomes and Dwarves.

There is no love lost between the two factions and as you travel the world, you'll find that the opposing faction's towns are not open and welcoming. They would slice you through rather than let you take a peek at their latest merchandise. Don't worry about that too much, however, it's possible to get a little revenge by sacking their town with a few dozen or more of your closest friends.

When a region is being attacked, a message can be seen either on the World Defense and Local Defense Channels. These channels can be a great way to choreograph the defense of your homeland.

After a PvP death you'll be forced to wait for a short period of time (2 mins) before resurrecting and jumping back into battle. A countdown timer appears letting you know just how long you have to wait. Generally, if you've had a relatively long run from the graveyard, you'll not have all that long left to wait.

Some spells have diminishing returns when used in PvP. These spells are Charm, Fear and Stun. All players are susceptible to all three of those spells save for Undead, though there are spells specifically for use against the Undead that have similar results. In the case of these spells, diminishing returns refers to casting the same spell type within 15 seconds of the first such spell wearing off. The second casting of the spell is reduced to 50% of the original duration. The third cast is reduced further to 75% and after the fourth cast of the same spell, the other player will be immune.

GENERAL STRATEGIES AND TIPS

There are some strategies that used in just about every type of PvP encounter within the game. It's important to keep them in mind whether you consider them honorable or dishonorable in nature. It's up to you what your own internal rules are, but knowing the available tactics that can (and will) be used by other players is a key to victory.

Bait Bait is when a lone enemy lures you into a trap in which either a higher-level player is waiting nearby or a group of players is waiting nearby. Baiting someone can be an easy way of getting a kill or splitting up a disorganized group.

Jump Before Being Jumped It's always better to do the jumping than be the one getting jumped. In this case, you pick the method of approach and the terrain in which to fight in as well as the timing of the fight. While it's not impossible to recover from being jumped by any means, it does tend to put a crimp in your usual fighting plan.

Corpse Camping Corpse camping, while not generally perceived as an honorable strategy, may be a tool you end up having to use. It sends the message that it's time for your enemy to move on, provided you let them get back up at some point.

Jumping Often this occurs when a player is engaged in some other activity and has no real chance of making a response. Some players use this when an enemy is killing mobs and at a disadvantage already. While this may be viewed as dishonorable, it may also be seen as the only necessary means for clearing a zone of the opposing faction. Besides, honor is defined differently by players and one may see it as a strategic advantage.

Buddy System This simply can't be stressed enough. Having a buddy to watch your back may make an enemy think twice before attacking. Seeing more than one player easily visible may make them think twice. However, there's something to be said for traveling with a stealthed Rogue and letting people think that you're the only one.

Use the Landscape When taking rests between PvE or PvP activity, don't sit out in the open. The tag over your head is a big enough indicator for your location; don't add to the advertisement by sitting in plain view. Dense foliage and trees do a reasonably good job at obscuring your presence. For those with stealth, make sure you use it. Using the landscape also means, getting out of the line of sight of casters and range combat classes. They can't hit what they can't see.

Use Buildings Use buildings both as line of sight obstructions and as places of rest. For two-story buildings, it's too easy to find you sitting on the first floor. If there is a second story, it may be best to go there so that someone just skimming through can't easily identify that you're there.

Control and Escape There are times when you know you have little hope of living through an encounter. These are the times you need to pull out the stops and find a way of controlling the situation just enough to make your escape. If possible, Fear your attacker, root them, stun them, whatever it takes. Use a speed enhancing technique whether natural Sprint, potions or engineered boots and run, don't walk, to the closest place of safety.

Dying Well There is a right way and a wrong way to die. If you have to die, do it in a place you can get to easily and resurrect in relative safety. Keep in mind the distance you have to work with and find a spot that is obscured from sight of enemies. If they try to camp your corpse, it will give you a chance to utilize your surroundings to resurrect and get out. Being able to rez behind a tree is a beautiful thing.

Be Creative Expand the boundaries of your imagination and think outside the box. (Just don't exploit.) There are countless of different ways to approach a situation and catching your enemy by surprise may be the best possible way of achieving victory. Even when being jumped, you may suddenly be hit with a little inspiration that can get you out of a bind.

Be Prepared Be prepared with potions, first aid and engineering for the times when you're encroaching on contested or opposite faction controlled areas. Having that extra mana or health could mean victory when it comes down to the wire on either nuking power or healing just enough to stay alive.

DOTs Damage over Time spells, poisons or abilities should always be the first thing used against an enemy and the last thing you put on them should they try to flee. Watching a severely weakened foe run away while still taking DOT damage is a feeling of pure joy.

Finish What you Start Unless you're the type to be merciful to your enemy, don't stop attacking until you have killed your opponent(s). That may sound harsh, but by allowing them to escape, it gives them time to regroup and call in friends. Killing them gives them a trip to the graveyard and a little bit of a "time out" rather than running rampantly back into battle.

Know When to Fight Don't get lured into a fight you aren't ready for. It's easy to get caught up in the moment and try to bite off more than you can chew. Realize your own limitations and know when it's best to fight or run the other way. Running isn't cowardly when it means you can come back more prepared and ready to fight on better footing. It's definitely not cowardly when faced with an obviously overwhelming force.

Hearthstone It may not be the fastest way to get out of a bad area, but using a Hearthstone may be the only way to escape a sticky situation. These can only be used once an hour so be careful in your choice of timing. However, if a town that you're currently based at is overrun and the flight master has been taken down, one of the easiest ways out is to stone home.

Ready your Mount/Sprint/Form If you have a faster means of travel than running, give yourself enough time to use it. Save your Sprint or other speedy means for when you need it most, either for chasing someone down for the final kill or for getting away when someone is about to get you. You can not mount while in active PvP so be sure to get far enough away to summon your mount and ride out—provided you have one. If you have a travel form, using it to get away from your enemy will be a big bonus for you. There are also Sprint potions available for those that do not have any other means of getting an immediate speed burst.

Hit and Run Be patient and use the Hit and Run method on opponents. This keeps them off balance and gives you a chance to recoup any lost health or mana. While the battle typically lasts longer, it will also be more enjoyable and the likelihood of your own survival goes up just a tad. Dash in, do some damage in range then back off a bit. Rinse and repeat as necessary.

Use Short Guild and Character Names While this may sound like an odd decision, your name/guild tag could easily be seen from both sides of a tree behind which you're trying to hide. Keeping your name and your guild tag short helps you remain hidden if that's your plan.

CLASS STRENGTHS IN PVP

Each class has their own strengths they need to utilize for direct one-on-one PvP. It's important to focus on these advantages. Here are some general ideas as to the kinds of abilities that the classes have available to them.

Druid: Druids are a grab bag of ability, a virtual jack-of-all-trades, master of none. They can heal, put out melee damage and inflict considerable ranged damage. They're not the masters of any of the three, however, their combined abilities make them a difficult target. If they toss on a root spell, be prepared to counter it or change into a ranged combat style as well, because it buys Druids the time they need to use their ranged abilities or heal. Even once you free yourself, be ready for an in-your-face battle.

Hunters: Hunters are distance fighters above all else. Between their long-range abilities and the addition of a pet, you'll need to get in close. Find a way to neutralize the pet if possible; two targets pose a much larger threat than the lone hunter. Even in melee, they aren't going to simply fall over because you want them to. Hunters have a few tricks that Rogues will particularly dislike such as traps and a Hunter's Mark which prevents you from going into stealth mode and getting away.

Mage: Mages can Sheep anyone that's not one of the Forsaken, which lends them a crowd control ability vital in neutralizing enemies. Their high damage output can ruin foes from a distance, but once they lose the advantage of range, a Mage can be an easy target, even with their Mana Shield, when faced with a high DPS enemy like Rogues or Warriors.

Paladin: "Kill me once, shame on you; kill me twice, shame on me." Paladins have their own tricks that make them very difficult to kill. Lay on Hands is just one edge they gain; it can be used once an hour and heals them to full health. They also have a couple abilities that focus on destroying Undead. Paladins are an Alliance-only class and despite what many think, they're a powerful force when joined by other Paladins. Overlapping abilities create an incredible fighting force.

Priest: Priests aren't your usual healing-only character. They have the ability to call up their Holy Word: Shield, which absorbs all damage up to a certain hit point count. While shielded, their casting cannot be interrupted. Priests have some impressive damage spells including a quite painful DoT and an instant nuke. When battling Undead, they can use Chain Undead to neutralize the threat and then heal up. Their Debuff strips off buffs on enemies and enchantments, like Polymorph, off of allies. Add Mana Drain or Mind Control to the mix and they'll quickly change your thoughts on the "typical" Priest.

Rogue: Rogues have a crowd control ability (Sap) that knocks opponents out of commission while they regenerate hit points. This isn't the biggest worry, however. They have a bag full of high DPS tricks that tear you up should you let them get in close quarters. Even a Priest or Mage shield can barely stand up to their torrential strikes. Rogues are deadliest when not seen. Should they get the first strikes, you'll find yourself on the wrong side of the battle in a hurry. While it's possible to survive such an attack, it requires solid gameplay and all your tricks to do so.

Shaman: Shaman are powder kegs. Their totems can be powerful instruments for healing and buffing, offensive attacks and ability prevention. They fall within the mid-range on hit points and armor and can put out a considerable amount of damage. Shaman are a Horde-only class. They get to wear mail at higher levels making them even more difficult to take down. Durability being a strength of theirs, you never know what you'll be up against when confronting a Shaman.

Warlock: Warlocks need time to let their spells work. They are not fast and heavy damage dealers. They do, however, have some nice crowd control abilities and various pets to keep other players in check. Imps toss fireballs, Voidwalkers suck up damage and Succubi dish it out! Warlocks, with the aid of two other players, can summon in extra troops as well as provide Soulstones for other players that are one-use resurrection items.

Warrior: Warriors may not be ranged damage dealers, but in close quarters they can take damage and deal it out in kind. Their Charge stuns casters quite well and disrupts any spells they were about to cast. Allowing a Warrior to get within striking distance spells serious trouble. They are a powerhouse and one of the more feared PvP foes. Even when locked down, they offer plink damage with their guns or bows.

NORMAL SERVERS

PvP is readily available on all the servers offered for the *World of Warcraft*, however, on a normal server there are no contested zones in which PvP can occur between the factions like on a PvP server. PvP must be triggered by one of four ways. In all of these cases, PvP is kept as a consensual act between players.

Dueling Players can type in the command /duel while targeting someone and fight another player.

Attacking Opposite faction NPCs By attacking an NPC from the opposite faction, you will be flagged for PvP and thus can be attacked by anyone wishing to defend.

Battlegrounds Battlegrounds are built for PvP. By walking into a battleground you are giving your consent to engage in PvP.

Arena In Stranglethorn Vale there is an Arena available for FFA (free for all) PvP.

FACTIONAL PVP SERVERS

PvP servers offer a more challenging atmosphere than the normal servers when it comes to getting around the world in any kind of relative safety.

Within the world there are areas broken down into three categories: Horde Controlled, Alliance Controlled and Contested. If you're a Horde player in the Alliance lands, you can be attacked at any time by anyone, but cannot be the first to attack (unless you're targeting someone who's flagged for PvP). The same is true for an Alliance member in Horde territory. In contested areas, all players are flagged for PvP and can be attacked by the opposite team.

Contested areas can make for a difficult time while questing if you go it alone, so be smart and use the buddy system. It may just save your life (over and over). Each of the three zone types has a color indicator on your mini-map and in the title of the name of a zone you have just entered.

Red indicates that you're in enemy territory and thus vulnerable to attack. However, you cannot attack another player character that hasn't been tagged for PvP. You can however attack NPCs. Once attacked, you may retaliate in kind.

Yellow indicates a contested zone. Players of either faction can attack the other at any time.

Green indicates that you're in a safe zone. You cannot be attacked unless you instigate the attack in some way either by attacking a player directly or aiding an NPC or PC engaged in PvP.

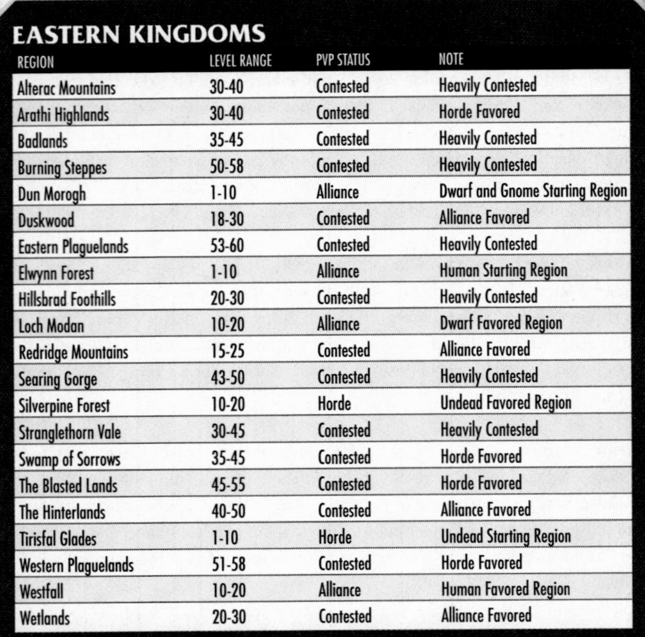

EASTERN KINGDOMS

REGION	LEVEL RANGE	PVP STATUS	NOTE
Alterac Mountains	30-40	Contested	Heavily Contested
Arathi Highlands	30-40	Contested	Horde Favored
Badlands	35-45	Contested	Heavily Contested
Burning Steppes	50-58	Contested	Heavily Contested
Dun Morogh	1-10	Alliance	Dwarf and Gnome Starting Region
Duskwood	18-30	Contested	Alliance Favored
Eastern Plaguelands	53-60	Contested	Heavily Contested
Elwynn Forest	1-10	Alliance	Human Starting Region
Hillsbrad Foothills	20-30	Contested	Heavily Contested
Loch Modan	10-20	Alliance	Dwarf Favored Region
Redridge Mountains	15-25	Contested	Alliance Favored
Searing Gorge	43-50	Contested	Heavily Contested
Silverpine Forest	10-20	Horde	Undead Favored Region
Stranglethorn Vale	30-45	Contested	Heavily Contested
Swamp of Sorrows	35-45	Contested	Horde Favored
The Blasted Lands	45-55	Contested	Horde Favored
The Hinterlands	40-50	Contested	Alliance Favored
Tirisfal Glades	1-10	Horde	Undead Starting Region
Western Plaguelands	51-58	Contested	Horde Favored
Westfall	10-20	Alliance	Human Favored Region
Wetlands	20-30	Contested	Alliance Favored

KALIMDOR

REGION	LEVEL RANGE	PVP STATUS	NOTE
Ashenvale Forest	18-30	Contested	Alliance Favored
Azshara	45-55	Contested	Alliance Favored
Darkshore	10-20	Alliance	Night Elf Favored
Desolace	30-40	Contested	Horde Favored
Durotar	1-10	Horde	Orc and Troll Starting Region
Dustwallow Marsh	34-45	Contested	Alliance Favored
Felwood	48-55	Contested	Heavily Contested
Feralas	40-50	Contested	Horde Favored
Mulgore	1-10	Horde	Tauren Starting Region
Stonetalon Mountains	15-27	Contested	Horde Favored
Tanaris Desert	40-50	Contested	Alliance Favored
Teldrassil	1-10	Alliance	Night Elf Starting Region
The Barrens	10-25	Horde	Horde Favored
Thousand Needles	25-35	Contested	Horde Favored
Un'Goro Crater	48-55	Contested	Heavily Contested
Winterspring	55-60	Contested	Alliance Favored

REWARDS, THE HONOR SYSTEM AND PVP GOALS

World of Warcraft is built for factional PvP; it's a world at war after all. By participating in PvP, players are able to earn points which help them gain favors in the game; some may earn special titles, some may earn a special tabard and it can even earn you a discount at some merchants—among other things.

The honor system works both in a positive and negative aspect. Those that kill NPCs or players that are much lower than their current level receive negative points. Over time, you may earn enough negative points to lose experience and even become KOS for your own faction (NPCs included). Those that attempt to gain honor by being involved in the defeat of players and NPCs of similar or higher levels gain rewards. With enough positive points, you may even earn the ability to gain access to special merchants and shops with items only available to a select few.

World of Warcraft is built on team play and team PvP; it's to be expected that there will be many team-oriented tasks within PvP to undertake. Achieving these goals will also net special rewards such as titles and even the possibility of a guild hall. The most nefarious of characters will attempt to go into the negative range to achieve infamy among all players. These will be the players to keep an eye out for since they will believe anyone is fair game thereafter.

PVP FLAGS AND TIMERS

It's important to take careful note of PvP flags and what they mean. Each side has a symbol that appears next to their character portrait that indicates whether or not they are in PvP mode. In order to be flagged for PvP, a player must be in duel mode, have been in (or are in) a contested area (including battlezones), or have assisted another player or NPC engaged in PvP.

Once you have been flagged as being in PvP, you must wait an additional 5 minutes after leaving a PvP area or engaging in PvP in a non-contested region before your flag will clear.

GROUP PVP

A well-oiled group can be a dominant force in nearly any situation unless matched by an evenly skilled and equipped force or outnumbered. Knowing and understanding your character as well as understanding the role of others around you can make all the difference between victory and defeat.

Party members will appear light green when they engage or are engaged in PvP. The two most important words to remember when being engaged in PvP are, "Don't Panic." When you feel that adrenaline rush begin to work it's way up into your face, try to take a deep breath and remain calm no matter how your palms may sweat. Whether you have been jumped or are among the jumpers, remaining calm keeps you focused on the job at hand.

Despite how fast it can all begin, the first and most important thing you can do is focus your efforts as a group on controlling and neutralizing one member at a time of the opposing force. Having one person in charge of letting everyone know who the target is works best. It's also important to choose whom you need to take down with some care. Each class has their own strengths and weaknesses and it's important to neutralize the stronger of the classes or members in a group first to ensure the members of your own survive the encounter.

The most effective groups are the ones that have worked together before. Hardly a word needs to be said to convey what needs to be done. For those times that something does need to be said, macros that have been built for use in PvE can just as easily be used in PvP if well constructed. A [/p attacking %t] macro can quickly and easily inform your party of who you're attacking at that moment and instruct them to focus their fire.

The best of groups are composed by at least one Priest, one Warrior, one Mage and any other variety of damage dealer or support class. While the Priest is busy trying to keep party members alive, it's important for the remaining party members to, in turn, protect the Priest. Once any healing classes in your party are taken out, all that is left to rely on are potions. However, there are very ingenious group make ups that can surprise others.

Seeing an odd group for the first time may catch you off guard. However, quickly assess their strengths and begin focusing on their weaknesses. If there's only one healer, the first target is obvious. If there is a Mage raining pain from outside of your range, either pull back out of their range or rush them. Seeing a group of five Mages sounds like an easy win, but the amount of damage and crowd control they can dish out would surprise many.

FOCUSING YOUR EFFORTS

It's important to keep in mind the most important targets to neutralize first. Learn the difference between "Soft" and "Hard" targets. Soft targets are generally cloth-wearing classes that can only take a minimum amount of damage before they die. A hard target is one that has to take a pounding before you gain any leverage and finally kill them. There are a few more considerations that you will need to make in a split second once the attack is on. Medium targets, as you can guess, are neither hard nor soft, thus surprisingly medium. These tend to be multi-ability leather wearers.

Caster classes tend to be soft targets, but when faced with many casters, there needs to be a prioritization put in place. Most often, Priests will be the first to be targeted. Given their ability to heal and shield (as well as resurrect), you do not want them to live to tell the tale of the battle when it's all said and done. Any class that heals is generally bad; by taking down the class that has the best healing capabilities you gain a bit of leverage. Mages tend to be the second target given their ability to crowd control by sheeping. They're glass cannons, however, and when engaged in close melee fall quickly and easily.

Soft Targets: Priests, Mages and Warlocks. These classes wear cloth and only have a limited number of hit points.

Medium Targets: Any leather-wearing class such as Rogues, Shaman, Druids and Hunters. Both Shaman and Hunters can wear mail in time bumping them into the edges of the Hard Target category.

Hard Targets: Warriors and Paladins. These are the heavy hitters that can give as well as they take. They take some time to kill and can do a lot of damage in the time that takes.

Most important of all is to work as a team in hunting down strays that try to get away. Letting yourself be baited into another trap does you and your group no good. If at all possible, the group should hunt down any stragglers that may be able to get with others to summon or that may be able to resurrect. Leave no enemy at your back and you may just make it out of the battle the victor—and alive.

DUELING

By selecting another player and typing in the command [/duel], players can fight each other one on one. A flag will drop between the duelers to indicate that a duel has begun. The fight ends not in a death, but in a near death. The defeated player takes on the prostrated stance of a supplicant and an announcement lets those in the area know who ended up the victor. Another way to instigate a duel is to right-click on a player's portrait and select the duel option.

The area in which players must fight is limited. Should you begin to stray, a warning box will appear. Should you not return to the dueling area, you will forfeit the duel.

There is a rule that most Rogues have that holds true for anyone. Being the first to issue the duel means you have no control over when the duel actually begins. That doesn't mean the other player can hold off for a long period of time; if the duel is not accepted within a reasonable amount of time, the duel option leaves. So, all good Rogues know, it's best to get the jump and control the timing of a fight than to be the one issuing the challenge.

THE ARENA

The arena is a free-for-all venue located in the heart of Stranglethorn Vale in the Eastern Kingdoms. By entering the area, all characters are able to kill any other character.

The arena is the same on any server and offers a venue in which many can come to compete in group or ladder competitions. As you enter, you'll notice that the location in your mini-map will have turned red indicating that you are vulnerable to attack. It's important that even as an observer, you keep on your toes. As in all arenas, fights may break out in the stands at any moment.

BATTLEGROUNDS

Battlegrounds act as a contested zone like the contested zones on the PvP server. They have quests and even team-based goals that need to be met just like any other area. They are a hotspot for PvP.

In each battleground you'll find a Horde town an Alliance town and various quests and monsters the same as you would in say a regular zone such as in Hillsbrad. Rewards will be commensurate with the risks involved and the goals achieved by either side, but overall experience should be higher than in any normal non-Battleground region.

It's important to work well as a team and create Raid groups in some cases in order to defeat another team's city, should that be your goal. Once the other city is defeated it's said to be razed to the ground. Battlegrounds foster and promote consistent excellence in teamwork and PvP by placing challenging situations before groups of players and guilds.

OPEN GROUND

Open ground fighting can be some of the most fun and challenging. Terrain can play a large part in how well you use line of sight to aid you in avoiding spells or catching your opponent off guard. Use the buddy system when out questing at the least. Having one other person with you may deter someone from deciding you are easy prey. Working in groups is always the best.

Undead have an advantage when it comes to working around water. They have no need to breathe and thus can use watery terrain to their advantage. For those that do breathe, remembering to watch your breath meter can be the difference between life and death at the hands of your enemy. Having a party member or a potion of underwater breathing can make all the difference in a pinch if you should find yourself at the disadvantage. It's best to avoid fighting near the water altogether however.

Casters will want to use distance and levels to fight. By finding the higher ground that takes some climbing to get to, they can sit in relative safety while their opponent either attempts to flee or attempts to scramble to reach them. More often than not, the caster will be raining down strikes the entire time.

Use the general channels to keep track of enemies in the zone. By letting others know of the enemy's whereabouts, they can be more alert for hostilities. Groups may be formed just to hunt them down and keep them from causing mischief. When in real need and unable to handle someone too high of level, it's best to call in some backup to come and clean things out. Communication can mean everything when out in an open zone. Enemies can hide anywhere and will take the opportunity to take the advantage at every chance they can.

TESTER PVP TIPS

There are many different strategies that players can use with their individual classes based on the talents and abilities they use. We have included some tester written strategies that may help you find your own PvP style.

TESTER TIP

PvP Tips as a Mage

by Terror

Survival

PvP is player on player combat. However, much of your adventuring in *Worlds of Warcraft* will have nothing to do with PvP interaction. There are quests, item gathering, instance hunting and just plain old experience gaining. Every player must take on these tasks, but doing simple tasks on a PvP server can sometimes change the whole dynamic. The biggest concern to most gamers who like PvP, but maybe are not as hardcore into it as others, is rather not how well they do in PvP, but how well they survive and even thrive in the environment. So this section is more about how to make the most of your time in a hostile setting, avoiding things like griefing so you can do other things the game requires.

First, there are some basic survival techniques for those travelers that try the encounters alone. In all things, you won't always have a small army to follow you around and protect you. Even while with friends, there are still times that your group can become the victim of a PvP raid or hunt. The way to protect yourself while you go about your non-PvP activity is to be smart. Much of the same things you would do in your normal life to avoid someone hostile, apply to your gaming environment as well. Safety is more assured in numbers. If you can take the opportunity to group in those areas you're unsure about, there's an increase in your chance to not only survive, but even best those hunting for someone to kill. Though being alone is most likely avoidable.

Always be aware of your surroundings. When you hunt, travel or even sit to rest, be sure to scan the area visually. With the exception of the Rogue class, you can see just about anyone coming for you and sometimes being aware of the attack. Removing that surprise can allow you to protect yourself or flee the danger. When I hunt, I like to use the terrain to my advantage. Much like the gun fighter who never sits with his back to the door, I employ the same theory when I hunt alone. I rest in the foliage. I rest with my back against a tree or hill. I find nooks and crannies to rest between my fights. The idea is simple, if you sit in the open, casually doing your thing, chances are someone will take that opportunity to attack you. Sometimes it's just smart to avoid the high traffic areas. You have a quest to do, at a place near a road that is often traveled by players. Instead of fighting near the road, find a more remote area to do your questing. This world is large and there are many things to do, just simply avoiding the high traffic areas can be enough to stave off the worst moments.

When you die, and you will, don't be in such a hurry to resurrect yourself and continue your business. Be smart approaching your corpse, look around for anyone camping your body looking to get another kill on you. Scout behind trees, rocks, etc. to see if they're hiding and waiting for you to pop up. Find the best possible distance and plan out a way to get away before you resurrect. Sometimes just thinking about the situation can help you avoid multiple deaths at the hand of a griefer.

Finally, if an area is just too over-populated with enemies, find something else to do. Remember, Azeroth is a large world, with many options for everyone. You don't need to spend hours attempting to do one quest and continually die at the hands of enemy players. Instead, find something else to do to make your gaming time more productive and fun. Dying a few times in a row via enemy attacks can be frustrating. It's much better to enjoy your time instead of becoming angry.

PvP Tips for a Mage

Looking to make your mark on the scene of PvP combat with your Mage? I have played a Mage almost my entire time during beta and I have some suggestions and concepts that have served me well. I don't claim to be the expert, obviously there are many opinions and viewpoints, and hopefully mine will help aspiring Mages become better PvPers.

Mages have three general types of spells, obviously you could fine tune this or call it something else, but this is my take on it. They are: Damage, Protection and Hampering spells. They make up the general basics of your spell pool in combat. It doesn't matter what line you might take, Arcane/Frost/Fire or a combo of them, you'll basically have the same type of spells. Combat with other players is very fast paced, some would say he who can twitch faster usually would win, but it's more than just twitching. A Mage who can correctly cast the right combination of spells will beat the twitch guy any day. There's a method to the encounters, each class has its weaknesses and strengths and some classes will always have a leg up on a Mage, just as a Mage will has its leg up on certain classes. The key is to correctly use your spells against your foe. What is that best combo? I say there are no right or wrong answers in combat. One time you may fight a Warrior that would attempt to use debuffs, snares and power blocks, that same Warrior might try to just out-damage you the next time. How you approach that fight depends on the situation; hopefully these tips help you correctly assess that situation.

Distance is your friend. A Mage who cannot keep his distance, usually ends up dead first. A Mage just doesn't have the ability to protect him/herself and no matter how fast you might guzzle a healing potion, it won't heal you enough to make a real difference. The fact is, the Mage is not meant to withstand much punishment; the Mage is meant to deal it. Keep your distance so that you can chew up casting time without being hit.

Also, a Mage has the ability to hamper and protect, though not great like a healer's ability to heal or shield, or a Shaman's ability to snare and buff resists, the Mage's hampering and protection is meant to be short lived and allow you to buy time to quickly out-damage your foe. A Mage can withstand a flurry of blows by casting Mana Shield, which absorbs some damage and allows you to root and gain distance on your foe to inflict more damage.

When fighting a melee type class, I want to root, snare and shield, in-between using my heaviest and quickest casting spells to damage them. Long casting spells do nothing but get you killed while you wait for any kind of damage output. Instant cast damage spells are great for PvP, as most can quickly put down your foe.

Against another caster, never underestimate a well-timed counter spell to mess up their rhythm. Casting requires a series of spells that you plan to use against your foe. When fighting another caster, anything that causes them to interrupt or block, can mean the difference in a fight. Remember, a caster requires line of sight for most spells, this can be a great advantage to even other casters—especially a Mage who has the ability to Blink.

Also, don't underestimate your ward spells. Having the ability to absorb fire or frost damage can come in handy when fighting casters that use those lines. (It also works for those melee fighters with imbued elemental effects on their weapons.) For example, a fire Mage that might attack you would have a hard time finishing you off if you a) take away some of their spell casts by casting fire ward, then b) Counterspell their next non-fire spell when they try to adapt. This forces them out of their rhythm and gives you the edge in the fight.

Don't forget other important spells like Dampen Magic against another caster or your Polymorph spell to buy you some time, regain your strategy and quickly unload your barrage.

There are some basic things I like to do. I prefer the fire damage line, mainly because I can gain Blastwave, add a stun to my fire spells, and decrease the duration of my instant Fire Blast. When I enter a fight, I like to Mana Shield for any pesky melee. I try to use distance against my opponents and strike from far away. If I have the advantage of surprise, I lead with Fireball, Fireblast and Scorch. If I think I can quickly kill them, I rush in after my Fireball to add in my Cone of Cold and Blastwave instant casts. Sometimes, I root at the end of that duration for that extra 100hp hit; that allows me to get another cast off.

When in a longer fight, I use the Scorch casts if I need to do anything. Usually all these spells, as well as my wand, are in my first bank so I can quickly cast them. I keep my secondary damage line spells on my second quick bar as well as some of my protection spells like Blink, Mana Shield, wards and heal potions. If I see a caster of any type make a long cast, I usually Counterspell it to mess up their timing. The best advice is don't be the victim; a Mage has to be quick on their feet at all times. Being cool in a fight and knowing what your basic plan of attack or defense is can win most encounters. Being caught by surprise is usually a sure way to end up dead. Enjoy!

TESTER TIP

PvP Tips for the Warlocks

by Ghoul

At this time, the Warlock is very strong in PvE but requires much planning, skill and zero mistakes to be successful in PvP. The Warlock thrives on use of their pet and DOTs, which takes time to kill their target. In PvP, another player will ignore the pet and go straight for the Warlock. The DOTs also make for a slow kill, so many players have time to heal or just flee. That is another issue I've found to be annoying playing this class in PvP. I can get the upper hand on players in many cases, but then they just run and I have no way to stop them. This has made my decision to take up Engineering to supplement my natural casting ability. The bombs stun and the Net-o-Matic stops enemies from running away.

Fear is the Warlock's greatest asset in PvP. It can keep your target off of you, allowing you to cast at will. The downside is that the target is also generally moving away from you, so if they're getting beat bad, they just keep on running. Also, you need to chase them to cast when they're Feared. A tactic I use is to try and Fear my target into an object like a wall or tree to plant it in place. Then I need not chase and can cast whatever I want.

Another trick up a Warlock's (spell) sleeve is the Curse of Tongues. At higher levels, this increases the target's casting time by 150%. This is very useful against casters and healers. The Warlock can also make Healthstones for an instant heal. A big problem in PvP is that a Warlock needs Soulshards to create the stones and summon pets. Shards do not stack, so it's hard to carry many and easy to use them up fast.

The last of the Warlock special spells is Banish. This takes a target out of the fight for 30 seconds. If you're alone and get attacked by multiple enemies make sure to Banish the healer.

The three combat-ready Warlock pets currently available have a wide range of abilities.

The Imp is a basic pet and requires no Shard to summon. This little guy gives a Weak Fire Shield to the summoner. It adds some Stamina to the group and has a low-end fire nuke. It's not a very impressive PvP pet.

The Voidwalker is the Warlock's main PvE soloing tank. It taunts and, if Sacrificed, gives a 10 second invulnerability. This pet does low melee damage and is virtually useless in PvP. It requires a Shard to summon.

Now, the Succubus is the third pet in the line and, in my opinion, is the most useful in PvP. They have an ability - Seduce - which sleeps a target for 10 seconds or until damage is done to it. This ability is very useful if a melee class or Rogue from stealth stuns you. Succubi can also go stealth themselves, so many times your opponent will think you're alone when you're not—surprise!

When in PvP I always hope to have my Succubus with me. If I'm attacked, I can Seduce my target right off then get in a free cast. If the target is a caster I lead off with Curse of Tongues. However, the rest of a standard battle spell set is as follows:

Immolate, Corruption, Curse of Agony (if it's a non-caster), Fear, Shadow Bolt, Shadow Bolt, Shadow Bolt, Fear, Shadow Bolt, Shadow Bolt. (Use bombs and Net-o-Matic as needed and if available.)

TESTER TIP

Shaman in PvP

by Shrikull

Strengths

Mobility: You get a 40% speed buff at 20; it's great for travel and scouting. It can be reduced to a 1 sec cast time via Talents and it's great for evasion if jumped.

Group Buffs via Totems: Shaman bring this to the group regardless of their level. A level 40 Shaman could easily offer many abilities to a group of level 60's (as an example).

Melee: Shaman can be formidable tanks with the Enhancement Talent spec.

Endurance: Shaman can simultaneously tank two or three mobs of equal level.

Limited CC: The AoE snare totem and insta DD snare can definitely be useful in a group situation.

PvP Tactics

Priest - Difficulty Rating: Easy

First, purge their shield and drop a snare totem. Then, feel free to tank a bit and use the insta DD snare or DD shock for spell interrupts.

Mage - Difficulty Rating: Medium (if they get the jump)

The best tactic is to drop a grounding totem and a fire or frost resist totem. Use DD shock for spell interrupts and purge any shield they bring up. Tank them, use the snare totem or DD snare to keep them from gaining distance.

Mages can be a pain, since they'll typically root you. At this point you have a few options: the grounding totem would be the best choice, followed by casting heal, a free action potion or chugging a heal potion as soon as you're damaged. If possible, Shock them to interrupt, but more than likely you won't have range for it. Once free from the root, close the distance and snare/interrupt or you're dead.

Paladin - Difficulty Rating: Easy to Medium

Use the snare totem coupled with DD snares. Kite them as long as you can while inflicting damage and then tank a bit when they're weak.

Paladins can offer a long fight. Try to get a snare on them, rush into melee and force them to use their shield. If they do, then back off and wait for it to expire and conserve mana. Kite them with snares until you're confident that you could handle a melee encounter and never count out their ability to Lay Hands when they're near death.

Druid - Difficulty Rating: Easy

Drop a snare totem, strip any buffs they may have, and then tank them. Follow this up with the insta DD snare and use the DD shock for interrupting their casts. The Druids offer a unique since they can root and heal. This can be problematic.

Rogue - Difficulty Rating: Medium to Hard

If they jump you, you're in deep trouble. Snare totem, chug a heal, shift into the ghost wolf and try to kite or just run outright. If you can jump them, Snare Totem, kite with DD snares, and melee once they're weak.

Warrior - Difficulty Rating: Hard

Even without constant stunning, Warriors are still our banes. Snare them, kite them with DDs and totems and only join into melee when you're feeling crazy. Run and come back with friends.

Warlock - Difficulty Rating: Easy

Snare them, ignore their pet, and jump into melee combat. They're currently on the low end of the totem pole when it comes to being dangerous.

Hunter - Difficulty Rating: ?

Unfortunately, I never fought one. I would close the distance as fast as possible, snare the pet in the process, and then jump into melee while using the DD snare on the Hunter.

General Tips

There are a few things to know when it comes to PvP. If you're going to melee, always have your Lightning Shield up. When it expires, recast it. Always drop a Stoneskin Totem for melee damage reduction and have a weapon proc up. I prefer Windfury, but Rockbiter is not bad either.

Depending on your Talent spec, you'll have more options. This spec gives you the ability to cast lesser heals for 1000hp with only a 25% chance of interrupt and insta cast 1 heal every 5 minutes for 1600hp at level 60. This may be able to allow us to beat down Warriors and any other classes will be cake.

I also recommend Alchemy/Herbalism. I use potions constantly and they are quite often the decision maker in many fights. Potions coupled with a decent Restoration spec make you very hard to kill.

TESTER TIP

A Warrior's Choices

by Indalamar

Forget all those bad memories of mindlessly beating on someone while the casters do all the work. This is *World of Warcraft* and here Warriors reign supreme. In the following write up, I'll explain how to play a Warrior against each of the classes. There are several fundamentals of a Warrior that do not change regardless of who you're fighting. Under ideal circumstances, you'll always be able to lead the fight with Charge, which gives you some Rage and allows you to close the distance to your target almost instantly. Secondly, always keep your target snared; fortunately, Warriors have the best snare in the game. Hamstring will quickly become your best friend; when upgraded, it can snare your opponent to 40% of his normal speed. Open every fight possible with the Charge + Hamstring combo. I will describe what to do in the event that you can't lead with this combo.

This write up is from the perspective of a level 60 Undead Warrior. My talent spec is as follows.

Arms

5 Deflection
5 Tactical Mastery
3 Improved Rend
3 Deep Wound
2 Impale
1 Improved Charge
1 Anger Management
5 Two Hand Weapon Specialization
1 Sweeping Strikes
2 Improved Hamstring
1 Mortal Strike

Fury

5 Cruelty
5 Improved Demoralizing Shout
5 Enrage
4 Improved Inner Rage
1 Piercing Howl

Vs. Druid

Druids are relatively easy to take down. They're part healer and part nuker leaving them slightly lacking in both departments. The one thing you need to watch out for when fighting a Druid is their root spell. A Druid's main form of damage is an instant cast nuke with a DOT attached. All of the spells that you need to concern yourself with are from the Nature line. Their root and heals are both nature spells which are easy to pick out due to the glowing green hands the Druid has when using them. They'll try to root you and throw in an occasional nuke. If you get rooted, pull out your ranged weapon and start shooting. Make sure that you watch the root duration closely; the second it breaks, rush in with a Hamstring. As with any healing class, the key to victory is to wait until you have them around 25% health and Pummel their heal. This shuts out all of their healing and defensive spells long enough to finish them off.

Vs. Hunter

Hunters can hurt if they get the jump on you. They have a couple of snare abilities and a self run speed buff. If a good Hunter catches you off guard, you'll be in for a difficult fight. If the Hunter is trying to kite you, Hamstring the pet to take it out of the fight while you chase the Hunter. If the Hunter is using his run speed buff, pause for a moment. When he turns to run, hit him with a range attack. The Hunters' run buff dazes them any time they're hit; Daze is a 50% snare. After you get your ranged attack in, they'll be snared—same as you. Continue this process while keeping Hamstring applied to the pet and you should be able to close the gap eventually. Once you manage to get in close, the fight's over and you win.

Vs. Mage

Mages are one of the toughest opponents you'll face as a Warrior. Mages have the ability to keep you rooted or snared for a considerable amount of time. Their upfront Damage is considerable. The moment you close the gap on a good Mage, he'll root you and Blink out of melee range. Pull out your ranged weapon and start shooting. As with the Druid's root, make sure you watch the root timer closely and make a mad dash for them the second it breaks. The Mage will more than likely be using Arcane Missiles on you while you're rooted or when you begin to run at them. Hit them with a Pummel the moment you're in range. This locks out their Arcane line which, in turn, shuts down Arcane Explosion, Blink, and Polymorph. If you can survive through the initial barrage of instant nukes that they'll throw in your face, you should be able to take them down relatively easy. Surviving the initial barrage is the hardest part though and comes down to your hit point pool and resist rates.

Vs. Paladin

Paladins don't pose any real threat to Warriors, even the Undead kind. Paladin battles tend to follow this trend. Warrior Hamstrings Paladin. Paladin begins to beat on Warrior and realizes he's losing. Paladin uses Invulnerability and heals himself. The Invulnerability wears off and the Paladin fights some more. Paladin then realizes he is still losing and uses his second Invulnerability and heals again. Invulnerability wears off and Paladin realizes he is still losing, Paladin dies. The worst thing that can happen here is the Paladin stuns you, throws up his shield and runs away. As long as you Pummel the first spell you see him cast to shut out his Holy line, there won't be anything to worry about.

Vs. Priest

Priests pose almost no threat to a Warrior. When you engage in melee, they'll use their AE fear. Make sure you get Hamstring on them before that happens and it'll be almost impossible for you to lose. They have two lines of spells: Shadow and Holy. Shadow spells are their damage spells and Holy are their healing. Don't Pummel their Shadow spells; wait until you see their hands glowing yellow and Pummel them. The yellow glowing means they're casting a holy spell. Regardless of which spell you stop, it shuts down their entire Holy line and prevents them from healing. As long as you keep them snared and in melee range, they won't put up any fight.

Vs. Rogue

The Rogues range from cakewalks to tough cookies. Rogues are very dependent on special attacks and, if they miss even one of their opening or finishing moves, they'll be relatively easy. As always, make sure you stick them with Hamstring immediately. Once they're snared, hit them with Rend so if they manage to slip into stealth or Vanish, it'll break when Rend does its DOT. Switch to Defensive stance, but just for long enough to disarm them and switch back to Battle Stance. Rogues can dish out the damage very fast, but they can't take a hit. There's a good chance that they'll have you snared with their poisons, so you have to make sure you don't let them get out of melee with you. If a Rogue gets away from you long enough to hide in stealth, and they'll hit you with Cheap Shot—then you're in trouble. Make sure to keep them engaged and snared at all times. As long as they don't get lucky with crits on their special attacks, you should be fine since their hps will give out before yours.

Vs. Shaman

Shaman can be a difficult fight because of their ability to snare you constantly. In addition, their grounding totem prevents some of your abilities from working on them. To make matters worse, most of their damage comes from instant nukes so they can continue to dish out the damage while running. This makes it very hard to get a Hamstring in. If you're unable to land Hamstring before they snare you, continue running towards them at all times, but quickly change your target to their Earthbind totem and crush it. With any luck, the Shaman will be too busy trying to stay away from you to realize that you aren't snared any more. Once you have the Shaman snared, he dies as fast as any other healer. Shaman only have one line of healing and it is Nature based. The moment you see their hands begin to glow green, hit them with a Pummel and that will seal their doom.

Vs. Warlock

Warlocks will, by far, be your hardest fight. Since Undead are immune to Fear, I have always made short work of Warlocks. However, for any other race there's almost nothing you can do to beat a good Warlock. You're only real hope is to engage them, use Inner Rage followed by Intimidating Shout and hope that the stun coupled with a Pummel will be enough to kill them. The most dangerous Warlock ability is their ability to keep you Feared until you die. Do not use Pummel until you see their hands glow black; this is their Darkness line that holds their Fear spell. If you can prevent them from getting off a Fear, you'll win.

Vs. Warrior

Their match up is simply about who has better gear and more skill. There are a few tips I can give when fighting other Warriors. First, make sure you keep them snared. If you get them snared before they snare you, run out of melee range and use your ranged weapon to try to get an hp advantage. Second, make sure you land Disarm as soon as possible. Third, try to get off your Intimidating Shout before they get theirs off.

I hope these basics help you in your adventures. The most important thing to remember, regardless of who you're fighting, is to always always always keep Hamstring applied to your target.

CRAFTING & PROFESSIONS

CHOOSING A PATH

Azeroth is full of many exciting discoveries and, for some, it comes in the form of its robust and interesting crafting system. Players can create various items and equipment as long as they have the right materials, tools and skill level.

You can pick two main Professions per character. Those choices are between: Alchemy, Blacksmithing, Enchanting, Engineering, Herbalism, Leatherworking, Mining, Skinning, and Tailoring. To complement these profession options, there are also secondary skills available to each character. There isn't a limit to the amount of these you may choose to incorporate into your character. They are: Cooking, First Aid, and Fishing.

Professions are a way to modify, or even improve, your character by offering more adventuring options beyond questing and grinding. The available products are wondrous: weapons and armor, potions and oils, bombs and shrinking devices, etc. True, you can't do all of them at once, so one of your first decisions is to decide which professions and secondary skills you'd like to have.

CONSIDER THE OPTIONS

Each class may, at first glance, look to be geared toward a certain profession. However, it would be a lie to say that Warriors never choose to be Tailors. You must decide what's more important to you. Do you wish to have a profession that can supplement your character class or one geared solely to the path of mercantilism? Are you interested in supplementing your combat (PvE and PvP) with gadgets and bombs or does having the ability to enchant your weapons to suit the occasion sound more interesting? You're not restricted to a specific profession based on your class. Mages can be Blacksmiths if they wish and Paladins can work with cloth; it's up to you.

BASIC CONCEPTS

Every profession focused on manufacturing (or enchanting) uses resources found in the game to create another product or service. All professions rely on other professions, or at least their products—some more heavily than others. The following table gives a brief description of each profession and trade skill while offering hints at which ones work well together.

PROFESSION QUICK LIST

PROFESSION	TYPICAL COMBO	PROFESSION TYPE	DESCRIPTION
Alchemist	Herbalism	Manufacturer	Makes potions and elixers with various attributes. Transmutation of metals and elements is also available to those that reach higher levels of Alchemy.
Blacksmith	Mining	Gatherer	Makes mail and plate armor, as well as metal weapons of all types, with the exception of what many consider "wooden weapons" like bows, crossbows, staves, etc.
Enchanter	Any	Producer	Enchants weapons with permanent spell effects. Disenchants items to attain resources, offering more options than simply selling items you may not use.
Engineer	Mining	Manufacturer	Engineers create gadgets, guns, bombs, etc. Many of the gadgets are usable only by other Engineers. They also create amazing mechanical pets and trinkets.
Herbalist	Alchemy	Gatherer	Tracking down herbs to be used in other professions is their specialty. Alchemists are always in need of herbs.
Leatherworker	Skinning	Manufacturer	Leather armor can only be made by those working in this profession. Leatherworkers also produce armor kits that strengthen all types of armor by increasing the AC.
Miner	Blacksmithing or Engineering	Gatherer	Discovering and mining deposits of ore is restricted to the Miners. In addition to the raw ore, a lucky Miner may discover a gem hidden in a vein.
Skinner	Leatherworking	Gatherer	Harvests the leather and hides from beasts slain in combat. Skinners supplement many professions and are in demand from many classes.
Tailor	Any	Manufacturer	Casters love tailors since they provide the cloth raiments of the land. Tailors also create bags usable by each class for more storage (both in the bank and on one's person).

SECONDARY SKILL QUICK LIST

TRADE SKILL	DESCRIPTION
Cook	Gather meats and parts of slain beasts and turn it all into tasty foods that replenish health. This often saves people from having to shop for food in towns.
First Aid	Heals adventurers with bandages maid from cloth. At higher levels, those with this skill also learn how to cure poisons which is often a life saver.
Fisher	Gathers fish and treasure from the bodies of water spread across Azeroth. Some fish are used in Alchemy and many are edible; pearls are used in Tailoring and Blacksmithing. However, the true prize is reeling in a chest of unknown treasure!

All items necessary to excel in your chosen line of work can be purchased from others in the game if necessary. It's very possible to be an Engineer and a Blacksmith if you have the gold to buy the ore and stone that you need. Guilds and friends are often key (exploited) in providing materials for such pursuits. Teamwork can be a huge advantage. One person producing ore to barter for armor and weapons is the foundation of a budding economy.

Of course, there's no rule saying that you must "make" something. Some players focus on gathering resources in exchange for gold and nothing more. There's plenty of room for herbalists, miners, skinners and fishers who wish to sell their wares and be done. The truth is, those with an abundance of gold are often willing to pay a premium in lieu of gathering the materials for themselves. Gathering raw resources is free, so anything you make is a profit. There will inevitably be continued debate on get rich quick schemes, but there's no doubting that gathering resources, in exchange for hard currency, is a viable option.

The obvious goal is to become the best crafter possible, regardless of which profession you choose. Maximizing your gold to do so in the cheapest and most efficient way possible is key. Everything available to crafters has a color. For example, Tailoring patterns and ore deposits each have a specific color depending on your level in the appropriate profession. Here's a breakdown.

GRAY is indicative of an easy thing to do. Whether creating something or harvesting, you won't receive any skill points for this.

GREEN is trivial and there's only a slight chance to gain a skill point by making/harvesting the item.

YELLOW is average and there's a good chance to skill up. This is often the best method for power leveling a craft since it offers cheaper components and quick rewards, but there's always the chance that you won't get level.

ORANGE offers a challenge. You have a 100% chance to gain a skill point, but there's a higher chance of failure. You won't lose any components on a failed attempt, you just have to continue trying until you succeed. Time is the only cost.

RED indicates that your skill level is to low and that it's impossible to harvest or create the item at that time.

It doesn't matter if you're Mining, Tailoring, Smithing, etc. Those colors always mean the same thing and represent the same chance of a skill up. The most assured way to level your skill is to make or harvest orange items. It could be more costly than working on yellows, but you'll definitely fly up the ranks.

Some items, with the same skill requirement, have better returns or use fewer materials. If you're trying to level up, focus on items that give a solid return while using as little of your resource pool as necessary. A good example of a trade off is when a yellow item uses two things and an orange one uses six. Sure, you'll get a point for the orange one, but by making the yellow, you have the potential for gaining three points with the same materials. However, there's also a slim risk that you'll make no progress.

Always watch for the change in color as you level. If you're just creating the same item over and over, it could very well change to green status and have no value beyond the item itself. It doesn't always happen on a set number, so pay attention. For this one reason, it's not always smart to hit the "create all" button. Follow this rule: If you're interested in skilling up, pay close attention; if you want the items, create as many as you'd like.

All professions have specific trainers that teach their craft. The big six cities typically house them all, but there are trainers hidden in the wild, in smaller towns, and even in dungeons/instances that may offer different recipes/patterns/plans/etc. It's important to visit the main trainers once every 5-10 ranks or so while starting out. After you begin attaining higher levels, pay attention to your rank and only visit when you must. As you learn new skills, they're automatically added to your menu. You need to advance in a profession to be able to learn better skills.

RANKS:

APPRENTICE: Requires Level 5 and allows you to gain skills up to 75.

JOURNEYMAN: Requires Apprentice and Level 10. Allows skills up to 150.

EXPERT: Requires Journeyman and Level 20. Allows skills up to 250.

ARTISAN: Requires Expert and Level 35. Allows skills up to 300.

TRAINER LEVEL	CAN TRAIN LEVEL
Journeyman	Apprentice
Expert	Journeyman and below
Artisan	Expert and below
Master	Artisan and below

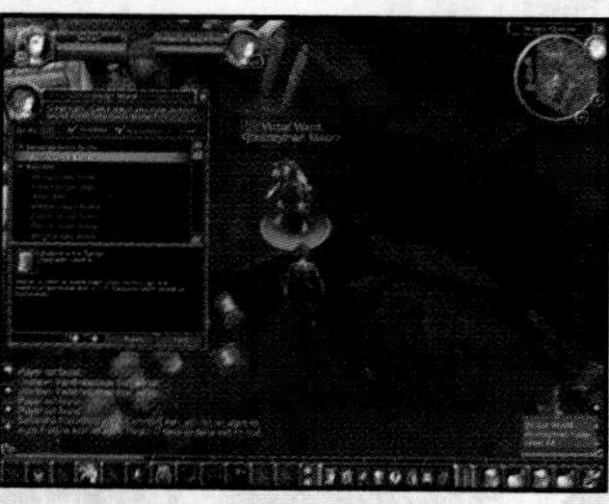

Not all trainers can teach you something new. As you level up, it's inevitable that you'll begin to surpass the knowledge of some trainers. Here's a breakdown of trainers and which levels of knowledge they offer.

Plans, recipes, and schematics can be purchased at your trainer. However, there are some that are dropped, received from quests, or purchased from hidden trainers around Azeroth. Some drops are extremely rare. Getting your hands on a rare set of plans and being the first to make that item for the market can make you rich quick. Dropped plans generally make an item much better than currently made items for that respective level. Rare plans, recipes, etc. are often some of the items that create the most voracious bidding. If you find a recipe or schematic as a drop, make sure to consult with someone before tossing it up at the auction house for a few silver.

EQUIPMENT AND TOOLS

Some professions require equipment and some don't. A Blacksmith needs a hammer (Blacksmith's Hammer) to make armor, but an Herbalist just needs their hands. There are three types of equipment geared toward the professions in the game.

STORE-BOUGHT

Items and components like Blacksmith's Hammers, Mining Picks, Skinning Knives, vials, thread, etc. are all purchasable from vendors. You can generally get most items at the general vendors and you only need to buy these once. In the case of equipment, they simply need to be in your packs (not your bank) and you'll draw the item once you initiate the action, whether it's mining ore or skinning a boar. However, for vials, thread, flux, etc., you'll need the item on you and you'll use the required amount depending on how many are required. That number will be drawn from your inventory.

PLAYER-MADE

Some skills, as you level, require the trader to use different, player-made items. This can be a potion for a Tailoring pattern or an Arclight Spanner for an Engineer, while Enchanters require Runed Rods. Keep the items in your packs when you wish to use them.

PERMANENT

Some items require you to travel to them. An Anvil isn't something that you can toss in your pack and carry around, nor is a forge. (However, if anyone will discover a way it's those crafty Gnomes.) When something like this is required, it will be noted in the recipe/pattern. You don't need to click the item, just get close enough to receive its effect.

GATHERER PROFESSIONS

The skills of Mining, Skinning and Herbalism are gathering skills. You won't be making anything, or need to make anything, to gather. These vocations supply other professions by providing resources necessary for them to ply their trades.

HERBALISM

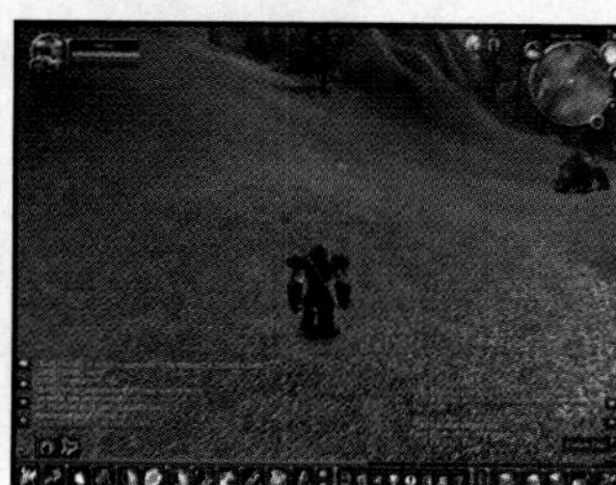

Your first skill is Find Herbs. Drag this icon from your ability book (P) into your hotkey bar, then hit the corresponding number or click it to activate it. Once you activate it you'll only need to refresh it on death or after logging in.

HERB	SKILL LEVEL
Peacebloom	1
Silverleaf	1
Earthroot	15
Mageroyal	50
Swiftthistle	50
Briarthorn	70
Stranglekelp	85
Bruiseweed	100
Wild Steelbloom	115
Grave Moss	120
Kingsblood	125
Liferoot	150
Fadeleaf	160
Goldthorn	170
Khadgar's Whisker	185
Wintersbite	195
Firebloom	205
Purple Lotus	210
Sungrass	230
Blindweed	235
Ghost Mushroom	245
Gromsblood	250
Dreamfoil	270
Plaguebloom	???

While out adventuring, yellow dots may appear on your mini map when any herbs are nearby, indicating their location.

If you mouse over the yellow dot on the mini map, you can discover which type of herbs are around.

When you're next to the plant, mouse over it to check the required skill level necessary to harvest it. Right-click on the plant to gather the herbs. It takes a few seconds and, if you're successful, a loot window opens with the herbs you found.

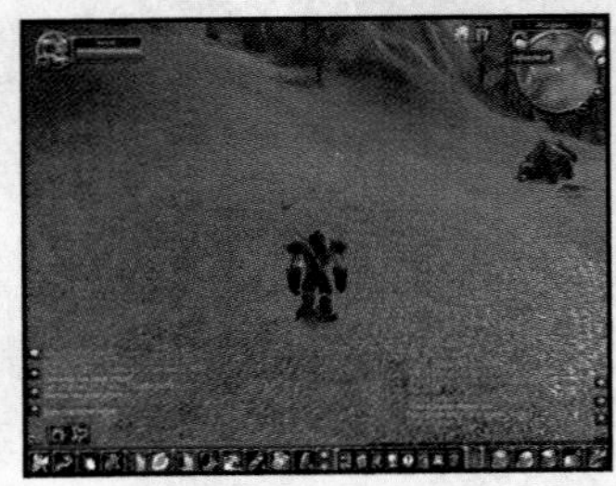

It's possible to get a few of the herbs from each plant and there are times when a bonus herb is included. (Swiftthistle is found on Mageroyal, Bruiseweed, Briarthorn, etc.)

MINING

Mining ore is crucial to the economy and, possibly, to another of your chosen professions. Copper, tin, on up are available at the swing of a pick, but jewels await the lucky. Find Minerals is the first skill granted to miners. Use it to go out and about to find your Copper. Drag the icon from your ability book (P) into your hotkey bar. Once you activate it, only death, logging, or choosing to hunt herbs removes its effect. A yellow dot appears on your mini map while you're out adventuring to indicate that there's ore to be found!

Mouse over the yellow dot on the mini map to discover what type of ore is available.

Once you reach a vein, mouse over it to check the skill level required to mine it.

Right-click the node to begin mining. After a few swings, your character will kneel down and check what you've found. However, a failure leaves your character standing over the node in an upright position. Right-click on the ore, stone, and - if you're lucky - gem, to place it into your backpack.

Even if you don't want the items, you need to remove them all from the node, otherwise, you'll continue to receive the same item. Repeat the process until the node disappears. Although you can swing at a vein multiple times, you only receive a point on the very first swing. Tapping a node multiple times will not level you up more quickly and it's good to share with other miners in your group if you're so inclined.

Once you gather a load of ore, return to a forge and smelt it into bars. Again, pull the Smelting icon from your ability menu (P) and drag it to your hotkey bar. While near the forge, you'll be able to change one ore into one bar. You may choose to do this all at once by selecting "create all," or one at a time if you want to manage your ore supply better.

MINING TABLE

PROCESS	SKILL LEVEL	SOURCE	COMPONENT(S)
Smelt Copper	1	Initial	1 Copper Ore
Smelt Bronze	65	Trained	1 Copper Bar, 1 Tin Bar
Smelt Tin	65	Trained	1 Tin Ore
Smelt Silver	75	Trained	1 Silver Ore
Smelt Iron	125	Trained	1 Iron Ore
Smelt Gold	155	Trained	1 Gold Ore
Smelt Steel	165	Trained	1 Iron Bar, 1 Coal
Smelt Mithril	175	Trained	1 Mithril Ore
Smelt Truesilver	230	Trained	1 Truesilver Ore
Smelt Thorium	250	Trained	1 Thorium Ore
Smelt Dark Iron	???	Unknown	8 Dark Iron Ore

SKINNING

When beasts are killed in the wild, Skinners swoop in to take their hides and any leather from their corpses. You'll need a Skinning Knife in your pack to do this. You must wait for the person who currently has looting rights to loot the animal. Once all the items are taken off the body, right-click it to begin skinning.

If you're successful, a loot window opens showing what you've managed to take off the body. The types of leather and hides depends on the level of the animal combined with a bit of randomness. Animals bordering the next tier may have a random Medium Leather hidden among the Light Leathers. Skinning higher level beasts offers better leather and hides.

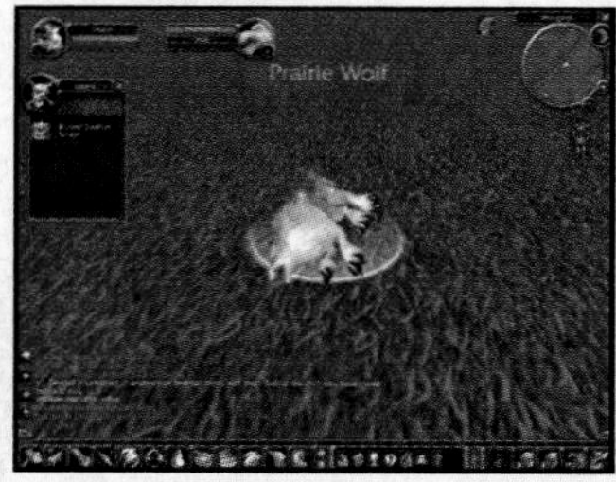

LAMB'S WOOL

Skinning sheep earns you wool, not leather. Keep this in mind if you have any friends who've chosen the path of a Tailor.

One thing you'll notice while hunting is that groups without a Skinner among them tend to leave beast corpses all around. It's a great idea to snag their skins while hunting on your own. It wouldn't be out of the ordinary to see a lone skinner trailing behind a solid group scavenging their leftovers.

MANUFACTURING PROFESSIONS

Making items is one of the most rewarding aspects of choosing a profession. The ability to take raw resources and use what knowledge you've gained to create potions or armor, or to enchant a sword to give it that fiery glow is something worth pursuing. Sure, it's not a bad way to increase the influx of gold either.

All the skills ramp up quickly at first, but as you gain higher levels, your progress slows to a more steady pace. As long as you continue to make items of appropriate levels, you'll continue to level up. Having a guild to supply you with gold or resources is a great way to whip through the early levels, but don't think that it's necessary. Even on your own, given the right career choices, you'll be able to become an artisan in your chosen field.

Along with the decrease in the rate of rank accumulation, you'll also notice that many of the higher level items have more required items to make them. A high end item may require that you adventure for a week to accumulate enough materials to create it. It's common to see a rare item sell for great money if it's part of a recipe or pattern. Pearls and gems are great examples. Black Pearls and Star Rubies are some of the most sought after commodities.

It's fair to say that if you bought all of the resources to create a high level item that someone, in return, is going to have to pay a pretty penny to have you create it for them. However, some items will require you to pay more for the resources than even the most interested of clients is willing to pay for the completed item. Be careful when choosing what to make and how much to pay for the resources.

There are times, however, when money is no object. If you can make a robe that can double a caster's current stat boosts, they're going to pay for it.

ALCHEMY

Taking herbs, mixing them up in a vial, and creating a potion sounds exciting, no? The low level potions are typically the least interesting, but that makes them no less useful. Low level adventurers would be glad to pay for Lesser, and even Minor, Healing and Mana Potions. However, it's the high end potions and elixers that really get people to dig into their pockets.

Invisibility Potions, Strength Potions, Defense Potions, Agility Potions—all of these are within reach of the alchemist. The list is huge and everyone loves the alchemist. Well, one that shares, anyway. There are no tools required for this profession, but you have to purchase vials whereas other vocations get away with not having to purchase materials constantly.

To create a potion, open your ability menu (P) and drag the Alchemy icon into your hotbar. Activating the icon opens the Alchemy menu and immediately displays which potions you have available to you.

Click on the name of the recipe to discover which reagents you'll need. It shows how many of each item also. Make sure you have all the appropriate ingredients (including the vials) in your bags before trying to create potions. The menu indicates which potions you can make and how many of each (depending on your resources) can be made as well. Mouse over the icon to see what the effects of the potion are.

As soon as you create a potion, it appears in your packs. To use it, either right-click it or drag it to your hotbar for easy access.

Alchemists have also learned how to transmute semi-rare ore and elements into rare types. Yes, you can transmute iron to gold, mithril to truesilver and more. You'll need to make your own Philosophers' Stone to do this and the ingredients are hard to find. However, this skill will be appreciated. You have to take 1-2 day breaks in-between doing these amazing feats.

It's really not too hard to level up this skill fast if you have Herbalism. The herbs you find are free and, as long you remember to have your Find Herbs skill up and running, you should have plenty of herbs. You'll use your potions constantly. Your groupmates, guildmates and strangers in the field will want them. They sell very well in the auction houses. It's not like you need to find someone who needs a potion; everyone wants them all the time.

This is a vocation that isn't tied down by having to return to town to work. If you keep a few empty vials on you, you can make potions while in the field.

Potions are generally used in combat and often have a 2 minute timer, whereas Elixers can often be used as often and as quickly as you'd like.

NO ROOM

If you're trying to create potions when your bags are full, you won't be able to add the potion to your inventory. This may become a problem at the lower levels when you've only got your backpack and a 6-slot or two. Storing all your resources in the bank is a good way to alleviate this problem. Continue piling up resources until you decide to create a bunch of potions. Then, transfer any stacks to your bank and continue creating them.

ALCHEMY

PRODUCT	SKILL LEVEL	SOURCE	REAGENT(S)
Elixir of Lion's Strength	1	Initial	1 Earthroot, 1 Silverleaf, 1 Empty Vial
Elixir of Minor Defense	1	Initial	2 Silverleaf, 1 Empty Vial
Minor Healing Potion	1	Initial	1 Peacebloom, 1 Silverleaf, 1 Empty Vial
Weak Troll's Blood Potion	15	Trained	1 Peacebloom, 2 Earthroot, 1 Empty Vial
Minor Mana Potion	25	Trained	1 Mageroyal, 1 Silverleaf, 1 Empty Vial
Minor Rejuvenation Potion	40	Trained	2 Mageroyal, 1 Peacebloom, 1 Empty Vial
Discolored Healing Potion	50	Found	1 Discolored Worg Heart, 1 Peacebloom, 1 Empty Vial
Elixir of Minor Agility	50	Found	1 Swiftthistle, 1 Silverleaf, 1 Empty Vial
Elixir of Minor Fortitude	50	Trained	2 Earthroot, 1 Peacebloom, 1 Empty Vial
Lesser Healing Potion	55	Trained	1 Minor Healing Potion, 1 Briarthorn
Rage Potion	60	Found	1 Sharp Claw, 1 Briarthorn, 1 Empty Vial
Swiftness Potion	60	Found	1 Swiftthistle, 1 Briarthorn, 1 Empty Vial
Elixir of Tongues	70	Found	2 Earthroot, 2 Mageroyal, 1 Empty Vial
Blackmouth Oil	80	Trained	2 Oily Blackmouth, 1 Empty Vial
Elixir of Giant Growth	90	Found	1 Deviate Fish, 1 Earthroot, 1 Empty Vial
Elixir of Water Breathing	90	Trained	1 Stranglekelp, 2 Blackmouth Oil, 1 Empty Vial
Elixir of Wisdom	90	Trained	1 Mageroyal, 2 Briarthorn, 1 Empty Vial
Holy Protection Potion	100	Found	1 Bruiseweed, 1 Swiftthistle, 1 Empty Vial
Swim Speed Potion	100	Trained	1 Swiftthistle, 1 Blackmouth Oil, 1 Empty Vial
Healing Potion	110	Trained	1 Bruiseweed, 1 Briarthorn, 1 Leaded Vial
Minor Magic Resistance Potion	110	Found	3 Mageroyal, 1 Wild Steelbloom, 1 Empty Vial
Elixir of Poison Resistance	120	Found	1 Large Venom Sac, 1 Bruiseweed, 1 Leaded Vial
Lesser Mana Potion	120	Trained	1 Mageroyal, 1 Stranglekelp, 1 Empty Vial
Cowardly Flight Potion	125	Found	1 Delicate Feather, 1 Kingsblood, 1 Leaded Vial
Strong Troll's Blood Potion	125	Trained	2 Bruiseweed, 2 Briarthorn, 1 Leaded Vial
Elixir of Defense	130	Trained	1 Wild Steelbloom, 1 Stranglekelp, 1 Leaded Vial
Fire Oil	130	Trained	2 Firefin Snapper, 1 Empty Vial
Shadow Protection Potion	135	Found	1 Grave Moss, 1 Kingsblood, 1 Leaded Vial
Elixir of Firepower	140	Trained	2 Fire Oil, 1 Kingsblood, 1 Leaded Vial
Elixir of Lesser Agility	140	Found	1 Wild Steelbloom, 1 Swiftthistle, 1 Leaded Vial
Elixir of Ogre's Strength	150	Found	1 Earthroot, 1 Kingsblood, 1 Leaded Vial
Free Action Potion	150	Found	2 Blackmouth Oil, 1 Stranglekelp, 1 Leaded Vial
Greater Healing Potion	155	Trained	1 Liferoot, 1 Kingsblood, 1 Leaded Vial
Mana Potion	160	Trained	1 Stranglekelp, 1 Kingsblood, 1 Leaded Vial
Fire Protection Potion	165	Found	1 Small Flame Sac, 1 Fire Oil, 1 Leaded Vial
Lesser Invisibility Potion	165	Trained	1 Fadeleaf, 1 Wild Steelbloom, 1 Leaded Vial
Shadow Oil	170	Trained	4 Fadeleaf, 4 Grave Moss, 1 Leaded Vial
Elixir of Fortitude	175	Trained	1 Wild Steelbloom, 1 Goldthorn, 1 Leaded Vial
Great Rage Potion	175	Found	1 Large Fang, 1 Kingsblood, 1 Leaded Vial
Mighty Troll's Blood Potion	180	Found	1 Liferoot, 1 Bruiseweed, 1 Leaded Vial
Elixir of Agility	185	Trained	1 Stranglekelp, 1 Goldthorn, 1 Leaded Vial
Frost Protection Potion	190	Found	1 Wintersbite, 1 Goldthorn, 1 Leaded Vial
Nature Protection Potion	190	Found	1 Liferoot, 1 Stranglekelp, 1 Leaded Vial
Elixir of Detect Lesser Invisibility	195	Found	1 Khadgar's Whisker, 1 Fadeleaf, 1 Leaded Vial
Elixir of Greater Defense	195	Trained	1 Wild Steelbloom, 1 Goldthorn, 1 Leaded Vial
Catseye Elixir	200	Trained	1 Goldthorn, 1 Fadeleaf, 1 Leaded Vial
Frost Oil	200	Trained	4 Khadgar's Whisker, 2 Wintersbite, 1 Leaded Vial
Greater Mana Potion	205	Trained	1 Khadgar's Whisker, 1 Goldthorn, 1 Leaded Vial
Oil of Immolation	205	Trained	1 Firebloom, 1 Goldthorn, 1 Crystal Vial
Goblin Rocket Fuel	210	Found	1 Firebloom, 1 Volatile Rum, 1 Leaded Vial
Magic Resistance Potion	210	Found	1 Khadgar's Whisker, 1 Purple Lotus, 1 Crystal Vial
Lesser Stoneshield Potion	215	Found	1 Mithril Ore, 1 Goldthorn, 1 Leaded Vial
Superior Healing Potion	215	Trained	1 Sungrass, 1 Khadgar's Whisker, 1 Crystal Vial
Philosophers' Stone	225	Found	4 Iron Bar, 1 Black Vitriol, 4 Purple Lotus, 4 Firebloom
Transmute: Iron to Gold	225	Found	1 Iron Bar
Transmute: Mithril to Truesilver	225	Found	1 Mithril Bar
Wildvine Potion	225	Found	1 Wildvine, 1 Purple Lotus, 1 Crystal Vial
Dreamless Sleep Potion	230	Trained	3 Purple Lotus, 1 Crystal Vial
Elixir of Detect Undead	230	Trained	1 Arthas' Tears, 1 Crystal Vial
Arcane Elixir	235	Trained	1 Blindweed, 1 Goldthorn, 1 Crystal Vial
Elixir of Greater Intellect	235	Trained	1 Blindweed, 1 Khadgar's Whisker, 1 Crystal Vial
Invisibility Potion	235	Found	1 Ghost Mushroom, 1 Sungrass, 1 Crystal Vial
Elixir of Dream Vision	240	Found	3 Purple Lotus, 1 Crystal Vial
Elixir of Greater Agility	240	Trained	1 Sungrass, 1 Goldthorn, 1 Crystal Vial
Gift of Arthas	240	Found	1 Arthas' Tears, 1 Blindweed, 1 Crystal Vial
Elixir of Giants	245	Found	1 Sungrass, 1 Gromsblood, 1 Crystal Vial
Ghost Dye	245	Found	2 Ghost Mushroom, 1 Purple Dye, 1 Crystal Vial
Elixir of Demonslaying	250	Found	1 Gromsblood, 1 Ghost Mushroom, 1 Crystal Vial
Elixir of Detect Demon	250	Trained	2 Gromsblood, 1 Crystal Vial
Elixir of Shadow Power	250	Found	3 Ghost Mushroom, 1 Crystal Vial
Limited Invulnerability Potion	250	Found	2 Blindweed, 1 Ghost Mushroom, 1 Crystal Vial
Stonescale Oil	250	Trained	1 Stonescale Eel, 1 Leaded Vial
Mighty Rage Potion	255	Found	3 Gromsblood, 1 Crystal Vial
Superior Mana Potion	260	Found	2 Sungrass, 2 Blindweed, 1 Crystal Vial
Elixir of Superior Defense	265	Found	2 Stonescale Oil, 1 Sungrass, 1 Crystal Vial
Elixir of the Sages	270	Found	1 Dreamfoil, 2 Plaguebloom, 1 Crystal Vial
Elixir of Brute Force	275	Found	2 Gromsblood, 2 Plaguebloom, 1 Crystal Vial
Major Healing Potion	275	Found	2 Golden Sansam, 1 Mountain Silversage, 1 Crystal Vial
Transmute: Air to Fire	275	Found	1 Essence of Air
Transmute: Arcanite	275	Found	1 Thorium Bar, 1 Arcane Crystal
Transmute: Earth to Water	275	Found	1 Essence of Earth
Transmute: Fire to Earth	275	Found	1 Essence of Fire
Transmute: Water to Air	275	Found	1 Essence of Water
Elixir of the Mongoose	280	Found	2 Mountain Silversage, 2 Plaguebloom, 1 Crystal Vial
Greater Stoneshield Potion	280	Found	3 Stonescale Oil, 1 Thorium Ore, 1 Crystal Vial
Greater Arcane Elixir	285	Found	3 Dreamfoil, 1 Mountain Silversage, 1 Crystal Vial
Purification Potion	285	Found	2 Icecap, 2 Plaguebloom, 1 Crystal Vial
Greater Arcane Protection Potion	290	Found	1 Dream Dust, 1 Dreamfoil, 1 Crystal Vial
Greater Fire Protection Potion	290	Found	1 Elemental Fire, 1 Dreamfoil, 1 Crystal Vial
Greater Frost Protection Potion	290	Found	1 Elemental Water, 1 Dreamfoil, 1 Crystal Vial
Greater Holy Protection Potion	290	Found	1 Elemental Air, 1 Dreamfoil, 1 Crystal Vial
Greater Nature Protection Potion	290	Found	1 Elemental Earth, 1 Dreamfoil, 1 Crystal Vial
Greater Shadow Protection Potion	290	Found	1 Shadow Oil, 1 Dreamfoil, 1 Crystal Vial
Major Mana Potion	295	Found	3 Dreamfoil, 2 Icecap, 1 Crystal Vial
Alchemist's Stone	300	Found	8 Essence of Fire, 8 Essence of Earth, 8 Essence of Air, 8 Essence of Water, 8 Living Essence, 2 Black Vitriol, 4 Black Lotus
Restorative Elixir	???	Quest	1 Elemental Earth, 1 Goldthorn, 1 Crystal Vial

BLACKSMITHING

Smiths are some of the most popular crafters. Not only do you create mail and plate armor, but weapons too! True, only four of the nine classes will ever require a Blacksmith for armoring needs, but each class could benefit from a new weapon now and then. Even Priests choose to learn how to use daggers now and then. However, the best Blacksmiths use leather, cloth, and even jewels, in their creations.

A Blacksmith's Hammer must be in your pack. Though that may sound obvious, it's often forgotten in the bank by an anxious smith wanting to try out a new pattern. You'll also need an anvil upon which to bang that hammer. Pull the Blacksmithing icon from your abilities menu (P) into your hotbar and activate it. This brings up your Blacksmithing menu and shows you all the plans you currently have available.

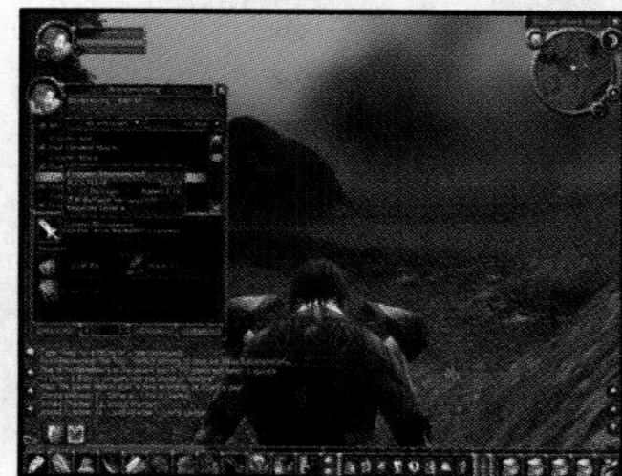

Click on the name of a plan to see what components you need. It shows you how many of each component you have in your bags and how many items of that plan you can make. It also gives you the option to make one or many in a row. Mouse over the icon of the desired item to find out the stats on it.

Once you've made an item, it drops into your packs automatically. At level 250, it's difficult to find a trainer in a main city that can train you. However, by finding dropped patterns and hidden trainers, you can continue your knowledge gathering. Some quests offer rewards for you as well. These require you to craft certain items and, in return, teach you new patterns as a quest reward. One of the quest lines leads you to the Mithril Order. It's not an easy quest chain, but the reward is the ability to craft a full set of mithril plate armor!

Once you've attained a high enough level, you must choose a new path. Decide whether you wish to focus on weapons and carry the title Weaponsmith, or become an Armorsmith. Both paths require quests and both are mutually exclusive. If you choose one path, the other is closed to you. If becoming a Weaponsmith interests you, you may be interested to discover that an even more specialized line allows you to choose between Hammersmith, Swordsmith, or Axesmith (again, mutually exclusive lines that require quests). Many high end patterns require the ability of an artisan in the appropriate line.

Blacksmithing is not a very fast skill to level up. You're often sharing ore available to Engineers and they're not scarce. Other Blacksmiths also compete for available ore in the auction houses. It's expensive to buy since the demand is so high. In the early stages, you may think that it's not too bad. However, as the resources become rarer, the prices and fervor that the items demand becomes even worse.

It's not a get rich quick profession, but some of the high end items sell for a ton and they're very desirable. Of course, it's because they're so difficult to make. Casual players can expect to either drop a good chunk of money on the resources or spend a couple weeks gathering all the materials required.

The good news is you can make some money. Every class needs something at a certain level. Rogues need daggers that you make that are hard to impossible to find through quests or drops at certain levels. Different classes will be desperate for a good weapon or piece of armor. The market demands that Blacksmiths fill these gaps and this gives you that extra surge of cash you'll need. You won't sell most of what you make early on, but you'll sell lots of certain pieces, especially if you find the rare dropped plans.

BLACKSMITHING

PRODUCT	SKILL LEVEL	SOURCE	COMPONENT(S)
Copper Bracers	1	Initial	2 Copper Bar
Copper Chain Pants	1	Trained	4 Copper Bar
Rough Copper Vest	1	Initial	4 Copper Bar
Rough Sharpening Stone	1	Initial	1 Rough Stone
Rough Weightstone	1	Initial	1 Rough Stone, 1 Linen Cloth
Copper Mace	15	Trained	6 Copper Bar, 1 Weak Flux, 2 Linen Cloth
Copper Axe	20	Trained	6 Copper Bar, 1 Weak Flux, 2 Linen Cloth
Copper Chain Boots	20	Trained	8 Copper Bar
Copper Shortsword	25	Trained	6 Copper Bar, 1 Weak Flux, 2 Linen Cloth
Rough Grinding Stone	25	Trained	2 Rough Stone
Copper Claymore	30	Trained	10 Copper Bar, 2 Weak Flux, 1 Rough Grinding Stone, 1 Light Leather
Copper Dagger	30	Trained	6 Copper Bar, 1 Weak Flux, 1 Rough Grinding Stone, 1 Light Leather
Copper Battle Axe	35	Trained	12 Copper Bar, 2 Weak Flux, 2 Malachite, 2 Rough Grinding Stone, 2 Light Leather
Copper Chain Belt	35	Trained	6 Copper Bar
Copper Chain Vest	35	Found	8 Copper Bar, 1 Malachite, 2 Rough Grinding Stone
Runed Copper Gauntlets	40	Trained	8 Copper Bar, 2 Rough Grinding Stone
Runed Copper Pants	45	Trained	8 Copper Bar, 2 Fine Thread, 3 Rough Grinding Stone
Gemmed Copper Gauntlets	60	Found	8 Copper Bar, 1 Tigerseye, 1 Malachite
Coarse Sharpening Stone	65	Trained	1 Coarse Stone
Coarse Weightstone	65	Trained	1 Coarse Stone, 1 Wool Cloth
Heavy Copper Maul	65	Trained	12 Copper Bar, 2 Weak Flux, 2 Light Leather
Ironforge Chain	70	Found	12 Copper Bar, 2 Malachite, 2 Rough Grinding Stone
Runed Copper Belt	70	Trained	10 Copper Bar
Thick War Axe	70	Trained	10 Copper Bar, 2 Weak Flux, 2 Silver Bar, 2 Rough Grinding Stone, 2 Light Leather
Coarse Grinding Stone	75	Trained	2 Coarse Stone
Runed Copper Breastplate	80	Found	12 Copper Bar, 1 Shadowgem, 2 Rough Grinding Stone
Runed Copper Bracers	90	Trained	10 Copper Bar, 3 Rough Grinding Stone
Heavy Copper Broadsword	95	Trained	14 Copper Bar, 2 Weak Flux, 2 Tigerseye, 2 Medium Leather
Rough Bronze Boots	95	Trained	6 Bronze Bar, 6 Rough Grinding Stone
Big Bronze Knife	100	Trained	6 Bronze Bar, 4 Weak Flux, 2 Rough Grinding Stone, 1 Tigerseye, 1 Medium Leather
Ironforge Breastplate	100	Found	16 Copper Bar, 2 Tigerseye, 3 Rough Grinding Stone
Rough Bronze Bracers	100	Found	4 Bronze Bar
Silver Rod	100	Trained	1 Silver Bar, 2 Rough Grinding Stone
Silver Skeleton Key	100	Trained	1 Silver Bar, 1 Rough Grinding Stone
Rough Bronze Cuirass	105	Trained	7 Bronze Bar
Rough Bronze Leggings	105	Trained	6 Bronze Bar
Bronze Mace	110	Trained	6 Bronze Bar, 4 Weak Flux, 1 Medium Leather
Pearl-handled Dagger	110	Trained	6 Bronze Bar, 1 Strong Flux, 2 Small Lustrous Pearl, 2 Coarse Grinding Stone
Rough Bronze Shoulders	110	Trained	5 Bronze Bar, 1 Shadowgem, 1 Coarse Grinding Stone
Bronze Axe	115	Trained	7 Bronze Bar, 4 Weak Flux, 1 Medium Leather
Bronze Shortsword	120	Trained	5 Bronze Bar, 4 Weak Flux, 2 Medium Leather
Patterned Bronze Bracers	120	Trained	5 Bronze Bar, 2 Coarse Grinding Stone
Bronze Warhammer	125	Trained	8 Bronze Bar, 1 Strong Flux, 1 Medium Leather
Deadly Bronze Poniard	125	Found	4 Bronze Bar, 1 Strong Flux, 1 Swiftness Potion, 2 Shadowgem, 2 Coarse Grinding Stone, 2 Medium Leather
Heavy Grinding Stone	125	Trained	3 Heavy Stone
Heavy Sharpening Stone	125	Trained	1 Heavy Stone
Heavy Weightstone	125	Trained	1 Heavy Stone, 1 Wool Cloth
Silvered Bronze Shoulders	125	Found	8 Bronze Bar, 2 Silver Bar, 2 Coarse Grinding Stone
Bronze Greatsword	130	Trained	12 Bronze Bar, 2 Strong Flux, 2 Medium Leather
Heavy Bronze Mace	130	Trained	8 Bronze Bar, 1 Strong Flux, 1 Moss Agate, 1 Shadowgem, 2 Coarse Grinding Stone, 2 Medium Leather
Silvered Bronze Boots	130	Trained	6 Bronze Bar, 1 Silver Bar, 2 Coarse Grinding Stone
Silvered Bronze Breastplate	130	Found	10 Bronze Bar, 2 Silver Bar, 2 Coarse Grinding Stone, 1 Lesser Moonstone
Bronze Battle Axe	135	Trained	14 Bronze Bar, 1 Strong Flux, 2 Medium Leather
Silvered Bronze Gauntlets	135	Trained	8 Bronze Bar, 1 Silver Bar, 2 Coarse Grinding Stone
Iridescent Hammer	140	Found	10 Bronze Bar, 1 Strong Flux, 1 Iridescent Pearl, 2 Coarse Grinding Stone, 2 Medium Leather
Ironforge Gauntlets	140	Found	8 Bronze Bar, 3 Shadowgem, 4 Coarse Grinding Stone
Green Iron Boots	145	Found	4 Iron Bar, 2 Lesser Moonstone, 2 Coarse Grinding Stone, 1 Green Dye

PRODUCT	SKILL LEVEL	SOURCE	COMPONENT(S)
Mighty Iron Hammer	145	Found	6 Iron Bar, 2 Strong Flux, 1 Elixir of Ogre's Strength, 2 Lesser Moonstone, 2 Coarse Grinding Stone, 2 Medium Leather
Shining Silver Breastplate	145	Trained	20 Bronze Bar, 2 Moss Agate, 2 Lesser Moonstone, 2 Iridescent Pearl, 4 Silver Bar
Golden Rod	150	Trained	1 Gold Bar, 2 Coarse Grinding Stone
Golden Skeleton Key	150	Trained	1 Gold Bar, 1 Heavy Grinding Stone
Green Iron Gauntlets	150	Found	4 Iron Bar, 2 Small Lustrous Pearl, 2 Coarse Grinding Stone, 1 Green Dye
Iron Buckle	150	Trained	1 Iron Bar
Iron Shield Spike	150	Found	6 Iron Bar, 4 Coarse Grinding Stone
Green Iron Leggings	155	Trained	8 Iron Bar, 1 Heavy Grinding Stone, 1 Green Dye
Silvered Bronze Leggings	155	Found	12 Bronze Bar, 4 Silver Bar, 2 Coarse Grinding Stone
Solid Iron Maul	155	Trained	8 Iron Bar, 2 Strong Flux, 1 Heavy Grinding Stone, 4 Silver Bar, 2 Heavy Leather
Barbaric Iron Breastplate	160	Found	20 Iron Bar, 4 Heavy Grinding Stone
Barbaric Iron Shoulders	160	Found	8 Iron Bar, 4 Sharp Claw, 2 Shadowgem, 2 Heavy Grinding Stone
Green Iron Shoulders	160	Found	7 Iron Bar, 1 Heavy Grinding Stone, 1 Green Dye
Hardened Iron Shortsword	160	Trained	6 Iron Bar, 2 Strong Flux, 1 Heavy Grinding Stone, 2 Lesser Moonstone, 3 Heavy Leather
Green Iron Bracers	165	Trained	6 Iron Bar, 1 Green Dye
Iron Counterweight	165	Found	4 Iron Bar, 2 Coarse Grinding Stone, 1 Lesser Moonstone
Golden Iron Destroyer	170	Found	10 Iron Bar, 4 Gold Bar, 2 Lesser Moonstone, 2 Strong Flux, 2 Heavy Leather, 2 Heavy Grinding Stone
Golden Scale Leggings	170	Found	10 Iron Bar, 2 Gold Bar, 1 Heavy Grinding Stone
Green Iron Helm	170	Trained	12 Iron Bar, 1 Citrine, 1 Green Dye
Barbaric Iron Helm	175	Found	10 Iron Bar, 2 Large Fang, 2 Sharp Claw
Golden Scale Shoulders	175	Found	6 Steel Bar, 2 Gold Bar, 1 Heavy Grinding Stone
Jade Serpentblade	175	Found	8 Iron Bar, 2 Strong Flux, 2 Heavy Grinding Stone, 2 Jade, 3 Heavy Leather
Barbaric Iron Boots	180	Found	12 Iron Bar, 4 Large Fang, 4 Tigerseye, 2 Heavy Grinding Stone
Glinting Steel Dagger	180	Trained	10 Steel Bar, 2 Strong Flux, 1 Moss Agate, 1 Elemental Earth, 1 Heavy Leather
Green Iron Hauberk	180	Trained	20 Iron Bar, 4 Heavy Grinding Stone, 2 Jade, 2 Moss Agate, 1 Green Leather Armor
Moonsteel Broadsword	180	Trained	8 Steel Bar, 2 Strong Flux, 2 Heavy Grinding Stone, 3 Lesser Moonstone, 3 Heavy Leather
Barbaric Iron Gloves	185	Found	14 Iron Bar, 3 Heavy Grinding Stone, 2 Large Fang
Golden Scale Bracers	185	Trained	5 Steel Bar, 2 Heavy Grinding Stone
Massive Iron Axe	185	Trained	14 Iron Bar, 2 Strong Flux, 2 Heavy Grinding Stone, 4 Gold Bar, 2 Heavy Leather
Polished Steel Boots	185	Found	8 Steel Bar, 1 Citrine, 1 Lesser Moonstone, 2 Heavy Grinding Stone
Golden Scale Coif	190	Found	8 Steel Bar, 2 Gold Bar, 2 Heavy Grinding Stone
Searing Golden Blade	190	Found	10 Steel Bar, 4 Gold Bar, 2 Elemental Fire, 2 Heavy Leather
Steel Weapon Chain	190	Found	8 Steel Bar, 2 Heavy Grinding Stone, 4 Heavy Leather
Golden Scale Cuirass	195	Found	12 Steel Bar, 2 Gold Bar, 4 Heavy Grinding Stone, 2 Jade
Frost Tiger Blade	200	Found	8 Steel Bar, 2 Strong Flux, 2 Heavy Grinding Stone, 2 Jade, 1 Frost Oil, 4 Heavy Leather
Golden Scale Boots	200	Found	10 Steel Bar, 4 Gold Bar, 4 Heavy Grinding Stone, 1 Citrine
Inlaid Mithril Cylinder	200	Found	5 Mithril Bar, 1 Gold Bar, 1 Truesilver Bar
Shadow Crescent Axe	200	Found	10 Steel Bar, 2 Strong Flux, 3 Heavy Grinding Stone, 2 Citrine, 1 Shadow Oil, 3 Heavy Leather
Solid Grinding Stone	200	Trained	4 Solid Stone
Solid Sharpening Stone	200	Trained	1 Solid Stone
Solid Weightstone	200	Trained	1 Solid Stone, 1 Silk Cloth
Steel Breastplate	200	Trained	16 Steel Bar, 3 Heavy Grinding Stone
Truesilver Rod	200	Trained	1 Truesilver Bar, 1 Heavy Grinding Stone
Truesilver Skeleton Key	200	Trained	1 Truesilver Bar, 1 Solid Grinding Stone
Golden Scale Gauntlets	205	Found	10 Steel Bar, 4 Gold Bar, 4 Heavy Grinding Stone, 1 Citrine
Heavy Mithril Gauntlet	205	Trained	6 Mithril Bar, 4 Mageweave Cloth
Heavy Mithril Shoulder	205	Trained	8 Mithril Bar, 6 Heavy Leather
Heavy Mithril Axe	210	Trained	12 Mithril Bar, 2 Citrine, 1 Solid Grinding Stone, 4 Heavy Leather
Heavy Mithril Pants	210	Found	10 Mithril Bar, 2 Lesser Moonstone

PRODUCT	SKILL LEVEL	SOURCE	COMPONENT(S)
Mithril Scale Pants	210	Trained	12 Mithril Bar
Mithril Scale Bracers	215	Found	8 Mithril Bar, 2 Citrine
Mithril Shield Spike	215	Found	4 Mithril Bar, 2 Truesilver Bar, 4 Solid Grinding Stone
Steel Plate Helm	215	Trained	14 Steel Bar, 1 Solid Grinding Stone
Blue Glittering Axe	220	Found	16 Mithril Bar, 2 Aquamarine, 1 Solid Grinding Stone, 4 Thick Leather
Mithril Scale Gloves	220	Found	8 Mithril Bar, 6 Heavy Leather, 4 Mageweave Cloth
Ornate Mithril Gloves	220	Found	10 Mithril Bar, 6 Mageweave Cloth, 1 Truesilver Bar, 1 Solid Grinding Stone
Ornate Mithril Pants	220	Found	12 Mithril Bar, 1 Truesilver Bar, 1 Solid Grinding Stone, 1 Aquamarine
Ornate Mithril Shoulders	225	Found	12 Mithril Bar, 1 Truesilver Bar, 6 Thick Leather
Truesilver Gauntlets	225	Trained	10 Mithril Bar, 8 Truesilver Bar, 3 Aquamarine, 3 Citrine, 1 Guardian Gloves, 2 Solid Grinding Stone
Wicked Mithril Blade	225	Found	14 Mithril Bar, 4 Truesilver Bar, 1 Solid Grinding Stone, 2 Thick Leather
Big Black Mace	230	Trained	16 Mithril Bar, 1 Black Pearl, 4 Shadowgem, 1 Solid Grinding Stone, 2 Thick Leather
Heavy Mithril Breastplate	230	Trained	16 Mithril Bar
Mithril Coif	230	Trained	10 Mithril Bar, 6 Mageweave Cloth
Orcish War Leggings	230	Found	12 Mithril Bar, 1 Elemental Earth
Heavy Mithril Boots	235	Trained	14 Mithril Bar, 4 Thick Leather
Mithril Scale Shoulders	235	Found	14 Mithril Bar, 4 Thick Leather, 4 Citrine
Mithril Spurs	235	Found	4 Mithril Bar, 3 Solid Grinding Stone
The Shatterer	235	Trained	24 Mithril Bar, 4 Core of Earth, 6 Truesilver Bar, 5 Citrine, 5 Jade, 4 Solid Grinding Stone, 4 Thick Leather
Dazzling Mithril Rapier	240	Found	14 Mithril Bar, 1 Aquamarine, 2 Lesser Moonstone, 2 Moss Agate, 1 Solid Grinding Stone, 2 Mageweave Cloth
Ornate Mithril Breastplate	240	Found	16 Mithril Bar, 6 Truesilver Bar, 1 Heart of Fire, 1 Solid Grinding Stone
Heavy Mithril Helm	245	Found	14 Mithril Bar, 1 Aquamarine
Ornate Mithril Boots	245	Found	14 Mithril Bar, 2 Truesilver Bar, 4 Thick Leather, 1 Solid Grinding Stone, 1 Aquamarine
Ornate Mithril Helm	245	Found	16 Mithril Bar, 2 Truesilver Bar, 1 Black Pearl, 1 Solid Grinding Stone
Phantom Blade	245	Trained	28 Mithril Bar, 6 Breath of Wind, 8 Truesilver Bar, 2 Lesser Invisibility Potion, 6 Aquamarine, 4 Solid Grinding Stone, 2 Thick Leather
Runed Mithril Hammer	245	Found	18 Mithril Bar, 2 Core of Earth, 1 Solid Grinding Stone, 4 Thick Leather
Truesilver Breastplate	245	Trained	12 Mithril Bar, 24 Truesilver Bar, 4 Star Ruby, 4 Black Pearl, 2 Solid Grinding Stone
Blight	250	Trained	28 Mithril Bar, 10 Ichor of Undeath, 10 Truesilver Bar, 6 Solid Grinding Stone, 6 Thick Leather
Dense Grinding Stone	250	Trained	4 Dense Stone
Dense Sharpening Stone	250	Trained	1 Dense Stone
Dense Weightstone	250	Trained	1 Dense Stone, 1 Runecloth
Thorium Armor	250	Found	16 Thorium Bar, 1 Blue Sapphire, 4 Yellow Power Crystal
Thorium Belt	250	Found	12 Thorium Bar, 4 Red Power Crystal
Ebon Shiv	255	Found	12 Mithril Bar, 6 Truesilver Bar, 2 Star Ruby, 1 Solid Grinding Stone, 2 Thick Leather
Thorium Bracers	255	Found	12 Thorium Bar, 4 Blue Power Crystal
Radiant Belt	260	Found	10 Thorium Bar, 2 Heart of Fire
Thorium Greatsword	260	Found	16 Thorium Bar, 2 Dense Grinding Stone, 4 Rugged Leather
Truesilver Champion	260	Trained	30, Mithril Bar, 16 Truesilver Bar, 6 Star Ruby, 4 Breath of Wind, 8 Solid Grinding Stone, 6 Thick Leather
Dark Iron Pulverizer	265	Found	18 Dark Iron Bar, 4 Heart of Fire
Imperial Plate Belt	265	Found	12 Thorium Bar, 1 Blue Sapphire
Imperial Plate Shoulders	265	Found	14 Thorium Bar, 6 Rugged Leather, 1 Blue Sapphire
Bleakwood Hew	270	Found	30, Thorium Bar, 6 Living Essence, 6 Wildvine, 6 Large Opal, 2 Dense Grinding Stone, 8 Rugged Leather
Dark Iron Mail	270	Found	10 Dark Iron Bar, 2 Heart of Fire
Imperial Plate Bracers	270	Found	16 Thorium Bar, 2 Aquamarine
Inlaid Thorium Hammer	270	Found	30, Thorium Bar, 4 Gold Bar, 2 Truesilver Bar, 2 Blue Sapphire, 4 Rugged Leather
Radiant Breastplate	270	Found	18 Thorium Bar, 2 Heart of Fire, 1 Star Ruby
Wildthorn Mail	270	Found	40 Thorium Bar, 2 Enchanted Thorium Bar, 4 Living Essence, 4 Wildvine, 1 Huge Emerald
Arcanite Rod	275	Trained	3 Arcanite Bar, 1 Dense Grinding Stone
Arcanite Skeleton Key	275	Trained	1 Arcanite Bar, 1 Dense Grinding Stone
Dark Iron Sunderer	275	Found	26 Dark Iron Bar, 4 Heart of Fire

PRODUCT	SKILL LEVEL	SOURCE	COMPONENT(S)
Dawn's Edge	275	Found	30, Thorium Bar, 4 Enchanted Thorium Bar, 4 Star Ruby, 4 Blue Sapphire, 2 Dense Grinding Stone, 4 Rugged Leather
Ornate Thorium Handaxe	275	Found	20 Thorium Bar, 2 Large Opal, 2 Dense Grinding Stone, 4 Rugged Leather
Thorium Shield Spike	275	Found	4 Thorium Bar, 4 Dense Grinding Stone, 2 Essence of Earth
Blazing Rapier	280	Found	10 Enchanted Thorium Bar, 4 Essence of Fire, 4 Heart of Fire, 2 Azerothian Diamond, 2 Dense Grinding Stone
Dark Iron Shoulders	280	Found	6 Dark Iron Bar, 1 Heart of Fire
Enchanted Battlehammer	280	Found	20 Thorium Bar, 6 Enchanted Thorium Bar, 2 Huge Emerald, 4 Powerful Mojo, 4 Rugged Leather
Huge Thorium Battleaxe	280	Found	40 Thorium Bar, 6 Dense Grinding Stone, 6 Rugged Leather
Thorium Boots	280	Found	20 Thorium Bar, 8 Rugged Leather, 4 Green Power Crystal
Thorium Helm	280	Found	24 Thorium Bar, 1 Star Ruby, 4 Yellow Power Crystal
Dark Iron Breastplate	285	Found	20 Dark Iron Bar, 8 Heart of Fire
Demon Forged Breastplate	285	Found	40 Thorium Bar, 10 Demonic Rune, 4 Blue Sapphire, 4 Star Ruby
Radiant Gloves	285	Found	18 Thorium Bar, 4 Heart of Fire
Rune Edge	285	Found	30, Thorium Bar, 2 Large Opal, 2 Dense Grinding Stone, 4 Rugged Leather
Serenity	285	Found	6 Enchanted Thorium Bar, 2 Arcanite Bar, 4 Powerful Mojo, 2 Large Opal, 2 Blue Sapphire, 1 Huge Emerald
Corruption	290	Found	40 Thorium Bar, 2 Arcanite Bar, 16 Demonic Rune, 8 Essence of Undeath, 2 Blue Sapphire, 2 Dense Grinding Stone, 4 Rugged Leather
Dawnbringer Shoulders	290	Found	20 Thorium Bar, 4 Arcanite Bar, 2 Huge Emerald, 2 Essence of Water
Fiery Plate Gauntlets	290	Found	20 Thorium Bar, 6 Enchanted Thorium Bar, 2 Essence of Fire, 4 Star Ruby
Radiant Boots	290	Found	14 Thorium Bar, 4 Heart of Fire
Volcanic Hammer	290	Found	30, Thorium Bar, 4 Heart of Fire, 4 Star Ruby, 4 Rugged Leather
Imperial Plate Boots	295	Found	30, Thorium Bar, 2 Blue Sapphire
Imperial Plate Helm	295	Found	30, Thorium Bar, 1 Huge Emerald, 2 Aquamarine
Radiant Circlet	295	Found	18 Thorium Bar, 4 Heart of Fire
Storm Gauntlets	295	Found	20 Thorium Bar, 4 Enchanted Thorium Bar, 4 Essence of Water, 4 Blue Sapphire
Annihilator	300	Found	40 Thorium Bar, 12 Arcanite Bar, 10 Essence of Undeath, 8 Huge Emerald, 2 Dense Grinding Stone, 4 Enchanted Leather
Arcanite Champion	300	Found	15 Arcanite Bar, 8 Azerothian Diamond, 1 Righteous Orb, 4 Large Opal, 8 Enchanted Leather, 2 Dense Grinding Stone
Arcanite Reaper	300	Found	20 Arcanite Bar, 6 Enchanted Leather, 2 Dense Grinding Stone
Blood Talon	300	Found	10 Enchanted Thorium Bar, 10 Arcanite Bar, 8 Demonic Rune, 10 Star Ruby, 2 Dense Grinding Stone
Enchanted Thorium Breastplate	300	Found	18 Enchanted Thorium Bar, 1 Essence of Earth
Enchanted Thorium Helm	300	Found	12 Enchanted Thorium Bar, 1 Essence of Earth
Enchanted Thorium Leggings	300	Found	12 Enchanted Thorium Bar, 1 Essence of Fire
Frostguard	300	Found	18 Arcanite Bar, 8 Blue Sapphire, 8 Azerothian Diamond, 4 Essence of Water, 2 Dense Grinding Stone, 4 Enchanted Leather
Hammer of the Titans	300	Found	50, Thorium Bar, 15 Arcanite Bar, 4 Guardian Stone, 6 Enchanted Leather, 10 Essence of Earth
Heartseeker	300	Found	10 Arcanite Bar, 10 Enchanted Thorium Bar, 2 Enchanted Leather, 6 Star Ruby, 6 Azerothian Diamond, 6 Large Opal, 4 Dense Grinding Stone
Helm of the Great Chief	300	Found	40 Thorium Bar, 4 Enchanted Thorium Bar, 60, Jet Black Feather, 6 Large Opal, 2 Huge Emerald
Imperial Plate Chest	300	Found	30, Thorium Bar, 1 Huge Emerald, 1 Blue Sapphire
Imperial Plate Leggings	300	Found	40 Thorium Bar, 2 Huge Emerald
Masterwork Stormhammer	300	Found	20 Enchanted Thorium Bar, 8 Huge Emerald, 8 Large Opal, 6 Essence of Earth, 4 Enchanted Leather
Radiant Leggings	300	Found	20 Thorium Bar, 4 Heart of Fire
Runic Breastplate	300	Found	40 Thorium Bar, 2 Arcanite Bar, 1 Star Ruby
Runic Plate Boots	300	Found	20 Thorium Bar, 2 Arcanite Bar, 10 Silver Bar
Runic Plate Helm	300	Found	30, Thorium Bar, 2 Arcanite Bar, 2 Truesilver Bar, 1 Huge Emerald
Runic Plate Leggings	300	Found	40 Thorium Bar, 2 Arcanite Bar, 1 Star Ruby
Runic Plate Shoulders	300	Found	20 Thorium Bar, 2 Arcanite Bar, 6 Gold Bar
Thorium Leggings	300	Found	26 Thorium Bar, 4 Red Power Crystal
Whitesoul Helm	300	Found	20 Thorium Bar, 4 Enchanted Thorium Bar, 6 Truesilver Bar, 6 Gold Bar, 2 Azerothian Diamond

ENCHANTING

This is probably the simplest skill, and yet, it's extremely costly to learn and master. Components are not gathered from the field or from dead beasts; instead, you must disenchant items of worth. This, of course, implies that you must find or purchase them. This process destroys the original item and leaves you with components necessary to ply your trade. It goes without saying that better items disenchant into better materials.

ONLY THE GOOD STUFF, UNFORTUNATELY

Only items with a quality of Good or above (Superior, Epic, Legendary, etc.) can be disenchanted for resources. You're not going to be able to get anything worthwhile from standard or inferior items.

Every magical item can be disenchanted. The difficult part about this method of resource gathering is that you really need to think twice about destroying some items. If an item was given to you from a quest and it's soulbound, but you can't use it, it's still not an easy choice. Those items typically sell for good money. However, it's safe to say that your enchantments will earn quite a return as well.

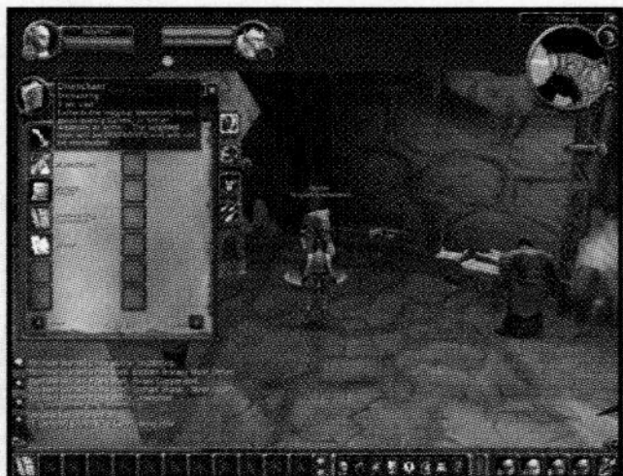

If you are with a party while hunting that doesn't need a certain item that can be disenchanted, ask for it and you'll often discover that you can grab some solid items that way. It's a standard to see a guild Enchanter snagging anything that someone doesn't immediately need. The Enchanter needs to keep everyone's weapon glowing, but that's a fair trade for resources that are typically hard to come by.

To disenchant an item open your skill book using "P" and find the disenchant skill.

Once you've dragged the icon into your hotbar, activate it to open the menu. Look in your packs to find an item that you wish to disenchant. Use the Disenchant skill and then click on the item. Remove the contents from the loot menu.

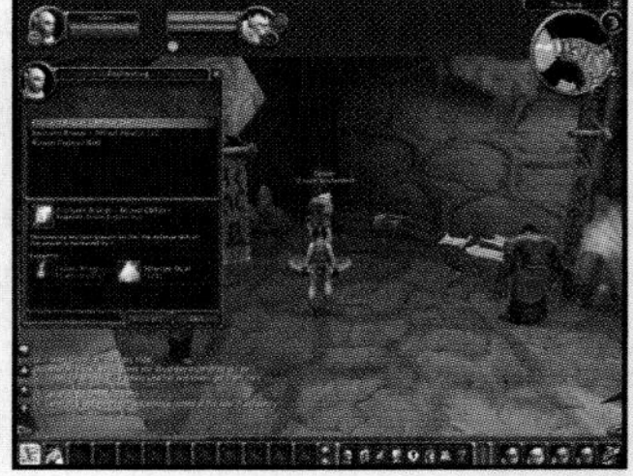

Once you've obtained a steady amount of resources, bring the Enchant icon down into your hotbar and select the enchantment you wish to apply.

Click on any recipe to see the components required. To enchant a weapon, either place it in your inventory or have someone place it in the bottom slot in the trade menu. Activate the appropriate enchantment and voila! Enchantments are permanent until replaced. If you wish to replace an enchantment, it will erase the one currently on in favor of the one newest one.

SOULBOUND ITEMS

The only way to enchant another player's soulbound equipment is through the trade window.

The quickest way to master this profession is to have friends willing to offer items that they don't need. Whether this is through a guild or just a group of players you've begun to hang out with, it's nice to be up front and explain to them that you've chosen the path of the Enchanter. Be generous with your services and you're certain to receive goodwill in kind.

Low-level Enchanters underbid one another to level up quickly. However, by the time they reach a level with solid enchantments that people crave, the prices skyrocket. The resources aren't cheap and the enchantments are permanent. Imagine two Warriors. Each has attained Level 50 and they're wearing the same equipment, they've chosen the same talents and use their abilities the same. However, one has every possible item enchanted and the other is in their normal equipment. Who's going to win?

People are constantly trying to get an edge over their competition and enchantments are sure ways to do that. If you're planning on holding onto an item for a while, get it enchanted early on and really take advantage of it.

ENCHANTING

PRODUCT	SKILL LEVEL	SOURCE	COMPONENTS
Runed Copper Rod	1	Initial	1 Copper Rod, 1 Strange Dust, 1 Lesser Magic Essence
Lesser Magic Wand	10	Trained	1 Simple Wood, 1 Lesser Magic Essence
Greater Magic Wand	70	Trained	1 Simple Wood, 1 Greater Magic Essence
Runed Silver Rod	100	Trained	1 Silver Rod, 6 Strange Dust, 3 Greater Magic Essence, 1 Shadowgem
Runed Golden Rod	150	Trained	1 Golden Rod, 1 Iridescent Pearl, 2 Greater Astral Essence, 2 Soul Dust
Lesser Mystic Wand	155	Trained	1 Star Wood, 1 Lesser Mystic Essence, 1 Soul Dust
Greater Mystic Wand	175	Trained	1 Star Wood, 1 Greater Mystic Essence, 1 Vision Dust
Runed Truesilver Rod	200	Trained	1 Truesilver Rod, 1 Black Pearl, 2 Greater Mystic Essence, 2 Vision Dust
Enchanted Leather	250	Trained	1 Rugged Leather, 1 Lesser Eternal Essence
Enchanted Thorium	250	Trained	1 Thorium Bar, 3 Dream Dust
Smoking Heart of the Mountain	265	Found	1 Blood of the Mountain, 1 Essence of Fire, 3 Small Brilliant Shard
Runed Arcanite Rod	290	Found	1 Arcanite Rod, 1 Golden Pearl, 10 Illusion Dust, 4 Greater Eternal Essence, 4 Small Brilliant Shard, 2 Large Brilliant Shard

ENCHANTMENTS

ENCHANTMENT	SKILL LEVEL	REAGENT(S)
Enchant Bracer - Minor Health	?	1 Strange Dust
Enchant Bracer - Minor Deflect	?	1 Lesser Magic Essence, 1 Strange Dust
Lesser Magic Wand	10	1 Simple Wood, 1 Lesser Magic Essence
Enchant Chest - Minor Health	15	1 Strange Dust
Enchant Bracer - Minor Deflection	20	
Enchant Chest - Minor Mana	20	1 Lesser Magic Essence
Enchant Chest - Minor Absorption	40	2 Strange Dust, 1 Lesser Magic Essence
Enchant Cloak - Minor Resistance	45	1 Strange Dust
Enchant Bracer - Minor Stamina	50	2 Lesser Magic Essence, 3 Strange Dust
Journeyman Enchanting	50	
Imbue Chest - Spirit	60	
Enchant Chest - Lesser Health	60	2 Strange Dust, 2 Lesser Magic Essence
Enchant Bracer - Minor Spirit	60	2 Lesser Magic Essence
Imbue Chest - Minor Spirit	60	
Enchant Bracer - Minor Strength	80	5 Strange Dust
Enchant Bracer - Minor Agility	80	2 Strange Dust, 1 Greater Magic Essence
Enchant Chest - Lesser Mana	80	1 Greater Magic Essence, 1 Lesser Magic Essenc
Enchant Weapon - Minor Beast Slayer	90	
Imbue Cloak - Protection	90	
Enchant Weapon - Minor Striking	90	2 Strange Dust, 1 Greater Magic Essence, 1 Small Glimmering Shard
Enchant Weapon - Minor Beastslayer	90	4 Strange Dust, 2 Greater Magic Essence
Greater Magic Wand	91	1 Simple Wood, 1 Greater Magic Essence
Enchant Cloak - Minor Protection	91	3 Strange Dust, 1 Greater Magic Essence
Enchant 2H Weapon - Intellect	100	
Enchant 2H Weapon - Lesser Intellect	100	3 Greater Magic Essence
Enchant 2H Weapon - Minor Impact	100	4 Strange Dust, 1 Small Glimmering Shard
Runed Silver Rod	100	1 Silver Rod, 6 Strange Dust, 3 Greater Magic Essence, 1 Shadowgem
Enchant Shield - Minor Stamina	105	1 Lesser Astral Essence, 2 Strange Dust
Enchant 2H Weapon - Lesser Spirit	110	1 Lesser Astral Essence, 6 Strange Dust
Enchant Cloak - Minor Agility	110	1 Lesser Astral Essence
Enchant Cloak - Lesser Protection	115	6 Strange Dust, 1 Small Glimmering Shard
Enchant Shield - Lesser Protection	115	1 Lesser Astral Essence, 1 Strange Dust, 1 Small Glimmering Shard
Enchant Bracer - Lesser Spirit	120	2 Lesser Astral Essence
Enchant Chest - Health	120	4 Strange Dust, 1 Lesser Astral Essence
Enchant Boots - Minor Agility	125	6 Strange Dust, 2 Lesser Astral Essence
Expert Enchanting	125	
Enchant Boots - Minor Stamina	125	8 Strange Dust
Enchant Cloak - Lesser Fire Resistance	125	
Enchant Shield - Lesser Spirit	130	2 Lesser Astral Essence, 4 Strange Dust
Enchant Bracer - Lesser Stamina	130	2 Soul Dust
Enchant Cloak - Lesser Shadow Resist	135	1 Greater Astral Essence, 1 Shadow Protection Potion
Enchant Cloak - Resist Lesser Shadow	135	
Enchant Weapon - Lesser Striking	140	2 Soul Dust, 1 Large Glimmering Shard
Enchant Chest - Lesser Absorption	140	2 Strange Dust, 1 Greater Astral Essence, 1 Large Glimmering Shard
Enchant Gloves - Herb Gathering	145	
Enchant Gloves - Fishing	145	1 Soul Dust
Enchant Gloves - Mining	145	3 Blackmouth Oil
Enchant 2H Weapon - Lesser Impact	145	1 Soul Dust, 3 Iron Ore
Enchant Chest - Mana	145	3 Soul Dust, 1 Large Glimmering Shard
Runed Golden Rod	150	1 Greater Astral Essence, 2 Lesser Astral Essence
Enchant Chest - Minor Stats	150	1 Golden Rod, 1 Iridescent Pearl, 2 Greater Astral Essence, 2 Soul Dust
Enchant Bracer - Lesser Intellect	150	1 Greater Astral Essence, 1 Soul Dust, 1 Large Glimmering Shard
Enchant Shield - Lesser Stamina	155	2 Greater Astral Essence
Lesser Mystic Wand	155	1 Lesser Mystic Essence, 1 Soul Dust
Enchant Cloak - Defense	155	1 Star Wood, 1 Lesser Mystic Essence, 1 Soul Dust
Enchant Boots - Lesser Agility	160	1 Small Glowing Shard, 3 Soul Dust
Enchant Chest - Greater Health	160	1 Soul Dust, 1 Lesser Mystic Essence
Enchant Bracer - Spirit	165	3 Soul Dust
Enchant Boots - Lesser Stamina	170	1 Lesser Mystic Essence
Enchant Bracer - Stamina	170	4 Soul Dust
Greater Mystic Wand	175	6 Soul Dust
Enchant Weapon - Lesser Beast Slayer	175	1 Star Wood, 1 Greater Mystic Essence, 1 Vision Dust
Enchant Weapon - Lesser Elemental Slayer	175	1 Lesser Mystic Essence, 1 Elemental Earth, 1 Small Glowing Shard
Enchant Weapon - Lesser Beastslayer	175	1 Lesser Mystic Essence, 2 Large Fang, 1 Small Glowing Shard
Enchant Cloak - Fire Resistance	175	1 Lesser Mystic Essence, 1 Elemental Fire
Enchant Shield - Spirit	180	1 Greater Mystic Essence, 1 Vision Dust
Enchant Bracer - Strength	180	1 Vision Dust
Enchant Chest - Greater Mana	185	1 Greater Mystic Essence
Enchant Boots - Lesser Spirit	190	1 Greater Mystic Essence, 2 Lesser Mystic Essence
Enchant Shield - Lesser Block	195	2 Greater Mystic Essence, 2 Vision Dust, 1 Large Glowing Shard
Enchant Weapon - Striking	195	2 Greater Mystic Essence, 1 Large Glowing Shard
Artisan Enchanting	200	
Enchant 2H Weapon - Impact	200	4 Vision Dust, 1 Large Glowing Shard
Enchant Gloves - Skinning	200	1 Vision Dust, 3 Green Whelp Scale
Enchant Chest - Lesser Stats	200	2 Greater Mystic Essence, 2 Vision Dust, 1 Large Glowing Shard
Runed Truesilver Rod	200	1 Truesilver Rod, 1 Black Pearl, 2 Greater Mystic Essence, 2 Vision Dust
Enchant Cloak - Greater Defense	205	3 Vision Dust
Enchant Cloak - Resistance	205	1 Lesser Nether Essence
Enchant Shield - Stamina	210	5 Vision Dust
Enchant Gloves - Agility	210	1 Lesser Nether Essence, 1 Vision Dust
Enchant Bracer - Intellect	210	1 Lesser Nether Essence
Enchant Gloves - Advanced Mining	215	3 Vision Dust, 3 Truesilver Bar
Enchant Boots - Stamina	215	4 Vision Dust
Enchant Bracer - Greater Spirit	220	3 Lesser Nether Essence, 1 Vision Dust
Enchant Chest - Superior Health	220	6 Vision Dust
Enchant Cloak - Lesser Agility	225	2 Lesser Nether Essence

ENCHANTMENT	SKILL LEVEL	REAGENT(S)
Enchant Gloves - Advanced Herbalism	225	3 Vision Dust, 3 Sungrass
Enchant Gloves - Strength	225	1 Lesser Nether Essence, 3 Vision Dust
Enchant Boots - Minor Speed	225	1 Small Radiant Shard, 1 Aquamarine, 1 Lesser Nether Essence
Enchant Shield - Greater Spirit	230	1 Greater Nether Essence, 1 Dream Dust
Enchant Chest - Superior Mana	230	1 Greater Nether Essence
Enchant Weapon - Demonslaying	230	1 Small Radiant Shard, 2 Dream Dust, 1 Elixir of Demonslaying
Enchant Boots - Agility	235	2 Greater Nether Essence
Enchant Shield - Frost Reflection	235	
Enchant Bracer - Greater Strength	240	2 Dream Dust
Enchant 2H Weapon - Greater Impact	240	1 Large Radiant Shard, 2 Dream Dust
Enchant Bracer - Greater Stamina	245	3 Dream Dust
Enchant Chest - Stats	245	1 Large Radiant Shard, 1 Dream Dust, 1 Greater Nether Essence
Enchant Weapon - Greater Striking	245	2 Large Radiant Shard, 1 Greater Nether Essence
Enchanted Thorium	250	1 Thorium Bar, 2 Dream Dust
Enchant Gloves - Minor Haste	250	2 Large Radiant Shard, 1 Wildvine
Enchant Gloves - Riding Skill	250	
Enchanted Leather	250	1 Rugged Leather, 1 Lesser Nether Essence
Enchant Weapon - Fiery Weapon	265	3 Large Radiant Shard, 1 Essence of Fire
Smoking Heart of the Mountain	265	1 Blood of the Mountain, 1 Heart of Fire, 1 Large Radiant Shard
Enchant Gloves - Herbalism	?	1 Soul Dust, 3 Kingsblood
Enchant Cloak - Lesser Fire Resist	?	1 Fire Oil, 1 Lesser Astral Essence
Enchant Chest - Absorption	?	2 Strange Dust, 1 Greater Astral Essence, 1 Large Glimmering Shard
Enchant Cloak - Minor Resist	?	1 Strange Dust, 2 Lesser Magic Essence
Enchant Cloak - Lesser Shadow Resistance	?	1 Greater Astral Essence, 1 Shadow Protection Potion

ENGINEERING

If you like toys, gadgets and thing that go BOOM!, become an Engineer. It's a great match if you've already chosen to be a miner since you'll use a ton of stone and ore. Also, gems are used constantly in Engineering and miners are the only players with ready access (as rare as it may be). Engineers create bombs, guns, animals that are pets and those that explode, special goggles and all sorts of other goodies. It's definitely not a boring profession.

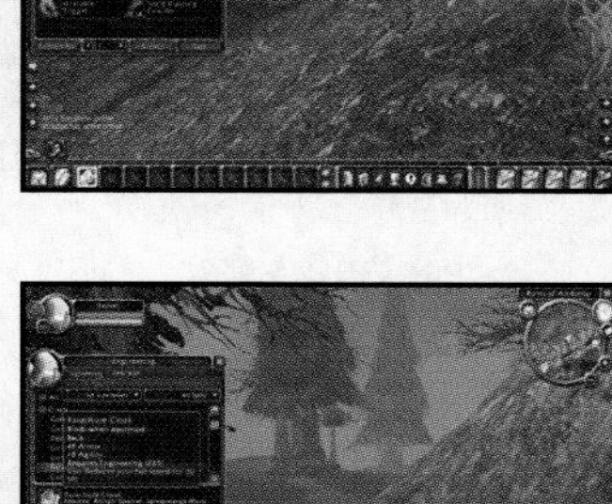

Snag the Engineering icon from your abilities menu (P) and place it in your hotbar. Activate it to see what you've learned and which schematics you've collected.

Click on the name of the schematic to see what components are needed. You can choose to make one item or a bunch of them. Yep! Tons of bombs!

Once an item is constructed it goes into your backpack.

Bombs and Dynamite: Right-click the icon if it's in your packs or use your hotbar for easy and quick access. A green circle will appear once you've activated it. Choose the area of effect and left-click to toss your creation at the enemy. As a sidenote, anything that stuns an enemy is a good thing—even if it's only for a few seconds.

Pets: Pets work from your pack or hotkey bars too. Battle chickens, Mithril Dragonlings, Explosive Sheep and the like appear when you click on them. Target dummies work like bombs in that you click where you want them and they activate in that spot.

Trinkets: Many items constructed at higher levels are trinkets. There are two trinket spots on your character. They must be equipped on your character to be used. You can click them on your character screen or put them in a hotkey bar. All trinkets have a timer ranging from 5 minutes to 1 hour. If you have a lot of trinkets, it's best to switch them out as you use them. The timer works whether it's equipped or in your bag. However, even if you carried five of the same item, say five Battle Chickens, they all have the same timer. So, using one activates all the timers. There's no need to have more than any of one trinket equipped at the same time.

At skill level 150, you get to pick either Goblin Engineering or Gnome Engineering. Goblins are more of the blow 'em up type and Gnomes love to make gadgets and trinkets. Either takes a quest to get and once you learn one, you can't learn the other. Blood oaths and everything!

Engineering is the anti-wealth skill. Just about everything you make can only be used by other Engineers and there's a good chance that they can make their own. Rare schematics are the only things that give you a bit of an edge over other Engineers. Hold onto those and try to get as much as you can from this career. This path is all about improving your character. You'll be making bombs, pets, goggles, parachutes, lasers, and all kinds of things that blow up and burn. It's what the killers and the hard-core people like to use. You'll be broke, but you'll be a walking time bomb with a bag full of tricks to pull out for a multitude of different reasons.

ENGINEERING

GADGET	SKILL LEVEL	SOURCE	COMPONENT(S)
Crafted Light Shot	1	Initial	1 Rough Blasting Powder, 1 Copper Bar
Rough Blasting Powder	1	Initial	1 Rough Stone
Rough Dynamite	1	Initial	2 Rough Blasting Powder, 1 Linen Cloth
Handful of Copper Bolts	30	Trained	1 Copper Bar
Rough Copper Bomb	30	Trained	1 Copper Bar, 1 Handful of Copper Bolts, 2 Rough Blasting Powder, 1 Linen Cloth
Arclight Spanner	50	Trained	6 Copper Bar
Copper Tube	50	Trained	2 Copper Bar, 1 Weak Flux
Rough Boomstick	50	Trained	1 Copper Tube, 1 Handful of Copper Bolts, 1 Wooden Stock
Crude Scope	60	Trained	1 Copper Tube, 1 Malachite, 1 Handful of Copper Bolts
Copper Modulator	65	Trained	2 Handful of Copper Bolts, 1 Copper Bar, 2 Linen Cloth
Coarse Blasting Powder	75	Trained	1 Coarse Stone
Coarse Dynamite	75	Trained	3 Coarse Blasting Powder, 1 Linen Cloth
Crafted Heavy Shot	75	Trained	1 Coarse Blasting Powder, 1 Copper Bar
Mechanical Squirrel	75	Found	1 Copper Modulator, 1 Handful of Copper Bolts, 1 Copper Bar, 2 Malachite
Target Dummy	85	Trained	1 Copper Modulator, 2 Handful of Copper Bolts, 1 Bronze Bar, 1 Wool Cloth
Silver Contact	90	Trained	1 Silver Bar
EZ-Thro Dynamite	100	Found	4 Coarse Blasting Powder, 1 Wool Cloth
Flying Tiger Goggles	100	Trained	6 Light Leather, 2 Tigerseye
Practice Lock	100	Trained	1 Bronze Bar, 2 Handful of Copper Bolts, 1 Weak Flux
Small Seaforium Charge	100	Found	2 Coarse Blasting Powder, 1 Copper Modulator, 1 Light Leather, 1 Refreshing Spring Water
Bronze Tube	105	Trained	2 Bronze Bar, 1 Weak Flux
Deadly Blunderbuss	105	Trained	2 Copper Tube, 4 Handful of Copper Bolts, 1 Wooden Stock, 2 Medium Leather
Large Copper Bomb	105	Trained	3 Copper Bar, 4 Coarse Blasting Powder, 1 Silver Contact
Standard Scope	110	Trained	1 Bronze Tube, 1 Moss Agate
Lovingly Crafted Boomstick	120	Trained	2 Bronze Tube, 2 Handful of Copper Bolts, 1 Heavy Stock, 3 Moss Agate
Shadow Goggles	120	Found	4 Medium Leather, 2 Shadowgem
Small Bronze Bomb	120	Trained	4 Coarse Blasting Powder, 2 Bronze Bar, 1 Silver Contact, 1 Wool Cloth
Crafted Solid Shot	125	Trained	1 Heavy Blasting Powder, 1 Bronze Bar
Flame Deflector	125	Found	1 Whirring Bronze Gizmo, 1 Small Flame Sac
Gnomish Universal Remote	125	Found	6 Bronze Bar, 1 Whirring Bronze Gizmo, 2 Flask of Oil, 1 Tigerseye, 1 Malachite
Heavy Blasting Powder	125	Trained	1 Heavy Stone
Heavy Dynamite	125	Trained	2 Heavy Blasting Powder, 1 Wool Cloth
Whirring Bronze Gizmo	125	Trained	2 Bronze Bar, 1 Wool Cloth
Silver-plated Shotgun	130	Trained	2 Bronze Tube, 2 Whirring Bronze Gizmo, 1 Heavy Stock, 3 Silver Bar
Ornate Spyglass	135	Trained	2 Bronze Tube, 2 Whirring Bronze Gizmo, 1 Copper Modulator, 1 Moss Agate
Big Bronze Bomb	140	Trained	2 Heavy Blasting Powder, 3 Bronze Bar, 1 Silver Contact
Minor Recombobulator	140	Trained	1 Bronze Tube, 2 Whirring Bronze Gizmo, 2 Medium Leather, 1 Moss Agate
Bronze Framework	145	Trained	2 Bronze Bar, 1 Medium Leather, 1 Wool Cloth
Moonsight Rifle	145	Found	3 Bronze Tube, 3 Whirring Bronze Gizmo, 1 Heavy Stock, 2 Lesser Moonstone
Aquadynamic Fish Attractor	150	Trained	2 Bronze Bar, 1 Nightcrawlers, 1 Coarse Blasting Powder
Explosive Sheep	150	Trained	1 Bronze Framework, 1 Whirring Bronze Gizmo, 2 Heavy Blasting Powder, 2 Wool Cloth
Gold Power Core	150	Trained	1 Gold Bar
Green Tinted Goggles	150	Trained	4 Medium Leather, 2 Moss Agate, 1 Flying Tiger Goggles
Ice Deflector	155	Trained	1 Whirring Bronze Gizmo, 1 Frost Oil

GADGET	SKILL LEVEL	SOURCE	COMPONENT(S)
Discombobulator Ray	160	Found	3 Whirring Bronze Gizmo, 2 Silk Cloth, 1 Jade, 1 Bronze Tube
Iron Strut	160	Trained	2 Iron Bar
Goblin Jumper Cables	165	Found	6 Iron Bar, 2 Whirring Bronze Gizmo, 2 Flask of Oil, 2 Silk Cloth, 2 Shadowgem, 1 Fused Wiring
Portable Bronze Mortar	165	Found	4 Bronze Tube, 1 Iron Strut, 4 Heavy Blasting Powder, 4 Medium Leather
Gyrochronatom	170	Trained	1 Iron Bar, 1 Gold Power Core
Bright-Eye Goggles	175	Found	6 Heavy Leather, 2 Citrine
Compact Harvest Reaper Kit	175	Trained	2 Iron Strut, 1 Bronze Framework, 2 Gyrochronatom, 4 Heavy Leather
Iron Grenade	175	Trained	1 Iron Bar, 1 Heavy Blasting Powder, 1 Silk Cloth
Samophlange Micro-adjustor	175	Trained	4 Steel Bar
Solid Blasting Powder	175	Trained	2 Solid Stone
Solid Dynamite	175	Trained	1 Solid Blasting Powder, 1 Silk Cloth
Accurate Scope	180	Trained	1 Bronze Tube, 1 Jade, 1 Citrine
Advanced Target Dummy	185	Trained	1 Iron Strut, 1 Bronze Framework, 1 Gyrochronatom, 4 Heavy Leather
Craftsman's Monocle	185	Found	6 Heavy Leather, 2 Citrine
Flash Bomb	185	Found	1 Blue Pearl, 1 Heavy Blasting Powder, 1 Silk Cloth
Big Iron Bomb	190	Trained	3 Iron Bar, 3 Heavy Blasting Powder, 1 Silver Contact
Goblin Land Mine	195	Found	3 Heavy Blasting Powder, 2 Iron Bar, 1 Gyrochronatom
Mithril Tube	195	Trained	3 Mithril Bar
Gnomish Cloaking Device	200	Trained	4 Gyrochronatom, 2 Jade, 2 Lesser Moonstone, 2 Citrine, 1 Fused Wiring
Large Seaforium Charge	200	Found	2 Solid Blasting Powder, 2 Heavy Leather, 1 Refreshing Spring Water
Mechanical Dragonling	200	Trained	1 Bronze Framework, 4 Iron Strut, 4 Gyrochronatom, 2 Citrine, 1 Fused Wiring
Mechanical Repair Kit	200	Trained	1 Mithril Bar, 1 Mageweave Cloth, 1 Solid Blasting Powder
Unstable Trigger	200	Trained	1 Mithril Bar, 1 Mageweave Cloth, 1 Solid Blasting Powder
Fire Goggles	205	Trained	1 Green Tinted Goggles, 2 Citrine, 2 Elemental Fire, 4 Heavy Leather
Gnomish Shrink Ray	205	Trained	1 Mithril Tube, 1 Unstable Trigger, 4 Mithril Bar, 4 Flask of Mojo, 2 Jade
Goblin Construction Hat	205	Trained	8 Mithril Bar, 1 Citrine, 4 Elemental Fire
Goblin Mining Helmet	205	Trained	8 Mithril Bar, 1 Citrine, 4 Elemental Earth
Goblin Mortar	205	Trained	2 Mithril Tube, 4 Mithril Bar, 5 Solid Blasting Powder, 1 Gold Power Core, 1 Elemental Fire
Goblin Rocket Fuel Recipe	205	Trained	1 Blank Parchment, 1 Engineer's Ink
Goblin Sapper Charge	205	Trained	1 Mageweave Cloth, 3 Solid Blasting Powder, 1 Unstable Trigger
Inlaid Mithril Cylinder Plans	205	Trained	1 Blank Parchment, 1 Engineer's Ink
Lil' Smoky	205	Found	1 Core of Earth, 2 Gyrochronatom, 1 Fused Wiring, 2 Mithril Bar, 1 Truesilver Bar
Mithril Blunderbuss	205	Trained	1 Mithril Tube, 1 Unstable Trigger, 1 Heavy Stock, 4 Mithril Bar, 2 Elemental Fire
Pet Bombling	205	Found	1 Big Iron Bomb, 1 Heart of Fire, 1 Fused Wiring, 6 Mithril Bar
Deadly Scope	210	Found	1 Mithril Tube, 2 Aquamarine, 2 Thick Leather
Gnomish Goggles	210	Trained	1 Fire Goggles, 1 Mithril Tube, 2 Gold Power Core, 2 Flask of Mojo, 2 Heavy Leather
Gnomish Net-o-Matic Projector	210	Trained	1 Mithril Tube, 2 Shadow Silk, 4 Thick Spider's Silk, 2 Solid Blasting Powder, 4 Mithril Bar
Hi-Impact Mithril Slugs	210	Trained	1 Mithril Bar, 1 Solid Blasting Powder
Gnomish Harm Prevention Belt	215	Trained	1 Dusky Belt, 4 Mithril Bar, 2 Truesilver Bar, 1 Unstable Trigger, 2 Aquamarine
Mithril Casing	215	Trained	3 Mithril Bar
Mithril Frag Bomb	215	Trained	1 Mithril Casing, 1 Unstable Trigger, 1 Solid Blasting Powder
Catseye Ultra Goggles	220	Found	4 Thick Leather, 2 Aquamarine, 1 Catseye Elixir
Mithril Heavy-bore Rifle	220	Found	2 Mithril Tube, 1 Unstable Trigger, 1 Heavy Stock, 6 Mithril Bar, 2 Citrine
Gnomish Rocket Boots	225	Trained	1 Black Mageweave Boots, 2 Mithril Tube, 4 Heavy Leather, 8 Solid Blasting Powder, 4 Gyrochronatom
Goblin Rocket Boots	225	Trained	1 Black Mageweave Boots, 2 Mithril Tube, 4 Heavy Leather, 2 Goblin Rocket Fuel, 1 Unstable Trigger
Parachute Cloak	225	Found	4 Bolt of Mageweave, 2 Shadow Silk, 1 Unstable Trigger, 4 Solid Blasting Powder
Spellpower Goggles Xtreme	225	Found	4 Thick Leather, 2 Star Ruby
Deepdive Helmet	230	Found	8 Mithril Bar, 1 Mithril Casing, 1 Truesilver Bar, 4 Tigerseye, 4 Malachite
Gnomish Battle Chicken	230	Trained	1 Mithril Casing, 6 Truesilver Bar, 6 Mithril Bar, 2 Inlaid Mithril Cylinder, 1 Gold Power Core, 2 Jade
Goblin Bomb Dispenser	230	Trained	2 Mithril Casing, 4 Solid Blasting Powder, 6 Truesilver Bar, 1 Unstable Trigger, 2 Accurate Scope
Rose Colored Goggles	230	Trained	6 Thick Leather, 2 Star Ruby
Gnomish Mind Control Cap	235	Trained	10 Mithril Bar, 4 Truesilver Bar, 1 Gold Power Core, 2 Star Ruby, 4 Mageweave Cloth
Hi-Explosive Bomb	235	Trained	2 Mithril Casing, 1 Unstable Trigger, 2 Solid Blasting Powder
The Big One	235	Trained	1 Mithril Casing, 1 Goblin Rocket Fuel, 6 Solid Dynamite, 1 Unstable Trigger
Gnomish Death Ray	240	Trained	2 Mithril Tube, 1 Unstable Trigger, 1 Soulstone, 4 Ichor of Undeath, 1 Inlaid Mithril Cylinder
Goblin Dragon Gun	240	Trained	2 Mithril Tube, 4 Goblin Rocket Fuel, 6 Mithril Bar, 6 Truesilver Bar, 1 Unstable Trigger
Sniper Scope	240	Found	1 Mithril Tube, 1 Star Ruby, 2 Truesilver Bar
Goblin Rocket Helmet	245	Trained	1 Goblin Construction Helmet, 4 Goblin Rocket Fuel, 4 Mithril Bar, 1 Unstable Trigger
Green Lens	245	Trained	8 Thick Leather, 2 Jade, 2 Heart of the Wild, 2 Wildvine
Mithril Gyro-Shot	245	Trained	2 Mithril Bar, 2 Solid Blasting Powder
Dense Blasting Powder	250	Trained	2 Dense Stone
Mithril Mechanical Dragonling	250	Found	14 Mithril Bar, 4 Heart of Fire, 4 Truesilver Bar, 2 Inlaid Mithril Cylinder, 2 Goblin Rocket Fuel, 2 Star Ruby
Salt Shaker	250	Trained	1 Mithril Casing, 6 Thorium Bar, 1 Gold Power Core, 4 Unstable Trigger
Thorium Grenade	260	Found	1 Thorium Widget, 3 Thorium Bar, 3 Dense Blasting Powder, 3 Runecloth
Thorium Rifle	260	Found	2 Mithril Tube, 2 Mithril Casing, 2 Thorium Widget, 4 Thorium Bar, 1 Deadly Scope
Thorium Widget	260	Found	3 Thorium Bar, 1 Runecloth
Lifelike Mechanical Toad	265	Found	1 Living Essence, 4 Thorium Widget, 1 Gold Power Core, 1 Rugged Leather
Spellpower Goggles Xtreme Plus	270	Found	1 Spellpower Goggles Xtreme, 4 Star Ruby, 2 Enchanted Leather, 8 Runecloth
Dark Iron Rifle	275	Found	2 Thorium Tube, 6 Dark Iron Bar, 2 Deadly Scope, 2 Blue Sapphire, 2 Large Opal, 4 Rugged Leather
Masterwork Target Dummy	275	Found	1 Mithril Casing, 1 Thorium Tube, 2 Thorium Widget, 1 Truesilver Bar, 2 Rugged Leather, 4 Runecloth
Thorium Tube	275	Found	6 Thorium Bar
Dark Iron Bomb	285	Found	2 Thorium Widget, 1 Dark Iron Bar, 3 Dense Blasting Powder, 3 Runecloth
Delicate Arcanite Converter	285	Found	1 Arcanite Bar, 1 Ironweb Spider Silk
Thorium Shells	285	Found	2 Thorium Bar, 1 Dense Blasting Powder
Master Engineer's Goggles	290	Found	1 Fire Goggles, 2 Huge Emerald, 4 Enchanted Leather
Voice Amplification Modulator	290	Found	2 Delicate Arcanite Converter, 1 Gold Power Core, 1 Thorium Widget, 1 Large Opal
Arcanite Dragonling	300	Found	1 Mithril Mechanical Dragonling, 8 Delicate Arcanite Converter, 10 Enchanted Thorium Bar, 6 Thorium Widget, 4 Gold Power Core, 6 Enchanted Leather
Flawless Arcanite Rifle	300	Found	10 Arcanite Bar, 2 Thorium Tube, 2 Essence of Fire, 2 Essence of Earth, 2 Azerothian Diamond, 2 Enchanted Leather

LEATHERWORKING

Leather armor is something that almost half of the classes long for and need desperately (at least early on while Shaman and Hunters haven't gained access to their mail armor). Skinning, obviously, is a fantastic second profession to take. Controlling your own resources is a great way to gain an edge over those wishing to buy from other players.

Open your abilities menu up (P) and pull the Leatherworking icon into your hotbar. At first, you won't know much, but that changes quickly. Once you begin to make even the simplest of armor pieces, you'll need to visit the trainer constantly. After a while, you'll be able to take a breath as your skill leveling slows a bit. Once you've created an item, it's dropped into your packs.

At rank 225, you have three classes of Leatherworking to pursue: Tribal, Elemental and Dragonscale. Each one requires a quest and you can only learn one. Tribal is all leather; the Spirit and Intellect buffs in this line make it nicely suited for Druids and Shaman. Elemental Leatherworking, with the Agility and Stamina increases, seems great for Rogues and Hunters. Dragonscale is all mail and lends itself to the higher level Shaman and Hunters.

Leatherworking combined with Skinning is a very easy skill to level up. There's no hunting for herbs or ore; you're killing what you'd kill anyway to get the items, finish quests, etc. If you take Skinning and Leatherworking at Level 5, the minimum level necessary, the skill levels up without much effort. Leatherworkers are not as popular as Blacksmiths. Smiths make armor and weapons while you're focused on armor. However, there is one advantage. Leatherworkers make armor kits and everyone loves those. A boost to your AC is a nice thing to have.

There's also another bonus to being a less-flashy professional. Chances are that when you're in a group, you'll be the only person collecting skins. The armor you make is for very popular classes (Rogues, Shaman, Hunters, & Druids) who are always looking for good gear. So your items will sell. Plus, if you actually wear the armor you make, you're always wearing the latest and greatest. End game gear is very hard to make, asking for some of the toughest items to find and in high quanities. But the end results are very worth it. It's so hard to make that very few are sold. And, when something is put up in the auction house or over the trade channel during peak hours, bidding wars are sure to happen.

LEATHERWORKING

PRODUCT	SKILL LEVEL	SOURCE	COMPONENT(S)
Handstitched Leather Boots	1	Initial	2 Light Leather, 1 Coarse Thread
Handstitched Leather Bracers	1	Initial	2 Light Leather, 3 Coarse Thread
Handstitched Leather Cloak	1	Initial	2 Light Leather, 1 Coarse Thread
Handstitched Leather Vest	1	Initial	3 Light Leather, 1 Coarse Thread
Light Armor Kit	1	Initial	1 Light Leather
Light Leather	1	Initial	3 Ruined Leather Scraps
Handstitched Leather Pants	15	Trained	4 Light Leather, 1 Coarse Thread
Handstitched Leather Belt	25	Trained	6 Light Leather, 1 Coarse Thread
Light Leather Quiver	30	Trained	4 Light Leather, 2 Coarse Thread
Small Leather Ammo Pouch	30	Trained	3 Light Leather, 4 Coarse Thread
Cured Light Hide	35	Trained	1 Light Hide, 1 Salt
Rugged Leather Pants	35	Found	5 Light Leather, 5 Coarse Thread
Embossed Leather Vest	40	Trained	8 Light Leather, 4 Coarse Thread
Kodo Hide Bag	40	Found	3 Thin Kodo Leather, 4 Light Leather, 1 Coarse Thread
Embossed Leather Boots	55	Trained	8 Light Leather, 5 Coarse Thread
Embossed Leather Gloves	55	Trained	3 Light Leather, 2 Coarse Thread
Embossed Leather Cloak	60	Trained	5 Light Leather, 2 Coarse Thread
White Leather Jerkin	60	Found	8 Light Leather, 2 Coarse Thread, 1 Bleach
Light Leather Bracers	70	Trained	6 Light Leather, 4 Coarse Thread
Embossed Leather Pants	75	Trained	1 Cured Light Hide, 6 Light Leather, 2 Coarse Thread
Fine Leather Gloves	75	Found	1 Cured Light Hide, 4 Light Leather, 2 Coarse Thread
Fine Leather Belt	80	Trained	6 Light Leather, 2 Coarse Thread
Fine Leather Cloak	85	Trained	10 Light Leather, 2 Fine Thread
Fine Leather Tunic	85	Trained	3 Cured Light Hide, 6 Light Leather, 4 Coarse Thread
Deviate Scale Cloak	90	Found	8 Deviate Scale, 1 Cured Light Hide, 1 Fine Thread
Fine Leather Boots	90	Found	7 Light Leather, 2 Coarse Thread
Moonglow Vest	90	Found	6 Light Leather, 1 Cured Light Hide, 4 Coarse Thread, 1 Small Lustrous Pearl
Murloc Scale Belt	90	Found	8 Slimy Murloc Scale, 6 Light Leather, 1 Fine Thread
Light Leather Pants	95	Trained	10 Light Leather, 1 Cured Light Hide, 1 Fine Thread
Murloc Scale Breastplate	95	Found	12 Slimy Murloc Scale, 1 Cured Light Hide, 8 Light Leather, 1 Fine Thread
Black Whelp Cloak	100	Found	12 Black Whelp Scale, 4 Medium Leather, 1 Fine Thread
Cured Medium Hide	100	Trained	1 Medium Hide, 1 Salt
Dark Leather Boots	100	Trained	4 Medium Leather, 2 Fine Thread, 1 Gray Dye
Dark Leather Tunic	100	Found	6 Medium Leather, 1 Fine Thread, 1 Gray Dye
Hillman's Leather Vest	100	Found	1 Fine Leather Tunic, 2 Cured Light Hide, 2 Coarse Thread
Medium Armor Kit	100	Trained	4 Medium Leather, 1 Coarse Thread
Deviate Scale Gloves	105	Found	2 Perfect Deviate Scale, 6 Deviate Scale, 2 Fine Thread
Fine Leather Pants	105	Found	8 Medium Leather, 1 Bolt of Woolen Cloth, 1 Fine Thread
Dark Leather Cloak	110	Trained	8 Medium Leather, 1 Fine Thread, 1 Gray Dye
Dark Leather Pants	115	Trained	12 Medium Leather, 1 Gray Dye, 1 Fine ThreadDeviate
Scale Belt	115	Found	10 Perfect Deviate Scale, 10 Deviate Scale, 2 Fine Thread
Dark Leather Gloves	120	Found	1 Fine Leather Gloves, 1 Cured Medium Hide, 1 Fine Thread, 1 Gray Dye
Hillman's Belt	120	Found	8 Medium Leather, 1 Elixir of Wisdom, 2 Fine Thread
Nimble Leather Gloves	120	Trained	1 Elixir of Minor Agility, 6 Medium Leather, 1 Fine Thread
Red Whelp Gloves	120	Found	6 Red Whelp Scale, 4 Medium Leather, 1 Fine Thread
Toughened Leather Armor	120	Trained	10 Medium Leather, 2 Cured Light Hide, 2 Fine Thread
Dark Leather Belt	125	Trained	1 Fine Leather Belt, 1 Cured Medium Hide, 2 Fine Thread, 1 Gray Dye
Fletcher's Gloves	125	Trained	8 Medium Leather, 4 Long Tail Feather, 2 Fine Thread
Guardian Cloak	125	Found	14 Heavy Leather, 2 Bolt of Silk Cloth, 2 Silken Thread
Hillman's Shoulders	130	Trained	1 Cured Medium Hide, 4 Medium Leather, 1 Fine Thread
Earthen Leather Shoulders	135	Found	6 Medium Leather, 1 Elemental Earth, 2 Fine Thread
Herbalist's Gloves	135	Found	8 Medium Leather, 4 Kingsblood, 2 Fine Thread
Toughened Leather Gloves	135	Trained	4 Medium Leather, 2 Cured Medium Hide, 2 Elixir of Defense, 2 Spider's Silk, 2 Fine Thread
Dark Leather Shoulders	140	Found	12 Medium Leather, 1 Elixir of Lesser Agility, 1 Gray Dye, 2 Fine Thread
Pilferer's Gloves	140	Found	10 Medium Leather, 2 Lucky Charm, 2 Fine Thread
Heavy Earthen Gloves	145	Found	12 Medium Leather, 2 Elemental Earth, 2 Bolt of Woolen Cloth, 2 Fine Thread
Hillman's Leather Gloves	145	Trained	14 Medium Leather, 4 Fine Thread
Barbaric Gloves	150	Found	6 Heavy Leather, 2 Large Fang, 1 Fine Thread
Cured Heavy Hide	150	Trained	1 Heavy Hide, 3 Salt
Heavy Armor Kit	150	Trained	5 Heavy Leather, 1 Fine Thread
Heavy Leather Ammo Pouch	150	Trained	8 Heavy Leather, 2 Fine Thread
Heavy Quiver	150	Trained	8 Heavy Leather, 2 Fine Thread
Hillman's Cloak	150	Trained	5 Heavy Leather, 2 Fine Thread
Green Leather Armor	155	Trained	9 Heavy Leather, 2 Green Dye, 4 Fine Thread
Green Leather Belt	160	Trained	1 Cured Heavy Hide, 5 Heavy Leather, 1 Fine Thread, 1 Green Dye, 1 Iron Buckle
Guardian Pants	160	Trained	12 Heavy Leather, 2 Bolt of Silk Cloth, 2 Fine Thread
Dusky Leather Leggings	165	Found	10 Heavy Leather, 1 Black Dye, 2 Fine Thread
Raptor Hide Belt	165	Trained	4 Raptor Hide, 4 Heavy Leather, 2 Fine Thread
Raptor Hide Harness	165	Trained	6 Raptor Hide, 4 Heavy Leather, 2 Fine Thread
Barbaric Leggings	170	Found	10 Heavy Leather, 2 Fine Thread, 1 Moss Agate
Guardian Belt	170	Found	2 Cured Heavy Hide, 4 Heavy Leather, 1 Fine Thread, 1 Iron Buckle
Thick Murloc Armor	170	Found	12 Thick Murloc Scale, 1 Cured Heavy Hide, 10 Heavy Leather, 3 Fine Thread
Barbaric Shoulders	175	Trained	8 Heavy Leather, 1 Cured Heavy Hide, 2 Fine Thread
Dusky Leather Armor	175	Trained	10 Heavy Leather, 1 Shadow Oil, 2 Fine Thread
Green Whelp Armor	175	Found	4 Green Whelp Scale, 10 Heavy Leather, 2 Fine Thread
Guardian Armor	175	Found	2 Cured Heavy Hide, 12 Heavy Leather, 1 Shadow Oil, 2 Fine Thread
Frost Leather Cloak	180	Trained	6 Heavy Leather, 2 Elemental Earth, 2 Elemental Water, 2 Fine Thread
Green Leather Bracers	180	Trained	2 Cured Heavy Hide, 6 Heavy Leather, 1 Green Dye, 1 Fine Thread
Dusky Bracers	185	Trained	16 Heavy Leather, 1 Black Dye, 2 Silken Thread
Gem-studded Leather Belt	185	Trained	4 Cured Heavy Hide, 2 Iridescent Pearl, 2 Jade, 1 Citrine, 1 Fine Thread
Barbaric Harness	190	Trained	14 Heavy Leather, 2 Fine Thread, 1 Iron Buckle
Green Whelp Bracers	190	Found	6 Green Whelp Scale, 8 Heavy Leather, 2 Silken Thread
Guardian Gloves	190	Trained	4 Heavy Leather, 1 Cured Heavy Hide, 1 Silken Thread
Murloc Scale Bracers	190	Found	16 Thick Murloc Scale, 1 Cured Heavy Hide, 14 Heavy Leather, 1 Silken Thread
Dusky Belt	195	Trained	10 Heavy Leather, 2 Bolt of Silk Cloth, 2 Black Dye, 1 Iron Buckle
Guardian Leather Bracers	195	Found	6 Heavy Leather, 2 Cured Heavy Hide, 1 Silken Thread
Barbaric Belt	200	Found	6 Heavy Leather, 2 Cured Heavy Hide, 2 Coarse Gorilla Hair, 1 Great Rage Potion, 1 Silken Thread, 1 Iron Buckle
Comfortable Leather Hat	200	Found	12 Heavy Leather, 2 Cured Heavy Hide, 2 Silken Thread
Cured Thick Hide	200	Trained	1 Thick Hide, 1 Deeprock Salt
Dusky Boots	200	Found	8 Heavy Leather, 2 Shadowcat Hide, 1 Shadow Oil, 2 Silken Thread
Swift Boots	200	Found	10 Heavy Leather, 2 Swiftness Potion, 2 Thick Spider's Silk, 1 Silken Thread
Thick Armor Kit	200	Trained	5 Thick Leather, 1 Silken Thread
Nightscape Headband	205	Trained	5 Thick Leather, 2 Silken Thread
Nightscape Tunic	205	Trained	7 Thick Leather, 2 Silken Thread
Turtle Scale Gloves	205	Found	6 Thick Leather, 8 Turtle Scale, 1 Heavy Silken Thread
Nightscape Shoulders	210	Found	8 Thick Leather, 6 Mageweave Cloth, 3 Silken Thread
Turtle Scale Bracers	210	Trained	8 Thick Leather, 12 Turtle Scale, 1 Heavy Silken Thread
Turtle Scale Breastplate	210	Trained	6 Thick Leather, 12 Turtle Scale, 1 Heavy Silken Thread
Big Voodoo Robe	215	Found	10 Thick Leather, 4 Flask of Mojo, 1 Heavy Silken Thread
Big Voodoo Mask	220	Found	8 Thick Leather, 6 Flask of Mojo, 1 Heavy Silken Thread
Tough Scorpid Bracers	220	Found	10 Thick Leather, 4 Scorpid Scale, 2 Silken Thread

PRODUCT	SKILL LEVEL	SOURCE	COMPONENT(S)
Tough Scorpid Breastplate	220	Found	12 Thick Leather, 12 Scorpid Scale, 4 Silken Thread
Wild Leather Shoulders	220	Found	10 Thick Leather, 1 Wildvine, 1 Cured Thick Hide
Dragonscale Gauntlets	225	Trained	24 Thick Leather, 12 Worn Dragonscale, 4 Heavy Silken Thread, 2 Cured Thick Hide
Quickdraw Quiver	225	Trained	12 Thick Leather, 1 Thick Hide, 1 Elixir of Agility, 4 Silken Thread
Thick Leather Ammo Pouch	225	Trained	10 Thick Leather, 1 Cured Thick Hide, 1 Elixir of Greater Defense, 6 Silken Thread
Tough Scorpid Gloves	225	Found	6 Thick Leather, 8 Scorpid Scale, 2 Silken Thread
Wild Leather Helmet	225	Found	10 Thick Leather, 2 Wildvine, 1 Cured Thick Hide
Wild Leather Vest	225	Found	12 Thick Leather, 2 Wildvine, 1 Cured Thick Hide
Wolfshead Helm	225	Trained	18 Thick Leather, 2 Thick Wolfhide, 8 Wicked Claw, 4 Heavy Silken Thread, 2 Cured Thick Hide
Gauntlets of the Sea	230	Trained	20 Thick Leather, 8 Globe of Water, 2 Core of Earth, 1 Cured Thick Hide, 4 Heavy Silken Thread
Nightscape Cloak	230	Found	12 Thick Leather, 4 Silken Thread
Nightscape Pants	230	Trained	14 Thick Leather, 4 Silken Thread
Turtle Scale Helm	230	Trained	14 Thick Leather, 24 Turtle Scale, 1 Heavy Silken Thread
Nightscape Boots	235	Trained	16 Thick Leather, 2 Heavy Silken Thread
Tough Scorpid Boots	235	Found	12 Thick Leather, 12 Scorpid Scale, 6 Silken Thread
Turtle Scale Leggings	235	Trained	14 Thick Leather, 28 Turtle Scale, 1 Heavy Silken Thread
Big Voodoo Cloak	240	Found	14 Thick Leather, 4 Flask of Big Mojo, 2 Heavy Silken Thread
Big Voodoo Pants	240	Found	10 Thick Leather, 6 Flask of Big Mojo, 2 Heavy Silken Thread
Tough Scorpid Shoulders	240	Found	12 Thick Leather, 16 Scorpid Scale, 2 Heavy Silken Thread
Tough Scorpid Leggings	245	Found	14 Thick Leather, 8 Scorpid Scale, 2 Heavy Silken Thread
Wild Leather Boots	245	Found	14 Thick Leather, 4 Wildvine, 2 Cured Thick Hide
Cured Rugged Hide	250	Trained	1 Rugged Hide, 1 Refined Deeprock Salt
Feathered Breastplate	250	Trained	40 Thick Leather, 40 Jet Black Feather, 2 Black Pearl, 4 Cured Thick Hide, 4 Heavy Silken Thread
Helm of Fire	250	Trained	40 Thick Leather, 12 Heart of Fire, 4 Core of Earth, 2 Cured Thick Hide, 4 Heavy Silken Thread
Rugged Armor Kit	250	Trained	5 Rugged Leather
Tough Scorpid Helm	250	Found	10 Thick Leather, 20 Scorpid Scale, 2 Heavy Silken Thread
Wild Leather Cloak	250	Found	16 Thick Leather, 6 Wildvine, 2 Cured Thick Hide
Wild Leather Leggings	250	Found	16 Thick Leather, 6 Wildvine, 2 Cured Thick Hide
Dragonscale Breastplate	255	Trained	40 Thick Leather, 30, Worn Dragonscale, 4 Heavy Silken Thread, 4 Cured Thick Hide
Heavy Scorpid Bracers	255	Found	4 Rugged Leather, 4 Heavy Scorpid Scale, 1 Rune Thread
Green Dragonscale Breastplate	260	Found	20 Rugged Leather, 25 Green Dragonscale, 2 Rune Thread
Wicked Leather Gauntlets	260	Found	8 Rugged Leather, 1 Black Dye, 1 Rune Thread
Chimeric Gloves	265	Found	6 Rugged Leather, 6 Chimera Leather, 1 Rune Thread
Heavy Scorpid Vest	265	Found	6 Rugged Leather, 6 Heavy Scorpid Scale, 1 Rune Thread
Wicked Leather Bracers	265	Found	8 Rugged Leather, 1 Black Dye, 1 Rune Thread
Green Dragonscale Leggings	270	Found	20 Rugged Leather, 25 Green Dragonscale, 1 Rune Thread
Ironfeather Shoulders	270	Found	24 Rugged Leather, 80, Ironfeather, 2 Jade, 1 Rune Thread
Living Shoulders	270	Found	12 Rugged Leather, 4 Living Essence, 1 Rune Thread
Runic Leather Gauntlets	270	Found	10 Rugged Leather, 6 Runecloth, 1 Rune Thread
Volcanic Leggings	270	Found	6 Rugged Leather, 1 Essence of Fire, 1 Core of Earth, 1 Rune Thread
Chimeric Boots	275	Found	4 Rugged Leather, 8 Chimera Leather, 1 Rune Thread
Frostsaber Boots	275	Found	4 Rugged Leather, 6 Frostsaber Leather, 1 Rune Thread
Heavy Scorpid Gauntlets	275	Found	6 Rugged Leather, 8 Heavy Scorpid Scale, 1 Rune Thread
Runic Leather Bracers	275	Found	6 Rugged Leather, 1 Black Pearl, 6 Runecloth, 1 Rune Thread
Stormshroud Pants	275	Found	16 Rugged Leather, 2 Essence of Water, 2 Essence of Air, 1 Rune Thread
Warbear Harness	275	Found	28 Rugged Leather, 12 Warbear Leather, 1 Rune Thread
Chimeric Leggings	280	Found	8 Rugged Leather, 8 Chimera Leather, 1 Rune Thread
Heavy Scorpid Belt	280	Found	6 Rugged Leather, 8 Heavy Scorpid Scale, 1 Rune Thread
Runic Leather Belt	280	Found	12 Rugged Leather, 10 Runecloth, 1 Rune Thread
Wicked Leather Headband	280	Found	12 Rugged Leather, 1 Black Dye, 1 Rune Thread
Blue Dragonscale Breastplate	285	Found	28 Rugged Leather, 30, Blue Dragonscale, 1 Cured Rugged Hide, 1 Rune Thread
Frostsaber Leggings	285	Found	6 Rugged Leather, 8 Frostsaber Leather, 1 Rune Thread
Heavy Scorpid Leggings	285	Found	8 Rugged Leather, 12 Heavy Scorpid Scale, 1 Rune Thread
Living Leggings	285	Found	16 Rugged Leather, 6 Living Essence, 1 Cured Rugged Hide, 1 Rune Thread
Stormshroud Armor	285	Found	16 Rugged Leather, 3 Essence of Water, 3 Essence of Air, 1 Cured Rugged Hide, 1 Rune Thread
Volcanic Breastplate	285	Found	8 Rugged Leather, 1 Essence of Fire, 1 Essence of Earth, 1 Rune Thread
Warbear Woolies	285	Found	24 Rugged Leather, 14 Warbear Leather, 1 Rune Thread
Black Dragonscale Breastplate	290	Found	40 Rugged Leather, 60, Black Dragonscale, 1 Cured Rugged Hide, 2 Rune Thread
Chimeric Vest	290	Found	10 Rugged Leather, 10 Chimera Leather, 1 Rune Thread
Devilsaur Gauntlets	290	Found	30, Rugged Leather, 8 Devilsaur Leather, 1 Rune Thread
Ironfeather Breastplate	290	Found	40 Rugged Leather, 120 Ironfeather, 1 Jade, 1 Cured Rugged Hide, 1 Rune Thread
Runic Leather Headband	290	Found	14 Rugged Leather, 10 Runecloth, 1 Rune Thread
Wicked Leather Pants	290	Found	16 Rugged Leather, 1 Cured Rugged Hide, 3 Black Dye, 1 Rune Thread
Blue Dragonscale Shoulders	295	Found	28 Rugged Leather, 30, Blue Dragonscale, 2 Enchanted Leather, 1 Cured Rugged Hide, 1 Rune Thread
Frostsaber Gloves	295	Found	6 Rugged Leather, 10 Frostsaber Leather, 1 Rune Thread
Heavy Scorpid Helm	295	Found	8 Rugged Leather, 12 Heavy Scorpid Scale, 1 Cured Rugged Hide, 1 Rune Thread
Stormshroud Shoulders	295	Found	12 Rugged Leather, 3 Essence of Water, 3 Essence of Air, 2 Enchanted Leather, 1 Rune Thread
Black Dragonscale Leggings	300	Found	40 Rugged Leather, 60, Black Dragonscale, 4 Enchanted Leather, 1 Cured Rugged Hide, 2 Rune Thread
Black Dragonscale Shoulders	300	Found	44 Rugged Leather, 45 Black Dragonscale, 2 Enchanted Leather, 1 Cured Rugged Hide, 1 Rune Thread
Devilsaur Leggings	300	Found	30, Rugged Leather, 14 Devilsaur Leather, 1 Cured Rugged Hide, 1 Rune Thread
Frostsaber Tunic	300	Found	12 Rugged Leather, 12 Frostsaber Leather, 1 Cured Rugged Hide, 2 Rune Thread
Heavy Scorpid Shoulders	300	Found	14 Rugged Leather, 14 Heavy Scorpid Scale, 1 Cured Rugged Hide, 2 Rune Thread
Living Breastplate	300	Found	16 Rugged Leather, 8 Living Essence, 2 Mooncloth, 1 Cured Rugged Hide, 2 Rune Thread
Red Dragonscale Breastplate	300	Found	40 Rugged Leather, 30, Red Dragonscale, 1 Rune Thread
Runic Leather Armor	300	Found	22 Rugged Leather, 4 Enchanted Leather, 16 Runecloth, 1 Cured Rugged Hide, 2 Rune Thread
Runic Leather Pants	300	Found	18 Rugged Leather, 12 Runecloth, 2 Enchanted Leather, 1 Rune Thread
Runic Leather Shoulders	300	Found	16 Rugged Leather, 4 Enchanted Leather, 18 Runecloth, 1 Cured Rugged Hide, 2 Rune Thread
Volcanic Shoulders	300	Found	10 Rugged Leather, 1 Essence of Fire, 1 Essence of Earth, 2 Rune Thread
Wicked Leather Armor	300	Found	20 Rugged Leather, 2 Cured Rugged Hide, 6 Felcloth, 4 Black Dye, 2 Rune Thread
Wicked Leather Belt	300	Found	14 Rugged Leather, 2 Black Dye, 2 Rune Thread

TAILORING

When people think of Tailors they immediately think of cloth armor. However, when a non-caster thinks of Tailors, they think of bags! Sure, Tailors make cloth armor and casters chase after them in droves trying to pick up some of the nicer equipment, but bags and cloaks are used by each class. Nice, huh?

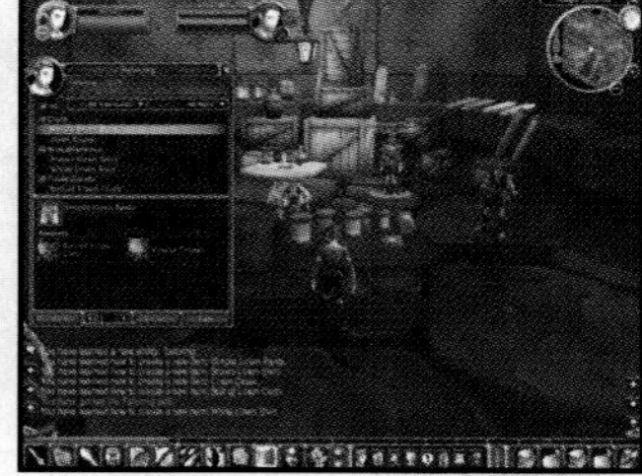

Open your abilities menu (P) and bring the Tailoring icon into your hotbar. Open the menu to see what you've got available.

Click on the name of a plan to see what components you need. It will show you how many of each component you have in your bags and how many items of that pattern you can make. It gives you the option to make 1 or many in a row. To see what the plan makes mouse over the picture, it'll give you the description of the item you're making. Once an item is made it goes into your backpack.

There really is no secondary skill needed for tailoring. The main supplies for this skill are cloth which is all dropped off humanoid mobs. By focusing on humanoid mobs, which is inevitable, you'll have a supply of cloth in no time. Tailors also buy tons of thread and dye from the vendors, however. So, you'll be spending more gold than you might expect on supplies. However, since you need no second profession to make the Tailor a viable profession, you have an opportunity to take a cash bringing gathering skill to supplement your income.

Taking Mining or Herbalism as a resource skill can make you a ton of money. Just put whatever you gather on the auctioneer and set a low minimum bid. It doesn't matter what it sells for, as it was free anyways and will offset all the dye and thread you need to buy. In most circumstances, it'll do a lot more then offset your costs, as resources are always in demand. Many casters take this skill to outfit themselves, especially since the components are so easy to find. This is one of the skills you do for yourself to wear the items you make.

In addition to the obvious, Tailors get to add a bit of flavor into the lives of role-players and those wishing to add a bit of flare to their toon. Tailors can make Tuxedo Jackets, Shirts and Pants and Wedding Dresses as well. No kidding. They also provide shirts and some are extremely sought after since they're hard to come by.

TAILORING

PRODUCT	SKILL LEVEL	SOURCE	COMPONENT(S)
Bolt of Linen Cloth	1	Initial	2 Linen Cloth
Brown Linen Shirt	1	Initial	1 Bolt of Linen Cloth, 1 Coarse Thread
Linen Cloak	1	Initial	1 Bolt of Linen Cloth, 1 Coarse Thread
Simple Linen Pants	1	Initial	1 Bolt of Linen Cloth, 1 Coarse Thread
White Linen Shirt	1	Trained	1 Bolt of Linen Cloth, 1 Coarse Thread, 1 Bleach
Brown Linen Vest	10	Trained	1 Bolt of Linen Cloth, 1 Coarse Thread
Linen Belt	15	Trained	1 Bolt of Linen Cloth, 1 Coarse Thread
Simple Linen Boots	20	Trained	2 Bolt of Linen Cloth, 1 Light Leather, 1 Coarse Thread
Brown Linen Pants	30	Trained	2 Bolt of Linen Cloth, 1 Coarse Thread
Brown Linen Robe	30	Trained	3 Bolt of Linen Cloth, 1 Coarse Thread
White Linen Robe	30	Trained	3 Bolt of Linen Cloth, 1 Coarse Thread, 1 Bleach
Heavy Linen Gloves	35	Trained	2 Bolt of Linen Cloth, 1 Coarse Thread
Blue Linen Shirt	40	Trained	2 Bolt of Linen Cloth, 1 Coarse Thread, 1 Blue Dye
Red Linen Robe	40	Found	3 Bolt of Linen Cloth, 2 Coarse Thread, 2 Red Dye
Red Linen Shirt	40	Trained	2 Bolt of Linen Cloth, 1 Coarse Thread, 1 Red Dye
Simple Dress	40	Trained	2 Bolt of Linen Cloth, 1 Coarse Thread, 1 Blue Dye, 1 Bleach
Linen Bag	45	Trained	3 Bolt of Linen Cloth, 3 Coarse Thread
Blue Linen Vest	55	Found	3 Bolt of Linen Cloth, 1 Coarse Thread, 1 Blue Dye
Red Linen Vest	55	Found	3 Bolt of Linen Cloth, 1 Coarse Thread, 1 Red Dye
Green Linen Bracers	60	Trained	3 Bolt of Linen Cloth, 2 Coarse Thread, 1 Green Dye
Reinforced Linen Cape	60	Trained	2 Bolt of Linen Cloth, 3 Coarse Thread
Linen Boots	65	Trained	3 Bolt of Linen Cloth, 1 Coarse Thread, 1 Light Leather
Barbaric Linen Vest	70	Trained	4 Bolt of Linen Cloth, 1 Light Leather, 1 Fine Thread
Blue Linen Robe	70	Found	4 Bolt of Linen Cloth, 2 Coarse Thread, 2 Blue Dye
Green Linen Shirt	70	Trained	3 Bolt of Linen Cloth, 1 Fine Thread, 1 Green Dye
Handstitched Linen Britches	70	Trained	4 Bolt of Linen Cloth, 2 Fine Thread
Red Linen Bag	70	Found	4 Bolt of Linen Cloth, 1 Fine Thread, 1 Red Dye
Bolt of Woolen Cloth	75	Trained	3 Wool Cloth
Simple Kilt	75	Trained	4 Bolt of Linen Cloth, 1 Fine Thread
Woolen Cape	75	Trained	1 Bolt of Woolen Cloth, 1 Fine Thread
Soft-soled Linen Boots	80	Trained	5 Bolt of Linen Cloth, 2 Light Leather, 1 Fine Thread
Woolen Bag	80	Trained	3 Bolt of Woolen Cloth, 1 Fine Thread
Green Woolen Vest	85	Trained	2 Bolt of Woolen Cloth, 2 Fine Thread, 1 Green Dye
Heavy Woolen Gloves	85	Trained	3 Bolt of Woolen Cloth, 1 Fine Thread
Green Woolen Robe	90	Found	3 Bolt of Woolen Cloth, 2 Fine Thread, 1 Green Dye
Pearl-clasped Cloak	90	Trained	3 Bolt of Woolen Cloth, 2 Fine Thread, 1 Small Lustrous Pearl
Green Woolen Bag	95	Found	4 Bolt of Woolen Cloth, 1 Green Dye, 1 Fine Thread
Red Woolen Boots	95	Found	4 Bolt of Woolen Cloth, 2 Light Leather, 1 Fine Thread, 2 Red Dye
Woolen Boots	95	Trained	4 Bolt of Woolen Cloth, 2 Fine Thread, 2 Light Leather
Blue Overalls	100	Found	4 Bolt of Woolen Cloth, 2 Fine Thread, 2 Blue Dye
Gray Woolen Shirt	100	Trained	2 Bolt of Woolen Cloth, 1 Fine Thread, 1 Gray Dye
Heavy Woolen Cloak	100	Found	3 Bolt of Woolen Cloth, 2 Fine Thread, 2 Small Lustrous Pearl
Gray Woolen Robe	105	Found	4 Bolt of Woolen Cloth, 3 Fine Thread, 1 Gray Dye
Double-stitched Woolen Shoulders	110	Trained	3 Bolt of Woolen Cloth, 2 Fine Thread
Heavy Woolen Pants	110	Trained	5 Bolt of Woolen Cloth, 4 Fine Thread
Stylish Red Shirt	110	Trained	3 Bolt of Woolen Cloth, 2 Red Dye, 1 Fine Thread
White Woolen Dress	110	Trained	3 Bolt of Woolen Cloth, 4 Bleach, 1 Fine Thread
Greater Adept's Robe	115	Found	5 Bolt of Woolen Cloth, 3 Fine Thread, 3 Red Dye
Red Woolen Bag	115	Found	4 Bolt of Woolen Cloth, 1 Red Dye, 1 Fine Thread
Colorful Kilt	120	Found	5 Bolt of Woolen Cloth, 3 Red Dye, 1 Fine Thread
Reinforced Woolen Shoulders	120	Found	6 Bolt of Woolen Cloth, 2 Medium Leather, 2 Fine Thread
Stylish Blue Shirt	120	Found	4 Bolt of Woolen Cloth, 2 Blue Dye, 1 Gray Dye, 1 Fine Thread
Stylish Green Shirt	120	Found	4 Bolt of Woolen Cloth, 2 Green Dye, 1 Gray Dye, 1 Fine Thread

PRODUCT	SKILL LEVEL	SOURCE	COMPONENT(S)
Bolt of Silk Cloth	125	Trained	4 Silk Cloth
Phoenix Gloves	125	Found	4 Bolt of Woolen Cloth, 1 Iridescent Pearl, 4 Fine Thread, 2 Bleach
Phoenix Pants	125	Found	6 Bolt of Woolen Cloth, 1 Iridescent Pearl, 3 Fine Thread
Spidersilk Boots	125	Trained	2 Bolt of Silk Cloth, 4 Medium Leather, 4 Spider's Silk, 2 Iridescent Pearl
Gloves of Meditation	130	Trained	4 Bolt of Woolen Cloth, 3 Fine Thread, 1 Elixir of Wisdom
Bright Yellow Shirt	135	Trained	1 Bolt of Silk Cloth, 1 Yellow Dye, 1 Fine Thread
Lesser Wizard's Robe	135	Trained	2 Bolt of Silk Cloth, 2 Fine Thread, 2 Spider's Silk
Azure Silk Pants	140	Trained	4 Bolt of Silk Cloth, 2 Blue Dye, 3 Fine Thread
Boots of Darkness	140	Found	3 Bolt of Silk Cloth, 2 Medium Leather, 1 Shadow Protection Potion, 2 Fine Thread
Spider Silk Slippers	140	Found	3 Bolt of Silk Cloth, 1 Spider's Silk, 2 Fine Thread
Azure Silk Gloves	145	Found	3 Bolt of Silk Cloth, 2 Heavy Leather, 2 Blue Dye, 2 Fine Thread
Azure Silk Hood	145	Trained	2 Bolt of Silk Cloth, 2 Blue Dye, 1 Fine Thread
Hands of Darkness	145	Found	3 Bolt of Silk Cloth, 2 Heavy Leather, 2 Shadow Protection Potion, 2 Fine Thread
Azure Silk Vest	150	Trained	5 Bolt of Silk Cloth, 4 Blue Dye
Gloves of the Devout	150	Found	3 Bolt of Silk Cloth, 2 Heavy Leather, 4 Healing Potion, 1 Fine Thread
Robes of Arcana	150	Found	4 Bolt of Silk Cloth, 2 Fine Thread, 2 Spider's Silk
Small Silk Pack	150	Trained	3 Bolt of Silk Cloth, 2 Heavy Leather, 3 Fine Thread
Dark Silk Shirt	155	Trained	2 Bolt of Silk Cloth, 2 Gray Dye, 1 Fine Thread
Silk Headband	160	Trained	3 Bolt of Silk Cloth, 2 Fine Thread
White Swashbuckler's Shirt	160	Trained	3 Bolt of Silk Cloth, 2 Bleach, 1 Silken Thread
Enchanter's Cowl	165	Trained	3 Bolt of Silk Cloth, 2 Fine Thread, 2 Thick Spider's Silk
Green Silk Armor	165	Found	5 Bolt of Silk Cloth, 2 Green Dye, 1 Silken Thread
Earthen Vest	170	Trained	3 Bolt of Silk Cloth, 1 Elemental Earth, 2 Fine Thread
Formal White Shirt	170	Trained	3 Bolt of Silk Cloth, 2 Bleach, 1 Fine Thread
Shadow Hood	170	Found	4 Bolt of Silk Cloth, 1 Silken Thread, 1 Shadow Oil
Azure Silk Belt	175	Trained	4 Bolt of Silk Cloth, 1 Elemental Water, 2 Blue Dye, 2 Fine Thread, 1 Iron Buckle
Azure Silk Cloak	175	Found	3 Bolt of Silk Cloth, 2 Blue Dye, 2 Fine Thread
Bolt of Mageweave	175	Trained	5 Mageweave Cloth
Boots of the Enchanter	175	Found	4 Bolt of Silk Cloth, 1 Silken Thread, 2 Thick Spider's Silk
Crimson Silk Belt	175	Trained	4 Bolt of Silk Cloth, 1 Iron Buckle, 2 Red Dye, 1 Silken Thread
Green Silk Pack	175	Found	4 Bolt of Silk Cloth, 3 Heavy Leather, 3 Fine Thread, 1 Green Dye
Red Swashbuckler's Shirt	175	Trained	3 Bolt of Silk Cloth, 2 Red Dye, 1 Silken Thread
Crimson Silk Cloak	180	Found	5 Bolt of Silk Cloth, 2 Red Dye, 2 Fire Oil, 1 Silken Thread
Green Silken Shoulders	180	Trained	5 Bolt of Silk Cloth, 2 Silken Thread
Spider Belt	180	Found	4 Bolt of Silk Cloth, 2 Thick Spider's Silk, 1 Iron Buckle
Black Silk Pack	185	Found	5 Bolt of Silk Cloth, 1 Black Dye, 4 Fine Thread
Crimson Silk Vest	185	Trained	4 Bolt of Silk Cloth, 2 Red Dye, 2 Fine Thread
Long Silken Cloak	185	Trained	4 Bolt of Silk Cloth, 1 Mana Potion, 1 Silken Thread
Rich Purple Silk Shirt	185	Found	4 Bolt of Silk Cloth, 1 Purple Dye, 1 Silken Thread
Azure Shoulders	190	Found	6 Bolt of Silk Cloth, 2 Naga Scale, 2 Blue Dye, 2 Silken Thread
Crimson Silk Shoulders	190	Found	5 Bolt of Silk Cloth, 2 Fire Oil, 2 Red Dye, 2 Silken Thread
Robe of Power	190	Trained	2 Bolt of Mageweave, 2 Elemental Earth, 2 Elemental Water, 2 Elemental Fire, 2 Elemental Air, 2 Silken Thread
Crimson Silk Pantaloons	195	Trained	4 Bolt of Silk Cloth, 2 Red Dye, 2 Silken Thread
Earthen Silk Belt	195	Found	5 Bolt of Silk Cloth, 4 Elemental Earth, 4 Heavy Leather, 1 Iron Buckle, 2 Silken Thread
Black Swashbuckler's Shirt	200	Trained	5 Bolt of Silk Cloth, 1 Black Dye, 1 Silken Thread
Icy Cloak	200	Found	3 Bolt of Mageweave, 2 Silken Thread, 1 Frost Oil, 2 Thick Spider's Silk
Star Belt	200	Found	4 Bolt of Mageweave, 4 Heavy Leather, 1 Citrine, 1 Iron Buckle, 1 Silken Thread
Black Mageweave Leggings	205	Trained	2 Bolt of Mageweave, 3 Silken Thread
Black Mageweave Vest	205	Trained	2 Bolt of Mageweave, 3 Silken Thread
Crimson Silk Robe	205	Found	8 Bolt of Silk Cloth, 4 Elemental Fire, 2 Mana Potion, 4 Red Dye, 1 Silken Thread
Black Mageweave Robe	210	Trained	3 Bolt of Mageweave, 1 Heavy Silken Thread
Crimson Silk Gloves	210	Trained	6 Bolt of Silk Cloth, 2 Elemental Fire, 2 Fire Oil, 2 Thick Leather, 4 Red Dye, 2 Silken Thread
Shadoweave Pants	210	Trained	3 Bolt of Mageweave, 2 Shadow Silk, 1 Heavy Silken Thread
Black Mageweave Gloves	215	Trained	2 Bolt of Mageweave, 2 Heavy Silken Thread
Orange Mageweave Shirt	215	Trained	1 Bolt of Mageweave, 1 Orange Dye, 1 Heavy Silken Thread
Red Mageweave Pants	215	Found	3 Bolt of Mageweave, 2 Red Dye, 1 Heavy Silken Thread
Red Mageweave Vest	215	Found	3 Bolt of Mageweave, 2 Red Dye, 1 Heavy Silken Thread
Shadoweave Robe	215	Trained	3 Bolt of Mageweave, 2 Shadow Silk, 1 Heavy Silken Thread
White Bandit Mask	215	Found	1 Bolt of Mageweave, 1 Bleach, 1 Heavy Silken Thread
Orange Martial Shirt	220	Found	2 Bolt of Mageweave, 2 Orange Dye, 1 Heavy Silken Thread
Cindercloth Robe	225	Trained	5 Bolt of Mageweave, 2 Heart of Fire, 2 Heavy Silken Thread
Dreamweave Gloves	225	Trained	4 Bolt of Mageweave, 4 Wildvine, 2 Heart of the Wild, 2 Heavy Silken Thread
Dreamweave Vest	225	Trained	6 Bolt of Mageweave, 6 Wildvine, 2 Heart of the Wild, 2 Heavy Silken Thread
Mageweave Bag	225	Trained	4 Bolt of Mageweave, 2 Silken Thread
Red Mageweave Gloves	225	Found	3 Bolt of Mageweave, 2 Red Dye, 2 Heavy Silken Thread
Shadoweave Gloves	225	Trained	5 Bolt of Mageweave, 5 Shadow Silk, 2 Heavy Silken Thread
Black Mageweave Boots	230	Trained	3 Bolt of Mageweave, 2 Heavy Silken Thread, 2 Thick Leather
Black Mageweave Headband	230	Trained	3 Bolt of Mageweave, 2 Heavy Silken Thread
Black Mageweave Shoulders	230	Trained	3 Bolt of Mageweave, 2 Heavy Silken Thread
Lavender Mageweave Shirt	230	Found	2 Bolt of Mageweave, 2 Purple Dye, 2 Heavy Silken Thread
Pink Mageweave Shirt	235	Found	3 Bolt of Mageweave, 1 Pink Dye, 1 Heavy Silken Thread
Red Mageweave Bag	235	Trained	4 Bolt of Mageweave, 2 Red Dye, 2 Heavy Silken Thread
Red Mageweave Shoulders	235	Found	4 Bolt of Mageweave, 2 Red Dye, 3 Heavy Silken Thread
Shadoweave Shoulders	235	Trained	5 Bolt of Mageweave, 4 Shadow Silk, 2 Heavy Silken Thread
Simple Black Dress	235	Trained	3 Bolt of Mageweave, 1 Black Dye, 1 Heavy Silken Thread, 1 Bleach
Admiral's Hat	240	Found	3 Bolt of Mageweave, 6 Long Elegant Feather, 2 Heavy Silken Thread
Red Mageweave Headband	240	Found	4 Bolt of Mageweave, 2 Red Dye, 2 Heavy Silken Thread
Shadoweave Boots	240	Trained	6 Bolt of Mageweave, 6 Shadow Silk, 3 Heavy Silken Thread, 2 Thick Leather
Tuxedo Shirt	240	Found	4 Bolt of Mageweave, 2 Heavy Silken Thread
Cindercloth Boots	245	Trained	5 Bolt of Mageweave, 1 Heart of Fire, 3 Heavy Silken Thread, 2 Thick Leather
Shadoweave Mask	245	Found	2 Bolt of Mageweave, 8 Shadow Silk, 2 Heavy Silken Thread
Tuxedo Pants	245	Found	4 Bolt of Mageweave, 3 Heavy Silken Thread
Bolt of Runecloth	250	Trained	5 Runecloth
Dreamweave Circlet	250	Trained	8 Bolt of Mageweave, 4 Wildvine, 2 Heart of the Wild, 3 Heavy Silken Thread, 1 Truesilver Bar, 1 Jade
Mooncloth	250	Found	2 Felcloth
Tuxedo Jacket	250	Found	5 Bolt of Mageweave, 3 Heavy Silken Thread
White Wedding Dress	250	Found	5 Bolt of Mageweave, 3 Heavy Silken Thread, 1 Bleach
Frostweave Robe	255	Found	5 Bolt of Runecloth, 2 Globe of Water, 1 Rune Thread
Frostweave Tunic	255	Found	5 Bolt of Runecloth, 2 Globe of Water, 1 Rune Thread
Runecloth Belt	255	Trained	3 Bolt of Runecloth, 1 Rune Thread
Cindercloth Vest	260	Found	5 Bolt of Runecloth, 3 Heart of Fire, 1 Rune Thread
Runecloth Bag	260	Found	5 Bolt of Runecloth, 2 Rugged Leather, 1 Rune Thread
Runecloth Robe	260	Found	5 Bolt of Runecloth, 1 Ironweb Spider Silk, 1 Rune Thread
Runecloth Tunic	260	Found	5 Bolt of Runecloth, 1 Ironweb Spider Silk, 1 Rune Thread
Frostweave Gloves	265	Found	3 Bolt of Runecloth, 1 Essence of Water, 1 Rune Thread
Ghostweave Belt	265	Found	3 Bolt of Runecloth, 2 Ghost Dye, 1 Ironweb Spider Silk, 1 Rune Thread
Runecloth Cloak	265	Found	4 Bolt of Runecloth, 1 Ironweb Spider Silk, 1 Rune Thread
Brightcloth Gloves	270	Found	4 Bolt of Runecloth, 2 Gold Bar, 1 Rune Thread
Brightcloth Robe	270	Found	5 Bolt of Runecloth, 2 Gold Bar, 1 Rune Thread
Cindercloth Gloves	270	Found	4 Bolt of Runecloth, 3 Heart of Fire, 1 Rune Thread
Ghostweave Gloves	270	Found	4 Bolt of Runecloth, 2 Ghost Dye, 1 Ironweb Spider Silk, 1 Rune Thread
Brightcloth Cloak	275	Found	4 Bolt of Runecloth, 2 Gold Bar, 1 Rune Thread
Cindercloth Cloak	275	Found	5 Bolt of Runecloth, 1 Essence of Fire, 1 Rune Thread
Cloak of Fire	275	Found	6 Bolt of Runecloth, 4 Essence of Fire, 4 Heart of Fire, 4 Elemental Fire, 1 Rune Thread
Felcloth Pants	275	Found	5 Bolt of Runecloth, 4 Felcloth, 1 Rune Thread
Ghostweave Vest	275	Found	6 Bolt of Runecloth, 4 Ghost Dye, 1 Ironweb Spider Silk, 1 Rune Thread
Runecloth Gloves	275	Found	4 Bolt of Runecloth, 4 Rugged Leather, 1 Rune Thread
Wizardweave Leggings	275	Found	6 Bolt of Runecloth, 1 Dream Dust, 1 Rune Thread
Cindercloth Pants	280	Found	6 Bolt of Runecloth, 1 Essence of Fire, 1 Rune Thread

IX

PRODUCT	SKILL LEVEL	SOURCE	COMPONENT(S)
Frostweave Pants	280	Found	6 Bolt of Runecloth, 1 Essence of Water, 1 Rune Thread
Runecloth Boots	280	Found	4 Bolt of Runecloth, 2 Ironweb Spider Silk, 4 Rugged Leather, 1 Rune Thread
Felcloth Boots	285	Found	6 Bolt of Runecloth, 4 Felcloth, 4 Rugged Leather, 1 Rune Thread
Robe of Winter Night	285	Found	10 Bolt of Runecloth, 12 Felcloth, 4 Essence of Undeath, 4 Essence of Water, 1 Rune Thread
Runecloth Pants	285	Found	6 Bolt of Runecloth, 4 Ironweb Spider Silk, 1 Rune Thread
Brightcloth Pants	290	Found	6 Bolt of Runecloth, 4 Gold Bar, 1 Ironweb Spider Silk, 1 Rune Thread
Felcloth Hood	290	Found	5 Bolt of Runecloth, 4 Felcloth, 1 Rune Thread
Ghostweave Pants	290	Found	6 Bolt of Runecloth, 4 Ghost Dye, 1 Rune Thread
Mooncloth Leggings	290	Found	6 Bolt of Runecloth, 4 Mooncloth, 1 Rune Thread
Runecloth Headband	295	Found	4 Bolt of Runecloth, 4 Ironweb Spider Silk, 1 Rune Thread
Felcloth Robe	300	Found	8 Bolt of Runecloth, 8 Felcloth, 4 Demonic Rune, 2 Rune Thread
Felcloth Shoulders	300	Found	7 Bolt of Runecloth, 6 Felcloth, 4 Demonic Rune, 4 Rugged Leather, 2 Rune Thread
Mooncloth Bag	300	Found	4 Bolt of Runecloth, 2 Mooncloth, 1 Rune Thread
Mooncloth Circlet	300	Found	4 Bolt of Runecloth, 6 Mooncloth, 1 Azerothian Diamond, 2 Enchanted Leather, 2 Rune Thread
Mooncloth Shoulders	300	Found	5 Bolt of Runecloth, 5 Mooncloth, 1 Rune Thread
Mooncloth Vest	300	Found	6 Bolt of Runecloth, 4 Mooncloth, 1 Rune Thread
Runecloth Shoulders	300	Found	7 Bolt of Runecloth, 4 Ironweb Spider Silk, 4 Rugged Leather, 1 Rune Thread
Wizardweave Robe	300	Found	8 Bolt of Runecloth, 2 Dream Dust, 1 Rune Thread
Wizardweave Turban	300	Found	6 Bolt of Runecloth, 4 Dream Dust, 1 Star Ruby, 1 Rune Thread
Mooncloth Boots	???	Unknown	6 Bolt of Runecloth, 4 Mooncloth, 2 Black Pearl, 1 Rune Thread

SECONDARY SKILLS

Secondary skills have no restrictions on how many a player can take. Anyone can learn them and they don't count against your maximum of two professions. So, if you wish to take all three, go nuts! These skills generally reduce your downtime and/or help your cash flow.

COOKING

Raw meat is often found on the beasts of Azeroth. However, turning the piles of flesh, legs, ribs, eggs, etc. into delicacies is the cook's advantage! The food that cooks create often heals at a better rate than store-bought food. Animals drop all sorts of ingredients for the avid cook. Cooks can also make mana-regenerating drinks and a tea that replenishes a Rogue's Energy bar.

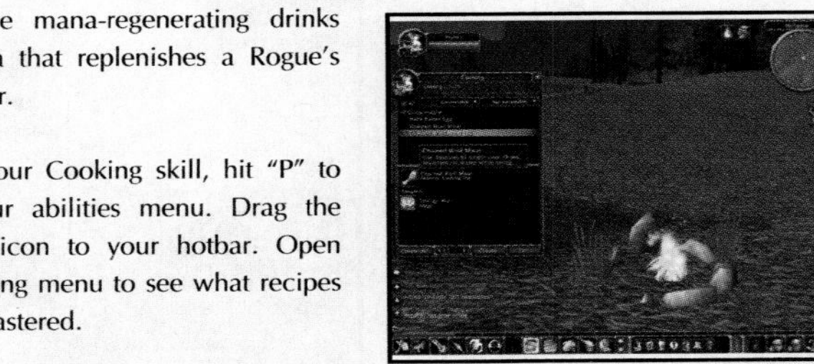

To use your Cooking skill, hit "P" to open your abilities menu. Drag the Cooking icon to your hotbar. Open the Cooking menu to see what recipes you've mastered.

Click on the name of a recipe to see what ingredients you need. It shows you how many of each ingredient you have in your bags and how many items you can cook up.

Your snacks are dropped into your packs once you've created them. You always need a fire when you cook. To make a fire, buy Simple Wood and Tinder from a general goods vendor.

Many Cooking recipes give short Stamina and Spirit bonuses. This makes the meals produced with the Cooking skill much more efficient than vendor food.

COOKING

FOOD	SKILL LEVEL	SOURCE	REAGENT(S)
Brilliant Smallfish	1	Found	1 Raw Brilliant Smallfish
Charred Wolf Meat	1	Initial	1 Stringy Wolf Meat
Crispy Bat Wing	1	Found	1 Meaty Bat Wing, 1 Mild Spices
Herb Baked Egg	1	Found	1 Small Egg, 1 Mild Spices
Roasted Boar Meat	1	Initial	1 Chunk of Boar Meat
Slitherskin Mackerel	1	Found	1 Raw Slitherskin Mackerel
Kaldorei Spider Kabob	10	Found	1 Small Spider Leg
Spiced Wolf Meat	10	Trained	1 Stringy Wolf Meat, 1 Mild Spices
Scorpid Surprise	20	Found	1 Scorpid Stinger
Beer Basted Boar Ribs	25	Found	1 Crag Boar Rib, 1 Rhapsody Malt
Roasted Kodo Meat	35	Found	1 Kodo Meat, 1 Mild Spices
Smoked Bear Meat	40	Found	1 Bear Meat
Boiled Clams	50	Trained	1 Clam Meat, 1 Refreshing Spring Water
Coyote Steak	50	Trained	1 Coyote Meat
Fillet of Frenzy	50	Found	1 Soft Frenzy Flesh, 1 Mild Spices
Goretusk Liver Pie	50	Found	1 Goretusk Liver, 1 Mild Spices
Loch Frenzy Delight	50	Found	1 Raw Loch Frenzy, 1 Mild Spices
Longjaw Mud Snapper	50	Found	1 Raw Longjaw Mud Snapper
Rainbow Fin Albacore	50	Found	1 Raw Rainbow Fin Albacore
Strider Stew	50	Found	1 Strider Meat, 1 Shiny Red Apple
Blood Sausage	60	Found	1 Bear Meat, 1 Boar Intestines, 1 Spider Ichor
Thistle Tea	60	Found	1 Swiftthistle, 1 Refreshing Spring Water
Crab Cake	75	Trained	1 Crawler Meat, 1 Mild Spices
Westfall Stew	75	Found	1 Stringy Vulture Meat, 1 Murloc Eye, 1 Goretusk Snout
Crocolisk Steak	80	Found	1 Crocolisk Meat, 1 Mild Spices
Dry Pork Ribs	80	Trained	1 Boar Ribs, 1 Mild Spices
Cooked Crab Claw	85	Found	1 Crawler Claw, 1 Mild Spices
Savory Deviate Delight	85	Found	1 Deviate Fish, 1 Mild Spices
Clam Chowder	90	Found	1 Clam Meat, 1 Ice Cold Milk, 1 Mild Spices
Dig Rat Stew	90	Found	1 Dig Rat
Murloc Fin Soup	90	Found	2 Murloc Fin, 1 Hot Spices
Bristle Whisker Catfish	100	Found	1 Raw Bristle Whisker Catfish
Crispy Lizard Tail	100	Found	1 Thunder Lizard Tail, 1 Hot Spices
Redridge Goulash	100	Found	1 Crisp Spider Meat, 1 Tough Condor Meat
Seasoned Wolf Kabob	100	Found	2 Lean Wolf Flank, 1 Stormwind Seasoning Herbs
Big Bear Steak	110	Found	1 Big Bear Meat, 1 Hot Spices
Gooey Spider Cake	110	Found	2 Gooey Spider Leg, 1 Hot Spices
Lean Venison	110	Found	1 Stag Meat, 4 Mild Spices
Succulent Pork Ribs	110	Found	2 Boar Ribs, 1 Hot Spices
Crocolisk Gumbo	120	Found	1 Tender Crocolisk Meat, 1 Hot Spices
Goblin Deviled Clams	125	Trained	1 Tangy Clam Meat, 1 Hot Spices
Hot Lion Chops	125	Found	1 Lion Meat, 1 Hot Spices
Lean Wolf Steak	125	Found	1 Lean Wolf Flank, 1 Mild Spices
Curiously Tasty Omelet	130	Found	1 Raptor Egg, 1 Hot Spices
Tasty Lion Steak	150	Found	2 Lion Meat, 1 Soothing Spices
Barbecued Buzzard Wing	175	Trained	1 Buzzard Wing, 1 Hot Spices
Carrion Surprise	175	Found	1 Mystery Meat, 1 Hot Spices
Giant Clam Scorcho	175	Found	1 Giant Clam Meat, 1 Hot Spices
Hot Wolf Ribs	175	Found	1 Red Wolf Meat, 1 Hot Spices
Jungle Stew	175	Found	1 Tiger Meat, 1 Refreshing Spring Water, 2 Shiny Red Apple
Mystery Stew	175	Found	1 Mystery Meat, 1 Skin of Dwarven Stout
Roast Raptor	175	Found	1 Raptor Flesh, 1 Hot Spices
Rockscale Cod	175	Found	1 Raw Rockscale Cod
Soothing Turtle Bisque	175	Found	1 Turtle Meat, 1 Soothing Spices
Dragonbreath Chilli	200	Found	1 Mystery Meat, 1 Small Flame Sac, 1 Hot Spices
Heavy Kodo Stew	200	Found	2 Heavy Kodo Meat, 1 Soothing Spices, 1 Refreshing Spring Water
Cooked Glossy Mightfish	225	Found	1 Raw Glossy Mightfish, 1 Soothing Spices
Fillet of Redgill	225	Found	1 Raw Redgill
Monster Omlette	225	Unknown	1 Giant Egg, 2 Soothing Spices
Spiced Chili Crab	225	Trained	1 Tender Crab Meat, 2 Hot Spices
Spotted Yellowtail	225	Found	1 Raw Spotted Yellowtail
Grilled Squid	240	Found	1 Winter Squid, 1 Soothing Spices
Hot Smoked Bass	240	Found	1 Raw Summer Bass, 2 Hot Spices
Nightfin Soup	250	Found	1 Raw Nightfin Snapper, 1 Refreshing Spring Water
Poached Sunscale Salmon	250	Found	1 Raw Sunscale Salmon
Baked Salmon	275	Found	1 Raw Whitescale Salmon, 1 Soothing Spices
Lobster Stew	275	Found	1 Darkclaw Lobster, 1 Refreshing Spring Water
Mightfish Steak	275	Found	1 Large Raw Mightfish, 1 Hot Spices, 1 Soothing Spices
Goldthorn Tea	???	R.Downs	1 Goldthorn, 1 Refreshing Spring Water

FIRST AID

First Aid offers non-healers the opportunity to heal themselves and others. No, it's not as amazing as the magical healing abilities of the Priest, Druid, Shaman or Paladin, but it's something! It's great for those non-healers while they're soloing or for a quick fix when your main healer goes down. Bandages of all types can heal wounds and lessen downtime. Also, Anti-Venom is a great ability for those adventurers wishing to solo in spider-laden areas.

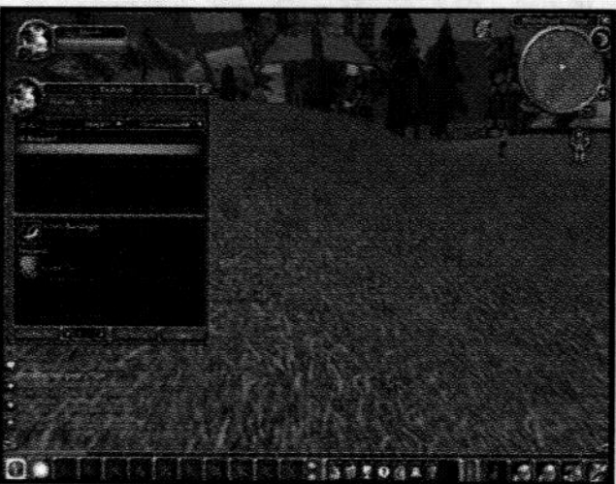

When you apply a bandage, it activates instantly, but takes a few seconds to heal. A player can only be bandaged once every 60 sec. First Aid is a stop-gap or emergency measure and isn't intended to be the focus of a player's battle time. If you're hit at anytime while the bandage is working, it stops healing. So, don't think that four characters can keep using First Aid on their tank to keep them standing.

Pull the First Aid icon into your hotbar from the abilities menu (P) and open the First Aid menu to choose which item you wish to create.

You never have enough cloth. There will be times when you know you'll never turn all the cloth you have into bandages and use them all, just to run out the next day. Some players keep a minimum of 100 cloth banked and 40 bandages on them. Bandages are best used after a fight and perfect for soloing. Applying one right after a fight can keep you going endlessly for some easy experience. Remember, if you get hit while applying the bandage, you lose the healing, but retain the 60 second cooldown timer. Once you learn the next level of bandage and get a good supply of them, dump the lower level bandages. You may think you may use them again, but you probably won't.

FIRST AID

ITEM	SKILL LEVEL	SOURCE	COMPONENT(S)
Linen Bandage	1	Initial	1 Linen Cloth
Heavy Linen Bandage	40	Trained	2 Linen Cloth
Anti-Venom	80	Trained	1 Small Venom Sac
Wool Bandage	80	Trained	1 Wool Cloth
Heavy Wool Bandage	115	Trained	2 Wool Cloth
Strong Anti-Venom	130	Found	1 Large Venom Sac
Silk Bandage	150	Trained	1 Silk Cloth
Heavy Silk Bandage	180	Found	2 Silk Cloth
Mageweave Bandage	210	Found	1 Mageweave Cloth
Heavy Mageweave Bandage	240	Trained	2 Mageweave Cloth
Runecloth Bandage	260	Trained	1 Runecloth
Heavy Runecloth Bandage	290	Trained	2 Runecloth

FISHING

Fishing has two really nice factors with it. The general ability is to catch fish. You can use the fish as food or cook it to make it even better. It's great for Hunters with pets that are always hungry. Some skills, like Alchemy, actually need certain types of fish for recipes they have. You can also catch clams, boxes, chests and mollusks that may have something of value inside of them. Most of the time, nothing but clam meat pops up. However, once in a while you get that pearl or some magical boots that just make you want to catch some more and try your luck again!

Pop open the abilities menu (P) and drag the Fishing icon into your hotbar. To Fish, activate the icon. Of course, you'll need to actually equip a fishing pole. This is the single profession/skill that requires you to actually have the item in your hands. When you've reached a body of water, whether it's a lake, pond, or ocean, hit the icon. Watch as you cast your bobber into the water.

FISHING POLES

M LEV	WEAPON NAME	VENDOR VALUE	NOTES
1	Fishing Pole	4	
1	Blump Family Fishing Pole	1 87	Fishing Skill +3
5	Strong Fishing Pole	1 80	Fishing Skill +5
15	Darkwood Fishing Pole	10 66	Fishing Skill +15
25	Big Iron Fishing Pole	33 78	Fishing Skill +20

Keep your mouse on the bobber and, as soon as it dips up and down, right-click it! If you were successful, take your reward from the loot window.

FISHING POLES DON'T MAKE GOOD WEAPONS

Since you actually have to equip the fishing pole to fish, there may come a time when you're caught off guard and forced to do battle. However, the first thing to do is to swap out that pole for a real weapon. (Check the weapon tables for the combat stats on fishing poles to see why.)

Fresh water and ocean waters have different types of fish. There are even bodies of water that are famous for dropping certain types of goodies more so than others. The best way to skill up is to fish in areas equal to your skill level. As an amateur fisher, stay in a starting area—Levels 1-10. As you progress, move farther out into the world. You may even be surprised at some of the odd places to fish.

GUILDS

CREATING A GUILD

Creating a guild is a simple enough process requiring only that you get together with nine other friends and purchase a charter. Charters cost 10 silver and can be bought from any Guildmaster in any of the six main cities throughout Azeroth. You'll be asked to input a name for your guild at the same time as making your purchase.

WHAT'S IN A NAME?

It's important not to rush into choosing a name for your guild. It should reflect the attitude of the guild and also stay within the naming conventions that Blizzard has set up. Getting the GM's attention for your name probably won't be the best way to garner their favor when you need them most. Remember, your guild name can make you famous or infamous.

Once you've purchased a guild charter, target the potential members one at a time and click the "Request a Signature" button in order to get members to sign it. Once it's signed, return to the Guildmaster and turn it in. Congratulations! You now have a guild to manage.

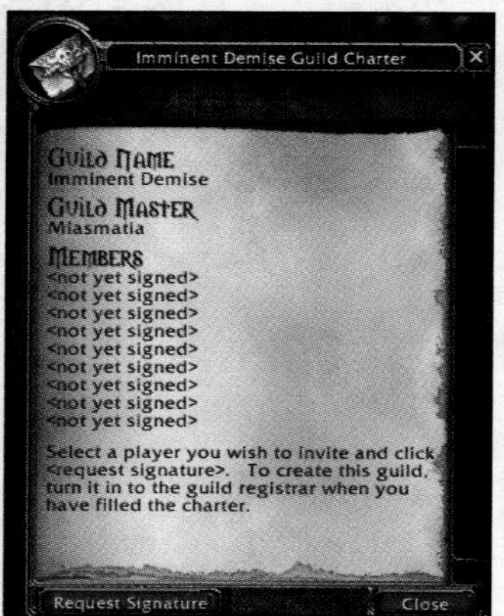

TYPES OF GUILDS

Guilds, also sometimes referred to as clans, are often comprised of a group of people with similar likes, personalities and gaming styles that join together for mutual benefit. While there may be plenty of guilds to choose from, choosing the right guild for your play style isn't always as easy as it sounds.

Large Guilds A large guild can offer a constant flow of equipment and supplies. There are always groups to join and someone is always around to help. They can also be impersonal in nature and it can be easy to get lost among the many. Seeing people with the same guild tag and not recognizing their name is a common occurrence.

Small Guilds A small guild can offer the intimacy that a large guild normally can't. Generally, everyone knows each other and relationships are closer in nature. On the negative side, it's often more difficult to find other members to group up with or help you along if you're on different play schedules.

Role-play Centric Some guilds focus on fostering a role-play atmosphere among their members. These sorts of guilds often plan and carry out events within the game, have members that rarely break character and are often very active on the storyboards of their home board as well as the boards of others.

PvP Centric Player vs. Player competition is sometimes the central focus of a guild. Being the best means killing the enemy and doing it well. If you don't have the "killer" instinct, you may want avoid guilds focused mainly on this aspect of the game.

PvE/Powerlevelers These types of guilds strive for excellence in beating the AI of the game, getting the very best items and maximizing their PvE experiences down to a science. They often level faster than other players and guilds and have some of the very best items the game can offer.

Casual Gaming Some guilds are made up just of other casual gamers. They schedule their playtimes to coincide with others in the guild so that they can have others to play with. While they may not achieve some of the higher game content goals, this can be a rewarding and fun atmosphere to take part in. A growing trend is the formation of guilds made up of families (parents and their children). They foster a smaller, more understanding community.

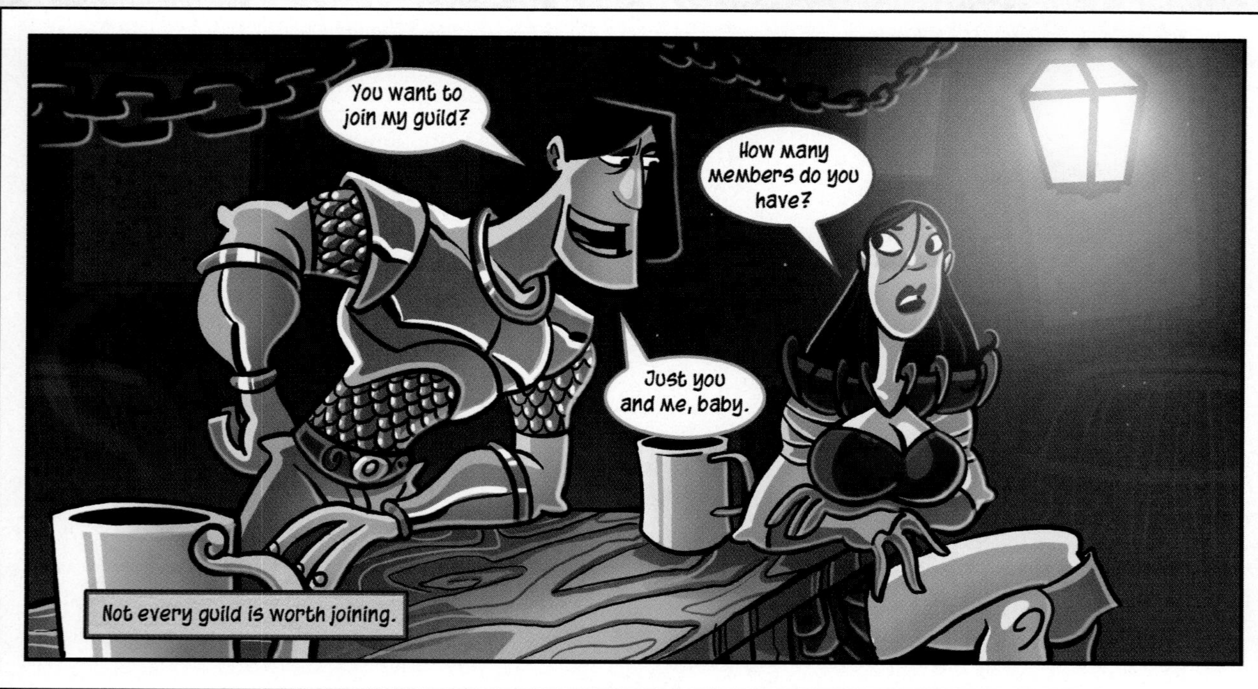

PvE/PvP/RP Some guilds strive for a very real balance between all the elements of the game. They have a varied membership and yet still manage to find common goals to push them forward. They may not necessarily have any strict rules that they have their membership abide by and are often more of a gathering spot.

When deciding on a guild to either join or create, it's important to keep all of these things in mind for what you most would like to be a part of. While not all PvP-centric guilds are without RP, not all RP guilds are without PvP and in many cases the two can co-exist on equal footing if it is the right kind of guild.

MANAGING A GUILD

There are many tools that are inherent in the guild management screen for guildmasters and members. The amount of control that any particular member has is up to the Guildmaster as well based on the settings they assign to each rank.

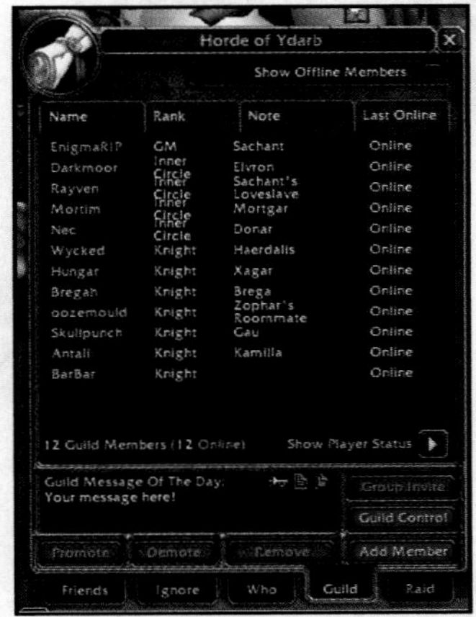

Take a look at your guild screen by using the social button on your toolbar or using the hotkey "O." Click the guild tab to see all the available commands for working with your guild.

You'll see a listing of all the members of your guild and whether they're currently online. Close the menu by clicking the tab at the top. Sorting members is also as easy as clicking the tab headers above each part.

As Guildmaster, you'll have access to every command without restriction. There are two different modes of viewing members of the guild that any member of the guild can access. One is a View Players mode and the other is a View Guild Status mode. Viewing players shows their name, zone, level, class and if they are a part of a group. Viewing a player's guild status shows their name, rank, any notes and when they were last online/or currently are online. This can be a handy feature for monitoring the activity of members.

GUILD SCREEN FEATURES

Guild Message of the Day (Trumpet Icon) This allows you to set a short message (60 characters max) letting the guild know of upcoming events or announcements.

Public Notes Those with access to this ability can set a note for a player that anyone in the guild can see. This is a useful tool for noting alternate characters belonging to a certain player and will stave off the usual confusion of who is who that many guilds face.

Officer Notes These are notes that only those given officer access can read. This is a good way to notate guild members that are either excelling or on warning for behavior.

Promote Promote members to new ranks with this option. Only the GM can promote a non-officer to officer, however. Regular officers can only promote others to the rank below them.

Demote This allows someone with this power to demote a member. They cannot however, demote another player of equal rank. Only the GM will be able to demote someone of an officer rank.

Remove Someone with access to this ability can remove other players from the guide. Only the GM can remove and officer and others can only dismiss those who rank below them.

Group Invite Any member of the guild can use the group invite option. This is not a guild only command.

Guild Control Guild control opens up the ranking structures for manipulation. Only the Guildmaster has access to this tool.

Add Member Any member that has been given access to this option can add any other player they wish by using this option.

Guildmasters get to toy with a few other extra features by being able to create and delete ranks in the guild as well as assign powers to select members.

There are predefined ranks already listed in the ranking structure that cannot be deleted. However, these ranks can have their name changed to reflect the flavor of the guild. Changes can be typed in the guild label box and then the Accept box clicked to lock it in.

Each rank can be customized with guild accessibility levels. The available options and what they give access to are as follows:

Guildchat Listen Listen to guildchat.

Guildchat Speak Speak in guildchat.

Officerchat Listen Listen to Officer Chat.

Officerchat Speak Speak in officer chat.

Promote Promote a member up to a rank below himself or herself.

Demote Demote a member a rank below himself or herself.

Invite Member Invite another player to join the guild.

Remove Member Remove a lower ranked member from the guild.

Set MOTD Set the Message of the Day.

Edit Public Note Edit someone's public note.

View Officer Note View an officer's note.

Edit Officer Note Edit an officer's note.

Clicking the small "plus sign" next to the ranking listing can create additional ranks. Any new ranks will be set at the lowest setting as compared to the other ranks and cannot be reordered to a higher position, so plan accordingly.

To remove a rank, select it and use the minus sign. Make sure that no member is assigned to the rank first, however, otherwise you'll be unable to remove it.

PLANNING YOUR RANKS

For those guilds that have officers that rank evenly, you'll find that you may want to use the generic officer ranking under GM to define them and then place a public note as to their specific rank. This keeps them all within the same power level and structure as each other and negates the need to try to shuffle around other ranks.

There are other things that you may want to do beyond the spectrum of the game. Running a guild can be a fun and rewarding experience, provided it is well organized and the members understand what is expected of them.

Take the time to create a guild charter By taking the time to create a guild charter, you can define the kind of guild that you want to be a part of and allow others to understand more of what you stand for as well.

Create a Website There are many different sites that will even host a guild should you not have any budding or full-fledged webmasters among you. A website and forum can be a vital way of keeping the members informed and active, even when they can't be within the game.

Create a Structure Structure your guild with a type of governing style as well as a ranking system. The game mechanics give a bit more play to defining roles within the guild and it creates a chain of command that others are willing to follow. It also helps foster a strong sense of organization.

Create a Recruiting Method If you choose to recruit new members, it's a wise idea to create some sort of method to go along with it. By doing so, you'll be able to better define the role of your members in the guild as well as define the kinds of people you feel best fit into the guild.

Have Fun The most successful guilds are successful for a reason. They are there to have fun and experience the game to their full potential. Losing site of the 'fun' factor will make you lose members quickly, while keeping it firmly in mind helps retain them and gathers new members as well.

OTHER GUILD COMMANDS

There are other guild commands that can be utilized by the members, officers and the guildmaster of a guild in the slash commands.

/ginfo Gives the start date, number of players and number of accounts in your guild.

/g Sends a message to your guild channel.

/o Sends a message to the officer channel of the guild.

/ginvite Invites another player to join your guild

/gremove Removes a player from your guild

/gpromote Promotes a player one rank within your guild

/gdemote Demotes a player one rank within your guild

/gmotd Sets the guild's message of the day

/gquit Quits you from your guild

/groster Gives an entire guild roster (This is an officer and guildmaster command only)

/gleader Allows the current guild leader to transfer leadership to another online player.

/gdisband Allows a guild leader to disband the guild.

GUILD TABARDS

Guildmasters have the option of creating a guild tabard that the members can purchase and wear. (Or, if the guild's well-established, one can be awarded to members as a badge of office upon inclusion into the guild.) A tabard is worn in the chest slot; it's specifically designed to hold one. Tabards do not have any special statistics to them, however, they do exhibit the guild colors and symbol that the guildmaster chooses.

The guildmaster needs to visit the Guild Tabard Designer that should be standing nearby the Guildmaster you had to do the guild charter and registration with.

Take the time to carefully consider all of the options that are offered. Once a tabard has been created, it cannot be changed. There are many different color combinations and symbols to choose from and it may take awhile to find just the right one.

The most important thing will be drumming up the 10 gold that it costs to even create a tabard. It's possible to incorporate a tax for your members so that one can be created or just pay it as the guildmaster. The more members you have to start with, the less of a burden the cost becomes.

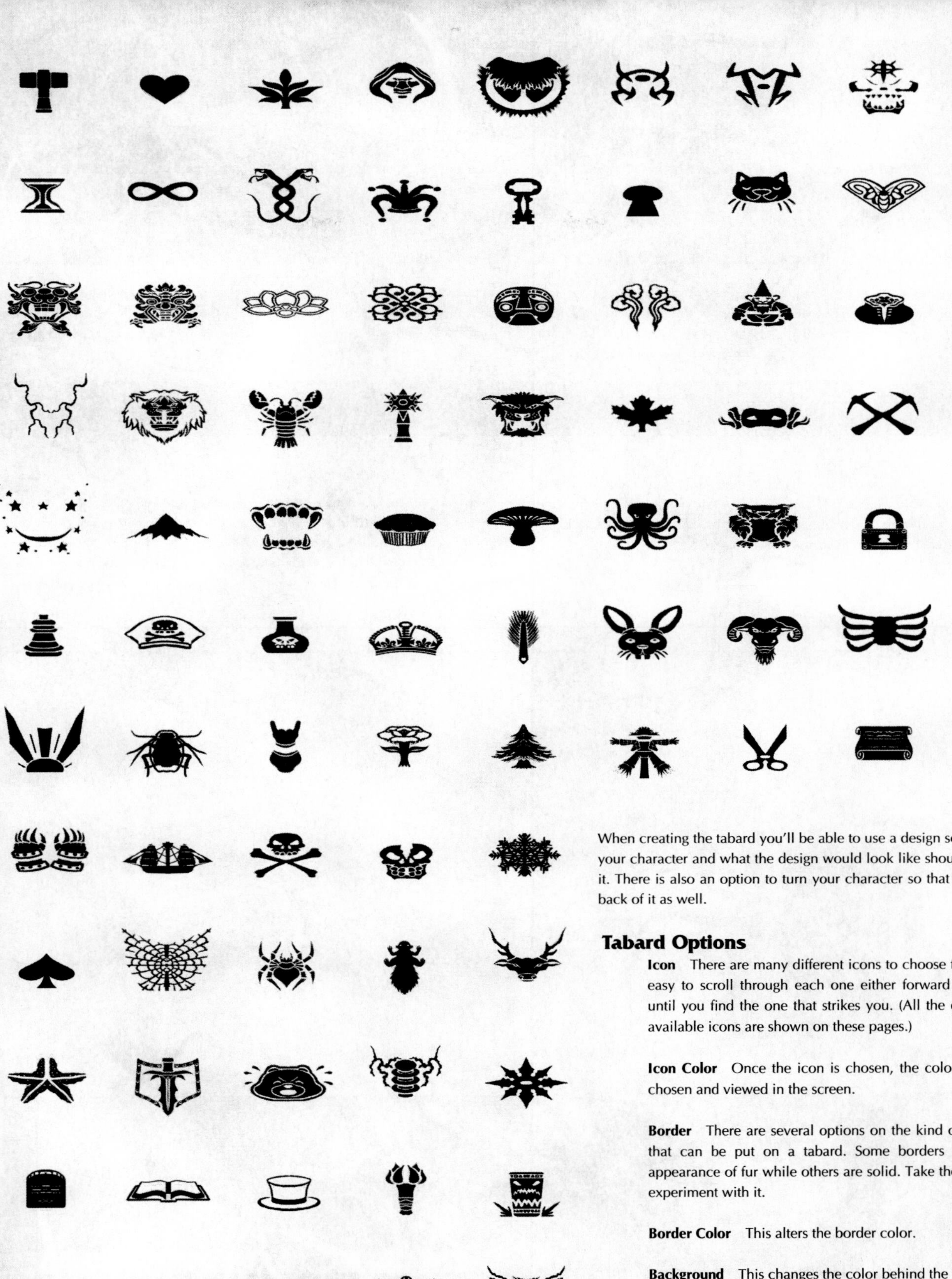

When creating the tabard you'll be able to use a design screen that shows your character and what the design would look like should you purchase it. There is also an option to turn your character so that you can see the back of it as well.

Tabard Options

Icon There are many different icons to choose from. It's easy to scroll through each one either forward or back until you find the one that strikes you. (All the currently available icons are shown on these pages.)

Icon Color Once the icon is chosen, the color can be chosen and viewed in the screen.

Border There are several options on the kind of border that can be put on a tabard. Some borders give the appearance of fur while others are solid. Take the time to experiment with it.

Border Color This alters the border color.

Background This changes the color behind the icon and border.

Once you have created the design that you like best, simply click on the "Accept" option. The price of the design will be deducted from your account and make buying a tabard available from the Tabard Vendor. Each individual member that chooses to purchase a tabard will need to pay one gold per tabard.

A guild that designs and purchases a tabard can show a unity on the battlefield that can either inspire fear or humor depending on the choices made in the design. It is a great way to show off the personality of the guild as well.

THE WORLD OF AZEROTH

HOW TO USE THIS SECTION

At first glance, one might immediately be overwhelmed with the amount of content in this section. Yes, there is an abundance of information, but it's ordered in the best way to give you the most information. Each Region section is broken up into the smaller Zone sections that form the regions. For example, the region of Khaz Modan is broken up into the following zones: Ironforge, Badlands, Dun Morogh, Loch Modan, Searing Gorge, and Wetlands. Beyond that, each element of the zone sections is described in detail to give you a clear idea on how best the sections will work for you.

REGION SECTIONS

Each region section (as marked below on the maps) is comprised of a varying amount of zones. When in game, players won't often say that they're in a specific region ("Hey, I'm in Khaz Modan.") However, they will frequently refer to the zone that they're in or heading to. The region section is just an easy way for players to get a general idea where they are in the big scheme of things.

ZONES

The zones of which each region is comprised are ordered alphabetically within the corresponding region section. However, instead of including the major cities within the body of the region sections, we've pulled them to the front for easy access. (Northern Kalimdor is the exception since to major cities lie within its borders: Darnassus and Orgrimmar.) Here is a list of each region, the cities and zones.

NORTHERN KALIMDOR

- Darnassus
- Orgrimmar
- Ashenvale
- Azshara
- Darkshore
- Desolace
- Durotar
- Felwood
- Moonglade
- Stonetalon Mountains
- Teldrassil
- The Barrens
- Winterspring

SOUTHERN KALIMDOR

- Thunder Bluff
- Dustwallow Marsh
- Feralas
- Mulgore
- Tanaris
- Thousand Needles
- Un'Goro Crater

AZEROTH

- Stormwind
- Blasted Lands
- Burning Steppes
- Duskwood
- Elwynn Forest
- Redridge Mountains
- Stranglethorn Vale
- Swamp of Sorrows
- Westfall

KHAZ MODAN

- Ironforge
- Badlands
- Dun Morogh
- Loch Modan
- Searing Gorge
- Wetlands

LORDAERON

- Undercity
- Alterac Mountains
- Arathi Highlands
- Eastern Plaguelands
- Hillsbrad Foothills
- Silverpine Forest
- The Hinterlands
- Tirisfal Glades
- Western Plaguelands

ZONE SECTIONS

As previously mentioned, each region section is broken up into the zones located within. In this guide, each zone gets its own corresponding section with an emblem, a map, a legend, and a quest list. Within non-city zones, a resource list is also included. Each item within the sections is fully described in this How To section. Refer back to these two pages if you ever need clarification on what something is or means.

THE EMBLEM

KHAZ MODAN

In the top left of each zone opener, there's an emblem which indicates two things: 1) the region in which the zone is located and 2) the status of the region. Each emblem can be one of three colors: green, yellow, and red.

GREEN indicates ALLIANCE controlled territory.

YELLOW indicates CONTESTED territory.

RED indicates HORDE controlled territory.

> Although we've chosen these colors to distinguish who holds certain territories, the colors mean something else entirely in the game. GREEN indicates a friendly territory and RED is an enemy held territory. YELLOW remains a contested territory.

MAPS

The maps and legends are exhaustively annotated. The maps themselves are the same as those used in the game, so you can pull up the in-game map and discover where you are in relation to what you're looking for.

CALLOUTS

The callouts on the maps correlate directly with the legends. However, instead of overlapping hundreds of icons on the same map, each callout represents a general area. The legends display everything and everyone within these areas.

RESOURCE LISTS

Directly below the maps, on non-city areas, a source list gives you a quick reference of which resources can be found in each zone. Within each section, the ore, herb and skinning resources are quickly outlined.

HERBALISM

HERB	AVAILABILITY
Peacebloom	Abundant
Silverleaf	Abundant
Earthroot	Abundant

LEGEND

1 GNOMEREGAN
Entrance to Gnomeregan Instance
Elder Crag Boars 7-8
Ice Claw Bear 7-8
Leper Gnome 8-10
Snow Leopard 7-8

2 FROSTMANE HOLD
Elder Crag Boars 7-8
Frostmane Headhunter 8-9
Frostmane Snowstrider 8-9
Frostmane Troll 7-8

The legends can be intimidating at first, but they're broken up in a very intuitive manner. First, they're broken up into areas that correspond to callouts on the maps. Under each area header, the NPCs and mobs that can be found in each area are listed.

QUESTS

The quest tables are sure to be one of the most used resources in this guide. Each quest list shows a vast amount of information. The quests for the zone are ordered alphabetically; only the quests that appear in your Quest Log for a specific zone will appear in the corresponding section in the guide.

COLUMNS

M LEV The minimum level you need to be to pick up the quest.

Q LEV The actual level of the quest.

QUEST LAUNCHER Who (or what) begins the quest.

QUEST FINISHER Who (or what) allows the quest to be completed.

CHAIN? Whether or not the quest BEGINS or CONTINUES a chain. The quests that end are not marked with a "Y" so as not to reveal too much of the storyline.

XP--- through XP+++ These six columns show the lowest amount (XP---) of experience that can be received and the highest (XP+++). The XP reward is determined by comparing your level with the quest level. For example, if you complete a quest at the minimum level for which it's allowed, you'll gain the max XP.

CASH REWARD The money (if any) awarded for completing the quest.

QUEST	M LEV	Q LEV	QUEST LAUNCHER	QUEST FINISHER	CHAIN?	XP---	XP--	XP-	XP+	XP++	XP+++	CASH REWARD
A Favor for Evershine	2	8	Rejold Barleybrew	Rejold Barleybrew	Y	55	110	210	320	420	525	None
A New Threat	1	2	Balir Frosthammer	Balir Frosthammer	N	15	35	70	100	140	170	None
CHOICE OF: 1 Bear Shawl or 1 Rustic Belt or 1 Snow Boots												
A Pilot's Revenge	8	11	A Dwarven Corpse (06)	Pilot Hammerfoot	N	65	130	260	400	525	650	None
CHOICE OF: 1 Craftsman's Dagger or 1 Compact Hammer												

REWARD LINES

The beige lines underneath the associated quest indicate that a reward is offered in addition to any XP or cash bonuses. There are two types of rewards: static and choices.

STATIC Static rewards (REWARD:) are granted upon the completion of the quest. If there is more than one static reward, you receive all of them.

CHOICE Some quests force you to choose (CHOICE OF:) between items. You are given the option to take Item A or Item B. Many quests offer more than two options.

ICONS

We've incorporated an icon system to help you quickly identify each type of reward offered in a given zone. You can quickly find out if there are any items that you're interested in just by skimming the quest tables for icons. They're broken up into armor icons (divided by which slot the item can be equipped in), weapon icons (two-handed weapons are indicated) and item icons. Further, for each armor type, there are multiple colors used to indicate each one.

CLOTH ARMOR
= Cloth Chest
= Cloth Feet
= Cloth Hand
= Cloth Head
= Cloth Legs
= Cloth Shoulders
= Cloth Wrist
= Cloth Waist

LEATHER ARMOR
= Leather Chest
= Leather Feet
= Leather Hand
= Leather Head
= Leather Legs
= Leather Shoulders
= Leather Wrist
= Leather Waist

MAIL ARMOR
= Mail Chest
= Mail Feet
= Mail Hand
= Mail Head
= Mail Legs
= Mail Shoulders
= Mail Wrist
= Mail Waist

PLATE ARMOR
= Plate Chest
= Plate Feet
= Plate Hand
= Plate Head
= Plate Legs
= Plate Shoulders
= Plate Wrist
= Plate Waist

WEAPONS
= 1H Axe
= 2H Axe
= Bow
= Crossbow
= Dagger
= Fist Weapon
= Fishing Pole
= Gun
= 1H Mace
= 2H Mace
= Polearm
= Spear
= Staff
= 1H Sword
= 2H Sword
= Throwing Weapon
= Wand

CLOAKS
= Cloak

SHIELDS
= Shield

ITEMS
= Necklace
= Ring
= Trinket

STORMWIND

Stormwind is one of the few great Humans cities that remains after many wars. Threatened on all sides by Gnolls, Orcs, and Undead, Stormwind offers a measure of protection and hope to the people of the east. Within the mighty walls, beyond the Valley of Heroes, is a city where violence and struggle is only found in pockets. The underground Stockades, is a dangerous place to wander because of constant riots and outright attacks, but the rest of the city of often calm. Children play in the streets, vendors hawk their wares, and life continues despite the hardships of Azeroth.

MAGE'S QUARTER

1 ENCHANTING SHOP
Betty Quin 25 Journeyman Enchanter
Jessara Cordell 30 Enchanting Supplies
Lucan Cordell 35 Expert Enchanter

2 THE STOCKADES
Entrance to the Stockades World Dungeon
Injured Stockade Grunt 45
Nurse Lillian 30
Stockade Archer 45
Stockade Grunt 45
Warden Thelwater 30 Quest

3 ACADEMY OF ARTS AND SCIENCE
Acolyte Dellis 15
Adair Gilroy 60 Librarian
Mazen Mac'Nadir 44

4 PYROTECHNICS
Darian Singh 30 Fireworks Vendor

5 THE SLAUGHTERED LAMB
Demisette Cloyce 60 Warlock Trainer
Gakin the Darkbinder 50
Jalane Ayrole 45 Master Shadoweave Tailor
Jarel Moor 30 Bartender
Sandahl 50 Warlock Trainer
Spackle Thornberry 40 Felhunter Trainer
Ursula Deline 40 Warlock Trainer
Zardeth of the Black Claw 70

6 OUTER AREAS
Archmage Malin 40
Crier Goodman 3
Erich Lohan 5
Karlie Chaddis 25
Stormwind City Patroller 75
Tannysa 35 Herbalism Trainer

7 ESSENTIAL COMPONENTS
Owen Vaughn 30 Reagent Vendor

8 LARSON CLOTHIERS
Evan Larson 30 Hatter
Sellandus 31 Expert Tailor
Thurman Schnedier 2
Wynne Larson 30 Robe Merchant

9 WIZARD'S SANCTUM
Elsharin 50 Mage Trainer
High Sorcerer Andromath 65
Jennea Cannon 40 Mage Trainer
Larimaine Purdue 50 Portal Trainer
Maginor Dumas 60 Master Mage

10 THE BLUE RECLUSE
Angus Stern 60 Head Chef
Connor Rivers 25 Apprentice Chef
Joachim Brenlow 30 Arcane Bartender
Steven Lohan 5

11 ALCHEMY NEEDS
Eldraelith 30 Herbalism Supplier
Lylyssia Nightbreeze 35 Journeyman Alchemist
Maria Lumere 30 Alchemy Supplies
Tel'Athir 31 Journeyman Alchemist

12 DUNCAN'S TEXTILES
Alexandra Bolero 30 Tailoring Supplies
Duncan Cullen 30 Light Armor Merchant
Georgio Bolero 46 Artisan Tailor
Lawrence Schneider 25 Journeyman Tailor

THE PARK

13 CANAL AREA
Caretaker Folsom 30 Quest

14 INSIDE THE PARK
Argos Nightwhisper 20
Imelda 25
Kelly Grant 40
Kimberly Grant 35
Maldryn 40 Druid Trainer
Shailea 35
Sheldras Moontree 60 Druid Trainer
Sylista 30 Stable Master
Theridran 50 Druid Trainer

15 HERBALISM STORE
Shylamiir 35 Herbalism Trainer

THE CATHEDRAL

16 CANAL AREA
Brandon 1
Justin 1
Morris Lawry 1
Roman 1
Stormwind City Patroller 75

17 THE FINEST THREAD

18 CATHEDRAL SQUARE

BROTHER KRISTOFF 40 QUEST

STORMWIND CITY PATROLLER 75

19 THE ARGENT DAWN

20 CITY HALL
Baros Alexston 30 City Architect Quest
Royal Factor Bathrilor 40 Stormwind Census

21 RIGHTEOUS PLATES
Agustus Moulaine 30 Mail Armor Merchant
Theresa Moulaine 30 Robe Vendor

22 JUST MACES
Gregory Ardus 30 Staff/Mace Merchant

23 CATHEDRAL OF LIGHT
Archbishop Benedictus 50
Arthur the Faithful 40 Paladin Trainer
Bishop Farthing 40
Brother Anton 50 Scarlet Crusade Quest
Brother Banjamin 40 Priest Trainer
Brother Cassius 30 Reagent Vendor
Brother Joshua 50 Priest Trainer
Brother Samo 55
Duthorian Rall 60
Gazin Tenorm 9
Katherine the Pure 50 Paladin Trainer
Lord Grayson Shadowbreaker 60 Paladin Trainer
Shaina Fuller 35 First Aid Trainer
Thomas 1 Quest

THE TRADE DISTRICT

24 CANAL AREA
Adam 1
Arnold Leland 35 Fishing Trainer
Billy 1
Catherine Leland 30 Fishing Supplier
Ol' Emma 2

25 CANAL TAILOR AND FIT SHOP
Lisbeth Schneider 30 Clothier
Rema Schneider 35 Quest

26 GALLINA WINERY
Julia Gallina 30 Wine Vendor
Roberto Pupellyverbos 30 Merlot Connoisseur
Suzetta Gallina 30

27 THE GILDED ROSE
Innkeeper Allison 30 Innkeeper

28 THE BANK
Bank Tellers
Stormwind City Guard 50

29 LIONHEART ARMORY
Aldric Moore 30 Mail Armor Merchant
Carla Granger 30 Cloth Armor Merchant
Harlan Bagley 12 Quest
Lara Moore 30 Leather Armor Merchant

30 WELLER'S ARSENAL
Gunther Weller 30 Weapon Merchant
Marda Weller 30 Weapon Merchant

31 STORMWIND VISITOR'S CENTER
Aldwin Laughlin 50 Guild Master
Rebecca Laughlin 25 Tabard Vendor

32 PESTLE'S APOTHECARY
Keldric Boucher 30 Arcane Goods Vendor
Kyra Boucher 30 Reagent Vendor
Morgan Pestle 30 Quest
Renato Gallina 45 Quest

33 TRIAS' CHEESE
Ben Trias 25
Corbett Schneider 5
Elaine Trias 30
Elling Trias 30

34 EVERYDAY MERCHANDISE
Edna Mulby 30 Trade Supplier
Stephanie Turner 5
Thurman Mulby 30 General Goods Vendor

35 GRYPHON AERIE
Dungar Longdrink 55 Elite Gryphon Master

36 THE EMPTY QUIVER
Frederick Stover 30 Bow/Arrow Merchant
Lina Stover 30 Arrow Merchant
Topper McNabb 1

37 FRAGRANT FLOWERS
Bernard Gump 30 Florist
Felicia Gump 30 Herbalism Supplier

OLD TOWN

38 THE SILVER SHIELD
Bryan Cross 30 Shield Merchant

39 THANE'S BOOTS
Mayda Thane 30 Cobbler

40 THE PROTECTIVE HIDE
Alyssa Griffith 30 Bag Vendor
Jillian Tanner 30 Leatherworking Supplies
Maris Granger 35 Skinning Trainer
Randal Worth 24 Journeyman Leatherworker
Seoman Griffith 30 Leather Armor Merchant
Simon Tanner 35 Expert Leatherworker

41 THE BARRACKS
Ander Germaine 60 Warrior Trainer
Doc Mixilpixil 45 Quest
Horatio Montogomery Statue
Ilsa Corbin 49 Warrior Trainer
Jasper Fel 30 Shady Dealer
Master Mathias Shaw 70 Quest
Master Wood 60 Elite
Osborne the Night Man 60 Rogue Trainer
Renzik "The Shiv" 40 Quest
Sloan McCoy 25 Poison Supplier
Woo Ping 50 Elite Weapon Master
Wu Shen 50 Warrior Trainer

42 LIMITED IMMUNITY
Nikova Raskol 5
Osric Strang 30 Heavy Armor Merchant
Wilhelm Strang 30 Mail Armor Merchant

43 HONEST BLADES
Heinrich Stone 30 Blade Merchant

44 PIG AND WHISTLE TAVERN
Aedis Brom 30
Bartleby 10 Drunk Quest
Christoph Faral 30
David Langston 5
Elly Langston 60 Barmaid
Erika Tate 30 Cooking Supplier
Harry Burlguard 50 Quest
Jenn Langston 5 Quest
Kendor Kabonka 50 Cooking Recipe Master
Reese Langstone 30 Tavernkeeper
Stephen Ryback Cooking Trainer

45 HEAVY HANDED WEAPONS
Gerik Koen 30 Two-Handed Weapon Merchant

46 THE FIVE DEADLY VENOMS
Dashel Stonefist 26
Lenny "Fingers" McCoy 35
Ol' Beasley 10

THE DWARVEN DISTRICT

47 OUT IN THE OPEN
Billibub Cogspinner 30 Engineering Supplier
Dane Lindgren 30 Journeyman Blacksmith
Furen Longbeard 40 Quest
Hank the Hammer 50 The Mithril Order
Kaita Deepforge 30 Blacksmithing Supplier
Lilliam Sparkspindle 35 Expert Engineer
Morgg Stormshot 53
Sprite Jumpsprocket 24 Journeyman Engineer
Therum Deepforge 33 Expert Blacksmith

48 UNMARKED TAVERN
Brohann Caskbelly 40
Wilder Thistlenettle 20

49 GUN STORE
Thulman Flintcrag 30 Gun Vendor

50 WEAPON STORE
Borgus Steelhand 60 Weapon Crafter
Grimand Elmore 50 Quest
Kathrum Axehand 30 Axe Merchant

51 MINER'S GUILD
Brooke Stonebraid 30 Mining Supplier
Gelman Stonehand 35 Mining Trainer

52 HUNTER'S GUILD
Einris Brightspear 60 Hunter Trainer
Jenova Stoneshield 30 Stable Master
Thorfin Stoneshield 40 Hunter Trainer
Ulfir Ironbeard 50 Hunter Trainer

53 TRAM STATION

STORMWIND KEEP

54 PALACE HALLS
Stormwind Royal Guard 75

55 LIBRARY WING
Donyal Tovald 15 Librarian
Lord Gregor Lescovar 31
Milton Sheaf 15 Librarian Quest
Tyrion 37
Tyrion's Spybot 25

56 PETITIONER'S CHAMBER
Caledra Dawnbreeze 60
Count Remington Ridgewell 40
Lord Baurles K. Wishock 10

57 THE KING'S CHAMBERS
Anduin Wrynn 5 King
Bishop DeLavey 32 Quest
Grand Admiral Jes-Tereth 90
Highlord Bolvar Fordragon 90
Lady Katrana Prestor 75
Major Samuelson 50 Quest
Mithras Ironhill 90
Stormwind Royal Guard 75

QUESTS

QUEST	M LEV	Q LEV	QUEST LAUNCHER	QUEST FINISHER	CHAIN?	XP---	XP--	XP-	XP+	XP++	XP+++	CASH REWARD
A Call to Arms: The Plaguelands!	50	50	Crier Goodman	Commander Ashlam Valorfist	Y	45	95	190	280	380	470	None
A Meal Served Cold	35	40	Angus Stern	Angus Stern	N	470	950	1900	2800	3750	4700	1 50 00
A Noble Brew	25	30	Zardeth of the Black Claw	Lord Baurles K. Wishock	N	250	490	975	1450	1950	2450	25 00
A Noble Brew	25	30	Zardeth of the Black Claw	Zardeth of the Black Claw	Y	250	490	975	1450	1950	2450	25 00
An Audience with the King	16	31	Baros Alexston	Lady Katrana Prestor	N	380	750	1500	2250	3000	3750	None
REWARD: Seal of Wrynn												
Assisting Arch Druid Staghelm	47	50	Innkeeper Allison	Arch Druid Fandral Staghelm	Y	45	95	190	280	380	470	None
Bazil Thredd	16	22	Baros Alexston	Warden Thelwater	Y	45	85	170	260	350	440	None
Bring the Light	39	42	Archbishop Benedictus	Archbishop Benedictus	N	430	850	1700	2600	3450	4300	None
REWARD: Vanquisher's Sword, Amberglow Talisman												
Brother Paxton	20	24	Milton Sheaf	Brother Paxton	Y	50	95	190	290	390	490	None
Brotherhood's End	16	31	Master Mathias Shaw	Baros Alexston	Y	65	130	250	380	500	625	None
Collecting Memories	14	18	Wilder Thistlenettle	Wilder Thistlenettle	N	140	270	550	800	1100	1350	None
CHOICE OF: 1 Tunneler's Boots or 1 Dusty Mining Gloves												
Elmore's Task	9	15	Verner Osgood	Grimand Elmore	N	10	20	40	65	85	110	None
Elmore's Task	9	15	Donal Osgood	Grimand Elmore	N	10	20	40	65	85	110	None
Elmore's Task	9	15	Smith Argus	Grimand Elmore	N	10	20	40	65	85	110	None
Good Natured Emma	50	52	Royal Factor Bathrilor	Ol' Emma	Y	500	1000	2050	3050	4100	5100	None
Harlan Needs a Resupply	1	2	Harlan Bagley	Rema Schneider	N	10	15	35	50	70	85	17
Humble Beginnings	10	15	Baros Alexston	Baros Alexston	N	110	210	420	625	850	1050	7 00
In Search of The Temple	38	43	Brohann Caskbelly	Brohann Caskbelly	Y	360	725	1450	2150	2900	3600	None
Infiltrating the Castle	16	31	Elling Trias	Tyrion	Y	25	50	100	150	200	250	None
Ink Supplies	20	24	Brother Paxton	Foreman Oslow	Y	50	95	190	290	390	490	None
Into The Temple of Atal'Hakkar	38	50	Brohann Caskbelly	Brohann Caskbelly	N	700	1400	2850	4250	5700	7100	None
REWARD: Guardian Talisman												
Items of Some Consequence	16	31		Tyrion	N	65	130	250	380	500	625	None
James Hyal	30	35	Connor Rivers	Vincent Hyal	Y	70	140	280	410	550	700	None
Jonespyre's Request	47	50	Tannysa	Quintis Jonespyre	Y	45	95	190	280	380	470	None
Look to an Old Friend	16	31	Master Mathias Shaw	Elling Trias	Y	25	50	100	150	200	250	None
Malin's Request	30	32	Archmage Malin	Skuerto	N	200	390	775	1150	1550	1950	None
Mazen's Behest	37	41	Acolyte Dellis	Watcher Mahar Ba	N	330	650	1300	2000	2650	3300	None
CHOICE OF: 1 Teacher's Sash or 1 Wanderlust Boots												
Mazen's Behest	37	41	Mazen Mac'Nadir	Acolyte Dellis	Y	35	65	130	200	260	330	None
Oh Brother...	15	20	Wilder Thistlenettle	Wilder Thistlenettle	N	160	310	625	925	1250	1550	None
REWARD: Miner's Revenge												
Package for Thurman	1	2	Rema Schneider	Thurman Schneider	N	15	25	50	80	100	130	None
Preserving Knowledge	20	38	Loremaster Dibbs	Loremaster Dibbs	Y	360	700	1400	2150	2850	3550	None
Quell The Uprising	22	26	Warden Thelwater	Warden Thelwater	N	270	525	1050	1600	2100	2650	40 00
Rethban Ore	20	24	Foreman Oslow	Brother Paxton	Y	95	190	390	575	775	975	None
Return to Kristoff	20	24	Brother Paxton	Brother Kristoff	N	200	390	775	1150	1550	1950	None
REWARD: Wandering Boots												

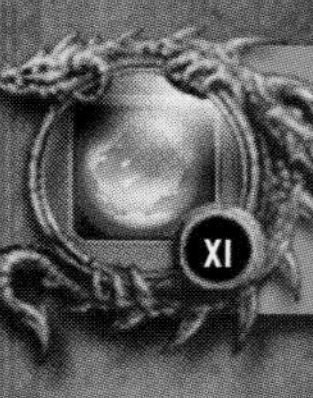

QUESTS continued

QUEST	M LEV	Q LEV	QUEST LAUNCHER	QUEST FINISHER	CHAIN?	XP---	XP--	XP-	XP+	XP++	XP+++	CASH REWARD
Return to Milton	20	38	Loremaster Dibbs	Milton Sheaf	N	360	700	1400	2150	2850	3550	85 00
Shadow of the Past	16	29	Baros Alexston	Master Mathias Shaw	Y	60	120	240	350	470	600	None
Southshore	20	38	Milton Sheaf	Loremaster Dibbs	Y	70	140	280	430	575	700	None
Speaking of Fortitude	20	24	Brother Kristoff	Milton Sheaf	Y	20	40	80	120	160	200	None
Stormpike's Delivery	9	15	Grimand Elmore	Mountaineer Stormpike	N	110	210	420	625	850	1050	7 00
Stormwind Library	1	1	Donyal Tovald	Donyal Tovald	N	0	0	0	0	0	0	None
CHOICE OF: 1 The Story of Morgan Ladimore or 1 Legends of the Gurubashi, Volume 3												
The Attack!	16	31		Elling Trias	Y	190	380	750	1150	1500	1900	None
The Color of Blood	22	26	Nikova Raskol	Nikova Raskol	N	270	525	1050	1600	2100	2650	40 00
The Corruption Abroad	18	24	Argos Nightwhisper	Gershala Nightwhisper	Y	150	290	575	875	1150	1450	13 00
The Curious Visitor	16	29	Warden Thelwater	Baros Alexston	Y	60	120	240	350	470	600	None
The Head of the Beast	16	31	Elling Trias	Master Mathias Shaw	Y	25	50	100	150	200	250	None
The Missing Diplomat	28	28	Thomas	Bishop DeLavey	Y	25	45	90	140	180	230	None
The Missing Diplomat	28	28		Bishop DeLavey	Y	25	45	90	140	180	230	None
The Missing Diplomat	28	28	Bishop DeLavey	Jorgen	Y	25	45	90	140	180	230	None
The Missing Diplomat	28	28	Jorgen	Elling Trias	Y	25	45	90	140	180	230	None
The Missing Diplomat	28	28	Elling Trias	Watcher Backus	Y	25	45	90	140	180	230	None
The Missing Diplomat	28	30	Watcher Backus	Watcher Backus	Y	250	490	975	1450	1950	2450	None
The Missing Diplomat	28	30	Watcher Backus	Elling Trias	Y	25	50	100	150	200	250	None
The Missing Diplomat	28	31	Dashel Stonefist	Dashel Stonefist	Y	130	250	500	750	1000	1250	None
The Missing Diplomat	28	31	Dashel Stonefist	Elling Trias	Y	25	50	100	150	200	250	None
The Missing Diplomat	28	31	Watcher Backus	Dashel Stonefist	Y	25	50	100	150	200	250	None
The Missing Diplomat	28	31	Elling Trias	Dashel Stonefist	Y	25	50	100	150	200	250	None
The Missing Diplomat	28	33	Mikhail	Mikhail	N	130	260	525	775	1050	1300	None
The Missing Diplomat	28	33	Elling Trias	Mikhail	Y	65	130	260	400	525	650	None
The Missing Diplomat	28	33	Tapoke Slim" Jahn"	Mikhail	Y	25	55	110	160	210	270	None
The Missing Diplomat	28	33	Mikhail	Commander Samaul	Y	130	260	525	775	1050	1300	None
The Missing Diplomat	28	35	Commander Samaul	Archmage Tervosh	Y	30	55	110	170	220	280	None
The Missing Diplomat	28	36	Archmage Tervosh	Private Hendel	N	70	140	280	420	550	700	None
The Missing Diplomat	28	38	Private Hendel	Archmage Tervosh	N	220	430	850	1300	1700	2150	None
The Missing Diplomat	28	38	Lady Jaina Proudmoore	Lady Jaina Proudmoore	N	430	850	1700	2600	3450	4300	1 30 00
REWARD: Jaina's Signet Ring												
The Perenolde Tiara	30	40	Count Remington Ridgewell	Count Remington Ridgewell	N	470	950	1900	2800	3750	4700	1 50 00
The Stockade Riots	16	29	Warden Thelwater	Warden Thelwater	Y	240	470	950	1400	1900	2350	25 00
To The Hinterlands	38	43	Brohann Caskbelly	Falstad Wildhammer	Y	180	360	725	1100	1450	1800	None
Underground Assault	15	20	Shoni the Shilent	Shoni the Shilent	N	160	310	625	925	1250	1550	None
CHOICE OF: 1 Polar Gauntlets or 1 Sable Wand												
Wine Shop Advert	1	2	Renato Gallina	Suzetta Gallina	N	15	25	50	80	100	130	None
REWARD: Bottle of Pinot Noir												
You Have Served Us Well	25	30	Zardeth of the Black Claw	Zggi	N	25	50	100	150	200	250	None
REWARD: Dread Mage Hat												

BLASTED LANDS

The Burning Legion was able to warp several places in the world to match its hatred and power, and the Blasted Lands have suffered much in this way. The Dark Portal sits here, ominous in its presence and guarded by those who seek the demons' return. Ogres, cultists, and warped beasts walk through the Blasted Lands almost unchecked, save for an Alliance stronghold, Nethergarde Keep. Though well stocked with people and provisions, this outpost of Humans and their allies is scarcely enough to hold back the tide of danger from the rest of the southern lands. Who can say what would happen if enough Warlocks gathered at the portal one day?

Dreadmaul Hold
Deadwind Pass
Nethergarde Keep
The Dark Portal
The Tainted Scar
Stranglethorn Vale
1
2
3
4
5
6
7
8
9

LOCAL RESOURCES

MINING

METAL	AVAILABILITY
Mithril	Abundant
Thorium	Moderate

HERBALISM

HERB	AVAILABILITY
Firebloom	Abundant
Sungrass	Abundant
Gromsblood	Moderate

SKINNING

Quantity of Skinnable Creatures: Moderate

Levels of Skinnable Creatures: 47-53 (Skinning 235-265)

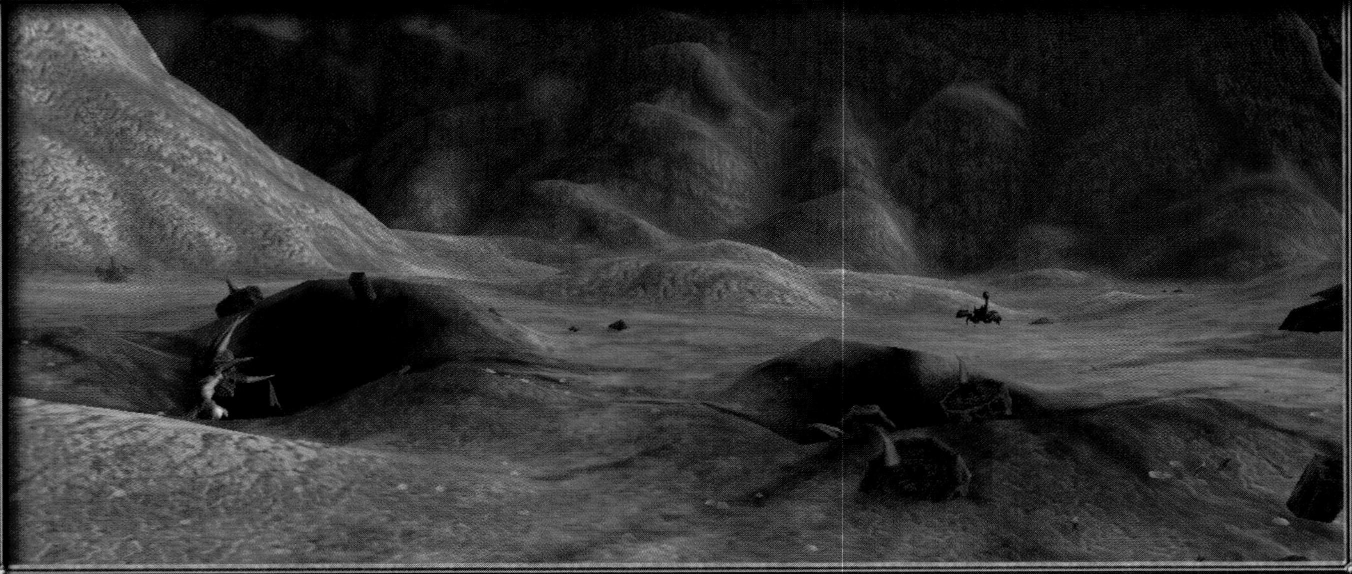

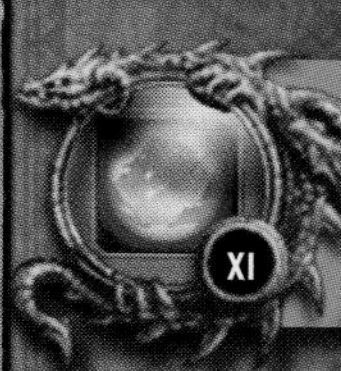

MAP LEGEND

1 THE TAINTED SCAR

2 DREADMAUL POST
- Dreadmaul Mauler 53-54
- Dreadmaul Warlock 53-54
- Servant of Grol 53-54

3 RISE OF THE DEFILER/CENTRAL BLASTED LANDS
- **Kum'isha the Collector Quest**
- **Black Slayer 47-48**
- **Felbeast 50-51**
- **Hellboar 52-53**
- **Portal Seaker 52-53**
- **Redstone Basilisk 47-48**
- **Redstone Crystalhide 50-51**
- **Scorpok Stinger 51**
- **Starving Snickerfang 46**

4 ALTAR OF STORMS
- Lady Sevine 59 Elite
- Servant of Sevine 56
- Shadowsworn Dreadweaver 53-55
- Shadowsworn Enforcer 54
- Shadowsworn Warlock 53-55

5 DREADMAUL HOLD
- Dreadmaul Brute 46-47
- Dreadmaul Ogre Mage 46-47
- Grol the Destroyer 58 Quest Target
- Scorpok Stinger 50-51
- Servant of Grol 53
- Starving Snickerfang 45-46
- Wretched Lost One 46

6 THE DARK PORTAL
- Felguard Elite 60 Elite
- Felguard Sentry 55
- Felhound 55
- Hellboar 52-53
- Manahound 60 Elite
- Redstone Crystalhide 51
- Scorpok Stinger 50-51
- Servant of Razelikh 57
- Razelikh the Defiler 60

7 SERPENT'S COIL
- Ashmane Boar 47-49
- Black Slayer 48
- Redstone Basilisk 47-48
- Servant of Allistarj 54
- Shadowsworn Adept 52-53
- Shadowsworn Cultist 52
- Shadowsworn Thug 52-53

8 NETHERGARDE ARMORY
- Nethergarde Engineer 47-48
- Nethergarde Forman 46-48
- Nethergarde Miner 47-48

9 NETHERGARDE KEEP
- **Alexandra Constantine 55 Elite Gryphon Master**
- **Ambassador Ardalan 55 Quest**
- **Enohar Thunderbrew 50 Quest**
- **Watcher Mahar Ba 45**
- Nethergarde Analyst 50
- Nethergarde Cleric 49-51
- Nethergarde Elite 55 Elite
- Nethergarde Officer 50
- Nethergarde Riftwatcher 49-51
- Nethergarde Soldier 49-51
- Quartermaster Lungertz 54

QUESTS

QUEST	M LEV	Q LEV	QUEST LAUNCHER	QUEST FINISHER	CHAIN?	XP---	XP--	XP-	XP+	XP++	XP+++	CASH REWARD
A Boar's Vitality	45	50	Bloodmage Drazial	Bloodmage Drazial	N	470	950	1900	2800	3750	4700	None
REWARD: Lung Juice Cocktail												
A Tale of Sorrow	45	57	Fallen Hero of the Horde	Fallen Hero of the Horde	Y	60	120	240	360	480	600	None
Everything Counts In Large Amounts	45	55	Kum'isha the Collector	Kum'isha the Collector	Y	575	1150	2250	3400	4500	5650	None
REWARD: Kum'isha's Junk												
Fall From Grace	45	45	Fallen Hero of the Horde	Fallen Hero of the Horde	Y	40	80	160	230	310	390	None
Heroes of Old	45	57	Corporal Thund Splithoof	Spectral Lockbox (Obj)	N	600	1200	2400	3600	4800	6000	None
REWARD: Shard of Afrasa												
Heroes of Old	45	57	Fallen Hero of the Horde	Corporal Thund Splithoof	Y	300	600	1200	1800	2400	3000	None
Infallible Mind	45	50	Bloodmage Lynnore	Bloodmage Lynnore	N	0	0	0	0	0	0	None
REWARD: Cerebral Cortex Compound												
Kirith	45	58	Fallen Hero of the Horde	Spirit of Kirith	Y	625	1250	2500	3700	4950	6200	None
Kum'isha's Endeavors	45	55	Kum'isha the Collector	Kum'isha the Collector	N	575	1150	2250	3400	4500	5650	None
REWARD: Emerald Encrusted Chest												
One Draenei's Junk...	45	55	Kum'isha the Collector	Kum'isha the Collector	N	0	0	0	0	0	0	None
REWARD: Kum'isha's Junk												
Petty Squabbles	50	57	Ambassador Ardalan	Fallen Hero of the Horde	Y	450	900	1800	2700	3600	4500	None
Rage of Ages	45	50	Bloodmage Drazial	Bloodmage Drazial	N	0	0	0	0	0	0	None
REWARD: R.O.I.D.S.												
Salt of the Scorpok	45	50	Bloodmage Drazial	Bloodmage Drazial	N	0	0	0	0	0	0	None
REWARD: Ground Scorpok Assay												
Snickerfang Jowls	45	50	Bloodmage Drazial	Bloodmage Drazial	N	470	950	1900	2800	3750	4700	None
REWARD: R.O.I.D.S.												
Spirit of the Boar	45	50	Bloodmage Drazial	Bloodmage Drazial	N	0	0	0	0	0	0	None
REWARD: Lung Juice Cocktail												
Spiritual Domination	45	50	Bloodmage Lynnore	Bloodmage Lynnore	N	0	0	0	0	0	0	None
REWARD: Gizzard Gum												
The Basilisk's Bite	45	50	Bloodmage Lynnore	Bloodmage Lynnore	N	470	950	1900	2800	3750	4700	None
REWARD: Cerebral Cortex Compound												
The Cover of Darkness	45	60	Spirit of Kirith	Fallen Hero of the Horde	Y	330	650	1300	2000	2650	3300	None
The Decisive Striker	45	50	Bloodmage Drazial	Bloodmage Drazial	N	470	950	1900	2800	3750	4700	None
REWARD: Ground Scorpok Assay												
The Demon Hunter	45	60	Fallen Hero of the Horde	Loramus Thalipedes	Y	650	1300	2650	3950	5300	6600	None
The Disgraced One	45	50	Fallen Hero of the Horde	Dispatch Commander Ruag	Y	120	240	480	725	950	1200	None
The Stones That Bind Us	45	57	Fallen Hero of the Horde	Fallen Hero of the Horde	Y	750	1500	3000	4550	6050	7550	None
To Serve Kum'isha	45	55	Kum'isha the Collector	Kum'isha the Collector	N	850	1700	3400	5050	6750	8450	None
REWARD: Emerald Encrusted Chest												
Uniting the Shattered Amulet	45	60	Fallen Hero of the Horde	Fallen Hero of the Horde	Y	825	1650	3300	5000	6650	8300	None
Vulture's Vigor	45	50	Bloodmage Lynnore	Bloodmage Lynnore	N	470	950	1900	2800	3750	4700	None
REWARD: Gizzard Gum												
You Are Rakh'likh, Demon	45	60	Fallen Hero of the Horde	Fallen Hero of the Horde	N	1000	2000	4000	5950	7950	9950	2 70 00
REWARD: Necklace of Sanctuary, Demon's Blood, Demon Hide Sack												

BURNING STEPPES

The Burning Steppes are more dangerous than almost any realm in the east, save perhaps for the Plaguelands, where the Scourge is located. In the Burning Steppes, massive Drakes, Whelps, and Dragonkin thrive in the heat, ash, and shadow of Blackrock Mountain, and other great mountains that line the area's perimeter. Passage into the Steppes is mainly possible through the road up from Lakeshire, in Redridge, but the creatures are so terrible in this land that few dare to approach.

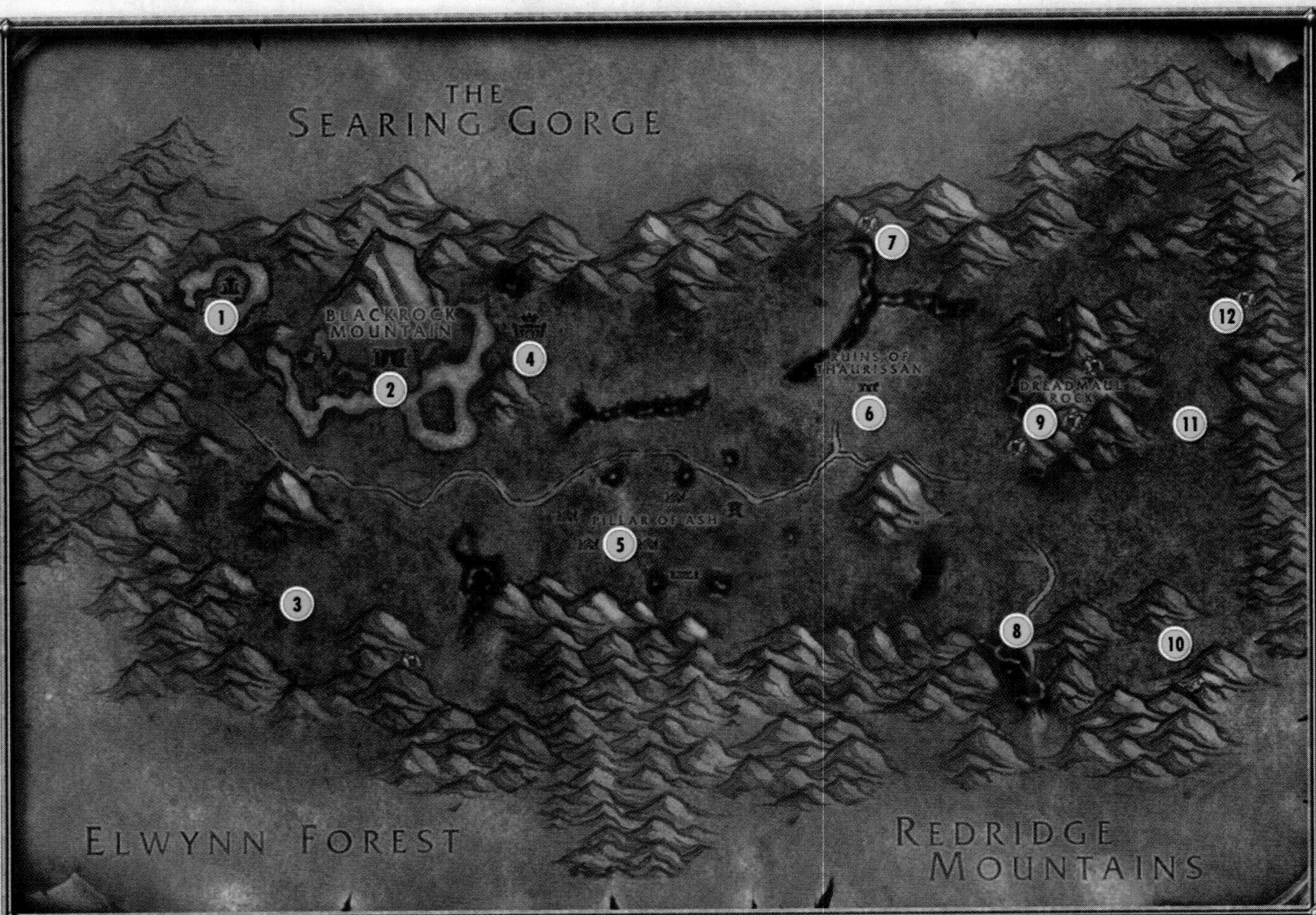

THE SEARING GORGE
BLACKROCK MOUNTAIN
RUINS OF THAURISSAN
DREADMAUL ROCK
PILLAR OF ASH
ELWYNN FOREST
REDRIDGE MOUNTAINS
1
2
3
4
5
6
7
8
9
10
11
12

LOCAL RESOURCES

MINING

METAL	AVAILABILITY
Mithril	Moderate
Thorium	Abundant

HERBALISM

HERB	AVAILABILITY
Sungrass	Trivial
Dreamfoil	Moderate

SKINNING

Quantity of Skinnable Creatures: Trivial

Levels of Skinnable Creatures: 48-58 (240-290)

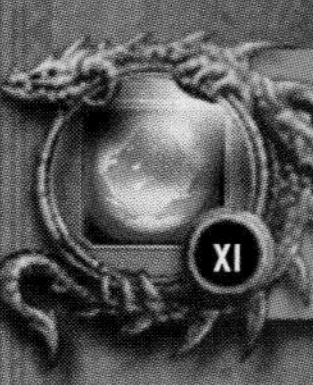

MAP LEGEND

1 ALTAR OF STORMS
Blackrock Warlock 55-57

2 BLACKROCK MOUNTAIN
Black Wyrmkin 51-54

3 DRACO'DAR
Firetail Scorpid 56-57
Flamescale Broodling 55-56
Flamescale Dragonspawn 56-57 Elite
Flamescale Wyrmkin 57-58 Elite
Giant Ember Worg 55-56
Scalding Broodling 51-54
Scalding Drake 52-55 Elite
Searscale Drake 55-58 Elite

4 BLACKROCK STRONGHOLD
Grark Lorkrub 56 Elite Quest
Blackrock Slayer 54-57
Blackrock Soldier 53-56
Blackrock Sorcerer 53-56
Blackrock Warlock 55-57

5 PILLAR OF ASH
Blackrock Slayer 54-57
Blackrock Soldier 53-56
Blackrock Sorcerer 53-56
Blackrock Warlock 55–57
Deathlash Scorpid 53-55
Flamekin Rager 54-56
Flamekin Spitter 50-53
Flamekin Sprite 51-53
Flamekin Torcher 54-56
Greater Obsidian Elemental 55-57
Obsidian Elemental 50-53
Slavering Ember Worg 53-54

6 RUINS OF THAURISSAN
Black Broodling 48-52
Black Dragonspawn 50-53 Elite
Black Drake 48-52 Elite
Black Wyrmkin 51-54 Elite
Flamekin Rager 54-56
Flamekin Spitter 50-53
Flamekin Sprite 51-53
Flamekin Torcher 54-56
Greater Obsidian Elemental 55-57
Obsidian Elemental 50-53
Thaurisan Agent 54-55
Thaurisan Firewalker 53-55
Thaurisan Spy 53-54
War Reaver 53-55

7 FLAME CREST
Kibler 56 Quest
Mathredis Firestar 60 Quest
Maxwort Umberglint 42 Quest
Ragged Jon 57 Quest
Tinkee Steamboil 53 Quest
Yuka Screwspigot 53 Quest
Deathlash Scorpid 53-55

8 BLACKROCK PASS
Venomtip Scorpid 50-53

9 DREADMAUL ROCK
Remains of Sha'ni Proudtusks Quest
Firegut Brute 50-53
Firegut Ogre Mage 48-52
Firegut Ogre 48-51

10 MORGAN'S VIGIL
Helendis Riverhorn 55 Quest
Marshal Maxwell 55 Quest
Mayara Brightwing 55 Quest
Oralius 55 Quest

11 TERROR WING PATH
Ember Worg 49-52
Venomtip Scorpid 50-53

12 SLITHER ROCK
Cyrus Therepantous 52 Quest
Flamescale Wyrmkin 57-58 Elite

QUESTS

QUEST	M LEV	Q LEV	QUEST LAUNCHER	QUEST FINISHER	CHAIN?	XP---	XP--	XP-	XP+	XP++	XP+++	CASH REWARD
A Taste of Flame	52	54	Cyrus Therepentous	Cyrus Therepentous	Y	550	1100	2200	3250	4350	5450	None
A Taste of Flame	52	54	Cyrus Therepentous	Cyrus Therepentous	Y	550	1100	2200	3250	4350	5450	None
Broodling Essence	50	52	Tinkee Steamboil	Tinkee Steamboil	Y	500	1000	2050	3050	4100	5100	75 00
Dark Iron Legacy	48	52	Franclorn Forgewright	Franclorn Forgewright	Y	50	100	200	310	410	500	None
Dragonkin Menace	48	54	Helendis Riverhorn	Helendis Riverhorn	Y	550	1100	2200	3250	4350	5450	1 65 00
Extinguish the Firegut	48	52	Oralius	Oralius	Y	500	1000	2050	3050	4100	5100	None
Felnok Steelspring	50	54	Tinkee Steamboil	Felnok Steelspring	Y	270	550	1100	1600	2150	2700	None
FIFTY! YEP!	50	56	Oralius	Oralius	N	575	1150	2300	3500	4650	5800	85 00
Gor'tesh the Brute Lord	48	53	Oralius	Oralius	Y	525	1050	2100	3150	4200	5250	None
Grark Lorkrub	52	58	Lexlort	Grark Lorkrub	N	625	1250	2500	3700	4950	6200	None
Krom'Grul	48	53	Sha'ni Proudtusk	Thal'trak Proudtusk	N	525	1050	2100	3150	4200	5250	None
REWARD: Sha'ni's Ring												
Leonid Barthalomew	57	60	Tinkee Steamboil	Leonid Barthalomew the Revered	Y	500	1000	2000	2950	3950	4950	None
Libram of Constitution	50	55		Mathredis Firestar	N	0	0	0	0	0	0	None
REWARD: Lesser Arcanum of Constitution												
Libram of Resilience	50	55		Mathredis Firestar	N	0	0	0	0	0	0	None
REWARD: Lesser Arcanum of Resilience												
Libram of Rumination	50	55		Mathredis Firestar	N	0	0	0	0	0	0	None
REWARD: Lesser Arcanum of Rumination												
Libram of Tenacity	50	55		Mathredis Firestar	N	0	0	0	0	0	0	None
REWARD: Lesser Arcanum of Tenacity												
Libram of Voracity	50	55		Mathredis Firestar	N	0	0	0	0	0	0	None
CHOICE OF: 1 Lesser Arcanum of Voracity (Choose the stat)												
Ogre Head On A Stick = Party	48	53	Oralius	Oralius	N	525	1050	2100	3150	4200	5250	2 40 00
CHOICE OF: 1 Maddening Gauntlets or 1 Choking Band												
Precarious Predicament	52	58	Grark Lorkrub	Lexlort	N	775	1550	3100	4650	6200	7750	2 65 00
Tablet of the Seven	50	50	Maxwort Uberglint	Maxwort Uberglint	N	240	470	950	1400	1900	2350	75 00
The Rise of the Machines	52	54	Hierophant Theodora Mulvadania	Hierophant Theodora Mulvadania	Y	550	1100	2200	3250	4350	5450	1 65 00
The True Masters	48	54	Helendis Riverhorn	Magistrate Solomon	Y	410	825	1650	2450	3300	4100	None
The True Masters	48	54	Magistrate Solomon	Highlord Bolvar Fordragon	Y	410	825	1650	2450	3300	4100	None
The True Masters	48	54	Highlord Bolvar Fordragon	Highlord Bolvar Fordragon	Y	55	110	220	320	430	550	None
The True Masters	48	54	Highlord Bolvar Fordragon	Magistrate Solomon	Y	550	1100	2200	3250	4350	5450	None
The True Masters	48	54	Magistrate Solomon	Marshal Maxwell	Y	55	110	220	320	430	550	None
The True Masters	48	54	Marshal Maxwell	Marshal Maxwell	Y	55	110	220	320	430	550	None

DUSKWOOD

Duskwood has always been a place of quiet refuge for those who don't like the hustle and bustle of life in Elwynn Forest. At the moment, it has become quiet for other reasons; the silent dead now wander through this once tranquil forest, slaying the living and threatening to overwhelm the town of Darkshire. People of that town speak of Raven Hill, a western town whose people have all but disappeared. And through it all, a force of great power wanders about the woods, calling to the people of Duskwood, "I hunger!"

LOCAL RESOURCES

MINING

METAL	AVAILABILITY
Copper	Moderate
Tin	Abundant
Iron	Moderate

HERBALISM

HERB	AVAILABILITY
Mageroyal	Trivial
Briarthorn	Moderate
Bruiseweed	Moderate
Kingsblood	Abundant
Wild Steelbloom	Trivial

SKINNING

Quantity of Skinnable Creatures: Abundant

Levels of Skinnable Creatures: 19-30 (Skinning 95-150)

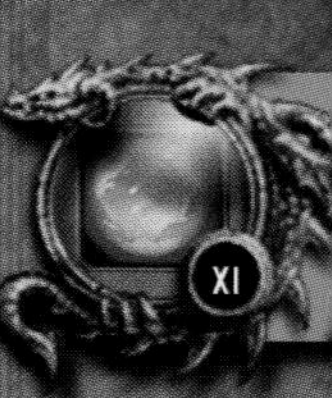

MAP LEGEND

1 THE HUSHED BANK
Sven Yorgen 20 Quest
Green Recluse 21-22
Pygmy Venom Web Spider 18-19
Rabid Dire Wolf 20-21
Starving Dire Wolf 19-20
Venom Web Spider 19-20

2 ADDLE'S STEAD
Defias Enchanter 26-27
Defias Night Blade 25-26
Defias Night Runner 25-26
Pygmy Venom Web Spider 18-19
Rabid Dire Wolf 20-21
Venom Web Spider 19-20

3 RAVEN HILL
Jitters 25 Quest

4 RAVEN HILL CEMETERY
Abercrombie 35 Quest
Bone Chewer 26-27
Carrion Recluse 25-26
Flesh Eater 24-25
Mor'ladrim 35 Elite Quest Target
Rotted One 25-26
Skeletal Fiend 24-25
Skeletal Raider 27-28

5 DAWNING WOODS CATACOMBS
Brain Eater 28-29
Plague Spreader 27-28
Skeletal Warder 28-29

6 FORLORN ROWE
Brain Eater 28-29
Morbent Fel 35 Elite Quest Target
Plague Spreader 28
Skeletal Healer 26-27
Skeletal Raider 27-28

7 THE DARKENED BANK
Black Widow Hatchling 24-25
Green Recluse 21-22
Pygmy Venom Web Spider 18-19
Rabid Dire Wolf 20-21
Starving Dire Wolf 19-20

8 VUL'GOR OGRE MOUND
Splinter Fist Enslaver 30-31
Splinter Fist Firemonger 28-29
Splinter Fist Taskmaster 27-28
Splinter Fist Warrior 29-30

9 CROSSROAD
Watcher Dodds 29 Quest
Black Ravager Mastiff 25-26
Black Ravager 25-26
Stitches 35 Elite
Young Black Ravager 23-24

10 YORGEN FARMSTEAD
Defias Enchanter 26-27
Defias Night Blade 25-26
Defias Night Runner 24-25
Young Black Ravager 23-24

11 TWILIGHT GROVE

12 THE ROTTING ORCHARD
Nightbane Shadow Weaver 27-28
Nightbane Dark Runner 28-29

13 BRIGHTWOOD GROVE
Black Ravager Mastiff 25-26
Black Ravager 25-26
Nightbane Dark Runner 28-29
Nightbane Shadow Weaver 27-28
Nightbane Worgen 26-27
Young Black Ravager 23-24

14 MANOR MISTMANTLE
Fetid Corpse 29-30
Stalven Mistmantle 35 Elite Quest Target

15 DARKSHIRE
Ambassador Berrybuck 30 Quest
Calor 20 Quest
Chef Grual 30 Quest
Clarise Gnarltree 31 Expert Blacksmith
Clerk Daltry 31 Quest
Commander Althea Ebonlocke 45 Quest
Councilman Millstipe 28 Quest
Danielle Zipstitch 27 Specialty Tailor
Felicia Maline 55 Gryphon Master
Finbus Geargrind 31 Expert Engineer
Innkeeper Trelayne 30 Innkeeper
Jonathon Carevin 25 Quest
Lord Ello Ebonlocke 30 Quest
Madame Eva 25 Quest
Sirra Von'Indi 24 Quest
Steven Black 30 Stable Master
Tavernkeeper Smitts 22 Quest
Viktori Prism'Antras 28 Quest
Watcher Backus 42 Quest

16 SPIDER CAVE
Black Widow Hatchling 24-25

17 BLIND MARY'S HAUNT
Blind Mary 40 Quest
Black Widow Hatchling 24-25
Skeletal Horror 23-24

18 TRANQUIL GARDENS CEMETERY
Insane Ghoul 26 Quest Target
Skeletal Mage 22-23
Skeletal Warrior 21-22

19 ROLAND'S DOOM
Gutspill 32
Nightbane Tainted One 30-31
Nightbane Vile Fang 29-30

QUESTS

QUEST	M LEV	Q LEV	QUEST LAUNCHER	QUEST FINISHER	CHAIN?	XP---	XP--	XP-	XP+	XP++	XP+++	CASH REWARD
A Daughter's Love	28	35	Watcher Ladimore	A Weathered Grave (Obj)	N	140	270	550	800	1100	1350	None
REWARD: Archeus												
Ambushed In The Forest	23	29		Ambassador Berrybuck	N	240	470	950	1400	1900	2350	25 00
Armed and Ready	20	29	Grimand Elmore	Sven Yorgen	Y	60	120	240	350	470	600	None
Awaiting Word	17	21		Watcher Callahan	N	40	85	170	250	330	420	None
Blessed Arm	20	29	Glorin Steelbrow	Grimand Elmore	Y	120	240	480	725	950	1200	None
Bride of the Embalmer	20	30	Lord Ello Ebonlocke	Lord Ello Ebonlocke	N	370	725	1450	2200	2900	3650	None
REWARD: Mantle of Honor, Crest of Darkshire												
Crime and Punishment	22	26	Councilman Millstipe	Councilman Millstipe	N	210	420	850	1250	1700	2100	None
CHOICE OF: 1 Ambassador's Boots or 1 Darkshire Mail Leggings												
Deliver the Thread	20	24	Madame Eva	Abercrombie	Y	150	290	575	875	1150	1450	13 00
Deliveries to Sven	17	23	Elaine Carevin	Sven Yorgen	N	90	180	370	550	725	925	8 00
Digging Through the Dirt	20	35	Eliza's Grave Dirt (Obj)	Eliza's Tombstone (Obj)	N	0	0	0	0	0	0	None
Dusky Crab Cakes	17	20	Chef Grual	Chef Grual	Y	80	160	310	470	625	775	None
REWARD: Recipe: Gooey Spider Cake												
Eight-Legged Menaces	17	21	Watcher Dodds	Watcher Dodds	N	130	250	500	750	1000	1250	None
REWARD: Night Watch Gauntlets												
Finding the Shadowy Figure	20	25	Tavernkeep Smitts	Jitters	Y	100	200	400	600	800	1000	None
Four-Legged Menaces	17	21		Watcher Callahan	N	130	250	500	750	1000	1250	10 00
Gather Rot Blossoms	20	24	Tavernkeep Smitts	Tavernkeep Smitts	Y	95	190	390	575	775	975	None
Ghost Hair Thread	20	24	Madame Eva	Blind Mary	Y	50	95	190	290	390	490	None
Ghoulish Effigy	20	27	Abercrombie	Abercrombie	Y	170	330	650	1000	1300	1650	22 00
Inquire at the Inn	20	25	Clerk Daltry	Tavernkeep Smitts	Y	20	40	80	120	160	200	None
Jitters' Growling Gut	17	20	Jitters	Chef Grual	Y	40	80	160	230	310	390	None
Juice Delivery	20	24	Tavernkeep Smitts	Abercrombie	Y	95	190	390	575	775	975	17 00
Lightforge Ingots	20	29	Glorin Steelbrow	Glorin Steelbrow	Y	180	350	700	1050	1400	1750	None
Lightforge Iron	20	29	Glorin Steelbrow	Waterlogged Chest (Obj)	Y	60	120	240	350	470	600	None
REWARD: Lightforge Ingot												
Look To The Stars	20	25	Viktori Prism'Antras	Viktori Prism'Antras	Y	200	400	800	1200	1600	2000	None
Look To The Stars	20	25	Viktori Prism'Antras	Blind Mary	Y	100	200	400	600	800	1000	None
Look To The Stars	20	25	Blind Mary	Viktori Prism'Antras	Y	150	300	600	900	1200	1500	None
Look To The Stars	20	33	Viktori Prism'Antras	Viktori Prism'Antras	N	270	525	1050	1600	2100	2650	None
CHOICE OF: 1 Zodiac Gloves or 1 Belt of the Stars												
Morbent Fel	20	33	Sven Yorgen	Sven Yorgen	N	400	800	1600	2350	3150	3950	None
REWARD: Torch of Holy FlameCHOICE OF: 1 Night Watch Pantaloons or 1 Watch Master's Cloak or 1 Sparkmetal Coif												
Morgan Ladimore	28	35	Sirra Von'Indi	Commander Althea Ebonlocke	Y	30	55	110	170	220	280	None
REWARD: The Story of Morgan Ladimore												
Morgan Ladimore	28	35		Commander Althea Ebonlocke	Y	30	55	110	170	220	280	None
REWARD: The Story of Morgan Ladimore												

QUESTS continued

QUEST	M LEV	Q LEV	QUEST LAUNCHER	QUEST FINISHER	CHAIN?	XP---	XP--	XP-	XP+	XP++	XP+++	CASH REWARD
Mor'Ladim	28	35	Commander Althea Ebonlocke	Commander Althea Ebonlocke	Y	210	410	825	1250	1650	2050	35 00
Note to the Mayor	20	30	Abercrombie	Lord Ello Ebonlocke	Y	60	120	240	370	490	600	None
Nothing But The Truth	37	42	Apothecary Faustin	Apothecary Faustin	N	430	850	1700	2600	3450	4300	None
CHOICE OF: 1 Cloak of Blight or 1 Cragwood Maul												
Nothing But The Truth	37	42	Deathstalker Zraedus	Infiltrator Marksen	N	260	500	1000	1550	2050	2550	None
Nothing But The Truth	37	42	Deathstalker Zraedus	Apothecary Faustin	Y	35	70	140	210	280	350	None
Nothing But The Truth	37	42	Apothecary Faustin	Deathstalker Zraedus	Y	35	70	140	210	280	350	None
Ogre Thieves	20	30	Abercrombie	Abercrombie	Y	120	240	480	725	950	1200	14 00
Proving Your Worth	20	28	Sven Yorgen	Sven Yorgen	Y	230	460	925	1400	1850	2300	18 00
Raven Hill	17	20	Elaine Carevin	Jitters	N	40	80	160	230	310	390	None
Return the Comb	20	24	Blind Mary	Madame Eva	Y	20	40	80	120	160	200	1 75
Return to Jitters	17	20	Chef Grual	Jitters	N	80	160	310	470	625	775	12 00
Return to Sven	20	25	Jitters	Sven Yorgen	Y	50	100	200	310	410	500	None
Seasoned Wolf Kabobs	18	25	Chef Grual	Chef Grual	N	200	400	800	1200	1600	2000	18 00
REWARD: 4 Seasoned Wolf Kabob, Recipe: Seasoned Wolf Kabob												
Seeking Wisdom	20	29	Sven Yorgen	Bishop Farthing	Y	60	120	240	350	470	600	None
Sirra is Busy	20	30		Sirra Von'Indi	N	0	0	0	0	0	0	None
Supplies from Darkshire	20	24	Abercrombie	Madame Eva	Y	50	95	190	290	390	490	None
Sven's Camp	20	25	Mound of loose dirt (Obj)	Sven Yorgen	Y	100	200	400	600	800	1000	None
Sven's Revenge	20	25	Sven Yorgen	Mound of loose dirt (Obj)	Y	100	200	400	600	800	1000	None
The Daughter Who Lived	28	35	Commander Althea Ebonlocke	Watcher Ladimore	Y	30	55	110	170	220	280	None
The Doomed Fleet	20	29	Bishop Farthing	Glorin Steelbrow	Y	120	240	480	725	950	1200	None
The Hermit	17	25	Elaine Carevin	Abercrombie	N	100	200	400	600	800	1000	None
The Legend of Stalvan	22	28	Madame Eva	Clerk Daltry	Y	25	45	90	140	180	230	None
The Legend of Stalvan	22	28	Clerk Daltry	Old Footlocker (Obj)	Y	120	230	460	700	925	1150	None
The Legend of Stalvan	22	28	Old Footlocker (Obj)	Clerk Daltry	Y	170	340	675	1000	1350	1700	None
The Legend of Stalvan	22	28	Clerk Daltry	Innkeeper Farley	Y	55	110	230	340	460	575	None
The Legend of Stalvan	22	28	Innkeeper Farley	Caretaker Folsom	Y	170	340	675	1000	1350	1700	None
The Legend of Stalvan	22	28	Caretaker Folsom	Sealed Crate (Obj)	Y	25	45	90	140	180	230	None
The Legend of Stalvan	22	28	Sealed Crate (Obj)	Marshal Haggard	Y	120	230	460	700	925	1150	None
The Legend of Stalvan	22	28	Marshal Haggard	Marshal Haggard	Y	120	230	460	700	925	1150	None
The Legend of Stalvan	22	28	Marshal Haggard	Tavernkeep Smitts	Y	55	110	230	340	460	575	None
The Legend of Stalvan	22	28	Tavernkeep Smitts	Commander Althea Ebonlocke	Y	25	45	90	140	180	230	None
REWARD: A Bloodstained Journal Page												
The Legend of Stalvan	22	28	Commander Althea Ebonlocke	Clerk Daltry	Y	25	45	90	140	180	230	None
The Legend of Stalvan	22	28	Clerk Daltry	Commander Althea Ebonlocke	Y	25	45	90	140	180	230	None
The Legend of Stalvan	22	35	Commander Althea Ebonlocke	Madame Eva	N	410	825	1650	2450	3300	4100	None
CHOICE OF: 1 Crescent of Forlorn Spirits or 1 Ring of Forlorn Spirits												
The Lost Ingots	20	29	Waterlogged Chest (Obj)	Glorin Steelbrow	Y	180	350	700	1050	1400	1750	None
The Night Watch	18	24	Commander Althea Ebonlocke	Commander Althea Ebonlocke	Y	150	290	575	875	1150	1450	17 00
The Night Watch	18	26	Commander Althea Ebonlocke	Commander Althea Ebonlocke	Y	210	420	850	1250	1700	2100	20 00
The Night Watch	18	30	Commander Althea Ebonlocke	Commander Althea Ebonlocke	N	250	490	975	1450	1950	2450	25 00
CHOICE OF: 1 Bandolier of the Night Watch or 1 Quiver of the Night Watch or 1 Gunnysack of the Night Watch												
The Shadowy Figure	20	25	Sven Yorgen	Madame Eva	Y	50	100	200	310	410	500	None
The Shadowy Search Continues	20	25	Madame Eva	Clerk Daltry	Y	20	40	80	120	160	200	None
The Totem of Infliction	18	25	Madame Eva	Madame Eva	N	260	500	1000	1550	2050	2550	None
REWARD: Totem of Infliction												
The Weathered Grave	28	35	A Weathered Grave (Obj)	Sirra Von'Indi	Y	70	140	280	410	550	700	None
Translate Abercrombie's Note	20	30	Lord Ello Ebonlocke	Sirra Von'Indi	N	25	50	100	150	200	250	None
Translation to Ello	20	30	Sirra Von'Indi	Lord Ello Ebonlocke	N	25	50	100	150	200	250	None
REWARD: Translated Letter from The Embalmer												
Translation to Ello	20	30		Lord Ello Ebonlocke	N	25	50	100	150	200	250	None
REWARD: Translated Letter from The Embalmer												
Wait for Sirra to Finish	20	30	Sirra Von'Indi	Sirra Von'Indi	Y	190	370	750	1100	1500	1850	None
Wolves at Our Heels	19	21	Lars	Lars	N	130	250	500	750	1000	1250	None
REWARD: 5 Flash Bundles												
Worgen in the Woods	23	28	Calor	Calor	Y	170	340	675	1000	1350	1700	18 00
Worgen in the Woods	23	29	Calor	Calor	Y	180	350	700	1050	1400	1750	19 00
Worgen in the Woods	23	31	Calor	Jonathan Carevin	N	0	0	0	0	0	0	None
REWARD: Consecrated Wand and CHOICE OF: 1 Cloak of the Faith or 1Shield of the Faith												
Worgen in the Woods	23	31	Calor	Calor	Y	190	380	750	1150	1500	1900	22 00
Zombie Juice	20	24	Abercrombie	Tavernkeep Smitts	Y	50	95	190	290	390	490	None

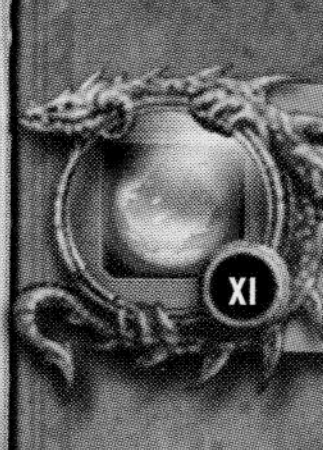

ELWYNN FOREST

Elwynn Forest has been a quiet land for some time, but pressing attacks from the Defias Gang and nearby Gnolls have made the Humans here nervous. It seems that the times of peace are over, because only the mighty city of Stormwind seems immune to the presence of foul beasts and aggressive bandits. The once great copper mines of Elwynn are plagued with Kobolds now, and the people of Goldshire have had to arm themselves against the wild beasts of the valley.

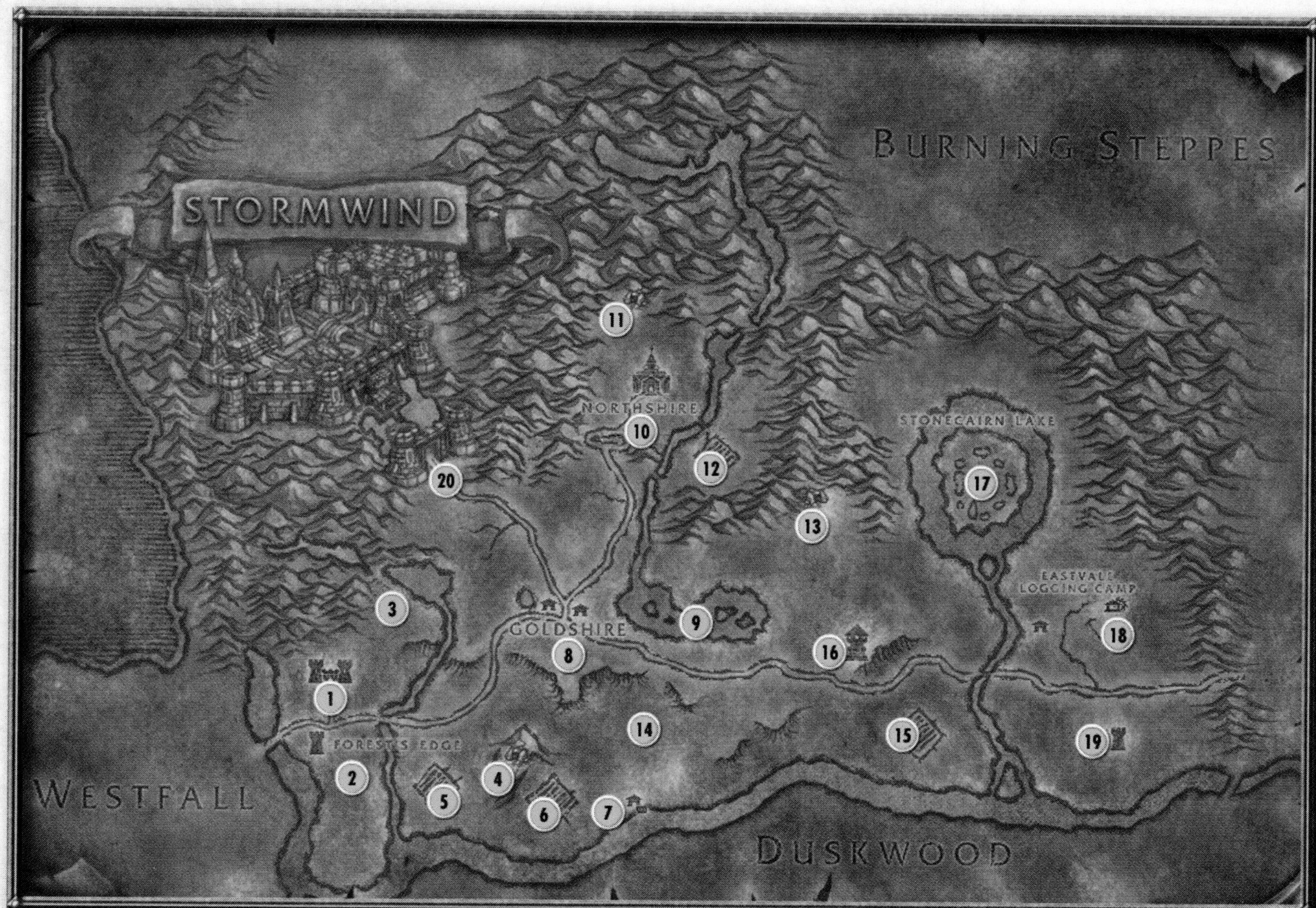

LOCAL RESOURCES

MINING

METAL	AVAILABILITY
Copper	Abundant

HERBALISM

HERB	AVAILABILITY
Peacebloom	Abundant
Silverleaf	Abundant
Earthroot	Common

SKINNING

Quantity of Skinnable Creatures: Abundant

Levels of Skinnable Creatures: 1-10 (Skinning 1-50)

MAP LEGEND

1 WESTBROOK GARRISON
- **Deputy Rainer 10 Quest**

2 FOREST'S EDGE
- Hogger 11+ Quest Target
- Longsnout 10-11
- Riverpaw Outrunner 9-10
- Riverpaw Runt 8-9
- Young Forest Bear 9

3 MIRROR LAKE ORCHARD
- Defias Bandit 8-9
- Defias Cutpurse 6
- Defias Rogue Wizard 9
- Mangy Wolf 5

4 FARGODEEP MINE
- Goldtooth 8
- Kobold Miner 7
- Kobold Taskmaster 10 Rare
- Kobold Tunneler 5-6

5 THE STONEFIELD FARM
- **"Auntie" Bernice Stonefield 6 Quest**
- **Gramma Stonefield 3 Quest**
- **Ma Stonefield 3 Quest**
- **Tommy Joe Stonefield 2 Quest**
- Stonetusk Boar 5-6
- Young Forest Bear 8-9

6 THE MACLURE VINEYARDS
- **Billy Maclure 1 Quest**
- **Joshua Maclure 5 Vendor**
- **Maybell Maclure 2 Quest**
- Stonetusk Boar 5-6
- Rockhide Boar 8

7 JEROD'S LANDING
- **Defias Dockmaster 10**
- **Rockhide Boar 8**

8 GOLDSHIRE
- **Adele Fielder 22 Leatherworker**
- **Helene Peltskinner 12 Skinner**
- **Innkeeper Farley 30 Innkeeper**
- **Marshal Dughan 25 Quest**
- **Michelle Belle 11 Physician**
- **Remy "Two Times" 5 Quest**
- **Smith Argus 24 Blacksmith Quest**
- **Tomas 10 Cook**
- **William Pestle 6 Quest**

9 CRYSTAL LAKE
- **Lee Brown 8 Fisher**
- Defias Bandit 8-9
- Grey Forest Wolf 7-8
- Mangy Wolf 5-6
- Murloc Steamrunner 6-7
- Murloc 7

10 NORTHSHIRE VALLEY
- **Deputy Willem 18 Quest**
- **Eagan Peltskinner 3 Quest**
- **Falkhaan Isenstrider 10 Quest**
- **Marshal McBride 20 Quest**
- **Milly Oswroth 2 Quest**
- Young Wolf 1-2

11 ECHO RIDGE MINE
- Kobold Laborer 4
- Kobold Vermin 1-2
- Kobold Worker 3

12 NORTHSHIRE VINEYARDS
- Defias Thug 3-4
- Garrick Padfoot 5 Quest Target

13 JASPERLODE MINE
- Kobold Geomancer 7-8
- Kobold Miner 6-7
- Mine Spider 9

14 SOUTHERN ELWYNN FOREST
- Rockhide Boar 7-8
- Young Forest Bear 8

15 BRACKWELL PUMPKIN PATCH
- **Ripe Pumpkin (Ground Spawn)**
- Defias Bandit 8-9
- Erlan Drudgemoor 8
- Morgan the Collector 10
- Porcine Entourage 7
- Princess 9
- Rockhide Boar 7-8
- Surena Caledon 9

16 TOWER OF AZORA
- **Dawn Brightstar 35 Arcane Goods**
- **Kitta Firewind 44 Enchanter**
- **Morley Eberlein 10 Vendor**
- **Servant of Azora 8-9**
- **Theocritus 24 Quest**

17 STONE CAIRN LAKE AND HERO'S VIGIL
- Defias Rogue Wizard 9-10
- Murloc Lurker 9-10

18 EASTVALE LOGGING CAMP
- **Katie Hunter 10 Vendor**
- **Marshal Haggard 20 Quest**
- **Sara Timberlain 5 Quest**
- **Supervisor Raelen 15 Quest**
- **Terry Palin 11 Vendor**
- Prowler 9-10

19 RIDGEPOINT TOWER
- Dead-tooth Jack 11 Quest Target
- Defias Bandit 8-9
- Prowler 9-10
- Young Forest Bear 8-9

QUESTS

QUEST	M LEV	Q LEV	QUEST LAUNCHER	QUEST FINISHER	CHAIN?	XP---	XP--	XP-	XP+	XP++	XP+++	CASH REWARD
A Bundle of Trouble	5	9	Supervisor Raelen	Supervisor Raelen	N	80	160	310	470	625	775	3 00
A Fishy Peril	7	10	Remy Two Times	Marshal Dughan	Y	10	15	35	50	70	85	None
A Threat Within	1	1	Deputy Willem	Marshal McBride	Y	5	10	15	25	30	40	None
Back to Billy	5	6	Auntie" Bernice Stonefield"	Billy Maclure	Y	15	25	55	80	110	140	None
Bounty on Garrick Padfoot	4	5	Deputy Willem	Deputy Willem	N	35	65	130	200	270	340	None
CHOICE OF: 1 Tapered Pants or 1 Layered Tunic or 1 Ensign Cloak												
Bounty on Murlocs	7	10	Guard Thomas	Guard Thomas	N	85	170	340	500	675	850	None
CHOICE OF: 1 Long Bayonet or 1 Solid Metal Club or 1 Well-used Sword												
Brotherhood of Thieves	2	4	Deputy Willem	Deputy Willem	N	35	70	140	210	280	360	None
CHOICE OF: 1 Militia Dagger or 1 Militia Hammer or 1 Militia Shortsword or 1 Militia Warhammer or 1 Militia Quarterstaff												
Cloth and Leather Armor	7	10	Marshal Dughan	Sara Timberlain	N	20	40	85	130	170	210	None
CHOICE OF: 1 Well-stitched Robe or 1 Patched Pants												
Collecting Kelp	5	7	William Pestle	William Pestle	N	30	65	130	190	250	320	None
Deliver Thomas' Report	7	10	Guard Thomas	Marshal Dughan	Y	110	210	420	625	850	1050	7 00
Discover Rolf's Fate	7	10	A half-eaten body (Obj)	Rolf's corpse (Obj)	Y	40	85	170	250	340	420	None
Eagan Peltskinner	1	2	Deputy Willem	Eagan Peltskinner	Y	10	15	35	50	70	85	None
Find the Lost Guards	7	10	Guard Thomas	A half-eaten body (Obj)	Y	20	40	85	130	170	210	None
Further Concerns	7	10	Marshal Dughan	Guard Thomas	Y	40	85	170	250	340	420	None
Give Gerard a Drink	1	1	Gerard Tiller	Gerard Tiller	N	0	0	0	0	0	0	None
REWARD: Shiny Red Apple												
Gold Dust Exchange	4	7	Remy Two Times	Remy Two Times	N	65	130	250	380	500	625	1 75
REWARD: Bag of Marbles												
Goldtooth	5	8	Billy Maclure	Auntie" Bernice Stonefield"	N	90	180	350	525	700	875	None
REWARD: Lion-stamped Gloves												
Grape Manifest	2	4	Milly Osworth	Brother Neals	N	35	70	140	210	280	360	None
CHOICE OF: 1 Wine-stained Cloak or 1 Latched Belt												
Investigate Echo Ridge	1	3	Marshal McBride	Marshal McBride	Y	25	50	100	150	200	250	40
Kobold Camp Cleanup	1	2	Quest Chest (Obj)	Marshal McBride	N	15	35	70	100	140	170	25
Kobold Camp Cleanup	1	2	Marshal McBride	Marshal McBride	N	15	35	70	100	140	170	25
Kobold Candles	3	7	William Pestle	William Pestle	Y	50	95	190	290	380	480	1 25
REWARD: 5 Glowing Wax Stick												
Lost Necklace	5	6	Quest Chest (Obj)	Billy Maclure	Y	15	25	55	80	110	140	None
Lost Necklace	5	6	Auntie" Bernice Stonefield"	Billy Maclure	Y	15	25	55	80	110	140	None
Manhunt	7	10	Marshal Dughan	Marshal Dughan	N	85	170	340	500	675	850	None
CHOICE OF: 1 Stormwind Chain Gloves or 1 Elastic Wristguards												
Manhunt	7	10		Marshal Dughan	N	85	170	340	500	675	850	None
CHOICE OF: 1 Stormwind Chain Gloves or 1 Elastic Wristguards												
Milly Osworth	2	4	Eagan Peltskinner	Milly Osworth	Y	5	5	15	20	30	35	None

QUESTS continued

QUEST	M LEV	Q LEV	QUEST LAUNCHER	QUEST FINISHER	CHAIN?	XP---	XP--	XP-	XP+	XP++	XP+++	CASH REWARD
Milly's Harvest	2	4	Milly Osworth	Milly Osworth	Y	20	35	70	110	140	180	None
Note to William	5	6	Gramma Stonefield	William Pestle	Y	15	25	55	80	110	140	None
Pie for Billy	5	6	Billy Maclure	Auntie" Bernice Stonefield"	Y	40	80	160	240	320	410	None
Princess Must Die!	6	9	Ma Stonefield	Ma Stonefield	N	80	160	310	470	625	775	None
CHOICE OF: 1 Weather-worn Boots or 1 Brass-studded Bracers or 1 Farmer's Boots												
Protect the Frontier	7	10	Guard Thomas	Guard Thomas	N	65	130	250	380	500	625	2 50
REWARD: 2 Lesser Healing Potion												
Red Linen Goods	4	9	Sara Timberlain	Sara Timberlain	N	80	160	310	470	625	775	None
REWARD: Red Linen Shirt, Red Linen Sash												
Report to Goldshire	1	5	Marshal McBride	Marshal Dughan	N	25	45	90	140	180	230	None
REWARD: Pikeman Shield												
Report to Gryan Stoutmantle	9	10	Marshal Haggard	Gryan Stoutmantle	N	65	130	250	380	500	625	2 50
Report to Gryan Stoutmantle	9	10	Guard Thomas	Gryan Stoutmantle	N	65	130	250	380	500	625	2 50
Report to Gryan Stoutmantle	9	10	Farmer Saldean	Gryan Stoutmantle	N	65	130	250	380	500	625	2 50
Report to Gryan Stoutmantle	9	10	Deputy Rainer	Gryan Stoutmantle	N	65	130	250	380	500	625	2 50
Report to Gryan Stoutmantle	9	10	Marshal Dughan	Gryan Stoutmantle	N	65	130	250	380	500	625	2 50
Report to Gryan Stoutmantle	9	10	Farmer Furlbrow	Gryan Stoutmantle	N	65	130	250	380	500	625	2 50
Report to Thomas	7	10	Rolf's corpse (Obj)	Guard Thomas	Y	20	40	85	130	170	210	None
Rest and Relaxation	1	1	Falkhaan Isenstrider	Innkeeper Farley	N	0	0	5	5	10	10	None
CHOICE OF: 5 Small Pumpkin or 5 Refreshing Spring Water												
Riverpaw Gnoll Bounty	6	10	Deputy Rainer	Deputy Rainer	N	85	170	340	500	675	850	None
CHOICE OF: 1 Militia Buckler or 1 Urchin's Pants												
Shipment to Stormwind	3	7	William Pestle	Morgan Pestle	N	80	160	320	470	625	800	3 50
CHOICE OF: 15 Explosive Rocket or 5 Oil of Olaf or 2 Elixir of Lion's Strength												
Skirmish at Echo Ridge	1	5	Marshal McBride	Marshal McBride	N	45	90	180	270	360	450	None
CHOICE OF: 1 Outfitter Belt or 1 Outfitter Boots or 1 Outfitter Gloves												
Speak with Gramma	5	6	Tommy Joe Stonefield	Gramma Stonefield	Y	15	25	55	80	110	140	None
The Escape	5	7	William Pestle	Maybell Maclure	N	80	160	320	470	625	800	None
REWARD: 5 Minor Healing Potion												
The Fargodeep Mine	4	7	Marshal Dughan	Marshal Dughan	Y	50	95	190	290	380	480	1 25
The Jasperlode Mine	4	10	Marshal Dughan	Marshal Dughan	N	85	170	340	500	675	850	3 50
Wanted: Hogger	5	11	Wanted Poster (Obj)	Marshal Dughan	N	90	180	350	525	700	875	None
CHOICE OF: 1 Footman Tunic or 1 Stormwind Guard Leggings or 1 Balanced Fighting Stick												
Westbrook Garrison Needs Help!	6	10	Marshal Dughan	Deputy Rainer	Y	20	40	85	130	170	210	None
Wolves Across the Border	1	2	Eagan Peltskinner	Eagan Peltskinner	N	15	35	70	100	140	170	None
CHOICE OF: 1 Soft Fur-lined Shoes or 1 Wolfskin Bracers												
Young Lovers	5	6	Maybell Maclure	Tommy Joe Stonefield	Y	15	25	55	80	110	140	None

REDRIDGE MOUNTAINS

East of Stormwind and Elwynn Forest is the town of Lakeshire, placed in the middle of the Redridge Mountains. Under siege by eastern Orc clans and hassled by Gnolls, things aren't simple for the people of Lakeshire currently. A great bridge that spans Lake Everstill is under repairs, even as enemy catapults lie in ruins along the southern ridgeline. To the north are Orcish Champions, known for their power and bravery, while the eastern groups have even greater leadership. Stonewatch Keep, on the far side of Lake Everstill sits as a constant reminder that peace has collapsed into a drawn-out war in Redridge.

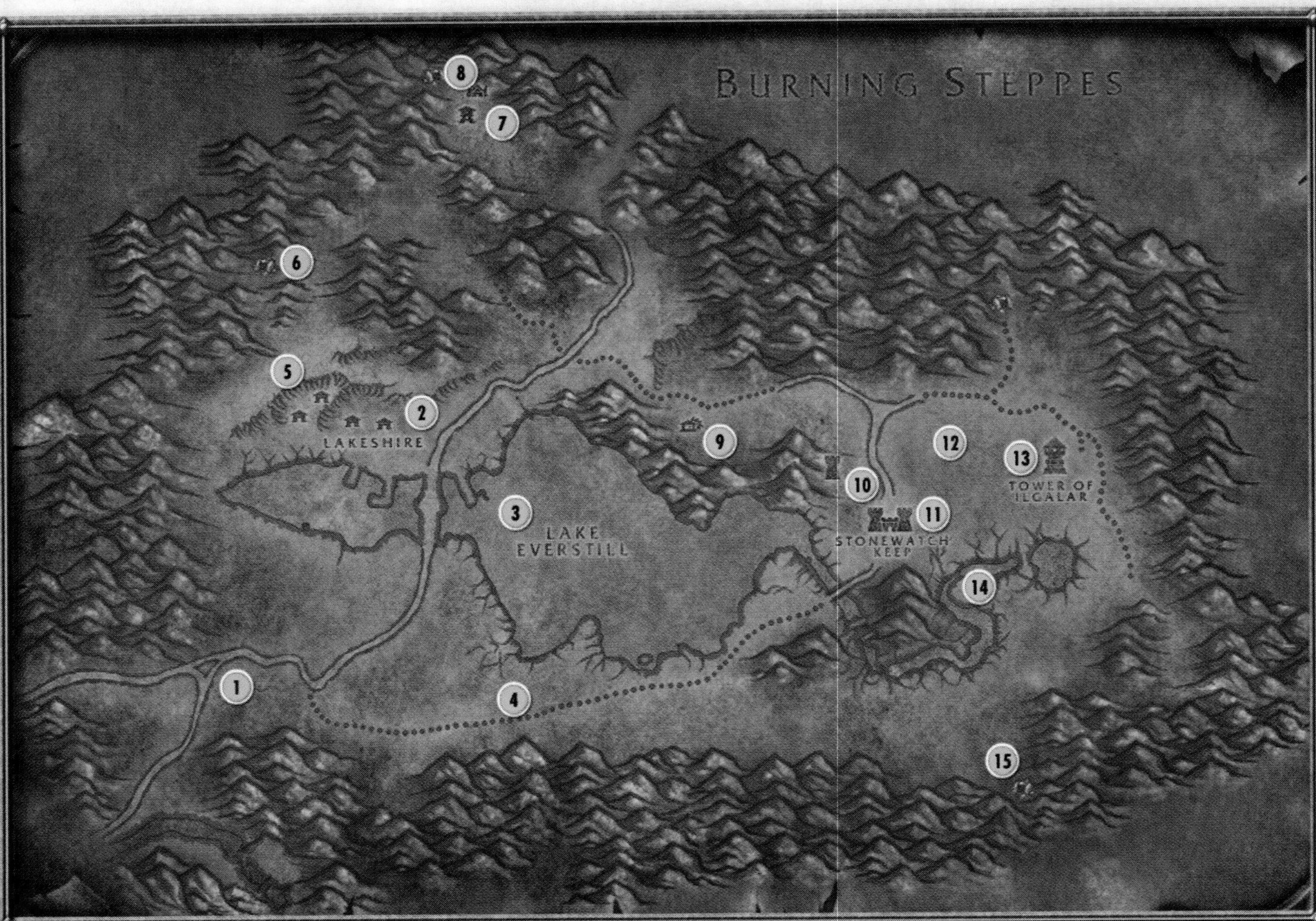

BURNING STEPPES
LAKESHIRE
LAKE EVERSTILL
STONEWATCH KEEP
TOWER OF ILGALAR
1 2 3 4 5 6 7 8 9 10 11 12 13 14 15

LOCAL RESOURCES

MINING

METAL	AVAILABILITY
Copper	Moderate
Tin	Moderate

HERBALISM

HERB	AVAILABILITY
Earthroot	Trivial
Mageroyal	Trivial
Briarthorn	Moderate
Bruiseweed	Moderate
Kingsblood	Trivial

SKINNING

Quantity of Skinnable Creatures: Moderate

Levels of Skinnable Creatures: 16-24 (Skinning 80-120)

MAP LEGEND

1 THREE CORNERS
Guard Parker 30 Quest
Black Dragon Whelp 17-18
Great Goretusk 16-17
Redridge Mongrel 15-16
Redridge Thrasher 14-15
Tarantula 15-16

2 LAKESHIRE
Alma Jainrose 20 Herbalism Trainer
Ariena Stormfeather 55 Gryphon Master
Chef Breanna 19 Quest
Crystal Boughman 22 Cooking Trainer
Darcy 15 Quest
Deputy Feldon 33 Quest
Foreman Oslow 20 Quest
Innkeeper Brianna 30 Innkeeper
Magistrate Solomon 36 Quest
Marshal Marris 35 Quest
Martie Jainrose 20 Quest
Verner Osgood 25 Quest
Bellygrub 24
Blackrock Outrunner 20-21
Great Goretusk 16-17

3 LAKE EVERSTILL
Great Goretusk 16-17
Murloc Flesheater 18-19
Murloc Minor Tidecaller 17-18
Murloc Scout 18-19
Murloc Shorestriker 16-17
Murloc Tidecaller 19-20

4 LAKERIDGE HIGHWAY
Black Dragon Whelp 17-18
Dire Condor 18-19
Great Goretusk 16-17
Murloc Minor Tidecaller 17-18
Murloc Shorestriker 16-17
Redridge Mongrel 16-17
Redridge Poacher 16-17

5 REDRIDGE CANYONS
Great Goretusk 16-17
Redridge Alpha 21-22
Redridge Basher 19-20
Redridge Brute 17-18
Redridge Mystic 18-19
Yowler 25 Quest Target

6 RETHBAN CAVERNS
Redridge Basher 19-20
Redridge Drudger 20-21

7 RENDER'S CAMP
Corporal Keeshan 25 Elite
Blackrock Champion 24-25
Blackrock Outrunner 20-21
Blackrock Renegade 21-22
Blackrock Summoner 22-23
Blackrock Tracker 23-24

8 RENDER'S ROCK
Blackrock Champion 24-25
Blackrock Summoner 22-23
Blackrock Tracker 23-24

9 ALTHER'S MILL
Black Dragon Whelp 17-18
Dire Condor 18-19
Great Goretusk 16-17
Greater Tarantula 19-20

10 STONEWATCH TOWER
Blackrock Grunt 19-20
Blackrock Outrunner 19-20
Blackrock Scout 20 Elite
Blackrock Sentry 21-22 Elite
Blackrock Shadowcaster 22-23 Elite

11 STONEWATCH KEEP
Blackrock Gladiator 25 Elite
Blackrock Hunter 24 Elite
Blackrock Shadowcaster 22-23 Elite
Gath'Ilzogg 26 Elite Quest Target
Tharil'zun 24 Elite Quest Target

12 GALARDELL VALLEY
Rabid Shadowhide Gnoll 21-22
Shadowhide Brute 23-23
Shadowhide Darkweaver 25-26
Shadowhide Gnoll 22-23
Shadowhide Slayer 25-26
Shadowhide Warrior 24-25

13 TOWER OF ILGALAR
Shadowhide Darkweaver 25-26
Shadowhide Slayer 25-26
Shadowhide Warrior 24-25

14 STONEWATCH FALLS
Murloc Nightcrawler 21
Murloc Tidecaller 19-20
Shadowhide Darkweaver 25-26
Shadowhide Slayer 25-26
Shadowhide Warrior 24-25

15 RENDER'S VALLEY
Blackrock Outrunner 21
Blackrock Renegade 21-22

QUESTS

QUEST	M LEV	Q LEV	QUEST LAUNCHER	QUEST FINISHER	CHAIN?	XP---	XP--	XP-	XP+	XP++	XP+++	CASH REWARD
A Baying of Gnolls	15	20	Verner Osgood	Verner Osgood	Y	120	230	460	700	925	1150	9 00
A Baying of Gnolls	15	20	Donal Osgood	Verner Osgood	Y	120	230	460	700	925	1150	9 00
A Free Lunch	12	15	Darcy	Guard Parker	Y	55	110	220	320	430	550	None
A Watchful Eye	20	21	Theocritus	Old Lion Statue (Obj)	Y	130	250	500	750	1000	1250	None
An Unwelcome Guest	18	24	Martie Jainrose	Martie Jainrose	N	200	390	775	1150	1550	1950	17 00
REWARD: Bouquet of Scarlet Begonias												
Assessing the Threat	11	17	Deputy Feldon	Deputy Feldon	N	95	190	380	575	750	950	7 00
Blackrock Bounty	20	25	Guard Howe	Guard Howe	N	200	400	800	1200	1600	2000	18 00
Blackrock Menace	18	21	Marshal Marris	Marshal Marris	Y	170	330	650	1000	1300	1650	13 00
Delivering Daffodils	12	15	Martie Jainrose	Darcy	N	25	55	110	160	220	270	None
REWARD: 10 Sauteed Sunfish												
Dry Times	12	15	Barkeep Daniels	Barkeep Daniels	N	110	210	420	625	850	1050	None
REWARD: Finely Woven Cloak, A Bulging Coin Purse												
Encroaching Gnolls	11	16	Guard Parker	Deputy Feldon	Y	30	60	120	170	230	290	2 00
Hilary's Necklace	12	15	Shawn	Hilary	N	110	210	420	625	850	1050	None
Howling in the Hills	15	25	Verner Osgood	Verner Osgood	N	200	400	800	1200	1600	2000	None
CHOICE OF: 1 Ring of Iron Will or 1 Gold Militia Boots												
Howling in the Hills	15	25	Donal Osgood	Verner Osgood	N	200	400	800	1200	1600	2000	None
CHOICE OF: 1 Ring of Iron Will or 1 Gold Militia Boots												
Looking Further	20	22	Old Lion Statue (Obj)	An Empty Jar (Obj)	N	130	260	525	775	1050	1300	None
Looking Further	20	22	Theocritus	An Empty Jar (Obj)	N	130	260	525	775	1050	1300	None
Messenger to Darkshire	18	18	Lord Ello Ebonlocke	Magistrate Solomon	N	35	70	140	200	270	340	2 50
Messenger to Darkshire	18	18	Magistrate Solomon	Lord Ello Ebonlocke	Y	100	200	400	600	800	1000	None
Messenger to Stormwind	14	14	General Marcus Jonathan	Magistrate Solomon	N	25	50	100	150	200	250	1 50
Messenger to Stormwind	14	14	Magistrate Solomon	General Marcus Jonathan	Y	50	100	200	290	390	490	None
Messenger to Westfall	14	14	Gryan Stoutmantle	Magistrate Solomon	N	25	50	100	150	200	250	1 50
Messenger to Westfall	14	14	Magistrate Solomon	Gryan Stoutmantle	Y	50	100	200	290	390	490	None
Missing In Action	19	25	Corporal Keeshan	Marshal Marris	N	260	500	1000	1550	2050	2550	None
CHOICE OF: 1 Robe of Solomon or 1 Deputy Chain Coat or 1 Bone-studded Leather												
Morganth	20	27	Old Lion Statue (Obj)	Theocritus	N	280	550	1100	1650	2200	2750	None
REWARD: Rose Mantle												
Morganth	20	27	Theocritus	Theocritus	N	280	550	1100	1650	2200	2750	None
REWARD: Rose Mantle												
Murloc Poachers	20	20	Dockmaster Baren	Dockmaster Baren	N	160	310	625	925	1250	1550	None
REWARD: Dwarven Fishing Pole												
Redridge Goulash	15	18	Chef Breanna	Chef Breanna	N	140	270	550	800	1100	1350	10 00
REWARD: 5 Redridge Goulash, Recipe: Redridge Goulash												
Return to Verner	13	18	Smith Argus	Verner Osgood	N	70	140	270	410	550	675	5 00
Selling Fish	16	21	Dockmaster Baren	Dockmaster Baren	N	130	250	500	750	1000	1250	10 00
REWARD: Murloc Fin Soup, Recipe: Murloc Fin Soup, 5 Fishliver Oil												
Shadow Magic	18	23	Marshal Marris	Marshal Marris	N	230	460	925	1400	1850	2300	30 00
Solomon's Law	17	23	Bailiff Conacher	Bailiff Conacher	N	190	370	750	1100	1500	1850	15 00
Tharil'zun	18	25	Marshal Marris	Marshal Marris	Y	260	500	1000	1550	2050	2550	None
CHOICE OF: 1 Fire Hardened Buckler or 1 Orc Crusher												
The Everstill Bridge	15	20	Foreman Oslow	Foreman Oslow	N	160	310	625	925	1250	1550	None
CHOICE OF: 1 Smith's Trousers or 1 Bridgeworker's Gloves or 1 Riding Gloves												
The Lost Tools	15	16	Foreman Oslow	Foreman Oslow	N	90	180	350	525	700	875	None
REWARD: 2 Medium Armor Kit												
The Price of Shoes	14	18	Verner Osgood	Smith Argus	Y	35	70	140	200	270	340	None
Underbelly Scales	14	18	Verner Osgood	Verner Osgood	N	170	340	675	1000	1350	1700	None
CHOICE OF: 1 Black Whelp Boots or 1 Black Whelp Gloves												
Visit the Herbalist	12	15	Guard Parker	Martie Jainrose	Y	25	55	110	160	220	270	None
Wanted: Gath'Ilzogg	15	26	Wanted: Gath'Ilzogg (Obj)	Magistrate Solomon	N	270	525	1050	1600	2100	2650	40 00
Wanted: Lieutenant Fangore	15	26	Wanted: Lieutenant Fangore (Obj)	Magistrate Solomon	N	270	525	1050	1600	2100	2650	40 00
What Comes Around...	22	25	Guard Berton	Guard Berton	N	200	400	800	1200	1600	2000	None
CHOICE OF: 1 Lucine Longsword or 1 Hardened Root Staff												

STRANGLETHORN VALE

At the southern end of the Eastern Kingdoms is an area of rivers, jungle, and coastline known as Stranglethorn Vale. This gigantic section of the continent is home to many beasts, and it is also a place where Goblins have and pirates are found in great numbers. The Horde settlement of Grom'Gol is here, along the western coast (accessed via Blimps from Orgrimmar and Undercity). To the south is Booty Bay, a neutral town that is truly a place where anything goes. Some of the finest hunters of big game in all of Azeroth come to Stranglethorn in hope of fighting the rarest of felines, apes, and raptors.

LOCAL RESOURCES

MINING

METAL	AVAILABILITY
Tin	Trivial
Iron	Abundant
Mithril	Moderate

HERBALISM

HERB	AVAILABILITY
Stranglekelp	Trivial
Bruiseweed	Moderate
Kingsblood	Trivial
Liferoot	Moderate
Fadeleaf	Trivial
Khadgar's Whiskers	Moderate
Goldthorn	Trivial

SKINNING

Quantity of Skinnable Creatures: Abundant

Levels of Skinnable Creatures: 30-50 (Skinning 150-250)

MAP LEGEND

1 REBEL CAMP
Brother Nimetz 40 Quest
Corporal Bluth 40 Vendor
Corporal Kaleb 40 Quest
Lieutenant Doren 40 Quest

2 KURZEN'S COMPOUND
Kurzen Commando 34
Kurzen Jungle Fighter 32-33
Kurzen Medicine Man 32-33
Kurzen War Panther 32-33
Kurzen War Tiger 32
Kurzen Wrangler 34

3 THE STOCKPILE
Colonel Kurzen 40 Elite Quest Target
Kurzen Commando 34-35
Kurzen Elite 36-37
Kurzen Headshrinker 34-35
Kurzen Shadow Hunter 38
Kurzen Subchief 38
Kurzen Witch Doctor 36

4 NORTHERN STRANGLETHORN VALE
Galvan the Ancient 60 Quest
Bloodscalp Beastmaster 34
Bloodscalp Hunter 35
Bloodscalp Scavenger 33
Elder Stranglethorn Tiger 34-35
Lastail Raptor 35
Mistvale Gorilla 32-33
Panther 32-33
River Crocolisk 31
Shadowmaw Panther 38
Sharptooth Frenzy 31
Stone Maw Basilisk 32
Stranglethorn Tiger 33
Stranglethorn Tigress 37-38
Venture Company Mechanic 34
Venture Company Miner 34-35
Young Panther 30-31
Young Stranglethorn Tiger 30-31

5 NESINGWARY'S EXPEDITION
Ajeck Rouack 40 Quest
Barnil Stonepot 40 Quest
Hemet Nesingwary 40 Quest
Jaquilina Dramet 39 Axe Vendor
Sir S. J. Erigadin 40 Quest
River Crocolisk 30-31
Young Stranglethorn Tiger 30-31

6 RUINS OF ZUL'KUNDA
Bloodscalp Beastmaster 34-35
Bloodscalp Berserker 36-37
Bloodscalp Headhunter 36-37
Bloodscalp Hunter 34-35
Bloodscalp Mystic 35
Bloodscalp Scout 34-35
Bloodscalp Tiger 35
Bloodscalp Witch Doctor 37
Nezzliok the Dire 40 Quest Target

7 ZUULDAIA RUINS
Bloodscalp Berserker 36-37
Bloodscalp Headhunter 36-37
Bloodscalp Witch Doctor 37

8 THE SAVAGE COAST
Bloodscalp Axethrower 33
Bloodscalp Shaman 34
Crystal Spine Basilisk 34
Elder Saltwater Crocolisk 38
Lashtail Raptor 35
Saltwater Crocolisk 35-36

9 BAL'LAL RUINS
Bloodscalp Axe Thrower 33
Bloodscalp Shaman 33-34
Bloodscalp Warrior 33-34

10 TKASHI RUINS
Bloodscalp Axe Thrower 34
Bloodscalp Shaman 33-34
Bloodscalp Warrior 33-34
Sin'Dall 37 Quest Target

11 LAKE NAZFERITI
Snapjaw Crocolisk 35-36
Sharptooth Frenzy 31-32

12 VENTURE COMPANY OPERATIONS CENTER
Foreman Cozzle 38 Quest Target
Venture Company Geologist 35-36
Venture Company Mechanic 35

13 VENTURE COMPANY BASE CAMP
Venture Company Geologist 35-36
Venture Company Mechanic 34
Venture Company Shredder 37

14 MOSH'OGG OGRE MOUND
Bhag'thera 40 Quest Target
Mosh'Ogg Lord 45 Elite
Mosh'Ogg Mauler 43 Elite
Mosh'Ogg Shaman 43 Elite
Mosh'Ogg Spellcrafter 43-44 Elite
Mosh'Ogg Warmonger 41-42 Elite

15 MIZJAH RUINS
Mosh'Ogg Brute 36-37
Mosh'Ogg Witchdoctor 37

16 SOUTHERN STRANGLETHORN
Se'Jib 50 Tribal Leatherworker
Cold Eye Basilisk 39
Jungle Thunderer 37-38
King Bangalash 43 Elite Quest Target
Shadowmaw Panther 37
Sharptooth Frenzy 32
Stranglethorn Tigress 37-38

17 BALIA'MAH RUINS
Skullsplitter Mystic 39
Skullsplitter Axe Thrower 39-40
Skullsplitter Warrior 39-40

18 RUINS OF ZUL'MAMWE
Ana'thek the Cruel 45
Kurzen Mindslave 44
Mogh the Undying 44 Elite
Skullsplitter Axe Thrower 39-40
Skullsplitter Beastmaster 42
Skullsplitter Berserker 43-44
Skullsplitter Headhunter 43-44
Skullsplitter Hunter 41-42
Skullsplitter Mystic 39-40
Skullsplitter Panther 41-42
Skullsplitter Scout 41-42
Skullsplitter Spiritchaster 44
Skullsplitter Warrior 39-40
Skullsplitter Witch Doctor 41-42

19 VENTURE COMPANY MINE
Venture Company Foreman 42
Venture Company Strip Miner 40-41
Venture Company Tinkerer 41

20 THE CAPE OF STRANGLETHORN
Jungle Stalker 40-41
Shadowmaw Panther 37
Thrashtail Basilisk 41-42

21 SOUTHERN SAVAGE COAST
Bloodsail Mage 40-41
Bloodsail Raider 40-41
Cold Eye Basilisk 39-40
Jungle Stalker 40-41
Naga Explorer 43-44

22 GURUBASHI ARENA
Jungle Stalker 40-41

23 BLOODSAIL COMPOUND
Bloodsail Swashbuckler 42
Bloodsail Warlock 42-43
Jungle Stalker 40-41

24 RUINS OF JUBUWAL
Jon-Jon the Crow 44
Zanzil Hunter 44
Zanzil Zombie 44

25 CRYSTALVEIN MINE
Ironjaw Basilisk 43-44

26 RUINS OF ABORAZ
Yenniku 41 Quest
Chucky "Ten Thumbs" 43
Zanzil Hunter 44
Zanzil Naga 44
Zanzil Witch Doctor 44
Zanzil Zombie 43

27 THE CRYSTAL SHORE
Silverback Patriarch 43

28 MISTVALE VALLEY
Witch Doctor Unbagwa 50 Quest
Elder Mistvale Gorilla 40-41
Gorlash 47 Elite Quest Target

29 NEK'MANI WELLSPRING
Naga Explorer 43-44

30 BOOTY BAY
"Sea Wolf" MacKinley 44 Quest
"Shaky" Phillips 44 Quest
Baron Revilgaz 60 Quest
Brikk Keencraft 54 Blacksmith
Captain Hecklebury Smotts 37 Quest
Crank Fizzlebub 34 Quest
Drizzlik 45 Quest
First Mate Crazz 44 Quest
Flora Silverwind 44 Herbalist
Gramik Goodstitch 34 Tailor
Gringer 55 Wind Rider Master
Gyll 55 Gryphon Master
Innkeeper Skindle 46 Innkeeper
Kebok 35 Quest
Krazek 35 Quest
Narkk 42 Pet Vendor
Oglethorpe Obnoticus 50 Gnome Engineer/Quest
Rikqiz 43 Leatherworker
Xizk Goodstitch 43 Tailor

31 WILD SHORE
Bloodsail Deckhand 43-44
Bloodsail Elder Magus 44
Bloodsail Mage 40-41
Bloodsail Seadog 44-45
Bloodsail Swabby 44
Bloodsail Swashbuckler 42-43
Bloodsail Warlock 42-43
Brutus 43
Captain Keelhaul 47
Fleet Master Firallon 48
Garr Salthoof 43
Ironpatch 43
Southern Sand Crawler 40-41

32 JAGUERO ISLE
Princess Poobah 50 Quest
Jaguero Stalker 50
King Mukla 55 Quest Target
Skymane Gorilla 50

33 JANEIRO'S POINT
Mok'rash 50 Elite Quest Target

34 KAL'AL RUINS
Murkgill Forager 35
Murkgill Hunter 35-36
Murkgill Lord 37
Murkgill Warrior 35-36

35 GROM'GOL BASE CAMP
Angrun 40 Herbalist
Brawn 35 Leatherworker
Commander Aggro'gosh 55 Quest
Far Seer Mok'thardin 45 Quest
Kin'weelay 39 Quest
Mudduk 40 Cook
Nimboya 41 Quest
Thysta 55 Wind Rider Master
Zeppelin Master Nez'raz 60 Zeppelin Master

36 Tethis 43 Elite Quest Target

QUESTS

QUEST	M LEV	Q LEV	QUEST LAUNCHER	QUEST FINISHER	CHAIN?	XP---	XP--	XP-	XP+	XP++	XP+++	CASH REWARD
Akiris by the Bundle	38	43	Privateer Bloads	Privateer Bloads	N	360	725	1450	2150	2900	3600	60 00
REWARD: Scorching Sash												
Akiris by the Bundle	38	43	Privateer Bloads	Privateer Groy	N	450	900	1800	2650	3550	4450	1 20 00
Ansirem's Key	32	37	Archmage Ansirem Runeweaver	Catelyn the Blade	Y	140	280	550	850	1100	1400	None
Bad Medicine	30	34	Sergeant Yohwa	Sergeant Yohwa	N	270	550	1100	1600	2150	2700	None
CHOICE OF: 1 Palm Frond Mantle or 1 Guerrilla Cleaver												
Big Game Hunter	28	45	Hemet Nesingwary	Hemet Nesingwary	N	575	1150	2350	3500	4700	5850	None
CHOICE OF: 1 Master Hunter's Bow or 1 Master Hunter's Rifle												
Bloodscalp Clan Heads	30	41	Nimboya	Bubbling Cauldron (Obj)	N	330	650	1300	2000	2650	3300	None
Bloodscalp Ears	30	35	Kebok	Kebok	N	280	550	1100	1650	2200	2750	35 00
REWARD: 8 Goblin Fishing Pole												

QUESTS continued

QUEST	M LEV	Q LEV	QUEST LAUNCHER	QUEST FINISHER	CHAIN?	XP---	XP--	XP-	XP+	XP++	XP+++	CASH REWARD
Bloody Bone Necklaces	30	37	Kin'weelay	Kin'weelay	N	290	575	1150	1700	2300	2850	None
REWARD: Bloodbone Band												
Bookie Herod	30	35	Lieutenant Doren	Bookie Herod's Records (Obj)	Y	210	410	825	1250	1650	2050	None
Chapter I	30	40	Barnil Stonepot	Barnil Stonepot	N	160	310	625	925	1250	1550	None
REWARD: Green Hills of Stranglethorn - Chapter I												
Chapter II	30	40	Barnil Stonepot	Barnil Stonepot	N	160	310	625	925	1250	1550	None
REWARD: Green Hills of Stranglethorn - Chapter II												
Chapter III	30	40	Barnil Stonepot	Barnil Stonepot	N	160	310	625	925	1250	1550	None
REWARD: Green Hills of Stranglethorn - Chapter III												
Chapter IV	30	40	Barnil Stonepot	Barnil Stonepot	N	160	310	625	925	1250	1550	None
REWARD: Green Hills of Stranglethorn - Chapter IV												
Colonel Kurzen	30	40	Lieutenant Doren	Lieutenant Doren	N	320	625	1250	1900	2500	3150	None
REWARD: Shrapnel Blaster												
Cortello's Riddle	35	43	A Soggy Scroll (Obj)	Musty Scroll (Obj)	Y	360	725	1450	2150	2900	3600	None
Cortello's Riddle	35	51	Musty Scroll (Obj)	Cortello's Treasure (Obj)	N	600	1200	2450	3650	4900	6100	None
REWARD: Explorer's Knapsack												
Cracking Maury's Foot	30	44	Sea Wolf" MacKinley"	Sea Wolf" MacKinley"	N	470	925	1850	2800	3700	4650	None
REWARD: Collection Plate												
Enchanted Azsharite Fel Weaponry	45	58	Galvan the Ancient	Galvan the Ancient	Y	60	120	250	370	500	625	None
CHOICE OF: 1 Enchanted Azsharite Felbane Dagger or 1 Enchanted Azsharite Felbane Staff or 1 Enchanted Azsharite Felbane Sword												
Enticing Negolash	1	45	Ruined Lifeboat (Obj)	Ruined Lifeboat (Obj)	N	0	0	0	0	0	0	None
Excelsior	31	38	Drizzlik	Drizzlik	N	290	575	1150	1700	2300	2850	None
REWARD: Excelsior Boots												
Facing Negolash	35	50	Sprogger	Captain Hecklebury Smotts	N	700	1400	2850	4250	5700	7100	None
REWARD: Smotts' Compass												
Favor for Krazek	32	37	Krazek	Krazek	Y	210	420	850	1250	1700	2100	30 00
Filling the Soul Gem	1	46		Yenniku	N	0	0	0	0	0	0	None
REWARD: Filled Soul Gem												
Fool's Stout	35	44	Crank Fizzlebub	Crank Fizzlebub	N	0	0	0	0	0	0	None
REWARD: Fool's Stout												
Headhunting	30	37	Nimboya	Nimboya	N	290	575	1150	1700	2300	2850	None
CHOICE OF: 1 Darkspear Cuffs or 1 Darkspear Armsplints												
Hostile Takeover	31	36	Kebok	Kebok	N	280	550	1100	1700	2250	2800	None
REWARD: Gemmed Gloves												
Hunt for Yenniku	30	34	Nimboya	Nimboya	Y	270	550	1100	1600	2150	2700	None
Investigate the Camp	28	32	Krazek	Krazek	N	130	260	525	775	1050	1300	16 00
Journey to Booty Bay!	1	1	Cap'n Copyright	Cap'n Copyright	N	0	0	0	0	0	0	None
Journey to Orgrimmar!	1	1		Nez'raz	N	0	0	0	0	0	0	None
Journey to Ratchet!	1	1	Captain Obvious	Captain Obvious	N	0	0	0	0	0	0	None
Journey to the Undercity!	1	1		Nez'raz	N	0	0	0	0	0	0	None
Jungle Secrets	30	33		Lieutenant Doren	Y	130	260	525	775	1050	1300	None
Keep An Eye Out	37	42	Dizzy One-Eye	Dizzy One-Eye	N	430	850	1700	2600	3450	4300	None
REWARD: Darktide Cape												
Krazek's Cookery	32	37	Corporal Kaleb	Krazek	Y	140	280	550	850	1100	1400	None
Kurzen's Mystery	30	38	Brother Nimetz	Brother Nimetz	Y	360	700	1400	2150	2850	3550	None
Magical Analysis	32	37	Baron Revilgaz	Archmage Ansirem Runeweaver	N	140	280	550	850	1100	1400	None
Mai'Zoth	30	43	Brother Nimetz	Brother Nimetz	N	450	900	1800	2650	3550	4450	None
REWARD: Tranquil Orb												
Message in a Bottle	45	55	Princess Poobah	Princess Poobah	N	850	1700	3400	5050	6750	8450	None
REWARD: Poobah's Nose Ring												
Mok'Thardin's Enchantment	33	38	Far Seer Mok'thardin	Far Seer Mok'thardin	Y	290	575	1150	1700	2300	2850	None
Mok'Thardin's Enchantment	33	41	Far Seer Mok'thardin	Far Seer Mok'thardin	Y	330	650	1300	2000	2650	3300	None
Mok'Thardin's Enchantment	33	41	Far Seer Mok'thardin	Far Seer Mok'thardin	Y	330	650	1300	2000	2650	3300	None
Mok'Thardin's Enchantment	33	44	Far Seer Mok'thardin	Far Seer Mok'thardin	N	470	925	1850	2800	3700	4650	None
REWARD: Choker of the High Shaman												
Panther Mastery	28	31	Sir S. J. Erlgadin	Sir S. J. Erlgadin	Y	190	380	750	1150	1500	1900	None
Panther Mastery	28	33	Sir S. J. Erlgadin	Sir S. J. Erlgadin	Y	200	390	775	1150	1550	1950	None
Panther Mastery	28	38	Sir S. J. Erlgadin	Sir S. J. Erlgadin	Y	220	430	850	1300	1700	2150	None
Panther Mastery	28	40	Sir S. J. Erlgadin	Sir S. J. Erlgadin	N	320	625	1250	1900	2500	3150	None
REWARD: Panther Hunter Leggings												
Patrol Schedules	30	37	Lieutenant Doren	Corporal Sethman	Y	30	55	110	170	230	290	None
Pretty Boy" Duncan"	32	39	Catelyn the Blade	Catelyn the Blade	Y	300	600	1200	1800	2400	3000	None
Raptor Mastery	28	34	Hemet Nesingwary	Hemet Nesingwary	Y	200	400	800	1200	1600	2000	None
Raptor Mastery	28	36	Hemet Nesingwary	Hemet Nesingwary	Y	210	420	850	1250	1700	2100	None
Raptor Mastery	28	41	Hemet Nesingwary	Hemet Nesingwary	Y	250	490	975	1450	1950	2450	None
Raptor Mastery	28	43	Hemet Nesingwary	Hemet Nesingwary	N	360	725	1450	2150	2900	3600	None
REWARD: Raptor Hunter Tunic												
Report to Doren	30	37	Corporal Sethman	Lieutenant Doren	N	290	575	1150	1700	2300	2850	None
CHOICE OF: 1 Junglewalker Sandals or 1 Frost Metal Pauldrons												
Report to Doren	30	37		Lieutenant Doren	N	290	575	1150	1700	2300	2850	None
CHOICE OF: 1 Junglewalker Sandals or 1 Frost Metal Pauldrons												

QUESTS continued

QUEST	M LEV	Q LEV	QUEST LAUNCHER	QUEST FINISHER	CHAIN?	XP---	XP--	XP-	XP+	XP++	XP+++	CASH REWARD
Return to Corporal Kaleb	32	37	Krazek	Corporal Kaleb	N	290	575	1150	1700	2300	2850	None
REWARD: Cap of Harmony												
Return to MacKinley	30	41	Shaky" Phillipe"	Sea Wolf" MacKinley"	Y	250	490	975	1450	1950	2450	40 00
Return to the Blasted Lands	45	58	Galvan the Ancient	Fallen Hero of the Horde	Y	160	310	625	925	1250	1550	None
Saving Yenniku	30	46	Kin'weelay	Nimboya	N	500	1000	2000	3050	4050	5050	None
CHOICE OF: 1 Nimboya's Mystical Staff or 1 Medal of Courage												
Scaring Shaky	30	41	Sea Wolf" MacKinley"	Shaky" Phillipe"	Y	80	160	330	490	650	825	None
Singing Blue Shards	30	35	Crank Fizzlebub	Crank Fizzlebub	Y	280	550	1100	1650	2200	2750	35 00
Skullsplitter Tusks	37	42	Kebok	Kebok	N	350	700	1400	2050	2750	3450	55 00
Some Assembly Required	31	36	Drizzlik	Drizzlik	Y	280	550	1100	1700	2250	2800	40 00
Speaking with Gan'zulah	30	46	Bubbling Cauldron (Obj)	Bubbling Cauldron (Obj)	N	410	800	1600	2450	3250	4050	None
Speaking with Nezzliok	30	40	Bubbling Cauldron (Obj)	Bubbling Cauldron (Obj)	N	240	470	950	1400	1900	2350	None
Special Forces	30	38	Sergeant Yohwa	Lieutenant Doren	Y	290	575	1150	1700	2300	2850	None
Split Bone Necklace	30	42	Kin'weelay	Kin'weelay	N	350	700	1400	2050	2750	3450	None
CHOICE OF: 1 Darkspear Shoes or 1 Darkspear Boots												
Stranglethorn Fever	32	35	Witch Doctor Unbagwa	Witch Doctor Unbagwa	N	0	0	0	0	0	0	None
Stranglethorn Fever	40	45	Fin Fizracket	Fin Fizracket	N	575	1150	2350	3500	4700	5850	None
REWARD: Medicine Blanket												
Supplies to Private Thorsen	30	32	Krazek	Private Thorsen	N	130	260	525	775	1050	1300	16 00
Supply and Demand	26	31	Drizzlik	Drizzlik	N	250	500	1000	1500	2000	2500	30 00
The Blade	32	40		Catelyn the Blade	N	240	470	950	1400	1900	2350	35 00
The Bloodsail Buccaneers	37	41	First Mate Crazz	Bloodsail Correspondence (Obj)	Y	250	490	975	1450	1950	2450	40 00
The Bloodsail Buccaneers	37	41	Bloodsail Correspondence (Obj)	First Mate Crazz	Y	250	490	975	1450	1950	2450	None
The Bloodsail Buccaneers	37	41	First Mate Crazz	Fleet Master Seahorn	Y	80	160	330	490	650	825	None
The Bloodsail Buccaneers	37	43	Fleet Master Seahorn	Fleet Master Seahorn	Y	360	725	1450	2150	2900	3600	None
The Bloodsail Buccaneers	37	45	Fleet Master Seahorn	Fleet Master Seahorn	N	490	975	1950	2900	3900	4850	None
REWARD: Blackwater Tunic												
The Captain's Chest	35	45	Captain Hecklebury Smotts	Captain Hecklebury Smotts	N	290	575	1150	1750	2300	2900	None
REWARD: Bloodband Bracers												
The Captain's Cutlass	35	45	Captain Hecklebury Smotts	Sprogger	Y	40	80	160	230	310	390	None
The Curse of the Tides	32	40	Catelyn the Blade	Baron Revilgaz	N	390	775	1550	2350	3100	3900	None
REWARD: Robe of Crystal Waters												
The Defense of Grom'gol	33	36	Commander Aggro'gosh	Commander Aggro'gosh	Y	280	550	1100	1700	2250	2800	40 00
The Defense of Grom'gol	33	37	Commander Aggro'gosh	Commander Aggro'gosh	N	290	575	1150	1700	2300	2850	None
REWARD: Grom'gol Buckler												
The Fate of Yenniku	30	45	Bubbling Cauldron (Obj)	Kin'weelay	Y	40	80	160	230	310	390	None
The Green Hills of Stranglethorn	30	40	Barnil Stonepot	Barnil Stonepot	N	470	950	1900	2800	3750	4700	None
REWARD: Olmann Sewar												
The Haunted Isle	32	37	Krazek	Baron Revilgaz	Y	30	55	110	170	230	290	None
The Hidden Key	30	37	Bookie Herod's Records (Obj)	Bookie Herod's Strongbox (Obj)	Y	140	280	550	850	1100	1400	None
REWARD: Bookmaker's Scepter												
The Mind's Eye	30	46	Kin'weelay	Kin'weelay	N	500	1000	2000	3050	4050	5050	None
The Second Rebellion	30	33	Sergeant Yohwa	Sergeant Yohwa	N	200	390	775	1150	1550	1950	None
The Singing Crystals	30	45	Kin'weelay	Kin'weelay	Y	390	775	1550	2350	3100	3900	None
The Spy Revealed!	30	37	Bookie Herod's Strongbox (Obj)	Lieutenant Doren	Y	140	280	550	850	1100	1400	None
The Stone of the Tides	32	37	Baron Revilgaz	Baron Revilgaz	Y	290	575	1150	1700	2300	2850	40 00
The Vile Reef	30	37	Kin'weelay	Kin'weelay	N	290	575	1150	1700	2300	2850	None
Tiger Mastery	28	31	Ajeck Rouack	Ajeck Rouack	Y	190	380	750	1150	1500	1900	None
Tiger Mastery	28	33	Ajeck Rouack	Ajeck Rouack	Y	200	390	775	1150	1550	1950	None
Tiger Mastery	28	35	Ajeck Rouack	Ajeck Rouack	Y	210	410	825	1250	1650	2050	None
Tiger Mastery	28	37	Ajeck Rouack	Ajeck Rouack	N	290	575	1150	1700	2300	2850	None
REWARD: Tiger Hunter Gloves												
Troll Witchery	30	40	Brother Nimetz	Brother Nimetz	N	320	625	1250	1900	2500	3150	None
Trollbane	32	37	Nimboya	Zengu	Y	70	140	280	430	575	700	None
Up to Snuff	37	41	Deeg	Deeg	N	330	650	1300	2000	2650	3300	None
Venture Company Mining	30	41	Crank Fizzlebub	Crank Fizzlebub	N	330	650	1300	2000	2650	3300	None
CHOICE OF: 1 Goblin Igniter or 1 Silver Spade												
Voodoo Dues	30	44	Sea Wolf" MacKinley"	Sea Wolf" MacKinley"	N	380	750	1500	2250	3000	3750	65 00
Water Elementals	32	37	Baron Revilgaz	Baron Revilgaz	Y	290	575	1150	1700	2300	2850	40 00
Welcome to the Jungle	28	30	Barnil Stonepot	Hemet Nesingwary	N	25	50	100	150	200	250	None
Whiskey Slim's Lost Grog	40	50	Whiskey Slim	Whiskey Slim	N	470	950	1900	2800	3750	4700	None
Zanzil's Secret	35	44	Crank Fizzlebub	Crank Fizzlebub	N	380	750	1500	2250	3000	3750	65 00
REWARD: Belt of Corruption												

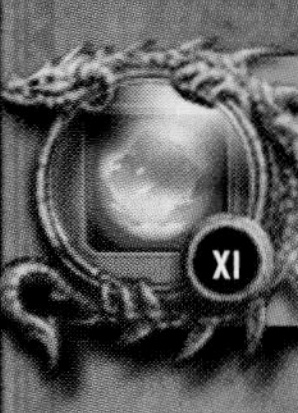

SWAMP OF SORROWS

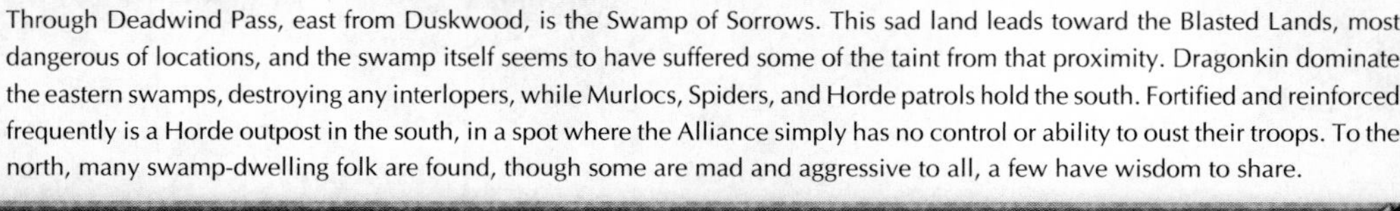

Through Deadwind Pass, east from Duskwood, is the Swamp of Sorrows. This sad land leads toward the Blasted Lands, most dangerous of locations, and the swamp itself seems to have suffered some of the taint from that proximity. Dragonkin dominate the eastern swamps, destroying any interlopers, while Murlocs, Spiders, and Horde patrols hold the south. Fortified and reinforced frequently is a Horde outpost in the south, in a spot where the Alliance simply has no control or ability to oust their troops. To the north, many swamp-dwelling folk are found, though some are mad and aggressive to all, a few have wisdom to share.

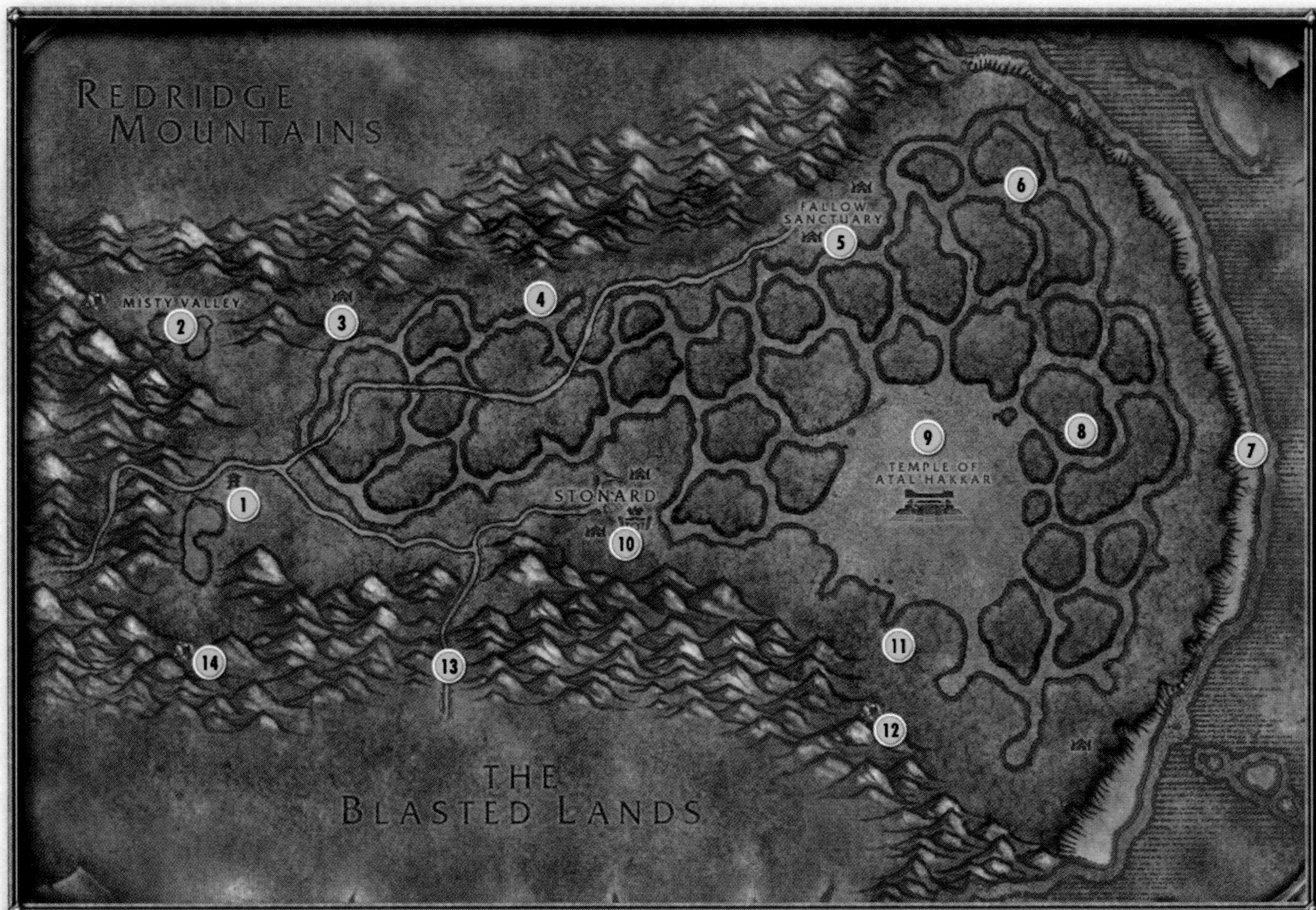

Redridge Mountains
Misty Valley
Fallow Sanctuary
Stonard
Temple of Atal'Hakkar
The Blasted Lands
1 2 3 4 5 6 7 8 9 10 11 12 13 14

LOCAL RESOURCES

MINING

METAL	AVAILABILITY
Iron	Moderate
Mithril	Moderate

HERBALISM

HERB	AVAILABILITY
Goldthorn	Moderate
Fadeleaf	Moderate
Khadgar's Whisker	Abundant
Blindweed	Abundant

SKINNING

Quantity of Skinnable Creatures: Moderate

Levels of Skinnable Creatures: 35-45 (Skinning 175-225)

MAP LEGEND

1 SPLINTERSPEAR JUNCTION
Sorrow Spinner 36
Stonard Scout 37
Swamp Jaguar 36

2 MISTY VALLEY
Mire Lord 42
Swampwalker Elder 39-40
Swampwalker 38-39
Tangled Horror 40-41

3 THE HARBORAGE
Magtoor 42 Quest
Masat T'andr 44 Vendor
Draenel Exile 42
Swamp Jaguar 37
Young Sawtooth Crocolisk 35-36

4 THE SHIFTING MIRE
Lost One Fisherman 36
Lost One Muckdweller 36-37
Lost One Mudlurker 34
Noboru the Cudgel 39 Quest Target
Sawtooth Crocolisk 38
Sorrow Spinner 36-37
Swamp Jaguar 36-37
Swampwalker 39
Tangled Horror 40

5 FALLOW SANCTUARY
Galan Goodward 37 Quest
Lost One Chieftain 39
Lost One Cook 37
Lost One Fisherman 36
Lost One Hunter 36-37
Lost One Muckdweller 36-37
Lost One Riftseeker 37-38
Lost One Seer 38
Stonard Explorer 37-38

6 NORTHERN SWAMP OF SORROWS
Sawtooth Crocolisk 38-39
Shadow Panther 39-40
Tangled Horror 40

7 MISTY REED STRAND
Marsh Flesheater 43-44
Marsh Inkspewer 42-43
Marsh Murloc 41
Monstrous Crawler 43
Sawtooth Snapper 42
Silt Crawler 40-41
Stonard Explorer 38

8 SORROWMURK
Elder Dragonkin 45 Elite
Sawtooth Snapper 41-42
Scalebane Captain 43-44 Elite

9 POOL OF TEARS
Green Scalebane 42 Elite
Green Wyrmkin 42 Elite
Scalebane Captain 43-44 Elite

10 STONARD
Breyk 55 Wind Rider Master
Dispatch Commander Ruag 60 Quest
Fel'zerul 60 Quest
Grunt Tharlak 55 Quest
Grunt Zuul 55 Quest
Helgrum the Swift 60 Quest
Rogvar 53 Alchemist
Stonard Cartographer 52
Stonard Grunt 55
Stonard Orc 50
Stonard Wayfinder 50-51
Zun'dartha 60 Quest

11 STAGALBOG
Deathstrike Tarantula 40-41
Marsh Flesheater 43
Marsh Inkspewer 42-43

12 STAGALBOG CAVE
Marsh Flesheater 43
Marsh Inkspewer 42-43
Marsh Oracle 45

13 PASS TO BLASTED LANDS
Fallen Hero of the Horde 60 Quest

14 ITHARIUS' CAVE
Itharius 45 Quest

QUESTS

QUEST	M LEV	Q LEV	QUEST LAUNCHER	QUEST FINISHER	CHAIN?	XP---	XP--	XP-	XP+	XP++	XP+++	CASH REWARD
Continued Threat	35	45	Katar	Katar	N	390	775	1550	2350	3100	3900	None
Deliver the Shipment	30	42	Watcher Biggs	Quartermaster Lungertz	N	260	500	1000	1550	2050	2550	None
Draenethyst Crystals	30	35	Magtoor	Magtoor	N	280	550	1100	1650	2200	2750	None
Driftwood	30	42	Watcher Biggs	Watcher Biggs	Y	350	700	1400	2050	2750	3450	None
Encroaching Wildlife	30	37	Watcher Biggs	Watcher Biggs	Y	290	575	1150	1700	2300	2850	None
Fresh Meat	35	44	Dar	Dar	N	380	750	1500	2250	3000	3750	None
REWARD: 10 Grilled King Crawler Legs, Leather Chef's Belt												
Galen's Escape	30	38	Galen Goodward	Galen's Strongbox (Obj)	N	290	575	1150	1700	2300	2850	None
REWARD: Visionary Buckler												
Lack of Surplus	35	40	Dar	Tok'Kar	Y	320	625	1250	1900	2500	3150	None
Lack of Surplus	35	42	Tok'Kar	Tok'Kar	Y	350	700	1400	2050	2750	3450	None
Neeka Bloodscar	30	35	Helgrum the Swift	Neeka Bloodscar	Y	140	270	550	800	1100	1350	None
Pool of Tears	38	43	Fel'zerul	Fel'zerul	Y	450	900	1800	2650	3550	4450	1 20 00
The Atal'ai Exile	38	44	Fel'zerul	Atal'ai Exile	Y	380	750	1500	2250	3000	3750	None
The Lost Caravan	30	35	Watcher Biggs	Watcher Biggs	Y	280	550	1100	1650	2200	2750	None
The Missing Orders	45	50	Dispatch Commander Ruag	Bengor	Y	120	240	480	725	950	1200	None
The Swamp Talker	45	55	Bengor	Fallen Hero of the Horde	N	575	1150	2250	3400	4500	5650	None
The Temple of Atal'Hakkar	38	50	Fel'zerul	Fel'zerul	N	600	1200	2350	3550	4700	5900	None
REWARD: Guardian Talisman												
Threat From the Sea	35	43	Katar	Tok'Kar	N	360	725	1450	2150	2900	3600	None
CHOICE OF: 1 Tok'kar's Murloc Shanker or 1 Tok'kar's Murloc Basher or 1 Tok'kar's Murloc Chopper												
Threat From the Sea	35	43	Katar	Katar	Y	450	900	1800	2650	3550	4450	None
Threat From the Sea	35	45	Tok'Kar	Katar	Y	0	0	0	0	0	0	None

WESTFALL

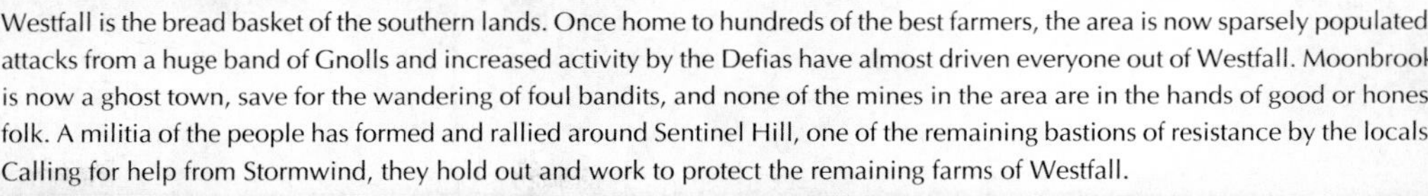

Westfall is the bread basket of the southern lands. Once home to hundreds of the best farmers, the area is now sparsely populated; attacks from a huge band of Gnolls and increased activity by the Defias have almost driven everyone out of Westfall. Moonbrook is now a ghost town, save for the wandering of foul bandits, and none of the mines in the area are in the hands of good or honest folk. A militia of the people has formed and rallied around Sentinel Hill, one of the remaining bastions of resistance by the locals. Calling for help from Stormwind, they hold out and work to protect the remaining farms of Westfall.

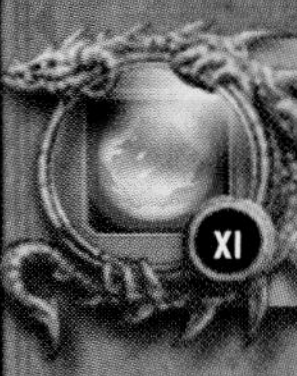

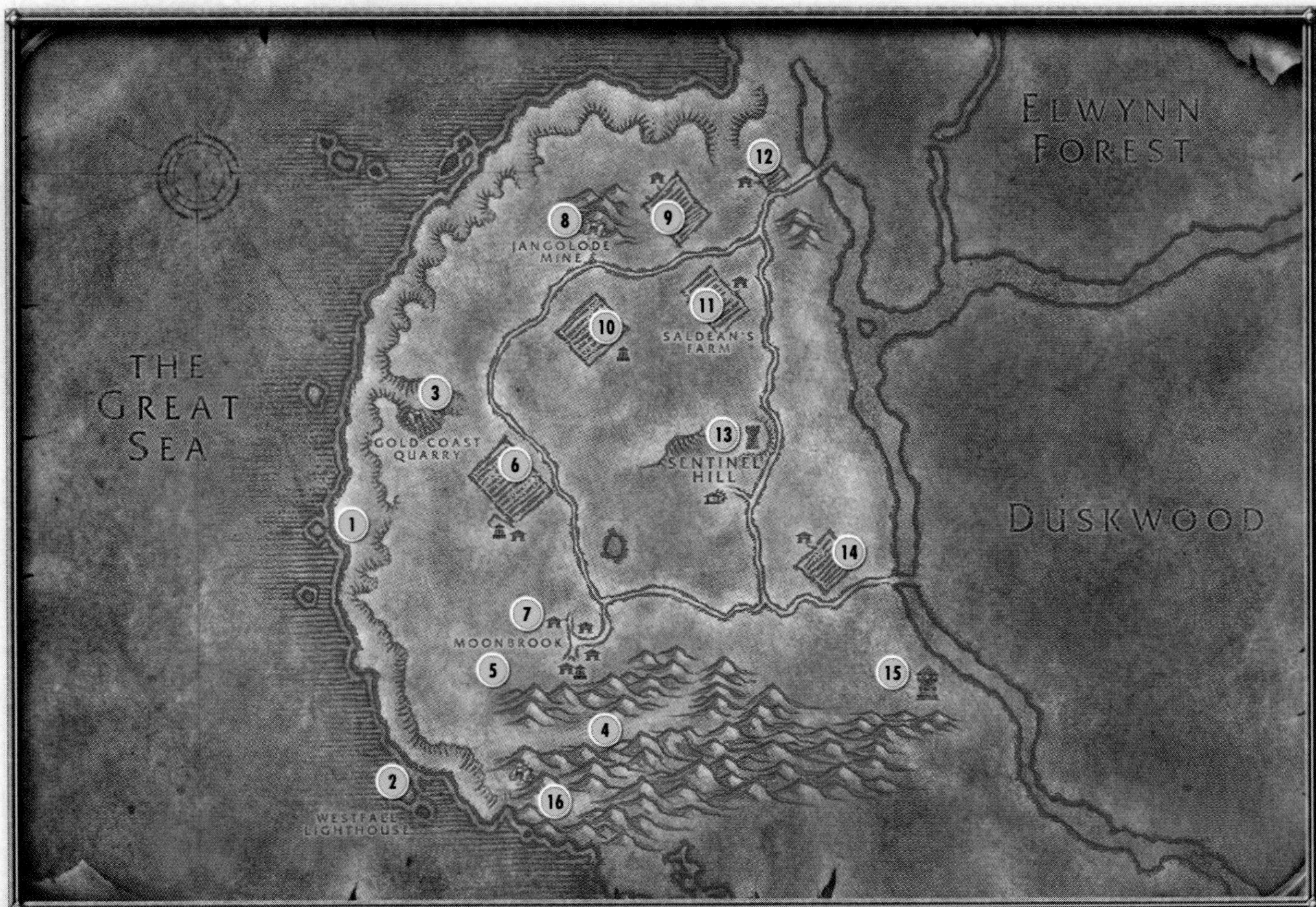

LOCAL RESOURCES

MINING

METAL	AVAILABILITY
Copper	Abundant
Tin	Moderate

HERBALISM

HERB	AVAILABILITY
Peacebloom	Trivial
Silverleaf	Moderate
Earthroot	Moderate
Mageroyal	Moderate
Briarthorn	Moderate
Bruiseweed	Moderate

SKINNING

Quantity of Skinnable Creatures: Moderate

Levels of Skinnable Creatures: 10-16 (Skinning 50-80)

MAP LEGEND

1 LONGSHORE
Crawler 11-12
Greater Fleshripper 16-17
Murloc Coastrunner 12-13
Murloc Hunter 16-17
Murloc Minor Oracle 13-14
Murloc Netter 14-15
Murloc Oracle 17-18
Murloc Raider 11-12
Murloc Tidehunter 17-19
Murloc Warrior 15-16
Old Murk-Eye 20 Elite Quest Target
Riverpaw Herbalist 14-15
Riverpaw Mongrel 13-14
Sand Crawler 13-14
Sea Crawler 15-16
Shore Crawler 17-18

2 WESTFALL LIGHTHOUSE
Captain Grayson 30 Quest

3 GOLD COAST QUARRY
Coyote Packleader 12-13
Coyote 10-11
Defias Looter 13-14
Defias Looter 13-14
Defias Pillager 14-15
Defias Trapper 12-13
Fleshripper 13
Goretusk 14-15
Harvest Golem 11-12
Riverpaw Miner 14-15
Young Goretusk 12-13

4 THE DAGGER HILLS
Grimbooze Thunderbrew 20 Quest
Defias Highwayman 17-18
Defias Knuckleduster 16-17
Defias Pathstalker 15-16

5 DEMONT'S PLACE
Defias Knuckleduster 16-17
Defias Pathstalker 15-16
Defias Pillager 14-15
Fleshripper 13-14
Goretusk 14-15
Riverpaw Brute 15-16
Riverpaw Herbalist 14-15

6 ALEXSTON FARMSTEAD
Defias Looter 13-14
Defias Pillager 14-15
Defias Smuggler 11-12
Defias Trapper 13
Dust Devil 18-19
Foe Reaper 4000 20
Harvest Golem 11-12
Harvest Watcher 14-15

7 MOONBROOK
Entrance to Deadmines Instance
Defias Looter 13-14
Defias Pillager 14-15
Fleshripper 13-14
Harvest Golem 11-12

8 JANGOLODE MINE
Coyote Packleader 12
Coyote 10-11
Defias Smuggler 11-12
Defias Trapper 12-13
Kobold Digger 12-13
Young Fleshripper 10-11

9 FURLBROW'S PUMPKIN FARM
Benny Blaanco 15
Coyote 10-11
Defias Looter 13-14
Defias Pillager 14-15
Defias Smuggler 11-12
Defias Trapper 12-13
Fleshripper 13-14
Harvest Watcher 14-15
Young Fleshripper 10-11
Young Goretusk 12-13

10 THE MOLSEN FARM
Coyote 10-11
Harvest Golem 11-12
Harvest Watcher 14-15
Young Fleshripper 10-11

11 SALDEAN'S FARM
Farmer Saldean 20 Quest
Salma Saldean 20 Quest
Coyote 10-11
Harvest Golem 11-12
Harvest Watcher 14-15
Young Fleshripper 10-11
Young Goretusk 12-13

12 THE JANSEN STEAD
Farmer Furlbrow 20 Quest
Verna Furlbrow 20 Quest
Coyote 10-11
Defias Footpad 10-11
Riverpaw Gnoll 11-12
Rusty Harvest Golem 9-10
Young Fleshripper 11-12
Young Goretusk 12-13

13 SENTINEL HILL
Captain Danuvin 33 Quest
Defias Traitor 15 Quest
Gryan Stoutmantle 35 Quest
Innkeeper Heather 30 Innkeeper
Kirk Maxwell 30 Stable Master
Protector Bialon 30 Quest
Scout Galiaan 30 Quest
Thor 55 Griffon Master
Defias Looter 13-14
Defias Pillager 14-15
Fleshripper 13-14
Goretusk 14-15
Great Goretusk 16-17
Greater Fleshripper 16-17
Young Fleshripper 10-11
Young Goretusk 12-13

14 THE DEAD ACRE
Defias Knuckleduster 16-17
Great Goretusk 16-17
Greater Fleshripper 16-17
Harvest Reaper 17-18

15 THE DUST PLAINS
Defias Tower Patroller 24
Defias Tower Sentry 24-25
Dust Devil 18-19
Great Goretusk 16-17
Klaven Mortwake 26 Elite Quest target
Riverpaw Bandit 16-17
Riverpaw Mystic 18-19
Riverpaw Taskmaster 17-18
Venture Co. Drone 22

16 STILWELL FARM
Daphne Stilwell 20

QUESTS

QUEST	M LEV	Q LEV	QUEST LAUNCHER	QUEST FINISHER	CHAIN?	XP---	XP--	XP-	XP+	XP++	XP+++	CASH REWARD
Captain Sander's Hidden Treasure	10	16	Old Jug (Obj)	Locked Chest (Obj)	N	120	230	460	700	925	1150	8 00
REWARD: Silver Bar, Captain Sander's Shirt, Captain Sander's Sash, Captain Sander's Booty Bag												
Captain Sander's Hidden Treasure	10	16	Captain's Footlocker (Obj)	Broken Barrel (Obj)	Y	60	120	230	350	460	575	None
Captain Sander's Hidden Treasure	10	16	Broken Barrel (Obj)	Old Jug (Obj)	Y	60	120	230	350	460	575	None
Goretusk Liver Pie	9	12	Salma Saldean	Salma Saldean	N	90	180	360	550	725	900	None
REWARD: 3 Goretusk Liver Pie, Recipe: Goretusk Liver Pie												
Keeper of the Flame	10	16	Captain Grayson	Captain Grayson	N	120	230	460	700	925	1150	6 00
REWARD: Scroll of Intellect, Scroll of Stamina and CHOICE OF: 3 Minor Mana Potion or 3 Minor Healing Potion												
Patrolling Westfall	8	14	Captain Danuvin	Captain Danuvin	N	100	200	390	600	775	975	None
CHOICE OF: 1 Belt of the People's Militia or 1 Bracers of the People's Militia												
Poor Old Blanchy	9	13	Verna Furlbrow	Verna Furlbrow	N	90	180	360	550	725	900	None
REWARD: Old Blanchy's Blanket, Old Blanchy's Feed Pouch												
Red Leather Bandanas	10	15	Scout Galiaan	Scout Galiaan	N	110	210	420	625	850	1050	None
CHOICE OF: 1 Cloak of the People's Militia or 1 Greaves of the People's Militia or 1 Leggings of the People's Militia												
Red Silk Bandanas	14	17	Scout Riell	Scout Riell	N	130	250	500	750	1000	1250	None
CHOICE OF: 1 Solid Shortblade or 1 Scrimshaw Dagger or 1 Piercing Axe												
Sweet Amber	40	44	Grimbooze Thunderbrew	Grimbooze Thunderbrew	N	550	1100	2250	3350	4500	5600	None
REWARD: Thunderbrew's Boot Flask												
Sweet Amber	40	44	Grimbooze Thunderbrew	Grimbooze Thunderbrew	Y	380	750	1500	2250	3000	3750	65 00
Sweet Amber	40	44	Grimbooze Thunderbrew	Grimbooze Thunderbrew	Y	470	925	1850	2800	3700	4650	1 25 00
Sweet Amber	40	44	Grimbooze Thunderbrew	Grimbooze Thunderbrew	Y	470	925	1850	2800	3700	4650	1 25 00
Sweet Amber	40	44	Grimbooze Thunderbrew	Grimbooze Thunderbrew	Y	470	925	1850	2800	3700	4650	1 25 00
The Coast Isn't Clear	10	19	Captain Grayson	Captain Grayson	N	150	290	575	875	1150	1450	11 00

QUESTS continued

QUEST	M LEV	Q LEV	QUEST LAUNCHER	QUEST FINISHER	CHAIN?	XP---	XP--	XP-	XP+	XP++	XP+++	CASH REWARD
The Coastal Menace	15	20	Captain Grayson	Captain Grayson	N	160	310	625	925	1250	1550	None
CHOICE OF: 1 Grayson's Torch or 1 Buckler of the Seas or 1 Torchlight Wand												
The Defias Brotherhood	14	18	Gryan Stoutmantle	Gryan Stoutmantle	N	140	270	550	800	1100	1350	None
The Defias Brotherhood	14	18	Gryan Stoutmantle	Wiley the Black	Y	140	270	550	800	1100	1350	None
The Defias Brotherhood	14	18	Wiley the Black	Gryan Stoutmantle	Y	70	140	270	410	550	675	None
The Defias Brotherhood	14	18	Gryan Stoutmantle	Master Mathias Shaw	Y	70	140	270	410	550	675	None
The Defias Brotherhood	14	18	Master Mathias Shaw	Gryan Stoutmantle	Y	35	70	140	200	270	340	None
The Defias Brotherhood	14	18	The Defias Traitor	Gryan Stoutmantle	Y	170	340	675	1000	1350	1700	None
The Defias Brotherhood	14	22	Gryan Stoutmantle	Gryan Stoutmantle	N	260	525	1050	1550	2100	2600	None
CHOICE OF: 1 Chausses of Westfall or 1 Tunic of Westfall or 1 Staff of Westfall												
The Forgotten Heirloom	9	12	Farmer Furlbrow	Farmer Furlbrow	N	90	180	360	550	725	900	None
REWARD: 10 Freshly Baked Bread, 10 Ice Cold Milk												
The Killing Fields	8	15	Farmer Saldean	Farmer Saldean	N	110	210	420	625	850	1050	None
CHOICE OF: 1 Harvester's Pants or 1 Harvester's Robe												
The People's Militia	9	12	Gryan Stoutmantle	Gryan Stoutmantle	Y	90	180	360	550	725	900	5 00
The People's Militia	9	14	Gryan Stoutmantle	Gryan Stoutmantle	Y	100	200	390	600	775	975	6 00
The People's Militia	9	17	Gryan Stoutmantle	Gryan Stoutmantle	N	160	320	650	950	1300	1600	None
CHOICE OF: 1 Edge of the People's Militia or 1 Fist of the People's Militia or 1 Spark of the People's Militia												
Thunderbrew Lager	0	15	Grimbooze Thunderbrew	Grimbooze Thunderbrew	N	0	0	0	0	0	0	None
REWARD: Keg of Thunderbrew Lager												
Westfall Stew	9	10	Verna Furlbrow	Salma Saldean	N	40	85	170	250	340	420	None
Westfall Stew	9	13	Salma Saldean	Salma Saldean	N	90	180	360	550	725	900	None
REWARD: 3 Westfall Stew, Recipe: Westfall Stew, Salma's Oven Mitts, Sharp Kitchen Knife												

IRONFORGE

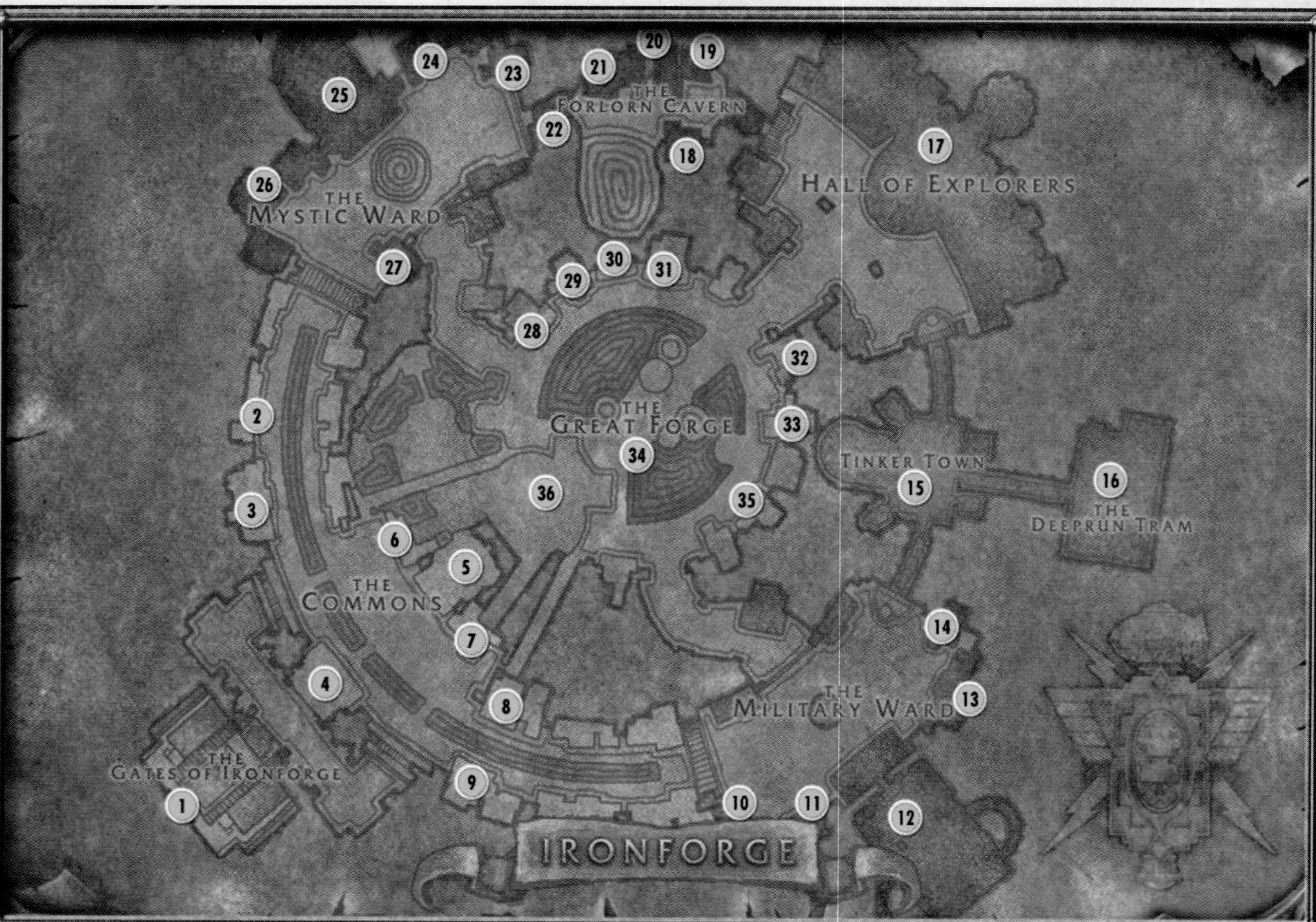

THE FORLORN CAVERN
HALL OF EXPLORERS
THE MYSTIC WARD
THE GREAT FORGE
TINKER TOWN
THE DEEPRUN TRAM
THE COMMONS
THE MILITARY WARD
THE GATES OF IRONFORGE
IRONFORGE

High above Dun Morogh is the city of Ironforge. A gem in the eye of Dwarves and Gnomes alike, this city embodies protection, craftsmanship, and stability for the Dwarven Empire. Though the Gnomes have lost their nearby capital of Gnomeregan, life here is good and few enemies dare to draw close. The greatest threat, in the eyes of the Dwarves, comes from within. The Dark Iron Dwarves and any traitors who side with their cause threaten to subvert whatever they touch. Ironforge's loyal servants are always in the lookout for these perils.

MAP LEGEND

THE GATES OF IRONFORGE

1 ENTRANCE
- Ironforge Guard 75
- Jordan Stilwell 30

THE COMMONS

2 STONEFIRE TAVERN
- Gwenna Firebrew 30 Barmaid
- Innkeeper Firebrew 30 Innkeeper

3 BARIM'S REAGENTS
- Barim Jurgenstaad 30 Reagent Vendor

4 THE AUCTION HOUSE
- Auctioneers

5 THE BANK
- Bank Tellers

6 IRONFORGE ARMORY
- Bromlir Ormsen 30 Heavy Armor Merchant
- Mangorn Flinthammer 30 Heavy Armor Merchant

7 STEELFURY'S WEAPON EMPORIUM
- Dolman Steelfury 30 Weapon Merchant
- Grenil Steelfury 30 Weapon Merchant

8 FIZZLESPINNER'S GENERAL GOODS
- Bryllia Ironbrand 30 General Goods
- Fillus Fizzlespinner 30 Trade Supplier
- Pithwick 30 Bag Vendor

9 IRONFORGE VISITOR'S CENTER
- Jondor Steelbrow 60 Guild Master
- Lyesa Steelbrow 25 Guild Tabard Vendor

THE MILITARY WARD

10 CRAGHELM'S PLATE AND CHAIN
- Dolkin Craghelm 30 Mail Armor Merchant
- Lissyphus Finespindle 30 Light Armor Merchant
- Olthran Craghelm 30 Heavy Armor Merchant

11 TIMBERLINE ARMS
- Brenwyn Wintersteel 30 Blade Merchant
- Hegnar Swiftaxe 30 Axe Merchant
- Kelomir Ironhand 30 Mace/Staff Merchant
- Thalgus Thunderfist 30 Two-Handed Weapon Merchant

12 HALL OF ARMS
- Belia Thundergranite 40 Pet Trainer
- Bilban Tosslespanner 45 Warrior Trainer
- Demnul Farmountain 45
- Ironforge Guard 75
- Kelstrum Stonebreaker 45 Warrior Trainer
- Olmin Burningbeard 50 Hunter Trainer
- Pilot Longbeard 23
- Regnus Thundergranite 40 Hunter Trainer
- Ulbrek Firehand 30 Stable Master
- Xiggs Fuselighter 45

13 BRUUK'S CORNER
- Bruuk Barleybeard 50 Bartender
- Edris Barleybeard 30 Barmaid
- Tisa Martine 30

14 GOLDFURY'S HUNTING SUPPLIES
- Bretta Goldfury 30 Gun Merchant
- Skolmin Goldfury 30 Bow Merchant

TINKER TOWN

15 GENERAL AREA
- Courier Hammerfall 3
- Fizzlebang Booms 40 Firework Vendor
- Gearcutter Cogspinner 30 Engineering Supplier
- Gnoarn 20 Quest
- High Tinker Makkatorque 55 Gnome King
- Jemma Quikswitch 24 Journeyman Engineer
- Klockmort Spannerspan 45
- Lomac Gearstrip 29 Quest
- Master Mechanic Castpipe 57 Quest
- Soolie Berryfizz 30 Alchemy Supplier
- Springspindle Fizzlegear 45 Artisan Enginner
- Tally Berryfizz 35 Expert Alchemist
- Tinkmaster Overspark 57 Master Engineer
- Trixie Quikswitch 31 Expert Engineer
- Vosur Brakthel 30 Journeyman Alchemist

16 DEEPRUN TRAM

HALL OF EXPLORERS

17 THE LIBRARY
- Advisor Belgrum 40 Quest
- Curator Thorius 45 Quest
- High Explorer Magelias 60 Quest
- Historian Karnik 20
- Krom Stoutarm 20
- Laris Geardawdle 50 Quest
- Libraryian Mae Paledust 30
- Lyon Mountainheart 40
- Prospector Stormpike 30 Quest
- Roettern Stonehammer 40 Quest

THE FORLORN CAVERN

18 SHADY BUILDING
- Durtham Greldon 40 Fist Weapon's Trainer
- Fenthwick 40 Rogue Trainer
- Hulfdan Blackbeard 60 Rogue Trainer
- Ormyr Flinteye 50 Rogue Trainer
- Tynnus Venomsprout 30 Shady Dealer

19 WARLOCK'S HOME
- Jubahl Corpseeker 60 Felhunter Trainer

20 WARLOCK'S GUILD
- Alexander Calder 60 Warlock Trainer
- Briarthorn 50 Warlock Trainer
- Gerrig Bonegrip 30 Quest
- Thistleheart 40 Warlock Trainer

21 TRAVELING FISHERMAN
- Grimnur Stonebrand 35 Fishing Trainer
- Lago Blackwrench 30
- Tansy Puddlefizz 30 Fishing Supplier

22 STONEBLADE'S PLACE
- Binny Springblade 40 Dagger Trainer
- Hjoldir Stoneblade 30 Blade Merchant
- Prynne 40 Thrown Weapon Trainer

THE MYSTIC WARD

23 MAEVA'S MYSTICAL APPAREL
- Ingrys Stonebrow 30 Cloth Armor Merchant
- Maeva Snowbraid 30 Robe Merchant

24 MAGE TYMOR'S HOME
- Mage Tymor 35 Quest

25 HALL OF MYSTERIES
- Beldruk Doombrow 50 Paladin Trainer
- Bink 40 Mage Trainer
- Braenna Flintcrag 50 Priest Trainer
- Brandur Ironhammer 50 Paladin Trainer
- Dink 40 Mage Trainer
- High Priest Rohan 60
- Ironforge Guard 75
- Juli Stormkettle 50 Mage Trainer
- Milstaff Stormeye 45 Portal Trainer
- Toldren Deepiron 40 Priest Trainer

26 THE FIGHTING WIZARD
- Bingus 30 Staff Merchant
- Harick Boulderdrum 30 Wands Merchant

27 LONGBERRY'S REAGENTS
- Ginny Longberry 30 Reagent Vendor

THE GREAT FORGE

28 LEATHER SHOP
- Balthus Stoneflayer 35 Skinning Trainer
- Bombus Finespindle 30 Leatherworking Supplies
- Fimble Finespindle 35 Expert Leatherworker
- Gretta Finespindle 24 Journeyman Leatherworker

29 TAILOR'S SHOP
- Jormund Stonebrow 35 Expert Tailor
- Outfitter Eric 35 Specialty Tailoring Supplies
- Poranna Snowbraid 30 Tailor Supplies
- Uthrar Threx 24 Journeyman Tailor

30 BURBIK'S SUPPLIES
- Burbik Gearspanner 30 Trade Supplier

31 DEEP MOUNTAIN MINING GUILD
- Geogram Bouldertoe 35 Mining Trainer
- Golnir Bouldertoe 30 Mining Supplier

32 THE BRONZE KETTLE
- Daryl Riknussun 35 Cooking Trainer
- Emrul Riknussun 30 Cooking Supplier

33 THIZZLEFUZZ ARCANERY
- Gimble Thistlefuzz 35 Expert Enchanter
- Thonus Pillarstone 25 Journeyman Enchanter
- Tilli Thistlefuzz 30 Enchanting Supplier

34 CENTRAL FORGE
- Bengus Deepforge 45 Artisan Blacksmith
- Brombar Higgleby 40 Keymaster
- Groum Stonebeard 25 Journeyman Blacksmith
- Grumnus Steelshaper 60 Armor Crafter
- Gryth Thurden 55 Elite Gryphon Master
- Ironus Coldsteel 54 Specialty Weapon Crafter
- Myolor Sunderfury 53 Quest
- Rotgath Stonebeard 31 Expert Blacksmith
- Thurgrum Deepforge 30 Blacksmith Supplier
- Tormus Deepforge 30

35 IRONFORGE PHYSICIAN
- Gwina Stonebranch 30 Herbalism Supplies
- Nissa Firestone 35 First Aid Trainer
- Reyna Stonebranch 35 Herbalism Trainer

36 THE HIGH SEAT
- King Magni Bronzebeard 90 Lord of Ironforge
- Royal Historian Archesonus 50
- Senator Barin Redstone 50 Quest

QUESTS

QUEST	M LEV	Q LEV	QUEST LAUNCHER	QUEST FINISHER	CHAIN?	XP---	XP--	XP-	XP+	XP++	XP+++	CASH REWARD
A Call to Arms: The Plaguelands!	50	50	Courier Hammerfall	Commander Ashlam Valorfist	Y	45	95	190	280	380	470	None
A Future Task	45	50	Historian Karnik	High Explorer Magellas	N	470	950	1900	2800	3750	4700	2 20 00
A King's Tribute	25	30	King Magni Bronzebeard	Grand Mason Marblesten	Y	120	240	480	725	950	1200	None
A King's Tribute	25	31	Grand Mason Marblesten	Grand Mason Marblesten	N	250	500	1000	1500	2000	2500	None
A King's Tribute	25	31	Grand Mason Marblesten	King Magni Bronzebeard	N	250	500	1000	1500	2000	2500	None
REWARD: Ironforge Memorial Ring												
A Little Slime Goes a Long Way	48	52	Laris Geardawdle	Laris Geardawdle	N	625	1250	2550	3800	5100	6350	75 00
A Little Slime Goes a Long Way	48	54	Laris Geardawdle	Laris Geardawdle	N	675	1350	2700	4100	5450	6800	40 00
CHOICE OF: 1 Hazecover Boots or 1 Brazen Gauntlets												
An Easy Pickup	45	52	Mage Tymor	Xiggs Fuselighter	Y	50	100	200	310	410	500	None
Arcane Runes	45	52	Mage Tymor	Pilot Xiggs Fuselighter	Y	260	500	1000	1550	2050	2550	None
Assisting Arch Druid Staghelm	47	50	Innkeeper Firebrew	Arch Druid Fandral Staghelm	Y	45	95	190	280	380	470	None
At Last!	40	48	Curator Thorius	Mountaineer Pebblebitty	N	440	875	1750	2650	3500	4400	None
REWARD: Key to Searing Gorge												
Dwarven Justice	40	55	Curator Thorius	Dying Archaeologist	Y	575	1150	2250	3400	4500	5650	None
Find Bingles	12	15	Gnoarn	Bingles Blastenheimer	Y	25	55	110	160	220	270	None
Gnome Improvement	28	35	Talvash del Kissel	Talvash del Kissel	N	140	270	550	800	1100	1350	None
REWARD: Talvash's Gold Ring												
Ironband Wants You!	30	37	Prospector Stormpike	Prospector Ironband	Y	70	140	280	430	575	700	None
Mythology of the Titans	28	38	Librarian Mae Paledust	Librarian Mae Paledust	N	360	700	1400	2150	2850	3550	None
REWARD: Explorers' League Commendation												
Passing the Burden	45	52	Historian Karnik	Mage Tymor	Y	50	100	200	310	410	500	None
Portents of Uldum	45	50	High Explorer Magellas	Historian Karnik	Y	45	95	190	280	380	470	None
Reclaimed Treasures	33	43	Krom Stoutarm	Krom Stoutarm	N	360	725	1450	2150	2900	3600	60 00
Reclaimers' Business in Desolace	30	33	Roetten Stonehammer	Kreldig Ungor	N	130	260	525	775	1050	1300	None
Return to Ironforge	45	50	Uldum Pedestal (Obj)	Historian Karnik	Y	45	95	190	280	380	470	None
Return to Mage Tymor	45	52	Pilot Xiggs Fuselighter	Mage Tymor	N	750	1500	3050	4550	6100	7600	None
CHOICE OF: 1 Steelsmith Greaves or 1 Skullspell Orb												
Sara Balloo's Plea	25	30	Sara Balloo	King Magni Bronzebeard	N	120	240	480	725	950	1200	None
Seeing What Happens	45	50	Historian Karnik	Uldum Pedestal (Obj)	N	470	950	1900	2800	3750	4700	None
Signal for Pickup	45	52	Xiggs Fuselighter	Xiggs Fuselighter	N	50	100	200	310	410	500	None
REWARD: Standard Issue Flare Gun												
Signal for Pickup	45	52	Burns	Xiggs Fuselighter	N	50	100	200	310	410	500	None
REWARD: Standard Issue Flare Gun												
Signal for Pickup	45	52	Xiggs Fuselighter	Xiggs Fuselighter	N	0	0	0	0	0	0	None
REWARD: Standard Issue Flare Gun												
Signal for Pickup	45	52	Burns	Xiggs Fuselighter	N	0	0	0	0	0	0	None
REWARD: Standard Issue Flare Gun												
Speak with Shoni	15	15	Gnoarn	Shoni the Shilent	Y	25	55	110	160	220	270	None
The Lost Dwarves	35	40	Prospector Stormpike	Baelog	Y	30	65	130	190	250	320	5 00
The Platinum Discs	40	47	High Explorer Magellas	Dinita Stonemantle	N	40	85	170	250	340	420	None
REWARD: Thawpelt Sack and CHOICE OF: 5 Superior Healing Potion or 5 Greater Mana Potion												
The Smoldering Ruins of Thaurissan	50	54	Royal Historian Archesonus	Royal Historian Archesonus	N	550	1100	2200	3250	4350	5450	1 65 00
REWARD: Ring of the Aristocrat												
The Smoldering Ruins of Thaurissan	50	54	Royal Historian Archesonus	Royal Historian Archesonus	Y	55	110	220	320	430	550	None

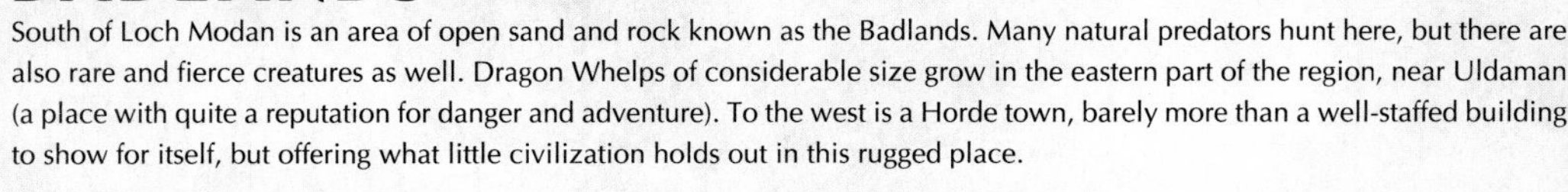

BADLANDS

South of Loch Modan is an area of open sand and rock known as the Badlands. Many natural predators hunt here, but there are also rare and fierce creatures as well. Dragon Whelps of considerable size grow in the eastern part of the region, near Uldaman (a place with quite a reputation for danger and adventure). To the west is a Horde town, barely more than a well-staffed building to show for itself, but offering what little civilization holds out in this rugged place.

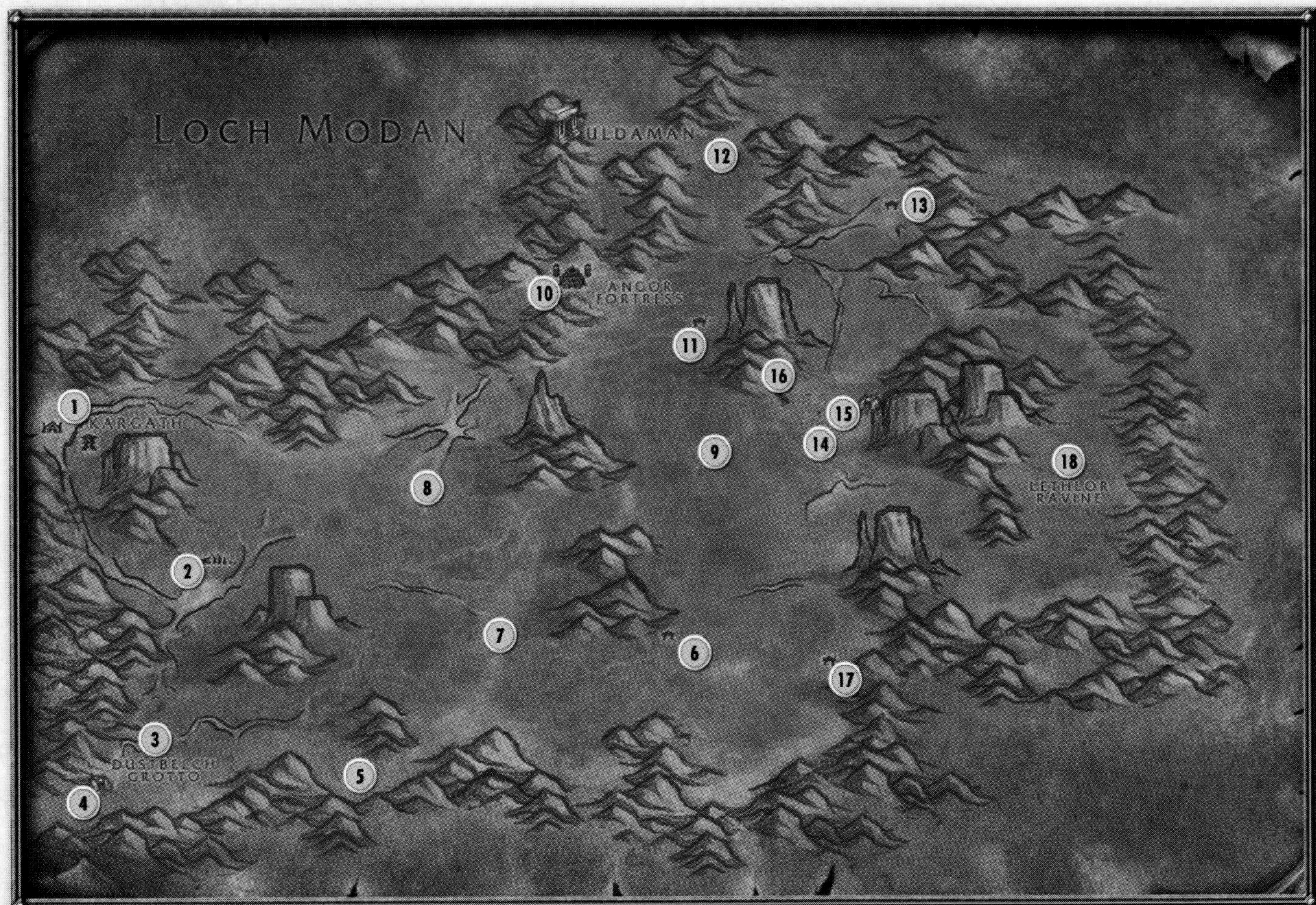

LOCAL RESOURCES

MINING

METAL	AVAILABILITY
Tin	Moderate
Iron	Moderate
Mithril	Trivial

HERBALISM

HERB	AVAILABILITY
Kingsblood	Abundant
Wild Steelbloom	Moderate
Khadgar's Whiskers	Moderate
Firebloom	Trivial

SKINNING

Quantity of Skinnable Creatures: Abundant

Levels of Skinnable Creatures: 35-45 (Skinning 175-225)

MAP LEGEND

1 KARGATH
Gorrick 55 Wind Rider Master
Greth 30 Stable Master
Grunt Gargal 52 Quest
Initiate Amakkar 52 Quest
Innkeeper Shul'kar 30 Innkeeper
Razal'blade 52 Quest
Shadowmage Vivian Lagrave 60 Quest
Thal'trak Proudtusk 55 Quest
Thunderheart 52 Quest

2 APOCRYPHAN'S REST
Elder Crag Coyote 39-40
Giant Buzzard 39-40
Ridge Stalker Patriarch 40-41

3 CAMP CAGG
Boss Tho'grun 41 Quest Target
Dustbelcher Mauler 41-42
Dustbelcher Mystic 37
Dustbelcher Shaman 41-42
Dustbelcher Wyrmhunter 40-41
Greater Rock Elemental 42-44

4 DUSTBELCH GROTTO
Dustbelcher Lord 44
Dustbelcher Ogre Mage 44

5 MIRAGE FLATS
Elder Crag Coyote 39-40
Giant Buzzard 39-40
Ridge Stalker Patriach 40-41
Zaricotl 55 Elite

6 AGMOND'S END
Agmond's Body Quest
Theldurin the Lost 30 Quest
Buzzard 37-38
Feral Crag Coyote 37-38
Murdaloc 42 Quest Target
Ridge Huntress 39
Rock Elemental 39-40
Stonevault Shaman 40-41
Stonevault Stonesnapper 39-40

7 CAMP WURG
Dustbelcher Brute 39
Dustbelcher Ogre 38-39
Elder Crag Coyote 39-40
Ridge Stalker Patriarch 41

8 THE DUSTBOWL
Lotwil Veriatus 36 Quest
Lucien Tosselwrench 31 Quest
Elder Crag Coyote 39-40
Giant Buzzard 39-40
Lesser Rock Elementals 37-39
Ridge Stalker Patriarch 41

9 VALLEY OF FANGS
Jazzrik 38 Vendor
Martek the Exiled 42 Quest
Rigglefuzz 37 Quest
Crag Coyote 35-36
Ridge Huntress 38-39

10 ANGOR FORTRESS
Crag Coyote 35
Ridge Stalker 36-37
Shadowforge Chanter 38-39
Shadowforge Warrior 38
Stone Golem 38-39

11 HAMMERTOE'S DIGSITE
Prospector Ryedol 35 Quest
Sigrun Ironhew 40 Quest
Crag Coyote 35-36
Ridge Stalker 35-36
Shadowforge Darkweaver 36-37
Shadowforge Tunneler 35-36
Starving Buzzard 35-36

12 THE MAKER'S TERRACE
Entrance to Uldaman World Dungeon
Shadowforge Digger 35-36 Elite
Shadowforge Ruffian 36-37 Elite
Shadowforge Surveyor 35-36 Elite

13 CAMP KOSH
Dustbelcher Mystic 37
Dustbelcher Warrior 36-37

14 DUSTWIND GULCH
Garek 50 Quest
Thorkaf Dragoneye 50 Master Dragonscale Leatherworker
Buzzard 37-38
Feral Crag Coyote 37-38
Ridge Stalker 35-36
Starving Buzzard 35-36

15 DUSTWIND GULCH CAVE
Entrance to Uldaman World Dungeon
Stonevault Basher 40 Elite
Stonevault Seer 39-40 Elite

16 CRYPT

17 CAMP BOFF
Dustbelcher Brute 39-40
Dustbelcher Ogre 38-39
Feral Crag Coyote 37-38

18 LETHLOR RAVINE
Large Gray Pillar
Pillar of Amethyst
Pillar of Diamond
Blacklash 50 Elite
Hematus 50 Elite
Scalding Whelp 42-43
Scorched Guardian 43-45 Elite

QUESTS

QUEST	M LEV	Q LEV	QUEST LAUNCHER	QUEST FINISHER	CHAIN?	XP---	XP--	XP-	XP+	XP++	XP+++	CASH REWARD
A Dwarf and His Tools	35	35	Prospector Ryedol	Prospector Ryedol	N	280	550	1100	1650	2200	2750	None
REWARD: Ryedol's Hammer												
A Sign of Hope	35	35	Crumpled Map (Obj)	Prospector Ryedol	Y	140	270	550	800	1100	1350	None
A Sign of Hope	35	35	Prospector Ryedol	Hammertoe Grez	Y	280	550	1100	1650	2200	2750	None
Agmond's Fate	30	38	Prospector Ironband	Prospector Ironband	N	290	575	1150	1700	2300	2850	None
REWARD: Prospector Gloves												
Amulet of Secrets	35	40	Hammertoe Grez	Hammertoe Grez	Y	320	625	1250	1900	2500	3150	None
An Ambassador of Evil	35	44	Historian Karnik	Advisor Belgrum	N	470	925	1850	2800	3700	4650	1 25 00
REWARD: Dwarf Captain's Sword												
Badlands Reagent Run	36	39	Jarkal Mossmeld	Jarkal Mossmeld	Y	300	600	1200	1800	2400	3000	45 00
Barbecued Buzzard Wings	33	40	Rigglefuzz	Rigglefuzz	N	240	470	950	1400	1900	2350	None
REWARD: 2 Barbecued Buzzard Wing, Recipe: Barbecued Buzzard Wing												
Broken Alliances	40	43	Gorn	Gorn	Y	360	725	1450	2150	2900	3600	None
Broken Alliances	40	50	Gorn	Gorn	N	600	1200	2350	3550	4700	5900	None
CHOICE OF: 1 Blazewind Breastplate or 1 Prismscale Hauberk or 1 Warforged Chestplate or 1 Mindburst Medallion												
Coolant Heads Prevail	35	37	Lotwil Veriatus	Lotwil Veriatus	Y	290	575	1150	1700	2300	2850	None
Coyote Thieves	30	40	Neeka Bloodscar	Neeka Bloodscar	Y	320	625	1250	1900	2500	3150	None
Dreadmaul Rock	48	52	Thal'trak Proudtusk	Sha'ni Proudtusk	Y	500	1000	2050	3050	4100	5100	None
Fiery Enchantments	40	45	Sigrun Ironhew	Sigrun Ironhew	N	390	775	1550	2350	3100	3900	None
REWARD: Fiery Enchantment												
Find Agmond	30	38	Prospector Ironband	Battered Dwarven Skeleton (Obj)	Y	150	290	575	875	1150	1450	4 00
REWARD: Ripped Prospector Belt, Jade, 2 Gold Ore												
Forbidden Knowledge	30	40	Gerrig Bonegrip	Theldurin the Lost	N	240	470	950	1400	1900	2350	None
REWARD: Skull of Impending Doom												
Forbidden Knowledge	30	40	Keeper Bel'dugur	Theldurin the Lost	N	240	470	950	1400	1900	2350	None
REWARD: Skull of Impending Doom												
Gyro... What?	35	37	Lotwil Veriatus	Lotwil Veriatus	N	290	575	1150	1700	2300	2850	None
Liquid Stone	35	37	Lucien Tosselwrench	Lucien Tosselwrench	N	210	420	850	1250	1700	2100	None
REWARD: Recipe: Lesser Stoneshield Potion, 2 Lesser Stoneshield Potion												
Mirages	35	38	Sigrun Ironhew	Sigrun Ironhew	Y	220	430	850	1300	1700	2150	None
Murdaloc	30	42	Battered Dwarven Skeleton (Obj)	Prospector Ironband	Y	350	700	1400	2050	2750	3450	None
REWARD: Rock Pulverizer												
Passing Word of a Threat	35	40	Historian Karnik	Advisor Belgrum	Y	160	310	625	925	1250	1550	None
Passing Word of a Threat	35	40	Advisor Belgrum	Historian Karnik	Y	240	470	950	1400	1900	2350	None

QUESTS continued

QUEST	M LEV	Q LEV	QUEST LAUNCHER	QUEST FINISHER	CHAIN?	XP---	XP--	XP-	XP+	XP++	XP+++	CASH REWARD
Pearl Diving	30	37	Rigglefuzz	Rigglefuzz	N	360	700	1400	2150	2850	3550	None
REWARD: Flash Bomb and CHOICE OF: 1 Flash Rifle or 1 Flash Wand												
Prospect of Faith	35	40	Prospector Ryedol	Historian Karnik	N	320	625	1250	1900	2500	3150	None
Prospect of Faith	35	40	Hammertoe Grez	Prospector Ryedol	Y	240	470	950	1400	1900	2350	None
Report to Helgrum	30	40	Neeka Bloodscar	Helgrum the Swift	N	240	470	950	1400	1900	2350	None
Scrounging	35	40	Sigrun Ironhew	Sigrun Ironhew	N	320	625	1250	1900	2500	3150	None
CHOICE OF: 1 Salbac Shield or 1 Ironheel Boots												
Seal of the Earth	40	50	Seal of the Earth (Obj)	Seal of the Earth (Obj)	N	0	0	0	0	0	0	None
Seal of the Earth	40	50	Seal of the Earth (Obj)	Seal of the Earth (Obj)	N	0	0	0	0	0	0	None
Solution to Doom	30	40	Theldurin the Lost	Theldurin the Lost	N	320	625	1250	1900	2500	3150	None
REWARD: Doomsayer's Robe												
Stone Is Better than Cloth	35	42	Lucien Tosselwrench	Lucien Tosselwrench	N	260	500	1000	1550	2050	2550	None
REWARD: Enchanted Stonecloth Bracers												
Study of the Elements: Rock	35	37	Lotwil Veriatus	Lotwil Veriatus	Y	290	575	1150	1700	2300	2850	None
Study of the Elements: Rock	35	39	Lotwil Veriatus	Lotwil Veriatus	Y	300	600	1200	1800	2400	3000	None
Study of the Elements: Rock	35	42	Lotwil Veriatus	Lotwil Veriatus	N	350	700	1400	2050	2750	3450	None
The Lost Tablets of Will	35	45	Advisor Belgrum	Advisor Belgrum	N	575	1150	2350	3500	4700	5850	1 30 00
REWARD: Medal of Courage												
The Rise of the Machines	52	54	Hierophant Theodora Mulvadania	Lotwil Veriatus	Y	140	270	550	800	1100	1350	None
The Star, the Hand and the Heart	30	44	Gerrig Bonegrip	Gerrig Bonegrip	Y	550	1100	2250	3350	4500	5600	None
This Is Going to Be Hard	35	42	Lotwil Veriatus	Lucien Tosselwrench	Y	0	0	0	0	0	0	None
This Is Going to Be Hard	35	42	Lucien Tosselwrench	Lotwil Veriatus	Y	0	0	0	0	0	0	None
This Is Going to Be Hard	35	45	Lotwil Veriatus	Lotwil Veriatus	N	490	975	1950	2900	3900	4850	None
REWARD: Nifty Stopwatch												
To Ironforge for Yagyin's Digest	30	40	Theldurin the Lost	Gerrig Bonegrip	Y	80	160	310	470	625	775	None
To the Undercity for Yagyin's Digest	30	40	Theldurin the Lost	Keeper Bel'dugur	Y	80	160	310	470	625	775	None
Tremors of the Earth	40	43	Garek	Garek	Y	360	725	1450	2150	2900	3600	None
Tremors of the Earth	40	50	Garek	Garek	N	600	1200	2350	3550	4700	5900	None
CHOICE OF: 1 Blazewind Breastplate or 1 Prismscale Hauberk or 1 Warforged Chestplate or 1 Mindburst Medallion												
Uldaman Reagent Run	36	42	Jarkal Mossmeld	Jarkal Mossmeld	N	350	700	1400	2050	2750	3450	55 00
REWARD: 5 Restorative Elixirs												

DUN MOROGH

Dun Morogh rests in the highlands between the Wetlands and the Searing Gorge. Blocked from reaching either because of the impassable cliffs of stone and ice that surround it, Dun Morogh is only traversable over land via the route through Loch Modan. This is the home of the Dwarven Capitol, Ironforge. Though Wolves, Troggs, and a small pocket of resistance from Dark Iron Dwarves are found here, few greater threats exist. The most dangerous part of Dun Morogh is located in the north-west, where the Gnome capitol of Gnomeregan once bustled with activity. A failed experiment in weaponry has altered the capitol into a nightmare of disease and poison, avoided by many.

WETLANDS
IRONFORGE
BREWNALL VILLAGE
KHARANOS
GOL'BOLAR QUARRY
COLDRIDGE VALLEY
THE SEARING GORGE
1 2 3 4 5 6 7 8 9 10 11 12 13 14 15 16 17 18 19 20 21 22 23

LOCAL RESOURCES

MINING

METAL	AVAILABILITY
Copper	Abundant

HERBALISM

HERB	AVAILABILITY
Peacebloom	Abundant
Silverleaf	Abundant
Earthroot	Abundant

SKINNING

Quantity of Skinnable Creatures: Abundant

Levels of Skinnable Creatures: 1-10 (Skinning 1-50)

HOW TO
AZEROTH
KHAZ MODAN
LORDAERON
NORTHERN KALIMDOR
SOUTHERN KALIMDOR

MAP LEGEND

1 GNOMEREGAN
- **Entrance to Gnomeregan Instance**
- Elder Crag Boars 7-8
- Ice Claw Bear 7-8
- Leper Gnome 8-10
- Snow Leopard 7-8

2 FROSTMANE HOLD
- Elder Crag Boars 7-8
- Frostmane Headhunter 8-9
- Frostmane Snowstrider 8-9
- Frostmane Troll 7-8
- Ice Claw Bear 7-8
- Snow Leopard 7-8

3 SOUTHWESTERN DUN MOROGH
- Crag Boar 5-6
- Juvenile Snow Leopard 5-6
- Young Black Bear 5-6

4 CHILL BREEZE VALLEY
- **Tundra MacGrann 20 Quest**
- Large Crag Boar 6-7
- Old Icebeard 11+

5 THE GRIZZLED DEN
- Wendigo 6-7
- Young Wendigo 5

6 KHARANOS
- **Golorn Frostbeard 10 Vendor**
- **Gremlock Pilsnor 10 Cook**
- **Innkeeper Belm 30 Innkeeper**
- **Jarven Thunderbrew 15 Quest**
- **Ozzie Togglevolt 10 Quest**
- **Ragnar Thunderbrew 30 Quest**
- **Razzle Sprysprocket 20 Quest**
- **Senir Whitebeard 12 Quest**
- **Shelby Stoneflint 30 Stable Master**
- **Thammer Pol 11 Physician**
- **Tharek Blackstone 12 Quest**
- **Tognus Flintfire 30 Blacksmith**

7 STEELGRILL'S DEPOT
- **Beldin Steelgrill 12 Quest**
- **Bronk Guzzlegear 24 Engineer**
- **Milli Featherwhistle 50 Mechanostrider Merchant**
- **Pilot Bellowfiz 18 Quest**
- **Pilot Stonegear 20 Quest**
- **Yarr Hammerstone 10 Miner**

8 COLDRIDGE PASS
- Rockjaw Raider 3-4

9 COLDRIDGE VALLEY
- **Grelin Whitebeard 5 Quest**
- **Talin Keeneye 5 Quest**
- Burly Rockjaw Trogg 2
- Frostmane Novice 3-4
- Frostmane Troll Whelps 3-4
- Grik'nir the Cold 5 Quest Target
- Ragged Young Wolf 1-2
- Rockjaw Troggs 1-2
- Small Crag Boar 3

10 ANVILMAR
- **Adlin Pridedrift 5 Quest**
- **Felix Whindlebolt 2 Quest**
- **Sten Stoutarm 5 Quest**

11 ICEFLOW LAKE
- Elder Crag Boars 7-8
- Ice Claw Bear 7-8
- Snow Leopard 7-8

12 SHIMMER RIDGE
- Frostmane Headhunter 8-9
- Frostmane Seer 8
- Frostmane Snowstrider 8-9
- Frostmane Troll 7-8

13 EASTERN DUN MOROGH
- Elder Crag Boar 7-8
- Snow Tracker Wolf 6-7

14 MISTY PINE REFUGE
- **Father Gavin 15 Argent Dawn**

15 AMBERSTILL RANCH
- **Rudra Amberstill 10 Quest**
- **Turuk Amberstill 10 Vendor**
- Vagash 12+ Quest Target

16 GOL'BOLAR QUARRY AND MINE
- **Foreman Stonebrow 12 Quest**
- **Senator Mehr Stonehallow 50 Quest**
- Rockjaw Bonesnapper 8-9
- Rockjaw Skullthumper 8-9

17 FAR EASTERN DUN MOROGH
- Elder Crag Boars 8-9
- Rockjaw Ambusher 9-10
- Scarred Crag Boar 9-10

18 HELM'S BED LAKE
- Captain Beld 11 Quest Target
- Dark Iron Spy 9-10
- Rockjaw Backbreaker 11-12
- Rockjaw Bonesnapper 8-9
- Scarred Crag Boar 9-10

19 NORTH GATE PASS
- Elder Crag Boars 8-9
- Ice Claw Bears 8-9
- Scarred Crag Boar 9-10

20 NORTH GATE OUTPOST
- **Pilot Hammerfoot 17 Quest**
- Snow Leopard 8
- Mangeclaw 11 Quest Target

QUEST	M LEV	Q LEV	QUEST LAUNCHER	QUEST FINISHER	CHAIN?	XP---	XP--	XP-	XP+	XP++	XP+++	CASH REWARD
A Favor for Evershine	2	8	Rejold Barleybrew	Rejold Barleybrew	Y	55	110	210	320	420	525	None
A New Threat	1	2	Balir Frosthammer	Balir Frosthammer	N	15	35	70	100	140	170	None
CHOICE OF: 1 Bear Shawl or 1 Rustic Belt or 1 Snow Boots												
A Pilot's Revenge	8	11	A Dwarven Corpse (Obj)	Pilot Hammerfoot	N	65	130	260	400	525	650	None
CHOICE OF: 1 Craftsman's Dagger or 1 Compact Hammer												
A Refugee's Quandry	1	3	Felix Whindlebolt	Felix Whindlebolt	N	25	50	100	150	200	250	40
Ammo for Rumbleshot	5	6	Loslor Rudge	Hegnar Rumbleshot	N	55	110	220	320	430	550	1 25
Beer Basted Boar Ribs	5	7	Ragnar Thunderbrew	Ragnar Thunderbrew	N	65	130	250	380	500	625	1 75
REWARD: 5 Beer Basted Boar Ribs, Recipe: Beer Basted Boar Ribs												
Bitter Rivals	2	6	Marleth Barleybrew	Unguarded Thunderbrew ale barrel (Obj)	Y	15	25	55	80	110	140	None
Bring Back the Mug	2	3	Durnan Furcutter	Adlin Pridedrift	N	25	50	100	150	200	250	25
Coldridge Valley Mail Delivery	1	3	Sten Stoutarm	Talin Keeneye	Y	20	40	75	110	150	190	None
Coldridge Valley Mail Delivery	1	4	Talin Keeneye	Grelin Whitebeard	N	25	55	110	160	220	270	7
Distracting Jarven	1	7		Jarven Thunderbrew	N	0	0	0	0	0	0	None
Dwarven Outfitters	1	1	Sten Stoutarm	Sten Stoutarm	N	10	15	30	50	65	80	None
CHOICE OF: 1 Rabbit Handler Gloves or 1 Wolf Handler Gloves or 1 Boar Handler Gloves												
Evershine	2	7	Pilot Bellowfiz	Rejold Barleybrew	Y	15	30	65	95	130	160	None
Frostmane Hold	7	9	Senir Whitebeard	Senir Whitebeard	Y	60	120	240	350	470	600	None
CHOICE OF: 1 Warm Winter Robe or 1 Stone Buckler												
Guarded Thunderbrew Barrel	1	1	Guarded Thunderbrew ale barrel (Obj)	Guarded Thunderbrew ale barrel (Obj)	N	0	0	0	0	0	0	None
Operation Recombobulation	7	10	Razzle Sprysprocket	Razzle Sprysprocket	N	85	170	340	500	675	850	None
CHOICE OF: 1 Driving Gloves or 1 Oil-stained Cloak												
Protecting the Herd	6	12	Rudra Amberstill	Rudra Amberstill	N	90	180	360	550	725	900	None
CHOICE OF: 1 Rancher's Trousers or 1 Soft Leather Tunic or 1 Coldridge Hammer												
Rejold's New Brew	8	10	Tharek Blackstone	Rejold Barleybrew	Y	10	15	35	50	70	85	None
REWARD: Mug of Shimmer Stout												
Rejold's New Brew	8	10	Pilot Bellowfiz	Rejold Barleybrew	Y	10	15	35	50	70	85	None
REWARD: Mug of Shimmer Stout												
Return to Bellowfiz	2	8	Rejold Barleybrew	Pilot Bellowfiz	N	90	180	350	525	700	875	None
CHOICE OF: 1 Sharp Axe or 1 Gnarled Short Staff or 1 Camping Knife												
Return to Marleth	2	7	Guarded Thunderbrew ale barrel (Obj)	Marleth Barleybrew	N	65	130	250	380	500	625	1 75
Return to Marleth	2	7	Unguarded Thunderbrew ale barrel (Obj)	Marleth Barleybrew	N	65	130	250	380	500	625	1 75
Scalding Mornbrew Delivery	2	3	Adlin Pridedrift	Durnan Furcutter	N	15	25	50	75	100	130	None
Search for Incendicite	20	22	Pilot Stonegear	Pilot Stonegear	N	180	350	700	1050	1400	1750	None
REWARD: Beerstained Gloves												
Senir's Observations	1	5	Mountaineer Thalos	Senir Whitebeard	N	35	65	130	200	270	340	None
Senir's Observations	1	5	Grelin Whitebeard	Mountaineer Thalos	Y	35	65	130	200	270	340	None
Shimmer Stout	8	10	Rejold Barleybrew	Mountaineer Barleybrew	Y	40	85	170	250	340	420	None
Stocking Jetsteam	2	6	Pilot Bellowfiz	Pilot Bellowfiz	Y	70	140	270	410	550	675	2 50
Stonegear's Search	20	23	Mountaineer Kadrell	Pilot Stonegear	Y	45	90	180	280	370	460	None
Stonegear's Search	20	23	Pilot Longbeard	Pilot Stonegear	Y	45	90	180	280	370	460	None
Stout to Kadrell	8	10	Mountaineer Barleybrew	Mountaineer Kadrell	N	65	130	250	380	500	625	None
Supplies to Tannok	1	5	Hands Springsprocket	Tannok Frosthammer	N	10	20	45	65	90	110	None
CHOICE OF: 5 Tough Jerky or 5 Refreshing Spring Water												
The Boar Hunter	1	3	Talin Keeneye	Talin Keeneye	N	25	50	100	150	200	250	None
CHOICE OF: 1 Dwarven Cloth Britches or 1 Dwarven Leather Pants												
The Grizzled Den	4	7	Pilot Stonegear	Pilot Stonegear	N	65	130	250	380	500	625	1 75
The Lost Pilot	8	10	Pilot Hammerfoot	A Dwarven Corpse (Obj)	Y	40	85	170	250	340	420	None
REWARD: Siege Brigade Vest												
The Perfect Stout	5	9	Rejold Barleybrew	Rejold Barleybrew	N	80	160	310	470	625	775	None
CHOICE OF: 1 Goat Fur Cloak or 1 Ivy-weave Bracers												
The Public Servant	6	11	Senator Mehr Stonehallow	Senator Mehr Stonehallow	N	65	130	260	400	525	650	3 00
The Reports	1	10	Senir Whitebeard	Senator Barin Redstone	N	40	85	170	250	340	420	1 75
The Stolen Journal	1	5	Grelin Whitebeard	Grelin Whitebeard	Y	55	110	220	340	450	550	None
CHOICE OF: 1 Dwarven Kite Shield or 1 Smooth Walking Staff												
The Troll Cave	1	4	Quest Chest (Obj)	Grelin Whitebeard	Y	35	70	140	210	280	360	None
REWARD: 3 Healing Herb and CHOICE OF: 1 Anvilmar Hand Axe or 1 Anvilmar Hammer or 1 Anvilmar Knife or 1 Anvilmar Sledge or 1 Anvilmar Musket												
The Troll Cave	1	4	Grelin Whitebeard	Grelin Whitebeard	Y	35	70	140	210	280	360	None
REWARD: 3 Healing Herb and CHOICE OF: 1 Anvilmar Hand Axe or 1 Anvilmar Hammer or 1 Anvilmar Knife or 1 Anvilmar Sledge or 1 Anvilmar Musket												
Those Blasted Troggs!	5	9	Foreman Stonebrow	Foreman Stonebrow	N	60	120	240	350	470	600	2 00
Tools for Steelgrill	2	5	Tharek Blackstone	Beldin Steelgrill	N	10	20	45	65	90	110	25
Tundra MacGrann's Stolen Stash	7	12	Tundra MacGrann	Tundra MacGrann	N	90	180	360	550	725	900	None
CHOICE OF: 1 Ironwrought Bracers or 1 Wooly Mittens												

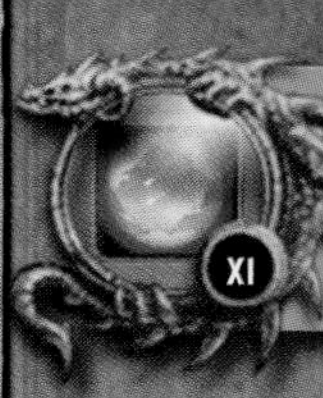

LOCH MODAN

Loch Modan is a large lake, created by the presence of the Stonewrought Dam and large meltoffs from the surrounding cliffs. Offering a blast of color and warmer weather to the Dwarves coming from Dun Morogh, this is a place of comfort. Yet, the presence of many militant Troggs and the recent ingress of Orc tribes to the north has put things on edge in Loch Modan. The Dwarves have concentrated more of their efforts here, and hope to fight the good fight against these enemies (and perhaps the dangerous Ogres in the northeast as well), but setbacks occur at every angle. Could there be traitors in the ranks?

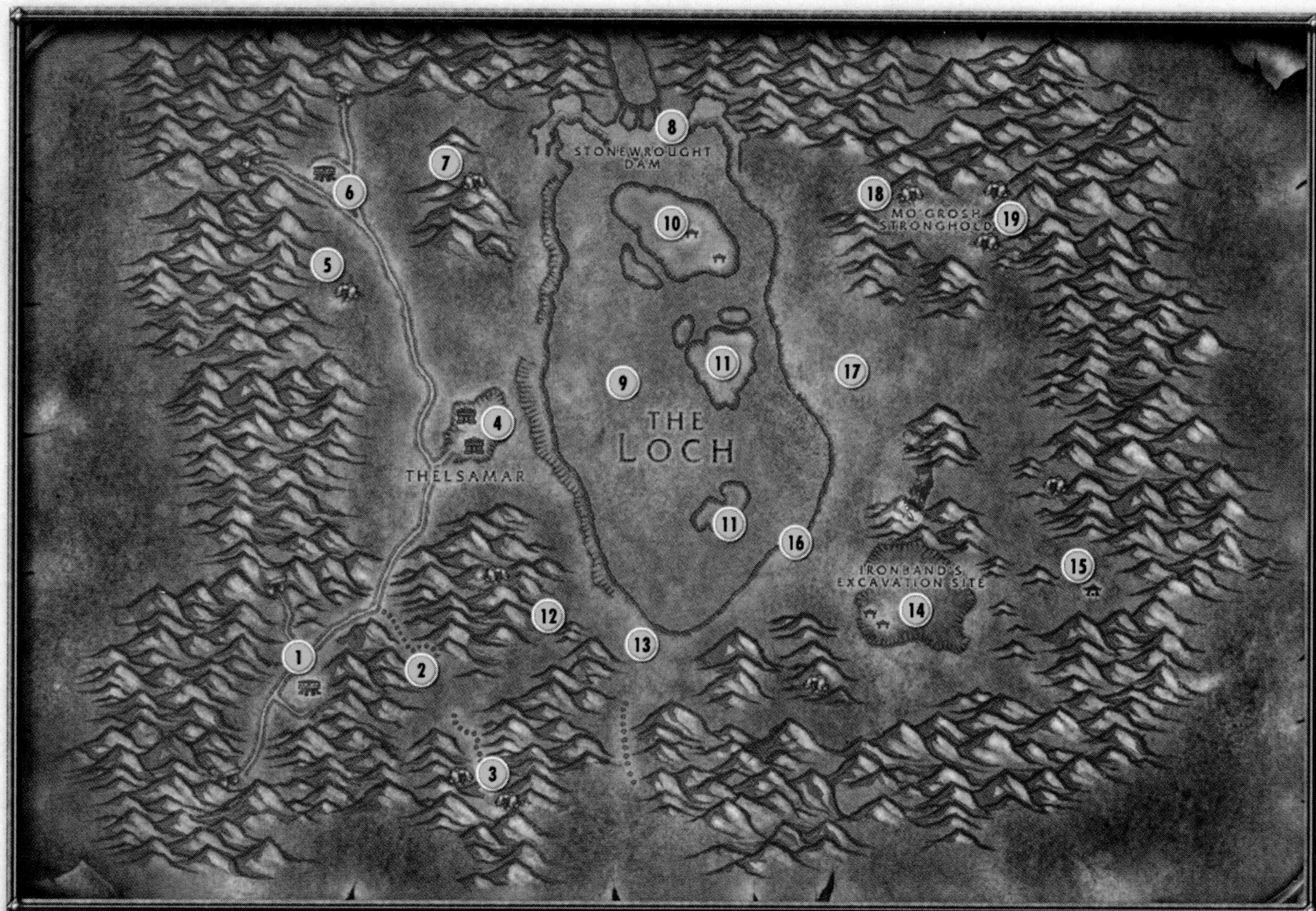

LOCAL RESOURCES

MINING

METAL	AVAILABILITY
Copper	Abundant
Tin	Moderate

HERBALISM

HERB	AVAILABILITY
Peacebloom	Trivial
Silverleaf	Abundant
Earthroot	Trivial
Mageroyal	Abundant
Briarthorn	Moderate
Bruiseweed	Trivial

SKINNING

Quantity of Skinnable Creatures: Abundant

Levels of Skinnable Creatures: 10-20 (Skinning 50-100)

MAP LEGEND

1 VALLEY OF KINGS
- **Captain Rugelfuss 40 Quest**
- **Mountaineer Cobbleflint 30 Quest**
- **Mountaineer Gravelgaw 30 Quest**
- **Mountaineer Pebblebitty 44 Quest**
- Elder Black Bear 11-12
- Forest Lurker 10-11

2 STONESPLINTER VALLEY
- Stonesplinter Bonesnapper 15-16
- Stonesplinter Scout 11-12
- Stonesplinter Seer 13-14
- Stonesplinter Shaman 15-16
- Stonesplinter Skullthumper 13-14
- Stonesplinter Trogg 11-12

3 STONESPLINTER CAVES
- Brawler 16
- Gnasher 16
- Grawmug 17 Quest Target
- Stonesplinter Bonesnapper 15-16
- Stonesplinter Seer 13-14
- Stonesplinter Shaman 15-16
- Stonesplinter Skullthumper 13-14

4 THELSAMAR
- **Brock Stoneseeker 15 Mining Trainer**
- **Dakk Blunderblast 15 Quest**
- **Ghak Healtouch 25 Quest**
- **Innkeeper Hearthstove 30 Innkeeper**
- **Kali Healtouch 14 Herbalism Trainer**
- **Lina Hearthstove 30 Stable Master**
- **Magistrate Bluntnose 20 Quest**
- **Mountaineer Kadrell 30 Quest**
- **Mountaineer Langarr 30 Quest**
- **Mountaineer Stenn 30 Quest**
- **Thorgrum Borrelson 55 Gryphon Master**
- **Torren Squarejaw 15 Quest**
- **Vidra Hearthstove 10 Quest**
- Elder Black Bear 11-12
- Forest Lurker 10-11
- Mountain Boar 10-11
- Stonesplinter Scout 11-12
- Stonesplinter Trogg 11-12

5 TUNNEL RAT CAVE
- Tunnel Rat Scout 10-11
- Tunnel Rat Vermin 10-11

6 ALGAZ STATION
- **Mountaineer Stormpike 30 Quest**
- Elder Black Bear 11-12
- Forest Lurker 10-11
- Mountain Boar 10-11

7 SILVER STREAM MINE
- Elder Black Bear 11-12
- Forest Lurker 10-11
- Mountain Boar 10-11
- Tunnel Rat Digger 12-13
- Tunnel Rat Forager 11-12
- Tunnel Rat Geomancer 12-13
- Tunnel Rat Kobold 11-12
- Tunnel Rat Vermin 10-11

8 STONEWROUGHT DAM
- **Chief Enginneer Hinderweir VII 40 Quest**
- **Deek Fizzlebizz 27 Journeyman Engineer**
- Dark Iron Insurgent 18
- Dark Iron Sapper 17

9 THE LOCH
- Cliff Lurker 13-14
- Loch Frenzy 12-13
- Mangy Mountain Boar 14-15
- Young Threshadon 19-20

10 TROGG ISLANDS
- **Bingles' Tools (Ground Spawn)**
- Stonesplinter Bonesnapper 15-16
- Stonesplinter Bonesnapper 15-16
- Stonesplinter Seer 13-14
- Stonesplinter Shaman 15-16
- Stonesplinter Skullthumper 13-14

11 CROCOLISK ISLANDS
- Loch Crocolisk 14-15

12 GRIZZLEPAW RIDGE
- Black Bear Patriarch 16-17
- Grizzled Black Bear 13-14
- Mangy Mountain Boar 14-15
- Ol' Sooty 20 Elite Quest Target

13 CARAVAN
- **Huldar 15 Quest**
- **Miran 15 Quest**
- Dark Iron Ambusher 10
- Saean 10

14 IRONBAND'S EXCAVATION SITE
- **Prospector Ironband 15 Quest**
- Berserk Trogg 19-20
- Grizzled Black Bear 13-14
- Mangy Mountain Boar 14-15
- Stonesplinter Digger 18-19
- Stonesplinter Geomancer 18-19

15 FARSTRIDER LODGE
- **Daryl the Youngling 15 Quest**
- **Vyrin Swiftwind 15 Quest**
- Cliff Hadin 15 Bowyer Vendor
- Irene Sureshot 15 Gunsmith Vendor
- Grizzled Black Bear 13-14
- Mangy Mountain Boar 14-15
- Mountain Buzzard 15-16

16 BINGLES' CRASH SITE
- **Bingles Blastenheimer 20 Quest**

17 HUNTING GROUNDS
- Black Bear Patriarch 16-17
- Elder Mountain Boar 16-17
- Wood Lurker 17-18

18 MO'GROSH STRONGHOLD
- Mo'grosh Enforcer 18-19 Elite
- Mo'grosh Orge 18-19 Elite
- Mo'grosh Shaman 18-19 Elite

19 MO'GROSH CAVERN
- Chok'sul 22 Elite Quest Target
- Mo'grosh Brute 19-20 Elite
- Mo'grosh Mystic 19-20 Elite

QUESTS

QUEST	M LEV	Q LEV	QUEST LAUNCHER	QUEST FINISHER	CHAIN?	XP---	XP--	XP-	XP+	XP++	XP+++	CASH REWARD
A Dark Threat Looms	16	18	Suspicious Barrel (Obj)	Chief Engineer Hinderweir VII	Y	140	270	550	800	1100	1350	None
A Dark Threat Looms	16	18	Chief Engineer Hinderweir VII	Suspicious Barrel (Obj)	Y	70	140	270	410	550	675	None
A Dark Threat Looms	16	18	Chief Engineer Hinderweir VII	Ashlan Stonesmirk	Y	140	270	550	800	1100	1350	None
A Dark Threat Looms	16	18	Ashlan Stonesmirk	Chief Engineer Hinderweir VII	Y	35	70	140	200	270	340	None
A Dark Threat Looms	16	18	Chief Engineer Hinderweir VII	Chief Engineer Hinderweir VII	Y	140	270	550	800	1100	1350	None
A Dark Threat Looms	16	18	Chief Engineer Hinderweir VII	Explosive Charge (Obj)	Y	70	140	270	410	550	675	None
A Dark Threat Looms	16	20	Explosive Charge (Obj)	Chief Engineer Hinderweir VII	N	200	390	775	1150	1550	1950	None
CHOICE OF: 1 Dwarven Tree Chopper or 1 Thornblade												
A Hunter's Boast	11	16	Daryl the Youngling	Daryl the Youngling	Y	90	180	350	525	700	875	None
CHOICE OF: 1 Daryl's Hunting Bow or 1 Daryl's Hunting Rifle												
A Hunter's Challenge	11	17	Daryl the Youngling	Daryl the Youngling	N	95	190	380	575	750	950	None
REWARD: Fine Cloth Shirt, Daryl's Shortsword												
After the Ambush	10	15	Huldar	Miran	N	10	20	40	65	85	110	None
Badlands Reagent Run	36	39	Ghak Healtouch	Ghak Healtouch	N	300	600	1200	1800	2400	3000	45 00
Bingles' Missing Supplies	12	15	Bingles Blastenheimer	Bingles Blastenheimer	N	110	210	420	625	850	1050	7 00
REWARD: Bingles' Flying Gloves												
Crocolisk Hunting	10	15	Marek Ironheart	Marek Ironheart	N	110	210	420	625	850	1050	None
REWARD: Recipe: Crocolisk Steak, Rugged Cape												
Excavation Progress Report	10	15	Prospector Ironband	Jern Hornhelm	Y	25	55	110	160	220	270	None
Filthy Paws	9	15	Mountaineer Stormpike	Mountaineer Stormpike	N	140	270	550	800	1100	1350	None
CHOICE OF: 1 Ironheart Chain or 1 Robe of the Keeper or 1 Ironplate Buckler												
Gathering Idols	13	18	Magmar Fellhew	Magmar Fellhew	N	140	270	550	800	1100	1350	None
CHOICE OF: 1 Dwarven Flamestick or 1 Trogg Slicer or 1 Thelsamar Axe												
In Defense of the King's Lands	10	12	Mountaineer Cobbleflint	Mountaineer Cobbleflint	N	90	180	360	550	725	900	5 00
REWARD: 5 Dalaran Sharp												
In Defense of the King's Lands	10	15	Mountaineer Gravelgaw	Mountaineer Gravelgaw	N	110	210	420	625	850	1050	7 00
REWARD: 3 Lesser Healing Potion												
In Defense of the King's Lands	10	15	Mountaineer Wallbang	Mountaineer Wallbang	N	110	210	420	625	850	1050	7 00
REWARD: 3 Coarse Sharpening Stone												
In Defense of the King's Lands	10	17	Captain Rugelfuss	Captain Rugelfuss	N	160	320	650	950	1300	1600	None
CHOICE OF: 1 Frontier Britches or 1 Dwarven Defender or 1 Lucky Trousers												
Ironband's Excavation	13	18	Jern Hornhelm	Magmar Fellhew	Y	35	70	140	200	270	340	None
Mercenaries	15	19	Magistrate Bluntnose	Magistrate Bluntnose	N	180	360	725	1100	1450	1800	20 00
Mountaineer Stormpike's Task	9	15	Mountaineer Kadrell	Mountaineer Stormpike	Y	55	110	220	320	430	550	None
Powder to Ironband	10	15	Prospector Stormpike	Jern Hornhelm	Y	25	55	110	160	220	270	None
Proof of Deed	40	48	Mountaineer Pebblebitty	Curator Thorius	N	440	875	1750	2650	3500	4400	1 40 00
Protecting the Shipment	10	15	Miran	Prospector Ironband	N	110	210	420	625	850	1050	None
CHOICE OF: 1 Foreman Belt or 1 Mud Stompers												
Rat Catching	10	11	Mountaineer Kadrell	Mountaineer Kadrell	N	90	180	350	525	700	875	4 00
CHOICE OF: 1 Burnt Hide Bracers or 1 Cavalier's Boots												
Report to Ironforge	10	15	Jern Hornhelm	Prospector Stormpike	Y	55	110	220	320	430	550	1 75
Resupplying the Excavation	10	15	Jern Hornhelm	Huldar	Y	25	55	110	160	220	270	None
Stonesplinter Trogg Disguise	10	12		Mountaineer Cobbleflint	N	25	45	90	140	180	230	None
REWARD: Knowledge: Stonesplinter Disguise												
Stormpike's Order	9	14	Mountaineer Stormpike	Furen Longbeard	N	100	200	390	600	775	975	6 00
The Head of Ol' Sooty	1	15		Vyrin Swiftwind	N	0	0	0	0	0	0	None
The Head of Ol' Sooty	1	15		Marek Ironheart	N	0	0	0	0	0	0	None
The Trogg Threat	10	12	Captain Rugelfuss	Captain Rugelfuss	N	90	180	360	550	725	900	5 00
Thelsamar Blood Sausages	7	11	Vidra Hearthstove	Vidra Hearthstove	N	90	180	350	525	700	875	4 00
REWARD: 5 Blood Sausage, Recipe: Blood Sausage												
Uldaman Reagent Run	38	42	Ghak Healtouch	Ghak Healtouch	N	350	700	1400	2050	2750	3450	55 00
REWARD: 5 Restorative Elixir												
Vyrin's Revenge	15	20	Daryl the Youngling	Vyrin Swiftwind	N	160	310	625	925	1250	1550	None
CHOICE OF: 1 Hunting Ammo Sack or 1 Hunting Quiver												
Vyrin's Revenge	15	20	Vyrin Swiftwind	Daryl the Youngling	Y	80	160	310	470	625	775	None
WANTED: Chok'sul	17	22	Wanted Poster (Obj)	Magistrate Bluntnose	N	180	350	700	1050	1400	1750	None
REWARD: Minor Channeling Ring and CHOICE OF: 1 Durable Chain Shoulders or 1 Kimbra Boots												

SEARING GORGE

West from the Badlands is the Searing Gorge, fed by lava flows. There are Dark Iron Dwarves and Elementals throughout the region, seeking the rare metals and sheer power that oozes from Azeroth all through the Gorge. A strange cult lives in the northwest, holding true to ceremonies and beliefs that are foreign to most of the east, and these people are not interested in making friends with any who draw near. Those who seek fame, fortune, mithril, and thorium are drawn here as moths to the flame.

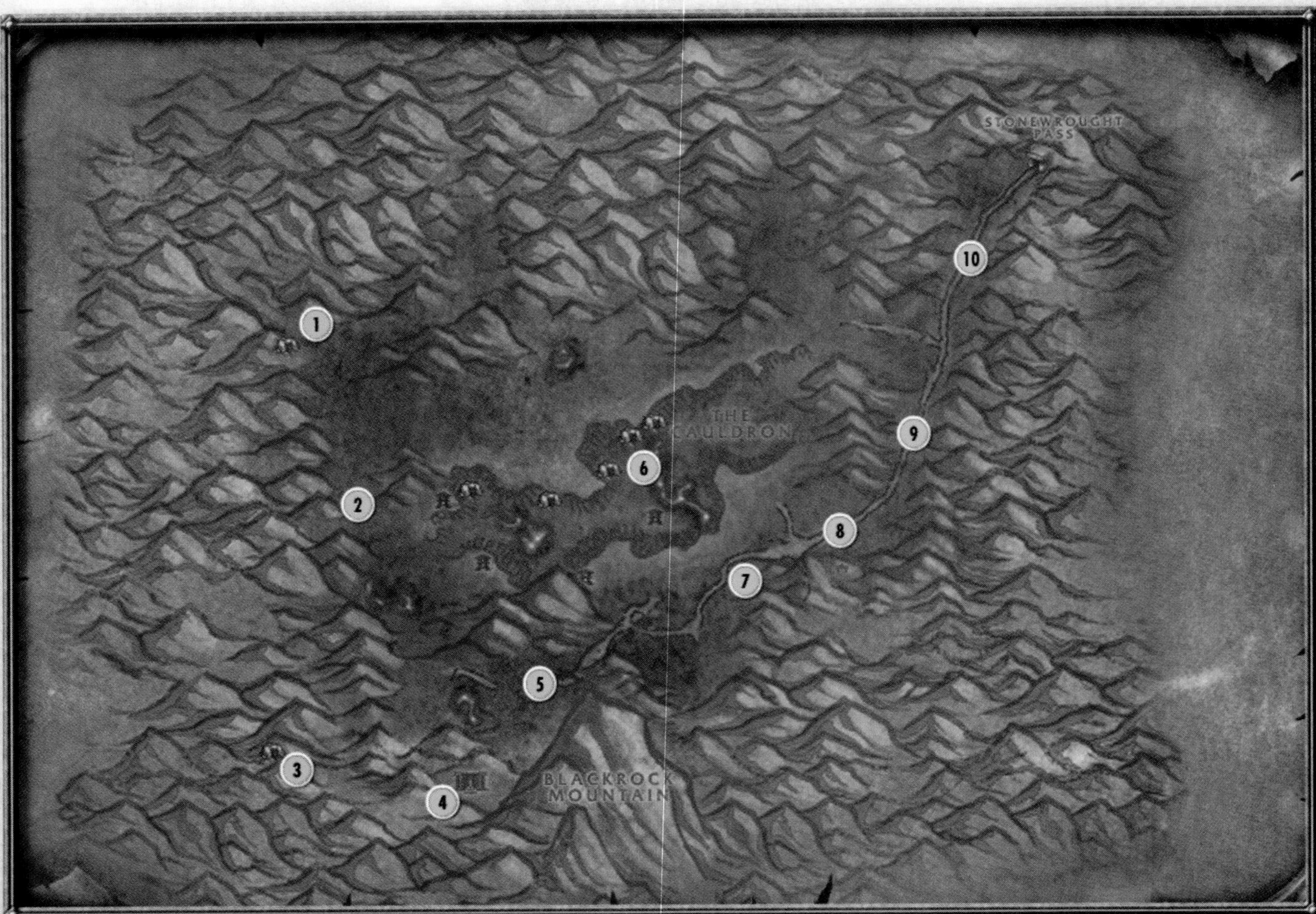

LOCAL RESOURCES

MINING

METAL	AVAILABILITY
Mithril	Abundant
Thorium	Moderate

HERBALISM

HERB	AVAILABILITY
Firebloom	Abundant

SKINNING

Quantity of Skinnable Creatures: None

Levels of Skinnable Creatures: N/A

HOW TO
AZEROTH
KHAZ MODAN
LORDAERON
NORTHERN KALIMDOR
SOUTHERN KALIMDOR

MAP LEGEND

1 FIREWATCH RIDGE
Twilight Dark Shaman 47-48 Elite
Twilight Fire Guard 48-49 Elite
Twilight Geomancer 50 Elite
Twilight Idolater 50 Elite

2 WESTERN SEARING GORGE
Greater Lava Spider 47-48
Inferno Elemental 49
Magma Elemental 46-47

3 BLACKCHAR CAVE
Greater Lava Spider 48-49

4 BLACKROCK MOUNTAIN
Entrance to Blackrock World Dungeon

5 SW SEAR GORGE
Graw Cornerstone 58 Vendor
Graw Cornerstone's Guardian 48
Greater Lava Spider 47-48
Magma Elemental 46-48
Searing Elemental 49

6 THE CAULDRON
Blazing Elemental 45-47
Dark Iron Slaver 45-46
Dark Iron Taskmaster 47
Heavy War Golem 48-49
Magma Elemental 47-48
Shadowsilk Poachers 47-48
Slaved Worker 45-47

7 THE SEA OF CINDERS
Magma Elemental 47-48
Searing Lava Spider 45-47

8 TANNER CAMP
Sarah Tanner 50 Master Elemental Leatherworker
Glassweb Spider 43-45

9 GRIMSILT DIG SITE
Dark Iron Geologist 43
Dark Iron Watchman 44
Glassweb Spider 43-35
Tempered War Golem 45-46

10 DUSTFIRE VALLEY
Locked Door to Loch Modan
Dark Iron Geologist 43
Dark Iron Watchman 44
Glassweb Spider 43-35
Tempered War Golem 45-46

QUESTS

QUEST	M LEV	Q LEV	QUEST LAUNCHER	QUEST FINISHER	CHAIN?	XP---	XP--	XP-	XP+	XP++	XP+++	CASH REWARD
Bijou's Belongings	55	59	Bijou	Bijou	Y	650	1300	2550	3850	5100	6400	None
Bijou's Belongings	55	59	Bijou	Bijou	Y	650	1300	2550	3850	5100	6400	None
Bijou's Reconnaissance Report	55	59	Bijou	Lexlort	N	650	1300	2550	3850	5100	6400	1 80 00
CHOICE OF: 1 Freewind Gloves or 1 Seapost Girdle												
Delivery to Ridgewell	57	60	Mayara Brightwing	Count Remington Ridgewell	N	650	1300	2650	3950	5300	6600	2 70 00
CHOICE OF: 1 Swiftfoot Treads or 1 Blinkstrike Armguards												
Disharmony of Flame	48	52	Thunderheart	Thunderheart	Y	500	1000	2050	3050	4100	5100	1 55 00
Divine Retribution	40	48	Kalaran Windblade	Kalaran Windblade	N	45	90	180	260	350	440	None
Doomrigger's Clasp	57	60	Mayara Brightwing	Mayara Brightwing	Y	170	330	650	1000	1300	1650	None
Egg Collection	57	60	Tinkee Steamboil	Tinkee Steamboil	N	1000	2000	4000	5950	7950	9950	2 70 00
Egg Freezing	57	60	Tinkee Steamboil	Tinkee Steamboil	N	825	1650	3300	5000	6650	8300	1 80 00
REWARD: Eggscilloscope												
En-Ay-Es-Tee-Why	55	59	Kibler	Kibler	N	650	1300	2550	3850	5100	6400	90 00
REWARD: Smolderweb Carrier												

QUESTS continued

QUEST	M LEV	Q LEV	QUEST LAUNCHER	QUEST FINISHER	CHAIN?	XP---	XP--	XP-	XP+	XP++	XP+++	CASH REWARD
Finkle Einhorn, At Your Service!	57	62		Malyfous Darkhammer	N	700	1400	2800	4250	5650	7050	None
For The Horde!	55	63	Thrall	Thrall	N	1100	2200	4350	6550	8700	10900	2● 85● 00●
CHOICE OF: 1 Mark of Tyranny or 1 Eye of the Beast or 1 Blackhand's Breadth												
Forging the Shaft	40	48	Kalaran Windblade	Kalaran Windblade	Y	440	875	1750	2650	3500	4400	1● 40● 00●
General Drakkisath's Demise	55	63	Marshal Maxwell	Marshal Maxwell	N	1100	2200	4350	6550	8700	10900	2● 85● 00●
CHOICE OF: 1 Mark of Tyranny or 1 Eye of the Beast or 1 Blackhand's Breadth												
Kibler's Exotic Pets	55	59	Kibler	Kibler	N	650	1300	2550	3850	5100	6400	90● 00●
REWARD: Worg Carrier												
Ledger from Tanaris	43	46	Wooden Outhouse (Obj)	Krinkle Goodsteel	N	500	1000	2000	3050	4050	5050	None
CHOICE OF: 1 Charged Lightning Rod or 1 Girdle of Reprisal												
Locked In	43	45	Wooden Outhouse (Obj)	Wooden Outhouse (Obj)	Y	390	775	1550	2350	3100	3900	None
Maxwell's Mission	55	61	Marshal Maxwell	Marshal Maxwell	N	850	1700	3400	5150	6850	8550	1● 85● 00●
CHOICE OF: 1 Wyrmthalak's Shackles or 1 Omokk's Girth Restrainer or 1 Halycon's Muzzle or 1 Vosh'gajin's Strand or 1 Voone's Vice Grips												
Mayara Brightwing	57	60	Count Remington Ridgewell	Mayara Brightwing	Y	65	130	260	400	525	650	None
Message to Maxwell	55	59	Bijou	Marshal Maxwell	Y	650	1300	2550	3850	5100	6400	1● 80● 00●
Mother's Milk	55	60	Ragged John	Ragged John	N	1000	2000	4000	5950	7950	9950	1● 80● 00●
REWARD: Ragged John's Neverending Cup												
Operative Bijou	55	59	Lexlort	Bijou	Y	650	1300	2550	3850	5100	6400	None
Overmaster Pyron	48	52	Jalinda Sprig	Jalinda Sprig	Y	500	1000	2050	3050	4100	5100	1● 55● 00●
Prayer to Elune	40	50	Zamael Lunthistle	Astarii Starseeker	N	600	1200	2350	3550	4700	5900	1● 45● 00●
CHOICE OF: 1 Kaylari Shoulders or 1 Runesteel Vambraces												
Prayer to Elune	40	50	Zamael Lunthistle	Zamael Lunthistle	Y	45	95	190	280	380	470	None
Put Her Down	55	59	Helendis Riverhorn	Helendis Riverhorn	N	650	1300	2550	3850	5100	6400	1● 80● 00●
CHOICE OF: 1 Astoria Robes or 1 Traphook Jerkin or 1 Jadescale Breastplate												
Release Them	40	52	Dying Archaeologist	Altar of Suntara (Obj)	N	500	1000	2050	3050	4100	5100	None
Rise, Obsidion!	40	52	Dying Archaeologist	Curator Thorius	N	750	1500	3050	4550	6100	7600	1● 55● 00●
CHOICE OF: 1 Centurion Legplates or 1 Lordrec Helmet or 1 Ring of Fortitude												
Seal of Ascension	57	60		Vaelan	Y	825	1650	3300	5000	6650	8300	None
Seal of Ascension	57	61		Vaelan	N	1050	2050	4100	6150	8200	10250	None
REWARD: Seal of Ascension												
Set Them Ablaze!	40	52	Squire Maltrake	Squire Maltrake	N	750	1500	3050	4550	6100	7600	2● 30● 00●
CHOICE OF: 1 Dragonflight Leggings or 1 Drakefire Headguard or 1 Axe of the Ebon Drake												
Shadoweaver	40	50	Nilith Lokrav	Nilith Lokrav	Y	470	950	1900	2800	3750	4700	1● 45● 00●
REWARD: Shadowy Bracers												
Squire Maltrake	40	50	Kalaran Windblade	Squire Maltrake	Y	45	95	190	280	380	470	None
Suntara Stones	40	48	Dorius Stonetender	Singed Letter (Obj)	Y	440	875	1750	2650	3500	4400	None
Suntara Stones	40	48	Singed Letter (Obj)	Curator Thorius	Y	440	875	1750	2650	3500	4400	1● 40● 00●
The Darkstone Tablet	57	60	Shadowmage Vivian Lagrave	Shadowmage Vivian Lagrave	N	825	1650	3300	5000	6650	8300	2● 70● 00●
CHOICE OF: 1 Swiftfoot Treads or 1 Blinkstrike Armguards												
The Demon Forge	55	61	Lorax	Lorax	N	850	1700	3400	5150	6850	8550	None
REWARD: Plans: Demon Forged Breastplate, 5 Elixirs of Demonslaying, Demon Kissed Sack												
The Final Tablets	40	58	Prospector Ironboot	Prospector Ironboot	N	775	1550	3100	4650	6200	7750	None
The Flame's Casing	40	50	Kalaran Windblade	Kalaran Windblade	Y	470	950	1900	2800	3750	4700	75● 00●
The Flawless Flame	40	48	Kalaran Windblade	Kalaran Windblade	Y	440	875	1750	2650	3500	4400	1● 40● 00●
The Matron Protectrate	57	62		Haleh	Y	700	1400	2800	4250	5650	7050	None
The Pack Mistress	55	59	Galamav the Marksman	Galamav the Marksman	N	650	1300	2550	3850	5100	6400	1● 80● 00●
CHOICE OF: 1 Astoria Robes or 1 Traphook Jerkin or 1 Jadescale Breastplate												
The Torch of Retribution	40	50	Kalaran Windblade	Torch of Retribution (Obj)	N	470	950	1900	2800	3750	4700	None
REWARD: Torch of Retribution												
The Torch of Retribution	40	50	Kalaran Windblade	Kalaran Windblade	Y	45	95	190	280	380	470	None
The Undermarket	40	50	Nilith Lokrav	Vizzklick	N	470	950	1900	2800	3750	4700	75● 00●
REWARD: Pattern: Shadoweave Mask												
The Undermarket	40	50	Nilith Lokrav	Nilith Lokrav	Y	470	950	1900	2800	3750	4700	None
REWARD: Shadowy Belt, Kovic's Trading Satchel												
Tinkee Steamboil	57	60	Felnok Steelspring	Tinkee Steamboil	Y	65	130	260	400	525	650	None
Trinkets...	40	50	Hoard of the Black Dragonflight	Hoard of the Black Dragonflight (Obj)	N	45	95	190	280	380	470	None
REWARD: Hoard of the Black Dragonflight												
Urok Doomhowl	55	60	Warosh the Redeemed	Warosh	N	1000	2000	4000	5950	7950	9950	None
REWARD: Prismcharm												
Urok Doomhowl	55	60	Warosh	Warosh	N	1000	2000	4000	5950	7950	9950	None
REWARD: Prismcharm												
Vivian Lagrave and the Darkstone Tablet	57	60	Apothecary Zinge	Shadowmage Vivian Lagrave	Y	65	130	260	400	525	650	None

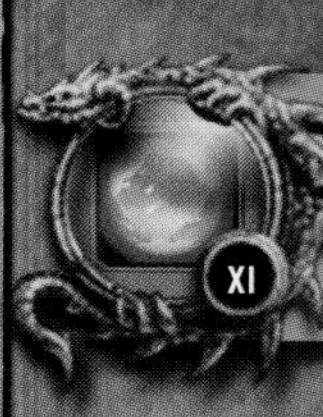

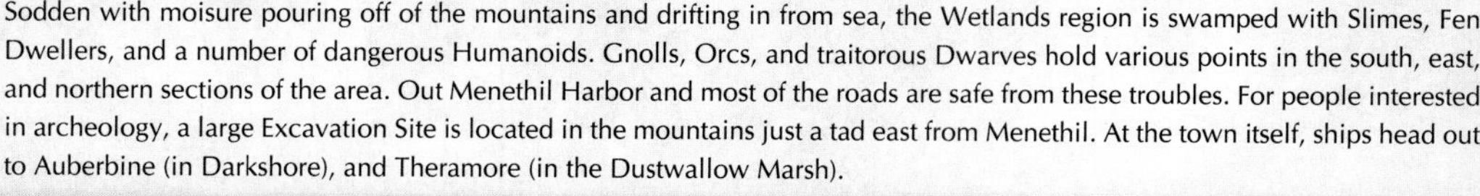

WETLANDS

Sodden with moisture pouring off of the mountains and drifting in from sea, the Wetlands region is swamped with Slimes, Fen Dwellers, and a number of dangerous Humanoids. Gnolls, Orcs, and traitorous Dwarves hold various points in the south, east, and northern sections of the area. Out Menethil Harbor and most of the roads are safe from these troubles. For people interested in archeology, a large Excavation Site is located in the mountains just a tad east from Menethil. At the town itself, ships head out to Auberbine (in Darkshore), and Theramore (in the Dustwallow Marsh).

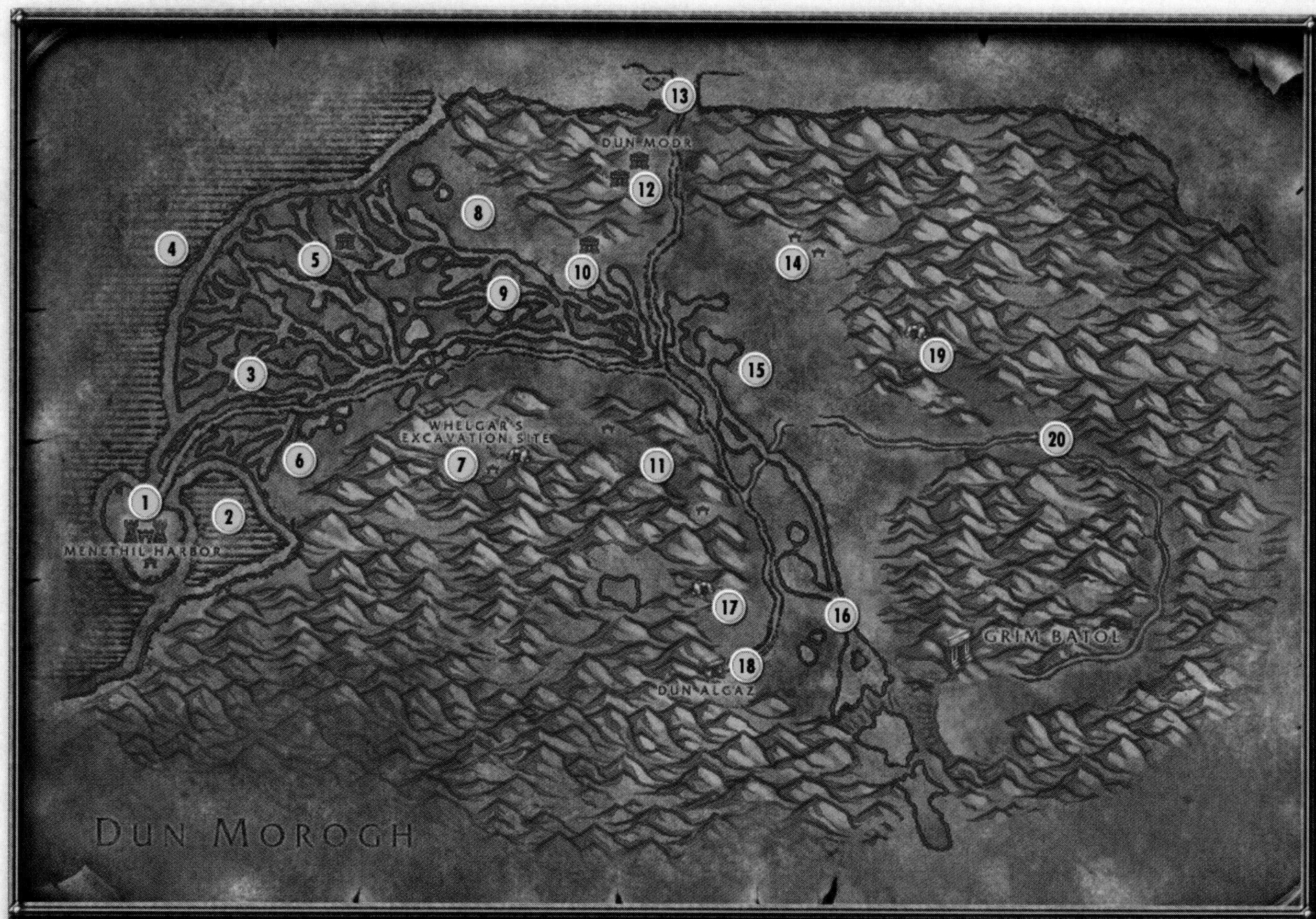

LOCAL RESOURCES

MINING

METAL	AVAILABILITY
Copper	Moderate
Tin	Abundant
Iron	Trivial

HERBALISM

HERB	AVAILABILITY
Peacebloom	Trivial
Earthroot	Trivial
Mageroyal	Trivial
Stranglekelp	Trivial
Briarthorn	Moderate
Kingsblood	Moderate
Wild Steelbloom	Trivial
Liferoot	Moderate

SKINNING

Quantity of Skinnable Creatures: Moderate

Levels of Skinnable Creatures: 21-30 (Skinning 105-150) From 48-54 for Dragonmaw Gates

MAP LEGEND

1 MENETHIL
- Archaeologist Flagongut 44 Quest
- Bethaine Flinthammer 30 Stable Master
- Captain Stoutfist 35 Quest
- First Mate Fitzsimmons 30 Quest
- Fremal Doohickey 30 First Aid
- Glorin Steelbrow 25 Quest
- Harlo Barnaby 25 Quest
- Harold Riggs 25 Fishing
- James Halloran 25 Quest
- Junder Brokk 20 Quest
- Mikhail 30 Quest
- Red Jack Flint 22 Quest
- Shellei Brondir 55 Gryphon Master
- Sida 20 Quest
- Tapoke "Slim" Jahn 34 Quest
- Telurinon Moonshadow 25 Herbalism
- Unger Statforth 25 Horse Vendor
- Vincent Hyal 30 Quest

2 MENETHIL BAY
- Bluegill Raider 28-29
- Fen Dweller 20
- Giant Wetlands Crocolisk 25-26
- Wetlands Crocolisk 23-24
- Young Wetlands Crocolisk 21-22

3 BLUEGILL MARSH
- Bluegill Forager 22
- Bluegill Muckdweller 23-24
- Bluegill Murloc 20-21
- Bluegill Oracle 26
- Bluegill Puddlejumper 21-22
- Bluegill Warrior 24-25
- Fen Creeper 24-25
- Fen Dweller 20-21
- Giant Welands Crocolisk 25-26
- Gobbler 22 Quest Target

4 THE LOST FLEET
- Captain Halyndor 30 Quest Target
- Cursed Marine 27-28
- Cursed Sailor 26-27
- First Mate Snellig 29 Quest Target

5 SUNDOWN MARSH
- Fradd Swiftgear 24 Engineer Vendor
- Wenna Silkbeard 29 Recipe Vendor
- Fen Creeper 24-25
- Giant Wetlands Crocolisk 25-26
- Mosshide Alpha 27
- Mosshide Brute 24-25
- Mosshide Fenrunner 22
- Mosshide Mystic 25-26
- Mosshide Trapper 23-24
- Wetlands Crocolisk 23-24
- Young Wetlands Crocoolisk 21-22

6 BLACK CHANNEL MARSH
- Black Ooze 23
- Mottled Raptor 22-23
- Mottled Screecher 24-25

7 WHELGAR'S EXCAVATION SITE
- Merrin Rockweaver 30 Quest
- Ormer Ironbraid 25 Quest
- Prospector Whelgar 30 Quest
- Mottled Razormaw 25-26
- Mottled Scytheclaw 25-26
- Sarltooth 29 Quest Target

8 SALTSPRAY GLEN
- Elder Razormaw 29
- Fen Creeper 24
- Fen Dweller 21
- Fen Lord 26
- Giant Wetlands Crocolisk 25-26
- Highland Lashtail 24-25
- Highland Raptor 23-24
- Highland Razormaw 27-28
- Highland Scytheclaw 25-26
- Wetlands Crocolisk 23-24

9 CENTRAL WETLANDS
- Kixxie 25 Vendor
- Black Slime 20
- Fen Creeper 24
- Fen Dweller 21
- Fen Lord 26
- Giant Wetlands Crocolisk 25-26
- Mosshide Alpha 27
- Mosshide Brute 24-25
- Mosshide Fenrunner 22
- Mosshide Mystic 25-26
- Mosshide Trapper 23-24
- Wetlands Crocolisk 23-24
- Young Wetlands Crocoolisk 21-22

10 IRONBEARD'S TOMB
- Black Ooze 23-24
- Crimson Ooze 24-25

11 ANGERFANG ENCAMPMENT
- Chieftain Nek'rosh 32 Elite
- Dragonmaw Battlemaster 30
- Dragonmaw Bonewarder 27-28
- Dragonmaw Centurion 29
- Dragonmaw Raider 26-27
- Dragonmaw Shadowwarder 29
- Dragonmaw Swamprunner 28

12 DUN MODR
- Dark Iron Entrepreneur 30 Vendor
- Longbraid the Grim 35 Quest
- Rhag Garmason 25 Quest
- Dark Iron Demolitionist 30-31 Elite
- Dark Iron Dwarf 27-28 Elite
- Dark Iron Rifleman 27-28 Elite
- Dark Iron Saboteur 28-29 Elite
- Dark Iron Tunneler 29-30 Elite

13 THANDOL SPAN
- Comar Villard 22 Quest

14 DIREFORGE HILL
- Balgaras the Foul 34 Elite Quest Target
- Black Ooze 24
- Dark Iron Demolitionist 31 Elite
- Dark Iron Dwarf 27-28 Elite
- Dark Iron Saboteur 28-29 Elite
- Dark Iron Tunneler 29-30 Elite
- Highland Lashtail 25
- Highland Raptor 24
- Highland Scytheclaw 26

15 THE GREEN BELT
- Rethiel the Greenwarden 30 Quest
- Black Ooze 24
- Crimson Whelp 25-26
- Highland Raptor 23-24
- Lost Whelp 24-25
- Red Whelp 24

16 MOSSHIDE FEN
- Black Ooze 23
- Black Slime 21
- Dark Iron Insurgent 18-19
- Fen Dweller 20
- Mosshide Fenrunner 22-23
- Mosshide Gnoll 20-21
- Mosshide Mistweaver 22
- Mosshide Mongrel 22
- Young Wetlands Crocolisk 21-22

17 THELGEN ROCK
- Cave Stalker 21-22
- Leech Stalker 21

18 DUN ALGAZ
- Dragonmaw Scout 19-20
- Dragonmaw Grunt 20-21
- Ma'ruk Wyrmscale 23

19 RAPTOR RIDGE
- Elder Razormaw 29
- Highland Razormaw 27-28

20 DRAGONMAW GATES
- Red Dragonspawn 47-48
- Red Scalebane 49
- Red Wyrmkin 48-49
- Scalebane Lieutenant 51-52
- Scalebane Royal Guard 53-54
- Wyrmkin Firebrand 52

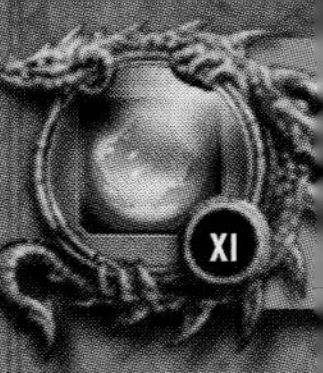

QUEST	M LEV	Q LEV	QUEST LAUNCHER	QUEST FINISHER	CHAIN?	XP---	XP--	XP-	XP+	XP++	XP+++	CASH REWARD
A Grim Task	26	34	Longbraid the Grim	Longbraid the Grim	N	340	675	1350	2000	2700	3350	None
CHOICE OF: 1 Gold Lion Shield or 1 Tranquil Ring												
Apprentice's Duties	18	26	James Halloran	James Halloran	N	210	420	850	1250	1700	2100	None
REWARD: Recipe: Crocolisk Gumbo and CHOICE OF: 1 Malleable Chain Leggings or 1 Resilient Poncho												
Blisters on The Land	20	26	Rethiel the Greenwarden	Rethiel the Greenwarden	N	270	525	1050	1600	2100	2650	None
CHOICE OF: 1 Fen Keeper Robe or 1 Forest Chain or 1 Phytoblade												
Claws from the Deep	20	22	Karl Boran	Karl Boran	Y	180	350	700	1050	1400	1750	14 00
Cleansing the Eye	22	30	Glorin Steelbrow	Archbishop Benedictus	N	250	490	975	1450	1950	2450	None
REWARD: Eye of Paleth												
Daily Delivery	18	21	Einar Stonegrip	James Halloran	N	85	170	330	500	675	825	7 00
Dark Iron Disguise	25	30		Roggo Harlbarrow	N	60	120	240	370	490	600	None
REWARD: Knowledge: Dark Iron Dwarf Disguise												
Defeat Nek'rosh	23	32	Dragonmaw Catapult (Obj)	Captain Stoutfist	N	260	500	1000	1550	2050	2550	None
CHOICE OF: 1 Ancient War Sword or 1 Barreling Reaper												
Defeat Nek'rosh	23	32	Captain Stoutfist	Captain Stoutfist	N	260	500	1000	1550	2050	2550	None
CHOICE OF: 1 Ancient War Sword or 1 Barreling Reaper												
Digging Through the Ooze	19	24	Sida	Sida	N	240	480	950	1450	1900	2400	35 00
REWARD: Ooze-covered Bag												
Fall of Dun Modr	25	25	Harlo Barnaby	Longbraid the Grim	N	100	200	400	600	800	1000	None
Fiora Longears	18	20	Red Jack Flint	Fiora Longears	Y	80	160	310	470	625	775	None
Fire Taboo	20	23	Rethiel the Greenwarden	Rethiel the Greenwarden	Y	190	370	750	1100	1500	1850	None
REWARD: 10 Spongy Morel												
In Search of The Excavation Team	21	24	Merrin Rockweaver	Tarrel Rockweaver	N	50	95	190	290	390	490	None
In Search of The Excavation Team	21	24	Tarrel Rockweaver	Merrin Rockweaver	Y	95	190	390	575	775	975	None
James Hyal	30	35	Vincent Hyal	Clerk Lendry	N	70	140	280	410	550	700	None
Journey to Auberdine!	1	1	Captain Placeholder	Captain Placeholder	N	0	0	0	0	0	0	None
Journey to Menethil!	1	1	Captain Noteo	Captain Noteo	N	0	0	0	0	0	0	None
Journey to Theramore!	1	1	Captain Noteo	Captain Placeholder	N	0	0	0	0	0	0	None
Journey to Theramore!	1	1	Captain Placeholder	Captain Placeholder	N	0	0	0	0	0	0	None
Lifting the Curse	22	30	First Mate Fitzsimmons	Intrepid's Locked Strongbox (Obj)	Y	120	240	480	725	950	1200	None
MacKreel's Moonshine	28	30	Foggy MacKreel	Brewmeister Bilger	N	310	600	1200	1850	2450	3050	55 00
Nek'rosh's Gambit	23	31	Captain Stoutfist	Dragonmaw Catapult (Obj)	Y	190	380	750	1150	1500	1900	None
Ormer's Revenge	22	24	Ormer Ironbraid	Ormer Ironbraid	Y	200	390	775	1150	1550	1950	17 00
Ormer's Revenge	22	27	Ormer Ironbraid	Ormer Ironbraid	Y	220	440	875	1300	1750	2200	22 00
Ormer's Revenge	22	29	Ormer Ironbraid	Ormer Ironbraid	N	300	600	1200	1750	2350	2950	None
REWARD: Recipe: Curiously Tasty Omelet and CHOICE OF: 1 Raptor's End or 1 Raptorbane Armor or 1 Excavation Rod												
Plea To The Alliance	28	31	Rhag Garmason	Captain Nials	N	130	250	500	750	1000	1250	None
Reclaiming Goods	20	25	Karl Boran	Damaged Crate (Obj)	Y	50	100	200	310	410	500	None
REWARD: 5 Healing Potion												
Report to Captain Stoutfist	23	28	Valstag Ironjaw	Captain Stoutfist	Y	25	45	90	140	180	230	None
Report to Mountaineer Rockgar	20	21	Mountaineer Kadrell	Mountaineer Rockgar	Y	15	35	65	100	130	170	None
Return the Statuette	20	25	Half-buried Barrel (Obj)	Karl Boran	N	150	300	600	900	1200	1500	None
CHOICE OF: 1 Icicle Rod or 1 Mariner Boots												
Search More Hovels	20	25	Sealed Barrel (Obj)	Half-buried Barrel (Obj)	Y	100	200	400	600	800	1000	None
The Algaz Gauntlet	20	21	Mountaineer Rockgar	Valstag Ironjaw	N	130	250	500	750	1000	1250	10 00
The Cursed Crew	22	29	First Mate Fitzsimmons	First Mate Fitzsimmons	Y	180	350	700	1050	1400	1750	19 00
The Dark Iron War	25	30	Motley Garmason	Motley Garmason	N	250	490	975	1450	1950	2450	25 00
The Eye of Paleth	22	30	Intrepid's Locked Strongbox (Obj)	Glorin Steelbrow	Y	120	240	480	725	950	1200	None
The Fury Runs Deep	22	27	Motley Garmason	Motley Garmason	N	280	550	1100	1650	2200	2750	None
CHOICE OF: 1 Belt of Vindication or 1 Headbasher												
The Greenwarden	20	21	First Mate Fitzsimmons	Rethiel the Greenwarden	Y	85	170	330	500	675	825	None
The Search Continues	20	25	Damaged Crate (Obj)	Sealed Barrel (Obj)	Y	50	100	200	310	410	500	None
REWARD: 10 Dwarven Mild												
The Thandol Span	28	31	Rhag Garmason	Ebenezer Rustlocke's Corpse (Obj)	Y	250	500	1000	1500	2000	2500	None
The Thandol Span	28	31	Ebenezer Rustlocke's Corpse (Obj)	Rhag Garmason	Y	250	500	1000	1500	2000	2500	None
The Thandol Span	28	31	Rhag Garmason	Rhag Garmason	Y	250	500	1000	1500	2000	2500	None
CHOICE OF: 1 Dwarven Guard Cloak or 1 Swampland Trousers												
The Third Fleet	22	27	First Mate Fitzsimmons	First Mate Fitzsimmons	Y	20	45	90	130	180	220	None
Tramping Paws	20	21	Rethiel the Greenwarden	Rethiel the Greenwarden	Y	130	250	500	750	1000	1250	None
Uncovering the Past	25	28	Prospector Whelgar	Prospector Whelgar	N	230	460	925	1400	1850	2300	25 00
REWARD: Silk Mantle of Gamn												
War Banners	23	28	Captain Stoutfist	Captain Stoutfist	Y	230	460	925	1400	1850	2300	25 00
Young Crocolisk Skins	18	22	James Halloran	James Halloran	Y	180	350	700	1050	1400	1750	14 00

UNDERCITY

The Ruins of Lordaeron

The War Quarter

The Magic Quarter

The Sewers

The Apothecarium

The Rogues' Quarter

Undercity

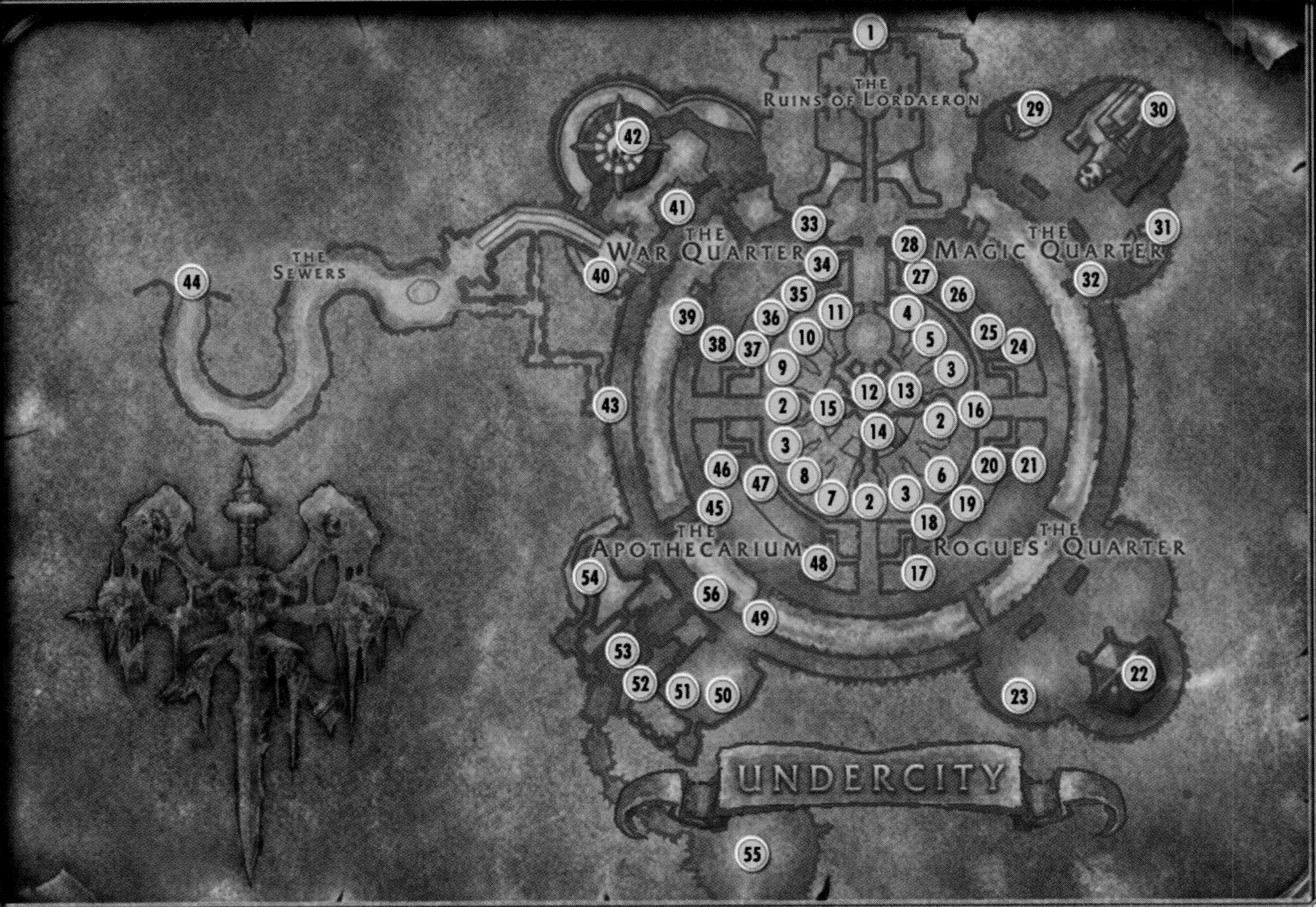

The seat of Lordaeron, where Humans sat in power and majesty has become a silent place. Beneath the abandoned streets of this lost capital, however, there is "life" anew, as the Undead build their own capital. This Undercity is home of the Forsaken, caught between the mindless death of the Scourge and the equal foulness of life that they have happily left behind. These Undead are sentient, willful, and prepared to fight against both the Human crusaders that seek to destroy them AND the Scourge that would enslave them at a moment's weakness.

RUINS OF LORDAERON ENTRANCE
1 ENTRANCE

ELEVATORS
2 ELEVATORS
Undercity Guardians 75

3 TRADE QUARTER- UPPER TIER
Undercity Guardians 75
Tawny Grisette 30 Mushroom Vendor

4 INN
Anya Maulray 30 Stable Keeper
Innkeeper Norman 30 Innkeeper

5 REAGENTS
Thomas Mordan 30 Reagent Vendor

6 GENERAL GOODS
Eleanor Rusk 30 General Goods Vendor

7 GENERAL TRADE GOODS
Felicia Doan 30 General Trade Goods Vendor
Genevie Gallow 32 Quest

8 BAT HANDLER
Michael Garrette 55 Bat Handler
Patrick Garrette 15 Quest

9 WEAPONS MERCHANT
Gorden Wendham 30 Weapons Merchant
Louis Warren 30 Weapons Merchant

10 HEAVY ARMOR MERCHANT
Timothy Weldon 30 Heavy Armor Merchant
Velora Nitely 45
Walter Ellingson 30 Heavy Armor Merchant

11 GENERAL TRADE AND LIGHT ARMOR
Lauren Newcomb 30 Light Armor Merchant
Daniel Bartlett 30 General Trade Supplier

12 BANK
Bankers 40

13 GUILD CREATION AND TABARDS
Royal Overseer Bauhaus 40 Undercity Census
Edward Remington 25 Guild Tabard Designer
Christopher Drakul 50 Guild Master
Merill Pleasance 25 Tabard Vendor

14 UNDER STEPS
Jeremiah Payson 30 Cockroach Vendor

15 COOKING
Eunice Burch 35 Cooking Trainer
Ronald Burch 30 Cooking Supplier
Raleigh Andrean 14 Ex-Chef Quest

16 CANALS (WANDERERS)
Apothecary Katrina 20 Royal Apothecary Society
Apothecary Vallia 20 Royal Apothecary Society
Edrick Killian 20
Mattie Alred 20
Harbinger Balthazad 3
Selina Pickman 20
Reginald Grimsford 20
Davitt Hickson 20

ROGUE QUARTER
17 BAG VENDOR
Jonathan Chambers 30 Bag Vendor

18 LEATHER WORK
Killian Hagey 35 Skinning Trainer
Joseph Moore 30 Leatherworking Supplies
Gillian Moore 30 Leather Armor Merchant
Arthur Moore 35 Expert Leatherworker
Dan Golthas 23 Journeyman Leatherworker

19 FIRST AID
Mary Edris 35 First Aid

20 POISON
Ezekiel Graves 30 Poison Vendor

21 DAGGERS
Charles Seaton 30 Blade Merchant
Nathaniel Steenwick 30 Thrown Weapons Vendor

22 ROGUE TRAINER BUILDING
Gothard Winslow 35
Mennet Carkad 30 Quest
Miles Dexter 50 Rogue Trainer
Carolyn Ward 50 Rogue Trainer
Gregory Charles 60 Rogue Trainer

23 ENGINEERING
Estelle Gendry 25 Quest
Lucian Fenner 35
Franklyn Lloyd 33 Expert Engineer
Elizabeth Van Talen 30 Engineering Supplier
Graham Van Talen 26 Journeyman Engineer

MAGIC QUARTER
24 BOOK DEALER
Salazar Boch 30 Book Dealer

25 CARTOGRAPHY
Jorah Annison 20

26 RESEARCH LIBRARY
Andrew Brownell 40 Quest
Samantha Shackelton 20
Oran Snakewrithe 50 Quest

27 TAILOR
Sheldon Van Croy 30 Cloth Armor Merchant
Victor Ward 24 Journeyman Tailor Trainer
Rhiannon Davis 32 Expert Tailor
Josef Gregorian 45 Artisan Tailor
Millie Gregorian 30 Tailoring Supplies
Lucile Castleton 30 Robe Vendor

28 STAFF MERCHANT
Zane Bradford 10 Wand Vendor
Sydney Upton 30 Staff Vendor

29 DEMON CIRCLE
Victor Bartholomew 20
Jezelle Pruitt 40
Adrian Bartlett 20

30 MAGIC TRAINER BUILDING
Hannah Akeley 30 Reagent Supplier
Silas Zimmer 30
Godrick Farsan 15
Kaelystia 60 Mage Trainer
Pierce Shackleton 50 Mage Trainer
Martha Strain 20 Demon Trainer
Kaal Soulreaper 60 Warlock Trainer
Luther Pickman 50 Warlock Trainer
Richard Kerwin 40 Warlock Trainer
Bethor Iceshard 60 Quest
Lexington Mortaim 35 Portal Trainer

31 SUMMONING CIRCLE
Carendin Halgar 50 Quest

32 FISHING PIER
Armand Cromwell 35 Fishing Trainer
Lizbeth Cromwell 30 Fishing Supplier

WARRIOR QUARTER
33 Helena Atwood 20

34 GUNSMITH
Nicholas Atwood 30 Gun Merchant

35 BLACKSMITH
Mirelle Tremane 30 Heavy Armor Merchant
Samuel Van Brunt 30 Blacksmith Supplier
James Van Brunt 35 Expert Blacksmith
Basil Frye 26 Journeyman Blacksmith

36 WEAPONS MERCHANTS
Francis Eliot 30 Axe Merchant
Benijah Fenner 30 Mace Merchant
Geoffrey Hartwell 30 Blade Merchant
Archibald 50 Elite Weapon Master

37 MINING
Sarah Killian 30 Mining Supplier
Brom Killian 35 Mining Trainer

38 BOW MERCHANT
Abigail Sawyer 30 Bow Merchant

39 GATHERING OF NPCS
Leona Tharpe 40
Joanna Whitehall 40
Gerard Abernathy 40
Theresa 5 Gerard's Mindslave (wanders)

40 WARRIOR TRAINING
Sergeant Houser 40 Sergeant
Travist Bosk 20
Eldin Partridge 20
Alyssa Blaye 20
Sergeant Rutgar 65 Sergeant

41 CROWD
Richard Van Brunt 20
Robert Grossom 20
Andrew Hartwell 20
Tyler 20
Edward 20
Riley Walker 20
Chloe Curthas 20
Marla Fowler 20
Brother Malach 20
Lysta Bancroft 30

42 WARRIOR AND PRIEST BUILDING
Father Lankester 40 Priest Trainer
Aelthalysta 60 Priest Trainer
Father Lazarus 50 Priest Trainer
Baltus Fowler 40 Warrior Trainer
Angela Curthas 50 Warrior Trainer
Christoph Walker 60 Warrior Trainer

43 ENTRANCE TO SEWERS

44 EXIT TO TIRISFAL GLADES

APOTHECARIUM
45 Keeper Bel'dugur

46 HERBALIST
Martha Alliestar 35 Herbalism Trainer
Katrina Alliestar 30 Herbalism Supplier

47 BLUE MOON ODDS AND ENDS
Allesandro Luca 25 Quest

48 ENCHANTMENT
Malcomb Wynn 23 Journeyman Enchanter
Thaddeus Webb 30 Enchanting Supplies
Lavinia Crowe 35 Expert Enchanter

49 PARQUAL FINTALLAS

50 Andron Gant 15 Quest

51 ALCHEMY
Algernon 30 Alchemy Supplies
Doctor Marsh 35 Expert Alchemist

52 ALCHEMIST
Doctor Herbert Halsey 50 Artisan Chemist
Chemist Fuely 30

53 APOTHECARIUM
Doctor Martin Felben 25 Journeyman Alchemist Trainer
Theodore Griffs 50
Chemist Cuely 30 Quest
Thersa Windsong 45
Master Apothecary Faranell 50 Royal Apothecary Society
Apothecary Zinge 29 Royal Apothecary Society Quest
Apothecary Keever 20 Royal Apothecary Society

54 Ganoosh 8

55 ROYAL QUARTER
Varimathras 100 Quest
Sharlindra 25
Lady Sylvanus Windrunner 63 Elite Banshee Queen

56 Boyle

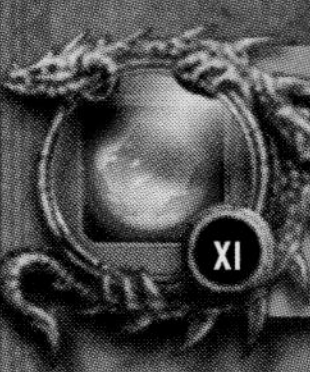

QUESTS

QUEST	M LEV	Q LEV	QUEST LAUNCHER	QUEST FINISHER	CHAIN?	XP---	XP--	XP-	XP+	XP++	XP+++	CASH REWARD
Another Power Source?	38	46	Chief Engineer Bilgewhizzle	Chief Engineer Bilgewhizzle	N	0	0	0	0	0	0	None
REWARD: Model 4711-FTZ Power Source												
Bring the End	37	42	Andrew Brownell	Andrew Brownell	N	430	850	1700	2600	3450	4300	None
REWARD: Vanquisher's Sword, Amberglow Talisman												
Errand for Apothecary Zinge	38	45	Apothecary Zinge	Alessandro Luca	Y	40	80	160	230	310	390	None
Errand for Apothecary Zinge	38	45	Alessandro Luca	Apothecary Zinge	Y	40	80	160	230	310	390	None
Going, Going, Guano!	30	33	Master Apothecary Faranell	Master Apothecary Faranell	Y	330	650	1300	2000	2650	3300	None
Hearts of Zeal	30	33	Master Apothecary Faranell	Master Apothecary Faranell	N	330	650	1300	2000	2650	3300	None
Into the Field	38	46	Apothecary Zinge	Chief Engineer Bilgewhizzle	Y	200	400	800	1200	1600	2000	None
Into The Scarlet Monastery	33	42	Varimathras	Varimathras	N	525	1050	2050	3100	4100	5150	None
CHOICE OF: 1 Sword of Omen or 1 Prophetic Cane or 1 Dragon's Blood Necklace												
Journey to Grom'gol!	1	1		Hin Denburg	N	0	0	0	0	0	0	None
Journey to Orgrimmar!	1	1		Hin Denburg	N	0	0	0	0	0	0	None
Lines of Communication	42	47	Oran Snakewrithe	Oran Snakewrithe	N	320	625	1250	1900	2500	3150	70 00
Reclaimed Treasures	33	43	Patrick Garrett	Patrick Garrett	N	360	725	1450	2150	2900	3600	60 00
Return to Apothecary Zinge	38	46	Chief Engineer Bilgewhizzle	Apothecary Zinge	N	500	1000	2000	3050	4050	5050	1 30 00
CHOICE OF: 1 Skilled Handling Gloves or 1 Master Apothecary Cape or 1 Loreskin Shoulders												
Sample for Helbrim	10	15	Apothecary Zinge	Apothecary Helbrim	N	110	210	420	625	850	1050	None
CHOICE OF: 1 Brewer's Gloves or 1 Long Draping Cape												
Seeping Corruption	45	52	Chemist Cuely	Thersa Windsong	N	50	100	200	310	410	500	None
Seeping Corruption	45	52	Chemist Cuely	Thersa Windsong	N	50	100	200	310	410	500	None
Seeping Corruption	45	52	Chemist Cuely	Chemist Cuely	N	260	500	1000	1550	2050	2550	40 00
Seeping Corruption	45	52	Chemist Cuely	Chemist Cuely	N	500	1000	2050	3050	4100	5100	75 00
Slake That Thirst	38	46	Chief Engineer Bilgewhizzle	Chief Engineer Bilgewhizzle	N	310	600	1200	1850	2450	3050	None
REWARD: Model 4711-FTZ Power Source												
The Book of Ur	16	26	Keeper Bel'dugur	Keeper Bel'dugur	N	210	420	850	1250	1700	2100	None
CHOICE OF: 1 Grizzled Boots or 1 Steel-clasped Bracers												
The Crown of Will	33	38	Sharlindra	Melisara	Y	30	55	110	170	230	290	None
The Lich's Identity	5	8	Bethor Iceshard	Bethor Iceshard	Y	55	110	210	320	420	525	1 75
The Star, the Hand and the Heart	30	44	Keeper Bel'dugur	Keeper Bel'dugur	Y	550	1100	2250	3350	4500	5600	None
To Steal From Thieves	27	36	Genavie Callow	Genavie Callow	N	280	550	1100	1700	2250	2800	None
CHOICE OF: 1 Grim Pauldrons or 1 Gallan Cuffs												
Zinge's Delivery	10	15	Apothecary Renferrel	Apothecary Zinge	Y	10	20	40	65	85	110	None

ALTERAC MOUNTAINS

The Alterac Mountains are home to many powerful Ogres and to the Dalarans (a group of mystics who use old and dangerous Elven magic to wreak vengeance against the Undead). While standing on the northwest shores of the area, a person can see over to the grim canopy of Silverpine Forest, a land filled with the walking dead. Yeti hold many of the high, snow-filled areas of Alterac, while the Dalarans and the dangerous Syndicate control the lowlands.

LOCAL RESOURCES

MINING

METAL	AVAILABILITY
Iron	Abundant
Mithril	Abundant

HERBALISM

HERB	AVAILABILITY
Goldthorn	Abundant
Fadeleaf	Moderate
Khadgar's Whisker	Trivial
Wintersbite	Abundant

SKINNING

Quantity of Skinnable Creatures: Moderate

Levels of Skinnable Creatures: 30-34 (Skinning 150-170)

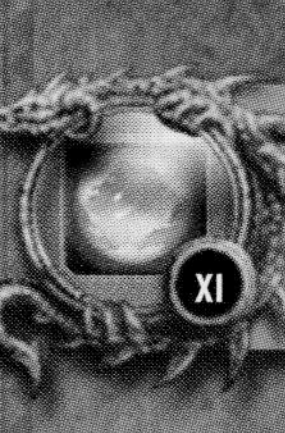

MAP LEGEND

1 LORDAMERE INTERNMENT CAMP
- Alina 33 Quest Target
- Dalaran Shield Guard 31-32
- Dalaran Theurgist 32-33
- Dermot 34 Quest Target
- Elder Gray Bear 25-26
- Giant Moss Creeper 24-25
- Mountain Lion 32-33
- Ricter 33 Quest Target

2 DALARAN
- Archmage Ansirem Runeweaver 40
- Dalaran Shield Guard 32
- Dalaran Summoner 34-35
- Dalaran Theurgist 33
- Dalaran Worker 33-34
- Elder Gray Bear 25-26
- Elemental Slave 33-34
- Gavin's Naze
- Giant Moss Creeper 25-26
- Giant Moss Creeper 25-26
- Hulking Mountain Lion 33-34
- Mountain Lion 32-33
- Snapjaw 30-31

3 THE HEADLAND
- Mountain Lion 32-33

4 CORRAHN'S DAGGER
- Hulking Mountain Lion 33-34
- Mountain Lion 32-33
- Syndicate Footpad 33
- Syndicate Thief 33-34

5 GROWLESS CAVE
- Giant Yeti 33-34
- Mountian Yeti 32-33

6 RUINS OF ALTERAC
- **Bro'kin 49 Speciality Alchemist**
- Crushridge Enforcer 38-39 Elite
- Crushridge Mage 37-38 Elite
- Crushridge Mauler 37-38 Elite
- Crushridge Warmonger 39-40 Elite
- Mudrake 40 Elite

7 THE UPLANDS
- Argus Shadow Mage 36
- Giant Yeti 33-34
- Grandpa Vishas 34 Elite
- Hulking Mountain Lion 33-34
- Nancy Vishas 33 Elite
- Syndicate Saboteur 37-38
- Syndicate Sentry 36-37

8 MISTY SHORE
- Snapjaw 30-31

9 DANDRED'S FORD
- Hulking Mountain Lion 33-34
- Snapjaw 30-31
- Syndicate Assassin 38-39
- Syndicate Enforcer 39-40

10 SLAUGHTER HOLLOW
- Crushridge Brute 35-36
- Crushridge Ogre 34-35

11 CRUSHRIDGE HOLD
- Crushridge Brute 35-36
- Crushridge Ogre 34-35

12 GALLOWS' CORNER
- Crushridge Brute 35
- Crushridge Ogre 35

13 STRAHNBAD
- Syndicate Spy 35
- Syndicate Wizard 35

14 CHILLWIND POINT
- **Bath'rah the Windcatcher 35 Quest**
- Hulking Mountain Lion 33-34
- Mountain Lion 32-33
- Snapjaw 30-31
- Stonefury 37

15 SOFERA'S NAZE
- Henchman Valik 30
- Syndicate Footpad 32
- Syndicate Thief 33-34

QUESTS

QUEST	M LEV	Q LEV	QUEST LAUNCHER	QUEST FINISHER	CHAIN?	XP---	XP--	XP-	XP+	XP++	XP+++	CASH REWARD
Baron's Demise	30	40	Magistrate Henry Maleb	Magistrate Henry Maleb	N	390	775	1550	2350	3100	3900	1 00 00
Barov Family Fortune	52	60	Alexi Barov	Alexi Barov	Y	650	1300	2650	3950	5300	6600	1 80 00
Barov Family Fortune	52	60	Weldon Barov	Weldon Barov	Y	650	1300	2650	3950	5300	6600	1 80 00
Betina Bigglezink	57	60	Leonid Barthalomew the Revered	Betina Bigglezink	Y	170	330	650	1000	1300	1650	None
Crushridge Bounty	30	36	Marshal Redpath	Marshal Redpath	Y	350	700	1400	2100	2800	3500	75 00
Crushridge Warmongers	30	40	Marshal Redpath	Marshal Redpath	N	470	950	1900	2800	3750	4700	None
CHOICE OF: 1 Burning Sliver or 1 Lunar Buckler												
Dark Council	30	40	Magistrate Henry Maleb	Magistrate Henry Maleb	N	320	625	1250	1900	2500	3150	50 00
Doctor Theolen Krastinov, the Butcher	55	60	Eva Sarkhoff	Eva Sarkhoff	Y	650	1300	2650	3950	5300	6600	None
Encrypted Letter	30	34	Syndicate Documents (Obj)	Loremaster Dibbs	Y	140	270	550	800	1100	1350	None
Encrypted Letter	30	34	Syndicate Documents (Obj)	Loremaster Dibbs	Y	140	270	550	800	1100	1350	None
Encrypted Letter	30	34	Syndicate Documents (Obj)	Loremaster Dibbs	Y	140	270	550	800	1100	1350	None
Foreboding Plans	26	34	Syndicate Documents (Obj)	Magistrate Henry Maleb	Y	140	270	550	800	1100	1350	None
Foreboding Plans	26	34	Syndicate Documents (Obj)	Magistrate Henry Maleb	Y	140	270	550	800	1100	1350	None
Foreboding Plans	26	34	Syndicate Documents (Obj)	Magistrate Henry Maleb	Y	140	270	550	800	1100	1350	None
Further Mysteries	30	34	Prospector Stormpike	Magistrate Henry Maleb	Y	140	270	550	800	1100	1350	None
Kirtonos the Herald	55	60	Eva Sarkhoff	Eva Sarkhoff	N	825	1650	3300	5000	6650	8300	None
REWARD: Spectral Essence and CHOICE OF: 1 Penelope's Rose or 1 Mirah's Song												
Krastinov's Bag of Horrors	55	60		Eva Sarkhoff	Y	650	1300	2650	3950	5300	6600	None
Krastinov's Bag of Horrors	55	60	Eva Sarkhoff	Eva Sarkhoff	Y	650	1300	2650	3950	5300	6600	None
Letter to Stormpike	30	34	Loremaster Dibbs	Prospector Stormpike	Y	140	270	550	800	1100	1350	None
Noble Deaths	26	36	Magistrate Henry Maleb	Magistrate Henry Maleb	N	280	550	1100	1700	2250	2800	40 00
Plagued Hatchlings	55	58	Betina Bigglezink	Betina Bigglezink	N	625	1250	2500	3700	4950	6200	90 00
Stormpike's Deciphering	28	40	Loremaster Dibbs	Prospector Stormpike	N	160	310	625	925	1250	1550	None
Syndicate Assassins	26	33	Magistrate Henry Maleb	Magistrate Henry Maleb	N	200	390	775	1150	1550	1950	None
CHOICE OF: 1 Crusader Belt or 1 Insulated Sage Gloves												
The Lich, Ras Frostwhisper	57	63	Magistrate Marduke	Magistrate Marduke	N	1100	2200	4350	6550	8700	10900	None
REWARD: Darrowshire Strongguard and CHOICE OF: 1 Warblade of Caer Darrow or 1 Crown of Caer Darrow or 1 Darrowspike												
Valik	29	34	Henchman Valik	Henchman Valik	N	25	55	110	160	220	270	None
REWARD: Syndicate Missive												

ARATHI HIGHLANDS

A fragrant wind of pollen, grass, and other living things blows over those who enter the Highlands of Arathi. People from both the Horde and Alliance settle here, trying to farm the arable land of the north and struggle against the many natural dangers of the land. Raptors walk across the flatlands, hunting for prey, and there are many aggressive Ogres and Trolls out in the wild as well. Beware the deadly elementals that spawn near old and forgotten shrines, for they have tremendous power. Seek Hammerfall in the northeast for safety (as the Horde), or walk into the small gorge of Refuge Point (as Alliance) in the center of the Highlands.

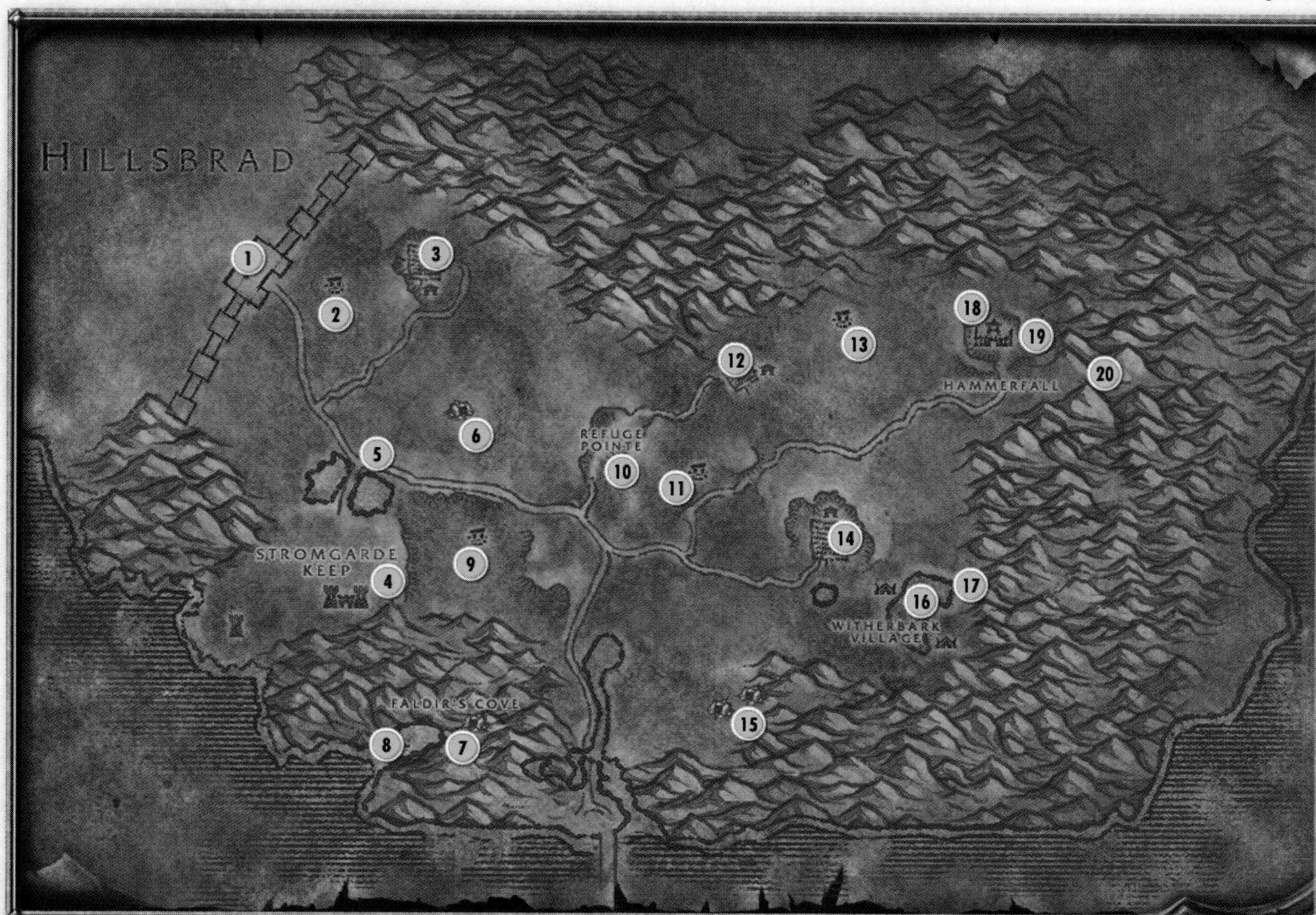

LOCAL RESOURCES

MINING

METAL	AVAILABILITY
Tin	Trivial
Iron	Moderate
Mithril	Trivial

HERBALISM

HERB	AVAILABILITY
Kingsblood	Moderate
Wild Steelbloom	Abundant
Liferoot	Trivial

SKINNING

Quantity of Skinnable Creatures: Moderate

Levels of Skinnable Creatures: 30-36 (Skinning 150-180)

MAP LEGEND

1 THORADIN'S WALL
Highland Strider 30-31
Plains Creeper 32-33
Young Mesa Buzzard 31-32

2 CIRCLE OF WEST BINDING
Burning Exile 38-39

3 NORTHFOLD MANOR
Plains Creeper 32-33
Syndicate Highwayman 30-31
Syndicate Mercenary 31-32
Syndicate Pathstalker 32-33
Young Mesa Buzzard 21-32

4 STROMGARDE KEEP
Boulderfist Lord 39-40 Elite
Boulderfist Mauler 37-38 Elite
Boulderfist Shaman 38-39 Elite
Lord Falconcrest 40 Elite
Otto 38 Elite
Prince Galen Trollbane 44 Elite
Stromgarde Defender 38-39 Elite
Stromgarde Troll Hunter 37-38 Elite
Stromgarde Vindicator 40 Elite
Syndicate Conjurer 36 Elite
Syndicate Magus 38 Elite
Syndicate Prowler 36 Elite

5 ARATHI HIGHWAY
Forsaken Courier 35
Forsaken Bodyguard 35
Lieutenant Valorcall 38 Elite
Stromgarde Cavalryman 37-38 Elite

5 BOULDER'GOR
Boulderfist Ogre 32-33
Highland Thrasher 33-34
Witherbark Troll 31-30

6 BOULDERFIST OUTPOST
Boulderfist Enforcer 33-34
Witherbark Witch Doctor 33

7 FALDIR'S COVE
Lolo the Lookout 39 Quest
Shakes O'Breen 40 Quest

8 THE DROWNED REEF
Daggerspine Raider 38-39
Daggerspine Sorceress 39-40

9 CIRCLE OF INNER BINDING
Highland Thrasher 33-34
Mesa Buzzard 34-35
Rumbling Exile 38-39

10 REFUGE POINTE
Apprentice Kryten 30 Quest
Captain Nials 41 Quest
Cedrick Prose 55 Gryphon Master
Highland Strider 30-31
Young Mesa Buzzard 31-32

11 CIRCLE OF OUTER BINDING
Thundering Exile 38-39

12 DABYRIE'S FARMSTEAD
Dabyrie Laborer 30-31
Dabyrie's Militia 31-32
Fardel Dabyrie 33 Quest Target
Marcel Dabyrie 34 Quest Target

13 CIRCLE OF EAST BINDING
Shards of Myzrael

14 GO'SHEK FARM
Kinelory 38 Quest
Quae 38 Quest
Giant Plains Creeper 35-36
Hammerfall Grunt 34-35
Hammerfall Peon 33-34
Mesa Buzzard 34-35

15 BOULDERFIST HALL
Boulderfist Brute 35-36
Boulderfist Magus 37
Highland Fleshstalker 36-37
Kor'gresh
Mesa Buzzard 34-35
Witherbark Berserker 36-37 Elite

16 WITHERBARK VILLAGE
Giant Plains Creeper 35-36
Witherbark Axe Thrower 32-33
Witherbark Head Hunter 34-35
Witherbark Witchdoctor 33-34

17 WITHERBARK CAVE
Witherbark Headhunter 34-35
Witherbark Shadow Hunter 35-36

18 HAMMERFALL
Drum Fel 30 Quest
Gor'mul 40 Quest
Innkeeper Adegwa 30 Innkeeper
Slagg 38 Superior Butcher
Tharlidun 30 Stable Master
Tor'gan 40 Quest
Urda 55 Wind Rider Master
Zaruk 60 Quest
Zengu 40 Quest
Highland Strider 30-31

19 DRYWHISKER GORGE
Drywhisker Kobold 35-36

20 DRYWHISKER CAVE
Drywhisker Digger 36-37
Drywhisker Surveyor 37-38

QUESTS

QUEST	M LEV	Q LEV	QUEST LAUNCHER	QUEST FINISHER	CHAIN?	XP---	XP--	XP-	XP+	XP++	XP+++	CASH REWARD
An Apprentice's Enchantment	30	39	Apprentice Kryten	Skuerto	Y	30	60	120	180	240	300	None
Attack on the Tower	30	39	Skuerto	Skuerto	Y	300	600	1200	1800	2400	3000	None
Breaking the Keystone	30	42	Iridescent Shards (Obj)	Keystone (Obj)	N	350	700	1400	2050	2750	3450	None
Breaking the Keystone	30	42	Stone of Inner Binding (Obj)	Keystone (Obj)	N	350	700	1400	2050	2750	3450	None
Call to Arms	30	32	Drum Fel	Drum Fel	Y	260	500	1000	1550	2050	2550	None
Call to Arms	30	38	Drum Fel	Drum Fel	Y	290	575	1150	1700	2300	2850	None
Call to Arms	30	40	Drum Fel	Drum Fel	N	320	625	1250	1900	2500	3150	50 00
CHOICE OF: 1 Silent Hunter or 1 Skullsplitter												
Death From Below	35	44	Shakes O'Breen	Shakes O'Breen	N	470	925	1850	2800	3700	4650	None
CHOICE OF: 1 Coldwater Ring or 1 Seafire Band												
Deep Sea Salvage	35	40	First Mate Nilzlix	First Mate Nilzlix	N	320	625	1250	1900	2500	3150	None
REWARD: Black Water Hammer												
Drowned Sorrows	35	40	Captain Steelgut	Captain Steelgut	N	320	625	1250	1900	2500	3150	None
REWARD: Seawolf Gloves												
Foul Magics	30	33	Tor'gan	Tor'gan	N	270	525	1050	1600	2100	2650	None
Foul Magics	35	40	Tor'gan	Tor'gan	N	320	625	1250	1900	2500	3150	None
CHOICE OF: 1 White Drakeskin Cap or 1 Radiant Silver Bracers												
Guile of the Raptor	29	37	Tor'gan	Gor'mul	N	30	55	110	170	230	290	None
Guile of the Raptor	29	37	Gor'mul	Tor'gan	N	290	575	1150	1700	2300	2850	None
REWARD: Call of the Raptor												
Guile of the Raptor	29	37	Tor'gan	Tor'gan	Y	290	575	1150	1700	2300	2850	None
Hammerfall	29	34	Gor'mul	Tor'gan	Y	25	55	110	160	220	270	None
Land Ho!	35	35	Lolo the Lookout	Shakes O'Breen	N	70	140	280	410	550	700	None
Malin's Request	30	39	Skuerto	Archmage Malin	N	380	750	1500	2250	3000	3750	90 00
CHOICE OF: 1 Vigilant Buckler or 1 Wingborne Boots												
Myzrael's Allies	30	40	Iridescent Shards (Obj)	Gerrig Bonegrip	Y	240	470	950	1400	1900	2350	None
Myzrael's Allies	30	40	Keystone (Obj)	Gerrig Bonegrip	Y	240	470	950	1400	1900	2350	None
Myzrael's Allies	30	40	Keystone (Obj)	Zaruk	Y	240	470	950	1400	1900	2350	None
Myzrael's Allies	30	40	Shards of Myzrael (Obj)	Gerrig Bonegrip	Y	240	470	950	1400	1900	2350	None
Myzrael's Allies	30	40	Stone of Inner Binding (Obj)	Gerrig Bonegrip	Y	240	470	950	1400	1900	2350	None
Northfold Manor	30	31	Captain Nials	Captain Nials	N	250	500	1000	1500	2000	2500	None
Raising Spirits	29	34	Tor'gan	Tor'gan	Y	270	550	1100	1600	2150	2700	None
Raising Spirits	29	34	Tor'gan	Gor'mul	Y	25	55	110	160	220	270	None
Raising Spirits	29	34	Gor'mul	Tor'gan	Y	25	55	110	160	220	270	None
Sigil of Arathor	32	41	Zengu	Zengu	Y	330	650	1300	2000	2650	3300	55 00
Sigil of Strom	32	37	Zengu	Zengu	Y	290	575	1150	1700	2300	2850	40 00
Sigil of Thoradin	32	40	Tor'gan	Zengu	Y	30	65	130	190	250	320	None
Sigil of Trollbane	32	42	Zengu	Zengu	Y	350	700	1400	2050	2750	3450	55 00
Stones of Binding	30	38	Iridescent Shards (Obj)	Stone of Inner Binding (Obj)	Y	290	575	1150	1700	2300	2850	None
Stones of Binding	30	38	Shards of Myzrael (Obj)	Stone of Inner Binding (Obj)	Y	290	575	1150	1700	2300	2850	None
Stromgarde Badges	30	37	Captain Nials	Captain Nials	N	360	700	1400	2150	2850	3550	None
REWARD: Stromgarde Cavalry Leggings												
Summoning the Princess	30	50	Theldurin the Lost	Shards of Myzrael (Obj)	N	700	1400	2850	4250	5700	7100	None
REWARD: Pulsating Crystalline Shard												
Sunken Treasure	35	40	Fleet Master Seahorn	Shakes O'Breen	N	320	625	1250	1900	2500	3150	None
Sunken Treasure	35	40	Professor Phizzlethorpe	Doctor Draxlegauge	Y	320	625	1250	1900	2500	3150	None
Sunken Treasure	35	40	Doctor Draxlegauge	Doctor Draxlegauge	Y	390	775	1550	2350	3100	3900	None
CHOICE OF: 1 Gnomish Zapper or 1 Servomechanic Sledgehammer												
Sunken Treasure	35	40	Doctor Draxlegauge	Shakes O'Breen	Y	160	310	625	925	1250	1550	None
Sunken Treasure	35	40	Shakes O'Breen	Fleet Master Seahorn	Y	320	625	1250	1900	2500	3150	None
The Broken Sigil	32	40	Zengu	Tor'gan	N	320	625	1250	1900	2500	3150	50 00
The Lost Fragments	30	41	Theldurin the Lost	Theldurin the Lost	N	330	650	1300	2000	2650	3300	None
The Princess Trapped	30	37	Shards of Myzrael (Obj)	Iridescent Shards (Obj)	Y	290	575	1150	1700	2300	2850	None
The Real Threat	30	40	Korin Fel	Korin Fel	N	390	775	1550	2350	3100	3900	None
CHOICE OF: 1 Mistspray Kilt or 1 Sword of Hammerfall												
Theldurin the Lost	30	40	Gerrig Bonegrip	Theldurin the Lost	Y	160	310	625	925	1250	1550	None
Theldurin the Lost	30	40	Zaruk	Theldurin the Lost	Y	160	310	625	925	1250	1550	None
Trelane's Defenses	30	39	Skuerto	Apprentice Kryten	Y	300	600	1200	1800	2400	3000	None
Trol'kalar	32	42	Trollbane's Tomb (Obj)	Zengu	N	430	850	1700	2600	3450	4300	None
CHOICE OF: 1 Blood-tinged Armor or 1 Pit Fighter's Shield												
Trol'kalar	32	42	Zengu	Trollbane's Tomb (Obj)	Y	85	170	340	525	700	850	None
Wand over Fist	30	39	Skuerto	Skuerto	N	300	600	1200	1800	2400	3000	None
Wanted! Marez Cowl	30	39	Wanted Board (Obj)	Captain Nials	N	380	750	1500	2250	3000	3750	None
REWARD: Arcane Runed Bracers												
Wanted! Otto and Falconcrest	30	40	Wanted Board (Obj)	Captain Nials	N	390	775	1550	2350	3100	3900	None
CHOICE OF: 1 Rod of Sorrow or 1 War Rider Bracers												
Worth Its Weight in Gold	30	36	Apprentice Kryten	Apprentice Kryten	N	350	700	1400	2100	2800	3500	None

THE EASTERN PLAGUELANDS

Beyond Darrowmere Lake are the Eastern Plaguelands, home of disease, sorrow, and some of the Scourge's greatest troops. Powerful spirits and spidery beings of magic have changed the land to suit their purposes, growing massive and poisonous fungal towers to promote their plague. Poison fills the air and the water is dangerous. Only the Scarlet Crusaders and the Argent Dawn are brave (or foolish) enough to stay here and fight against impossible odds. All wise adventurers avoid the Scarlet Crusade, who see the taint in everything, but the Argent Dawn camp, in the east, is a safe haven for the Alliance.

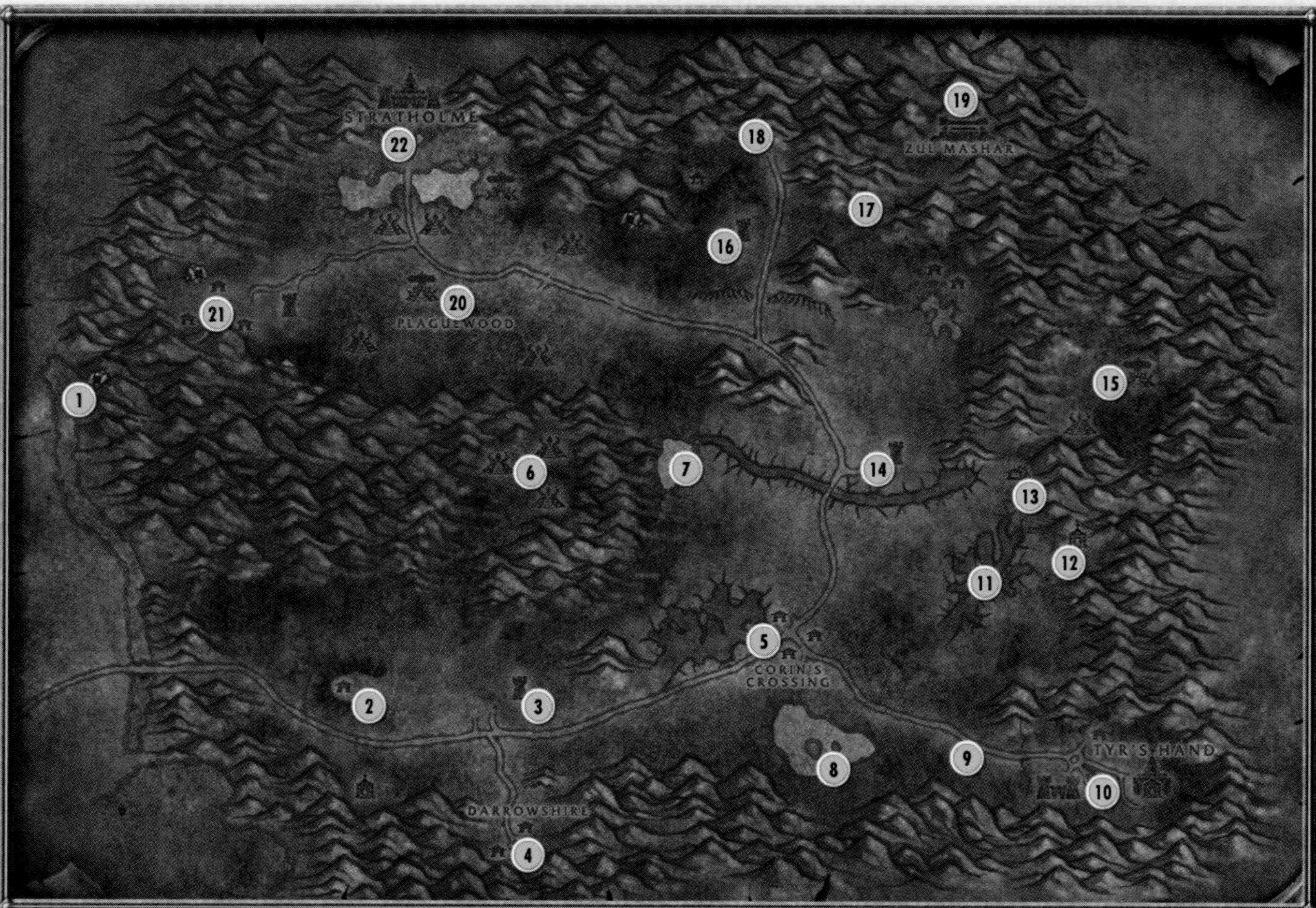

LOCAL RESOURCES

MINING

METAL	AVAILABILITY
Thorium	Moderate

HERBALISM: NONE

SKINNING

Quantity of Skinnable Creatures: Trivial

Levels of Skinnable Creatures: 53-56 (Skinning 265-280)

HOW TO
AZEROTH
KHAZ MODAN
LORDAERON
NORTHERN KALIMDOR
SOUTHERN KALIMDOR

MAP LEGEND

1 THONDRORIL RIVER
Tirion Fordring 61 Quest
Carrion Grub 54-55
Plaguebat 54
Plaguehound Runt 53-54

2 THE MARRIS STEAD
Abomination 59-60
Death Singer 57-59
Diseased Flayer 59
Duskwing 60 Elite
Eyeless Watcher 58
Scourge Champion 60

3 CROWN GUARD TOWER
Carrion Grub 55
Noxious Plaguebat 55-56
Plaguehound 55-56

4 DARROWSHIRE
Carrion Grub 55
Plaguebat 53
Plaguehound Runt 53-54
Putrid Gargoyle 56

5 CORIN'S CROSSING
Dark Caster 56
Gibbering Ghoul 57
Hate Shrieker 55-57
Scourge Warder 56
Stitched Horror 58
Unseen Servant 55
Vile Tutor 56-57

6 THE FUNGAL VALE
Abomination 59-60
Crypt Slayer 58-59
Dark Adept 57
Death Singer 59
Diseased Flayer 59
Eyeless Watcher 58
Scourge Champion 59-60
Shadowmage 59-60

7 BLACKWOOD LAKE
Blighted Horror 56-57
Plague Monstrosity 58

8 LAKE MERELDAR
Plague Ravager 55-56

9 SCARLET BASE CAMP
Scarlet Cleric 54 Elite
Scarlet Enchanter 55 Elite
Scarlet Warder 53-54 Elite

10 TYR'S HAND
Scarlet Archmage 55-57 Elite
Scarlet Cleric 54-55 Elite
Scarlet Curate 55-56 Elite
Scarlet Enchanter 53-55 Elite
Scarlet Praetorian 56-57 Elite
Scarlet Warder 53-54 Elite

11 PESTILENT SCAR
Living Decay 55-56
Rotting Sludge 54-55

12 LIGHT'S HOPE CHAPEL
Argent Guard 55
Argent Rider 55
Betina Bigglezink 57
Carlin Redpath 58
Duke Nicholas Zuerenhoff 60
Leonid Barthalomew the Revered 60
Lord Maxwell Tyrosus 61
Quartermaster Miranda Breechlock 60
Smokey LaRue 55

13 BROWMAN MILL
Death Singer 58-59
Diseased Flayer 58
Dread Weaver 58-59
Scourge Champion 59-60

14 EASTWALL TOWER
Borelgore 61 Elite
Carrion Grub 55
Crypt Horror 57-58
Diseased Flayer 59
Noxious Plaguebat 55-56
Plaguehound 55-56
Scourge Guard 57-58

15 THE NOXIOUS GLADE
Crypt Slayer 58-59
Death Singer 59
Diseased Flayer 59
Dread Weaver 59
Scourge Champion 60

16 NORTHPASS TOWER
Aurora Skycaller 62
Kriss Goldenlight 60
Carrion Grub 55
Noxious Plaguebat 55-56
Plaguehound 55-56

17 NORTHDALE
Death Singer 57-59
Eyeless Watcher 57-58
Frenzied Plaguehound 57
Plague Monstrosity 58

18 QUEL'LITHIEN LODGE
Pathstrider 57-58
Ranger 59-60
Ranger Lord Hawkspear 60 Elite
Woodsman 58-59

19 ZUL'MASHAR
Mossflayer Cannibal 57-59
Mossflayer Scout 57-58
Mossflayer Shadowhunter 58-59

20 PLAGUEWOOD
Cannibal Ghoul 54
Cursed Mage 54-55
Putrid Gargoyle 56
Scourge Soldier 53-54
Scourge Warder 56
Stitched Horror 57

21 TERRORDALE
Carrion Devourer 56
Crypt Fiend 53-54
Crypt Walker 55-56
Dark Caster 56
Gibbering Ghoul 57
Hate Shrieker 55-57
Scourge Soldier 53
Scourge Warder 56
Stitched Horror 57-58
Stitched Horror 58
Torn Screamer 53-55
Unseen Servant 55
Vile Tutor 56-57

22 STRATHOLME
Entrance to Stratholme World Dungeon
Hate Shrieker 55-56
Necromancer 54
Stitched Horror 58
Torn Screamer 53-55

QUESTS

QUEST	M LEV	Q LEV	QUEST LAUNCHER	QUEST FINISHER	CHAIN?	XP---	XP--	XP-	XP+	XP++	XP+++	CASH REWARD
A Strange Historian	50	56	Marlene Redpath	Chromie	Y	440	875	1750	2600	3500	4350	None
Argent Dawn Commission	50	55	Duke Nicholas Zverenhoff	Duke Nicholas Zverenhoff	N	55	110	220	340	450	550	None
REWARD: Argent Dawn Commission												
Augustus' Receipt Book	50	55	Augustus the Touched	Augustus the Touched	N	280	550	1100	1700	2250	2800	None
Auntie Marlene	50	56	Pamela Redpath	Marlene Redpath	Y	290	575	1150	1750	2300	2900	None
Brother Carlin	50	56	Chromie	Carlin Redpath	Y	290	575	1150	1750	2300	2900	None
Corruptor's Scourgestones	50	55	Duke Nicholas Zverenhoff	Duke Nicholas Zverenhoff	N	55	110	220	340	450	550	None
REWARD: Argent Dawn Valor Token												
Defenders of Darrowshire	50	55	Carlin Redpath	Carlin Redpath	N	575	1150	2250	3400	4500	5650	None
Fragments of the Past	53	56	Aurora Skycaller	Aurora Skycaller	Y	575	1150	2300	3500	4650	5800	None
Hameya's Plea	54	60	Torn Scroll (Obj)	Mound of Dirt (Obj)	N	650	1300	2650	3950	5300	6600	90 00
REWARD: Hameya's Slayer, Hameya's Cloak												
Heroes of Darrowshire	50	56	Carlin Redpath	Carlin Redpath	N	0	0	0	0	0	0	None
Hidden Treasures	50	60	Pamela Redpath	Joseph's Chest (Obj)	N	1000	2000	4000	5950	7950	9950	None
REWARD: Ring of Protection, Archlight Talisman, Magebane Scion												
Invader's Scourgestones	50	55	Duke Nicholas Zverenhoff	Duke Nicholas Zverenhoff	N	55	110	220	340	450	550	None
REWARD: Argent Dawn Valor Token												
Little Pamela	50	55	Marlene Redpath	Pamela Redpath	Y	280	550	1100	1700	2250	2800	None
Lord Maxwell Tyrosus	55	62	Duke Nicholas Zverenhoff	Lord Maxwell Tyrosus	Y	700	1400	2800	4250	5650	7050	None
Marauders of Darrowshire	50	60	Carlin Redpath	Carlin Redpath	Y	650	1300	2650	3950	5300	6600	None
Menethil's Gift	57	62	Menethil's Gift (Obj)	Leonid Barthalomew the Revered	Y	875	1750	3500	5300	7050	8800	None
Minion's Scourgestones	50	55	Duke Nicholas Zverenhoff	Duke Nicholas Zverenhoff	N	55	110	220	340	450	550	None
REWARD: Argent Dawn Valor Token												
Pamela's Doll	50	55	Pamela Redpath	Pamela Redpath	N	280	550	1100	1700	2250	2800	None
Return to Chromie	50	60	Carlin Redpath	Chromie	Y	330	650	1300	2000	2650	3300	None
Sister Pamela	50	55	Jessica Redpath	Pamela Redpath	Y	55	110	220	340	450	550	None
The Annals of Darrowshire	50	56	Chromie	Chromie	N	575	1150	2300	3500	4650	5800	None
The Argent Hold	55	62	Lord Maxwell Tyrosus	The Argent Hold (Obj)	N	1050	2100	4200	6350	8450	10550	2 80 00
CHOICE OF: 1 Argent Avenger or 1 Argent Defender or 1 Argent Crusader												
The Battle of Darrowshire	55	60	Chromie	Pamela Redpath	Y	825	1650	3300	5000	6650	8300	None
REWARD: Tea with Sugar												
The Lost Tablets of Mosh'aru	40	58	Prospector Ironboot	Prospector Ironboot	Y	775	1550	3100	4650	6200	7750	None
The Restless Souls	55	61	Caretaker Alen	Egan	Y	675	1350	2750	4100	5500	6850	None
Tormented By the Past	53	58	Aurora Skycaller	Remorseful Highborne	Y	470	925	1850	2800	3700	4650	None
Uncle Carlin	50	56	Pamela Redpath	Carlin Redpath	N	290	575	1150	1750	2300	2900	None
Zaeldarr the Outcast	50	55	Caretaker Alen	Caretaker Alen	N	420	850	1700	2500	3350	4200	85 00

HILLSBRAD FOOTHILLS

The gentle foothills around Hillsbrad would have stayed peaceful if not for the fall of Lordaeron. Now, these farmlands have become the frontlines for the war between the Alliance of the Undead of the Forsaken. Tarren Mill is a Horde town in the northeast with strong connections to the Undercity. Southshore, loyal to the Alliance, is settled in the south, along the river. Tension is high in Hillsbrad itself, to the northwest, and its people are constantly under attack by Undead and Horde troops. There is no escape from this by land, and neither does the sea offer salvation (Sirens and Murlocs wander the strands, settling freely while their enemies fight amongst themselves).

LOCAL RESOURCES

MINING

METAL	AVAILABILITY
Copper	Trivial
Tin	Moderate
Iron	Moderate
Mithril	Trivial

HERBALISM

HERB	AVAILABILITY
Mageroyal	Moderate
Briarthorn	Abundant
Swiftthistle	Abundant
Stranglekelp	Moderate
Bruiseweed	Abundant
Wild Steelbloom	Abundant
Kingsblood	Abundant
Liferoot	Moderate

SKINNING

Quantity of Skinnable Creatures: Abundant

Levels of Skinnable Creatures: 20-31 (Skinning 100-155)

MAP LEGEND

1 SOUTHPOINT TOWER
Deathstalker Lesh 32
Elder Gray Bear 25-26
Forest Moss Creeper 20-21

2 AZURELODE MINE
Elder Gray Bear 25-26
Giant Moss Creeper 25-26
Hillsbrad Foreman 28
Hillsbrad Miner 26-27
Hillsbrad Sentry 27-28
Miner Hackett 29 Quest target

3 WESTERN STRAND
Torn Fin Coastrunner 29-30
Torn Fin Muckdweller 28-29
Torn Fin Oracle 30-31
Torn Fin Tidehunter 31-32

4 HILLSBRAD FIELDS
Hillsbrad Tailor 24 Tailor (Alliance)
Blacksmith Verringtan 26 Quest Target
Blacksmith (Alliance)
Clerk Horace Whitesteed 26 Quest Target
Farmer Ray 23 Quest Target
Forest Moss Creeper 20-21
Gray Bear 21-22
Hillsbrad Apprentice Blacksmith 24-25
Hillsbrad Councilman 25-26
Hillsbrad Farmer 23-24
Hillsbrad Farmhand 22-23
Hillsbrad Footman 25-26
Hillsbrad Peasant 24-25
Magistrate Burnside 30
Starving Mountain Lion 23-24
Vicious Gray Bear 23-24

5 DARROW HILL
Cave Yeti 30-31
Starving Mountain Lion 23-24
Vicious Gray Bear 22-23

6 YETI CAVE
Cave Yeti 30-31

7 SOUTHSHORE
Bartolo Ginsetti 32 Quest
Chef Jessen 35 Quest
Darren Malvew 30 Quest
Innkeeper Anderson 30 Innkeeper
Lieutenant Farren Orinelle 25 Quest
Loremaster Dibbs 30 Quest
Magistrate Henry Maleb 30 Quest
Marshal Redpath 41 Quest
Merideth Carlson 32 Horse Trainer
Phin Odelic 36 Quest
Wesley 30 Stable Master
Snapjaw 30-31
Starving Mountain Lion 23-24
Vicious Gray Bear 22-23

8 TARREN MILL
Apothecary Lydon 35 Quest
Arachne Venomblood 29 Herbalist
Daryl Stack 56 Master Tailor
Deathguard Humbert 32 Quest
Deathguard Samsa 32 Quest
High Executor Darthalia 50 Quest
Innkeeper Shay 30 Innkeeper
Kayren Soothsallow 30
Keeper Bel'varil 34 Quest
Krusk 25 Quest
Magus Wordeen Voidglare 42 Quest
Melisara 25 Quest
Novice Thaivand 30 Quest
Serge Hinnot 32 Expert Alchemist
Tallow 27 Quest
Theodore Mon Claire 30 Stable Master
Zarise 55 Bat Handler
Elder Gray Bear 25-26
Forest Moss Creeper 20-21
Giant Moss Creeper 24-25
Gray Bear 21-22
Snapjaw 30-31

9 DURNHOLDE KEEP
Elder Gray Bear 25-26
Forest Moss Creeper 20-21
Giant Moss Creeper 24-25
Syndicate Rogue 21-22
Syndicate Shadow Mage 21-22
Syndicate Watchman 20-21
Vicious Gray Bear 22-23

10 THORADIN'S WALL
Elder Gray Bear 25-26
Elder Moss Creeper 26-27
Giant Moss Creeper 24-25

11 NETHANDER STEAD
Elder Gray Bear 25-26
Elder Moss Creeper 26-27
Feral Mountain Lion 27-28
Giant Moss Creeper 24-25
Mudsnout Gnoll 26-28
Mudsnout Shaman 27-28
Snapjaw 30-31
Syndicate Rogue 21-22
Syndicate Shadow Mage 21-22
Syndicate Watchman 20-21

12 DUN GAROK
Dun Garok Mountaineer 28-29 Elite
Dun Garok Priest 29-30 Elite
Dun Garok Rifleman 29-30 Elite
Elder Moss Creeper 26-27
Feral Mountain Lion 27-28

13 EASTERN STRAND
Daggerspine Screamer 29-30
Daggerspine Shorehunter 30-31
Daggerspine Shorestalker 29-30
Daggerspine Siren 30

PURGATION ISLE
Judge Thelgram 34 Friendly to Alliance
Cursed Paladin 30-31
Cursed Acolyte 30-31
Condemned Monk 31-32
Writhing Mage 31-32
Cursed Justicar 33
Arados the Damned 35 Quest Target
Condemned Cleric 31-32

QUESTS

QUEST	M LEV	Q LEV	QUEST LAUNCHER	QUEST FINISHER	CHAIN?	XP---	XP--	XP-	XP+	XP++	XP+++	CASH REWARD
Bartolo's Yeti Fur Cloak	29	34	Bartolo Ginsetti	Bartolo Ginsetti	N	270	550	1100	1600	2150	2700	None
REWARD: Yeti Fur Cloak												
Battle of Hillsbrad	19	24	High Executor Darthalia	High Executor Darthalia	Y	200	390	775	1150	1550	1950	17 00
Battle of Hillsbrad	19	25	High Executor Darthalia	High Executor Darthalia	Y	200	400	800	1200	1600	2000	18 00
Battle of Hillsbrad	19	26	High Executor Darthalia	High Executor Darthalia	Y	210	420	850	1250	1700	2100	20 00
Battle of Hillsbrad	19	26	High Executor Darthalia	High Executor Darthalia	Y	210	420	850	1250	1700	2100	20 00
Battle of Hillsbrad	19	28	High Executor Darthalia	High Executor Darthalia	Y	230	460	925	1400	1850	2300	25 00
Battle of Hillsbrad	19	30	High Executor Darthalia	High Executor Darthalia	Y	250	490	975	1450	1950	2450	25 00
Battle of Hillsbrad	19	32	High Executor Darthalia	Varimathras	N	260	500	1000	1550	2050	2550	None
REWARD: Band of the Undercity and CHOICE OF: 1 Sacred Burial Trousers or 1 Deadskull Shield or 1 Runic Darkblade 2H												
Blackmoore's Legacy	29	36	Gol'dir	Krusk	Y	210	420	850	1250	1700	2100	30 00
Bracers of Binding	30	34	Keeper Bel'varil	Keeper Bel'varil	N	270	550	1100	1600	2150	2700	35 00
Costly Menace	30	34	Darren Malvew	Darren Malvew	N	270	550	1100	1600	2150	2700	None
REWARD: Recipe: Tasty Lion Steak, 5 Tasty Lion Steak and CHOICE OF: 1 Shepherd's Girdle or 1 Shepherd's Gloves												
Dalaran Patrols	30	35	Magus Wordeen Voidglare	Magus Wordeen Voidglare	N	210	410	825	1250	1650	2050	25 00
Dangerous!	19	28	Dangerous! (Obj)	High Executor Darthalia	N	230	460	925	1400	1850	2300	None
REWARD: Hooded Cowl and CHOICE OF: 1 Bow of Plunder or 1 Sentry Buckler or 1 Charred Wand												
Down the Coast	25	30	Lieutenant Farren Orinelle	Lieutenant Farren Orinelle	Y	190	370	750	1100	1500	1850	21 00
Elixir of Agony	24	28	Apothecary Lydon	Apothecary Lydon	Y	230	460	925	1400	1850	2300	25 00
REWARD: 3 Swiftness Potion, 5 Healing Potion												
Elixir of Agony	24	28	Apothecary Lydon	Master Apothecary Faranell	Y	120	230	460	700	925	1150	None
Elixir of Agony	24	30	Apothecary Lydon	Dusty Rug (Obj)	N	370	725	1450	2200	2900	3650	None
Elixir of Agony	24	30	Master Apothecary Faranell	Apothecary Lydon	Y	310	600	1200	1850	2450	3050	None
CHOICE OF: 1 High Apothecary Cloak or 1 Meditative Sash												
Elixir of Agony	24	30	Apothecary Lydon	Apothecary Lydon	Y	120	240	480	725	950	1200	None
Elixir of Pain	21	24	Apothecary Lydon	Stanley's Dish (Obj)	N	150	290	575	875	1150	1450	None
Elixir of Pain	21	24	Apothecary Lydon	Apothecary Lydon	Y	200	390	775	1150	1550	1950	None
REWARD: Recipe: Hot Lion Chops and CHOICE OF: 1 Gloves of Brawn or 1 Stomping Boots or 1 Firewalker Boots												
Elixir of Suffering	19	22	Apothecary Lydon	Umpi	N	180	350	700	1050	1400	1750	None
Elixir of Suffering	19	22	Apothecary Lydon	Apothecary Lydon	Y	20	35	70	110	140	180	1 50
Farren's Proof	25	32	Lieutenant Farren Orinelle	Lieutenant Farren Orinelle	Y	260	500	1000	1550	2050	2550	30 00
Farren's Proof	25	32	Lieutenant Farren Orinelle	Marshal Redpath	Y	25	50	100	150	200	260	None
Farren's Proof	25	32	Marshal Redpath	Lieutenant Farren Orinelle	Y	25	50	100	150	200	260	None
Gol'dir	29	36	Krusk	Gol'dir	Y	280	550	1100	1700	2250	2800	None
Helcular's Revenge	29	33	Novice Thaivand	Helcular's Grave (Obj)	N	330	650	1300	2000	2650	3300	None
Helcular's Revenge	29	33	Novice Thaivand	Novice Thaivand	Y	270	525	1050	1600	2100	2650	None
Hints of a New Plague?	30	33	Phin Odelic	Quae	Y	130	260	525	775	1050	1300	None
Hints of a New Plague?	30	36	Quae	Kinelory	N	0	0	0	0	0	0	None
Hints of a New Plague?	30	36	Quae	Quae	Y	280	550	1100	1700	2250	2800	None
Hints of a New Plague?	30	37	Quae	Phin Odelic	N	360	700	1400	2150	2850	3550	None
CHOICE OF: 1 Dustfall Robes or 1 Lightstep Leggings												
Hints of a New Plague?	30	37	Kinelory	Quae	Y	290	575	1150	1700	2300	2850	None
Humbert's Sword	26	30	Deathguard Humbert	Deathguard Humbert	N	310	600	1200	1850	2450	3050	None
CHOICE OF: 1 Ribbed Breastplate or 1 Mercenary Leggings												
In the Name of the Light	34	40	Raleigh the Devout	Raleigh the Devout	N	470	950	1900	2800	3750	4700	None
CHOICE OF: 1 Sword of Serenity or 1 Bonebiter 2H or 1 Black Menace or 1 Orb of Lorica												
Infiltration	29	34	Krusk	Krusk	Y	270	550	1100	1600	2150	2700	35 00
Lord Aliden Perenolde	29	40	Krusk	Elysa	Y	320	625	1250	1900	2500	3150	None
Prison Break In	30	34	Magus Wordeen Voidglare	Magus Wordeen Voidglare	Y	340	675	1350	2000	2700	3350	70 00
Reassignment	25	32	Lieutenant Farren Orinelle	Major Samuelson	N	320	650	1300	1900	2550	3200	None
Soothing Turtle Bisque	28	31	Chef Jessen	Chef Jessen	N	250	500	1000	1500	2000	2500	30 00
REWARD: Recipe: Soothing Turtle Bisque, 3 Soothing Turtle Bisque												
Souvenirs of Death	20	25	Deathguard Samsa	Deathguard Samsa	N	260	500	1000	1550	2050	2550	None
REWARD: Skull Ring												
Stone Tokens	30	32	Keeper Bel'varil	Keeper Bel'varil	N	260	500	1000	1550	2050	2550	30 00
Stormwind Ho!	25	32	Lieutenant Farren Orinelle	Lieutenant Farren Orinelle	Y	200	390	775	1150	1550	1950	None
REWARD: Fish Gutter												
Taretha's Gift	29	40	Elysa	Krusk	N	390	775	1550	2350	3100	3900	None
CHOICE OF: 1 Mantis Boots or 1 Pillager's Pauldrons												
The Crown of Will	34	39	Melisara	Melisara	Y	230	450	900	1350	1800	2250	None
The Crown of Will	34	41	Melisara	Melisara	Y	330	650	1300	2000	2650	3300	None
The Crown of Will	34	43	Melisara	Sharlindra	N	360	725	1450	2150	2900	3600	None
REWARD: Ethereal Talisman												
The Crown of Will	34	43	Melisara	Melisara	Y	450	900	1800	2650	3550	4450	None
The Hammer May Fall	30	32	Tallow	Drum Fel	Y	260	500	1000	1550	2050	2550	30 00
The Rescue	17	22	Krusk	Krusk	N	220	440	875	1300	1750	2200	None
REWARD: Recipe: Big Bear Steak and CHOICE OF: 1 Grunt Vest or 1 Orcish War Chain												
Time To Strike	19	20	Deathstalker Lesh	High Executor Darthalia	N	80	160	310	470	625	775	6 00
WANTED: Baron Vardus	35	40	Wanted Poster (Obj)	High Executor Darthalia	N	320	625	1250	1900	2500	3150	None
REWARD: Inferno Robe												
WANTED: Syndicate Personnel	17	22	Wanted Poster (Obj)	High Executor Darthalia	N	180	350	700	1050	1400	1750	14 00

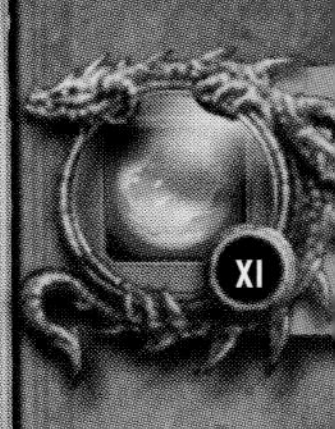

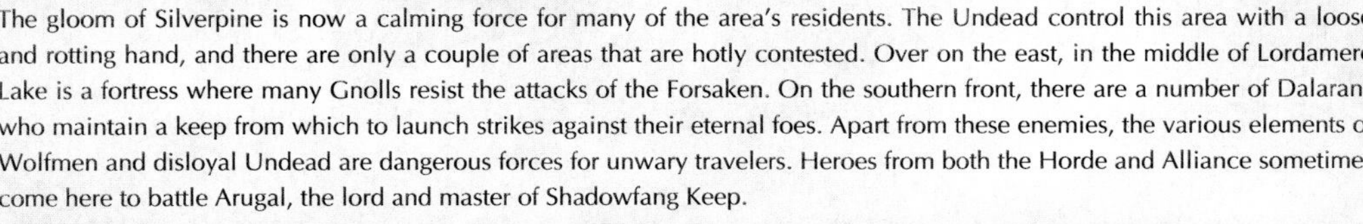

SILVERPINE FOREST

The gloom of Silverpine is now a calming force for many of the area's residents. The Undead control this area with a loose and rotting hand, and there are only a couple of areas that are hotly contested. Over on the east, in the middle of Lordamere Lake is a fortress where many Gnolls resist the attacks of the Forsaken. On the southern front, there are a number of Dalarans who maintain a keep from which to launch strikes against their eternal foes. Apart from these enemies, the various elements of Wolfmen and disloyal Undead are dangerous forces for unwary travelers. Heroes from both the Horde and Alliance sometimes come here to battle Arugal, the lord and master of Shadowfang Keep.

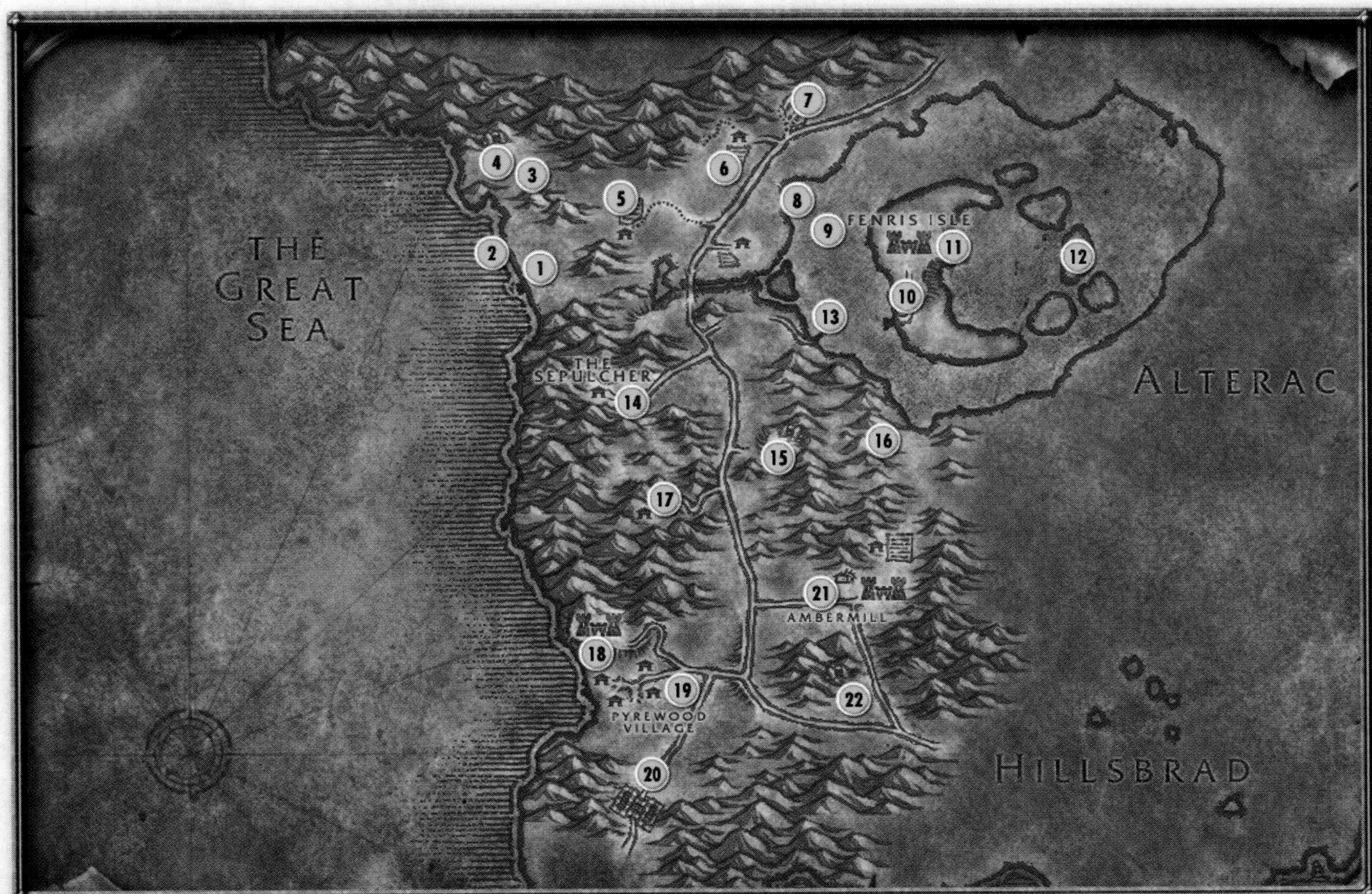

THE GREAT SEA
FENRIS ISLE
THE SEPULCHER
ALTERAC
AMBERMILL
PYREWOOD VILLAGE
HILLSBRAD

LOCAL RESOURCES

MINING

METAL	AVAILABILITY
Copper	Abundant
Tin	Moderate

HERBALISM

HERB	AVAILABILITY
Peacebloom	Abundant
Silverleaf	Abundant
Earthroot	Moderate
Mageroyal	Trivial
Briarthorn	Trivial
Bruiseweed	Trivial

SKINNING

Quantity of Skinnable Creatures: Abundant

Levels of Skinnable Creatures: 10-21 (Skinning 50-105)

MAP LEGEND

1 NORTH TIDE'S HOLLOW
Moonrage Darksoul 13-14
Moonrage Glutton 12-13

2 NORTH TIDE'S RUN
Moonrage Darksoul 13-14
Moonrage Glutton 12-13

3 THE SKITTERING DARK
Giant Grizzled Bear 12-13
Moss Stalker 12-13

4 SKITTERING DARK CAVE
Mist Creeper 13-14
Moss Stalker 12-13

5 THE DEAD FIELD
Ferocious Grizzled Bear 11-12
Giant Grizzled Bear 12-13
Moonrage Glutton 12-13
Mottled Worg 11-12
Nightlash 14 Quest Target
Rothide Gladerunner 11-12
Rothide Mystic 12-13

6 THE IVAR PATCH
Quinn Yorick 14 Quest
Rane Yorick 15 Quest
Mottled Worg 11-12
Ravenclaw Slave 11-12

7 MAIDEN'S ORCHARD
Deathstalker Erland 11 Quest
Mottled Worg 11-12
Worg 10-11

8 THE SHINING STRAND
Vile Fin Shredder 12-13
Vile Fin Tidehunter 13-14

9 LORDAMERE LAKE
Vile Fin Lakestalker 18-19
Vile Fin Oracle 19-20

10 FENRIS ISLE
Elder Lake Skulker 16-17
Lake Skulker 15-16
Rot Hide Brute 16-17
Rot Hide Plague Weaver 17
Rot Hide Savage 18-19
Vile Fin Lakestalker 18-19
Vile Fin Oracle 19-20

11 FENRIS KEEP
Raging Rot Hide 18-19
Rot Hide Savage 18-19

12 THE DAWNING ISLES
Elder Lake Creeper 18-19
Elder Lake Skulker 16-17
Lake Creeper 17-18
Lake Skulker 15-16
Vile Fin Shorecreeper 16-17
Vile Fin Tidecaller 17-18

13 THE DECREPIT FERRY
Fenwick Thatros 16
Hand of Ravenclaw 15-16
Ravenclaw Champion 14-15
Ravenclaw Servant 13-14

14 THE SEPULCHER
Apothecary Renferrel 14 Quest
Dalar Dawnweaver 21 Quest
Guillaume Sorouy 28 Journeyman Blacksmith
High Executor Hadrec 30 Quest
Innkeeper Bates 30 Innkeeper
Johan Focht 19 Miner Trainer
Karos Razok 55 Bat Handler
Sarah Goode 30 Stable Master
Shadow Priest Allistar 20 Quest
Yuriv's Tombstone Quest Target
Ferocious Grizzled Bear 11-12
Moonrage Whitescalp 10-11

15 DEEP ELM MINE
Ferocious Grizzled Bear 11-12
Grimson the Pale 15 Quest Target
Moonrage Darksoul 13-14
Moonrage Glutton 12-13

16 DEEP ELM CANYONS
Dalaran Wizard 19-20
Moonrage Bloodhowler 15-16
Moonrage Darksoul 13-14
Vile Fin Lakestalker 18-19
Vile Fin Oracle 19-20

17 OLSEN'S FARTHING
Ravenclaw Raider 12-13
Ravenclaw Slave 11-12

18 SHADOWFANG KEEP
Entrance to Shadowfang Keep World Dungeon

19 PYREWOOD VILLAGE
Dalaran Apprentice 13-14
Giant Grizzled Bear 12-13
Pyrewood Elder 14-15 Elite
Pyrewood Sentry 15 Elite
Pyrewood Watcher 14 Elite

20 GREYMANE WALL
Bloodsnout Worg 16-17
Haggard Refugee 18-19
Moonrage Bloodhowler 15-16
Sickly Refugee 19-29
Valdred Moray 21 Quest Target

21 AMBERMILL
Archmage Arateic 18 Quest Target
Dalaran Conjurer 17-18
Dalaran Protector 14-15
Dalaran Warder 16-17
Dalaran Watcher 18-19
Dalaran Wizard 19-20

22 BEREN'S PERIL
Dalaran Watcher 18-19
Dalaran Wizard 18-19
Ravenclaw Drudger 19-20
Ravenclaw Guardian 20-21

QUESTS

QUEST	M LEV	Q LEV	QUEST LAUNCHER	QUEST FINISHER	CHAIN?	XP---	XP--	XP-	XP+	XP++	XP+++	CASH REWARD
A Husband's Revenge	10	20	Raleigh Andrean	Raleigh Andrean	N	160	310	625	925	1250	1550	12 00
REWARD: Ring of Scorn												
A Recipe For Death	9	12	Apothecary Renferrel	Master Apothecary Faranell	Y	90	180	360	550	725	900	5 00
REWARD: 5 Senggin Root												
A Recipe For Death	9	15	Master Apothecary Faranell	Apothecary Renferrel	Y	140	270	550	800	1100	1350	14 00
A Recipe For Death	9	18	Apothecary Renferrel	Master Apothecary Faranell	N	210	410	825	1250	1650	2050	None
REWARD: Elixir of Minor Fortitude, Swiftness Potion and CHOICE OF: 1 Nightglow Concoction or 1 Acidproof Cloak												
Ambermill Investigations	10	16	Shadow Priest Allister	Shadow Priest Allister	Y	120	230	460	700	925	1150	8 00
Arugal Must Die	18	27	Dalar Dawnweaver	Dalar Dawnweaver	N	330	650	1300	2000	2650	3300	None
REWARD: Seal of Sylvanas												
Arugal's Folly	9	11	Dalar Dawnweaver	Dalar Dawnweaver	Y	90	180	350	525	700	875	None
Arugal's Folly	9	14	Dalar Dawnweaver	Dalar Dawnweaver	Y	100	200	390	600	775	975	6 00
Arugal's Folly	9	15	Dalar Dawnweaver	Dalar Dawnweaver	N	140	270	550	800	1100	1350	None
CHOICE OF: 1 Logsplitter or 1 Bonegrinding Pestle or 1 Cinder Wand												
Arugal's Folly	9	15	Dalar Dawnweaver	Dalar Dawnweaver	Y	110	210	420	625	850	1050	7 00
Assault on Fenris Isle	10	24	High Executor Hadrec	High Executor Hadrec	N	200	390	775	1150	1550	1950	None
CHOICE OF: 1 High Robe of the Adjudicator or 1 Talonstrike												
Beren's Peril	16	21	Shadow Priest Allister	Shadow Priest Allister	N	130	250	500	750	1000	1250	None
REWARD: Wand of Decay												
Border Crossings	10	14	Shadow Priest Allister	Dalaran Crate (Obj)	Y	100	200	390	600	775	975	None
Dalaran's Intentions	10	14	Dalar Dawnweaver	Shadow Priest Allister	Y	10	20	40	60	80	100	None
Dalar's Analysis	10	14	Shadow Priest Allister	Dalar Dawnweaver	Y	10	20	40	60	80	100	None
Deathstalkers in Shadowfang	18	25	High Executor Hadrec	Deathstalker Vincent	N	200	400	800	1200	1600	2000	18 00
REWARD: Ghostly Mantle												
Escorting Erland	10	11	Deathstalker Erland	Rane Yorick	Y	90	180	350	525	700	875	None
REWARD: Deathstalker Shortsword												
Ivar the Foul	10	12	Rane Yorick	Rane Yorick	N	70	140	270	410	550	675	3 50
CHOICE OF: 1 Quilted Bracers or 1 Weathered Belt												
Journey to Hillsbrad Foothills	19	20	Apothecary Renferrel	Apothecary Lydon	N	120	230	460	700	925	1150	9 00
Lost Deathstalkers	10	12	High Executor Hadrec	Rane Yorick	Y	25	45	90	140	180	230	None
Maps and Runes	10	14	Dalaran Crate (Obj)	Shadow Priest Allister	Y	75	150	300	440	600	750	5 00
Prove Your Worth	9	10	Dalar Dawnweaver	Dalar Dawnweaver	Y	85	170	340	500	675	850	3 50
Pyrewood Ambush	12	15	Deathstalker Faerleia	Deathstalker Faerleia	N	140	270	550	800	1100	1350	14 00
CHOICE OF: 1 Faerleia's Shield or 1 Stretched Leather Trousers or 1 Mystic Shawl												
Raleigh and the Undercity	10	16	Magistrate Sevren	Raleigh Andrean	Y	60	120	230	350	460	575	None
Report to Hadrec	10	16	Apothecary Renferrel	High Executor Hadrec	Y	60	120	230	350	460	575	None
REWARD: Medium Armor Kit and CHOICE OF: 5 Coarse Weightstone or 5 Coarse Sharpening Stone												
Return to Quinn	10	11	Apothecary Renferrel	Quinn Yorick	N	65	130	260	400	525	650	None
Rot Hide Clues	10	16	Corpse Laden Boat (Obj)	High Executor Hadrec	Y	30	60	120	170	230	290	None
Rot Hide Ichor	10	17	High Executor Hadrec	Apothecary Renferrel	Y	130	250	500	750	1000	1250	9 00
Rot Hide Origins	10	17	Apothecary Renferrel	Bethor Iceshard	N	30	65	130	190	250	320	None
Speak with Renferrel	10	12	High Executor Hadrec	Apothecary Renferrel	Y	10	20	35	55	70	90	None
The Dead Fields	10	14	High Executor Hadrec	High Executor Hadrec	Y	100	200	390	600	775	975	6 00
REWARD: Reconnaissance Boots												
The Deathstalkers' Report	10	11	Rane Yorick	High Executor Hadrec	Y	45	90	180	260	350	440	2 00
The Decrepit Ferry	10	16	High Executor Hadrec	Corpse Laden Boat (Obj)	Y	90	180	350	525	700	875	None
The Engraved Ring	10	16	High Executor Hadrec	Magistrate Sevren	Y	60	120	230	350	460	575	None
The Hidden Niche	12	18	Shallow Grave (Obj)	Dusty Shelf (Obj)	Y	70	140	270	410	550	675	5 00
The Weaver	10	22	Shadow Priest Allister	Shadow Priest Allister	N	180	350	700	1050	1400	1750	None
CHOICE OF: 1 Ceranium Rod or 1 Camouflaged Tunic												
Thule Ravenclaw	10	16	Bethor Iceshard	Apothecary Renferrel	Y	30	60	120	170	230	290	None
REWARD: Bethor's Potion												
Wand to Bethor	12	18	Dusty Shelf (Obj)	Bethor Iceshard	N	170	340	675	1000	1350	1700	None
CHOICE OF: 1 Stamped Trousers or 1 Rugged Mail Gloves or 1 Serrated Knife												
Wild Hearts	10	11	Rane Yorick	Apothecary Renferrel	Y	45	90	180	260	350	440	None
REWARD: Recipe: Discolored Healing Potion, Discolored Healing Potion												

THE HINTERLANDS

In the far northeast is a land that is almost forgotten by those who fight for survival throughout the Eastern Kingdoms. The Hinterlands is an expanse of pine trees and valleys where Wolves, Owlbeasts, and even Dragonkin live. On the southern ridgeline are many outposts of Trolls, all powerful and very much steeped in a bloody philosophy that even divides them from the Horde's Trolls. Along the northwest end are Dwarves and Elves who also live on their own, apart from the aid or interference of the Alliance. Hunting up in Hinterlands is usually safe and quiet, making it a place beloved by crafters throughout the world.

LOCAL RESOURCES

MINING

METAL	AVAILABILITY
Iron	Trivial
Mithril	Abundant

HERBALISM

HERB	AVAILABILITY
Goldthorn	Moderate
Khadgar's Whiskers	Moderate
Sungrass	Abundant

SKINNING

Quantity of Skinnable Creatures: Abundant

Levels of Skinnable Creatures: 40-49 (Skinning 200-245)

MAP LEGEND

1 AERIE PEAK
Falstad Wildhammer 50
Killium Bouldertug 50 Stable Master
Wildhammer Sentry 55
Mangy Silvermane 41-42
Razorbeak Gryphon 45
Trained Razorbeak 40-41

2 HIRI'WATHA
Witherbark Hideskinner 42-43
Witherbark Venomblood 43

3 QUEL'DANIL LODGE
Highvale Marksman 45-46
Highvale Outrunner 43-44
Highvale Ranger 46-47
Highvale Scout 44-45

4 AGOL'WATHA
Cerulean Dragonspawn 48-49
Green Sludge 46-47
Jade Ooze 48
Primitive Owlbeast 44

5 SKULK ROCK
Green Sludge 46-47
Jade Ooze 47-48
Savage Owlbeast 46-47

6 SERADANE

7 JINTHA'ALOR
Silvermane Stalker 47-48
Vilebranch Warrior 46 Elite
Vilebranch Witch Doctor 46-47 Elite

8 SHAOL'WATHA
Silvermane Stalker 47-48

9 THE TEMPLE OF ZUL
Morta'Gya The Keeper 50 Elite
Qiaga The Keeper 52 Elite Quest Target
Vilebrach Soothsayer 47
Vilebranch Axe Thrower 46
Vilebranch Scalper 47
Vilebranch Wolf Pup 46-47

10 VALORWIND LAKE
Primitive Owlbeast 44-45
Razorbeak Gryphon 45
Silvermane Howler 46

11 THE CREEPING RUIN
Green Sludge 46-47
Jade Ooze 48

12 SHADRA'ALOR
Atal'ai Exile 45 Quest
Witherbark Broodguard 44-45
Witherbark Caller 45-46
Witherbark Sadist 44-45

13 THE OVERLOOK CLIFFS
Gammerita 48 Elite Quest Target
Saltwater Snapjaw 49-50

QUESTS

QUEST	M LEV	Q LEV	QUEST LAUNCHER	QUEST FINISHER	CHAIN?	XP---	XP--	XP-	XP+	XP++	XP+++	CASH REWARD
Consult Master Gadrin	40	45	Apothecary Lydon	Master Gadrin	Y	290	575	1150	1750	2300	2900	None
Grim Message	35	42	Nimboya	Nimboya	N	350	700	1400	2050	2750	3450	55 00
Gryphon Master Talonaxe	38	43	Falstad Wildhammer	Gryphon Master Talonaxe	Y	90	180	360	525	700	900	None
Jammal'an the Prophet	38	53	Atal'ai Exile	Atal'ai Exile	N	650	1300	2600	3950	5250	6550	None
CHOICE OF: 1 Rainstrider Leggings or 1 Helm of Exile												
Nekrum's Medallion	40	47	Thadius Grimshade	Thadius Grimshade	Y	525	1050	2100	3150	4200	5250	70 00
Rescue OOX-09/HL!	43	48	Homing Robot OOX-09/HL	Oglethorpe Obnoticus	N	550	1100	2200	3250	4350	5450	None
CHOICE OF: 1 Gnomish Inventor Boots or 1 Gnomish Water Sinking Device												
Return to Fel'Zerul	38	44	Atal'ai Exile	Fel'zerul	Y	380	750	1500	2250	3000	3750	None
Return to the Hinterlands	40	47	Thadius Grimshade	Gryphon Master Talonaxe	Y	210	420	850	1250	1700	2100	None
Rhapsody Shindigger	38	43	Gryphon Master Talonaxe	Rhapsody Shindigger	Y	180	360	725	1100	1450	1800	None
Rhapsody's Kalimdor Kocktail	38	43	Rhapsody Shindigger	Rhapsody Shindigger	N	360	725	1450	2150	2900	3600	None
Rhapsody's Tale	38	43	Rhapsody Shindigger	Brohann Caskbelly	Y	270	550	1100	1600	2150	2700	None
Rin'ji is Trapped!	42	47	Rin'ji	Rin'ji's Secret (Obj)	Y	420	850	1700	2500	3350	4200	None
Rin'ji's Secret	42	47	Rin'ji's Secret (Obj)	Oran Snakewrithe	N	210	420	850	1250	1700	2100	None
Saving Sharpbeak	40	53	Gryphon Master Talonaxe	Gryphon Master Talonaxe	N	800	1600	3150	4750	6300	7900	2 40 00
CHOICE OF: 1 Gryphon Rider's Stormhammer or 1 Gryphon Rider's Leggings												
Skulk Rock Clean-up	40	48	Fraggar Thundermantle	Fraggar Thundermantle	N	440	875	1750	2650	3500	4400	50 00
Summoning Shadra	40	50	Master Gadrin	Apothecary Lydon	N	700	1400	2850	4250	5700	7100	None
Thadius Grimshade	40	47	Gryphon Master Talonaxe	Thadius Grimshade	Y	210	420	850	1250	1700	2100	None
The Altar of Zul	40	48	Gryphon Master Talonaxe	Gryphon Master Talonaxe	Y	440	875	1750	2650	3500	4400	None
The Ancient Egg	40	50	Yeh'kinya	Yeh'kinya	Y	600	1200	2350	3550	4700	5900	None
The Divination	40	47	Thadius Grimshade	Thadius Grimshade	Y	110	210	420	625	850	1050	None
Troll Necklace Bounty	40	45	Fraggar Thundermantle	Fraggar Thundermantle	N	40	80	160	230	310	390	None
Troll Necklace Bounty	40	45	Fraggar Thundermantle	Fraggar Thundermantle	N	390	775	1550	2350	3100	3900	65 00
Undamaged Venom Sac	40	45	Apothecary Lydon	Apothecary Lydon	Y	390	775	1550	2350	3100	3900	None
Venom Bottles	40	43	Venom Bottle (Obj)	Apothecary Lydon	Y	360	725	1450	2150	2900	3600	None
Venom to the Undercity	40	55	Apothecary Lydon	Master Apothecary Faranell	N	850	1700	3400	5050	6750	8450	2 50 00
CHOICE OF: 1 Royal Highmark Vestments or 1 Honorguard Chestpiece or 1 Aegis of Battle												
Witherbark Cages	40	45	Gryphon Master Talonaxe	Gryphon Master Talonaxe	Y	390	775	1550	2350	3100	3900	None

TIRISFAL GLADES

Tirisfal Glades has seen the ravages of plague and the Scourge. The once vibrant villages and grand city of Lordaeron lay in ruins. Remnants of the Scourge still roam the land and the Undead who have awakened of their own free will are hunted by the Scarlet Crusade. Murlocs infect the northern shore and Rothide Gnolls have been seen taking over a farmstead just south of it. It is a land in constant turmoil.

LOCAL RESOURCES

MINING

METAL	AVAILABILITY
Copper	Abundant

HERBALISM

HERB	AVAILABILITY
Peacebloom	Abundant
Silverleaf	Abundant
Earthroot	Common

SKINNING

Quantity of Skinnable Creatures: Abundant

Levels of Skinnable Creatures: 1-10 (Skinning 1-50)

MAP LEGEND

1 DEATHKNELL
Undertaker Mordo 5 Quest
Executor Arren 5 Quest
Deathguard Saltain 75 Quest
Duskbat 1-2
Young Scavenger 1-2
Wretched Zombie 1-2
Mindless Zombie 1-2
Rattlecage Skeleton 2-3
Mangy Duskbat 3-4
Ragged Scavenger 2-3
Scarlet Convert 3
Mevin Korgal 5
Calvin Montague 5 Quest

2 NIGHT WEB'S HOLLOW
Young Night Web Spider 2-3
Night Web Spider 3-4

3 SOLLIDEN FARMSTEAD
Deathguard Simmer 23 Quest
Greater Duskbat 6-7
Decrepit Darkhound 5-6
Tirisfal Farmhand 5-6
Tirisfal Farmer 7
Scarlet Warrior 6-7

4 NIGHTMARE VALE
Decrepit Hound 5-6
Greater Duskbat 6-7
Cursed Darkhound 7-8
Scarlet Zealot 8-9
Scarlet Missionary 7-8
Captain Perrine 9

5 STILLWATER POND
Decrepit Darkhound 5-6
Cursed Darkhound 7-8
Greater Duskbat 6-7
Rotting Dead 5- 6
Ravaged Corpse 6-7

6 AGAMAND MILLS
Cursed Darkhound 7-8
Rattlecage Soldier 6-7
Lost Soul 6
Devlin Agamand 9
Darkbone Caster 7-8
Cracked Skull Soldier 8-9
Nissa Agamand 10
Thurman Agamand 10
Gregor Agamand 10
Rotting Ancestor 10-11
Wailing Ancestor 9-11

7 COLD HEARTH MANOR
Bowen Brisboi 24 Journeyman Tailor
Ravaged Corpse 6-7
Rotting Dead 5-6
Vampiric Duskbat 8-9
Cursed Darkhound 7-8
Greater Duskbat 6-7

8 BRILL
Deathguard Dillinger 22 Quest
Junior Apothecary Holland 20 Quest
Faruza 5 Apprentice Herbalist
Morganus 30 Stable Master
Zachariah Post 30 Undead Horse Merchant
Velma Warnam 30 Undead Horse Riding Instructor
Executor Zygand 14 Quest
Eliza Callen 12 Leather Armor Merchant
Abigail Shiel 9 Trade Supplies
Mrs. Winters 10 General Supplies
Selina Weston 12 Alchemy & Herbalism Supplies

9 GARREN'S HAUNT
Rot Hide Gnoll 6-7
Rot Hide Graverobber 6-7
Rot Hide Mongrel 7-8
Maggot Eye 10

10 RUINS OF LORDAERON

11 UNDERCITY

12 BRIGHTWATER LAKE
Clyde Kellen 16 Fisherman
Cursed Darkhound 7-8
Vampiric Duskbat 8-9

13 BALNIR FARMSTEAD
Cursed Darkhound 7-8
Vampiric Bat 8-9
Bleeding Horror 9-11
Wandering Spirit 10-11

14 THE BULWARK
Argent Quartermaster Hasana 58 Quest
Argent Officer Garush 60 Quest
High Executor Derrington 61 Quest
Apothecary Dithers 58 Quest
Shadow Priestess Vandis 60 Quest
Alexi Barov 60 Quest

15 CRUSADER OUTPOST
Scarlet Zealot 8-9
Scarlet Friar 9-10
Captain Vachon 11

16 VENOMWEB VALE
Vampiric Duskbat 8-9
Ravenous Darkhound 9-10
Vicious Nightweb Spider 9-10

17 FAOL'S REST
Ravenous Darkhound 9-10

18 WHISPERING GARDENS-ENTRANCE TO SCARLET MONASTERY INSTANCE
Scarlet Scout 29-30+
Scarlet Magician 29-30+
Scarlet Preserver 29-30+

19 SCARLET WATCH POST
Scarlet Friar 9-10
Scarlet Vanguard 10-11
Scarlet Bodyguard 10-11
Scarlet Neophyte 10-11
Captain Melrache 12

20 ZEPPLIN TO ORGRIMMAR AND GROM'GOL-OUTPOST
Deathguard Linnea 22 Quest
Shelene Rhobart 25 Jouneyman Leatherworker
Rand Rhobart 13 Skinner
Martine Tramblay 15 Fishing Supplies

21 NORTH COAST
Vile Fin Minor Oracle 9-9
Vile Fin Puddlejumper 7-8
Vile Fin Muckdweller 9-10

22 GUNTHER'S RETREAT
Gunther Arcanus 53 Quest
Shambling Horror 7-8
Hungering Dead 7-8
Gunther's Minion 7-8

QUEST	M LEV	Q LEV	QUEST LAUNCHER	QUEST FINISHER	CHAIN?	XP---	XP--	XP-	XP+	XP++	XP+++	CASH REWARD
A New Plague	6	6	Apothecary Johaan	Apothecary Johaan	Y	55	110	220	320	430	550	1 25
REWARD: 3 Weak Troll's Blood Potion												
A New Plague	6	9	Apothecary Johaan	Apothecary Johaan	Y	80	160	310	470	625	775	3 00
REWARD: 5 Slumber Sand												
A New Plague	6	11	Apothecary Johaan	Captured Mountaineer	N	90	180	350	525	700	875	None
A New Plague	6	11	Apothecary Johaan	Apothecary Johaan	Y	20	45	90	130	180	220	None
REWARD: Apprentice Sash												
A Plague Upon Thee	48	55	Mickey Levine	Mickey Levine	N	575	1150	2250	3400	4500	5650	85 00
A Plague Upon Thee	48	55	Mickey Levine	Mickey Levine	Y	575	1150	2250	3400	4500	5650	85 00
A Putrid Task	4	6	Deathguard Dillinger	Deathguard Dillinger	N	40	80	160	240	320	410	1 00
A Rogue's Deal	1	5	Calvin Montague	Innkeeper Renee	N	10	20	45	65	90	110	None
CHOICE OF: 5 Forest Mushroom Cap or 5 Refreshing Spring Water												
A Rogue's Deal	1	5		Innkeeper Renee	N	10	20	45	65	90	110	None
CHOICE OF: 5 Forest Mushroom Cap or 5 Refreshing Spring Water												
A Rogue's Deal	1	5	Calvin Montague	Calvin Montague	N	10	20	45	65	90	110	25
At War With The Scarlet Crusade	5	8	Executor Zygand	Executor Zygand	Y	70	140	280	420	550	700	2 25
At War With The Scarlet Crusade	5	9	Executor Zygand	Executor Zygand	Y	80	160	310	470	625	775	3 00
At War With The Scarlet Crusade	5	10	Executor Zygand	Executor Zygand	Y	85	170	340	500	675	850	3 50
At War With The Scarlet Crusade	5	12	Executor Zygand	Executor Zygand	N	90	180	360	550	725	900	None
CHOICE OF: 1 Ceremonial Knife or 1 Striking Hatchet												
Candles of Beckoning	5	10	Crate of Candles (Obj)	Crate of Candles (Obj)	N	0	0	0	0	0	0	None
REWARD: Candle of Beckoning												
Deaths in the Family	7	11	Coleman Farthing	Coleman Farthing	N	90	180	350	525	700	875	4 00
Delivery to Silverpine Forest	9	10	Apothecary Johaan	Apothecary Renferrel	N	65	130	250	380	500	625	2 50
Doom Weed	5	6	Junior Apothecary Holland	Junior Apothecary Holland	N	55	110	220	320	430	550	1 25
Fields of Grief	4	7	Apothecary Johaan	Captured Scarlet Zealot	N	15	30	65	95	130	160	None
Fields of Grief	4	7	Deathguard Simmer	Apothecary Johaan	Y	65	130	250	380	500	625	1 75
Forsaken Duties	6	9	Magistrate Sevren	Deathguard Linnea	Y	20	40	80	120	160	200	None
Gordo's Task	5	5	Gordo	Junior Apothecary Holland	Y	25	45	90	140	180	230	None
Graverobbers	4	8	Magistrate Sevren	Magistrate Sevren	N	70	140	280	420	550	700	2 25
CHOICE OF: 1 Cold Steel Gauntlets or 1 Zombie Skin Boots												
Night Web's Hollow	2	4	Executor Arren	Executor Arren	Y	35	70	140	210	280	360	None
CHOICE OF: 1 Flax Vest or 1 Rugged Mail Vest or 1 Zombie Skin Leggings												
Proof of Demise	5	7	Deathguard Burgess	Deathguard Burgess	N	65	130	250	380	500	625	1 75
CHOICE OF: 1 Zombie Skin Bracers or 1 Clasped Belt or 1 Netted Gloves												
Proving Allegiance	5	12	Gunther Arcanus	Gunther Arcanus	Y	70	140	270	410	550	675	None
Rattling the Rattlecages	1	3	Shadow Priest Sarvis	Shadow Priest Sarvis	N	25	50	100	150	200	250	None
CHOICE OF: 1 Flax Boots or 1 Scavenger Tunic or 1 Roamer's Leggings												
Rear Guard Patrol	6	11	Deathguard Linnea	Deathguard Linnea	N	65	130	260	400	525	650	3 00
Return the Book	5	8	Bethor Iceshard	Gunther Arcanus	Y	35	70	140	210	280	350	None
Return to the Magistrate	6	9	Deathguard Linnea	Magistrate Sevren	N	40	80	160	230	310	390	1 50
Rude Awakening	1	1	Undertaker Mordo	Shadow Priest Sarvis	Y	5	10	15	25	30	40	None
Scavenging Deathknell	2	3	Deathguard Saltain	Deathguard Saltain	N	30	65	130	190	250	320	None
CHOICE OF: 1 Flax Belt or 1 Rustmetal Bracers or 1 Short Duskbat Cape												
Speak with Sevren	7	10	Coleman Farthing	Magistrate Sevren	Y	10	15	35	50	70	85	None
The Chill of Death	7	8	Gretchen Dedmar	Gretchen Dedmar	N	70	140	280	420	550	700	2 25
CHOICE OF: 1 Adept's Cloak or 1 Sewing Gloves												
The Damned	1	2	Novice Elreth	Novice Elreth	N	15	35	70	100	140	170	None
CHOICE OF: 1 Flax Bracers or 1 Old Leather Belt												
The Dormant Shade	5	10	Lillith's Dinner Table (Obj)	Lillith's Dinner Table (Obj)	N	0	0	0	0	0	0	None
The Family Crypt	7	13	Magistrate Sevren	Magistrate Sevren	N	90	180	360	550	725	900	None
CHOICE OF: 1 Darkwood Staff or 1 Bonecracker												
The Haunted Mills	7	10	Coleman Farthing	Coleman Farthing	N	40	85	170	250	340	420	None
The Mills Overrun	6	8	Deathguard Dillinger	Deathguard Dillinger	N	90	180	350	525	700	875	4 50
CHOICE OF: 1 Cryptwalker Boots or 1 Sturdy Cloth Trousers												
The Mindless Ones	1	2	Shadow Priest Sarvis	Shadow Priest Sarvis	N	15	35	70	100	140	170	None
CHOICE OF: 1 Flax Gloves or 1 Battered Cloak												
The Prodigal Lich	5	8	Magistrate Sevren	Bethor Iceshard	Y	20	35	70	110	140	180	None
The Prodigal Lich Returns	5	12	Gunther Arcanus	Bethor Iceshard	N	90	180	360	550	725	900	5 00
REWARD: Bone Buckler												
The Red Messenger	2	5	Executor Arren	Executor Arren	Y	65	130	270	400	525	675	None
CHOICE OF: 1 Executor Staff or 1 Deathguard Buckler												
The Scarlet Crusade	2	4	Executor Arren	Executor Arren	Y	35	70	140	210	280	360	None
REWARD: 5 Refreshing Spring Water and CHOICE OF: 1 Forsaken Dagger or 1 Forsaken Maul or 1 Forsaken Shortsword or 1 Forsaken Bastard Sword												
Vital Intelligence	2	5	Executor Arren	Executor Zygand	N	35	65	130	200	270	340	75
Wanted: Maggot Eye	6	10	Wanted! (Obj)	Executor Zygand	N	85	170	340	500	675	850	3 50
CHOICE OF: 1 Brass Scale Pants or 1 Tiller's Vest												

XI

THE WESTERN PLAGUELANDS

Above the Alterac Mountains is the entrance to the Western Plaguelands. Tainted beasts, vicious Humans from the Scarlet Crusade, and a number of Scourge Undead live there. Cauldrons of bubbling liquids are guarded by the mindless dead. The Horde and the Alliance, so seldom to agree on matters, are both at war with the dangers posed by the Scourge, and this is the frontline of that battle. To the east is Darrowmere Lake, where Scholomance sits quietly in a deserted town. Walk here not, lest your group face trials of epic and deadly proportions.

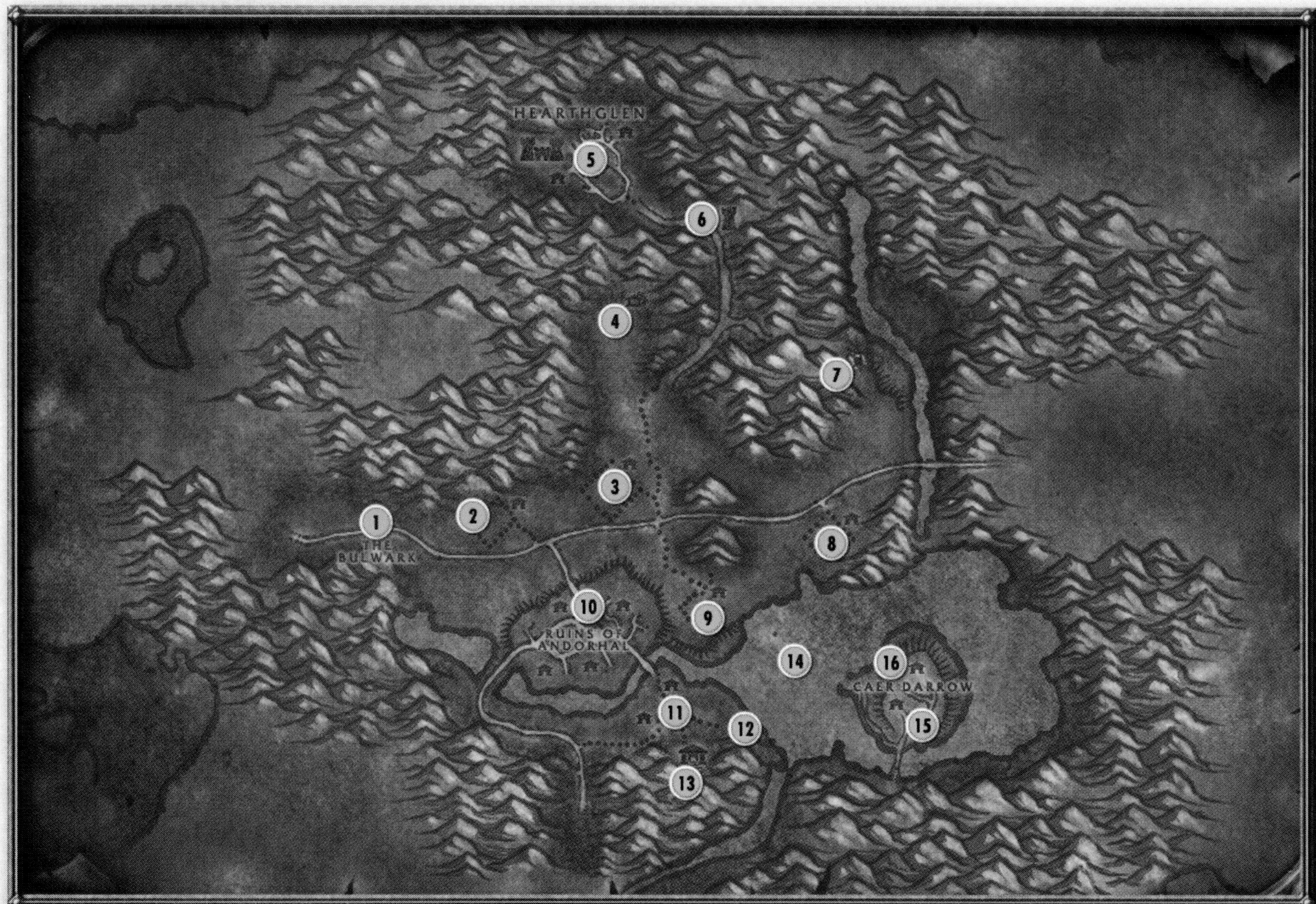

LOCAL RESOURCES

MINING: NONE

HERBS: NONE

SKINNING

Quantity of Skinnable Creatures: Trivial

Levels of Skinnable Creatures: 51-54 (Skinning 255-270)

MAP LEGEND

1 THE BULWARK
- Carrion Vultures 52-53
- Diseased Black Bears 51-52
- Venom Mist Lurkers 51-52

2 FELSTONE FIELDS
- Scarlet Hound 52-54
- Scarlet Hunter 52-54
- Scarlet Ivoker 52-54
- Scarlet Medic 52-54
- Skelatal Flayer 50-52
- Skeletal Sorcerer 50-52
- Slavering Ghoul 50-52

3 DALSON'S TEARS
- Blighted Zombie 52-54
- Carrion Lurker 53-54
- Diseased Wolf 53-54
- Rotting Cadaver 52-54
- Skeletal Terror 52-54

4 NORTHRIDGE LUMBER
- Carrion Lurker 56-57
- Scarlet Knight 54-56
- Scarlet Lumberjack 54-56

5 HEARTHGLEN
- Foremen Jerris 62 Elite
- High Protector Lorik 61 Elite
- Scarlet Paladin 55-56 Elite
- Scarlet Priest 56-57 Elite
- Scarlet Sentinel 55-56 Elite
- Scarlet Worker 55-57 Elite

6 SCARLET TOWER
- High Clerist 63 Elite
- Scarlet Avenger 56-57
- Scarlet Knight 54-55
- Scarlet Mage 55-56
- Scarlet Spellbinder 57-58

7 THE WEEPING CAVE
- Decaying Horror 55-56
- Devouring Ooze 55-56
- Plague Lurker 54-55
- Rotting Behemoth 55-56
- Vile Slime 54-55

8 GAHRRON'S WITHERING
- Hungering Wraith 56-58
- Plague Lurkers 54-55
- Taunting Vision 56-58
- Waling Death 56-58

9 THE WRITHING HAUNT
- Fetid Zombie 55-56
- Freezing Ghoul 55-56
- Plague Lurker 54-55
- Rotting Ghoul 55-56

10 RUINS OF ANDERHOL
- Cold Wraith 54-56 Elite
- Decrepit Guardian 56-57 Elite
- Flesh Golem 56-57 Elite
- Screaming Haunt 54-56 Elite
- Searing Ghoul 54-56 Elite
- Skeletal Acolyte 54-56 Elite
- Skeletal Executioner 55-56 Elite
- Skeletal Warlord 55-56 Elite
- Soulless Ghoul 54-56 Elite

11 SORROW HILL
- Skeletal Flayers 50-51
- Slavering Ghouls 50-51

12 UTHER'S TOMB
- High Priest Thel'Danis 65

13 SORROW HILL (CRYPT)
- Lord Maldazzar
- Skeletal Flayers 50-51
- Skeletal Sorcerer 51-52
- Slavering Ghouls 50-51

14 DARROWMERE LAKE

15 CAER DARROW

16 ENTRANCE TO SCHOLOMANCE WORLD DUNGEON

QUESTS

QUEST	M LEV	Q LEV	QUEST LAUNCHER	QUEST FINISHER	CHAIN?	XP---	XP--	XP-	XP+	XP++	XP+++	CASH REWARD
A Call to Arms: The Plaguelands!	50	50	Warcaller Gorlach	High Executor Derrington	Y	45	95	190	280	380	470	None
A Call to Arms: The Plaguelands!	50	50	Harbinger Balthazad	High Executor Derrington	Y	45	95	190	280	380	470	None
A Call to Arms: The Plaguelands!	50	50	Bluff Runner Windstrider	High Executor Derrington	Y	45	95	190	280	380	470	None
A Matter of Time	53	56	Chromie	Chromie	N	575	1150	2300	3500	4650	5800	None
CHOICE OF: 1 Orchid Amice or 1 Gold Link Belt												
A Plague Upon Thee	48	55	Nathaniel Dumah	Nathaniel Dumah	N	575	1150	2250	3400	4500	5650	85 00
A Plague Upon Thee	48	55	Nathaniel Dumah	Nathaniel Dumah	Y	575	1150	2250	3400	4500	5650	85 00
All Along the Watchtowers	50	56	Commander Ashlam Valorfist	Commander Ashlam Valorfist	N	575	1150	2300	3500	4650	5800	85 00
All Along the Watchtowers	50	56	High Executor Derrington	High Executor Derrington	N	575	1150	2300	3500	4650	5800	85 00
Araj's Scarab	55	60	Alchemist Arbington	Alchemist Arbington	N	500	1000	2000	2950	3950	4950	None
Araj's Scarab	55	60	Apothecary Dithers	Apothecary Dithers	N	500	1000	2000	2950	3950	4950	None
Argent Dawn Commission	50	55	Argent Officer Pureheart	Argent Officer Pureheart	N	55	110	220	340	450	550	None
REWARD: Argent Dawn Commission												
Argent Dawn Commission	50	55	Argent Officer Garush	Argent Officer Garush	N	55	110	220	340	450	550	None
REWARD: Argent Dawn Commission												
Better Late Than Never	50	52	Janice Felstone	Janice's Parcel (Obj)	N	260	500	1000	1550	2050	2550	None
Better Late Than Never	50	52	Janice's Parcel (Obj)	Royal Factor Bathrilor	Y	260	500	1000	1550	2050	2550	None
Better Late Than Never	50	52	Janice's Parcel (Obj)	Royal Overseer Bauhaus	Y	260	500	1000	1550	2050	2550	None
Blood Tinged Skies	52	56	Tirion Fordring	Tirion Fordring	N	575	1150	2300	3500	4650	5800	None
Blood Tinged Skies	52	56	Lord Tirion Fordring	Tirion Fordring	N	575	1150	2300	3500	4650	5800	None
Breastplate of the Chromatic Flight	57	62	Catalogue of the Wayward (Obj)	Jeziba	N	1050	2100	4200	6350	8450	10550	None
REWARD: Breastplate of the Chromatic Flight												
Carrion Grubbage	52	56	Tirion Fordring	Tirion Fordring	N	575	1150	2300	3500	4650	5800	None
Carrion Grubbage	52	56	Lord Tirion Fordring	Tirion Fordring	N	575	1150	2300	3500	4650	5800	None
Catalogue of the Wayward	57	62	Jeziba	Catalogue of the Wayward (Obj)	N	70	140	280	420	550	700	None
Clear the Way	50	52	Commander Ashlam Valorfist	Commander Ashlam Valorfist	N	500	1000	2050	3050	4100	5100	75 00
Corruptor's Scourgestones	50	55	Argent Officer Pureheart	Argent Officer Pureheart	N	55	110	220	340	450	550	None
REWARD: Argent Dawn Valor Token												
Corruptor's Scourgestones	50	55	Argent Officer Garush	Argent Officer Garush	N	55	110	220	340	450	550	None
REWARD: Argent Dawn Valor Token												
Counting Out Time	53	56	Chromie	Chromie	N	575	1150	2300	3500	4650	5800	None
REWARD: Attuned Dampener												
Counting Out Time	53	56	Chromie	Chromie	N	60	120	230	350	460	575	None
REWARD: Attuned Dampener												
Dalson's Tears Cauldron	50	55	Scourge Cauldron (Obj)	Scourge Cauldron (Obj)	N	55	110	220	340	450	550	None
Demon Dogs	52	56	Tirion Fordring	Tirion Fordring	N	575	1150	2300	3500	4650	5800	None
Demon Dogs	52	56	Lord Tirion Fordring	Tirion Fordring	N	575	1150	2300	3500	4650	5800	None
Felstone Field Cauldron	50	53	Scourge Cauldron (Obj)	Scourge Cauldron (Obj)	N	55	110	210	320	420	525	None
Gahrron's Withering Cauldron	50	58	Scourge Cauldron (Obj)	Scourge Cauldron (Obj)	N	60	120	250	370	500	625	None
Glyphed Oaken Branch	51	56	Mulgris Deepriver	Mathrengyl Bearwalker	N	575	1150	2300	3500	4650	5800	None
REWARD: Cerise Drape												
Glyphed Oaken Branch	51	56	Mulgris Deepriver	Nara Wildmane	N	575	1150	2300	3500	4650	5800	None
REWARD: Cerise Drape												

QUEST	M LEV	Q LEV	QUEST LAUNCHER	QUEST FINISHER	CHAIN?	XP---	XP--	XP-	XP+	XP++	XP+++	CASH REWARD
Good Luck Charm	50	52	Ol' Emma	Janice Felstone	Y	260	500	1000	1550	2050	2550	None
Good Luck Charm	50	52	Jeremiah Payson	Janice Felstone	Y	260	500	1000	1550	2050	2550	None
Invader's Scourgestones	50	55	Argent Officer Pureheart	Argent Officer Pureheart	N	55	110	220	340	450	550	None
REWARD: Argent Dawn Valor Token												
Invader's Scourgestones	50	55	Argent Officer Garush	Argent Officer Garush	N	55	110	220	340	450	550	None
REWARD: Argent Dawn Valor Token												
Legplates of the Chromatic Defier	57	62	Catalogue of the Wayward (Obj)	Jeziba	N	1050	2100	4200	6350	8450	10550	None
CHOICE OF: 1 Legguards of the Chromatic Defier or 1 Legplates of the Chromatic Defier												
Locked Away	52	55	Locked Cabinet (Obj)	Locked Cabinet (Obj)	N	700	1400	2800	4250	5650	7050	2 50 00
REWARD: Farmer Dalson's Shotgun, Dalson Family Wedding Ring												
Locked Away	52	55	Outhouse (Obj)	Outhouse (Obj)	N	0	0	0	0	0	0	None
Minion's Scourgestones	50	55	Argent Officer Pureheart	Argent Officer Pureheart	N	55	110	220	340	450	550	None
REWARD: Argent Dawn Valor Token												
Minion's Scourgestones	50	55	Argent Officer Garush	Argent Officer Garush	N	55	110	220	340	450	550	None
REWARD: Argent Dawn Valor Token												
Mission Accomplished!	50	58	Commander Ashlam Valorfist	Commander Ashlam Valorfist	N	925	1850	3700	5600	7450	9300	None
REWARD: Heroic Commendation Medal and CHOICE OF: 1 Valiant Shortsword or 1 Intrepid Shortsword												
Mission Accomplished!	50	58	High Executor Derrington	High Executor Derrington	N	925	1850	3700	5600	7450	9300	None
REWARD: Heroic Commendation Medal and CHOICE OF: 1 Valiant Shortsword or 1 Intrepid Shortsword												
Mold Rhymes With...	55	57	Alchemist Arbington	Krinkle Goodsteel	Y	60	120	240	360	480	600	None
Mold Rhymes With...	55	57	Apothecary Dithers	Krinkle Goodsteel	Y	60	120	240	360	480	600	None
Mrs. Dalson's Diary	52	55	Mrs. Dalson's Diary (Obj)	Mrs. Dalson's Diary (Obj)	N	0	0	0	0	0	0	None
Return to Chillwind Point	50	53	Scourge Cauldron (Obj)	High Priestess MacDonnell	Y	270	525	1050	1600	2100	2650	80 00
Return to Chillwind Point	50	55	Scourge Cauldron (Obj)	High Priestess MacDonnell	Y	280	550	1100	1700	2250	2800	85 00
Return to Chillwind Point	50	55	Scourge Cauldron (Obj)	High Priestess MacDonnell	Y	280	550	1100	1700	2250	2800	85 00
Return to Chillwind Point	50	58	Scourge Cauldron (Obj)	High Priestess MacDonnell	N	310	625	1250	1850	2500	3100	90 00
Return to the Bulwark	50	53	Scourge Cauldron (Obj)	Shadow Priestess Vandis	Y	270	525	1050	1600	2100	2650	80 00
Return to the Bulwark	50	55	Scourge Cauldron (Obj)	Shadow Priestess Vandis	Y	280	550	1100	1700	2250	2800	85 00
Return to the Bulwark	50	55	Scourge Cauldron (Obj)	Shadow Priestess Vandis	Y	280	550	1100	1700	2250	2800	85 00
Return to the Bulwark	50	58	Scourge Cauldron (Obj)	Shadow Priestess Vandis	N	310	625	1250	1850	2500	3100	90 00
Scarlet Diversions	50	53	High Executor Derrington	High Executor Derrington	N	525	1050	2100	3150	4200	5250	80 00
Scholomance	55	55	High Executor Derrington	Apothecary Dithers	Y	55	110	220	340	450	550	None
Scholomance	55	55	Commander Ashlam Valorfist	Alchemist Arbington	Y	55	110	220	340	450	550	None
Skeletal Fragments	55	57	Apothecary Dithers	Apothecary Dithers	Y	450	900	1800	2700	3600	4500	None
Skeletal Fragments	55	57	Alchemist Arbington	Alchemist Arbington	Y	450	900	1800	2700	3600	4500	None
Soulbound Keepsake	57	62	Leonid Barthalomew the Revered	Magistrate Marduke	Y	525	1050	2100	3200	4250	5300	None
Target: Dalson's Tears	50	55	High Priestess MacDonnell	Scourge Cauldron (Obj)	Y	575	1150	2250	3400	4500	5650	None
Target: Dalson's Tears	50	55	Slitherblade Tide Priestess	Scourge Cauldron (Obj)	Y	575	1150	2250	3400	4500	5650	None
Target: Dalson's Tears	50	55	Shadow Priestess Vandis	Scourge Cauldron (Obj)	Y	575	1150	2250	3400	4500	5650	None
Target: Felstone Field	50	53	High Priestess MacDonnell	Scourge Cauldron (Obj)	Y	525	1050	2100	3150	4200	5250	None
Target: Felstone Field	50	53	Slitherblade Tide Priestess	Scourge Cauldron (Obj)	Y	525	1050	2100	3150	4200	5250	None
Target: Felstone Field	50	53	Shadow Priestess Vandis	Scourge Cauldron (Obj)	Y	525	1050	2100	3150	4200	5250	None
Target: Gahrron's Withering	50	58	High Priestess MacDonnell	Scourge Cauldron (Obj)	Y	625	1250	2500	3700	4950	6200	None
Target: Gahrron's Withering	50	58	Slitherblade Tide Priestess	Scourge Cauldron (Obj)	Y	625	1250	2500	3700	4950	6200	None
Target: Gahrron's Withering	50	58	Shadow Priestess Vandis	Scourge Cauldron (Obj)	Y	625	1250	2500	3700	4950	6200	None
Target: Writhing Haunt	50	55	High Priestess MacDonnell	Scourge Cauldron (Obj)	Y	575	1150	2250	3400	4500	5650	None
Target: Writhing Haunt	50	55	Slitherblade Tide Priestess	Scourge Cauldron (Obj)	Y	575	1150	2250	3400	4500	5650	None
Target: Writhing Haunt	50	55	Shadow Priestess Vandis	Scourge Cauldron (Obj)	Y	575	1150	2250	3400	4500	5650	None
The Dying, Ras Frostwhisper	57	62	Magistrate Marduke	Leonid Barthalomew the Revered	Y	525	1050	2100	3200	4250	5300	None
The Human, Ras Frostwhisper	57	62	Magistrate Marduke	Magistrate Marduke	Y	700	1400	2800	4250	5650	7050	None
The Key to Scholomance	55	60	Alchemist Arbington	Alchemist Arbington	N	1000	2000	4000	5950	7950	9950	None
REWARD: Skeleton Key												
The Key to Scholomance	55	60	Apothecary Dithers	Apothecary Dithers	N	1000	2000	4000	5950	7950	9950	None
REWARD: Skeleton Key												
The Last Barov	52	62	Alexi Barov	Alexi Barov	N	875	1750	3500	5300	7050	8800	1 85 00
REWARD: Barov Peasant Caller												
The Last Barov	52	62	Weldon Barov	Weldon Barov	N	875	1750	3500	5300	7050	8800	1 85 00
REWARD: Barov Peasant Caller												
The Scourge Cauldrons	50	53	Commander Ashlam Valorfist	High Priestess MacDonnell	Y	55	110	210	320	420	525	None
The Scourge Cauldrons	50	53	High Executor Derrington	Shadow Priestess Vandis	Y	55	110	210	320	420	525	None
The Wildlife Suffers Too	51	54	Mulgris Deepriver	Mulgris Deepriver	Y	410	825	1650	2450	3300	4100	None
The Wildlife Suffers Too	51	56	Mulgris Deepriver	Mulgris Deepriver	N	440	875	1750	2600	3500	4350	None
Two Halves Become One	50	54	Janice Felstone	Janice Felstone	N	550	1100	2200	3250	4350	5450	None
REWARD: Felstone Good Luck Charm												
Unfinished Business	50	56	Kirsta Deepshadow	Kirsta Deepshadow	Y	575	1150	2300	3500	4650	5800	65 00
Unfinished Business	50	57	Kirsta Deepshadow	Kirsta Deepshadow	Y	600	1200	2400	3600	4800	6000	65 00
Unfinished Business	50	58	Kirsta Deepshadow	Kirsta Deepshadow	N	625	1250	2500	3700	4950	6200	1 75 00
Villains of Darrowshire	50	57	Carlin Redpath	Carlin Redpath	N	600	1200	2400	3600	4800	6000	None
Wrath of the Blue Flight	57	62	Haleh	Jeziba	Y	700	1400	2800	4250	5650	7050	None
Writhing Haunt Cauldron	50	55	Scourge Cauldron (Obj)	Scourge Cauldron (Obj)	N	55	110	220	340	450	550	None

DARNASSUS

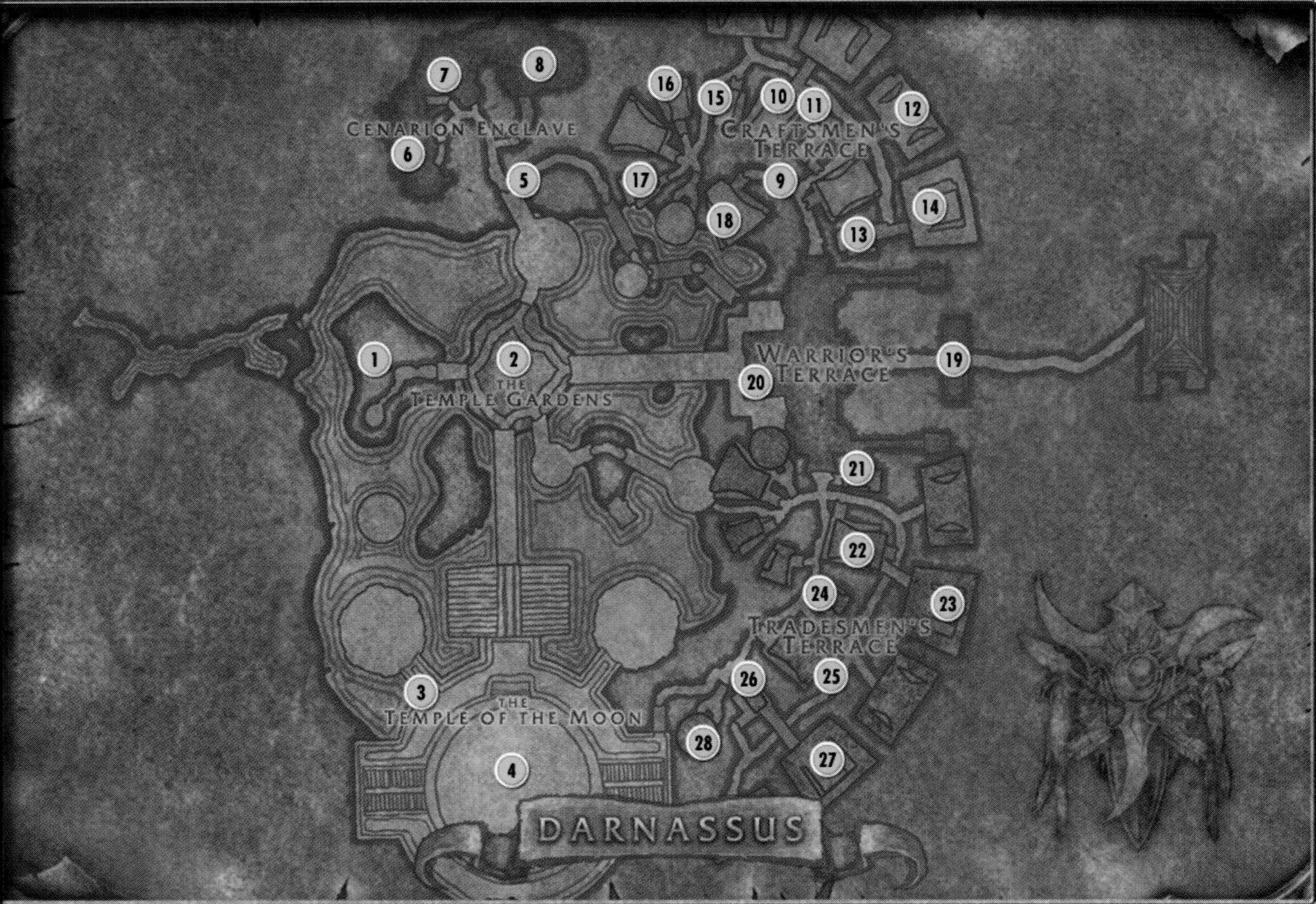

CENARION ENCLAVE
CRAFTSMEN'S TERRACE
WARRIOR'S TERRACE
THE TEMPLE GARDENS
TRADESMEN'S TERRACE
THE TEMPLE OF THE MOON
DARNASSUS

The Night Elves have lost much, but they have not lost their hope! Darnassus is the rallying point where the Elves meet to plan their healing and restoration of the land. Locked away from many battles, safe on Teldrassil, this is an ideal place for quiet meditation and reflection. Even visitors feel safe under the boughs of the ancient trees, many of whom are wise and powerful, sworn to protect the Night Elven people. With all this to speak for the city's safety, there are still Druids who fear that the taint left by the Burning Legion could affect the forest and its creatures even in Teldrassil.

MAP LEGEND

THE TEMPLE GARDENS

1 TELEPORTER
Teleporter to Rut'theran Village
Sarin Starlight 55
Sister Aquinne 15 Quest

2 BANK
Bankers 35
Darnassus Sentinel 75

TEMPLE OF THE MOON

3 OUTSIDE TEMPLE
Chief Archeologist Greywhisker 40 Quest
Darnassus Sentinel 75

4 INSIDE TEMPLE
Astaril Starseeker 60 Priest
Elissa Dumas 35 Portal Trainer
Gracina Spiritmight 55
Jandria 50 Priest Trainer
Larila 40 Priest Trainer
Priestess A'moora 20
Priestess Alathea 60
Sentinel Dalia Sunblade 44 Quest
Tyrande Whisperwind 70 Quest
Wisp 15

CENARION ENCLAVE

5 CENTRAL PATH
Crildor 55 Elite
Darnassian Protector 75
Dendrythis 30 Fruit Vendor
Jartsam 35 Nightsaber Instructor
Lelanai 35 Tiger Handler
Rellian Greenspyre 17 Quest

6 SHADY TREE (LEFT)
Anishar 50 Rogue Trainer
Erion Shadewhisper 60 Rogue Trainer
Faelyssa 35
Kyrai 30 Poison Vendor
Syurna 40 Rogue Trainer

7 DRUID TREE (MIDDLE)
Arch Druid Fandral Staghelm 70 Quest
Cyroen 50 Reagent Vendor
Denatharion 50 Druid Trainer
Fylerian Nightwing 40 Druid Trainer
Mathrengyl Bearwalker 60 Druid Trainer

8 HUNTER'S TREE (RIGHT)
Alassin 30 Stable Master
Corand 35
Dorion 50 Hunter Trainer
Jeen'ra Nightrunner 60 Hunter Trainer
Jocaste 40 Hunter Trainer
Nightshade 50 Pet of Jeen'ra
Shadow 30 Pet of Dorion
Silvaria 40 Pet Trainer

CRAFTSMEN'S TERRACE

9 ON THE STREETS
Ancient of Lore 90

10 ENCHANTING SHOP
Lalina Summermoon 27 Journeyman Enchanter
Taladan 35 Expert Enchanter
Vaean 30 Enchanting Supplies

11 GENERAL TRADE
Mythrin'dir 30 General Trade

12 INN
Mailbox
Innkeeper Saelienne 30 Innkeeper

13 TAILOR/LEATHERWORKING STORE
Darianna 24 Journeyman Leatherworker
Eladriel 35 Skinning Trainer
Elynna 30 Tailoring Supplies
Faldron 32 Expert Leatherworker
Lotherias 35
Me'lynn 35 Expert Tailor
Saenorion 30 Leatherworking Supplies
Telonis 46 Artisan Leatherworker
Trianna 25 Journeyman Tailor

14 GUILD BUILDING
Lysheana 60 Guild Master
Shalumon 25 Tabard Vendor

15 PRIVATE RESIDENCE
Aftermath of Second War Book

16 FIRST AID TRAINER
Dannelor 35 First Aid Trainer

17 RESTAURANT
Alegon 35 Cooking Trainer
Fyldan 30 Cooking Supplier

18 ALCHEMY/ARGENT DAWN EMBASSY
Ainethil 46 Artisan Alchemy
Argent Guard Manados 23 Argent Dawn
Dawnwatcher Selgorm 25 Argent Dawn
Milla Fairancora 24 Journeyman Alchemist
Sylvanna Forestmoon 32 Expert Alchemist
Ulthir 30 Alchemy Supplies

WARRIOR'S TERRACE

19 COURTYARD
Ancient of War 90
Ancient Protector 75
Mydrannul 30 General Goods Vendor
Shylenai 30 Owl TrainerFyrenna 30 Fruit Vendor

20 MAIN TERRACE
Arias'ta Bladesinger 60 Warrior Trainer
Ariyell Skyshadow 30 Weapon Merchant
Cylania 30 Armorer
Darnassus Sentinel 75
Darnath Bladesinger 55
Elanaria 65
Ilyenia Moonfire 50 Elite Weapon Master
Mathiel 33 Quest
Sildanair 40 Warrior Trainer
Thyn'tel Bladeweaver 60 Quest

TRADESMEN'S TERRACE

21 GENERAL STORE
Ellandrieth 30 General Goods
Yidan 30 Bag Merchant

22 WEAPON STORE
Glorandiir 30 Axe Merchant
Kieran 30 Weapon Merchant
Merelyssa 30 Blade Merchant
Mythidan 30 Mace/Staff Merchant

23 UPSTAIRS ROOM
Treshala Fallowbrook 20

24 FLETCHER AND THROWN WEAPONS
Landria 30 Bow Merchant
Turian 30 Thrown Weapon Merchant

25 CLOTH ARMOR AND TWO-HANDED WEAPONS
Ealyshia Dewwhisper 50 Two-Handed Weapon Merchant
Vinasia 30 Cloth Armor Merchant

26 MAIL ARMOR AND SHIELDS
Caynrus 30 Shield Merchant
Melea 30 Mail Merchant

27 STAVES AND ROBES
Anadyia 30 Robe Vendor
Andrus 30 Staff Merchant

28 LEATHER ARMOR DEALERS
Cyridan 30 Leather Armor Merchant

QUESTS

QUEST	M LEV	Q LEV	QUEST LAUNCHER	QUEST FINISHER	CHAIN?	XP---	XP--	XP-	XP+	XP++	XP+++	CASH REWARD
A Call to Arms: The Plaguelands!	50	50	Herald Moonstalker	Commander Ashlam Valorfist	Y	45	95	190	280	380	470	None
Assisting Arch Druid Staghelm	47	50	Innkeeper Saelienne	Arch Druid Fandral Staghelm	Y	45	95	190	280	380	470	None
Calm Before the Storm	50	54	Gracina Spiritmight	Idriana	N	825	1650	3250	4900	6500	8150	None
CHOICE OF: 1 Oblivion Orb or 1 Snarkshaw Spaulders or 1 Eschewal Greaves												
Grove of the Ancients	6	11	Arch Druid Fandral Staghelm	Onu	N	90	180	350	525	700	875	None
In Search of Thaelrid	18	24	Dawnwatcher Shaedlass	Argent Guard Thaelrid	Y	240	480	950	1450	1900	2400	None
March of the Silithid	50	53	Gracina Spiritmight	Alchemist Pestlezugg	Y	55	110	210	320	420	525	None
Morrowgrain Research	47	50	Mathrengyl Bearwalker	Mathrengyl Bearwalker	N	470	950	1900	2800	3750	4700	None
REWARD: Cenarion Circle Cache												
Morrowgrain Research	47	50	Arch Druid Fandral Staghelm	Mathrengyl Bearwalker	Y	45	95	190	280	380	470	None
REWARD: 20 Packets of Tharlendris Seeds												
Morrowgrain to Thunder Bluff	47	50	Mathrengyl Bearwalker	Mathrengyl Bearwalker	N	45	95	190	280	380	470	None
REWARD: Cenarion Circle Cache												
Sathrah's Sacrifice	5	12	Priestess A'moora	Priestess A'moora	N	90	180	360	550	725	900	None
CHOICE OF: 1 Lace Pants or 1 Cushioned Boots												
Tears of the Moon	5	12	Priestess A'moora	Priestess A'moora	Y	120	230	460	700	925	1150	10 00
The Temple of the Moon	5	10	Sister Aquinne	Priestess A'moora	Y	10	15	35	50	70	85	None
Trouble In Darkshore?	14	14	Chief Archaeologist Greywhisker	Archaeologist Hollee	Y	50	100	200	290	390	490	None
Twilight Falls	20	25	Argent Guard Manados	Argent Guard Manados	N	260	500	1000	1550	2050	2550	None
REWARD: Nimbus Boots, Heartwood Girdle												
Un'Goro Soil	47	50	Arch Druid Fandral Staghelm	Jenal	N	470	950	1900	2800	3750	4700	1 45 00

ORGRIMMAR

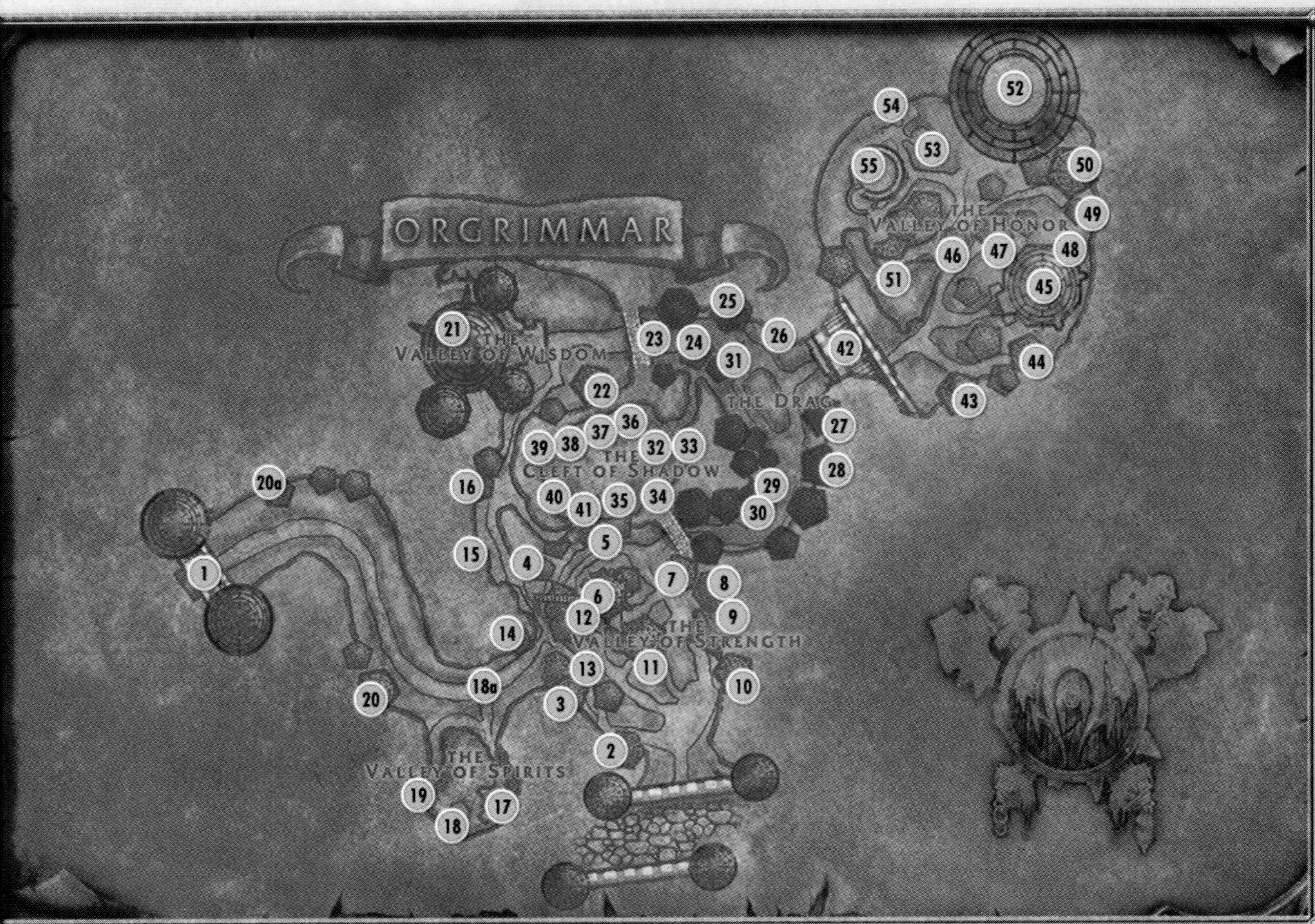

Orgrimmar never lacked for wood, stone, or defenders. Orcs understand the importance of a strong presentation, and Orgrimmar makes anyone think twice before causing problems near its walls. At the far end of this city, Thrall holds court, ever trying to promote unity between the many tribes of the Horde. Frustrated by internal conflicts, setbacks with the Alliance, and the tenuous "friendship" with the Forsaken, the Orcish leaders have much on their minds. One pressing concern is the rise in cults, especially those sworn to demonic magics. Orcs are well versed in the horrors of demons and their power of mortal beings; any who brook with the occult are a great risk to the Horde.

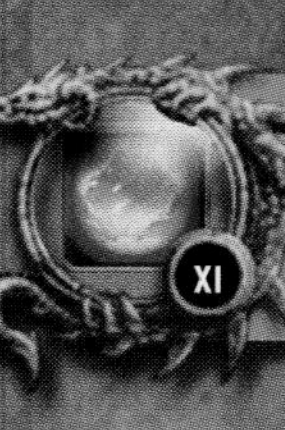

MAP LEGEND

ORGRIMMAR ENTRANCE

1 ENTRANCE
Orgrimmar Grunts 75

VALLEY OF STRENGTH

2 ORGRIMMAR GENERAL STORE
Trak'gen 30 General Goods Merchant
Shimra 30 General Trade Goods Merchant

3 HORDE EMBASSY
Urtran Clanbringer 45 Guild Master
Garyl 30 Tabard Vendor

4 PASSAGE TO VALLEY OF SPIRITS
Orgrimmar Grunt 75

5 SPIRITFURY REAGENTS
Horthus 30 Reagents Vendor

6 THE SKYTOWER
Ogrimmar Grunt 75
Doras 55 Elite Wind Rider Master

7 BOOMSTICK IMPORTS
Kaja 30 Guns and Ammo Merchant

8 OGRIMMAR AUCTION HOUSE
Auctioneers 50

9 INN
Innkeeper Gryshka 30 Innkeeper
Gamon 12
Zazo 14
Goma 12
Doyo'da 11
Barkeep Morag 13
Kozish 12
Sarok 25

10 SORAM'S LEATHER AND STEEL ARMORY
Sana 30 Mail Merchant
Morgum 30 Leather Armor Merchant
Ollanus 30 Light Armor Merchant

11 BANK OF ORGRIMMAR
Bankers 35-40
Mailbox

12 THE SHATTERED AXE
Urtharo 30 Weapon Merchant

13 THE CHOPHOUSE
Olvia 50 Meat Vendor

14 OFFICER'S QUARTERS

15 ZANKAJA 15 QUEST

16 STRANGLETHORN IMPORTED FRUITS
Shan'ti 35 Fruit Vendor

VALLEY OF SPIRITS

17 DARKBRIAR LODGE
Enyo 50 Mage Trainer
Uthel'nay 40 Mage Trainer
Deino 40 Mage Trainer Quest
Pephredo 60 Mage Trainer
Thuul 45 Portal Trainer

18 SPIRIT LODGE
Witch Doctor Mau'ri 55
Ur'kyo 40 Priest Trainer

18A Xan'tish 30 Snake Vendor (wanders)

19 SURVIVAL OF THE FITTEST
Arnok 35 First Aid Trainer

20 SKYFURY STAVES
Ukra'nor 30 Staff Merchant

20A Keldran 38 Quest

VALLEY OF WISDOM

21 THRALL'S FORTRESS- GROMMASH HOLD
Ogrimmar Grunt 75
Zor Lonetree 65 Elder Far Seer Quest
Grelkor 50 Shaman Trainer
Kandris Dreamseeker 60 Shaman Trainer
Searn Firewarder 15 Quest
Sian'tsu 40 Shaman Trainer
Eitrigg 20
Vol'jin 60 Elite
Thrall 63 Warchief
Nazgrel 65 Adviser to Thrall Quest

22 ASORAN'S MARKET
Asoran 30 General Goods
Magenius 30 Reagents Vendor

THE DRAG

23 Warcaller Gorlach 3 (Wanderer)

24 GODAN'S RUNEWORKS
Kithas 35 Enchanting Supplies
Godan 35 Expert Enchanter
Jhag 26 Journeyman Enchanter

25 YELMAK'S ALCHEMY AND POTIONS
Kor'geld 30 Alchemy Supplies
Whuut 23 Journeyman Alchemist
Yelmak 35 Expert Alchemist
Jes'rimon 50 Quest

26 DROFFERS AND SONS SALVAGE
Dan Droffers 45 Droffers and Sons Salvage Quest
Malton Droffers 40 Droffers and Sons Salvage Quest

27 KODOHIDE LEATHERWORKERS
Karolek 35 Expert Leatherworker
Handor 30 Cloth and Leather Merchant
Thuwd 35 Skinning Trainer
Tamar 30 Leatherworking Supplies

28 MAGAR'S CLOTH GOODS
Snang 24 Journeyman Tailor
Magar 35 Expert Tailor
Kamari 26 Journeyman Leatherworker
Tor'phan 30 Cloth and Leather Armor Merchant
Borya 30 Tailoring Supplies

29 GOTRI'S TRAVELING GEAR
Gotri 30 Bag Vendor

30 BORSTANS FIREPIT
Zamja 35 Cooking Trainer
Borstan 30 Meat Vendor
Xen'to 30 Cooking Supplier

31 JANDI'S ARBORETUM
Zeal'aya 30 Herbalism Supplier
Jandi 35 Herbalism Trainer

THE CLEFT OF SHADOW

32 Neeru Fireblade 37 Quest

33 RAGEFIRE CHASM 13+ INSTANCE DUNGEON

34 DARK EARTH FUNGUS AND MUSHROOMS
Kor'jus 30 Mushroom Vendor

35 Kor'ghan Quest

36 DARKFIRE ENCLAVE
Mirket 50 Warlock Trainer
Zevrost 50 Warlock Trainer
Gan'rul Bloodeye 40 Quest
Grol'dar 50 Warlock Trainer
Kurgul 45 Demon Trainer
Succubus 45 Kurgul's Minion
Cazul 40 Quest

37 SHADOWDEEP REAGENTS
Hagrus 30 Reagent Vendor

38 IRONWOOD STAVES AND WANDS
Maragus 30 Staff Merchant
Katis 30 Wand Merchant

39 REKKUL'S POISONS
Rekkul 30 Poison Vendor
Gest 40 Rogue Trainer

40 SHADOWSWIFT BROTHERHOOD
Shenthul 60 Rogue Trainer
Therzok 20 Quest
Zando'zan 35 Quest
Ormok 50 Rogue Trainer

41 THE SLOW BLADE
Kareth 30 Blade Merchant

THE VALLEY OF HONOR

42 ENTRANCE TO THE VALLEY OF HONOR
Orgrimmar Grunt 75

43 KIRO'S HARNESSES
Kiro 30 War Harness Maker

44 ORGRIMMAR BOWYER
Jin'sora 30 Bow Merchant

45 HALL OF THE BRAVE
Sorek 50 Warrior Trainer
Grezz Razorfist 60 Warrior Trainer
Sayoc 50 Elite Weapon Master
Grinning Dog 48 Elite
Zel'mak 40 Warrior Trainer

46 RED CANYON MINING
Gorina 30 Mining Supplier
Makaru 35 Mining Trainer

47 NOGG'S MACHINE SHOP
Sovik 30 Engineering Supplies
Nogg 35 Expert Engineer
Roxxik 46 Artisan Engineer
Thund 23 Journeyman Engineer

48 BLACKSMITHING
Orokk Omosh 45 Quest
Krathok Moltenfist 53 Quest
Okothos Ironrager 52 Armorsmith
Ox 53 The Mithril Order Quest
Ugh'thok 25 Journeyman Blacksmith
Aturk the Anvil 50 Quest
Shayis Steelfury 60 Armor Crafter
Borgosh Corebender 51 Weaponsmith

49 THE BURNING ANVIL
Sara Steelfury 45 Artisan Blacksmith
Tumi 30 Heavy Armor Merchant
Sumi 30 Blacksmithing Supplier

50 ARMS OF LEGEND
Zendo'jian 30 Axe Vendor
Shoma 30 Blade Merchant
Galthuk 8 Two-Handed Weapons Merchant
Kelgruk Bloodaxe 60 Weapon Crafter
Koru 30 Maces and Staves Vendor

51 LUMAK'S FISHING
Lumak 35 Fishing Trainer
Shankys 30 Fishing Supplier

52 THE RING OF VALOR
Belgrom Rockmaul 35 Quest
Ogrimmar Grunt 75

53 Xon'cha 30 Stable Master

54 WOLF RIDERS
Kildar 50 Wolf Riding Instructor
Ogunaro Wolfrunner 45 Wolf Master
Riding Wolves 10

55 HUNTER'S HALL
Xoa'tsu 40 Pet Trainer
Sian'dur 40 Hunter Trainer
Xor'Juul 50 Hunter Trainer
Ormak Grimshot 60 Hunter Trainer
Shim'la 35

QUEST	M LEV	Q LEV	QUEST LAUNCHER	QUEST FINISHER	CHAIN?	XP---	XP--	XP-	XP+	XP++	XP+++	CASH REWARD
A Threat in Feralas	38	43	Belgrom Rockmaul	Rok Orhan	Y	90	180	360	525	700	900	None
Alliance Relations	30	30	Keldran	Takata Steelblade	N	120	240	480	725	950	1200	None
Alliance Relations	30	30	Craven Drok	Keldran	Y	60	120	240	370	490	600	None
Alliance Relations	30	33	Takata Steelblade	Keldran	N	270	525	1050	1600	2100	2650	None
CHOICE OF: 1 Gloves of Kapelan or 1 Swiftrunner Cape												
Alliance Relations	30	33	Takata Steelblade	Maurin Bonesplitter	Y	25	55	110	160	210	270	None
Assisting Arch Druid Runetotem	47	50	Innkeeper Gryshka	Arch Druid Hamuul Runetotem	Y	45	95	190	280	380	470	None
Befouled by Satyr	25	33	Takata Steelblade	Takata Steelblade	N	270	525	1050	1600	2100	2650	None
Betrayed	44	53	Belgrom Rockmaul	Ag'tor Bloodfist	Y	270	525	1050	1600	2100	2650	None
Betrayed	44	53	Ag'tor Bloodfist	Kaldorei Tome of Summoning (Obj)	Y	400	800	1600	2350	3150	3950	None
Betrayed	44	56	Ag'tor Bloodfist	Belgrom Rockmaul	N	725	1450	2900	4400	5850	7300	None
CHOICE OF: 1 Pyrestone Orb or 1 Belgrom's Hammer												
Betrayed	44	56	Kaldorei Tome of Summoning (Obj)	Ag'tor Bloodfist	Y	440	875	1750	2600	3500	4350	None
Bone-Bladed Weapons	48	52	Jes'rimon	Jes'rimon	N	500	1000	2050	3050	4100	5100	40 00
CHOICE OF: 1 White Bone Band or 1 White Bone Shredder or 1 White Bone Spear												
Cache of Mau'ari	55	60	Witch Doctor Mau'ari	Witch Doctor Mau'ari	N	0	0	0	0	0	0	None
REWARD: Cache of Mau'ari												
Calm Before the Storm	50	54	Zilzibin Drumlore	Karus	N	825	1650	3250	4900	6500	8150	None
CHOICE OF: 1 Oblivion Orb or 1 Snarkshaw Spaulders or 1 Eschewal Greaves												
Chillwind E'ko	55	60	Witch Doctor Mau'ari	Witch Doctor Mau'ari	N	0	0	0	0	0	0	None
REWARD: 3 Juju Chill												
Deliver the Gems	37	44	Jarkal Mossmeld	Dran Droffers	Y	190	370	750	1100	1500	1850	1 25 00
Eitrigg's Wisdom	55	61	Warlord Goretooth	Thrall	Y	675	1350	2750	4100	5500	6850	None
Find the Gems and Power Source	37	44	Jarkal Mossmeld	Jarkal Mossmeld	N	380	750	1500	2250	3000	3750	None
Frostmaul E'ko	55	60	Witch Doctor Mau'ari	Witch Doctor Mau'ari	N	0	0	0	0	0	0	None
REWARD: 3 Juju Might												
Frostsaber E'ko	55	60	Witch Doctor Mau'ari	Witch Doctor Mau'ari	N	0	0	0	0	0	0	None
REWARD: 3 Juju Flurry												
Hidden Enemies	9	12	Thrall	Thrall	N	90	180	360	550	725	900	2 50
Hidden Enemies	9	12	Thrall	Thrall	Y	45	90	180	270	360	460	None
Hidden Enemies	9	15	Thrall	Neeru Fireblade	Y	10	20	40	65	85	110	None
Hidden Enemies	9	16	Neeru Fireblade	Thrall	N	150	290	575	875	1150	1450	None
CHOICE OF: 1 Kris of Orgrimmar or 1 Hammer of Orgrimmar or 1 Axe of Orgrimmar or 1 Staff of Orgrimmar												
Hidden Enemies	9	16	Thrall	Thrall	Y	120	230	460	700	925	1150	8 00
Ice Thistle E'ko	55	60	Witch Doctor Mau'ari	Witch Doctor Mau'ari	N	0	0	0	0	0	0	None
REWARD: 3 Juju Escape												
Journey to Grom'gol	1	1	Torc the Orc	Torc the Orc	N	0	0	0	0	0	0	None
Journey to the Undercity!	1	1	Torc the Orc	Torc the Orc	N	0	0	0	0	0	0	None
Luck Be With You	55	60	Witch Doctor Mau'ari	Witch Doctor Mau'ari	Y	650	1300	2650	3950	5300	6600	90 00
March of the Silithid	50	53	Zilzibin Drumlore	Alchemist Pestlezugg	Y	55	110	210	320	420	525	None
Necklace Recovery	37	41	Dran Droffers	Dran Droffers	Y	250	490	975	1450	1950	2450	None
Necklace Recovery, Take 2	37	41	Dran Droffers	Remains of a Paladin	Y	250	490	975	1450	1950	2450	None
Necklace Recovery, Take 3	37	44	Dran Droffers	Jarkal Mossmeld	N	550	1100	2250	3350	4500	5600	None
REWARD: Jarkal's Enhancing Necklace												
Nogg's Ring Redo	28	35	Nogg	Nogg	N	140	270	550	800	1100	1350	None
REWARD: Nogg's Gold Ring												
Returning the Lost Satchel	9	16	Maur Grimtotem	Rahauro	N	150	290	575	875	1150	1450	None
CHOICE OF: 1 Featherbead Bracers or 1 Savannah Bracers												
Ripple Delivery	42	48	Gilveradin Sunchaser	Dran Droffers	N	440	875	1750	2650	3500	4400	1 40 00
Ripple Recovery	42	48	Malton Droffers	Gilveradin Sunchaser	Y	440	875	1750	2650	3500	4400	None
Ripple Recovery	42	48	Dran Droffers	Malton Droffers	Y	45	90	180	260	350	440	None
Searching for the Lost Satchel	9	16	Rahauro	Maur Grimtotem	Y	90	180	350	525	700	875	None
Shardtooth E'ko	55	60	Witch Doctor Mau'ari	Witch Doctor Mau'ari	N	0	0	0	0	0	0	None
REWARD: 3 Juju Embers												
Slaying the Beast	9	16	Neeru Fireblade	Neeru Fireblade	N	120	230	460	700	925	1150	8 00
Testing an Enemies Strength.	9	15	Rahauro	Rahauro	N	110	210	420	625	850	1050	7 00
The Burning of Spirits	25	33	Maurin Bonesplitter	Maurin Bonesplitter	N	270	525	1050	1600	2100	2650	None
The Power to Destroy...	9	16	Varimathras	Varimathras	N	150	290	575	875	1150	1450	None
CHOICE OF: 1 Ghastly Trousers or 1 Dredgemire Leggings or 1 Gargoyle Leggings												
The Swarm Grows	29	33	Belgrom Rockmaul	Moktar Krin	Y	200	390	775	1150	1550	1950	None
Translating the Journal	37	42	Jarkal Mossmeld	Jarkal Mossmeld	N	35	70	140	210	280	350	None
Translating the Journal	37	42	Remains of a Paladin	Jarkal Mossmeld	Y	350	700	1400	2050	2750	3450	None
Wildkin E'ko	55	60	Witch Doctor Mau'ari	Witch Doctor Mau'ari	N	0	0	0	0	0	0	None
REWARD: 3 Juju Guile												
Winterfall E'ko	55	60	Witch Doctor Mau'ari	Witch Doctor Mau'ari	N	0	0	0	0	0	0	None
REWARD: 3 Juju Power												

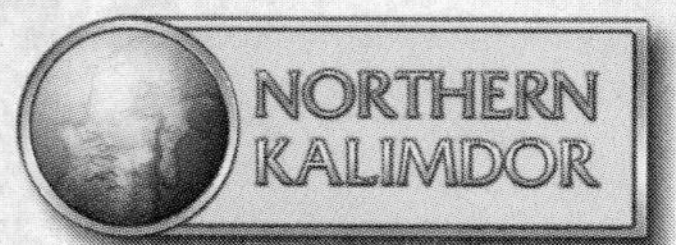

ASHENVALE

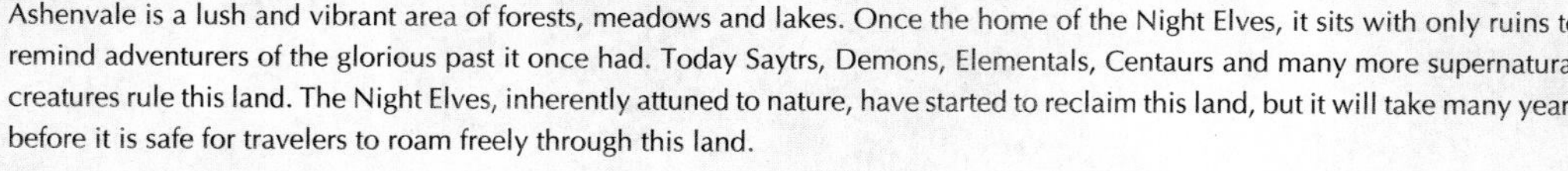

Ashenvale is a lush and vibrant area of forests, meadows and lakes. Once the home of the Night Elves, it sits with only ruins to remind adventurers of the glorious past it once had. Today Saytrs, Demons, Elementals, Centaurs and many more supernatural creatures rule this land. The Night Elves, inherently attuned to nature, have started to reclaim this land, but it will take many years before it is safe for travelers to roam freely through this land.

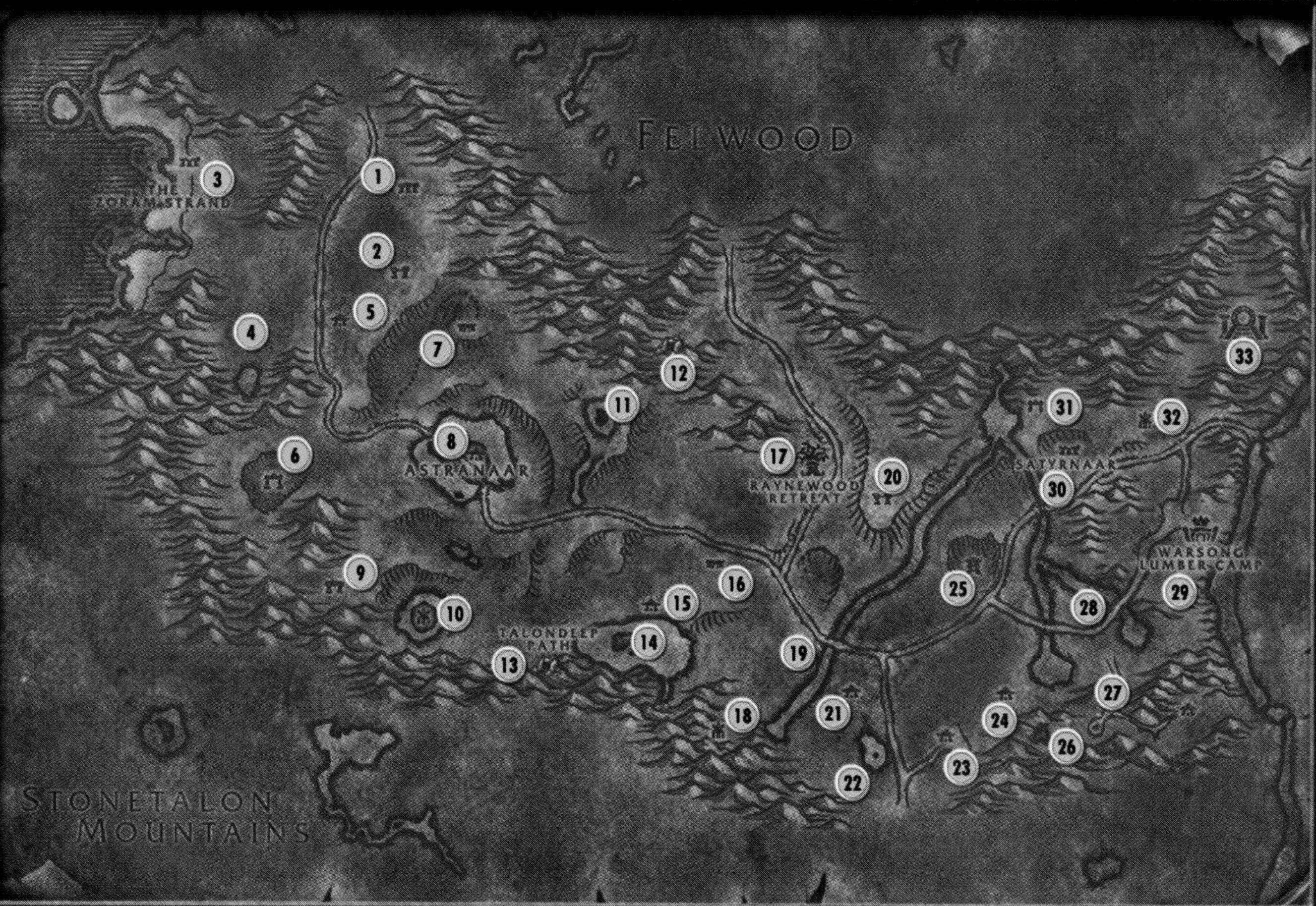

FELWOOD
THE ZORAM STRAND
ASTRANAAR
RAYNEWOOD RETREAT
SATYRNAAR
WARSONG LUMBER CAMP
TALONDEEP PATH
STONETALON MOUNTAINS

LOCAL RESOURCES

MINING

METAL	AVAILABILITY
Silver	Rare
Tin	Rare
Iron	Rare

HERBALISM

HERB	AVAILABILITY
Stranglekelp	Moderate
Briarthorn	Moderate

SKINNING

Quantity of Skinnable Creatures: Abundant

Levels of Skinnable Creatures: 18-20 (Skinning 75-150)

MAP LEGEND

1 BATHRAN'S HAUNT
Forsaken Seeker 18-19
Forsaken Herbalist 18-19
Forsaken Thug 20

2 THE RUINS OF ORDIL'
Dark Strand Cultist 18-19
Imp (Minion) 18-19
Dark Strand Adept 18-19
Voidwalker Minion 18-19

3 THE ZORAM STRAND
Andruk 55 Wind Rider Master
Clattering Crawler 19-20
Mystlash Hydra 20
Spined Crawler 20-21
Wrathtail Sorceress 18-19
Wrathtail WaveRider 18-19
Ghostpaw Runner 19-20
Wild Buck 18-19
Deeps World Dungeon
Entrance to Blackfathom

3A FISHING VILLAGE
Talen 17 Quest
Andruk 55 Elite Wind Rider Master

4 LAKE FALATHIM
Ghostpaw Runner 19-20
Mugglefin 23+
Saltspittle Muckdweller 20-21
Saltspittle Oracle 20-21
Saltspittle Puddlejumper 19-20
Wild Buck 18-19

5 MAESTRA'S POST
Feero Ironhand 20 Quest
Delgren the Purifier 19 Quest
Orendil Broadleaf 27 Quest
Liladris Moonriver 42 Quest
Sentinel Onaeya 20 Quest
Wild Buck 18-19

6 THE SHRINE OF AESSINA
Illiyana 24 Quest
Therysil 17 Quest
Sentinel Melyria Frostshadow Quest
Lilyn Darkriver Quest

7 THISTLEFUR VILLAGE
Dal Bloodclaw 25
Thistlefur Shaman 22-23
Thistlefur Avenger 22-23
Thistlefur Pathfinder 22-23

8 ASTRANAAR
Pelturas Whitemoon 21 Quest
Nantar 21 Baker
Maluressian 30 Stable Master
Raene Wolfrunner 25 Quest
Dagri 23 Raene Wolfrunner's Pet
Fahran Silentblade 28 Tools and Supplies
Maliynn 19 Grocer
Korra 20 Tiger
Haljan Oakheart 26 General Goods
Kimlya 30 Innkeeper
Dalria 24 Trade Goods
Xai'ander 35 Weaponsmith
Aayndia Floralwind 37 Leatherworker
Faldreas Goeth'shael 19 Quest
Sentinel Thenysil 23 Quest
Shindrell Swiftfire 25
Daelyshia 55 Hippogriff Master
Lardan 25 Leatherworking
Llana 25 Reagent Supplies
Tandaan Lightmane 23 Leather Armor Merchant
Aeolynn 22 Clothier
Astranaar Sentinenl 40

9 FIRE SCAR SHRINE
Felslayer 22-23
Burning Legionnaire 23-24

10 RUINS OF STARDUST
Shadethicket Raincaller 23-24
Shadethicket Woodshaper 23-24

11 IRIS LAKE
Shadethicket Moss Eater 21-23

12 THE HOWLING VALE
Terrorwulf Fleshripper 28-29
Terrorwulf Shadow Weaver 29-30

13 TALONDEEP PATH
Shadowhorn Stag 21-22
Ashenvale Bear 21-22

14 MYSTRAL LAKE
Befouled Water Elementals 23-25

15 SILVERWIND REFUGE
Harklan Moongrove 24 Alchemy Supplies
Shandrina 24 Trade Goods
Ulthaan 26 Butcher
Danlaar Nightstride 35 Hunter Trainer
Jayla 23 Skinner Trainer
Bhaldaran Ravenshade 34 Bowyer
Cylania Rootstalker 24 Herbalist
Kylanna 31 Alchemist
Sentinel Velene Starstrike 25 Quest

16 GREENPAW VILLAGE
Foulweald Totemic 23-24
Foulweald Ursa 23-24
Foulweald Shaman 23-24
Foulweald Warrior 23-24
Foulweald Den Watcher 23-24
Foulweald Pathfinder 23-24

17 RAYNEWOOD RETREAT
Keeper Ordanus 29
Laughing Sister 24-25
Cenarion Protector 25-26
Cenarion Vindicator 26-27

18 BLOODTOOTH CAMP
Ran Bloodtooth 30
Bloodtooth Guard 27-28
Ghostpaw Runner 19-20
Ashenvale Bear 21-22

19 MOONWELL
Blink Dragon 26
Ghostpaw Howler 23
Wildthorn Venomspitter 24

20 NIGHT RUN
Wildthorn Venomspitter 24-25
Elder Ashenvale Bear 24-25
Felmusk Satyr 25-26
Felmusk Rogue 26-27
Felmusk Felsworn 27-28
Felmusk Shadowstalker 26-27

21 SILVERWING OUTPOST
Ashenvale Sentinel 40
Ashenvale Warriror 40

22 FALLEN SKY LAKE
Shadethicket Stone Mover 25-26
Shadethicket Bark Ripper 26-27
Wildthorn Stalker 20-21

23 NIGHTSONG WOODS
Wildthorn Stalker 20-21
Warsong Shredder 27
Rotting Slime 20-22
Ghostpaw Runner 19-20
Horde Shaman 28-29
Horde Grunt 29-30

24 THE DOR'DANIL BARROW DEN
Uthil Mooncaller 32
Rotting Slime (Outside) 21-22
Forsaken Infiltrator 28-29
Forsaken Intruder 28-29
Forsaken Stalker 28-29
Forsaken Assasin 28-29
Severed Druid 28-29
Severed Dreamer 29-30
Severed Keeper 29-30
Severed Sleeper 29-30

25 SPLINTERTREE POST

26 MONUMENT TO GROM HELLSCREAM
Felguard 29-31
Legion Hound 29-31
Searing Infernal 29-31

27 DEMON FALL CANYON
Legion Hound 29-30
Mannoroc Lasher 29-30
Searing Infernal 29-30
Felguard 29-30

28 FELFIRE HILL
Mannoroc Lasher 29-30
Searing Infernal 29-30
Felguard 29-30

29 WARSONG LUMBER CAMP
Loruk Foreststrider 44 Banker
Horde Grunt 29-30
Horde Shaman 28-29
Warsong Shredder 27-28
Horde Scout 26-27
Horde Peon 26-27

30 SATYRNAAR
Bleakheart Trickster 26-28
Bleakheart Shadowstalker 26-28
Bleakheart Saytr 26-28
Bleakheart Hellcaller 26-28

31 XAVIAN
Galtharis 32
Xavian Felsworn 28-30
Xavian Betrayer 28-30
Xavian Hellcaller 28-30
Xavian Rogue 28-30

32 FOREST SONG
Kayneth Stillwind 31 Quest
Giant Ashenvale Bear 29-30
Wildthorn Lurker 29-30

33 BOUGH SHADOW

QUESTS

QUEST	M LEV	Q LEV	QUEST LAUNCHER	QUEST FINISHER	CHAIN?	XP---	XP--	XP-	XP+	XP++	XP+++	CASH REWARD
An Aggressive Defense	18	24	Raene Wolfrunner	Raene Wolfrunner	N	200	390	775	1150	1550	1950	17 00
REWARD: 10 Moist Cornbreads, 10 Melon Juice												
Answered Questions	25	30	Jonathan Carevin	Thyn'tel Bladeweaver	N	310	600	1200	1850	2450	3050	None
CHOICE OF: 1 Lunaris Bow or 1 Moonbeam Wand												
Bathran's Hair	20	20	Orendil Broadleaf	Orendil Broadleaf	N	80	160	310	470	625	775	None
Culling the Threat	18	25	Raene Wolfrunner	Raene Wolfrunner	N	200	400	800	1200	1600	2000	18 00
REWARD: 2 Restoring Balm												
Elemental Bracers	20	24	Sentinel Velene Starstrike	Sentinel Velene Starstrike	Y	200	390	775	1150	1550	1950	None
Elune's Tear	20	22	Pelturas Whitemoon	Pelturas Whitemoon	N	180	350	700	1050	1400	1750	14 00
Fallen Sky Lake	20	30	Pelturas Whitemoon	Pelturas Whitemoon	N	310	600	1200	1850	2450	3050	None
CHOICE OF: 1 Snapbrook Armor or 1 Beastial Manacles												
Forsaken Diseases	24	29	Kayneth Stillwind	Kayneth Stillwind	N	240	470	950	1400	1900	2350	None
Insane Druids	24	32	Kayneth Stillwind	Kayneth Stillwind	N	320	650	1300	1900	2550	3200	None
REWARD: Emil's Brand												
Journey to Stonetalon Peak	18	18	Faldreas Goeth'Shael	Keeper Albagorm	N	70	140	270	410	550	675	None
Kayneth Stillwind	24	29	Shindrell Swiftfire	Kayneth Stillwind	N	60	120	240	350	470	600	None
Mage Summoner	20	25	Sentinel Velene Starstrike	Sentinel Velene Starstrike	N	260	500	1000	1550	2050	2550	None
REWARD: Light of Elune												
Mage Summoner	20	25	Sentinel Velene Starstrike	Sentinel Velene Starstrike	N	260	500	1000	1550	2050	2550	None
REWARD: Light of Elune												
On Guard in Stonetalon	17	21	Kaela Shadowspear	Gaxim Rustfizzle	Y	15	35	65	100	130	170	None
On Guard in Stonetalon	17	21	Sentinel Thenysil	Kaela Shadowspear	Y	85	170	330	500	675	825	None
Orendil's Cure	20	20	Orendil Broadleaf	Pelturas Whitemoon	N	200	390	775	1150	1550	1950	25 00
Passage to Booty Bay	25	30	Wharfmaster Dizzywig	Caravaneer Ruzzgot	Y	60	120	240	370	490	600	None
Pridewings of Stonetalon	18	21	Shindrell Swiftfire	Shindrell Swiftfire	N	170	330	650	1000	1300	1650	13 00
Raene's Cleansing	18	19	Raene Wolfrunner	Teronis' Corpse	Y	150	290	575	875	1150	1450	None
Raene's Cleansing	18	21	Teronis' Corpse	Raene Wolfrunner	N	130	250	500	750	1000	1250	None
Raene's Cleansing	18	21	Raene Wolfrunner	Shael'dryn	Y	85	170	330	500	675	825	None
Raene's Cleansing	18	27	Shael'dryn	Shael'dryn	Y	220	440	875	1300	1750	2200	None
Raene's Cleansing	18	28	Shael'dryn	Shael'dryn	Y	230	460	925	1400	1850	2300	None
Raene's Cleansing	18	28	Hidden Shrine (Obj)	Shael'dryn	Y	25	45	90	140	180	230	None
Raene's Cleansing	18	28	Shael'dryn	Raene Wolfrunner	Y	25	45	90	140	180	230	None
Raene's Cleansing	18	28	Raene Wolfrunner	Krolg	Y	170	340	675	1000	1350	1700	None
Raene's Cleansing	18	28	Shael'dryn	Hidden Shrine (Obj)	Y	170	340	675	1000	1350	1700	None
REWARD: Dartol's Rod of Transformation												
Raene's Cleansing	18	30	Krolg	Raene Wolfrunner	N	310	600	1200	1850	2450	3050	None
REWARD: Glacial Stone, Ring of Pure Silver												
Raene's Cleansing	18	30	Krolg	Krolg	Y	250	490	975	1450	1950	2450	None
Ruuzel	20	25	Talen	Talen	N	260	500	1000	1550	2050	2550	None
REWARD: Robes of Antiquity												
Satyr Slaying!	22	27		Illiyana	N	0	0	0	0	0	0	None
Supplies to Auberdine	19	24	Feero Ironhand	Delgren the Purifier	N	290	575	1150	1750	2300	2900	50 00
CHOICE OF: 1 Everglow Lantern or 1 Chestplate of Kor												
The Ancient Statuette	19	20	Talen	Talen	N	120	230	460	700	925	1150	9 00
The Barrens Port	25	30	Thyn'tel Bladeweaver	Wharfmaster Dizzywig	Y	120	240	480	725	950	1200	None
The Branch of Cenarius	26	32	Anilia	Illiyana	N	260	500	1000	1550	2050	2550	None
CHOICE OF: 1 Faerie Mantle or 1 Brightscale Girdle												
The Caravan Road	25	30	Caravaneer Ruzzgot	Clerk Daltry	Y	120	240	480	725	950	1200	None
The Carevin Family	25	30	Clerk Daltry	Jonathan Carevin	Y	25	50	100	150	200	250	None
The Howling Vale	25	30	Sentinel Melyria Frostshadow	Sentinel Melyria Frostshadow	Y	250	490	975	1450	1950	2450	25 00
The Ruins of Stardust	20	23	Pelturas Whitemoon	Pelturas Whitemoon	N	190	370	750	1100	1500	1850	15 00
The Scythe of Elune	25	30	Jonathan Carevin	Jonathan Carevin	Y	250	490	975	1450	1950	2450	25 00
The Zoram Strand	14	19	Shindrell Swiftfire	Shindrell Swiftfire	N	150	290	575	875	1150	1450	11 00
Trek to Ashenvale	15	19	Sentinel Selarin	Raene Wolfrunner	N	35	75	150	220	290	370	None
Velinde Starsong	25	30	Sentinel Melyria Frostshadow	Thyn'tel Bladeweaver	Y	60	120	240	370	490	600	None
Velinde's Effects	25	30	Thyn'tel Bladeweaver	Thyn'tel Bladeweaver	Y	60	120	240	370	490	600	None
Vile Satyr! Dryads in Danger!	26	32	Illiyana	Anilia	Y	260	500	1000	1550	2050	2550	None

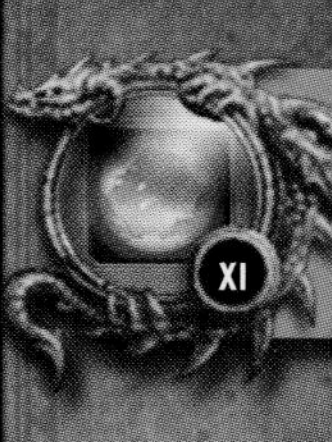

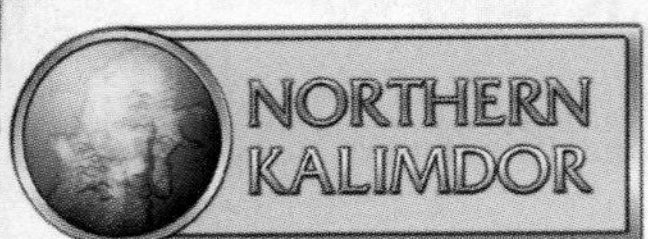

AZSHARA

Azshara is located to the east of Ashenvale. Named after Queen Azshara that was corrupted and transformed into a Naga, the Naga still make this land their home along with many other denizens that have flooded in. This zone has progressive level increases of mobs as you travel through the area. To the south, creatures can be found in the mid to high ranges and they become more dangerous as you continue north.

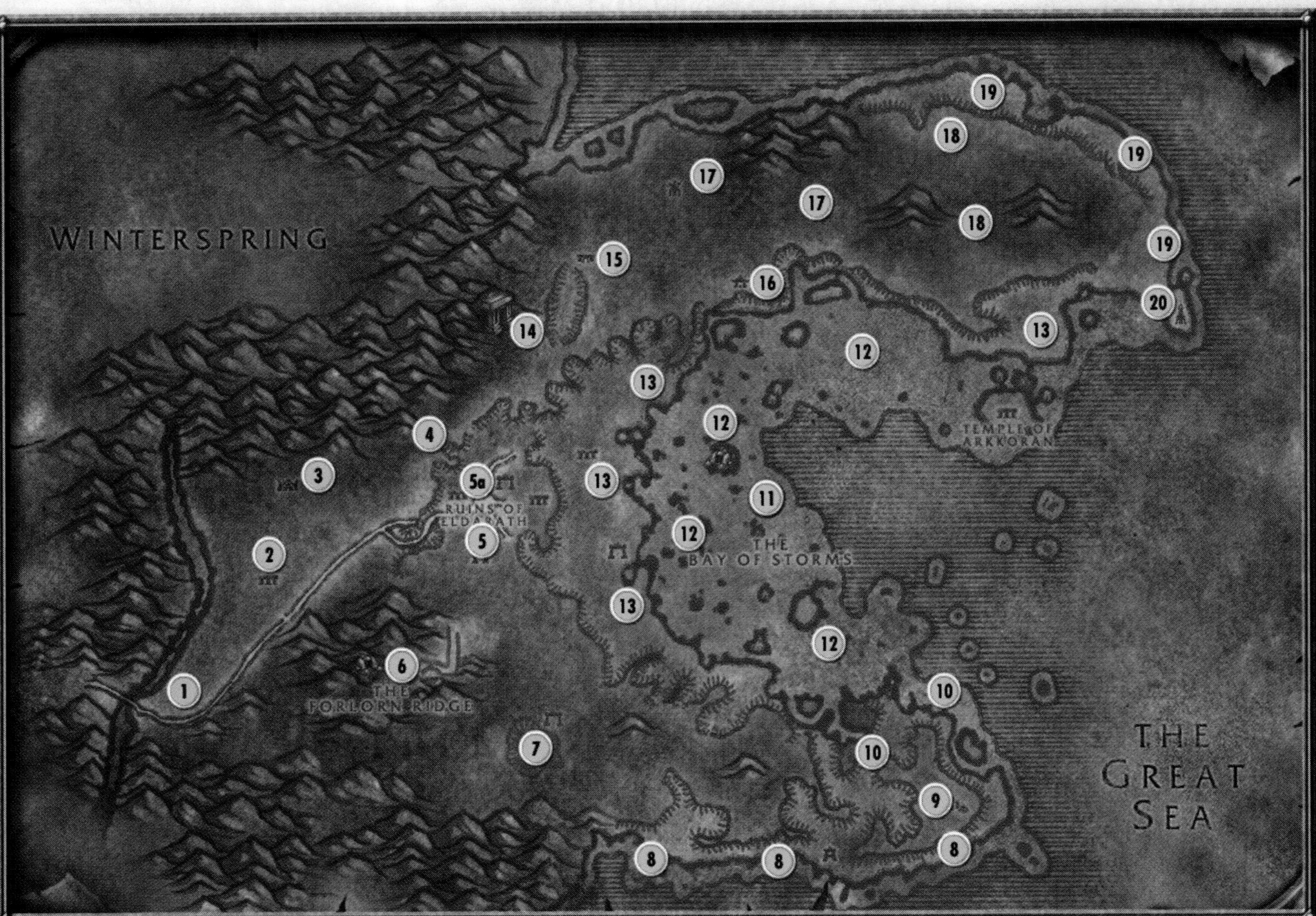

LOCAL RESOURCES

MINING

METAL	AVAILABILITY
Mithril	Abundant
Thorium	Moderate

HERBALISM

HERB	AVAILABILITY
Purple Lotus	Common
Sungrass	Rare
Stranglekelp	Rare
Dreamfoil	Rare

SKINNING

Quantity of Skinnable Creatures: Abundant

Levels of Skinnable Creatures: 45-55 (Skinning 200-275)

MAP LEGEND

1 SHADOWSONG SHRINE
- Highborn Apparition 45-47
- Highborn Lichling 45-57
- Mosshoof Runner 45-46

2 HALDARR ENCAMPMENT
- Cliff Walker 53-54 Elite
- Haldarr Felsworn 45-46
- Haldar Satyr 45-46
- Haldarr Trickster 45-46
- Mosshoof Runner 45-47
- Sentinel Keldara Sunblade 45
- Thunderhead Hippogryph 46-48

3 VALORMOK
- **Ag'Tor Bloodfist 45 Quest**
- **Haggrum Bloodfist 45**
- **Jediga 49 Quest**
- **Kroum 55 Elite Flight Master**
- Mosshoff Runner 45-46

4 BEAR'S HEAD
- Cliff Walker 53 Elite
- Timbermaw Pathfinder 47-48
- Timberweb Recluse 47-48
- Timbermaw Totemic 47-48
- Timbermaw Warrior 47-48

5 RUINS OF ELDARATH
- Lady Sesspira 51 Elite
- Lingering Highborne 48-50
- Spitelash Screamer 46-48
- Spitelash Siren 51-52
- Spitelash Serpent Guard 48-49
- Spitelash Warrior 46-48
- Thunderhead Stagwing 49-60
- Timberweb Recluse 47-48

5A. TEMPLE OF ZIN-MALOR
- Spitelash Serpent Guard 48-49
- Spitelash Siren 51-52
- Warlord Krellian 55

6 FORLORN RIDGE
- Forest ooze 52-53
- Mosshoof Courser 53-54

7 LAKE MINNAR
- Blue Dragon Spawn 50-51
- Blue Scalebane 52-53
- Draconic Magelord 53-54
- Draconic Mageweaver 51-52
- Mosshoof Courser 52-53

8 THE RUINED REACHES
- **Horizon Scout Crewman 42**
- **Jubie GadgetSpring 44 Engineer Supplier, Rare Schematics**
- Coralshell Lurker 53-54
- Great Wavethrasher 53-54
- Makrinni Razorclaw 54-55
- Storm Bay Oracle 54-55

9 RAVENCREST MONUMENT
- Spitelash Battlemaster 53-54
- Spitelash Enchantress 54-55

10 SOUTH RIDGE BEACH
- Coralshell Lurker 53-54
- Makrinni Razorclaw 54-55
- Great Wavethrasher 53-54
- Storm Bay Oracle 54-55

11 HETAERA'S CLUTCH
- Servant of Arkkoroc 53-55 Elite

12 BAY OF STORMS
- **Lormus Thalipedes 60 Quest**
- **Rataf 50 Elite Lormus' pet**
- **Shatllar 50 Elite Lormus' pet**
- **Zaman 50 Elite Lormus' pet**
- Servant of Arkkoroc 53-55 Elite

13 THE SHATTERED STRAND
- Coralshell Lurker 53-54
- Great Wavethrasher 53-54
- Makrinni Razorclaw 54-55
- Spitelash Myrmidon 50-51
- Spitelash Siren 51-52
- Arkkoran Clacker 53-54
- Arkkoran Muckdweller 53-54
- Arkkoran Oracle 53-54

14 TIMBERMAW HOLD
- Cliff Walker 53-54Elite
- Timberweb Recluse 47-48
- Timbermaw Pathfinder 46-47
- Timbermaw Shaman 50-51
- Thunderhead Stagwing 49-50
- Timbermaw Watcher 49-50
- Timbermaw Warrior 47-48

15 URSOLAN
- Timbermaw Shaman 50-51
- Thunderhead Skystormer 51-52
- Timbermaw Ursa 51-52
- Timbermaw Watcher 49-50

16 THALASSIAN BASE CAMP
- Blood Elf Reclaimer 52-53
- Blood Elf Surveyor 51-52
- Thunderhead Skystormer 51-52

17 LEGASH ENCAMPMENT
- Cliff Breaker 54-55 Elite
- Cliff Walker 52-53 Elite
- Forest Ooze 52-53
- Legashi Hellcaller 52-53
- Legashi Rogue 52-53
- Legashi Satyr 51-52
- Mosshoof Courser 51-52
- Thunderhead Consort 53-54
- Thunderhead Skystormer 51-52

18 BITTER REACHES
- Cliff Breaker 54-55 Elite
- Cliff Thunderer 54-55 Elite
- Cliff Walker 52-53 Elite
- Forest Ooze 52-53
- Mistwalker Ravager 52-53
- Mosshoof Courser 51-52
- Thunderhead Skystormer 51-52
- Thunderhead Consort 53-54
- Thunderhead Patriarch 54-55

19 JAGGED REACHES
- Coralshell Lurker 53-54
- Makrinni Scrabbler 52-53
- Storm Bay Warrior 51-52
- Wavethrasher 52-53

20 TOWER OF ELPARA
- Coralshell Lurker 53-54
- Makrinni Scrabbler 52-53
- Storm Bay Warrior 51-52
- Wavethrasher 52-53

21 TEMPLE OF ARKKORAN
- Arkkoran Clacker 53-54
- Arkkoran Oracle 54-55
- Arkkoran Pincer 54-55
- **Arkkoran Muckdweller 53-54**
- **Lord Arkkoran 60 Elite**

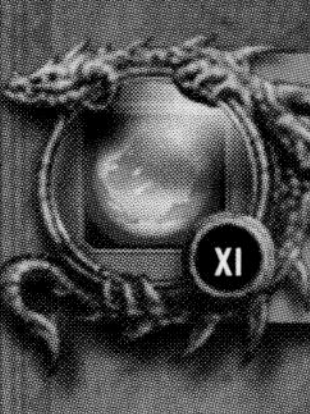

QUESTS

QUEST	M LEV	Q LEV	QUEST LAUNCHER	QUEST FINISHER	CHAIN?	XP---	XP--	XP-	XP+	XP++	XP+++	CASH REWARD
A Crew Under Fire	48	57	Captain Vanessa Beltis	Captain Vanessa Beltis	N	60	120	240	360	480	600	None
A Land Filled with Hatred	45	47	Loh'atu	Loh'atu	N	420	850	1700	2500	3350	4200	70 00
A Meeting with the Master	45	48	Sanath Lim-yo	Sanath Lim-yo	N	220	440	875	1300	1750	2200	None
Andron's Payment to Jediga	45	52	Andron Gant	Jediga	N	380	750	1500	2300	3050	3800	75 00
Azsharite	45	58	Loramus Thalipedes	Loramus Thalipedes	N	775	1550	3100	4650	6200	7750	2 65 00
Breaking the Ward	45	58	Loramus Thalipedes	Loramus Thalipedes	Y	310	625	1250	1850	2500	3100	None
Delivery to Andron Gant	45	52	Jediga	Andron Gant	Y	260	500	1000	1550	2050	2550	60 00
Delivery to Archmage Xylem	45	52	Jediga	Archmage Xylem	Y	260	500	1000	1550	2050	2550	40 00
Delivery to Jes'rimon	45	52	Jediga	Jes'rimon	Y	260	500	1000	1550	2050	2550	40 00
Delivery to Magatha	45	52	Jediga	Magatha Grimtotem	Y	260	500	1000	1550	2050	2550	None
Jes'rimon's Payment to Jediga	45	52	Jes'rimon	Jediga	N	380	750	1500	2300	3050	3800	60 00
Kim'jael Indeed!	47	53	Kim'jael	Kim'jael	N	650	1300	2600	3950	5250	6550	8 00
REWARD: 3 M73 Frag Grenades												
Kim'jael's Missing" Equipment"	47	53	Kim'jael	Kim'jael	N	650	1300	2600	3950	5250	6550	1 60 00
Loramus	45	57	Loramus Thalipedes	Loramus Thalipedes	Y	60	120	240	360	480	600	None
Magatha's Payment to Jediga	45	52	Magatha Grimtotem	Jediga	N	380	750	1500	2300	3050	3800	60 00
Meeting with the Master	45	55	Sanath Lim-yo	Sanath Lim-yo	N	0	0	0	0	0	0	None
Return Trip	45	55	Nyrill	Nyrill	N	0	0	0	0	0	0	None
Spiritual Unrest	45	47	Loh'atu	Loh'atu	N	420	850	1700	2500	3350	4200	50 00
Stealing Knowledge	45	52	Jediga	Jediga	N	500	1000	2050	3050	4100	5100	None
The Formation of Felbane	45	58	Loramus Thalipedes	Galvan the Ancient	Y	470	925	1850	2800	3700	4650	None
The Name of the Beast	45	58	Loramus Thalipedes	Lord Arkkoroc	Y	625	1250	2500	3700	4950	6200	None
The Name of the Beast	45	58	Lord Arkkoroc	Lord Arkkoroc	Y	625	1250	2500	3700	4950	6200	2 65 00
The Name of the Beast	45	58	Lord Arkkoroc	Loramus Thalipedes	Y	310	625	1250	1850	2500	3100	None
Xylem's Payment to Jediga	45	52	Archmage Xylem	Jediga	N	380	750	1500	2300	3050	3800	60 00

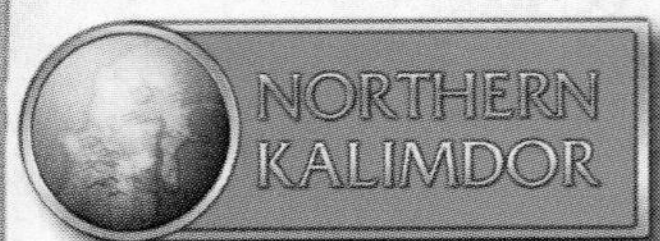

DARKSHORE

Darkshore is the first port of call for Night Elves leaving their beloved Darnassus behind. This zone can easily support those characters wishing to create a home until they gain a bit of experience. As a zone on the sea, it has many beaches and the perils to go with them. While it's not as large a metropolis as Stormwind or Ironforge, Auberdeen does a good job of supporting the adventurers and boasts a fine dock in which ships ferry travelers into more dangerous territories.

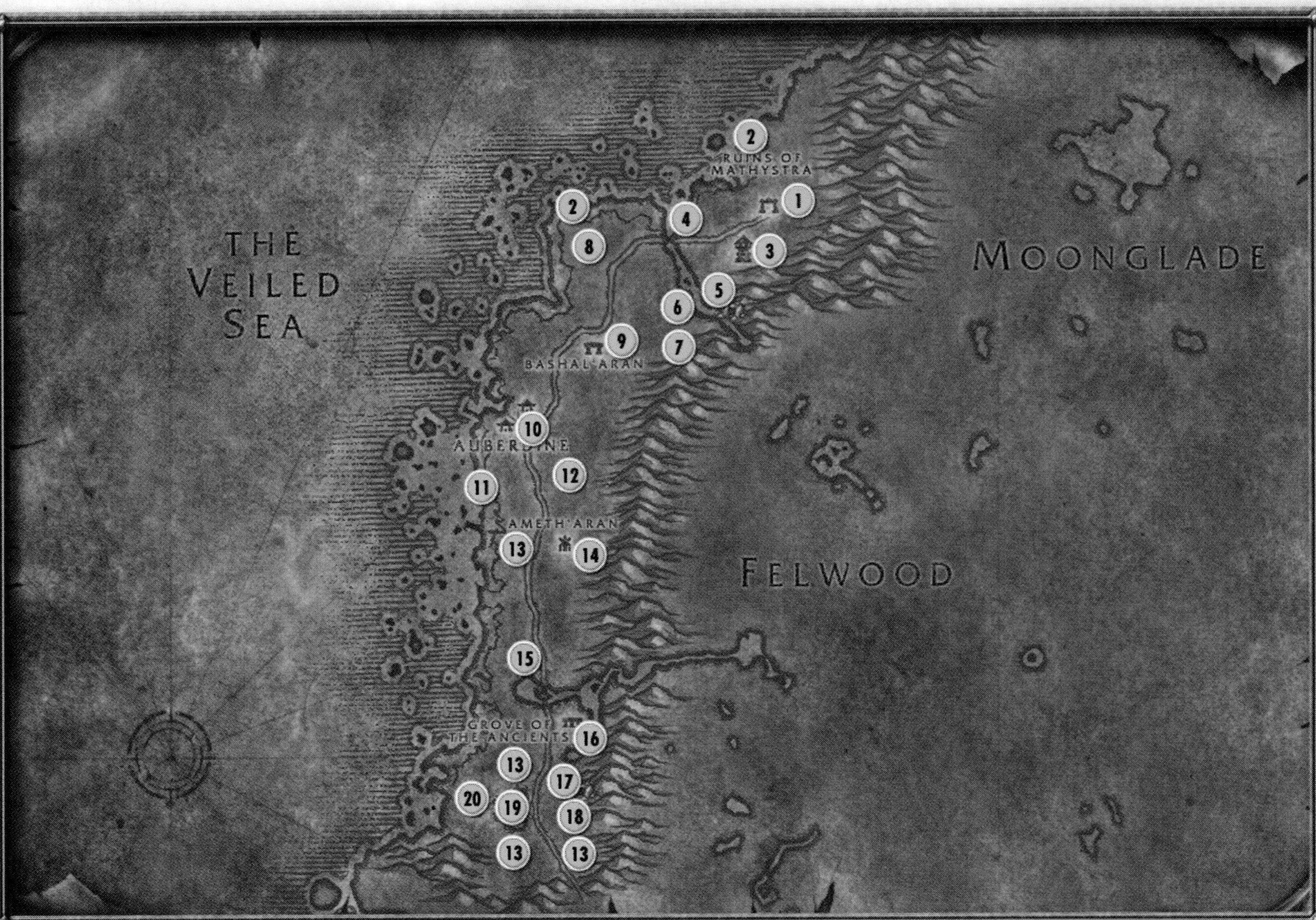

The Veiled Sea
Ruins of Mathystra
Moonglade
Bashal'Aran
Auberdine
Ameth'Aran
Felwood
Grove of the Ancients

LOCAL RESOURCES

MINING

METAL	AVAILABILITY
Copper	Abundant
Tin	Rare

HERBALISM

HERB	AVAILABILITY
Peacebloom	Abundant
Silverleaf	Abundant
Briarthorn	Abundant
Bruiseweed	Rare

SKINNING

Quantity of Skinnable Creatures: High

Levels of Skinnable Creatures: 10-16 (Skinning 50-80)

MAP LEGEND

1 RUINS OF MATHYSTRA
Giant Forestrider 17-19
Moonstalker Matriarch 19-20
Moonstalker Sire 18-19
Moonstalker Runt 16 Moonstalker Matriarch's Minion
Stormscale Myrmidon 18-19
Stormscale Sorceress 19-20
Stormscale Warrior 20-21

2 MYSTS EDGE
Gelkak Gyromist 18 Quest
Raging Reef Crawler 20-21
Greymist Tidehunter 19
Greymist Oracle 18-19
Elder Darkshore Thresher 16-17

3 TOWER OF ALTHALAXX
Dark Strand Fanatic 16-17
Delmanis the Hated 17
Dark Strand Voidcaller 28-29
Dark Strand Voidcaller's Minion 28-29
Balthule Shadowstrike 15

4 CLIFFSPRING RIVER
Encrusted Tide Crawler 18-20
Reef Crawler 15-17
Moonstalker 14-15
Rabid Thistle Bear 13-15
Forestrider 14-16

5 CLIFFSPRING FALLS
Stormscale Wave Rider 15-16
Stormscale Siren 16-17

6 BLACKWOOD VILLAGE
Blackwood Warrior 16-17
Blackwood Totemic 18

7 THISTLE BEAR DEN
Thistle Cub 10
Den Mother 18

8 DARKSHORE GENERAL
Thistle Bear 11-12
Rabid Thistle Bear 13-14
Moonstalker Runt 10-11
Moonstalker 14-15
Forestrider Fledgling 11-13

9 BASHAL'ARAN
Asterion 15 Quest
Vile Sprite 10-11
Wild Grell 11-12
Deth'ryll Satyr 12-13

10 AUBERDINE
Auberdine Sentinel 40
Tharnarian Treetender 18 Quest
Terenthis 15 Quest
Grimclaw 13 Quest
Sentinel Elissa Starbreeze 20 Quest
Gershala Nightwhisper 20 Quest
Thelgrum Stonehammer 30 Mining Supplier
Jenna Lemkenilli 26 Journeyman Engineer
Kurdram Stonehammer 35 Mining Trainer
Delfrum Flintbeard 25 Journeyman Blacksmith
Elisa Steelhand 30 Blacksmithing Supplier
Gorbold Steelhand 30 General Trade Supplier
Valdaron 14 Tailoring Supplies
Grondal Moonbreeze 29 Journeyman Tailor
Shaldyn 15 Clothier
Alanndarian 22
Dalmond 17 General Goods
Naram Longclaw 20 Weaponsmith
Thundris Windreaver 15
Mavralyn 18 Leather Armor and Leatherworking Supplies
Harlon Thornguard 25 Armorer & Shieldsmith
Archeologist Hollee 12 Explorer's League Quest
Sentinel Glynda Nal'Shea 45 Quest
Barithras Moonshade 14 Quest
Allyndia 15 Grocer
Taldan 16 Drink Vendor
Innkeeper Shaussiy 30 Innkeeper
Kyndri 13 Baker
Laird 14 Fish Vendor
Wizbang Cranktoggle 15 Quest
Cerellean Whiteclaw 15 Quest
Boats to Teldrassil and Menethil
Gwennyth Bly'Leggonde 21
Caylais Moonfeather 55 Elite Hippogryph Master
Yalda 51
Jaelysa 30 Stable Master
Gubber Blump 15 Quest

11 THE LONG WASH
Pygmy Tide Crawler 9-10
Greymist Raider 11-12
Greymist Coast Runner 12-13
Young Reef Crawler 10-11
Darkshore Thresher 13

12 MOONKIN CAVE
Moonkin 12-13
Young Moonkin 11-12

13 TWILIGHT VALE
Blackwood Windtalker 13-14
Blackwood Pathfinder 12-13
Moonstalker 14-15
Rabid Thistle Bear 13-14
Grizzled Thistle Bear 16-17
Foreststrider 15
Blackwood Warrior 16-17
Blackwood Totemic 17-18
Giant Foreststrider 17-19
Moonstalker Sire 18-19
Moonstalker Matriarch 19-20
Moonstalker Runt 16 Moonstalker Matriarch's Minion

14 AMETH'ARAN
Anaya Dawnrunner 16 Quest
Cursed Highborn 10-11
Writhing Highborn 11-12
Wailing Highborn 12-13

15 WILDBEND RIVER

16 GROVE OF THE ANCIENTS
Onu 55 Ancient of Lore Quest
Tiyana 15 Grocer
Ullana 15 Trade Supplies

17 Grimclaw 13 Quest

18 BLACKWOOD DEN
Blackwood Ursa 18-19
Blackwood Shaman 19-20

19 THE MASTER'S GLAIVE
Twilight Disciple 16-17
Twilight Thug 17-18

20 REMTRAVEL'S EXCAVATION
Prospector Remtravel 16 Explorer's League Quest
Cracked Golem 18-19

21 Sentinel Aynasha 20 Quest

QUESTS

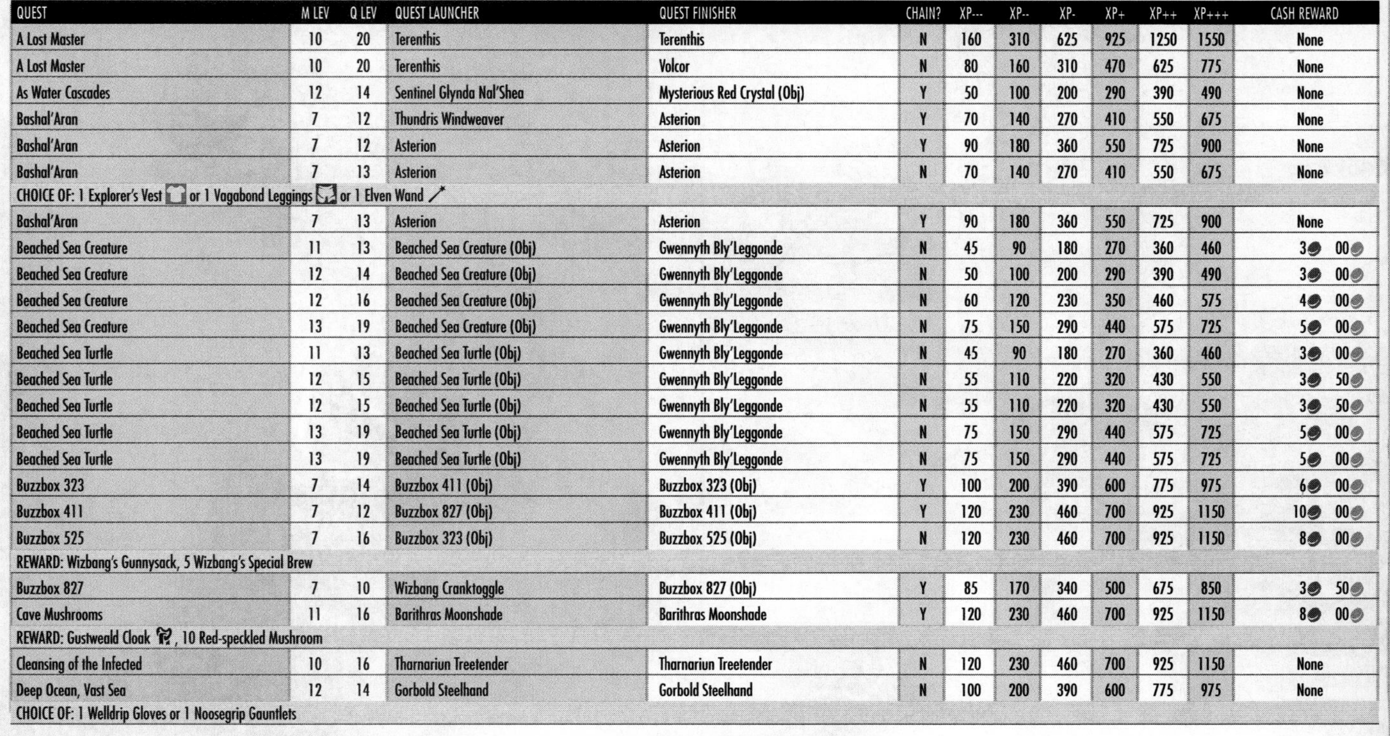

QUEST	M LEV	Q LEV	QUEST LAUNCHER	QUEST FINISHER	CHAIN?	XP---	XP--	XP-	XP+	XP++	XP+++	CASH REWARD
A Lost Master	10	20	Terenthis	Terenthis	N	160	310	625	925	1250	1550	None
A Lost Master	10	20	Terenthis	Volcor	N	80	160	310	470	625	775	None
As Water Cascades	12	14	Sentinel Glynda Nal'Shea	Mysterious Red Crystal (Obj)	Y	50	100	200	290	390	490	None
Bashal'Aran	7	12	Thundris Windweaver	Asterion	Y	70	140	270	410	550	675	None
Bashal'Aran	7	12	Asterion	Asterion	Y	90	180	360	550	725	900	None
Bashal'Aran	7	13	Asterion	Asterion	N	70	140	270	410	550	675	None
CHOICE OF: 1 Explorer's Vest or 1 Vagabond Leggings or 1 Elven Wand												
Bashal'Aran	7	13	Asterion	Asterion	Y	90	180	360	550	725	900	None
Beached Sea Creature	11	13	Beached Sea Creature (Obj)	Gwennyth Bly'Leggonde	N	45	90	180	270	360	460	3 00
Beached Sea Creature	12	14	Beached Sea Creature (Obj)	Gwennyth Bly'Leggonde	N	50	100	200	290	390	490	3 00
Beached Sea Creature	12	16	Beached Sea Creature (Obj)	Gwennyth Bly'Leggonde	N	60	120	230	350	460	575	4 00
Beached Sea Creature	13	19	Beached Sea Creature (Obj)	Gwennyth Bly'Leggonde	N	75	150	290	440	575	725	5 00
Beached Sea Turtle	11	13	Beached Sea Turtle (Obj)	Gwennyth Bly'Leggonde	N	45	90	180	270	360	460	3 00
Beached Sea Turtle	12	15	Beached Sea Turtle (Obj)	Gwennyth Bly'Leggonde	N	55	110	220	320	430	550	3 50
Beached Sea Turtle	12	15	Beached Sea Turtle (Obj)	Gwennyth Bly'Leggonde	N	55	110	220	320	430	550	3 50
Beached Sea Turtle	13	19	Beached Sea Turtle (Obj)	Gwennyth Bly'Leggonde	N	75	150	290	440	575	725	5 00
Beached Sea Turtle	13	19	Beached Sea Turtle (Obj)	Gwennyth Bly'Leggonde	N	75	150	290	440	575	725	5 00
Buzzbox 323	7	14	Buzzbox 411 (Obj)	Buzzbox 323 (Obj)	Y	100	200	390	600	775	975	6 00
Buzzbox 411	7	12	Buzzbox 827 (Obj)	Buzzbox 411 (Obj)	Y	120	230	460	700	925	1150	10 00
Buzzbox 525	7	16	Buzzbox 323 (Obj)	Buzzbox 525 (Obj)	N	120	230	460	700	925	1150	8 00
REWARD: Wizbang's Gunnysack, 5 Wizbang's Special Brew												
Buzzbox 827	7	10	Wizbang Cranktoggle	Buzzbox 827 (Obj)	Y	85	170	340	500	675	850	3 50
Cave Mushrooms	11	16	Barithras Moonshade	Barithras Moonshade	Y	120	230	460	700	925	1150	8 00
REWARD: Gustweald Cloak, 10 Red-speckled Mushroom												
Cleansing of the Infected	10	16	Tharnariun Treetender	Tharnariun Treetender	N	120	230	460	700	925	1150	None
Deep Ocean, Vast Sea	12	14	Gorbold Steelhand	Gorbold Steelhand	N	100	200	390	600	775	975	None
CHOICE OF: 1 Welldrip Gloves or 1 Noosegrip Gauntlets												

QUEST	M LEV	Q LEV	QUEST LAUNCHER	QUEST FINISHER	CHAIN?	XP---	XP--	XP-	XP+	XP++	XP+++	CASH REWARD
Easy Strider Living	9	12	Alanndarian Nightsong	Alanndarian Nightsong	N	90	180	360	550	725	900	None
REWARD: Recipe: Strider Stew, 5 Strider Stew												
Escape Through Force	10	22	Volcor	Terenthis	N	180	350	700	1050	1400	1750	14 00
REWARD: Steadfast Cinch												
Escape Through Force	10	22		Volcor	Y	0	0	0	0	0	0	None
Escape Through Stealth	10	20	Volcor	Terenthis	N	80	160	310	470	625	775	6 00
REWARD: Scarab Trousers												
Escape Through Stealth	10	20		Volcor	Y	0	0	0	0	0	0	None
For Love Eternal	11	16	Cerellean Whiteclaw	Cerellean Whiteclaw	N	90	180	350	525	700	875	None
REWARD: Tear of Grief												
Fruit of the Sea	15	17	Gubber Blump	Gubber Blump	N	130	250	500	750	1000	1250	None
CHOICE OF: 1 Shucking Gloves or 1 Crustacean Boots												
Gyromast's Retrieval	14	20	Gelkak Gyromast	Gelkak Gyromast	Y	160	310	625	925	1250	1550	12 00
Gyromast's Revenge	14	20	Gelkak Gyromast	Gelkak Gyromast	N	120	230	460	700	925	1150	9 00
REWARD: 5 Elixir of Water Breathing												
How Big a Threat?	10	14	Terenthis	Terenthis	N	100	200	390	600	775	975	None
How Big a Threat?	10	14	Terenthis	Terenthis	Y	75	150	300	440	600	750	None
Journey to Darkshore!	1	1	Captain Quirk	Captain Quirk	N	0	0	0	0	0	0	None
Journey to Menethil Harbor!	1	1	Captain Quirk	Captain Quirk	N	0	0	0	0	0	0	None
Mathystra Relics	11	20	Onu	Onu	N	200	390	775	1150	1550	1950	None
CHOICE OF: 1 Hardwood Cudgel or 1 Woodsman Sword												
Onu	11	16	Barithras Moonshade	Onu	Y	60	120	230	350	460	575	None
Onu is meditating	1	1	Onu	Onu	N	0	0	0	0	0	0	None
REWARD: Phial of Scrying												
Onu is meditating	1	1	Onu	Onu	N	0	0	0	0	0	0	None
REWARD: Phial of Scrying												
Plagued Lands	10	14	Tharnariun Treetender	Tharnariun Treetender	Y	100	200	390	600	775	975	6 00
Return to Onu	11	17	Twilight Tome (Obj)	Onu	N	95	190	380	575	750	950	7 00
Tharnariun's Hope	10	18	Tharnariun Treetender	Tharnariun Treetender	N	140	270	550	800	1100	1350	None
CHOICE OF: 1 Evergreen Gloves or 1 Timberland Cape												
The Absent Minded Prospector	15	20	Archaeologist Hollee	Prospector Remtravel	N	120	230	460	700	925	1150	None
The Absent Minded Prospector	15	20	Archaeologist Flagongut	Archaeologist Flagongut	N	200	390	775	1150	1550	1950	None
CHOICE OF: 1 Relic Blade or 1 Skullchipper												
The Absent Minded Prospector	15	20	Prospector Remtravel	Archaeologist Hollee	Y	200	390	775	1150	1550	1950	None
The Absent Minded Prospector	15	20	Archaeologist Hollee	Chief Archaeologist Greywhisker	Y	120	230	460	700	925	1150	None
CHOICE OF: 1 Hammerfist Gloves or 1 Windfelt Gloves or 1 Relic Hunter Belt												
The Absent Minded Prospector	15	20	Chief Archaeologist Greywhisker	Archaeologist Flagongut	Y	160	310	625	925	1250	1550	None
The Blackwood Corrupted	15	18	Thundris Windweaver	Thundris Windweaver	N	170	340	675	1000	1350	1700	20 00
CHOICE OF: 1 Moonstone Wand or 1 Wildkeeper Leggings or 1 Guststorm Legguards												
The Cliffspring River	11	15	Thundris Windweaver	Thundris Windweaver	N	80	160	320	480	650	800	None
The Fall of Ameth'Aran	9	12	Sentinel Tysha Moonblade	Sentinel Tysha Moonblade	N	90	180	360	550	725	900	5 00
The Family and the Fishing Pole	10	14	Gubber Blump	Gubber Blump	N	100	200	390	600	775	975	None
REWARD: Blump Family Fishing Pole												
The Fragments Within	12	14	Mysterious Red Crystal (Obj)	Sentinel Glynda Nal'Shea	N	100	200	390	600	775	975	None
CHOICE OF: 1 Briarsteel Shortsword or 1 Curvewood Dagger or 1 Oakthrush Staff												
The Master's Glaive	11	17	Onu	Scrying Bowl (Obj)	Y	65	130	250	380	500	625	None
The Red Crystal	12	14	Sentinel Glynda Nal'Shea	Sentinel Glynda Nal'Shea	Y	50	100	200	290	390	490	6 00
The Sleeper Has Awakened	17	20	Kerlonian Evershade	Liladris Moonriver	N	160	310	625	925	1250	1550	None
CHOICE OF: 1 Owlsight Rifle or 1 Jadefinger Baton or 1 Steelcap Shield												
The Tower of Althalaxx	13	18	Sentinel Elissa Starbreeze	Balthule Shadowstrike	Y	70	140	270	410	550	675	None
The Tower of Althalaxx	13	18	Balthule Shadowstrike	Balthule Shadowstrike	Y	140	270	550	800	1100	1350	10 00
The Tower of Althalaxx	13	18	Balthule Shadowstrike	Delgren the Purifier	Y	100	200	400	600	800	1000	None
The Tower of Althalaxx	13	21	Delgren the Purifier	Delgren the Purifier	N	170	330	650	1000	1300	1650	None
The Tower of Althalaxx	13	24	Delgren the Purifier	Delgren the Purifier	Y	200	390	775	1150	1550	1950	None
CHOICE OF: 1 Clergy Ring or 1 Staff of the Purifier												
The Tower of Althalaxx	13	28	Delgren the Purifier	Balthule Shadowstrike	Y	55	110	230	340	460	575	None
The Tower of Althalaxx	13	28	Delgren the Purifier	Delgren the Purifier	Y	230	460	925	1400	1850	2300	None
The Tower of Althalaxx	13	31	Balthule Shadowstrike	Delgren the Purifier	N	250	500	1000	1500	2000	2500	None
CHOICE OF: 1 Pious Legwraps or 1 Seraph's Strike												
The Tower of Althalaxx	13	31	Balthule Shadowstrike	Balthule Shadowstrike	Y	250	500	1000	1500	2000	2500	None
The Twilight Camp	11	17	Scrying Bowl (Obj)	Twilight Tome	Y	130	250	500	750	1000	1250	9 00
Therylune's Escape	10	18	Therylune	Therysil	N	140	270	550	800	1100	1350	10 00
Thundris Windweaver	11	15	Terenthis	Thundris Windweaver	Y	10	20	40	65	85	110	None
Tools of the Highborne	9	12	Thundris Windweaver	Thundris Windweaver	N	90	180	360	550	725	900	5 00
REWARD: Ivy Cuffs												
WANTED: Murkdeep!	15	18	WANTED: Murkdeep! (Obj)	Sentinel Glynda Nal'Shea	N	170	340	675	1000	1350	1700	None
CHOICE OF: 1 Timberland Armguards or 1 Ridgeback Bracers or 1 Breakwater Girdle												
Washed Ashore	11	13	Gwennyth Bly'Leggonde	Gwennyth Bly'Leggonde	Y	70	140	270	410	550	675	4 00
Washed Ashore	11	14	Gwennyth Bly'Leggonde	Gwennyth Bly'Leggonde	N	100	200	390	600	775	975	None
CHOICE OF: 1 Sandcomber Boots or 1 Dryweed Belt or 1 Clamshell Bracers												

DESOLACE

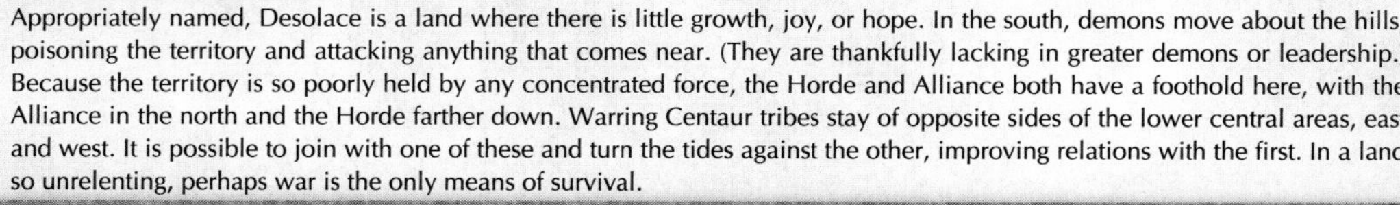

Appropriately named, Desolace is a land where there is little growth, joy, or hope. In the south, demons move about the hills, poisoning the territory and attacking anything that comes near. (They are thankfully lacking in greater demons or leadership.) Because the territory is so poorly held by any concentrated force, the Horde and Alliance both have a foothold here, with the Alliance in the north and the Horde farther down. Warring Centaur tribes stay of opposite sides of the lower central areas, east and west. It is possible to join with one of these and turn the tides against the other, improving relations with the first. In a land so unrelenting, perhaps war is the only means of survival.

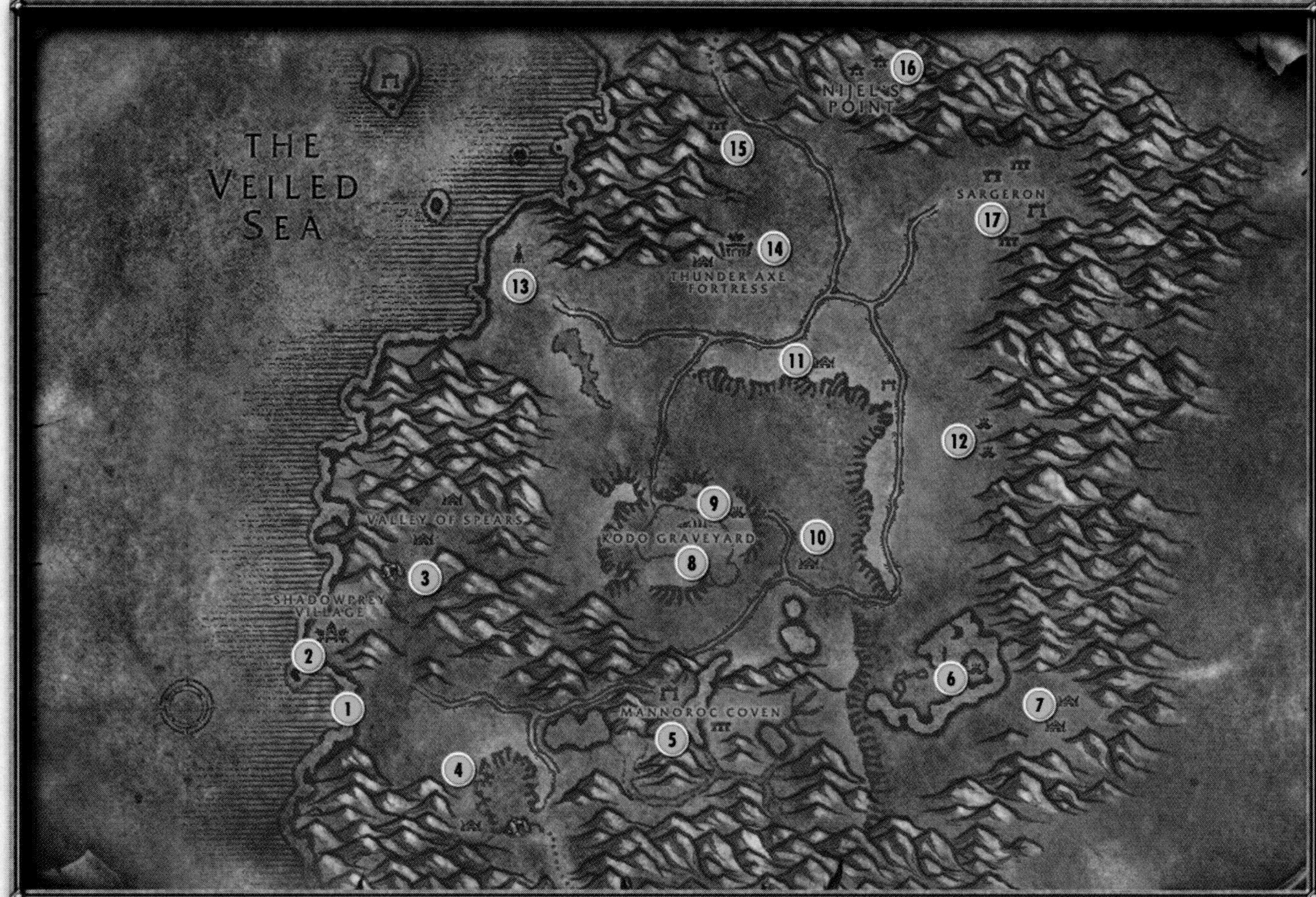

LOCAL RESOURCES

MINING

METAL	AVAILABILITY
Mithril	Rare

HERBALISM: NONE

SKINNING

Quantity of Skinnable Creatures: Abundant

Levels of Skinnable Creatures: 30-40 (Skinning 100-175)

MAP LEGEND

1 SAR'THERIS STRAND
- Drysnap Crawler 33-34
- Drysnap Pincer 34-35
- Elder Thunder Lizard 34-38
- Dread Ripper 37-40
- Scorpashi Lasher 34-35
- Scorpashi Snapper 30-32

2 SHADOWSPREY VILLAGE
- **Thalon 55+ Wind Rider Master**
- **Jinar'Zillen 40 Quest**
- **Roon Wildmane 45 Quest**
- **Inkeeper Sikewa 30 Innkeeper**
- **Aboda 30 Stable Master**
- **Taiga Wiseman 60 Quest**

3 VALLEY OF SPEARS
- Maraudine Bonepaw 37-38+
- Maraudine Khan Advisor 38-39+
- Maraudine Khan Guard 39-40+
- Maraudine Marauder 39-40+
- Maraudine Mauler 38-39+
- Maraudine Pack Runner 39+
- Maraudine Scout 37-38
- Maraudine Windchaser 38-39
- Maraudine Wrangler 37-38

4 GELKIS VILLAGE
- Gelkis Earthcaller 34-35
- Gelkis Marauder 35-36
- Gelkis Mauler 35-36
- Gelkis Outrunner 32-33
- Gelkis Scout 32-33
- Gelkis Stamper 33-34
- Gelkis Windchaser 33-34
- Dread Ripper 37-40
- Elder Thunder Lizard 34-38

5 MANNOROC COVEN
- Scorpashi Lasher 34-35
- Scorpashi Snapper 30-32
- Elder Thunder Lizard 34-38
- Ley Hunter 39-40
- Doomwarder 37-38
- Doomwarder Captain 38-39
- Doomwarder Lord 39-40
- Lesser Infernal 36-37
- Nether Maiden 37-38
- Mage Hunter 38-39

6 MAGRAM VILLAGE
- **Warug 44 Quest**
- Magram Bonepaw 37-38
- Magram Marauder 35-36
- Elder Thunder Lizard 34-38
- Dread Ripper 37-40
- Whirlwind Shredder 32-34

7 SHADOWBREAK RAVINE

8 KODO GRAVEYARD
- Aged Kodo 33-35
- Ancient Kodo 37-38
- Dying Kodo 37
- Carrion Horror 35-38

9 GHOST WALKER POST
- **Gurda Wildmane 35 Quest**
- **Felgur Twocuts 44 Quest**
- **Superior Macecrafter 40**
- **Nataka Longhorn 40 Quest**
- **Narv Hidecrafter 42 Expert Leathercrafter**
- Takata Steelblade 40 Quest
- Maurin Bonesplitter 35 Quest
- Harnor 40 Food & Drink
- Kireena 41 Trade Goods
- Ghost Walker Brave 50

10 SCRABBLESCREWS CAMP
- **Smeed Scrabblescrews 45**
- Gizelton Caravan Kodo 35
- Tamed Kodo 34-35

11 KORMEK'S HUT
- **Bibbly F'utzbuckle 45 Quest**
- **Cork Gizelton 38 Quest**
- **Rigger Gizelton 36 Quest**
- Gizelton Caravan Kodo 35
- Hulking Gritjaw Basilisk 37-38
- Elder Thunder Lizard 34-38
- Bonepaw Hyena 30-32
- Whirlwind Stormwalker 36-38
- Dread Flyer 34-38
- Scorpashi Lasher 34-35
- Scorpashi Snapper 30-32

12 KOLKAR VILLAGE
- Elder Thunder Lizard 34-38
- Raging Thunder Lizard 31-34
- Dread Swoop 31-33
- Kolkar Battle Lord 32-33
- Kolkar Centaur 30-31
- Kolkar Destroyer 32-33
- Kolkar Mauler 31-32
- Kolkar Scout 30-31
- Kolkar Windchaser 31-32

13 ETHEL RETHOR
- **Azore Aldamort 60 Quest**
- Scorpashi Lasher 34-35
- Scorpashi Snapper 30-32
- Hulking Gritjaw Basilisk 37-38
- Whirlwind Stormwalker 35-37
- Whirlwind Ripper 32-34
- Dread Swoop 30-33
- Slitherblade Myrmidon 34-35
- Slitherblade Naga 32-33
- Slitherblade Oracle 34-35
- Slitherblade Razortail 35-36
- Slitherblade Sea Witch 35-36
- Slitherblade Tidehunter 36-37
- Slitherblade Warrior 33-34

14 THUNDER AXE FORTRESS
- Burning Blade Adept 31-32
- Burning Blade Augur 30-31
- Burning Blade Felsworn 31-32
- Burning Blade Invoker 38-39
- Burning Blade Reaver 30-31
- Burning Blade Shadowmage 32-33
- Burning Blade Summoner 38-39

15 TETHRIS ARAN

16 NIJEL'S POINT
- **Vahlarriel Demonslayer 37 Quest**
- **Corporal Melkins 39**
- **Captain Pentigast 42**
- **Kreldig Ungar 35 Reclaimers Inc. Quest**
- **Innkeeper Lyshaera 30 Innkeeper**
- **Janet Hommers 40 Food & Drink**
- **Shelgrayn 30 Stable Master**
- **Baritanas Skyriver 55 Hyppogryph Master**
- Nijel's Point Guard 45

17 SARGERON
- Hatefury Betrayer 32-33
- Hatefury Felsworn 30-32
- Hatefury Hellcaller 31-33
- Hatefury Rogue 30-32
- Hatefury Shadowstalker 32-33
- Hatefury Trickster 31-32

QUESTS

QUEST	M LEV	Q LEV	QUEST LAUNCHER	QUEST FINISHER	CHAIN?	XP---	XP--	XP-	XP+	XP++	XP+++	CASH REWARD
Assault on the Kolkar	30	32	Warug	Warug	Y	260	500	1000	1550	2050	2550	None
Bodyguard for Hire	30	35	Cork Gizelton	Smeed Scrabblescrew	N	280	550	1100	1650	2200	2750	None
REWARD: Trader's Ring												
Bone Collector	33	39	Bibbly F'utzbuckle	Bibbly F'utzbuckle	N	230	450	900	1350	1800	2250	None
REWARD: Kodobone Necklace												
Book of the Ancients	34	40	Azore Aldamort	Azore Aldamort	N	390	775	1550	2350	3100	3900	50 00
Broken Tears	30	33	Warug	Warug	Y	270	525	1050	1600	2100	2650	None
Brother Anton	34	39	Brother Crowley	Brother Anton	Y	30	60	120	180	240	300	None
Brutal Politics	30	35	Captain Pentigast	Warug	Y	210	410	825	1250	1650	2050	None
Catch of the Day	32	37	Nataka Longhorn	Nataka Longhorn	N	210	420	850	1250	1700	2100	None
CHOICE OF: 3 Mithril Ore or 5 Thick Leather or 5 Mageweave Cloth												
Centaur Bounty	30	31	Felgur Twocuts	Felgur Twocuts	N	320	625	1250	1900	2500	3150	None
CHOICE OF: 1 Lilac Sash or 1 Braced Handguards												
Centaur Bounty	30	31	Corporal Melkins	Corporal Melkins	N	380	750	1500	2250	3000	3750	None
REWARD: Ring of Calm												
Claim Rackmore's Treasure!	30	36	Rackmore's Log (Obj)	Rackmore's Chest (Obj)	N	280	550	1100	1700	2250	2800	1 15 00
Clam Bait	31	35	Mai'Lahii	Mai'Lahii	N	280	550	1100	1650	2200	2750	None
Down the Scarlet Path	34	39	Brother Anton	Brother Anton	Y	300	600	1200	1800	2400	3000	45 00
Down the Scarlet Path	34	40	Brother Anton	Raleigh the Devout	N	160	310	625	925	1250	1550	None
Family Tree	32	35	Cliffwatcher Longhorn	Nataka Longhorn	N	210	410	825	1250	1650	2050	25 00
Fish in a Bucket	1	1	Jinar'Zillen	Jinar'Zillen	N	0	0	0	0	0	0	50
REWARD: Bloodbelly Fish												
Gelkis Alliance	30	33	Gurda Wildmane	Uthek the Wise	Y	65	130	260	400	525	650	None
Get Me Out of Here!	34	39	Melizza Brimbuzzle	Hornizz Brimbuzzle	N	230	450	900	1350	1800	2250	45 00
Ghost-o-plasm Round Up	34	39	Hornizz Brimbuzzle	Hornizz Brimbuzzle	N	230	450	900	1350	1800	2250	45 00
CHOICE OF: 1 Condor Bracers or 1 Anchorhold Buckler												
Gizelton Caravan	32	38	Rigger Gizelton	Smeed Scrabblescrew	N	290	575	1150	1700	2300	2850	None
CHOICE OF: 1 Sidegunner Shottie or 1 Kodo Brander or 1 Studded Ring Shield												
Gizmo for Warug	30	35	Warug	Warug	N	210	410	825	1250	1650	2050	None
Hand of Iruxos	32	38	Taiga Wisemane	Taiga Wisemane	Y	290	575	1150	1700	2300	2850	45 00
Hunting in Stranglethorn	28	31	Roon Wildmane	Hemet Nesingwary	N	130	250	500	750	1000	1250	None
Khan Dez'hepah	30	35	Felgur Twocuts	Felgur Twocuts	N	350	700	1400	2050	2750	3450	None
Khan Hratha	30	42	Uthek the Wise	Uthek the Wise	N	430	850	1700	2600	3450	4300	None
CHOICE OF: 1 Gelkis Marauder Chain or 1 Uthek's Finger												
Khan Hratha	30	42	Warug	Warug	N	430	850	1700	2600	3450	4300	None
CHOICE OF: 1 Magram Hunter's Belt or 1 Ceremonial Centaur Blanket												
Khan Jehn	30	37	Uthek the Wise	Uthek the Wise	Y	290	575	1150	1700	2300	2850	None
Khan Shaka	30	37	Warug	Warug	Y	290	575	1150	1700	2300	2850	None

XI

QUESTS continued

QUEST	M LEV	Q LEV	QUEST LAUNCHER	QUEST FINISHER	CHAIN?	XP---	XP--	XP-	XP+	XP++	XP+++	CASH REWARD
Kodo Roundup	30	34	Smeed Scrabblescrew	Smeed Scrabblescrew	N	200	400	800	1200	1600	2000	None
CHOICE OF: 1 Kodo Rustler Boots or 1 Wrangling Spaulders												
Magram Alliance	30	33	Gurda Wildmane	Warug	Y	65	130	260	400	525	650	None
Ongeku	30	37	Uthek the Wise	Uthek the Wise	Y	290	575	1150	1700	2300	2850	None
Other Fish to Fry	32	36	Drulzegar Skraghook	Drulzegar Skraghook	N	280	550	1100	1700	2250	2800	None
Portals of the Legion	32	38	Taiga Wisemane	Taiga Wisemane	N	360	700	1400	2150	2850	3550	45● 00●
CHOICE OF: 1 Pardoc Grips or 1 Ringtail Girdle or 1 Bracesteel Belt												
Raid on the Kolkar	30	32	Uthek the Wise	Uthek the Wise	Y	260	500	1000	1550	2050	2550	None
Reagents for Reclaimers Inc.	30	33	Kreldig Ungor	Kreldig Ungor	Y	270	525	1050	1600	2100	2650	35● 00●
Reagents for Reclaimers Inc.	30	35	Kreldig Ungor	Kreldig Ungor	Y	280	550	1100	1650	2200	2750	25● 00●
Reagents for Reclaimers Inc.	30	40	Kreldig Ungor	Roetten Stonehammer	N	320	625	1250	1900	2500	3150	35● 00●
CHOICE OF: 1 Auric Bracers or 1 Stormfire Gauntlets												
Reagents for Reclaimers Inc.	30	40	Kreldig Ungor	Kreldig Ungor	Y	320	625	1250	1900	2500	3150	35● 00●
Regthar Deathgate	30	32	Nazgrel	Regthar Deathgate	Y	65	130	260	380	500	650	None
Regthar Deathgate	30	32	Belgrom Rockmaul	Regthar Deathgate	Y	65	130	260	380	500	650	None
Regthar Deathgate	30	32	Krusk	Regthar Deathgate	Y	65	130	260	380	500	650	None
Return to Vahlarriel	30	33	Dalinda Malem	Vahlarriel Demonslayer	N	330	650	1300	2000	2650	3300	None
CHOICE OF: 1 Grappler's Belt or 1 Gloves of Insight or 1 Garrison Cloak or 1 Moonlit Amice												
Sceptre of Light	34	40	Azore Aldamort	Azore Aldamort	Y	320	625	1250	1900	2500	3150	50● 00●
Search for Tyranis	30	33	Dalinda Malem	Dalinda Malem	N	270	525	1050	1600	2100	2650	None
Stealing Supplies	30	35	Uthek the Wise	Uthek the Wise	Y	140	270	550	800	1100	1350	None
CHOICE OF: 200 Silver Star or 200 Feathered Arrow or 200 Exploding Shot												
Strange Alliance	30	35	Captain Pentigast	Uthek the Wise	Y	210	410	825	1250	1650	2050	None
The Corrupter	25	33	Maurin Bonesplitter	Takata Steelblade	N	25	55	110	160	210	270	None
The Corrupter	25	33	Maurin Bonesplitter	Maurin Bonesplitter	Y	270	525	1050	1600	2100	2650	None
The Corrupter	25	35	Maurin Bonesplitter	Maurin Bonesplitter	N	280	550	1100	1650	2200	2750	None
The Corrupter	25	40	Takata Steelblade	Takata Steelblade	N	390	775	1550	2350	3100	3900	None
CHOICE OF: 1 Basalt Buckler or 1 Enforcer Pauldrons												
The Karnitol Shipwreck	30	39	Kreldig Ungor	Roetten Stonehammer	N	230	450	900	1350	1800	2250	None
CHOICE OF: 1 Hellion Boots or 1 Sanguine Pauldrons												
The Karnitol Shipwreck	30	39	Kreldig Ungor	Karnitol's Chest (Obj)	Y	300	600	1200	1800	2400	3000	None
The Karnitol Shipwreck	30	39	Karnitol's Chest (Obj)	Kreldig Ungor	Y	150	300	600	900	1200	1500	None
The Karnitol Shipwreck	30	39	Kreldig Ungor	Kreldig Ungor	Y	300	600	1200	1800	2400	3000	None
The Kolkar of Desolace	30	32	Regthar Deathgate	Felgur Twocuts	N	65	130	260	380	500	650	[illegible]
Vahlarriel's Search	30	33	Malem Chest (Obj)	Vahlarriel Demonslayer	Y	200	390	775	1150	1550	1950	[illegible]
Vahlarriel's Search	30	33	Vahlarriel Demonslayer	Dalinda Malem	Y	270	525	1050	1600	2100	2650	[illegible]
Vahlarriel's Search	30	33	Vahlarriel Demonslayer	Malem Chest (Obj)	Y	200	390	775	1150	1550	1950	None

DUROTAR

Azeroth's Orcs and Trolls call Durotar their home. The Valley of Trials begins to temper the characters with its rugged and demanding landscape. Sen'jin is to the south and Razor Hill lies to the north. Orgrimmar, the capitol city of the Orcs, is at the exteme northern edge of the region. A new dungeon was recently discovered within Orgrimmar itself and adventurers trying to prove themselves often venture there before even leaving Durotar for far off lands.

ORGRIMMAR
THE BARRENS
RAZOR HILL
VALLEY OF TRIALS
SEN'JIN VILLAGE
ECHO ISLES
THE GREAT SEA

LOCAL RESOURCES

MINING

METAL	AVAILABILITY
Copper	Abundant

HERBALISM

HERB	AVAILABILITY
Silverleaf	Abundant
Peacebloom	Abundant
Earthroot	Moderate

SKINNING

Quantity of Skinnable Creatures: Abundant

Levels of Skinnable Creatures: 1-11 (Skinning 1-50)

MAP LEGEND

1 THE VALLEY OF TRIALS
Kzan Thornslash 34 Weaponsmith
Rarc 10 Armorer & Shieldcrafter
Huklah 11 Cloth & Leather Armor
Rwag 8 Rogue Trainer
Gornek 5 Quest
Den Grunt 75
Ken'Jai 10 Priest Trainer
Shikrik 10 Shaman Trainer
Canaga Earthcaller 8 Quest
Mai'ah 10 Mage Trainer
Ruzan 10 Quest
Zureetha Fargaze 12 Quest
Jen'shan 8 Hunter Trainer
Frang 11 Warrior Trainer
Magga 5
Duokna 10 General Goods
Zlagk 9 Butcher
Galgar 8
Kaltunk 20
Mottled Boar 1-2
Sarkoth 4
Scorpid Worker 3
Vile Familiar 3-4
Felstalker 3-4

2 BURNING BLADE COVE
Yarrog Baneshadow 5
Vile Familiar 3-4
Felstalker 3-4

3 KOLKAR CRAG
Kolkar Drudge 6-7
Kolkar Outrunner 7-8

4 SEN'JIN VILLAGE/DARKSPEAR STRAND
Ukor 4 Quest
Sen'jin Watcher 25-30
Miao'zan 25 Journeyman Alchemist
Hai'zan 14 Butcher
Vel'rin Fang 7 Quest
Master Vornal 11 Quest
Master Gadrin 12
K'waii 11 General Goods
Tai'tasi 12 Trade Supplies
Xur'gyl 40 Axe Trainer
Trayexir 40 Bow Trainer
Zansoa 14 Fishing Supplies
Xar'Ti 50 Raptor Rider Trainer
Zjolnir 45 Raptor handler
Un'Thuwa 14 Mage Trainer
Bom'bay 8 Witch Doctor in Training
Mishiki 14 Herbalist
Clattering Scorpid 5-6
Dire Mottled Boar 6-7
Pygmy Surf Crawler 5-8
Makura Clacker 6-7
Makura Shellhide 6-7

5 ECHO ISLES
Zalazane 10
Durotar Tiger 5-8
Bloodtalon Taillasher 6-8
Makrura Clacker 5-8
Surf Crawler 7-8
Hexed Troll 8-9
Voodoo Troll 8-9

6 TIRAGARDE KEEP
Lieutenant Benedict 8
Kul Tiras Marine 6-7
Kul Tiras Sailor 5-6

7 SCUTTLE COAST
Pygmy Surf Crawler 5-6
Makura Clacker 6-7
Makura Shellhide 6-7

8 RAZOR HILL
Razor Hill Grunt 28-32
Orgnil Soulscar 18 Quest
Thotar 16 Hunter Trainer
Gar'Thok 10 Quest
Kaplak 14 Rogue Trainer
Takrin Pathseeker 30 Quest
Grimtak 14 Butcher
Cook Torka 6 Quest
Showja'my 30 Stable Master
Innkeeper Grosk 30 Innkeeper
Yelnagi Blackarm 16
Wuark 16 Armorer & Shieldcrafter
Krunn 16 Miner
Dwukk 27 Journeyman Blacksmith
Uhgar 15 Weaponsmith
Ghrawt 13 Bowyer
Cutac 14 Cloth & Leather Armor Merchant
Dhugru Gorelust 37 Warlock Trainer
Ophek 10
Kitha 17 Demon Trainer
Voidwalker 17 Kitha's Minion
Flakk 15 Trade Supplies
Rawrk 15 First Aid Trainer
Jark 14 General Goods
Swart 15 Shaman Trainer
Tai'jin 18 Priest Trainer
Tarshaw Jaggedscar 43 Warrior Trainer
Furl Scornbrow 6 Quest

9 DRYGULCH RAVINE
Dustwind Harpy 7-8
Dustwind Pillager 7-8
Dustwind Savage 9-10
Dustwind Storm Witch 10-11

10 MARGOZ' CAMP
Margoz 18 Quest

11 SKULL ROCK
Gazz'uz 14
Burning Blade Thug 8-9
Burning Blade Apprentice 10-11

12 Rezlak 5 Tinker's Union

13 DEAD EYE SHORE
Makrura Snapclaw 8-9
Encrusted Surf Crawler 7-10
Corrupted Surf Crawler 10-11
Elder Mottled Boar 8-9
Venomtail Scorpid 9-10
Bloodtalon Scythemaw 8

14 ROCKTUSK FARM
Swine 3
Elder Mottled Boar 8-9
Venomtail Scorpid 9-10
Bloodtalon Scythemaw 8

15 JAGGEDSWINE FARM
Swine 3
Elder Mottled Boar 8-9
Venomtail Scorpid 9-10
Bloodtalon Scythemaw 8-10

16 ZEPPELIN TO GROM'GOL BASE CAMP AND UNDERCITY

17 BLADEFIST BAY
Makrura Snapclaw 8-9
Encrusted Surf Crawler 7-10
Corrupted Surf Crawler 10-11
Elder Mottled Boar 8-9
Venomtail Scorpid 9-10
Bloodtalon Scythemaw 8

18 SOUTHFURY RIVER
Bloodtalon Scythemaw 8-10
Bloodtalon Taillasher 5-10
Armored Scorpid 8-10
Corrupted Bloodtalon Scythemaw 10-11
Dreadmaw Crockilisk 9-11
Elder Mottled Boar 8-9

19 Misha Tor'kren 5 Quest

20 RAZORMANE GROUNDS
Dire Mottled Boar 6-7
Razormane Dustrunner 8-9
Razormane Battleguard 9-10
Razormane Scout 7-8
Razormane Quillboar 6-7
Bloodtalon Taillasher 6-8
Armored Scorpid 7

21 THUNDER RIDGE
Fizzle Darkstorm 12
Voidwalker Minion 10
Lightning Hide 10-11
Thunder Lizard 9-10
Burning Blade Apprentice 10-11
Burning Blade Fanatic 9-10

QUESTS

QUEST	M LEV	Q LEV	QUEST LAUNCHER	QUEST FINISHER	CHAIN?	XP---	XP--	XP-	XP+	XP++	XP+++	CASH REWARD
A Peon's Burden	1	5	Ukor	Innkeeper Grosk	N	10	20	45	65	90	110	None
CHOICE OF: 5 Tough Hunks of Bread or 5 Refreshing Spring Water												
A Solvent Spirit	5	7	Master Vornal	Master Vornal	N	65	130	250	380	500	625	1 75
REWARD: 10 Really Sticky Glue												
A Strategic Alliance	5	8		Lar Prowltusk	Y	35	70	140	210	280	350	None
Ak'Zeloth	4	13	Neeru Fireblade	Ak'Zeloth	Y	45	90	180	270	360	460	None
Break a Few Eggs	6	8	Cook Torka	Cook Torka	N	70	140	280	420	550	700	2 25
REWARD: 5 Tough Hunk of Bread, 5 Tough Jerky												
Burning Blade Medallion	1	5	Zureetha Fargaze	Zureetha Fargaze	Y	65	130	270	400	525	675	None
REWARD: Minor Healing Potion and CHOICE OF: 1 Dust-covered Leggings or 1 Jagged Chain Vest or 1 Ripped Pants												
Carry Your Weight	4	7	Furl Scornbrow	Furl Scornbrow	N	65	130	250	380	500	625	None
REWARD: Handmade Leather Bag												
Conscript of the Horde	10	12	Takrin Pathseeker	Kargal Battlescar	Y	45	90	180	270	360	460	None
Crossroads Conscription	10	12	Kargal Battlescar	Sergra Darkthorn	N	90	180	360	550	725	900	None
Cutting Teeth	1	2	Gornek	Gornek	N	15	35	70	100	140	170	None
CHOICE OF: 1 Soft Wool Boots or 1 Battleworn Leather Gloves												
Dark Storms	4	12	Orgnil Soulscar	Orgnil Soulscar	N	90	180	360	550	725	900	None
REWARD: Tiger Hide Boots												
Encroachment	6	10	Gar'Thok	Gar'Thok	N	65	130	250	380	500	625	2 50
Finding the Antidote	7	9	Kor'ghan	Kor'ghan	N	0	0	0	0	0	0	None
REWARD: Venomtail Antidote												
Flawed Power Stone	1	14	Flawed Power Stone (Obj)	Flawed Power Stone (Obj)	N	0	0	0	0	0	0	None
REWARD: Flawed Power Stone												
Flawed Power Stone	1	14	Flawed Power Stones (Obj)	Flawed Power Stone (Obj)	N	0	0	0	0	0	0	None
REWARD: Flawed Power Stone												
Flawed Power Stone	1	14	Flawed Power Stones (Obj)	Flawed Power Stone (Obj)	N	0	0	0	0	0	0	None
REWARD: Flawed Power Stone												
From The Wreckage...	3	8	Gar'Thok	Gar'Thok	N	70	140	280	420	550	700	None
CHOICE OF: 1 Dirt-trodden Boots or 1 Sandrunner Wristguards or 1 Wide Metal Girdle												
Galgar's Cactus Apple Surprise	1	3	Galgar	Galgar	N	40	75	150	230	300	380	50
REWARD: 10 Cactus Apple Surprise												
Lost But Not Forgotten	8	11	Misha Tor'kren	Misha Tor'kren	N	90	180	350	525	700	875	None
REWARD: Handsewn Cloak												
Margoz	4	12	Orgnil Soulscar	Margoz	Y	10	20	35	55	70	90	None
Minshina's Skull	4	9	Master Gadrin	Master Gadrin	N	80	160	310	470	625	775	None
REWARD: Faintly Glowing Skull												
Need for a Cure	7	9	Rhinag	Rhinag	N	100	200	390	600	775	975	None
CHOICE OF: 1 Charging Buckler or 1 Light Scorpid Armor												
Neeru Fireblade	4	12	Margoz	Neeru Fireblade	Y	45	90	180	270	360	460	None
Practical Prey	5	8	Vel'rin Fang	Vel'rin Fang	N	70	140	280	420	550	700	2 25
Report to Orgnil	4	7	Master Gadrin	Orgnil Soulscar	N	30	65	130	190	250	320	None
Report to Sen'jin Village	1	5	Zureetha Fargaze	Master Gadrin	N	25	45	90	140	180	230	None
Sarkoth	1	4	Hana'zua	Gornek	N	10	20	35	55	70	90	None
CHOICE OF: 1 Soft Wool Vest or 1 Battleworn Chain Leggings												
Sarkoth	1	4	Hana'zua	Hana'zua	Y	35	70	140	210	280	360	None
Securing the Lines	7	11	Rezlak	Rezlak	N	90	180	350	525	700	875	None
CHOICE OF: 1 Harpy Wing Clipper or 1 Hickory Shortbow or 1 Blemished Wooden Staff												
Skull Rock	4	12	Margoz	Margoz	N	90	180	360	550	725	900	None
CHOICE OF: 1 Jagged Dagger or 1 Steady Bastard Sword or 1 Stinging Mace												
Sting of the Scorpid	1	3	Gornek	Gornek	N	25	50	100	150	200	250	None
CHOICE OF: 1 Soft Wool Belt or 1 Battleworn Leather Cape												
The Admiral's Orders	1	7	Gar'Thok	Nazgrel	N	65	130	250	380	500	625	1 75
The Demon Seed	9	14	Ak'Zeloth	Ak'Zeloth	N	130	250	500	750	1000	1250	None
REWARD: Banshee Armor												
The New Horde	1	1		Gornek	Y	5	10	15	25	30	40	None
Thwarting Kolkar Aggression	5	8	Lar Prowltusk	Lar Prowltusk	N	70	140	280	420	550	700	None
CHOICE OF: 1 Seasoned Fighter's Cloak or 1 Heavy Cord Bracers												
Vanquish the Betrayers	3	7	Gar'Thok	Gar'Thok	Y	65	130	250	380	500	625	1 75
Vile Familiars	2	4	Zureetha Fargaze	Zureetha Fargaze	Y	45	90	180	270	360	450	None
CHOICE OF: 1 Primitive Club or 1 Primitive Hand Blade or 1 Primitive Hatchet or 1 Primitive Walking Stick or 1 Primitive Bow												
Winds in the Desert	7	9	Rezlak	Rezlak	Y	80	160	310	470	625	775	3 00
Your Place In The World	1	1	Kaltunk	Gornek	Y	5	10	15	25	30	40	None
Zalazane	4	10	Master Gadrin	Master Gadrin	N	85	170	340	500	675	850	None
CHOICE OF: 1 Lightweight Boots or 1 Veiled Grips												

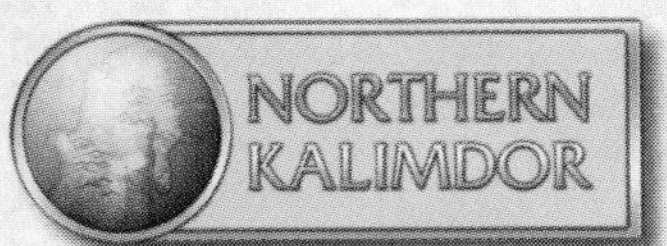

FELWOOD

Felwood is rife with corruption. The once green of the land is now filled predominantly with shades of ominous brown. The Emerald Circle works hard to push out the corruption that has taken over this land however, their efforts seem miniscule compared to the sheer devastation that surrounds them. This zone is located to the north of Ashenvale and serves as a passageway to both Moonglade and Winterspring. This area is a higher-level region best for those from Level 45 and up.

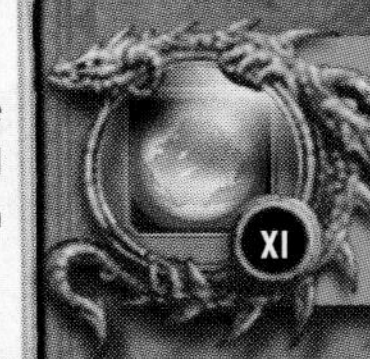

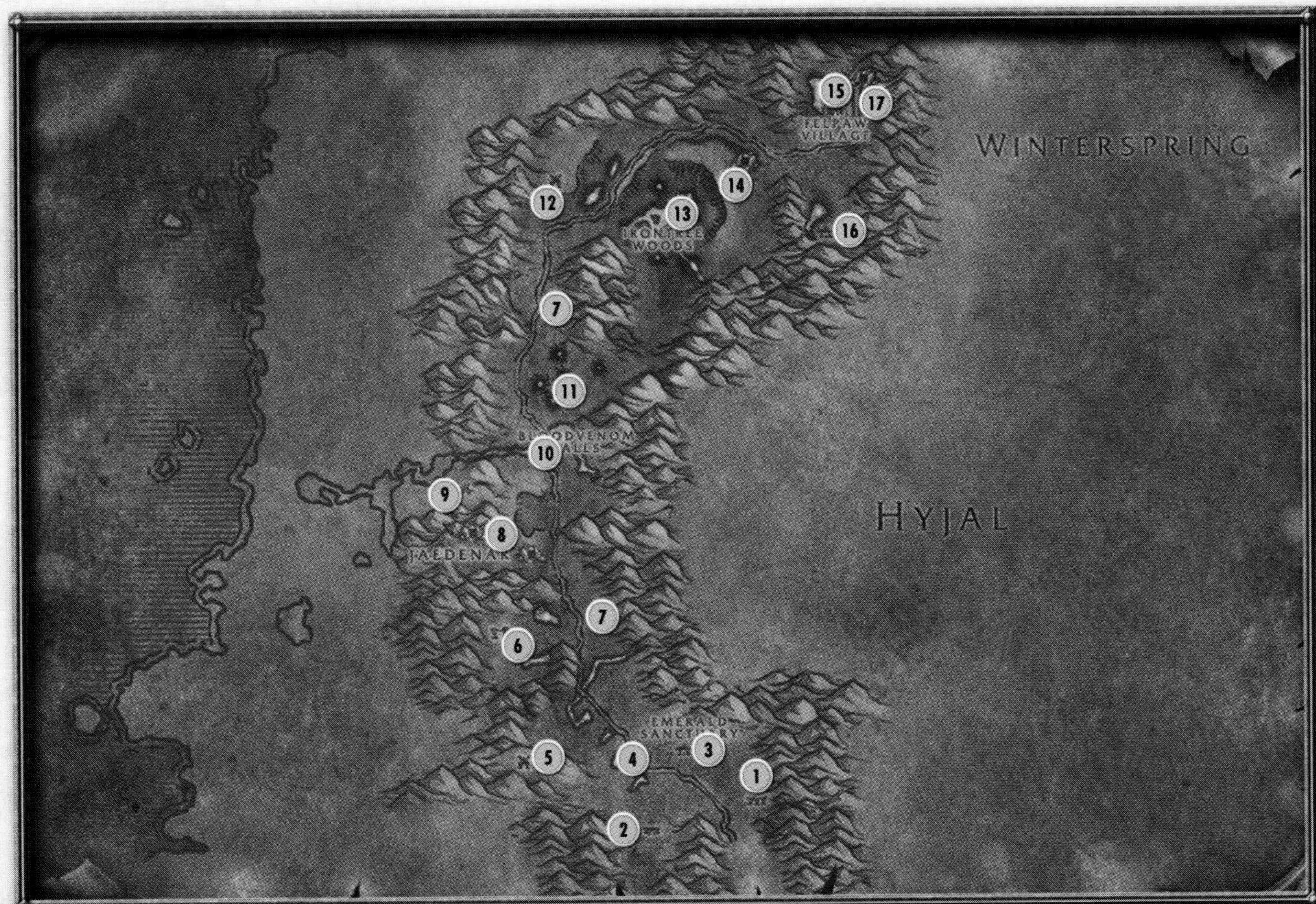

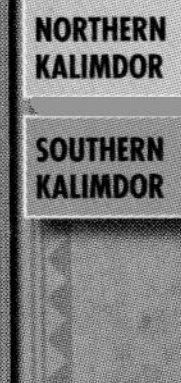

15
17
FELPAW VILLAGE
WINTERSPRING
14
12
13
IRONTREE WOODS
16
7
11
BLOODVENOM FALLS
10
9
8
JAEDENAR
HYJAL
7
6
EMERALD SANCTUARY
5
4
3
1
2

LOCAL RESOURCES

MINING

METAL	AVAILABILITY
Mithril	Moderate
Thorium	Rare

HERBALISM

None save for quest plants that grant bonuses.

SKINNING

Quantity of Skinnable Creatures: Abundant

Levels of Skinnable Creatures: 48-53 (Skinning 175-250)

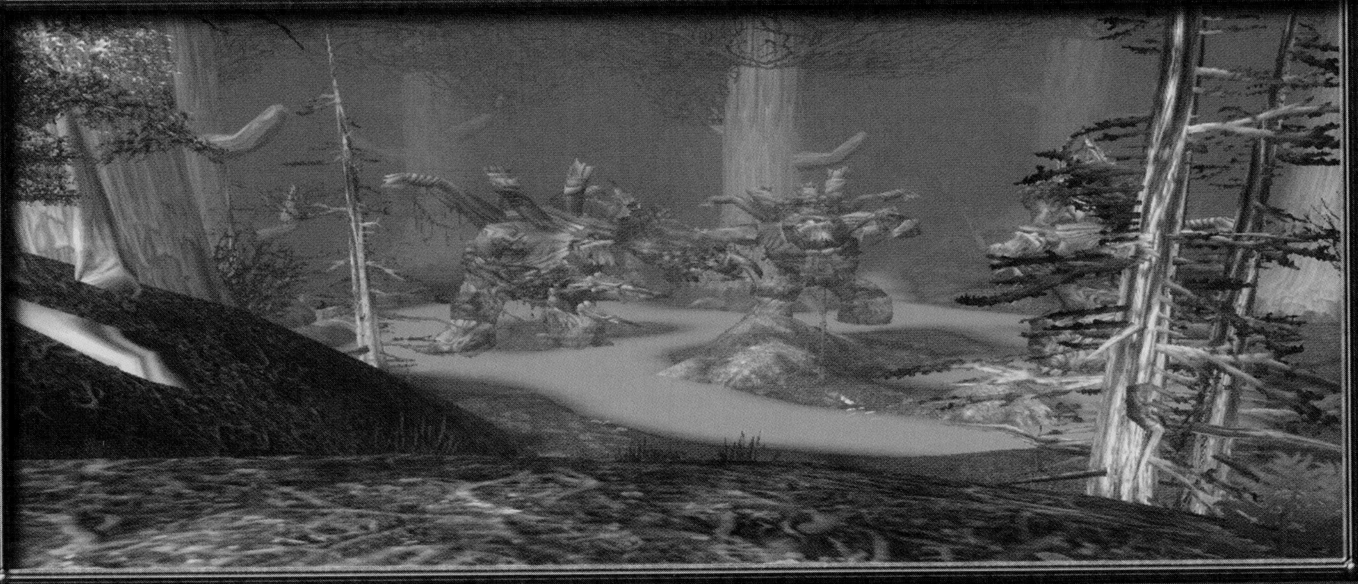

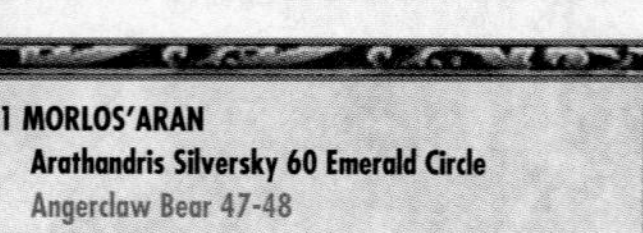

MAP LEGEND

1 MORLOS'ARAN
Arathandris Silversky 60 Emerald Circle
Angerclaw Bear 47-48
Ironbeak Owl 48-49
Felpaw Wolf 47-48

2 DEADWOOD VILLAGE
Felpaw Wolf 47-48
Deadwood Warrior 48-49
Deadwood Pathfinder 49-50
Deadwood Gardener 48-49
Ironbeak Owl 48-49

3 EMERALD CIRCLE
Jessir Moonbow 50
Della 49 Jessir's Pet
Greta Mosshoof 59 Emerald Circle
Tenell Leafrunner 62 Emerald Circle
Kelek Skysweeper 57 Emerald Circle
Eriden Bluewind 57 Emerald Circle
Taronn Redfeather 50 Emerald Circle
Ivy Leafrunner 63 Emerald Circle
Ironbeak Owl 48-49
Angerclaw Bear 47-48
Felpaw Wolf 47-48

4 Maybess Riverbreeze 60 Emerald Circle

5 JADEFIRE GLEN
Jadefire Satyr 49-50
Jadefire Felsworn 49-51
Felpaw Wolf 47-48

6 RUINS OF CONSTELLAS
Xavathras 54
Cursed Ooze 49-50
Felpaw Wolf 47-48
Angerclaw Bear 47-48
Jadefire Shadowstalker 51-52
Jadefire Rogue 50
Jadefire Felsworn 50-51

7 FELWOOD (GENERAL)
Felpaw Wolf 47-48
Angerclaw Bear 47-48
Angerclaw Mauler 49-50
Ironbeak Hunter 50-51
Felpaw Scavenger 49-50

8 JAEDENAR
Tainted Ooze 51-52
Jaedenar Hound 50-51
Jaedenar Guardian 50-51
Jaedenar Adept 51-52
Ironbeak Hunter 50-51
Jaedenar Cultist 51-52

9 BLOODVENOM POST
Bloodvenom Post Brave 65
Storm Shadowhoof 60 Quest
Trull Failbane 55 Quest
Bale 55 General Goods
Brakkar 55 Elite Wind Rider Master

10 BLOODVENOM FALLS
Tainted Ooze 51-52
Angerclaw Mauler 49-50
Ironbeak Hunter 50-51

11 SHATTER SCAR VALE
Entropic Horror 54
Entropic Beast 51-52
Infernal Bodyguard 54 Elite
Infernal Sentry 52-53 Elite

12 JADEFIRE RUN
Jadefire Trickster 52-53
Jadefire Betrayer 52
Jadefire Hellcaller 53-54
Felpaw Scavenger 49-50
Angerclaw Mauler 49-50

13 IRONTREE WOODS
Arei 56 Quest
Irontree Stomper 52-53
Toxic Horror 54

14 IRONTREE CAVERN
Warped Shredder 53
Warpwood Moss Flayer 52-53

15 FELPAW VILLAGE
Felpaw Ravager 51-53
Deadwood Den Watcher 53-54
Deadwood Shaman 53-54
Deadwood Avenger 54-55
Winterfall Runner 57
Chieftain Bloodpaw 56

16 TALONBRANCH GLADE
Golhine the Hooded 60 Druid Trainer
Kaerbrus 57 Hunter Trainer
Shi'alune 56 Kaerbrus' Pet
Malygen 55 General Goods
Ironbeak Screecher 53

17 TIMBERMAW HOLD/PASSAGE TO WINTERSPRING AND MOONGLADE
Grazle 55 Quest

QUESTS

QUEST	M LEV	Q LEV	QUEST LAUNCHER	QUEST FINISHER	CHAIN?	XP---	XP--	XP-	XP+	XP++	XP+++	CASH REWARD
A Final Blow	48	58	Greta Mosshoof	Greta Mosshoof	N	925	1850	3700	5600	7450	9300	None
CHOICE OF: 1 Brantwood Sash or 1 Blight Leather Gloves or 1 Gearforge Girdle												
A Husband's Last Battle	46	51	Dreka'Sur	Dreka'Sur	N	490	975	1950	2950	3900	4900	75 00
Ancient Spirit	49	56	Arei	Kayneth Stillwind	N	725	1450	2900	4400	5850	7300	None
CHOICE OF: 1 Ethereal Mist Cape or 1 Clouddrift Mantle												
Brumeran of the Chillwind	53	58	Storm Shadowhoof	Storm Shadowhoof	Y	625	1250	2500	3700	4950	6200	None
Cleansed Water Returns to Felwood	48	54	Islen Waterseer	Greta Mosshoof	Y	270	550	1100	1600	2150	2700	None
Cleansing Felwood	48	55	Arathandris Silversky	Arathandris Silversky	N	575	1150	2250	3400	4500	5650	None
Cleansing Felwood	48	55	Maybess Riverbreeze	Maybess Riverbreeze	N	575	1150	2250	3400	4500	5650	None
Collection of the Corrupt Water	48	52	Greta Mosshoof	Greta Mosshoof	Y	380	750	1500	2300	3050	3800	None
Corrupted Night Dragon	48	55	Corrupted Night Dragon (Obj)	Corrupted Night Dragon (Obj)	N	55	110	220	340	450	550	None
Corrupted Night Dragon	48	55	Corrupted Night Dragon (Obj)	Corrupted Night Dragon (Obj)	N	55	110	220	340	450	550	None
Corrupted Night Dragon	48	55	Corrupted Night Dragon (Obj)	Corrupted Night Dragon (Obj)	N	55	110	220	340	450	550	None
Corrupted Night Dragon	48	55	Corrupted Night Dragon (Obj)	Corrupted Night Dragon (Obj)	N	55	110	220	340	450	550	None
Corrupted Sabers	49	54	Winna Hazzard	Winna Hazzard	N	550	1100	2200	3250	4350	5450	60 00
Corrupted Songflower	48	55	Corrupted Songflower (Obj)	Corrupted Songflower (Obj)	N	55	110	220	340	450	550	None
Corrupted Songflower	48	55	Corrupted Songflower (Obj)	Corrupted Songflower (Obj)	N	55	110	220	340	450	550	None
Corrupted Songflower	48	55	Corrupted Songflower (Obj)	Corrupted Songflower (Obj)	N	55	110	220	340	450	550	None
Corrupted Songflower	48	55	Corrupted Songflower (Obj)	Corrupted Songflower (Obj)	N	55	110	220	340	450	550	None
Corrupted Songflower	48	55	Corrupted Songflower (Obj)	Corrupted Songflower (Obj)	N	55	110	220	340	450	550	None
Corrupted Songflower	48	55	Corrupted Songflower (Obj)	Corrupted Songflower (Obj)	N	55	110	220	340	450	550	None
Corrupted Songflower	48	55	Corrupted Songflower (Obj)	Corrupted Songflower (Obj)	N	55	110	220	340	450	550	None
Corrupted Songflower	48	55	Corrupted Songflower (Obj)	Corrupted Songflower (Obj)	N	55	110	220	340	450	550	None
Corrupted Songflower	48	55	Corrupted Songflower (Obj)	Corrupted Songflower (Obj)	N	55	110	220	340	450	550	None
Corrupted Whipper Root	48	55	Corrupted Whipper Root (Obj)	Corrupted Whipper Root (Obj)	N	55	110	220	340	450	550	None
Corrupted Whipper Root	48	55	Corrupted Whipper Root (Obj)	Corrupted Whipper Root (Obj)	N	55	110	220	340	450	550	None
Corrupted Whipper Root	48	55	Corrupted Whipper Root (Obj)	Corrupted Whipper Root (Obj)	N	55	110	220	340	450	550	None
Corrupted Whipper Root	48	55	Corrupted Whipper Root (Obj)	Corrupted Whipper Root (Obj)	N	55	110	220	340	450	550	None

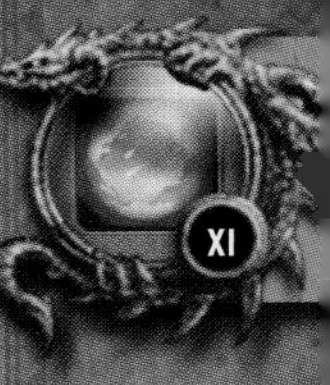

HOW TO
AZEROTH
KHAZ MODAN
LORDAERON
NORTHERN KALIMDOR
SOUTHERN KALIMDOR

Corrupted Whipper Root	48	55	Corrupted Whipper Root (Obj)	Corrupted Whipper Root (Obj)	N	55	110	220	340	450	550	None
Corrupted Whipper Root	48	55	Corrupted Whipper Root (Obj)	Corrupted Whipper Root (Obj)	N	55	110	220	340	450	550	None
Corrupted Windblossom	48	55	Corrupted Windblossom (Obj)	Corrupted Windblossom (Obj)	N	55	110	220	340	450	550	None
Corrupted Windblossom	48	55	Corrupted Windblossom (Obj)	Corrupted Windblossom (Obj)	N	55	110	220	340	450	550	None
Corrupted Windblossom	48	55	Corrupted Windblossom (Obj)	Corrupted Windblossom (Obj)	N	55	110	220	340	450	550	None
Corrupted Windblossom	48	55	Corrupted Windblossom (Obj)	Corrupted Windblossom (Obj)	N	55	110	220	340	450	550	None
Corrupted Windblossom	48	55	Corrupted Windblossom (Obj)	Corrupted Windblossom (Obj)	N	55	110	220	340	450	550	None
Corrupted Windblossom	48	55	Corrupted Windblossom (Obj)	Corrupted Windblossom (Obj)	N	55	110	220	340	450	550	None
Corrupted Windblossom	48	55	Corrupted Windblossom (Obj)	Corrupted Windblossom (Obj)	N	55	110	220	340	450	550	None
Corrupted Windblossom	48	55	Corrupted Windblossom (Obj)	Corrupted Windblossom (Obj)	N	55	110	220	340	450	550	None
Corrupted Windblossom	48	55	Corrupted Windblossom (Obj)	Corrupted Windblossom (Obj)	N	55	110	220	340	450	550	None
Past Endeavors	53	60	Storm Shadowhoof	Melor Stonehoof	N	330	650	1300	2000	2650	3300	None
REWARD: Hunter's Insignia Medal												
Purified!	49	54	Eridan Bluewind	Eridan Bluewind	N	550	1100	2200	3250	4350	5450	None
REWARD: Flute of the Ancients												
Rescue From Jaedenar	49	55	Captured Arko'narin	Jessir Moonbow	Y	575	1150	2250	3400	4500	5650	None
Retribution of the Light	49	57	Jessir Moonbow	Remains of Trey Lightforge	Y	450	900	1800	2700	3600	4500	None
REWARD: Remains of Trey Lightforge												
Salve via Disenchanting	48	55	Arathandris Silversky	Arathandris Silversky	N	0	0	0	0	0	0	None
REWARD: 2 Cenarion Plant Salve												
Salve via Disenchanting	48	55	Maybess Riverbreeze	Maybess Riverbreeze	N	0	0	0	0	0	0	None
REWARD: 2 Cenarion Plant Salve												
Salve via Disenchanting	48	55	Arathandris Silversky	Arathandris Silversky	N	420	850	1700	2500	3350	4200	None
REWARD: 2 Cenarion Plant Salve												
Salve via Disenchanting	48	55	Maybess Riverbreeze	Maybess Riverbreeze	N	420	850	1700	2500	3350	4200	None
REWARD: 2 Cenarion Plant Salve												
Salve via Gathering	48	55	Arathandris Silversky	Arathandris Silversky	N	0	0	0	0	0	0	None
REWARD: 2 Cenarion Plant Salve												
Salve via Gathering	48	55	Maybess Riverbreeze	Maybess Riverbreeze	N	0	0	0	0	0	0	None
REWARD: 2 Cenarion Plant Salve												
Salve via Gathering	48	55	Arathandris Silversky	Arathandris Silversky	N	420	850	1700	2500	3350	4200	None
REWARD: 2 Cenarion Plant Salve												
Salve via Gathering	48	55	Maybess Riverbreeze	Maybess Riverbreeze	N	420	850	1700	2500	3350	4200	None
REWARD: 2 Cenarion Plant Salve												
Salve via Hunting	48	55	Arathandris Silversky	Arathandris Silversky	N	0	0	0	0	0	0	None
REWARD: 2 Cenarion Plant Salve												
Salve via Hunting	48	55	Maybess Riverbreeze	Maybess Riverbreeze	N	0	0	0	0	0	0	None
REWARD: 2 Cenarion Plant Salve												
Salve via Hunting	48	55	Arathandris Silversky	Arathandris Silversky	N	420	850	1700	2500	3350	4200	None
REWARD: 2 Cenarion Plant Salve												
Salve via Hunting	48	55	Maybess Riverbreeze	Maybess Riverbreeze	N	420	850	1700	2500	3350	4200	None
REWARD: 2 Cenarion Plant Salve												
Salve via Mining	48	55	Arathandris Silversky	Arathandris Silversky	N	0	0	0	0	0	0	None
REWARD: 2 Cenarion Plant Salve												
Salve via Mining	48	55	Maybess Riverbreeze	Maybess Riverbreeze	N	0	0	0	0	0	0	None
REWARD: 2 Cenarion Plant Salve												
Salve via Mining	48	55	Arathandris Silversky	Arathandris Silversky	N	420	850	1700	2500	3350	4200	None
REWARD: 2 Cenarion Plant Salve												
Salve via Mining	48	55	Maybess Riverbreeze	Maybess Riverbreeze	N	420	850	1700	2500	3350	4200	None
REWARD: 2 Cenarion Plant Salve												
Salve via Skinning	48	55	Arathandris Silversky	Arathandris Silversky	N	0	0	0	0	0	0	None
REWARD: 2 Cenarion Plant Salve												
Salve via Skinning	48	55	Maybess Riverbreeze	Maybess Riverbreeze	N	0	0	0	0	0	0	None
REWARD: 2 Cenarion Plant Salve												
Salve via Skinning	48	55	Arathandris Silversky	Arathandris Silversky	N	420	850	1700	2500	3350	4200	None
REWARD: 2 Cenarion Plant Salve												
Salve via Skinning	48	55	Maybess Riverbreeze	Maybess Riverbreeze	N	420	850	1700	2500	3350	4200	None
REWARD: 2 Cenarion Plant Salve												
Seeking Spiritual Aid	48	52	Greta Mosshoof	Islen Waterseer	N	260	500	1000	1550	2050	2550	None
Shy-Rotam	53	60	Storm Shadowhoof	Storm Shadowhoof	N	825	1650	3300	5000	6650	8300	None
CHOICE OF: 1 Beasthunter Dagger or 1 Beaststalker Blade												
The Corruption of the Jadefire	49	54	Eridan Bluewind	Eridan Bluewind	N	550	1100	2200	3250	4350	5450	None
The Remains of Trey Lightforge	49	57	Remains of Trey Lightforge	Jessir Moonbow	N	750	1500	3000	4550	6050	7550	22 00
CHOICE OF: 1 Hunt Tracker Blade or 1 Tidecrest Blade												
The Remains of Trey Lightforge	49	57	Spirit of Trey Lightforge	Jessir Moonbow	N	750	1500	3000	4550	6050	7550	22 00
CHOICE OF: 1 Hunt Tracker Blade or 1 Tidecrest Blade												
To Winterspring!	53	56	Ivy Leafrunner	Wynd Nightchaser	Y	60	120	230	350	460	575	None
Ursius of the Shardtooth	53	56	Storm Shadowhoof	Storm Shadowhoof	Y	575	1150	2300	3500	4650	5800	None
Verifying the Corruption	48	54	Taronn Redfeather	Taronn Redfeather	N	675	1350	2700	4100	5450	6800	1 65 00
Well of Corruption	49	54	Winna Hazzard	Winna Hazzard	N	550	1100	2200	3250	4350	5450	None
Wild Guardians	52	56	Trull Failbane	Trull Failbane	Y	575	1150	2300	3500	4650	5800	85 00
Wild Guardians	52	58	Trull Failbane	Trull Failbane	Y	625	1250	2500	3700	4950	6200	90 00
Wild Guardians	52	59	Trull Failbane	Trull Failbane	N	650	1300	2550	3850	5100	6400	1 80 00

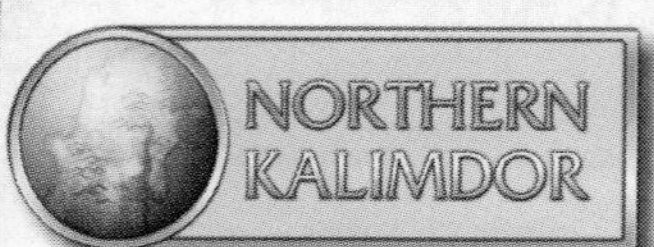

MOONGLADE

Moonglade is a peaceful and serene setting with a small village named Nighthaven looking down on it. There isn't much here as of yet, but the way in is dangerous if you aren't friendly with the Timbermaws that guard the way in.

SHRINE OF REMULOS
NIGHTHAVEN
LAKE ELUNE'ARA
STORMRAGE BARROW DENS
1
2
3

LOCAL RESOURCES

MINING: NONE **HERBALISM: NONE** **SKINNING: NONE**

MAP LEGEND

1 Bunthen Plainswind 60

2 SHRINE OF REMULOS
- Keeper Remulos 62 Quest

3 NIGHTHAVEN
- Bessany Plainswind 60
- Genia Sunshadow 51 Specialty Dress Maker
- Darnall 53 Tailoring Supplies
- Mylentha Riverbend 60
- Dendrite Starblaze 60
- Moren Riverbend 60
- Keeper Remulos 62
- Rabine Saturna 60
- Silva Fil'naveth 60
- Celes Earthborn 60
- Tajarri 60

4 STORMRAGE BARROW DEN

GETTING THERE

In order to get into Moonglade you need to make your way down through the passageways of Timbermaw Hold. If you get friendly with the Timbermaws that guard the way, this can be an extremely easy task. If you're not so friendly, you'll find yourself either stealthing through, dying through or killing through to get there.

NIGHTHAVEN

Nighthaven is the only town currently within Moonglade. It offers a few select high level vendors including a specialty dress maker that does indeed have a wedding dress for sale should that special day arrive for a lady of Azeroth.

STORMRAGE BARROW DENS

There are three entrances to Stormrage Barrow Dens that lead into the catacombs of the dens. There is currently nothing within the Dens but it can be expected that some high level mobs will soon be waiting for your visit.

STONETALON MOUNTAINS

Stonetalon Mountains can be found in the mountains between the Barrens and Desolace. The Tauren outpost of Sun Rock Retreat lies off the beaten path near the middle of the mountain and provides the Horde with the only local inn. The Peak itself houses an Alliance flight path and an Alliance vendor. Though home to many beasts, the wilderness is constantly being cut back by expanding goblin deforesters. In addition to the Barrens and Desolace, explorers can travel to and from Ashenvale forest via a secret tunnel that burrows through the foothills.

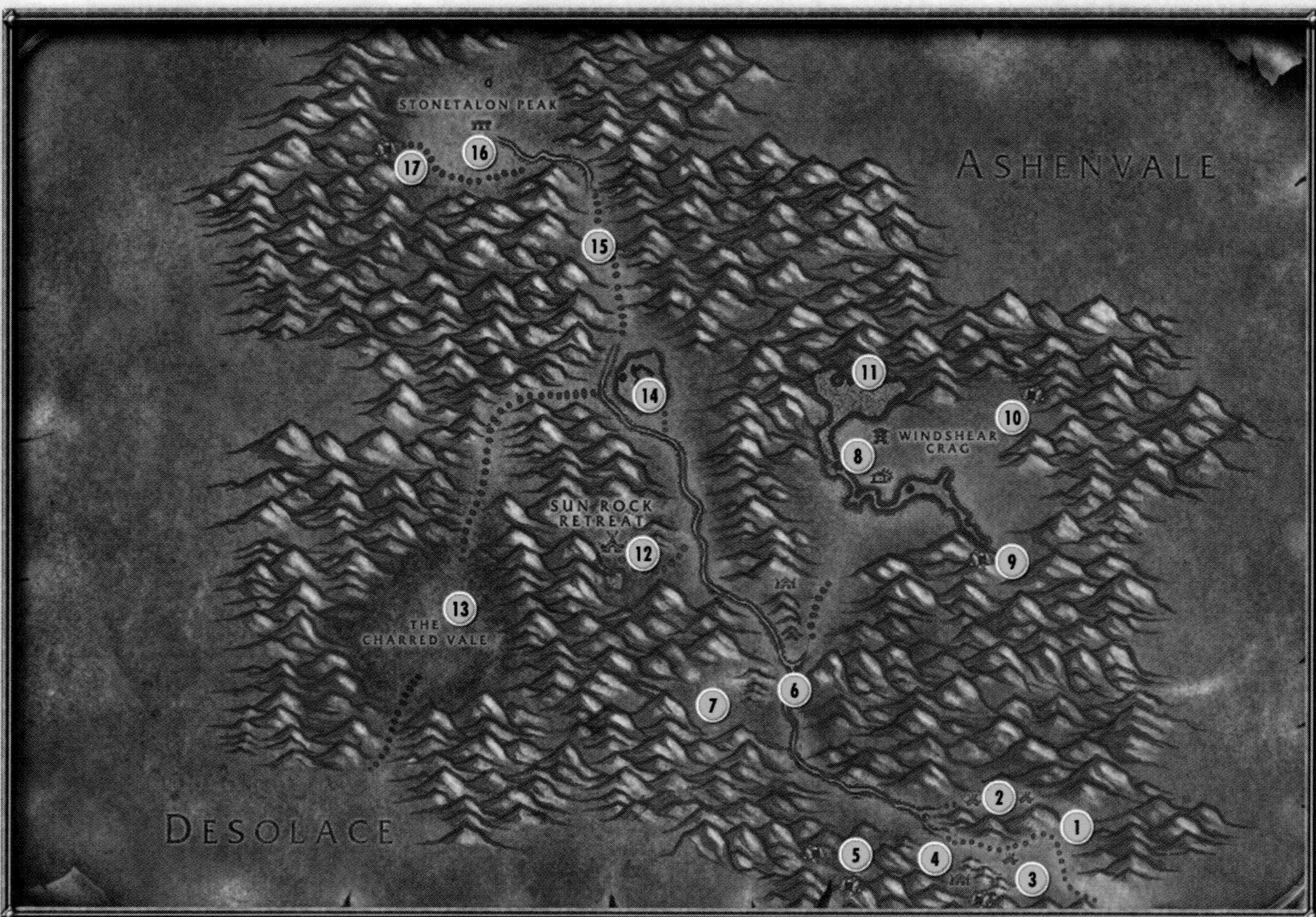

LOCAL RESOURCES

MINING

METAL	AVAILABILITY
Copper	Abundant
Tin	Abundant
Silver	Abundant
Iron	Moderate
Mithril	Rare

HERBALISM

HERB	AVAILABILITY
Kingsblood	Abundant
Bruiseweed	Abundant
Briarthorn	Abundant
Mageroyal	Abundant
Wild Steelbloom	Abundant

SKINNING

Quantity of Skinnable Creatures: Abundant

Levels of Skinnable Creatures: 18-26 (Skinning: 75-125)

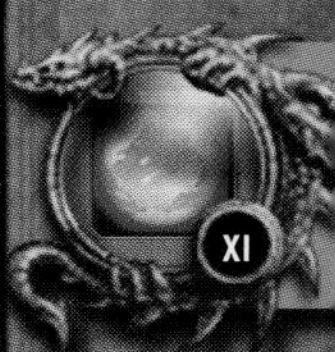

HOW TO
AZEROTH
KHAZ MODAN
LORDAERON
NORTHERN KALIMDOR
SOUTHERN KALIMDOR

MAP LEGEND

1 CAMP APARAJE

2 GRIMTOTEM POST

3 GREATWOOD VALE

4 MALAKA'JIN
Witch Doctor Jin'Zil 25 Quest
Ken'Zigla 20 Quest
Borand 30 Bowyer

5 BOULDERSLIDE RAVINE

6 WEB WINDER PATH
Gaxim Rustfizzle 30 Quest
Kaela Shadowspear 23 Quest
Deepmoss Creeper 17-18
Deepmoss Venomspitter 18-19

7 SISHIR CANYON

8 WINDSHEAR CRAG
Ziz Fizziks 20 Quest
Cliff Stormer 18-19
Raging Cliff Stormer 19-20
Deepmoss Venomspitter 18-19
Deepmoss Webspinner 20-21
Young Pridewing 19
Venture Company Logger 19-20
Venture Company Deforester 20
Venture Company Operator 20,21
XT:4 23
XT:9 23

9 WINDSHEAR MINE
Piznik 20 Quest
Windshear Digger 21-22
Windshear Geomancer 21-22
Windshear Overlord 22-23
Windshear Tunnelrat 21

10 TALONDEEP PATH
Braug Dimspirit 35 Quest

11 CRAGPOOL LAKE
Nizzik 24 Vendor
Venture Company Builder 22
Venture Company Engineer 21-22
Venture Company Machine Smith 22-23
Gerenzo Wrenchwhistle 27
Compact Harvest Reaper 22

12 SUN ROCK RETREAT
Innkeeper Jayka 30 Innkeeper
Tharm 55 Wind Ride Master
Gereck Stable Master
Jeeda 24 Vendor
Krond 27 Butcher
Grawnal 32 General Goods
Stonetalon Grunt

13 THE CHARRED VALE
Blackened Basilisk 24
Scorched Basilisk 28
Singed Basilisk 25
Rogue Flame Spirit 24
Burning Ravager 24-25
Burning Destroyer 25-26
Charred Ancient 25
Blackened Ancient 28
Furious Stone Spirit 24-27
Young Chimaera 24
Fledgling Chimaera 25-27
Chimaera Matriarch 28
Bloodfury Harpy 23-24
Bloodfury Ambusher 23-24
Bloodfury Slayer 25-26
Bloodfury Rogue Feather 25-26
Bloodfury Windcaller 24
Bloodfury Storm Witch 26-27

14 MIRKFALLON LAKE
Pridewing Wyvern 21-22
Pridewing Consort 22-23
Pridewing Skyhunter 23-24
Deepmoss Venomspitter 18-19
Raging Cliff Stormer 19-20
Antlered Courser 22
Blackened Basilisk 24
Rogue Flame Spirit 23

15 STONETALON MOUNTAIN
Braelyn Firehand 30 Quest
Antlered Courser 22-23

16 STONETALON PEAK
Teloren Hippogryph Master
Chylina 24 Vendor
Keeper Albagorm 30 Quest
Sap Beast 22-23
Corrosive Sap Beast 25
Antlered Courser 22-23
Great Courser 25
Fey Dragon 24
Wily Fey Dragon 26
Twilight Hunter 23-24
Son of Cenarius 25
Daughter of Cenarius 23-25
Cenarion Botanist 23-24
Treant Ally 23

17 THE TALON DEN
Cenarion Druid 26-27 Elite
Cenarion Caretaker 25-26 Elite
Mirkfallon Dryad 25 Elite
Gatekeeper Kordurus 25 Elite

QUESTS

QUEST	M LEV	Q LEV	QUEST LAUNCHER	QUEST FINISHER	CHAIN?	XP---	XP--	XP-	XP+	XP++	XP+++	CASH REWARD
A Gnome's Respite	17	21	Gaxim Rustfizzle	Gaxim Rustfizzle	N	170	330	650	1000	1300	1650	None
A Scroll from Mauren	17	21	Gaxim Rustfizzle	Collin Mauren	Y	85	170	330	500	675	825	None
An Old Colleague	17	21	Gaxim Rustfizzle	Lomac Gearstrip	Y	85	170	330	500	675	825	None
Cenarius' Legacy	20	25	Braelyn Firehand	Braelyn Firehand	Y	150	300	600	900	1200	1500	None
Covert Ops - Alpha	17	22	Gaxim Rustfizzle	Gaxim Rustfizzle	N	220	440	875	1300	1750	2200	None
Covert Ops - Beta	17	22	Gaxim Rustfizzle	Gaxim Rustfizzle	N	220	440	875	1300	1750	2200	None
Devils in Westfall	17	21	Collin Mauren	Collin Mauren	N	170	330	650	1000	1300	1650	None
Enraged Spirits	20	26	Kaela Shadowspear	Kaela Shadowspear	N	210	420	850	1250	1700	2100	20 00
Further Instructions	16	21	Ziz Fizziks	Sputtervalve	Y	85	170	330	500	675	825	None
Further Instructions	16	27	Sputtervalve	Ziz Fizziks	Y	110	220	440	650	875	1100	None
Gerenzo Wrenchwhistle	16	27	Ziz Fizziks	Ziz Fizziks	N	220	440	875	1300	1750	2200	22 00
CHOICE OF: 1 Engineer's Cloak or 1 Draftsman Boots												
Gerenzo's Orders	17	22	Piznik	Ziz Fizziks	N	130	260	525	775	1050	1300	None
REWARD: Dredge Boots												
Gerenzo's Orders	17	22	Piznik	Piznik	Y	220	440	875	1300	1750	2200	None
Goblin Invaders	13	19	Seereth Stonebreak	Seereth Stonebreak	N	150	290	575	875	1150	1450	11 00
Ineptitude + Chemicals = Fun	17	21	Lomac Gearstrip	Gaxim Rustfizzle	N	85	170	330	500	675	825	None
Ineptitude + Chemicals = Fun	17	21	Lomac Gearstrip	Lomac Gearstrip	Y	170	330	650	1000	1300	1650	None
Jin'Zil's Forest Magic	20	26	Witch Doctor Jin'Zil	Witch Doctor Jin'Zil	N	210	420	850	1250	1700	2100	None
CHOICE OF: 1 Voodoo Mantle or 1 Hexed Bracers												
Kaela's Update	17	22	Gaxim Rustfizzle	Kaela Shadowspear	N	20	35	70	110	140	180	None
Ordanus	20	29	Braelyn Firehand	Braelyn Firehand	Y	240	470	950	1400	1900	2350	None
Reception from Tyrande	17	28	Sentinel Thenysil	Tyrande Whisperwind	N	340	675	1350	2050	2700	3400	None
REWARD: Band of Elven Grace and CHOICE OF: 1 Efflorescent Robe or 1 Grizzly Tunic or 1 Wildwood Chain												
Reclaiming the Charred Vale	20	27	Keeper Albagorm	Falfindel Waywarder	N	220	440	875	1300	1750	2200	None
CHOICE OF: 1 Tempered Bracers or 1 Constable Buckler												
Reclaiming the Charred Vale	20	27	Keeper Albagorm	Keeper Albagorm	Y	220	440	875	1300	1750	2200	None
Retrieval for Mauren	17	26	Collin Mauren	Collin Mauren	N	210	420	850	1250	1700	2100	None
REWARD: Spellcrafter Wand												
Shredding Machines	13	23	Seereth Stonebreak	Seereth Stonebreak	N	190	370	750	1100	1500	1850	15 00
Special Delivery for Gaxim	17	21	Collin Mauren	Gaxim Rustfizzle	N	85	170	330	500	675	825	None
Super Reaper 6000	16	21	Ziz Fizziks	Ziz Fizziks	Y	170	330	650	1000	1300	1650	None
The Den	20	29	Braelyn Firehand	Talon Den Hoard (Obj)	N	300	600	1200	1750	2350	2950	None
REWARD: Sacred Band, Panther Armor, Juggernaut Leggings												
The Elder Crone	13	18	Seereth Stonebreak	Magatha Grimtotem	N	70	140	270	410	550	675	None
The Spirits of Stonetalon	13	17	Zor Lonetree	Seereth Stonebreak	Y	30	65	130	190	250	320	None
Update for Sentinel Thenysil	17	22	Kaela Shadowspear	Sentinel Thenysil	Y	85	170	350	525	700	875	None
Wounded Ancients	22	28	Kaela Shadowspear	Kaela Shadowspear	N	230	460	925	1400	1850	2300	25 00

TELDRASSIL

Teldrassil is the new home of the Night Elves. This distant homeland is far away from the safety of the Alliance lands, yet they are free from the focus of many enemies. Undead are not tolerated in this forest of life and beauty, and the Night Elves have many protectors that guard the land from any Demonic taint. Beware though; the Firbolg and Timberlings who once existed in perfect balance with this land, have grown aggressive of late. The Druids of Teldrassil seek answers before the beasts and people of the land suffer their own madness.

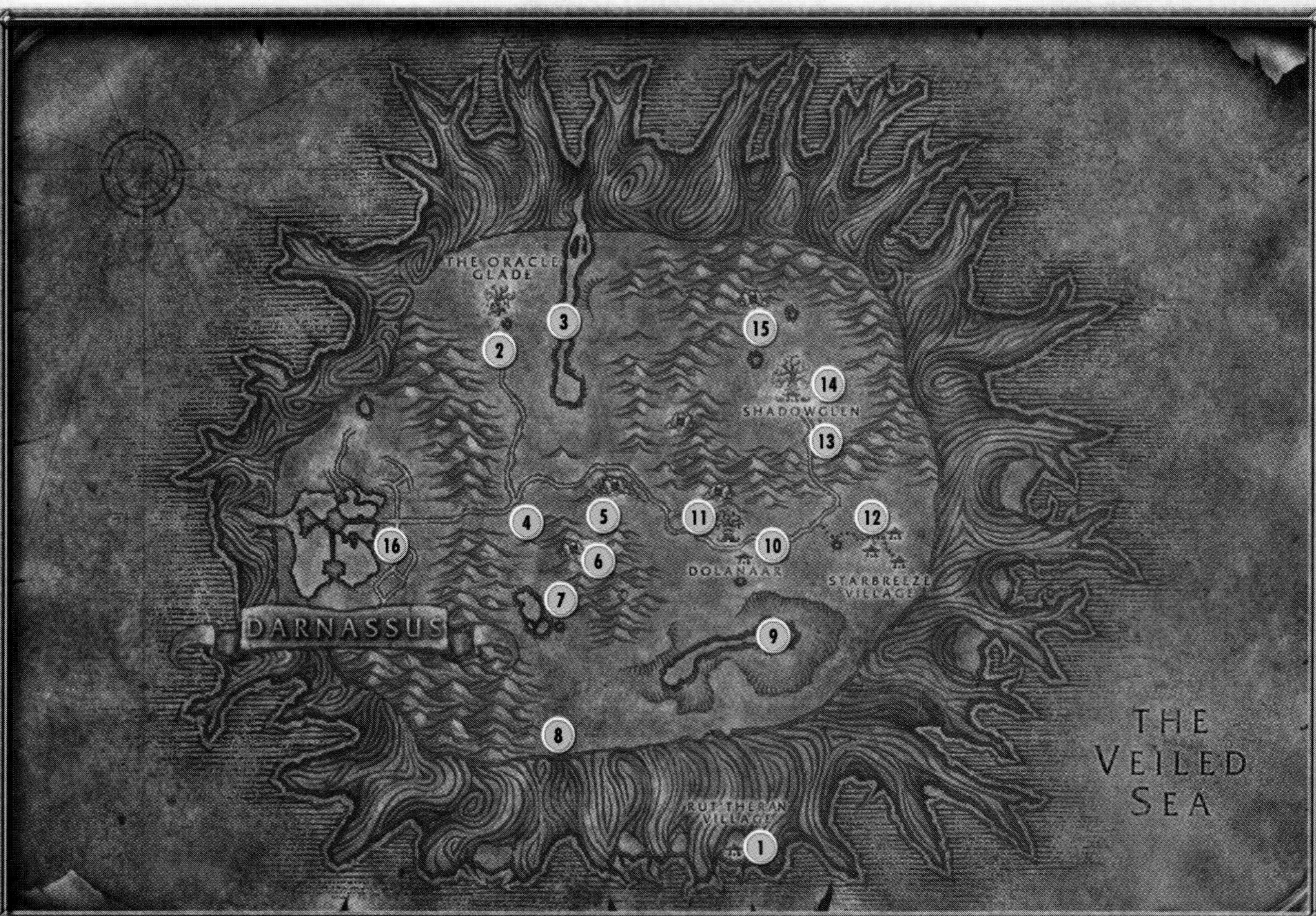

LOCAL RESOURCES

MINING: NONE

HERBALISM

HERB	AVAILABILITY
Peacebloom	Abundant
Silverleaf	Abundant
Earthroot	Common

SKINNING

Quantity of Skinnable Creatures: Abundant

Levels of Skinnable Creatures: 1-10 (Skinning 1-50)

MAP LEGEND

1 RUT'THERAN VILLAGE
Boat to Auberdine
Daryn Lightwind 30 Quest
Erelas Ambersky 30 Quest
Vesprystus 55 Hippogryph Master

2 THE ORACLE GLADE
Alanna Raveneye 29 Enchanter
Mist 10 Quest
Sentinel Arynia Cloudsbreak 10 Quest
Strange-Leafed Plant
Bloodfeather Fury 9-10
Bloodfeather Harpy 8-9
Bloodfeather Matriarch 11
Bloodfeather Rogue 9
Bloodfeather Sorceress 9
Elder Nightsaber 8-9
Feral Nightsaber 11
Lady Sarthrah 12
Minion of Sethir 10
Sethir the Ancient 13 Quest Target
Strigid Hunter 8-9
Strigid Screecher 7-8
Webwood Silkspinner 9

3 WELLSPRING RIVER
Blackmoss the Fetid 13 Quest Target
Elder Timberling 11
Timberling Mire Beast 9

4 ROAD TO DARNASSUS
Nadyia Maneweaver 30 Leatherworker
Radnaal Maneweaver 19 Skinner
Nightsaber Stalker 7-8
Strigid Screecher 7-8
Webwood Venomfang 7-8

5 BAN'ETHIL HOLLOW
Agal 8 Quest Target
Gnarlpine Ambusher 6-7
Gnarlpine Defender 7
Gnarlpine Shaman 8
Webwood Venomfang 7-8

6 BAN'ETHIL BARROW DEN
Oben Rageclaw 40 Quest
Gnarlpine Augur 9
Gnarlpine Defender 7
Gnarlpine Shaman 8
Rageclaw 10 Quest Target

7 POOLS OF ARLITHRIEN
Nightsaber Stalker 7-8
Strigid Screecher 7-8
Webwood Venomfang 7-8

8 GNARLPINE HOLD
Strange-Fruited Plant
Gnarlpine Avenger 10
Gnarlpine Pathfinder 9-10
Ursal the Mauler 12 Quest Target

9 LAKE AL'AMETH
Denalan 11 Quest
Fel Cone (Ground Spawns)
Timberling Seed (Ground Spawns)
Oakenscowl 9+ Quest Target
Timberling Bark Ripper 7-8
Timberling Tramplers 8-9
Timberling 5-6

10 DOLANAAR
Arthridas Bearmantle 11 Quest
Byancie 22 First Aid
Corithras Moonrage 10 Quest
Cyndra Kindwhisper 28 Alchemist
Innkeeper Keldamyr 30 Innkeeper
Malorne Bladeleaf 17 Herbalist
Sentinel Kyra Starsong 12 Quest
Syral Bladeleaf 12 Quest
Tallonkai Swiftroot 11 Quest
Zarrin 13 Cook

11 FEL ROCK
Dark Sprite 6-7
Lord Melenas 8 Quest Target
Rascal Sprite 5-6
Shadow Sprite 5-6
Vicious Grell 7

12 STARBREEZE VILLAGE
Gaerolas Talvethren 7 Quest
Zenn Foulhoof 7 Quest
Ferocitas Dream Eater 8 Quest Target
Gnarlpine Gardener 5
Gnarlpine Mystic 6-7
Gnarlpine Ursa 5-6
Gnarlpine Warrior 6-7

13 SHADOWGLEN
Iverron 5 Quest
Tarindrella 7 Quest
Grell 2-3
Grellkin 3-4
Mangy Nightsaber 2-3
Thistle Boar 2-3
Webwood Spider 3-4
Young Nightsaber 1-2
Young Thistleboar 1-2

14 ALDRASSIL
Conservator Ilthalaine 4 Quest
Dirania Silvershine 8 Quest
Gilshalan Windwalker 9 Quest
Tenaron Stormgrip 10 Quest

15 SHADOWTHREAD CAVE
Webwood Egg (Ground Spawn)
Githyliss the Vile 5 Quest Target
Webwood Spider 3-4

QUESTS

QUEST	M LEV	Q LEV	QUEST LAUNCHER	QUEST FINISHER	CHAIN?	XP---	XP--	XP-	XP+	XP++	XP+++	CASH REWARD
A Friend in Need	2	4	Iverron	Dirania Silvershine	Y	10	20	35	55	70	90	None
A Good Friend	2	4	Dirania Silvershine	Iverron	N	25	55	110	160	220	270	None
A Troubling Breeze	4	6	Athridas Bearmantle	Gaerolas Talvethren	Y	25	55	110	160	220	270	None
Crown of the Earth	1	5	Tenaron Stormgrip	Tenaron Stormgrip	Y	35	65	130	200	270	340	None
Crown of the Earth	1	5	Tenaron Stormgrip	Corithras Moonrage	Y	25	45	90	140	180	230	None
Crown of the Earth	1	5	Corithras Moonrage	Corithras Moonrage	Y	35	65	130	200	270	340	None
Crown of the Earth	1	9	Corithras Moonrage	Corithras Moonrage	Y	80	160	310	470	625	775	None
Crown of the Earth	1	11	Corithras Moonrage	Arch Druid Fandral Staghelm	N	110	220	440	650	875	1100	None
CHOICE OF: 1 Ashwood Bow or 1 Thicket Hammer												

QUESTS continued

QUEST	M LEV	Q LEV	QUEST LAUNCHER	QUEST FINISHER	CHAIN?	XP---	XP--	XP-	XP+	XP++	XP+++	CASH REWARD
Crown of the Earth	1	11	Corithras Moonrage	Corithras Moonrage	Y	65	130	260	400	525	650	None
Denalan's Earth	4	5	Syral Bladeleaf	Denalan	N	25	45	90	140	180	230	50
Dolanaar Delivery	1	5	Porthannius	Innkeeper Keldamyr	N	10	20	45	65	90	110	None
CHOICE OF: 5 Darnassian Bleu or 5 Refreshing Spring Water												
Druid of the Claw	3	10	Oben Rageclaw	Oben Rageclaw	N	110	210	420	625	850	1050	None
CHOICE OF: 1 Sleeping Robes or 1 Brushwood Blade												
Favored of Elune?	42	47	Erelas Ambersky	Erelas Ambersky	N	420	850	1700	2500	3350	4200	1 35 00
Ferocitas the Dream Eater	1	8	Tallonkai Swiftroot	Tallonkai Swiftroot	N	90	180	350	525	700	875	4 50
Find Ranshalla	52	57	Erelas Ambersky	Ranshalla	N	300	600	1200	1800	2400	3000	None
Gnarlpine Corruption	4	6	Gaerolas Talvethren	Athridas Bearmantle	Y	55	110	220	320	430	550	1 25
Iverron's Antidote	2	4	Dirania Silvershine	Iverron	N	45	90	180	270	360	450	None
CHOICE OF: 1 Sedgeweed Britches or 1 Barkmail Vest												
Iverron's Antidote	2	4	Dirania Silvershine	Dirania Silvershine	Y	35	70	140	210	280	360	None
Mist	6	11	Mist	Sentinel Arynia Cloudsbreak	N	90	180	350	525	700	875	None
CHOICE OF: 1 Cord Bracers or 1 Crag Buckler or 1 Scout's Cloak												
Moontouched Wildkin	52	55	Erelas Ambersky	Erelas Ambersky	Y	575	1150	2250	3400	4500	5650	85 00
Nighthaven Village	53	56	Daryn Lightwind	Wynd Nightchaser	Y	60	120	230	350	460	575	None
Oakenscowl	4	9	Denalan	Denalan	N	100	200	390	600	775	975	6 00
CHOICE OF: 1 Dirtwood Belt or 1 Moss-covered Gauntlets												
Planting the Heart	9	12	Denalan	Denalan's Planter (Obj)	N	90	180	360	550	725	900	None
REWARD: Cleansed Timberling Heart												
Protection of the Grove	5	7		Sentinel Shayla Nightbreeze	N	65	130	250	380	500	625	None
Recipe of the Kaldorei	2	7	Zarrin	Zarrin	N	65	130	250	380	500	625	85
REWARD: Recipe: Kaldorei Spider Kabob, 3 Kaldorei Spider Kabob												
Rellian Greenspyre	4	7	Denalan	Rellian Greenspyre	Y	30	65	130	190	250	320	None
Return to Denalan	4	9	Rellian Greenspyre	Denalan	Y	10	15	30	50	65	80	None
Seek Redemption!	4	7	Syral Bladeleaf	Zenn Foulhoof	N	65	130	250	380	500	625	1 75
Seek Redemption!	4	7	Moon Priestess Amara	Zenn Foulhoof	N	65	130	250	380	500	625	1 75
Seek Redemption!	4	7	Sentinel Shayla Nightbreeze	Zenn Foulhoof	N	65	130	250	380	500	625	1 75
Seek Redemption!	4	7	Sentinel Kyra Starsong	Zenn Foulhoof	N	65	130	250	380	500	625	1 75
Teldrassil	6	11	Sentinel Arynia Cloudsbreak	Arch Druid Fandral Staghelm	Y	45	90	180	260	350	440	None
Teldrassil	6	11		Arch Druid Fandral Staghelm	Y	45	90	180	260	350	440	None
Tenaron's Summons	1	5	Gilshalan Windwalker	Tenaron Stormgrip	Y	5	10	20	25	35	45	None
Tenaron's Summons	1	5	Melithar Staghelm	Tenaron Stormgrip	Y	5	10	20	25	35	45	None
The Balance of Nature	1	2	Conservator Ilthalaine	Conservator Ilthalaine	N	15	35	70	100	140	170	35
CHOICE OF: 1 Archery Training Gloves or 1 Stemleaf Bracers												
The Balance of Nature	1	3	Conservator Ilthalaine	Conservator Ilthalaine	N	25	50	100	150	200	250	50
CHOICE OF: 1 Draped Cloak or 1 Blackened Leather Belt												
The Emerald Dreamcatcher	1	6	Tallonkai Swiftroot	Tallonkai Swiftroot	Y	40	80	160	240	320	410	1 00
The Enchanted Glade	6	11	Sentinel Arynia Cloudsbreak	Sentinel Arynia Cloudsbreak	N	45	90	180	260	350	440	None
CHOICE OF: 1 Shackled Girdle or 1 Rain-spotted Cape												
The Glowing Fruit	4	10	Strange Fruited Plant (Obj)	Denalan	N	85	170	340	500	675	850	3 50
The Relics of Wakening	4	9	Athridas Bearmantle	Athridas Bearmantle	Y	80	160	310	470	625	775	3 00
CHOICE OF: 1 Barkmail Leggings or 1 Gritroot Staff												
The Road to Darnassus	5	8	Moon Priestess Amara	Moon Priestess Amara	N	70	140	280	420	550	700	2 25
The Shimmering Frond	4	10	Strange Fronded Plant (Obj)	Denalan	N	85	170	340	500	675	850	3 50
The Sleeping Druid	3	8	Oben Rageclaw	Oben Rageclaw	Y	70	140	280	420	550	700	None
The Sprouted Fronds	4	10	Sprouted Frond (Obj)	Sprouted Frond (Obj)	N	10	15	35	50	70	85	None
REWARD: 5 Sprouted Fronds												
The Woodland Protector	1	1	Melithar Staghelm	Tarindrella	Y	5	10	15	25	30	40	None
The Woodland Protector	1	3	Tarindrella	Tarindrella	N	25	50	100	150	200	250	None
REWARD: 3 Healing Herb CHOICE OF: 1 Canopy Leggings or 1 Tracking Boots or 1 Viny Gloves												
Timberling Seeds	4	7	Denalan	Denalan	Y	65	130	250	380	500	625	None
REWARD: 10 Forest Mushroom Caps												
Timberling Sprouts	4	7	Denalan	Denalan	N	80	160	320	470	625	800	3 50
CHOICE OF: 1 Gardening Gloves or 1 Graystone Bracers												
Tumors	4	9	Rellian Greenspyre	Rellian Greenspyre	N	100	200	390	600	775	975	6 00
REWARD: Pruning Knife												
Twisted Hatred	4	7	Tallonkai Swiftroot	Tallonkai Swiftroot	N	65	130	250	380	500	625	None
CHOICE OF: 1 Feral Bracers or 1 Viny Wrappings												
Ursal the Mauler	4	12	Athridas Bearmantle	Athridas Bearmantle	N	120	230	460	700	925	1150	None
CHOICE OF: 1 Defender Axe or 1 Thornroot Club												
Webwood Egg	1	5	Gilshalan Windwalker	Gilshalan Windwalker	N	55	110	220	340	450	550	None
CHOICE OF: 1 Woodland Shield or 1 Woodland Tunic or 1 Woodland Robes												
Webwood Venom	1	3	Gilshalan Windwalker	Gilshalan Windwalker	Y	25	50	100	150	200	250	None
CHOICE OF: 1 Thistlewood Axe or 1 Thistlewood Dagger or 1 Thistlewood Staff or 1 Thistlewood Blade or 1 Thistlewood Maul or 1 Thistlewood Bow												
Zenn's Bidding	4	5	Zenn Foulhoof	Zenn Foulhoof	N	45	90	180	270	360	450	1 00
REWARD: 5 Severed Voodoo Claw												

THE BARRENS

The Barrens are one of the largest zones and a central hub for travel between regions. Savannah Prowlers roam the land and remain hidden from younger adventurers, while Raptors, Centaurs, Harpies and all sorts of other wildlife can be seen hunting or foraging. This provides plenty of skinning opportunities. Ore and herbs are also all across the landscape. Three dungeons are within the zone: The Wailing Caverns, Razorfen Downs, and Razorfen Kraul. The Barrens offers access to many other zones including Stonetalon, Thousand Needles, Durotar, and Dustwallow Marsh; of course, that doesn't mention the Wyvern paths or the port town of Ratchet where adventurers can book passage on a ship.

LOCAL RESOURCES

MINING

METAL	AVAILABILITY
Copper	Abundant
Tin	Abundant
Silver	Uncommon
Iron	Rare
Mithril	Rare

HERBALISM

HERB	AVAILABILITY
Peacebloom	Abundant
Briarthorn	Abundant
Earthroot	Abundant
Silverleaf	Abundant
Mageroyal	Abundant
Bruiseweed	Uncommon
Kingsblood	Uncommon
Wild Steelbloom	Rare
Grave Moss	Rare

SKINNING

Quantity of Skinnable Creatures: Abundant

Levels of Skinnable Creatures: 12-24 (Skinning 50-100)

1 BAEL MODAN
Bael'dun Excavator 21-22
Bael'dun Foreman 22-23
Bael'dun Officer 26
Bael'dun Rifleman 24,25
Bael'dun Soldier 23,24
Digger Flameforge 24
General Twinbraid 30
Lord Cyrik Blackforge 23
Malgin Barleybrew 25
Prospector Khazgorm 26
Captain Gerogg Hammertoe 27 Elite

2 BLACKTHORN RIDGE
Razormane Pathfinder 20,21
Razormane Seer 23,24
Razormane Stalker 22,23
Razormane Warfrenzy 24,25
Kuz Orcbane 21
Nak Orcbane 23
Lok Orcbane 25
Hagg Taurenbane 26 Elite

3 SOUTHERN BARRENS
Gann Stonespire 18 Quest
Hannah Bladeleaf 24 Elite
Marcus Bel 24 Elite
Thora Feathermoon 25 Elite
Brontus 27 Elite
Barrens Kodo 19,20
Greater Barrens Kodo 24,25
Wooly Kodo 25,26
Greater Thunderhawk 23,24
Hecklefang Stalker 22,23
Stormhide 22,23
Thunderstomp 24
Washte Pawne 25

4 SILITHID MOUNDS 18-24
Hannah Bladeleaf 24 Elite
Marcus Bel 24 Elite
Thora Feathermoon 25 Elite
Brontus 27 Elite
Silithid Creeper 20,21
Silithid Grub 20
Silithid Harvester 24
Silithid Protector 18,19
Silithid Swarmer 21,22
Barrens Kodo 19,20
Wooly Kodo 25,26
Greater Barrens Kodo 24,25

5 FIELD OF GIANTS
Azzere the Skyblade 25
Owatanka 24
Brontus 27 Elite
Hannah Bladeleaf 24 Elite
Marcus Bel 24 Elite
Thora Feathermoon 25 Elite
Thunderhead 20-21
Wooly Kodo 25-26
Zhevra Courser 20-21
Thunderhawk Cloudscraper 20-21
Greater Barrens Kodo 24-25
Gazelle 2
Barrens Kodo 19120
Zhevra Courser 20-21

6 CAMP TAURAJO
Kelsuwa 30 Stablemaster
Innkeeper Byula 30 Innkeeper
Dranh 15 Skinner
Jorn Skyseer 32 Quest
Yonada 25 Tailoring & Leatherworking Supplies
Mahani 31 Expert Tailor
Krulmoo Fullmoon 42 Expert Leatherworker
Gahroot 25 Butcher
Ruga Ragetotem 30 Quest
Grunt Logmar 20 Quest
Grunt Dogran 20 Quest
Mangletooth 17 Quest
Kirge Sternhorn 22
Tatternack Steelforge 14
Takar the Seer 45 Quest

7 BRAMBLESCAR
Bristleback Geomancer 19-20
Bristleback Hunter 18-19
Bristleback Thornweaver 17-18

8 RAPTOR GROUNDS
Sunscale Scytheclaw 15-16
Sunscale Screecher 13-15
Sunscale Lashtail 11-13
Fleeting Plainstrider 12-13
Hecklefang Hyena 15-16
Ornery Plainstrider 16-17
Zhevra Charger 17-18

9 MIDDLE BARRENS
Hannah Bladeleaf- 24 Elite
Marcus Bel 24 Elite
Thora Feathermoon 25 Elite
Barrens Giraffe 15-16
Wandering Barrens Giraffe 18-19
Barrens Kodo 19-20
Hecklefang Snarler 18-19
Thunderhawk Hatchling 18-20
Gazelle 2
Stormsnout 18-19

10 AGAMA'GOR
Bristleback Geomancer 19-20
Bristleback Hunter 18-19
Bristleback Thornweaver 17-18
Bristleback Water Seeker 16-17
Geopriest Gukk'rok 19
Swinegart Spearhide 22 Elite

11 NORTHWATCH HOLD
Gilthares Firebough 17 Quest
Theramore Marine 15-16
Theramore Preserver 16-17
Cannoneer Smythe 19
Cannoneer Whessan 19
Captain Fairmount 20

12 THE MERCHANT COAST
Klannoc Macleod 65 The Islander, Quest
Islen Waterseer 37 Quest
Mahren Skyseer 32 Quest
Southsea Brigand 12-13
Southsea Cannoneer 13-14
Southsea Cutthroat 24-15
Southsea Privateer 14-15
Polly 18
Tazan 13
Baron Longshore 16
Slimeshell Makrura 18-19
Isha Awak 27

13 RATCHET
Brewmaster Drohn 9 Quest
Captain Thalo'thas Brightsun 25 Quest
Wrenix the Wretched 20 Quest
Vazario Linkgrease 40 Master Goblin Engineer, Quest Giver
Tinkerwiz 25 Journeyman Engineer
Gagsprocket 20 Engineering Goods
Gazlowe 60 Quest Giver
Sputtervalve 15 Tinkers' Union, Quest Giver
Crane Operator Bigglefuzz 18 Quest Giver
Zikkel 30 Banker
Fuzruckle 27 Banker
Mebok Mizzyrix 17 Quest Giver
Ironzar 23 Weaponsmith
Wharfmaster Dizzywig 15 Quest Giver
Shipmaster Grimble 45 Shipmaster
Kilxx 24 Fisherman
Liv Rizzlefix 17 Workshop Assistant
Grazlix 25 Armorer & Shieldcrafter
Vexspindle 24 Cloth & Leather Armor Merchant
Ranik 22 Trade Supplies
Jazzik 22 General Supplies
Zizzek 22 Fisherman
Reggifuz 35 Stablemaster
Innkeeper Wiley 35 Innkeeper
Menara Voidrender 50 Quest Giver
Strahad Farsan 60 Quest Giver
Acolyte Magaz 20 Quest Giver
Acolyte Fenrick 20 Quest Giver
Acolyte Wytula 20 Quest Giver

14 NORTH RATCHET PLAIN
Thun'grim Firegaze 29 Quest
Ornery Plainstrider 16,17
Savannah Matriarch 17,18
Sunscale Scytheclaw 15,16
Zhevra Charger 17,18
Ishamuhale 19
Swiftmane 21 Elite
Humar the Pridelord 23 Elite

15 STAGNANT OASIS
Kolkar Marauder 15-16
Kolkar Pack Runner 14-15
Kolkar Packhound 13
Kolkar Stormer 13-14
Kolkar Wrangler 12-13
Oasis Snapjaw 15-16
Brokespear 17
Verog the Dervish 18
Rocklance 17 Elite

16 LUSHWATER OASIS/WAILING CAVERNS
Falla Sagewind 25 Quest
Kalldan Felmoon 27 Specialist Leatherworking Supplies
Nalpak 14 Disciple of Naralex, Quest
Ebru 14 Disciple of Naralex, Quest
Waldor 28 Journeyman Leatherworker
Deviate Coiler 15,16 Elite
Deviate Creeper 15,16 Elite
Deviate Lurker 16,17 Elite
Deviate Slayer 16,17 Elite
Deviate Stalker 15,16,17 Elite
Deviate Stinglash 17 Elite
Devouring Ectoplasm 16,17 Elite
Cloned Ectoplasm 16,17 Elite
Mad Magglish 18 Elite
Kolkar Marauder 15-16
Kolkar Pack Runner 14-15
Kolkar Packhound 13
Kolkar Stormer 13-14
Kolkar Wrangler 12-13
Oasis Snapjaw 15-16
Hezrul Bloodmark 19
Gesharahan 20 Elite

17 CROSSROADS
Innkeeper Boorand Plainswind 30 Innkeeper
Larhka 18 Beverage Merchant
Zargh 16 Butcher
Moorane Hearthgrain 18 Baker
Lizzarik 19 Weapon Dealer
Sergra Darkthorn 34 Quest Giver
Kil'hala 25 Journeyman Tailor
Wrahk 18 Tailoring Supplies
Halija Whitestrider 19 Clothier
Tonga Runetotem 22 Quest
Kaltimah Stormcloud 23 Bags and Sacks
Mankrik 15 Quest
Thork 42 Quest
Devrak 55 Wind Rider Master
Hula'mahi 30 Reagents and Herbs
Korran 12 Quest
Uthrok 16 Bowyer and Gunsmith
Jahan Hawkwing 21 Leather & Mail Armor Merchant
Nargal Deatheye 35 Weaponsmith
Traugh 31 Expert Blacksmith
Sikwa 30 Stable Master
Barg 14 General Goods Vendor
Tari'Qa 14 Trade Supplies
Gazrog 25 Quest
Apothecary Helbrim 22 Quest
Tarban Hearthgrain 22 Baker
Grub 13 Quest Giver
Duhng 18 Cook
Kranal Fiss 15 Quest Giver

18 ORC RAMPART
Lanti'gah 4
Regthar Deathgate 28 Quest
Kolkar Invader 16-17
Kolkar Storm Seer 15-16
Warlord Krom'zar 20

19 CENTRAL BARRENS
Barrens Giraffe 15-16
Gazelle 2
Hecklefang Hyena 15-16
Lost Barrens Kodo 14-15
Ornery Plainstrider 16-17
Savannah Prowler 14-15
Sunscale Screecher 13-15
Zhevra Charger 17-18
Snort the Heckler 17

20 HONOR'S STAND
Ornery Plainstrider 16-17
Sunscale Scytheclaw 15-16
Zhevra Charger 17-18

21 THE FORGOTTEN POOLS
Kolkar Stormer 13,14
Kolkar Wrangler 12,13
Barak Kodobane 16
Stonearm 15

22 THORN HILL
Razormane Defender 12,13
Razormane Geomancer 12,13
Razormane Hunter 11,12
Razormane Mystic 13,14
Razormane Thornweaver 10,11
Razormane Water Seeker 10,11
Kreenig Snarlsnout 15
Elder Mystic Razorsnout 15 Elite

23 FAR WATCH POST
Ak'Zeloth 22 Quest
Kargal Battlescar 15 Quest
Uzzek 20 Quest

24 KODO BONES
Savannah Huntress 11-12
Savannah Prowler 14-15
Echeyakee 16
25 Dreadmist Peak
Burning Blade Acolyte 11-12
Burning Blade Bruiser 10-11
Rathorian 15

26 THE MOR'SHAN RAMPART
Vrang Wildgore 48 Weaponsmith & Armorcrafter
Wenikee Boltbucket 19
Ornery Plainstrider 16-17
Savannah Patriarch 15-16
Sunscale Scytheclaw 15-16
Zhevra Charger 17-18

27 THE DRY HILLS
Witchwing Ambusher 17,18
Witchwing Harpy 14,15
Witchwing Roguefeather 15,16
Witchwing Slayer 16,17
Witchwing Windcaller 17,18
Sister Rathtalon 19 Elite

28 NORTHERN BARRENS
Barrens Giraffe 15,16
Fleeting Plainstrider 12,13
Hecklefang Hyena 15,16
Lost Barrens Kodo 14,15
Savannah Prowler 14,15
Sunscale Screecher 13,14,15
Zhevra Runner 13,14
Gazelle 2

29 VENTURE COMPANY OPERATIONS
Taskmaster Fizzule 35 Elite Quest
Venture Co. Peon 13-14
Venture Co. Drudger 14-15
Tinkerer Sniggles 16

30 SLUDGE FENS
Venture Co. Mercenary 15-16
Venture Co. Drudger 14-15
Engineer Whirleygig 19
Foreman Grills" 19
Formeman Silixiz 25
Overseer Glibby 16
Grand Foreman Puzik Gallywix 26 Elite

31 NORTHERN PLAIN
Ornery Plainstrider 16-17
Sunscale Scytheclaw 15-16
Zhevra Charger 17-18
Takk the Leaper 19 Elite

32 BOULDER LODE MINE
Venture Co. Enforcer 16-17
Venture Co. Overseer 17-18
Boss Copperplug 19

33 SOUTHFURY RIVER
Dreadmaw Crocolisk 9-11

QUESTS

QUEST	M LEV	Q LEV	QUEST LAUNCHER	QUEST FINISHER	CHAIN?	XP---	XP--	XP-	XP+	XP++	XP+++	CASH REWARD
A New Ore Sample	25	29	Tatternack Steelforge	Tatternack Steelforge	N	240	470	950	1400	1900	2350	25 00
REWARD: Orcish War Sword												
Agamaggan's Agility	14	20	Mangletooth	Mangletooth	N	0	0	0	0	0	0	None
Agamaggan's Strength	14	20	Mangletooth	Mangletooth	N	0	0	0	0	0	0	None
Altered Beings	10	16	Tonga Runetotem	Tonga Runetotem	N	120	230	460	700	925	1150	8 00
Apothecary Zamah	10	15	Apothecary Helbrim	Apothecary Zamah	N	80	160	320	480	650	800	None
REWARD: Cauldron Stirrer and CHOICE OF: 4 Elixirs of Minor Fortitude or 4 Elixirs of Minor Agility or 3 Minor Rejuvenation Potions or 2 Swiftness Potions												
Betrayal from Within	17	25	Mangletooth	Thork	N	310	600	1200	1850	2450	3050	None
CHOICE OF: 1 Barkshell Tunic or 1 Dry Moss Tunic												
Betrayal from Within	17	25	Mangletooth	Mangletooth	Y	150	300	600	900	1200	1500	None
Blood Shards of Agamaggan	14	21	Mangletooth	Mangletooth	N	130	250	500	750	1000	1250	None
Blueleaf Tubers	20	26	Mebok Mizzyrix	Mebok Mizzyrix	N	210	420	850	1250	1700	2100	None
REWARD: A Small Container of Gems												
Centaur Bracers	9	14	Regthar Deathgate	Regthar Deathgate	N	130	250	500	750	1000	1250	None
CHOICE OF: 1 Orcish Battle Bow or 1 Pointed Axe or 1 Stonewood Hammer												
Chen's Empty Keg	11	15	Brewmaster Drohn	Brewmaster Drohn	Y	140	270	550	800	1100	1350	None
REWARD: 5 Stormstout												
Chen's Empty Keg	11	24	Brewmaster Drohn	Brewmaster Drohn	N	200	390	775	1150	1550	1950	None
REWARD: 5 Trogg Ales												
Consumed by Hatred	14	20	Mankrik	Mankrik	N	200	390	775	1150	1550	1950	None
CHOICE OF: 1 Boar Hunter's Cape or 1 Grassland Sash												
Counterattack!	11	20	Regthar Deathgate	Regthar Deathgate	N	200	390	775	1150	1550	1950	25 00
Cry of the Thunderhawk	10	20	Jorn Skyseer	Jorn Skyseer	Y	200	390	775	1150	1550	1950	None
REWARD: Gloves of the Moon and CHOICE OF: 1 Cobalt Buckler or 1 Wind Rider Staff												
Deepmoss Spider Eggs	17	20	Mebok Mizzyrix	Mebok Mizzyrix	N	200	390	775	1150	1550	1950	25 00
Dig Rat Stew	15	23	Grub	Grub	N	190	370	750	1100	1500	1850	None
REWARD: Recipe: Dig Rat Stew, 5 Dig Rat Stew, Apothecary Gloves												
Disrupt the Attacks	9	12	Thork	Thork	N	90	180	360	550	725	900	None
Echeyakee	10	16	Sergra Darkthorn	Sergra Darkthorn	Y	150	290	575	875	1150	1450	None
Egg Hunt	17	22	Korran	Korran	N	180	350	700	1050	1400	1750	None
CHOICE OF: 1 Harlequin Robes or 1 Violet Scale Armor												
Enraged Thunder Lizards	10	18	Jorn Skyseer	Jorn Skyseer	Y	170	340	675	1000	1350	1700	None
Free From the Hold	13	20	Gilthares Firebough	Captain Thalo'thas Brightsun	N	200	390	775	1150	1550	1950	25 00
CHOICE OF: 1 Buckled Boots or 1 Riveted Gauntlets												
Fungal Spores	10	15	Apothecary Helbrim	Apothecary Helbrim	N	110	210	420	625	850	1050	7 00
Gann's Reclamation	17	23	Gann Stonespire	Gann Stonespire	Y	190	370	750	1100	1500	1850	15 00
Hamuul Runetotem	10	16	Tonga Runetotem	Arch Druid Hamuul Runetotem	Y	30	60	120	170	230	290	None
Harpy Lieutenants	12	16	Darsok Swiftdagger	Darsok Swiftdagger	Y	120	230	460	700	925	1150	8 00
Harpy Raiders	12	15	Darsok Swiftdagger	Darsok Swiftdagger	Y	110	210	420	625	850	1050	7 00
Hezrul Bloodmark	11	19	Regthar Deathgate	Regthar Deathgate	N	110	220	440	650	875	1100	8 00
REWARD: Bounty Hunter's Ring												
Horde Presence	15	29	Kadrak	Kadrak	N	300	600	1200	1750	2350	2950	None
CHOICE OF: 1 Trailblazer Boots or 1 Jutebraid Gloves												

QUEST	M LEV	Q LEV	QUEST LAUNCHER	QUEST FINISHER	CHAIN?	XP---	XP--	XP-	XP+	XP++	XP+++	CASH REWARD
Ignition	13	18	Wizzlecrank's Shredder	Wizzlecrank's Shredder	N	140	270	550	800	1100	1350	None
In Nightmares	10	25	Falla Sagewind	Arch Druid Hamuul Runetotem	N	200	400	800	1200	1600	2000	None
CHOICE OF: 1 Talbar Mantle or 1 Quagmire Galoshes												
In Nightmares	10	25	Falla Sagewind	Mathrengyl Bearwalker	N	200	400	800	1200	1600	2000	None
CHOICE OF: 1 Talbar Mantle or 1 Quagmire Galoshes												
Industrial Espionage	13	18		Sputtervalve	N	0	0	0	0	0	0	None
Isha Awak	10	27	Mahren Skyseer	Mahren Skyseer	N	280	550	1100	1650	2200	2750	None
REWARD: Beastmaster's Girdle and CHOICE OF: 1 Branding Rod or 1 Ward of the Vale												
Ishamuhale	10	19	Jorn Skyseer	Jorn Skyseer	Y	180	360	725	1100	1450	1800	None
Jorn Skyseer	10	18	Sergra Darkthorn	Jorn Skyseer	Y	15	25	55	80	110	140	None
Kolkar Leaders	11	16	Regthar Deathgate	Regthar Deathgate	N	90	180	350	525	700	875	8 00
Letter to Jin'Zil	15	20	Darsok Swiftdagger	Witch Doctor Jin'Zil	N	160	310	625	925	1250	1550	None
Lost in Battle	14	20	Mankrik	Mankrik	N	120	230	460	700	925	1150	9 00
Mahren Skyseer	9	27	Jorn Skyseer	Mahren Skyseer	Y	55	110	220	330	440	550	None
Miner's Fortune	13	18	Wharfmaster Dizzywig	Wharfmaster Dizzywig	N	170	340	675	1000	1350	1700	None
REWARD: A Sack of Coins												
Mura Runetotem	10	15	Tonga Runetotem	Mura Runetotem	N	110	210	420	625	850	1050	None
CHOICE OF: 1 Jackseed Belt or 1 Sower's Cloak												
Nara Wildmane	10	16	Arch Druid Hamuul Runetotem	Nara Wildmane	Y	10	25	45	70	90	120	None
Nugget Slugs	10	15	Wenikee Boltbucket	Wenikee Boltbucket	N	110	210	420	625	850	1050	None
Plainstrider Menace	10	12	Sergra Darkthorn	Sergra Darkthorn	Y	90	180	360	550	725	900	5 00
Prowlers of the Barrens	10	15	Sergra Darkthorn	Sergra Darkthorn	Y	110	210	420	625	850	1050	7 00
Raptor Horns	13	18	Mebok Mizzyrix	Mebok Mizzyrix	N	140	270	550	800	1100	1350	None
REWARD: 5 Raptor Punch, Barkeeper's Cloak												
Raptor Thieves	9	13	Gazrog	Gazrog	Y	90	180	360	550	725	900	6 00
Razorhide	14	20	Mangletooth	Mangletooth	N	0	0	0	0	0	0	None
Revenge of Gann	17	26	Gann Stonespire	Gann Stonespire	N	210	420	850	1250	1700	2100	20 00
REWARD: Totemic Clan Ring												
Revenge of Gann	17	26	Gann Stonespire	Gann Stonespire	Y	210	420	850	1250	1700	2100	20 00
Rilli Greasygob	10	18	Wenikee Boltbucket	Rilli Greasygob	Y	35	70	140	200	270	340	None
Rising Spirit	14	20	Mangletooth	Mangletooth	N	0	0	0	0	0	0	None
Samophlange	10	14	Sputtervalve	Control Console (Obj)	Y	75	150	300	440	600	750	None
Samophlange	10	14	Control Console (Obj)	Control Console (Obj)	Y	50	100	200	290	390	490	None
Samophlange	10	14	Control Console (Obj)	Control Console (Obj)	Y	75	150	300	440	600	750	None
Samophlange	10	16	Control Console (Obj)	Sputtervalve	N	120	230	460	700	925	1150	None
CHOICE OF: 1 Engineer's Hammer or 1 Welding Shield												
Samophlange Manual	10	19	Rilli Greasygob	Rilli Greasygob	N	180	360	725	1100	1450	1800	None
CHOICE OF: 1 Tork Wrench or 1 Samophlange Screwdriver												
Serena Bloodfeather	12	20	Darsok Swiftdagger	Darsok Swiftdagger	N	200	390	775	1150	1550	1950	None
CHOICE OF: 1 Elegant Shortsword or 1 Harpy Skinner or 1 Zhovur Axe												
Sergra Darkthorn	10	10	Melor Stonehoof	Sergra Darkthorn	Y	65	130	250	380	500	625	None
Southsea Freebooters	9	14	Gazlowe	Gazlowe	Y	75	150	300	440	600	750	5 00
Spirit of the Wind	14	20	Mangletooth	Mangletooth	N	0	0	0	0	0	0	None
Stolen Booty	9	16	Gazlowe	Gazlowe	N	120	230	460	700	925	1150	8 00
CHOICE OF: 1 Wayfaring Gloves or 1 Padded Lamellar Boots												
Stolen Silver	9	18	Gazrog	Gazrog	N	140	270	550	800	1100	1350	10 00
CHOICE OF: 1 Rambling Boots or 1 Settler's Leggings												
Supplies for the Crossroads	9	12	Thork	Thork	N	90	180	360	550	725	900	5 00
The Angry Scytheclaws	10	17	Sergra Darkthorn	Sergra Darkthorn	Y	130	250	500	750	1000	1250	9 00
The Barrens Oases	10	10	Arch Druid Hamuul Runetotem	Tonga Runetotem	Y	40	85	170	250	340	420	None
The Disruption Ends	9	15	Thork	Thork	N	110	210	420	625	850	1050	None
CHOICE OF: 1 Binding Girdle or 1 Cinched Belt												
The Escape	13	18	Wizzlecrank's Shredder	Sputtervalve	N	170	340	675	1000	1350	1700	20 00
CHOICE OF: 1 Flaring Baton or 1 Greasy Tinker's Pants												
The Forgotten Pools	10	13	Tonga Runetotem	Tonga Runetotem	Y	70	140	270	410	550	675	None
The Guns of Northwatch	13	20	Captain Thalo'thas Brightsun	Captain Thalo'thas Brightsun	N	160	310	625	925	1250	1550	None
CHOICE OF: 1 Privateer Musket or 1 Sea Dog Britches												
The Missing Shipment	9	14	Wharfmaster Dizzywig	Gazlowe	Y	10	20	40	60	80	100	None
The Missing Shipment	9	14	Gazlowe	Wharfmaster Dizzywig	Y	10	20	40	60	80	100	None
The Stagnant Oasis	10	16	Tonga Runetotem	Tonga Runetotem	Y	120	230	460	700	925	1150	None
The Swarm Grows	29	33	Korran	Belgrom Rockmaul	Y	130	260	525	775	1050	1300	None
The Tear of the Moons	22	30	Feegly the Exiled	Feegly the Exiled	N	250	490	975	1450	1950	2450	25 00
The Zhevra	10	13	Sergra Darkthorn	Sergra Darkthorn	Y	90	180	360	550	725	900	6 00
Tribes at War	14	21	Mangletooth	Mangletooth	N	170	330	650	1000	1300	1650	None
Verog the Dervish	11	18	Regthar Deathgate	Regthar Deathgate	Y	100	200	400	600	800	1000	10 00
WANTED: Baron Longshore	11	16	Wanted Poster (Obj)	Gazlowe	N	120	230	460	700	925	1150	8 00
Weapons of Choice	17	24	Tatternack Steelforge	Tatternack Steelforge	N	200	390	775	1150	1550	1950	None
CHOICE OF: 1 Demolition Hammer or 1 Everglow Lantern												
Wenikee Boltbucket	10	14	Sputtervalve	Wenikee Boltbucket	Y	50	100	200	290	390	490	None
Wharfmaster Dizzywig	9	11	Apothecary Helbrim	Wharfmaster Dizzywig	N	45	90	180	260	350	440	None
Wisdom of Agamaggan	14	20	Mangletooth	Mangletooth	N	0	0	0	0	0	0	None
Ziz Fizziks	16	21	Sputtervalve	Ziz Fizziks	Y	40	85	170	250	330	420	None

WINTERSPRING

The northern land of Winterspring is reached through a dangerous tunnel out of Felwood. The Furbolg who live there are hard to befriend, and have a natural tendency to attack anything that hasn't been at war with their mutual enemies for quite some time. On the other side of the tunnel is Winterspring itself, where snow falls, geysers blast into the sky, and some of the greatest Yetis in all of Azeroth dwell. To escape from the cold and the monsters of Winterspring, look toward the center of the valley and speak with the Goblins who hold a neutral town there.

LOCAL RESOURCES

MINING

METAL	AVAILABILITY
Thorium	Abundant

HERBALISM

HERB	AVAILABILITY
Ice Caps	Abundant

SKINNING

Quantity of Skinnable Creatures: Abundant

Levels of Skinnable Creatures: 55-60 (Skinning 250-300)

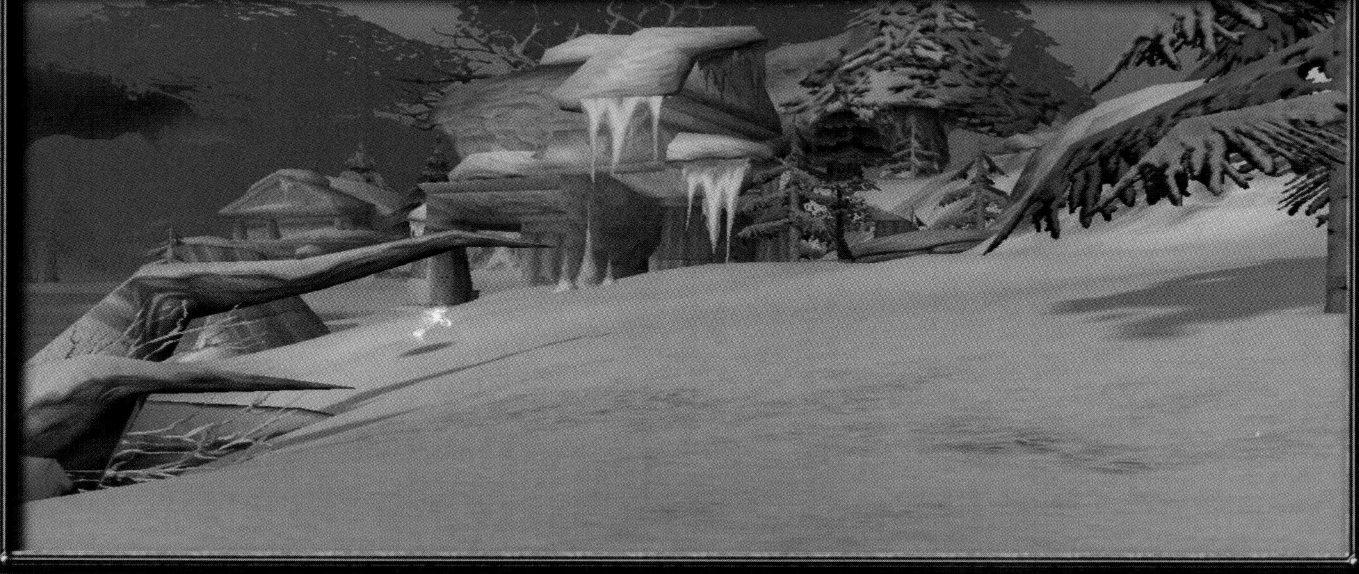

MAP LEGEND

❶ FROSTFIRE HOT SPRINGS
Fledgling Chillwind 54-55
Ragged Owlbeast 53-55
Rogue Ice Thistle 53-54
Shardtooth Bear 53-54
Winterfall Totemic 54-55
Winterfall Pathfinder 53-54
Winterfall Den Watcher 55-56

❷ TIMBERMAW POST
Winterfall Totemic 54-55
Winterfall Pathfinder 53-54
Winterfall Den Watcher 55-56

❸ THE RUINS OF KEL'THERIL
Anguished Highborn 55-56
Suffering Highborn 54-55

❹ LAKE KEL'THERIL
Anguished Highborn 55-56
Suffering Highborn 54-55

❺ MAZTHORIL
Brumeran 58 Elite
Chillwind Chimera 55
Cobalt Broodlings 55-56
Cobalt Scalebane 56-57 Elite
Cobalt Mageweaver 57-58 Elite
Cobalt Welps 54
Cobalt Wyrmkin 55-56 Elite
Shardtooth Mauler 55
Spell Eater 55-56
Spellmaw 56 Elite
Manaclaw 58 Elite
Scryer 59 Elite
Winterspring Owl 54-56

❻ DUN MANDARR
Berserker Owlbeast 57-58
Crazed Owlbeast 58
Elder Shardtooth 57-58
Moontouched Owlbeast 58
Winterspring Screecher 57-58

❼ FROSTWHISPER GORGE
Frostmaul Preserver 59-60 Elite
Frostmaul Giant 59-60 Elite

❽ DARKWHISPER GORGE
Hederine Manstalker 59-60 Elite
Hedereine Slayer 59-60 Elite

❾ OWLWING THICKET
Ranshalla 58
Berserk Owl Beast 58-59
Chillwind Ravager 59
Crazed Owl Beast 56-57
Moontouched Owl Beast 57-58

❿ ICE THISTLE HILLS
Chillwing Chimaera 55-57
Ice Thistle Yeti 55-56
Ice Thistle Patriarch 57-58
Ice Thistle Matriarch 56-57
Shardtooth Mauler 55-56
Winterspring Owl 55-56

⓫ WINTERFALL VILLAGE
Shardtooth 54-55
Winterspring Owl 54-55
Winterfall Ursa 57-58
Winterfall Shaman 56-57
Winterfall Den Watcher 55-56

⓬ EVERLOOK
Everlook Bruiser 65
Maethrya 55 Elite Alliance Flight Master
Yaugrek 55 Elite Horde Flight Master
Meggi Peppinrocker 60
Malyfous Darkhammer 55 The Thorium Brotherhood Quest
Evie Whirlbrew 58 Alchemy Supplies Rare recipes
Umi Rumplesnicker 57 Quest
Azzleby 30 Stable Master
Seril Scourbane 57
Lilith the Lithe 55
Qia Trade good supplies Rare Patterns
Kilram 58
Blixxrak 55 Light Armor Merchant
Nixxrak 54 Heavy Armor Merchant
Wixxrap 55 Weaponsmith And Gunsmith
Jack Sterling 50
Umaron Stragarelm 42
Lunnix Sprocketslip 54 Mining supplier
Felnok Steelspring 54
Legacki 57
Himmik 60 Food and Drink
Jessica Redpath 50
Gregor Greystone 55 Argent Dawn
Innkeeper Vizzie 30
Gogo 58
Harco Wigglesworth 54
Xizzer Fizzbolt 55 Engineer Supplier
Chillwind Chimaera 57
Shardtooth Mauler 56

⓭ THE HIDDEN GROVE
Berserk Owl Beast 58-59
Crazed Owl beast 56-57
Moontouch Owl Beast 57-58

⓮ FROSTSABER ROCK
Frostsaber Stalker 59-60
Frostsaber Huntress 58-59
Frostsaber Pride Watcher 60
Frostsaber Cub 55-56
Frostsaber 55-56

⓯ STARFALL VILLAGE
Syvrana 55 Trade Goods
Lyranne Feathersong 56 Food and Drink
Wynd Nightchaser 62
Jaron Stoneshapper 55 Explorers' Club
Natheril Raincaller 57 General Goods

QUESTS

QUEST	M LEV	Q LEV	QUEST LAUNCHER	QUEST FINISHER	CHAIN?	XP---	XP--	XP-	XP+	XP++	XP+++	CASH REWARD
Are We There, Yeti?	52	56	Umi Rumplesnicker	Umi Rumplesnicker	Y	440	875	1750	2600	3500	4350	85 00
Are We There, Yeti?	52	58	Umi Rumplesnicker	Umi Rumplesnicker	N	775	1550	3100	4650	6200	7750	90 00
REWARD: Mechanical Yeti												
Are We There, Yeti?	52	58	Umi Rumplesnicker	Umi Rumplesnicker	Y	470	925	1850	2800	3700	4650	90 00
Breastplate of Bloodthirst	57	62	Malyfous's Catalogue (Obj)	Malyfous Darkhammer	N	0	0	0	0	0	0	None
REWARD: Breastplate of Bloodthirst												
Cap of the Scarlet Savant	57	62	Malyfous's Catalogue (Obj)	Malyfous Darkhammer	N	0	0	0	0	0	0	None
REWARD: Cap of the Scarlet Savant												
Chillwind Horns	50	54	Felnok Steelspring	Felnok Steelspring	Y	550	1100	2200	3250	4350	5450	None
Duke Nicholas Zverenhoff	50	52	Gregor Greystone	Duke Nicholas Zverenhoff	N	260	500	1000	1550	2050	2550	40 00
Enraged Wildkin	53	59	Jaron's Wagon (Obj)	Jaron Stoneshaper	N	650	1300	2550	3850	5100	6400	90 00
Enraged Wildkin	53	59	Jaron Stoneshaper	Damaged Crate (Obj)	Y	320	650	1300	1900	2550	3200	None
Enraged Wildkin	53	59	Damaged Crate (Obj)	Jaron's Wagon (Obj)	Y	320	650	1300	1900	2550	3200	None
Falling to Corruption	52	56	Donova Snowden	Deadwood Cauldron (Obj)	Y	440	875	1750	2600	3500	4350	None
Fiery Plate Gauntlets	55	60	Malyfous Darkhammer	Malyfous Darkhammer	N	825	1650	3300	5000	6650	8300	None
REWARD: Plans: Fiery Plate Gauntlets, Fiery Plate Gauntlets												
Guarding Secrets	52	59	Trull Failbane	Nara Wildmane	N	650	1300	2550	3850	5100	6400	None
CHOICE OF: 1 Seaspray Bracers or 1 Shining Armplates												
High Chief Winterfall	52	59	Donova Snowden	Donova Snowden	N	650	1300	2550	3850	5100	6400	None
CHOICE OF: 1 Crystal Breeze Mantle or 1 Fernpulse Jerkin or 1 Willow Band Hauberk												
Leggings of Arcana	57	62	Malyfous's Catalogue (Obj)	Malyfous Darkhammer	N	0	0	0	0	0	0	None
REWARD: Leggings of Arcana												
Lorax's Tale	55	61	Lorax	Lorax	N	70	140	270	410	550	675	None
Mystery Goo	52	56	Deadwood Cauldron (Obj)	Donova Snowden	Y	440	875	1750	2600	3500	4350	None
Remorseful Highborne	53	58	Remorseful Highborne	Wynd Nightchaser	Y	470	925	1850	2800	3700	4650	None
Return to Tinkee	50	54	Felnok Steelspring	Tinkee Steamboil	N	270	550	1100	1600	2150	2700	None
CHOICE OF: 1 Blitzcleaver or 1 Grave Scepter												
Strange Sources	51	56	Donova Snowden	Donova Snowden	N	575	1150	2300	3500	4650	5800	None
REWARD: Deep River Cloak												
The Crystal of Zin-Malor	53	58	Wynd Nightchaser	Arch Druid Fandral Staghelm	N	625	1250	2500	3700	4950	6200	None
CHOICE OF: 1 Turquoise Sash or 1 Plow Wood Spaulders or 1 Emerald Mist Gauntlets												
The Everlook Report	50	52	Gregor Greystone	Argent Officer Pureheart	N	260	500	1000	1550	2050	2550	40 00
The Everlook Report	50	52	Gregor Greystone	Argent Officer Garush	N	260	500	1000	1550	2050	2550	40 00
The Ruins of Kel'Theril	53	56	Wynd Nightchaser	Jaron Stoneshaper	Y	60	120	230	350	460	575	None
The Ruins of Kel'Theril	53	56	Jaron Stoneshaper	Aurora Skycaller	Y	575	1150	2300	3500	4650	5800	None
Threat of the Winterfall	52	56	Donova Snowden	Donova Snowden	N	575	1150	2300	3500	4650	5800	85 00
Toxic Horrors	52	56	Donova Snowden	Donova Snowden	Y	575	1150	2300	3500	4650	5800	None
Winterfall Runners	52	57	Donova Snowden	Donova Snowden	Y	600	1200	2400	3600	4800	6000	None
Words of the High Chief	52	59	Donova Snowden	Kelek Skykeeper	N	650	1300	2550	3850	5100	6400	None
Wrath of the Blue Flight	57	62	Haleh	Haleh	Y	70	140	280	420	550	700	None

THUNDER BLUFF

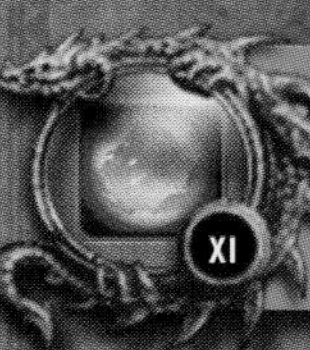

THUNDER BLUFF
THE SPIRIT RISE
THE ELDER RISE
THE HUNTER RISE

Rising on the strength of thick ropes and heavy counterweights, the elevators of Thunder Bluff enter into a city that mocks assault and lives halfway between earth and sky. The Tauren welcome their allies to visit and dance or plan with them. The watchful eye of the Cairne Bloodhoof is always looking out toward the valley. The Centaurs of Kalimdor once fought hard against the Tauren, attempting to destroy them and their homes. Though this enmity remains, the Tauren have regrouped and are ready to push back against their foes, assisting the Horde in bringing Kalimdor back under a flag of leadership and strength.

MAP LEGEND

THUNDER BLUFF ELEVATOR

1 ELEVATOR
Bluff Watchers 50 (Throughout City)

THUNDER BLUFF MAIN LEVEL

2 THUNDER BLUFF CIVIC INFORMATION
Krumn 50 Guildmaster
Thrumn 25 Tabard Vendor

3 KURUK'S GOODS
Kuruk 30 General Goods Vendor
Pakwa 30 Bag Vendor

4 TRADE GOODS AND SUPPLIES
Shadi Mistrunner 30 Trade Goods Supplier

5 THUNDER BLUFF WEAPONS
Jyn Stonehoof 30 Weapons Merchant

6 INN
Innkeeper Pala 30 Innkeeper

7 PASSAGE TO THE HUNTERS RISE

8 BANK
Bulrug 30 Stable Master
Bankers 45
Mailbox

9 HEWA'S ARMORY
Elki 30 Mail Armor Merchant
Hewa 30 Cloth Armor Merchant
Ahanu 30 Leather Armor Merchant

10 TOWER
Tal 55 Elite Wind Rider Master

11 BREAD AND GRAINS
Fyr Mistrunner 30 Bread Vendor

12 KARN'S SMITHY
Taur Stonehoof 30 Blacksmithing Supplier
Karn Stonehoof 35 Expert Blacksmith
Orm Stonehoof 45 Quest
Thrag Stonehoof 24 Journeyman Blacksmith

13 PASSAGE TO SPIRIT RISE
Sage Truthseeker 30 Quest

14 STONEHOOF GEOLOGY
Kurm Stonehoof 40 Mining Supplier
Brek Stonehoof 35 Miner Trainer

15 STONESPIRE TENT
Auld Stonespire 28 Quest

16 Eyahn Eagletalon 12 Quest

17 Chepi 30 Reagent Vendor (Wanderer)

THUNDER BLUFF SECOND LEVEL

18 THUNDERHORN ARCHERY
Kuna Thunderhorn 30 Bowyer & Fletching Goods

19 FRUITS AND VEGETABLES
Nan Mistrunner 30 Fruit Vendor

20 HOLISTIC HERBALISM
Nida Winterhoof 30 Herbalism Supplier
Komin Winterhoof 35 Herbalism Trainer

21 PASSAGE TO ELDER RISE

22 CLOUDWEAVER'S BASKETS
Tand 30 Basket Weaver

23 BENA'S ALCHEMY
Mani Winterhoof 30 Alchemy Supplies
Bena Winterhoof 35 Expert Alchemist
Kray 25 Journeyman Alchemist

24 DAWNSTRIDER'S ENCHANTERS
Teg Dawnstrider 35 Expert Enchanter
Nata Dawnstrider 30 Enchanting Supplies
Mot Dawnstrider 21 Journeyman Enchanter

25 PASSAGE TO SPIRIT RISE

26 THUNDER BLUFF ARMORERS
Mooranta 35 Skinning Trainer
Vhan 26 Journeyman Tailor
Veren Tailstrider 21 Quest
Tepa 35 Expert Tailor
Mahu 30 Leatherworking & Tailoring Supplies
Tagain 30 Cloth Armor Merchant
Fela 30 Heavy Armor Merchant
Grod 30 Leather Armor Merchant
Mak 24 Journeyman Leatherworker
Una 46 Artisan Leatherworker
Tarn 36 Expert Leatherworker

THUNDER BLUFF TOP LEVEL

27 RAINSTICKS
Sunn Ragetotem 30 Staff Merchant

28 KODO STEAK AND RIBS
Kaga Mistrunner 30 Meat Vendor

29 WINTERHOOF TOTEMS
Tah Winterhoof 30

30 MOUNTAINTOP BAIT & TACKLE
Sewa Mistrunner 40 Fishing Supplier
Kah Mistrunner 45 Fishing Trainer

31 PASSAGE TO ELDER RISE

32 CHIEF'S TENT
Cairne Bloodhoof 63 Elite High Chieftain

33 PASSAGE TO THE HUNTER RISE

34 THUNDERHOOF'S FIREARMS
Hogor Thunderhoof 30 Guns Merchant

35 RAGETOTEM ARMS
Delgo Ragetotem 30 Axe Merchant
Etu Ragetotem 30 Mace & Staff Merchant
Ohanako 30 Two-Handed Weapon Merchant
Kard Ragetotem 30 Sword & Dagger Merchant

36 HARNESSES
Sura Wildmane 30 War Harness Vendor

37 ASKA'S KITCHEN
Naal Mistrunner 40 Cooking Supplier
Aska Mistrunner 45 Cooking Trainer

38 AUDITORIUM
Zangen Stonehoof 25 Quest

THE HUNTER RISE

39 MOSARN'S TENT
Mosarn 30

40 HESUWA'S TENT
Hesuwa Thunderhorn 40 Pet Trainer

41 DRAYL'S TENT
Drayl 35

42 ANSEKHWA'S TENT
Ansekhwa 50 Elite Weapon Master

43 HUNTER'S HALL
Henen Ragetotem 65
Urek Thunderhorn 40 Hunter Trainer
Ker Ragetotem 40 Warrior Trainer
Kary Thunderhorn 50 Hunter Trainer
Torm Ragetotem 50 Warrior Trainer
Holt Thunderhorn 60 Hunter Trainer
Sark Ragetotem 60 Warrior Trainer

44 Melor Stonehoof 68 Quest

45 SAERN PRIDERUNNER'S TENT
Saern Priderunner 50

46 Kon Yelloweyes 25

ELDER RISE

47 BASHANA'S TENT
Bashana Runetotem 35

48 MAGATHA'S TENT
Magatha Grimtotem 95 Elder Crone
Cor Grimtotem 75
Gorm Grimtotem 75
Rahauro 20 Magatha's Servant

49 HALL OF ELDERS
Turak Runetotem 50 Druid Trainer
Sheal Runetotem 60 Druid Trainer
Arch Druid Hamuul Runetotem 65 Quest
Kym Wildmane 40 Druid Trainer
Nara Wildmane 55 Quest

50 Ghede 25

51 ELDER RISE DRUMS
Sheza Wildmane 30

SPIRIT RISE

52 SPIRITUAL HEALING
Pand Stonebinder 35 First Aid Trainer

53 HALL OF SPIRITS
Xanis Flameweaver 15
Tigor Skychaser 40 Shaman Trainer
Beram Skychaser 60 Shaman Trainer
Slin Skychaser 50 Shaman Trainer

54 Pawe Mistrunner 24

55 THE POOLS OF VISION
Clarice Foster 17 Quest
Miles Welsh 40 Priest Trainer
Ursyn Ghull 40 Mage Trainer
Malakai Cross 50 Priest Trainer
Apothecary Zamah 22 Royal Apothecary Society Quest
Brigitte Cranston 45 Portal Trainer
Archmage Shymm 60 Mage Trainer
Father Cobb 60 Priest Trainer
Thurston Zane 60 Mage Trainer

QUESTS

QUEST	M LEV	Q LEV	QUEST LAUNCHER	QUEST FINISHER	CHAIN?	XP---	XP--	XP-	XP+	XP++	XP+++	CASH REWARD
A Future Task	45	50	Nara Wildmane	Sage Truthseeker	N	470	950	1900	2800	3750	4700	2 20 00
A Vengeful Fate	29	34	Auld Stonespire	Auld Stonespire	N	410	800	1600	2450	3250	4050	None
CHOICE OF: 1 Berylline Pads or 1 Stonefist Girdle or 1 Marbled Buckler												
Assisting Arch Druid Runetotem	47	50	Innkeeper Pala	Arch Druid Hamuul Runetotem	Y	45	95	190	280	380	470	None
Blood of Innocents	13	23	Apothecary Lydon	Apothecary Lydon	N	190	370	750	1100	1500	1850	None
Compendium of the Fallen	28	38	Sage Truthseeker	Sage Truthseeker	N	360	700	1400	2150	2850	3550	None
CHOICE OF: 1 Vile Protector or 1 Forcestone Buckler or 1 Omega Orb												
Forsaken Aid	13	18	Magatha Grimtotem	Apothecary Zamah	Y	35	70	140	200	270	340	None
Frostmaw	26	37	Melor Stonehoof	Melor Stonehoof	N	430	850	1700	2550	3400	4250	None
REWARD: Spirit Hunter Headdress												
Gathering Leather	4	8	Veren Tallstrider	Veren Tallstrider	N	90	180	350	525	700	875	None
CHOICE OF: 1 Animal Skin Belt or 1 Double-layered Gloves												
Journey to Tarren Mill	13	18	Apothecary Zamah	Apothecary Lydon	Y	140	270	550	800	1100	1350	None
Kodo Hide Bag	4	10	Veren Tallstrider	Veren Tallstrider	N	40	85	170	250	340	420	None
REWARD: Pattern: Kodo Hide Bag												
Melor Sends Word	20	30	Jorn Skyseer	Melor Stonehoof	Y	0	0	0	0	0	0	None
Morrowgrain Research	47	50	Bashana Runetotem	Bashana Runetotem	N	470	950	1900	2800	3750	4700	None
REWARD: Cenarion Circle Cache												
Morrowgrain Research	47	50	Arch Druid Hamuul Runetotem	Bashana Runetotem	Y	45	95	190	280	380	470	None
REWARD: 20 Packets of Tharlendris Seeds												
Morrowgrain to Thunder Bluff	47	50	Bashana Runetotem	Bashana Runetotem	N	45	95	190	280	380	470	None
REWARD: Cenarion Circle Cache												
Plainsrunning	40	40		Saern Priderunner	N	0	0	0	0	0	0	None
Portents of Uldum	45	50	Sage Truthseeker	Nara Wildmane	Y	45	95	190	280	380	470	None
Preparation for Ceremony	7	11	Eyahn Eagletalon	Eyahn Eagletalon	N	90	180	350	525	700	875	None
CHOICE OF: 1 Bound Harness or 1 Tribal Warrior's Shield												
Return to Thunder Bluff	13	23	Apothecary Lydon	Apothecary Zamah	N	140	280	550	850	1100	1400	None
Return to Thunder Bluff	45	50	Uldum Pedestal (Obj)	Nara Wildmane	Y	45	95	190	280	380	470	None
Seeing What Happens	45	50	Nara Wildmane	Uldum Pedestal (Obj)	N	470	950	1900	2800	3750	4700	None
Serpentbloom	14	18	Apothecary Zamah	Apothecary Zamah	N	170	340	675	1000	1350	1700	20 00
REWARD: Apothecary Gloves												
Steelsnap	20	30	Melor Stonehoof	Melor Stonehoof	N	250	490	975	1450	1950	2450	None
The Flying Machine Airport	13	23	Apothecary Zamah	Apothecary Zamah	N	230	460	925	1400	1850	2300	30 00
The Platinum Discs	40	47	Sage Truthseeker	Bena Winterhoof	N	40	85	170	250	340	420	None
REWARD: Thawpelt Sack and CHOICE OF: 5 Superior Healing Potion or 5 Greater Mana Potion												
The Sacred Flame	20	25	Zangen Stonehoof	Zangen Stonehoof	Y	260	500	1000	1550	2050	2550	35 00
The Sacred Flame	20	29	Rau Cliffrunner	Rau Cliffrunner	N	240	470	950	1400	1900	2350	None
CHOICE OF: 1 Cliffrunner's Aim or 1 Azure Sash												
The Sacred Flame	20	29	Zangen Stonehoof	Rau Cliffrunner	Y	60	120	240	350	470	600	None
Un'Goro Soil	47	50	Arch Druid Hamuul Runetotem	Ghede	N	470	950	1900	2800	3750	4700	1 45 00
Until Death Do Us Part	12	15	Clarice Foster	Yuriv's Tombstone (Obj)	N	55	110	220	320	430	550	None

DUSTWALLOW MARSH

Watery murky pools scattered among the land are the biggest indication that you're in Dustwallow Marsh. Theramore, an Alliance City, has a few trainers and vendors and there are many travel options including a flight path and a boat going to Menethil on the Eastern Kingdoms continent. This is a dangerous area and only adventurers reaching the mid to highest levels of their training can wander here in safety. However, the Horde is making a push into the region and has set up Brackenwall Village with their own flight path. There are plenty of quests for either faction to take part in, but be careful. The creatures in the marsh tend to attack in packs, so be cautious while you travel through.

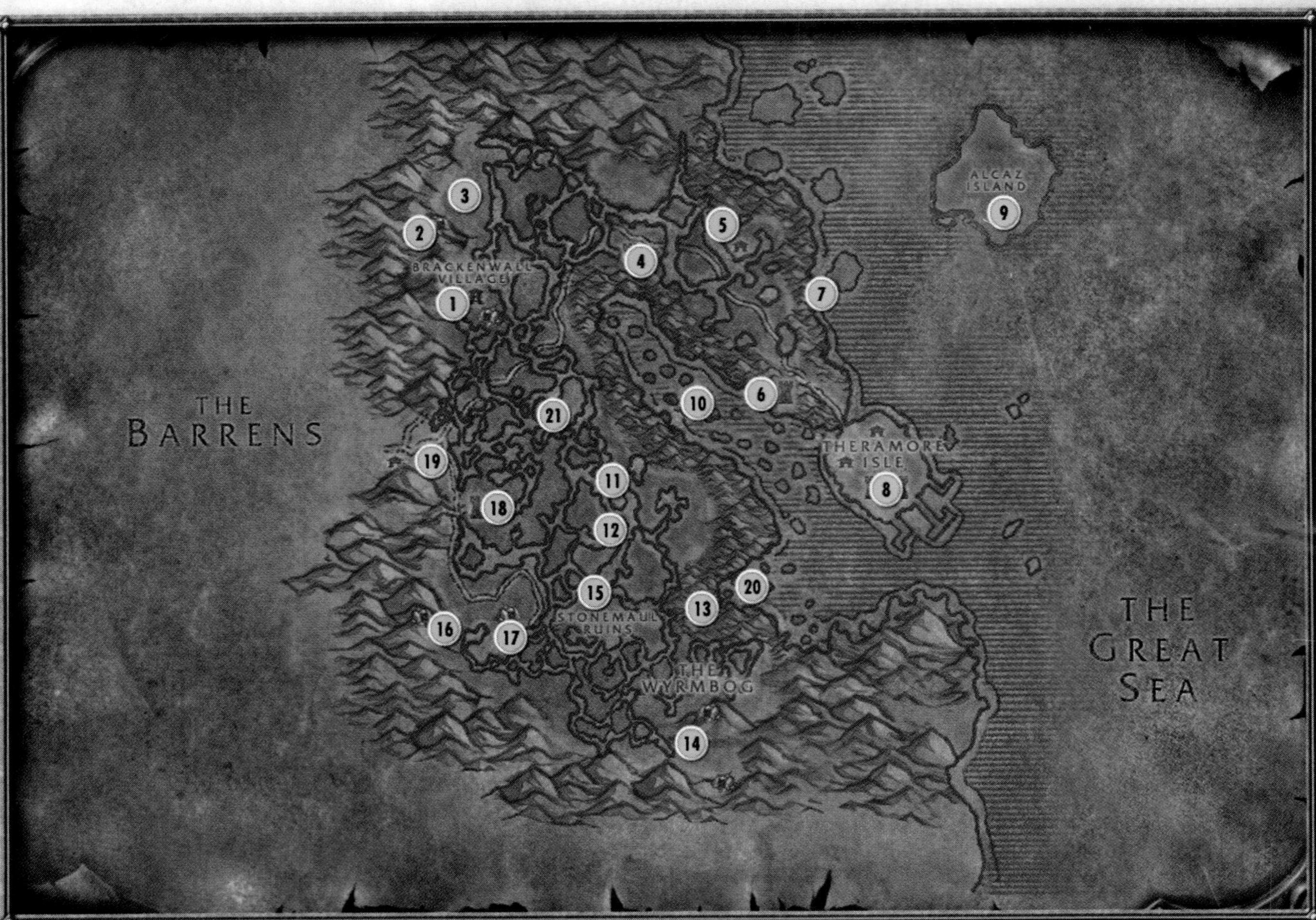

LOCAL RESOURCES

MINING: NONE

HERBALISM

HERB	AVAILABILITY
Kingsblood	Moderate

SKINNING

Quantity of Skinnable Creatures: Abundant

Levels of Skinnable Creatures: 35-60(Skinning 150-300)

MAP LEGEND

1 BRACKENWALL VILLAGE
- Mudcrush Durtfeet 42 Quest
- Brackenwall Enforcer 55
- Nazeer Bloodpike 48 Quest
- Ghok'ka 43 Tailoring Supplies
- Shardi 55 Elite Wind Rider Master
- Zanara 43 Bowyer
- Zulrg 43 Weaponsmith
- Overlord Mok'Morokk Quest
- Krog 40 Quest
- Krak 43 Armorer
- Do'gol 30
- Ogg'mar 40 Butcher
- Draz'Zilb 40 Quest
- Tharg 44 Quest

2 DARK MIST CAVERN
- Darkmist Recluse 36-37
- Darkmist Spider 35-36

3 BLUEFEN
- Drywallow Crocolisk 35-36
- Bloodfen Raptor 35-36
- Drywallow Vicejaw 36-37
- Darkfang Spider 35-36
- Darkfang Lurker 36
- Withervine Bark Ripper 36-37 Elemental
- Theramore Infiltrator 36
- Withervine Creeper 35-36

4 NORTH SENTRY POINT
- Theramore Sentry 35-36

5 WITCH HILL
- 'Swamp Eye' Jarl 42 Quest
- Drywallow Crocolisk 35-36
- Bloodfen Raptor 35-36
- Bloodfen Screecher 36-37
- Drywallow Vicejaw 36-37
- Withervine Creeper 35-36

6 SENTRY POINT
- Sentry Point Guard 32-33

7 DREADMURK SHORE
- Mirefin Coastrunner 36-37
- Mirefin Muckdweller 36-
- Murdrock Spikeshell 37-38
- Murdrock Tortoise 37

8 THERAMORE ISLE
- Theramore Guard 53-57
- Theramore Lieutenant 52
- Michael 30 Stable Master
- Morgan Stern 36
- Fiora Longears 26
- Innkeeper Janene 30 Innkeeper
- Bartender Lillian 45 Bartender
- Craig Nollward 32 Cook
- Ingo Woolybush 39 Explorer's League
- Guard Byron 40
- Medic Tamberlyn 51
- Captain Thomas 53 Blue Team Captain
- Guard Kahill 50
- Guard Narrisha 50
- Combat Master Szigeti 55
- Combat Master Criton 55
- Medic Helaina 51
- Guard Jarad 50
- Captain Andrews 53 Red Team Captain
- Guard Tark 50
- Spot 35
- Theramore Practicing Guard 48-49
- Brother Karman 45 Paladin Trainer
- Dwane Wertle 28 Chef
- Piter Verance 41 Weaponsmith & Armorer
- Clerk Lendry 20
- Captain Evencane 45 Warrior Trainer
- Command Samaul 40
- Captain Garran Vimes 50
- Adjutant Tesoran 35
- Alchemist Narett 37 Expert Alchemist
- Uma Bartulm 37 Herbalism & Alchemy Supplies
- Marie Holdston 37 Weaponsmith
- Hans Weston 37 Armorer & Shieldsmith
- Caz Twosprocket 35
- Gregor MacVince 35 Horse Breeder
- Helenia Olden 34 Trade Supplies
- Timothy Worthington 51 Master Tailor
- Baldruc 55 Elite Gryphon Master

9 ALCAZ ISLAND
- Strashaz Hydra 59-60 Elite
- Strashaz Siren 59 Elite
- Strashaz Sorceress 61 Elite

10 DUST WALLOW BAY
- Mottled Drywallow Crocolisk 38-39
- Drywallow Snapper 37
- Drywallow Daggermaw 40-41 Elite

11 THE QUAGMIRE
- Darkfang Creeper 38

12 Tabetha Quest NPC

13 THE DRAGONMURK
- Mottled Drywallow Crocolisk 38-39
- Drywallow Snapper 37
- Drywallow Daggermaw 40-41 Elite
- Searing Whelp 42

14 THE WYRMBOG
- Firemane Scalebane 43-44 Elite
- Searing Hatchling 41-42
- Firemane Flamecaller 44 Elite
- Giant Darkfang Spider 41
- Entrance to Onyxia's Lair World Dungeon

15 STONEMAUL RUINS
- Firemane Ashe Tail 42-43 Elite
- Firemane Scout 41-42 Elite
- Searing Hatchling 41-42

16 BLOODFEN BURROW
- Bloodfen Lashtail 40-41

17 THE DEN OF FLAME
- Firemane Ash Tail 42-43 Elite
- Firemane Scout 41-42 Elite

18 LOST POINT
- Theramore Deserter 37
- Swamp Ooze 38
- Bloodfen Scytheclaw 37
- Darkfang Venomspitter 38
- Mottled Drywallow Crocolisk 38-39

19 SHADY REST INN

20 TIDEFURY COVE
- Muckshell Pincer 42
- Muckshell Scrabbler 42

21 BEEZIL'S WRECK
- Acidic Swamp Ooze 39-41
- Corrosive Swamp Ooze 38

QUESTS

QUEST	M LEV	Q LEV	QUEST LAUNCHER	QUEST FINISHER	CHAIN?	XP---	XP--	XP-	XP+	XP++	XP+++	CASH REWARD
... and Bugs	33	40	Morgan Stern	Morgan Stern	N	320	625	1250	1900	2500	3150	None
REWARD: Baroque Apron												
Army of the Black Dragon	38	43	Tharg	Tharg	N	450	900	1800	2650	3550	4450	None
CHOICE OF: 1 Tharg's Shoelace or 1 Tharg's Frisbee												
Captain Vimes	30	35	Theramore Lieutenant	Captain Garran Vimes	N	280	550	1100	1650	2200	2750	None
Challenge Overlord Mok'Morokk	38	45	Overlord Mok'Morokk	Draz'Zilb	N	490	975	1950	2900	3900	4850	None
CHOICE OF: 1 Fiendish Skiv or 1 Chillnail Splinter												
Daelin's Men	30	38	Adjutant Tesoran	Captain Garran Vimes	Y	30	55	110	170	230	290	None
Deadmire	35	45	Melor Stonehoof	Melor Stonehoof	N	390	775	1550	2350	3100	3900	None
Feast at the Blue Recluse	30	37	Angus Stern	Angus Stern	N	0	0	0	0	0	0	None
REWARD: Moist Towelette												
Finding Reethe	30	37		Krog	N	0	0	0	0	0	0	None
Fire at the Shady Rest	30	35		Captain Garran Vimes	N	0	0	0	0	0	0	None
Highperch Venom	25	30	Fiora Longears	Fiora Longears	N	370	725	1450	2200	2900	3650	None
REWARD: Windborne Belt												
Hungry!	32	36	Mudcrush Durtfeet	Mudcrush Durtfeet	N	280	550	1100	1700	2250	2800	None
CHOICE OF: 1 Mud's Crushers or 1 Durtfeet Stompers												
Identifying the Brood	38	43	Draz'Zilb	Draz'Zilb	N	525	1050	2150	3200	4300	5350	None
CHOICE OF: 1 Scorched Cape or 1 Rustler Gloves												
Jarl Needs a Blade	30	35	Swamp Eye" Jarl"	Swamp Eye" Jarl"	N	350	700	1400	2050	2750	3450	35 00
REWARD: Reedknot Ring, Artisan's Trousers												
Jarl Needs Eyes	30	35	Swamp Eye" Jarl"	Swamp Eye" Jarl"	Y	280	550	1100	1650	2200	2750	None
Jim's Song	30	35		Smiling Jim	N	0	0	0	0	0	0	None
Journey to Astranaar	18	20	Fiora Longears	Shindrell Swiftfire	N	0	0	0	0	0	0	None
Journey to Theramore!	1	1		Captain Noteo	N	0	0	0	0	0	0	None
Lieutenant Paval Reethe	30	37	Theramore Guard Badge (Obj)	Krog	N	70	140	280	430	575	700	None
Lieutenant Paval Reethe	30	40	Theramore Guard Badge (Obj)	Captain Garran Vimes	Y	80	160	310	470	625	775	None
Lieutenant Paval Reethe	30	40	Captain Garran Vimes	Adjutant Tesoran	Y	30	65	130	190	250	320	None
Marg Speaks	30	35	Bubbling Cauldron (Obj)	Nazeer Bloodpike	Y	280	550	1100	1650	2200	2750	None
Morgan Stern	33	38	Angus Stern	Morgan Stern	Y	70	140	280	430	575	700	None
Mudrock Soup and Bugs	33	38	Morgan Stern	Morgan Stern	Y	290	575	1150	1700	2300	2850	None
Overlord Mok'Morokk's Concern	38	43	Overlord Mok'Morokk	Overlord Mok'Morokk	N	450	900	1800	2650	3550	4450	None
REWARD: Enormous Ogre Boots												
Questioning Reethe	30	37	Ogron	Krog	N	360	700	1400	2150	2850	3550	None
CHOICE OF: 1 Eyepoker or 1 Blasting Hackbut												
Report to Zor	30	35	Nazeer Bloodpike	Zor Lonetree	N	280	550	1100	1650	2200	2750	None
Soothing Spices	30	35	Swamp Eye" Jarl"	Swamp Eye" Jarl"	Y	140	270	550	800	1100	1350	None
REWARD: 20 Frog Leg Stew												
Stinky's Escape	30	37	Stinky" Ignatz"	Morgan Stern	N	290	575	1150	1700	2300	2850	40 00
REWARD: Elixir of Fortitude												
Stinky's Escape	30	37	Stinky" Ignatz"	Mebok Mizzyrix	N	290	575	1150	1700	2300	2850	40 00
REWARD: Elixir of Fortitude												
Suspicious Hoofprints	30	35	Hoofprints (Obj)	Krog	N	140	270	550	800	1100	1350	None
Suspicious Hoofprints	30	35	Hoofprints (Obj)	Krog	N	140	270	550	800	1100	1350	None
Suspicious Hoofprints	30	35	Hoofprints (Obj)	Captain Garran Vimes	N	140	270	550	800	1100	1350	None
Suspicious Hoofprints	30	35	Hoofprints (Obj)	Captain Garran Vimes	N	140	270	550	800	1100	1350	None
The Black Shield	30	35	Caz Twosprocket	Captain Garran Vimes	N	140	270	550	800	1100	1350	None
The Black Shield	30	35	Black Shield (Obj)	Captain Garran Vimes	Y	70	140	280	410	550	700	None
The Black Shield	30	35	Captain Garran Vimes	Caz Twosprocket	Y	30	55	110	170	220	280	None
The Black Shield	30	35	Krog	Do'gol	Y	30	55	110	170	220	280	None
The Black Shield	30	37	Krog	Mosarn	N	140	280	550	850	1100	1400	None
The Black Shield	30	37	Do'gol	Krog	N	140	280	550	850	1100	1400	None
The Black Shield	30	37	Do'gol	Do'gol	Y	290	575	1150	1700	2300	2850	None
The Black Shield	30	35	Black Shield (Obj)	Krog	Y	70	140	280	410	550	700	None
The Brood of Onyxia	38	43	Draz'Zilb	Overlord Mok'Morokk	Y	35	70	140	220	290	360	None
The Brood of Onyxia	38	43	Overlord Mok'Morokk	Draz'Zilb	Y	35	70	140	220	290	360	None
The Brood of Onyxia	38	45	Draz'Zilb	Draz'Zilb	N	490	975	1950	2900	3900	4850	None
CHOICE OF: 1 Encarmine Boots or 1 Boots of Zua'tec												
The Burning Inn	30	35		Krog	N	0	0	0	0	0	0	None
The Deserters	30	38		Captain Garran Vimes	N	290	575	1150	1700	2300	2850	None
The Deserters	30	38	Captain Garran Vimes	Balos Jacken	Y	290	575	1150	1700	2300	2850	None
The Lost Report	30	35	Loose Dirt (Obj)	Nazeer Bloodpike	N	210	410	825	1250	1650	2050	None
The Orc Report	30	35	Loose Dirt (Obj)	Theramore Lieutenant	Y	70	140	280	410	550	700	None
The Severed Head	30	35	Loose Dirt (Obj)	Nazeer Bloodpike	Y	210	410	825	1250	1650	2050	None
The Theramore Docks	30	35	Nazeer Bloodpike	Nazeer Bloodpike	N	280	550	1100	1650	2200	2750	None
The Troll Witchdoctor	30	35	Nazeer Bloodpike	Kin'weelay	N	280	550	1100	1650	2200	2750	None
Theramore Spies	30	35	Nazeer Bloodpike	Nazeer Bloodpike	Y	280	550	1100	1650	2200	2750	None
They Call Him Smiling Jim	30	35	Guard Byron	Captain Garran Vimes	N	30	55	110	170	220	280	None
Vimes's Report	30	38	Captain Garran Vimes	Lady Jaina Proudmoore	Y	30	55	110	170	230	290	None

FERALAS

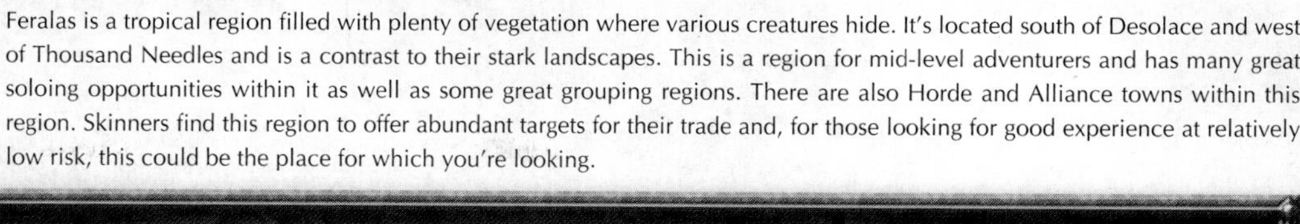

Feralas is a tropical region filled with plenty of vegetation where various creatures hide. It's located south of Desolace and west of Thousand Needles and is a contrast to their stark landscapes. This is a region for mid-level adventurers and has many great soloing opportunities within it as well as some great grouping regions. There are also Horde and Alliance towns within this region. Skinners find this region to offer abundant targets for their trade and, for those looking for good experience at relatively low risk, this could be the place for which you're looking.

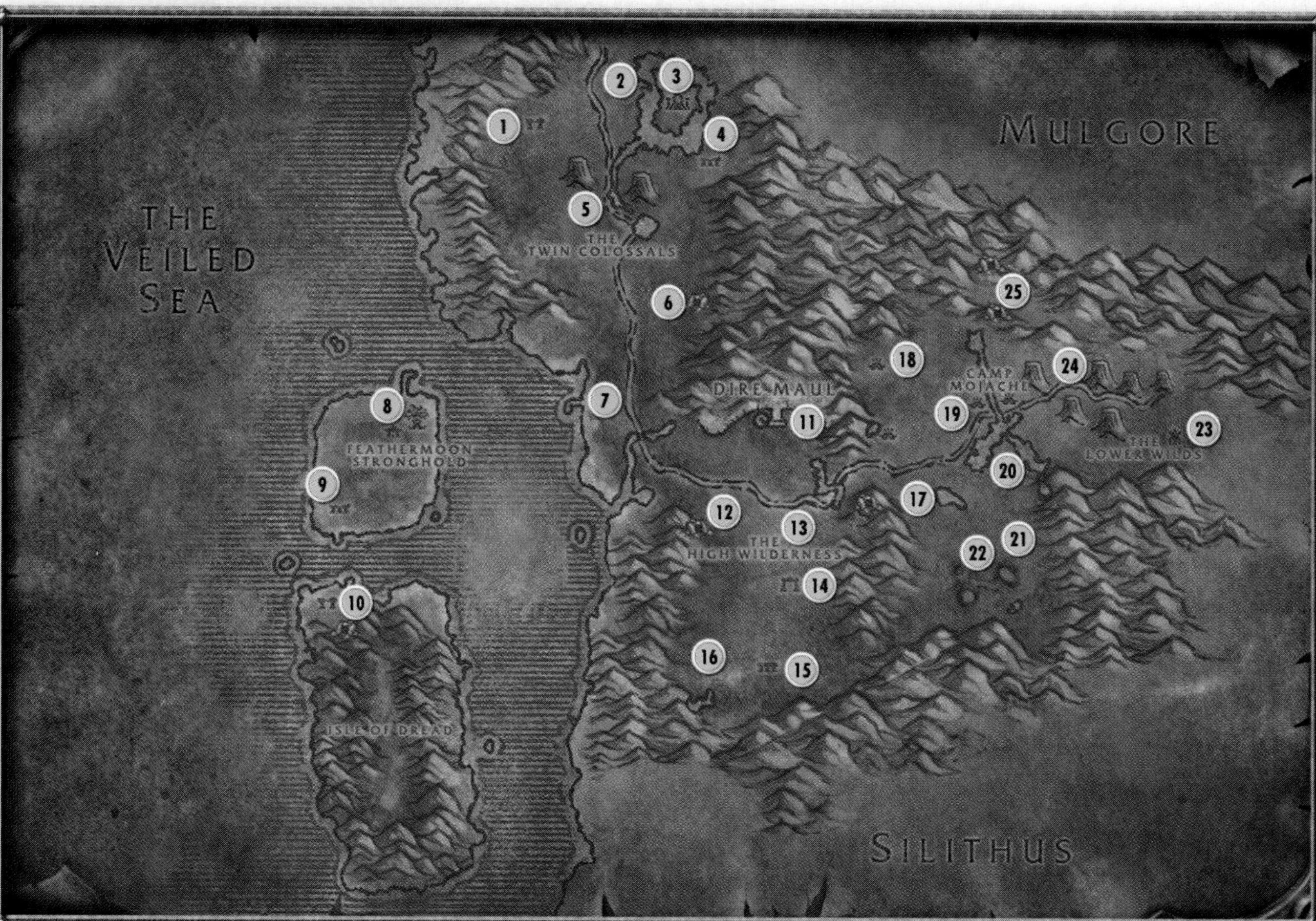

LOCAL RESOURCES

MINING

METAL	AVAILABILITY
Mithril	Abundant

HERBALISM

HERB	AVAILABILITY
Sungrass	Abundant
Goldthorn	Moderate
Purple Lotus	Rare

SKINNING

Quantity of Skinnable Creatures: Abundant

Levels of Skinnable Creatures: 40-45 (Skinning 150-175)

MAP LEGEND

1 RUINS OF RAVENWIND
Northspring Roguefeather 48-49
Northspring Windcaller 49-50
Northspring Slayer 49-50

2 JADEMIR LAKE
Jademir Dragonspawn 60 elite

3 DREAM BOUGH
Jademir Dragonspawn 60 elite
4 Oneiros
Jademir Dragonspawn 60 elite

5 THE TWIN COLOSSALS
Milbon Snarltooth 50
Ironfur Patriarch 48-49
Rabid Longtooth 47-48
Groddoc Thunderer 49-50
Sprite Dragon 48-50
Rockbiter 45
Land Walker 48-49 elite
Cliff Giant 49-50 elite
Wandering Forest Walker 45 elite

6 RAGE SCAR HOLD
Ferocious Rage Scar 47-48
Rage Scar yeti 46-47
Elder rage Scar 48-49

7 THE FORGOTTEN COAST
Rogue Vale Screecher 44-46
Sea Elelmental 48-49
Deep Strider 47 elite
Shore Strider 48-48 elite
Wave Strider 48
Sea Spray 47-48

8 FEATHERMOON STRONGHOLD-ALLIANCE CAMP(SARDOR ISLE)
Innkeeper Shyria 30
Feathermoon Sentinel 65
Fyldren Moonfeather 55 elite
Pratt McGrubben Leatherworker 55
Brannock 52 fisherman
Antarius 30 stablemaster
Logannas 52 alchemy supplier
Vivianna 52 trade supplies
Madrack Greenwell 54 food and drink
Faralorn 53 General supplies

9 RUINS OF SOLARSAL
Hatecrest Warrior 42-43
Hatecrest Screamer 41-42
Hatecrest Siren 42
Hatecrest Waverider 41-42

10 ISLE OF DREAD
Hatecrest Myrmidon 43-44
Hatecrest Sorceress 43-44
Hatecrest Serpentguard 44-45
Lord Shalzaru 47

11 ENTRANCE TO DIRE MAUL WORLD DUNGEON
Rogue vale Screecher 45
Longtooth Howler 44
Grizzled Ironfur Bear 44-45
Gordok Brute 60 elite

12 FERAL SCAR VALE
Feral Scar Yeti 43-44
Enraged Feral Scar 44-45
Hulking Feral Scar 46
Lurking Feral Scar 46
Vale Screecher 42

13 HIGH WILDERNESS
Grizzled Ironfur Bear 44
Rogue Vale Screecher 46
Longtooth Howler 44

14 RUINS OF ISILDIEN-NORTH
Gordunni Brute 42-43
Gordunni Mauler 43
Gordunni Warlock 43-44
Vale Screecher 41
Ironfur Bear 41-42
Groddoc Ape 42-43

15 RUINS OF ISILDIEN-SOUTH
Gordunni Mauler 43-44
Gordunni Warlock 43-44
Gordunni Shaman 45
Gordunni Mage-lord 45-46
Gordunni Warlord 46-47
Gordunni Battlemaster 45-45

16 FRAYFEATHER HIGHLANDS
Frayfeather Stagwing 44-45
Frayfeather Hippogryph 43
Frayfeather Skystormer 45-46
Cursed Sycamore 45 elite
Frayfeather Patriarch 46-47
17 Lower Wilds-west
Grimtotem Shaman 43-44
Sprite Darter 44-45
Ironfur Bear 42
Grimtotem Naturalist 41-42
Grimtotem Raider 42-43
Longtooth Runner 40

18 GRIMTOTEM COMPOUND
Grimtototem Naturalist 41-42
Grimtotem Shaman 43-44
Grimtotem Raider 42-43

19 CAMP MOJACHE
Rok Orhan 40
Witch Doctor Uzer'I 50
Shyrka Wolfrunner 30 stablemaster
Kulleg Stonehorn 41 skinning trainer
Hahrana Ironhide 55 Master Leatherworker
Worb Strongstitch 46 leatehrworking supplies
Sheendra Tallgrass 42 trade supplies
Hodoken Swiftstrider 45
Sage Palerunner 44
Ruw 44 herbalism trainer
Bronk 45 alchemy trainer
Jannos Lighthoof 43 druid trainer
Camp Mojache Brave 65
Orik'andi 42
Talo thornhoof 50
Loorana 43 food and drink
Orwin Gizzmick 50
Shyn 55 elite wind rider master
Blaise Montgomery 47
Innkeeper Gruel 30
Cawind Trueaim 46 gunsmith and Bowyer

20 WILDWING LAKE

21 WOODPAW HILLS
Woodpaw Brute 41-42
Woodpaw trapper 40-41
Woodpaw Mongrel lvl 40-41
Woodpaw Alpha 43-44
Woodpaw Reaver 42-43
Woodpaw Mystic 42-43

22 THE WRITHING DEEP
Grizzled Ironfur Bear 44-45
Longtooth Howler 43-44
Zukk'ash Wasp 44-45
Zukk'ash Worker 44-45

23 LOWER WILDS
Longtooth Howler 44
Groddoc Ape 41-43
Ironfur Bear 42
Longtooth runner 41
Woodpaw Trapper 41-42
Woodpaw Brute 41-42
Woodpaw Mongrel 40-41

24 LARISS PAVILION
Ironfur Bear 41-42
Longtooth Runner 41

25 GORDUNNI OUTPOST
Gordunni Brute 41-43
Gordunni Ogre 40-41
Gordunni Ogre-mage 41-42

QUESTS

QUEST	M LEV	Q LEV	QUEST LAUNCHER	QUEST FINISHER	CHAIN?	XP---	XP--	XP-	XP+	XP++	XP+++	CASH REWARD
A Hero's Welcome	40	46	Ginro Hearthkindle	Shandris Feathermoon	Y	600	1200	2400	3650	4850	6050	None
CHOICE OF: 1 Ceremonial Elven Blade or 1 Sanctimonial Rod												
A Short Incubation	38	47	Quentin	Quentin	N	210	420	850	1250	1700	2100	None
A Strange Request	40	45	Witch Doctor Uzer'i	Neeru Fireblade	Y	200	390	775	1150	1550	1950	None
Against Lord Shalzaru	40	45	Latronicus Moonspear	Latronicus Moonspear	Y	290	575	1150	1750	2300	2900	50 00
Against the Hatecrest	40	43	Shandris Feathermoon	Latronicus Moonspear	Y	35	70	140	220	290	360	None
Against the Hatecrest	40	43	Latronicus Moonspear	Latronicus Moonspear	Y	270	550	1100	1600	2150	2700	45 00
Alpha Strike	39	43	Hadoken Swiftstrider	Hadoken Swiftstrider	Y	270	550	1100	1600	2150	2700	45 00
An Orphan Looking For a Home	38	47	Kindal Moonweaver	Quentin	Y	110	210	420	625	850	1050	None
An Orphan Looking For a Home	38	47		Quentin	Y	110	210	420	625	850	1050	None
Becoming a Parent	37	48	Agnar Beastamer	Agnar Beastamer	N	45	90	180	260	350	440	None
REWARD: Sprite Darter Egg												

QUESTS continued

QUEST	M LEV	Q LEV	QUEST LAUNCHER	QUEST FINISHER	CHAIN?	XP---	XP--	XP-	XP+	XP++	XP+++	CASH REWARD
Boat Wreckage	40	44	Wrecked Row Boat (Obj)	Ginro Hearthkindle	Y	40	75	150	230	300	380	None
Corrupted Songflower	48	55	Corrupted Songflower (Obj)	Corrupted Songflower (Obj)	N	55	110	220	340	450	550	None
Dark Ceremony	38	46	Rok Orhan	Rok Orhan	Y	410	800	1600	2450	3250	4050	None
Dark Heart	45	50	Talo Thornhoof	Talo Thornhoof	N	600	1200	2350	3550	4700	5900	None
CHOICE OF: 1 Wingcrest Gloves or 1 Stronghorn Girdle												
Delivering the Relic	40	45	Latronicus Moonspear	Vestia Moonspear	N	390	775	1550	2350	3100	3900	None
CHOICE OF: 1 Dawnrider's Chestpiece or 1 Sentinel's Guard												
Doling Justice	38	47	Jer'kai Moonweaver	Jer'kai Moonweaver	N	320	625	1250	1900	2500	3150	None
Doling Justice	38	47	Jer'kai Moonweaver	Tyrande Whisperwind	N	525	1050	2100	3150	4200	5250	None
CHOICE OF: 1 Firwillow Wristbands or 1 Nightscale Girdle												
Escaping the Hive	40	46	Zukk'ash Pod (Obj)	Ginro Hearthkindle	Y	410	800	1600	2450	3250	4050	None
Faerie Dragon Muisek	40	50	Witch Doctor Uzer'i	Witch Doctor Uzer'i	Y	470	950	1900	2800	3750	4700	None
Feralas: A History	42	47	Feralas: A History (Obj)	Daryn Lightwind	Y	40	85	170	250	340	420	None
Food for Baby	38	47	Agnar Beastamer	Agnar Beastamer	Y	420	850	1700	2500	3350	4200	None
Freedom for All Creatures	38	47	Kindal Moonweaver	Kindal Moonweaver	N	320	625	1250	1900	2500	3150	None
Gordunni Cobalt	38	43	Orwin Gizzmick	Orwin Gizzmick	N	360	725	1450	2150	2900	3600	None
CHOICE OF: 1 Boots of the Maharishi or 1 Stargazer Cloak												
Hippogryph Muisek	40	47	Witch Doctor Uzer'i	Witch Doctor Uzer'i	Y	420	850	1700	2500	3350	4200	None
In Search of Knowledge	42	47	Troyas Moonbreeze	Daryn Lightwind	N	40	85	170	250	340	420	None
Jonespyre's Request	47	50	Innkeeper Shyria	Quintis Jonespyre	Y	45	95	190	280	380	470	None
Morrowgrain to Feathermoon Stronghold	47	50	Quintis Jonespyre	Quintis Jonespyre	N	45	95	190	280	380	470	None
REWARD: 5 Packets of Tharlendris Seeds												
Mountain Giant Muisek	40	50	Witch Doctor Uzer'i	Witch Doctor Uzer'i	N	470	950	1900	2800	3750	4700	None
Natural Materials	40	50	Witch Doctor Uzer'i	Witch Doctor Uzer'i	N	470	950	1900	2800	3750	4700	None
Psychometric Reading	40	44	Quintis Jonespyre	Ginro Hearthkindle	Y	40	75	150	230	300	380	None
Rescue OOX-22/FE!	40	45	Homing Robot OOX-22/FE	Oglethorpe Obnoticus	N	490	975	1950	2900	3900	4850	None
CHOICE OF: 1 Failed Flying Experiment or 1 Chainlink Towel												
Return to Feathermoon Stronghold	40	43	Solarsal Gazebo (Obj)	Shandris Feathermoon	N	180	360	725	1100	1450	1800	45 00
Return to Troyas	42	48	Daryn Lightwind	Troyas Moonbreeze	N	330	650	1300	2000	2650	3300	None
Return to Witch Doctor Uzer'i	40	45	Neeru Fireblade	Witch Doctor Uzer'i	N	95	190	390	575	775	975	None
Rise of the Silithid	40	46	Shandris Feathermoon	Gracina Spiritmight	N	40	80	160	240	320	410	None
Testing the Vessel	40	47	Witch Doctor Uzer'i	Witch Doctor Uzer'i	Y	420	850	1700	2500	3350	4200	None
The Battle Plans	39	43	Woodpaw Battle Map (Obj)	Hadoken Swiftstrider	N	360	725	1450	2150	2900	3600	None
CHOICE OF: 1 Earthclasp Barrier or 1 Rushridge Boots												
The Borrower	42	48	Daryn Lightwind	Curgle Cranklehop	Y	110	220	440	650	875	1100	None
The Giant Guardian	44	49	Rockbiter	Shay Leafrunner	Y	340	675	1350	2050	2700	3400	None
The Gordunni Orb	38	47	Rok Orhan	Uthel'nay	N	210	420	850	1250	1700	2100	None
The High Wilderness	39	44	Angelas Moonbreeze	Angelas Moonbreeze	N	380	750	1500	2250	3000	3750	65 00
The Knife Revealed	40	44	Ginro Hearthkindle	Quintis Jonespyre	N	40	75	150	230	300	380	None
The Mark of Quality	40	46	Pratt McGrubben	Pratt McGrubben	N	410	800	1600	2450	3250	4050	None
CHOICE OF: 1 Pratt's Handcrafted Boots or 1 Pratt's Handcrafted Gloves												
The Mark of Quality	40	46	Jangdor Swiftstrider	Jangdor Swiftstrider	N	410	800	1600	2450	3250	4050	None
CHOICE OF: 1 Jangdor's Handcrafted Boots or 1 Jangdor's Handcrafted Gloves												
The Missing Courier	40	43	Latronicus Moonspear	Ginro Hearthkindle	Y	35	70	140	220	290	360	None
The Missing Courier	40	43	Ginro Hearthkindle	Wrecked Row Boat (Obj)	Y	270	550	1100	1600	2150	2700	None
The Morrow Stone	42	50	Equinex Monolith (Obj)	Troyas Moonbreeze	N	470	950	1900	2800	3750	4700	None
CHOICE OF: 1 Cairnstone Sliver or 1 Seedtime Hoop												
The Mystery of Morrowgrain	47	50	Quintis Jonespyre	Quintis Jonespyre	N	470	950	1900	2800	3750	4700	None
CHOICE OF: 1 Quintis' Research Gloves or 1 Bark Iron Pauldrons												
The Newest Member of the Family	38	47	Quentin	Agnar Beastamer	Y	420	850	1700	2500	3350	4200	None
The Ogres of Feralas	38	43	Rok Orhan	Rok Orhan	Y	270	550	1100	1600	2150	2700	45 00
The Ogres of Feralas	38	44	Rok Orhan	Rok Orhan	N	380	750	1500	2250	3000	3750	1 25 00
The Ruins of Solarsal	40	43	Shandris Feathermoon	Solarsal Gazebo (Obj)	Y	270	550	1100	1600	2150	2700	None
The Stave of Equinex	42	50	Troyas Moonbreeze	Equinex Monolith (Obj)	Y	470	950	1900	2800	3750	4700	None
REWARD: A Sparkling Stone												
The Strength of Corruption	47	52	Talo Thornhoof	Talo Thornhoof	N	500	1000	2050	3050	4100	5100	None
The Sunken Temple	46	51	Angelas Moonbreeze	Marvon Rivetseeker	Y	370	725	1450	2200	2900	3650	None
The Super Snapper FX	42	48	Curgle Cranklehop	Daryn Lightwind	Y	440	875	1750	2650	3500	4400	None
The Woodpaw Gnolls	40	44	Ginro Hearthkindle	Large Leather Backpacks (Obj)	Y	0	0	0	0	0	0	None
The Writhing Deep	40	46	Large Leather Backpacks (Obj)	Zukk'ash Pod (Obj)	Y	0	0	0	0	0	0	None
To the Top	25	25	Marli Wishrunner	Marli Wishrunner	N	0	0	0	0	0	0	None
Treant Muisek	40	50	Witch Doctor Uzer'i	Witch Doctor Uzer'i	Y	470	950	1900	2800	3750	4700	None
Vengeance on the Northspring	45	50	Talo Thornhoof	Talo Thornhoof	N	360	700	1400	2150	2850	3550	55 00
Wandering Shay	44	49	Shay Leafrunner	Rockbiter	N	460	900	1800	2750	3650	4550	None
CHOICE OF: 1 Granite Grips or 1 Vinehedge Cinch												
War on the Woodpaw	39	42	Hadoken Swiftstrider	Hadoken Swiftstrider	Y	260	500	1000	1550	2050	2550	45 00
Weapons of Spirit	40	50	Witch Doctor Uzer'i	Witch Doctor Uzer'i	N	470	950	1900	2800	3750	4700	None
CHOICE OF: 1 Force of the Hippogryph or 1 Spirit of the Faerie Dragon or 1 Strength of the Treant or 1 Will of the Mountain Giant												
Woodpaw Investigation	39	43	Hadoken Swiftstrider	Woodpaw Battle Map (Obj)	Y	180	360	725	1100	1450	1800	None

MULGORE

Mulgore is the starting region for the Tauren. The largest portion of the land is made up of open plains ringed by mountains and the mesas that make up the capitol city of Thunder Bluff to the north. Wild Kodo Beasts roam the land and there is a rumor that a massive patriarch walks among them. Harpies have taken residence along the hillsides and the Venture Co. is trying to strip the land around Thunder Bluff and Bloodhoof Village. However, among even those dangerous adversaries, there are heroes. Cairne Bloodhoof sits in Thunder Bluff waiting for those willing to defend the land to join him.

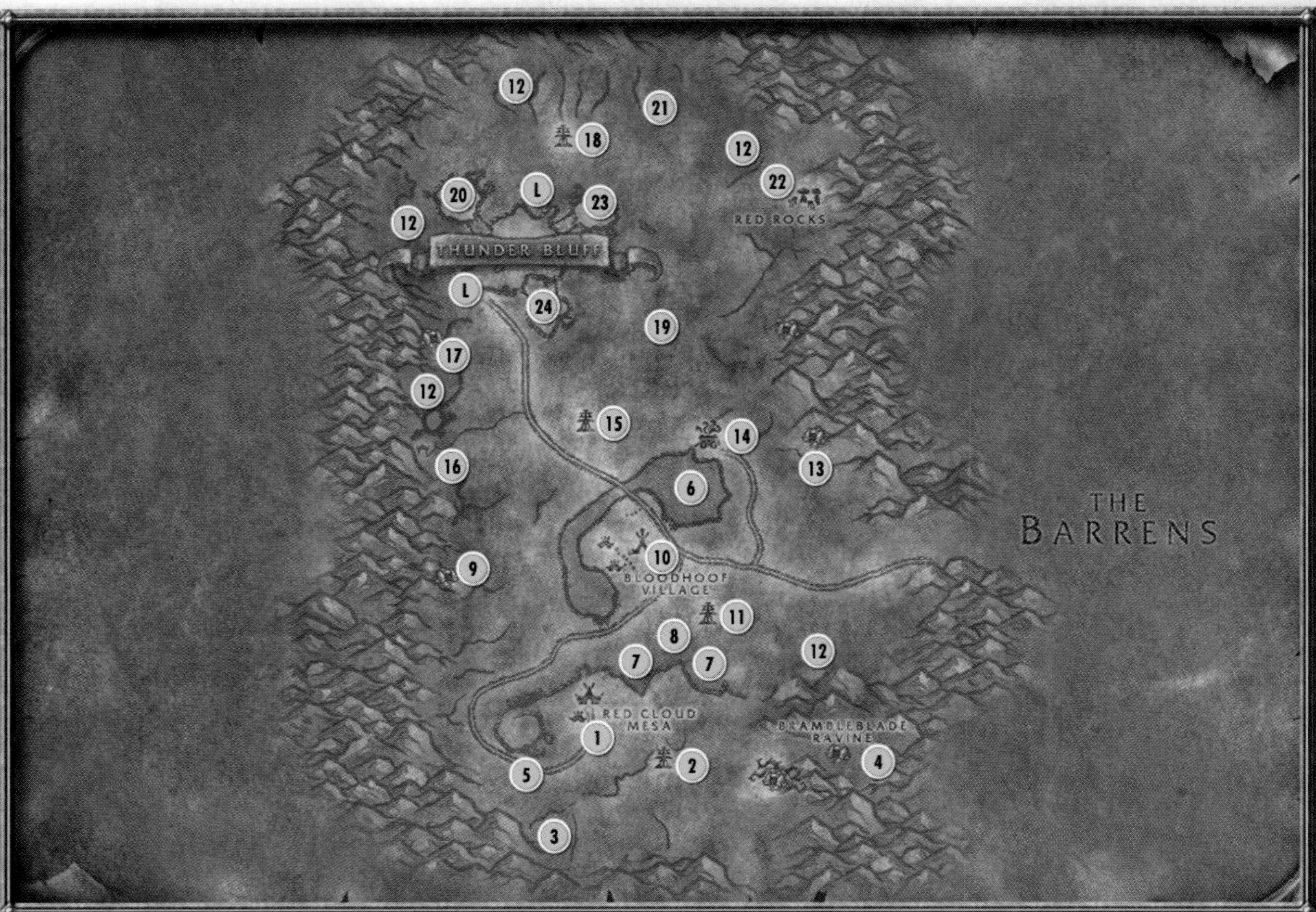

LOCAL RESOURCES

MINING

METAL	AVAILABILITY
Copper	Abundant

HERBALISM

HERB	AVAILABILITY
Peacebloom	Abundant
Silverleaf	Abundant
Earthroot	Abundant

SKINNING

Quantity of Skinnable Creatures: Abundant

Levels of Skinnable Creatures: 1-12 (Skinning 1-50)

MAP LEGEND

L LIFT

1 CAMP NARACHE
- Moodan Sungrain 11 Baker
- Brave Windfeather 13 Quest NPC
- Vorn Skyseer 5
- Bronk Stoolrage 10 Armorer and shieldcrafter
- Marjak Keenblade 9 Weaponsmith
- Varia Hardhide 7 Leather Armor Merchant
- Grull Hawkwind 4 Quest
- Chief Hawkwind 36 Quest
- Harutt Thunderhorn 10 Warrior Trainer
- Lanka Farshot 11 Hunter Trainer
- Seer Ravenfeather 10
- Meela Dawnstrider 10 Shaman Trainer
- Gart Mistrunner 9 Druid Trainer
- Hawnie Softbreeze 8 General Goods
- Brave Lightning Horn 15
- Brave Proudsnout 16
- Brave Greathoof 13
- Brave Running Wolf 12

2 WELL/RED CLOUD MESA
- GreatMother Hawkwind 9 Quest
- Mountain Cougar 3
- Plainstrider 1-2
- Battleboar 3-4

3 Seer Graytongue 8 Quest

4 BRAMBLEBLADE RAVINE
- Chief Sharptusk 5
- Bristleback Quilboar 3-4
- Bristleback Battleboar 4-5
- Bristleback Shaman 4

5 Antur Fallow 3 Quest

6 STONEBULL LAKE

7 PALEMANE CAMPS
- Palemane Tanner 5-6
- Palemane Skinner 6-7
- Palemane Poacher 7-8

8 THE ROLLING PLAINS
- Prairie Wolf 5-10
- Taloned Swoop 8-9
- Elder Plainstrider 8- 9
- Galak Centaur 10
- Galak Outrunner 9
- Flatland Cougar 7-8
- Prairie Stalker 7-8
- Swoop 7-9
- Adult Plainstrider 6-7
- Flatland Prowler 9

9 PALEMANE ROCK
- Palemane Tanner 5-6
- Palemane Skinner 6-7
- Palemane Poacher 7-8

10 BLOODHOOF VILLAGE
- Brave Rainchaser 14
- Krang Stonehoof 14 Warrior Trainer
- Gennia Runetotem 12 Druid trainer
- Narm Skychaser 13 Shaman Trainer
- Harken Windtotem 21 Quest
- Zarlman Two-Moons 7
- Brave Wildrunner 14
- Brave Strongbash 14
- Brave Ironhorn 14
- Brave Cloudmane 14
- Brave Dawneagle 14
- Yaw Sharpmane 11 Hunter Trainer
- Harn Longcast 9 Fishing Supplies
- Wunna Darkmane 10 Trade Goods
- Moorat Longstride 12 General Goods
- Yonn Deepcut 8 Skinner Trainer
- Chaw Stronghide 23 Leatherworking Trainer
- Pyall Silenstride 12 Cooking Trainer
- Kennah Hawkeye 10 Gunsmith Supplier
- Mahnott Roughwound 11 Weaponsmith
- Harant Ironbrace 13 Armorer and Shieldcrafter
- Skorn Whitecloud 21 Story Teller
- Seikwa 30 Stable Master
- Magrin Rivermane 6
- Innkeeper Kauth 30
- Vira Younghoof 13 First Aid Trainer
- Varg Windwhisper 14 Leather Armor Merchant
- Ruul Eagletalon 9 Quest
- Jhawna Oatwind 13 Baker
- Morin Cloudstalker 10 Quest

11 WINTERHOOF WATERWELL
- Venture Co. Hireling 5-6
- Vencure Co. Laborer 6

12 WINDFURY HARPIES
- Windfury Harpy 7-8
- Windfury Wind Witch 9
- Windfury Matriarch 10-11
- Windfury Sorceress 9-10

13 THE VENTURE CO. MINE
- Venture Co. Worker 8-9
- Venture Co. Supervisor 9-10

14 RAVAGED CARAVAN
- Flatland Cougar 7-8
- Adult Plainstrider 6-7
- Prairie Stalker 7-8
- Venture Co. Laborer 7
- Venture Co. Taskmaster 7-8
- Swoop 7-9

15 THUNDERHORN WATER WELL
- Flatland Cougar 7-8
- Elder Plainstrider 8-9
- Adult Plainstrider 6-7
- Swoop 7-9
- Praire Stalker 7-8
- Venture Co. Laborer 6-7
- Venture Co. Taskmaster 8

16 BAEL'DUN DIGSITE
- Bael'dun Digger 7-8
- Bael'dun Appraiser 8-9

17 Seer Wiserunner

18 WILDMANE WATER WELL
- Prairie Wolf Alpha 9-10
- Flatland Prowler 9
- Elder Plainstrider 8-9
- Venture Co. Worker 8-9
- Venture Co. Supervisor 9
- Windfury Matriarch 10-11
- Windfury Sorceress 9-10
- Taloned Swoop 8-10

19 THE GOLDEN PLAINS
- Kodo Calf 7
- Kodo Bull 7-11
- Kodo Matriarch 11-12
- Prairie Stalker 7-8
- Swoop 7-9
- Taloned Swoop 8-10
- Adult Plainstrider 6-7
- Elder Plainstrider 8-9
- Flatland Prowler 9
- Prairie Wolf Alpha 9-10
- Flatland Cougar 7-8
- The Rake 10

20 WINDFURY RIDGE
- Windfury Matriarch 10-11
- Windfury Sorceress 9-10

21 RED ROCKS: SACRED BURIAL GROUND
- Lorekeeper Raintotem 8 Quest
- Ancestral Spirit 9 Quest
- Flatland Prowler 9
- Taloned Swoop 8-10
- Prairie Wolf Alpha 9-10
- Elder Plainstrider 8-9
- Kodo Matriarch 11-12
- Kodo Bull 10
- Bristleback Interloper 9-10

22 VENTURE CO BUILDINGS
- Enforcer Emilgund 11
- Venture Co. Worker 8-9

QUESTS

QUEST	M LEV	Q LEV	QUEST LAUNCHER	QUEST FINISHER	CHAIN?	XP---	XP--	XP-	XP+	XP++	XP+++	CASH REWARD
A Humble Task	1	2	Chief Hawkwind	Greatmother Hawkwind	Y	10	15	35	50	70	85	17
A Humble Task	1	3	Greatmother Hawkwind	Chief Hawkwind	Y	20	40	75	110	150	190	40
A Sacred Burial	7	10	Lorekeeper Raintotem	Lorekeeper Raintotem	N	65	130	250	380	500	625	2 50
A Task Unfinished	1	5	Antur Fallow	Innkeeper Kauth	N	10	20	45	65	90	110	None
CHOICE OF: 5 Tough Hunk of Bread or 5 Refreshing Spring Water												
Break Sharptusk!	3	5	Brave Windfeather	Brave Windfeather	N	65	130	270	400	525	675	None
CHOICE OF: 1 Painted Chain Leggings or 1 Nomadic Gloves												
Dangers of the Windfury	5	8	Ruul Eagletalon	Ruul Eagletalon	N	70	140	280	420	550	700	2 25
Dwarven Digging	6	8	Baine Bloodhoof	Baine Bloodhoof	N	70	140	280	420	550	700	None
CHOICE OF: 1 Fortified Bindings or 1 Rough-hewn Kodo Leggings												
Journey into Thunder Bluff	3	10	Ancestral Spirit	Cairne Bloodhoof	Y	40	85	170	250	340	420	None
Journey to the Crossroads	9	12	Kirge Sternhorn	Thork	N	25	45	90	140	180	230	None
Mazzranache	5	8	Maur Raincaller	Maur Raincaller	N	70	140	280	420	550	700	None
CHOICE OF: 1 Cliff Runner Boots or 1 Plains Hunter Wristguards												
Poison Water	4	5	Mull Thunderhorn	Mull Thunderhorn	N	45	90	180	270	360	450	None
Rite of Strength	1	4	Seer Graytongue	Chief Hawkwind	Y	45	90	180	270	360	450	None
CHOICE OF: 1 Rock Mace or 1 Stone Tomahawk or 1 Whittling Knife or 1 Elder's Cane or 1 Brave's Axe or 1 Light Hunting Rifle												
Rite of Vision	3	6	Baine Bloodhoof	Zarlman Two-Moons	Y	5	10	20	35	45	55	None
Rite of Vision	3	7	Zarlman Two-Moons	Zarlman Two-Moons	N	65	130	250	380	500	625	None
Rite of Vision	3	7	Zarlman Two-Moons	Seer Wiserunner	Y	50	95	190	290	380	480	None
CHOICE OF: 1 Rainwalker Boots or 1 Sun-beaten Cloak												
Rite of Wisdom	3	10	Seer Wiserunner	Ancestral Spirit	Y	85	170	340	500	675	850	None
Rites of the Earthmother	1	3	Chief Hawkwind	Seer Graytongue	Y	25	50	100	150	200	250	None
Rites of the Earthmother	1	5	Chief Hawkwind	Baine Bloodhoof	N	35	65	130	200	270	340	None
Rites of the Earthmother	3	14	Cairne Bloodhoof	Cairne Bloodhoof	N	130	250	500	750	1000	1250	None
REWARD: Kodo Hunter's Leggings												
Sharing the Land	1	6	Baine Bloodhoof	Baine Bloodhoof	N	55	110	220	320	430	550	1 25
REWARD: 25 Flash Pellet												
Supervisor Fizsprocket	5	12	Morin Cloudstalker	Morin Cloudstalker	N	90	180	360	550	725	900	None
CHOICE OF: 1 Compact Fighting Knife or 1 Goblin Smasher												
Swoop Hunting	4	6	Harken Windtotem	Harken Windtotem	N	70	140	270	410	550	675	2 50
The Battleboars	1	4	Grull Hawkwind	Grull Hawkwind	N	45	90	180	270	360	450	None
REWARD: Nomadic Vest, 10 Tough Hunk of Bread												
The Hunt Begins	1	2	Grull Hawkwind	Grull Hawkwind	N	15	35	70	100	140	170	None
CHOICE OF: 1 Nomadic Belt or 1 Painted Chain Gloves												
The Hunt Continues	1	3	Grull Hawkwind	Grull Hawkwind	Y	25	50	100	150	200	250	None
CHOICE OF: 1 Nomadic Bracers or 1 Painted Chain Belt												
The Hunter's Way	10	10	Skorn Whitecloud	Melor Stonehoof	Y	85	170	340	500	675	850	None
The Ravaged Caravan	5	8	Sealed Supply Crate (Obj)	Morin Cloudstalker	N	55	110	210	320	420	525	None
The Ravaged Caravan	5	8	Morin Cloudstalker	Sealed Supply Crate (Obj)	Y	55	110	210	320	420	525	None
The Venture Co.	5	10	Morin Cloudstalker	Morin Cloudstalker	N	65	130	250	380	500	625	2 50
Thunderhorn Cleansing	4	8	Mull Thunderhorn	Mull Thunderhorn	N	70	140	280	420	550	700	None
REWARD: Thunderhorn Cloak												
Thunderhorn Totem	4	7	Mull Thunderhorn	Mull Thunderhorn	N	65	130	250	380	500	625	None
Whitecloud's Story	1	4		Skorn Whitecloud	N	0	0	0	0	0	0	None
Wildmane Cleansing	4	10	Mull Thunderhorn	Mull Thunderhorn	N	110	210	420	625	850	1050	None
CHOICE OF: 1 Ceremonial Tomahawk or 1 Dreamwatcher Staff												
Wildmane Totem	4	10	Mull Thunderhorn	Mull Thunderhorn	N	85	170	340	500	675	850	None
Winterhoof Cleansing	4	6	Mull Thunderhorn	Mull Thunderhorn	N	55	110	220	320	430	550	None

TANARIS

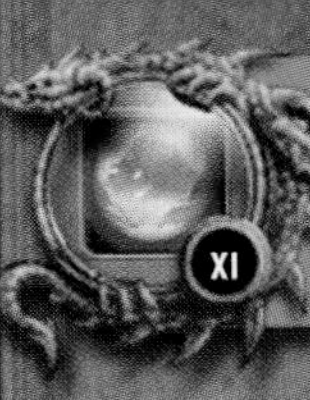

Gadgetzan is one big desert with all the desert creatures you have come to expect by now. It has lizards, buzzards, elementals and more. There are also Dragons, Ogres and humans along with an instanced dungeon to test the mighty. If that's not enough, head north and check out the pirates, they always put on a good show. It's a good place to solo - especially to farm things you need like leather or cloth. Some great rare items drop here (Julie's Dagger). Beyond that, the zone is huge and easily shareable with others. There's a place right by the crater where the mobs drop herbs, so you can kill for the herbs instead of looking for them.

Zul'Farrak
Steamwheedle Port
Un'Goro Crater
Gadgetzan
Abyssal Sands
Caverns of Time
The Great Sea
Uldum
1 2 3 4 5 6 7 8 9 10 11 12 13 14 15 16 17 18 19 20 21

LOCAL RESOURCES

MINING

METAL	AVAILABILITY
Mithril	Moderate
Truesilver	Moderate
Thorium	Moderate

HERBALISM

HERB	AVAILABILITY
Firebloom	Abundant
Purple Lotus	Abundant

SKINNING

Quantity of Skinnable Creatures: Abundant

Levels of Skinnable Creatures: 40-55 (Skinning 225-275)

MAP LEGEND

1 GADGETZAN
- Senior Surveyor Fizzledowser 50 Quest
- Tran'rek 45 Quest
- Nixx Sprocketspring 55 Goblin Engineer
- Buzzek Bracketswing 55 Master Engineer
- Spigot Operator Luglunket 40 Quest
- Trenton Lighthammer 55 Quest
- Pikkle 45 Mining Trainer

2 NOONSHADE RUINS
- Wastewander Bandit 41-42
- Wastewander Thief 40-41

3 STEAMWHEEDLE PORT
- Yeh'ikinya 40 Quest
- Prospector Ironboot 45 Quest
- Stoley 30 Quest
- Torta 45 Quest

4 WATERSPRING FIELD
- Wastewander Bandit 41-43
- Caliph Scorpidsting 46
- Wastewander Thief 40-42
- Wastewander Shadow Mage 40-43
- Wastewander Rogue 42-44
- Wastewander Assassin 43-46
- Scorpid Tail Lasher 44-45 Fire Roc 43-44
- Blisterpaw Hyena 43-45
- Glasshide Gazer 44-46

5 ZALASHJI'S DEN
- Zalashji 45

6 WAVESTRIDER BEACH

7 ENTRANCE TO CAVERNS OF TIME EPIC WORLD DUNGEON
- Occulus 50 Elite

8 LOST RIGGER COVE
- Southsea Pirate 44-46
- Southsea Freebooter 43-45
- Andre Firebeard 45
- Southsea Dock Worker 44-46
- Southsea Swashbuckler 44-45

9 SOUTH BREAK SHORE
- Coast Strider 48 Elite Giant
- Surf Glider 48-50

10 LANDS END BEACH
- Giant Surf Glider 48-50 Elite

11 THE GAPING CHASM
- Glasshide Glazer 45
- Hazzali Sandreaver 49-51
- Hazzali Stinger 49
- Hazzali Stormer 49-50
- Hazzali Tunneler 48-49
- Hazzali Wasp 48
- Hazzali Worker 47-49

12 BROKEN PILLAR
- Marvon Rivetseeker Quest NPC
- Blisterpaw Hyena 43-46
- Fire Roc 44-45
- Glasshide Gazer 43-45
- Scorpid Tail Lasher 43-46
- Scorpid Dunestalker 45-47
- Gusting Vortex 44-46

13 EAST MOON RUINS
- Rabid Blisterpaw 45-48
- Dunemaul Ogre 45-47
- Dunemaul Brute 45-48
- Dunemaul Enforcer 45-47
- Dunemaul Ogre Mage 45-48
- Dunemaul Warlock 45-48
- Glasshide Gazer 44-47
- Glasshide Petrifier 48-49

14 SOUTH MOON RUINS
- Dunemaul Enforcer 45-47
- Dunemaul Ogre Mage 45-48
- Dunemaul Warlock 45-48
- Dune Smasher 48-49
- Glasshide Petrifier 47-49
- Searing Roc 47-48
- Scorpid Dunestalker 46-47

15 VALLEY OF THE WATCHERS
- Prospector Gunstan 45 Explorers' League Quest
- Dune Smasher 48-49 Elite Giant
- Raging Dune Smasher 50 Elite
- Blisterpaw Hyena 43-46
- Glasshides Petrifier 47-49

16 THISTLESHRUB VALLEY
- Glasshide Petrifier 47-49
- Scorpid Dunestalker 46-47
- Thistleshrub Rootshaper 49-50
- Thistleshrub Dew Collector 48-49
- Gnarled Thistleshrub 48-50

17 DUNEMAUL COMPOUND
- Rabid Blisterpaw 45-48
- Dunemaul Ogre 45-47
- Dunemaul Brute 45-48
- Dunemaul Enforcer 45-47
- Dunemaul Ogre Mage 45-48
- Dunemaul Warlock 45-48
- Glasshide Gazer 44-47

18 THE NOXIOUS LAIR
- Centipaar Stinger 48-50
- Centipaar Swarmer 49-50
- Centipaar Wasp 47-49

19 ABYSSAL SANDS
- Blisterpaw Hyena 44-46
- Scorpid Tail Lasher 43-44
- Fire Roc 43-45
- Glasshide Basilisk 43-
- Scorpid Dunecrawler 46-47
- Glasshide Gazer 45-46
- Land Rager 45-46

20 SANDSORROW WATCH
- Ground Pounder 41-42
- Glasshide Basilisk 42-43
- Starving Blisterpaw 41-42
- Sandfury Hideskinner 42-43 Elite
- Sandfury Axe Thrower 42-44 Elite
- Sandfury Firecaller 43-44 Elite
- Sandfury Shadowcaster 43-44 Elite

21 ENTRANCE TO ZUL'FARRAK WORLD DUNGEON

QUESTS

QUEST	M LEV	Q LEV	QUEST LAUNCHER	QUEST FINISHER	CHAIN?	XP---	XP--	XP-	XP+	XP++	XP+++	CASH REWARD
A Bad Egg	42	47	Curgle Cranklehop	Curgle Cranklehop	N	40	85	170	250	340	420	7 00
A Fine Egg	42	47	Curgle Cranklehop	Curgle Cranklehop	N	210	420	850	1250	1700	2100	None
REWARD: Box of Spells												
An Extraordinary Egg	42	47	Curgle Cranklehop	Curgle Cranklehop	N	420	850	1700	2500	3350	4200	None
REWARD: Box of Goodies												
An Ordinary Egg	42	47	Curgle Cranklehop	Curgle Cranklehop	N	110	210	420	625	850	1050	None
REWARD: Box of Rations												
Bungle in the Jungle	50	53	Alchemist Pestlezugg	Alchemist Pestlezugg	N	525	1050	2100	3150	4200	5250	None
Calm Before the Storm	50	54	Alchemist Pestlezugg	Gracina Spiritmight	Y	55	110	220	320	430	550	None
Calm Before the Storm	50	54	Alchemist Pestlezugg	Zilzibin Drumlore	Y	55	110	220	320	430	550	None
Deliver to MacKinley	40	45	Stoley	Sea Wolf" MacKinley"	N	390	775	1550	2350	3100	3900	50 00
CHOICE OF: 1 Swashbuckler Sash or 1 Shinkicker Boots												
Delivery for Marin	44	49	Sprinkle	Marin Noggenfogger	Y	45	90	180	270	360	460	None
Fire Plume Forged	55	57	Krinkle Goodsteel	Alchemist Arbington	Y	450	900	1800	2700	3600	4500	None
Fire Plume Forged	55	57	Krinkle Goodsteel	Apothecary Dithers	Y	450	900	1800	2700	3600	4500	None
Gadgetzan Water Survey	38	46	Senior Surveyor Fizzledowser	Senior Surveyor Fizzledowser	Y	310	600	1200	1850	2450	3050	35 00
Gahz'ridian	43	48	Marvon Rivetseeker	Marvon Rivetseeker	N	440	875	1750	2650	3500	4400	None
CHOICE OF: 1 Surveyor's Tunic or 1 Staff of Lore												
Handle With Care	42	47	Curgle Cranklehop	Erelas Ambersky	N	210	420	850	1250	1700	2100	50 00
In Good Taste	44	49	Marin Noggenfogger	Sprinkle	Y	45	90	180	270	360	460	None
Insect Part Analysis	39	48	Alchemist Pestlezugg	Senior Surveyor Fizzledowser	N	45	90	180	260	350	440	70 00
Insect Part Analysis	39	48	Senior Surveyor Fizzledowser	Alchemist Pestlezugg	Y	45	90	180	260	350	440	None
Into the Depths	46	51	Marvon Rivetseeker	Altar of Hakkar (Obj)	N	490	975	1950	2950	3900	4900	None
More Wastewander Justice	40	44	Chief Engineer Bilgewhizzle	Chief Engineer Bilgewhizzle	N	380	750	1500	2250	3000	3750	65 00
Noggenfogger Elixir	44	49	Marin Noggenfogger	Marin Noggenfogger	N	0	0	0	0	0	0	70 00
REWARD: 5 Noggenfogger Elixir												
Noxious Lair Investigation	39	47	Placeholder - Darkhollow Mine	Alchemist Pestlezugg	N	320	625	1250	1900	2500	3150	50 00
Noxious Lair Investigation	39	47	Senior Surveyor Fizzledowser	Alchemist Pestlezugg	N	320	625	1250	1900	2500	3150	50 00
Pawn Captures Queen	50	54	Alchemist Pestlezugg	Alchemist Pestlezugg	N	550	1100	2200	3250	4350	5450	None
Rescue OOX-17/TN!	43	48	Homing Robot OOX-17/TN	Oglethorpe Obnoticus	N	550	1100	2200	3250	4350	5450	None
CHOICE OF: 1 Optomatic Deflector or 1 Thermotastic Egg Timer												
Rise of the Silithid	39	48	Senior Surveyor Fizzledowser	Zilzibin Drumlore	N	550	1100	2200	3250	4350	5450	None
Rise of the Silithid	39	49	Senior Surveyor Fizzledowser	Gracina Spiritmight	N	575	1150	2300	3400	4550	5700	None
Screecher Spirits	40	44	Yeh'kinya	Yeh'kinya	Y	380	750	1500	2250	3000	3750	None
Secret of the Circle	46	51	Marvon Rivetseeker	Idol of Hakkar (Obj)	N	600	1200	2450	3650	4900	6100	None
REWARD: Hakkar'i Urn												
Sprinkle's Secret Ingredient	44	49	Sprinkle	Sprinkle	N	460	900	1800	2750	3650	4550	None
Stoley's Debt	40	45	Sea Wolf" MacKinley"	Stoley	Y	40	80	160	230	310	390	None
Stoley's Shipment	40	45	Stoley	Stoley	Y	390	775	1550	2350	3100	3900	50 00
Super Sticky	48	54	Tran'rek	Tran'rek	N	550	1100	2200	3250	4350	5450	1 65 00
The Scrimshank Redemption	39	48	Senior Surveyor Fizzledowser	Senior Surveyor Fizzledowser	Y	440	875	1750	2650	3500	4400	None
The Stone Circle	46	51	Marvon Rivetseeker	Marvon Rivetseeker	N	490	975	1950	2950	3900	4900	None
The Stone Watcher	45	50	Uldum Pedestal (Obj)	Uldum Pedestal (Obj)	N	470	950	1900	2800	3750	4700	None
The Stone Watcher	45	50	Stone Watcher of Norgannon	Uldum Pedestal (Obj)	N	470	950	1900	2800	3750	4700	None
The Super Egg-O-Matic	42	47	Egg-O-Matic (Obj)	Egg-O-Matic (Obj)	N	110	210	420	625	850	1050	None
REWARD: Egg Crate												
The Thirsty Goblin	44	49	Marin Noggenfogger	Marin Noggenfogger	Y	460	900	1800	2750	3650	4550	70 00
Thistleshrub Valley	45	50	Tran'rek	Tran'rek	N	470	950	1900	2800	3750	4700	75 00
Tooga's Quest	40	50	Tooga	Torta	N	600	1200	2350	3550	4700	5900	None
CHOICE OF: 1 Chelonian Cuffs or 1 Band of the Great Tortoise												
WANTED: Andre Firebeard	40	45	Wanted Poster (Obj)	Security Chief Bilgewhizzle	N	390	775	1550	2350	3100	3900	1 30 00
WANTED: Andre Firebeard	40	45	WANTED: Caliph Scorpidsting (Obj)	Security Chief Bilgewhizzle	N	390	775	1550	2350	3100	3900	1 30 00
WANTED: Caliph Scorpidsting	39	46	Wanted Poster (Obj)	Chief Engineer Bilgewhizzle	N	500	1000	2000	3050	4050	5050	1 30 00
WANTED: Caliph Scorpidsting	39	46	WANTED: Caliph Scorpidsting (Obj)	Chief Engineer Bilgewhizzle	N	500	1000	2000	3050	4050	5050	1 30 00
Wastewander Justice	40	43	Chief Engineer Bilgewhizzle	Chief Engineer Bilgewhizzle	Y	360	725	1450	2150	2900	3600	60 00
Water Pouch Bounty	40	44	Spigot Operator Luglunket	Spigot Operator Luglunket	N	190	370	750	1100	1500	1850	None
REWARD: Gadgetzan Water Co. Care Package												
Water Pouch Bounty	40	44	Spigot Operator Luglunket	Spigot Operator Luglunket	N	40	75	150	230	300	380	None
REWARD: Gadgetzan Water Co. Care Package												

THOUSAND NEEDLES

This region is located beyond the Barrens in southern Kalimdor. It's a large, winding valley dotted with tall mesas all around, save for the area to the southeast. It's completely flat down there and perfect for some questing. High atop the mesas, the Tauren have built a network of rope bridges and lifts to convey customers to vendors and quest givers. There are no guardrails to keep you safe; you can easily fall over the edge while taking a peek.

LOCAL RESOURCES

MINING

METAL	AVAILABILITY
Copper	Abundant
Tin	Common
Iron	Common
Silver	Rare
Gold	Very Rare

HERBALISM

HERB	AVAILABILITY
Kingsblood	Common
Bruiseweed	Rare

SKINNING

Quantity of Skinnable Creatures: Abundant

Levels of Skinnable Creatures: 25-35 (Skinning 75-125)

MAP LEGEND

1 CAMP E'THOK
Galak Mauler 27-28
Galak Marauder 26-27
Galak Stormer 26-28
Pesterhide Snarler 28-29
Needles Cougar 28-29

2 HIGHPERCH
Highperch Wyvern 28-29

3 WHITEREACH POST
Wizlo Bearingshiner 31 Quest
Laer Steprunner 42 Food and drink
Pesterhide Snarler 28-29
Motega Fireman 28

4 DARKCLOUD PINNACLE (BOTTOM AREA)
Boiling Elemental 27-28
Scaulding Elemental 28-29

5 DARKCLOUD PINNACLE (ENTRANCE TO TOP)
Grimtotem Bandit 25-26
Grimtotem Stomper 26-27
Grimtotem Geomancer 25-27
Grimtotem Reaver 28

6 THE SCREECHING CANYON
Screeching Roguefeather 29-30
Screeching Harpy 28-29

7 ROGUEFEATHER DEN
Screeching Roguefeather 29-30
Screeching Harpy 28-29
Screeching Windcaller 30
Grenka Bloodscreech 31

8 SPLITHOOF CRAG
Galak Wrangler 25-26
Galak Windchaser 24-25
Galak Packrunner 26
Galak Packhound 24-25
Galak Scout 24-25

9 SPLITHOOF HOLD
Galak Scout 24-25
Galak Mauler 27-28
Galak Stormer 26-27
Galak Marauder 27-28
Galak Flame Guard 30

10 FREEWIND POST ENTRANCE (HORDE TOWN)
Freewind Brave 45
Nyse 55 Elite Flight Master
Elv 28 Quest
Inkeeper Abeqwa 30 Innkeeper
Dandia 37 Trade supplies
Rau Cliffrunner 30
Thalia Aberhide 30
Jawn Highmesa 35 General Goods
Awenasa 30 Stable Master
Turhaw 40 Butcher Food & Water
Guard Wachabe 45
Montarr Lorkeeper 45 Rare Items
Starn 37 Gunsmith and Bower

11 WINDBREAKER CANYON
Elder Cloud Serpent 27-29
Pesterhide Snarler 28-29
Needles Cougar 28-29

12 THE WEATHERED NOOK
Prate Cloudseeker 37
Dorn Plainstalker 29 Quest

13 AN ORC CAMP QUESTS
Krueg Skullsplitter 37
Tarkrev Shadowstalker 35
Nag'Zhen 35
Mortkar Krin 35
Bok'Zhen 35
War Party Kobo 29-20

14 SNAPPER SPAWNS
Sparkshell Snapper 34-35
Sparkshell Tortoise 31-32

15 SCAVENGER SPAWNS
Salt Flat Scavenger 30-31

16 SALTSTONE SPAWNS
Saltstone Grazer 34-35
Saltstone Crystalhide 32-33

17 THE RUSTMAUL DIG SITE
Silithid Hive Drone 33-34
Silithid Invader 34-35
Silithid Searcher 32-33

18 SCORPID SPAWNS
Scorpid Terror 33-34
Scorpid Reaver 32-33

19 MIRAGE RACEWAY
Brivelthwerp 35 Ice Cream Vendor
Gnome Pit Boss 35
Gnome Pit Crewman 30
Crazzle Sprysprocket 35 Gnome Ticket Vendor
Jinky Twizzlefixxit 30 Engineer Supplier
Kravel Koalbeard 29 Quest
Fizzle Brassbolts 30 Quest
Wizzle Brassbolts 31 Quest
Daisy 15 Race Start Girl
Goblin Pit Crewman 30
Goblin Pit Boss 35
Rugfizzle 35 Goblin Ticket Vendor
Razzeric 30
Pozzik 30
Riznek 35 Drink vendor
Drag Master Miglen
Track Master Zherin 30est
Zuzubeb 35 Race Announcer
Rizzlle Brassbolts 31
Magus Tirth 51 Chicken Vendor
Quenting 40
Zamek 30

QUESTS

QUEST	M LEV	Q LEV	QUEST LAUNCHER	QUEST FINISHER	CHAIN?	XP---	XP--	XP-	XP+	XP++	XP+++	CASH REWARD
A Bump in the Road	28	33	Trackmaster Zherin	Trackmaster Zherin	N	200	390	775	1150	1550	1950	None
A Grim Discovery	37	45	Krueg Skullsplitter	Belgrom Rockmaul	N	490	975	1950	2900	3900	4850	65 00
CHOICE OF: 1 Battlemaster Cape or 1 Jademoon Orb												
A Grim Discovery	38	45	Krueg Skullsplitter	Krueg Skullsplitter	Y	390	775	1550	2350	3100	3900	65 00
A New Cloak's Sheen	38	45	Krueg Skullsplitter	Krueg Skullsplitter	Y	390	775	1550	2350	3100	3900	65 00
Alexstrasza	25	30	Braug Dimspirit	Braug Dimspirit	N	0	0	0	0	0	0	None
Alien Egg	24	26	Hagar Lightninghoof	Hagar Lightninghoof	N	210	420	850	1250	1700	2100	15 00
Arikara	24	28	Magatha Grimtotem	Motega Firemane	N	230	460	925	1400	1850	2300	25 00
CHOICE OF: 1 Brute Hammer or 1 Stingshot Wand or 1 Clink Shield												
Back to Booty Bay	35	43	Kravel Koalbeard	Crank Fizzlebub	N	90	180	360	525	700	900	None
Delivery to the Gnomes	30	36	Kravel Koalbeard	Fizzle Brassbolts	N	70	140	280	420	550	700	10 00
Dream Dust in the Swamp	30	36	Krazek	Krazek	Y	350	700	1400	2100	2800	3500	None
Encrusted Tail Fins	30	35	Wizzle Brassbolts	Wizzle Brassbolts	N	350	700	1400	2050	2750	3450	75 00
Final Passage	25	36	Parqual Fintallas	Dorn Plainstalker	N	420	850	1700	2500	3350	4200	None
CHOICE OF: 1 Windstorm Hammer or 1 Dancing Flame												
Free at Last	25	29	Lakota Windsong	Thalia Amberhide	N	240	470	950	1400	1900	2350	None
CHOICE OF: 1 Windsong Cinch or 1 Windsong Drape												
Free at Last	25	29		Thalia Amberhide	N	240	470	950	1400	1900	2350	None
CHOICE OF: 1 Windsong Cinch or 1 Windsong Drape												
Get the Gnomes Drun	35	44	Kravel Koalbeard	Gnome Pit Boss	N	40	75	150	230	300	380	None
Get the Goblins Drunk	35	44	Kravel Koalbeard	Goblin Pit Boss	N	40	75	150	230	300	380	None
Gnomes Win!	1	1		Crazzle Sprysprocket	N	0	0	0	0	0	0	None
REWARD: Gnome Prize Box												
Goblin Sponsorship	29	37	Pozzik	Gazlowe	Y	70	140	280	430	575	700	None
Goblin Sponsorship	29	37	Gazlowe	Wharfmaster Lozgil	Y	70	140	280	430	575	700	None
Goblin Sponsorship	29	37	Wharfmaster Lozgil	Baron Revilgaz	Y	30	55	110	170	230	290	None
Goblin Sponsorship	29	37	Baron Revilgaz	Baron Revilgaz	Y	290	575	1150	1700	2300	2850	40 00
Goblin Sponsorship	29	37	Baron Revilgaz	Pozzik	Y	70	140	280	430	575	700	None
Goblins Win!	1	1		Rugfizzle	N	0	0	0	0	0	0	None
REWARD: Goblin Prize Box												
Grimtotem Spying	24	28	Cliffwatcher Longhorn	Cliffwatcher Longhorn	N	230	460	925	1400	1850	2300	None
CHOICE OF: 1 Desert Shoulders or 1 Tundra Boots or 1 Grimtoll Wristguards												
Grimtotem Spying	24	28		Cliffwatcher Longhorn	N	230	460	925	1400	1850	2300	None
CHOICE OF: 1 Desert Shoulders or 1 Tundra Boots or 1 Grimtoll Wristguards												
Gul'dan	25	36	Parqual Fintallas	Parqual Fintallas	N	0	0	0	0	0	0	None
Hardened Shells	30	30	Wizzle Brassbolts	Wizzle Brassbolts	N	250	490	975	1450	1950	2450	25 00
Hemet Nesignwary	28	31	Kravel Koalbeard	Hemet Nesingwary	N	130	250	500	750	1000	1250	30 00
Homeward Bound	25	29	Pao'ka Swiftmountain	Motega Firemane	N	240	470	950	1400	1900	2350	19 00

QUEST	M LEV	Q LEV	QUEST LAUNCHER	QUEST FINISHER	CHAIN?	XP---	XP--	XP-	XP+	XP++	XP+++	CASH REWARD
Hypercapacitor Gizmo	24	30	Wizlo Bearingshiner	Wizlo Bearingshiner	N	310	600	1200	1850	2450	3050	None
REWARD: Inventor's League Ring												
Hypercapacitor Gizmo	24	30		Wizlo Bearingshiner	N	310	600	1200	1850	2450	3050	None
REWARD: Inventor's League Ring												
Indurium	30	35	Martek the Exiled	Martek the Exiled	N	280	550	1100	1650	2200	2750	None
Indurium Ore	29	42	Pozzik	Pozzik	N	0	0	0	0	0	0	None
Keeping Pace	29	41	Pozzik	Rizzle's Plans (Obj)	Y	170	330	650	1000	1300	1650	None
Kel'Thuzad	25	36	Parqual Fintallas	Parqual Fintallas	N	0	0	0	0	0	0	None
Kil'jaeden	25	36	Parqual Fintallas	Parqual Fintallas	N	0	0	0	0	0	0	None
Load Lightening	29	30	Pozzik	Pozzik	Y	250	490	975	1450	1950	2450	25 00
Malygos	25	30	Braug Dimspirit	Braug Dimspirit	N	0	0	0	0	0	0	None
Martek the Exiled	26	35	Fizzle Brassbolts	Martek the Exiled	Y	140	270	550	800	1100	1350	None
Message to Freewind Post	23	25	Brave Moonhorn	Cliffwatcher Longhorn	Y	50	100	200	310	410	500	1 75
Neltharion	25	30	Braug Dimspirit	Braug Dimspirit	Y	310	600	1200	1850	2450	3050	None
Ner'zhul	25	36	Parqual Fintallas	Parqual Fintallas	Y	350	700	1400	2100	2800	3500	None
News for Fizzle	30	38	Martek the Exiled	Fizzle Brassbolts	N	150	290	575	875	1150	1450	None
CHOICE OF: 1 Fizzle's Zippy Lighter or 1 Gnomish Mechanic's Gloves												
Ore for the Races	30	42	Fizzle Brassbolts	Fizzle Brassbolts	N	0	0	0	0	0	0	None
Pacify the Centaur	23	25	Cliffwatcher Longhorn	Cliffwatcher Longhorn	N	200	400	800	1200	1600	2000	18 00
Parts for Kravel	30	31	Wharfmaster Dizzywig	Kravel Koalbeard	N	130	250	500	750	1000	1250	15 00
Parts of the Swarm	28	35	Korran	Belgrom Rockmaul	N	140	270	550	800	1100	1350	18 00
CHOICE OF: 1 Dryleaf Pants or 1 Bleeding Crescent												
Protect Kanati Greycloud	23	25	Kanati Greycloud	Kanati Greycloud	N	200	400	800	1200	1600	2000	None
CHOICE OF: 1 Lightheel Boots or 1 Loamflake Bracers or 1 Palestrider Gloves												
Razzeric's Tweaking	29	41	Razzeric	Razzeric	Y	330	650	1300	2000	2650	3300	55 00
Report Back to Fizzlebub	35	44	Kravel Koalbeard	Crank Fizzlebub	N	190	370	750	1100	1500	1850	None
Rizzle's Schematics	29	41	Rizzle's Plans (Obj)	Pozzik	N	170	330	650	1000	1300	1650	None
Rocket Car Parts	30	31	Kravel Koalbeard	Kravel Koalbeard	N	250	500	1000	1500	2000	2500	30 00
Rumors for Kravel	30	36	Krazek	Kravel Koalbeard	N	350	700	1400	2100	2800	3500	75 00
Sacred Fire	24	27	Motega Firemane	Magatha Grimtotem	N	220	440	875	1300	1750	2200	22 00
Safety First	29	41	Shreev	Razzeric	N	80	160	330	490	650	825	None
CHOICE OF: 1 Razzeric's Customized Seatbelt or 1 Razzeric's Racing Grips												
Safety First	29	41	Razzeric	Shreev	Y	80	160	330	490	650	825	None
Salt Flat Venom	30	30	Fizzle Brassbolts	Fizzle Brassbolts	N	250	490	975	1450	1950	2450	25 00
Serpent Wild	24	26	Hagar Lightninghoof	Motega Firemane	Y	110	210	420	625	850	1050	None
Serpent Wild	24	26		Motega Firemane	Y	110	210	420	625	850	1050	None
Test of Endurance	25	30	Dorn Plainstalker	Dorn Plainstalker	Y	250	490	975	1450	1950	2450	None
Test of Faith	25	26	Dorn Plainstalker	Dorn Plainstalker	Y	110	210	420	625	850	1050	None
Test of Lore	25	30	Braug Dimspirit	Braug Dimspirit	N	190	370	750	1100	1500	1850	None
Test of Lore	25	30	Dorn Plainstalker	Braug Dimspirit	Y	120	240	480	725	950	1200	None
Test of Lore	25	30	Braug Dimspirit	Parqual Fintallas	Y	120	240	480	725	950	1200	None
Test of Lore	25	36	Parqual Fintallas	Parqual Fintallas	N	210	420	850	1250	1700	2100	None
Test of Strength	25	30	Dorn Plainstalker	Dorn Plainstalker	Y	310	600	1200	1850	2450	3050	None
The Brassbolts Brothers	30	30	Pilot Longbeard	Wizzle Brassbolts	N	250	490	975	1450	1950	2450	None
The Brassbolts Brothers	40	46	Klockmort Spannerspan	Wizzle Brassbolts	Y	40	80	160	240	320	410	None
The Crone of the Kraul	29	34	Falfindel Waywarder	Falfindel Waywarder	N	340	675	1350	2000	2700	3350	None
REWARD: "Mage-Eye" Blunderbuss and CHOICE OF: 1 Berylline Pads or 1 Stonefist Girdle or 1 Marbled Buckler												
The Eighteenth Pilot	29	37	Pozzik	Razzeric	Y	30	55	110	170	230	290	None
The Gnome Pit Crew is Thirsty	35	44	Gnome Pit Boss	Gnome Pit Boss	N	0	0	0	0	0	0	None
The Goblin Pit Crew is Thirsty	35	44	Goblin Pit Boss	Goblin Pit Boss	N	0	0	0	0	0	0	None
The Rumormonger	30	36	Kravel Koalbeard	Krazek	Y	140	280	550	850	1100	1400	None
The Swarm Grows	29	35	Moktar Krin	Moktar Krin	N	280	550	1100	1650	2200	2750	35 00
Wanted: Arnak Grimtotem	25	29	Wanted Poster - Arnak Grimtotem (Obj)	Cliffwatcher Longhorn	N	240	470	950	1400	1900	2350	None
CHOICE OF: 1 Brawnhide Armor or 1 Plainsguard Leggings												
Wharfmaster Dizzywig	30	36	Kravel Koalbeard	Wharfmaster Dizzywig	Y	140	280	550	850	1100	1400	None
Wind Rider	25	29	Elu	Elu	N	180	350	700	1050	1400	1750	19 00
REWARD: 2 Heavy Armor Kit												
Ysera	25	30	Braug Dimspirit	Braug Dimspirit	N	0	0	0	0	0	0	None
Zamek's Distraction	29	41	Zamek	Zamek	N	0	0	0	0	0	0	None
Zanzil's Mixture and a Fool's Stout	35	44	Crank Fizzlebub	Kravel Koalbeard	N	380	750	1500	2250	3000	3750	None

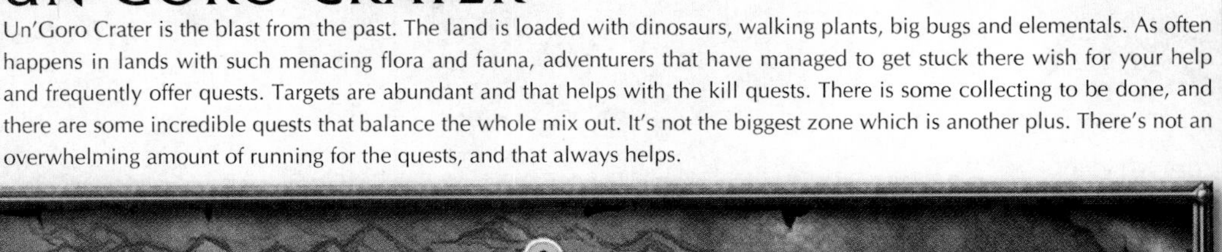

UN'GORO CRATER

Un'Goro Crater is the blast from the past. The land is loaded with dinosaurs, walking plants, big bugs and elementals. As often happens in lands with such menacing flora and fauna, adventurers that have managed to get stuck there wish for your help and frequently offer quests. Targets are abundant and that helps with the kill quests. There is some collecting to be done, and there are some incredible quests that balance the whole mix out. It's not the biggest zone which is another plus. There's not an overwhelming amount of running for the quests, and that always helps.

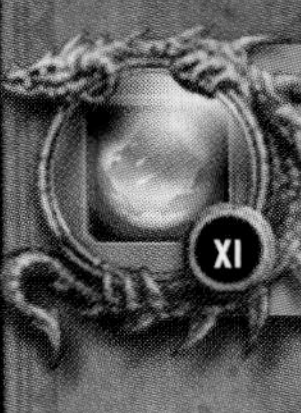

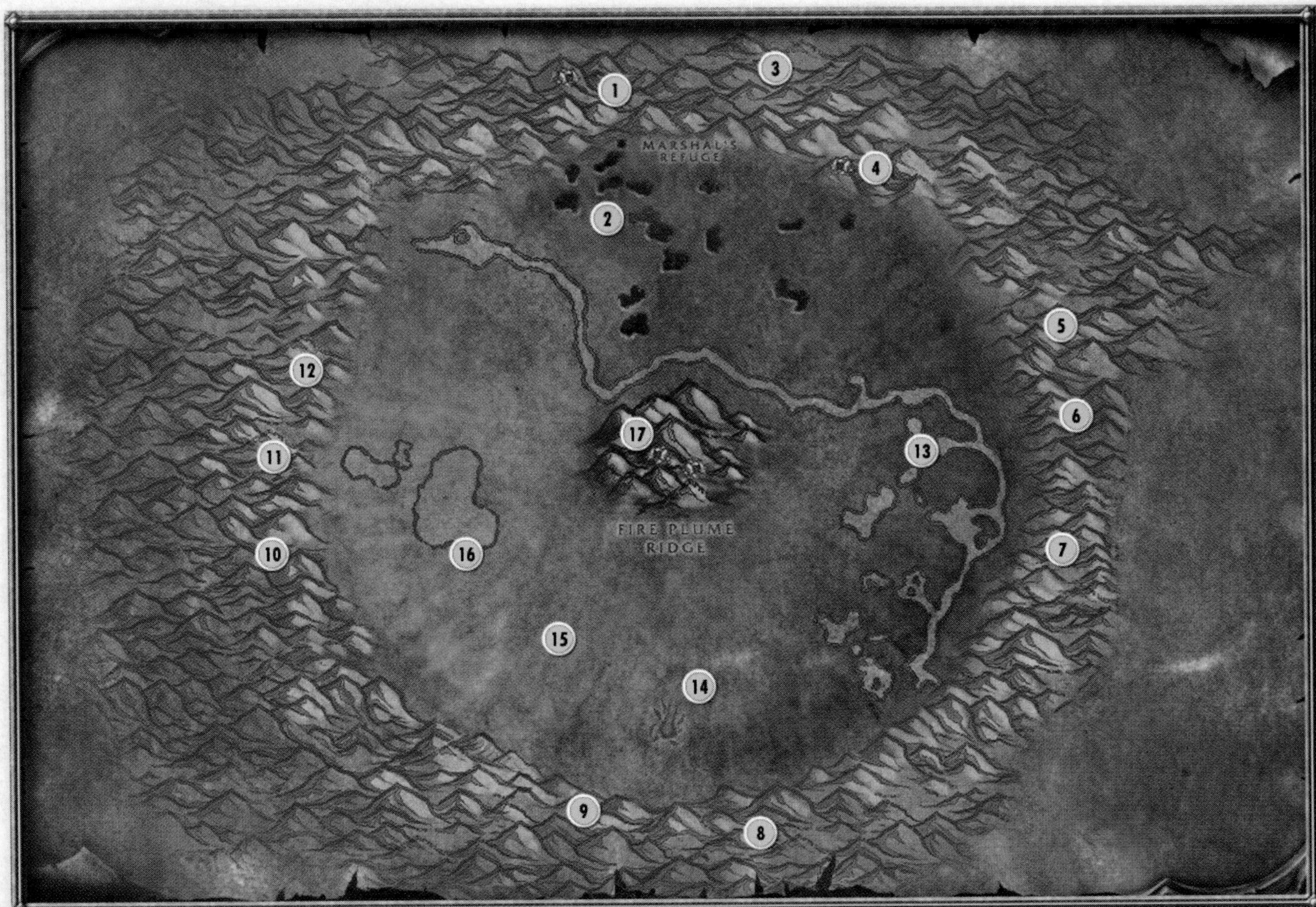

LOCAL RESOURCES

MINING

METAL	AVAILABILITY
Thorium	Common
True Silver Rare	

HERBALISM

Mobs drop a variety of med-high end herbs

SKINNING

Quantity of Skinnable Creatures: Abundant

Levels of Skinnable Creatures: 40-55 (Skinning 225-275)

MAP LEGEND

1 MARSHAL'S REFUGE
- Shizzle 40 Quest
- Quixxil 40 Quest
- Muigin 51 Quest
- Petra Grossen 46 Quest
- Dadanga 45 Quest
- Hol'Anyee Marshal 45 Quest
- Williden Marshal 48 Quest
- Linken 40 Quest
- Bloodpetal Pests 30-35

2 LAKKARI TAR PITS
- Karna Remtravel 45 Quest
- Mor'Vek 60 "Ravasaur Trainer"
- Tar Lurker 53-54
- Tar Lord 53-54
- Tar Beast 51-52
- Tar Creeper 51-52
- Primal ooze 50-51
- Bloodpetal Flayer 51-52
- Piemetradon 51-52
- Stone Guardian 59-50 Elite
- Young Diemetradon 50-51

3 NORTHERN CRYSTAL PYLON
- Pterrordax 50-51

4 FUNGAL ROCK
- A-Me 01 48 Quest
- Un'Goro Gorilla 50-51
- Un'Goro Stomper 51-52
- Un'Goro Thunderer 52-53
- U'Cha 55

5 IRONSTONE PLATEAU
- Fledgling Pterrordax 50

6 EASTERN STONE PYLON

7 FLEDGLING PTERRORDAX 50

8 PTERRORDAX 50-52

9 PTERRORDAX 50-52

10 WESTERN CRYSTAL PYLON
- Frenzied Pterrordax 52-53

11 FRENZIED PTERRORDAX 52-53

12 FRENZIED PTERRORDAX 52-53

13 THE MARSHLANDS
- Ravasaur 48-49
- Ravasaur Runner 49-50
- Venomhide Ravasaur 50-51
- Tyannodon 55Elite
- Bloodpetal Lasher 49-50

14 THE SLITHERING SCAR
- Gorishi Wasp 51-52
- Gorishi Worker 51-52
- Gorishi Reaver 52-53
- Gorishi Stinger 52-53
- Gorishi Tunneler 52-53

15 TERROR RUN
- Glutinous Ooze 53-54
- Bloodpetal Trapper 53-54
- Elder Diemetradon 54-55
- Spike Stegodon 53 Elite
- Thunderstomp Stegodon 55 Elite
- Plated Stegodon 53 Elite

16 GOLAKKA HOT SPRINGS
- Elder Diemetradon 54-55
- Bloodpetal Trapper 53-54
- Glutinous Ooze 52-54
- Krakle 60 Quest
- Spiked Stegodon 52-54 Elite
- Stegodon 53 Elite

17 FIRE PLUME RIDGE
- Scorching Elemental 53-54
- Living Blaze 54-55
- Blazerunner 56 Elite
- Ironhide DevilSaur 55 Elite

QUESTS

QUEST	M LEV	Q LEV	QUEST LAUNCHER	QUEST FINISHER	CHAIN?	XP---	XP--	XP-	XP+	XP++	XP+++	CASH REWARD
A Little Help From My Friends	50	55	Ringo	Spraggle Frock	N	575	1150	2250	3400	4500	5650	None
CHOICE OF: 1 Bejeweled Legguards or 1 Treetop Leggings or 1 Clayridge Helm												
A Visit to Gregan	47	52	Muigin	Gregan Brewspewer	Y	380	750	1500	2300	3050	3800	None
Alien Ecology	48	52	Hol'anyee Marshal	Hol'anyee Marshal	N	500	1000	2050	3050	4100	5100	40 00
Beware of Pterrordax	49	55	Beware of Pterrordax (Obj)	Spraggle Frock	N	575	1150	2250	3400	4500	5650	None
CHOICE OF: 1 Grotslab Gloves or 1 Cragplate Greaves												
Bloodpetal Sprouts	47	53	Muigin	Muigin	N	400	800	1600	2350	3150	3950	None
Bloodpetal Zapper	47	53	Larion	Larion	N	400	800	1600	2350	3150	3950	None
REWARD: Bloodpetal Zapper												
Chasing A-Me 01	48	53	A-Me 01	A-Me 01	N	400	800	1600	2350	3150	3950	None
Chasing A-Me 01	48	53	A-Me 01	Karna Remtravel	N	650	1300	2600	3950	5250	6550	1 60 00
Chasing A-Me 01	48	53	Karna Remtravel	A-Me 01	Y	270	525	1050	1600	2100	2650	None
Crystal Charge	47	53	Northern Crystal Pylon (Obj)	Northern Crystal Pylon (Obj)	N	0	0	0	0	0	0	None
REWARD: 5 Crystal Charge												
Crystal Force	47	53	Eastern Crystal Pylon (Obj)	Eastern Crystal Pylon (Obj)	N	0	0	0	0	0	0	None
REWARD: 3 Crystal Force												
Crystal Restore	47	53	Northern Crystal Pylon (Obj)	Northern Crystal Pylon (Obj)	N	0	0	0	0	0	0	None
REWARD: 5 Crystal Restore												
Crystal Spire	47	53	Eastern Crystal Pylon (Obj)	Eastern Crystal Pylon (Obj)	N	0	0	0	0	0	0	None
REWARD: 3 Crystal Spire												
Crystal Ward	47	53	Western Crystal Pylon (Obj)	Western Crystal Pylon (Obj)	N	0	0	0	0	0	0	None
REWARD: 3 Crystal Ward												
Crystal Yield	47	53	Western Crystal Pylon (Obj)	Western Crystal Pylon (Obj)	N	0	0	0	0	0	0	None
REWARD: 5 Crystal Yield												
Crystals of Power	47	53	J.D. Collie	J.D. Collie	N	525	1050	2100	3150	4200	5250	80 00
Dadanga is Hungry!	47	55	Dadanga	Dadanga	N	0	0	0	0	0	0	None
REWARD: Small Brown-wrapped Package												
Expedition Salvation	48	53	Williden Marshal	Williden Marshal	N	525	1050	2100	3150	4200	5250	40 00
Finding the Source	51	55	Krakle	Krakle	Y	575	1150	2250	3400	4500	5650	None
Haze of Evil	47	52	Gregan Brewspewer	Muigin	N	500	1000	2050	3050	4100	5100	75 00
Larion and Muigin	47	52	Larion	Larion	Y	500	1000	2050	3050	4100	5100	75 00
Lost!	50	55	Spraggle Frock	Ringo	N	280	550	1100	1700	2250	2800	None
Making Sense of It	47	53	J.D. Collie	J.D. Collie	N	55	110	210	320	420	525	None
REWARD: Crystal Pylon User's Manual												
Marvon's Workshop	47	52	Larion	Liv Rizzlefix	Y	260	500	1000	1550	2050	2550	None
Muigin and Larion	47	52	Muigin	Muigin	Y	500	1000	2050	3050	4100	5100	None
Roll the Bones	49	54	Spark Nilminer	Spark Nilminer	N	550	1100	2200	3250	4350	5450	None
CHOICE OF: 1 Archaeologist's Quarry Boots or 1 Excavator's Utility Belt												
Shizzle's Flyer	49	55	Shizzle	Shizzle	N	575	1150	2250	3400	4500	5650	None
CHOICE OF: 1 Shizzle's Drizzle Blocker or 1 Shizzle's Muzzle or 1 Shizzle's Nozzle Wiper												
The Apes of Un'Goro	47	55	Torwa Pathfinder	Torwa Pathfinder	N	575	1150	2250	3400	4500	5650	85 00
The Bait for Lar'korwi	48	56	Torwa Pathfinder	Torwa Pathfinder	N	725	1450	2900	4400	5850	7300	None
CHOICE OF: 1 Plainstalker Tunic or 1 Outrider Leggings												
The Eastern Pylon	47	53	J.D. Collie	J.D. Collie	N	400	800	1600	2350	3150	3950	None
The Fare of Lar'korwi	48	53	Torwa Pathfinder	Torwa Pathfinder	Y	525	1050	2100	3150	4200	5250	None
The Mighty U'cha	50	55	Torwa Pathfinder	Torwa Pathfinder	N	575	1150	2250	3400	4500	5650	None
CHOICE OF: 1 Beastsmasher or 1 Beastslayer												
The New Springs	51	55	Krakle	Donova Snowden	Y	280	550	1100	1700	2250	2800	None
The Northern Pylon	47	53	J.D. Collie	J.D. Collie	N	400	800	1600	2350	3150	3950	None
The Scent of Lar'korwi	48	53	Torwa Pathfinder	Torwa Pathfinder	Y	525	1050	2100	3150	4200	5250	None
The Western Pylon	47	53	J.D. Collie	J.D. Collie	N	400	800	1600	2350	3150	3950	None
Volcanic Activity	49	55	Liv Rizzlefix	Liv Rizzlefix	N	575	1150	2250	3400	4500	5650	85 00
Zapper Fuel	47	52	Liv Rizzlefix	Larion	N	500	1000	2050	3050	4100	5100	None

ARMOR

CLOTH CHEST ARMOR

EPIC CLOTH CHEST ARMOR

M LEV	ARMOR NAME	LEV	BIND	AC	VENDOR PURCHASE VALUE		
42	Robes of Insight	47	BoE	123	1	25	65
▶	**SPELL** Reduces Cost of next spell by up to 500						
50	Embrace of the Wind Serpent	55	BoA	143	2	02	74
▶	**SPELL** Nature Resist +12						
57	Alanna's Embrace	62	BoA	161	3	02	22
▶	**SPELL** Increase spell Dmg 10						
57	Robe of the Archmage	62	BoA	161	2	88	15
▶	**SPELL** Increase spell Dmg 20						
57	Robe of the Void	62	BoA	161	2	89	20
▶	**SPELL** Increase Shadow Dmg 28						
57	Vestments of the Devout	62	BoA	161	2	90	28
▶	**SPELL** Increase Healing 66						

SUPERIOR CLOTH CHEST ARMOR

M LEV	ARMOR NAME	LEV	BIND	AC	VENDOR PURCHASE VALUE		
19	Corsair's Overshirt	24	BoA	68		11	47
19	Tree Bark Jacket	24	BoE	68		12	02
20	Necrology Robes	25	BoE	70		13	34
▶	**SPELL** Shadow Resist +5						
21	Black Velvet Robes	26	BoE	71		15	25
24	Robes of Arugal	29	BoA	76		18	92
26	Mechbuilder's Overalls	31	BoE	79		23	52
▶	**SPELL** Arcane Resist +5						
29	Beguiler Robes	34	BoE	83		32	23
N/A	Civinad Robes	37	BoA	89		41	98
N/A	Enchanted Gold Bloodrobe	38	BoA	92		46	85
33	Robe of Power	38	BoA	92		47	00
▶	**SPELL** Increase spell Dmg 7						
35	Death's Head Vestment	40	BoE	96		53	10
35	Robe of the Magi	40	BoE	96		50	67
▶	**SPELL** Increase spell Dmg 11						
36	Elemental Raiment	41	BoE	99		56	48
▶	**SPELL** Increase spell Dam 11, Arcane, Fire, Frost, Nature & Shadow Resist +5						
39	Robes of the Lich	44	BoA	106		69	03
40	Dreamweave Vest	45	BoE	108		79	46
▶	**SPELL** Increase spell Dam 9 Random						
42	Grimlok's Tribal Vestments	47	BoA	113		89	97
46	Funeral Pyre Vestment	51	BoE	122	1	23	56
▶	**SPELL** Fire & Shadow Resist +10						
50	Vestments of the Atal'ai Prophet	55	BoA	131	1	51	46
52	Robe of Winter Night	57	BoE	136	1	70	25
▶	**SPELL** Increase Shadow Dmg 24						
55	Mooncloth Vest	60	BoE	143	2	00	42
55	Robes of the Royal Crown	60	BoA	143	2	04	75
56	Necropile Robe	61	BoA	145	2	07	32
56	The Postmaster's Tunic	61	BoA	145	2	11	17
57	Freezing Lich Robes	62	BoA	148	2	17	78
▶	**SPELL** Increase Frost Dmg 25, Frost Resist +15						
58	Robes of the Exalted	63	BoA	150	2	31	18
▶	**SPELL** Increase Healing 62						
58	Widow's Clutch	63	BoA	150	2	25	12
▶	**SPELL** Arcane Resist +13						

GOOD CLOTH CHEST ARMOR

M LEV	ARMOR NAME	LEV	BIND	AC	VENDOR PURCHASE VALUE	
5	Brown Linen Robe	10	BoE	30		98
5	Red Linen Robe	10	BoE	30		99
N/A	Sleeping Robes	10	BoA	30		94
5	White Linen Robe	10	BoE	30		99
6	Beaded Robe	11	BoE	33	1	19
6	Beaded Wraps	11	BoE	33	1	21
6	Foreman Vest	11	BoE	33	1	31
6	Journeyman's Robe	11	BoE	33	1	21
6	Journeyman's Vest	11	BoE	33	1	19
7	Blue Linen Vest	12	BoE	36	1	61
7	Red Linen Vest	12	BoE	36	1	60
8	Ancestral Robe	13	BoE	39	1	87
8	Ancestral Tunic	13	BoE	39	2	03
8	Disciple's Robe	13	BoE	39	1	91
8	Disciple's Vest	13	BoE	39	2	05
N/A	Banshee Armor	14	BoA	42	2	27
9	Barbaric Linen Vest	14	BoE	42	2	24
9	Blue Linen Robe	14	BoE	42	2	43
N/A	Harvester's Robe	15	BoA	45	2	68
10	Jester's Blouse	15	BoE	45	2	75
10	Jester's Robe	15	BoE	45	2	74
N/A	Manaweave Robe	15	BoA	45	2	75
N/A	Robe of the Keeper	15	BoA	45	2	94
N/A	Spell fire Robes	15	BoA	45	2	76
11	Native Robe	16	BoE	47	3	41
11	Native Vest	16	BoE	47	3	25
12	Magister's Robe	17	BoE	49	3	58
12	Magister's Vest	17	BoE	49	3	81
13	Green Woolen Robe	18	BoE	51	4	45
13	Noble's Robe	18	BoE	51	4	23
13	Robe of Evocation	18	BoA	51	4	20
13	Runic Cloth Robe	18	BoE	51	4	17
13	Runic Cloth Vest	18	BoE	51	4	42
13	Solstice Robe	18	BoE	51	4	15
14	Willow Robe	19	BoE	53	4	92
14	Willow Vest	19	BoE	53	4	88
15	Aboriginal Robe	20	BoE	55	5	77
15	Aboriginal Vest	20	BoE	55	5	42
15	Blue Overalls	20	BoE	55	5	89
15	Whispering Vest	20	BoE	55	5	47
16	Gray Woolen Robe	21	BoE	57	6	38
16	Seer's Padded Armor	21	BoE	57	6	75
16	Seer's Robe	21	BoE	57	6	48
N/A	Grunt Vest	22	BoA	59	7	45
N/A	Harlequin Robes	22	BoA	59	7	62
17	Robe of the Moccasin	22	BoA	59	7	68
18	Bloody Apron	23	BoA	60	8	90
18	Buccaneer's Robes	23	BoE	60	8	37
18	Buccaneer's Vest	23	BoE	60	8	47
18	Greater Adept's Robe	23	BoE	60	8	84
18	Mystic's Robe	23	BoE	60	8	15
18	Mystic's Wrap	23	BoE	60	8	09
N/A	High Robe of the Adjudicator	24	BoA	62	10	05
19	Ritual Shroud	24	BoE	62	9	99
19	Ritual Tunic	24	BoE	62	9	50
N/A	Fen Keeper Robe	25	BoA	63	10	44
N/A	Robe of Solomon	25	BoA	63	10	32
N/A	Robes of Antiquity	25	BoA	63	11	29
20	Scholarly Robes	25	BoE	63	10	35
20	Shimmering Armor	25	BoE	63	10	36
20	Shimmering Robe	25	BoE	63	10	44
N/A	Astral Knot Blouse	26	BoA	65	12	85
N/A	Astral Knot Robe	26	BoA	65	12	03
N/A	Nether-lace Robe	26	BoA	65	12	07
N/A	Nether-lace Tunic	26	BoA	65	12	48
21	Pagan Vest	26	BoE	65	12	36
21	Pagan Wraps	26	BoE	65	11	68
21	Smoldering Robe	26	BoE	65	12	07

GOOD CLOTH CHEST ARMOR continued

M LEV	ARMOR NAME	LEV	BIND	AC	VENDOR PURCHASE VALUE (silver)	(copper)
21	Vicar's Robe	26	BoE	65	12	62
22	Druidic Robe	27	BoE	67	13	69
22	Druidic Vest	27	BoE	67	13	74
22	Lesser Wizard's Robe	27	BoE	67	13	38
22	Sacrificial Robes	27	BoE	67	13	22
22	Sunfire Armor	27	BoE	67	13	28
22	Sunfire Robe	27	BoE	67	14	12
N/A	Efflorescent Robe	28	BoA	68	15	44
23	Sanguine Armor	28	BoE	68	14	30
23	Sanguine Robe	28	BoE	68	14	73
24	Enchantress Robe	29	BoE	69	16	86
24	Enchantress Wraps	29	BoE	69	16	44
25	Azure Silk Vest	30	BoE	71	18	74
▶	**SPELL** Increase Frost Dam 4					
25	Nightwalker Armor	30	BoE	71	18	06
25	Robes of Arcana	30	BoE	71	18	07
25	Watcher's Jerkin	30	BoE	71	18	70
25	Watcher's Robes	30	BoE	71	17	16
26	Death Speaker Robes	31	BoA	72	19	00
26	Raincaller Robes	31	BoE	72	19	46
26	Raincaller Vest	31	BoE	72	19	32
26	Robes of the Shadowcaster	31	BoE	72	20	38
26	Silver-thread Armor	31	BoE	72	20	69
26	Silver-thread Robe	31	BoE	72	19	88
27	Sage's Cloth	32	BoE	73	21	48
27	Sage's Robe	32	BoE	73	21	56
28	Green Silk Armor	33	BoE	75	23	98
28	Satyr's Robe	33	BoE	75	24	80
28	Satyr's Tunic	33	BoE	75	23	55
29	Beastwalker Robe	34	BoE	76	27	34
29	Earthen Vest	34	BoE	76	26	96
29	Pressed Felt Robe	34	BoE	76	25	38
29	Siren's Drape	34	BoE	76	27	26
29	Siren's Gown	34	BoE	76	26	00
30	Elder's Padded Armor	35	BoE	77	29	98
30	Elder's Robe	35	BoE	77	29	55
31	Thistlefur Jerkin	36	BoE	79	33	36
31	Thistlefur Robe	36	BoE	79	30	41
32	Dryad's Raiment	37	BoE	81	35	53
32	Dryad's Tunic	37	BoE	81	35	79
N/A	Dustfall Robes	37	BoA	81	33	39
32	Stormcloud Armor	37	BoE	81	33	29
32	Stormcloud Robe	37	BoE	81	35	62
33	Conjurer's Robe	38	BoE	83	38	20
33	Conjurer's Vest	38	BoE	83	37	09
33	Robe of Doan	38	BoA	83	39	03
34	Stonecloth Robe	39	BoE	85	39	47
34	Stonecloth Vest	39	BoE	85	42	66
N/A	Baroque Apron	40	BoA	88	44	56
N/A	Doomsayer's Robe	40	BoA	88	43	24
N/A	Inferno Robe	40	BoA	88	43	86
▶	**SPELL** Increase Fire Dmg 13					
N/A	Robe of Crystal Waters	40	BoA	88	41	92
35	Twilight Armor	40	BoE	88	46	20
35	Twilight Robe	40	BoE	88	41	94
36	Aurora Armor	41	BoE	90	45	47
36	Aurora Robe	41	BoE	90	45	65
36	Black Mageweave Vest	41	BoE	90	48	15
36	Crimson Silk Robe	41	BoE	90	47	41
36	Geomancer's Jerkin	41	BoE	90	48	87
36	Geomancer's Wraps	41	BoE	90	46	94
37	Black Mageweave Robe	42	BoE	92	52	57
37	Embersilk Robes	42	BoE	92	52	40
37	Embersilk Tunic	42	BoE	92	51	64
38	Red Mageweave Vest	43	BoE	94	57	99
38	Shadoweave Robe	43	BoE	94	57	38
▶	**SPELL** Increase Shadow Dmg 13					
38	Sorcerer Drape	43	BoE	94	58	01
38	Sorcerer Robe	43	BoE	94	54	48
39	Silksand Tunic	44	BoE	96	58	88
39	Silksand Wraps	44	BoE	96	62	23
40	Cindercloth Robe	45	BoE	98	66	44
▶	**SPELL** Increase Fire Dmg 16					
40	Regal Armor	45	BoE	98	66	92
40	Regal Robe	45	BoE	98	67	63
40	Stormcloth Vest	45	BoE	98	65	97
▶	**SPELL** Increase Healing 26					
41	Darkmist Armor	46	BoE	100	72	06

GOOD CLOTH CHEST ARMOR continued

M LEV	ARMOR NAME	LEV	BIND	AC	VENDOR PURCHASE VALUE (gold)	(silver)	(copper)
41	Darkmist Wraps	46	BoE	100		68	70
41	Mistscape Armor	46	BoE	100		67	07
41	Mistscape Robe	46	BoE	100		70	16
42	Lunar Raiment	47	BoE	103		76	98
42	Lunar Vest	47	BoE	103		75	59
43	Royal Blouse	48	BoE	105		82	51
43	Royal Gown	48	BoE	105		84	90
44	Windchaser Robes	49	BoE	107		87	06
44	Windchaser Wraps	49	BoE	107		91	24
45	Gossamer Robe	50	BoE	109		94	06
45	Gossamer Tunic	50	BoE	109		93	72
N/A	Mage Dragon Robe	50	BoA	109		90	58
46	Bloodwoven Jerkin	51	BoE	111		99	26
46	Bloodwoven Wraps	51	BoE	111		98	53
46	Frostweave Robe	51	BoE	111		96	65
▶	**SPELL** Increase Frost Dmg 14						
46	Frostweave Tunic	51	BoE	111		97	02
▶	**SPELL** Increase Frost Dam 14						
45	Hibernal Armor	51	BoE	111	1	04	38
46	Hibernal Robe	51	BoE	111		96	94
47	Cindercloth Vest	52	BoE	113	1	05	61
▶	**SPELL** Increase Fire Dam 14						
47	Gaea's Raiment	52	BoE	113	1	11	15
47	Gaea's Tunic	52	BoE	113	1	01	31
47	Runecloth Robe	52	BoE	113	1	09	17
47	Runecloth Tunic	52	BoE	113	1	08	78
48	Illusionary Robe	53	BoE	115	1	12	71
48	Illusionary Wraps	53	BoE	115	1	13	96
49	Brightcloth Robe	54	BoE	117	1	20	89
▶	**SPELL** Frost Resist +16, Shadow Resist +15						
49	Venomshroud Chestguard	54	BoE	117	1	20	02
49	Venomshroud Silk Robes	54	BoE	117	1	23	53
50	Duskwoven Robe	55	BoE	120	1	21	53
50	Duskwoven Tunic	55	BoE	120	1	27	11
50	Ghostweave Vest	55	BoE	120	1	28	59
▶	**SPELL** Restores 7 MP Every 5 Sec						
N/A	Royal Highmark Vestments	55	BoA	120	1	32	29
51	High Arcane Robe	56	BoE	122	1	36	22
51	High Arcane Tunic	56	BoE	122	1	29	22
51	Necrotic Drape	56	BoE	122	1	32	82
51	Necrotic Silk Robes	56	BoE	122	1	31	35
52	Arachnidian Armor	57	BoE	124	1	41	32
52	Arachnidian Robes	57	BoE	124	1	35	56
53	Mystical Armor	58	BoE	126	1	46	40
53	Mystical Robe	58	BoE	126	1	44	75
N/A	Astoria Robes	59	BoA	128	1	50	61
54	Fay Robes	59	BoE	128	1	50	20
54	Fay Vest	59	BoE	128	1	51	37
54	Highborne Padded Armor	59	BoE	128	1	57	92
54	Highborne Robes	59	BoE	128	1	56	77
55	Bonecaster's Shroud	60	BoE	130	1	62	09
55	Bonecaster's Vest	60	BoE	130	1	68	30
55	Coldtouch Phantom Wraps	60	BoA	130	1	68	29
▶	**SPELL** Arcane Resist +13, Frost Resist +20						
55	Wizardweave Robe	60	BoE	130	1	60	93
▶	**SPELL** Arcane Resist +17, Fire Resist +18						
56	Celestial Silk Robes	61	BoE	132	1	66	33
56	Celestial Tunic	61	BoE	132	1	77	99
56	Felcloth Robe	61	BoE	132	1	80	53
▶	**SPELL** Increase Shadow Dmg 21						
56	Zephyr Armor	61	BoE	132	1	71	38
56	Zephyr Robe	61	BoE	132	1	75	85
57	Nova Armor	62	BoE	134	1	75	89
57	Nova Robes	62	BoE	134	1	73	87
58	Demonskin Chestpiece	63	BoE	136	1	84	08
58	Demonskin Robes	63	BoE	136	1	94	79
59	Elunarian Silk Robes	64	BoE	139	2	08	22
59	Elunarian Vest	64	BoE	139	2	02	30
59	Empyreal Armor	64	BoE	139	2	06	63
59	Empyreal Robe	64	BoE	139	1	97	72
60	Eternal Chestguard	65	BoE	140	2	16	33
60	Eternal Wraps	65	BoE	140	2	01	37
60	Lich's Armor	65	BoE	140	2	15	42
60	Lich's Robe	65	BoE	140	2	21	64

STANDARD CLOTH CHEST ARMOR

M LEV	ARMOR NAME	LEV	BIND	AC	VENDOR PURCHASE VALUE		
N/A	Gamemaster's Robe	1	BoA	3			1
1	Light Magesmith Robe	4	None	12			6
1	Scarlet Initiate Robes	4	None	12			6
N/A	Flax Vest	5	BoA	15			10
N/A	Soft Wool Vest	5	BoA	15			9
1	Tattered Cloth Vest	5	None	15			9
1	Thin Cloth Armor	5	None	15			10
N/A	Woodland Robes	5	None	15			10
3	Brown Linen Vest	8	None	23			31
3	Plain Robe	8	None	23			32
3	Snowy Robe	8	None	23			31
4	Spider Web Robe	9	None	26			46
4	Violet Robes	9	None	26			44
5	Knitted Tunic	10	None	29			56
N/A	Warm Winter Robe	10	BoA	29			55
N/A	Well-stitched Robe	10	BoA	29			55
5	Woven Vest	10	None	29			59
8	Double-stitched Robes	13	None	37		1	21
12	Green Woolen Vest	17	None	47		2	16
12	Heavy Weave Armor	17	None	47		2	24
12	Robe of Apprenticeship	17	None	47		2	32
12	Stonesplinter Rags	17	None	47		2	23
13	Dalaran Wizard's Robe	18	None	49		2	57
17	Thick Cloth Vest	22	None	56		4	54
17	White Woolen Dress	22	None	56		4	66
18	Shimmering Silk Robes	23	None	57		5	31
22	Padded Armor	27	None	63		8	32
24	Chromatic Robe	29	None	66		10	18
32	Burning Robes	37	None	77		21	98

STANDARD CLOTH CHEST ARMOR continued

M LEV	ARMOR NAME	LEV	BIND	AC	VENDOR PURCHASE VALUE		
32	Crimson Silk Vest	37	None	77		20	52
32	Russet Vest	37	None	77		20	27
45	Embroidered Armor	50	None	103		55	36
45	Silver Dress Robes	50	None	103		53	27

INFERIOR CLOTH CHEST ARMOR

M LEV	ARMOR NAME	LEV	BIND	AC	VENDOR PURCHASE VALUE		
1	Acolyte's Robe	1	None	3			1
1	Acolyte's Robe	1	None	3			1
1	Apprentice's Robe	1	None	3			1
1	Apprentice's Robe	1	None	3			1
1	Apprentice's Robe	1	None	3			1
1	Neophyte's Robe	1	None	3			1
1	Neophyte's Robe	1	None	3			1
1	Neophyte's Robe	1	None	3			1
1	Novice's Robe	1	None	3			1
1	Novice's Robe	1	None	3			1
1	Frayed Robe	4	None	11			4
2	Patchwork Armor	7	None	19			14
8	Calico Tunic	13	None	35			80
12	Canvas Vest	17	None	44		1	43
18	Brocade Vest	23	None	54		3	37
24	Cross-stitched Vest	29	None	62		6	83
32	Interlaced Vest	37	None	73		14	60
38	Crochet Vest	43	None	85		22	44
52	Twill Vest	57	None	111		58	97
61	Mesh Armor	66	None	128		88	43

CLOTH CLOAKS

EPIC CLOTH CLOAKS

M LEV	ARMOR NAME	LEV	BIND	AC	VENDOR PURCHASE VALUE		
60	Cloak of Flames	65	BoE	84	2	60	18
▸	**SPELL** Fire Resist +5, Deals 10 Dam to Melee Attackers						

SUPERIOR CLOTH CLOAKS

M LEV	ARMOR NAME	LEV	BIND	AC	VENDOR PURCHASE VALUE		
16	Firebane Cloak	21	BoE	31		6	17
▸	**SPELL** Fire Resist +5						
17	Glowing Lizardscale Cloak	22	BoA	32		7	01
19	Sentry Cloak	24	BoE	34		8	63
20	Cape of the Brotherhood	25	BoA	35		9	40
23	Amy's Blanket	28	BoE	37		13	31
24	Glowing Thresher Cape	29	BoA	38		15	23
29	Tigerstrike Mantle	34	BoE	42		24	46
32	Dark Hooded Cape	37	BoE	45		31	59
33	Wing of the Whelping	38	BoE	46		34	28
34	Energy Cloak	39	BoE	47		36	72
▸	**SPELL** Restores 375-425 Mana (1 Hr Cooldown)						
35	Icy Cloak	40	BoE	48		37	88
▸	**SPELL** Frost Resist +11						
35	Silky Spider Cape	42	BoA	51		47	99
41	Blackmetal Cape	46	BoE	55		63	41

SUPERIOR CLOTH CLOAKS continued

M LEV	ARMOR NAME	LEV	BIND	AC	VENDOR PURCHASE VALUE		
44	Blackflame Cape	49	BoE	59		81	52
▸	**SPELL** Fire & Shadow Resist +5						
48	Nightfall Drape	53	BoA	63	1	02	61
49	Featherskin Cape	54	BoA	65	1	05	95
50	Blisterbane Wrap	55	BoE	66	1	09	80
▸	**SPELL** Shadow Resist +6						
50	Cloak of Fire	55	BoE	66	1	12	80
▸	**SPELL** Cloak of Fire, Fire Resist +6						
50	Dark Phantom Cape	55	BoE	66	1	14	89
51	Stoneshield Cloak	56	BoE	67	1	15	94
▸	**SPELL** Increased Armor 150						
53	Cape of the Fire Salamander	58	BoA	69	1	39	79
▸	**SPELL** Fire Resist +7						
53	Mageflame Cloak	58	BoE	69	1	35	85
▸	**SPELL** Increase Fire Dam 13, Fire Resist +10						
54	Royal Tribunal Cloak	59	BoA	70	1	37	38
55	Onyxia Scale Cloak	60	BoE	72	1	51	98
▸	**SPELL** Fire Resist +16						
55	The Emperor's New Cape	60	BoA	72	1	45	88
56	Stoneskin Gargoyle Cape	61	BoA	73	1	52	01
▸	**SPELL** Attack Power 20						
58	Bloodmoon Cloak	63	BoA	75	1	68	84
▸	**SPELL** Arcane Resist +7						
58	Cape of the Black Baron	63	BoA	75	1	64	98
58	Frostweaver Cape	63	BoA	75	1	69	48
▸	**SPELL** Frost Resist +10						
N/A	Shroud of the Exile	63	BoA	75	1	78	55

GOOD CLOTH CLOAKS

M LEV	ARMOR NAME	LEV	BIND	AC	VENDOR PURCHASE VALUE
9	Aboriginal Cape	14	BoE	21	1 76
10	Buckskin Cape	15	BoE	22	2 51
N/A	Cloak of the People's Militia	15	BoA	22	2 67
10	Feral Cloak	15	BoE	22	2 20
10	Fine Leather Cloak	15	BoE	22	2 67
N/A	Finely Woven Cloak	15	BoA	22	2 13
N/A	Gustweald Cloak	15	BoA	22	2 08
10	Harvest Cloak	15	BoE	22	2 64
N/A	Long Draping Cape	15	BoA	22	2 63
N/A	Mystic Shawl	15	BoA	22	2 07
10	Rat Cloth Cloak	15	BoE	22	2 11
10	Rathorian's Cape	15	BoE	22	3 20
N/A	Sower's Cloak	15	BoA	22	2 60
10	Willow Cape	15	BoE	22	2 19
11	Inscribed Leather Cloak	16	BoE	23	3 15
11	Raider's Cloak	16	BoE	23	2 34
11	War Paint Cloak	16	BoE	23	2 32
12	Outrunner's Cloak	17	BoE	24	2 67
12	Prospector's Cloak	17	BoE	24	2 67
12	Ritual Cape	17	BoE	24	2 87
12	Seer's Cape	17	BoE	24	2 92
N/A	Acidproof Cloak	18	BoA	26	4 74
13	Bandit Cloak	18	BoE	26	4 18
N/A	Barkeeper's Cloak	18	BoA	26	4 62
13	Burnished Cloak	18	BoE	26	3 27
13	Deviate Scale Cloak	18	BoE	26	4 13
13	Pagan Cape	18	BoE	26	3 37
13	Stonemason Cloak	18	BoE	26	4 08
13	Subterranean Cape	18	BoA	26	3 07
N/A	Timberland Cape	18	BoA	26	4 80
14	Buccaneer's Cape	19	BoE	26	3 58
14	Grunt's Cape	19	BoE	26	3 53
14	Miner's Cape	19	BoA	26	5 48
14	Moonstalker's Cape	19	BoE	26	3 53
14	Pearl-clasped Cloak	19	BoE	26	3 70
14	Privateer's Cape	19	BoE	26	5 56
15	Black Whelp Cloak	20	BoE	27	5 19
N/A	Boar Hunter's Cape	20	BoA	27	5 28
15	Defender Cloak	20	BoE	27	4 31
15	Desperado Cape	20	BoE	27	6 15
15	Druidic Cloak	20	BoE	27	4 16
N/A	Enchanted Moonstalker Cloak	20	BoA	27	0
▶	**SPELL** Form of the Moonstalker (Quest)				
15	Feyscale Cloak	20	BoA	27	6 42
15	Hulking Cloak	20	BoE	27	4 07
15	Overseer's Cloak	20	BoE	27	6 30
15	Scouting Cloak	20	BoE	27	5 58
16	Bristlebark Cape	21	BoE	28	4 68
16	Heavy Woolen Cloak	21	BoE	28	4 75
16	Shimmering Cloak	21	BoE	28	5 12
17	Forest Leather Cloak	22	BoE	29	7 02
17	Fortified Cloak	22	BoE	29	5 70
17	Sanguine Cape	22	BoE	29	5 51
17	Wrangler's Cloak	22	BoE	29	5 38
18	Ancient Cloak	23	BoE	30	9 16
18	Hide of Lupos	23	BoE	30	7 81
18	Regent's Cloak	23	BoE	30	7 81
18	Spiked Chain Cloak	23	BoE	30	6 08
18	Spirit Cloak	23	BoE	30	6 55
18	Sporid Cape	23	BoA	30	6 30
18	Sunfire Cloak	23	BoE	30	6 25
19	Lambent Scale Cloak	24	BoE	31	6 87
19	Pirate's Cloak	24	BoE	31	8 87
19	Sentry's Cape	24	BoE	31	6 87
19	Sylvan Cloak	24	BoE	31	7 44
19	Watcher's Cape	24	BoE	31	7 47
20	Enchantress Cloak	25	BoE	32	8 29
20	Firemail Cloak	25	BoE	32	12 84
▶	**SPELL** Fire Resist +5				
20	Heavy Runed Cloak	25	BoE	32	11 66
20	Inferno Cloak	25	BoE	32	8 31
▶	**SPELL** Fire Resist +5				
20	Kodo Hide Cloak	25	BoE	32	7 76
20	Webwing Cloak	25	BoE	32	10 28
21	Battleforge Cloak	26	BoE	32	9 22
21	Cloak of Night	26	BoE	32	9 01
21	Dervish Cape	26	BoE	32	12 00
21	Feathered Cape	26	BoE	32	11 36

GOOD CLOTH CLOAKS continued

M LEV	ARMOR NAME	LEV	BIND	AC	VENDOR PURCHASE VALUE
21	Fenrus' Hide	26	BoA	32	8 75
N/A	Resilient Poncho	26	BoA	32	8 95
21	Silver-thread Cloak	26	BoE	32	9 26
22	Emblazoned Cloak	27	BoE	33	12 82
N/A	Engineer's Cloak	27	BoA	33	9 92
22	Pathfinder Cloak	27	BoE	33	9 65
N/A	Prelacy Cape	27	BoA	33	9 84
22	Raincaller Cloak	27	BoE	33	9 82
22	Slayer's Cape	27	BoE	33	9 65
22	Wolfmaster Cape	27	BoA	33	12 68
23	Cenarion Cape	28	BoE	34	10 62
23	Glimmering Mail Cloak	28	BoE	34	11 12
23	Sage's Cloak	28	BoE	34	11 20
23	Wicked Chain Cloak	28	BoE	34	10 62
24	Ambusher's Cloak	29	BoE	35	11 74
24	Basilisk Scale Cloak	29	BoE	35	11 68
24	Monk's Cloak	29	BoE	35	15 41
24	Satyr's Cape	29	BoE	35	12 15
24	Siren's Cape	29	BoE	35	11 92
N/A	Windsong Drape	29	BoA	35	12 07
N/A	Cloak of the Faith	30	BoA	35	13 05
25	Cutthroat's Cape	30	BoE	35	13 57
25	Elder's Cloak	30	BoE	35	14 11
N/A	High Apothecary Cloak	30	BoA	35	13 20
N/A	Mourning Shawl	30	BoA	35	14 11
25	Phalanx Cloak	30	BoE	35	13 26
N/A	Repairman's Cape	30	BoA	35	13 56
26	Cloak of Rot	31	BoE	36	14 25
N/A	Dwarven Guard Cloak	31	BoA	36	22 22
26	Infiltrator Cloak	31	BoE	36	17 69
26	Pillager's Cloak	31	BoE	36	14 13
26	Thistlefur Cloak	31	BoE	36	15 31
27	Burning Blade Cape	32	BoE	37	15 55
27	Dryad's Cape	32	BoE	37	16 36
27	Headhunter's Cloak	32	BoE	37	15 55
27	Insignia Cloak	32	BoE	37	21 18
27	Mail Combat Cloak	32	BoE	37	16 58
27	Stormcloud Cloak	32	BoE	37	16 76
28	Conjurer's Cloak	33	BoE	37	17 79
N/A	Garrison Cloak	33	BoA	37	27 30
28	Ghostwalker Cloak	33	BoE	37	17 10
N/A	Grimsteel Cape	33	BoA	37	27 48
28	Marauder's Cloak	33	BoE	37	17 10
28	Renegade Cloak	33	BoE	37	17 78
28	Stonecloth Cape	33	BoE	37	17 07
N/A	Swiftrunner Cape	33	BoA	37	22 39
28	Vibrant Silk Cape	33	BoE	37	17 78
N/A	Watch Master's Cloak	33	BoA	37	23 21
29	Archer's Cloak	34	BoE	38	23 82
29	Geomancer's Cloak	34	BoE	38	20 46
29	Knight's Cloak	34	BoE	38	20 00
N/A	Yeti Fur Cloak	34	BoA	38	23 52
30	Azure Silk Cloak	35	BoE	38	22 40
▶	**SPELL** Increase Frost Dam 6				
30	Hawkeye's Cloak	35	BoE	38	20 70
30	Sparkleshell Cloak	35	BoE	38	20 70
30	Twilight Cape	35	BoE	38	21 11
31	Chief Brigadier Cloak	36	BoE	39	23 40
31	Crimson Silk Cloak	36	BoE	39	23 14
▶	**SPELL** Fire Resist +7				
31	Embersilk Cloak	36	BoE	39	23 87
31	Frost Leather Cloak	36	BoE	39	22 69
▶	**SPELL** Increase Frost Dam 7				
31	Sentinel Cloak	36	BoE	39	30 92
31	Witch Doctor's Cloak	36	BoE	39	22 77
32	Aurora Cloak	37	BoE	41	25 36
32	Glyphed Cloak	37	BoE	41	32 90
32	Guardian Cloak	37	BoE	41	25 36
32	Long Silken Cloak	37	BoE	41	24 96
32	Nocturnal Cloak	37	BoE	41	25 04
32	Slithid Scale Cloak	37	BoE	41	25 04
33	Berserker Cloak	38	BoE	42	27 18
33	Elven Cape	38	BoE	42	36 48
33	Silksand Cape	38	BoE	42	28 89
33	Sorcerer Cloak	38	BoE	42	27 08
34	Captain's Cloak	39	BoE	43	30 15
34	Darkmist Cape	39	BoE	43	31 76
34	Ravager's Cloak	39	BoE	43	29 21

GOOD CLOTH CLOAKS continued

M LEV	ARMOR NAME	LEV	BIND	AC	VENDOR PURCHASE VALUE		
34	Warden's Cloak	39	BoE	43		29	21
35	Lunar Cloak	40	BoE	44		33	32
35	Ranger Cloak	40	BoE	44		42	38
35	Regal Cloak	40	BoE	44		32	81
36	Ancient Cloak	41	BoE	45		34	07
36	Brigade Cloak	41	BoE	45		36	62
36	Brilliant Red Cloak	41	BoE	45		44	32
36	Imperial Leather Cloak	41	BoE	45		46	77
36	Mistscape Cloak	41	BoE	45		36	21
36	Wolf Rider's Cloak	41	BoE	45		34	07
37	Assassin's Cape	42	BoE	46		36	80
37	Blackforge Cape	42	BoE	46		38	25
N/A	Ceremonial Centaur Blanket	42	BoA	46		40	12
N/A	Cloak of Blight	42	BoA	46		37	69
N/A	Darktide Cape	42	BoA	46		58	26
37	Windchaser Cloak	42	BoE	46		36	86
38	Bloodwoven Cloak	43	BoE	47		40	44
38	Bonelink Cape	43	BoE	47		39	74
38	Royal Cape	43	BoE	47		42	57
N/A	Scorched Cape	43	BoA	47		64	37
N/A	Stargazer Cloak	43	BoA	47		63	70
38	Tracker's Cloak	43	BoE	47		51	49
39	Cabalist Cloak	44	BoE	48		55	57
39	Champion's Cape	44	BoE	48		42	96
39	Gossamer Cape	44	BoE	48		42	97
39	Khan's Cloak	44	BoE	48		42	92
39	Scorpashi Cape	44	BoE	48		42	92
39	Well Oiled Cloak	44	BoE	48		44	83
N/A	Battlemaster Cape	45	BoA	49		69	85
▸	**SPELL** Attack Power 10						
40	Gaea's Cloak	45	BoE	49		48	77
40	Gryphon Mail Cloak	45	BoE	49		49	71
40	Heraldic Cloak	45	BoE	49		62	07
N/A	Master Apothecary Cape	45	BoA	49		47	13
N/A	Medicine Blanket	45	BoA	49		48	53
N/A	Parachute Cloak	45	BoE	49		46	96
▸	**SPELL** Reduces Fall Speed for 30 Sec (30 Min Cooldown)						
40	Rageclaw Cloak	45	BoE	49		46	36
40	Warmonger's Cloak	45	BoE	49		48	03
41	Emberscale Cape	46	BoA	50		76	99
41	Hibernal Cloak	46	BoE	50		50	11
41	Icebrand Cape	46	BoE	50		50	07
41	Nightscape Cloak	46	BoE	50		52	63
41	Vampiric Cape	46	BoE	50		50	07
41	Venomshroud Cape	46	BoE	50		53	47
42	Chieftain's Cloak	47	BoE	51		67	95
42	Thunderscale Cape	47	BoE	51		59	37
43	Big Voodoo Cloak	48	BoE	52		63	23
N/A	Chainlink Towel	48	BoA	52		96	31
43	Illusionary Cloak	48	BoE	52		60	29
43	Keeper's Cloak	48	BoE	52		58	40
43	Lord's Cape	48	BoE	52		63	70
43	Necrotic Cape	48	BoE	52		59	19
43	Protector Cape	48	BoE	52		58	40
44	Arachnidian Cape	49	BoE	53		67	95
44	Duskwoven Cape	49	BoE	53		66	67
44	Ironhide Cloak	49	BoE	53		62	49
44	Jadefire Cloak	49	BoE	53		62	49
44	Righteous Cloak	49	BoE	53		80	63
45	Crusader's Cloak	50	BoE	54		73	45
45	High Arcane Cloak	50	BoE	54		70	32
45	Praetorian Cloak	50	BoE	54		66	86
45	Serpentskin Cloak	50	BoE	54		91	44
45	Wild Leather Cloak	50	BoE	54		90	17
46	Daemonic Cloak	51	BoE	55		71	54
46	Ebonhold Cloak	51	BoE	55		74	68
46	Highborne Cloak	51	BoE	55		73	64
46	Infernal Cape	51	BoE	55		92	65
47	Bloodlust Cape	52	BoE	57		75	84
47	Bonecaster's Cape	52	BoE	57		76	85
47	Mystical Cape	52	BoE	57		81	21
47	Pridelord Cape	52	BoE	57		75	84
47	Spritecaster Cape	52	BoA	57		83	33
47	Wingveil Cloak	52	BoA	57		78	31
48	Angelic Cloak	53	BoE	58	1	02	54
48	Blackveil Cape	53	BoA	58	1	01	02
48	Divine Cloak	53	BoE	58		87	97
48	Fay Cloak	53	BoE	58		87	36

GOOD CLOTH CLOAKS continued

M LEV	ARMOR NAME	LEV	BIND	AC	VENDOR PURCHASE VALUE		
48	Runecloth Cloak	53	BoE	58		87	41
49	Celestial Cape	54	BoE	59		92	98
49	Impenetrable Cloak	54	BoE	59		85	21
49	Stormhide Cloak	54	BoE	59		85	36
50	Abyssal Cape	55	BoE	60		98	15
50	Brightcloth Cloak	55	BoE	60		97	16
▸	**SPELL** Increase Frost Dam 6, Frost & Shadow Resist +7						
N/A	Chemist's Smock	55	BoA	60		90	32
50	Cindercloth Cloak	55	BoE	60		95	03
▸	**SPELL** Increase Fire Dam 8						
50	Demonskin Cloak	55	BoE	60		94	38
50	Graverot Cape	55	BoA	60	1	36	09
50	Nether Runed Cloak	55	BoE	60		90	32
50	Spiritwalker Cloak	55	BoE	60	1	13	91
50	Zephyr Cloak	55	BoE	60		94	27
N/A	Cerise Drape	56	BoA	61		95	74
N/A	Deep River Cloak	56	BoA	61		95	74
N/A	Ethereal Mist Cape	56	BoA	61		96	61
51	Hellcaller Cloak	56	BoE	61		95	74
N/A	Sunborne Cape	56	BoA	61	1	04	43
▸	**SPELL** Increase Fire Dam 10						
52	Elunarian Cloak	57	BoE	62	1	07	98
52	Nightmare Cloak	57	BoE	62	1	34	44
52	Nova Cloak	57	BoE	62	1	10	69
52	Tempest Cape	57	BoE	62	1	05	13
52	Warlord's Cape	57	BoE	62	1	01	49
53	Butcher's Apron	58	BoA	63	1	37	83
53	Eternal Cloak	58	BoE	63	1	16	54
53	Phantasmal Cloak	58	BoE	63	1	40	92
N/A	Raincaster Drape	58	BoA	63	1	16	10
▸	**SPELL** Increase Healing 20						
N/A	Shaleskin Cape	58	BoA	63	1	67	98
53	Triumphant Cloak	58	BoE	63	1	07	58
54	Arch Druid's Cloak	59	BoE	64	1	12	96
54	Empyreal Cloak	59	BoE	64	1	22	74
54	Mercurial Cloak	59	BoE	64	1	14	44
55	Armswake Cloak	60	BoA	65	1	94	98
N/A	Hameya's Cloak	60	BoA	65	1	18	60
▸	**SPELL** Arcane Resist +15						
55	Hellfire Cape	60	BoE	65	1	53	65
56	Archivist Cape	61	BoA	66	1	63	76
56	Kraken Cape	61	BoE	66	1	33	37
56	Lich's Cloak	61	BoE	66	1	34	35
56	Seraphim Cape	61	BoE	66	1	24	53
56	Wildfire Cape	61	BoA	66	1	36	33
▸	**SPELL** Fire Resist +15						

STANDARD CLOTH CLOAKS

M LEV	ARMOR NAME	LEV	BIND	AC	VENDOR PURCHASE VALUE
N/A	Battered Cloak	5	BoA	7	11
N/A	Battleworn Leather Cape	5	BoA	7	9
N/A	Bear Shawl	5	BoA	7	9
N/A	Draped Cloak	5	BoA	7	7
N/A	Ensign Cloak	5	BoA	7	11
N/A	Short Duskbat Cape	5	BoA	7	8
1	Webbed Cloak	5	None	7	7
N/A	Wine-stained Cloak	5	BoA	7	7
1	Linen Cloak	6	None	9	11
1	Wispy Cloak	6	None	9	11
N/A	Adept's Cloak	8	BoA	12	24
3	Beaded Cloak	8	None	12	24
3	Burnt Leather Cloak	8	None	12	28
3	Charger's Cloak	8	None	12	22
3	Journeyman's Cloak	8	None	12	24
3	Primal Cape	8	None	12	22
N/A	Sun-beaten Cloak	8	BoA	12	36
N/A	Thunderhorn Cloak	8	BoA	12	30
3	Warrior's Cloak	8	None	12	23
4	Ancestral Cloak	9	None	13	32
4	Battle Chain Cloak	9	None	13	32
4	Handstitched Leather Cloak	9	None	13	34
4	Infantry Cloak	9	None	13	34
N/A	Oil-stained Cloak	9	BoA	13	33
4	Pioneer Cloak	9	None	13	41

STANDARD CLOTH CLOAKS continued

M LEV	ARMOR NAME	LEV	BIND	AC	VENDOR PURCHASE VALUE
N/A	Seasoned Fighter's Cloak	9	BoA	13	48
4	Tribal Cloak	9	None	13	32
4	Wendigo Fur Cloak	9	None	13	43
5	Disciple's Cloak	10	None	14	42
N/A	Goat Fur Cloak	10	BoA	14	53
5	Grizzly Cape	10	None	14	41
5	Native Cloak	10	None	14	43
N/A	Old Blanchy's Blanket	10	BoA	14	45
5	War Torn Cape	10	None	14	41
6	Cadet Cloak	11	None	16	58
6	Demon Scarred Cloak	11	BoA	16	0
6	Gypsy Cloak	11	None	16	70
6	Jester's Cape	11	None	16	54
N/A	Rain-spotted Cape	11	BoA	16	67
N/A	Scout's Cloak	11	BoA	16	86
6	Warm Cloak	11	None	16	70
7	Ceremonial Leather Cloak	12	BoE	17	68
N/A	Handsewn Cloak	12	BoA	17	72
7	Melrache's Cape	12	None	17	1 01
7	Reinforced Linen Cape	12	None	17	67
7	Runic Cloth Cloak	12	BoE	17	67
7	Twain TEST Cloak	12	None	17	67
7	Veteran Cloak	12	None	17	70
8	Brackwater Cloak	13	BoE	19	91
8	Embossed Leather Cloak	13	None	19	1 12
8	Hunting Cloak	13	None	19	1 06
8	Lupine Cloak	13	None	19	84
8	Magister's Cloak	13	None	19	92
9	Bard's Cloak	14	None	20	1 30
9	Bloodspattered Cloak	14	None	20	1 01
9	Soldier's Cloak	14	None	20	1 01
10	Mystic's Cape	15	BoE	21	1 28
N/A	Rugged Cape	15	BoA	21	1 51
11	Woolen Cape	16	None	22	1 42
17	Dark Leather Cloak	22	None	28	4 08
25	Hillman's Cloak	30	None	34	10 27

INFERIOR CLOTH CLOAKS

M LEV	ARMOR NAME	LEV	BIND	AC	VENDOR PURCHASE VALUE
1	Ragged Leather Cloak	3	None	4	2
1	Flimsy Chain Cloak	5	None	7	7
1	Frayed Cloak	5	None	7	4
1	Loose Chain Cloak	6	None	8	11
1	Patchwork Cloak	6	None	8	7
5	Worn Leather Cloak	10	None	14	36
7	Warped Leather Cloak	12	None	16	61
9	Calico Cloak	14	None	19	71
10	Worn Mail Cloak	15	None	20	1 33
11	Patched Leather Cloak	16	None	21	1 17
12	Laced Mail Cloak	17	None	22	1 69
13	Canvas Cloak	18	None	23	1 31
17	Rawhide Cloak	22	None	26	2 79
18	Linked Chain Cloak	23	None	27	3 96
19	Brocade Cloak	24	None	28	2 81
23	Tough Leather Cloak	28	None	31	5 82
24	Reinforced Chain Cloak	29	None	31	7 28
25	Cross-stitched Cloak	30	None	32	5 41
31	Interlaced Cloak	36	None	36	9 81
32	Double Mail Cloak	37	None	37	16 04
33	Hardened Leather Cloak	38	None	37	13 58
41	Thick Leather Cloak	46	None	45	26 59
42	Crochet Cloak	47	None	46	22 56
44	Overlinked Chain Cloak	49	None	48	40 90
47	Twill Cloak	52	None	51	32 58
51	Smooth Leather Cloak	56	None	55	48 64
52	Laminated Scale Cloak	57	None	56	62 84
57	Mesh Cloak	62	None	60	53 75
57	Strapped Cloak	62	None	60	68 44
63	Sterling Chain Cloak	68	None	66	1 06 87

CLOTH FOOT ARMOR

SUPERIOR CLOTH FOOT ARMOR

M LEV	ARMOR NAME	LEV	BIND	AC	VENDOR PURCHASE VALUE
20	Spidersilk Boots	25	BoE	48	9 79
24	Moccasins of the White Hare	29	BoE	52	14 31
27	Acidic Walkers	32	BoA	55	19 84
▸	**SPELL** Nature Resist +5				
33	Thoughtcast Boots	38	BoE	63	33 77
39	Furen's Boots	44	BoE	73	54 21
45	Mistwalker Boots	50	BoE	82	80 66
51	Mooncloth Boots	56	BoE	92	1 16 48
54	High Priestess Boots	59	BoA	97	1 43 17
▸	**SPELL** Shadow Resist +10				
54	Ogreseer Tower Boots	59	BoA	97	1 36 84
54	Wolfrunner Shoes	59	BoE	97	1 43 18
56	The Postmaster's Treads	61	BoA	100	1 64 25
58	Fire Striders	63	BoA	103	1 75 26
▸	**SPELL** Increase Fire Dam 17, Fire Resist +15				

GOOD CLOTH FOOT ARMOR

M LEV	ARMOR NAME	LEV	BIND	AC	VENDOR PURCHASE VALUE
10	Willow Boots	15	BoE	31	2 10
11	Aboriginal Footwraps	16	BoE	32	2 42
11	Soft-soled Linen Boots	16	BoE	32	2 37
12	Seer's Boots	17	BoE	34	2 80
13	Mystic's Slippers	18	BoE	35	3 24
13	Walking Boots	18	BoE	35	3 24
14	Buccaneer's Boots	19	BoE	36	3 68
14	Woolen Boots	19	BoE	36	3 59
15	Red Woolen Boots	20	BoE	38	4 16
15	Ritual Sandals	20	BoE	38	4 15
16	Bluegill Sandals	21	BoE	39	5 13
16	Foreman's Boots	21	BoE	39	4 69
16	Shimmering Boots	21	BoE	39	5 08
17	Pagan Shoes	22	BoE	40	5 70
18	Druidic Sandals	23	BoE	41	6 16
N/A	Kimbra Boots	23	BoA	41	6 15
N/A	Rat Stompers	23	BoA	41	6 34
18	Smoldering Boots	23	BoE	41	6 36
18	Sunfire Boots	23	BoE	41	6 58
N/A	Firewalker Boots	24	BoA	43	7 28
19	Sanguine Sandels	24	BoE	43	6 99
N/A	Wandering Boots	24	BoA	43	6 88

GOOD CLOTH FOOT ARMOR continued

M LEV	ARMOR NAME	LEV	BIND	AC	VENDOR PURCHASE VALUE		
20	Dark Runner Boots	25	BoE	44		8	12
20	Enchantress Slippers	25	BoE	44		8	23
N/A	Lightheel Boots	25	BoA	44		7	76
N/A	Nimbus Boots	25	BoA	44		7	74
21	Watcher's Boots	26	BoE	45		9	20
22	Silver-thread Boots	27	BoE	46		10	41
23	Boots of Darkness	28	BoE	47		11	25
▶	**SPELL** Increase Shadow Dam 4						
23	Sage's Boots	28	BoE	47		11	12
23	Spider Silk Slippers	28	BoE	47		11	20
24	Raincaller Boots	29	BoE	48		12	52
26	Satyr's Boots	31	BoE	50		14	65
26	Siren's Slippers	31	BoE	50		15	41
27	Thistlefur Sandals	32	BoE	50		16	73
28	Elder's Boots	33	BoE	51		18	64
29	Dryad's Footpads	34	BoE	52		20	09
29	Stormcloud Boots	34	BoE	52		19	70
30	Boots of the Enchanter	35	BoE	53		22	72
30	Conjurer's Shoes	35	BoE	53		21	36
30	Stonecloth Boots	35	BoE	53		22	75
N/A	Durtfeet Stompers	36	BoA	54		22	88
N/A	Everlast Boots	36	BoA	54		24	30
32	Geomancer's Boots	37	BoE	56		27	13
N/A	Junglewalker Sandals	37	BoA	56		27	49
32	Twilight Boots	37	BoE	56		25	36
33	Aurora Boots	38	BoE	57		27	28
33	Embersilk Boots	38	BoE	57		29	09
N/A	Kodo Rustler Boots	38	BoA	57		28	25
34	Silksand Boots	39	BoE	59		30	98
N/A	Wingborne Boots	39	BoA	59		31	88
N/A	Hellion Boots	40	BoA	60		34	64
N/A	Mantis Boots	40	BoA	60		31	81
35	Sorcerer Slippers	40	BoE	60		31	46
36	Darkmist Boots	41	BoE	62		36	91
36	Regal Boots	41	BoE	62		34	23
N/A	Darkspear Shoes	42	BoA	63		40	10
37	Lunar Slippers	42	BoE	63		38	72
N/A	Boots of the Maharishi	43	BoA	65		40	86
38	Mistscape Boots	43	BoE	65		39	59
39	Royal Boots	44	BoE	66		45	81
39	Windchaser Footpads	44	BoE	66		47	17
N/A	Encarmine Boots	45	BoA	68		49	83
N/A	Gnomish Rocket Boots	45	BoE	68		46	96
▶	**SPELL** Increase Run Speed for 30 Sec						
N/A	Goblin Rocket Boots	45	BoE	68		47	12
▶	**SPELL** Increase Run Speed for 30 Sec						
40	Gossamer Boots	45	BoE	68		49	62
41	Black Mageweave Boots	46	BoE	69		54	59
41	Bloodwoven Boots	46	BoE	69		50	56
42	Gaea's Slippers	47	BoE	71		56	69
42	Hibernal Boots	47	BoE	71		59	38
43	Shadoweave Boots	48	BoE	72		60	30
▶	**SPELL** Increase Shadow Dam 8						
43	Venomshroud Boots	48	BoE	72		61	92
44	Cindercloth Boots	49	BoE	73		67	65
▶	**SPELL** Increase Fire Dam 13						
N/A	Gnomish Inventor Boots	49	BoA	73		67	68
44	Illusionary Boots	49	BoE	73		64	03
45	Duskwoven Sandals	50	BoE	75		70	83
45	Necrotic Slippers	50	BoE	75		69	05
45	Stormcloth Boots	50	BoE	75		71	10
▶	**SPELL** Increase Nature Dam 9						
46	Arachnidian Footpads	51	BoE	76		77	25
47	High Arcane Boots	52	BoE	78		79	17
48	Highborne Footpads	53	BoE	79		88	01
N/A	Rancor Boots	53	BoA	79		87	08
49	Bonecaster's Boots	54	BoE	81		86	02
N/A	Hazecover Boots	54	BoA	81		89	63
49	Mystical Boots	54	BoE	81		86	32
N/A	Archaeologist's Quarry Boots	55	BoA	82		98	86
51	Fay Boots	56	BoE	84	1	02	95
51	Runecloth Boots	56	BoE	84		95	53

GOOD CLOTH FOOT ARMOR continued

M LEV	ARMOR NAME	LEV	BIND	AC	VENDOR PURCHASE VALUE		
52	Felcloth Boots	57	BoE	85	1	11	12
▶	**SPELL** Increase Fire Dam 10						
52	Zephyr Boots	57	BoE	85	1	05	14
53	Celestial Slippers	58	BoE	87	1	16	15
54	Demonskin Boots	59	BoE	88	1	14	01
54	Nova Boots	59	BoE	88	1	22	76
54	Omnicast Boots	59	BoA	88	1	17	94
▶	**SPELL** Increase spell Dam 11						
55	Elunarian Boots	60	BoE	89	1	25	73
56	Empyreal Boots	61	BoE	91	1	34	84
56	Fangdrip Runners	61	BoA	91	1	24	53
▶	**SPELL** Nature Resist +20						
56	Necropile Boots	61	BoA	91	1	35	42
57	Eternal Boots	62	BoE	92	1	40	66
58	Lich's Boots	63	BoE	94	1	47	07

STANDARD CLOTH FOOT ARMOR

M LEV	ARMOR NAME	LEV	BIND	AC	VENDOR PURCHASE VALUE		
N/A	Gamemaster's Slippers	1	BoA	2			1
N/A	Flax Boots	5	BoA	10			7
N/A	Snow Boots	5	BoA	10			7
N/A	Soft Fur-lined Shoes	5	BoA	10			7
N/A	Soft Wool Boots	5	BoA	10			7
1	Tattered Cloth Boots	5	None	10			7
1	Thin Cloth Shoes	5	None	10			7
N/A	Viny Wrappings	7	BoA	14			16
N/A	Dirt-trodden Boots	8	BoA	16			23
4	Bog Boots	9	None	18			32
4	Journeyman's Boots	9	None	18			32
4	Simple Linen Boots	9	None	18			32
5	Beaded Sandals	10	None	20			45
N/A	Farmer's Boots	10	None	20			45
5	Knitted Sandals	10	None	20			41
5	Web-covered Boots	10	None	20			44
5	Woven Boots	10	None	20			44
6	Ancestral Boots	11	None	22			57
6	Disciple's Boots	11	None	22			58
7	Jester's Shoes	12	None	24			67
N/A	Cavalier's Boots	13	BoA	25			89
8	Linen Boots	13	None	25			87
8	Native Sandals	13	None	25			84
9	Magister's Boots	14	None	27		1	08
N/A	Reconnaissance Boots	14	BoA	27		1	05
N/A	Sandcomber Boots	14	BoA	27		1	01
10	Runic Cloth Boots	15	BoE	29		1	29
12	Heavy Weave Shoes	17	None	32		1	70
17	Thick Cloth Shoes	22	None	38		3	42
22	Padded Boots	27	None	44		6	15
32	Russet Boots	37	None	53		15	38
45	Embroidered Boots	50	None	71		41	99

INFERIOR CLOTH FOOT ARMOR

M LEV	ARMOR NAME	LEV	BIND	AC	VENDOR PURCHASE VALUE		
1	Frayed Shoes	4	None	8			3
5	Patchwork Shoes	10	None	19			29
8	Calico Shoes	13	None	24			58
12	Canvas Shoes	17	None	30		1	13
18	Brocade Shoes	23	None	37		2	47
24	Cross-stitched Sandals	29	None	43		4	89
27	Interlaced Boots	32	None	45		6	48
41	Crochet Boots	46	None	62		20	18
50	Twill Boots	55	None	74		38	52
59	Mesh Boots	64	None	86		63	27

CLOTH HAND ARMOR

EPIC CLOTH HAND ARMOR

M LEV	ARMOR NAME	LEV	BIND	AC	VENDOR PURCHASE VALUE
57	Gloves of spell Mastery	62	BoE	101	1 40 84
▶	**SPELL** Increased Critical Spell				

SUPERIOR CLOTH HAND ARMOR

M LEV	ARMOR NAME	LEV	BIND	AC	VENDOR PURCHASE VALUE
15	Magefist Gloves	20	BoE	38	3 55
27	Hotshot Pilot's Gloves	32	BoE	50	13 08
29	Gloves of Old	34	BoE	52	15 65
40	Dreamweave Gloves	45	BoE	68	39 44
▶	**SPELL** Increase spell Dam 9 Random				
47	Atal'ai Gloves	52	BoA	78	63 82
▶	**SPELL** Increase spell Dam 5				
50	Gloves of the Atal'ai Prophet	55	BoA	82	76 29
52	Demonskin Gloves	57	BoA	85	87 97
54	Hands of the Exalted Herald	59	BoA	88	94 74
▶	**SPELL** Increase Healing 30				
55	Hands of Power	60	BoA	89	99 83
▶	**SPELL** Increase spell Dam 13				

GOOD CLOTH HAND ARMOR

M LEV	ARMOR NAME	LEV	BIND	AC	VENDOR PURCHASE VALUE
10	Adept's Gloves	15	BoE	28	1 39
N/A	Brewer's Gloves	15	BoA	28	1 39
10	Coppercloth Gloves	15	BoE	28	1 39
11	Aboriginal Gloves	16	BoE	29	1 63
N/A	Wayfaring Gloves	16	BoA	29	1 67
11	Willow Gloves	16	BoE	29	1 63
12	Heavy Woolen Gloves	17	BoE	31	1 80
N/A	Apothecary Gloves	18	BoA	32	2 14
N/A	Evergreen Gloves	18	BoA	32	2 11
13	Seer's Gloves	18	BoE	32	2 15
14	Mystic's Gloves	19	BoE	33	2 51
N/A	Beerstained Gloves	20	BoA	34	2 80
15	Buccaneer's Gloves	20	BoE	34	2 75
N/A	Riding Gloves	20	BoA	34	2 79
15	Ritual Gloves	20	BoE	34	2 92
17	Gnoll Casting Gloves	22	BoE	37	3 69
▶	**SPELL** Increase spell Dam 3				
17	Gold-flecked Gloves	22	BoA	37	3 64
17	Raven's Claws	22	BoE	37	3 70
17	Shimmering Gloves	22	BoE	37	3 93
18	Pagan Mitts	23	BoE	38	4 45
18	Serpent Gloves	23	BoA	38	4 18
19	Smoldering Gloves	24	BoE	39	4 76
19	Sunfire Gloves	24	BoE	39	4 97
20	Druidic Gloves	25	BoE	40	5 32
20	Phoenix Gloves	25	BoE	40	5 26
▶	**SPELL** Increase Fire Dam 5				
21	Enchantress Gloves	26	BoE	41	6 26
21	Gloves of Meditation	26	BoE	41	6 10
21	Sanguine Handwraps	26	BoE	41	6 02
23	Silver-thread Gloves	28	BoE	43	7 60
23	Watcher's Handwraps	28	BoE	43	7 75
24	Azure Silk Gloves	29	BoE	43	8 15
▶	**SPELL** Increase Frost Dam 6				
24	Hands of Darkness	29	BoE	43	8 24
▶	**SPELL** Increase Shadow Dam 5				
24	Sage's Gloves	29	BoE	43	8 24
25	Gloves of the Devout	30	BoE	44	9 14
▶	**SPELL** Increase Healing 14				
25	Raincaller Mitts	30	BoE	44	8 81
N/A	Jutebraid Gloves	31	BoA	45	9 65
26	Satyr's Handgrips	31	BoE	45	10 17
N/A	Shilly Mitts	31	BoA	45	10 09
26	Siren's Gloves	31	BoE	45	9 65
27	Elder's Gloves	32	BoE	46	10 98
N/A	Gloves of Kapelan	33	BoA	47	11 90
N/A	Insulated Sage Gloves	33	BoA	47	12 16

GOOD CLOTH HAND ARMOR

M LEV	ARMOR NAME	LEV	BIND	AC	VENDOR PURCHASE VALUE
28	Thistlefur Gloves	33	BoE	47	12 40
N/A	Zodiac Gloves	33	BoA	47	12 34
29	Dryad's Handwraps	34	BoE	47	13 25
29	Stormcloud Gloves	34	BoE	47	13 47
N/A	Gemmed Gloves	35	BoA	48	13 80
N/A	Pardoc Grips	35	BoA	48	13 79
30	Stonecloth Gloves	35	BoE	48	13 87
31	Conjurer's Gloves	36	BoE	49	15 84
32	Geomancer's Gloves	37	BoE	51	18 34
32	Twilight Gloves	37	BoE	51	16 84
33	Embersilk Mitts	38	BoE	52	19 04
34	Aurora Gloves	39	BoE	53	21 07
35	Engineering Gloves	40	BoE	55	21 36
35	Revelosh's Gloves	40	BoA	55	21 46
35	Silksand Gloves	40	BoE	55	22 62
35	Sorcerer Gloves	40	BoE	55	21 30
36	Darkmist Handguards	41	BoE	56	23 11
37	Crimson Silk Gloves	42	BoE	57	25 69
▶	**SPELL** Increase Fire Dam 8				
37	Regal Gloves	42	BoE	57	24 55
38	Black Mageweave Gloves	43	BoE	59	28 59
▶	**SPELL** Increase spell Dam 8				
38	Lunar Handwraps	43	BoE	59	28 19
38	Mistscape Gloves	43	BoE	59	27 95
39	Royal Gloves	44	BoE	60	30 87
39	Stormcloth Gloves	44	BoE	60	28 75
▶	**SPELL** Increase spell Dam 8				
39	Windchaser Handguards	44	BoE	60	28 77
40	Bloodwoven Mitts	45	BoE	61	31 56
40	Red Mageweave Gloves	45	BoE	61	32 75
▶	**SPELL** Increase spell Dam 5				
40	Shadoweave Gloves	45	BoE	61	33 34
▶	**SPELL** Increase Shadow Dam 10				
41	Gossamer Gloves	46	BoE	63	35 60
N/A	Skilled Handling Gloves	46	BoA	63	33 81
42	Gaea's Handwraps	47	BoE	64	38 20
42	Hibernal Gloves	47	BoE	64	36 22
44	Illusionary Gloves	49	BoE	67	43 17
44	Venomshroud Mitts	49	BoE	67	44 81
45	Necrotic Gloves	50	BoE	68	45 52
N/A	Quintis' Research Gloves	50	BoA	68	44 57
N/A	Wingcrest Gloves	50	BoA	68	48 26
46	Arachnidian Gloves	51	BoE	69	52 23
46	Duskwoven Gloves	51	BoE	69	47 58
47	High Arcane Gloves	52	BoE	71	53 36
47	Frostweave Gloves	53	BoE	72	54 71
▶	**SPELL** Increase Frost Dam 13				
48	Highborne Gloves	53	BoE	72	55 36
49	Brightcloth Gloves	54	BoE	73	60 66
▶	**SPELL** Frost Resist +12, Shadow Resist +11				
49	Cindercloth Gloves	54	BoE	73	59 55
▶	**SPELL** Increase Fire Dam 10				
49	Ghostweave Gloves	54	BoE	73	60 87
▶	**SPELL** Increased Mana Regen				
49	Mystical Gloves	54	BoE	73	56 89
49	Silkweb Gloves	54	BoA	73	58 86
50	Fay Gloves	55	BoE	75	65 67
50	Runecloth Gloves	55	BoE	75	66 17
▶	**SPELL** Increase spell Dam 6				
51	Bonecaster's Gloves	56	BoE	76	65 17
52	Zephyr Gloves	57	BoE	77	70 87
53	Celestial Handwraps	58	BoE	79	78 54
N/A	Freewind Gloves	59	BoA	80	75 30
54	Nova Gloves	59	BoE	80	82 71
55	Demonskin Handwraps	60	BoE	81	83 22
56	Empyreal Gloves	61	BoE	83	90 85
57	Darkbind Fingers	62	BoA	84	86 98
▶	**SPELL** Shadow Resist +20				
57	Darkshade Gloves	62	BoA	84	87 17
▶	**SPELL** Arcane Resist +15, Shadow Resist +10				
57	Elunarian Handgrips	62	BoE	84	93 42
58	Eternal Gloves	63	BoE	85	99 87
58	Lich's Gloves	63	BoE	85	99 46

STANDARD CLOTH HAND ARMOR

M LEV	ARMOR NAME	LEV	BIND	AC	VENDOR PURCHASE VALUE
N/A	Flax Gloves	5	BoA	9	5
N/A	Outfitter Gloves	5	BoA	9	4
N/A	Rabbit Handler Gloves	5	BoA	9	4
1	Tattered Cloth Gloves	5	None	9	5
1	Thin Cloth Gloves	5	None	9	4
N/A	Viny Gloves	5	BoA	9	5
N/A	Netted Gloves	8	BoA	14	16
N/A	Gardening Gloves	9	BoA	16	23
4	Journeyman's Gloves	9	None	16	21
5	Beaded Gloves	10	None	18	30
5	Heavy Linen Gloves	10	None	18	29
5	Knitted Gloves	10	None	18	27
5	Woven Gloves	10	None	18	30
6	Disciple's Gloves	11	None	20	37
6	Fingerless Gloves	11	None	20	35
7	Ancestral Gloves	12	None	21	48
N/A	Salma's Oven Mitts	12	BoA	21	47
N/A	Wooly Mittens	12	BoA	21	48
8	Jester's Gloves	13	None	23	56
8	Native Handwraps	13	None	23	60
9	Magister's Gloves	14	None	25	72
N/A	Welldrip Gloves	14	BoA	25	67

STANDARD CLOTH HAND ARMOR continued

M LEV	ARMOR NAME	LEV	BIND	AC	VENDOR PURCHASE VALUE
10	Runic Cloth Gloves	15	BoE	27	86
12	Heavy Weave Gloves	17	None	29	1 13
17	Thick Cloth Gloves	22	None	35	2 29
22	Padded Gloves	27	None	40	4 13
32	Russet Gloves	37	None	48	10 33
45	Embroidered Gloves	50	None	65	28 19

INFERIOR CLOTH HAND ARMOR

M LEV	ARMOR NAME	LEV	BIND	AC	VENDOR PURCHASE VALUE
1	Frayed Gloves	3	None	5	1
2	Patchwork Gloves	7	None	12	7
10	Calico Gloves	15	None	25	57
14	Canvas Gloves	19	None	30	1 01
20	Brocade Gloves	25	None	36	2 12
21	Cross-stitched Gloves	26	None	37	2 47
28	Interlaced Gloves	33	None	42	4 93
43	Crochet Gloves	48	None	59	16 30
53	Twill Gloves	58	None	71	30 92
58	Mesh Gloves	63	None	77	37 76

CLOTH HEAD ARMOR

EPIC CLOTH HEAD ARMOR

M LEV	ARMOR NAME	LEV	BIND	AC	VENDOR PURCHASE VALUE
49	Eye of Flame	55	BoE	117	1 50 73
▶	**SPELL** Increase Fire Dam 25, Fire Resist +15				
54	Circle of Flame	59	BoA	125	1 92 92
▶	**SPELL** Fire Resist +15, Channels 300 HP to MP on Use				
N/A	Cap of the Scarlet Savant	62	BoA	131	2 29 07
▶	**SPELL** Increase Dam and healing by spells + 18				

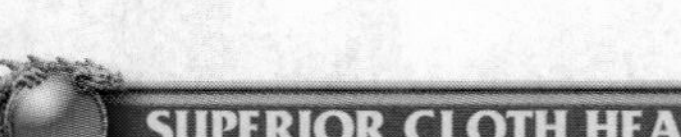

SUPERIOR CLOTH HEAD ARMOR

M LEV	ARMOR NAME	LEV	BIND	AC	VENDOR PURCHASE VALUE
27	Holy Shroud	32	BoE	65	19 82
▶	**SPELL** Increase Healing 30				
30	Embalmed Shroud	35	BoA	69	26 89
32	Electromagnetic Gigaflux Reactivator	37	BoA	73	31 72
▶	**SPELL** Deals 147-167 Nature dam/Shields User				
35	Corpseshroud	40	BoE	78	37 75
38	Papal Fez	43	BoE	84	48 85
▶	**SPELL** Increase Healing 20				
39	Miner's Hat of the Deep	44	BoE	86	52 36
39	Whitemane's Chapeau	44	BoA	86	53 56
42	Cassandra's Grace	47	BoE	92	68 79
▶	**SPELL** Increase Healing 30				
44	Bad Mojo Mask	49	BoA	95	78 58
▶	**SPELL** Increase Shadow Dam 8				
N/A	Green Lens	49	BoE	95	77 70
46	Soulcatcher Halo	51	BoE	99	86 64
N/A	Gemburst Circlet	54	BoA	105	1 06 34
50	Chief Architect's Monocle	55	BoA	107	1 11 91
55	Starfire Tiara	60	BoA	116	1 43 68
▶	**SPELL** Fire Resist +10				
56	The Postmaster's Band	61	BoA	118	1 63 67
▶	**SPELL** Malown's Rally				
57	Dreadmaster's Shroud	62	BoA	120	1 72 48
▶	**SPELL** Increase spell Dam 12				
57	Mooncloth Circlet	62	BoE	120	1 66 93
N/A	Crown of Caer Darrow	63	BoA	122	1 74 69
▶	**SPELL** Frost Resist +15				

GOOD CLOTH HEAD ARMOR

M LEV	ARMOR NAME	LEV	BIND	AC	VENDOR PURCHASE VALUE
N/A	Flying Tiger Goggles	20	BoE	45	4 08
N/A	Shadow Goggles	24	BoE	50	7 22
N/A	Dread Mage Hat	30	BoA	57	12 85
N/A	Green Tinted Goggles	30	BoE	57	14 10
26	Sage's Circlet	31	BoE	59	14 10
26	Watcher's Cap	31	BoE	59	15 32
27	Raincaller Cap	32	BoE	60	15 88
27	Siren's Circlet	32	BoE	60	15 57
38	Enchanter's Cowl	33	BoE	61	18 10
28	Satyr's Cap	33	BoE	61	17 86
29	Elder's Hat	34	BoE	62	18 75
29	Shadow Hood	34	BoE	62	19 99
▶	**SPELL** Increase Shadow Dam 4				
N/A	Bright-Eye Goggles	35	BoE	62	21 05
30	Stormcloud Cowl	35	BoE	62	22 15
30	Thistlefur Cap	35	BoE	62	22 58
31	Conjurer's Cap	36	BoE	64	23 85
31	Cowl of Necromancy	36	BoE	64	23 57
31	Dryad's Headband	36	BoE	64	23 16
32	Craftsman's Monocle	37	BoE	66	26 32
32	Nimar's Tribal Headdress	37	BoE	66	26 03
32	Silk Wizard Hat	37	BoE	66	27 20
33	Circlet of the Order	38	BoE	68	29 26
33	Stonecloth Circlet	38	BoE	68	27 09
33	Twilight Cowl	38	BoE	68	27 17
34	Augural Shroud	39	BoE	69	30 13
34	Aurora Cowl	39	BoE	69	31 49
35	First Mate Hat	40	BoE	71	34 49
35	Geomancer's Cap	40	BoE	71	34 42
35	Living Cowl	40	BoE	71	34 63
36	Embersilk Coronet	41	BoE	73	35 59
N/A	Fire Goggles	41	BoE	73	34 78
▶	**SPELL** Fire Resist +17				
N/A	Goblin Construction Helmet	41	BoA	73	35 17
▶	**SPELL** Fire Protection, Fire Resist +15				
36	Holy Diadem	41	BoE	73	35 54
36	Sorcerer Circlet	41	BoE	73	34 24
N/A	Gnomish Goggles	42	BoA	75	39 29
37	Regal Wizard Hat	42	BoE	75	36 68
37	Silksand Circlet	42	BoE	75	39 45
37	Thinking Cap	42	BoE	75	38 52
N/A	**SPELL**power Goggles Xtreme	43	BoE	76	40 88
▶	**SPELL** Increase spell Dam 11				
N/A	Catseye Ultra Goggles	44	BoE	78	43 98
▶	**SPELL** Increases Stealth Detect by 18				

GOOD CLOTH HEAD ARMOR continued

M LEV	ARMOR NAME	LEV	BIND	AC	VENDOR PURCHASE VALUE
39	Darkmist Wizard Hat	44	BoE	78	44 51
39	Mistscape Wizard Hat	44	BoE	78	45 44
40	Lunar Coronet	45	BoE	80	49 14
40	Royal Headband	45	BoE	80	50 91
41	Black Mageweave Headband	46	BoE	82	54 21
N/A	Deepdive Helmet	46	BoE	82	52 27
▶	**SPELL** Allows Underwater Breathing				
N/A	Rose Colored Goggles	46	BoE	82	51 69
41	Windchaser Coronet	46	BoE	82	52 70
N/A	Gnomish Mind Control Cap	47	BoE	83	55 20
▶	**SPELL** Attempts to Mind Control a Humanoid for 20 sec				
N/A	Goblin Rocket Helmet	47	BoE	83	58 34
▶	**SPELL** Use: Stuns Player, Mezs Enemy for 30 sec				
42	Gossamer Headpiece	47	BoE	83	57 47
43	Admiral's Hat	48	BoE	85	60 07
▶	**SPELL** Increases Stamina of Party Members by 10				
43	Bloodwoven Mask	48	BoE	85	59 87
43	Hibernal Cowl	48	BoE	85	59 80
43	Red Mageweave Headband	48	BoE	85	60 75
43	Stormcloth Headband	48	BoE	85	60 52
▶	**SPELL** Increase Nature Dam 8				
44	Gaea's Circlet	49	BoE	87	65 99
44	Shadoweave Mask	49	BoE	87	67 90
▶	**SPELL** Increase Shadow Dam 14				
45	Dreamweave Circlet	50	BoE	88	71 61
▶	**SPELL** Increase spell Dam 8				
45	Illusionary Coronet	50	BoE	88	69 54
N/A	Speedy Racer Goggles	50	BoA	88	67 45
45	Venomshroud Mask	50	BoE	88	71 66
46	Duskwoven Cowl	51	BoE	90	76 61
48	High Arcane Circle	53	BoE	94	86 39
48	Necrotic Crown	53	BoE	94	81 78
N/A	Spell power Goggles Xtreme Plus	54	BoE	95	90 02
▶	**SPELL** Increase spell Dam 14				
50	Arachnidian Circlet	55	BoE	97	98 57
N/A	Hakkar'i Shroud	55	BoA	97	45 38
50	Mystical Crown	55	BoE	97	90 10
52	Fay Wreath	57	BoE	100	1 09 91
52	Highborne Crown	57	BoE	100	1 01 25
53	Felcloth Hood	58	BoE	102	1 07 75
▶	**SPELL** Increase Shadow Dam 18				

GOOD CLOTH HEAD ARMOR continued

M LEV	ARMOR NAME	LEV	BIND	AC	VENDOR PURCHASE VALUE
N/A	Master Engineer's Goggles	58	BoE	102	1 17 39
53	Zephyr Cover	58	BoE	102	1 14 76
54	Bonecaster's Crown	59	BoE	104	1 20 64
54	Runecloth Headband	59	BoE	104	1 13 58
N/A	Bloodsail Admiral's Hat	60	BoE	106	1 28 95
▶	**SPELL** Summon Blood Parrot				
55	Nova Circlet	60	BoE	106	1 20 11
56	Celestial Crown	61	BoE	107	1 35 41
N/A	Crown of the Penitent	61	BoA	107	1 32 50
▶	**SPELL** Aura of Penitence				
N/A	Shawn's Super Special Swami Hat	61	BoE	107	1 35 84
56	Wizardweave Turban	61	BoE	107	1 27 68
▶	**SPELL** Arcane & Fire Resist +18				
57	Demonskin Circlet	62	BoE	109	1 37 12
57	Empyreal Diadem	62	BoE	109	1 42 58
58	Elunarian Diadem	63	BoE	111	1 46 61
58	Lich's Crown	63	BoE	111	1 48 66
59	Eternal Crown	64	BoE	113	1 56 74

STANDARD CLOTH HEAD ARMOR

M LEV	ARMOR NAME	LEV	BIND	AC	VENDOR PURCHASE VALUE
N/A	Gamemaster Hood	1	BoA	2	1
15	Lucky Fishing Hat	20	None	42	2 44
▶	**SPELL** Fishing Skill +5				
24	Azure Silk Hood	29	None	54	7 45
N/A	Hooded Cowl	30	BoA	55	8 01
27	Silk Headband	32	None	57	9 99
32	Russet Hat	37	None	63	15 84
38	White Bandit Mask	43	None	73	26 19
45	Embroidered Hat	50	None	84	43 88

INFERIOR CLOTH HEAD ARMOR

M LEV	ARMOR NAME	LEV	BIND	AC	VENDOR PURCHASE VALUE
28	Interlaced Cowl	33	None	54	6 82
38	Crochet Hat	43	None	69	16 03
51	Twill Cover	56	None	89	39 37

CLOTH LEG ARMOR

SUPERIOR CLOTH LEG ARMOR

M LEV	ARMOR NAME	LEV	BIND	AC	VENDOR PURCHASE VALUE
17	Darkweave Breeches	22	BoE	56	9 06
26	Leech Pants	31	BoA	69	22 98
30	Blighted Leggings	35	BoA	74	35 59
▶	**SPELL** Increase Shadow Dam 6				
30	Necromancer Leggings	35	BoE	74	36 20
▶	**SPELL** Increase Shadow Dam 6				
35	Stoneweaver Leggings	40	BoA	84	50 94
45	**SPELL**shock Leggings	50	BoE	105	1 09 62
▶	**SPELL** Increase spell Dam 12				
47	Dalewind Trousers	52	BoE	109	1 28 15
50	Kilt of the Atal'ai Prophet	55	BoA	115	1 52 02
N/A	Rainstrider Leggings	55	BoA	115	1 50 37
52	Haunting Specter Leggings	57	BoA	119	1 65 81
53	Mooncloth Leggings	58	BoE	121	1 81 13
55	Skyshroud Leggings	60	BoA	125	1 92 30
▶	**SPELL** Increase spell Dam 17				
56	Skullsmoke Pants	61	BoA	127	2 15 85
▶	**SPELL** Fire Resist +10, Shadow Resist +5				
56	The Postmaster's Trousers	61	BoA	127	2 17 46
56	Wolfshear Leggings	61	BoA	127	1 98 80
58	Spiritshroud Leggings	63	BoA	131	2 23 44

GOOD CLOTH LEG ARMOR

M LEV	ARMOR NAME	LEV	BIND	AC	VENDOR PURCHASE VALUE
5	Journeyman's Pants	10	BoE	26	94
6	Beaded Britches	11	BoE	29	1 19
6	Foreman Pants	11	BoE	29	1 19
7	Disciple's Pants	12	BoE	31	1 49
N/A	Rancher's Trousers	12	BoA	31	1 62
8	Ancestral Woollies	13	BoE	34	2 02
9	Handstitched Linen Britches	14	BoE	37	2 26
9	Jester's Britches	14	BoE	37	2 27
9	Native Pants	14	BoE	37	2 36
N/A	Leggings of the People's Militia	15	BoA	39	2 82
11	Magister's Pants	16	BoE	41	3 33
11	Runic Loincloth	16	BoE	41	3 33
12	Aboriginal Loincloth	17	BoE	43	3 78
N/A	Lucky Trousers	17	BoA	43	3 62
N/A	Ghastly Trousers	18	BoA	45	4 25
13	Silk-threaded Trousers	18	BoE	45	4 34
N/A	Stamped Trousers	18	BoA	45	4 44
13	Willow Pants	18	BoE	45	4 31
14	Mystic's Woolies	19	BoE	46	4 72
N/A	Scarab Trousers	20	BoA	48	5 41
15	Scarecrow Trousers	20	BoE	48	5 72
N/A	Sea Dog Britches	20	BoA	48	5 55
15	Seafarer's Pantaloons	20	BoE	48	5 57
15	Seer's Pants	20	BoE	48	5 65
16	Ritual Kilt	21	BoE	50	6 76
17	Buccaneer's Pants	22	BoE	51	7 38

GOOD CLOTH LEG ARMOR continued

M LEV	ARMOR NAME	LEV	BIND	AC	VENDOR PURCHASE VALUE		
17	Heavy Woolen Pants	22	BoE	51		7	43
14	Colorful Kilt	24	BoE	54		9	35
19	Shimmering Trousers	24	BoE	54		9	20
20	Pagan Britches	25	BoE	56		10	41
20	Phoenix Pants	25	BoE	56		10	76
▶	**SPELL** Increase Fire Dam 6						
21	Smoldering Pants	26	BoE	57		12	11
▶	**SPELL** Increase Fire Dam 8						
21	Sunfire Pants	26	BoE	57		12	75
22	Druidic Leggings	27	BoE	58		13	28
23	Azure Silk Pants	28	BoE	60		14	94
▶	**SPELL** Increase Frost Dam 6						
23	Enchantress Pants	28	BoE	60		15	28
23	Gaze Dreamer Pants	28	BoA	60		15	49
24	Humbert's Pants	29	BoE	61		17	03
24	Sanguine Trousers	29	BoE	61		16	15
25	Silver-thread Pants	30	BoE	62		18	21
25	Watcher's Leggings	30	BoE	62		17	10
N/A	Pious Legwraps	31	BoA	63		20	33
26	Raincaller Pants	31	BoE	63		20	06
N/A	Swampland Trousers	31	BoA	63		19	74
N/A	Sacred Burial Trousers	32	BoA	64		22	43
27	Sage's Pants	32	BoE	64		22	03
N/A	Night Watch Pantaloons	33	BoA	65		24	85
28	Satyr's Leggings	33	BoE	65		24	71
28	Siren's Pants	33	BoE	65		23	55
29	Elder's Pants	34	BoE	66		26	77
N/A	Artisan's Trousers	35	BoA	67		29	55
N/A	Dryleaf Pants	35	BoA	67		28	05
30	Thistlefur Pants	35	BoE	67		27	54
31	Dryad's Leggings	36	BoE	69		30	76
31	Stormcloud Trousers	36	BoE	69		31	67
32	Conjurer's Breeches	37	BoE	71		35	24
32	Stonecloth Britches	37	BoE	71		34	10
34	Geomancer's Trousers	39	BoE	75		39	01
34	Twilight Pants	39	BoE	75		38	99
35	Aurora Pants	40	BoE	77		45	84
35	Embersilk Leggings	40	BoE	77		44	76
36	Black Mageweave Leggings	41	BoE	78		48	32
37	Shadoweave Pants	42	BoE	80		52	76
▶	**SPELL** Increase Shadow Dam 13						
37	Silksand Legwraps	42	BoE	80		53	16
37	Sorcerer Pants	42	BoE	80		50	26
38	Darkmist Pants	43	BoE	82		54	13
38	Red Mageweave Pants	43	BoE	82		52	84
▶	**SPELL** Increase spell Dam 7						
39	Regal Leggings	44	BoE	84		62	84
39	Stormcloth Pants	44	BoE	84		57	29
▶	**SPELL** Increase Nature Dam 6						
40	Lunar Leggings	45	BoE	86		61	94
40	Mistscape Pants	45	BoE	86		67	83
41	Pale Leggings	46	BoE	88		69	97
41	Royal Trousers	46	BoE	88		72	28
41	Windchaser Woolies	46	BoE	88		67	64
42	Gossamer Pants	47	BoE	90		76	35
43	Bloodwoven Pants	48	BoE	92		80	13
44	Cindercloth Leggings	49	BoE	93		87	65
▶	**SPELL** Increase Fire Dam 11						
44	Hibernal Pants	49	BoE	93		84	36
45	Illusionary Pants	50	BoE	95		93	41
N/A	Dragonflight Leggings	51	BoA	97		95	89
46	Gaea's Leggings	51	BoE	97	1	04	48
47	Venomshroud Leggings	52	BoE	99	1	09	55
48	Duskwoven Pants	53	BoE	101	1	07	74
49	High Arcane Pants	54	BoE	103	1	20	80
49	Necrotic Britches	54	BoE	103	1	16	46
50	Arachnidian Legguards	55	BoE	105	1	32	36
50	Felcloth Pants	55	BoE	105	1	31	40
▶	**SPELL** Increase Shadow Dam 15						
50	Senior Designer's Pantaloons	55	BoA	105	1	25	27
N/A	Treetop Leggings	55	BoA	105	1	23	92
50	Wizardweave Leggings	55	BoE	105	1	24	41
▶	**SPELL** Arcane & Fire Resist +16						
51	Cindercloth Pants	56	BoE	106	1	34	80
▶	**SPELL** Increase Fire Dam 15						
51	Frostweave Pants	56	BoE	106	1	34	36
▶	**SPELL** Increase Frost Dam 15						
51	Highborne Pants	56	BoE	106	1	36	83

GOOD CLOTH LEG ARMOR continued

M LEV	ARMOR NAME	LEV	BIND	AC	VENDOR PURCHASE VALUE		
51	Mystical Leggings	56	BoE	106	1	28	33
52	Bonecaster's Sarong	57	BoE	108	1	43	49
52	Runecloth Pants	57	BoE	108	1	35	55
53	Brightcloth Pants	58	BoE	110	1	54	84
▶	**SPELL** Frost Resist +17, Shadow Resist +16						
53	Fay Trousers	58	BoE	110	1	57	56
53	Ghostweave Pants	58	BoE	110	1	43	74
▶	**SPELL** Restores 7 MP Every 5 sec						
54	Celestial Kilt	59	BoE	112	1	65	50
55	Demonskin Sarong	60	BoE	114	1	67	06
N/A	Whispersilk Leggings	60	BoA	114	1	68	85
▶	**SPELL** Increase spell Dam 8						
55	Zephyr Leggings	60	BoE	114	1	66	88
56	Necropile Leggings	61	BoA	116	1	81	21
56	Nova Leggings	61	BoE	116	1	66	88
57	Elunarian Sarong	62	BoE	118	1	87	51
58	Empyreal Leggings	63	BoE	119	2	01	03
58	Eternal Sarong	63	BoE	119	2	00	44
59	Lich's Leggings	64	BoE	121	2	09	59

STANDARD CLOTH LEG ARMOR

M LEV	ARMOR NAME	LEV	BIND	AC	VENDOR PURCHASE VALUE		
1	Webbed Pants	3	None	8			4
N/A	Dwarven Cloth Britches	5	BoA	13			10
N/A	Ripped Pants	5	BoA	13			10
N/A	Sedgeweed Britches	5	BoA	13			9
N/A	Tapered Pants	5	BoA	13			9
1	Tattered Cloth Pants	5	None	13			9
1	Thin Cloth Pants	5	None	13			10
2	Simple Linen Pants	7	None	18			23
3	Solliden's Trousers	8	None	20			31
N/A	Sturdy Cloth Trousers	8	BoA	20			32
5	Brown Linen Pants	10	None	25			60
5	Knitted Pants	10	None	25			55
N/A	Urchin's Pants	10	BoA	25			60
5	Woven Pants	10	None	25			59
N/A	Lace Pants	12	BoA	30			93
10	Simple Kilt	15	None	37		1	64
12	Heavy Weave Pants	17	None	41		2	25
17	Thick Cloth Pants	22	None	49		4	55
22	Padded Pants	27	None	55		8	29
32	Russet Pants	37	None	67		20	43
34	Crimson Silk Pantaloons	39	None	71		24	30
45	Embroidered Pants	50	None	91		55	78

INFERIOR CLOTH LEG ARMOR

M LEV	ARMOR NAME	LEV	BIND	AC	VENDOR PURCHASE VALUE		
1	Acolyte's Pants	1	None	3			1
1	Apprentice's Pants	1	None	3			1
1	Brawler's Pants	1	None	3			1
1	Footpad's Pants	1	None	3			1
1	Neophyte's Pants	1	None	3			1
1	Novice's Pants	1	None	3			1
1	Recruit's Pants	1	None	3			1
1	Recruit's Pants	1	None	3			1
1	Rugged Trapper's Pants	1	None	3			1
1	Squire's Pants	1	None	3			1
1	Squire's Pants	1	None	3			1
1	Thug Pants	1	None	3			1
1	Thug Pants	1	None	3			1
1	Trapper's Pants	1	None	3			1
1	Frayed Pants	2	None	5			1
3	Patchwork Pants	8	None	19			20
6	Calico Pants	11	None	26			51
15	Canvas Pants	20	None	43		2	17
16	Brocade Pants	21	None	45		2	57
22	Cross-stitched Pants	27	None	52		5	46
34	Interlaced Pants	39	None	67		16	92
40	Crochet Pants	45	None	77		25	98
54	Twill Pants	59	None	101		65	17
62	Mesh Pants	67	None	114		92	16

CLOTH SHOULDER ARMOR

SUPERIOR CLOTH SHOULDER ARMOR

M LEV	ARMOR NAME	LEV	BIND	AC	VENDOR PURCHASE VALUE		
20	Magician's Mantle	25	BoE	52		10	20
▶	**SPELL** Increase spell Dmg 2						
22	Slime-encrusted Pads	27	BoA	55		11	90
▶	**SPELL** Restores 3 HP Every 4 sec						
23	Feline Mantle	28	BoA	56		13	04
27	Batwing Mantle	32	BoA	60		20	41
N/A	Berylline Pads	36	BoA	65		27	65
33	Pads of the Venom Spider	38	BoE	69		34	53
42	Flameseer Mantle	47	BoA	85		65	98
▶	**SPELL** Increase Fire Dmg 8						
51	Elder Wizard's Mantle	56	BoE	100	1	23	55
▶	**SPELL** Increase spell Dmg 5						
52	Boreal Mantle	57	BoA	102	1	27	20
▶	**SPELL** Increase Frost Dmg 17, Frost Resist +10						
55	Soulstealer Mantle	60	BoA	107	1	43	15
56	Mooncloth Shoulders	61	BoE	109	1	58	40
56	Sunderseer Mantle	61	BoA	109	1	64	22

GOOD CLOTH SHOULDER ARMOR

M LEV	ARMOR NAME	LEV	BIND	AC	VENDOR PURCHASE VALUE		
17	Buccaneer's Mantle	22	BoE	44		5	51
21	Druidic Mantle	26	BoE	49		9	64
21	Sunfire Mantle	26	BoE	49		9	29
N/A	Talbar Mantle	26	BoA	49		9	33
N/A	Voodoo Mantle	26	BoA	49		8	92
22	Enchantress Mantle	27	BoE	50		10	38
N/A	Rose Mantle	27	BoA	50		10	03
22	Sanguine Mantle	27	BoE	50		9	97
N/A	Desert Shoulders	28	BoA	51		10	62
N/A	Ghostly Mantle	28	BoA	51		11	19
N/A	Silk Mantle of Gamn	28	BoA	51		11	53
23	Watcher's Mantle	28	BoE	51		11	67
24	Raincaller Mantle	29	BoE	52		11	79
24	Silver-thread Amice	29	BoE	52		12	64
25	Death Speaker Mantle	30	BoA	53		13	10
N/A	Fairywing Mantle	30	BoA	53		14	11
25	Sage's Mantle	30	BoE	53		13	71
N/A	Faerie Mantle	32	BoA	55		16	22
27	Satyr's Mantle	32	BoE	55		16	00
27	Siren's Amice	32	BoE	55		15	99
28	Elder's Mantle	33	BoE	56		18	18
N/A	Mantle of Woe	33	BoA	56		17	12
N/A	Moonlit Amice	33	BoA	56		17	10
N/A	Palm Frond Mantle	34	BoA	57		18	75
29	Thistlefur Mantle	34	BoE	57		20	60
30	Bloodmage Mantle	35	BoA	58		21	84
30	Dryad's Amice	35	BoE	58		21	94
N/A	Mantle of Honor	35	BoA	58		21	02
30	Stormcloud Mantle	35	BoE	58		22	23
31	Conjurer's Mantle	36	BoE	59		23	94
31	Green Silken Shoulders	36	BoE	59		23	23
31	Stonecloth Epaulets	36	BoE	59		22	98
33	Azure Shoulders	38	BoE	62		27	91
▶	**SPELL** Increase Frost Dmg 8						
33	Crimson Silk Shoulders	38	BoE	62		27	81
33	Geomancer's Spaulders	38	BoE	62		26	98
33	Mantle of Doan	38	BoA	62		29	38
33	Twilight Mantle	38	BoE	62		27	49
34	Aurora Mantle	39	BoE	64		30	36
34	Embersilk Mantle	39	BoE	64		30	97
35	Silksand Shoulder Pads	40	BoE	66		34	06
36	Sorcerer Mantle	41	BoE	67		34	64
37	Regal Mantle	42	BoE	69		37	10
38	Darkmist Mantle	43	BoE	71		40	75
38	Mistscape Mantle	43	BoE	71		42	08
39	Lunar Mantle	44	BoE	72		44	67
40	Royal Amice	45	BoE	74		50	37

GOOD CLOTH SHOULDER ARMOR continued

M LEV	ARMOR NAME	LEV	BIND	AC	VENDOR PURCHASE VALUE		
40	Windchaser Amice	45	BoE	74		46	79
41	Black Mageweave Shoulders	46	BoE	75		54	79
41	Gossamer Shoulderpads	46	BoE	75		49	93
42	Bloodwoven Pads	47	BoE	77		56	06
42	Red Mageweave Shoulders	47	BoE	77		53	91
42	Shadoweave Shoulders	47	BoE	77		59	38
▶	**SPELL** Increase Shadow Dmg 10						
43	Gaea's Amice	48	BoE	78		63	74
43	Hibernal Mantle	48	BoE	78		58	90
44	Illusionary Mantle	49	BoE	80		65	23
44	Stormcloth Shoulders	49	BoE	80		66	20
▶	**SPELL** Increase Shadow Dmg 13						
44	Venomshroud Mantle	49	BoE	80		67	45
45	Necrotic Mantle	50	BoE	82		67	25
46	Duskwoven Amice	51	BoE	83		71	65
47	Arachnidian Pauldrons	52	BoE	85		75	68
47	High Arcane Mantle	52	BoE	85		80	34
47	Kentic Amice	52	BoA	85		75	66
49	Highborne Pauldrons	54	BoE	88		88	36
50	Mystical Mantle	55	BoE	90		96	03
51	Bonecaster's Spaulders	56	BoE	91		96	28
N/A	Orchid Amice	56	BoA	91		95	74
52	Fay Amice	57	BoE	93	1	11	08
N/A	Azure Moon Amice	58	BoA	94	1	07	58
54	Celestial Pauldrons	59	BoE	96	1	12	71
N/A	Crystal Breeze Mantle	59	BoA	96	1	15	41
54	Zephyr Pads	59	BoE	96	1	18	76
55	Nova Mantle	60	BoE	98	1	28	45
65	Demonskin Epaulets	61	BoE	99	1	32	04
56	Necropile Mantle	61	BoA	99	1	36	39
56	Runecloth Shoulders	61	BoE	99	1	25	70
57	Deadwalker Mantle	62	BoA	101	1	42	18
57	Elunarian Spaulders	62	BoE	101	1	41	14
57	Empyreal Mantle	62	BoE	101	1	34	01
57	Felcloth Shoulders	62	BoE	101	1	35	09
▶	**SPELL** Increase Shadow Dmg 15						
58	Eternal Spaulders	63	BoE	102	1	50	86
58	Lich's Mantle	63	BoE	102	1	50	24

STANDARD CLOTH SHOULDER ARMOR

M LEV	ARMOR NAME	LEV	BIND	AC	VENDOR PURCHASE VALUE		
16	Aboriginal Shoulder Pads	21	None	40		2	86
16	Seer's Mantle	21	None	40		3	01
17	Double-stitched Woolen Shoulders	22	None	42		3	31
17	Mystic's Shoulder Pads	22	None	42		3	46
18	Ritual Amice	23	None	43		3	96
19	Pagan Mantle	24	None	44		4	33
19	Reinforced Woolen Shoulders	24	None	44		4	25
19	Shimmering Amice	24	None	44		4	11

INFERIOR

M LEV	ARMOR NAME	LEV	BIND	AC	VENDOR PURCHASE VALUE		
15	Canvas Shoulderpads	20	None	37		1	63
17	Brocade Shoulderpads	22	None	40		2	22
23	Cross-stitched Shoulderpads	28	None	46		4	64
30	Interlaced Shoulderpads	35	None	52		9	02
44	Crochet Shoulderpads	49	None	72		26	36
51	Twill Shoulderpads	56	None	82		41	57
64	Mesh Mantle	69	None	101		76	49

CLOTH WAIST ARMOR

SUPERIOR CLOTH WAIST ARMOR

M LEV	ARMOR NAME	LEV	BIND	AC	VENDOR PURCHASE VALUE		
18	Keller's Girdle	23	BoE	37		5	24
24	Belt of Arugal	29	BoA	43		10	00
32	Sutarn's Ring	37	BoE	50		21	47
36	Deathmage Sash	41	BoA	55		29	10
48	Dawnspire Cord	53	BoA	71		68	65
48	Serenity Belt	53	BoE	71		68	65
53	Sash of the Burning Heart	58	BoA	78		91	53
▸	**SPELL** Increase Fire Dmg 8						
54	Grimgore Noose	59	BoA	79		94	01
56	Clutch of Andros	61	BoA	82	1	09	50
56	Dustfeather Sash	61	BoA	82	1	02	51

GOOD CLOTH WAIST ARMOR

M LEV	ARMOR NAME	LEV	BIND	AC	VENDOR PURCHASE VALUE		
10	Aboriginal Sash	15	BoE	25		1	39
N/A	Captain Sander's Sash	15	BoA	25		1	45
N/A	Foreman Belt	15	BoA	25		1	34
N/A	Jackseed Belt	15	BoA	25		1	38
10	Rat Cloth Belt	15	BoE	25		1	40
11	Willow Belt	16	BoE	26		1	62
12	Mystic's Belt	17	BoE	28		1	88
13	Girdle of Nobility	18	BoE	29		2	09
13	Seer's Belt	18	BoE	29		2	21
14	Ritual Belt	19	BoE	30		2	42
15	Buccaneer's Cord	20	BoE	31		2	81
N/A	Grassland Sash	20	BoA	31		2	74
N/A	Relic Hunter Belt	20	BoA	31		2	84
15	Wise Man's Belt	20	BoE	31		2	78
16	Jewel-encrusted Sash	21	BoE	32		3	31
16	Pagan Belt	21	BoE	32		3	12
17	Druidic Sash	22	BoE	33		3	61
17	Lesser Belt of the Spire	22	BoE	33		3	90
17	Shimmering Sash	22	BoE	33		3	63
18	Tarantula Silk Sash	23	BoE	34		4	24
19	Brimstone Belt	24	BoE	35		4	69
19	Sunfire Belt	24	BoE	35		4	61
20	Ghamoo-ra's Bind	25	BoA	36		5	22
20	Sanguine Belt	25	BoE	36		5	24
21	Enchantress Sash	26	BoE	37		6	35
22	Nightwind Belt	27	BoE	37		6	84
22	Silver-thread Sash	27	BoE	37		6	81
22	Watcher's Cinch	27	BoE	37		6	47
23	Raincaller Cord	28	BoE	38		7	56
23	Wizard's Belt	28	BoE	38		7	49
24	Dreamer's Belt	29	BoE	39		8	30
24	Sage's Sash	29	BoE	39		8	12
25	Satyr's Cord	30	BoE	40		9	35
25	Siren's Sash	30	BoE	40		8	64
26	Beaded Raptor Collar	31	BoE	41		9	53
26	Elder's Sash	31	BoE	41		10	12
27	Thistlefur Belt	32	BoE	41		10	42
28	Dryad's Sash	33	BoE	42		11	96
28	Stormcloud Sash	33	BoE	42		12	34
29	Conjurer's Cinch	34	BoE	43		13	68
29	Stonecloth Belt	34	BoE	43		12	76
30	Azure Silk Belt	35	BoE	43		14	88
▸	**SPELL** 15% Increased Swim Speed						
30	Crimson Silk Belt	35	BoE	43		15	03
31	Geomancer's Cord	36	BoE	44		16	38
N/A	Lilac Sash	36	BoA	44		15	60
31	Spider Belt	36	BoE	44		15	24
▸	**SPELL** Use: Removes Root/Makes You Immune for 5 sec						
31	Twilight Belt	36	BoE	44		15	60
32	Aurora Sash	37	BoE	46		16	97
32	Embersilk Cord	37	BoE	46		17	89
34	Earthen Silk Belt	39	BoE	48		20	17
34	Silksand Girdle	39	BoE	48		21	25
34	Sorcerer Sash	39	BoE	48		21	39
35	Monogrammed Sash	40	BoA	49			0
35	Regal Sash	40	BoE	49		22	03
35	Star Belt	40	BoE	49		21	20
▸	**SPELL** Increase SPELL Dmg 6						
36	Darkmist Girdle	41	BoE	50		23	46
N/A	Razzeric's Customized Seatbelt	41	BoA	50		23	88
N/A	Teacher's Sash	41	BoA	50		23	27
36	Lunar Belt	42	BoE	52		26	28
37	Mistscape Sash	42	BoE	52		26	16

GOOD CLOTH WAIST ARMOR

M LEV	ARMOR NAME	LEV	BIND	AC	VENDOR PURCHASE VALUE		
38	Windchaser Cinch	43	BoE	53		27	78
39	Royal Sash	44	BoE	54		30	43
N/A	Scorching Sash	44	BoA	54		31	19
▸	**SPELL** Increase Fire Dmg 8						
40	Bloodwoven Cord	45	BoE	55		31	09
N/A	Swashbuckler Sash	45	BoA	55		31	54
41	Gossamer Belt	46	BoE	56		33	67
42	Gaea's Belt	47	BoE	58		35	98
42	Hibernal Sash	47	BoE	58		36	77
N/A	Shadowy Belt	47	BoA	58		36	08
43	Illusionary Sash	48	BoE	59		41	24
43	Venomshroud Waistband	48	BoE	59		42	48
44	Duskwoven Sash	49	BoE	60		42	20
45	Necrotic Waistband	50	BoE	61		46	20
46	Arachnidian Girdle	51	BoE	62		51	31
46	High Arcane Sash	51	BoE	62		51	07
46	Runecloth Belt	51	BoE	62		51	12
47	Mystical Belt	52	BoE	64		51	41
48	Ghostweave Belt	53	BoE	65		57	63
▸	**SPELL** Restores 7 MP Every 5 sec						
48	Highborne Cord	53	BoE	65		55	98
49	Ban'thok Sash	54	BoA	66		56	81
49	Fay Sash	54	BoE	66		56	87
50	Bonecaster's Waistband	55	BoE	67		61	94
51	Celestial Belt	56	BoE	68		68	66
51	Zephyr Sash	56	BoE	68		67	84
N/A	Brantwood Sash	58	BoA	71		71	72
53	Demonskin Belt	58	BoE	71		76	59
53	Nova Belt	58	BoE	71		71	80
N/A	Turquoise Sash	58	BoA	71		71	72
N/A	Valconian Sash	58	BoA	71		73	48
55	Elunarian Belt	60	BoE	73		85	96
55	Empyreal Sash	60	BoE	73		81	64
56	Eternal Cord	61	BoE	74		85	46
57	Lich's Sash	62	BoE	76		89	34

STANDARD CLOTH WAIST ARMOR

M LEV	ARMOR NAME	LEV	BIND	AC	VENDOR PURCHASE VALUE		
N/A	Flax Belt	5	BoA	8			4
N/A	Soft Wool Belt	5	BoA	8			5
1	Tattered Cloth Belt	5	None	8			4
1	Thin Cloth Belt	5	None	8			4
4	Beaded Cord	9	None	15			21
4	Bonecaster Sash	9	None	15			22
4	Journeyman's Belt	9	None	15			23
4	Linen Belt	9	None	15			22
N/A	Red Linen Sash	9	BoA	15			21
5	Ancestral Belt	10	None	16			28
N/A	Dirtwood Belt	10	BoA	16			27
5	Disciple's Sash	10	None	16			28
5	Knitted Belt	10	None	16			29
5	Woven Belt	10	None	16			29
N/A	Apprentice Sash	12	BoA	19			44
7	Jester's Cord	12	None	19			49
7	Native Sash	12	None	19			47
8	Magister's Belt	13	None	21			61
9	Runic Cloth Belt	14	BoE	22			67
12	Heavy Weave Belt	17	None	26		1	15
17	Thick Cloth Belt	22	None	31		2	16
22	Padded Belt	27	None	36		4	19
32	Russet Belt	37	None	43		10	95
45	Embroidered Belt	50	None	58		28	62

INFERIOR CLOTH WAIST ARMOR

M LEV	ARMOR NAME	LEV	BIND	AC	VENDOR PURCHASE VALUE		
1	Frayed Belt	3	None	5			1
3	Patchwork Belt	8	None	12			10
9	Calico Belt	14	None	21			45
13	Canvas Belt	18	None	26			86
16	Brocade Belt	21	None	29		1	32
25	Cross-stitched Belt	30	None	36		3	65
29	Interlaced Belt	34	None	38		5	21
37	Crochet Belt	42	None	47		9	85
48	Twill Belt	53	None	58		22	77
63	Mesh Belt	68	None	74		51	09

XII

CLOTH WRIST ARMOR

SUPERIOR CLOTH WRIST ARMOR

M LEV	ARMOR NAME	LEV	BIND	AC	VENDOR PURCHASE VALUE		
17	Mindthrust Bracers	22	BoE	28		4	64
26	Glowing Magical Bracelets	31	BoE	35		12	16
41	Forgotten Wraps	46	BoE	48		41	33
49	Aristocratic Cuffs	54	BoE	57		74	63
N/A	Manacle Cuffs	55	BoA	58		79	39
52	Flameweave Cuffs	57	BoA	60		86	06
▶	**SPELL** Fire Resist +10						
52	Tearfall Bracers	57	BoA	60		81	19
54	Funeral Cuffs	59	BoA	62		91	91
▶	**SPELL** Shadow Resist +10						
N/A	Wyrmthalak's Shackles	60	BoA	63		95	05
57	Magiskull Cuffs	62	BoE	65	1	12	91

GOOD CLOTH WRIST ARMOR

M LEV	ARMOR NAME	LEV	BIND	AC	VENDOR PURCHASE VALUE		
10	Willow Bracers	15	BoE	20		1	47
12	Mystic's Bracelets	17	BoE	21		1	89
12	Seer's Cuffs	17	BoE	21		1	89
13	Crystalline Cuffs	18	BoA	22		2	08
N/A	Featherbead Bracers	18	BoA	22		2	05
13	Ritual Bands	18	BoE	22		2	19
N/A	Timberland Armguards	18	BoA	22		2	13
14	Buccaneer's Bracers	19	BoE	23		2	38
14	Pagan Bands	19	BoE	23		2	51
15	Shimmering Bracers	20	BoE	24		2	95
16	Druidic Bracers	21	BoE	25		3	17
18	Sunfire Bracers	23	BoE	26		4	33
20	Enchantress Bracelets	25	BoE	28		5	50
20	Sanguine Cuffs	25	BoE	28		5	28
21	Watcher's Cuffs	26	BoE	28		6	31
22	Silver-thread Cuffs	27	BoE	29		6	81
23	Fingerbone Bracers	28	BoE	30		7	68
23	Raincaller Cuffs	28	BoE	30		7	17
23	Sage's Bracers	28	BoE	30		7	44
24	Satyr's Bands	29	BoE	30		8	37
25	Siren's Bracelets	30	BoE	31		8	71
25	Thistlefur Bands	30	BoE	31		9	25
26	Elder's Bracers	31	BoE	32		10	31
27	Dryad's Bracelets	32	BoE	32		10	46
28	Frost Bracers	33	BoE	33		11	97
▶	**SPELL** Frost Resist +7						
28	Spidertank Oilrag	33	BoA	33		11	54
28	Stormcloud Wristbands	33	BoE	33		11	98
29	Stonecloth Bindings	34	BoE	33		12	85
30	Conjurer's Bracers	35	BoE	34		14	29
30	Geomancer's Bracers	35	BoE	34		15	10
N/A	Gallan Cuffs	36	BoA	35		16	65
31	Twilight Cuffs	36	BoE	35		15	54
N/A	Darkspear Cuffs	37	BoA	35		17	94
32	Embersilk Bracelets	37	BoE	35		17	31
33	Aurora Bracers	38	BoE	36		19	58
33	Silksand Bracers	38	BoE	36		19	19
N/A	Arcane Runed Bracers	39	BoA	37		19	86
N/A	Condor Bracers	39	BoA	37		19	47
34	Sorcerer Bracelets	39	BoE	37		19	64
35	Darkmist Bands	40	BoE	38		22	94
N/A	Radiant Silver Bracers	40	BoA	38		22	02
36	Lunar Bindings	41	BoE	39		23	72
36	Regal Cuffs	41	BoE	39		23	71
N/A	Enchanted Stonecloth Bracers	42	BoA	40		25	87
37	Mistscape Bracers	42	BoE	40		26	83
38	Royal Bands	43	BoE	41		28	48
38	Windchaser Cuffs	43	BoE	41		26	44
39	Bloodwoven Bracers	44	BoE	42		29	00
40	Gossamer Bracers	45	BoE	43		31	06
N/A	Shadowy Bracers	45	BoA	43		30	82
▶	**SPELL** Increase Shadow Dmg 3						
N/A	Bloodband Bracers	46	BoA	44		35	63
41	Gaea's Cuffs	46	BoE	44		34	86
N/A	Firwillow Wristbands	47	BoA	45		36	66
42	Hibernal Bracers	47	BoE	45		35	94
42	Venomshroud Armguards	47	BoE	45		38	36
43	Illusionary Bands	48	BoE	46		40	04
44	Necrotic Bracers	49	BoE	47		42	06
45	Arachnidian Bracelets	50	BoE	48		48	30
45	Duskwoven Bracers	50	BoE	48		47	39
N/A	Scorched Bands	50	BoA	48		45	46
46	High Arcane Bracers	51	BoE	49		49	97
47	Highborne Bracelets	52	BoE	50		55	55
48	Bonecaster's Bindings	53	BoE	50		54	51
48	Mystical Bracers	53	BoE	50		57	18
N/A	Breezecloud Bracers	54	BoA	51		57	76
49	Fay Cuffs	54	BoE	51		61	30
50	Celestial Bindings	55	BoE	52		65	24
N/A	Shizzle's Nozzle Wiper	55	BoA	52		63	34
51	Zephyr Bands	56	BoE	53		66	37
52	Demonskin Bracelets	57	BoE	54		68	55
52	Incendic Bracers	57	BoA	54		67	66
▶	**SPELL** Fire Resist +14						
53	Elunarian Cuffs	58	BoE	55		75	75
53	Nova Bracers	58	BoE	55		78	50
55	Empyreal Bracers	60	BoE	57		85	30
56	Eternal Bindings	61	BoE	58		89	62
56	Necropile Cuffs	61	BoA	58		89	65
57	Lich's Bracers	62	BoE	59		93	71

STANDARD CLOTH WRIST ARMOR

M LEV	ARMOR NAME	LEV	BIND	AC	VENDOR PURCHASE VALUE		
N/A	Flax Bracers	5	BoA	6			4
N/A	Stemleaf Bracers	5	BoA	6			5
1	Tattered Cloth Bracers	5	None	6			4
1	Thin Cloth Bracers	5	None	6			4
3	Beaded Cuffs	8	None	10			16
3	Ghostly Bracers	8	None	10			15
3	Journeyman's Bracers	8	None	10			15
4	Ancestral Bracers	9	None	11			22
5	Disciple's Bracers	10	None	13			29
N/A	Elastic Wristguards	10	BoA	13			29
N/A	Heavy Cord Bracers	10	BoA	13			28
N/A	Ivy-weave Bracers	10	BoA	13			29
5	Knitted Bracers	10	None	13			29
5	Silver-lined Bracers	10	None	13			28
5	Woven Bracers	10	None	13			29
N/A	Cord Bracers	11	BoA	14			35
6	Native Bands	11	None	14			36
7	Green Linen Bracers	12	None	15			45
7	Jester's Bands	12	None	15			44
N/A	Quilted Bracers	12	BoA	15			46
7	Runic Cloth Bracers	12	BoE	15			47
9	Aboriginal Bands	14	None	17			70
N/A	Bracers of the People's Militia	14	BoA	17			72
9	Magister's Bracers	14	None	17			71
12	Heavy Weave Bracers	17	None	20		1	15
17	Thick Cloth Bracers	22	None	24		2	17
22	Padded Bracers	27	None	28		4	20
32	Russet Bracers	37	None	34		10	99
45	Embroidered Bracers	50	None	45		28	73

INFERIOR CLOTH WRIST ARMOR

M LEV	ARMOR NAME	LEV	BIND	AC	VENDOR PURCHASE VALUE		
1	Frayed Bracers	5	None	6			3
4	Patchwork Bracers	9	None	11			14
7	Calico Bracers	12	None	14			30
14	Canvas Bracers	19	None	21			99
17	Brocade Bracers	22	None	23		1	52
23	Cross-stitched Bracers	28	None	27		3	03
33	Interlaced Bracers	38	None	33		7	74
39	Crochet Bracers	44	None	38		11	89
49	Twill Bracers	54	None	46		24	31
60	Mesh Bracers	65	None	55		41	33

LEATHER CHEST ARMOR

EPIC LEATHER CHEST ARMOR

M LEV	ARMOR NAME	LEV	BIND	AC	VENDOR PURCHASE VALUE		
N/A	Breastplate of Bloodthirst	62	BoA	286	3	51	92
▶	**SPELL** Adds 2% Crit and 1% Dodge						

SUPERIOR LEATHER CHEST ARMOR

M LEV	ARMOR NAME	LEV	BIND	AC	VENDOR PURCHASE VALUE		
17	Starsight Tunic	22	BoE	116		11	37
19	Blackened Defias Armor	24	BoA	126		14	67
N/A	Tunic of Westfall	24	BoA	126		14	12
20	Gloomshroud Armor	25	BoE	130		15	53
30	Spirewind Fetter	35	BoE	154		41	61
31	Wolffear Tunic	36	BoE	158		49	68
34	Quilward Harness	39	BoE	171		61	91
44	Jinxed Hoodoo Skin	49	BoA	211	1	32	41
45	Feathered Breastplate	50	BoE	214	1	44	78
46	Cow King's Hide	51	BoE	218	1	51	67
▶	**SPELL** Arcane, Fire, Frost, Nature & Shadow Resist +10						
48	Flamestrider Robes	53	BoA	227	1	66	59
▶	**SPELL** Fire Resist +10						
50	Warbear Harness	55	BoE	235	1	97	17
52	Stormshroud Armor	57	BoE	243	2	09	66
▶	**SPELL** Adds 2% Crit						
53	Ironfeather Breastplate	58	BoE	247	2	36	50
53	Songbird Blouse	58	BoA	247	2	19	72
55	Living Breastplate	60	BoE	254	2	47	76
▶	**SPELL** Increase Healing 24, Nature Resist +10						
56	Cadaverous Armor	61	BoA	258	2	50	48
▶	**SPELL** Attack Power 60						
56	Nightbrace Tunic	61	BoA	258	2	50	48
▶	**SPELL** Attack Power 50, Fire & Shadow Resist +10						
57	Tombstone Breastplate	62	BoA	262	2	68	08
▶	**SPELL** Adds 2% Crit						
58	Dragonstalker Tunic	63	BoA	266	3	01	73
▶	**SPELL** Increase spell Dmg 9						

GOOD LEATHER CHEST ARMOR

M LEV	ARMOR NAME	LEV	BIND	AC	VENDOR PURCHASE VALUE		
5	Brood Mother Carapace	10	BoE	61		1	19
5	Sleek Feathered Tunic	10	BoE	61		1	19
6	Burnt Leather Vest	11	BoE	66		1	55
6	Primal Wraps	11	BoE	66		1	49
7	Embossed Leather Vest	12	BoE	72		1	92
N/A	Soft Leather Tunic	12	BoA	72		2	01
N/A	Footman Tunic	13	BoA	77		2	43
8	Hard Crawler Carapace	13	BoE	77		2	52
8	Pioneer Tunic	13	BoE	77		2	34
8	Riverpaw Leather Vest	13	BoE	77		2	49
8	Tribal Vest	13	BoE	77		2	50
10	Gnoll War Harness	15	BoE	87		3	47
10	Gypsy Tunic	15	BoE	87		3	63
N/A	Spore-covered Tunic	15	BoA	87		3	68
11	Grizzly Jerkin	16	BoE	93		4	14
12	Fine Leather Tunic	17	BoE	98		4	61
12	Hunting Tunic	17	BoE	98		4	84
13	Ceremonial Leather Harness	18	BoE	103		5	19
13	Moonglow Vest	18	BoE	103		5	45
14	Bard's Tunic	19	BoE	109		6	01
14	Murloc Scale Breastplate	19	BoE	109		6	01
15	Dark Leather Tunic	20	BoE	96		6	89
15	Hillman's Leather Vest	20	BoE	96		7	23
15	Lupine Vest	20	BoE	96		6	78
16	Inscribed Leather Breastplate	21	BoE	101		8	22
N/A	Camouflaged Tunic	22	BoA	105		9	53
17	Feral Tunic	22	BoE	105		8	97
17	Loch Croc Hide Vest	22	BoE	105		9	29
18	Armor of the Fang	23	BoA	110		10	10
18	Bandit Jerkin	23	BoE	110		11	13
18	Prospector's Chestpiece	23	BoE	110		10	14
N/A	Barkshell Tunic	25	BoA	118		13	55

GOOD LEATHER CHEST ARMOR continued

M LEV	ARMOR NAME	LEV	BIND	AC	VENDOR PURCHASE VALUE		
N/A	Bone-studded Leather	25	BoA	118		13	35
N/A	Dry Moss Tunic	25	BoA	118		13	60
20	Scouting Tunic	25	BoE	118		14	16
21	Forest Leather Chestpiece	26	BoE	123		15	26
21	Moonstalker's Gown	26	BoE	123		14	63
N/A	Panther Armor	27	BoA	128		16	72
23	Bristlebark Blouse	28	BoE	132		17	70
N/A	Grizzly Tunic	28	BoA	132		19	37
23	Pirate's Rag	28	BoE	132		18	55
N/A	Brawnhide Armor	29	BoA	137		19	47
N/A	Raptorbane Armor	29	BoA	137		20	23
▶	**SPELL** Adds 30 Attack Power Vs. Beasts						
24	Wrangler's Wraps	29	BoE	137		19	47
25	Dervish Tunic	30	BoE	121		23	34
N/A	Ninja Armor	30	BoA	121		22	60
N/A	Ribbed Breastplate	30	BoA	121		22	09
N/A	Snapbrook Armor	30	BoA	121		23	51
26	Green Leather Armor	31	BoE	125		23	66
26	Kodo Hide Chestguard	31	BoE	125		23	56
27	Emblazoned Chestpiece	32	BoE	129		28	14
27	Pathfinder Vest	32	BoE	129		25	92
28	Cenarion Chestguard	33	BoE	132		28	51
28	Monk's Vest	33	BoE	132		30	53
28	Raptor Hide Harness	33	BoE	132		30	96
29	Cutthroat's Vest	34	BoE	136		31	36
29	Thick Murloc Armor	34	BoE	136		32	11
30	Dusky Leather Armor	35	BoE	140		37	60
30	Green Whelp Armor	35	BoE	140		37	73
▶	**SPELL** 5% Chance to Sleep Attackers (30 sec)						
30	Guardian Armor	35	BoE	140		34	77
30	Infiltrator Armor	35	BoE	140		36	66
31	Headhunter's Armor	36	BoE	144		37	95
31	Insignia Chestguard	36	BoE	144		40	32
32	Ghostwalker Rags	37	BoE	148		41	74
33	Archer's Jerkin	38	BoE	152		49	35
35	Hawkeye's Tunic	40	BoE	158		52	59
35	Sentinel Breastplate	40	BoE	158		54	25
36	Glyphed Breastplate	41	BoE	162		60	56
36	Nightscape Tunic	41	BoE	162		59	71
36	Witch Doctor's Silk Robes	41	BoE	162		56	79
37	Nocturnal Tunic	42	BoE	166		61	34
38	Big Voodoo Robe	43	BoE	170		72	75
38	Elven Armor	43	BoE	170		70	71
N/A	Raptor Hunter Tunic	43	BoA	170		72	71
39	Warden's Wraps	44	BoE	173		71	54
40	Ranger Tunic	45	BoE	177		81	24
40	Wild Leather Vest	45	BoE	177		80	02
41	Imperial Leather Breastplate	46	BoE	181		90	98
41	Wolf Rider's Padded Armor	46	BoE	181		83	45
42	Assassin's Tunic	47	BoE	185		90	13
N/A	Surveyor's Tunic	48	BoA	188	1	02	38
43	Tracker's Tunic	48	BoE	188	1	02	76
44	Scorpashi Breastplate	49	BoE	192	1	04	15
45	Cabalist Chestpiece	50	BoE	195	1	12	84
46	Heraldic Breastplate	51	BoE	199	1	27	25
46	Rageclaw Chestguard	51	BoE	199	1	19	24
47	Vampiric Armor	52	BoE	202	1	26	40
48	Chieftain's Breastplate	53	BoE	206	1	34	18
49	Keeper's Armor	54	BoE	210	1	42	02
N/A	Hakkar'i Breastplate	55	BoA	213	1	50	71
50	Mixologist's Tunic	55	BoA	213	1	65	38
50	Righteous Armor	55	BoE	213	1	54	82
51	Jadefire Chestguard	56	BoE	217	1	59	57
N/A	Plainstalker Tunic	56	BoA	217	1	62	87
51	Serpentskin Armor	56	BoE	217	1	73	96
N/A	Blazewind Breastplate	57	BoA	221	1	69	38
52	Praetorian Padded Armor	57	BoE	221	1	69	15
52	Volcanic Breastplate	57	BoE	221	1	72	75
▶	**SPELL** Increased Armor 120, Fire Resist +20						
53	Chimeric Vest	58	BoE	224	1	84	49
▶	**SPELL** Arcane Resist +16, Nature Resist +17						
53	Infernal Breastplate	58	BoE	224	1	83	70
N/A	Fernpulse Jerkin	59	BoA	228	1	88	26
54	Pridelord Gown	59	BoE	228	1	88	26

GOOD LEATHER CHEST ARMOR continued

M LEV	ARMOR NAME	LEV	BIND	AC	VENDOR PURCHASE VALUE		
N/A	Traphook Jerkin	59	BoA	228	1	93	02
55	Angelic Armor	60	BoE	231	1	99	42
N/A	Brindlethorn Tunic	60	BoA	231	2	08	79
▶	SPELL Attack Power 20						
56	Spiritwalker Jerkin	61	BoE	234	2	08	61
56	Stormhide Armor	61	BoE	234	2	07	56
56	Wicked Leather Armor	61	BoE	234	2	27	32
57	Frostsaber Tunic	62	BoE	238	2	18	35
▶	SPELL Frost & Shadow Resist +18						
57	Nether Runed Chestpiece	62	BoE	238	2	17	94
57	Runic Leather Armor	62	BoE	238	2	20	02
58	Nightmare Tunic	63	BoE	242	2	32	63
59	Arch Druid's Chestpiece	64	BoE	245	2	40	28
59	Phantasmal Tunic	64	BoE	245	2	54	56
60	Hellfire Tunic	65	BoE	249	2	67	29
60	Seraphim Chestguard	65	BoE	249	2	52	29

INFERIOR LEATHER CHEST ARMOR

M LEV	ARMOR NAME	LEV	BIND	AC	VENDOR PURCHASE VALUE		
1	Ragged Leather Vest	5	None	28			8
4	Worn Leather Vest	9	None	50			37
6	Warped Leather Vest	11	None	60			59
15	Patched Leather Jerkin	20	None	86		2	77
16	Rawhide Tunic	21	None	91		3	37
22	Tough Leather Armor	27	None	115		6	48
28	Hardened Leather Tunic	33	None	119		11	62
40	Thick Leather Tunic	45	None	159		33	31
52	Smooth Leather Armor	57	None	199		69	78
59	Strapped Armor	64	None	221	1	02	09

STANDARD LEATHER CHEST ARMOR

M LEV	ARMOR NAME	LEV	BIND	AC	VENDOR PURCHASE VALUE		
1	Frostmane Leather Vest	4	None	24			8
1	Cracked Leather Vest	5	None	30			12
1	Dirty Leather Vest	5	None	30			12
N/A	Layered Tunic	5	BoA	30			12
N/A	Nomadic Vest	5	BoA	30			13
N/A	Scavenger Tunic	5	BoA	30			12
N/A	Woodland Tunic	5	BoA	30			13
3	Handstitched Leather Vest	8	None	47			40
N/A	Light Scorpid Armor	9	BoA	53			58
4	Lumberjack Jerkin	9	None	53			54
5	Battered Leather Harness	10	None	58			75
5	Rough Leather Vest	10	None	58			71
N/A	Bound Harness	11	BoA	63			90
N/A	Tiller's Vest	11	BoA	63			90
7	Black Bear Hide Vest	12	None	68		1	21
8	White Leather Jerkin	13	None	73		1	50
12	Buckled Harness	17	None	93		2	84
12	Tanned Leather Jerkin	17	None	93		2	90
17	Cured Leather Armor	22	None	100		5	59
17	Studded Leather Harness	22	None	100		5	74
19	Toughened Leather Armor	24	None	109		7	43
22	Cuirboulli Vest	27	None	121		10	44
22	Grunt's Harness	27	None	121		10	33
32	Battle Harness	37	None	140		24	97
32	Studded Doublet	37	None	140		27	39
33	Barbaric Harness	38	None	144		27	38
45	Reinforced Leather Vest	50	None	185		67	90

LEATHER FOOT ARMOR

SUPERIOR LEATHER FOOT ARMOR

M LEV	ARMOR NAME	LEV	BIND	AC	VENDOR PURCHASE VALUE		
19	Feet of the Lynx	24	BoE	87		10	75
25	Harbinger Boots	30	BoE	91		19	59
31	Briar Tredders	36	BoE	109		36	06
32	Swampwalker Boots	37	BoE	112		40	93
42	Sandstalker Ankleguards	47	BoA	140		87	84
47	Slitherscale Boots	52	BoA	153	1	17	04
49	Sandals of the Insurgent	54	BoE	159	1	39	93
54	Swiftwalker Boots	59	BoA	172	1	76	99
55	Pads of the Dread Wolf	60	BoA	175	1	80	24
▶	SPELL Attack Power 40						
56	Boots of the Shrieker	61	BoA	177	1	90	74
▶	SPELL Shadow Resist +10						
57	Verdant Footpads	62	BoA	180	2	14	06
▶	SPELL Increase Healing 34						

GOOD LEATHER FOOT ARMOR

M LEV	ARMOR NAME	LEV	BIND	AC	VENDOR PURCHASE VALUE		
10	Embossed Leather Boots	15	None	60		2	68
10	Rugged Boots	15	BoE	60		2	59
11	Bard's Boots	16	BoE	64		3	02
11	Lupine Slippers	16	BoE	64		2	90
N/A	Black Whelp Boots	18	BoA	71		4	20
13	Blackened Defias Boots	18	BoE	71		3	85
13	Feral Shoes	18	BoE	71		3	84
13	Inscribed Leather Boots	18	BoE	71		4	08
N/A	Rambling Boots	18	BoA	71		3	88
13	Stable Boots	18	BoE	71		3	99
14	Prospector's Boots	19	BoE	75		4	42
15	Agile Boots	20	BoE	66		5	26
15	Bandit Boots	20	BoE	66		5	47
N/A	Buckled Boots	21	BoA	69		6	01
16	Moonstalker's Sandels	21	BoE	69		5	85
17	Scouting Boots	22	BoE	72		7	31
18	Bristlebark Boots	23	BoE	75		7	60
18	Footpads of the Fang	23	BoA	75		7	87

GOOD LEATHER FOOT ARMOR continued

M LEV	ARMOR NAME	LEV	BIND	AC	VENDOR PURCHASE VALUE		
N/A	Darkstalker Boots	24	BoA	79		9	00
19	Forest Leather Boots	24	BoE	79		9	03
N/A	Stomping Boots	24	BoA	79		9	22
N/A	Ambassador's Boots	25	BoA	81		9	67
N/A	Mariner Boots	25	BoA	81		10	39
20	VanCleef's Boots	25	BoE	81		9	79
20	Wrangler's Boots	25	BoE	81		9	71
21	Pirate's Boots	26	BoE	85		12	04
N/A	Draftsman Boots	27	BoA	88		12	45
23	Dervish Boots	28	BoE	91		14	37
23	Kodo Hide Boots	28	BoE	91		13	27
N/A	Tundra Boots	28	BoA	91		13	27
N/A	Grizzled Boots	29	BoA	94		15	81
25	Emblazoned Boots	30	BoE	83		16	69
N/A	Lancer Boots	30	BoA	83		16	01
N/A	Ninja Boots	30	BoA	83		16	06
25	Pathfinder Footpads	30	BoE	83		16	06
N/A	Trailblazer Boots	30	BoA	83		16	39
N/A	Vorrel's Boots	30	BoA	83		16	14
26	Cenarion Footpads	31	BoE	86		17	91
26	Monk's Footpads	31	BoE	86		18	45
27	Cutthroat's Boots	32	BoE	88		19	44
28	Gnomebot Operating Boots	33	BoA	91		21	81
28	Infiltrator Boots	33	BoE	91		22	89
29	Headhunter's Slippers	34	BoE	94		23	52
29	Insignia Boots	34	BoE	94		24	81
30	Ghostwalker Boots	35	BoE	96		25	87
31	Archer's Boots	36	BoE	99		28	39
32	Hawkeye's Shoes	37	BoE	101		31	30
32	Sentinel Boots	37	BoE	101		33	77
33	Tromping Miner's Boots	38	BoE	104		36	07
34	Glyphed Boots	39	BoE	107		37	39
34	Witch Doctor's Slippers	39	BoE	107		36	52
35	Dusky Boots	40	BoE	109		42	37
▶	SPELL Add 7 Subtlety						
35	Elven Boots	40	BoE	109		41	79
35	Swift Boots	40	BoE	109		42	53
▶	SPELL Use: Increases Run Speed by 40% for 15 sec						

GOOD LEATHER FOOT ARMOR continued

M LEV	ARMOR NAME	LEV	BIND	AC	VENDOR PURCHASE VALUE		
N/A	Excelsior Boots	41	BoA	111		43	93
36	Nocturnal Shoes	41	BoE	111		42	59
N/A	Wanderlust Boots	41	BoA	111		43	80
37	Ranger Boots	42	BoE	114		49	08
37	Warden's Footpads	42	BoE	114		46	00
N/A	Enormous Ogre Boots	43	BoA	117		53	79
38	Imperial Leather Boots	43	BoE	117		54	36
39	Tracker's Boots	44	BoE	119		55	19
39	Wolf Rider's Boots	44	BoE	119		53	66
40	Assassin's Boots	45	BoE	122		57	95
N/A	Jangdor's Handcrafted Boots	45	BoA	122		58	47
N/A	Pratt's Handcrafted Boots	45	BoA	122		57	80
41	Cabalist Boots	46	BoE	124		64	34
41	Scorpashi Slippers	46	BoE	124		62	59
42	Heraldic Boots	47	BoE	127		71	61
42	Nightscape Boots	47	BoE	127		71	58
43	Rageclaw Boots	48	BoE	129		73	00
44	Chieftain's Boots	49	BoE	132		83	65
44	Wild Leather Boots	49	BoE	132		81	50
45	Vampiric Boots	50	BoE	134		83	58
46	Keeper's Hooves	51	BoE	137		89	43
46	Righteous Boots	51	BoE	137		91	28
47	Serpentskin Boots	52	BoE	139	1	02	61
48	Jadefire Sabatons	53	BoE	142	1	00	48
49	Infernal Boots	54	BoE	144	1	09	54
50	Chimeric Boots	55	BoE	147	1	15	30
▶	**SPELL** Arcane & Nature Resist +12						
50	Frostsaber Boots	55	BoE	147	1	14	43
▶	**SPELL** Frost & Shadow Resist +12						
50	Praetorian Boots	55	BoE	147	1	12	90
50	Shadefiend Boots	55	BoA	147	1	20	53
51	Angelic Boots	56	BoE	149	1	21	20
51	Pridelord Boots	56	BoE	149	1	19	68
52	Spiritwalker Boots	57	BoE	152	1	26	51
53	Stormhide Boots	58	BoE	154	1	34	47
54	Nightmare Boots	59	BoE	157	1	44	62
55	Nether Runed Boots	60	BoE	159	1	48	26
55	Springtide Boots	60	BoA	159	1	61	14
▶	**SPELL** Increase Healing 20						
N/A	Swiftfoot Treads	60	BoA	159	1	49	69
56	Cadaverous Walkers	61	BoA	161	1	58	95
56	Phantasmal Boots	61	BoE	161	1	61	94
57	Arch Druid's Sandels	62	BoE	164	1	63	45
57	Hellfire Boots	62	BoE	164	1	68	77
58	Seraphim Shoes	63	BoE	166	1	71	63

STANDARD LEATHER FOOT ARMOR

M LEV	ARMOR NAME	LEV	BIND	AC	VENDOR PURCHASE VALUE		
1	Cracked Leather Boots	5	None	20			9
1	Dirty Leather Boots	5	None	20			9
N/A	Rainwalker Boots	7	BoA	28			21
3	Handstitched Leather Boots	8	None	32			29
N/A	Zombie Skin Boots	8	BoA	32			30
4	Burnt Leather Boots	9	None	36			41
4	Gray Fur Booties	9	None	36			41
4	Primal Sandels	9	None	36			39
5	Battered Leather Boots	10	None	40			51
5	Lithe Boots	10	None	40			54
5	Rough Leather Boots	10	None	40			52
N/A	Weather-worn Boots	10	BoA	40			52
6	Pioneer Boots	11	None	43			70
N/A	Cushioned Boots	12	BoA	47			87
7	Gypsy Sandals	12	None	47			86
N/A	Tiger Hide Boots	12	BoA	47			89
7	Tribal Boots	12	None	47			88
8	Grizzly Slippers	13	None	50		1	05
9	Hunting Boots	14	None	54		1	28
10	Ceremonial Leather Ankleguards	15	BoE	57		1	52
12	Tanned Leather Boots	17	None	64		2	15
13	Fine Leather Boots	18	None	67		2	43
15	Dark Leather Boots	20	None	63		3	07
17	Cured Leather Boots	22	None	69		4	22
22	Cuirboulli Boots	27	None	83		7	88
32	Studded Boots	37	None	96		18	86
35	Worn Running Boots	40	None	103		24	88
45	Reinforced Leather Boots	50	None	127		51	50

INFERIOR LEATHER FOOT ARMOR

M LEV	ARMOR NAME	LEV	BIND	AC	VENDOR PURCHASE VALUE		
1	Ragged Leather Boots	3	None	12			2
3	Worn Leather Boots	8	None	31			19
10	Warped Leather Boots	15	None	54		1	09
14	Patched Leather Boots	19	None	67		1	76
20	Rawhide Boots	25	None	73		4	00
21	Tough Leather Boots	26	None	76		4	78
30	Hardened Leather Boots	35	None	87		10	31
43	Thick Leather Boots	48	None	116		30	79
49	Smooth Leather Boots	54	None	130		42	96
64	Strapped Boots	69	None	163		95	60

LEATHER HAND ARMOR

EPIC LEATHER HAND ARMOR

M LEV	ARMOR NAME	LEV	BIND	AC	VENDOR PURCHASE VALUE		
37	Gloves of Holy Might	42	BoE	125		53	44
▶	**SPELL** Add 1% Crit, 20 Attack Power/30 for Undead						

SUPERIOR LEATHER HAND ARMOR

M LEV	ARMOR NAME	LEV	BIND	AC	VENDOR PURCHASE VALUE		
22	Naga Battle Gloves	27	BoA	88		9	80
22	Toughened Leather Gloves	27	BoE	88		9	62
22	Wolfclaw Gloves	27	BoE	88		9	80
23	Brawler Gloves	28	BoE	91		10	70
30	Ebon Vise	35	BoA	96		22	32
37	Arachnid Gloves	42	BoA	114		40	14
▶	**SPELL** Nature Resist +10						
41	Gauntlets of the Sea	46	BoE	124		53	63
▶	**SPELL** Use: Heals Target for 300-500						
45	Elven Spirit Claws	50	BoE	134		68	17
▶	**SPELL** Increase Nature Dmg 13						
48	Bloodfire Talons	53	BoA	142		85	20
▶	**SPELL** Increase spell Dmg 9, Fire Resist +10						
51	Mar Alom's Grip	56	BoE	149	1	05	19
▶	**SPELL** Increase Healing 20						
53	Devilsaur Gauntlets	58	BoE	154	1	17	01
▶	**SPELL** Attack Power 28						

SUPERIOR LEATHER HAND ARMOR continued

M LEV	ARMOR NAME	LEV	BIND	AC	VENDOR PURCHASE VALUE		
54	Skul's Fingerbone Claws	59	BoA	157	1	14	03
▶	**SPELL** Add 1% Crit						
56	Fallbrush Handgrips	61	BoA	161	1	36	38
56	Gargoyle Slashers	61	BoA	161	1	24	27
▶	**SPELL** Attack Power 42						
56	Slaghide Gauntlets	61	BoA	161	1	33	43
▶	**SPELL** Increased Armor 100						

GOOD LEATHER HAND ARMOR

M LEV	ARMOR NAME	LEV	BIND	AC	VENDOR PURCHASE VALUE		
N/A	Bingles' Flying Gloves	15	BoA	54		1	82
10	Fine Leather Gloves	15	BoE	54		1	81
10	Hunting Gloves	15	BoE	54		1	71
11	Lupine Handwraps	16	BoE	58		1	93
12	Bard's Gloves	17	BoE	61		2	29
N/A	Shucking Gloves	17	BoA	61		2	22
N/A	Black Whelp Gloves	18	BoA	65		2	62
13	Blackened Defias Gloves	18	BoE	65		2	55
N/A	Dusty Mining Gloves	18	BoA	65		2	58
13	Feral Gloves	18	BoE	65		2	56
13	Metalworking Gloves	18	BoE	65		2	59

XII

GOOD LEATHER HAND ARMOR

M LEV	ARMOR NAME	LEV	BIND	AC	VENDOR PURCHASE VALUE
13	Woodworking Gloves	18	BoE	65	2s 67c
14	Gloves of the Fang	19	BoE	68	3s 07c
14	Inscribed Leather Gloves	19	BoE	68	3s 14c
14	Prospector's Mitts	19	BoE	68	2s 94c
15	Bandit Gloves	20	BoE	60	3s 69c
15	Foreman's Gloves	20	BoE	60	3s 39c
15	Ghoul Fingers	20	BoE	60	3s 62c
N/A	Gloves of the Moon	20	BoA	60	3s 59c
N/A	Hammerfist Gloves	20	BoA	60	3s 47c
N/A	Windfelt Gloves	20	BoA	60	3s 48c
16	Deviate Scale Gloves	21	BoE	63	4s 20c
17	Moonstalker's Gloves	22	BoE	66	4s 48c
18	Scouting Gloves	23	BoE	69	5s 05c
19	Bristlebark Gloves	24	BoE	71	5s 72c
19	Nimble Leather Gloves	24	BoE	71	5s 88c
19	Red Whelp Gloves	24	BoE	71	5s 86c
▶	**SPELL** 5% Chance to deal 15-25 Dam on hit				
20	Fletcher's Gloves	25	BoE	74	6s 90c
▶	**SPELL** Add 1% Missile Crit				
20	Forest Leather Gloves	25	BoE	74	6s 82c
21	Dark Leather Gloves	26	BoE	77	7s 91c
▶	**SPELL** Add 5 Lockpicking				
22	Herbalist's Gloves	27	BoE	80	8s 61c
▶	**SPELL** Add 5 Herbalism				
22	Pirate's Gloves	27	BoE	80	8s 33c
22	Wrangler's Gloves	27	BoE	80	8s 04c
23	Dervish Gloves	28	BoE	83	9s 71c
23	Pilferer's Gloves	28	BoE	83	8s 85c
▶	**SPELL** Add 7 Subtlety				
24	Emblazoned Gloves	29	BoE	86	9s 85c
24	Heavy Earthen Gloves	29	BoE	86	9s 78c
▶	**SPELL** Attack Power 16				
24	Hillman's Leather Gloves	29	BoE	86	10s 49c
24	Kodo Hide Handwraps	29	BoE	86	9s 73c
25	Barbaric Gloves	30	BoE	75	10s 71c
N/A	Ninja Gloves	30	BoA	75	11s 34c
▶	**SPELL** Nature Resist +8				
25	Pathfinder Gloves	30	BoE	75	10s 71c
26	Monk's Handwraps	31	BoE	78	12s 48c
27	Cenarion Handgrips	32	BoE	80	12s 96c
27	Infiltrator Gloves	32	BoE	80	13s 02c
28	Cutthroat's Mitts	33	BoE	83	14s 25c
N/A	Gloves of Insight	33	BoA	83	15s 04c
N/A	Shepherd's Gloves	33	BoA	83	14s 92c
29	Headhunter's Mitts	34	BoE	85	15s 68c
29	Insignia Gloves	34	BoE	85	16s 54c
30	Archer's Gloves	35	BoE	88	17s 53c
N/A	Braced Handguards	36	BoA	90	20s 31c
31	Ghostwalker Gloves	36	BoE	90	18s 97c
N/A	Mud's Crushers	36	BoA	90	18s 99c
32	Hawkeye's Gloves	37	BoE	92	20s 87c
N/A	Prospector Gloves	37	BoA	92	22s 09c
32	Sentinel Gloves	37	BoE	92	22s 43c
N/A	Tiger Hunter Gloves	37	BoA	92	21s 36c
33	Glyphed Mitts	38	BoE	95	22s 99c
N/A	Gnomish Mechanic's Gloves	38	BoA	95	24s 21c
33	Witch Doctor's Handwraps	38	BoE	95	22s 54c
34	Nocturnal Gloves	39	BoE	97	24s 34c
34	Swine Fists	39	BoA	97	24s 28c
35	Elven Gloves	40	BoE	99	28s 57c
N/A	Seawolf Gloves	40	BoA	99	27s 94c
N/A	Stormfire Gauntlets	40	BoA	99	26s 41c
36	Ranger Gloves	41	BoE	101	30s 19c
N/A	Razzeric's Racing Grips	41	BoA	101	29s 96c
36	Warden's Gloves	41	BoE	101	28s 39c
38	Bonefingers	43	BoA	106	33s 67c
38	Imperial Leather Gloves	43	BoE	106	35s 96c
N/A	Rustler Gloves	43	BoA	106	35s 73c
38	Wolf Rider's Gloves	43	BoE	106	33s 12c
39	Tracker's Gloves	44	BoE	108	37s 21c
40	Assassin's Gloves	45	BoE	111	38s 63c
N/A	Jangdor's Handcrafted Gloves	45	BoA	111	38s 83c
N/A	Pratt's Handcrafted Gloves	45	BoA	111	38s 68c
41	Cabalist Gloves	46	BoE	113	42s 73c
41	Scorpashi Gloves	46	BoE	113	41s 72c
42	Heraldic Gloves	47	BoE	115	48s 43c
43	Rageclaw Gloves	48	BoE	118	53s 13c
44	Chieftain's Gloves	49	BoE	120	52s 55c

GOOD LEATHER HAND ARMOR continued

M LEV	ARMOR NAME	LEV	BIND	AC	VENDOR PURCHASE VALUE
45	Vampiric Gloves	50	BoE	122	55s 72c
46	Keeper's Gloves	51	BoE	124	59s 62c
46	Righteous Gloves	51	BoE	124	61s 77c
47	Jadefire Gloves	52	BoE	126	63s 20c
47	Serpentskin Gloves	52	BoE	126	69s 38c
47	Wicked Leather Gauntlets	52	BoE	126	68s 72c
48	Chimeric Gloves	53	BoE	129	68s 67c
▶	**SPELL** Arcane Resist +11, Nature Resist +12				
48	Infernal Gloves	53	BoE	129	69s 66c
49	Ogreseer Fists	54	BoA	131	71s 10c
49	Praetorian Gloves	54	BoE	131	71s 01c
49	Runic Leather Gauntlets	54	BoE	131	71s 95c
50	Angelic Gloves	55	BoE	133	79s 47c
N/A	Nightfall Gloves	56	BoA	136	87s 34c
51	Pridelord Gloves	56	BoE	136	79s 78c
52	Spiritwalker Gloves	57	BoE	138	85s 65c
N/A	Blight Leather Gloves	58	BoA	140	89s 65c
53	Stormhide Gloves	58	BoE	140	89s 65c
54	Frostsaber Gloves	59	BoE	143	95s 04c
▶	**SPELL** Frost Resist +13, Shadow Resist +12				
54	Nightmare Gloves	59	BoE	143	1g 00s 12c
55	Nether Runed Handgrips	60	BoE	144	98s 84c
56	Cadaverous Gloves	61	BoA	147	1g 05s 56c
56	Phantasmal Handguards	61	BoE	147	1g 09s 15c
57	Arch Druid's Mitts	62	BoE	149	1g 08s 97c
58	Hellfire Gloves	63	BoE	151	1g 19s 45c
58	Seraphim Gloves	63	BoE	151	1g 14s 41c

XII

CLOTH ARMOR

LEATHER ARMOR

MAIL ARMOR

PLATE ARMOR

SHIELDS

WEAPONS

STANDARD LEATHER HAND ARMOR°

M LEV	ARMOR NAME	LEV	BIND	AC	VENDOR PURCHASE VALUE
N/A	Archery Training Gloves	5	BoA	19	6c
N/A	Battleworn Leather Gloves	5	BoA	19	5c
1	Cracked Leather Gloves	5	None	19	6c
1	Dirty Leather Gloves	5	None	19	6c
N/A	Nomadic Gloves	5	BoA	19	5c
N/A	Wolf Handler Gloves	5	BoA	19	6c
N/A	Double-layered Gloves	8	BoA	29	20c
N/A	Lion-stamped Gloves	8	BoA	29	19c
N/A	Sewing Gloves	8	BoA	29	20c
N/A	Driving Gloves	9	BoA	33	28c
5	Battered Leather Gloves	10	None	36	34c
5	Burnt Leather Gloves	10	None	36	36c
5	Primal Mitts	10	None	36	34c
5	Rough Leather Gloves	10	None	36	35c
N/A	Veiled Grips	10	BoA	36	36c
5	White Wolf Gloves	10	None	36	36c
6	Pioneer Gloves	11	None	39	47c
7	Tribal Gloves	12	None	43	59c
8	Embossed Leather Gloves	13	None	46	71c
8	Gypsy Gloves	13	None	46	73c
9	Grizzly Gloves	14	None	49	84c
10	Ceremonial Leather Gloves	15	BoE	52	1s 02c
12	Tanned Leather Gloves	17	None	58	1s 44c
17	Cured Leather Gloves	22	None	62	2s 82c
22	Cuirboulli Gloves	27	None	76	5s 29c
29	Dog Training Gloves	34	None	81	9s 63c
▶	**SPELL** Add 30 Attack Power Vs. Beasts				
32	Studded Gloves	37	None	88	12s 66c
33	Guardian Gloves	38	None	90	13s 74c
45	Reinforced Leather Gloves	50	None	116	34s 59c

INFERIOR LEATHER HAND ARMOR

M LEV	ARMOR NAME	LEV	BIND	AC	VENDOR PURCHASE VALUE
1	Ragged Leather Gloves	4	None	14	2c
1	Worn Leather Gloves	6	None	21	6c
8	Warped Leather Gloves	13	None	43	51c
12	Patched Leather Gloves	17	None	55	90c
18	Rawhide Gloves	23	None	62	2s 11c
24	Tough Leather Gloves	29	None	77	3s 87c
31	Hardened Leather Gloves	36	None	81	7s 65c
44	Thick Leather Gloves	49	None	108	22s 21c
53	Smooth Leather Gloves	58	None	126	36s 57c
63	Strapped Gloves	68	None	146	61s 37c

LEATHER HEAD ARMOR

SUPERIOR LEATHER HEAD ARMOR

M LEV	ARMOR NAME	LEV	BIND	AC	VENDOR PURCHASE VALUE		
28	Enduring Cap	33	BoE	118		26	55
32	Adventurer's Pith Helmet	37	BoE	132		40	83
33	Expert Goldminer's Helmet	38	BoE	135		42	20
▶	**SPELL** Adds 7 to 1H Axe						
40	Wolfshead Helm	45	BoE	158		74	21
▶	**SPELL** On Shift: Adds 20 Energy or 5 Rage						
N/A	Engineer's Guild Headpiece	47	BoA	165		88	47
43	Winged Helm	48	BoE	168		96	24
45	Embrace of the Lycan	50	BoA	174	1	08	58
▶	**SPELL** Attack Power 32						
45	Helm of Fire	50	BoE	174	1	08	19
▶	**SPELL** Fireball, Fire Resist +5						
52	Ghostshroud	57	BoA	197	1	64	84
▶	**SPELL** Shadow Resist +5						
52	Mask of the Unforgiven	57	BoA	197	1	58	95
▶	**SPELL** Adds 2% Hit 1% Crit						
52	Ragefury Eyepatch	57	BoA	197	1	66	69
▶	**SPELL** Adds 2% Crit						
58	Eye of Rend	63	BoA	216	2	10	31
▶	**SPELL** Adds 2% Crit						
58	Feathermoon Headress	63	BoE	216	2	05	46

GOOD LEATHER HEAD ARMOR

M LEV	ARMOR NAME	LEV	BIND	AC	VENDOR PURCHASE VALUE		
25	Humbert's Helm	30	BoE	98		17	63
N/A	Ninja Mask	30	BoA	98		16	06
25	Ringed Helm	30	BoE	98		16	63
26	Emblazoned Hat	31	BoE	101		17	67
26	Kodo Hide Helm	31	BoE	101		17	67
26	Ruffled Chaplet	31	BoE	101		18	84
27	Monk's Cap	32	BoE	105		19	76
27	Tribal Worg Helm	32	BoE	105		20	65
27	Whisperwind Headdress	32	BoA	105		20	59
28	Infiltrator Cap	33	BoE	108		21	57
29	Pathfinder Hat	34	BoE	111		23	52
30	Cenarion Coronet	35	BoE	114		26	73
30	Insignia Cap	35	BoE	114		26	99
31	Archer's Cap	36	BoE	117		28	71
31	Feathered Headdress	36	BoE	117		28	46
32	Cutthroat's Hat	37	BoE	120		31	30
N/A	Spirit Hunter Headdress	37	BoA	120		32	18
33	Cloaked Hood	38	BoE	123		36	96
33	Headhunter's Headress	38	BoE	123		33	81
33	Sentinel Cap	38	BoE	123		35	14
34	Ghostwalker Crown	39	BoE	126		36	52
34	Glyphed Helm	39	BoE	126		37	68
N/A	Cap of Harmony	40	BoA	129		39	91
35	Comfortable Leather Hat	40	BoE	129		41	31
35	Elven Cap	40	BoE	129		42	40
35	Hawkeye's Helm	40	BoE	129		39	44
25	Humbert's Helm	30	BoE	98		17	63
N/A	White Drakeskin Cap	40	BoA	129		40	98

GOOD LEATHER HEAD ARMOR continued

M LEV	ARMOR NAME	LEV	BIND	AC	VENDOR PURCHASE VALUE		
36	Nightscape Headband	41	BoE	132		44	95
37	Ranger Helm	42	BoE	135		48	73
37	Witch Doctor's Headress	42	BoE	135		46	00
38	Imperial Leather Helm	43	BoE	138		49	53
38	Nocturnal Skullcap	43	BoE	138		49	68
39	Big Voodoo Mask	44	BoE	141		53	50
40	Tracker's Headband	45	BoE	144		60	50
40	Warden's Wizard Hat	45	BoE	144		57	95
40	Wild Leather Helmet	45	BoE	144		62	30
42	Cabalist Helm	47	BoE	150		68	97
42	Wolf Rider's Skullcap	47	BoE	150		67	59
43	Assassin's Visor	48	BoE	153		73	00
43	Heraldic Headpiece	48	BoE	153		78	75
44	Scorpashi Skullcap	49	BoE	156		78	11
45	Chieftain's Headdress	50	BoE	158		84	67
45	Rageclaw Helm	50	BoE	158		83	58
46	Vampiric Headress	51	BoE	161		89	43
47	Righteous Helmet	52	BoE	164		98	58
48	Keeper's Wreath	53	BoE	167	1	00	48
N/A	Lordrec Helmet	53	BoA	167	1	00	63
49	Serpentskin Helm	54	BoE	171	1	06	17
50	Infernal Cap	55	BoE	173	1	17	85
51	Jadefire Crown	56	BoE	176	1	19	68
51	Wicked Leather Headband	56	BoE	176	1	31	54
52	Angelic Halo	57	BoE	179	1	34	44
52	Praetorian Coif	57	BoE	179	1	26	86
53	Pridelord Halo	58	BoE	182	1	34	47
53	Runic Leather Headband	58	BoE	182	1	41	55
54	Spiritwalker Headpiece	59	BoE	185	1	43	53
55	Stormhide Helm	60	BoE	188	1	48	26
56	Nightmare Helmet	61	BoE	191	1	66	16
57	Bone Ring Helm	62	BoA	194	1	78	36
57	Nether Runed Crown	62	BoE	194	1	63	45
57	Phantasmal Headdress	62	BoE	194	1	72	54
58	Arch Druid's Headress	63	BoE	196	1	83	27
58	Hellfire Helm	63	BoE	196	1	79	85
58	Tribal War Feathers	63	BoA	196	1	71	25
▶	**SPELL** Increase Nature Dmg 13						
59	Seraphim Crown	64	BoE	199	1	80	21

STANDARD LEATHER HEAD ARMOR

M LEV	ARMOR NAME	LEV	BIND	AC	VENDOR PURCHASE VALUE		
32	Studded Hat	37	None	114		20	40
45	Reinforced Leather Cap	50	None	150		55	04

INFERIOR LEATHER HEAD ARMOR

M LEV	ARMOR NAME	LEV	BIND	AC	VENDOR PURCHASE VALUE		
30	Hardened Leather Helm	35	None	102		10	36
37	Thick Leather Hat	42	None	121		18	63
52	Smooth Leather Helmet	57	None	161		51	98

LEATHER LEG ARMOR

EPIC LEATHER LEG ARMOR

M LEV	ARMOR NAME	LEV	BIND	AC	VENDOR PURCHASE VALUE		
N/A	Leggings of Arcana	62	BoA	250	3	50	57
▶	**SPELL** Increase spell Dmg 9						

SUPERIOR LEATHER LEG ARMOR

M LEV	ARMOR NAME	LEV	BIND	AC	VENDOR PURCHASE VALUE		
18	Leggings of the Fang	23	BoA	106		12	56
25	Petrolspill Leggings	30	BoE	116		26	83
▶	**SPELL** Fire Resist -10						
25	Troll's Bane Leggings	30	BoE	116		25	74
N/A	Triprunner Dungarees	37	BoA	142		52	67
34	Warchief Kilt	39	BoE	149		60	74
38	Basilisk Hide Pants	43	BoE	163		80	40

SUPERIOR LEATHER LEG ARMOR continued

M LEV	ARMOR NAME	LEV	BIND	AC	VENDOR PURCHASE VALUE		
44	Jinxed Hoodoo Kilt	49	BoA	185	1	32	90
49	Windscale Sarong	54	BoA	202	1	75	95
50	Stormshroud Pants	55	BoE	205	1	87	28
▶	**SPELL** Increased Critical 2						
52	Living Leggings	57	BoE	212	2	12	77
▶	**SPELL** Increase Healing 24, Nature Resist +8						
52	Warbear Woolies	57	BoE	212	2	22	33
53	Warstrife Leggings	58	BoA	216	2	23	84
▶	**SPELL** Increased Dodge 2						
55	Devilsaur Leggings	60	BoE	222	2	57	09
▶	**SPELL** Attack Power 46						
55	Earthborn Kilt	60	BoE	222	2	53	08
55	Tressermane Leggings	60	BoA	222	2	39	48
58	Blademaster Leggings	63	BoA	233	2	77	17

GOOD LEATHER LEG ARMOR

M LEV	ARMOR NAME	LEV	BIND	AC	VENDOR PURCHASE VALUE		
5	Burnt Leather Breeches	10	BoE	53		1	20
6	Primal Kilt	11	BoE	58		1	49
6	Rugged Leather Pants	11	BoE	58		1	62
7	Pioneer Trousers	12	BoE	63		1	93
7	Tribal Pants	12	BoE	63		1	99
N/A	Vagabond Leggings	13	BoA	67		2	47
9	Grizzly Pants	14	BoE	72		2	80
9	Gypsy Trousers	14	BoE	72		2	94
10	Embossed Leather Pants	15	BoE	76		3	47
N/A	Harvester's Pants	15	BoA	76		3	39
N/A	Kodo Hunter's Leggings	15	BoA	76		3	68
N/A	Stretched Leather Trousers	15	BoA	76		3	63
11	Hunting Pants	16	BoE	81		3	92
12	Ceremonial Leather Loincloth	17	BoE	86		4	54
N/A	Frontier Britches	17	BoA	86		4	58
13	Bard's Trousers	18	BoE	90		5	25
13	Blackened Defias Leggings	18	BoE	90		5	63
N/A	Dredgemire Leggings	18	BoA	90		5	12
N/A	Greasy Tinker's Pants	18	BoA	90		5	19
N/A	Wildkeeper Leggings	18	BoA	90		5	12
14	Light Leather Pants	19	BoE	95		5	99
14	Lupine Leggings	19	BoE	95		5	90
15	Brambleweed Leggings	20	BoE	84		6	92
15	Feral Leggings	20	BoE	84		6	78
15	Inscribed Leather Pants	20	BoE	84		7	18
N/A	Slick Deviate Leggings	20	BoA	84		7	13
N/A	Smith's Trousers	20	BoA	84		7	15
15	Stonemason Trousers	20	BoE	84		7	31
16	Fine Leather Pants	21	BoE	88		8	29
16	Prospector's Woolies	21	BoE	88		7	80
16	Smelting Pants	21	BoA	88		8	04
17	Bandit Pants	22	BoE	92		9	82
18	Bluegill Breeches	23	BoE	96		10	85
18	Dark Leather Pants	23	BoE	96		10	89
19	Moonstalker's Leggings	24	BoE	100		11	45
19	Scouting Trousers	24	BoE	100		11	46
21	Bristlebark Britches	26	BoE	108		14	63
21	Forest Leather Pants	26	BoE	108		15	32
21	Stalking Pants	26	BoE	108		15	71
22	Shadow Weaver Leggings	27	BoE	112		16	90
22	Wrangler's Leggings	27	BoE	112		16	09
23	Pirate's Pantaloons	28	BoE	116		18	48
23	Saber Leggings	28	BoE	116		18	94
24	Kodo Hide Leggings	29	BoE	120		19	47
24	Mystic Sarong	29	BoE	120		20	99
25	Dervish Leggings	30	BoE	106		22	02
N/A	Ninja Pants	30	BoA	106		22	52
▶	**SPELL** Frost Resist +11						
26	Emblazoned Leggings	31	BoE	109		23	74
26	Pathfinder Pants	31	BoE	109		23	56
27	Cenarion Kilt	32	BoE	113		25	92
27	Guardian Pants	32	BoE	113		27	94
28	Cutthroat's Loincloth	33	BoE	116		28	51
28	Dusky Leather Leggings	33	BoE	116		30	97
28	Monk's Pants	33	BoE	116		30	31
29	Barbaric Leggings	34	BoE	119		31	51
29	Ferine Leggings	34	BoA	119		33	46
29	Infiltrator Pants	34	BoE	119		31	75
30	Headhunter's Woolies	35	BoE	123		34	50
30	Insignia Leggings	35	BoE	123		36	25
31	Ghostwalker Legguards	36	BoE	126		37	95
32	Archer's Trousers	37	BoE	129		42	60
N/A	Lightstep Leggings	37	BoA	129		44	42
33	Hawkeye's Breeches	38	BoE	133		45	08
34	Sentinel Trousers	39	BoE	136		50	42
35	Glyphed Leggings	40	BoE	139		56	48
N/A	Mistspray Kilt	40	BoA	139		54	86
N/A	Panther Hunter Leggings	40	BoA	139		54	03
35	Witch Doctor's Loincloth	40	BoE	139		52	59
36	Nocturnal Leggings	41	BoE	142		56	79
37	Elven Leggings	42	BoE	145		66	89
38	Ranger Leggings	43	BoE	149		69	91
38	Warden's Woolies	43	BoE	149		66	24
39	Wolf Rider's Leggings	44	BoE	152		71	54
40	Assassin's Pants	45	BoE	155		77	27
40	Imperial Leather Pants	45	BoE	155		83	59
41	Nightscape Pants	46	BoE	158		87	08
41	Oilskin Leggings	46	BoA	158		86	45
41	Tracker's Leggings	46	BoE	158		87	45
42	Big Voodoo Pants	47	BoE	161		90	22
42	Scorpashi Leggings	47	BoE	161		90	13
43	Cabalist Leggings	48	BoE	165		98	94
44	Heraldic Leggings	49	BoE	168	1	12	75

GOOD LEATHER LEG ARMOR continued

M LEV	ARMOR NAME	LEV	BIND	AC	VENDOR PURCHASE VALUE		
44	Ragedaw Leggings	49	BoE	168	1	04	15
45	Vampiric Pants	50	BoE	171	1	11	44
45	Wild Leather Leggings	50	BoE	171	1	15	85
46	Chieftain's Leggings	51	BoE	174	1	21	25
47	Atal'ai Leggings	52	BoA	177	1	32	00
47	Keeper's Woolies	52	BoE	177	1	26	40
N/A	Gryphon Rider's Leggings	53	BoA	180	1	34	66
48	Righteous Leggings	53	BoE	180	1	39	85
49	Jadefire Pants	54	BoE	184	1	42	02
49	Serpentskin Leggings	54	BoE	184	1	46	05
49	Volcanic Leggings	54	BoE	184	1	45	59
▶	**SPELL** Increased Armor 80, Fire Resist +20						
N/A	Windshear Leggings	54	BoA	184	1	44	46
50	Praetorian Leggings	55	BoE	187	1	50	54
51	Chimeric Leggings	56	BoE	190	1	62	33
▶	**SPELL** Arcane & Nature Resist +16						
51	Infernal Leggings	56	BoE	190	1	67	17
52	Frostsaber Leggings	57	BoE	193	1	70	12
▶	**SPELL** Frost Resist +17, Shadow Resist +16						
53	Angelic Leggings	58	BoE	196	1	90	71
53	Pridelord Pants	58	BoE	196	1	79	30
53	Wicked Leather Pants	58	BoE	196	1	78	92
54	Luminary Kilt	59	BoA	200	1	97	30
54	Stormhide Leggings	59	BoE	200	1	88	26
55	Runic Leather Pants	60	BoE	202	2	08	85
55	Spiritwalker Leggings	60	BoE	202	2	01	72
56	Cadaverous Kilt	61	BoA	205	2	09	54
56	Crypt Stalker Leggings	61	BoA	205	2	11	91
▶	**SPELL** Nature & Shadow Resist +18						
56	Nether Runed Legguards	61	BoE	205	2	07	56
57	Arch Druid's Kilt	62	BoE	208	2	17	94
57	Ghostloom Leggings	62	BoA	208	2	19	97
57	Nightmare Leggings	62	BoE	208	2	33	48
58	Phantasmal Leggings	63	BoE	212	2	43	33
58	Seraphim Legguards	63	BoE	212	2	28	84
59	Hellfire Legguards	64	BoE	215	2	52	72

STANDARD LEATHER LEG ARMOR

M LEV	ARMOR NAME	LEV	BIND	AC	VENDOR PURCHASE VALUE		
N/A	Canopy Leggings	5	BoA	26			13
1	Cracked Leather Pants	5	None	26			11
1	Dirty Leather Pants	5	None	26			12
N/A	Dust-covered Leggings	5	BoA	26			12
N/A	Dwarven Leather Pants	5	BoA	26			12
N/A	Zombie Skin Leggings	5	BoA	26			13
N/A	Rough-hewn Kodo Leggings	9	BoA	46			54
5	Battered Leather Pants	10	None	51			68
5	Handstitched Leather Pants	10	None	51			71
N/A	Patched Pants	10	BoA	51			75
5	Rough Leather Pants	10	None	51			70
12	Tanned Leather Pants	17	None	82		2	89
17	Cured Leather Pants	22	None	87		5	61
22	Cuirboulli Pants	27	None	106		9	61
32	Studded Pants	37	None	123		24	95
45	Reinforced Leather Pants	50	None	162		68	42

INFERIOR LEATHER LEG ARMOR

M LEV	ARMOR NAME	LEV	BIND	AC	VENDOR PURCHASE VALUE		
1	Primitive Kilt	1	None	5			1
1	Primitive Kilt	1	None	5			1
1	Ragged Leather Pants	2	None	10			2
2	Worn Leather Pants	7	None	34			18
9	Warped Leather Pants	14	None	65		1	23
13	Patched Leather Pants	18	None	81		2	08
19	Rawhide Pants	24	None	90		4	79
25	Tough Leather Pants	30	None	95		8	56
27	Hardened Leather Pants	32	None	101		10	49
37	Thick Leather Pants	42	None	131		26	25
48	Smooth Leather Pants	53	None	162		54	86
61	Strapped Pants	66	None	199	1	11	75

LEATHER SHOULDER ARMOR

SUPERIOR LEATHER SHOULDER ARMOR

M LEV	ARMOR NAME	LEV	BIND	AC	VENDOR PURCHASE VALUE		
25	Mantle of Thieves	30	BoE	100		19	57
26	Forest Tracker Epaulets	31	BoE	103		23	26
27	Watchman Pauldrons	32	BoE	106		24	88
33	Flintrock Shoulders	38	BoE	125		41	40
37	Fleshhide Shoulders	42	BoA	137		59	57
40	Sheepshear Mantle	45	BoE	146		69	90
47	Atal'ai Spaulders	52	BoA	167	1	14	76
▶	**SPELL** Increased Armor 80						
49	Ironfeather Shoulders	54	BoE	173	1	27	58
49	Living Shoulders	54	BoE	173	1	38	03
▶	**SPELL** Increase Healing 28, Nature Resist +8						
54	Demonic Runed Spaulders	59	BoA	188	1	80	88
N/A	Halycon's Muzzle	60	BoA	190	1	80	28
▶	**SPELL** Arcane Resist +10						
56	Spaulders of the Unseen	61	BoE	193	1	93	70
56	Truestrike Shoulders	61	BoA	193	1	91	49
▶	**SPELL** Adds 2% Hit, 24 Attack Power						
57	Death's Clutch	62	BoA	197	1	96	52
58	Wyrmtongue Shoulders	63	BoA	199	2	10	36

GOOD LEATHER SHOULDER ARMOR

M LEV	ARMOR NAME	LEV	BIND	AC	VENDOR PURCHASE VALUE		
20	Forest Leather Mantle	25	BoE	89		9	82
21	Hillman's Shoulders	26	BoE	92		11	99
21	Moonstalker's Shoulder Pads	26	BoE	92		11	63
22	Bristlebark Amice	27	BoE	96		12	07
22	Earthen Leather Shoulders	27	BoE	96		13	06
22	Pirate's Shoulders	27	BoE	96		12	55
23	Dark Leather Shoulders	28	BoE	99		14	57
23	Wrangler's Mantle	28	BoE	99		13	27
24	Dervish Spaulders	29	BoE	103		14	84
25	Emblazoned Shoulders	30	BoE	90		16	39
25	Kodo Hide Pauldrons	30	BoE	90		16	06
26	Pathfinder Shoulder Pads	31	BoE	93		17	67
27	Cenarion Mantle	32	BoE	97		19	44
27	Monk's Shoulders	32	BoE	97		20	74
28	Infiltrator Shoulders	33	BoE	99		22	81
29	Cutthroat's Mantle	34	BoE	102		23	52
30	Barbaric Shoulders	35	BoE	105		26	09
30	Headhunter's Spaulders	35	BoE	105		25	87
30	Insignia Mantle	35	BoE	105		28	09
31	Ghostwalker Pads	36	BoE	108		28	46
32	Archer's Shoulderpads	37	BoE	111		32	07
32	Boulder Pads	37	BoE	111		33	51
33	Hawkeye's Epaulets	38	BoE	114		33	81
33	Sentinel Shoulders	38	BoE	114		36	60
34	Glyphed Epaulets	39	BoE	116		38	24
34	Witch Doctor's Pauldrons	39	BoE	116		36	52
35	Nocturnal Shoulder Pads	40	BoE	119		39	44
36	Elven Shoulders	41	BoE	122		46	61
36	Revelosh's Spaulders	41	BoA	122		43	31
36	Warden's Mantle	41	BoE	122		42	59
37	Nightscape Shoulders	42	BoE	125		47	82
37	Ranger Shoulders	42	BoE	125		49	26
38	Wolf Rider's Shoulder Pads	43	BoE	127		49	68
39	Assassin's Shoulders Pads	44	BoE	130		53	66
39	Imperial Leather Spaulders	44	BoE	130		57	43
39	Wild Leather Shoulders	44	BoE	130		55	37
40	Tracker's Shoulderpads	45	BoE	133		60	95
N/A	Loreskin Shoulders	46	BoA	135		65	10
42	Cabalist Spaulders	47	BoE	138		69	75
42	Scorpashi Shoulder Pads	47	BoE	138		67	59
N/A	Failed Flying Experiment	48	BoA	141		79	62
43	Heraldic Spaulders	48	BoE	141		79	32
43	Rageclaw Shoulder Pads	48	BoE	141		73	00
44	Vampiric Shoulder Pads	49	BoE	144		78	11
45	Chieftain's Shoulders	50	BoE	146		85	30
N/A	Kaylari Shoulders	50	BoA	146		84	98
46	Keeper's Mantle	51	BoE	149		89	43
46	Righteous Spaulders	51	BoE	149		93	69

GOOD LEATHER SHOULDER ARMOR continued

M LEV	ARMOR NAME	LEV	BIND	AC	VENDOR PURCHASE VALUE		
48	Jadefire Epaulets	53	BoE	154	1	00	48
N/A	Penance Spaulders	53	BoA	154	1	00	25
48	Serpentskin Spaulders	53	BoE	154	1	03	73
49	Praetorian Pauldrons	54	BoE	157	1	06	51
N/A	Snarkshaw Spaulders	54	BoA	157	1	06	51
50	Infernal Shoulderpads	55	BoE	160	1	18	72
N/A	Shadowskin Spaulders	55	BoA	160	1	12	90
N/A	Shizzle's Muzzle	55	BoA	160	1	18	34
50	Splinthide Shoulders	55	BoA	160	1	16	17
N/A	Clouddrift Mantle	56	BoA	163	1	19	68
52	Angelic Shoulders	57	BoE	166	1	35	41
52	Pridelord Pauldrons	57	BoE	166	1	26	86
N/A	Plow Wood Spaulders	58	BoA	168	1	41	54
53	Stormhide Shoulders	58	BoE	168	1	34	47
N/A	Wyrmhide Spaulders	58	BoA	168	1	37	26
▶	**SPELL** Adds 2% Hit						
54	Nether Runed Shoulder Pads	59	BoE	171	1	41	20
54	Spiritwalker Spaulders	59	BoE	171	1	44	63
54	Stormshroud Shoulders	59	BoE	171	1	46	92
▶	**SPELL** Adds 1% Crit						
55	Nightmare Spaulders	60	BoE	173	1	59	40
56	Arch Druid's Epaulets	61	BoE	176	1	55	67
56	Volcanic Shoulders	61	BoE	176	1	60	19
▶	**SPELL** Increased Armor 50, Fire Resist +18						
57	Phantasmal Spaulders	62	BoE	179	1	74	44
57	Runic Leather Shoulders	62	BoE	179	1	73	32
58	Hellfire Shoulders	63	BoE	181	1	81	16
58	Seraphim Shoulder Pads	63	BoE	181	1	71	63

STANDARD LEATHER SHOULDER ARMOR

M LEV	ARMOR NAME	LEV	BIND	AC	VENDOR PURCHASE VALUE		
15	Bashing Pauldrons	20	None	68		3	23
15	Rugged Spaulders	20	None	68		3	08
16	Inscribed Leather Spaulders	21	None	72		3	79
16	Lupine Mantle	21	None	72		3	50
17	Bandit Shoulders	22	None	75		4	03
18	Rigid Shoulderpads	23	None	78		4	69
18	Scouting Spaulders	23	None	78		4	58
19	Feral Shoulder Pads	24	None	82		5	15
20	Prospector's Pads	25	None	84		5	82

INFERIOR LEATHER SHOULDER ARMOR

M LEV	ARMOR NAME	LEV	BIND	AC	VENDOR PURCHASE VALUE		
15	Patched Leather Shoulderpads	20	None	65		2	07
20	Rawhide Shoulderpads	25	None	80		4	18
21	Tough Leather Shoulderpads	26	None	83		4	40
32	Hardened Leather Shoulderpads	37	None	100		12	71
42	Thick Leather Shoulderpads	47	None	125		29	03
47	Smooth Leather Shoulderpads	52	None	137		38	96
60	Strapped Shoulderpads	65	None	168		80	10

EPIC LEATHER WAIST ARMOR

M LEV	ARMOR NAME	LEV	BIND	AC	VENDOR PURCHASE VALUE		
56	Sash of Mercy	61	BoA	158	1	77	33
▶	SPELL Increase Healing 48						

SUPERIOR LEATHER WAIST ARMOR

M LEV	ARMOR NAME	LEV	BIND	AC	VENDOR PURCHASE VALUE		
18	Deviate Scale Belt	23	BoE	68		6	58
22	Silver-lined Belt	27	BoE	79		10	31
26	Moss Cinch	31	BoA	77		14	42
32	Gem-studded Leather Belt	37	BoE	91		26	52
▶	SPELL Use: Heals Player for 225-375						
37	Ogron's Sash	42	BoE	103		38	30
50	Girdle of Beastial Fury	55	BoA	132		93	29
▶	SPELL Attack Power 30						
N/A	Nagmara's Whipping Belt	55	BoA	132		98	19
52	Serpentine Sash	57	BoE	137	1	06	01
55	Cloudrunner Girdle	60	BoA	143	1	24	34
▶	SPELL Increased Armor 90						
N/A	Vosh'gajin's Strand	60	BoA	143	1	20	64
▶	SPELL Adds 1% Crit						
56	Crystallized Girdle	61	BoA	145	1	26	68
57	Frostbite Girdle	62	BoA	147	1	30	51
▶	SPELL Frost Resist +10						

GOOD LEATHER WAIST ARMOR

M LEV	ARMOR NAME	LEV	BIND	AC	VENDOR PURCHASE VALUE		
N/A	Dryweed Belt	14	BoA	46		1	51
10	Bard's Belt	15	BoE	49		1	80
N/A	Binding Girdle	15	BoA	49		1	75
10	Wendigo Collar	15	BoE	49		1	69
12	Feral Cord	17	BoE	55		2	22
12	Inscribed Leather Belt	17	BoE	55		2	44
13	Prospector's Sash	18	BoE	58		2	56
14	Bandit Cinch	19	BoE	61		3	15
15	Moonstalker's Belt	20	BoE	54		3	39
16	Belt of the Fang	21	BoA	57		4	05
16	Scouting Belt	21	BoE	57		4	22
17	Blackened Defias Belt	22	BoE	59		4	51
N/A	Steadfast Cinch	22	BoA	59		4	47
17	Support Girdle	22	BoE	59		4	69
18	Bristlebark Belt	23	BoE	62		5	07
18	Forest Leather Belt	23	BoE	62		5	23
18	Ruffian Belt	23	BoE	62		5	32
19	Guardsman Belt	24	BoE	64		5	86
19	Wrangler's Belt	24	BoE	64		5	72
20	Dark Leather Belt	25	BoE	67		7	03
N/A	Heartwood Girdle	25	BoA	67		6	50
20	Hillman's Belt	25	BoE	67		7	05
20	Pirate's Belt	25	BoE	67		7	08
21	Girdle of the Blindwatcher	26	BoA	69		8	03
21	Kodo Hide Girdle	26	BoE	69		7	31
N/A	Belt of Vindication	27	BoA	72		8	23
22	Dervish Belt	27	BoE	72		8	67
N/A	Beastmaster's Girdle	28	BoA	74		9	47
23	Pathfinder Belt	28	BoE	74		9	55
N/A	Azure Sash	29	BoA	77		10	00
24	Cenarion Cord	29	BoE	77		9	73
24	Emblazoned Belt	29	BoE	77		9	89
N/A	Windsong Cinch	29	BoA	77		9	73
▶	SPELL Attack Power 12						
N/A	Meditative Sash	30	BoA	68		10	92
25	Monk's Waistband	30	BoE	68		11	14
N/A	Ninja Belt	30	BoA	68		11	21
N/A	Windborne Belt	30	BoA	68		10	97
26	Cutthroat's Belt	31	BoE	70		11	78
27	Green Leather Belt	32	BoE	72		13	11
27	Infiltrator Cord	32	BoE	72		13	72
N/A	Grappler's Belt	33	BoA	75		15	54
28	Headhunter's Belt	33	BoE	75		14	25

GOOD LEATHER WAIST ARMOR continued

M LEV	ARMOR NAME	LEV	BIND	AC	VENDOR PURCHASE VALUE		
28	Raptor Hide Belt	33	BoE	75		15	53
29	Ghostwalker Belt	34	BoE	77		15	68
29	Guardian Belt	34	BoE	77		15	92
29	Insignia Belt	34	BoE	77		16	60
N/A	Shepherd's Girdle	34	BoA	77		16	35
30	Archer's Belt	35	BoE	79		18	95
N/A	Ringtail Girdle	35	BoA	79		17	25
▶	SPELL Attack Power 16						
31	Hawkeye's Cord	36	BoE	81		18	97
31	Sentinel Girdle	36	BoE	81		20	76
32	Witch Doctor's Waistband	37	BoE	83		20	87
33	Glyphed Belt	38	BoE	85		23	17
33	Nocturnal Sash	38	BoE	85		22	54
34	Dusky Belt	39	BoE	87		25	87
34	Elven Belt	39	BoE	87		26	36
35	Barbaric Belt	40	BoE	89		28	04
▶	SPELL Use: Adds 30 Rage						
35	Warden's Waistband	40	BoE	89		26	29
36	Ranger Cord	41	BoE	91		30	73
37	Imperial Leather Belt	42	BoE	93		32	94
N/A	Magram Hunter's Belt	42	BoA	93		33	31
37	Wolf Rider's Belt	42	BoE	93		30	67
38	Assassin's Belt	43	BoE	96		33	12
N/A	Gnomish Harm Prevention Belt	43	BoE	96		33	17
▶	SPELL Use: Shields User from 500 Dam						
N/A	Tharg's Shoelace	43	BoA	96		35	86
N/A	Belt of Corruption	44	BoA	98		38	15
N/A	Leather Chef's Belt	44	BoA	98		38	31
39	Tracker's Belt	44	BoE	98		35	66
40	Scorpashi Sash	45	BoE	99		38	63
41	Cabalist Belt	46	BoE	102		43	53
41	Rageclaw Belt	46	BoE	102		41	72
42	Heraldic Belt	47	BoE	104		46	32
42	Vampiric Bindings	47	BoE	104		45	06
43	Chieftain's Belt	48	BoE	106		51	93
44	Keeper's Cord	49	BoE	108		52	07
44	Righteous Waistguard	49	BoE	108		52	95
N/A	Vinehedge Cinch	49	BoA	108		53	33
45	Serpentskin Girdle	50	BoE	110		60	10
47	Infernal Belt	52	BoE	114		66	69
47	Jadefire Belt	52	BoE	114		63	20
48	Praetorian Girdle	53	BoE	116		66	99
49	Angelic Belt	54	BoE	118		72	73
N/A	Excavator's Utility Belt	55	BoA	120		75	27
50	Pridelord Girdle	55	BoE	120		75	27
51	Runic Leather Belt	56	BoE	122		83	68
51	Spiritwalker Belt	56	BoE	122		85	42
51	Stormhide Belt	56	BoE	122		80	24
52	Nether Runed Belt	57	BoE	124		84	57
53	Nightmare Girdle	58	BoE	126		91	48
54	Phantasmal Girdle	59	BoE	128		97	55
55	Arch Druid's Belt	60	BoE	130		98	84
55	Wicked Leather Belt	60	BoE	130		99	01
56	Cadaverous Belt	61	BoA	132	1	03	96
56	Seraphim Sash	61	BoE	132	1	03	78
57	Flamescarred Girdle	62	BoA	134	1	08	97
▶	SPELL Fire Resist +20						

STANDARD LEATHER WAIST ARMOR

M LEV	ARMOR NAME	LEV	BIND	AC	VENDOR PURCHASE VALUE		
N/A	Blackened Leather Belt	5	BoA	17			6
1	Cracked Leather Belt	5	None	17			6
1	Dirty Leather Belt	5	None	17			6
N/A	Nomadic Belt	5	BoA	17			6
N/A	Old Leather Belt	5	BoA	17			6
N/A	Outfitter Belt	5	BoA	17			6
1	Squealer's Belt	7	None	23			13
N/A	Animal Skin Belt	8	BoA	26			19
3	Primal Belt	8	None	26			18
4	Burnt Leather Belt	9	None	30			26
5	Battered Leather Belt	10	None	33			37
5	Handstitched Leather Belt	10	None	33			34

STANDARD LEATHER WAIST ARMOR continued

M LEV	ARMOR NAME	LEV	BIND	AC	VENDOR PURCHASE VALUE		
5	Pioneer Belt	10	None	33			35
5	Ratty Old Belt	10	None	33			37
5	Rough Leather Belt	10	None	33			36
5	Tribal Belt	10	None	33			35
6	Grizzly Belt	11	None	35			44
7	Gypsy Sash	12	None	38			57
N/A	Weathered Belt	12	BoA	38			57
8	Hunting Belt	13	None	41			71
9	Ceremonial Leather Belt	14	BoE	44			86
10	Lupine Cord	15	BoE	47		1	01
11	Fine Leather Belt	16	None	50		1	25
12	Tanned Leather Belt	17	None	52		1	45
13	Murloc Scale Belt	18	None	55		1	56
17	Cured Leather Belt	22	None	56		2	77
22	Cuirboulli Belt	27	None	68		5	24
32	Studded Belt	37	None	79		13	74
45	Reinforced Leather Belt	50	None	104		34	08

INFERIOR LEATHER WAIST ARMOR

M LEV	ARMOR NAME	LEV	BIND	AC	VENDOR PURCHASE VALUE		
1	Ragged Leather Belt	5	None	16			4
2	Worn Leather Belt	7	None	22			9
9	Warped Leather Belt	14	None	42			60
13	Patched Leather Belt	18	None	52		1	02
19	Rawhide Belt	24	None	58		2	35
25	Tough Leather Belt	30	None	61		4	65
N/A	Ripped Prospector Belt	38	BoA	77		9	61
34	Hardened Leather Belt	39	None	79		10	68
39	Thick Leather Belt	44	None	88		15	03
50	Smooth Leather Belt	55	None	108		32	56
58	Strapped Belt	63	None	122		47	38

LEATHER WRIST ARMOR

EPIC LEATHER WRIST ARMOR

M LEV	ARMOR NAME	LEV	BIND	AC	VENDOR PURCHASE VALUE		
44	Bladebane Armguards	49	BoE	101		88	02

SUPERIOR LEATHER WRIST ARMOR

M LEV	ARMOR NAME	LEV	BIND	AC	VENDOR PURCHASE VALUE		
20	Drakewing Bands	25	BoE	57		8	53
28	Emissary Cuffs	33	BoA	64		18	25
▶	**SPELL** Arcane Resist +5						
30	Unearthed Bands	35	BoE	67		20	96
▶	**SPELL** Attack Power 08						
34	Enchanted Kodo Bracers	39	BoE	75		30	63
47	Darkwater Bracers	52	BoA	97		75	62
▶	**SPELL** Shadow Resist +7						
50	Deepfury Bracers	55	BoE	103		95	05
52	Cinderhide Armsplints	57	BoA	106	1	03	98
▶	**SPELL** Fire Resist +10						
56	Bleak Howler Armguards	61	BoA	113	1	25	20
58	Blackmist Armguards	63	BoA	116	1	40	18
▶	**SPELL** Increased Hit Chance 1, Shadow Resist +10						

GOOD LEATHER WRIST ARMOR continued

M LEV	ARMOR NAME	LEV	BIND	AC	VENDOR PURCHASE VALUE		
10	Bard's Bracers	15	BoE	38		1	74
11	Feral Bindings	16	BoE	41		1	93
12	Inscribed Leather Bracers	17	BoE	43		2	29
12	Prospector's Cuffs	17	BoE	43		2	22
N/A	Ridgeback Bracers	18	BoA	45		2	79
N/A	Savannah Bracers	18	BoA	45		2	56
14	Bandit Bracers	19	BoE	48		3	18
15	Moonstalker's Bracelets	20	BoE	42		3	54
16	Scouting Bracers	21	BoE	44		4	25
17	Bristlebark Bindings	22	BoE	46		4	72
18	Wrangler's Wristbands	23	BoE	48		5	07
19	Forest Leather Bracers	24	BoE	50		5	84
20	Bear Bracers	25	BoE	52		7	05
20	Kodo Hide Cuffs	25	BoE	52		6	47
N/A	Loamflake Bracers	25	BoA	52		6	47
20	Owl Bracers	25	BoE	52		7	08
20	Wolf Bracers	25	BoE	52		7	03
21	Black Wolf Bracers	26	BoA	54		7	68
21	Deepwood Bracers	26	BoE	54		7	51
21	Pathfinder Bracers	26	BoE	54		7	31

GOOD LEATHER WRIST ARMOR continued

M LEV	ARMOR NAME	LEV	BIND	AC	VENDOR PURCHASE VALUE		
21	Pirate's Bracers	26	BoE	54		7	29
22	Bands of Serra'kis	27	BoA	56		8	77
22	Cenarion Cuffs	27	BoE	56		8	04
22	Dervish Bracers	27	BoE	56		8	73
23	Emblazoned Bracers	28	BoE	58		8	88
23	Glowing Leather Bracers	28	BoE	58		8	95
24	Cutthroat's Armguards	29	BoE	60		9	73
24	Madwolf Bracers	29	BoE	60		10	22
24	Monk's Wristbands	29	BoE	60		10	20
25	Headhunter's Bands	30	BoE	53		10	71
25	Jurassic Wristguards	30	BoE	53		11	13
26	Infiltrator Bracers	31	BoE	55		11	74
28	Ghostwalker Bindings	33	BoE	58		14	25
28	Insignia Bracers	33	BoE	58		15	14
29	Archer's Bracers	34	BoE	60		15	70
30	Hawkeye's Bracers	35	BoE	61		18	21
31	Green Leather Bracers	36	BoE	63		19	34
31	Sentinel Bracers	36	BoE	63		20	68
32	Dusky Bracers	37	BoE	65		21	46
32	Glyphed Bracers	37	BoE	65		22	33
33	Green Whelp Bracers	38	BoE	66		23	87
33	Murloc Scale Bracers	38	BoE	66		23	16
33	Witch Doctor's Bindings	38	BoE	66		22	54
34	Elven Bands	39	BoE	68		25	89
34	Guardian Leather Bracers	39	BoE	68		25	59
34	Nocturnal Wristbands	39	BoE	68		24	34
35	Warden's Wristbands	40	BoE	69		26	29
36	Ranger Wristguards	41	BoE	71		30	62
37	Imperial Leather Bracers	42	BoE	73		33	06
37	Wolf Rider's Wristbands	42	BoE	73		30	67
38	Assassin's Bands	43	BoE	74		33	12
39	Scorpashi Wristbands	44	BoE	76		35	77
39	Tracker's Wristguards	44	BoE	76		37	89
40	Cabalist Bracers	45	BoE	77		40	16
41	Heraldic Bracers	46	BoE	79		44	36
41	Rageclaw Bracers	46	BoE	79		41	72
42	Vampiric Bands	47	BoE	81		45	06
43	Chieftain's Bracers	48	BoE	82		48	55
43	Keeper's Bindings	48	BoE	82		48	67
44	Righteous Bracers	49	BoE	84		53	35
45	Jadefire Bracelets	50	BoE	85		55	72
45	Serpentskin Bracers	50	BoE	85		60	53
46	Praetorian Wristbands	51	BoE	87		59	62
47	Infernal Armsplints	52	BoE	89		65	23
48	Pridelord Bands	53	BoE	90		66	99
48	Wicked Leather Bracers	53	BoE	90		73	11

GOOD LEATHER WRIST ARMOR continued

M LEV	ARMOR NAME	LEV	BIND	AC	VENDOR PURCHASE VALUE		
49	Angelic Bracers	54	BoE	92		72	18
50	Runic Leather Bracers	55	BoE	93		76	56
50	Stormhide Bracers	55	BoE	93		75	27
51	Spiritwalker Bracers	56	BoE	95		79	88
52	Nether Runed Armguards	57	BoE	97		84	57
53	Nightmare Armguards	58	BoE	98		94	66
54	Arch Druid's Armguards	59	BoE	100		94	13
55	Chillhide Bracers	60	BoA	101		98	84
▶	**SPELL** Frost Resist +15						
55	Phantasmal Armsplints	60	BoE	101	1	03	19
55	Seraphim Bindings	60	BoE	101		98	84
56	Hellfire Bracers	61	BoE	103	1	06	75

STANDARD LEATHER WRIST ARMOR

M LEV	ARMOR NAME	LEV	BIND	AC	VENDOR PURCHASE VALUE		
1	Cracked Leather Bracers	5	None	13			6
1	Dirty Leather Bracers	5	None	13			6
N/A	Nomadic Bracers	5	BoA	13			6
N/A	Wolfskin Bracers	5	BoA	13			6
N/A	Feral Bracers	7	BoA	18			13
3	Burnt Leather Bracers	8	None	21			19
N/A	Sandrunner Wristguards	8	BoA	21			20
N/A	Zombie Skin Bracers	8	BoA	21			19
4	Handstitched Leather Bracers	9	None	23			28
4	Primal Bands	9	None	23			26
5	Battered Leather Bracers	10	None	25			34
5	Pioneer Bracers	10	None	25			36
N/A	Plains Hunter Wristguards	10	BoA	25			35

STANDARD continued

M LEV	ARMOR NAME	LEV	BIND	AC	VENDOR PURCHASE VALUE		
5	Rough Leather Bracers	10	None	25			37
5	Sturdy Leather Bracers	10	None	25			36
5	Tribal Bracers	10	None	25			36
6	Grizzly Bracers	11	None	28			44
N/A	Burnt Hide Bracers	12	BoA	30			60
7	Gypsy Bands	12	None	30			57
7	Ice-covered Bracers	12	None	30			58
8	Ceremonial Leather Bracers	13	BoE	32			70
N/A	Ivy Cuffs	13	BoA	32			72
9	Gnoll Kindred Bracers	14	None	34			87
9	Hunting Bracers	14	None	34			87
9	Light Leather Bracers	14	None	34			84
9	Lupine Cuffs	14	BoE	34			84
12	Tanned Leather Bracers	17	None	41		1	45
17	Cured Leather Bracers	22	None	44		2	78
22	Cuirboulli Bracers	27	None	53		5	27
32	Studded Bracers	37	None	61		12	62
45	Reinforced Leather Bracers	50	None	81		34	46

INFERIOR LEATHER WRIST ARMOR

M LEV	ARMOR NAME	LEV	BIND	AC	VENDOR PURCHASE VALUE		
1	Ragged Leather Bracers	4	None	10			2
4	Worn Leather Bracers	9	None	22			18
6	Warped Leather Bracers	11	None	26			32
15	Patched Leather Bracers	20	None	38		1	36
16	Rawhide Bracers	21	None	40		1	61
22	Tough Leather Bracers	27	None	50		3	51
29	Hardened Leather Bracers	34	None	54		6	27
38	Thick Leather Bracers	43	None	67		14	02
54	Smooth Leather Bracers	59	None	90		38	11

MAIL CHEST ARMOR

EPIC MAIL CHEST ARMOR

M LEV	ARMOR NAME	LEV	BIND	AC	VENDOR PURCHASE VALUE		
39	Icemail Jerkin	44	BoE	344	1	41	13
▶	**SPELL** Frost Resist +10						
52	Savage Gladiator Chain	57	BoA	441	3	35	33
▶	**SPELL** Adds +20 Defense, +2% Crit						
57	Onyxia Scale Breastplate	62	BoE	480	4	19	37
▶	**SPELL** Increased Armor 150, Fire Resist +9						
57	Invulnerable Mail	63	BoE	487	4	38	36
▶	**SPELL** Adds 150 Armor, 20 Defense, and Negates 5% of Physical Attacks						

SUPERIOR MAIL CHEST ARMOR

M LEV	ARMOR NAME	LEV	BIND	AC	VENDOR PURCHASE VALUE		
20	Phantom Armor	25	BoA	220		18	80
20	Tortoise Armor	25	BoA	220		18	72
▶	**SPELL** Increased Armor 110						
21	Martyr's Chain	26	BoE	229		22	13
23	Mutant Scale Breastplate	28	BoA	246		26	20
24	Shining Silver Breastplate	29	BoE	255		29	35
N/A	Brutal Hauberk	30	BoA	226		30	98
▶	**SPELL** Use: Adds 30 Rage						
25	Double Link Tunic	30	BoE	226		31	08
▶	**SPELL** Increased Armor 60						
N/A	Fire Hardened Hauberk	30	BoA	226		32	42
▶	**SPELL** Use: Adds 30 Rage						
26	Avenger's Armor	31	BoE	234		33	79
30	Ironspine's Ribcage	35	BoA	263		53	20

SUPERIOR MAIL CHEST ARMOR

M LEV	ARMOR NAME	LEV	BIND	AC	VENDOR PURCHASE VALUE		
31	Green Iron Hauberk	36	BoE	270		56	58
▶	**SPELL** Increased Armor 120						
33	Archon Chestpiece	38	BoE	282		67	23
34	Scarlet Chestpiece	39	BoE	287		69	92
39	Deathchill Armor	44	BoA	315	1	04	34
39	Polished Jazeraint Armor	44	BoE	315	1	03	01
43	Gahz'rilla Scale Armor	48	BoA	342	1	46	34
46	Dragonscale Breastplate	51	BoE	363	1	84	55
▶	**SPELL** Fire & Frost Resist +13, Shadow Resist +12, Use: Absorb 600 Magic Dam						
47	Atal'ai Breastplate	52	BoA	370	1	84	32
▶	**SPELL** Attack Power 22						
47	Green Dragonscale Breastplate	52	BoE	370	1	99	38
▶	**SPELL** Nature Resist +11						
49	Wildthorn Mail	54	BoE	384	2	06	42
▶	**SPELL** Increase Nature Dmg 20						
52	Blue Dragonscale Breastplate	57	BoE	405	2	44	09
▶	**SPELL** Arcane Resist +8						
52	Deathdealer Breastplate	57	BoA	405	2	45	90
▶	**SPELL** Adds 2% Crit						
53	Black Dragonscale Breastplate	58	BoE	412	2	60	71
▶	**SPELL** Attack Power 50, Fire Resist +8						
56	Bloodmail Hauberk	61	BoA	433	3	25	09
▶	**SPELL** Adds 1% Dodge						
56	Red Dragonscale Breastplate	61	BoE	433	2	98	36
▶	**SPELL** Increase Healing 60, Fire Resist +12						
57	Bonebrace Hauberk	62	BoA	440	3	38	84
▶	**SPELL** Attack Power 56						
57	Dreamwalker Chestpiece	62	BoE	440	3	33	87
58	Breastplate of the Chosen	63	BoA	446	3	59	55

GOOD MAIL CHEST ARMOR

M LEV	ARMOR NAME	LEV	BIND	AC	VENDOR PURCHASE VALUE		
5	Copper Chain Vest	10	BoE	97		1	42
6	Charger's Armor	11	BoE	107		1	79
6	Warrior's Tunic	11	BoE	107		1	89
8	Battle Chain Tunic	13	BoE	125		2	95
8	Dargol's Hauberk	13	BoE	125		2	81
N/A	Explorer's Vest	13	BoA	125		2	85
8	Infantry Tunic	13	BoE	125		3	05
10	Cadet Vest	15	BoE	143		4	06
10	Guerrilla Armor	15	BoE	143		4	36
N/A	Ironheart Chain	15	BoA	143		4	07
10	Slarkskin	15	BoE	143		4	23
10	Wax-polished Armor	15	BoE	143		4	16
11	Ironforge Chain	16	BoE	153		4	96
11	Veteran Armor	16	BoE	153		4	76
11	War Torn Tunic	16	BoE	153		4	65
13	Brackwater Vest	18	BoE	171		6	53
13	Runed Copper Breastplate	18	BoE	171		6	30
13	Soldier's Armor	18	BoE	171		6	75
15	Ironforge Breastplate	20	BoE	161		8	71
▶	**SPELL** Increased Armor 30						
15	Raider's Chestpiece	20	BoE	161		8	11
16	Bloodspattered Surcoat	21	BoE	169		9	36
16	Burnished Tunic	21	BoE	169		10	01
N/A	Violet Scale Armor	22	BoA	177		11	40
18	Defender Tunic	23	BoE	185		13	12
N/A	Orcish War Chain	23	BoA	185		12	69
18	War Paint Chestpiece	23	BoE	185		12	16
N/A	Chestplate of Kor	24	BoA	193		14	18
19	Outrunner's Chestguard	24	BoE	193		13	74
N/A	Wildwood Chain	24	BoA	193		15	09
N/A	Deputy Chain Coat	25	BoA	200		16	68
N/A	Forest Chain	25	BoA	200		16	56
20	Fortified Chain	25	BoE	200		16	82
21	Dusty Chain Armor	26	BoE	208		17	69
21	Grunt's Chestpiece	26	BoE	208		17	55
21	Silvered Bronze Breastplate	26	BoE	208		18	31
22	Husk of Naraxis	27	BoE	216		19	91
22	Lambent Scale Breastplate	27	BoE	216		21	19
23	Hulking Chestguard	28	BoE	224		21	24
23	Humbert's Chestpiece	28	BoE	224		21	40
24	Battleforge Armor	29	BoE	232		24	47
25	Large Ogre Chain Armor	30	BoE	206		26	69
25	Spiked Chain Breastplate	30	BoE	206		25	70
26	Glimmering Mail Breastplate	31	BoE	213		29	39
26	Sentry's Surcoat	31	BoE	213		28	27
27	Barbaric Iron Breastplate	32	None	219		33	30
28	Ambusher's Chestguard	33	BoE	226		36	77
28	Slayer's Surcoat	33	BoE	226		34	21
29	Wicked Chain Chestpiece	34	BoE	233		37	63
30	Onyx Shredder Plate	35	BoE	240		41	27
30	Phalanx Breastplate	35	BoE	240		42	56
31	Basilisk Scale Breastplate	36	BoE	245		45	54
31	Mail Combat Armor	36	BoE	245		47	85
32	Pillager's Chestguard	37	BoE	251		50	09
33	Renegade Chestguard	38	BoE	256		56	05
34	Burning Blade Breastplate	39	BoE	261		58	43
34	Knight's Breastplate	39	BoE	261		59	15
35	Golden Scale Cuirass	40	BoE	266		65	58
35	Marauder's Tunic	40	BoE	266		63	10
35	Steel Breastplate	40	BoE	266		64	88
▶	**SPELL** Increased Armor 150						
36	Chief Brigadier Armor	41	BoE	272		72	68
36	Sparkleshell Breastplate	41	BoE	272		68	15
37	Berserker Chestguard	42	BoE	277		73	68
N/A	Blood-tinged Armor	42	BoA	277		77	93
N/A	Gelkis Marauder Chain	42	BoA	277		73	66
37	Turtle Scale Breastplate	42	BoE	277		75	67
38	Slithid Scale Chestguard	43	BoE	282		79	49
39	Captain's Breastplate	44	BoE	287		93	25
39	Ravager's Armor	44	BoE	287		85	85
39	Tough Scorpid Breastplate	44	BoE	287		86	28
N/A	Blackwater Tunic	45	BoA	291	1	01	40
40	Brigade Breastplate	45	BoE	291		99	30
N/A	Dawnrider's Chestpiece	45	BoA	291		99	69
41	Ancient Chestpiece	46	BoE	298	1	00	14
41	Drake-scale Vest	46	BoE	298	1	00	93
42	Blackforge Breastplate	47	BoE	304	1	16	99
42	Bonelink Armor	47	BoE	304	1	08	15

GOOD MAIL CHEST ARMOR continued

M LEV	ARMOR NAME	LEV	BIND	AC	VENDOR PURCHASE VALUE		
43	Champion's Armor	48	BoE	311	1	23	22
44	Khan's Chestpiece	49	BoE	317	1	24	98
45	Warmonger's Chestpiece	50	BoE	323	1	37	53
46	Gryphon Mail Breastplate	51	BoE	330	1	48	34
46	Thunderscale Breastplate	51	BoE	330	1	56	56
47	Icebrand Chestpiece	52	BoE	336	1	51	68
48	Heavy Scorpid Vest	53	BoE	343	1	66	04
48	Lord's Breastplate	53	BoE	343	1	69	68
N/A	Splintsteel Armor	53	BoA	343	1	68	50
49	Protector Breastplate	54	BoE	349	1	70	43
49	Radiant Breastplate	54	BoE	349	1	70	03
▶	**SPELL** Frost & Shadow Resist +16						
50	Crusader's Armor	55	BoE	355	1	97	75
N/A	Honorguard Chestpiece	55	BoA	355	1	80	16
51	Dark Iron Mail	56	BoE	362	1	92	55
51	Ebonhold Armor	56	BoE	362	1	99	14
51	Ironhide Breastplate	56	BoE	362	1	91	49
52	Daemonic Surcoat	57	BoE	368	2	02	98
N/A	Prismscale Hauberk	57	BoA	368	2	04	04
N/A	Basaltscale Armor	58	BoA	374	2	30	54
53	Divine Breastplate	58	BoE	374	2	33	81
53	Royal Decorated Armor	58	BoA	374	2	15	16
54	Bloodlust Breastplate	59	BoE	381	2	25	92
N/A	Jadescale Breastplate	59	BoA	381	2	25	92
N/A	Willow Band Hauberk	59	BoA	381	2	25	92
55	Abyssal Breastplate	60	BoE	387	2	56	86
56	Impenetrable Breastplate	61	BoE	393	2	49	07
57	Hellcaller Chestguard	62	BoE	400	2	61	53
57	Savage Mail Tunic	62	BoE	400	2	75	10
57	Tempest Breastplate	62	BoE	400	2	69	89
59	Mercurial Breastplate	64	BoE	412	3	12	16
59	Warlord's Chestguard	64	BoE	412	2	88	34
60	Kraken Breastplate	65	BoE	419	3	23	10
60	Triumphant Chestpiece	65	BoE	419	3	02	75

STANDARD MAIL CHEST ARMOR

M LEV	ARMOR NAME	LEV	BIND	AC	VENDOR PURCHASE VALUE		
N/A	Barkmail Vest	5	BoA	47			14
1	Frostmane Chain Vest	5	None	47			14
N/A	Jagged Chain Vest	5	BoA	47			15
N/A	Rugged Mail Vest	5	BoA	47			15
1	Rusted Chain Vest	5	None	47			15
1	Tarnished Chain Vest	5	None	47			15
2	Mountaineer Chestpiece	7	None	65			32
2	Rough Copper Vest	7	None	65			32
5	Light Chain Armor	10	None	92			86
5	Light Mail Armor	10	None	92			82
N/A	Siege Brigade Vest	10	BoA	92			87
12	Chainmail Armor	17	None	154		3	49
17	Scalemail Vest	22	None	168		7	11
18	Rough Bronze Cuirass	23	None	175		7	52
22	Polished Scale Vest	27	None	205		11	85
32	Augmented Chain Vest	37	None	238		31	34
45	Brigandine Vest	50	None	307		85	54

INFERIOR MAIL CHEST ARMOR

M LEV	ARMOR NAME	LEV	BIND	AC	VENDOR PURCHASE VALUE		
1	Flimsy Chain Vest	5	None	45			9
5	Loose Chain Vest	10	None	88			58
9	Worn Mail Vest	14	None	121		1	39
11	Laced Mail Vest	16	None	137		1	98
17	Linked Chain Vest	22	None	159		4	39
23	Reinforced Chain Vest	28	None	201		8	92
28	Double Mail Vest	33	None	203		14	75
40	Overlinked Chain Armor	45	None	262		36	96
49	Laminated Scale Armor	54	None	314		71	09
57	Sterling Chain Armor	62	None	360	1	07	47

MAIL FOOT ARMOR

SUPERIOR MAIL FOOT ARMOR

M LEV	ARMOR NAME	LEV	BIND	AC	VENDOR PURCHASE VALUE		
16	Silver-linked Footguards	21	BoE	128		8	50
27	Caverndeep Trudgers	32	BoE	166		29	45
30	Scarlet Boots	35	BoE	181		37	90
30	Ravasaur Scale Boots	35	BoE	181		39	96
32	Black Ogre Kickers	37	BoE	190		45	81
45	Elven Chain Boots	50	BoE	244	1	29	54
49	Bloodshot Greaves	54	BoA	264	1	61	43
52	Savage Gladiator Greaves	57	BoA	278	1	93	00
54	Timmy's Galoshes	59	BoA	288	2	11	68
56	Wind Dancer Boots	61	BoA	297	2	25	61
▶	**SPELL** Adds 1% Dodge						
56	Windreaver Greaves	61	BoA	297	2	33	38

GOOD MAIL FOOT ARMOR

M LEV	ARMOR NAME	LEV	BIND	AC	VENDOR PURCHASE VALUE		
N/A	Greaves of the People's Militia	15	BoA	98		3	31
N/A	Mud Stompers	15	BoA	98		3	05
11	Bloodspattered Sabatons	16	BoE	105		3	50
N/A	Padded Lamellar Boots	16	BoA	105		3	72
N/A	Crustacean Boots	17	BoA	111		4	03
12	Soldier's Boots	17	BoE	111		4	09
12	War Paint Boots	17	BoE	111		4	03
N/A	Tunneler's Boots	18	BoA	118		4	69
14	Blackrock Boots	19	BoE	124		5	68
14	Raider's Boots	19	BoE	124		5	33
15	Outrunner's Slippers	20	BoE	110		6	13
16	Burnished Boots	21	BoE	116		7	05
16	Grunt's Boots	21	BoE	116		7	05
N/A	Dredge Boots	22	BoA	122		8	30
18	Defender Boots	23	BoE	127		9	38
18	Savage Trodders	23	BoA	127		9	34
19	Hulking Boots	24	BoE	132		10	35
20	Fortified Boots	25	BoE	138		12	31
N/A	Gold Militia Boots	25	BoA	138		12	57
N/A	Quagmire Galoshes	25	BoA	138		12	49
21	Silvered Bronze Boots	26	BoE	143		13	17
22	Dragonmaw Chain Boots	27	BoE	149		15	73
22	Lambent Scale Boots	27	BoE	149		15	73
22	Spiked Chain Greaves	27	BoE	149		14	54
23	Sentry's Sabatons	28	BoE	154		16	00
24	Battleforge Boots	29	BoE	159		18	30
24	Green Iron Boots	29	BoE	159		17	67
24	Slayer's Slippers	29	BoE	159		17	60
26	Glimmering Mail Greaves	31	BoE	146		22	30
26	Wicked Chain Boots	31	BoE	146		21	30
27	Ambusher's Boots	32	BoE	151		24	09
27	Basilisk Scale Sabatons	32	BoE	151		23	43
27	Trouncing Boots	32	BoE	151		23	80
28	Pillager's Boots	33	BoE	155		25	77
29	Phalanx Boots	34	BoE	160		29	03
30	Mail Combat Boots	35	BoE	165		33	01
31	Barbaric Iron Boots	36	BoE	169		37	00
31	Renegade Boots	36	BoE	169		35	27
32	Burning Blade Boots	37	BoE	172		37	73
32	Knight's Boots	37	BoE	172		39	83
32	Polished Steel Boots	37	BoE	172		39	37
33	Marauder's Gauntlets	38	BoE	176		40	75
34	Chief Brigadier Boots	39	BoE	180		47	11
34	Sparkleshell Sabatons	39	BoE	180		44	01
35	Berserker Boots	40	BoE	183		52	21
35	Golden Scale Boots	40	BoE	183		49	77
36	Slithid Scale Boots	41	BoE	187		51	34
37	Captain's Boots	42	BoE	190		56	80
N/A	Darkspear Boots	42	BoA	190		60	21
37	Ravager's Boots	42	BoE	190		55	54
38	Brigade Boots	43	BoE	194		63	68
39	Ancient Greaves	44	BoE	197		64	67
40	Blackforge Greaves	45	BoE	200		72	33
40	Bonelink Sabatons	45	BoE	200		69	85
N/A	Boots of Zua'tec	45	BoA	200		75	36
N/A	Ironheel Boots	45	BoA	200		71	78
41	Champion's Greaves	46	BoE	205		82	84

GOOD MAIL FOOT ARMOR continued

M LEV	ARMOR NAME	LEV	BIND	AC	VENDOR PURCHASE VALUE		
41	Khan's Greaves	46	BoE	205		75	44
42	Gryphon Mail Greaves	47	BoE	209		87	98
42	Tough Scorpid Boots	47	BoE	209		83	75
43	Warmonger's Greaves	48	BoE	213		92	18
44	Icebrand Sabatons	49	BoE	218		94	15
44	Thunderscale Greaves	49	BoE	218		94	58
45	Protector Sabatons	50	BoE	222	1	00	74
46	Lord's Boots	51	BoE	227	1	07	52
47	Atal'ai Boots	52	BoA	231	1	19	77
47	Ironhide Greaves	52	BoE	231	1	14	26
48	Crusader's Boots	53	BoE	236	1	32	12
48	Fleetfoot Greaves	53	BoA	236	1	21	12
49	Daemonic Greaves	54	BoE	240	1	28	39
50	Ebonhold Boots	55	BoE	244	1	43	62
52	Divine Greaves	57	BoE	253	1	66	76
53	Abyssal Boots	58	BoE	257	1	78	01
53	Bloodlust Boots	58	BoE	257	1	62	09
53	Radiant Boots	58	BoE	257	1	64	21
▶	**SPELL** Frost & Shadow Resist +15						
54	Impenetrable Sabatons	59	BoE	262	1	70	19
54	Swiftdart Battleboots	59	BoA	262	1	73	12
55	Hellcaller Greaves	60	BoE	266	1	78	70
55	Tempest Boots	60	BoE	266	1	87	17
56	Bloodmail Boots	61	BoA	270	1	87	99
56	Mercurial Greaves	61	BoE	270	2	01	68
57	Warlord's Sabatons	62	BoE	275	1	97	02
58	Kraken Boots	63	BoE	279	2	23	96
58	Savage Mail Boots	63	BoE	279	2	18	41
58	Triumphant Sabatons	63	BoE	279	2	06	87

STANDARD MAIL FOOT ARMOR

M LEV	ARMOR NAME	LEV	BIND	AC	VENDOR PURCHASE VALUE	
N/A	Outfitter Boots	5	BoA	33		10
1	Rusted Chain Boots	5	None	33		11
1	Tarnished Chain Boots	5	None	33		11
N/A	Tracking Boots	5	BoA	33		11
N/A	Cryptwalker Boots	8	BoA	51		34
4	Copper Chain Boots	9	None	57		49
4	Perrine's Boots	9	None	57		48
5	Charger's Boots	10	None	64		62
N/A	Cliff Runner Boots	10	BoA	64		64
5	Light Chain Boots	10	None	64		66
5	Light Mail Boots	10	None	64		64
N/A	Lightweight Boots	10	BoA	64		67
5	Warrior's Boots	10	None	64		66
6	Infantry Boots	11	None	70		87
7	Battle Chain Boots	12	None	76	1	05
8	Cadet Boots	13	None	81	1	38
8	War Torn Slippers	13	None	81	1	27
9	Veteran Boots	14	None	87	1	57
10	Brackwater Boots	15	BoE	94	1	91
12	Chainmail Boots	17	None	106	2	65
13	Rough Bronze Boots	18	None	112	2	95
17	Scalemail Boots	22	None	116	4	88
22	Polished Scale Boots	27	None	141	8	79
32	Augmented Chain Boots	37	None	164	23	87
45	Brigandine Boots	50	None	211	65	13

INFERIOR MAIL FOOT ARMOR

M LEV	ARMOR NAME	LEV	BIND	AC	VENDOR PURCHASE VALUE	
1	Flimsy Chain Boots	3	None	19		3
4	Loose Chain Boots	9	None	54		33
8	Worn Mail Boots	13	None	77		92
15	Laced Mail Boots	20	None	99	2	55
16	Linked Chain Boots	21	None	105	3	02
22	Reinforced Chain Boots	27	None	134	5	97
27	Double Mail Boots	32	None	136	9	62
41	Overlinked Chain Boots	46	None	184	31	70
48	Laminated Scale Boots	53	None	212	49	40
60	Sterling Chain Boots	65	None	259	91	61

MAIL HAND ARMOR

EPIC MAIL HAND ARMOR

M LEV	ARMOR NAME	LEV	BIND	AC	VENDOR PURCHASE VALUE		
44	Edgemaster's Handguards	49	BoE	238	1	06	01
▶	**SPELL** Increased 1H Axe						

SUPERIOR MAIL HAND ARMOR

M LEV	ARMOR NAME	LEV	BIND	AC	VENDOR PURCHASE VALUE		
18	Thorbia's Gauntlets	23	BoE	127		7	87
23	Algae Fists	28	BoA	154		12	75
29	Grubbis Paws	34	BoA	160		22	60
31	Reticulated Bone Gauntlets	36	BoE	169		29	16
31	Stormgale Fists	36	BoE	169		29	05
39	Gauntlets of Divinity	44	BoA	197		54	36
▶	**SPELL** Attack Power 32						
40	Dragonscale Gauntlets	45	BoE	200		59	79
▶	**SPELL** Adds 1% Crit						
41	Murkwater Gauntlets	46	BoE	205		60	86
48	Battlecaller Gauntlets	53	BoE	236	1	03	74
52	Savage Gladiator Grips	57	BoA	253	1	27	62
53	Molten Fists	58	BoA	257	1	30	83
▶	**SPELL** Firebolt, Fire Resist +10						
54	Storm Gauntlets	59	BoE	262	1	40	99
▶	**SPELL** Fire Resist +10, Add 3 Dam, Add 13 to Nature spells						
N/A	Voone's Vice Grips	60	BoA	266	1	45	33
▶	**SPELL** Adds 2% Crit						
58	Dracorian Gauntlets	63	BoA	279	1	72	10

GOOD MAIL HAND ARMOR

M LEV	ARMOR NAME	LEV	BIND	AC	VENDOR PURCHASE VALUE		
10	Gemmed Copper Gauntlets	15	BoE	90		2	16
10	Veteran Gloves	15	BoE	90		2	09
12	Sapper's Gloves	17	BoE	101		2	89
12	Skeletal Gauntlets	17	BoE	101		2	78
12	Soldier's Gauntlets	17	BoE	101		2	67
N/A	Rugged Mail Gloves	18	BoA	107		3	34
13	War Paint Gloves	18	BoE	107		3	07
14	Raider's Gauntlets	19	BoE	113		3	58
15	Blackrock Gauntlets	20	BoE	100		4	05
N/A	Bridgeworker's Gloves	20	BoA	100		4	18
15	Burnished Gloves	20	BoE	100		4	08
15	Outrunner's Gloves	20	BoE	100		4	07
N/A	Riveted Gauntlets	20	BoA	100		4	19
16	Grunt's Handwraps	21	BoE	106		4	68
N/A	Night Watch Gauntlets	21	BoA	106		4	73
N/A	Polar Gauntlets	22	BoA	111		5	57
N/A	Dagmire Gauntlets	23	BoA	115		6	41
18	Defender Gauntlets	23	BoE	115		6	49
18	Hulking Gauntlets	23	BoE	115		6	08
N/A	Gloves of Brawn	24	BoA	120		7	14
N/A	Hedgeseed Gauntlets	24	BoA	120		7	22
20	Fortified Gauntlets	25	BoE	125		8	25
N/A	Palestrider Gloves	25	BoA	125		7	87
21	Spiked Chain Gauntlets	26	BoE	130		8	77
22	Lambent Scale Gloves	27	BoE	135		10	52
22	Sentry's Gloves	27	BoE	135		9	65
22	Silvered Bronze Gauntlets	27	BoE	135		9	65
23	Battleforge Gauntlets	28	BoE	140		11	24
23	Ironforge Gauntlets	28	BoE	140		11	45
▶	**SPELL** Attack Power 12						
24	Slayer's Gloves	29	BoE	145		11	68
25	Glimmering Mail Gauntlets	30	BoE	129		13	40
25	Green Iron Gauntlets	30	BoE	129		12	95
25	Wicked Chain Gauntlets	30	BoE	129		12	85
26	Ambusher's Gauntlets	31	BoE	133		14	26
N/A	Brutal Gauntlets	31	BoA	133		15	46
N/A	Fire Hardened Gauntlets	31	BoA	133		14	97
27	Basilisk Scale Gauntlets	32	BoE	137		15	55
27	Bonefist Gauntlets	32	BoE	137		15	85
27	Gauntlets of Ogre Strength	32	BoE	137		16	21
▶	**SPELL** Attack Power 16						
28	Phalanx Gauntlets	33	BoE	141		17	78

GOOD MAIL HAND ARMOR continued

M LEV	ARMOR NAME	LEV	BIND	AC	VENDOR PURCHASE VALUE		
29	Mail Combat Gauntlets	34	BoE	146		19	84
29	Pillager's Gloves	34	BoE	146		18	81
30	Burning Blade Gauntlets	35	BoE	150		20	70
30	Renegade Gauntlets	35	BoE	150		21	60
31	Marauder's Gauntlets	36	BoE	153		22	77
32	Barbaric Iron Gloves	37	BoE	157		27	11
32	Knight's Gauntlets	37	BoE	157		25	64
33	Chief Brigadier Gauntlets	38	BoE	160		28	52
33	Scarlet Gauntlets	38	BoE	160		27	28
33	Sparkleshell Gauntlets	38	BoE	160		27	05
34	Slithid Scale Gloves	39	BoE	163		29	21
35	Berserker Gauntlets	40	BoE	167		31	95
35	Ravager's Handwraps	40	BoE	167		31	55
36	Captain's Gauntlets	41	BoE	170		37	40
36	Golden Scale Gauntlets	41	BoE	170		36	89
36	Turtle Scale Gloves	41	BoE	170		34	77
37	Ancient Gauntlets	42	BoE	173		36	80
38	Brigade Gauntlets	43	BoE	176		42	87
39	Blackforge Gauntlets	44	BoE	179		43	28
39	Bonelink Gauntlets	44	BoE	179		42	92
39	Mithril Scale Gloves	44	BoE	179		44	47
40	Khan's Gloves	45	BoE	182		46	36
40	Tough Scorpid Gloves	45	BoE	182		46	76
41	Champion's Gauntlets	46	BoE	186		54	79
42	Gryphon Mail Gauntlets	47	BoE	190		58	18
42	Warmonger's Gauntlets	47	BoE	190		56	23
43	Icebrand Gauntlets	48	BoE	194		58	40
44	Thunderscale Gauntlets	49	BoE	198		62	29
45	Lord's Gauntlets	50	BoE	202		73	19
45	Protector Gauntlets	50	BoE	202		66	86
47	Crusader's Gauntlets	52	BoE	210		75	93
47	Ironhide Gauntlets	52	BoE	210		75	84
48	Daemonic Gauntlets	53	BoE	214		80	39
N/A	Maddening Gauntlets	53	BoA	214		80	39
N/A	Brazen Gauntlets	54	BoA	218		89	96
49	Ebonhold Gauntlets	54	BoE	218		89	27
50	Bloodlust Gauntlets	55	BoE	222		90	32
N/A	Bricksteel Gauntlets	55	BoA	222		91	91
N/A	Grotslab Gloves	55	BoA	222		95	37
50	Heavy Scorpid Gauntlet	55	BoE	222		96	49
51	Divine Gauntlets	56	BoE	226	1	05	15
52	Impenetrable Gauntlets	57	BoE	230	1	01	49
52	Radiant Gloves	57	BoE	230	1	02	42
▶	**SPELL** Frost & Shadow Resist +12						
53	Abyssal Gauntlets	58	BoE	234	1	17	32
54	Tempest Gauntlets	59	BoE	238	1	17	43
54	Trueaim Gauntlets	59	BoA	238	1	19	72
▶	**SPELL** Adds 8 to Bow						
55	Gilded Gauntlets	60	BoA	242	1	20	68
55	Hellcaller Gauntlets	60	BoE	242	1	18	60
56	Bloodmail Gauntlets	61	BoA	246	1	24	30
56	Darkspinner Claws	61	BoA	246	1	27	62
▶	**SPELL** Nature & Shadow Resist +13						
56	Mercurial Gauntlets	61	BoE	246	1	27	13
57	Warlord's Gauntlets	62	BoE	250	1	30	76
58	Kraken Gauntlets	63	BoE	254	1	47	58
58	Triumphant Gauntlets	63	BoE	254	1	37	30

STANDARD MAIL HAND ARMOR

M LEV	ARMOR NAME	LEV	BIND	AC	VENDOR PURCHASE VALUE		
N/A	Boar Handler Gloves	5	BoA	30			7
N/A	Painted Chain Gloves	5	BoA	30			7
1	Rusted Chain Gloves	5	None	30			7
1	Tarnished Chain Gloves	5	None	30			7
N/A	Cold Steel Gauntlets	8	BoA	46			23
4	Warrior's Gloves	9	None	52			33
5	Charger's Handwraps	10	None	58			41
5	Light Chain Gloves	10	None	58			44
5	Light Mail Gloves	10	None	58			43
N/A	Moss-covered Gauntlets	10	BoA	58			41

STANDARD MAIL HAND ARMOR continued

M LEV	ARMOR NAME	LEV	BIND	AC	VENDOR PURCHASE VALUE		
N/A	Stormwind Chain Gloves	10	BoA	58			42
6	Battle Chain Gloves	11	None	63			56
6	Infantry Gauntlets	11	None	63			54
7	Runed Copper Gauntlets	12	None	69			71
7	War Torn Handgrips	12	None	69			67
8	Cadet Gauntlets	13	None	74			92
9	Brackwater Gauntlets	14	BoE	80		1	06
N/A	Noosegrip Gauntlets	14	BoA	80		1	01
10	Bloodspattered Gloves	15	BoE	85		1	21
12	Chainmail Gloves	17	None	96		1	76
17	Scalemail Gloves	22	None	105		3	22
22	Polished Scale Gloves	27	None	128		5	88
32	Augmented Chain Gloves	37	None	149		15	96
45	Brigandine Gloves	50	None	192		40	44

INFERIOR MAIL HAND ARMOR

M LEV	ARMOR NAME	LEV	BIND	AC	VENDOR PURCHASE VALUE		
1	Flimsy Chain Gloves	4	None	23			3
2	Loose Chain Gloves	7	None	39			11
6	Worn Mail Gloves	11	None	60			39
13	Laced Mail Gloves	18	None	96		1	29
19	Linked Chain Gloves	24	None	108		2	98
25	Reinforced Chain Gloves	30	None	116		5	34
31	Double Mail Gloves	36	None	138		9	71
42	Overlinked Chain Gloves	47	None	171		23	57
54	Laminated Scale Gloves	59	None	214		46	59
62	Sterling Chain Gloves	67	None	243		67	81

CLOTH ARMOR

LEATHER ARMOR

MAIL ARMOR

PLATE ARMOR

SHIELDS

WEAPONS

MAIL HEAD ARMOR

EPIC MAIL HEAD ARMOR

M LEV	ARMOR NAME	LEV	BIND	AC	VENDOR PURCHASE VALUE		
54	Helm of Narv	59	BoE	371	2	76	36

SUPERIOR MAIL HEAD ARMOR

M LEV	ARMOR NAME	LEV	BIND	AC	VENDOR PURCHASE VALUE		
27	Frostreaver Crown	32	BoE	196		30	21
28	Sunblaze Coif	33	BoE	202		32	01
▶	**SPELL** Fire Resist +10						
37	Raging Berserker's Helm	42	BoA	247		68	63
▶	**SPELL** Adds 1% Crit						
42	High Bergg Helm	47	BoE	272	1	05	43
47	Braincage	52	BoE	300	1	36	69
N/A	Helm of Exile	55	BoA	317	1	69	80
51	Horns of Eranikus	56	BoA	323		85	97
52	Savage Gladiator Helm	57	BoA	329	1	90	73
56	Helm of the Great Chief	61	BoE	352	2	42	85
▶	**SPELL** Aura of Resolve						
58	Crown of Tyranny	63	BoA	363	2	53	36
▶	**SPELL** Adds 40 to Group Attack Power, lowers Spirit by 10.						

GOOD MAIL HEAD ARMOR

M LEV	ARMOR NAME	LEV	BIND	AC	VENDOR PURCHASE VALUE		
N/A	Brutal Helm	31	BoA	173		23	28
N/A	Fire Hardened Coif	31	BoA	173		22	21
26	Glimmering Mail Coif	31	BoE	173		22	45
26	Sentry's Headress	31	BoE	173		21	20
27	Ambusher's Helm	32	BoE	178		23	90
28	Phalanx Headguard	33	BoE	184		26	58
28	Slayer's Skullcap	33	BoE	184		25	66
N/A	Sparkmetal Coif	33	BoA	184		28	25
28	Tusken Helm	33	BoA	184		26	27
29	Green Iron Helm	34	BoE	189		30	53
29	Wicked Chain Helmet	34	BoE	189		28	22
30	Barbaric Iron Helm	35	BoE	195		33	37
30	Basilisk Scale Crown	35	BoE	195		31	05
30	Mail Combat Headguard	35	BoE	195		32	98
31	Renegade Circlet	36	BoE	199		36	86
32	Pillager's Crown	37	BoE	204		37	57
33	Burning Blade Circlet	38	BoE	208		40	57
33	Golden Scale Coif	38	BoE	208		44	05
33	Knight's Headguard	38	BoE	208		41	39
34	Chief Brigadier Coif	39	BoE	212		46	72
34	Marauder's Helmet	39	BoE	212		43	82
35	Sparkleshell Crown	40	BoE	216		47	33
36	Berserker Coif	41	BoE	221		53	57
N/A	Goblin Mining Helmet	41	BoA	221		52	55
▶	**SPELL** Adds 5 to Mining						
37	Captain's Circlet	42	BoE	225		60	38
37	Slithid Scale Coronet	42	BoE	225		55	20
38	Ravager's Crown	43	BoE	229		59	62
38	Skullsplitter Helm	43	BoE	229		61	72

GOOD MAIL HEAD ARMOR continued

M LEV	ARMOR NAME	LEV	BIND	AC	VENDOR PURCHASE VALUE		
39	Brigade Circlet	44	BoE	233		69	95
40	Ancient Crown	45	BoE	237		69	54
40	Blackforge Cowl	45	BoE	237		74	69
41	Bonelink Helmet	46	BoE	242		75	10
41	Mithril Coif	46	BoE	242		79	55
41	Turtle Scale Helm	46	BoE	242		77	80
42	Champion's Helmet	47	BoE	247		88	45
43	Khan's Helmet	48	BoE	252		87	60
43	Warmonger's Circlet	48	BoE	252		92	11
45	Gryphon Mail Crown	50	BoE	263	1	07	15
45	Thunderscale Helm	50	BoE	263	1	01	15
45	Tough Scorpid Helm	50	BoE	263	1	02	72
N/A	Drakefire Headguard	51	BoA	268	1	08	30
46	Lord's Crown	51	BoE	268	1	07	45
47	Icebrand Circlet	52	BoE	273	1	13	76
48	Crusader's Helm	53	BoE	278	1	21	67
48	Protector Helm	53	BoE	278	1	20	58
N/A	Conservator Helm	54	BoA	283	1	38	42
N/A	Clayridge Helm	55	BoA	289	1	40	44
50	Ebonhold Helmet	55	BoE	289	1	43	51
50	Ironhide Helmet	55	BoE	289	1	35	49
51	Daemonic Crown	56	BoE	294	1	43	62
52	Divine Circlet	57	BoE	299	1	52	39
53	Bloodlust Coif	58	BoE	304	1	61	37
54	Abyssal Helm	59	BoE	309	1	68	96
54	Heavy Scorpid Helm	59	BoE	309	1	82	30
54	Radiant Circlet	59	BoE	309	1	70	34
▶	**SPELL** Frost & Shadow Resist +18						
55	Impenetrable Helmet	60	BoE	314	1	77	91
55	Tempest Band	60	BoE	314	1	87	03
56	Hellcaller Helmet	61	BoE	320	1	86	80
57	Mercurial Circlet	62	BoE	325	1	99	48
58	Dragoneye Coif	63	BoA	330	2	15	84
▶	**SPELL** Attack Power 28						
58	Kraken Helm	63	BoE	330	2	08	65
58	Warlord's Helmet	63	BoE	330	2	05	95
59	Triumphant Skullcap	64	BoE	335	2	16	25

STANDARD MAIL HEAD ARMOR

M LEV	ARMOR NAME	LEV	BIND	AC	VENDOR PURCHASE VALUE		
32	Augmented Chain Helm	37	None	194		24	56
45	Brigandine Helm	50	None	250		59	97

INFERIOR MAIL HEAD ARMOR

M LEV	ARMOR NAME	LEV	BIND	AC	VENDOR PURCHASE VALUE		
25	Double Mail Coif	30	None	150		7	71
39	Overlinked Coif	44	None	210		26	18
49	Laminated Scale Helm	54	None	255		51	12

MAIL LEG ARMOR

EPIC MAIL LEG ARMOR

M LEV	ARMOR NAME	LEV	BIND	AC	VENDOR PURCHASE VALUE		
N/A	Legguards of the Chromatic Defier	62	BoA	420	4	54	82
N/A	Legplates of the Chromatic Defier	62	BoA	420	4	25	65

SUPERIOR MAIL LEG ARMOR

M LEV	ARMOR NAME	LEV	BIND	AC	VENDOR PURCHASE VALUE		
N/A	Chausses of Westfall	24	BoA	185		17	27
21	Dreamsinger Legguards	26	BoE	200		22	41
N/A	Dual Reinforced Leggings	37	BoA	241		63	44
▶	**SPELL** Increased Armor 180						
34	Legguards of the Vault	39	BoE	252		73	19
34	Firemane Leggings	39	BoE	252		76	21
▶	**SPELL** Fire Resist +10						
38	Scarlet Leggings	43	BoA	271		95	87
48	Searingscale Leggings	53	BoA	330	2	01	41
▶	**SPELL** Fire Resist +10						
49	Green Dragonscale Leggings	54	BoE	336	2	24	82
▶	**SPELL** Nature Resist +11						
51	Windrunner Legguards	56	BoE	348	2	50	65
52	Savage Gladiator Leggings	57	BoA	354	2	53	36
53	Woollies of the Prancing Minstrel	58	BoA	360	2	68	64
▶	**SPELL** Adds 2% Dodge						
57	Maelstrom Leggings	62	BoA	385	3	13	18
57	Black Dragonscale Leggings	62	BoE	385	3	19	33
▶	**SPELL** Attack Power 54, Fire Resist +8						
58	Tristam Legguards	63	BoA	391	3	33	88
▶	**SPELL** Attack Power 34						

GOOD MAIL LEG ARMOR

M LEV	ARMOR NAME	LEV	BIND	AC	VENDOR PURCHASE VALUE		
N/A	Barkmail Leggings	10	BoA	85		1	42
5	Warrior's Pants	10	BoE	85		1	46
6	Charger's Pants	11	BoE	93		1	79
7	Battle Chain Pants	12	BoE	101		2	35
7	Infantry Leggings	12	BoE	101		2	45
8	Runed Copper Pants	13	BoE	109		2	99
N/A	Stormwind Guard Leggings	13	BoA	109		2	90
9	Cadet Leggings	14	BoE	117		3	36
9	War Torn Kilt	14	BoE	117		3	37
10	Veteran Leggings	15	BoE	125		4	15
11	Brackwater Leggings	16	BoE	134		4	92
N/A	Settler's Leggings	17	BoA	142		5	39
12	Soldier's Leggings	17	BoE	142		5	33
13	Bloodspattered Britches	18	BoE	150		6	15
N/A	Gargoyle Leggings	18	BoA	150		6	15
N/A	Guststorm Legguards	18	BoA	150		6	15
14	Goblin Mail Leggings	19	BoE	158		7	13
14	Raider's Legguards	19	BoE	158		7	41
14	War Paint Legguards	19	BoE	158		7	07
15	Foreman's Leggings	20	BoE	140		8	10
16	Burnished Leggings	21	BoE	148		9	33
16	Rough Bronze Leggings	21	BoE	148		9	62
17	Outrunner's Legguards	22	BoE	155		10	76
18	Defender Leggings	23	BoE	161		13	02
18	Mighty Chain Pants	23	BoE	161		12	21
19	Grunt's Legguards	24	BoE	168		13	74
19	Legionnaire's Leggings	24	BoE	168		15	03
20	Fortified Leggings	25	BoE	175		16	64
20	Hulking Leggings	25	BoE	175		15	53
N/A	Darkshire Mail Leggings	26	BoA	182		18	10
21	Lambent Scale Legguards	26	BoE	182		19	19
N/A	Malleable Chain Leggings	26	BoA	182		17	96
N/A	Juggernaut Leggings	27	BoA	189		20	68
22	Spiked Chain Leggings	27	BoE	189		19	31

GOOD MAIL LEG ARMOR continued

M LEV	ARMOR NAME	LEV	BIND	AC	VENDOR PURCHASE VALUE		
23	Battleforge Legguards	28	BoE	196		22	58
N/A	Brutal Legguards	29	BoA	203		23	38
N/A	Fire Hardened Leggings	29	BoA	203		24	65
N/A	Plainsguard Leggings	29	BoA	203		23	37
24	Sentry's Leggings	29	BoE	203		23	37
25	Glimmering Mail Legguards	30	BoE	180		26	92
N/A	Mercenary Leggings	30	BoA	180		26	61
26	Green Iron Leggings	31	BoE	186		29	06
26	Silvered Bronze Leggings	31	BoE	186		28	42
27	Ambusher's Leggings	32	BoE	192		31	63
27	Slayer's Pants	32	BoE	192		32	98
28	Wicked Chain Legguards	33	BoE	198		34	21
29	Golden Scale Leggings	34	BoE	204		38	82
29	Phalanx Leggings	34	BoE	204		39	41
30	Basilisk Scale Legguards	35	BoE	210		41	40
31	Mail Combat Leggings	36	BoE	215		46	99
31	Pillager's Leggings	36	BoE	215		45	54
32	Burning Blade Breeches	37	BoE	219		50	09
32	Renegade Leggings	37	BoE	219		54	25
N/A	Stromgarde Cavalry Leggings	37	BoA	219		54	38
33	Marauder's Leggings	38	BoE	224		54	10
34	Knight's Legguards	39	BoE	229		59	37
35	Chief Brigadier Leggings	40	BoE	233		67	53
35	Sparkleshell Legguards	40	BoE	233		63	10
36	Slithid Scale Legplates	41	BoE	238		68	15
37	Berserker Leggings	42	BoE	242		77	42
37	Mithril Scale Pants	42	BoE	242		80	53
▶	**SPELL** Adds 1% Dodge						
37	Orcish War Leggings	42	BoE	242		77	39
38	Captain's Leggings	43	BoE	246		86	65
38	Ravager's Woolies	43	BoE	246		79	49
39	Ancient Legguards	44	BoE	251		85	85
40	Brigade Leggings	45	BoE	255		93	94
40	Iridescent Scale Leggings	45	BoE	255	1	01	76
▶	**SPELL** Fire & Frost Resist +13						
41	Blackforge Leggings	46	BoE	261	1	01	36
41	Bonelink Legplates	46	BoE	261	1	00	14
42	Khan's Legguards	47	BoE	266	1	08	15
42	Turtle Scale Leggings	47	BoE	266	1	09	52
43	Champion's Leggings	48	BoE	272	1	26	92
44	Tough Scorpid Leggings	49	BoE	277	1	27	04
44	Warmonger's Leggings	49	BoE	277	1	31	90
45	Gryphon Mail Legguards	50	BoE	283	1	44	93
46	Icebrand Legguards	51	BoE	289	1	43	09
46	Thunderscale Leggings	51	BoE	289	1	44	85
47	Lord's Legguards	52	BoE	294	1	52	46
48	Protector Legguards	53	BoE	300	1	60	78
49	Crusader's Leggings	54	BoE	305	1	72	61
50	Ironhide Legguards	55	BoE	311	1	80	65
51	Daemonic Legguards	56	BoE	316	1	91	49
51	Ebonhold Leggings	56	BoE	316	2	03	58
N/A	Outrider Leggings	56	BoA	316	2	05	20
52	Bloodlust Britches	57	BoE	322	2	02	98
52	Divine Legguards	57	BoE	322	2	03	96
52	Heavy Scorpid Leggings	57	BoE	322	2	17	60
54	Abyssal Leggings	59	BoE	333	2	26	15
55	Impenetrable Legguards	60	BoE	338	2	37	21
N/A	Pridemail Leggings	60	BoA	338	2	51	44
▶	**SPELL** Increase Nature Dmg 17						
56	Bloodmail Legguards	61	BoA	344	2	71	85
56	Hellcaller Leggings	61	BoE	344	2	49	07
56	Radiant Leggings	61	BoE	344	2	53	30
▶	**SPELL** Frost & Shadow Resist +18						
56	Tempest Leggings	61	BoE	344	2	62	78
57	Warlord's Legguards	62	BoE	350	2	61	53
58	Mercurial Legguards	63	BoE	355	2	81	37
58	Triumphant Legplates	63	BoE	355	2	74	61
59	Kraken Legplates	64	BoE	361	2	93	23

STANDARD MAIL LEG ARMOR

M LEV	ARMOR NAME	LEV	BIND	AC	VENDOR PURCHASE VALUE		
N/A	Battleworn Chain Leggings	5	BoA	41			14
N/A	Painted Chain Leggings	5	BoA	41			14
N/A	Roamer's Leggings	5	BoA	41			14
1	Rusted Chain Leggings	5	None	41			15
1	Tarnished Chain Leggings	5	None	41			15
4	Copper Chain Pants	9	None	73			67
5	Light Chain Leggings	10	None	81			87
5	Light Mail Leggings	10	None	81			83
N/A	Brass Scale Pants	11	BoA	89		1	15
12	Chainmail Pants	17	None	135		3	51
17	Scalemail Pants	22	None	147		6	45
22	Polished Scale Leggings	27	None	180		11	81
32	Augmented Chain Leggings	37	None	208		31	46
45	Brigandine Leggings	50	None	269		86	15

INFERIOR MAIL LEG ARMOR

M LEV	ARMOR NAME	LEV	BIND	AC	VENDOR PURCHASE VALUE		
1	Flimsy Chain Pants	2	None	16			2
3	Loose Chain Pants	8	None	62			31
7	Worn Mail Pants	12	None	91			89
14	Laced Mail Pants	19	None	142		2	99
20	Linked Chain Pants	25	None	158		6	76
21	Reinforced Chain Pants	26	None	164		7	32
30	Double Mail Pants	35	None	189		17	72
38	Overlinked Chain Pants	43	None	222		34	77
51	Laminated Scale Pants	56	None	285		79	29
59	Sterling Chain Pants	64	None	325	1	17	59

MAIL SHOULDER ARMOR

SUPERIOR MAIL SHOULDER ARMOR

M LEV	ARMOR NAME	LEV	BIND	AC	VENDOR PURCHASE VALUE		
24	Sparkleshell Mantle	29	BoE	191		23	12
37	Herod's Shoulder	42	BoA	228		68	67
38	Skeletal Shoulders	43	BoE	232		73	40
40	Spaulders of a Lost Age	45	BoE	240		85	53
50	Dregmetal Spauders	55	BoA	293	1	66	10
54	Blue Dragonscale Shoulders	59	BoE	314	2	05	43
▶	**SPELL** Arcane Resist +6						
55	Black Dragonscale Shoulders	60	BoE	319	2	17	36
▶	**SPELL** Attack Power 40, Fire Resist +6						
56	Drakesfire Epaulets	61	BoE	325	2	30	83
▶	**SPELL** Fire Resist +10						
58	Bonespike Shoulder	63	BoA	335	2	54	46
▶	**SPELL** Deals 60-90 Dam Vs. Attackers Who Crit						

GOOD MAIL SHOULDER ARMOR

M LEV	ARMOR NAME	LEV	BIND	AC	VENDOR PURCHASE VALUE		
20	Cutthroat Pauldrons	25	BoE	150		12	66
20	Silvered Bronze Shoulders	25	BoE	150		12	84
21	Fortified Spaulders	26	BoE	156		14	26
21	Hulking Spaulders	26	BoE	156		13	22
22	Lambent Scale Pauldrons	27	BoE	162		14	49
22	Spiked Chain Shoulder Pads	27	BoE	162		14	54
23	Battleforge Shoulderguards	28	BoE	168		17	07
23	Glorious Shoulders	28	BoE	168		17	31
25	Elite Shoulders	30	BoE	154		21	10
25	Glimmering Mail Pauldrons	30	BoE	154		20	43
25	Sentry's Shoulderguards	30	BoE	154		19	36
26	Slayer's Shoulder Pads	31	BoE	159		21	30
27	Ambusher's Pauldrons	32	BoE	165		23	91
27	Barbaric Iron Shoulders	32	BoE	165		25	00
27	Green Iron Shoulders	32	BoE	165		25	71
27	Wicked Chain Shoulder Pads	32	BoE	165		23	43
28	Phalanx Spaulders	33	BoE	170		27	09
29	Basilisk Scale Shoulder Pads	34	BoE	175		28	35
30	Golden Scale Shoulders	35	BoE	180		31	06
30	Mail Combat Spaulders	35	BoE	180		32	42
N/A	Grim Pauldrons	36	BoA	184		34	72
31	Pillager's Pauldrons	36	BoE	184		34	30
N/A	Frost Metal Pauldrons	37	BoA	188		38	04
32	Renegade Pauldrons	37	BoE	188		41	01
33	Burning Blade Pauldrons	38	BoE	192		40	75
33	Knight's Pauldrons	38	BoE	192		43	17
N/A	Wrangling Spaulders	38	BoA	192		40	75
35	Chief Brigadier Pauldrons	40	BoE	200		47	36

GOOD MAIL SHOULDER ARMOR continued

M LEV	ARMOR NAME	LEV	BIND	AC	VENDOR PURCHASE VALUE		
N/A	Enforcer Pauldrons	40	BoA	200		50	15
35	Marauder's Shoulder Pads	40	BoE	200		47	54
N/A	Pillager's Pauldrons	40	BoA	200		48	11
N/A	Sanguine Pauldrons	40	BoA	200		47	38
36	Berserker Pauldrons	41	BoE	204		54	20
36	Sparkleshell Shoulder Pads	41	BoE	204		51	34
37	Slithid Scale Shoulder Pads	42	BoE	208		55	45
38	Captain's Shoulderguards	43	BoE	211		61	58
38	Ravager's Mantle	43	BoE	211		59	88
39	Ancient Pauldrons	44	BoE	215		64	67
39	Brigade Pauldrons	44	BoE	215		65	77
40	Bonelink Epaulets	45	BoE	219		69	85
40	Rockshard Pauldrons	45	BoA	219		71	56
41	Blackforge Pauldrons	46	BoE	223		79	57
42	Champion's Pauldrons	47	BoE	228		81	23
42	Khan's Mantle	47	BoE	228		81	47
42	Mithril Scale Shoulder	47	BoE	228		86	61
43	Gryphon Mail Pauldrons	48	BoE	233		95	70
43	Tough Scorpid Shoulders	48	BoE	233		89	78
44	Icebrand Shoulder Pads	49	BoE	238		94	15
44	Warmonger's Pauldrons	49	BoE	238		99	73
45	Thunderscale Pauldrons	50	BoE	242	1	05	17
46	Protector Pads	51	BoE	247	1	07	79
47	Lord's Pauldrons	52	BoE	252	1	15	29
48	Crusader's Pauldrons	53	BoE	257	1	23	14
48	Ironhide Pauldrons	53	BoE	257	1	21	12
49	Daemonic Epaulets	54	BoE	262	1	28	39
49	Ebonhold Shoulderpads	54	BoE	262	1	36	97
50	Lead Surveyor's Mantle	55	BoA	266	1	36	09
51	Divine Pauldrons	56	BoE	271	1	45	51
52	Bloodlust Epaulets	57	BoE	276	1	52	91
53	Abyssal Pauldrons	58	BoE	281	1	62	87
54	Impenetrable Pauldrons	59	BoE	285	1	70	19
55	Tempest Pauldrons	60	BoE	290	1	94	19
55	Windshrieker Pauldrons	60	BoA	290	1	92	23
▶	**SPELL** Arcane Resist +20						
56	Heavy Scorpid Shoulders	61	BoE	295	2	02	61
56	Hellcaller Shoulder Pads	61	BoE	295	1	87	63
57	Mercurial Pauldrons	62	BoE	300	2	02	64
57	Royal Cap Spaulders	62	BoA	300	2	06	60
57	Warlord's Shoulder Pads	62	BoE	300	1	97	02
58	Kraken Pauldrons	63	BoE	304	2	11	18
58	Savage Mail Shoulders	63	BoE	304	2	19	19
58	Triumphant Shoulder Pads	63	BoE	304	2	06	87

STANDARD MAIL SHOULDER ARMOR

M LEV	ARMOR NAME	LEV	BIND	AC	VENDOR PURCHASE VALUE		
16	Bloodspattered Shoulder Pads	21	None	120		4	23
16	Raider's Shoulderpads	21	None	120		4	31
17	Burnished Pauldrons	22	None	126		5	15
17	Rough Bronze Shoulders	22	None	126		5	32
17	War Paint Shoulder Pads	22	None	126		4	86
18	Blackrock Pauldrons	23	None	131		5	83
18	Outrunner's Pauldrons	23	None	131		5	49
19	Defender Spaulders	24	None	137		6	67
N/A	Durable Chain Shoulders	24	BoA	137		6	24
20	Grunt's Pauldrons	25	None	143		7	02

INFERIOR MAIL SHOULDER ARMOR

M LEV	ARMOR NAME	LEV	BIND	AC	VENDOR PURCHASE VALUE		
15	Laced Mail Shoulderpads	20	None	108		2	60
16	Linked Chain Shoulderpads	21	None	114		2	86
22	Reinforced Chain Shoulderpads	27	None	146		6	09
34	Double Mail Shoulderpads	39	None	176		18	91
37	Overlinked Chain Shoulderpads	42	None	187		24	34
50	Laminated Scale Shoulderpads	55	None	240		56	56
64	Sterling Chain Shoulderpads	69	None	300	1	13	49

MAIL WAIST ARMOR

SUPERIOR MAIL WAIST ARMOR

M LEV	ARMOR NAME	LEV	BIND	AC	VENDOR PURCHASE VALUE		
15	Stormbringer Belt	20	BoE	99		5	34
19	Cobrahn's Grasp	24	BoA	119		8	44
28	Girdle of Golem Strength	33	BoE	140		20	55
▶	**SPELL** Adds 5 Defense						
N/A	Stonefist Girdle	36	BoA	152		28	30
▶	**SPELL** Increased Armor 100						
37	Boar Champion's Belt	42	BoA	171		45	41
44	Belt of the Gladiator	49	BoE	196		77	16
52	Chillsteel Girdle	57	BoA	228	1	27	67
▶	**SPELL** Frost Resist +10						
55	Chiselbrand Girdle	60	BoA	239	1	53	10
▶	**SPELL** Attack Power 44						
57	Detention Strap	62	BoA	247	1	64	47

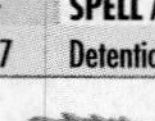

GOOD MAIL WAIST ARMOR

M LEV	ARMOR NAME	LEV	BIND	AC	VENDOR PURCHASE VALUE		
N/A	Cinched Belt	15	BoA	81		2	05
10	Silver Defias Belt	15	BoE	81		2	03
11	Soldier's Girdle	16	BoE	86		2	33
12	War Paint Waistband	17	BoE	91		2	67
N/A	Breakwater Girdle	18	BoA	96		3	37
13	Raider's Belt	18	BoE	96		3	12
14	Outrunner's Cord	19	BoE	101		3	53
15	Burnished Girdle	20	BoE	90		4	35
15	Grunt's Belt	20	BoE	90		4	07
15	Runescale Girdle	20	BoE	90		4	19
17	Defender Girdle	22	BoE	100		5	72
17	Hulking Belt	22	BoE	100		5	38
18	Warchief's Girdle	23	BoE	104		6	41
19	Fortified Belt	24	BoE	108		7	33
20	Spiked Chain Belt	25	BoE	113		7	76
21	Lambent Scale Girdle	26	BoE	117		8	81
21	Sentry's Sash	26	BoE	117		8	77
23	Battleforge Girdle	28	BoE	126		11	20
23	Slayer's Sash	28	BoE	126		11	18
24	Garneg's War Belt	29	BoE	130		12	23
24	Glimmering Mail Girdle	29	BoE	130		12	28
25	Wicked Chain Waistband	30	BoE	116		12	85
26	Ambusher's Girdle	31	BoE	120		14	32
26	Basilisk Scale Belt	31	BoE	120		14	13
N/A	Brightscale Girdle	32	BoA	123		16	96
27	Phalanx Girdle	32	BoE	123		16	22
N/A	Belt of the Stars	33	BoA	127		18	58
N/A	Crusader Belt	33	BoA	127		18	17
28	Pillager's Girdle	33	BoE	127		17	10
29	Burning Blade Belt	34	BoE	131		18	81
29	Mail Combat Belt	34	BoE	131		20	14
N/A	Bracesteel Belt	35	BoA	135		20	70
30	Marauder's Belt	35	BoE	135		20	70
30	Renegade Belt	35	BoE	135		22	25
31	Sparkleshell Belt	36	BoE	138		23	00
32	Knight's Girdle	37	BoE	141		26	82
32	Scarlet Belt	37	BoE	141		25	07
33	Chief Brigadier Girdle	38	BoE	144		27	91
33	Slithid Scale Armguards	38	BoE	144		27	63
34	Ravager's Cord	39	BoE	147		29	21

GOOD MAIL WAIST ARMOR continued

M LEV	ARMOR NAME	LEV	BIND	AC	VENDOR PURCHASE VALUE		
35	Berserker Belt	40	BoE	150		32	94
36	Ancient Belt	41	BoE	153		34	07
36	Captain's Waistguard	41	BoE	153		35	43
37	Bonelink Belt	42	BoE	156		36	80
37	Heavy Notched Belt	42	BoE	156		38	85
38	Brigade Girdle	43	BoE	158		43	03
39	Blackforge Girdle	44	BoE	161		44	78
39	Serpent Clasp Belt	44	BoE	161		45	49
▶	**SPELL** Adds 1% Crit						
41	Champion's Girdle	46	BoE	168		50	50
N/A	Girdle of Reprisal	46	BoA	168		52	07
▶	**SPELL** Deals 75-125 Dam When Struck (1% Chance)						
41	Khan's Belt	46	BoE	168		50	07
N/A	Nightscale Girdle	47	BoA	171		55	21
42	Warmonger's Belt	47	BoE	171		56	44
43	Gryphon Mail Belt	48	BoE	175		59	87
44	Icebrand Belt	49	BoE	178		62	49
44	Thunderscale Girdle	49	BoE	178		62	53
45	Lord's Girdle	50	BoE	182		73	45
45	Protector Waistband	50	BoE	182		66	86
N/A	Stronghorn Girdle	50	BoA	182		72	66
46	Ironhide Belt	51	BoE	186		71	54
47	Crusader's Belt	52	BoE	189		76	23
47	Radiant Belt	52	BoE	189		75	95
▶	**SPELL** Frost & Shadow Resist +12						
49	Daemonic Belt	54	BoE	196		85	21
49	Ebonhold Girdle	54	BoE	196		89	60
50	Bloodlust Belt	55	BoE	200		90	32
50	Divine Girdle	55	BoE	200		90	07
N/A	Gold Link Belt	56	BoA	203		95	74
51	Heavy Scorpid Belt	56	BoE	203	1	03	75
51	Impenetrable Belt	56	BoE	203		95	74
52	Abyssal Girdle	57	BoE	207	1	11	06
53	Hellcaller Belt	58	BoE	211	1	07	58
N/A	Seapost Girdle	59	BoA	214	1	12	96
54	Tempest Belt	59	BoE	214	1	17	87
54	Warlord's Belt	59	BoE	214	1	12	96
55	Triumphant Girdle	60	BoE	218	1	18	60
56	Bloodmail Belt	61	BoA	221	1	36	89
56	Foresight Girdle	61	BoA	221	1	31	49
56	Mercurial Girdle	61	BoE	221	1	33	37
57	Kraken Girdle	62	BoE	225	1	41	06

STANDARD MAIL WAIST ARMOR

M LEV	ARMOR NAME	LEV	BIND	AC	VENDOR PURCHASE VALUE		
N/A	Latched Belt	5	BoA	27			7
N/A	Painted Chain Belt	5	BoA	27			7
1	Rusted Chain Belt	5	None	27			7
N/A	Rustic Belt	5	BoA	27			7
1	Tarnished Chain Belt	5	None	27			7
N/A	Clasped Belt	8	BoA	42			23
3	Warrior's Girdle	8	None	42			23
N/A	Wide Metal Girdle	8	BoA	42			23
4	Charger's Belt	9	None	47			31
5	Battle Chain Girdle	10	None	52			41

STANDARD MAIL WAIST ARMOR continued

M LEV	ARMOR NAME	LEV	BIND	AC	VENDOR PURCHASE VALUE		
5	Infantry Belt	10	None	52			44
5	Light Chain Belt	10	None	52			43
5	Light Mail Belt	10	None	52			41
6	Copper Chain Belt	11	None	57			56
6	Royal Frostmane Girdle	11	None	57			55
N/A	Shackled Girdle	11	BoA	57			54
7	Cadet Belt	12	None	62			72
8	War Torn Girdle	13	None	67			84
N/A	Belt of the People's Militia	14	BoA	72		1	02
9	Brackwater Girdle	14	BoE	72		1	09
9	Veteran Girdle	14	None	72		1	08
10	Bloodspattered Sash	15	BoE	77		1	27
12	Chainmail Belt	17	None	87		1	75
13	Runed Copper Belt	18	None	91		1	98
17	Scalemail Belt	22	None	95		3	38
22	Polished Scale Belt	27	None	116		5	81
32	Augmented Chain Belt	37	None	134		15	78
45	Brigandine Belt	50	None	173		42	92

INFERIOR MAIL WAIST ARMOR

M LEV	ARMOR NAME	LEV	BIND	AC	VENDOR PURCHASE VALUE		
1	Flimsy Chain Belt	2	None	10			1
3	Loose Chain Belt	8	None	40			16
7	Worn Mail Belt	12	None	59			48
14	Laced Mail Belt	19	None	91		1	47
20	Linked Chain Belt	25	None	101		3	32
21	Reinforced Chain Belt	26	None	105		3	59
29	Double Mail Belt	34	None	118		7	70
39	Overlinked Chain Belt	44	None	145		17	97
47	Laminated Scale Belt	52	None	170		30	82
58	Sterling Chain Belt	63	None	205		54	94

MAIL WRIST ARMOR

SUPERIOR MAIL WRIST ARMOR

M LEV	ARMOR NAME	LEV	BIND	AC	VENDOR PURCHASE VALUE		
21	Jimmied Handcuffs	26	BoA	100		10	98
22	Yorgen Bracers	27	BoE	104		12	41
25	Pugilist Bracers	30	BoE	99		16	92
36	Crushridge Bindings	41	BoE	131		43	98
37	Ironaya's Bracers	42	BoA	133		44	90
▸	**SPELL** Increased Armor 50						
44	Slimescale Bracers	49	BoE	153		76	24
52	Pyremail Wristguards	57	BoA	177	1	25	25
▸	**SPELL** Fire Resist +10						
54	Lordly Armguards	59	BoE	183	1	40	01
55	Brazecore Armguards	60	BoA	186	1	49	16
56	Loomguard Armbraces	61	BoA	189	1	60	19
▸	**SPELL** Increase Healing 30						

GOOD MAIL WRIST ARMOR

M LEV	ARMOR NAME	LEV	BIND	AC	VENDOR PURCHASE VALUE		
10	Bloodspattered Wristbands	15	BoE	63		2	20
10	Soldier's Wristguards	15	BoE	63		2	04
12	Raider's Bracers	17	BoE	71		2	68
12	War Paint Bindings	17	BoE	71		2	67
13	Cavedweller Bracers	18	BoA	75		3	11
13	Outrunner's Cuffs	18	BoE	75		3	07
14	Burnished Bracers	19	BoE	79		3	73
14	Grunt's Bracers	19	BoE	79		3	64
17	Defender Bracers	22	BoE	77		5	68
17	Hulking Bands	22	BoE	77		5	38
18	Rough Bronze Bracers	23	BoE	81		6	29
19	Fortified Bracers	24	BoE	84		7	25
20	Patterned Bronze Bracers	25	BoE	88		8	07
20	Rift Bracers	25	BoA	88		8	40
20	Spiked Chain Wristbands	25	BoE	88		8	50
N/A	Hexed Bracers	26	BoA	91		8	95
21	Lambent Scale Bracers	26	BoE	91		9	29
21	Sentry's Armsplints	26	BoE	91		8	77
22	Battleforge Wristguards	27	BoE	95		10	07
N/A	Beetle Clasps	27	BoA	95		9	81
N/A	Tempered Bracers	27	BoA	95		10	48
N/A	Grimtoll Wristguards	28	BoA	98		11	42
23	Slayer's Cuffs	28	BoE	98		10	62
24	Glimmering Mail Bracers	29	BoE	101		12	28
N/A	Steel-clasped Bracers	29	BoA	101		11	73
24	Wicked Chain Bracers	29	BoE	101		11	68
25	Ambusher's Bracers	30	BoE	90		12	87
25	Basilisk Scale Bracelets	30	BoE	90		12	85

GOOD MAIL WRIST ARMOR continued

M LEV	ARMOR NAME	LEV	BIND	AC	VENDOR PURCHASE VALUE		
N/A	Beastial Manacles	30	BoA	90		13	31
N/A	Fire-welded Bracers	30	BoA	90		14	06
26	Phalanx Bracers	31	BoE	93		14	42
27	Pillager's Bracers	32	BoE	96		15	55
28	Mail Combat Armguards	33	BoE	99		17	71
29	Burning Blade Bracers	34	BoE	102		18	81
29	Renegade Bracers	34	BoE	102		19	42
30	Marauder's Bracers	35	BoE	105		20	70
N/A	Duracin Bracers	36	BoA	107		24	21
31	Knight's Bracers	36	BoE	107		24	29
31	Scarlet Wristguards	36	BoE	107		23	14
31	Sparkleshell Bracers	36	BoE	107		22	77
32	Chief Brigadier Bracers	37	BoE	110		24	97
N/A	Darkspear Armsplints	37	BoA	110		26	81
32	Slithid Scale Bracelets	37	BoE	110		25	04
34	Berserker Bracers	39	BoE	114		29	13
N/A	Auric Bracers	40	BoA	117		31	57
35	Captain's Bracers	40	BoE	117		32	68
35	Ravager's Armguards	40	BoE	117		31	55
35	Revelosh's Armguards	40	BoA	117		31	96
N/A	War Rider Bracers	40	BoA	117		32	30
37	Ancient Vambraces	42	BoE	121		36	80
37	Brigade Bracers	42	BoE	121		39	27
37	Turtle Scale Bracers	42	BoE	121		40	13
▸	**SPELL** Increased Armor 100						
38	Blackforge Bracers	43	BoE	123		41	62
38	Bonelink Bracers	43	BoE	123		39	74
38	Mithril Scale Bracers	43	BoE	123		41	03
39	Tough Scorpid Bracers	44	BoE	125		43	46
40	Champion's Bracers	45	BoE	127		46	58
40	Khan's Bindings	45	BoE	127		46	36
41	Warmonger's Bracers	46	BoE	130		51	30
42	Gryphon Mail Bracelets	47	BoE	133		55	64
43	Icebrand Bracers	48	BoE	136		58	40
43	Thunderscale Bracers	48	BoE	136		63	67
44	Lord's Armguards	49	BoE	139		65	71
44	Protector Armguards	49	BoE	139		62	49
N/A	Chelonian Cuffs	50	BoA	141		68	75
45	Ironhide Bracers	50	BoE	141		66	86
N/A	Poobah's Nose Ring	50	BoA	141		73	13
46	Crusader's Armguards	51	BoE	144		77	77
46	Daemonic Bindings	51	BoE	144		71	54
46	Heavy Scorpid Bracers	51	BoE	144		76	15
47	Ebonhold Wristguards	52	BoE	147		78	57
48	Bloodlust Bracelets	53	BoE	150		80	39
49	Divine Bracers	54	BoE	153		88	65
50	Impenetrable Bindings	55	BoE	155		90	32

GOOD MAIL WRIST ARMOR continued

M LEV	ARMOR NAME	LEV	BIND	AC	VENDOR PURCHASE VALUE		
50	Rubicund Armguards	55	BoA	155		97	81
51	Abyssal Bracers	56	BoE	158	1	03	31
N/A	Crypt Demon Bracers	56	BoA	158	1	04	06
53	Hellcaller Bindings	58	BoE	164	1	07	58
53	Tempest Bracers	58	BoE	164	1	10	60
N/A	Seaspray Bracers	59	BoA	167	1	20	63
54	Warlord's Armsplints	59	BoE	167	1	12	96
55	Mercurial Bracers	60	BoE	169	1	27	94
55	Slashclaw Bracers	60	BoA	169	1	20	62
▶	**SPELL** Adds 1% Crit						
56	Triumphant Bracers	61	BoE	172	1	24	53
57	Kraken Bracers	62	BoE	175	1	39	04
57	Twilight Void Bracers	62	BoA	175	1	31	98
▶	**SPELL** Shadow Resist +15						

STANDARD MAIL WRIST ARMOR

M LEV	ARMOR NAME	LEV	BIND	AC	VENDOR PURCHASE VALUE		
1	Rusted Chain Bracers	5	None	21			7
N/A	Rustmetal Bracers	5	BoA	21			7
1	Tarnished Chain Bracers	5	None	21			7
2	Copper Bracers	7	None	29			17
3	Charger's Bindings	8	None	33			22
N/A	Graystone Bracers	8	BoA	33			23
4	Battle Chain Bracers	9	None	36			33
4	Warrior's Bracers	9	None	36			33
N/A	Brass-studded Bracers	10	BoA	40			44
N/A	Fortified Bindings	10	BoA	40			42
5	Infantry Bracers	10	None	40			44
5	Light Chain Bracers	10	None	40			43

STANDARD MAIL WRIST ARMOR continued

M LEV	ARMOR NAME	LEV	BIND	AC	VENDOR PURCHASE VALUE	
5	Light Mail Bracers	10	None	40		43
6	War Torn Bands	11	None	44		53
7	Brackwater Bracers	12	BoE	48		70
7	Cadet Bracers	12	None	48		73
N/A	Ironwrought Bracers	12	BoA	48		69
8	Veteran Bracers	13	None	52		89
N/A	Clamshell Bracers	14	BoA	56	1	01
12	Chainmail Bracers	17	None	67	1	76
14	Runed Copper Bracers	19	None	75	2	25
17	Scalemail Bracers	22	None	74	3	36
22	Polished Scale Bracers	27	None	90	5	86
28	Green Iron Bracers	33	None	94	11	06
32	Augmented Chain Bracers	37	None	104	15	90
32	Golden Scale Bracers	37	None	104	16	49
45	Brigandine Bracers	50	None	134	40	29

INFERIOR MAIL WRIST ARMOR

M LEV	ARMOR NAME	LEV	BIND	AC	VENDOR PURCHASE VALUE	
1	Flimsy Chain Bracers	4	None	16		3
5	Loose Chain Bracers	10	None	38		28
9	Worn Mail Bracers	14	None	53		73
11	Laced Mail Bracers	16	None	60		97
17	Linked Chain Bracers	22	None	70	2	32
23	Reinforced Chain Bracers	28	None	88	4	38
33	Double Mail Bracers	38	None	101	11	45
43	Overlinked Chain Bracers	48	None	122	24	63
53	Laminated Scale Bracers	58	None	147	44	04
61	Sterling Chain Bracers	66	None	167	64	09

PLATE CHEST ARMOR

EPIC PLATE CHEST ARMOR

M LEV	ARMOR NAME	LEV	BIND	AC	VENDOR PURCHASE VALUE		
N/A	Breastplate of the Chromatic Flight	62	BoA	702	2	94	61
▶	**SPELL** Fire Resist +15						

SUPERIOR PLATE CHEST ARMOR

M LEV	ARMOR NAME	LEV	BIND	AC	VENDOR PURCHASE VALUE		
40	Carapace of Tuten'kash	42	BoA	387		63	77
44	Truesilver Breastplate	49	BoE	507	1	08	99
▶	**SPELL** Heals 60-100 Dam when struck (3% Chance)						
49	Hydralick Armor	54	BoE	558	1	43	41
▶	**SPELL** Fire Resist +10						
49	Warrior's Embrace	54	BoA	558	1	42	33
▶	**SPELL** Adds 2% Dodge						
50	Carapace of Anub'shiah	55	BoA	569	1	55	96
52	Demon Forged Breastplate	57	BoE	590	1	66	40
▶	**SPELL** Steals 120 HP when struck (3% Chance)						
54	Dark Iron Plate	59	BoA	611	1	94	28
▶	**SPELL** Increased Armor 120						
54	Skul's Cold Embrace	59	BoA	611	1	81	76
▶	**SPELL** Frost Resist +10						
55	Plate of the Shaman King	60	BoA	622	1	90	85
56	Deathbone Chestplate	61	BoA	633	2	05	78
▶	**SPELL** Adds 25 Defense						
58	General's Ceremonial Plate	63	BoA	654	2	27	68
▶	**SPELL** Increased Armor 140						
N/A	Ornate Adamantium Breastplate	63	BoA	654	2	25	19
▶	**SPELL** Increased Defense						

GOOD PLATE CHEST ARMOR

M LEV	ARMOR NAME	LEV	BIND	AC	VENDOR PURCHASE VALUE		
40	Saltstone Surcoat	41	BoE	322		49	04
40	Jouster's Chestplate	42	BoE	352		51	97
40	Naga Scale Breastplate	43	BoE	383		52	90
40	Field Plate Armor	44	BoE	414		60	40
40	Embossed Plate Armor	45	BoE	424		67	43
41	Heavy Mithril Breastplate	46	BoE	433		70	45
▶	**SPELL** Increased Armor 90						
41	Warbringer's Chestguard	46	BoE	433		67	93
42	Chromite Chestplate	47	BoE	442		76	66
43	Ornate Mithril Breastplate	48	BoE	451		83	68
▶	**SPELL** Adds 1% Crit and 1% Dodge						
43	Tyrant's Chestpiece	48	BoE	451		81	92
44	Gothic Plate Armor	49	BoE	461		84	38
45	Prismatic Scale Breastplate	50	BoE	470		89	15
45	Thorium Armor	50	BoE	470		92	39
▶	**SPELL** Arcane, Fire, Frost, Nature & Shadow Resist +8						
46	Bloodforged Chestpiece	51	BoE	479		95	39
46	Valorous Chestguard	51	BoE	479	1	02	51
47	Overlord's Chestplate	52	BoE	488	1	03	97
48	Wyrm Scale Chestguard	53	BoE	498	1	07	18
49	Revenant Chestplate	54	BoE	507	1	19	07
49	Spiderfang Carapace	54	BoA	507	1	17	30
49	Sunscale Chestguard	54	BoE	507	1	13	62
50	Leviathan Chestpiece	55	BoE	517	1	25	76
51	High Chief's Armor	56	BoE	527	1	27	66
52	Jademir Scale Breastplate	57	BoE	536	1	35	32
52	Spectral Plate Chestpiece	57	BoE	536	1	48	10
N/A	Warforged Chestplate	57	BoA	536	1	36	55
53	Templar Chestplate	58	BoE	546	1	48	08
54	Valkyrie Breastplate	59	BoE	556	1	50	61
N/A	Boulderskin Breastplate	60	BoA	565	1	68	24
▶	**SPELL** Increased Armor 200						
55	Hydra Chestplate	60	BoE	565	1	62	04
55	Imperial Plate Chest	60	BoE	565	1	62	04

GOOD PLATE CHEST ARMOR continued

M LEV	ARMOR NAME	LEV	BIND	AC	VENDOR PURCHASE VALUE		
56	Glorious Breastplate	61	BoE	575	1	66	05
57	Dragonbone Armor	62	BoE	585	1	74	35
57	Nether Plate Armor	62	BoE	585	1	78	68
57	Runic Breastplate	62	BoE	585	1	82	05
▶	**SPELL** Increased Armor 150, Fire & Nature Resist +15						
58	Demon Plate Armor	63	BoE	594	1	94	66
58	Enchanted Thorium Breastplate	63	BoE	594	1	99	77
58	Titan's Breastplate	63	BoE	594	1	83	07
60	Exalted Harness	65	BoE	613	2	01	83
60	Hyperion Armor	65	BoE	613	2	03	70

STANDARD PLATE CHEST ARMOR

M LEV	ARMOR NAME	LEV	BIND	AC	VENDOR PURCHASE VALUE		
45	Platemail Vest	50	None	446		54	58
N/A	PVP Plate Breastplate Alliance	60	None	537		94	88

INFERIOR PLATE CHEST ARMOR

M LEV	ARMOR NAME	LEV	BIND	AC	VENDOR PURCHASE VALUE		
53	Light Plate Chestpiece	58	None	491		59	87

PLATE FOOT ARMOR

EPIC PLATE FOOT ARMOR

M LEV	ARMOR NAME	LEV	BIND	AC	VENDOR PURCHASE VALUE		
40	Boots of Avoidance	45	BoE	349		78	07
▶	**SPELL** Adds 2% Dodge						

SUPERIOR PLATE FOOT ARMOR

M LEV	ARMOR NAME	LEV	BIND	AC	VENDOR PURCHASE VALUE		
37	Obsidian Greaves	42	BoE	266		47	85
50	Battlechaser's Greaves	55	BoE	391	1	14	06
53	Sapphiron's Scale Boots	58	BoE	413	1	40	87
53	Shalehusk Boots	58	BoA	413	1	37	32
56	Master Cannoneer Boots	61	BoA	435	1	54	33
▶	**SPELL** Adds 2% Dodge						
56	Ribsteel Footguards	61	BoA	435	1	60	69

GOOD PLATE FOOT ARMOR

M LEV	ARMOR NAME	LEV	BIND	AC	VENDOR PURCHASE VALUE		
40	Jouster's Greaves	40	BoE	202		33	78
40	Saltstone Sabatons	40	BoE	202		34	18
40	Field Plate Boots	41	BoE	222		36	35
40	Revelosh's Boots	41	BoA	222		34	38
40	Embossed Plate Boots	42	BoE	242		37	27
40	Naga Scale Greaves	42	BoE	242		37	72
N/A	Rushridge Boots	43	BoA	263		42	58
40	Warbringer's Sabatons	43	BoE	263		40	59
40	Chromite Greaves	44	BoE	285		46	13
40	Tyrant's Greaves	44	BoE	285		47	01
40	Gothic Sabatons	45	BoE	291		47	49
N/A	Shinkicker Boots	45	BoA	291		47	49
41	Prismatic Scale Sabatons	46	BoE	298		50	07
42	Bloodforged Sabatons	47	BoE	304		59	02
42	Heavy Mithril Boots	47	BoE	304		57	69
▶	**SPELL** Increased Armor 70						
42	Valorous Greaves	47	BoE	304		54	77
43	Overlord's Greaves	48	BoE	310		59	60
N/A	Gnomish Water Sinking Device	49	BoA	317		67	91
44	Ornate Mithril Boots	49	BoE	317		67	39
▶	**SPELL** Adds 1% Dodge, Use: Negate Root/Immune to Root 5 Sec						
44	Wyrm Scale Greaves	49	BoE	317		62	49
45	Revenant Boots	50	BoE	323		70	85

GOOD PLATE FOOT ARMOR continued

M LEV	ARMOR NAME	LEV	BIND	AC	VENDOR PURCHASE VALUE		
45	Sunscale Sabatons	50	BoE	323		66	86
46	High Chief's Sabatons	51	BoE	329		71	54
47	Leviathan Boots	52	BoE	336		76	50
N/A	Steelsmith Greaves	52	BoA	336		77	72
48	Jademir Scale Sabatons	53	BoE	342		80	39
48	Spectral Plate Greaves	53	BoE	342		80	78
N/A	Eschewal Greaves	54	BoA	349		85	66
▶	**SPELL** Adds 1% Dodge						
N/A	Shieldplate Sabatons	54	BoA	349		85	21
49	Valkyrie Sabatons	54	BoE	349		85	21
N/A	Cragplate Greaves	55	BoA	355		90	32
50	Templar Boots	55	BoE	355		94	29
51	Glorious Sabatons	56	BoE	362		95	74
51	Hydra Sabatons	56	BoE	362		98	47
51	Thorium Boots	56	BoE	362	1	03	36
▶	**SPELL** Arcane, Fire, Frost, Nature & Shadow Resist +7						
53	Dragonbone Greaves	58	BoE	375	1	07	58
53	Nether Plate Greaves	58	BoE	375	1	11	49
54	Imperial Plate Boots	59	BoE	382	1	20	62
55	Demon Plate Boots	60	BoE	389	1	25	19
55	Runic Plate Boots	60	BoE	389	1	22	93
▶	**SPELL** Increased Armor 100, Fire & Nature Resist +10						
55	Titan's Greaves	60	BoE	389	1	18	60
56	Deathbone Sabatons	61	BoA	395	1	27	17
57	Corpselight Greaves	62	BoA	402	1	41	67
57	Hyperion Greaves	62	BoE	402	1	32	47
57	Lavawalker Greaves	62	BoA	402	1	31	49
▶	**SPELL** Fire Resist +20						
58	Exalted Sabatons	63	BoE	409	1	37	30

STANDARD PLATE FOOT ARMOR

M LEV	ARMOR NAME	LEV	BIND	AC	VENDOR PURCHASE VALUE		
45	Platemail Boots	50	None	307		40	16
N/A	PVP Plate Boots Alliance	60	None	369		72	70

INFERIOR PLATE FOOT ARMOR

M LEV	ARMOR NAME	LEV	BIND	AC	VENDOR PURCHASE VALUE		
47	Light Plate Boots	52	None	302		31	89

PLATE HAND ARMOR

EPIC PLATE HAND ARMOR

M LEV	ARMOR NAME	LEV	BIND	AC	VENDOR PURCHASE VALUE		
57	Stronghold Gauntlets	62	BoE	439	1	52	71
▶	**SPELL** Immune to Disarm						

SUPERIOR PLATE FOOT ARMOR

M LEV	ARMOR NAME	LEV	BIND	AC	VENDOR PURCHASE VALUE		
40	Cragfists	45	BoA	291		37	85
▶	**SPELL** Add 7 Defense						
40	Plated Fist of Hakoo	45	BoE	291		40	61
40	Truesilver Gauntlets	45	BoE	291		40	28
43	Vice Grips	48	BoA	310		48	40
▶	**SPELL** Attack Power 14						
53	Fiery Plate Gauntlets	58	BoE	375		89	19
▶	**SPELL** Add Fire Dmg - Weap 04, Fire Resist +10						
55	Backusarian Gauntlets	60	BoA	389	1	03	16
55	Stonegrip Gauntlets	60	BoE	389	1	04	26
▶	**SPELL** Add 15 Defense						
56	Reiver Claws	61	BoA	395	1	05	58
▶	**SPELL** Add 1% Crit						
57	Boneclenched Gauntlets	62	BoA	402	1	05	61
▶	**SPELL** Increased Armor 220, Frost Resist +10						

STANDARD PLATE FOOT ARMOR

M LEV	ARMOR NAME	LEV	BIND	AC	VENDOR PURCHASE VALUE		
45	Platemail Gloves	50	None	279		26	97
N/A	PVP Plate Gauntlets Alliance	60	None	336		48	28

INFERIOR PLATE FOOT ARMOR

M LEV	ARMOR NAME	LEV	BIND	AC	VENDOR PURCHASE VALUE		
51	Light Plate Gloves	56	None	296		27	03

GOOD PLATE FOOT ARMOR

M LEV	ARMOR NAME	LEV	BIND	AC	VENDOR PURCHASE VALUE		
40	Jouster's Gauntlets	40	BoE	184		22	36
40	Saltstone Gauntlets	40	BoE	184		22	86
40	Field Plate Gauntlets	41	BoE	201		24	06
40	Heavy Mithril Gauntlet	41	BoE	201		24	76
▶	**SPELL** Increased Armor 80						
40	Naga Scale Gauntlets	41	BoE	201		23	11
40	Warbringer's Gauntlets	42	BoE	220		25	24
40	Embossed Plate Gauntlets	43	BoE	239		29	00
40	Chromite Gauntlets	44	BoE	259		30	53
40	Ornate Mithril Gloves	44	BoE	259		29	87
▶	**SPELL** Add 1% Crit						
39	Tyrant's Gauntlets	44	BoE	259		29	88
40	Prismatic Scale Gauntlets	45	BoE	265		30	90
41	Gothic Plate Gauntlets	46	BoE	271		33	93
42	Bloodforged Gauntlets	47	BoE	276		36	05
42	Valorous Gauntlets	47	BoE	276		39	01
43	Wyrm Scale Gauntlets	48	BoE	282		38	93
N/A	Granite Grips	49	BoA	288		42	51
44	Overlord's Gauntlets	49	BoE	288		43	16
45	Revenant Gauntlets	50	BoE	294		46	89
45	Sunscale Gauntlets	50	BoE	294		44	57
47	High Chief's Gauntlets	52	BoE	305		50	56
47	Leviathan Gauntlets	52	BoE	305		53	18
48	Jademir Scale Gauntlets	53	BoE	311		55	98
48	Spectral Plate Gauntlets	53	BoE	311		53	44
50	Templar Gauntlets	55	BoE	323		62	40
50	Valkyrie Gauntlets	55	BoE	323		60	21
51	Fists of Phalanx	56	BoA	329		65	65
51	Glorious Gauntlets	56	BoE	329		63	83
52	Hydra Gauntlets	57	BoE	335		69	85
53	Dragonbone Gauntlets	58	BoE	341		71	72
N/A	Emerald Mist Gauntlets	58	BoA	341		71	72
N/A	Lavaplate Gauntlets	58	BoA	341		77	68
53	Nether Plate Gauntlets	58	BoE	341		73	77
55	Banshee's Touch	60	BoA	353		85	35
▶	**SPELL** Arcane & Frost Resist +13						
55	Demon Plate Gauntlets	60	BoE	353		84	68
55	Titan's Gauntlets	60	BoE	353		79	07
56	Deathbone Gauntlets	61	BoA	359		85	10
56	Exalted Gauntlets	61	BoE	359		83	02
57	Hyperion Gauntlets	62	BoE	365		88	65

PLATE HEAD ARMOR

EPIC PLATE HEAD ARMOR

M LEV	ARMOR NAME	LEV	BIND	AC	VENDOR PURCHASE VALUE		
56	Lionheart Helm	61	BoE	561	2	18	94
▶	**SPELL** Adds 2% Crit						

SUPERIOR PLATE HEAD ARMOR

M LEV	ARMOR NAME	LEV	BIND	AC	VENDOR PURCHASE VALUE		
40	Horned Viking Helmet	42	BoA	315		45	75
▶	**SPELL** Use: Charges Enemy, Stuns Player, and Mezs Enemy for 30 sec						
40	Icemetal Barbute	44	BoA	370		51	97
▶	**SPELL** Frost Resist +10						
47	Mugthol's Helm	52	BoE	436		90	80
N/A	Avenguard Helm	54	BoA	454	1	05	54
51	Golem Skull Helm	56	BoA	471	1	18	61
▶	**SPELL** Adds 11 Defense						
55	Whitesoul Helm	60	BoE	505	1	48	59
▶	**SPELL** Increased Armor 120						

GOOD PLATE HEAD ARMOR

M LEV	ARMOR NAME	LEV	BIND	AC	VENDOR PURCHASE VALUE		
40	Jouster's Visor	40	BoE	239		33	90
40	Saltstone Helm	41	BoE	262		37	31
40	Field Plate Helmet	42	BoE	286		39	40
40	Embossed Plate Helmet	43	BoE	311		39	64
40	Naga Scale Crown	43	BoE	311		41	20
40	Chromite Barbute	44	BoE	337		46	30
N/A	Sentinel's Guard	45	BoA	344		50	02
40	Warbringer's Crown	45	BoE	344		48	06
41	Gothic Plate Helmet	46	BoE	352		51	48
41	Tyrant's Helm	46	BoE	352		50	36
42	Heavy Mithril Helm	47	BoE	359		57	90
▶	**SPELL** Increased Armor 100						
43	Prismatic Scale Helmet	48	BoE	367		58	40
43	Valorous Helm	48	BoE	367		59	37
44	Ornate Mithril Helm	49	BoE	374		67	63
▶	**SPELL** Add 1% Crit						
44	Overlord's Helmet	49	BoE	374		66	95
45	Bloodforged Helmet	50	BoE	382		66	86
46	Revenant Helmet	51	BoE	389		76	08
47	Wyrm Scale Circlet	52	BoE	397		75	84
48	Leviathan Helm	53	BoE	405		84	25
48	Sunscale Crown	53	BoE	405		80	39

XII

GOOD PLATE HEAD ARMOR continued

M LEV	ARMOR NAME	LEV	BIND	AC	VENDOR PURCHASE VALUE		
49	Spectral Plate Helmet	54	BoE	412		85	95
50	High Chief's Crown	55	BoE	420		90	32
51	Templar Crown	56	BoE	428	1	00	32
51	Thorium Helm	56	BoE	428	1	03	72
▶	**SPELL** Arcane, Fire, Frost, Nature & Shadow Resist +10						
52	Jademir Scale Helm	57	BoE	436	1	01	49
53	Hydra Headpiece	58	BoE	444	1	11	88
53	Valkyrie Headress	58	BoE	444	1	07	58
54	Glorious Headress	59	BoE	451	1	12	96
54	Imperial Plate Helm	59	BoE	451	1	21	06
54	Nether Plate Helmet	59	BoE	451	1	17	50
55	Dragonbone Skullcap	60	BoE	459	1	18	60
56	Demon Plate Helm	61	BoE	467	1	32	90
56	Runic Plate Helm	61	BoE	467	1	29	56
▶	**SPELL** Increased Armor 150, Fire & Nature Resist +13						
57	Titan's Crown	62	BoE	475	1	30	76
57	Enchanted Thorium Helm	63	BoE	483	1	50	89
58	Hyperion Helm	63	BoE	483	1	40	68
58	Skull of Gyth	63	BoA	483	1	43	36
▶	**SPELL** Increased Armor 200						
59	Exalted Helmet	64	BoE	491	1	44	17

STANDARD PLATE HEAD ARMOR

M LEV	ARMOR NAME	LEV	BIND	AC	VENDOR PURCHASE VALUE		
40	Steel Plate Helm	43	None	295		23	77
▶	**SPELL** Increased Armor 60						
45	Platemail Helm	50	None	363		40	62
N/A	PVP Cloth Helm Horde	60	None	436		74	07
N/A	PVP Plate Helm Alliance	60	None	436		71	16

INFERIOR PLATE HEAD ARMOR

M LEV	ARMOR NAME	LEV	BIND	AC	VENDOR PURCHASE VALUE		
50	Light Plate Helmet	55	None	378		36	12

XII

CLOTH ARMOR
LEATHER ARMOR
MAIL ARMOR
PLATE ARMOR
SHIELDS
WEAPONS

PLATE LEG ARMOR

EPIC PLATE LEG ARMOR

M LEV	ARMOR NAME	LEV	BIND	AC	VENDOR PURCHASE VALUE		
57	Cloudkeeper Legplates	62	BoE	614	2	99	00
▶	**SPELL** Heaven's Blessing						

SUPERIOR PLATE LEG ARMOR

M LEV	ARMOR NAME	LEV	BIND	AC	VENDOR PURCHASE VALUE		
41	Golem Shard Leggings	46	BoE	417		80	24
▶	**SPELL** Add 9 Defense						
46	Silvershell Leggings	51	BoE	461	1	16	84
52	Legplates of the Eternal Guardian	57	BoA	516	1	64	56
▶	**SPELL** Increased Armor 220						
58	Direwing Legguards	63	BoE	572	2	20	90
58	Warmaster Legguards	63	BoA	572	2	31	96
▶	**SPELL** Add 2% Dodge						

GOOD PLATE LEG ARMOR

M LEV	ARMOR NAME	LEV	BIND	AC	VENDOR PURCHASE VALUE		
40	Saltstone Legplates	40	BoE	257		42	98
40	Jouster's Legplates	41	BoE	282		49	00
40	Heavy Mithril Pants	42	BoE	308		53	87
▶	**SPELL** Increased Armor 120						
40	Naga Scale Legplates	42	BoE	308		50	49
40	Field Plate Leggings	43	BoE	335		52	86
40	Embossed Plate Leggings	44	BoE	363		57	30
40	Ornate Mithril Pants	44	BoE	363		59	52
▶	**SPELL** Add 1% Dodge						
40	Warbringer's Legguards	45	BoE	371		64	32
41	Chromite Legplates	46	BoE	379		72	27
42	Gothic Plate Leggings	47	BoE	387		74	41
42	Tyrant's Legplates	47	BoE	387		79	25
43	Prismatic Scale Belt	48	BoE	395		81	95
44	Bloodforged Legplates	49	BoE	403		83	32
44	Valorous Legguards	49	BoE	403		85	03
45	Overlord's Legplates	50	BoE	411		95	86
46	Wyrm Scale Legplates	51	BoE	419		95	39
47	Revenant Leggings	52	BoE	427	1	07	92
47	Sunscale Legplates	52	BoE	427	1	01	12

GOOD PLATE LEG ARMOR continued

M LEV	ARMOR NAME	LEV	BIND	AC	VENDOR PURCHASE VALUE		
N/A	Centurion Legplates	53	BoA	436	1	06	92
49	High Chief's Legguards	54	BoE	444	1	13	62
49	Leviathan Leggings	54	BoE	444	1	20	39
N/A	Bejeweled Legguards	55	BoA	452	1	23	45
▶	**SPELL** Add 1% Dodge						
50	Jademir Scale Legguards	55	BoE	452	1	20	43
51	Spectral Plate Leggings	56	BoE	461	1	29	26
52	Templar Legplates	57	BoE	469	1	42	30
52	Valkyrie Legplates	57	BoE	469	1	35	32
53	Glorious Legplates	58	BoE	478	1	43	44
53	Lavacrest Leggings	58	BoA	478	1	49	80
54	Hydra Legplates	59	BoE	486	1	57	23
55	Thorium Leggings	60	BoE	495	1	73	76
▶	**SPELL** Arcane, Fire, Frost, Nature & Shadow Resist +10						
56	Deathbone Legguards	61	BoA	503	1	70	85
56	Dragonbone Legplates	61	BoE	503	1	66	05
56	Imperial Plate Leggings	61	BoE	503	1	79	23
56	Nether Plate Leggings	61	BoE	503	1	73	36
57	Demon Plate Leggings	62	BoE	512	1	88	08
57	Handcrafted Mastersmith Leggings	62	BoA	512	1	82	74
▶	**SPELL** Increased Armor 270						
57	Runic Plate Leggings	62	BoE	512	1	82	72
▶	**SPELL** Increased Armor 150, Fire & Nature Resist +14						
57	Titan's Legplates	62	BoE	512	1	74	35
58	Enchanted Thorium Leggings	63	BoE	520	2	00	48
58	Exalted Legplates	63	BoE	520	1	83	07
59	Hyperion Legplates	64	BoE	528	1	97	70

STANDARD PLATE LEG ARMOR

M LEV	ARMOR NAME	LEV	BIND	AC	VENDOR PURCHASE VALUE		
45	Platemail Leggings	50	None	390		54	37
N/A	PVP Plate Legplates Alliance	60	None	470		94	88

INFERIOR PLATE LEG ARMOR

M LEV	ARMOR NAME	LEV	BIND	AC	VENDOR PURCHASE VALUE		
50	Light Plate Pants	55	None	407		52	53

 PLATE SHOULDER ARMOR

EPIC PLATE SHOULDER ARMOR

M LEV	ARMOR NAME	LEV	BIND	AC	VENDOR PURCHASE VALUE		
50	Stockade Pauldrons	55	BoE	465	1	53	78
▶	**SPELL** Increased Defense						

SUPERIOR PLATE SHOULDER ARMOR

M LEV	ARMOR NAME	LEV	BIND	AC	VENDOR PURCHASE VALUE		
45	Big Bad Pauldrons	50	BoA	388		85	93
46	Wyrmslayer Spaulders	51	BoE	395		89	97
52	Wailing Nightbane Pauldrons	57	BoA	443	1	31	02
▶	**SPELL** Shadow Resist +10						
53	Dawnbringer Shoulders	58	BoE	451	1	30	80
▶	**SPELL** Increase Healing 30						
54	Ebonsteel Spaulders	59	BoA	458	1	43	68
55	Slamshot Shoulders	60	BoA	466	1	42	04
▶	**SPELL** Attack Power 20						
56	Stoneform Shoulders	61	BoA	474	1	63	67
▶	**SPELL** Increased Armor 210						

GOOD PLATE SHOULDER ARMOR

M LEV	ARMOR NAME	LEV	BIND	AC	VENDOR PURCHASE VALUE		
40	Heavy Mithril Shoulder	41	BoE	242		37	01
40	Jouster's Pauldrons	41	BoE	242		36	88
40	Saltstone Shoulder Pads	41	BoE	242		34	94
40	Field Plate Pauldrons	42	BoE	264		36	84
40	Naga Scale Pauldrons	42	BoE	264		38	01
40	Embossed Plate Pauldrons	43	BoE	287		39	95
40	Warbringer's Spaulders	43	BoE	287		41	51
40	Tyrant's Epaulets	44	BoE	311		42	84
40	Chromite Pauldrons	45	BoE	318		50	36
40	Ornate Mithril Shoulder	45	BoE	318		48	57
▶	**SPELL** Add 1% Dodge						
40	Prismatic Scale Pauldrons	45	BoE	318		46	36
N/A	Gemshale Pauldrons	46	BoA	325		52	64
42	Bloodforged Shoulder Pads	47	BoE	332		54	07
42	Gothic Plate Spaulders	47	BoE	332		56	02
43	Valorous Pauldrons	48	BoE	338		59	82
44	Wyrm Scale Epaulets	49	BoE	345		62	49

GOOD PLATE SHOULDER ARMOR continued

M LEV	ARMOR NAME	LEV	BIND	AC	VENDOR PURCHASE VALUE		
N/A	Bark Iron Pauldrons	50	BoA	352		73	45
45	Overlord's Spaulders	50	BoE	352		72	16
46	Revenant Shoulders	51	BoE	359		76	64
46	Sunscale Spaulders	51	BoE	359		71	54
47	Earthslag Shoulders	52	BoA	366		78	00
48	High Chief's Pauldrons	53	BoE	373		80	39
47	Imperial Plate Shoulders	53	BoE	373		86	46
48	Leviathan Pauldrons	53	BoE	373		85	48
49	Jademir Scale Shoulder Pads	54	BoE	381		85	21
50	Spectral Plate Pauldrons	55	BoE	388		91	81
51	Templar Pauldrons	56	BoE	395	1	01	05
51	Valkyrie Pauldrons	56	BoE	395		95	74
52	Glorious Shoulder Pads	57	BoE	402	1	01	49
53	Dark Iron Shoulders	58	BoE	410	1	07	76
▶	**SPELL** Increased Armor 130						
53	Hydra Pauldrons	58	BoE	410	1	12	72
54	Dragonbone Pauldrons	59	BoE	417	1	12	96
54	Nether Plate Pauldrons	59	BoE	417	1	18	37
55	Runic Plate Shoulders	60	BoE	424	1	22	47
▶	**SPELL** Increased Armor 100, Fire & Nature Resist +10						
56	Acid-etched Pauldrons	61	BoA	431	1	28	10
▶	**SPELL** Nature Resist +20						
56	Demon Plate Pauldrons	61	BoE	431	1	25	21
56	Titan's Shoulder Pads	61	BoE	431	1	24	53
57	Exalted Epaulets	62	BoE	439	1	30	76
58	Hyperion Pauldrons	63	BoE	446	1	41	75

STANDARD PLATE SHOULDER ARMOR

M LEV	ARMOR NAME	LEV	BIND	AC	VENDOR PURCHASE VALUE		
N/A	PVP Plate Shoulder Horde	60	None	403		71	16
N/A	PVP Plate Shoulder Alliance	60	None	403		72	97

INFERIOR PLATE SHOULDER ARMOR

M LEV	ARMOR NAME	LEV	BIND	AC	VENDOR PURCHASE VALUE		
49	Light Plate Shoulderpads	54	None	343		37	30

PLATE WAIST ARMOR

SUPERIOR PLATE WAIST ARMOR

M LEV	ARMOR NAME	LEV	BIND	AC	VENDOR PURCHASE VALUE		
35	Enormous Ogre Belt	40	BoE	182		27	04
46	Atal'alarion's Tusk Ring	51	BoA	296		62	63
52	Girdle of Uther	57	BoE	332		82	26
53	Rainbow Girdle	58	BoA	338		89	88
N/A	Omokk's Girth Restrainer	60	BoA	350		95	42
▶	**SPELL** Add 1% Crit						
58	Brigam Girdle	63	BoA	368	1	16	41
58	Handcrafted Mastersmith Girdle	63	BoA	368	1	19	87
▶	**SPELL** Increased Armor 150						

GOOD PLATE WAIST ARMOR

M LEV	ARMOR NAME	LEV	BIND	AC	VENDOR PURCHASE VALUE		
40	Jouster's Girdle	40	BoE	165		22	44
40	Saltstone Girdle	40	BoE	165		22	95
40	Field Plate Girdle	41	BoE	181		24	14
40	Naga Scale Belt	41	BoE	181		23	20
40	Embossed Plate Girdle	42	BoE	198		26	95
40	Warbringer's Belt	42	BoE	198		25	34
40	Chromite Girdle	43	BoE	215		28	37
40	Tyrant's Belt	43	BoE	215		28	92
39	Prismatic Scale Legguards	44	BoE	233		29	89
40	Gothic Plate Girdle	45	BoE	238		31	54

GOOD PLATE WAIST ARMOR continued

M LEV	ARMOR NAME	LEV	BIND	AC	VENDOR PURCHASE VALUE
41	Bloodforged Belt	46	BoE	244	33 38
41	Valorous Girdle	46	BoE	244	36 25
42	Wyrm Scale Belt	47	BoE	249	36 05
43	Overlord's Girdle	48	BoE	254	40 48
44	Sunscale Belt	49	BoE	259	41 66
45	Revenant Girdle	50	BoE	264	47 06
45	Thorium Belt	50	BoE	264	46 36
▶	**SPELL** Arcane, Fire, Frost, Nature & Shadow Resist +6				
46	High Chief's Belt	51	BoE	269	47 69
46	Leviathan Girdle	51	BoE	269	50 35
47	Atal'ai Girdle	52	BoA	275	53 38
47	Jademir Scale Belt	52	BoE	275	50 56
47	Spectral Plate Girdle	52	BoE	275	50 61
47	Imperial Plate Belt	53	BoE	280	55 33
49	Templar Girdle	54	BoE	285	59 08
49	Valkyrie Girdle	54	BoE	285	61 56
50	Glorious Belt	55	BoE	291	60 21
50	Hydra Girdle	55	BoE	291	62 39
50	Stonewall Girdle	55	BoA	291	61 48
▶	**SPELL** Increased Armor 160				
N/A	Stalwart Clutch	56	BoA	296	70 12
▶	**SPELL** Adds 12 Defense				
52	Dragonbone Girdle	57	BoE	302	67 66

GOOD PLATE WAIST ARMOR continued

M LEV	ARMOR NAME	LEV	BIND	AC	VENDOR PURCHASE VALUE
52	Nether Plate Girdle	57	BoE	302	69 85
N/A	Gearforge Girdle	58	BoA	307	71 72
▶	**SPELL** Increased Defense				
54	Demon Plate Girdle	59	BoE	313	80 94
54	Titan's Belt	59	BoE	313	75 30
55	Exalted Girdle	60	BoE	318	79 07
56	Deathbone Girdle	61	BoA	323	84 46
56	Hyperion Girdle	61	BoE	323	84 75

STANDARD PLATE WAIST ARMOR

M LEV	ARMOR NAME	LEV	BIND	AC	VENDOR PURCHASE VALUE
45	Platemail Belt	50	None	251	26 67

INFERIOR PLATE WAIST ARMOR

M LEV	ARMOR NAME	LEV	BIND	AC	VENDOR PURCHASE VALUE
52	Light Plate Belt	57	None	272	28 34

PLATE WRIST ARMOR

SUPERIOR PLATE WRIST ARMOR

M LEV	ARMOR NAME	LEV	BIND	AC	VENDOR PURCHASE VALUE
40	Skullplate Bracers	42	BoE	169	30 27
43	Giantslayer Cuffs	48	BoE	217	47 15
48	Runed Golem Shackles	53	BoE	240	64 64
▶	**SPELL** Adds 6 Defense				
52	Emberplate Armguards	57	BoA	258	86 37
▶	**SPELL** Fire Resist +10				
54	Vambraces of the Sadist	59	BoA	267	92 96
▶	**SPELL** Add 1% Crit				
57	Vigorsteel Vambraces	62	BoA	281	1 10 05
58	Battleborn Armbraces	63	BoA	286	1 16 40
▶	**SPELL** Adds 1% Crit and 1% Hit				

GOOD PLATE WRIST ARMOR

M LEV	ARMOR NAME	LEV	BIND	AC	VENDOR PURCHASE VALUE
40	Jouster's Wristguards	40	BoE	129	22 19
40	Saltstone Armsplints	40	BoE	129	21 73
40	Field Plate Vambraces	41	BoE	141	23 88
40	Naga Scale Vambraces	41	BoE	141	23 63
40	Embossed Plate Bracers	42	BoE	154	24 75
40	Warbringer's Armsplints	42	BoE	154	25 15
40	Chromite Bracers	43	BoE	167	28 07
40	Tyrant's Armguards	43	BoE	167	27 77
40	Prismatic Scale Armguards	44	BoE	181	28 61
40	Bloodforged Bindings	45	BoE	185	31 08
40	Gothic Plate Vambraces	45	BoE	185	33 11
41	Valorous Wristguards	46	BoE	189	35 74
41	Wyrm Scale Bracers	46	BoE	189	33 38
43	Overlord's Vambraces	48	BoE	197	39 88
43	Sunscale Wristguards	48	BoE	197	38 93
44	High Chief's Bindings	49	BoE	202	41 66
44	Revenant Bracers	49	BoE	202	43 50
45	Jademir Scale Armguards	50	BoE	206	44 57

GOOD PLATE WRIST ARMOR continued

M LEV	ARMOR NAME	LEV	BIND	AC	VENDOR PURCHASE VALUE
N/A	Runesteel Vambraces	50	BoA	206	45 49
46	Leviathan Vambraces	51	BoE	210	49 62
46	Thorium Bracers	51	BoE	210	49 98
▶	**SPELL** Arcane, Fire, Frost, Nature & Shadow Resist +5				
47	Valkyrie Vambraces	52	BoE	214	50 56
48	Spectral Plate Vambraces	53	BoE	218	58 44
49	Imperial Plate Bracers	54	BoE	222	60 44
49	Templar Bracers	54	BoE	222	60 18
50	Glorious Bindings	55	BoE	226	60 21
51	Dragonbone Bindings	56	BoE	231	63 83
51	Hydra Vambraces	56	BoE	231	67 12
52	Nether Plate Vambraces	57	BoE	235	71 16
53	Titan's Armsplints	58	BoE	239	71 72
54	Demon Plate Vambraces	59	BoE	243	79 78
54	Exalted Armsplints	59	BoE	243	75 30
N/A	Shining Armplates	59	BoA	243	75 30
N/A	Blinkstrike Armguards	60	BoA	247	79 07
▶	**SPELL** Add 1% Crit				
55	Hyperion Vambraces	60	BoE	247	81 93

STANDARD PLATE WRIST ARMOR

M LEV	ARMOR NAME	LEV	BIND	AC	VENDOR PURCHASE VALUE
45	Platemail Bracers	50	None	195	26 87
N/A	PVP Plate Wrist Alliance	60	None	235	47 44

INFERIOR PLATE WRIST ARMOR

M LEV	ARMOR NAME	LEV	BIND	AC	VENDOR PURCHASE VALUE
48	Light Plate Bracers	53	None	196	22 61

SHIELDS

EPIC SHIELDS

M LEV	ARMOR NAME	LEV	BIND	AC	VENDOR PURCHASE VALUE		
36	The Green Tower	41	BoE	738	1	25	77
▶	**SPELL** On Hit: 1% Chance for 3 Dmg Thorns and 50 Nature Resist						
41	Blackskull Shield	46	BoE	828	1	88	15
▶	**SPELL** Increased Armor 100, Shadow Resist +10						
45	Wall of the Dead	50	BoE	900	2	32	73
▶	**SPELL** On Hit: 3% Chance to Raise Armor by 150 (20 sec)						
54	Skullflame Shield	59	BoE	1062	4	22	96
▶	**SPELL** Fire & Shadow Resist +10, On Hit: 3% 35 Life Steal, 1% 75-125 AoE						

SUPERIOR SHIELDS

M LEV	ARMOR NAME	LEV	BIND	AC	VENDOR PURCHASE VALUE		
15	Kresh's Back	20	BoA	330		10	64
▶	**SPELL** Adds 6 Defense						
15	Gold-plated Buckler	20	BoA	330		10	67
19	Redbeard Crest	24	BoE	396		19	20
20	Seedcloud Buckler	25	BoA	413		20	67
23	Commander's Crest	28	BoA	462		27	11
N/A	Arctic Buckler	29	BoA	479		30	28
▶	**SPELL** Frost Resist +5						
25	Shield of Thorsen	30	BoE	495		33	59
▶	**SPELL** Increased Armor 50						
26	Resplendent Guardian	31	BoE	512		39	60
▶	**SPELL** Add 1% Block						
N/A	Marbled Buckler	36	BoA	594		61	05
31	Heart of Agamaggan	36	BoA	594		63	09
32	Thermaplugg's Central Core	37	BoA	611		69	17
▶	**SPELL** On Hit: 5% Chance to deal 35-65 Dmg to Attacker						
33	Skullance Shield	38	BoE	627		71	23
37	Olaf's All Purpose Shield	42	BoA	693		93	98
▶	**SPELL** Use: Slows Fall Speed for 30 sec						
37	Savage Boar's Guard	42	BoA	693		96	52
39	Aegis of the Scarlet Commander	44	BoA	726	1	16	81
41	Mountainside Buckler	46	BoE	759	1	32	35
43	Troll Protector	48	BoE	792	1	52	96
▶	**SPELL** Add 2% Block						
49	Aegis of Stormwind	54	BoE	891	2	35	05
51	Crest of Supremacy	56	BoA	924	2	46	45
53	Rock Golem Bulwark	58	BoA	957	2	90	82
▶	**SPELL** Arcane Resist +15						
55	Crest of Retribution	60	BoA	990	3	06	56
▶	**SPELL** On Block: Deals 5-35 Dmg						
56	Husk of Nerub'enkan	61	BoA	1007	3	23	03
▶	**SPELL** Nature Resist +15						
57	Garrett Family Crest	62	BoE	1023	3	46	94
56	Rhombeard Protector	61	BoA	1007	3	50	31
58	Draconian Deflector	63	BoA	1040	3	52	12
▶	**SPELL** Increased Defense, Fire Resist +10						
N/A	Argent Defender	62	BoA	1023	3	65	15
▶	**SPELL** On Hit: 1% Chance to Raise Block by 50% for 10 sec						
N/A	Darrowshire Strongguard	63	BoA	1040	3	67	20
▶	**SPELL** Frost & Nature Resist +10						

GOOD SHIELDS

M LEV	ARMOR NAME	LEV	BIND	AC	VENDOR PURCHASE VALUE		
7	Gypsy Buckler	12	BoE	161		2	48
7	War Torn Shield	12	BoE	161		2	45
8	Cadet Shield	13	BoE	185		3	00
8	Grizzly Buckler	13	BoE	185		3	05
9	Brackwater Shield	14	BoE	210		3	66
9	Hunting Buckler	14	BoE	210		3	64
10	Ceremonial Buckler	15	BoE	225		4	38
N/A	Faerleia's Shield	15	BoA	225		4	43
N/A	Ironplate Buckler	15	BoA	225		4	70
10	Veteran Shield	15	BoE	225		4	35
11	Bard's Buckler	16	BoE	240		5	33
N/A	Welding Shield	16	BoA	240		4	98
N/A	Dwarven Defender	17	BoA	255		6	13
12	Lupine Buckler	17	BoE	255		5	85
12	Soldier's Shield	17	BoE	255		6	15

GOOD SHIELDS continued

M LEV	ARMOR NAME	LEV	BIND	AC	VENDOR PURCHASE VALUE		
13	Bloodspattered Shield	18	BoE	270		6	56
13	Dust Bowl	18	BoE	270		7	15
13	Inscribed Buckler	18	BoE	270		6	54
14	Feral Buckler	19	BoE	285		8	15
14	Raider's Shield	19	BoE	285		7	94
15	Bandit Buckler	20	BoE	300		9	40
N/A	Buckler of the Seas	20	BoA	300		9	18
N/A	Cobalt Buckler	20	BoA	300		9	29
N/A	Furen's Favor	20	BoA	300		9	06
N/A	Ruga's Bulwark	20	BoA	300		8	95
N/A	Steelcap Shield	20	BoA	300		8	68
15	War Paint Shield	20	BoE	300		8	70
16	Burnished Shield	21	BoE	315		10	22
16	Green Carapace Shield	21	BoE	315		10	25
▶	**SPELL** Nature Resist +4						
16	Prospector's Buckler	21	BoE	315		9	98
17	Outrunner's Shield	22	BoE	330		11	68
17	Scouting Buckler	22	BoE	330		11	66
18	Bear Buckler	23	BoE	345		13	08
18	Defender Shield	23	BoE	345		13	23
18	Moonstalker's Buckler	23	BoE	345		13	61
18	Owl's Disk	23	BoE	345		13	49
19	Black Husk Shield	24	BoE	360		14	90
▶	**SPELL** Use: Attempt to Cure Multiple Poison Effects						
19	Forest Buckler	24	BoE	360		15	19
19	Grunt's Shield	24	BoE	360		15	78
19	Stormwind Guard Shield	24	BoE	360		14	85
N/A	Bastion of Stormwind	25	BoA	375		17	62
▶	**SPELL** Adds 5 Defense						
20	Bristlebark Buckler	25	BoE	375		16	57
20	Fortified Shield	25	BoE	375		17	81
20	Guardian Buckler	25	BoE	375		16	64
21	Hulking Shield	26	BoE	390		18	72
21	Pirate's Buckler	26	BoE	390		18	74
N/A	Constable Buckler	27	BoA	405		22	45
N/A	Fire Hardened Buckler	27	BoA	405		22	20
22	Lambent Scale Shield	27	BoE	405		21	16
N/A	Ward of the Vale	27	BoA	405		22	21
22	Wrangler's Buckler	27	BoE	405		22	63
N/A	Clink Shield	28	BoA	420		22	66
23	Dervish Buckler	28	BoE	420		24	26
23	Kodo Hide Buckler	28	BoE	420		24	63
N/A	Sentry Buckler	28	BoA	420		24	51
24	Battleforge Shield	29	BoE	435		26	78
24	Spiked Chain Shield	29	BoE	435		25	16
25	Emblazoned Buckler	30	BoE	450		29	87
25	Pathfinder Guard	30	BoE	450		29	07
N/A	Shield of the Faith	30	BoA	450		27	95
26	Cenarion Buckler	31	BoE	465		31	62
26	Glimmering Shield	31	BoE	465		30	89
26	Sentry's Shield	31	BoE	465		32	22
N/A	Deadskull Shield	32	BoA	480		33	06
27	Monk's Guard	32	BoE	480		34	89
27	Slayer's Shield	32	BoE	480		33	17
28	Ambusher's Shield	33	BoE	495		37	39
28	Cutthroat's Buckler	33	BoE	495		38	26
28	Infiltrator Buckler	33	BoE	495		39	23
N/A	Gold Lion Shield	34	BoA	510		44	05
29	Headhunter's Buckler	34	BoE	510		41	01
29	Nefarious Buckler	34	BoE	510		43	90
29	Phalanx Shield	34	BoE	510		43	30
29	Wicked Chain Shield	34	BoE	510		41	79
N/A	Crest of Darkshire	35	BoA	525		47	97
30	Insignia Buckler	35	BoE	525		48	45
31	Archer's Buckler	36	BoE	540		48	82
31	Basilisk Scale Shield	36	BoE	540		52	26
31	Combat Shield	36	BoE	540		53	11
N/A	Energized Stone Circle	36	BoA	540		49	38
31	Ghostwalker Buckler	36	BoE	540		49	43
N/A	Grom'gol Buckler	37	BoA	555		57	83
32	Hawkeye's Buckler	37	BoE	555		55	81
32	Pillager's Shield	37	BoE	555		53	43
32	Renegade Shield	37	BoE	555		58	28
33	Sentinel Buckler	38	BoE	570		62	02
N/A	Studded Ring Shield	38	BoA	570		57	71
N/A	Visionary Buckler	38	BoA	570		62	68
N/A	Anchorhold Buckler	39	BoA	585		65	62
34	Burning Shield	39	BoE	585		62	32
34	Glyphed Buckler	39	BoE	585		63	81

GOOD SHIELDS continued

M LEV	ARMOR NAME	LEV	BIND	AC	VENDOR PURCHASE VALUE		
34	Knight's Crest	39	BoE	585		67	47
N/A	Vigilant Buckler	39	BoA	585		64	77
▶	**SPELL** Add 1% Block						
34	Witch Doctor's Protector	39	BoE	585		62	46
N/A	Basalt Buckler	40	BoA	600		70	75
35	Chief Brigadier Shield	40	BoE	600		69	18
N/A	Lunar Buckler	40	BoA	600		67	61
35	Marauder's Crest	40	BoE	600		71	62
36	Jouster's Crest	41	BoE	615		75	27
▶	**SPELL** Increased Armor 50						
36	Saltstone Shield	41	BoE	615		74	82
36	Sparkleshell Shield	41	BoE	615		75	94
N/A	Vile Protector	41	BoA	615		77	54
▶	**SPELL** On Hit: 1% Chance to Deal 105-175 Dmg to Attacker						
37	Berserker Shield	42	BoE	630		79	20
N/A	Pit Fighter's Shield	42	BoA	630		82	82
N/A	Earthclasp Barrier	43	BoA	645		90	51
38	Field Plate Shield	43	BoE	645		88	82
40	Naga Scale Crest	43	BoE	645		85	95
▶	**SPELL** Increased Armor 50						
38	Slithid Scale Buckler	43	BoE	645		84	65
N/A	Tharg's Frisbee	43	BoA	645		92	12
39	Captain's Buckler	44	BoE	660		95	58
N/A	Collection Plate	44	BoA	660		94	44
39	Ravager's Shield	44	BoE	660		97	10
40	Brigade Defender	45	BoE	675	1	02	12
40	Embossed Plate Shield	45	BoE	675	1	00	97
N/A	Forcestone Buckler	45	BoA	675	1	08	62
N/A	Salbac Shield	45	BoA	675	1	01	26
41	Ancient Defender	46	BoE	690	1	11	58
41	Warbringer's Shield	46	BoE	690	1	11	98
41	Chromite Shield	46	BoE	690	1	12	34
42	Bonelink Wall Shield	47	BoE	705	1	17	82
42	Blackforge Buckler	47	BoE	705	1	19	00
43	Tyrant's Shield	48	BoE	720	1	24	83
43	Champion's Wall Shield	48	BoE	720	1	30	48
44	Gothic Shield	49	BoE	735	1	40	12
44	Khan's Buckler	49	BoE	735	1	42	89
45	Warmonger's Buckler	50	BoE	750	1	47	24
45	Prismatic Scale Shield	50	BoE	750	1	52	32
46	Bloodforged Shield	51	BoE	765	1	52	34
46	Valorous Shield	51	BoE	765	1	56	95
46	Gryphon Mail Buckler	51	BoE	765	1	57	66
N/A	Optomatic Deflector	51	BoA	765	1	59	88
▶	**SPELL** Add 2% Block						
46	Thunderscale Defender	51	BoE	765	1	59	93
47	Icebrand Crest	52	BoE	780	1	62	10
47	Overlord's Shield	52	BoE	780	1	64	49
47	Stoneshell Guard	52	BoA	780	1	65	78
▶	**SPELL** Increased Armor 100						
48	Wyrm Scale Deflector	53	BoE	795	1	72	54
48	Lord's Crest	53	BoE	795	1	86	42
49	Protector Buckler	54	BoE	810	1	87	81
49	Revenant Deflector	54	BoE	810	1	89	03
50	Crusader's Shield	55	BoE	825	1	92	21
N/A	Shizzle's Drizzle Blocker	55	BoA	825	1	92	70
49	Sunscale Shield	54	BoE	810	1	94	20
50	Leviathan Shield	55	BoE	825	1	98	88
N/A	Aegis of Battle	55	BoA	825	2	11	63
51	Astral Guard	56	BoA	840	2	15	69
51	High Chief's Shield	56	BoE	840	2	17	41
51	Ebonhold Buckler	56	BoE	840	2	20	28
52	Spectral Shield	57	BoE	855	2	20	92
51	Ironhide Shield	56	BoE	840	2	22	12
52	Daemonic Shield	57	BoE	855	2	26	25
52	Jademir Scale Shield	57	BoE	855	2	29	50
54	Valkyrie Shield	59	BoE	885	2	40	98
53	Divine Shield	58	BoE	870	2	47	60
53	Templar Shield	58	BoE	870	2	49	38
55	Glorious Shield	60	BoE	900	2	53	03
54	Bloodlust Buckler	59	BoE	885	2	58	26
54	Hydra Shield	59	BoE	885	2	62	76
56	Nether Shield	61	BoE	915	2	65	68
55	Abyssal Wall	60	BoE	900	2	73	96
57	Rattlecage Buckler	62	BoA	930	2	78	96
57	Dragonbone Guard	62	BoE	930	2	78	96
56	Impenetrable Wall	61	BoE	915	2	87	85
57	Hellcaller Guard	62	BoE	930	2	89	32
58	Titan's Shield	63	BoE	945	2	92	91
57	Tempest Shield	62	BoE	930	3	06	37
59	Mercurial Guard	64	BoE	960	3	10	40
59	Warlord's Buckler	64	BoE	960	3	20	07
58	Demon Guard	63	BoE	945	3	20	52

GOOD SHIELDS continued

M LEV	ARMOR NAME	LEV	BIND	AC	VENDOR PURCHASE VALUE		
60	Exalted Shield	65	BoE	975	3	22	94
60	Triumphant Shield	65	BoE	975	3	24	93
60	Kraken Shield	65	BoE	975	3	25	92
60	Hyperion Shield	65	BoE	975	3	29	71

STANDARD SHIELDS

M LEV	ARMOR NAME	LEV	BIND	AC	VENDOR PURCHASE VALUE		
N/A	Deathguard Buckler	5	BoA	38			15
N/A	Pikeman Shield	5	BoA	38			15
N/A	Dwarven Kite Shield	5	BoA	38			15
N/A	Thick Bark Buckler	5	BoA	38			15
1	Large Round Shield	5	None	38			15
1	Small Shield	5	None	38			15
N/A	Woodland Shield	5	BoA	38			16
1	Large Wooden Shield	5	None	38			16
1	Dented Buckler	5	None	38			16
3	Burnt Buckler	8	None	78			48
3	Charger's Shield	8	None	78			52
4	Warrior's Shield	9	None	95			70
N/A	Charging Buckler	9	BoA	95			71
4	Primal Buckler	9	None	95			72
5	Battle Shield	10	None	113			88
N/A	Stone Buckler	10	BoA	113			89
5	Worn Heater Shield	10	None	113			89
5	Round Buckler	10	None	113			89
N/A	Militia Buckler	10	BoA	113			91
5	Dull Heater Shield	10	None	113			94
5	Standard Issue Shield	10	None	113			94
5	Small Targe	10	None	113			96
5	Pioneer Buckler	10	None	113			96
6	Tribal Buckler	11	None	132		1	15
N/A	Tribal Warrior's Shield	11	BoA	132		1	16
N/A	Crag Buckler	11	BoA	132		1	16
6	Thuggish Shield	11	None	132		1	21
6	Infantry Shield	11	None	132		1	25
N/A	Bone Buckler	12	BoA	153		1	53
19	Razormane War Shield	24	BoA	342		2	33
12	Banded Buckler	17	None	242		3	55
12	Wall Shield	17	None	242		3	67
15	Worn Turtle Shell Shield	20	None	285		5	62
▶	**SPELL** Increased Armor 30						
17	Large Metal Shield	22	None	314		6	86
17	Ringed Buckler	22	None	314		7	29
21	Techbot CPU Shell	26	None	371		11	20
22	Kite Shield	27	None	385		12	36
22	Reinforced Targe	27	None	385		13	12
32	Heavy Pavise	37	None	527		32	31
32	Metal Buckler	37	None	527		34	17
35	Battered Viking Shield	40	None	570		44	36
45	Crested Heater Shield	50	None	713		87	25
45	Ornate Buckler	50	None	713		93	93

INFERIOR SHIELDS

M LEV	ARMOR NAME	LEV	BIND	AC	VENDOR PURCHASE VALUE		
1	Worn Wooden Buckler	1	None	4			1
1	Worn Wooden Shield	1	None	4			1
1	Battered Buckler	2	None	10			3
1	Bent Large Shield	4	None	26			7
1	Cracked Buckler	6	None	47			16
2	Worn Large Shield	7	None	60			24
6	Wooden Shield	11	None	125			81
10	Wooden Buckler	15	None	203		11	82
11	Simple Buckler	16	None	216		2	10
12	Rectangular Shield	17	None	230		2	43
17	Small Round Shield	22	None	297		4	57
18	Box Shield	23	None	311		5	19
23	Targe Shield	28	None	378		9	10
24	Tower Shield	29	None	392		10	05
28	Reinforced Buckler	33	None	446		15	85
31	Reflective Heater	36	None	486		21	02
37	Blocking Targe	42	None	567		31	54
43	Protective Pavise	48	None	648		53	32
48	Deflecting Tower	53	None	716		68	37
51	Crested Buckler	56	None	756		82	37
60	Plate Wall Shield	65	None	878	1	29	24
63	Plated Buckler	68	None	918	1	51	34

WEAPONS

ONE-HANDED AXES

EPIC AXES (1H)

M LEV	WEAPON NAME	LEV	BIND	DPS	SPEED	VENDOR PURCHASE VALUE		
42	Flurry Axe	47	BoE	35.33	1.5	2	96	27
▶	**SPELL/NOTE** On Attack: Chance for Extra Attack							
52	Axe of the Deep Woods	57	BoE	41.48	2.7	5	41	23
▶	**SPELL/NOTE** On Attack: Chance to Deal 90-126 Nature Dmg							

SUPERIOR AXES (1H)

M LEV	WEAPON NAME	LEV	BIND	DPS	SPEED	VENDOR PURCHASE VALUE		
15	Serpent's Kiss	20	BoE	13.40	2.5		16	86
▶	**SPELL/NOTE** On Attack: Chance to Deal 21 Poison Dmg Over 15 sec							
18	Guillotine Axe	23	BoE	15.00	2.7		24	52
▶	**SPELL/NOTE** Main Hand Only							
18	Razor's Edge	23	BoE	15.21	2.4		25	89
20	Butcher's Cleaver	25	BoA	16.18	1.7		33	00
20	Grimclaw	25	BoE	16.00	2		33	37
▶	**SPELL/NOTE** On Attack: Chance to Deal 30 Shadow Dmg							
22	Axe of the Enforcer	27	BoE	17.12	2.6		39	37
25	Bearded Boneaxe	30	BoE	18.95	1.9		51	43
▶	**SPELL/NOTE** Main Hand Only							
25	Headsplitter	30	BoE	18.91	2.3		56	05
25	Vibroblade	30	BoE	19.06	1.6		52	88
▶	**SPELL/NOTE** On Attack: Chance to Lower Target Armor by 100							
31	Pronged Reaver	36	BoA	23.96	2.4		97	88
32	Stalvan's Reaper	37	BoE	24.83	2.9	1	06	82
▶	**SPELL/NOTE** On Attack: Chance to Lower Enemy Attributes by 2							
33	Shovelphlange's Mining Axe	38	BoE	25.71	2.8	1	13	80
▶	**SPELL/NOTE** Attack Power 10							
33	Steelclaw Reaver	38	BoE	25.83	1.8	1	12	90
▶	**SPELL/NOTE** Main Hand Only							
34	Sickle Axe	39	BoE	26.54	2.6	1	16	85
40	Curve-bladed Ripper	45	BoE	30.26	1.9	1	97	78
▶	**SPELL/NOTE** Main Hand Only							
40	Digmaster 5000	45	BoE	30.28	1.8	1	85	60
43	Winter's Bite	48	BoE	32.14	2.1	2	47	48
▶	**SPELL/NOTE** Main Hand Only, On Hit: Chance for 20-30 Dmg/Snare for 50% Move Speed							
45	Ripsaw	50	BoA	33.33	2.7	2	88	53
▶	**SPELL/NOTE** Main Hand Only, On Attack: Chance to Wound for 75 Dmg							
48	Axe of Rin'ji	53	BoE	35.00	1.9	3	47	05
48	Ribsplitter	53	BoE	35.19	2.7	3	53	32
▶	**SPELL/NOTE** Main Hand Only, Attack Power 10							
50	Dawn's Edge	55	BoE	36.43	2.1	3	60	44
▶	**SPELL/NOTE** Add 1% Crit							
51	Tooth of Eranikus	56	BoA	37.08	2.4	3	88	01
▶	**SPELL/NOTE** Main Hand Only, Add 1% Hit							
52	Soul Breaker	57	BoA	37.50	1.6	4	41	42
▶	**SPELL/NOTE** Main Hand Only							
52	Wraith Scythe	57	BoA	37.73	2.2	4	31	76
▶	**SPELL/NOTE** Main Hand Only, On Attack: Chance to Steal 45 HP from Target							
53	Rivenspike	58	BoA	38.23	3.1	4	41	06
▶	**SPELL/NOTE** On Attack: Chance to Reduce Target Armor by 200							
55	Demonfork	60	BoA	39.46	2.8	4	73	39
▶	**SPELL/NOTE** Main Hand Only, On Attack: Chance to Transfer 50 HP over 25 sec							
N/A	Windreaper	60	BoA	39.55	3.3	5	14	18
56	Serathil	61	BoE	40.00	1.9	5	39	57
▶	**SPELL/NOTE** Increased Armor 100							
57	Iceblade Hacker	62	BoA	40.75	2	5	66	83
▶	**SPELL/NOTE** Main Hand Only							
58	Annihilator	63	BoE	41.47	1.7	5	71	50
▶	**SPELL/NOTE** Main Hand Only, On Attack: Chance to Reduce Target Armor by ww200							

GOOD AXES (1H)

M LEV	WEAPON NAME	LEV	BIND	DPS	SPEED	VENDOR PURCHASE VALUE	
6	Rodentia Flint Axe	11	BoE	6.00	2	3	00
▶	**SPELL/NOTE** Main Hand Only						
6	Scalping Tomahawk	11	BoE	5.83	1.8	3	09
▶	**SPELL/NOTE** Main Hand Only						
N/A	Defender Axe	13	BoA	6.96	2.3	4	72
▶	**SPELL/NOTE** Main Hand Only, +10 to Armor Class						
8	Stonesplinter Axe	13	BoE	6.82	2.2	4	77
▶	**SPELL/NOTE** Main Hand Only						
N/A	Pointed Axe	14	BoA	7.11	1.9	5	62
▶	**SPELL/NOTE** Main Hand Only						
10	Brutish Riverpaw Axe	15	BoE	7.86	2.8	7	32
▶	**SPELL/NOTE** Main Hand Only						
10	Deadmines Cleaver	15	BoE	7.88	2.6	6	90
▶	**SPELL/NOTE** Main Hand Only						
10	Dwarven Hatchet	15	BoE	7.50	2	7	42
▶	**SPELL/NOTE** Main Hand Only						
N/A	Elunite Axe	15	BoA	7.78	2.7	6	93
▶	**SPELL/NOTE** Main Hand Only						
N/A	Haggard's Axe	15	BoA	7.78	2.7	6	75
▶	**SPELL/NOTE** Main Hand Only						
N/A	Heirloom Axe	15	BoA	7.78	2.7	6	83
▶	**SPELL/NOTE** Main Hand Only						
10	Quilboar Tomahawk	15	BoE	7.80	2.5	6	85
▶	**SPELL/NOTE** Main Hand Only						
N/A	Thun'grim's Axe	15	BoA	7.78	2.7	6	96
▶	**SPELL/NOTE** Main Hand Only						
N/A	Umbral Axe	15	BoA	7.78	2.7	6	72
▶	**SPELL/NOTE** Main Hand Only						
12	Thick War Axe	17	BoE	8.60	2.5	9	37
▶	**SPELL/NOTE** Main Hand Only						
N/A	Thelsamar Axe	18	BoA	9.05	2.1	10	94
▶	**SPELL/NOTE** Main Hand Only						
16	Grunt Axe	21	BoE	10.65	2.3	16	94
16	Orcish Cleaver	21	BoE	10.56	1.8	17	06
▶	**SPELL/NOTE** Main Hand Only						
17	Smite's Reaver	22	BoA	11.05	1.9	18	30
18	Flesh Carver	23	BoE	11.52	2.3	20	68
▶	**SPELL/NOTE** Main Hand Only						
18	Forester's Axe	23	BoE	11.60	2.5	20	20
▶	**SPELL/NOTE** Main Hand Only						
19	Black Metal Axe	24	BoE	12.38	2.1	23	00
▶	**SPELL/NOTE** Main Hand Only						
19	Shadowhide Scalper	24	BoE	12.41	2.9	23	80
▶	**SPELL/NOTE** Main Hand Only						
20	Ridge Cleaver	25	BoE	12.73	2.2	27	55
▶	**SPELL/NOTE** Main Hand Only						
21	Marauder Axe	26	BoE	13.25	2	30	87
▶	**SPELL/NOTE** Main Hand Only						
22	Blurred Axe	27	BoE	13.82	1.7	33	71
▶	**SPELL/NOTE** Main Hand Only						
24	Callous Axe	29	BoE	15.00	2.8	40	94
▶	**SPELL/NOTE** Attack Power 08						
N/A	Shoni's Disarming Tool	31	BoA	16.05	1.9	50	28
▶	**SPELL/NOTE** Off-Hand Only, On Attack: 5% Chance for 5 sec Disarm						
26	Splitting Hatchet	31	BoE	16.11	1.8	50	33
N/A	Barreling Reaper	32	BoA	16.58	1.9	53	08
▶	**SPELL/NOTE** Main Hand Only						
N/A	Fish Gutter	32	BoA	16.67	2.1	54	47
▶	**SPELL/NOTE** Main Hand Only						
28	Hacking Cleaver	33	BoE	17.11	1.9	61	12
N/A	Guerrilla Cleaver	34	BoA	17.68	2.8	63	96
▶	**SPELL/NOTE** Main Hand Only						
29	Hillborne Axe	34	BoE	17.73	2.2	65	90
N/A	Bleeding Crescent	35	BoA	18.13	2.4	70	40
▶	**SPELL/NOTE** Main Hand Only						
N/A	Crescent of Forlorn Spirits	35	BoA	18.13	1.6	73	57
▶	**SPELL/NOTE** Main Hand Only						

GOOD AXES continued

M LEV	WEAPON NAME	LEV	BIND	DPS	SPEED	VENDOR PURCHASE VALUE		
32	Gloom Reaper	37	BoE	19.63	2.7		89	64
34	Savage Axe	39	BoE	21.43	2.8	1	04	76
▶	**SPELL/NOTE** Main Hand Only							
35	Greater Scythe	40	BoE	22.14	2.8	1	13	54
▶	**SPELL/NOTE** Main Hand Only							
36	Glutton's Cleaver	41	BoA	23.00	2	1	21	70
▶	**SPELL/NOTE** On Attack: 5% Chance to Deal 50 Dmg over 30 sec							
37	Heavy Mithril Axe	42	BoE	24.07	2.7	1	25	20
▶	**SPELL/NOTE** Main Hand Only							
39	Blue Glittering Axe	44	BoE	25.83	1.8	1	46	59
41	Ebonclaw Reaver	46	BoE	27.22	1.8	1	66	96
43	Crescent Edge	48	BoE	28.57	2.1	2	10	90
N/A	Axe of the Ebon Drake	51	BoA	30.26	1.9	2	41	59
▶	**SPELL/NOTE** Main Hand Only							
N/A	Force of the Hippogryph	51	BoA	30.42	2.4	2	57	29
▶	**SPELL/NOTE** Main Hand Only							
47	Moon Cleaver	52	BoE	30.91	2.2	2	74	85
N/A	Blitzcleaver	54	BoA	32.05	2.2	2	87	89
▶	**SPELL/NOTE** Attack Power 20							
49	Eater of the Dead	54	BoA	32.05	2.2	2	96	61
▶	**SPELL/NOTE** Main Hand Only, +30 Attack Power Vs. Undead							
50	Corpse Harvester	55	BoE	32.69	2.6	3	05	26
50	Grizzle's Skinner	55	BoA	32.92	2.4	3	06	27
▶	**SPELL/NOTE** Main Hand Only							
50	Ornate Thorium Handaxe	55	BoA	32.63	1.9	3	30	79
▶	**SPELL/NOTE** Main Hand Only							
52	Rune Edge	57	BoA	33.91	2.3	3	53	38
▶	**SPELL/NOTE** Main Hand Only							
53	Warlord's Axe	58	BoE	34.57	2.3	3	64	96
56	Felstone Reaver	61	BoE	36.50	2	4	24	09
59	Demon's Claw	64	BoE	38.26	2.3	4	92	81

INFERIOR AXES (1H)

M LEV	WEAPON NAME	LEV	BIND	DPS	SPEED	VENDOR PURCHASE VALUE		
4	Rusty Hatchet	9	None	2.86	2.1			72
▶	**SPELL/NOTE** Main Hand Only							
9	Worn Hatchet	14	None	4.29	2.1		2	37
▶	**SPELL/NOTE** Main Hand Only							
14	Unbalanced Axe	19	None	5.63	2.4		4	86
▶	**SPELL/NOTE** Main Hand Only							
17	Gouging Pick	22	None	6.67	1.8		7	68
▶	**SPELL/NOTE** Main Hand Only							
22	Meat Cleaver	27	None	8.33	2.4		12	82
▶	**SPELL/NOTE** Main Hand Only							
33	Keen Axe	38	None	12.27	2.2		36	50
▶	**SPELL/NOTE** Main Hand Only							
43	Heavy Flint Axe	48	None	17.17	2.3		83	36
▶	**SPELL/NOTE** Main Hand Only							
51	Jagged Axe	56	None	20.00	1.9	1	27	66
▶	**SPELL/NOTE** Main Hand Only							

STANDARD AXES (1H)

M LEV	WEAPON NAME	LEV	BIND	DPS	SPEED	VENDOR PURCHASE VALUE		
1	Worn Axe	2	None	1.00	2			7
▶	**SPELL/NOTE** Main Hand Only							
1	Deadman Cleaver	3	None	1.14	2.2			11
▶	**SPELL/NOTE** Main Hand Only							
N/A	Anvilmar Hand Axe	4	BoA	1.50	2			17
▶	**SPELL/NOTE** Main Hand Only							
1	Hand Axe	4	None	1.50	2			16
N/A	Primitive Hatchet	4	BoA	1.59	2.2			17
▶	**SPELL/NOTE** Main Hand Only							
N/A	Stone Tomahawk	4	BoA	1.67	2.1			16
▶	**SPELL/NOTE** Main Hand Only							
1	Trogg Hand Axe	4	None	1.50	2			16
▶	**SPELL/NOTE** Main Hand Only							
2	Kobold Excavation Pick	7	None	2.71	2.4			55
▶	**SPELL/NOTE** Main Hand Only							
N/A	Sharp Axe	8	BoA	3.27	2.6			80
▶	**SPELL/NOTE** Main Hand Only							
3	Skull Hatchet	8	None	3.25	2			81
▶	**SPELL/NOTE** Main Hand Only							
4	Copper Axe	9	None	3.95	1.9		1	09
▶	**SPELL/NOTE** Main Hand Only							
4	Frostmane Hand Axe	9	None	3.75	2		1	06
▶	**SPELL/NOTE** Main Hand Only							
4	Lumberjack Axe	9	None	3.85	2.6		1	13
▶	**SPELL/NOTE** Main Hand Only							
4	Tomahawk	9	None	3.82	1.7		1	08
▶	**SPELL/NOTE** Main Hand Only							
N/A	Ceremonial Tomahawk	10	BoA	4.41	1.7		1	38
▶	**SPELL/NOTE** Main Hand Only							
N/A	Striking Hatchet	12	BoA	5.29	1.7		2	31
▶	**SPELL/NOTE** Main Hand Only							
11	Hatchet	16	None	7.20	2.5		4	81
15	Cleaver	20	None	9.09	2.2		8	83
18	Bronze Axe	23	None	10.48	2.1		12	69
▶	**SPELL/NOTE** Main Hand Only							
19	Double Axe	24	None	11.00	2.5		13	90
30	Crescent Axe	35	None	17.12	2.6		45	09
41	Francisca	46	None	25.87	2.3	1	04	43

TWO-HANDED AXES

EPIC AXES (2H)

M LEV	WEAPON NAME	LEV	BIND	DPS	SPEED	VENDOR PURCHASE VALUE		
35	Fiery War Axe	40	BoE	40.34	2.9	2	15	28
▶	**SPELL/NOTE** On Attack: Chance to Deal 155-197 Dmg/24 More Over Time							
44	Kang the Decapitator	49	BoE	47.36	3.6	4	45	80
▶	**SPELL/NOTE** On Attack: Chance to Deal 560 Dmg Over 30 sec							
55	Brain Hacker	60	BoE	56.67	2.1	7	90	64
▶	**SPELL/NOTE** Adds 14 Fire Dmg							

SUPERIOR AXES (2H)

M LEV	WEAPON NAME	LEV	BIND	DPS	SPEED	VENDOR PURCHASE VALUE		
15	Boahn's Fang	20	BoE	17.60	2.5		20	84
15	Prospector Axe	20	BoE	17.50	2.4		22	05
18	Night Reaver	23	BoE	19.70	3.3		30	66
▶	**SPELL/NOTE** On Attack: Chance to Deal 60-90 Shadow Dmg							
18	Taskmaster Axe	23	BoA	19.63	2.7		30	79
21	Killmaim	26	BoE	21.72	3.2		47	71
▶	**SPELL/NOTE** On Attack: Chance to Deal 100 Dmg Over 30 sec							
23	Supercharger Battle Axe	28	BoE	23.04	2.8		54	83
▶	**SPELL/NOTE** On Attack: Chance to Deal 80-100 Nature Dmg							

SUPERIOR AXES (2H) continued

M LEV	WEAPON NAME	LEV	BIND	DPS	SPEED	VENDOR PURCHASE VALUE		
27	Bloodspiller	32	BoE	26.67	2.7		78	74
▶	**SPELL/NOTE** On Attack: Chance to Deal 130 Dmg Over 30 sec							
28	Burning War Axe	33	BoE	27.73	3.3		87	56
▶	**SPELL/NOTE** On Attack: Chance to Deal 86-110 Dmg/108 More Over Time							
29	Corpsemaker	34	BoA	28.95	3.8		99	30
32	Thermaplugg's Left Arm	37	BoA	32.59	2.7	1	35	60
34	Manslayer	39	BoE	34.53	3.2	1	58	75
▶	**SPELL/NOTE** Attack Power 38							
35	Hellslayer Battle Axe	40	BoE	35.52	2.9	1	72	09
▶	**SPELL/NOTE** Adds 66 Attack Power Vs. Undead							
35	Obsidian Cleaver	40	BoE	35.61	3.3	1	68	95
N/A	Whirlwind Axe	40	BoA	35.56	3.6	1	67	66
37	Ravager	42	BoA	37.29	3.5	1	89	23
▶	**SPELL/NOTE** On Attack: Chance to Begin an AoE Whirlwind							
N/A	Bonebiter	44	BoA	38.82	3.4	2	34	76
39	Pendulum of Doom	44	BoE	38.88	4	2	14	89
▶	**SPELL/NOTE** On Attack: Chance to Deal 250-350 Shadow Dmg							
43	Executioner's Cleaver	48	BoE	41.84	3.8	3	19	67
▶	**SPELL/NOTE** Add 1% Hit							
44	The Minotaur	49	BoE	42.66	3.2	3	40	67

SUPERIOR AXES (2H) continued

M LEV	WEAPON NAME	LEV	BIND	DPS	SPEED	VENDOR PURCHASE VALUE		
49	Bleakwood Hew	54	BoE	46.48	2.7	4	61	54
▸	SPELL/NOTE Bleakwood Curse							
51	Lord Alexander's Battle Axe	56	BoE	48.13	3.2	4	96	40
52	Dark Iron Sunderer	57	BoE	48.85	2.6	5	12	25
▸	SPELL/NOTE On Attack: Chance to Reduce Target Armor by 300							
54	The Nicker	59	BoA	50.50	4	5	76	71
▸	SPELL/NOTE On Attack:Chance to Deal 50-150 Dmg/150 More Over Time							
55	Dreadforge Retaliator	60	BoA	51.35	3.7	6	10	08
▸	SPELL/NOTE Add 1% Parry							
56	Gravestone War Axe	61	BoA	52.21	3.4	6	35	75
▸	SPELL/NOTE Creeping Mold							
58	Arcanite Reaper	63	BoE	53.82	3.8	7	30	36
▸	SPELL/NOTE Attack Power 62							

STANDARD AXES (2H)

M LEV	WEAPON NAME	LEV	BIND	DPS	SPEED	VENDOR PURCHASE VALUE		
1	Worn Battleaxe	2	None	1.38	2.9			8
N/A	Brave's Axe	4	BoA	2.12	3.3			20
1	Broad Axe	4	None	2.10	3.1			21
N/A	Thistlewood Axe	4	BoA	2.14	3.5			21
3	Large Axe	8	None	4.29	2.8			96
3	Wood Chopper	8	None	4.24	3.3			99
4	Vile Fin Battle Axe	9	None	5.00	3.1		1	40
9	Tabar	14	None	8.28	3.2		4	42
10	Rock Chipper	15	None	9.00	3.5		5	55
15	Bearded Axe	20	None	11.82	3.3		10	60
20	Battle Axe	25	None	15.26	3.8		19	56
22	Bronze Battle Axe	27	None	16.90	2.9		24	35
30	Bullova	35	None	22.37	3.8		56	57
39	Great Axe	44	None	31.25	3.6	1	12	33

INFERIOR AXES (2H)

M LEV	WEAPON NAME	LEV	BIND	DPS	SPEED	VENDOR PURCHASE VALUE		
3	Beaten Battle Axe	8	None	3.39	3.1			65
7	Crude Battle Axe	12	None	5.00	3		1	94
12	Short-handled Battle Axe	17	None	6.61	3.1		4	52
18	Shiny War Axe	23	None	8.96	2.4		11	04
22	Stone War Axe	27	None	10.77	2.6		16	09
27	Hefty War Axe	32	None	13.04	2.8		28	35
44	Splintering Battle Axe	49	None	22.88	3.3	1	11	89
54	Balanced War Axe	59	None	27.60	2.5	1	88	26

GOOD AXES (2H)

M LEV	WEAPON NAME	LEV	BIND	DPS	SPEED	VENDOR PURCHASE VALUE		
5	Severing Axe	10	BoE	7.03	3.2		2	98
8	Copper Battle Axe	13	BoE	9.06	3.2		6	13
N/A	Logsplitter	16	BoA	10.83	3.6		10	34
11	Twin-bladed Axe	16	BoE	10.74	2.7		10	24
12	Cold Iron Pick	17	BoE	11.33	3		12	23
N/A	Axe of Orgrimmar	18	BoA	11.82	3.3		14	04
13	Barbaric Battle Axe	18	BoE	11.94	3.6		13	72
N/A	Piercing Axe	18	BoA	11.82	3.3		12	78
14	Brashclaw's Chopper	19	BoE	12.50	3.4		14	92
14	Mo'grosh Can Opener	19	BoE	12.50	3.2		16	18
N/A	Dwarven Tree Chopper	20	BoA	13.03	3.3		17	55
▸	SPELL/NOTE Adds 2 to 2H Axe Skill							
15	Lupine Axe	20	BoE	13.04	2.3		18	07
N/A	Miner's Revenge	20	BoA	13.00	3.5		17	75
N/A	Skullchipper	20	BoA	13.00	3.5		17	17
N/A	Zhovur Axe	20	BoA	13.06	3.1		17	89
16	Rockslicer	21	BoA	13.79	3.3		20	11
17	Battle Slayer	22	BoE	14.55	3.3		22	62
18	Scythe Axe	23	BoE	15.14	3.6		26	64
18	Shadowhide Battle Axe	23	BoE	15.31	3.2		26	83
19	Blackrock Champion's Axe	24	BoE	16.09	3.2		29	31
19	Massive Battle Axe	24	BoE	16.06	3.3		30	36
20	Slayer's Battle Axe	25	BoE	16.90	2.9		33	87
21	Arced War Axe	26	BoA	17.58	3.3		38	57
22	Heavy Ogre War Axe	27	BoE	18.29	3.8		41	33
22	Reef Axe	27	BoA	18.33	3.3		40	10
23	Barbarian War Axe	28	BoE	19.03	3.1		44	96
23	Black Metal War Axe	28	BoE	18.97	2.9		44	43
24	Tunnel Pick	29	BoE	19.84	3.1		49	63
25	Brutal War Axe	30	BoE	20.28	3.6		56	26
26	Merciless Axe	31	BoE	21.09	3.2		60	39
29	Midnight Axe	34	BoE	22.96	2.7		80	68
▸	SPELL/NOTE On Attack: Chance to Deal Shadow Dmg							
32	Massive Iron Axe	37	BoE	25.57	3.5	1	12	48
35	Shadow Crescent Axe	40	BoE	29.00	2.5	1	42	21
N/A	Skullsplitter	41	BoA	30.17	2.9	1	43	82
N/A	Dwarven Charge	42	BoA	31.21	2.9	1	62	43
37	Monstrous War Axe	42	BoE	31.22	3.7	1	56	37
N/A	Tok'kar's Murloc Chopper	43	BoA	32.50	3.2	1	75	50
39	Headchopper	44	BoE	33.62	2.9	1	82	34
▸	SPELL/NOTE Add 1% Crit							
39	Lumbering Ogre Axe	44	BoE	33.72	3.9	1	92	05
41	Gigantic War Axe	46	BoE	35.63	3.2	2	27	75
44	Grinning Axe	49	BoE	38.04	2.8	2	84	60
N/A	Will of the Mountain Giant	51	BoA	39.46	2.8	3	03	08
N/A	Beastslayer	55	BoA	42.58	3.3	4	10	50
▸	SPELL/NOTE Adds 72 Attack Power Vs. Beasts							
N/A	Limb Cleaver	55	BoA	42.71	2.4	4	10	53
51	Colossal Great Axe	56	BoE	43.42	3.8	4	37	01
51	Huge Thorium Battleaxe	56	BoE	43.33	3.3	3	99	49
▸	SPELL/NOTE Adds to 2H Axe Skill							
53	Angerforge's Battle Axe	58	BoA	45.00	2.6	4	57	70
54	Razor's Edge	59	BoE	45.80	2.5	5	17	40
58	Death Striker	63	BoE	48.93	2.8	5	71	08

BOWS

EPIC BOWS

M LEV	WEAPON NAME	LEV	BIND	DPS	SPEED	VENDOR PURCHASE VALUE		
37	Bow of Searing Arrows	42	BoE	25.00	2.7	1	47	21
48	Hurricane	53	BoE	30.31	1.6	3	20	31

SUPERIOR BOWS

M LEV	WEAPON NAME	LEV	BIND	DPS	SPEED	VENDOR PURCHASE VALUE		
19	Venomstrike	24	BoA	9.58	2.4		22	40
20	Ranger Bow	25	BoE	12.59	2.7		24	21
27	Harpyclaw Short Bow	32	BoE	16.11	1.8		47	65
27	Nightstalker Bow	32	BoA	16.18	1.7		50	86
33	Quillshooter	38	BoE	15.89	2.8		87	25
34	Skystriker Bow	39	BoE	20.71	2.1		89	85
36	Monolithic Bow	41	BoE	21.85	2.7	1	02	75
42	Needle Threader	47	BoE	24.50	2	1	66	94
42	Stinging Bow	47	BoE	24.52	2.1	1	72	49
▸	SPELL/NOTE Attack Power 14							
48	Houndmaster's Bow	53	BoA	27.22	1.8	2	44	33
▸	SPELL/NOTE Adds 24 Attack Power Vs. Beasts							
50	Gyphonwing Long Bow	55	BoE	28.33	2.7	2	79	90
54	Riphook	59	BoA	30.23	2.2	3	63	18
▸	SPELL/NOTE Attack Power 22							
58	Truesilver Plated Long Bow	63	BoE	32.22	1.8	4	27	03

XII

GOOD BOWS

M LEV	WEAPON NAME	LEV	BIND	DPS	SPEED	VENDOR PURCHASE VALUE		
6	Hunting Bow	11	BoE	4.62	2.6		2	40
N/A	Orcish Battle Bow	14	BoA	5.53	1.9		4	25
N/A	Daryl's Hunting Bow	15	BoA	5.87	2.3		5	15
10	Heavy Shortbow	15	BoE	6.00	2.5		5	15
11	Centaur Longbow	16	BoE	6.14	2.2		6	09
11	Fine Shortbow	16	BoE	6.18	1.7		6	36
14	Fine Longbow	19	BoE	7.41	2.7		9	72
16	Light Bow	21	BoE	7.94	1.7		11	84
18	Short Ash Bow	23	BoE	9.21	1.9		16	10
21	Naga Heartpiercer	26	BoA	10.56	1.8		23	14
22	Precision Bow	27	BoE	10.96	2.6		24	26
N/A	Bow of Plunder	28	BoA	11.35	2.6		28	62
N/A	Cliffrunner's Aim	29	BoA	11.96	2.3		29	91
24	Long Battle Bow	29	BoE	11.82	2.2		30	39
N/A	Lunaris Bow	30	BoA	12.22	2.7		32	26
N/A	Raptor's End	30	BoA	12.07	2.9		34	26
27	Archer's Longbow	32	BoE	12.88	2.6		40	61
27	Ravenwood Bow	32	BoE	12.89	1.9		42	07
27	Sturdy Recurve	32	BoE	12.95	2.2		38	93
29	Whipwood Recurve Bow	34	BoE	13.61	1.8		48	14
30	Dense Shortbow	35	BoE	14.21	1.9		51	62
30	Long Redwood Bow	35	BoE	14.29	2.8		55	68
36	Trueshot Bow	41	BoE	18.16	1.9		87	22
40	Crusader Bow	45	BoE	20.91	2.2	1	25	16
N/A	Master Hunter's Bow	45	BoA	20.83	2.4	1	19	99
42	Massive Longbow	47	BoE	21.96	2.8	1	35	90
44	Sylvan Shortbow	49	BoE	22.75	2	1	57	65
46	Harpy Needler	51	BoE	23.70	2.7	1	95	91
48	Siege Bow	53	BoE	24.64	2.8	2	01	35
50	Quillfire Bow	55	BoE	25.65	2.3	2	27	12
55	Voone's Twitchbow	60	BoA	27.81	1.6	3	06	19
56	Blasthorn Bow	61	BoE	28.27	2.6	3	37	43
58	Hawkeye Bow	63	BoE	29.41	1.7	3	46	57
60	Archstrike Bow	65	BoE	30.22	2.3	4	11	61

STANDARD BOWS

M LEV	WEAPON NAME	LEV	BIND	DPS	SPEED	VENDOR PURCHASE VALUE	
1	Worn Shortbow	2	None	1.52	2.3		5
1	Polished Shortbow	4	None	1.75	2		11
N/A	Primitive Bow	4	BoA	1.85	2.7		12
N/A	Thistlewood Bow	4	BoA	1.96	2.3		12
1	Cadet's Bow	6	None	2.25	2		28
3	Hornwood Recurve Bow	8	None	2.38	2.1		57
N/A	Ashwood Bow	11	BoA	3.81	2.1	1	41
N/A	Hickory Shortbow	11	BoA	3.75	2	1	34
11	Laminated Recurve Bow	16	None	5.77	2.6	3	50
16	Reinforced Bow	21	None	7.50	2.2	7	62
20	Heavy Recurve Bow	25	None	9.17	2.4	12	69
29	Longbow	34	None	13.04	2.3	30	86
36	Baelog's Shortbow	41	None	16.52	2.3	54	14

INFERIOR BOWS

M LEV	WEAPON NAME	LEV	BIND	DPS	SPEED	VENDOR PURCHASE VALUE	
3	Cracked Shortbow	8	None	1.96	2.3		39
8	Feeble Shortbow	13	None	3.33	1.8	1	46
14	Light Hunting Bow	19	None	4.41	1.7	3	74
19	Mishandled Recurve Bow	24	None	5.63	2.4	7	51
23	Stiff Recurve Bow	28	None	6.79	2.8	10	62
26	Taut Compound Bow	31	None	7.60	2.5	15	41
40	Balanced Long Bow	45	None	12.22	1.8	50	70
45	Recurve Long Bow	55	None	15.20	2.5	90	15

CROSSBOWS

SUPERIOR CROSSBOWS

M LEV	WEAPON NAME	LEV	BIND	DPS	SPEED	VENDOR PURCHASE VALUE		
27	Crystalpine Stinger	32	BoE	14.46	2.8		47	29
35	Swiftwind	40	BoE	20.75	2		96	30
43	Skull Splitting Crossbow	48	BoE	25.19	2.6	1	78	92
▶	**SPELL/NOTE** Attack Power 14							
51	Heartseeking Crossbow	56	BoE	28.87	3.1	2	94	44
54	Blackcrow	59	BoA	34.22	3.2	3	60	55
▶	**SPELL/NOTE** Add 1% Hit							

GOOD CROSSBOWS

M LEV	WEAPON NAME	LEV	BIND	DPS	SPEED	VENDOR PURCHASE VALUE	
22	Steelarrow Crossbow	27	BoE	13.24	3.4	25	46

STANDARD CROSSBOWS

M LEV	WEAPON NAME	LEV	BIND	DPS	SPEED	VENDOR PURCHASE VALUE	
3	Light Crossbow	8	None	2.60	2.5		57
16	Fine Light Crossbow	21	None	7.41	2.7	7	02
29	Heavy Crossbow	34	None	13.04	2.8	28	22

DAGGERS

EPIC DAGGERS

M LEV	WEAPON NAME	LEV	BIND	DPS	SPEED	VENDOR PURCHASE VALUE		
40	Gut Ripper	45	BoE	33.89	1.8	2	70	31
▶	**SPELL/NOTE** On Attack: Chance for 95-121 Dmg							
48	Shadowblade	53	BoE	38.93	1.4	4	67	10
▶	**SPELL/NOTE** On Attack: Chance for 110-140 Shadow Dmg							
58	Alcor's Sunrazor	63	BoA	45.38	1.3	7	87	72
▶	**SPELL/NOTE** Fire Resist +10, On Attack: Chance for a Fire Bolt							
58	Deathstriker	63	BoA	45.59	1.7	7	56	24

SUPERIOR DAGGERS

M LEV	WEAPON NAME	LEV	BIND	DPS	SPEED	VENDOR PURCHASE VALUE	
18	Evocator's Blade	23	BoE	15.31	1.6	25	09
19	Assassin's Blade	24	BoE	15.53	1.9	29	74
20	Blackfang	25	BoE	16.33	1.5	33	86
▶	**SPELL/NOTE** Shadow Resist +5						
20	Doomspike	25	BoE	16.33	1.5	32	29

SUPERIOR DAGGERS continued

M LEV	WEAPON NAME	LEV	BIND	DPS	SPEED	VENDOR PURCHASE VALUE		
21	Blackvenom Blade	26	BoE	16.67	1.8		35	94
▶	**SPELL/NOTE** On Attack: Chance to Deal 15 Dmg Over 15 sec							
N/A	Black Menace	44	BoA	29.67	1.5	1	75	22
▶	**SPELL/NOTE** On Attack: Chance to Cast a Bolt							
N/A	Lifeforce Dirk	54	BoA	35.94	1.6	3	53	15
N/A	Darrowspike	63	BoA	41.33	1.5	5	78	06
21	Prison Shank	26	BoA	16.67	1.8		35	52
21	Talon of Vultros	26	BoE	16.75	2		38	00
23	Bite of Serra'kis	28	BoA	17.69	1.3		46	65
▶	**SPELL/NOTE** On Attack: Chance to Deal 40 Dmg Over 20 sec							
24	Meteor Shard	29	BoA	18.33	1.8		48	93
▶	**SPELL/NOTE** On Attack: Chance to Deal 35 Fire Dmg							
26	Vendetta	31	BoE	19.23	1.3		57	65
27	Claw of the Shadowmancer	32	BoE	20.53	1.9		67	31
▶	**SPELL/NOTE** On Attack: Chance to Deal 35 Shadow Dmg							
27	Toxic Revenger	32	BoA	20.53	1.9		65	92
▶	**SPELL/NOTE** On Attack: Chance for 15 Dmg AoE DOT							

SUPERIOR DAGGERS continued

M LEV	WEAPON NAME	LEV	BIND	DPS	SPEED	VENDOR PURCHASE VALUE		
29	Torturing Poker	34	BoA	17.65	1.7		76	78
30	Swinetusk Shank	35	BoA	23.00	1.5		88	66
31	Howling Blade	36	BoE	23.93	1.4		94	66
▶	**SPELL/NOTE** On Attack: Chance to Reduce Attack Power by 30							
31	Stonevault Shiv	36	BoE	24.00	1.5		97	89
32	Sliverblade	37	BoE	25.00	1.4	1	00	26
▶	**SPELL/NOTE** On Attack: Chance to Deal 45 Frost Dmg							
34	Hypnotic Blade	39	BoA	26.79	1.4	1	27	83
34	The Ziggler	39	BoE	26.47	1.7	1	24	72
▶	**SPELL/NOTE** On Attack: Chance to Deal 20-30 Nature Dmg							
39	Coldrage Dagger	44	BoA	29.67	1.5	1	71	93
▶	**SPELL/NOTE** On Attack: Chance for 20-30 Frost Dmg and 50% Snare							
42	Gutwrencher	47	BoE	31.56	1.6	2	27	38
▶	**SPELL/NOTE** On Attack: Chance for 80 Dmg Over 30 sec							
42	Widowmaker	47	BoE	31.58	1.9	2	24	79
44	Stealthblade	49	BoE	32.86	1.4	2	73	66
▶	**SPELL/NOTE** On Attack: Chance to Reduce Threat to All Enemies							
46	Searing Needle	51	BoE	33.89	1.8	2	88	83
▶	**SPELL/NOTE** On Attack: Chance for 69 Dmg and +10 Fire Exposure							
49	Hookfang Shanker	54	BoA	35.71	1.4	3	54	51
▶	**SPELL/NOTE** On Attack: Chance for 70 Dmg Over Time and 50 Armor Sunder							
50	Barman Shanker	55	BoA	36.50	2	3	94	11
▶	**SPELL/NOTE** Main Hand Only, On Hit: Chance for 100 Dmg Over 30 sec							
50	Julie's Dagger	55	BoE	36.54	1.3	3	61	57
▶	**SPELL/NOTE** On Attack: Chance to Heal User 78 Over 12 sec							
51	Dire Nail	56	BoA	36.67	1.5	4	04	27
▶	**SPELL/NOTE** Shadow Resist +5							
52	Blood-etched Blade	57	BoA	20.33	1.5	4	34	91
▶	**SPELL/NOTE** On Attack: Chance to Deal 120 Dmg/Convert to Mana							
55	Keris of Zul'Serak	60	BoA	39.44	1.8	5	11	99
▶	**SPELL/NOTE** On Attack: Chance for 50 Dmg/10% Attack Speed Debuff							
56	Fang of the Crystal Spider	61	BoA	40.31	1.6	5	33	88
▶	**SPELL/NOTE** On Attack: Chance to Slow Attack/SPELLs by 10%							
56	Frightalon	61	BoA	40.00	1.4	5	24	22
▶	**SPELL/NOTE** Adds 8 to Arcane SPELLs/Effects							
57	Finkle's Skinner	62	BoA	40.38	1.3	5	52	29
▶	**SPELL/NOTE** Add 10 to Skinning, Add 45 Attack Power Vs. Beasts							
57	Witchblade	62	BoA	40.63	1.6	5	23	06
▶	**SPELL/NOTE** Increase Arcane Dmg 8							
58	Bonescraper	63	BoA	41.43	1.4	5	82	10
▶	**SPELL/NOTE** Attack Power 30							
58	Gift of the Elven Magi	63	BoA	41.33	1.5	5	65	17
58	Heartseeker	63	BoE	41.47	1.7	5	82	15
▶	**SPELL/NOTE** Add 1% Crit							
58	Scarlet Kris	63	BoE	41.33	1.5	5	98	51

GOOD DAGGERS

M LEV	WEAPON NAME	LEV	BIND	DPS	SPEED	VENDOR PURCHASE VALUE		
5	Jeweled Dagger	10	BoE	5.31	1.6		2	51
6	Carving Knife	11	BoE	5.94	1.6		3	23
N/A	Jagged Dagger	11	BoA	6.00	1.5		3	25
6	Small Hand Blade	11	BoE	6.00	1.5		3	05
N/A	Compact Fighting Knife	12	BoA	6.33	1.5		3	88
N/A	Blade of Cunning	13	BoA	6.75	2		4	68
▶	**SPELL/NOTE** Add 1 to Subtlety							
N/A	Craftsman's Dagger	13	BoA	6.76	1.7		5	01
8	Stonesplinter Dagger	13	BoE	7.00	1.5		4	79
9	Curved Dagger	14	BoE	7.19	1.6		6	05
N/A	Curvewood Dagger	14	BoA	7.00	1.5		5	82
N/A	Elunite Dagger	15	BoA	7.65	1.7		7	01
10	Giant Tarantula Fang	15	BoE	7.50	1.4		7	03
N/A	Haggard's Dagger	15	BoA	7.65	1.7		6	77
N/A	Heirloom Dagger	15	BoA	7.65	1.7		6	85
10	Long Crawler Limb	15	BoE	7.50	1.6		7	29
10	Ritual Blade	15	BoE	7.50	1.4		7	30
N/A	Thun'grim's Dagger	15	BoA	7.65	1.7		6	98
N/A	Umbral Dagger	15	BoA	7.65	1.7		6	80
12	Slicer Blade	17	BoE	8.67	1.5		9	47
12	War Knife	17	BoE	8.53	1.7		9	79
13	Chanting Blade	18	BoA	9.00	1.5		10	55
13	Goblin Screwdriver	18	BoE	8.93	1.4		11	13
13	Hollowfang Blade	18	BoE	8.93	1.4		10	49
N/A	Kris of Orgrimmar	18	BoA	9.00	1.5		10	26
N/A	Scrimshaw Dagger	18	BoA	8.89	1.8		11	13
N/A	Serrated Knife	18	BoA	9.06	1.6		10	46
13	Spinner Fang	18	BoE	9.00	1.5		10	73
14	Brackclaw	19	BoE	9.64	1.4		12	81

GOOD DAGGERS continued

M LEV	WEAPON NAME	LEV	BIND	DPS	SPEED	VENDOR PURCHASE VALUE		
14	Venom Web Fang	19	BoE	9.67	1.5		12	48
▶	**SPELL/NOTE** On Attack: Chance to Poison for 15 Dmg over 15 sec							
14	Wicked Dagger	19	BoE	9.38	1.6		12	03
15	Big Bronze Knife	20	BoE	10.00	1.9		14	26
N/A	Harpy Skinner	20	BoA	9.64	1.4		14	36
15	Hook Dagger	20	BoE	10.00	1.5		13	94
N/A	Relic Blade	20	BoA	10.00	1.8		13	79
N/A	Thornblade	20	BoA	10.00	1.6		14	09
17	Spikelash Dagger	22	BoE	11.05	1.9		19	29
17	Tail Spike	22	BoA	11.11	1.8		19	42
18	Pearl-handled Dagger	23	BoE	11.47	1.7		21	07
20	Deadly Bronze Poniard	25	BoE	12.78	1.8		27	31
21	Battle Knife	26	BoE	13.44	1.6		30	12
21	Wyvern Tailspike	26	BoE	13.61	1.8		31	09
▶	**SPELL/NOTE** On Attack: Chance to Poison for 30 Dmg over 15 sec							
22	Naraxis' Fang	27	BoE	13.75	1.6		33	32
▶	**SPELL/NOTE** On Attack: Chance to Poison for 30 Dmg over 15 sec							
23	Cross Dagger	28	BoE	14.62	1.3		38	30
24	Flesh Piercer	29	BoE	15.25	2		39	86
▶	**SPELL/NOTE** On Attack: Chance to Deal 30 Dmg over 30 sec							
25	Honed Stiletto	30	BoE	15.71	1.4		44	26
27	Broad Bladed Knife	32	BoE	16.75	2		56	74
29	Daring Dirk	34	BoE	17.50	1.6		64	05
31	Deadly Kris	36	BoE	18.93	1.4		78	71
31	Glinting Steel Dagger	36	BoE	18.67	1.5		80	72
▶	**SPELL/NOTE** Attack Power 12							
33	Tigerbane	38	BoE	20.53	1.9		98	24
▶	**SPELL/NOTE** Adds 18 Attack Power Vs. Beasts							
34	Searing Golden Blade	39	BoE	21.43	1.4	1	03	95
▶	**SPELL/NOTE** Increase Fire Dmg 6							
35	Gemstone Dagger	40	BoE	22.33	1.5	1	07	70
▶	**SPELL/NOTE** Fire & Frost Resist +5							
N/A	Silent Hunter	41	BoA	23.06	1.8	1	14	61
37	Razor Blade	42	BoE	23.82	1.7	1	27	69
N/A	Tok'kar's Murloc Shanker	43	BoA	25.00	1.6	1	40	90
39	Sacrificial Kris	44	BoE	25.71	1.4	1	48	70
N/A	Ceremonial Elven Blade	45	BoA	26.67	1.8	1	57	75
N/A	Fiendish Skiv	45	BoA	26.58	1.9	1	67	92
42	Dreadblade	47	BoE	28.00	1.5	1	85	23
42	Gahz'rilla Fang	47	BoA	28.06	1.8	1	86	81
▶	**SPELL/NOTE** On Attack: Chance for a 10 Dmg Nature Shield							
45	Vorpal Dagger	50	BoE	29.69	1.6	2	32	84
46	Ebon Shiv	51	BoE	30.33	1.5	2	48	92
N/A	Hunt Tracker Blade	57	BoA	33.67	1.5	3	38	30
N/A	Beasthunter Dagger	60	BoA	35.59	1.7	4	32	92
▶	**SPELL/NOTE** Adds 33 Attack Power Vs. Beasts							
N/A	Enchanted Azsharite Felbane Dagger	60	BoA	35.67	1.5	4	20	44
▶	**SPELL/NOTE** Adds 33 Attack Power Vs. Demons							
N/A	Skilled Fighting Blade	60	BoA	35.71	1.4	4	03	65
▶	**SPELL/NOTE** Adds 4 to Dagger Skill							
57	Demon Blade	62	BoE	36.94	1.8	4	57	04
59	Bloodstrike Dagger	64	BoE	38.24	1.7	5	05	76

STANDARD DAGGERS

M LEV	WEAPON NAME	LEV	BIND	DPS	SPEED	VENDOR PURCHASE VALUE		
1	Worn Dagger	2	None	0.94	1.6			7
1	Deadman Dagger	3	None	1.07	1.4			10
1	Dirk	3	None	1.25	1.6			11
1	Trogg Dagger	3	None	1.00	1.5			10
N/A	Anvilmar Knife	4	BoA	1.25	1.6			16
N/A	Forsaken Dagger	4	BoA	1.25	1.6			17
N/A	Militia Dagger	4	BoA	1.33	1.5			16
N/A	Primitive Hand Blade	4	BoA	1.47	1.7			17
N/A	Thistlewood Dagger	4	BoA	1.47	1.7			16
N/A	Whittling Knife	4	BoA	1.33	1.5			16
1	Simple Dagger	6	None	2.50	1.8			38
N/A	Camping Knife	8	BoA	3.21	1.4			81
3	Stiletto	8	None	3.33	1.5			80
4	Bloodstained Knife	9	None	3.75	1.6		1	09
N/A	Long Bayonet	10	BoA	4.41	1.7		1	42
N/A	Pruning Knife	10	BoA	4.06	1.6		1	50
5	Small Green Dagger	10	None	4.33	1.5		1	46
6	Copper Dagger	11	None	5.00	1.5		1	94
N/A	Sharp Kitchen Knife	11	BoA	5.00	1.5		1	83
N/A	Ceremonial Knife	12	BoA	5.36	1.4		2	26
11	Jambiya	16	None	7.14	1.4		4	78
14	Poignard	19	None	8.46	1.3		7	30

STANDARD DAGGERS continued

M LEV	WEAPON NAME	LEV	BIND	DPS	SPEED	VENDOR PURCHASE VALUE		
16	Buzzer Blade	21	None	9.67	1.5		9	43
16	Razormane Backstabber	21	BoA	9.41	1.7		2	47
19	Kris	24	None	10.94	1.6		14	23
27	Shadow Hunter Knife	32	Quest	15.59	1.7			0
27	Thornspike	32	None	15.59	1.7		31	24
29	Main Gauche	34	None	16.56	1.6		38	67
39	Rondel	44	None	24.06	1.6		90	86

INFERIOR DAGGERS

M LEV	WEAPON NAME	LEV	BIND	DPS	SPEED	VENDOR PURCHASE VALUE		
2	Sharpened Letter Opener	7	None	2.06	1.7			38
9	Fisherman Knife	14	None	4.29	1.4		2	40
11	Threshadon Fang	16	None	5.00	1.5		3	17
13	Small Dagger	18	None	5.36	1.4		4	40
18	Hunting Knife	23	None	7.06	1.7		8	11
24	Deft Stiletto	29	None	8.93	1.4		15	64
34	Shiny Dirk	39	None	12.81	1.6		39	57
39	Fine Pointed Dagger	44	None	15.36	1.4		62	15
48	Spiked Dagger	53	None	19.06	1.6	1	07	18

FISHING POLES

FISHING POLES

M LEV	WEAPON NAME	LEV	BIND	DPS	SPEED	VENDOR PURCHASE VALUE		
N/A	Fishing Pole	1	None	1.00	3			4
N/A	Blump Family Fishing Pole	10	BoA	5.67	3		1	87
▶	**SPELL/NOTE** Fishing Skill +3							
5	Strong Fishing Pole	10	None	5.67	3		1	80
▶	**SPELL/NOTE** Fishing Skill +5							
15	Darkwood Fishing Pole	20	None	11.83	3		10	66
▶	**SPELL/NOTE** Fishing Skill +15							
25	Big Iron Fishing Pole	30	None	19.00	3		33	78
▶	**SPELL/NOTE** Fishing Skill +20							

FIST WEAPONS

SUPERIOR FIST WEAPONS

M LEV	WEAPON NAME	LEV	BIND	DPS	SPEED	VENDOR PURCHASE VALUE		
21	Iron Knuckles	26	BoA	16.47	1.7		36	63
▶	**SPELL/NOTE** On Attack: Chance to Deal 4 Dmg and Interrupt							
46	Vilerend Slicer	51	BoE	33.93	1.4	3	06	56
▶	**SPELL/NOTE** Main Hand Only, On Attack: Chance to Deal 75 Dmg							
51	Bloodfist	56	BoA	36.67	1.5	3	92	42
▶	**SPELL/NOTE** On Attack: Chance to Deal 20 Dmg							
55	Blood Talon	60	BoA	39.23	1.3	4	88	21
▶	**SPELL/NOTE** Main Hand Only, On Attack: Deals Dmg Over Time							
55	Hurd Smasher	60	BoA	39.44	1.8	5	08	51
▶	**SPELL/NOTE** On Attack: Chance for 2 sec Stun							
56	Gargoyle Shredder Talons	61	BoA	40.00	1.8	5	10	59
▶	**SPELL/NOTE** Off-Hand Only, On Attack: Chance to Deal 110 Dmg Over 30 sec							

GOOD FIST WEAPONS

M LEV	WEAPON NAME	LEV	BIND	DPS	SPEED	VENDOR PURCHASE VALUE		
N/A	White Bone Shredder	52	BoA	31.07	1.4	2	71	91
▶	**SPELL/NOTE** Off-Hand Only							
51	Rockfist	56	BoA	33.21	1.4	3	25	78

STANDARD FIST WEAPONS

M LEV	WEAPON NAME	LEV	BIND	DPS	SPEED	VENDOR PURCHASE VALUE		
10	Left-Handed Brass Knuckles	15	None	6.79	1.4		4	27
▶	**SPELL/NOTE** Off-Hand Only							
10	Right-Handed Brass Knuckles	15	None	6.79	1.4		4	26
▶	**SPELL/NOTE** Main Hand Only							
20	Left-Handed Claw	25	None	11.67	1.5		16	47
▶	**SPELL/NOTE** Off-Hand Only							
20	Right-Handed Claw	25	None	11.67	1.5		16	23
▶	**SPELL/NOTE** Main Hand Only							
29	Bloody Brass Knuckles	34	None	16.56	1.6		39	58
30	Left-Handed Blades	35	None	17.33	1.5		44	21
▶	**SPELL/NOTE** Off-Hand Only							
30	Right-Handed Blades	35	None	17.33	1.5		43	41
▶	**SPELL/NOTE** Main Hand Only							

GUNS

EPIC GUNS

M LEV	WEAPON NAME	LEV	BIND	DPS	SPEED	VENDOR PURCHASE VALUE		
43	Precisely Calibrated Boomstick	48	BoE	27.67	1.5	2	45	39
53	Dwarven Hand Cannon	58	BoE	32.76	2.9	4	50	40

SUPERIOR GUNS

M LEV	WEAPON NAME	LEV	BIND	DPS	SPEED	VENDOR PURCHASE VALUE		
16	Lil Timmy's Peashooter	21	BoE	10.96	2.6		14	56
22	Double-barreled Shotgun	27	BoE	13.26	2.3		30	20
24	Hi-tech Supergun	29	BoE	14.35	2.3		36	32
28	Chesterfall Musket	33	BoE	16.52	2.3		55	14
29	Ironweaver	34	BoE	17.31	2.6		58	74
30	Glass Shooter	35	BoA	17.93	2.9		66	52

SUPERIOR GUNS continued

M LEV	WEAPON NAME	LEV	BIND	DPS	SPEED	VENDOR PURCHASE VALUE		
37	The Silencer	42	BoE	22.32	2.8	1	15	32
▶	**SPELL/NOTE** Attack Power 14							
38	Shadowforge Bushmaster	43	BoE	22.76	2.9	1	30	52
▶	**SPELL/NOTE** Shadow Resist +7							
42	Galgann's Fireblaster	47	BoA	24.62	2.6	1	66	81
45	Guttbuster	50	BoE	26.11	2.7	2	10	29
48	Houndmaster's Rifle	53	BoA	27.39	2.3	2	45	27
▶	**SPELL/NOTE** Beast Slaying 24							
50	Dark Iron Rifle	55	BoE	28.38	3.4	2	91	52
51	Burstshot Harquebus	56	BoA	28.85	2.6	2	96	69
▶	**SPELL/NOTE** Attack Power 10							
53	Shell Launcher Shotgun	58	BoE	29.78	2.3	3	47	04
56	Flawless Arcanite Rifle	61	BoE	31.17	3	3	73	62
56	Willey's Portable Howitzer	61	BoA	31.25	2.4	3	84	43

GOOD GUNS

M LEV	WEAPON NAME	LEV	BIND	DPS	SPEED	VENDOR PURCHASE VALUE		
5	Rough Boomstick	10	BoE	4.13	2.3		1	87
N/A	Skorn's Rifle	12	BoA	5.00	1.9		2	97
8	Compact Shotgun	13	BoE	5.25	2		3	56
N/A	Daryl's Hunting Rifle	16	BoA	6.40	2.5		5	95
N/A	Dwarven Fishing Pole	19	BoA	7.37	1.9		9	22
14	Hunter's Muzzle Loader	19	BoE	7.50	1.8		9	40
N/A	Owlsight Rifle	20	BoA	7.88	2.6		10	63
N/A	Privateer Musket	20	BoA	7.83	2.3		10	38
16	Deadly Blunderbuss	21	BoE	8.27	2.6		11	79
19	Lovingly Crafted Boomstick	24	BoE	9.72	1.8		18	00
21	Silver-plated Shotgun	26	BoE	10.37	2.7		23	57
24	Moonsight Rifle	29	BoE	11.76	1.7		31	83
26	Mage-Eye" Blunderbuss"	31	BoE	12.50	2.8		37	69
28	BKP Sparrow" Smallbore"	33	BoE	13.24	1.7		45	77
N/A	Blasting Hackbut	37	BoA	15.36	2.8		63	86
32	Explosive Shotgun	37	BoE	15.24	2.1		64	14
N/A	Flash Rifle	37	BoA	15.28	1.8		63	86
N/A	Sidegunner Shottie	38	BoA	15.94	3.2		69	09
34	Smoothbore Gun	39	BoE	16.60	2.5		77	45
N/A	Shrapnel Blaster	40	BoA	17.37	1.9		80	73
36	Mithril Blunderbuss	41	BoE	17.93	2.9		89	58
39	Mithril Heavy-bore Rifle	44	BoE	20.15	3.4	1	13	69
39	Sniper Rifle	44	BoE	20.17	3	1	10	26
N/A	Master Hunter's Rifle	45	BoA	20.58	2.6	1	20	42
43	Ricochet Blunderbuss	48	BoE	22.39	2.3	1	50	60
45	Percussion Shotgun	50	BoE	23.26	2.3	1	77	91
47	Thorium Rifle	52	BoE	24.12	3.4	1	97	39
51	Burnside Rifle	56	BoE	26.00	2.5	2	55	65
N/A	Farmer Dalson's Shotgun	56	BoA	25.79	1.9	2	47	24
55	Sharpshooter Harquebus	60	BoE	27.95	2.2	3	17	84

STANDARD GUNS

M LEV	WEAPON NAME	LEV	BIND	DPS	SPEED	VENDOR PURCHASE VALUE		
1	Old Blunderbuss	2	None	1.52	2.3			5
1	Solid Blunderbuss	3	None	2.05	2.2			8
N/A	Anvilmar Musket	4	BoA	1.85	2.7			12
N/A	Light Hunting Rifle	4	BoA	1.84	1.9			12
2	Pellet Rifle	7	None	2.50	2.6			40
4	Hunting Rifle	9	None	2.96	2.7			79
4	Ornate Blunderbuss	9	None	2.95	2.2			82
9	Hunter's Boomstick	14	None	5.00	2.1		2	64
16	Large Bore Blunderbuss	21	None	7.40	2.5		7	54
21	BKP 2700 Enforcer""	26	None	9.63	2.7		14	19
31	BKP 42 Ultra""	36	None	13.81	2.1		36	95

INFERIOR GUNS

M LEV	WEAPON NAME	LEV	BIND	DPS	SPEED	VENDOR PURCHASE VALUE		
2	Rust-covered Blunderbuss	7	None	1.88	2.4			28
8	Cheap Blunderbuss	13	None	3.18	2.2		1	47
13	Dirty Blunderbuss	18	None	4.09	2.2		3	35
17	Shoddy Blunderbuss	22	None	5.00	2.1		5	90
24	Oiled Blunderbuss	29	None	7.00	2		11	73
28	Long-barreled Musket	33	None	7.88	2.6		18	77
38	Sentinel Musket	43	None	11.61	2.8		43	62
52	Primed Musket	57	None	15.83	1.8	1	01	49

ONE-HANDED MACES

EPIC MACES (1H)

M LEV	WEAPON NAME	LEV	BIND	DPS	SPEED	VENDOR PURCHASE VALUE		
38	Ardent Custodian	43	BoE	32.86	2.1	2	15	32
▸	**SPELL/NOTE** Main Hand Only, Adds 100 to Armor and 7 to Defense							
40	Hammer of Expertise	50	BoA	36.90	2.1			0
▸	**SPELL/NOTE** Main Hand Only							
49	Hammer of the Northern Wind	54	BoE	39.52	2.1	4	52	67
▸	**SPELL/NOTE** Main Hand Only, On Attack: Chance to Deal 20-30 Dmg and Slow by 50%							
55	Ironfoe	60	BoA	43.54	2.4	6	30	86
▸	**SPELL/NOTE** Main Hand Only, On Attack: Chance to Gain Increased Crit and Attack Speed							
57	Hand of Edward the Odd	62	BoE	45.00	1.6	7	05	54
▸	**SPELL/NOTE** Fiery Weapon, On Attack: Chance to Gain Instant Cast on Next spell							

SUPERIOR MACES (1H)

M LEV	WEAPON NAME	LEV	BIND	DPS	SPEED	VENDOR PURCHASE VALUE		
16	Face Smasher	21	BoE	14.04	2.6		20	25
19	Skeletal Club	24	BoE	15.58	2.6		29	96
▸	**SPELL/NOTE** Main Hand Only, On Attack: Chance to Deal 30 Shadow Dmg							
19	Stinging Viper	24	BoA	15.54	2.8		30	18
▸	**SPELL/NOTE** On Attack: Chance to Deal 35 Poison Dmg Over 15 sec							
20	Diamond Hammer	25	BoE	16.20	2.5		32	76
22	Crested Scepter	27	BoE	17.12	2.6		40	28
▸	**SPELL/NOTE** Main Hand Only							
23	Oscillating Power Hammer	28	BoE	17.50	2		44	19
24	Beazel's Basher	29	BoE	18.40	2.5		48	63
▸	**SPELL/NOTE** Main Hand Only							
26	Looming Gavel	31	BoE	19.79	2.4		59	71
▸	**SPELL/NOTE** Main Hand Only							
28	Death Speaker Scepter	33	BoA	17.14	2.8		73	24
▸	**SPELL/NOTE** Increase Healing 10, Main Hand Only							
28	Dreamslayer	33	BoE	21.43	2.1		69	02
▸	**SPELL/NOTE** Main Hand Only							
30	Ironspine's Fist	35	BoA	22.92	2.4		88	36
30	Royal Diplomatic Scepter	35	BoA	23.04	2.3		89	02
31	Excavator's Brand	36	BoE	24.04	2.6		98	59
▸	**SPELL/NOTE** On Attack: Chance to Deal 40 Fire Dmg + 9 Over Time							
32	Deadwood Sledge	37	BoE	25.00	1.9	1	04	64
▸	**SPELL/NOTE** Main Hand Only							

SUPERIOR MACES (1H) continued

M LEV	WEAPON NAME	LEV	BIND	DPS	SPEED	VENDOR PURCHASE VALUE		
32	Ebony Boneclub	37	BoE	25.00	1.8	1	09	27
▸	**SPELL/NOTE** Shadow Resist +5							
33	Midnight Mace	38	BoE	25.80	2.5	1	16	20
▸	**SPELL/NOTE** Shadow Resist +10							
34	Fight Club	39	BoE	26.59	2.2	1	19	70
37	Stonevault Bonebreaker	42	BoE	28.70	2.7	1	48	53
39	Hand of Righteousness	44	BoA	29.81	2.7	1	79	22
▸	**SPELL/NOTE** Increase Healing 14, Main Hand Only							
40	Heaven's Light	45	BoE	30.37	2.7	1	94	41
▸	**SPELL/NOTE** Main Hand Only							
40	Wirt's Third Leg	45	BoE	30.43	2.3	1	95	77
41	Mug O' Hurt	46	BoE	31.18	1.7	2	07	36
▸	**SPELL/NOTE** On Attack: Chance to Slow Opponent Movement by 50%							
42	The Shatterer	47	BoE	31.67	2.4	2	31	59
▸	**SPELL/NOTE** Main Hand Only, On Attack: Chance to Disarm Opponent							
43	The Hand of Antu'sul	48	BoA	32.22	2.7	2	41	11
▸	**SPELL/NOTE** Main Hand Only, On Attack: Chance to Deal 7 Dmg/Slow 4 Enemies							
48	Bonesnapper	53	BoE	35.19	2.7	3	38	32
▸	**SPELL/NOTE** Main Hand Only							
49	Might of Hakkar	54	BoA	35.83	2.4	3	46	65
▸	**SPELL/NOTE** Main Hand Only							
49	Viking Warhammer	54	BoE	35.83	2.4	3	58	15
▸	**SPELL/NOTE** Main Hand Only							
52	Serenity	57	BoE	37.50	2	4	27	21
▸	**SPELL/NOTE** Main Hand Only, On Attack: Chance to Dispel Magical Effect on Foe							
53	Rubidium Hammer	58	BoA	38.25	2	4	54	37
▸	**SPELL/NOTE** Increased Armor 120, Main Hand Only							
54	The Cruel Hand of Timmy	59	BoA	38.89	1.8	4	66	57
▸	**SPELL/NOTE** On Attack: Chance to Lower All Attributes by 15 for 1 min							
54	The Hammer of Grace	59	BoA	38.89	2.7	4	85	81
▸	**SPELL/NOTE** Increase Healing 28, Main Hand Only							
55	Venomspitter	60	BoA	39.47	1.9	5	17	71
▸	**SPELL/NOTE** On Attack: Chance to Deal 105 Poison Over 30 sec							
56	Bludstone Hammer	61	BoE	40.24	2.1	5	26	05
▸	**SPELL/NOTE** Main Hand Only							
57	Bonechill Hammer	62	BoA	40.63	2.4	5	32	22
▸	**SPELL/NOTE** On Attack: Chance to Deal 112 Frost Dmg							
57	Mass of McGowan	62	BoE	40.79	3.8	5	48	40
▸	**SPELL/NOTE** Main Hand Only							
57	Masterwork Stormhammer	63	BoE	41.50	2	5	63	04
▸	**SPELL/NOTE** Main Hand Only, On Attack: Chance to Launch Chain Lightning							
58	Scepter of the Unholy	63	BoA	41.25	2.4	5	84	28
▸	**SPELL/NOTE** Increase Shadow Dmg 14, Shadow Resist +7, Main Hand Only							

GOOD MACES (1H)

M LEV	WEAPON NAME	LEV	BIND	DPS	SPEED	VENDOR PURCHASE VALUE	
6	Frostmane Scepter	11	BoE	5.91	2.2	3	06
▶	**SPELL/NOTE** Main Hand Only						
N/A	Stinging Mace	11	BoA	5.87	2.3	3	26
▶	**SPELL/NOTE** Main Hand Only						
7	Cranial Thumper	12	BoE	6.43	2.8	3	98
▶	**SPELL/NOTE** Main Hand Only						
7	Priest's Mace	12	BoE	6.50	2	3	86
▶	**SPELL/NOTE** Main Hand Only						
N/A	Skorn's Hammer	12	BoA	6.48	2.7	3	83
▶	**SPELL/NOTE** Main Hand Only						
N/A	Compact Hammer	13	BoA	6.96	2.3	4	90
▶	**SPELL/NOTE** Main Hand Only						
N/A	Thornroot Club	13	BoA	6.90	2.1	5	12
▶	**SPELL/NOTE** Main Hand Only						
9	Staunch Hammer	14	BoE	7.27	2.2	6	12
▶	**SPELL/NOTE** Main Hand Only						
10	Driftwood Club	15	BoE	7.65	1.7	7	40
▶	**SPELL/NOTE** Main Hand Only						
N/A	Elunite Hammer	15	BoA	7.61	2.3	6	98
▶	**SPELL/NOTE** Main Hand Only						
N/A	Haggard's Hammer	15	BoA	7.61	2.3	6	85
▶	**SPELL/NOTE** Main Hand Only						
N/A	Heirloom Hammer	15	BoA	7.61	2.3	6	88
▶	**SPELL/NOTE** Main Hand Only						
10	Stonesplinter Mace	15	BoE	7.50	2	7	11
▶	**SPELL/NOTE** Main Hand Only						
N/A	Thun'grim's Mace	15	BoA	7.61	2.3	7	01
▶	**SPELL/NOTE** Main Hand Only						
N/A	Umbral Mace	15	BoA	7.61	2.3	6	83
▶	**SPELL/NOTE** Main Hand Only						
10	Weighted Sap	15	BoE	7.73	2.2	6	87
▶	**SPELL/NOTE** Main Hand Only						
N/A	Bonegrinding Pestle	16	BoA	8.13	2.4	8	39
▶	**SPELL/NOTE** Main Hand Only						
N/A	Engineer's Hammer	16	BoA	8.13	2.4	7	76
▶	**SPELL/NOTE** Main Hand Only						
N/A	Fist of the People's Militia	17	BoA	8.44	1.6	9	54
▶	**SPELL/NOTE** Main Hand Only						
12	Gnoll Punisher	17	BoE	8.54	2.4	9	30
▶	**SPELL/NOTE** Main Hand Only						
12	Petrified Shinbone	17	BoE	8.75	2	9	75
▶	**SPELL/NOTE** Main Hand Only						
12	Sergeant's Warhammer	17	BoE	8.57	2.1	9	33
12	Wicked Blackjack	17	BoE	8.70	2.3	9	71
▶	**SPELL/NOTE** Main Hand Only						
N/A	Hammer of Orgrimmar	18	BoA	9.14	2.9	11	27
▶	**SPELL/NOTE** Main Hand Only						
13	Mo'grosh Masher	18	BoE	9.20	2.5	11	17
▶	**SPELL/NOTE** Main Hand Only						
14	Barbed Club	19	BoE	9.57	2.3	12	19
▶	**SPELL/NOTE** Main Hand Only						
14	Gnoll Skull Basher	19	BoE	9.63	2.7	12	30
▶	**SPELL/NOTE** Main Hand Only						
N/A	Hardwood Cudgel	20	BoA	10.00	2.6	13	63
▶	**SPELL/NOTE** Main Hand Only						
16	Blackrock Mace	21	BoE	10.60	2.5	16	81
▶	**SPELL/NOTE** Main Hand Only						
16	Cookie's Tenderizer	21	BoA	10.54	2.8	15	97
17	Block Mallet	22	BoE	11.11	1.8	19	62
▶	**SPELL/NOTE** Main Hand Only						
17	Bruiser Club	22	BoE	11.14	2.2	17	88
▶	**SPELL/NOTE** Main Hand Only						
17	Shadowhide Mace	22	BoE	11.14	2.2	18	50
▶	**SPELL/NOTE** Main Hand Only						
17	Stout Battlehammer	22	BoE	10.87	2.3	19	69
▶	**SPELL/NOTE** Main Hand Only						
19	Jagged Star	24	BoE	12.32	2.8	23	76
▶	**SPELL/NOTE** Main Hand Only						
20	Baron's Scepter	25	BoA	12.71	2.4	26	11
▶	**SPELL/NOTE** Main Hand Only						
20	Battlesmasher	25	BoE	12.78	2.7	26	95
20	Heavy Bronze Mace	25	BoE	12.86	2.8	27	41
▶	**SPELL/NOTE** Main Hand Only						
20	Steelscale Crushfish	25	BoE	12.80	2.5	25	81
20	Wicked Spiked Mace	25	BoE	12.80	2.5	28	21
▶	**SPELL/NOTE** Main Hand Only						
23	Iridescent Hammer	28	BoE	14.44	1.8	36	93

GOOD MACES (1H) continued

M LEV	WEAPON NAME	LEV	BIND	DPS	SPEED	VENDOR PURCHASE VALUE		
25	Mighty Iron Hammer	30	BoE	15.54	2.8		45	52
▶	**SPELL/NOTE** Main Hand Only							
26	Leaden Mace	31	BoE	16.03	2.9		50	96
28	Sequoia Hammer	33	BoE	17.04	2.7		59	58
▶	**SPELL/NOTE** Main Hand Only							
30	Kovork's Rattle	35	BoE	18.33	3		72	27
N/A	Ryedol's Hammer	36	BoA	19.00	2.5		79	76
▶	**SPELL/NOTE** Main Hand Only							
N/A	Bookmaker's Scepter	37	BoA	19.57	2.3		83	84
▶	**SPELL/NOTE** Main Hand Only							
32	Giant Club	37	BoE	19.74	1.9		87	55
▶	**SPELL/NOTE** Main Hand Only							
34	Murphstar	39	BoE	21.43	2.1		98	92
N/A	Black Water Hammer	40	BoA	22.22	2.7	1	12	56
▶	**SPELL/NOTE** Main Hand Only							
N/A	Windstorm Hammer	40	BoA	22.14	2.1	1	12	62
▶	**SPELL/NOTE** Main Hand Only							
38	Goblin Nutcracker	43	BoE	25.00	2.2	1	38	77
41	Big Black Mace	46	BoE	27.50	2.4	1	72	91
▶	**SPELL/NOTE** Main Hand Only							
41	Galgann's Firehammer	46	BoA	27.50	2.2	1	80	76
▶	**SPELL/NOTE** On Attack: Chance to Deal 80-112 Dmg							
42	Skullcrusher Mace	47	BoE	28.15	2.7	1	89	40
44	Diamond-Tip Flail	49	BoE	29.17	2.4	2	19	25
44	Runed Mithril Hammer	49	BoE	29.25	2	2	16	60
▶	**SPELL/NOTE** Main Hand Only							
N/A	Spirit of the Faerie Dragon	51	BoA	30.38	2.6	2	59	14
▶	**SPELL/NOTE** Main Hand Only							
N/A	Gryphon Rider's Stormhammer	53	BoA	31.48	2.7	2	68	28
▶	**SPELL/NOTE** Main Hand Only, On Attack: Chance to Deal 91-125							
48	Smashing Star	53	BoE	31.61	2.8	2	83	08
49	Fist of the Damned	54	BoA	32.11	1.9	2	95	51
▶	**SPELL/NOTE** On Attack: Chance to Steal 30 HP							
N/A	Grave Scepter	54	BoA	32.19	1.6	2	88	96
▶	**SPELL/NOTE** Main Hand Only							
N/A	Beastsmasher	55	BoA	32.86	2.1	3	27	23
▶	**SPELL/NOTE** Main Hand Only, Adds 30 Attack Power Vs. Beasts							
N/A	Belgrom's Hammer	55	BoA	32.86	2.8	3	01	44
▶	**SPELL/NOTE** Main Hand Only							
50	Blesswind Hammer	55	BoE	32.86	2.1	3	19	24
N/A	Swiftstrike Cudgel	55	BoA	32.50	1.6	3	01	56
▶	**SPELL/NOTE** Main Hand Only, Add 1% Hit							
53	Volcanic Hammer	58	BoE	34.60	2.5	3	92	55
▶	**SPELL/NOTE** Main Hand Only, On Attack: Chance to Deal 100-128 + 18 Over Time							
55	Bashguuder	60	BoA	35.74	2.7	4	32	87
▶	**SPELL/NOTE** Main Hand Only, On Attack: Chance to Sunder Armor by 50							

STANDARD MACES (1H)

M LEV	WEAPON NAME	LEV	BIND	DPS	SPEED	VENDOR PURCHASE VALUE
1	Worn Mace	2	None	1.05	1.9	7
▶	**SPELL/NOTE** Main Hand Only					
1	Club	3	None	1.05	1.9	10
▶	**SPELL/NOTE** Main Hand Only					
1	Deadman Club	3	None	1.11	1.8	11
▶	**SPELL/NOTE** Main Hand Only					
1	Putrid Wooden Hammer	3	None	1.00	2	10
▶	**SPELL/NOTE** Main Hand Only					
N/A	Anvilmar Hammer	4	BoA	1.67	2.1	17
▶	**SPELL/NOTE** Main Hand Only					
N/A	Forsaken Maul	4	BoA	1.58	1.9	17
▶	**SPELL/NOTE** Main Hand Only					
N/A	Militia Hammer	4	BoA	1.52	2.3	17
▶	**SPELL/NOTE** Main Hand Only					
N/A	Primitive Club	4	BoA	1.67	2.1	17
▶	**SPELL/NOTE** Main Hand Only					
N/A	Rock Mace	4	BoA	1.58	1.9	16
▶	**SPELL/NOTE** Main Hand Only					
1	Small Wooden Hammer	4	None	1.58	1.9	16
▶	**SPELL/NOTE** Main Hand Only					
N/A	Thistlewood Maul	4	BoA	1.58	1.9	17
▶	**SPELL/NOTE** Main Hand Only					
2	Cudgel	7	None	2.78	1.8	56
▶	**SPELL/NOTE** Main Hand Only					
2	Flanged Mace	7	None	3.00	2	57
▶	**SPELL/NOTE** Main Hand Only					
2	Kobold Mining Mallet	7	None	2.83	2.3	58
▶	**SPELL/NOTE** Main Hand Only					

STANDARD MACES continued

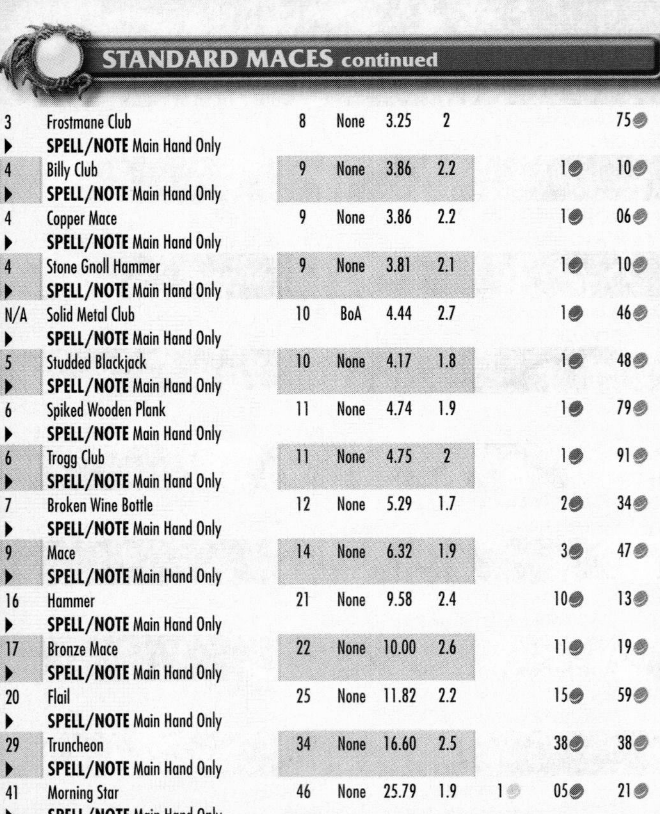

M LEV	WEAPON NAME	LEV	BIND	DPS	SPEED	VENDOR PURCHASE VALUE		
3	Frostmane Club	8	None	3.25	2			75
▶	**SPELL/NOTE** Main Hand Only							
4	Billy Club	9	None	3.86	2.2		1	10
▶	**SPELL/NOTE** Main Hand Only							
4	Copper Mace	9	None	3.86	2.2		1	06
▶	**SPELL/NOTE** Main Hand Only							
4	Stone Gnoll Hammer	9	None	3.81	2.1		1	10
▶	**SPELL/NOTE** Main Hand Only							
N/A	Solid Metal Club	10	BoA	4.44	2.7		1	46
▶	**SPELL/NOTE** Main Hand Only							
5	Studded Blackjack	10	None	4.17	1.8		1	48
▶	**SPELL/NOTE** Main Hand Only							
6	Spiked Wooden Plank	11	None	4.74	1.9		1	79
▶	**SPELL/NOTE** Main Hand Only							
6	Trogg Club	11	None	4.75	2		1	91
▶	**SPELL/NOTE** Main Hand Only							
7	Broken Wine Bottle	12	None	5.29	1.7		2	34
▶	**SPELL/NOTE** Main Hand Only							
9	Mace	14	None	6.32	1.9		3	47
▶	**SPELL/NOTE** Main Hand Only							
16	Hammer	21	None	9.58	2.4		10	13
▶	**SPELL/NOTE** Main Hand Only							
17	Bronze Mace	22	None	10.00	2.6		11	19
▶	**SPELL/NOTE** Main Hand Only							
20	Flail	25	None	11.82	2.2		15	59
▶	**SPELL/NOTE** Main Hand Only							
29	Truncheon	34	None	16.60	2.5		38	38
▶	**SPELL/NOTE** Main Hand Only							
41	Morning Star	46	None	25.79	1.9	1	05	21
▶	**SPELL/NOTE** Main Hand Only							

INFERIOR MACES (1H)

M LEV	WEAPON NAME	LEV	BIND	DPS	SPEED	VENDOR PURCHASE VALUE		
4	Carpenter's Mallet	9	None	2.94	1.7			72
▶	**SPELL/NOTE** Main Hand Only							
7	Heavy Hammer	12	None	3.75	2.4		1	50
▶	**SPELL/NOTE** Main Hand Only							
12	Ornamental Mace	17	None	5.18	2.8		3	66
▶	**SPELL/NOTE** Main Hand Only							
17	Bludgeoning Cudgel	22	None	6.67	1.8		7	79
▶	**SPELL/NOTE** Main Hand Only							
23	Bulky Bludgeon	28	None	8.75	2.8		15	48
▶	**SPELL/NOTE** Main Hand Only							
23	Large Bear Bone	28	None	8.75	2.4		14	84
▶	**SPELL/NOTE** Main Hand Only							
29	Noboru's Cudgel	34	BoA	10.48	2.1			0
▶	**SPELL/NOTE** Main Hand Only							
35	Stone Club	40	None	13.18	2.2		42	89
▶	**SPELL/NOTE** Main Hand Only							
41	Blunting Mace	46	None	16.43	2.1		71	98
▶	**SPELL/NOTE** Main Hand Only							
49	Clout Mace	54	None	19.35	2.3	1	13	62
▶	**SPELL/NOTE** Main Hand Only							

2H TWO-HANDED MACES

EPIC MACES (2H)

M LEV	WEAPON NAME	LEV	BIND	DPS	SPEED	VENDOR PURCHASE VALUE		
47	Taran Icebreaker	52	BoE	49.57	2.3	5	52	89
▶	**SPELL/NOTE** On Attack: Chance to Deal 180-220 Dmg/36 Over Time							

SUPERIOR MACES (2H)

M LEV	WEAPON NAME	LEV	BIND	DPS	SPEED	VENDOR PURCHASE VALUE		
16	Black Malice	21	BoE	18.33	3.3		24	95
▶	**SPELL/NOTE** On Attack: Chance to Deal 55-85 Shadow Dmg							
16	Rakzur Club	21	BoE	18.27	2.6		23	62
18	Smite's Mighty Hammer	23	BoE	19.71	3.5		31	03
23	Dense Triangle Mace	28	BoE	22.92	2.4		54	36
24	Slaghammer	29	BoE	23.75	2.8		63	40
N/A	Verigan's Fist	31	BoA	25.63	3.2		74	59
29	Cobalt Crusher	34	BoE	28.91	3.2	1	01	46
▶	**SPELL/NOTE** On Attack: Chance to Deal 110-120 Frost Dmg							
29	Manual Crowd Pummeler	34	BoA	29.00	2		95	64
▶	**SPELL/NOTE** On Attack: Chance to Add 50% Attack Speed for 30 sec							
30	Viscous Hammer	35	BoE	30.17	2.9	1	08	09
▶	**SPELL/NOTE** Attack Power 34							
32	The Pacifier	37	BoE	32.50	4	1	28	23
32	The Shoveler	37	BoE	32.50	3.4	1	28	31
▶	**SPELL/NOTE** Attack Power 20							
N/A	Whirlwind Warhammer	40	BoA	35.74	3.4	1	72	64
37	Thornstone Sledgehammer	42	BoE	37.19	3.2	1	94	07
▶	**SPELL/NOTE** Nature Resist +10							
39	Mograine's Might	44	BoA	38.93	2.8	2	25	67
40	The Jackhammer	45	BoE	39.60	2.5	2	54	63
▶	**SPELL/NOTE** On Attack: Chance to Add 30% Attack Speed							
44	The Rockpounder	49	BoA	42.70	3.7	3	22	48
▶	**SPELL/NOTE** Add 2% Crit							
45	Blanchard's Stout	50	BoE	43.39	3.1	3	50	42
▶	**SPELL/NOTE** Fire Resist +5							
45	Ragehammer	50	BoE	43.38	3.7	3	67	32
▶	**SPELL/NOTE** On Attack: Chance to Add 20 Dmg and 5% Attack Speed							
47	The Judge's Gavel	52	BoE	45.00	2.9	3	78	33
▶	**SPELL/NOTE** On Attack: Chance to Imprison Target (No Actions/No Dmg) for 10 sec							
50	Dark Iron Pulverizer	55	BoE	47.43	3.7	4	57	60
▶	**SPELL/NOTE** On Attack: Chance to Stun Foe for 8 sec							

SUPERIOR MACES (2H) continued

M LEV	WEAPON NAME	LEV	BIND	DPS	SPEED	VENDOR PURCHASE VALUE		
51	Enchanted Battlehammer	56	BoE	48.08	2.6	4	81	24
▶	**SPELL/NOTE** Add 1% Parry							
52	Impervious Giant	57	BoA	48.89	2.7	5	41	67
▶	**SPELL/NOTE** AC +30, Add 1% Hit							
53	Twig of the World Tree	58	BoE	49.73	3.7	5	65	88
55	Fist of Omokk	60	BoA	51.36	3.3	5	94	10
56	Malown's Slam	61	BoA	52.11	3.8	6	23	80
▶	**SPELL/NOTE** On Attack: Chance to Add 50 to User Strength and Daze Foe (2 sec)							
57	Frightskull Shaft	62	BoA	53.09	3.4	6	93	32
▶	**SPELL/NOTE** On Attack: Chance to Deal 120 Dmg Over Time and Reduce Strength							
58	Hammer of the Titans	63	BoE	53.82	3.8	7	09	12
▶	**SPELL/NOTE** On Attack: Chance to Stun Target for 3 sec							
58	Seeping Willow	63	BoA	53.94	3.3	7	08	84
▶	**SPELL/NOTE** On Attack: Chance to Deal 200 Dmg Over Time and Reduce All Stats							
N/A	Shimmering Platinum Warhammer	63	BoA	53.87	3.1	7	35	97

STANDARD MACES (2H)

M LEV	WEAPON NAME	LEV	BIND	DPS	SPEED	VENDOR PURCHASE VALUE		
1	Battleworn Hammer	2	None	1.38	2.9			9
1	Large Club	3	None	1.56	3.2			14
N/A	Anvilmar Sledge	4	BoA	2.10	3.1			20
N/A	Militia Warhammer	4	BoA	1.90	2.9			21
3	Kobold Mining Shovel	6	None	2.96	2.7			47
2	Farmer's Shovel	7	None	3.78	3.7			68
3	Beatstick	8	None	4.42	2.6			99
4	Wooden Mallet	9	None	5.00	2.6		1	40
N/A	Thicket Hammer	11	BoA	6.45	3.1		2	35
10	Giant Club	15	None	9.00	3.5		5	33
11	Heavy Copper Maul	16	None	9.46	2.8		5	95
15	Rhahk'Zor's Hammer	20	None	11.88	3.2		10	81
16	Rock Hammer	21	None	12.57	3.7		12	57
20	Bronze Warhammer	25	None	15.16	3.1		19	44
21	Maul	26	None	16.03	2.9		21	94
30	War Hammer	35	None	22.29	3.5		52	97
40	War Maul	45	None	32.42	3.3	1	22	21

GOOD MACES (2H)

M LEV	WEAPON NAME	LEV	BIND	DPS	SPEED	VENDOR PURCHASE VALUE (gold)	(silver)	(copper)
N/A	Coldridge Hammer	12	BoA	8.33	2.7		4	66
N/A	Goblin Smasher	12	BoA	8.23	3.1		5	03
7	Icepane Warhammer	12	BoE	8.48	3.3		5	06
N/A	Bonecracker	13	BoA	9.06	3.2		6	40
8	Spiked Club	13	BoE	9.03	3.1		6	10
N/A	Stonewood Hammer	14	BoA	9.53	3.2		7	05
10	Birchwood Maul	15	BoE	10.00	3.3		9	22
10	Burrowing Shovel	15	BoE	10.00	2.3		9	22
13	Ironwood Maul	18	BoE	11.79	2.8		14	08
14	Heavy Spiked Mace	19	BoE	12.50	3.4		14	70
16	Heavy Gnoll War Club	21	BoE	13.65	3.7		20	64
16	Oak Mallet	21	BoE	13.71	3.5		20	72
16	Trogg Beater	21	BoE	13.75	3.6		21	18
18	Battering Hammer	23	BoE	15.16	3.1		27	41
18	Shadowhide Maul	23	BoE	15.17	3		26	23
20	Hefty Battlehammer	25	BoE	16.88	3.2		33	06
20	Ironwood Treebranch	25	BoE	16.76	3.4		33	24
N/A	Demolition Hammer	26	BoA	17.61	2.3		40	16
N/A	Headbasher	26	BoA	17.61	2.3		36	71
22	Kazon's Maul	27	BoE	18.24	3.4		41	97
N/A	Orc Crusher	27	BoA	18.19	3.6		44	18
N/A	Brute Hammer	28	BoA	19.09	3.3		44	26
N/A	Glacial Stone	30	BoA	20.28	3.6		53	37
▸	**SPELL/NOTE** On Attack: Chance to Deal 65 Frost Dmg							
N/A	Mechanic's Pipehammer	30	BoA	20.36	2.8		56	32
26	Solid Iron Maul	31	BoE	21.14	3.5		62	58
29	Goblin Power Shovel	34	BoE	22.88	3.3		83	57
29	Golden Iron Destroyer	34	BoE	22.91	2.75		83	60
31	Ballast Maul	36	BoE	24.71	3.4	1	00	77
31	Huge Stone Club	36	BoE	24.72	3.6	1	02	61
31	Korg Bat	36	BoE	24.68	3.1		96	35
33	Rock Hammer	38	BoE	26.67	3	1	15	56
35	Sequoia Branch	40	BoE	28.95	3.8	1	35	30

GOOD MACES (2H) continued

M LEV	WEAPON NAME	LEV	BIND	DPS	SPEED	VENDOR PURCHASE VALUE (gold)	(silver)	(copper)
N/A	Servomechanic Sledgehammer	41	BoA	30.23	2.2	1	50	28
▸	**SPELL/NOTE** Adds 7 to 2H Mace Skill							
N/A	Silver Spade	41	BoA	30.14	3.7	1	45	87
N/A	Cragwood Maul	42	BoA	31.25	2.8	1	64	84
N/A	Rock Pulverizer	42	BoA	31.22	3.7	1	68	37
▸	**SPELL/NOTE** Attack Power 34							
N/A	Tok'kar's Murloc Basher	43	BoA	32.32	2.8	1	74	85
41	Greater Maul	46	BoE	35.74	3.4	2	15	52
43	Conk Hammer	48	BoE	37.29	3.5	2	53	78
45	Royal Mallet	50	BoE	38.70	2.7	2	88	89
49	Inlaid Thorium Hammer	54	BoE	41.83	3	3	88	71
51	Backbreaker	56	BoE	43.39	3.1	4	15	17
53	Force of Magma	58	BoA	45.00	3.2	4	69	83
▸	**SPELL/NOTE** On Attack: Chance to Deal 150 Fire Dmg							
53	Painbringer	58	BoE	44.82	2.8	4	68	23
56	Fierce Mauler	61	BoE	47.42	3.3	5	44	05
58	Brutehammer	63	BoE	48.97	3.4	6	02	03

INFERIOR MACES (2H)

M LEV	WEAPON NAME	LEV	BIND	DPS	SPEED	VENDOR PURCHASE VALUE (gold)	(silver)	(copper)
4	Cracked Sledge	9	None	3.79	3.3			97
9	Rusty Warhammer	14	None	5.67	3		2	94
14	Battered Mallet	19	None	7.41	2.9		6	03
17	Wooden Maul	22	None	8.62	2.9		9	63
22	Rock Maul	27	None	10.86	2.9		17	65
30	Large War Club	35	None	14.19	3.1		34	51
45	Crushing Maul	50	None	23.18	3.3	1	20	59
52	Bulky Maul	57	None	26.53	3.6	1	69	15

POLEARMS

SUPERIOR POLEARMS

M LEV	WEAPON NAME	LEV	BIND	DPS	SPEED	VENDOR PURCHASE VALUE (gold)	(silver)	(copper)
20	Gargoyle's Bite	22	BoE	18.97	2.9		28	54
▸	**SPELL/NOTE** AC +60							
23	Bloodpike	28	BoE	23.13	3.2		53	82
▸	**SPELL/NOTE** On Attack: Chance for 110 Dmg Over 30 sec							
31	Poison-tipped Bone Spear	36	BoE	31.30	2.3	1	21	83
▸	**SPELL/NOTE** On Attack: Chance for 150 Dmg Over 30 sec							
34	Ruthless Shiv	39	BoE	34.81	2.7	1	50	74
35	Grim Reaper	40	BoE	35.65	3.1	1	58	05
▸	**SPELL/NOTE** On Attack: Chance to Deal 130 Dmg							
39	Khoo's Point	44	BoE	38.80	2.5	2	18	33
42	Grimlok's Charge	47	BoA	40.93	2.7	2	82	18
43	Bonechewer	48	BoE	41.96	2.8	2	93	67
43	Eyegouger	48	BoE	41.83	3	3	17	25
44	Diabolic Skiver	49	BoA	42.76	2.9	3	33	46
▸	**SPELL/NOTE** On Attack: Chance for 160-180 Shadow Dmg							
45	Blight	50	BoE	43.33	2.7	3	38	57
▸	**SPELL/NOTE** On Attack: Chance for 50 Dmg and 180 Over Time							
46	Headspike	51	BoA	44.17	3	3	92	88
47	Stoneraven	52	BoE	44.85	3.3	3	87	19
49	Smoldering Claw	54	BoA	46.55	2.9	4	59	80
▸	**SPELL/NOTE** Fire Resist +10, On Attack: Chance for 135 Fire Dmg							
51	Frenzied Striker	56	BoA	48.21	2.8	4	83	30
▸	**SPELL/NOTE** Add 1% Parry							
53	Flame Wrath	58	BoA	49.70	3.3	5	76	26
▸	**SPELL/NOTE** On Attack: Chance for Fire Shield and 130-170 AoE							
55	Darkspear	60	BoE	51.25	3.2	6	26	25
55	The Needler	60	BoE	51.36	2.2	6	07	84
▸	**SPELL/NOTE** On Attack: Chance to Deal 75 Dmg							
56	Chillpike	61	BoA	52.32	2.8	6	26	29
▸	**SPELL/NOTE** On Attack: Chance to Deal 80-90 Frost Dmg							
58	Blackhand Doomsaw	63	BoA	54.00	3.5	7	43	46
▸	**SPELL/NOTE** On Attack: Chance to Deal 324-540 Dmg							

GOOD POLEARMS

M LEV	WEAPON NAME	LEV	BIND	DPS	SPEED	VENDOR PURCHASE VALUE (gold)	(silver)	(copper)
20	Pearl-encrusted Spear	21	BoE	13.75	3.2		20	79
20	Impaling Harpoon	22	BoA	14.38	2.4		23	23
24	Armor Piercer	29	BoA	19.81	2.6		48	52
31	Headhunting Spear	36	BoE	24.69	3.2	1	02	24
N/A	White Bone Spear	52	BoA	40.37	2.7	3	41	08

STANDARD POLEARMS

M LEV	WEAPON NAME	LEV	BIND	DPS	SPEED	VENDOR PURCHASE VALUE (gold)	(silver)	(copper)
20	Short Spear	25	None	15.15	3.3		20	29
30	Heavy Spear	35	None	22.37	3.8		54	26

INFERIOR POLEARMS

M LEV	WEAPON NAME	LEV	BIND	DPS	SPEED	VENDOR PURCHASE VALUE (gold)	(silver)	(copper)
20	Pitchfork	25	None	10.00	3.7		14	10

STAVES

EPIC STAVES

M LEV	WEAPON NAME	LEV	BIND	DPS	SPEED	VENDOR PURCHASE VALUE		
35	Staff of Jordan	40	BoE	40.41	3.7	2	17	70
▶	**SPELL/NOTE** Increase spell Dmg 13							
43	Warden Staff	48	BoE	46.46	2.4	4	28	63
▶	**SPELL/NOTE** Adds 15 Defense, AC +260							
49	Glowing Brightwood Staff	54	BoE	51.29	3.1	5	70	18
▶	**SPELL/NOTE** Nature Resist +15							
56	Elemental Mage Staff	61	BoE	57.50	3.2	8	30	00
▶	**SPELL/NOTE** Increase Fire Dmg 21, Fire & Frost Resist +20							
57	Headmaster's Charge	62	BoA	58.45	2.9	8	70	13

SUPERIOR STAVES

M LEV	WEAPON NAME	LEV	BIND	DPS	SPEED	VENDOR PURCHASE VALUE		
17	Witching Stave	22	BoE	19.17	3.6		29	22
▶	**SPELL/NOTE** Increase Shadow Dmg 7							
18	Emberstone Staff	23	BoA	19.67	3		31	61
18	Staff of the Blessed Seer	23	BoE	19.67	3		32	55
▶	**SPELL/NOTE** Increase Healing 22							
N/A	Crescent Staff	24	BoA	20.34	2.9		36	80
19	Staff of the Friar	24	BoE	20.38	2.6		35	98
N/A	Staff of Westfall	24	BoA	20.50	3		36	39
19	Twisted Chanter's Staff	24	BoE	20.44	3.4		35	17
20	Living Root	25	BoA	21.21	2.9		40	53
▶	**SPELL/NOTE** Nature Resist +5							
21	Odo's Ley Staff	26	BoA	21.72	2.9		48	02
22	Staff of the Shade	27	BoE	22.31	2.6		50	16
▶	**SPELL/NOTE** Increase Shadow Dmg 13							
24	Rod of the Sleepwalker	29	BoA	23.75	2.8		59	54
26	Gnarled Ash Staff	31	BoE	25.63	3.2		70	69
27	Hydrocane	32	BoA	21.61	2.8		82	10
▶	**SPELL/NOTE** Frost Resist +15, Allows Breathing Underwater							
27	Wind Spirit Staff	32	BoA	26.67	3.3		82	67
31	Loksey's Training Stick	36	BoA	31.29	3.1	1	22	79
▶	**SPELL/NOTE** Add 60 Attack Power Vs. Beasts							
32	Windweaver Staff	37	BoE	32.42	3.1	1	28	74
▶	**SPELL/NOTE** Increase Arcane Dmg 8							
33	Black Duskwood Staff	38	BoE	33.57	2.8	1	45	77
▶	**SPELL/NOTE** On Attack: Chance to Deal 110-140 Shadow Dmg							
34	Illusionary Rod	39	BoA	34.71	3.4	1	59	24
37	Ironshod Bludgeon	42	BoA	37.20	2.5	1	86	39
41	Tanglewood Staff	46	BoE	40.29	3.4	2	62	09
▶	**SPELL/NOTE** Increase Nature Dmg 8							
42	Bludgeon of the Grinning Dog	47	BoE	41.18	3.4	2	69	74
▶	**SPELL/NOTE** On Attack: Chance for a 3 sec Stun							
42	Witch Doctor's Cane	47	BoE	41.09	2.3	2	95	85
▶	**SPELL/NOTE** Increase Nature Dmg 19							
45	The Chief's Enforcer	50	BoA	43.53	3.4	3	59	36
▶	**SPELL/NOTE** On Attack: Chance for a 3 sec Stun							
48	Kindling Stave	53	BoA	45.86	2.9	4	32	34
▶	**SPELL/NOTE** Fire Resist +10							
49	Soulkeeper	54	BoE	46.58	3.8	4	34	20
N/A	Dancing Sliver	60	BoA	51.25	2.4	6	45	02
N/A	Argent Crusader	62	BoA	53.00	3	6	77	82
49	Spire of Hakkar	54	BoA	46.47	3.4	4	43	14
▶	**SPELL/NOTE** Increase **SPELL/NOTE** Dmg 9							
51	Spire of the Stoneshaper	56	BoE	48.24	3.4	4	85	01
▶	**SPELL/NOTE** On Use: Add 1000 Armor but Prevents spells/Melee Attacks							
55	Guiding Stave of Eternal Wisdom	60	BoA	51.36	3.3	6	12	38
▶	**SPELL/NOTE** Increases Group MP Regen by 10							
55	Slavedriver's Cane	60	BoA	51.32	3.4	6	37	69
▶	**SPELL/NOTE** Increases Group HP/MP Regen by 6							
56	Trindlehaven Staff	61	BoA	52.14	2.1	6	57	49
57	Staff of Hale Magefire	62	BoE	53.03	3.3	6	52	25

GOOD STAVES

M LEV	WEAPON NAME	LEV	BIND	DPS	SPEED	VENDOR PURCHASE VALUE		
N/A	Arcane Staff	10	BoA	7.07	2.9		3	06
N/A	Gritroot Staff	10	BoA	6.92	2.6		3	02
N/A	Ley Staff	10	BoA	7.07	2.9		3	05
N/A	Balanced Fighting Stick	13	BoA	8.86	2.2		6	01
N/A	Darkwood Staff	13	BoA	9.06	3.2		5	92
8	Sturdy Quarterstaff	13	BoE	8.93	2.8		6	31
N/A	Oakthrush Staff	14	BoA	9.46	2.8		7	02
N/A	Cauldron Stirrer	15	BoA	10.16	3.1		9	19
10	Staff of Conjuring	15	BoE	10.17	3		9	05
▶	**SPELL/NOTE** On Use: Summons Food to Eat							
11	Defias Mage Staff	16	BoE	10.71	2.8		9	95
12	Foamspittle Staff	17	BoE	11.41	3.2		11	84
13	Riverpaw Mystic Staff	18	BoE	11.83	3		13	92
13	Staff of Nobles	18	BoE	11.88	3.2		13	17
N/A	Staff of Orgrimmar	18	BoA	11.82	3.3		12	82
14	Gnarled Hermit's Staff	19	BoE	12.50	2.8		15	72
14	Medicine Staff	19	BoE	12.60	2.5		14	87
14	Riverside Staff	19	BoE	12.58	3.1		14	97
15	Channeler's Staff	20	BoE	13.09	3.4		18	55
15	Lesser Staff of the Spire	20	BoE	13.09	3.4		18	54
N/A	Wind Rider Staff	20	BoA	13.04	2.8		17	10
N/A	Ceranium Rod	22	BoA	14.44	2.7		23	22
18	Nightbane Staff	23	BoE	15.00	2.7		26	33
18	Staff of Horrors	23	BoE	15.15	3.4		26	92
▶	**SPELL/NOTE** On Attack: Reduce Target's Dmg by 5 for 2 min							
N/A	Staff of the Purifier	23	BoA	15.27	3.7		26	35
▶	**SPELL/NOTE** On Use: Remove 1 Poison/1 Disease From Target							
N/A	Brewing Rod	25	BoA	16.90	2.9		34	39
N/A	Hardened Root Staff	25	BoA	16.82	3.3		35	00
N/A	Icicle Rod	25	BoA	16.84	3.8		34	76
▶	**SPELL/NOTE** Increase Frost Dmg 6							
N/A	Staff of Soran'ruk	25	BoA	16.90	2.9		33	44
▶	**SPELL/NOTE** Increase Shadow Dmg 5							
21	Cryptbone Staff	26	BoE	17.41	2.9		36	44
22	Dwarven Magestaff	27	BoE	18.39	2.8		44	14
22	Kam's Walking Stick	27	BoE	18.39	2.8		40	23
22	Ogremage Staff	27	BoE	18.24	3.4		41	17
24	Magician Staff	29	BoE	19.67	3		50	59
28	Bloodscalp Channeling Staff	33	BoE	22.32	2.8		72	39
▶	**SPELL/NOTE** Increase Nature Dmg 11							
29	Acrobatic Staff	34	BoE	22.95	2.2		80	88
32	Big Stick	37	BoE	25.67	3	1	07	79
34	Staff of Protection	39	BoE	27.67	3	1	26	19
▶	**SPELL/NOTE** AC +100, Arcane, Fire, Frost, Nature, & Shadow Resist +6							
N/A	Celestial Stave	40	BoA	28.83	3	1	31	14
▶	**SPELL/NOTE** Increase Arcane Dmg 7							
N/A	Staff of Dar'Orahil	40	BoA	28.89	2.7	1	31	47
▶	**SPELL/NOTE** Increase Shadow Dmg 11							
N/A	Staff of Noh'Orahil	40	BoA	28.89	2.7	1	31	47
▶	**SPELL/NOTE** Increase Fire Dmg 11							
36	Spellforce Rod	41	BoE	30.16	3.2	1	46	95
▶	**SPELL/NOTE** Increase **SPELL** Dmg 10							
37	Monk's Staff	42	BoE	31.25	2.4	1	66	40
39	Spiritchaser Staff	44	BoE	33.57	2.8	1	91	39
N/A	Nimboya's Mystical Staff	46	BoA	35.65	2.3	2	24	95
N/A	Sanctimonial Rod	46	BoA	35.65	3.1	2	13	77
N/A	Spellbinder	46	BoA	35.74	2.7	2	16	13
N/A	Staff of Lore	48	BoA	37.26	3.1	2	55	01
N/A	Strength of the Treant	50	BoA	38.92	3.7	2	99	52
47	Diviner Long Staff	52	BoE	40.38	2.6	3	16	66
49	Thaumaturgist Staff	54	BoE	41.81	3.6	3	57	14
53	Magus Long Staff	58	BoE	45.00	3.4	4	52	63
N/A	Enchanted Azsharite Felbane Staff	60	BoA	46.61	2.8	5	27	47
▶	**SPELL/NOTE** Add 78 Attack Power Vs. Demons							
55	Solstice Staff	60	BoE	46.73	2.6	5	02	85

STANDARD STAVES

M LEV	WEAPON NAME	LEV	BIND	DPS	SPEED	VENDOR PURCHASE VALUE		
1	Bent Staff	2	None	1.38	2.9			9
1	Handcrafted Staff	2	None	1.38	2.9			9
1	Crooked Staff	3	None	1.67	3.3			14
N/A	Elder's Cane	4	BoA	2.14	3.5			20
N/A	Militia Quarterstaff	4	BoA	1.96	2.8			21
N/A	Primitive Walking Stick	4	BoA	2.10	3.1			20
1	Short Staff	4	None	2.03	3.2			20
N/A	Thistlewood Staff	4	BoA	2.10	3.1			21
N/A	Executor Staff	5	BoA	2.59	2.9			30
N/A	Smooth Walking Staff	5	BoA	2.73	3.3			32
3	Farmer's Broom	6	None	3.29	3.5			46
N/A	Gnarled Short Staff	8	BoA	4.29	2.8			99
3	Long Bo Staff	8	None	4.20	2.5		1	00
3	Walking Stick	8	None	4.20	2.5		1	00
4	Vile Fin Oracle Staff	9	None	5.00	2.9		1	41
N/A	Dreamwatcher Staff	10	BoA	5.63	3.2		1	83
5	Driftwood Branch	10	None	5.74	3.4		1	74
5	Frostbit Staff	10	None	5.74	2.7		1	86
5	Frostmane Staff	10	None	5.65	3.1		1	88

STANDARD STAVES continued

M LEV	WEAPON NAME	LEV	BIND	DPS	SPEED	VENDOR PURCHASE VALUE		
N/A	Blemished Wooden Staff	11	BoA	6.41	3.2		2	36
11	Quarter Staff	16	None	9.44	2.7		6	04
15	Gnarled Staff	20	None	11.90	2.9		11	08
20	Long Staff	25	None	15.17	3		19	72
31	Battle Staff	36	None	22.94	3.4		58	71
40	War Staff	45	None	32.42	3.3	1	23	11

INFERIOR STAVES

M LEV	WEAPON NAME	LEV	BIND	DPS	SPEED	VENDOR PURCHASE VALUE		
3	Withered Staff	8	None	3.33	3			68
7	Rough Wooden Staff	12	None	5.00	3.3		1	96
13	Chipped Quarterstaff	18	None	7.10	3.1		5	22
18	Cedar Walking Stick	23	None	9.11	2.8		10	96
23	Oaken War Staff	28	None	11.35	3.7		17	90
32	Metal Stave	37	None	15.32	3.1		42	08
42	Heavy War Staff	47	None	21.91	3.4		98	21
46	Stout War Staff	51	None	23.87	3.1	1	19	24

XII

CLOTH ARMOR

LEATHER ARMOR

MAIL ARMOR

PLATE ARMOR

SHIELDS

WEAPONS

ONE-HANDED SWORDS

EPIC SWORDS (1H)

M LEV	WEAPON NAME	LEV	BIND	DPS	SPEED	VENDOR PURCHASE VALUE		
36	Dazzling Longsword	41	BoE	31.47	1.7	1	85	29
▸	**SPELL/NOTE** Main Hand Only, On Attack: Chance to Sunder Armor 100/Prevent Stealth							
45	Bloodrazor	50	BoE	37.04	2.7	3	91	25
▸	**SPELL/NOTE** Main Hand Only, On Attack: Chance to Deal 120 Dmg Over 30 sec							
51	Krol Blade	56	BoE	40.89	2.8	5	18	57
▸	**SPELL/NOTE** Main Hand Only, Add 1% Crit							
52	Dragon's Call	57	BoA	41.40	2.5	5	69	21
▸	**SPELL/NOTE** On Attack: Chance to Summon Dragon Whelp (Up to 3/Battle)							
60	Teebu's Blazing Longsword	65	BoE	47.24	2.9	8	70	08
▸	**SPELL/NOTE** Main Hand Only, Deals 22-24 Fire Dmg							

SUPERIOR SWORDS (1H)

M LEV	WEAPON NAME	LEV	BIND	DPS	SPEED	VENDOR PURCHASE VALUE		
15	Ironpatch Blade	20	BoE	13.46	2.6		17	70
15	Night Watch Shortsword	20	BoE	13.46	2.6		17	42
19	Cruel Barb	24	BoA	15.54	2.8		29	64
▸	**SPELL/NOTE** Attack Power 12							
19	Shadowfang	24	BoE	15.56	2.7		29	64
▸	**SPELL/NOTE** Main Hand Only, On Attack: Chance to Deal 30 Shadow Dmg							
N/A	Wingblade	24	BoA	15.68	2.2		29	33
▸	**SPELL/NOTE** Main Hand Only							
21	Twisted Sabre	26	BoE	16.67	1.8		38	40
▸	**SPELL/NOTE** Main Hand Only							
22	Heavy Marauder Scimitar	27	BoE	17.08	2.4		39	22
▸	**SPELL/NOTE** Main Hand Only							
22	Sword of Corruption	27	BoE	17.14	2.1		41	38
▸	**SPELL/NOTE** On Attack: Chance to Deal 30 Dmg Over 3 sec							
N/A	Sword of Omen	44	BoA	29.74	1.9	1	82	55
N/A	Sword of Serenity	44	BoA	30.00	2.2	1	87	14
N/A	Mirah's Song	61	BoA	40.00	1.8	5	12	73
N/A	Argent Avenger	62	BoA	40.68	2.2	5	36	22
▸	**SPELL/NOTE** On Attack: Chance to Add 200 Attack Power Vs. Undead							
23	Sword of Decay	28	BoE	17.59	2.7		45	62
▸	**SPELL/NOTE** Main Hand Only, On Attack: Chance to Reduce Foe Strength by 10							
26	The Black Knight	31	BoE	19.74	1.9		61	05
▸	**SPELL/NOTE** Main Hand Only, On Attack: Chance to Deal 35-45 Dmg							
26	The Butcher	31	BoE	19.64	2.8		57	47
▸	**SPELL/NOTE** Main Hand Only							
29	Electrocutioner Leg	34	BoA	22.06	1.7		75	64
▸	**SPELL/NOTE** Main Hand Only, On Attack: Chance to Deal 10-20 Nature Dmg							
29	Zealot Blade	34	BoE	22.14	2.8		80	94
31	Tainted Pierce	36	BoE	24.21	1.9		92	22
▸	**SPELL/NOTE** On Attack: Chance to Deal 45 Dmg Over 3 sec							
32	Blade of the Basilisk	37	BoE	25.00	1.9	1	00	66
▸	**SPELL/NOTE** On Attack: Chance to Add 50 Defense for 5 sec							
33	Reforged Blade of Heroes	38	BoE	20.45	2.2	1	14	21
34	Scorpion Sting	39	BoE	26.46	2.4	1	17	74
▸	**SPELL/NOTE** On Attack: Chance to Deal 65 Poison Dmg Over 25 sec							

SUPERIOR SWORDS (1H) continued

M LEV	WEAPON NAME	LEV	BIND	DPS	SPEED	VENDOR PURCHASE VALUE		
35	Annealed Blade	40	BoE	27.22	1.8	1	29	80
36	Ginn-su Sword	41	BoE	27.94	1.7	1	35	94
36	Speedsteel Rapier	41	BoE	28.06	1.8	1	47	10
38	Nordic Longshank	43	BoA	29.32	2.2	1	69	01
41	Bloodletter Scalpel	46	BoE	31.11	1.8	2	10	60
▸	**SPELL/NOTE** On Attack: Chance to Deal 55 Dmg							
42	Shortsword of Vengeance	47	BoE	31.67	2.4	2	35	56
▸	**SPELL/NOTE** On Attack: Chance to Deal 30 Holy Dmg							
44	Phantom Blade	49	BoE	32.69	2.6	2	55	08
▸	**SPELL/NOTE** Main Hand Only, On Attack: Chance to Sunder Armor 100/Prevent Stealth							
44	Sang'thraze the Deflector	49	BoA	29.12	1.7	2	63	83
▸	**SPELL/NOTE** Add 1% Parry							
44	Serpent Slicer	49	BoE	32.80	2.5	2	51	41
▸	**SPELL/NOTE** On Attack: Chance to Deal 80 Poison Dmg Over 20 sec							
45	Jang'thraze the Protector	50	BoA	33.42	1.9	2	74	03
▸	**SPELL/NOTE** Main Hand Only, On Attack: Chance to Shield User for 55-85 Dmg							
48	Firebreather	53	BoA	35.23	2.2	3	50	69
▸	**SPELL/NOTE** On Attack: Chance to Deal 70 Dmg/9 More Over 6 sec							
49	Doomforged Straightedge	54	BoE	35.79	1.9	3	49	25
▸	**SPELL/NOTE** Attack Power 12							
50	Hanzo Sword	55	BoE	36.33	1.5	3	72	86
▸	**SPELL/NOTE** On Attack: Chance to Deal 75 Dmg							
51	Blazing Rapier	56	BoE	37.06	1.7	3	86	48
▸	**SPELL/NOTE** On Attack: Chance to Deal 100 Dmg Over 30 sec							
52	Arbiter's Blade	57	BoA	37.71	2.4	4	27	16
▸	**SPELL/NOTE** Main Hand Only							
52	Assassination Blade	57	BoE	37.59	2.7	4	09	88
▸	**SPELL/NOTE** Add 1% Crit							
53	Lord General's Sword	58	BoA	38.27	2.6	4	41	06
▸	**SPELL/NOTE** Main Hand Only, Adds 15 Attack Power to Group Members							
54	Ebon Hilt of Marduk	59	BoA	38.89	2.7	4	51	84
▸	**SPELL/NOTE** Main Hand Only, On Attack: Chance to Deal 210 Dmg Over 3 sec							
57	Silent Fang	62	BoA	40.63	1.6	5	68	80
▸	**SPELL/NOTE** Main Hand Only, On Attack: Chance to Silence Enemy Casters							
58	Dal'Rend's Sacred Charge	63	BoA	41.43	2.8	5	48	12
▸	**SPELL/NOTE** Main Hand Only, Add 1% Crit							
58	Dal'Rend's Tribal Guardian	63	BoA	41.39	1.8	6	03	63
▸	**SPELL/NOTE** Off-Hand Only, Adds 10 Defense and 100 Armor							
58	Frost Guard	63	BoE	41.30	2.3	5	69	43
▸	**SPELL/NOTE** Main Hand Only							
58	Skullforge Reaver	63	BoA	41.40	2.5	5	67	30
▸	**SPELL/NOTE** On Attack: Chance to Steal 2 HP/sec for 30 sec							
58	Sword of Zeal	63	BoE	41.43	2.8	5	54	00
▸	**SPELL/NOTE** Main Hand Only, Adds 1 Dmg and 10 Armor							

GOOD SWORDS (1H)

M LEV	WEAPON NAME	LEV	BIND	DPS	SPEED	VENDOR PURCHASE VALUE		
5	Notched Shortsword	10	BoE	5.48	2.1		2	44
7	Pale Skinner	12	BoE	6.59	2.2		3	86
▶	SPELL/NOTE Main Hand Only							
8	Feral Blade	13	BoE	6.92	2.6		4	81
▶	SPELL/NOTE Main Hand Only							
N/A	Briarsteel Shortsword	14	BoA	7.20	2.5		5	80
9	Enamelled Broadsword	14	BoE	7.29	2.4		5	75
▶	SPELL/NOTE Main Hand Only							
N/A	Elunite Sword	15	BoA	7.62	2.1		6	96
▶	SPELL/NOTE Main Hand Only							
N/A	Haggard's Sword	15	BoA	7.62	2.1		6	90
▶	SPELL/NOTE Main Hand Only							
N/A	Heirloom Sword	15	BoA	7.62	2.1		6	90
▶	SPELL/NOTE Main Hand Only							
N/A	Thun'grim's Sword	15	BoA	7.62	2.1		7	03
▶	SPELL/NOTE Main Hand Only							
N/A	Umbral Sword	15	BoA	7.62	2.1		6	88
▶	SPELL/NOTE Main Hand Only							
11	Defias Rapier	16	BoE	8.13	1.6		7	87
▶	SPELL/NOTE Main Hand Only							
11	Raider Shortsword	16	BoE	8.16	1.9		8	25
11	Redridge Machete	16	BoE	8.26	2.3		8	23
▶	SPELL/NOTE Main Hand Only							
N/A	Daryl's Shortsword	17	BoA	8.70	2.3		9	72
13	Cursed Felblade	18	BoA	9.04	2.6		10	32
▶	SPELL/NOTE Main Hand Only, On Attack: Chance to Reduce Foe Attack Power by 15							
13	Northern Shortsword	18	BoE	9.09	2.2		10	70
N/A	Solid Shortblade	18	BoA	9.20	2.5		10	54
14	Blackwater Cutlass	19	BoE	9.47	1.9		12	58
14	Scimitar of Atun	19	BoE	9.62	2.6		11	80
▶	SPELL/NOTE Main Hand Only							
N/A	Elegant Shortsword	20	BoA	10.00	2		14	84
16	Buzz Saw	21	BoA	10.42	2.4		17	00
17	Militant Shortsword	22	BoE	11.00	2.5		19	16
17	Thief's Blade	22	BoA	11.18	1.7		18	03
18	Butcher's Slicer	23	BoA	11.55	2.9		21	31
19	Bluegill Kukri	24	BoE	12.32	2.8		24	61
▶	SPELL/NOTE Main Hand Only							
19	Decapitating Sword	24	BoE	12.31	2.6		24	52
▶	SPELL/NOTE Main Hand Only							
19	Sword of the Night Sky	24	BoE	12.06	1.7		23	00
▶	SPELL/NOTE Main Hand Only							
N/A	Talonstrike	24	BoA	12.19	1.6		22	83
▶	SPELL/NOTE Main Hand Only							
N/A	Lucine Longsword	25	BoA	12.80	2.5		27	61
▶	SPELL/NOTE Main Hand Only							
N/A	Phytoblade	25	BoA	12.86	2.8		26	19
▶	SPELL/NOTE Main Hand Only, On Attack: Chance to Deal 35 Nature Dmg							
21	Black Metal Shortsword	26	BoE	13.53	1.7		29	49
▶	SPELL/NOTE Shadow Resist +4, Main Hand Only							
21	Darkwater Talwar	26	BoA	13.41	2.2		29	41
▶	SPELL/NOTE Main Hand Only, On Attack: Chance to Deal 25 Shadow Dmg							
22	Fighter Broadsword	27	BoE	13.93	2.8		34	50
▶	SPELL/NOTE Main Hand Only							
22	Skeletal Longsword	27	BoE	13.86	2.2		32	69
▶	SPELL/NOTE Main Hand Only							
23	Dragonmaw Shortsword	28	BoE	14.55	2.2		38	42
25	Viking Sword	30	BoE	15.56	2.7		44	36
▶	SPELL/NOTE Main Hand Only							
27	Hardened Iron Shortsword	32	BoE	16.67	1.8		54	68
▶	SPELL/NOTE Main Hand Only							
30	Jade Serpentblade	35	BoE	18.27	2.6		73	04
31	Mercenary Blade	36	BoE	18.75	2.4		81	65
31	Silithid Ripper	36	BoE	18.91	2.3		76	55
▶	SPELL/NOTE Main Hand Only, On Attack: Chance to Deal 45 Dmg Over 30 sec							
33	Knightly Longsword	38	BoE	20.33	1.5		97	16
35	Nobles Broadsword	40	BoE	22.14	2.1	1	13	56
N/A	Olmann Sewar	41	BoA	22.96	2.7	1	23	37
▶	SPELL/NOTE Main Hand Only							
N/A	Sword of Hammerfall	41	BoA	23.04	2.3	1	18	93
▶	SPELL/NOTE Main Hand Only							
38	Ebon Scimitar	43	BoE	25.00	1.9	1	39	79
N/A	Dwarf Captain's Sword	45	BoA	26.60	2.5	1	55	84
40	Furious Falchion	45	BoE	26.60	2.5	1	67	44
▶	SPELL/NOTE Main Hand Only							
N/A	Vanquisher's Sword	45	BoA	26.59	2.2	1	60	16
▶	SPELL/NOTE Attack Power 16							

GOOD SWORDS (1H) continued

M LEV	WEAPON NAME	LEV	BIND	DPS	SPEED	VENDOR PURCHASE VALUE		
40	Wicked Mithril Blade	45	BoE	26.74	2.3	1	58	91
▶	SPELL/NOTE Main Hand Only							
43	Dazzling Mithril Rapier	48	BoE	28.53	1.7	2	00	92
▶	SPELL/NOTE Main Hand Only							
46	Rune Sword	51	BoE	30.31	1.6	2	59	32
49	Blade of the Wretched	54	BoA	32.14	2.1	2	94	41
▶	SPELL/NOTE Main Hand Only, On Attack: Chance to Deal 90 Dmg Over 3 sec							
49	Widow Blade	54	BoE	32.25	2	3	09	96
N/A	Linken's Sword of Mastery	56	BoA	33.33	1.8	3	41	94
▶	SPELL/NOTE Main Hand Only, On Attack: Chance to Deal 45-75 Dmg							
52	Crystal Sword	57	BoE	33.91	2.3	3	70	47
52	Dimensional Blade	57	BoA	34.05	2.1	3	67	85
▶	SPELL/NOTE Off-Hand Only							
N/A	Tidecrest Blade	57	BoA	34.04	2.6	3	38	30
N/A	Intrepid Shortsword	58	BoA	34.52	2.1	3	60	82
N/A	Valiant Shortsword	58	BoA	34.52	2.1	3	58	60
54	Dimensional Blade	59	BoE	35.00	1.6	4	13	76
N/A	Beaststalker Blade	60	BoA	35.91	2.2	4	31	42
▶	SPELL/NOTE Adds 33 Attack Power Vs. Beasts							
N/A	Blade of Reckoning	60	BoA	35.83	2.4	4	02	12
▶	SPELL/NOTE Attack Power 22							
N/A	Enchanted Azsharite Felbane Sword	60	BoA	35.75	2	4	18	90
▶	SPELL/NOTE Main Hand Only, Adds 33 Attack Power Vs. Demons							
N/A	Hameya's Slayer	60	BoA	35.75	2	4	19	11
▶	SPELL/NOTE Adds 33 Attack Power Vs. Demons							
57	Battlefell Sabre	62	BoE	37.05	2.2	4	34	93
▶	SPELL/NOTE Main Hand Only							
60	Holy War Sword	65	BoE	38.64	2.2	5	19	46

STANDARD SWORDS (1H)

M LEV	WEAPON NAME	LEV	BIND	DPS	SPEED	VENDOR PURCHASE VALUE		
1	Worn Shortsword	2	None	1.05	1.9			7
▶	SPELL/NOTE Main Hand Only							
1	Deadman Blade	3	None	1.20	2.5			10
▶	SPELL/NOTE Main Hand Only							
1	Dull Blade	3	None	1.05	1.9			11
▶	SPELL/NOTE Main Hand Only							
1	Shortsword	3	None	1.15	2.6			10
▶	SPELL/NOTE Main Hand Only							
N/A	Forsaken Shortsword	4	BoA	1.67	2.1			17
▶	SPELL/NOTE Main Hand Only							
N/A	Militia Shortsword	4	BoA	1.40	2.5			17
▶	SPELL/NOTE Main Hand Only							
1	Pitted Defias Shortsword	4	None	1.50	2			16
▶	SPELL/NOTE Main Hand Only							
N/A	Thistlewood Blade	4	BoA	1.59	2.2			17
▶	SPELL/NOTE Main Hand Only							
1	Fine Scimitar	6	None	2.37	1.9			37
3	Frostmane Shortsword	8	None	3.25	2			83
▶	SPELL/NOTE Main Hand Only							
4	Copper Shortsword	9	None	3.81	2.1		1	10
▶	SPELL/NOTE Main Hand Only							
4	Gladius	9	None	3.81	2.1		1	07
▶	SPELL/NOTE Main Hand Only							
4	Rockjaw Blade	9	None	3.81	2.1		1	13
▶	SPELL/NOTE Main Hand Only							
4	Short Sabre	9	None	3.95	1.9		1	10
▶	SPELL/NOTE Main Hand Only							
5	Rodentia Shortsword	10	None	4.35	2.3		1	39
▶	SPELL/NOTE Main Hand Only							
5	Stonesplinter Blade	10	None	4.50	2		1	46
▶	SPELL/NOTE Main Hand Only							
N/A	Well-used Sword	10	BoA	4.29	2.1		1	44
▶	SPELL/NOTE Main Hand Only							
N/A	Deathstalker Shortsword	11	BoA	5.00	2.1		1	88
N/A	Harpy Wing Clipper	11	BoA	5.00	2.6		1	79
▶	SPELL/NOTE Main Hand Only							
10	Cutlass	15	None	6.82	2.2		4	04
▶	SPELL/NOTE Main Hand Only							
14	Scimitar	19	None	8.70	2.3		7	63
▶	SPELL/NOTE Main Hand Only							
19	Bronze Shortsword	24	None	11.19	2.1		14	39
▶	SPELL/NOTE Main Hand Only							
20	Smotts' Cutlass	25	Quest	11.58	1.9			0
▶	SPELL/NOTE Main Hand Only							

STANDARD SWORDS (1H) continued

M LEV	WEAPON NAME	LEV	BIND	DPS	SPEED	VENDOR PURCHASE VALUE		
21	Longsword	26	None	12.17	2.3		17	48
▶	**SPELL/NOTE** Main Hand Only							
31	Broadsword	36	None	17.61	2.3		49	25
▶	**SPELL/NOTE** Main Hand Only							
41	Falchion	46	None	25.68	2.2	1	03	67
▶	**SPELL/NOTE** Main Hand Only							

INFERIOR SWORDS (1H)

M LEV	WEAPON NAME	LEV	BIND	DPS	SPEED	VENDOR PURCHASE VALUE		
3	Feeble Sword	8	None	2.50	2			55
▶	**SPELL/NOTE** Main Hand Only							
8	Commoner's Sword	13	None	3.91	2.3		1	93
▶	**SPELL/NOTE** Main Hand Only							
14	Stock Shortsword	19	None	5.83	1.8		5	01
▶	**SPELL/NOTE** Main Hand Only							
19	Warped Blade	24	None	7.19	1.6		9	88
▶	**SPELL/NOTE** Main Hand Only							
24	Short Cutlass	29	None	9.07	2.7		15	63
▶	**SPELL/NOTE** Main Hand Only							
25	Aura Proc Damage Sword	30	BoE	9.50	2		17	20
▶	**SPELL/NOTE** Main Hand Only, On Attack: Chance to Add 4 Point Dmg Shield							
31	Light Scimitar	36	None	11.32	1.9		30	48
▶	**SPELL/NOTE** Main Hand Only							
41	Sharp Shortsword	46	None	16.39	1.8		69	10
▶	**SPELL/NOTE** Main Hand Only							
47	Fine Longsword	52	None	18.41	2.2	1	01	12
▶	**SPELL/NOTE** Main Hand Only							

2H TWO-HANDED SWORDS

EPIC SWORDS (2H)

M LEV	WEAPON NAME	LEV	BIND	DPS	SPEED	VENDOR PURCHASE VALUE		
39	Nightblade	44	BoE	43.39	2.8	2	95	13
▶	**SPELL/NOTE** On Attack: Chance to Deal 125-275 Shadow Dmg							
50	Sul'thraze the Lasher	55	BoA	52.12	2.6	6	19	36
▶	**SPELL/NOTE** On Attack: Chance to Lower Strength/Deal 90-210 Dmg +125 Over Time							
52	Destiny	57	BoE	53.85	2.6	7	00	24
▶	**SPELL/NOTE** On Attack: Chance to Add 300 Strength for 10 sec							
58	Blackblade of Shahram	63	BoA	59.35	2.3	9	52	41
58	Runeblade of Baron Rivendare	63	BoA	59.46	2.8	9	13	45
59	Blade of Hanna	64	BoE	60.24	2.1	10	47	29

SUPERIOR SWORDS (2H)

M LEV	WEAPON NAME	LEV	BIND	DPS	SPEED	VENDOR PURCHASE VALUE		
18	Searing Blade	23	BoE	19.60	2.5		32	60
▶	**SPELL/NOTE** On Attack: Chance to Deal 70 Fire Dmg/9 More Over Time							
20	Duskbringer	25	BoE	21.03	3.4		39	61
▶	**SPELL/NOTE** On Attack: Chance to Deal 60-100 Shadow Dmg							
21	Guardian Blade	26	BoE	21.72	2.9		45	16
▶	**SPELL/NOTE** Adds 13 Defense and 40 Armor							
21	Onyx Claymore	26	BoE	21.61	2.8		46	29
23	Pysan's Old Greatsword	28	BoE	22.88	3.3		57	44
26	Deanship Claymore	29	BoE	23.75	2.8		61	91
▶	**SPELL/NOTE** Add 15 Defense							
24	Gizmotron Megachopper	29	BoE	23.91	3.2		61	21
26	Strike of the Hydra	31	BoA	25.61	3.3		71	55
28	Claymore of the Martyr	33	BoE	27.76	2.9		85	24
30	Morbid Dawn	35	BoA	30.17	2.9	1	11	24
31	Ancient Defender	36	BoE	31.29	3.1	1	22	80
▶	**SPELL/NOTE** Add 15 Defense and 100 Armor							
32	Boneslasher	37	BoE	32.59	2.7	1	37	54
N/A	Whirlwind Sword	40	BoA	35.52	2.9	1	73	25
36	Sword of the Magistrate	41	BoE	36.52	3.3	1	75	96
35	X'caliboar	42	BoA	37.27	3.3	2	01	44
39	Witchfury	44	BoE	38.93	2.8	2	29	11
▶	**SPELL/NOTE** On Attack: Chance to Deal 150 Shadow Dmg							
42	Mutilator	47	BoA	41.20	2.5	2	91	79
43	Deathblow	48	BoE	41.96	2.8	2	92	45
▶	**SPELL/NOTE** On Attack: Chance to Deal 160 Dmg							
44	Blade of the Titans	49	BoE	42.58	3.3	3	23	89
44	Stoneslayer	49	BoA	42.69	3.9	3	28	51
▶	**SPELL/NOTE** On Attack: Chance to Add 10 Dmg for 8 sec							
47	Truesilver Champion	52	BoE	45.00	3	3	85	48
▶	**SPELL/NOTE** On Attack: Chance to Cast Holy Shield on User							
47	Warmonger	52	BoE	45.00	3	4	16	77
▶	**SPELL/NOTE** Add 3% Hit							
48	Drakefang Butcher	53	BoA	45.93	2.7	4	24	46
▶	**SPELL/NOTE** On Attack: Chance to Deal 150 Dmg Over 30 sec							
52	Demonslayer	57	BoE	48.87	3.1	5	28	00
▶	**SPELL/NOTE** Adds 99 Attack Power Vs. Demons							
53	Corruption	58	BoA	49.67	3	5	68	08

SUPERIOR SWORDS (2H) continued

M LEV	WEAPON NAME	LEV	BIND	DPS	SPEED	VENDOR PURCHASE VALUE		
53	Stone of the Earth	58	BoA	49.69	3.2	5	70	11
▶	**SPELL/NOTE** AC +280							
55	Doombringer	60	BoE	51.43	2.8	5	91	86
▶	**SPELL/NOTE** On Attack: Chance to Deal 125-275 Shadow Dmg							
56	Relentless Scythe	61	BoA	52.17	2.3	6	62	26
▶	**SPELL/NOTE** Add 1% Parry							
57	Barovian Family Sword	62	BoA	53.10	2.1	7	18	47
▶	**SPELL/NOTE** On Attack: Chance to Steal 150 HP Over 15 sec							
58	Arcanite Champion	63	BoE	53.83	3	7	46	19
▶	**SPELL/NOTE** On Attack: Chance to Heal 270-450 HP/Buff Strength by 120 for 30 sec							
58	Demonshear	63	BoA	53.91	2.3	7	27	69
▶	**SPELL/NOTE** On Attack: Chance to Deal 150 Shadow Dmg/120 Over 30 sec							
70	Juno's Redemption	63	BoA	53.94	3.3	7	25	10
N/A	Warblade of Caer Darrow	63	BoA	53.94	3.3	6	98	26

GOOD SWORDS (2H)

M LEV	WEAPON NAME	LEV	BIND	DPS	SPEED	VENDOR PURCHASE VALUE		
N/A	Brushwood Blade	10	BoA	7.17	3		3	00
5	Training Sword	10	BoE	7.14	3.5		3	06
N/A	Steady Bastard Sword	11	BoA	7.59	2.7		3	95
7	Short Bastard Sword	12	BoE	8.33	3		4	95
10	Coral Claymore	15	BoE	10.00	2.8		8	79
11	Merc Sword	16	BoE	10.71	2.8		10	49
12	Brashclaw's Skewer	17	BoE	11.41	3.2		11	33
N/A	Edge of the People's Militia	17	BoA	11.21	2.9		11	32
13	Edged Bastard Sword	18	BoE	11.77	3.1		13	77
13	Mo'grosh Toothpick	18	BoE	11.79	2.8		14	02
N/A	Trogg Slicer	18	BoA	11.91	3.4		13	72
14	Ghoulfang	19	BoE	12.50	3.6		15	78
▶	**SPELL/NOTE** On Attack: Chance to Deal 35 Shadow Dmg							
14	Heavy Copper Broadsword	19	BoE	12.59	2.7		14	98
N/A	Samophlange Screwdriver	19	BoA	12.60	2.5		14	94
15	Gleaming Claymore	20	BoE	13.10	2.9		17	91
15	Shadowhide Two-handed Sword	20	BoE	13.10	2.9		17	68
15	Shiver Blade	20	BoE	13.10	2.9		17	69
▶	**SPELL/NOTE** On Attack: Chance to Deal 35 Frost Dmg							
N/A	Woodsman Sword	20	BoA	13.03	3.3		17	76
17	Blessed Claymore	22	BoE	14.60	2.5		24	62
19	Executioner's Sword	24	BoE	15.88	3.4		28	54
21	Haunting Blade	26	BoA	17.50	3.8		36	75
21	Polished Zweihander	26	BoE	17.50	3.6		38	77
23	Cavalier Two-hander	28	BoE	18.97	2.9		45	82
24	Black Metal Greatsword	29	BoE	19.70	3.3		48	69
24	Huge Ogre Sword	29	BoE	19.74	3.8		50	37
25	Darksteel Bastard Sword	30	BoE	20.47	3.2		57	09
N/A	Seraph's Strike	31	BoA	21.09	3.2		61	47
N/A	Ancient War Sword	32	BoA	21.67	3.3		67	83
N/A	Emil's Brand	32	BoA	21.61	3.1		70	87
27	Glimmering Flamberge	32	BoE	21.72	3.2		68	94

GOOD SWORDS (2H) continued

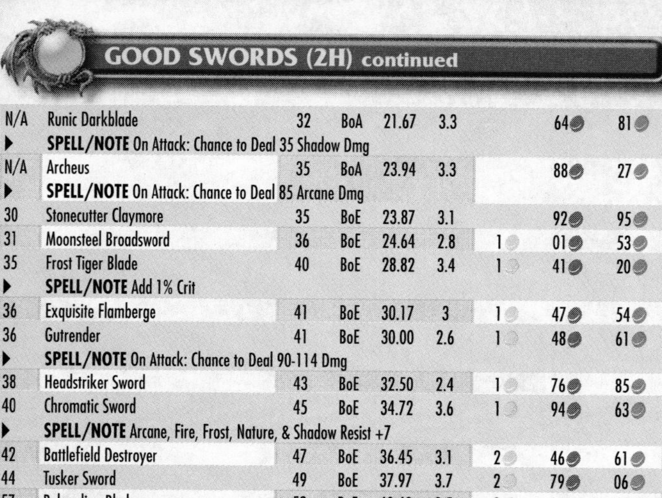

M LEV	WEAPON NAME	LEV	BIND	DPS	SPEED	VENDOR PURCHASE VALUE		
N/A	Runic Darkblade	32	BoA	21.67	3.3		64	81
▶	**SPELL/NOTE** On Attack: Chance to Deal 35 Shadow Dmg							
N/A	Archeus	35	BoA	23.94	3.3		88	27
▶	**SPELL/NOTE** On Attack: Chance to Deal 85 Arcane Dmg							
30	Stonecutter Claymore	35	BoE	23.87	3.1		92	95
31	Moonsteel Broadsword	36	BoE	24.64	2.8	1	01	53
35	Frost Tiger Blade	40	BoE	28.82	3.4	1	41	20
▶	**SPELL/NOTE** Add 1% Crit							
36	Exquisite Flamberge	41	BoE	30.17	3	1	47	54
36	Gutrender	41	BoE	30.00	2.6	1	48	61
▶	**SPELL/NOTE** On Attack: Chance to Deal 90-114 Dmg							
38	Headstriker Sword	43	BoE	32.50	2.4	1	76	85
40	Chromatic Sword	45	BoE	34.72	3.6	1	94	63
▶	**SPELL/NOTE** Arcane, Fire, Frost, Nature, & Shadow Resist +7							
42	Battlefield Destroyer	47	BoE	36.45	3.1	2	46	61
44	Tusker Sword	49	BoE	37.97	3.7	2	79	06
57	Beheading Blade	52	BoE	40.43	3.5	3	15	47
47	Thorium Greatsword	52	BoE	40.42	3.6	3	36	21
49	Dark Espadon	54	BoE	41.82	3.3	3	55	84
52	Gallant Flamberge	57	BoE	44.26	3.4	4	25	45
54	Massacre Sword	59	BoE	45.79	3.8	4	75	31
57	Shin Blade	62	BoE	47.95	2.2	5	52	34
60	Divine Warblade	65	BoE	50.56	2.7	6	41	85

STANDARD SWORDS (2H)

M LEV	WEAPON NAME	LEV	BIND	DPS	SPEED	VENDOR PURCHASE VALUE		
1	Tarnished Bastard Sword	3	None	1.56	3.2			13
1	Bastard Sword	4	None	2.17	3			20
N/A	Forsaken Bastard Sword	4	BoA	2.12	3.3			20
2	Practice Sword	7	None	3.75	3.2			71
2	Two-handed Sword	7	None	3.62	2.9			68
6	Copper Claymore	11	None	6.33	3		2	41
10	Claymore	15	None	9.06	3.2		5	35
16	Espadon	21	None	12.59	2.9		12	15
21	Bronze Greatsword	26	None	16.00	3		22	05
21	Dacian Falx	26	None	15.97	3.1		24	07
N/A	Orcish War Sword	29	BoA	18.23	3.1		30	14
31	Flamberge	36	None	23.13	3.2		61	79
41	Zweihander	46	None	33.57	2.8	1	30	06

INFERIOR SWORDS (2H)

M LEV	WEAPON NAME	LEV	BIND	DPS	SPEED	VENDOR PURCHASE VALUE		
2	Crude Bastard Sword	7	None	2.97	3.2			49
9	Old Greatsword	14	None	5.69	3.6		2	93
12	Blunt Claymore	17	None	6.61	3.1		4	51
19	Standard Claymore	24	None	9.67	3		12	21
23	Long Bastard Sword	28	None	11.41	3.2		17	83
29	Broad Claymore	34	None	13.79	3.3		31	25
37	Whetted Claymore	42	None	18.71	3.1		63	72
53	Tapered Greatsword	58	None	26.90	2.9	1	79	30

THROWN WEAPONS

SUPERIOR THROWN WEAPONS

M LEV	WEAPON NAME	LEV	BIND	DPS	SPEED	VENDOR PURCHASE VALUE
55	Flightblade Throwing Axe	60	BoA	35.59	1.7	11

GOOD THROWN WEAPONS

M LEV	WEAPON NAME	LEV	BIND	DPS	SPEED	VENDOR PURCHASE VALUE
N/A	Silver Star	37	BoA	17.5	2	9

INFERIOR THROWN WEAPONS

M LEV	WEAPON NAME	LEV	BIND	DPS	SPEED	VENDOR PURCHASE VALUE
3	Boot Knife	8	None	2.25	2	0

STANDARD THROWN WEAPONS

M LEV	WEAPON NAME	LEV	BIND	DPS	SPEED	VENDOR PURCHASE VALUE
1	Crude Throwing Axe	3	None	1	2	0
1	Small Throwing Knife	3	None	1	2	0
3	Balanced Throwing Dagger	8	None	3	2	0
3	Weighted Throwing Axe	8	None	3	2	0
11	Keen Throwing Knife	16	None	6.5	2	0
11	Sharp Throwing Axe	16	None	6.5	2	0
22	Deadly Throwing Axe	27	None	11.5	2	0
22	Heavy Throwing Dagger	27	None	11.5	2	0
35	Gleaming Throwing Axe	40	None	18.25	2	1
35	Wicked Throwing Dagger	40	None	18.33	1.8	1

WANDS

SUPERIOR WANDS

M LEV	WEAPON NAME	LEV	BIND	DPS	SPEED	VENDOR PURCHASE VALUE		
15	Firebelcher	20	BoA	20.29	1.7		13	12
16	Skycaller	21	BoE	21.56	1.6		14	22
17	Cookie's Stirring Rod	22	BoA	22.31	1.3		16	60
22	Thunderwood	27	BoE	27.11	1.9		29	91
N/A	Gravestone Scepter	29	BoA	29.00	1.5		35	35
▶	**SPELL/NOTE** Shadow Resist +5							
29	Starfaller	34	BoE	32.86	1.4		58	51
30	Necrotic Wand	35	BoA	33.21	1.4		66	49
33	Earthen Rod	38	BoE	35.59	1.7		86	28
34	Freezing Shard	39	BoE	35.77	1.3		95	92
▶	**SPELL/NOTE** Increase Frost Dmg 6							
35	Plaguerot Sprig	40	BoA	37.19	1.6		96	60
▶	**SPELL/NOTE** Shadow Resist +7							
37	Jaina's Firestarter	42	BoE	39.38	1.6	1	14	87
44	Flaming Incinerator	49	BoE	47.22	1.8	1	91	39
▶	**SPELL/NOTE** Fire Resist +8							
45	Wand of Allistarj	50	BoE	48.42	1.9	2	09	45
▶	**SPELL/NOTE** Arcane Resist +9							
48	Pyric Caduceus	53	BoA	52.50	1.8	2	50	83
▶	**SPELL/NOTE** Increase Fire Dmg 8							
51	Rod of Corrosion	56	BoA	55.00	1.3	2	89	89
▶	**SPELL/NOTE** Nature Resist +10							

SUPERIOR WANDS continued

M LEV	WEAPON NAME	LEV	BIND	DPS	SPEED	VENDOR PURCHASE VALUE		
53	Torch of Austen	58	BoE	56.79	1.4	3	35	90
▶	**SPELL/NOTE** Fire Resist +10							
54	Skul's Ghastly Touch	59	BoA	58.33	1.8	3	43	39
▶	**SPELL/NOTE** Increase Shadow Dmg 8							
55	Banshee Finger	60	BoA	59.74	1.9	3	77	27
▶	**SPELL/NOTE** Frost Resist +10							
55	Serpentine Skuller	60	BoA	59.64	1.4	3	60	56
▶	**SPELL/NOTE** Shadow Resist +10							
57	Bonecreeper Stylus	62	BoA	62.63	1.9	3	93	04
▶	**SPELL/NOTE** Increase spell Dmg 5							

GOOD WANDS

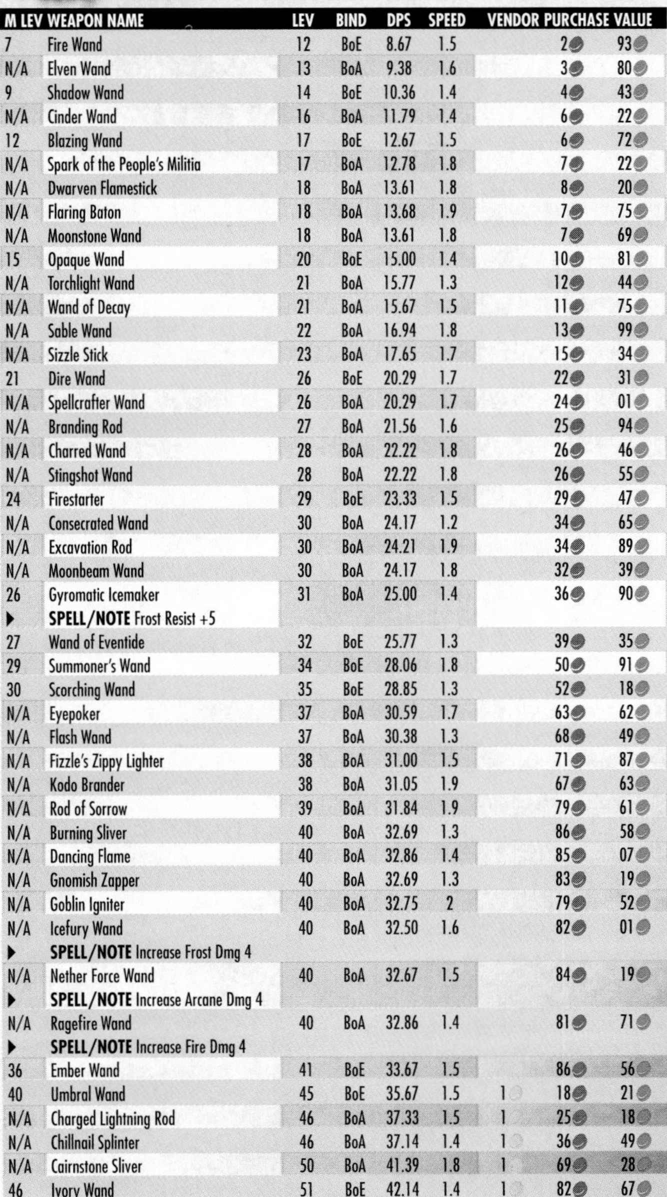

M LEV	WEAPON NAME	LEV	BIND	DPS	SPEED	VENDOR PURCHASE VALUE		
7	Fire Wand	12	BoE	8.67	1.5		2	93
N/A	Elven Wand	13	BoA	9.38	1.6		3	80
9	Shadow Wand	14	BoE	10.36	1.4		4	43
N/A	Cinder Wand	16	BoA	11.79	1.4		6	22
12	Blazing Wand	17	BoE	12.67	1.5		6	72
N/A	Spark of the People's Militia	17	BoA	12.78	1.8		7	22
N/A	Dwarven Flamestick	18	BoA	13.61	1.8		8	20
N/A	Flaring Baton	18	BoA	13.68	1.9		7	75
N/A	Moonstone Wand	18	BoA	13.61	1.8		7	69
15	Opaque Wand	20	BoE	15.00	1.4		10	81
N/A	Torchlight Wand	21	BoA	15.77	1.3		12	44
N/A	Wand of Decay	21	BoA	15.67	1.5		11	75
N/A	Sable Wand	22	BoA	16.94	1.8		13	99
N/A	Sizzle Stick	23	BoA	17.65	1.7		15	34
21	Dire Wand	26	BoE	20.29	1.7		22	31
N/A	Spellcrafter Wand	26	BoA	20.29	1.7		24	01
N/A	Branding Rod	27	BoA	21.56	1.6		25	94
N/A	Charred Wand	28	BoA	22.22	1.8		26	46
N/A	Stingshot Wand	28	BoA	22.22	1.8		26	55
24	Firestarter	29	BoE	23.33	1.5		29	47
N/A	Consecrated Wand	30	BoA	24.17	1.2		34	65
N/A	Excavation Rod	30	BoA	24.21	1.9		34	89
N/A	Moonbeam Wand	30	BoA	24.17	1.8		32	39
26	Gyromatic Icemaker	31	BoA	25.00	1.4		36	90
▶	**SPELL/NOTE** Frost Resist +5							
27	Wand of Eventide	32	BoE	25.77	1.3		39	35
29	Summoner's Wand	34	BoE	28.06	1.8		50	91
30	Scorching Wand	35	BoE	28.85	1.3		52	18
N/A	Eyepoker	37	BoA	30.59	1.7		63	62
N/A	Flash Wand	37	BoA	30.38	1.3		68	49
N/A	Fizzle's Zippy Lighter	38	BoA	31.00	1.5		71	87
N/A	Kodo Brander	38	BoA	31.05	1.9		67	63
N/A	Rod of Sorrow	39	BoA	31.84	1.9		79	61
N/A	Burning Sliver	40	BoA	32.69	1.3		86	58
N/A	Dancing Flame	40	BoA	32.86	1.4		85	07
N/A	Gnomish Zapper	40	BoA	32.69	1.3		83	19
N/A	Goblin Igniter	40	BoA	32.75	2		79	52
N/A	Icefury Wand	40	BoA	32.50	1.6		82	01
▶	**SPELL/NOTE** Increase Frost Dmg 4							
N/A	Nether Force Wand	40	BoA	32.67	1.5		84	19
▶	**SPELL/NOTE** Increase Arcane Dmg 4							
N/A	Ragefire Wand	40	BoA	32.86	1.4		81	71
▶	**SPELL/NOTE** Increase Fire Dmg 4							
36	Ember Wand	41	BoE	33.67	1.5		86	56
40	Umbral Wand	45	BoE	35.67	1.5	1	18	21
N/A	Charged Lightning Rod	46	BoA	37.33	1.5	1	25	18
N/A	Chillnail Splinter	46	BoA	37.14	1.4	1	36	49
N/A	Cairnstone Sliver	50	BoA	41.39	1.8	1	69	28
46	Ivory Wand	51	BoE	42.14	1.4	1	82	67
48	Wizard's Hand	53	BoE	44.44	1.8	2	06	03
52	Glowstar Rod	57	BoE	50.00	1.5	2	61	10
55	Dragon Finger	60	BoE	53.21	1.4	3	06	28
59	Lunar Wand	64	BoE	56.76	1.7	3	73	65

STANDARD WANDS

M LEV	WEAPON NAME	LEV	BIND	DPS	SPEED	VENDOR PURCHASE VALUE		
5	Lesser Magic Wand	10	None	5.67	1.5		1	04
13	Greater Magic Wand	18	None	11.94	1.8		4	65
15	Smoldering Wand	20	None	13.44	1.6		6	68
16	Gloom Wand	21	None	14.44	1.8		7	70
18	Charred Razormane Wand	23	BoA	15.67	1.5		2	40
20	Burning Wand	25	None	17.50	1.4		11	61
20	Dusk Wand	25	None	17.65	1.7		11	66
26	Lesser Mystic Wand	31	None	23.08	1.3		21	48
29	Combustible Wand	34	None	25.94	1.6		28	78
30	Greater Mystic Wand	35	None	27.25	2		31	57
30	Pestilent Wand	35	None	27.00	1.5		31	42
40	Pitchwood Wand	45	None	34.71	1.7		71	45
41	Blackbone Wand	46	None	35.31	1.6		77	46

OFF-HAND ITEMS

EPIC OFF-HAND ITEMS

M LEV	ARMOR NAME	LEV	BIND	AC	VENDOR PURCHASE VALUE		
58	Book of the Dead	63	BoA	0	1	04	52
▶	Spell Summon Skeleton						

SUPERIOR OFF-HAND ITEMS

M LEV	ARMOR NAME	LEV	BIND	AC	VENDOR PURCHASE VALUE		
23	Orb of Mistmantle	28	BoE	0		14	01
▶	**SPELL** Increase Healing 8						
15	Pulsating Hydra Heart	20	BoE	0		15	75
▶	**SPELL** Increase Fire Dmg 4						
30	Rod of Molten Fire	35	BoE	0		31	13
▶	**SPELL** Increase Fire Dmg 8, Fire Resist +6						
17	Antipodean Rod	22	BoE	0		31	21
▶	**SPELL** Increase Fire Dmg 3						
N/A	Prophetic Cane	44	BoA	0		48	85
N/A	Orb of Noh'Orahil	40	BoA	0		50	00
▶	**SPELL** Increase Fire Dmg 8						
N/A	Orb of Dar'Orahil	40	BoA	0		50	00
▶	Spell Increase Shadow Dmg 8						
N/A	Celestial Orb	40	BoA	0		53	82
▶	**SPELL** Increase Arcane Dmg 5						
33	Swampchill Fetish	38	BoE	0		54	68
▶	Spell Increase Frost Dmg 7, Frost & Shadow Resist +5						
33	Orb of the Forgotten Seer	38	BoA	0		54	68
▶	**SPELL** Increase Spell Dmg 6						
54	Lapidis Tankard of Tidesippe	59	BoE	0		55	37
▶	Spell Restores 1992 MP Over 30 sec (Drink)						
38	Umbral Crystal	43	BoE	0		56	13
▶	**SPELL** Increase Shadow Dmg 10						
36	Mordresh's Lifeless Skull	41	BoA	0		78	35
33	Beacon of Hope	38	BoE	0		78	82
▶	**SPELL** Increase Healing 20						
N/A	Orb of Lorica	44	BoA	0		81	42
42	Desertwalker Cane	47	BoA	0		84	09
49	Drakestone	54	BoA	0		89	82
▶	Spell Increase Spell Dmg 4						
48	Enthralled Sphere	53	BoA	0	1	04	52
54	Globe of D'sak	59	BoA	0	1	04	52
▶	Spell Shadow Resist +7						
57	Skull of Burning Shadows	62	BoA	0	1	24	58
▶	**SPELL** Fire Resist +15, Shadow Resist +10						
46	Basilisk Rod	51	BoE	0	1	31	13
▶	Spell Arcane, Fire, Frost, Nature & Shadow Resist +6						
53	Magmus Stone	58	BoA	0	1	31	62
▶	**SPELL** Fire Resist +15						
56	Tome of Knowledge	61	BoA	0	1	32	37
N/A	Penelope's Rose	61	BoA	0	1	46	62
N/A	Magebane Scion	60	BoA	0	1	53	35
▶	Spell Arcane, Fire & Frost Resist +10						
55	Thaurissan's Royal Scepter	60	BoA	0	2	20	45

GOOD OFF-HAND ITEMS

M LEV	ARMOR NAME	LEV	BIND	AC	VENDOR PURCHASE VALUE		
4	Beaded Orb	9	BoE	0		72	15
4	Journeyman's Stave	9	BoE	0		8	02
N/A	Arcane Orb	10	BoA	0		4	00
▶	**SPELL** Use: Restores 80-240 MP						
N/A	Ley Orb	10	BoA	0		4	00
▶	**SPELL** Use: Restores 80-240 MP						
7	Ancestral Orb	12	BoE	0		8	02
7	Disciple's Stein	12	BoE	0		5	27
10	Jester's Orb	15	BoE	0		5	27
10	Native Branch	15	BoE	0		72	15
N/A	Veildust Medicine Bag	15	BoA	0		5	62
▶	**SPELL** Mana Rejuvenation						
N/A	Tear of Grief	16	BoA	0		4	52
12	Magister's Orb	17	BoE	0		8	02
12	Runic Cane	17	BoE	0		6	66
N/A	Nightglow Concoction	18	BoA	0		6	07
13	Runic Stave	18	BoE	0		8	02
14	Eerie Stable Lantern	19	BoA	0		6	66

GOOD OFF-HAND ITEMS continued

M LEV	ARMOR NAME	LEV	BIND	AC	VENDOR PURCHASE VALUE		
N/A	Tork Wrench	19	BoA	30		7	82
14	Willow Branch	19	BoE	0		5	27
15	Aboriginal Rod	20	BoE	0		72	15
N/A	Jadefinger Baton	20	BoA	0		8	57
N/A	Grayson's Torch	21	BoA	15		9	68
16	Seer's Fine Stein	21	BoE	0		8	02
18	Buccaneer's Orb	23	BoE	0		5	27
18	Mystic's Sphere	23	BoE	0		8	02
19	Ritual Stein	24	BoE	0		72	15
N/A	Everglow Lantern	25	BoA	0		16	32
▶	**SPELL** Use: Heal 135-165 HP for Target						
N/A	Orb of Soran'ruk	25	BoA	0		41	32
▶	**SPELL** Increase Fire Dmg 3						
20	Shimmering Stave	25	BoE	0		20	27
N/A	Totem of Infliction	25	BoA	50		11	36
▶	**SPELL** Deals 75-125 Dmg Attacker (1% Chance)						
21	Orb of Power	26	BoE	0		20	00
21	Pagan Rod	26	BoE	0		72	15
22	Druidic Stave	27	BoE	0		5	27
22	Sunfire Sphere	27	BoE	0		8	02
23	Fireproof Orb	28	BoE	0		20	00
▶	**SPELL** Fire Resist +6						
23	Sanguine Star	28	BoE	0		8	02
24	Enchantress Orb	29	BoE	0		20	27
25	Strength of Will	30	BoE	0		20	00
25	Watcher's Star	30	BoE	0		72	15
26	Cursed Eye of Paleth	31	BoA	0			0
▶	**SPELL** Increase Shadow Dmg 6						
N/A	Eye of Paleth	31	BoA	0		5	37
▶	**SPELL** Increase Healing 12						
26	Raincaller Scepter	31	BoE	0		72	15
26	Silver-thread Rod	31	BoE	0		8	02
27	Sage's Stave	32	BoE	0		5	27
28	Satyr's Rod	33	BoE	0		8	02
N/A	Torch of Holy Flame	33	BoA	0		50	00
▶	**SPELL** Use: Decreases Target Armor by 50 for 1 Minute						
29	Siren's Rod	34	BoE	0		5	27
30	Elder's Amber Stave	35	BoE	0		72	15
31	Thistlefur Branch	36	BoE	0		72	15
32	Dryad's Stave	37	BoE	0		72	15
32	Stormcloud Orb	37	BoE	0		8	02
33	Conjurer's Sphere	38	BoE	0		72	15
34	Stonecloth Branch	39	BoE	0		8	02
35	Twilight Orb	40	BoE	0		75	57
36	Aurora Sphere	41	BoE	0		79	22
36	Geomancer's Rod	41	BoE	0		72	15
N/A	Omega Orb	41	BoA	0		48	85
▶	Spell Increase Spell Dmg 5						
N/A	Skull of Impending Doom	41	BoA	0		56	30
▶	**SPELL** Use: Increases Run Speed 60% but deals HP/MP Damage for 10 sec						
37	Embersilk Stave	42	BoE	0		72	15
N/A	Explorer's League Lodestar	42	BoA	0		25	42
N/A	Uthek's Finger	42	BoA	0		28	85
38	Sorcerer Sphere	43	BoE	0		75	57
N/A	Tranquil Orb	43	BoA	0		31	42
39	Silksand Star	44	BoE	0		79	22
N/A	Jademoon Orb	45	BoA	0		71	35
40	Regal Star	45	BoE	0		75	57
41	Darkmist Orb	46	BoE	0		72	15
41	Mistscape Stave	46	BoE	0		49	92
42	Lord Sakrasis' Scepter	47	BoE	0		55	37
42	Lunar Sphere	47	BoE	0		72	15
43	Royal Scepter	48	BoE	0		75	57
44	Windchaser Orb	49	BoE	0		49	92
45	Gossamer Rod	50	BoE	0		52	87
46	Bloodwoven Rod	51	BoE	0		72	15
46	Hibernal Sphere	51	BoE	0		79	22
N/A	Thermotastic Egg Timer	51	BoA	0		98	85
47	Gaea's Scepter	52	BoE	0		72	15
N/A	Skullspell Orb	52	BoA	0		89	82
48	Illusionary Orb	53	BoE	0		52	87
N/A	Oblivion Orb	54	BoA	0	1	02	87
49	Venomshroud Stein	54	BoE	0		79	22

GOOD OFF-HAND ITEMS continued

M LEV	ARMOR NAME	LEV	BIND	AC	VENDOR PURCHASE VALUE		
50	Duskwoven Branch	55	BoE	0		5	27
N/A	Pyrestone Orb	55	BoA	0	1	09	53
51	High Arcane Scepter	56	BoE	0		8	02
51	Necrotic Orb	56	BoE	0		72	15
N/A	Spirit of Aquementas	56	BoA	0	1	38	15
▶	**SPELL** Decreases MP Cost of Spells by 25						
52	Arachnidian Branch	57	BoE	0		72	15
51	High Arcane Scepter	56	BoE	0		8	02
51	Necrotic Orb	56	BoE	0		72	15
N/A	Spirit of Aquementas	56	BoA	0	1	38	15
▶	**SPELL** Decreases MP Cost of Spells by 25						
52	Arachnidian Branch	57	BoE	0		72	15
N/A	Father Flame	58	None	0		66	57
▶	**SPELL** Fire Resist +10						
53	Mystical Orb	58	BoE	0		5	27
54	Fay Star	59	BoE	0		5	27
54	Highborne Star	59	BoE	0		8	02
55	Bonecaster's Star	60	BoE	0		72	15
56	Celestial Orb	61	BoE	0		72	15
56	Zephyr Star	61	BoE	0		8	02
57	Nova Scepter	62	BoE	0		5	27
58	Demonskin Stave	63	BoE	0		72	15
59	Elunarian Sphere	64	BoE	0		8	02
59	Empyreal Stave	64	BoE	0		5	27
60	Eternal Rod	65	BoE	0		72	15
60	Lich's Rod	65	BoE	0		5	27

STANDARD OFF-HAND ITEMS

M LEV	ARMOR NAME	LEV	BIND	AC	VENDOR PURCHASE VALUE			
N/A	Silver Totem of Aquementas	0	Quest	0				0
▶	**SPELL** Dispel's Blazerunner's Aura (Quest)							
N/A	Smoky Torch	1	None	0				1
N/A	Blue Sparkler	10	None	0			2	50
5	Dim Torch	10	None	0				0
▶	**SPELL** Adds 4 Spirit to Group Members							
N/A	Red Sparkler	10	None	0			2	50
N/A	Simple Wildflowers	10	None	0				50
N/A	White Sparkler	10	None	0			2	50
N/A	Red Rose	20	None	0			1	25
N/A	Bouquet of Scarlet Begonias	23	None	0			5	75
N/A	Lesser Firestone	28	BoA	0				0
▶	**SPELL** Adds a 25-35 Fire Proc to a Weapon							
N/A	Beautiful Wildflowers	30	None	0			5	00
25	Stiches' Femur	30	BoA	50			6	25
N/A	Morbent's Bane	33	BoA	0				0
▶	**SPELL** Removes Enchantment's from Morbent Fel (Quest)							
N/A	Firestone	36	BoA	0				0
▶	**SPELL** Adds a 40-60 Fire Proc to a Weapon							
31	Spellstone	36	BoA	0				0
▶	**SPELL** Use: Absorbs 400 Magic Dmg for 1 min							
N/A	Black Rose	40	None	0			12	50
N/A	Greater Firestone	46	BoA	0				0
▶	**SPELL** Adds a 60-90 Fire Proc to a Weapon							
43	Greater SPELLstone	48	BoA	0				0
▶	**SPELL** Use: Absorbs 650 Magic Dmg for 1 min							
N/A	Bouquet of White Roses	50	None	0			50	00
N/A	Major Firestone	56	BoA	0				0
▶	**SPELL** Adds an 80-120 Fire Proc to a Weapon							
N/A	Bouquet of Black Roses	60	None	0	12		50	00
55	Major Spellstone	60	BoA	0				0
▶	**SPELL** Use: Absorbs 900 Magic Dmg for 1 min							

NECKLACES

EPIC NECKLACES

M LEV	ARMOR NAME	LEV	BIND	AC	VENDOR PURCHASE VALUE		
46	Lei of Lilies	51	BoE	0	1	30	00
▶	**SPELL** Conjures Lily Roots (that Restore HP/MP)						
55	Jeweled Amulet of Cainwyn	60	BoE	0	2	11	25
59	Lady Maye's Pendant	64	BoE	0	1	05	00

SUPERIOR NECKLACES

M LEV	ARMOR NAME	LEV	BIND	AC	VENDOR PURCHASE VALUE		
27	Stygian Bone Amulet	32	BoA	0		30	02
28	River Pride Choker	33	BoE	0		58	96
30	Ghostshard Talisman	35	BoA	0		34	82
30	Kaleidoscope Chain	35	BoE	0		66	14
36	Gazlowe's Charm	41	BoE	0		74	13
36	Glowing Eye of Mordresh	41	BoA	0		52	77
38	Necklace of Calisea	43	BoE	0		25	35
N/A	Dragon's Blood Necklace	44	BoA	0		83	77
39	Triune Amulet	44	BoA	0		92	95
N/A	Jarkal's Enhancing Necklace	47	BoA	0		89	90
N/A	Talvash's Enhancing Necklace	47	BoA	0		89	90
43	Lifeblood Amulet	48	BoA	0	1	30	41
44	Skibi's Pendent	49	BoE	0		80	39
46	Horizon Choker	51	BoE	0		91	37
51	Dragon's Eye	56	BoA	0	1	06	80
51	Verek's Collar	56	BoA	0	1	46	27
▶	**SPELL** Add 1% Dodge						
52	Medallion of Grand Marshal Morris	57	BoE	0	1	06	37
▶	**SPELL** Add 15 Defense						
N/A	Conqueror's Medallion	58	BoA	0	1	23	77
54	Lady Alizabeth's Pendant	59	BoE	0	1	46	17
N/A	Archlight Talisman	60	BoA	0		87	88
55	Imperial Jewel	60	BoA	0	1	96	46
▶	**SPELL** Attack Power 32						
56	Emberfury Talisman	61	BoA	0	1	96	46
▶	**SPELL** Fire Resist +7, Add 1% Crit						
56	Heart of the Fiend	61	BoA	0	1	28	28
N/A	Mark of Fordring	63	BoA	0	1	02	83
▶	**SPELL** Add 1% Crit						
58	Star of Mystaria	63	BoA	0	1	21	57
58	Tooth of Gnarr	63	BoA	0	1	20	93

GOOD NECKLACES continued

M LEV	ARMOR NAME	LEV	BIND	AC	VENDOR PURCHASE VALUE	
25	Glowing Green Talisman	30	BoE	0	15	35
25	Spectral Necklace	30	BoE	0	49	96
26	Crystal Starfire Medallion	31	BoE	0	17	13
26	Gnomeregan Amulet	31	BoA	0	37	78
26	Wolfpack Medallion	31	BoE	0	25	38
27	Basalt Necklace	32	BoE	0	40	07
27	Cerulean Talisman	32	BoE	0	42	20
28	Tundra Necklace	33	BoE	0	42	24
29	Necklace of Harmony	34	BoE	0	27	77
30	Embersparck Pendant	35	BoE	0	18	40
30	Greenstone Talisman	35	BoE	0	53	95
30	Mark of the Kirin Tor	35	BoE	0	18	06
30	Pendant of Myzrael	35	BoA	0		0
31	Thallium Choker	36	BoE	0	39	69
33	Forest Pendent	38	BoE	0	41	64
34	Jet Chain	39	BoE	0	71	43
N/A	Explorers' League Commendation	41	BoA	0	84	30
36	Iridium Chain	41	BoE	0	47	18
N/A	Kodobone Necklace	41	BoA	0	49	12
37	Marsh Chain	42	BoE	0	47	49
N/A	Ethereal Talisman	43	BoA	0	43	07
N/A	Choker of the High Shaman	44	BoA	0	41	82
39	Lodestone Necklace	44	BoE	0	78	94
N/A	Amberglow Talisman	45	BoA	0	59	30
N/A	Medal of Courage	45	BoA	0	81	55
40	Shriveled Heart	45	BoA	0		0
40	Tellurium Necklace	45	BoE	0	49	71
42	Desert Choker	47	BoE	0	53	96
42	Entwined Opaline Talisman	47	BoE	0	71	45
42	Fairy's Embrace	47	BoE	0	64	20
42	Talisman of the Naga Lord	47	BoE	0	52	82
42	Warrior's Honor	47	BoE	0	76	45
43	Onyx Choker	48	BoE	0	53	96
N/A	Pulsating Crystalline Shard	50	BoA	0	54	30
45	Vanadium Talisman	50	BoE	0	53	96
46	Arctic Pendent	51	BoE	0	51	45
47	Fire Opal Necklace	52	BoA	0	79	12
48	Marble Necklace	53	BoE	0	50	12

GOOD NECKLACES continued

M LEV	ARMOR NAME	LEV	BIND	AC	VENDOR PURCHASE VALUE		
N/A	Felstone Good Luck Charm	54	BoA	0		71	64
▶	**SPELL** Shadow Resist +13						
49	Selenium Chain	54	BoE	0		52	82
51	Swamp Pendent	56	BoE	0		77	67
N/A	Mindburst Medallion	57	BoA	0	1	68	75
52	Obsidian Pendent	57	BoE	0		55	13
N/A	Heroic Commendation Medal	58	BoA	0		71	08
N/A	Voice Amplification Modulator	58	BoE	0		59	30
▶	**SPELL** Resist Silence						
54	Quicksilver Pendent	59	BoE	0		77	57
55	Halycon's Spiked Collar	60	BoA	0	1	06	70
▶	**SPELL** Adds 45 Attack Power Vs. Beasts						
N/A	Hunter's Insignia Medal	60	BoA	0		61	45
55	Jungle Necklace	60	BoE	0		57	57
N/A	Necklace of Sanctuary	60	BoA	0	1	69	30
▶	**SPELL** Fire & Shadow Resist +10						
55	Talisman of Evasion	60	BoA	0	1	63	96
▶	**SPELL** Add 1% Dodge						
57	Granite Necklace	62	BoE	0		59	82
58	Vermilion Necklace	63	BoE	0		62	57
60	Prismatic Pendent	65	BoE	0		65	07

INFERIOR NECKLACES

M LEV	ARMOR NAME	LEV	BIND	AC	VENDOR PURCHASE VALUE		
N/A	Tarnished Silver Necklace	1	None	0			73

RINGS

EPIC RINGS

M LEV	ARMOR NAME	LEV	BIND	AC	VENDOR PURCHASE VALUE		
38	Underworld Band	43	BoE	0		62	00
▶	**SPELL** Increase Shadow Dmg 8						
41	Ring of Saviors	46	BoE	0	2	27	75
▶	**SPELL** Use: AoE Taunt, but 50% Dmg Increase for Enemies						
47	Freezing Band	52	BoE	0		45	00
▶	**SPELL** Increase Frost Dmg 13, Frost Resist +10						
53	Myrmidon's Signet	58	BoE	0	3	00	00
56	Mark of the Dragon Lord	61	BoA	0	2	13	72
▶	**SPELL** Use: Raises 500 Point Shield; Buffs MP Regen by 22						

SUPERIOR RINGS

M LEV	ARMOR NAME	LEV	BIND	AC	VENDOR PURCHASE VALUE		
17	Black Pearl Ring	22	BoE	0		11	53
17	Lavishly Jeweled Ring	22	BoA	0		8	12
17	Ring of Defense	22	BoE	20		11	53
▶	**SPELL** Adds 6 Defense						
18	Band of Purification	23	BoE	0		15	27
20	Ring of Precision	25	BoE	0		22	07
21	Deep Fathom Ring	26	BoA	0		15	27
21	Silverlaine's Family Seal	26	BoA	0		16	50
N/A	Sergeant's Insignia	28	BoA	0			0
24	Plains Ring	29	BoE	0		7	50
N/A	Seal of Sylvanas	29	BoA	0		20	55
24	Thunderbrow Ring	29	BoE	0		21	64
25	The Queen's Jewel	30	BoE	0		26	46
29	Electrocutioner Lagnut	34	BoA	0		32	37
30	Ironspine's Eye	35	BoA	0		43	08
31	Agamaggan's Clutch	36	BoA	0		18	16
31	Mark of Kern	36	BoE	0		87	46
▶	**SPELL** Increases Party Attack Power by 10						
31	Ring of the Underwood	36	BoE	0		6	56
32	Blush Ember Ring	37	BoE	0		33	81
32	Charged Gear	37	BoA	0		45	86
▶	**SPELL** Arcane & Nature Resist +5						
N/A	Dragonclaw Ring	38	BoA	0		61	30
39	Assault Band	44	BoE	0		66	46
▶	**SPELL** Attack Power 20						
41	Mindseye Circle	46	BoE	0	1	08	12
42	Archaedic Stone	47	BoA	50	1	07	95
N/A	Masons Fraternity Ring	47	BoA	0		70	92
43	Brainlash	48	BoE	0	1	58	12
45	Runed Ring	50	BoE	0	3	82	22
▶	**SPELL** Increase Spell Dmg 4						
48	Eye of Adaegus	53	BoE	0	1	11	57
49	Cyclopean Band	54	BoA	0	1	36	57
49	Drakeclaw Band	54	BoA	0		55	42
▶	**SPELL** Adds 6 Defense						

SUPERIOR RINGS continued

M LEV	ARMOR NAME	LEV	BIND	AC	VENDOR PURCHASE VALUE		
54	Naglering	59	BoA	0	1	71	57
▶	**SPELL** Arcane Resist +10, Adds 1% Hit, 3 Dmg Dealt to Attackers						
55	Band of Flesh	60	BoA	0	1	48	46
55	Band of the Heirophant	60	BoE	0		79	13
N/A	Eye of Orgrimmar	60	BoA	0		70	82
▶	**SPELL** Increase Spell Dmg 9						
N/A	Magni's Willl	60	BoA	0		71	02
▶	**SPELL** Add 1% Crit						
N/A	Ring of Protection	60	BoA	150		78	88
▶	**SPELL** Increased Armor 150						
55	Rosewine Circle	60	BoA	0	1	37	82
N/A	Songstone of Ironforge	60	BoA	0		71	56
▶	**SPELL** Increase Spell Dmg 9						
N/A	Thrall's Resolve	60	BoA	0		74	07
▶	**SPELL** Increased Armor 150						
55	Emperor's Seal	61	BoA	0	1	99	21
▶	**SPELL** Arcane & Frost Resist +6						
55	Maiden's Circle	61	BoE	0	1	06	48
▶	**SPELL** Increase Spell Dmg 9						
N/A	Seal of Ascension	61	BoA	0			0
▶	**SPELL** Fire, Frost & Nature Resist +10, Quest Item						
56	The Postmaster's Seal	61	BoA	0	1	22	11
N/A	Fordring's Seal	63	BoA	0	1	01	56
▶	**SPELL** Increase Healing 34						
58	Painweaver Band	63	BoA	0	1	52	82
▶	**SPELL** Adds 1% Crit, 16 Attack Power						
58	Seal of Rivendare	63	BoA	0	1	54	57

GOOD RINGS

M LEV	ARMOR NAME	LEV	BIND	AC	VENDOR PURCHASE VALUE		
10	The 1 Ring	15	BoE	0		11	30
N/A	Bounty Hunter's Ring	20	BoA	0		4	03
15	Lead Band	20	BoE	0		4	96
15	Overseer's Ring	20	BoE	0		6	25
15	Quartz Ring	20	BoE	0		4	64
N/A	Ring of Scorn	20	BoA	0		4	12
16	Ring of the Moon	21	BoE	0		8	37
16	Volcanic Rock Ring	21	BoE	0		8	37
17	Clay Ring	22	BoE	0		8	74
N/A	Clergy Ring	22	BoA	0		5	56
17	Meadow Ring	22	BoE	0		10	64
18	Viridian Band	23	BoE	0		10	62
18	Zircon Band	23	BoE	0		10	87
19	Black Widow Band	24	BoE	0		6	50
19	Blood Ring	24	BoE	0		8	37

GOOD RINGS continued

M LEV	ARMOR NAME	LEV	BIND	AC	VENDOR PURCHASE VALUE		
19	Demon Band	24	BoE	0		8	37
N/A	Minor Channeling Ring	24	BoA	0		18	75
20	Coral Band	25	BoE	0		13	12
20	Defias Renegade Ring	25	BoE	0		6	50
20	Prairie Ring	25	BoE	0		10	64
N/A	Ring of Iron Will	25	BoA	0		4	62
20	Ring of the Shadow	25	BoE	0		13	06
▶	**SPELL** Shadow Resist +5						
N/A	Sacred Band	25	BoA	0		13	78
N/A	Skull Ring	25	BoA	0		12	50
N/A	Sustaining Ring	25	BoA	0		14	62
N/A	Totemic Clan Ring	25	BoA	0		6	50
21	Amber Hoop	26	BoE	0		9	97
21	Chrome Ring	26	BoE	0		11	30
21	Defias Mage Ring	26	BoE	0			25
22	Azora's Will	27	BoE	0		10	52
22	Heart Ring	27	BoE	0		10	38
N/A	Band of Elven Grace	28	BoA	0		6	77
23	Ivory Band	28	BoE	0		9	14
23	Savannah Ring	28	BoE	0		8	95
24	Cobalt Ring	29	BoE	0		21	89
24	Jacinth Circle	29	BoE	0		17	21
25	Gnomeregan Band	30	BoA	0		12	43
26	Band of Thorns	31	BoE	0		16	32
N/A	Brilliant Gold Ring	31	BoA	0			0
N/A	Inventor's League Ring	31	BoA	0		86	30
N/A	Ironforge Memorial Ring	31	BoA	0		8	82
N/A	Monkey Ring	31	BoA	0		8	97
N/A	Ring of Pure Silver	31	BoA	0		12	50
N/A	Seal of Wrynn	31	BoA	0		37	50
N/A	Snake Hoop	31	BoA	0		8	97
N/A	Tiger Band	31	BoA	0		8	97
N/A	Band of the Undercity	32	BoA	0		15	00
N/A	Ring of Calm	32	BoA	0		15	40
N/A	Tranquil Ring	33	BoA	0		6	65
28	Tundra Ring	33	BoE	0		21	74
29	Basalt Ring	34	BoE	0		17	13
29	Spinel Ring	34	BoE	0		17	10
N/A	Bloodbone Band	35	BoA	0		11	30
30	Cerulean Ring	35	BoE	0		21	44
N/A	Nogg's Gold Ring	35	BoA	0		64	63
N/A	Reedknot Ring	35	BoA	0		56	65
N/A	Ring of Forlorn Spirits	35	BoA	0		15	00
N/A	Talvash's Gold Ring	35	BoA	0		64	63
N/A	Trader's Ring	35	BoA	0		40	40
31	Mindbender Loop	36	BoE	0		16	96
31	Ogremind Ring	36	BoE	0		21	00
32	Amethyst Band	37	BoE	0		39	69
32	Fen Ring	37	BoE	0		24	69
32	Voodoo Band	37	BoE	0		17	20
33	Greenstone Circle	38	BoE	0		64	69
N/A	Jaina's Signet Ring	38	BoA	0		46	30
34	Thallium Hoop	39	BoE	0		17	45
35	Carnelian Loop	40	BoE	0		46	49
35	Inscribed Gold Ring	40	BoE	0		18	03
35	Prismstone Ring	40	BoE	0		18	03
35	Welken Ring	40	BoE	0		19	12
36	Forest Hoop	41	BoE	0		46	49
37	Jet Loop	42	BoE	0		28	96
38	Hematite Link	43	BoE	0		39	71
38	Iridium Circle	43	BoE	0		28	85
39	Falcon's Hook	44	BoE	0		25	42
40	Marsh Ring	45	BoE	0		24	63
41	Aquamarine Ring	46	BoE	0		49	71
N/A	Coldwater Ring	46	BoA	0		20	92
41	Lodestone Hoop	46	BoE	0		55	38
N/A	Seafire Band	46	BoA	0		20	92
42	Tellurium Band	47	BoE	0		71	13
43	Band of the Unicorn	48	BoE	0		25	42
▶	**SPELL** Increase Spell Dmg 6						
44	Desert Ring	49	BoE	0		46	49
44	Topaz Ring	49	BoE	0		47	39
N/A	Band of the Great Tortoise	50	BoA	120		20	92
N/A	Burning Obsidian Band	50	BoA	0		36	57
45	Onyx Ring	50	BoE	0		49	71
N/A	Seedtime Hoop	50	BoA	0		70	92
46	Vanadium Loop	51	BoE	0		74	71

GOOD RINGS continued

M LEV	ARMOR NAME	LEV	BIND	AC	VENDOR PURCHASE VALUE		
47	Sardonyx Knuckle	52	BoE	0		77	78
47	Stardust Band	52	BoE	0		83	75
N/A	White Bone Band	52	BoA	0		70	42
▶	**SPELL** Attack Power 24						
48	Arctic Ring	53	BoE	0		62	89
N/A	Choking Band	53	BoA	0		65	42
48	Dark Iron Ring	53	BoA	0		65	92
N/A	Ring of Fortitude	53	BoA	0		52	92
N/A	Sha'ni's Ring	53	BoA	0		65	42
49	Marble Circle	54	BoE	0		63	22
N/A	Ring of the Aristocrat	54	BoA	0		90	42
N/A	Chemist's Ring	55	BoA	0		73	96
N/A	Dalson Family Wedding Ring	55	BoA	0		81	09
N/A	Mark of Hakkar	55	BoA	0		55	42
50	Selenium Loop	55	BoE	0		83	06
50	Serpentine Loop	55	BoE	0		78	96
51	Ring of the Heavens	56	BoE	0		83	75
52	Swamp Ring	57	BoE	0		88	11
53	Jasper Link	58	BoE	0		74	14
53	Obsidian Band	58	BoE	0		91	63
54	Magus Ring	59	BoA	0	1	49	07
54	Quicksilver Ring	59	BoE	0		63	17
55	Dragonscale Band	60	BoE	0		83	75
N/A	Band of the Penitent	61	BoA	0		88	14
▶	**SPELL** Add 1% Crit						
56	Jungle Ring	61	BoE	0		77	81
56	Perdiot Circle	61	BoE	0		74	71
56	Flaming Band	61	BoA	0	1	49	07
▶	**SPELL** Increase Fire Dmg 13						
57	Granite Ring	62	BoE	0		88	13
58	Vermilion Band	63	BoE	0		73	96
59	Demonic Bone Ring	64	BoE	0		83	76
59	Opal Ring	64	BoE	0	1	05	39
60	Prismatic Band	65	BoE	0		89	63
N/A	Lagrave's Seal	54	BoA	0		90	92

STANDARD RINGS

M LEV	ARMOR NAME	LEV	BIND	AC	VENDOR PURCHASE VALUE		
N/A	Mood Ring	10	None	0		25	00
N/A	Cubic Zirconia Ring	20	None	0	1	25	00
N/A	Silver Piffeny Band	30	None	0	2	50	00
N/A	Miniscule Diamond Ring	40	None	0	6	25	00
N/A	Flawless Diamond Solitaire	50	None	0	12	50	00
N/A	The Rock	60	None	0	25	00	00

TRINKETS

EPIC TRINKETS

M LEV	ARMOR NAME	LEV	BIND	AC	VENDOR PURCHASE VALUE
51	Lifestone	56	BoE	0	2 80 00
▶	**SPELL** Heals 10 HP/5 sec, On Use: Heals 300-700 HP				
58	The Lion Horn of Stormwind	63	BoE	0	1 78 80
▶	**SPELL** The Lion Horn of Stormwind				

SUPERIOR RINGS

M LEV	ARMOR NAME	LEV	BIND	AC	VENDOR PURCHASE VALUE
38	Blazing Emblem	43	BoE	0	16 25
▶	**SPELL** Fire Resist +15, On Use: Adds 50 Fire Resist and -25 to Fire Damage				
40	Ankh of Life	45	BoE	0	53 50
▶	**SPELL** On Use: Heals Target for 135-165 HP				
46	Six Demon Bag	51	BoE	0	1 54 95
▶	**SPELL** On Use: Attacks Enemies with Elemental Magic				
47	Uther's Strength	52	BoA	0	71 30
▶	**SPELL** On Hit: 2% Chance of Shielding You				
50	Smoking Heart of the Mountain	55	BoA	150	15 00
▶	**SPELL** Fire, Frost, Nature & Shadow Resist +7				
53	Burst of Knowledge	58	BoA	0	1 00 00
▶	**SPELL** Add 6 to Dmg/Healing Spells, On Use: Reduces MP Costs by 100				
53	Hand of Justice	58	BoA	0	1 00 00
▶	**SPELL** Adds 20 Attack Power, On Attack: 2% Chance of Extra Attack				
53	Piccolo of the Flaming Fire	58	BoA	0	1 07 34
54	Orb of Deception	59	BoE	0	46 18
▶	**SPELL** Shift into Form from Enemy Faction				
54	Second Wind	59	BoA	0	1 00 00
▶	**SPELL** Add 20 to Healing, On Use: Restores 300 MP Over 10 sec				
55	Briarwood Reed	60	BoA	0	1 00 00
▶	**SPELL** Increase Spells Dmg 15				
55	Force of Will	60	BoA	0	1 00 00
▶	**SPELL** Adds 10 Defense, On Hit: 1% Chance to Reduce Melee Dmg by 25				
N/A	Ragged John's Neverending Cup	60	BoA	0	81 44
55	Ramstein's Lightning Bolts	60	BoA	0	96 00
▶	**SPELL** On Use: Deals 500 Nature Dmg in an AoE				
55	Smolderweb's Eye	60	BoA	0	96 33
▶	**SPELL** On Use: Poison Target for 5 Dmg Every 2 sec				
56	Cannonball Runner	61	BoA	0	1 08 50
▶	**SPELL** On Use: Summons Cannon Pet				
56	Heart of the Scale	61	BoA	0	1 05 39
▶	**SPELL** On Use: Adds 20 Fire Resistance and Deals 20 Dmg to Attackers				
N/A	Seal of the Dawn	61	BoA	0	96 15
▶	**SPELL** Adds 81 Attack Power Vs. Undead				
N/A	Barov Peasant Caller	62	BoA	0	89 91
▶	**SPELL** On Use: Summons 3 Peasants				

SUPERIOR RINGS continued

M LEV	ARMOR NAME	LEV	BIND	AC	VENDOR PURCHASE VALUE
N/A	Barov Peasant Caller	62	BoA	0	89 91
▶	**SPELL** On Use: Summons 3 Peasants				
N/A	Blackhand's Breadth	63	BoA	0	1 62 50
▶	**SPELL** Add 2% Crit				
N/A	Eye of the Beast	63	BoA	0	1 62 50
▶	**SPELL** Adds 15 Spirit to Group Members				
N/A	Mark of Tyranny	63	BoA	0	1 62 50
▶	**SPELL** Increased Armor 180, Arcane Resist +10, Add 1% Dodge				

GOOD RINGS

M LEV	ARMOR NAME	LEV	BIND	AC	VENDOR PURCHASE VALUE
35	Cold Basilisk Eye	40	BoE	0	46 42
▶	**SPELL** On Use: Slow Target Attack by 5% for 15 sec				
36	Tidal Charm	41	BoA	0	1 03 06
▶	**SPELL** On Use: Stun Target for 3 sec				
N/A	Thunderbrew's Boot Flask	44	BoA	0	1 00 00
▶	**SPELL** On Use: Deals 250 AoE Dmg Over 5 sec				
N/A	Orb of Fire	46	BoA	0	39 87
N/A	Carrot on a Stick	50	BoA	0	71 62
▶	**SPELL** Adds 3% to Mount Speed				
N/A	Guardian Talisman	50	BoA	0	89 10
▶	**SPELL** On Hit: 2% Chance to Add 350 Armor for 15 sec				
N/A	Nifty Stopwatch	50	BoA	0	46 62
▶	**SPELL** On Use: Adds 40% Run Speed for 10 sec				
N/A	Smotts' Compass	50	BoA	0	21 71
▶	**SPELL** Add 1% Dodge				
N/A	Linken's Boomerang	56	BoA	0	62 03
▶	**SPELL** On Use: Deals 113-187 Dmg to Target (Chance to Disarm/Stun)				
N/A	Shard of Afrasa	57	BoA	0	46 62
▶	**SPELL** Adds 5 HP/MP Every 5 sec				
N/A	Chained Essence of Eranikus	60	BoA	0	64 64
▶	**SPELL** On Use: Deals 50 Dmg/5 sec in an AoE for 45 sec				
N/A	Demon's Blood	60	BoA	0	88 07
▶	**SPELL** Adds 5 Defense, 10 Shadow Resist, and Improves HP Regen				
N/A	Prismcharm	60	BoA	0	74 64
N/A	Spectral Essence	60	BoA	0	0
▶	**SPELL** Visions of the Past (Quest)				
N/A	Ward of the Elements	60	BoA	0	79 53
▶	**SPELL** Arcane, Fire, Frost, Nature & Shadow Resist +8				
N/A	Smokey's Lighter	61	BoA	0	70 00
▶	**SPELL** On Use: Deals 125 Fire Dmg to Targets In Front				

SHIRTS

STANDARD SHIRTS

M LEV	ARMOR NAME	LEV	BIND	AC	VENDOR PURCHASE VALUE
N/A	Acolyte's Shirt	1	None		1
N/A	Apprentice's Shirt	1	None		1
N/A	Brawler's Harness	1	None		1
N/A	Deprecated Rogue's Vest	1	None		1
N/A	Deprecated War Harness	1	None		1
N/A	Deprecated Work Shirt	1	None		1
N/A	Footpad's Shirt	1	None		1
N/A	Neophyte's Shirt	1	None		1
N/A	Primitive Mantle	1	None		1
N/A	Primitive Mantle	1	None		1
N/A	Recruit's Shirt	1	None		1
N/A	Recruit's Shirt	1	None		1
N/A	Rugged Trapper's Shirt	1	None		1
N/A	Sawbones Shirt	1	BoA		62 50
N/A	Squire's Shirt	1	None		1
N/A	Squire's Shirt	1	None		1
N/A	Thug Shirt	1	None		1
N/A	Thug Shirt	1	None		1
N/A	Trapper's Shirt	1	None		1
N/A	Tuxedo Shirt	1	None		25
N/A	Tuxedo Shirt	1	None		2 50

STANDARD SHIRTS continued

M LEV	ARMOR NAME	LEV	BIND	AC	VENDOR PURCHASE VALUE
N/A	Brown Linen Shirt	7	None		11
N/A	White Linen Shirt	7	None		75
N/A	Blue Linen Shirt	10	None		75
N/A	Red Linen Shirt	10	None		25
N/A	Deckhand's Shirt	14	None		1 39
N/A	Green Linen Shirt	14	None		37
N/A	Captain Sander's Shirt	15	None		1 37
N/A	Fine Cloth Shirt	17	None		87
N/A	Common Brown Shirt	20	None		1 00
N/A	Common Gray Shirt	20	None		1 00
N/A	Common White Shirt	20	None		1 00
N/A	Gray Woolen Shirt	20	None		2 00
N/A	Stylish Red Shirt	22	None		2 50
N/A	Stylish Blue Shirt	25	None		2 50
N/A	Stylish Green Shirt	25	None		2 50
N/A	Bright Yellow Shirt	27	None		5 00
N/A	Bold Yellow Shirt	30	None		10 00
N/A	Dark Silk Shirt	31	None		12 00
N/A	White Swashbuckler's Shirt	32	None		5 00
N/A	Formal White Shirt	34	None		5 50
N/A	Red Swashbuckler's Shirt	35	None		7 50

STANDARD SHIRTS continued

M LEV	ARMOR NAME	LEV	BIND	AC	VENDOR PURCHASE VALUE
N/A	Rich Purple Silk Shirt	37	None		15 00
N/A	Black Swashbuckler's Shirt	40	None		15 00
N/A	Orange Martial Shirt	40	None		15 00
N/A	Stylish Black Shirt	40	None		15 00
N/A	Orange Mageweave Shirt	43	None		15 00
N/A	Lavender Mageweave Shirt	46	None		15 00
N/A	Pink Mageweave Shirt	47	None		15 00
N/A	Master Builwder's Shirt	55	BoA		71 37

MISCELLANEOUS

SUPERIOR ITEMS

M LEV	ARMOR NAME	LEV	BIND	AC	VENDOR PURCHASE VALUE
56	Polychromatic Visionwrap	61	BoA		2 04 98
▶	**SPELL** Arcane, Fire, Frost, Nature & Shadow Resist +20				

STANDARD ITEMS

M LEV	ARMOR NAME	LEV	BIND	VENDOR PURCHASE VALUE
N/A	Acolyte's Shoes	1	None	1
N/A	Apprentice's Boots	1	None	1
N/A	Black Tuxedo	1	None	1
N/A	Brawler's Boots	1	None	1
N/A	Dress Shoes	1	None	1
N/A	Easter Dress (Robe)	1	None	1
N/A	Footpad's Shoes	1	None	1
N/A	Neophyte's Boots	1	None	1
N/A	Recruit's Boots	1	None	1
N/A	Recruit's Boots	1	None	1
N/A	Rugged Trapper's Boots	1	None	1
N/A	Squire's Boots	1	None	1
N/A	Thug Boots	1	None	1
N/A	Thug Boots	1	None	1

STANDARD ITEMS continued

M LEV	ARMOR NAME	LEV	BIND	AC	VENDOR PURCHASE VALUE
N/A	Trapper's Boots	1	None		1
N/A	Tuxedo Jacket	1	None		1
▶	**SPELL** Sharp Dresser				
N/A	Tuxedo Pants	1	None		1
1	Tuxedo Pants	1	None		1
N/A	White Wedding Dress (Robe)	1	None		1
N/A	Simple Dress (Robe)	10	None		59
N/A	White Traditional Hanbok (Robe)	10	None		5 95
N/A	Red Traditional Hanbok (Robe)	20	None		35 28
N/A	Blue Wedding Hanbok (Robe)	30	None		1 10 20
N/A	Green Wedding Hanbok (Robe)	40	None		2 74 42
N/A	Simple Black Dress (Robe)	47	None		44 99
N/A	Royal Dangui (Robe)	50	None		5 77 39
N/A	Formal Dangui (Robe)	60	None		10 13 24

INFERIOR ITEMS

M LEV	ARMOR NAME	LEV	BIND	VENDOR PURCHASE VALUE
N/A	Red Defias Mask	15	BoA	81

ALCOHOLIC BEVERAGES

ITEM NAME	REQ LEV	COOLDOWN	SELL PRICE	PURCHASE PRICE
Bottle of Pinot Noir	1		50	12
▶ A fairly weak alcoholic beverage.				
Cherry Grog	25		3 40	85
▶ A strong alcoholic beverage.				
Cuergo's Gold	0	1 sec	16 00	4 00
▶ A strong alcoholic beverage.				
Cuergo's Gold with Worm	0		16 00	4 00
▶ A potent alcoholic beverage.				
Dark Dwarven Lager	0		10 00	2 50
▶ A potent alcoholic beverage.				
Flagon of Mead	0		15 00	3 75
▶ A strong alcoholic beverage.				
Flask of Port	0		1 50	37
▶ A typical alcoholic beverage.				
Jug of Bourbon	0		20 00	5 00
▶ A strong alcoholic beverage.				
Junglevine Wine	0		3 00	75
▶ A strong alcoholic beverage.				
Keg of Thunderbrew Lager	0		4 45	1 11
▶ Increases STAM by 3 and gets you pretty drunk.				
Lung Juice Cocktail	0	1 sec	N/A	N/A
▶ Increases STAM by 50 when consumed. Effect lasts for 60 minutes.				
Mug of Shimmer Stout	0	1 hr	45	11
▶ Restores 140 to 180 mana.				
Rhapsody Malt	1	2 min	50	12
▶ A fairly weak alcoholic beverage.				
Skin of Dwarven Stout	0		1 20	30
▶ A typical alcoholic beverage.				
Southshore Stout	0		1 45	36
▶ A typical alcoholic beverage.				
Stormstout	0		2 55	63
▶ A powerful ale that increases your STR by 4 and decreases your INT by 5 for 5 min.				
Thunder Ale	1	1 sec	50	12
▶ A fairly weak alcoholic beverage.				
Trogg Ale	0		3 55	88
▶ Increases your health by 23 to 37, but decreases your SPI by 4 for 5 min.				
Volatile Rum	0	1 sec	16 00	4 00
▶ A strong alcoholic beverage.				
Watered-down Beer	1		N/A	N/A
▶ This weak beer increases your SPI by 1 and decreases your STAM by 1 for 10 min.				
Wizbang's Special Brew	0	1 sec	1 20	30
▶ A typical alcoholic beverage.				

DRINKS

ITEM NAME	REQ LEV	COOLDOWN	SELL PRICE	PURCHASE PRICE
Bubbling Water	15	10 sec	5 00	25
▶ Restores 835 mana over 24 sec. Must sit while drinking.				
Conjured Crystal Water	55	1 sec	N/A	N/A
▶ Restores 1213 mana over 40 sec. Must sit while drinking.				
Conjured Fresh Water	5	1 sec	N/A	N/A
▶ Restores 436 mana over 21 sec. Must sit while drinking.				
Conjured Mineral Water	35	1 sec	N/A	N/A
▶ Restores 1992 mana over 30 sec. Must sit while drinking.				
Conjured Purified Water	15	1 sec	N/A	N/A
▶ Restores 835 mana over 24 sec. Must sit while drinking.				
Conjured Sparkling Water	45	1 sec	N/A	N/A
▶ Restores 2934 mana over 30 sec. Must sit while drinking.				
Conjured Spring Water	25	1 sec	N/A	N/A
▶ Restores 1344 mana over 27 sec. Must sit while drinking.				
Conjured Water	1	1 sec	N/A	N/A
▶ Restores 151 mana over 18 sec. Must sit while drinking.				
Enchanted Water	25	1 sec	5 35	1 33
▶ Restores 1344 mana over 27 sec. Must sit while drinking.				
Goldthorn Tea	25	1 sec	3 40	85
▶ Restores 1344 mana over 27 sec. Must sit while drinking.				
Ice Cold Milk	5	1 sec	1 25	6
▶ Restores 436 mana over 21 sec. Must sit while drinking.				
Melon Juice	15	1 sec	5 00	25
▶ Restores 835 mana over 24 sec. Must sit while drinking.				
Moonberry Juice	35	1 sec	20 00	1 00
▶ Restores 1992 mana over 30 sec. Must sit while drinking.				
Morning Glory Dew	45	1 sec	40 00	2 00
▶ Restores 2934 mana over 30 sec. Must sit while drinking.				
Night Dragon's Breath	45	1 sec	N/A	N/A
Restores 394 to 456 mana and 394 to 456 health.				
Raptor Punch	0	1 min	3 55	88
▶ Increases your INT by 4 and decreases your STAM by 5 for 5 min.				
Refreshing Spring Water	1	1 sec	25	1
▶ Restores 151 mana over 18 sec. Must sit while drinking.				
Restoring Balm	0	1 sec	4 80	1 20
▶ Heals the target of 180 dmg over 12 sec.				
Sweet Nectar	25	3 min	10 00	50
▶ Restores 1344 mana over 27 sec. Must sit while drinking.				

FOOD

ITEM NAME	REQ LEV	COOLDOWN	SELL PRICE	PURCHASE PRICE
Alterac Swiss	45	1 sec	40 00	2 00
▶ Restores 2148 health over 30 sec. Must sit while eating.				
Baked Salmon	45	1 sec	32 00	1 60
▶ Restores 2148 health over 30 sec. Must sit while eating.				
Barbecued Buzzard Wing	25	1 sec	12 00	3 00
▶ Restores 1636 health over 27 sec. Must sit while eating. If you spend at least 10 seconds eating you will become well fed and gain a temporary STR and SPI buff.				
Beer Basted Boar Ribs	1	1 sec	40	10
▶ Restores 126 health over 18 sec. Must sit while eating. If you spend at least 10 seconds eating you will become well fed and gain a temporary STR and SPI buff.				
Big Bear Steak	15	1 sec	5 00	1 25
▶ Restores 1027 health over 24 sec. Must sit while eating. If you spend at least 10 seconds eating you will become well fed and gain a temporary STR and SPI buff.				
Blood Sausage	5	1 sec	1 60	40
▶ Restores 474 health over 21 sec. Must sit while eating. If you spend at least 10 seconds eating you will become well fed and gain a temporary STR and SPI buff.				
Bloodbelly Fish	25	1 sec	12 50	62
▶ Restores 1392 health over 30 sec. Must sit while eating.				
Bogling Root	0	1 sec	1 50	37
▶ Increases melee dmg by 1 for 10 min.				
Boiled Clams	5	10 min	80	20
▶ Restores 474 health over 21 sec. Must sit while eating. If you spend at least 10 seconds eating you will become well fed and gain a temporary STR and SPI buff.				
Brilliant Smallfish	1	1 sec	25	1
▶ Restores 61 health over 18 sec. Must sit while eating.				
Bristle Whisker Catfish	15	1 sec	5 00	25
▶ Restores 552 health over 24 sec. Must sit while eating.				
Cactus Apple Surprise	0	1 sec	25	1
▶ Restores 126 health over 18. Must sit while eating. If you spend at least 10 seconds eating you will become well fed and gain a temporary STR and SPI buff.				
Candy Bar	1	1 sec	40	10
▶ Restores 189 health over 21 sec. Must sit while eating. If you spend at least 10 seconds eating you will become well fed and gain a temporary STR and SPI buff.				
Carrion Surprise	25	1 sec	12 00	3 00
▶ Restores 1636 health over 27 sec. Must sit while eating. If you spend at least 10 seconds eating you will become well fed and gain a temporary STR and SPI buff.				
Charred Wolf Meat	1	1 sec	20	5
▶ Restores 61 health over 18 sec. Must sit while eating.				
Chocolate Square	1	1 sec	40	10
▶ Restores 189 health over 21 sec. Must sit while eating. If you spend at least 10 seconds eating you will become well fed and gain a temporary STR and SPI buff.				
Clam Chowder	10	1 sec	3 00	75
▶ Restores 552 health over 24 sec. Must sit while eating.				
Conjured Bread	5	1 sec	N/A	N/A
▶ Restores 243 health over 21 sec. Must sit while eating.				
Conjured Muffin	1	1 sec	N/A	N/A
▶ Restores 61 health over 18 sec. Must sit while eating.				
Conjured Pumpernickel	25	1 sec	N/A	N/A
▶ Restores 874 health over 27 sec. Must sit while eating.				
Conjured Rye	15	1 sec	N/A	N/A
▶ Restores 552 health over 24 sec. Must sit while eating.				
Conjured Sourdough	35	1 sec	N/A	N/A
▶ Restores 1392 health over 30 sec. Must sit while eating.				
Conjured Sweet Roll	45	1 sec	N/A	N/A
▶ Restores 2148 health over 30 sec. Must sit while eating.				
Cooked Crab Claw	5	1 sec	1 00	25
▶ Restores 294 health and 294 mana over 21 sec. Must sit while eating.				
Cooked Glossy Mightfish	35	1 sec	15 00	3 75
▶ Restores 874 health over 27. Must sit while eating. Also increases your STAM by 10 for 10 min.				
Coyote Steak	5	1 sec	80	20
▶ Restores 474 health over 21 sec. Must sit while eating. If you spend at least 10 seconds eating you will become well fed and gain a temporary STR and SPI buff.				
Crab Cake	5	1 sec	1 00	25
▶ Restores 474 health over 21 sec. Must sit while eating. If you spend at least 10 seconds eating you will become well fed and gain a temporary STR and SPI buff.				
Crispy Bat Wing	1	1 sec	40	10
▶ Restores 126 health over 18 sec. Must sit while eating. If you spend at least 10 seconds eating you will become well fed and gain a temporary STR and SPI buff.				
Crispy Lizard Tail	12	1 sec	5 00	1 25
▶ Restores 1027 health over 24 sec. Must sit while eating. If you spend at least 10 seconds eating you will become well fed and gain a temporary STR and SPI buff.				
Crocolisk Gumbo	15	1 sec	4 00	1 00
▶ Restores 1027 health over 24 sec. Must sit while eating. If you spend at least 10 seconds eating you will become well fed and gain a temporary STR and SPI buff.				
Crocolisk Steak	5	1 sec	1 00	25
▶ Restores 474 health over 21 sec. Must sit while eating. If you spend at least 10 seconds eating you will become well fed and gain a temporary STR and SPI buff.				
Cured Ham Steak	35	1 sec	20 00	1 00
▶ Restores 1392 health over 30 sec. Must sit while eating.				
Curiously Tasty Omelet	15	1 sec	6 00	1 50
▶ Restores 1027 health over 24 sec. Must sit while eating. If you spend at least 10 seconds eating you will become well fed and gain a temporary STR and SPI buff.				
Dalaran Sharp	5	1 sec	1 25	6
▶ Restores 243 health over 21 sec. Must sit while eating.				
Darkshore Grouper	5	1 sec	1 25	6
▶ Restores 243 health over 21 sec. Must sit while eating.				
Darnassian Bleu	1	1 sec	25	1
▶ Restores 61 health over 18 sec. Must sit while eating.				
Deep Fried Plantains	45	1 sec	40 00	2 00
▶ Restores 2148 health over 30 sec. Must sit while eating.				
Delicious Cave Mold	25	1 sec	10 00	50
▶ Restores 874 health over 27 sec. Must sit while eating.				
Dig Rat Stew	10	1 sec	2 80	70
▶ Restores 552 health over 24 sec. Must sit while eating.				
Dragonbreath Chilli	35	1 sec	12 00	3 00
▶ Occasionally belch flame at enemies struck in melee for the next 10 min.				
Dried King Bolete	45	1 sec	40 00	2 00
▶ Restores 2148 health over 30 sec. Must sit while eating.				
Dry Pork Ribs	5	1 sec	1 00	25
▶ Restores 474 health over 21 sec. Must sit while eating. If you spend at least 10 seconds eating you will become well fed and gain a temporary STR and SPI buff.				
Dwarven Mild	15	1 sec	5 00	25
▶ Restores 552 health over 24 sec. Must sit while eating.				
Filet of Redgill	35	1 sec	18 00	90
▶ Restores 1392 health over 30 sec. Must sit while eating.				

ITEM NAME	REQ LEV	COOLDOWN	SELL PRICE	PURCHASE PRICE
Fillet of Frenzy	5	1 sec	84	21
▶ Restores 474 health over 21 sec. Must sit while eating. If you spend at least 10 seconds eating you will become well fed and gain a temporary STR and SPI buff.				
Fine Aged Cheddar	35	1 sec	20 00	1 50
▶ Restores 1392 health over 30 sec. Must sit while eating.				
Fissure Plant	5	1 sec	85	21
▶ Restores 243 health over 21 sec. Must sit while eating.				
Flank of Meat	15	1 sec	N/A	N/A
▶ Restores 670 health over 30 sec. Must sit while eating.				
Forest Mushroom Cap	1	1 sec	25	1
▶ Restores 61 health over 18 sec. Must sit while eating.				
Freshly Baked Bread	5	1 sec	1 25	6
▶ Restores 243 health over 21 sec. Must sit while eating.				
Frog Leg Stew	0	1 sec	12 50	62
▶ Restores 874 health over 27. Must sit while eating.				
Giant Clam Scorcho	25	1 sec	12 50	3 12
▶ Restores 1636 health over 27 sec. Must sit while eating. If you spend at least 10 seconds eating you will become well fed and gain a temporary STR and SPI buff.				
Gizzard Gum	0	1 sec	N/A	N/A
▶ Increases SPI by 50 when consumed. Effect lasts for 60 minutes.				
Goblin Deviled Clams	15	1 hour	3 80	95
▶ Restores 1027 health over 24 sec. Must sit while eating. If you spend at least 10 seconds eating you will become well fed and gain a temporary STR and SPI buff.				
Goldenbark Apple	25	1 sec	10 00	50
▶ Restores 874 health over 27 sec. Must sit while eating.				
Gooey Spider Cake	15	1 sec	4 00	1 00
▶ Restores 1027 health over 24 sec. Must sit while eating. If you spend at least 10 seconds eating you will become well fed and gain a temporary STR and SPI buff.				
Goretusk Liver Pie	5	1 sec	1 00	25
▶ Restores 474 health over 21 sec. Must sit while eating. If you spend at least 10 seconds eating you will become well fed and gain a temporary STR and SPI buff.				
Green Tea Leaf	4	1 sec	56	14
▶ Instantly heals 30 dmg. Also restores 60 mana over 10 sec. Must sit while drinking.				
Grilled King Crawler Legs	35	1 sec	10 00	50
▶ Restores 1392 health over 30 sec. Must sit while eating.				
Grilled Squid	35	1 sec	14 00	3 50
▶ Restores 874 health over 27. Must sit while eating. Also increases your STAM by 10 for 10 min.				
Grim Guzzler Boar	45	1 sec	40 00	2 00
▶ Restores 2148 health over 30 sec. Must sit while eating.				
Ground Scorpok Assay	0	1 sec	N/A	N/A
▶ Increases AGI by 50 when consumed. Effect lasts for 60 minutes.				
Haunch of Meat	5	1 hour	1 25	6
▶ Restores 243 health over 21 sec. Must sit while eating.				
Healing Herb	0	1 sec	10	2
▶ Restores 61 health over 18 sec. Must sit while eating.				
Heavy Kodo Stew	35	1 sec	12 00	3 00
▶ Restores 2514 health over 30 sec. Must sit while eating. If you spend at least 10 seconds eating you will become well fed and gain a temporary STR and SPI buff.				
Herb Baked Egg	1	1 sec	40	10
▶ Restores 126 health over 18 sec. Must sit while eating. If you spend at least 10 seconds eating you will become well fed and gain a temporary STR and SPI buff.				
Homemade Cherry Pie	45	1 sec	40 00	2 00
▶ Restores 2148 health over 30 sec. Must sit while eating.				
Hot Lion Chops	15	1 sec	5 00	1 25
▶ Restores 1027 health over 24 sec. Must sit while eating. If you spend at least 10 seconds eating you will become well fed and gain a temporary STR and SPI buff.				
Hot Smoked Bass	35	1 sec	16 00	4 00
▶ Restores 874 health over 27 sec. Must sit while eating. Also increases your SPI by 10 for 10 min.				
Hot Wolf Ribs	25	1 sec	12 50	3 12
▶ Restores 1636 health over 27 sec. Must sit while eating. If you spend at least 10 seconds eating you will become well fed and gain a temporary STR and SPI buff.				
Jungle Stew	25	1 sec	12 00	3 00
▶ Restores 1636 health over 27 sec. Must sit while eating. If you spend at least 10 seconds eating you will become well fed and gain a temporary STR and SPI buff.				
Kaldorei Spider Kabob	1	1 sec	40	10
▶ Restores 126 health over 18 sec. Must sit while eating. If you spend at least 10 seconds eating you will become well fed and gain a temporary STR and SPI buff.				
Lean Venison	15	1 sec	3 80	95
▶ Restores 1027 health over 24 sec. Must sit while eating. If you spend at least 10 seconds eating you will become well fed and gain a temporary STR and SPI buff.				
Leg Meat	1	1 sec	25	1
▶ Restores 61 health over 18 sec. Must sit while eating.				
Lobster Stew	45	1 sec	36 00	1 80
▶ Restores 2148 health over 30 sec. Must sit while eating.				
Loch Frenzy Delight	5	1 sec	1 25	6
▶ Restores 243 health over 21 sec. Must sit while eating.				
Lollipop	1	1 sec	40	10
▶ Restores 189 health over 21 sec. Must sit while eating. If you spend at least 10 seconds eating you will become well fed and gain a temporary STR and SPI buff.				
Longjaw Mud Snapper	5	1 sec	1 25	6
▶ Restores 243 health over 21 sec. Must sit while eating.				
Mightfish Steak	45	1 sec	16 00	4 00
▶ Restores 1933 health over 27 sec. Must sit while eating. Also increases your STAM by 10 for 10 min.				
Mithril Head Trout	25	1 sec	12 50	62
▶ Restores 874 health over 27 sec. Must sit while eating.				
Moist Cornbread	15	1 sec	5 00	25
▶ Restores 552 health over 24 sec. Must sit while eating.				
Monster Omlette	40	1 sec	12 00	3 00
▶ Restores 2514 health over 30 sec. Must sit while eating. If you spend at least 10 seconds eating you will become well fed and gain a temporary STR and SPI buff.				
Moon Harvest Pumpkin	35	1 sec	20 00	1 00
▶ Restores 1392 health over 30 sec. Must sit while eating.				
Mulgore Spice Bread	25	1 sec	10 00	50
▶ Restores 874 health over 27 sec. Must sit while eating.				
Murloc Fin Soup	15	1 sec	5 00	1 25
▶ Restores 1027 health over 24 sec. Must sit while eating. If you spend at least 10 seconds eating you will become well fed and gain a temporary STR and SPI buff.				
Mutton Chop	15	1 sec	5 00	25
▶ Restores 552 health over 24 sec. Must sit while eating.				
Mystery Stew	25	1 sec	12 00	3 00
▶ Restores 1636 health over 27 sec. Must sit while eating. If you spend at least 10 seconds eating you will become well fed and gain a temporary STR and SPI buff.				
Nightfin Soup	35	1 sec	20 00	1 00
▶ Restores 874 health over 27 sec. Must sit while eating. Also restores 8 mana every 5 seconds for 10 min.				
Oil Covered Fish	5	1 sec	40	10
▶ Restores 61 health over 18 sec. Must sit while eating.				
Poached Sunscale Salmon	35	1 sec	18 00	90
▶ Restores 874health over 27 sec. Must sit while eating. Also restores 6 health every 5 seconds for 10 min.				
Rainbow Fin Albacore	5	1 sec	1 25	6
▶ Restores 243 health over 21 sec. Must sit while eating.				
Raw Black Truffle	35	1 sec	20 00	1 00
▶ Restores 1392 health over 30 sec. Must sit while eating.				
Raw Brilliant Smallfish	1	1 sec	20	1
▶ Restores 30 health over 15 sec. Must sit while eating.				
Raw Bristle Whisker Catfish	15	1 sec	4 00	20
▶ Restores 243 health over 21 sec. Must sit while eating.				
Raw Glossy Mightfish	35	1 sec	12 00	3 00
▶ Restores 874 health over 27 sec. Must sit while eating.				
Raw Loch Frenzy	5	1 sec	1 00	5
▶ Restores 61 health over 18 sec. Must sit while eating.				
Raw Longjaw Mud Snapper	5	1 sec	1 00	5
▶ Restores 61 health over 18 sec. Must sit while eating.				
Raw Mithril Head Trout	25	1 sec	10 00	50
▶ Restores 552 health over 24 sec. Must sit while eating.				
Raw Nightfin Snapper	35	1 sec	16 00	80
▶ Restores 874 health over 27 sec. Must sit while eating.				
Raw Rainbow Fin Albacore	5	1 sec	1 00	5
▶ Restores 61 health over 18 sec. Must sit while eating.				
Raw Redgill	35	1 sec	16 00	80
▶ Restores 874 health over 27 sec. Must sit while eating.				
Raw Rockscale Cod	25	1 sec	8 00	40
▶ Restores 552 health over 24 sec. Must sit while eating.				
Raw Slitherskin Mackerel	1	1 sec	20	1
▶ Restores 30 health over 15 sec. Must sit while eating.				
Raw Spinefin Halibut	45	1 sec	32 00	1 60
▶ Restores 1392 health over 30 sec. Must sit while eating.				
Raw Spotted Yellowtail	35	1 sec	16 00	80
▶ Restores 874 health over 27 sec. Must sit while eating.				
Raw Sunscale Salmon	35	1 sec	16 00	80
▶ Restores 874 health over 27 sec. Must sit while eating.				
Raw Whitescale Salmon	45	1 sec	32 00	1 60
▶ Restores 1392 health over 30 sec. Must sit while eating.				
Redridge Goulash	10	1 sec	6 00	1 50
▶ Restores 1027 health over 24 sec. Must sit while eating. If you spend at least 10 seconds eating you will become well fed and gain a temporary STR and SPI buff.				
Red-speckled Mushroom	5	1 sec	1 25	6
▶ Restores 243 health over 21 sec. Must sit while eating.				
Ripe Watermelon	1	1 sec	25	1
▶ Restores 61 health over 18 sec. Must sit while eating.				
Roast Raptor	25	1 sec	12 00	3 00
▶ Restores 1636 health over 27 sec. Must sit while eating. If you spend at least 10 seconds eating you will become well fed and gain a temporary STR and SPI buff.				
Roasted Boar Meat	1	1 sec	24	6
▶ Restores 61 health over 18 sec. Must sit while eating.				
Roasted Kodo Meat	1	1 sec	36	9
▶ Restores 126 health over 18 sec. Must sit while eating. If you spend at least 10 seconds eating you will become well fed and gain a temporary STR and SPI buff.				
Roasted Quail	45	1 sec	40 00	2 00
▶ Restores 2148 health over 30 sec. Must sit while eating.				
Rockscale Cod	25	1 sec	10 00	50
▶ Restores 874 health over 27 sec. Must sit while eating.				
Sauteed Sunfish	0	1 sec	40	10
▶ Restores 243 health over 21 sec. Must sit while eating.				

ITEM NAME	REQ LEV	COOLDOWN	SELL PRICE	PURCHASE PRICE
Savory Deviate Delight	0	1 sec	1 00	25
▶ Eat me.				
Scorpid Surprise	1	10 sec	40	10
▶ Heals 294 dmg over 21 sec, assuming you don't bite down on a poison sac.				
Seasoned Wolf Kabob	15	1 sec	4 00	1 00
▶ Restores 1027 health over 24 sec. Must sit while eating. If you spend at least 10 seconds eating you will become well fed and gain a temporary STR and SPI buff.				
Senggin Root	0	1 sec	45	11
▶ Restores 294 health and 294 mana over 21 sec. Must sit while eating.				
Shiny Red Apple	1	1 sec	25	1
▶ Restores 61 health over 18 sec. Must sit while eating.				
Sickly Looking Fish	1	1 sec	25	1
▶ Restores 30 health over 15 sec. Must sit while eating.				
Slitherskin Mackerel	1	1 sec	25	1
▶ Restores 61 health over 18 sec. Must sit while eating.				
Small Pumpkin	1	1 sec	25	1
▶ Restores 61 health over 18 sec. Must sit while eating.				
Smoked Bear Meat	5	1 sec	1 25	6
▶ Restores 243 health over 21 sec. Must sit while eating.				
Snapvine Watermelon	15	1 sec	5 00	25
▶ Restores 552 health over 24 sec. Must sit while eating.				
Soft Banana Bread	35	1 sec	20 00	1 00
▶ Restores 1392 health over 30 sec. Must sit while eating.				
Soothing Turtle Bisque	25	1 sec	12 00	3 00
▶ Restores 1636 health over 27 sec. Must sit while eating. If you spend at least 10 seconds eating you will become well fed and gain a temporary STR and SPI buff.				
Special Chicken Feed	1	1 sec	25	6
▶ Restores 30 health over 15 sec. Must sit while eating.				
Spiced Chilli Crab	40	1 sec	12 00	3 00
▶ Restores 2514 health over 30 sec. Must sit while eating. If you spend at least 10 seconds eating you will become well fed and gain a temporary STR and SPI buff.				
Spiced Wolf Meat	1	1 sec	40	10
▶ Restores 126 health over 18 sec. Must sit while eating. If you spend at least 10 seconds eating you will become well fed and gain a temporary STR and SPI buff.				
Spiced Wolf Ribs	25	1 sec	12 00	3 00
▶ Restores 1636 health over 27 sec. Must sit while eating. If you spend at least 10 seconds eating you will become well fed and gain a temporary STR and SPI buff.				

ITEM NAME	REQ LEV	COOLDOWN	SELL PRICE	PURCHASE PRICE
Spinefin Halibut	45	1 sec	40 00	2 00
▶ Restores 2148 health over 30 sec. Must sit while eating.				
Spongy Morel	15	1 sec	5 00	25
▶ Restores 552 health over 24 sec. Must sit while eating.				
Spotted Yellowtail	35	1 sec	20 00	1 00
▶ Restores 1392 health over 30 sec. Must sit while eating.				
Stormwind Brie	25	1 sec	10 00	62
▶ Restores 874 health over 27 sec. Must sit while eating.				
Strider Stew	5	1 sec	74	18
▶ Restores 474 health over 21 sec. Must sit while eating. If you spend at least 10 seconds eating you will become well fed and gain a temporary STR and SPI buff.				
Succulent Pork Ribs	10	1 sec	3 00	75
▶ Restores 552 health over 24 sec. Must sit while eating.				
Tasty Lion Steak	20	1 sec	12 00	3 00
▶ Restores 1636 health over 27 sec. Must sit while eating. If you spend at least 10 seconds eating you will become well fed and gain a temporary STR and SPI buff.				
Tel'Abim Banana	5	1 sec	1 25	6
▶ Restores 243 health over 21 sec. Must sit while eating.				
Tigule and Foror's Strawberry Ice Cream	15	1 sec	5 00	25
▶ Restores 552 health over 24 sec. Must sit while eating.				
Tough Hunk of Bread	1	1 sec	25	1
▶ Restores 61 health over 18 sec. Must sit while eating.				
Tough Jerky	1	1 sec	25	1
▶ Restores 61 health over 18 sec. Must sit while eating.				
Westfall Stew	5	1 sec	4 00	1 00
▶ Restores 552 health over 24 sec. Must sit while eating.				
Whipper Root Tuber	45	1 sec	N/A	N/A
▶ Restores 700 to 900 health.				
Wild Hog Shank	25	1 min	10 00	50
▶ Restores 874 health over 27 sec. Must sit while eating.				
Windblossom Berries	45	1 sec	N/A	N/A
▶ Restores 1933 health over 27 sec. Must sit while eating. Also increases your STAM by 10 for 10 min.				
Winter Squid	35	1 sec	14 00	3 50
▶ Restores 874 health over 27 sec. Must sit while eating.				

POISONS

ITEM NAME	REQ LEV	COOLDOWN	SELL PRICE	PURCHASE PRICE
Crippling Poison	20	3 min	52	13
▶ Coats a weapon with poison that lasts for 30 minutes. Each strike has a 30% chance of poisoning the enemy, slowing their movement speed to 50% of normal for 12 sec.				
Crippling Poison II	50		7 00	1 75
▶ Coats a weapon with poison that lasts for 30 minutes. Each strike has a 30% chance of poisoning the enemy, slowing their movement speed to 30% of normal for 12 sec.				
Deadly Poison	30		1 20	30
▶ Coats a weapon with poison that lasts for 30 minutes. Each strike has a 30% chance of poisoning the enemy for 36 Nature dmg over 12 sec. Stacks up to 5 times on a single target. 60 charges.				
Deadly Poison II	38		2 20	55
▶ Coats a weapon with poison that lasts for 30 minutes. Each strike has a 30% chance of poisoning the enemy for 52 Nature dmg over 12 sec. Stacks up to 5 times on a single target. 75 charges.				
Deadly Poison III	46		4 00	1 00
▶ Coats a weapon with poison that lasts for 30 minutes. Each strike has a 30% chance of poisoning the enemy for 88 Nature dmg over 12 sec. Stacks up to 5 times on a single target. 90 charges.				
Deadly Poison IV	54		6 00	1 50
▶ Coats a weapon with poison that lasts for 30 minutes. Each strike has a 30% chance of poisoning the enemy for 124 Nature dmg over 12 sec. Stacks up to 5 times on a single target. 105 charges.				
Instant Poison	20		22	5
▶ Coats a weapon with poison that lasts for 30 minutes. Each strike has a 20% chance of poisoning the enemy which instantly inflicts 19 to 25 Nature dmg. 40 charges.				
Instant Poison II	28		80	20
▶ Coats a weapon with poison that lasts for 30 minutes. Each strike has a 20% chance of poisoning the enemy which instantly inflicts 30 to 38 Nature dmg. 55 charges.				

ITEM NAME	REQ LEV	COOLDOWN	SELL PRICE	PURCHASE PRICE
Instant Poison III	36		1 20	30
▶ Coats a weapon with poison that lasts for 30 minutes. Each strike has a 20% chance of poisoning the enemy which instantly inflicts 44 to 56 Nature dmg. 70 charges.				
Instant Poison IV	44		3 00	75
▶ Coats a weapon with poison that lasts for 30 minutes. Each strike has a 20% chance of poisoning the enemy which instantly inflicts 67 to 85 Nature dmg. 85 charges.				
Instant Poison V	52		4 00	1 00
▶ Coats a weapon with poison that lasts for 30 minutes. Each strike has a 20% chance of poisoning the enemy which instantly inflicts 92 to 118 Nature dmg. 100 charges.				
Instant Poison VI	60		5 00	1 25
▶ Coats a weapon with poison that lasts for 30 minutes. Each strike has a 20% chance of poisoning the enemy which instantly inflicts 112 to 148 Nature dmg. 115 charges.				
Instant Toxin	24		4 00	1 00
▶ Coats a sword or dagger with poison that lasts for 30 minutes. Each strike has a chance of poisoning the enemy which instantly inflicts 10-30 dmg.				
Mind-numbing Poison	24	1 sec	72	18
▶ Coats a weapon with poison that lasts for 30 minutes. Each strike has a 20% chance of poisoning the enemy, Increasing their casting time by 40% for 10 sec. 50 charges.				
Mind-numbing Poison II	38		3 00	75
▶ Coats a weapon with poison that lasts for 30 minutes. Each strike has a 20% chance of poisoning the enemy, increasing their casting time by 50% for 12 sec. 75 charges.				
Mind-numbing Poison III	52		7 00	1 75
▶ Coats a weapon with poison that lasts for 30 minutes. Each strike has a 20% chance of poisoning the enemy, increasing their casting time by 60% for 14 sec. 100 charges.				

POTIONS

ITEM NAME	REQ LEV	COOLDOWN	SELL PRICE	PURCHASE PRICE
Arcane Elixir	37		16 00	4 00
▶ Increases spell dmg by 20 for 30 min.				
Catseye Elixir	30	3 sec	6 00	1 50
▶ Increases your stealth detection by 20 for 10 min.				
Cleansing Water	0	3 sec	71 43	17 85
▶ Purifies the friendly target, removing 1 disease effect and 1 poison effect.				
Cowardly Flight Potion	15	5 min	3 40	85
▶ You run in fear at a high speed from a nearby enemy in a random direction. If there are no enemies nearby you stand frozen in fear.				
Discolored Healing Potion	5	2 min	1 00	25
▶ Restores 140 to 180 health.				
Dreamless Sleep Potion	35	2 min	10 00	2 50
▶ Puts the imbiber in a dreamless sleep for 15 sec. During that time the imbiber heals 1200 health and 1200 mana.				
Elixir of Agility	27	2 min	8 00	2 00
▶ Increases AGI by 15 for 1 hour.				
Elixir of Defense	16	3 sec	1 60	40
▶ Increases armor by 150 for 1 hour.				
Elixir of Demonslaying	40	3 sec	28 00	7 00
▶ Increases attack power by 265 against demons. Lasts 5 min.				
Elixir of Detect Demon	40	3 sec	20 00	5 00
▶ Shows the location of all nearby demons on the minimap for 1 hour.				

ITEM NAME	REQ LEV	COOLDOWN	SELL PRICE	PURCHASE PRICE
Elixir of Detect Lesser Invisibility	29	3 sec	6 00	1 50
▶ Grants detect lesser invisibility for 10 min.				
Elixir of Detect Undead	36	3 sec	12 00	3 00
▶ Shows the location of all nearby undead on the minimap for 1 hour.				
Elixir of Dream Vision	38	3 sec	24 00	6 00
▶ Gives you a dream vision that lets you explore areas that are too dangerous to explore in person.				
Elixir of Firepower	18	3 sec	1 40	35
▶ Increases spell fire dmg by up to 10 for 30 min.				
Elixir of Fortitude	25	3 sec	4 40	1 10
▶ Increases the player's maximum health by 120 for 1 hour.				
Elixir of Giant Growth	8	3 sec	3 80	95
▶ Your size is increased and your STR goes up by 8 to match your new size. Lasts 2 min.				
Elixir of Giants	38	3 sec	28 00	7 00
▶ Increases your STR by 20, STAM by 20 and size for 20 min.				
Elixir of Greater Agility	38	3 sec	24 00	6 00
▶ Increases AGI by 30 for 1 hour.				
Elixir of Greater Defense	29	3 sec	8 00	2 00
▶ Increases armor by 300 for 1 hour.				
Elixir of Greater Intellect	37	3 sec	40 00	10 00
▶ Increases INT by 40 for 1 hour.				
Elixir of Lesser Agility	18	3 sec	1 40	35
▶ Increases AGI by 8 for 1 hour.				
Elixir of Lion's Strength	1	3 sec	80	20
▶ Increases STR by 4 for 1 hour.				
Elixir of Minor Agility	2	3 sec	60	15
▶ Increases AGI by 4 for 1 hour.				
Elixir of Minor Defense	1	3 sec	20	5
▶ Increases armor by 50 for 1 hour.				
Elixir of Minor Fortitude	2	3 sec	60	15
▶ Increases the player's maximum health by 27 for 1 hour.				
Elixir of Ogre's Strength	20	3 sec	80	20
▶ Increases STR by 8 for 1 hour.				
Elixir of Poison Resistance	14	3 sec	1 40	35
▶ Target is immune to poison for 1 min and is cured of any existing poisons.				
Elixir of Shadow Power	40	3 sec	1 40	35
▶ Increases spell shadow dmg by up to 40 for 30 min.				
Elixir of Superior Defense	43	3 sec	20 00	5 00
▶ Increases armor by 400 for 1 hour.				
Elixir of Water Breathing	8	3 sec	3 80	95
▶ Allows the Imbiber to breathe water for 30 min.				
Elixir of Wisdom	10	3 sec	4 00	1 00
▶ Increases INT by 6 for 1 hour.				
Fire Protection Potion	23	3 sec	6 80	1 70
▶ Absorbs 1024 to 1706 fire dmg. Lasts 1 hour.				
Fishliver Oil	0	2 min	2 75	68
▶ Increases your attack speed by 10% for 30 sec.				
Free Action Potion	20	5 min	3 00	75
▶ Makes you immune to Root, Snare and Stun effects for the next 30 sec.				
Frost Oil	30	2 min	6 00	1 50
▶ When applied to a melee weapon it gives a 10% chance of casting Frostbolt at the opponent when it hits. Lasts 30 minutes.				
Frost Protection Potion	28	1 sec	12 00	3 00
▶ Absorbs 1350 to 2250 Frost dmg. Lasts 1 hour.				
Great Rage Potion	25	2 min	6 00	1 50
▶ Increases Rage by 30 to 60.				
Greater Healing Potion	21	2 min	5 00	1 25
▶ Restores 455 to 585 health.				
Greater Mana Potion	31	2 min	4 80	1 20
▶ Restores 700 to 900 mana.				
Greater Stoneshield Potion	46	2 min	30 00	7 50
▶ Increases armor by 1500 for 1 min.				
Healing Potion	12	2 min	3 00	75
▶ Restores 280 to 360 health.				
Holy Protection Potion	10	2 min	2 50	62
▶ Absorbs 300 to 500 holy dmg. Lasts 1 hour.				
Invisibility Potion	37	2 min	20 00	5 00
▶ Gives the imbiber invisibility for 15 sec.				
Jungle Remedy	22	10 min	1 00	25
▶ Cures diseases and neutralizes poisons.				
Lesser Healing Potion	3	3 sec	1 00	25
▶ Restores 140 to 180 health.				
Lesser Invisibility Potion	23	2 min	4 00	1 00
▶ Gives the imbiber lesser invisibility for 15 sec.				
Lesser Mana Potion	14	10 min	1 20	30
▶ Restores 280 to 360 mana.				
Lesser Stoneshield Potion	33	2 min	15 00	3 75
▶ Increases armor by 1000 for 1 min.				
▶ Imbiber is immune to physical attacks for the next 10 sec.				
Magic Resistance Potion	32	2 min	80	20
▶ Increases your resistance to all schools of magic by 60 for 30 sec.				

ITEM NAME	REQ LEV	COOLDOWN	SELL PRICE	PURCHASE PRICE
Limited Invulnerability Potion	45	2 min	1 20	30
Major Healing Potion	45	2 min	40 00	10 00
▶ Restores 1050 to 1750 health.				
Major Mana Potion	49	2 min	40 00	10 00
▶ Restores 1350 to 2250 mana.				
Mana Potion	22	2 min	4 80	1 20
▶ Restores 455 to 585 mana.				
Mighty Troll's Blood Potion	26	2 min	4 20	1 05
▶ Regenerate 4 health every 5 sec for 1 hour.				
Minor Healing Potion	1	3 sec	20	5
▶ Restores 70 to 90 health.				
Minor Magic Resistance Potion	12	2 min	80	20
▶ Increases your resistance to all schools of magic by 30 for 30 sec.				
Minor Mana Potion	5	2 min	40	10
▶ Restores 140 to 180 mana.				
Minor Rejuvenation Potion	5	2 min	60	15
▶ Restores 90 to 150 mana and 90 to 150 health.				
Nature Protection Potion	28	2 min	12 00	3 00
▶ Absorbs 1350 to 2250 Nature dmg. Lasts 1 hour.				
Oil of Immolation	31	2 min	8 00	2 00
▶ Does 50 Fire dmg to any enemies within a 5 yard radius around the caster every 3 seconds for 15 sec.				
Oil of Olaf	0	3 sec	12	3
▶ Increases armor by 50 for 1 hour.				
Potion of Fervor	15	1 sec	40	10
▶ Increases STR by 14 and does 15 dmg to you every 3 sec for 1 min.				
Purification Potion	47	2 min	30 00	7 50
▶ Removes one Curse, one Disease and one Poison from the Imbiber.				
Rage Potion	4	2 min	1 20	30
▶ Increases Rage by 20 to 40.				
Restorative Elixir	32	2 min	8 00	2 00
▶ Removes all negative effects on you.				
Shadow Oil	24	3 sec	6 00	1 50
▶ When applied to a melee weapon it gives a 15% chance of casting Shadowbolt III at the opponent when it hits. Lasts 30 minutes.				
Shadow Protection Potion	17	1 sec	4 00	1 00
▶ Absorbs 675 to 1125 shadow dmg. Lasts 1 hour.				
Strong Troll's Blood Potion	15	2 min	1 60	40
▶ Regenerate 3 health every 5 sec for 1 hour.				
Superior Healing Potion	35	3 sec	10 00	2 50
▶ Restores 700 to 900 health.				
Superior Mana Potion	41	2 min	16 00	4 00
▶ Restores 900 to 1500 mana.				
Swiftness Potion	5	2 min	1 00	25
▶ Increases run speed by 50% for 15 sec.				
Swim Speed Potion	10	2 min	1 40	35
▶ Increases swim speed by 100% for 21 sec.				
Thistle Tea	5	2 min	1 20	30
▶ Instantly restores 100 energy.				
Weak Troll's Blood Potion	1	5 min	40	10
▶ Regenerate 1 health every 5 sec for 1 hour.				
Wildvine Potion	35	3 sec	10 00	2 50
▶ Restores 1 to 1000 health and 1 to 1000 mana.				
Winterfall Firewater	45	2 min	N/A	N/A
▶ Increases your attack power by 35 and size for 20 min.				

SCROLLS

ITEM NAME	REQ LEV	COOLDOWN	SELL PRICE	PURCHASE PRICE
Scroll of Agility	10		2 00	50
▶ Increases the target's AGI by 5 for 30 min.				
Scroll of Agility II	25	1 sec	3 50	87
▶ Increases the target's AGI by 9 for 30 min.				
Scroll of Agility III	40	1 sec	5 00	1 25
▶ Increases the target's AGI by 13 for 30 min.				
Scroll of Agility IV	55	1 sec	6 50	1 25
▶ Increases the target's AGI by 17 for 30 min.				
Scroll of Intellect	5	1 sec	1 50	37
▶ Increases the target's INT by 4 for 30 min.				
Scroll of Intellect II	20	1 sec	3 00	75
▶ Increases the target's INT by 8 for 30 min.				
Scroll of Intellect III	35	1 sec	4 50	1 12
▶ Increases the target's INT by 12 for 30 min.				
Scroll of Intellect IV	50	1 sec	6 00	1 12
▶ Increases the target's INT by 16 for 30 min.				
Scroll of Protection	1	1 sec	1 00	25
▶ Increases the target's Armor by 60 for 30 min.				
Scroll of Protection II	15	1 sec	2 50	62
▶ Increases the target's Armor by 120 for 30 min.				
Scroll of Protection III	30	1 sec	4 00	1 00
▶ Increases the target's Armor by 180 for 30 min.				
Scroll of Protection IV	45	1 sec	5 50	1 00
▶ Increases the target's Armor by 240 for 30 min.				
Scroll of Spirit	1	1 sec	1 00	25
▶ Increases the target's SPI by 3 for 30 min.				
Scroll of Spirit II	15	1 sec	2 50	62
▶ Increases the target's SPI by 7 for 30 min.				
Scroll of Spirit III	30	1 sec	4 00	1 00
▶ Increases the target's SPI by 11 for 30 min.				
Scroll of Spirit IV	45	1 sec	5 50	1 00
▶ Increases the target's SPI by 15 for 30 min.				
Scroll of Stamina	5	1 sec	1 50	37
▶ Increases the target's STAM by 4 for 30 min.				
Scroll of Stamina II	20	1 sec	3 00	75
▶ Increases the target's STAM by 8 for 30 min.				
Scroll of Stamina III	35	1 sec	4 50	1 12
▶ Increases the target's STAM by 12 for 30 min.				
Scroll of Stamina IV	50	1 sec	6 00	1 12
▶ Increases the target's STAM by 16 for 30 min.				
Scroll of Strength	10	1 sec	2 00	50
▶ Increases the target's STR by 5 for 30 min.				
Scroll of Strength II	25	1 sec	3 50	87
▶ Increases the target's STR by 9 for 30 min.				
Scroll of Strength III	40	1 sec	5 00	1 25
▶ Increases the target's STR by 13 for 30 min.				
Scroll of Strength IV	55	1 sec	6 50	1 25
▶ Increases the target's STR by 17 for 30 min.				

QUEST ITEMS

ITEM NAME	REQ LEV	COOLDOWN	DESCRIPTION
Dark Keeper Key	0	1 min	Use on the Dark Coffer in the Black Vault.
Eau de Mixilpixil	1		Cure for the Touch of Zanzil
Empty Canteen	0		This container should be filled with water from the corrupt moon well in Jaedenar.
Empty Cursed Ooze Jar	0		Fills an Empty Cursed Ooze Jar with a sample of Cursed Ooze. WARNING! Will likely destroy the creature's body.
Empty Pure Sample Jar	0		Fills an Empty Pure Sample Jar with a sample of pure ooze. WARNING! Will likely destroy the creature's body.
Empty Tainted Ooze Jar	0		Fills an Empty Tainted Ooze Jar with a sample of Tainted Ooze. WARNING! Will likely destroy the creature's body.
Empty Vial Labeled #1	0		This container should be filled with water from the first tide pool in Azshara.
Empty Vial Labeled #2	0		This container should be filled with water from the second tide pool in Azshara.
Empty Vial Labeled #3	0		This container should be filled with water from the third tide pool in Azshara.
Empty Vial Labeled #4	0		This container should be filled with water from the fourth tide pool in Azshara.
Executioner's Key	0		
Hinott's Oil	1		Cure for the Touch of Zanzil
Magic Knucklebone	0		Place 7 Magic Knucklebones in the Charm Pouch to create a Knucklebone Pouch.
Nimboya's Laden Pike	0		Place at a Witherbark village.
Samophlange Manual Page	0		Join the cover and 5 pages to create the Samophlange Manual.
Scooby Snack	1		
War Horn Mouthpiece	0		Place in the Maraudine War Horn, and blow.
Weegli's Barrel	0		Place near the Troll Door.

MISCELLANEOUS

ITEM NAME	REQ LEV	COOLDOWN	SELL PRICE	PURCHASE PRICE
Air Sapta	0		N/A	N/A
▶ Allows the shaman to see elemental SPIs.				
Aquadynamic Fish Lens	0	1 sec	1 00	25
▶ When applied to your fishing pole, increases Fishing by 50 for 10 minutes.				
Attuned Dampener	0		N/A	N/A
▶ Inflict 525 to 675 Arcane dmg on the attuned target, and lower the dmg it deals by 25%.				
Bag of Marbles	0	1 min	3 30	82
▶ Decreases target's chance to hit by 25% for 10 sec.				
Blue Firework	0	1 sec	50	12
▶ Shoots a firework into the air that bursts into a thousand blue stars.				
Bright Baubles	0		2 50	62
▶ When applied to your fishing pole, increases Fishing by 75 for 10 minutes.				
Burning Charm	25	1 sec	7 15	1 78
▶ Banishes a Thundering Exile				
Call of the Raptor	0		21 35	5 33
▶ Increases your AGI by 12 for 30 min.				
Cerebral Cortex Compound	0	1 sec	N/A	N/A
▶ Increases INT by 50 when consumed. Effect lasts for 60 minutes.				
Clutch of Foresight	55	1 hour	2 15 73	53 93
▶ Counters the enemy's spellcast, preventing any spell from that school of magic from being cast for 10 sec. Generates a high amount of threat.				
Colossal Parachute	0	3 min	20 00	5 00
▶ Slows falling speed for 30 sec.				
Crate With Holes	0	1 sec	N/A	N/A
▶ Use in Razorfen Kraul near buried tubers to summon a Snufflenose Gopher.				
Cresting Charm	25	10 sec	7 05	1 76
▶ Banishes a Burning Exile				
Crystal Basilisk Spine	25		3 25	81
▶ Increases Frost and Shadow resistance by 10 for 1 min.				
Dark Iron Ale Mug	0	5 min	6 00	1 50
▶ Throw near a patron of the Grim Guzzler				
Dog Whistle	25	30 sec	2 55 00	3 75
▶ Summons a tracking hound that will temporarily protect you.				
Earth Sapta	0		N/A	N/A
▶ Allows the shaman to see elemental SPIs.				
Explosive Rocket	0	3 min	30	7
▶ Inflicts 28 to 32 Fire dmg in a 20 yard radius.				
Eye of Arachnida	55	10 min	1 91 15	47 78
▶ Summons an Eye of Kilrogg and binds your vision to it. The eye is stealthy and quick, but very fragile.				
Faintly Glowing Skull	0	1 min	1 50	37
▶ Steals 75 to 125 life from target enemy.				
Fertile Bulb	5		1 52	38
▶ Inflicts 47 to 53 Nature dmg in a 10 yard radius.				
Fiery Enchantment	0	1 sec	26 00	6 50
▶ Enchants a weapon to have a 15% chance of casting Fiery Blaze when it strikes.				
Fire Sapta	0		N/A	N/A
▶ Allows the shaman to see elemental SPIs.				
Flash Bundle	0	1 min	1 00	25
▶ Calls down a pillar of fire, burning all enemies within the area for 55 to 71 Fire dmg and an additional 48 dmg over 8 sec.				
Flesh Eating Worm	0		2 50	62
▶ When applied to your fishing pole, increases Fishing by 75 for 10 minutes.				
Glowing Wax Stick	0	1 min	1 75	43
▶ Decrease the armor of the target by 50 for 30 sec. While affected, the target cannot stealth or turn invisible.				
Goblin Fishing Pole	0	3 min	8 50	2 12
▶ Inflicts 128 to 172 Fire dmg in a 5 yard radius.				
Green Firework	0	1 sec	50	12
▶ Shoots a firework into the air that bursts into a thousand green stars.				
Heavy Armor Kit	20		26 00	6 50
▶ Permanently increase the armor value of an item worn on the chest, legs, hands or feet by 24.				
Immature Venom Sac	0	1 sec	N/A	N/A
▶ Cures 1 poison effects.				

ITEM NAME	REQ LEV	COOLDOWN	SELL PRICE	PURCHASE PRICE
Large Rope Net	2		95	23
▶ Renders a target unable to move for 10 sec.				
Light Armor Kit	1	1 sec	60	15
▶ Permanently increase the armor value of an item worn on the chest, legs, hands or feet by 8.				
Light of Elune	0		16 20	4 05
▶ Grants immunity from all dmg and spells for 10 sec.				
M73 Frag Grenade	0	1 min	30 00	7 50
▶ Inflicts 149 to 201 Fire dmg and stuns targets in a 10 yard radius for 3 sec.				
Magic Candle	1	1 min	50	12
▶ Hurls a fiery ball that causes 14 to 22 Fire dmg and an additional 2 dmg over 4 sec.				
Magic Dust	10	1 min	8 55	2 13
▶ Puts the enemy target to sleep for up to 30 sec. Any dmg caused will awaken the target. Only one target can be asleep at a time.				
Mechanical Yeti	0	1 min	50 00	12 50
▶ Summons a mechanical yeti that will temporarily protect you.				
Medium Armor Kit	5	1 sec	8 00	2 00
▶ Permanently increase the armor value of an item worn on the chest, legs, hands or feet by 16.				
Moist Towelette	0	2 min	1 65	41
▶ Removes 1 negative spell effect from user. Cleans with the power of lemon.				
Nightcrawlers	0		1 00	25
▶ When applied to your fishing pole, increases Fishing by 50 for 10 min.				
Noggenfogger Elixir	35		35 00	8 75
▶ Drink Me.				
Party Grenade	0	3 min	1 00	25
▶ The ultimate party favor!				
R.O.I.D.S.	0	2 min	N/A	N/A
▶ Increases STR by 50 when consumed. Effect lasts for 60 minutes.				
Really Sticky Glue	0	3 min	45	11
▶ Renders a target unable to move for 10 sec.				
Red Firework	0	1 sec	50	12
▶ Shoots a firework into the air that bursts into a thousand red stars.				
Red Fireworks Rocket	0	1 sec	1 00	25
▶ Shoots a firework into the air that bursts into a thousand red stars.				
Red Streaks Firework	0	1 sec	1 00	25
▶ Shoots a firework into the air that bursts into red streaks.				
Red, White and Blue Firework	0	1 sec	2 50	62
▶ Shoots a firework into the air that bursts into red, white and blue stars.				
Rugged Armor Kit	40	1 sec	40 00	10 00
▶ Permanently increase the armor value of an item worn on the chest, legs, hands or feet by 40.				
Severed Voodoo Claw	0		95	23
▶ Physical dmg caused by the target is reduced by 5 for 2 min.				
Shadowforge Torch	0		28 46	7 11
Shiny Bauble	0		50	12
▶ When applied to your fishing pole, increases Fishing by 25 for 10 min.				
Slumber Sand	0	3 min	15	3
▶ Puts the enemy target to sleep for up to 20 sec. Any dmg caused will awaken the target. Only one target can be asleep at a time.				
Soulstone	0	3 min	N/A	N/A
▶ A Soulstone is used automatically 5 seconds after death, restoring its owner to life at 15% health and mana.				
Spiked Collar	20	10 min	43 25	10 81
▶ Summons a guardian felhunter that will temporarily protect you.				
Sprouted Frond	5	1 hour	1 25	31
▶ Heal your target for 71 to 85.				
Super Snuff	0	3 min	3 70	92
▶ Makes you sneeze!				
Thick Armor Kit	30	1 sec	40 00	10 00
▶ Permanently increase the armor value of an item worn on the chest, legs, hands or feet by 32.				
Thundering Charm	25	10 sec	7 40	1 85
▶ Banishes a Cresting Exile				
Unlit Poor Torch	0		10	2
Water Sapta	0		N/A	N/A
Allows the shaman to see elemental SPIs.				
Yellow Rose Firework	0	1 sec	1 50	37
▶ Shoots a firework into the air that bursts in a yellow pattern.				

ALCHEMY POTIONS

POTION	DESCRIPTION
Arcane Elixir	Adds 20 to Spell Damage for 30 mins
Blackmouth Oil	Used for Creating More Complex Potions
Catseye Elixir	Adds 25 to Stealth Detection for 10 mins
Discolored Healing Potion	Restores 140-180 Health
Dreamless Sleep Potion	Puts User to Sleep for 15 secs/Restores 1200 Health and Mana
Elixir of Agility	Adds 15 Agility for 1 hr
Elixir of Defense	Adds 150 Armor for 1 hr
Elixir of Demonslaying	Adds 344 Attack Power Vs. Demons for 5 mins
Elixir of Detect Demon	Shows Locations of Demons on Minimap for 1 hr
Elixir of Detect Lesser Invisibility	Grants User Detect Lesser Invisibility for 10 mins
Elixir of Detect Undead	Shows Locations of Undead on Minimap for 1 hr
Elixir of Dream Vision	Adds Farsight to User
Elixir of Firepower	Adds 10 to Spell Fire Damage for 30 mins
Elixir of Fortitude	Adds 138 to User's Maximum Health for 1 hr
Elixir of Giant Growth	Adds 8 Strength and Increases Size for 2 mins
Elixir of Giants	Adds 20 to Strength and Stamina for 20 mins
Elixir of Greater Agility	Adds 30 Agility for 1 hr
Elixir of Greater Defense	Adds 345 Armor for 1 hr
Elixir of Greater Intellect	Adds 40 Intellect for 1 hr
Elixir of Lesser Agility	Adds 8 Agility for 1 hr
Elixir of Lion's Strength	Adds 4 Strength for 1 hr
Elixir of Minor Agility	Adds 4 Agility for 1 hr
Elixir of Minor Defense	Adds 50 Armor for 1 hr
Elixir of Minor Fortitude	Adds 27 to User's Maximum Health for 1 hr
Elixir of Ogre's Strength	Adds 8 Strength for 1 hr
Elixir of Poison Resistance	Cures All Poisons and Makes User Immune to them for 1 min
Elixir of Shadow Power	Adds 40 to Shadow Spell Damage for 30 mins
Elixir of Superior Defense	Adds 400 Armor for 1 hr
Elixir of Water Breathing	Allows User to Breathe Water for 30 mins
Elixir of Wisdom	Adds 9 Intellect for 1 hr
Fire Oil	Used to Create More Compex Potions
Fire Protection Potion	Absorbs 975-1625 Fire Damage Over 1 hr
Free Action Potion	Makes User Immune to Root/Snare/Stun for 30 secs
Frost Oil	Adds a 10% Chance for a Weapon to Proc Frostbolt for 30 mins
Frost Protection Potion	Absorbs 1350-2250 Nature Damage Over 1 hr
Ghost Dye	Used in Leatherworking
Goblin Rocket Fuel	Used in Engineering Products
Great Rage Potion	Adds 30-60 Rage
Greater Healing Potion	Restores 455-585 Health
Greater Mana Potion	Restores 700-900 Mana
Greater Stoneshield Potion	Adds 1500 Armor for 1 min
Healing Potion	Restores 280-360 Health
Holy Protection Potion	Absorbs 300-500 Holy Damage Over 1 hr
Invisibility Potion	Grants User Invisibility for 15 secs
Lesser Healing Potion	Restores 140-180 Health
Lesser Invisibility Potion	Grants User Lesser Invisibility for 15 secs
Lesser Mana Potion	Restores 280-360 Mana
Lesser Stoneshield Potion	Adds 1300 Armor for 1 min
Magic Resistance Potion	Adds 66 to all Resistances for 30 secs
Major Healing Potion	Restores 1050-1750 Health
Major Mana Potion	Restores 1350-2250 Mana
Mana Potion	Restores 455-585 Mana
Mighty Troll's Blood Potion	Regenerates 5 Health/5 secs for 1 hr
Minor Healing Potion	Restores 70-90 Health
Minor Magic Resistance Potion	Adds 30 to All Resistances for 30 secs
Minor Mana Potion	Restores 140-180 Mana
Minor Rejuvenation Potion	Restores 90-150 Health and Mana
Nature Protection Potion	Absorbs 1417-2362 Frost Damage Over 1 hr
Oil of Immolation	Deals 65 Fire Damage/3 Sec for 15 Sec to All Enemies Within 5 Yards
Philosophers' Stone	Used in Transmuting Advanced Metals
Purification Potion	Removes 1 Curse, 1 Disease, and 1 Poison from User
Rage Potion	Adds 20-40 Rage
Shadow Oil	Adds a 15% Chance for a Weapon to Proc Shadowbolt 3 for 30 mins
Shadow Protection Potion	Absorbs 675-1125 Shadow Damage Over 1 hr
Stonescale Oil	Used to Create for Advanced Potions
Strong Troll's Blood Potion	Regenerates 3 Health/5 secs for 1 hr
Superior Healing Potion	Restores 700-900 Health
Superior Mana Potion	Restores 900-1500 Mana
Swiftness Potion	Increases Run Speed by 50% for 15 secs
Swim Speed Potion	Doubles Swim Speed for 20 secs
Transmute Arcanite	Creates Arcanite Bars From Thorium and Arcane Crystals
Transmute Iron to Gold	Turns a Bar of Iron into Gold (48 hr Cooldown)
Transmute Mithril to Truesilver	Turns a Bar of Mithril into Truesilver (48 hr Cooldown)
Weak Troll's Blood Potion	Regenerates 1 Health/5 secs for 1 hr
Wildvine Potion	Restores 1-1100 Health and Mana

ENCHANMENTS

POTION	DESCRIPTION
Enchant 2H Weapon - Greater Impact	Damage +7
Enchant 2H Weapon - Impact	Damage +5
Enchant 2H Weapon - Lesser Impact	Damage +3
Enchant 2H Weapon - Lesser Intellect	Intellect +3
Enchant 2H Weapon - Lesser Spirit	Spirit +3
Enchant 2H Weapon - Minor Impact	Damage +2
Enchant Boots - Agility	Agility +5
Enchant Boots - Lesser Agility	Agility +3
Enchant Boots - Lesser Spirit	Spirit +3
Enchant Boots - Lesser Stamina	Stamina +3
Enchant Boots - Minor Agility	Agility +1
Enchant Boots - Minor Speed	Slightly Raises Movement Speed
Enchant Boots - Minor Stamina	Stamina +1
Enchant Boots - Stamina	Stamina +5
Enchant Bracer - Greater Spirit	Spirit +7
Enchant Bracer - Greater Stamina	Stamina +7
Enchant Bracer - Greater Strength	Strength +7
Enchant Bracer - Intellect	Intellect +5
Enchant Bracer - Lesser Intellect	Intellect +3
Enchant Bracer - Lesser Spirit	Spirit +3
Enchant Bracer - Lesser Stamina	Stamina +3
Enchant Bracer - Minor Agility	Agility +1
Enchant Bracer - Minor Deflection	Defense +1
Enchant Bracer - Minor Spirit	Spirit +1
Enchant Bracer - Minor Stamina	Stamina +1
Enchant Bracer - Minor Strength	Strength +1
Enchant Bracer - Spirit	Spirit +5
Enchant Bracer - Stamina	Stamina +5
Enchant Bracer - Strength	Strength +5
Enchant Chest - Greater Health	Health +35
Enchant Chest - Greater Mana	Mana +50
Enchant Chest - Health	Health +25
Enchant Chest - Lesser Absorption	5% Chance to Absorb 25 dmg
Enchant Chest - Lesser Health	Health +15
Enchant Chest - Lesser Mana	Mana +20
Enchant Chest - Lesser Stats	All Attributes +2
Enchant Chest - Mana	Mana +30
Enchant Chest - Minor Absorption	2% Chance to Absorb 10 dmg
Enchant Chest - Minor Health	Health +5
Enchant Chest - Minor Mana	Mana +5
Enchant Chest - Minor Stats	All Attributes +1
Enchant Chest - Stats	All Attributes +3

POTION	DESCRIPTION
Enchant Chest - Superior Health	Health +50
Enchant Chest - Superior Mana	Mana +65
Enchant Cloak - Defense	Armor +30
Enchant Cloak - Fire Resistance	Fire Resistance +15
Enchant Cloak - Greater Defense	Armor +50
Enchant Cloak - Lesser Agility	Agility +3
Enchant Cloak - Lesser Fire Resistance	Fire Resistance +10
Enchant Cloak - Lesser Protection	Armor +20
Enchant Cloak - Lesser Shadow Resist	Shadow Resistance +10
Enchant Cloak - Minor Agility	Agility +1
Enchant Cloak - Minor Protection	Armor +10
Enchant Cloak - Minor Resistance	All Resists +2
Enchant Cloak - Resistance	Adds 5 to All Resistances
Enchant Gloves - Advanced Herbalism	Herbalism +5
Enchant Gloves - Advanced Mining	Mining +5
Enchant Gloves - Agility	Agility +5
Enchant Gloves - Fishing	Fishing +2
Enchant Gloves - Mining	Mining +2
Enchant Gloves - Minor Haste	Raises Attack Speed by 1%
Enchant Gloves - Riding Skill	Raises Mount Speed Slightly
Enchant Gloves - Skinning	Skinning +5
Enchant Gloves - Strength	Strength +5
Enchant Shield - Frost Reflection	Adds 1% Chance to Reflect Frost dmg
Enchant Shield - Greater Spirit	Spirit +7
Enchant Shield - Lesser Block	Block +2%
Enchant Shield - Lesser Protection	Armor +20
Enchant Shield - Lesser Spirit	Spirit +3
Enchant Shield - Lesser Stamina	Stamina +3
Enchant Shield - Minor Stamina	Stamina +1
Enchant Shield - Spirit	Spirit +5
Enchant Shield - Stamina	Stamina +5
Enchant Weapon - Demonslaying	Adds Ability to Stun Demons
Enchant Weapon - Fiery Weapon	Adds Chance to Proc for 40 Fire dmg
Enchant Weapon - Greater Striking	Damage +5
Enchant Weapon - Lesser Beastslayer	Damage +6 Vs. Beasts
Enchant Weapon - Lesser Elemental Slayer	Attack Power +40 Vs. Elementals
Enchant Weapon - Lesser Striking	Damage +2
Enchant Weapon - Minor Beastslayer	Damage +2 Vs. Beasts
Enchant Weapon - Minor Striking	Damage +1
Enchant Weapon - Striking	Damage +3

ENGINEERING GADGETS

ITEM	DURATION	RANGE	COOLDOWN	DESCRIPTION
Accurate Scope	N/A	N/A	N/A	Adds 3 dmg/shot to a Bow or Gun
Advanced Target Dummy	3 mins	Short	1 min	Taunts Nearby Monsters
Aquadynamic Fish Attractor	5 mins	Self	None	Adds 100 to Your Fishing Skill
Arclight Spanner	N/A	N/A	N/A	Used to Craft Other Engineering Items
Big Bronze Bomb	2 sec	20 yd	1 min	Use: Inflicts 85 to 115 Fire dmg/disorients targets in a 5 yard radius for 2 sec
Big Iron Bomb	3 sec	20 yd	1 min	Use: Inflicts 149 to 201 Fire dmg/disorients targets in a 5 yard radius for 3 sec
Bright-Eye Goggles	N/A	N/A	N/A	Cloth Helm: 62 Armor, +9 Stamina, +9 Spirit
Bronze Framework	N/A	N/A	N/A	Component
Bronze Tube	N/A	N/A	N/A	Component
Catseye Ultra Goggles	N/A	N/A	N/A	Cloth Head: 78 Armor, +18 Stealth Detection
Coarse Blasting Powder	N/A	N/A	N/A	Component
Coarse Dynamite	Instant	20 yd	1 min	Use: Inflicts 51 to 69 Fire dmg in a 5 yard radius
Compact Harvest Reaper Kit	10 mins	Short	1 min	Creates a Combative Pet
Copper Modulator	N/A	N/A	N/A	Component
Copper Tube	N/A	N/A	N/A	Component
Crafted Heavy Shot	N/A	N/A	N/A	Adds 5 DPS to a Gun
Crafted Light Shot	N/A	N/A	N/A	Adds 2.5 DPS to a Gun
Crafted Solid Shot	N/A	N/A	N/A	Adds 9 DPS to a Gun
Craftsman's Monocle	N/A	N/A	N/A	Cloth Helm: 66 Armor, +15 Intellect
Crude Scope	N/A	N/A	N/A	Adds 1 dmg/shot to Bows and Guns
Deadly Blunderbuss	N/A	N/A	N/A	8.3 DPS Gun (2.6 Speed)
Deadly Scope	N/A	N/A	N/A	Adds 5 dmg/shot to a Bow or Gun
Deepdive Helmet	N/A	N/A	N/A	Cloth Head: 82 Armor, +15 Stamina, Allows Underwater Breathing
Discombobulator Ray	12 sec	20 yd	3 mins	Reduces Target Attack Rate by 50% and Movement by 30%
Explosive Sheep	3 mins	20 yd	1 min	Use: Summons an Explosive Sheep which will charge at a nearby enemy and explode for 135 to 165 dmg
EZ-Thro Dynamite	Instant	20 yd	1 min	Use: Inflicts 51 to 69 Fire dmg in a 5 yard radius (Usable by Non-Engineers)
Fire Goggles	N/A	N/A	N/A	Cloth Head: 73 Armor, 17 Fire Resistance
Flame Deflector	15 sec	Self	None	Increases Fire Resistance by 15 for 15 secs
Flash Bomb	10 sec	20 yd	3 mins	Causes All Beasts in a 5 yard Radius to Flee
Flying Tiger Goggles	N/A	N/A	N/A	Cloth Helm: 45 Armor, +4 Stamina, +4 Spirit
Gnomish Battle Chicken	90 sec	Short	1 min	Summons a Combative Chicken
Gnomish Cloaking Device	10 sec	Self	1 hr	Makes the User Invisible

ITEM	DURATION	RANGE	COOLDOWN	DESCRIPTION
Gnomish Death Ray	N/A	N/A	10 mins	Trinket: Use: Can Do Serious Harm to Target (or User)
Gnomish Goggles	N/A	N/A	N/A	Cloth Helm: 75 Armor, +9 Agility,.+9 Stamina, +9 Spirit
Gnomish Harm Prevention Belt	10 mins	Self	N/A	Leather Waist: 96 Armor, +6 Stamina, Use: Shield User from 500 dmg
Gnomish Mind Control Cap	20 sec	20 yd	60 mins	Cloth Head: 83 Armor, +14 Spirit, Use: Attempts to Mind Control a Humanoid Target
Gnomish Net-o-Matic Projector	20 sec	20 yd	10 mins	Attempts to Root Target (May Root User)
Gnomish Rocket Boots	20 sec	Self	5 mins	Cloth Feet: 68 Armor, Use: Chance to Boost Speed
Gnomish Shrink Ray	N/A	20 yd	5 mins	Trinket That Reduces Target Attack Power by 250
Gnomish Universal Remote	Instant	20 yd	3 mins	Attempts to Mind Controll a Machine (May Root/Taunt Instead)
Goblin Bomb Dispenser	Instant	20 yd	30 mins	Trinket: Use to Create a Mobile Bomb that Seeks a Target and Deals 315-385 Fire dmg
Goblin Construction Hat	N/A	N/A	N/A	Cloth Helm: 73 Armor, 15 Fire Resistance, Use: Aborbs 300-500 Fire dmg
Goblin Dragon Gun	10 sec	Forward Cone	1 min	Deals 61-69 Fire dmg/sec For 10 secs
Goblin Jumper Cables	Instant	Short	30 mins	Attempts to Resurrect a Target (May Explode)
Goblin Land Mine	Long	Short	1 min	Explodes for 450 Fire dmg When an Enemy Steps on It
Goblin Mining Helmet	N/A	N/A	N/A	Mail Helm: 221 Armor, +5 Mining, +15 Stamina
Goblin Mortar	3 sec	20 yd	10 mins	Deals 383 to 517 Fire dmg/Stuns Targets in a 10 Yard Radius for 3 sec
Goblin Rocket Boots	20 sec	Self	5 mins	Cloth Boots: 68 Armor, Use: Adds to Your Run Speed (Or Explodes)
Goblin Rocket Fuel Recipe	N/A	N/A	N/A	Component
Goblin Rocket Helmet	30 sec	20 yd	3 mins	Cloth Helm: 83 Armor, +15 Stamina, Use: Charge an Enemy and Mez Them
Goblin Sapper Charge	Instant	Self	1 min	Deals 450 to 750 Fire dmg to Enemies Nearby and 375-625 dmg to User
Gold Power Core	N/A	N/A	N/A	Component
Green Lens	N/A	N/A	N/A	Cloth Head: 95 Armor, +10 Stamina, + Random Enchantment
Green Tinted Goggles	N/A	N/A	N/A	Cloth Head: 57 Armor, +8 Stamina, +7 Spirit
Gyrochronatom	N/A	N/A	N/A	Component
Handful of Copper Bolts	N/A	N/A	N/A	Component
Heavy Blasting Powder	N/A	N/A	N/A	Component
Heavy Dynamite	Instant	20 yd	1 min	Use: Inflicts 128 to 172 Fire dmg in a 5 yard radius
Hi-Explosive Bomb	3 sec	20 yd	1 min	Use: Inflicts 255-345 Fire dmg/Disorients Targets in a 3 Yard Radius for 3 sec
Hi-Impact Mithril Slugs	N/A	N/A	N/A	Adds 13 DPS to a Gun
Ice Deflector	15 sec	Self	5 mins	Increases Frost Resistance by 18
Inlaid Mithril Cylinder	N/A	N/A	N/A	Component
Iron Grenade	Instant	20 yd	1 min	Use: Inflicts 132 to 218 Fire dmg/disorients targets in a 3 yard radius for 3 sec
Iron Strut	N/A	N/A	N/A	Component
Large Copper Bomb	1 sec	20 yd	1 min	Use: Inflicts 43 to 57 Fire dmg/disorients targets in a 5 yard radius for 1 sec
Large Seaforium Charge	Instant	Short	None	Opens Difficult Locked Doors
Lil' Smoky	N/A	N/A	N/A	Summons a Friendly Robot
Lovingly Crafted Boomstick	N/A	N/A	N/A	9.7 DPS Gun (1.8 Speed)
Mechanical Dragonling	1 min	Short	1 hr	Summons a Combative Pet
Mechanical Repair Kit	Instant	20 yd	None	Restores 700 Health to a Friendly Mechanical Target
Mechanical Squirrel	None	N/A	1 sec	Summons a Mechanical Pet
Minor Recombobulator	Instant	20 yd	None	Dispels Polymorph on a Friendly Target
Mithril Blunderbuss	N/A	N/A	N/A	17.9 DPS Gun (2.9 Speed)
Mithril Casing	N/A	N/A	N/A	Component
Mithril Frag Bomb	2 sec	20 yd	1 min	Deals 149-201 Fire dmg in an 8 Yard Radius/Disorients Targets for 2 sec
Mithril Gyro-Shot	N/A	N/A	N/A	Adds 15.5 DPS to a Gun
Mithril Heavy-bore Rifle	N/A	N/A	N/A	20.1 DPS Gun (3.4 Speed)
Mithril Mechanical Dragonling	1 min	Short	1 hr	Summons a Combative Pet
Mithril Tube	N/A	N/A	N/A	Component
Moonsight Rifle	N/A	N/A	N/A	11.8 DPS Gun (1.7 Speed)
Ornate Spyglass	Instant	N/A	N/A	Looks at a Distant Point
Parachute Cloak	30 sec	Self	30 mins	Back: 49 Armor, +8 Agility, Use: Reduce Fall Speed
Pet Bombling	N/A	N/A	N/A	Summons a Pet Bomb
Portable Bronze Mortar	Instant	20 yd	30 secs	Use: Inflicts 85 to 115 Fire dmg/disorients targets in a 5 yard radius for 2 sec
Practice Lock	N/A	N/A	N/A	Used to Raise Lockpicking
Rose Colored Goggles	N/A	N/A	N/A	Cloth Head: 82 Armor, +12 Intellect, +13 Spirit
Rough Blasting Powder	N/A	N/A	N/A	Component
Rough Boomstick	N/A	N/A	N/A	4.1 DPS Gun (Speed 2.3)
Rough Copper Bomb	1 sec	20 yd	1 min	Use: Inflicts 22 to 28 Fire dmg/disorients targets in a 3 yard radius for 1 sec
Rough Dynamite	Instant	20 yd	1 min	Use: Inflicts 26 to 34 Fire dmg in a 5 yard radius
Samophlange Micro-adjustor	N/A	N/A	N/A	Component
Shadow Goggles	N/A	N/A	N/A	Cloth Helm: 50 Armor, +5 Intellect, +6 Spirit
Silver Contact	N/A	N/A	N/A	Component
Silver-plated Shotgun	N/A	N/A	N/A	10.4 DPS Gun (2.7 Speed)
Small Bronze Bomb	2 sec	20 yd	1 min	Use: Inflicts 73 to 97 Fire dmg/disorients targets in a 3 yard radius for 2 sec
Small Seaforium Charge	Instant	Short	None	Opens Simple, Locked Doors
Sniper Scope	N/A	N/A	N/A	Adds 7 dmg/shot to a Bow or Gun
Solid Blasting Powder	N/A	N/A	N/A	Component
Solid Dynamite	Instant	20 yd	1 min	Use: Inflicts 213 to 285 Fire dmg in a 5 yard radius
Spellpower Goggles Xtreme	N/A	N/A	N/A	Cloth Head: 76 Armor, Increases dmg and Healing of Spells by 11
Standard Scope	N/A	N/A	N/A	Adds 2 dmg/shot to Bows and Guns
Target Dummy	3 mins	Short	1 min	Taunts Nearby Monsters
The Big One	5 sec	20 yd	1 min	Use: Inflicts 340-460 Fire dmg/Disorients Targets in a 10 Yard Radius for 5 sec
Unstable Trigger	N/A	N/A	N/A	Component
Whirring Bronze Gizmo	N/A	N/A	N/A	Component

BESTIARY

ALTERAC MOUNTAINS

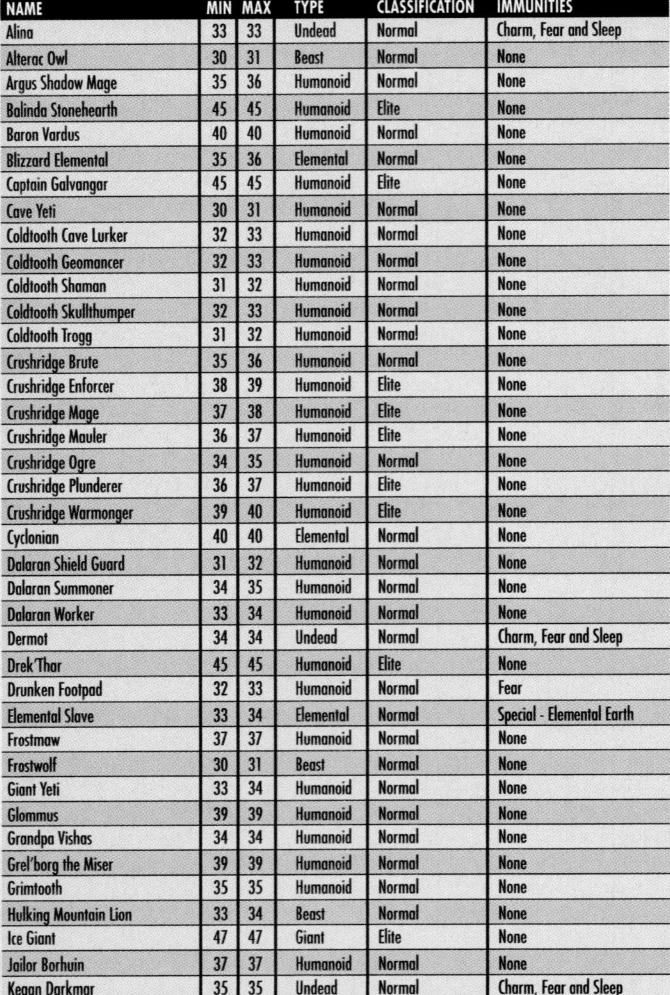

NAME	MIN	MAX	TYPE	CLASSIFICATION	IMMUNITIES
Alina	33	33	Undead	Normal	Charm, Fear and Sleep
Alterac Owl	30	31	Beast	Normal	None
Argus Shadow Mage	35	36	Humanoid	Normal	None
Balinda Stonehearth	45	45	Humanoid	Elite	None
Baron Vardus	40	40	Humanoid	Normal	None
Blizzard Elemental	35	36	Elemental	Normal	None
Captain Galvangar	45	45	Humanoid	Elite	None
Cave Yeti	30	31	Humanoid	Normal	None
Coldtooth Cave Lurker	32	33	Humanoid	Normal	None
Coldtooth Geomancer	32	33	Humanoid	Normal	None
Coldtooth Shaman	31	32	Humanoid	Normal	None
Coldtooth Skullthumper	32	33	Humanoid	Normal	None
Coldtooth Trogg	31	32	Humanoid	Normal	None
Crushridge Brute	35	36	Humanoid	Normal	None
Crushridge Enforcer	38	39	Humanoid	Elite	None
Crushridge Mage	37	38	Humanoid	Elite	None
Crushridge Mauler	36	37	Humanoid	Elite	None
Crushridge Ogre	34	35	Humanoid	Normal	None
Crushridge Plunderer	36	37	Humanoid	Elite	None
Crushridge Warmonger	39	40	Humanoid	Elite	None
Cyclonian	40	40	Elemental	Normal	None
Dalaran Shield Guard	31	32	Humanoid	Normal	None
Dalaran Summoner	34	35	Humanoid	Normal	None
Dalaran Worker	33	34	Humanoid	Normal	None
Dermot	34	34	Undead	Normal	Charm, Fear and Sleep
Drek'Thar	45	45	Humanoid	Elite	None
Drunken Footpad	32	33	Humanoid	Normal	Fear
Elemental Slave	33	34	Elemental	Normal	Special - Elemental Earth
Frostmaw	37	37	Humanoid	Normal	None
Frostwolf	30	31	Beast	Normal	None
Giant Yeti	33	34	Humanoid	Normal	None
Glommus	39	39	Humanoid	Normal	None
Grandpa Vishas	34	34	Humanoid	Normal	None
Grel'borg the Miser	39	39	Humanoid	Normal	None
Grimtooth	35	35	Humanoid	Normal	None
Hulking Mountain Lion	33	34	Beast	Normal	None
Ice Giant	47	47	Giant	Elite	None
Jailor Borhuin	37	37	Humanoid	Normal	None
Kegan Darkmar	35	35	Undead	Normal	Charm, Fear and Sleep
Lo'Grosh	39	39	Humanoid	Rare Spawn	None

NAME	MIN	MAX	TYPE	CLASSIFICATION	IMMUNITIES
Lord Aliden Perenolde	42	42	Humanoid	Normal	None
Morloch	34	34	Humanoid	Normal	None
Mountain Lion	32	33	Beast	Normal	None
Mountain Yeti	32	33	Humanoid	Normal	None
Muckrake	40	40	Humanoid	Elite	None
Mug'thol	43	43	Humanoid	Normal	None
Nagaz	40	40	Humanoid	Normal	None
Narillasanz	44	44	Dragon	Elite	Special - Fire Dragon
Ricter	33	33	Undead	Normal	Charm, Fear and Sleep
Skhowl	36	36	Humanoid	Rare Spawn	None
Snapjaw	30	31	Beast	Normal	None
Snowblind Ambusher	35	36	Humanoid	Normal	None
Snowblind Harpy	35	36	Humanoid	Normal	None
Snowblind Windcaller	35	36	Humanoid	Normal	None
Stone Fury	37	37	Elemental	Normal	Special - Elemental Earth
Syndicate Assassin	38	39	Humanoid	Normal	None
Syndicate Enforcer	39	40	Humanoid	Normal	None
Syndicate Footpad	32	33	Humanoid	Normal	None
Syndicate Saboteur	37	38	Humanoid	Normal	None
Syndicate Sentry	36	37	Humanoid	Normal	None
Syndicate Spy	35	36	Humanoid	Normal	None
Syndicate Thief	33	34	Humanoid	Normal	None
Syndicate Wizard	34	35	Humanoid	Normal	None
Targ	41	41	Humanoid	Elite	None
Taskmaster Snivvle	34	34	Humanoid	Normal	None
Vanndar Stormpike	45	45	Humanoid	Elite	None
Warden Belamoore	36	36	Humanoid	Normal	None
Whitewhisker Digger	31	32	Humanoid	Normal	None
Whitewhisker Geomancer	32	33	Humanoid	Normal	None
Whitewhisker Overseer	32	33	Humanoid	Normal	None
Whitewhisker Tunnel Rat	32	33	Humanoid	Normal	None
Whitewhisker Vermin	31	32	Humanoid	Normal	None
Wildpaw Alpha	32	33	Humanoid	Normal	None
Wildpaw Brute	32	33	Humanoid	Normal	None
Wildpaw Gnoll	31	32	Humanoid	Normal	None
Wildpaw Mystic	32	33	Humanoid	Normal	None
Wildpaw Shaman	31	32	Humanoid	Normal	None
Winterax Berserker	40	41	Humanoid	Elite	None
Winterax Shadowcaster	40	41	Humanoid	Elite	None
Winterax Troll	40	41	Humanoid	Elite	None

ARATHI HIGHLANDS

NAME	MIN	MAX	TYPE	CLASSIFICATION	IMMUNITIES
Apothecary Jorell	36	36	Undead	Normal	Charm, Fear and Sleep
Blackwater Deckhand	38	39	Humanoid	Normal	None
Boulderfist Brute	35	36	Humanoid	Normal	None
Boulderfist Enforcer	33	34	Humanoid	Normal	None
Boulderfist Lord	39	40	Humanoid	Elite	None
Boulderfist Magus	36	37	Humanoid	Normal	None
Boulderfist Mauler	37	38	Humanoid	Elite	None
Boulderfist Ogre	32	33	Humanoid	Normal	None
Boulderfist Shaman	38	39	Humanoid	Elite	None
Burning Exile	38	39	Elemental	Normal	Special - Elemental Fire
Caretaker Alaric	41	41	Humanoid	Elite	None
Caretaker Nevlin	41	41	Humanoid	Elite	None
Caretaker Weston	41	41	Humanoid	Elite	None
Cresting Exile	38	39	Elemental	Normal	Special - Elemental Water
Daggerspine Marauder	40	41	Humanoid	Normal	None
Daggerspine Raider	38	39	Humanoid	Normal	None
Daggerspine Sorceress	39	40	Humanoid	Normal	None
Darbel Montrose	39	39	Humanoid	Rare Spawn Elite	None
Dark Iron Bombardier	30	31	Humanoid	Normal	None
Dark Iron Supplier	31	32	Humanoid	Normal	None
Drywhisker Digger	36	37	Humanoid	Normal	None
Drywhisker Kobold	35	36	Humanoid	Normal	None
Drywhisker Surveyor	37	38	Humanoid	Normal	None

NAME	MIN	MAX	TYPE	CLASSIFICATION	IMMUNITIES
Elder Mesa Buzzard	37	38	Beast	Normal	None
Fardel Dabyrie	33	33	Humanoid	Normal	None
Feeboz	39	39	Humanoid	Normal	None
Forsaken Bodyguard	35	35	Undead	Normal	Charm, Fear and Sleep
Forsaken Courier	35	35	Undead	Normal	Charm, Fear and Sleep
Foulbelly	42	42	Humanoid	Rare Spawn Elite	None
Fozruk	42	42	Giant	Elite	None
Geomancer Flintdagger	40	40	Humanoid	Rare Spawn	None
Giant Plains Creeper	35	36	Beast	Normal	None
Hammerfall Grunt	34	35	Humanoid	Normal	None
Hammerfall Guardian	50	50	Humanoid	Normal	None
Hammerfall Peon	33	34	Humanoid	Normal	None
Highland Fleshstalker	36	37	Beast	Normal	None
Highland Strider	30	31	Beast	Normal	None
Highland Thrasher	33	34	Beast	Normal	None
Kenata Dabyrie	35	35	Humanoid	Normal	None
Kor'gresh Coldrage	39	39	Humanoid	Normal	None
Kovork	36	36	Humanoid	Rare Spawn	None
Lord Falconcrest	40	40	Humanoid	Elite	None
Marcel Dabyrie	34	34	Humanoid	Normal	None
Marez Cowl	40	40	Humanoid	Elite	None
Mesa Buzzard	34	35	Beast	Normal	None
Molok the Crusher	39	39	Humanoid	Rare Spawn	None

XIV

ALT-DUR

DUR-HIN

LOC-STR

SWA-WIN

ARATHI HIGHLANDS

NAME	MIN	MAX	TYPE	CLASSIFICATION	IMMUNITIES
Myzrael	50	50	Elemental	Elite	Special
Nimar the Slayer	37	37	Humanoid	Rare Spawn	None
Or'Kalar	40	40	Humanoid	Normal	None
Otto	38	38	Humanoid	Elite	None
Plains Creeper	32	33	Beast	Normal	None
Prince Nazjak	41	41	Humanoid	Rare Spawn	None
Rumbling Exile	38	39	Elemental	Normal	Special - Elemental Earth
Ruul Onestone	39	39	Humanoid	Rare Spawn Elite	None
Shakes O'Breen	40	40	Humanoid	Normal	None
Singer	34	34	Humanoid	Rare Spawn	None
Sleeby	40	40	Humanoid	Normal	None
Stromgarde Cavalryman	36	37	Humanoid	Normal	None
Summoned Guardian	38	38	Elemental	Elite	Special - Elemental Water
Syndicate Conjuror	35	36	Humanoid	Elite	None
Syndicate Highwayman	30	31	Humanoid	Normal	None
Syndicate Magus	37	38	Humanoid	Elite	None
Syndicate Mercenary	31	32	Humanoid	Normal	None
Syndicate Pathstalker	32	33	Humanoid	Normal	None
Syndicate Prowler	36	37	Humanoid	Elite	None
Thenan	42	42	Giant	Elite	None
Thundering Exile	38	39	Elemental	Normal	Special - Elemental Air
Vengeful Surge	40	40	Elemental	Normal	Special - Elemental Water
Witherbark Axe Thrower	32	33	Humanoid	Normal	None
Witherbark Berserker	36	37	Humanoid	Elite	None
Witherbark Headhunter	34	35	Humanoid	Normal	None
Witherbark Shadow Hunter	35	36	Humanoid	Normal	None
Witherbark Shadowcaster	31	32	Humanoid	Normal	None
Witherbark Troll	30	31	Humanoid	Normal	None
Witherbark Witch Doctor	33	34	Humanoid	Normal	None
Young Mesa Buzzard	31	32	Beast	Normal	None
Zalas Witherbark	40	40	Humanoid	Normal	None
Znort	39	39	Humanoid	Normal	None

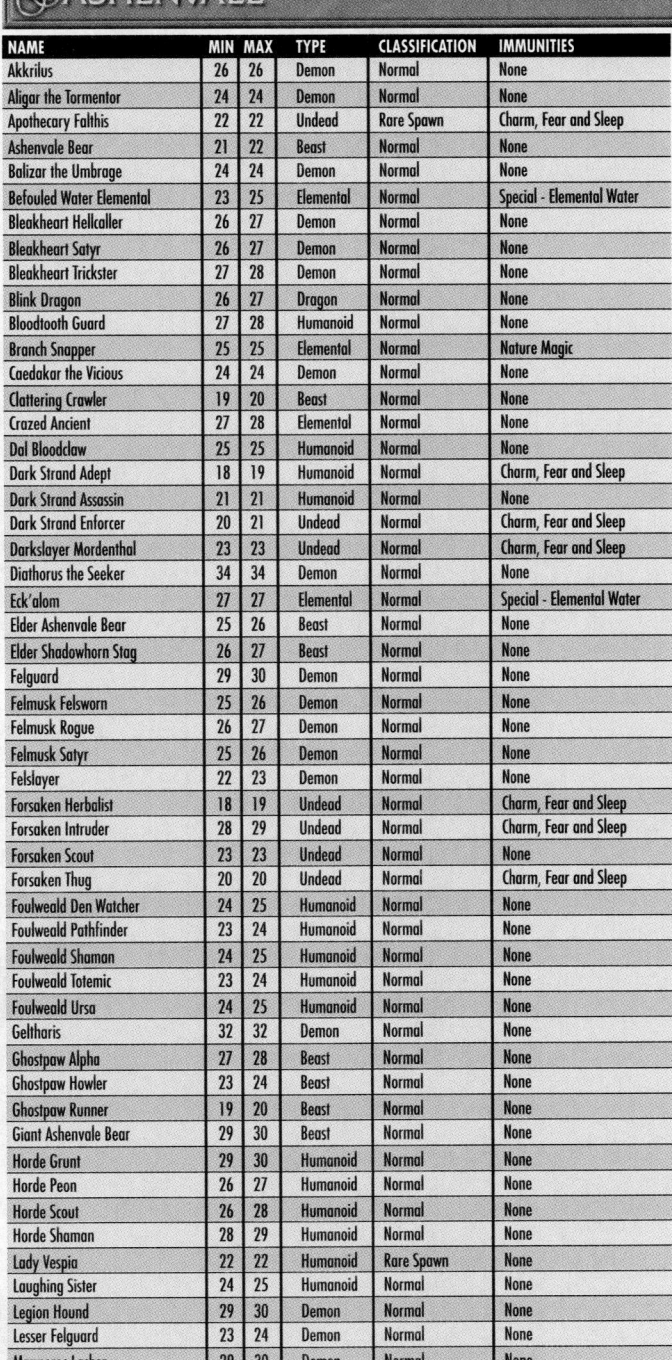

ASHENVALE

NAME	MIN	MAX	TYPE	CLASSIFICATION	IMMUNITIES
Akkrilus	26	26	Demon	Normal	None
Aligar the Tormentor	24	24	Demon	Normal	None
Apothecary Falthis	22	22	Undead	Rare Spawn	Charm, Fear and Sleep
Ashenvale Bear	21	22	Beast	Normal	None
Balizar the Umbrage	24	24	Demon	Normal	None
Befouled Water Elemental	23	25	Elemental	Normal	Special - Elemental Water
Bleakheart Hellcaller	26	27	Demon	Normal	None
Bleakheart Satyr	26	27	Demon	Normal	None
Bleakheart Trickster	27	28	Demon	Normal	None
Blink Dragon	26	27	Dragon	Normal	None
Bloodtooth Guard	27	28	Humanoid	Normal	None
Branch Snapper	25	25	Elemental	Normal	Nature Magic
Caedakar the Vicious	24	24	Demon	Normal	None
Clattering Crawler	19	20	Beast	Normal	None
Crazed Ancient	27	28	Elemental	Normal	None
Dal Bloodclaw	25	25	Humanoid	Normal	None
Dark Strand Adept	18	19	Humanoid	Normal	Charm, Fear and Sleep
Dark Strand Assassin	21	21	Humanoid	Normal	None
Dark Strand Enforcer	20	21	Undead	Normal	Charm, Fear and Sleep
Darkslayer Mordenthal	23	23	Undead	Normal	Charm, Fear and Sleep
Diathorus the Seeker	34	34	Demon	Normal	None
Eck'alom	27	27	Elemental	Normal	Special - Elemental Water
Elder Ashenvale Bear	25	26	Beast	Normal	None
Elder Shadowhorn Stag	26	27	Beast	Normal	None
Felguard	29	30	Demon	Normal	None
Felmusk Felsworn	25	26	Demon	Normal	None
Felmusk Rogue	26	27	Demon	Normal	None
Felmusk Satyr	25	26	Demon	Normal	None
Felslayer	22	23	Demon	Normal	None
Forsaken Herbalist	18	19	Undead	Normal	Charm, Fear and Sleep
Forsaken Intruder	28	29	Undead	Normal	Charm, Fear and Sleep
Forsaken Scout	23	23	Undead	Normal	None
Forsaken Thug	20	20	Undead	Normal	Charm, Fear and Sleep
Foulweald Den Watcher	24	25	Humanoid	Normal	None
Foulweald Pathfinder	23	24	Humanoid	Normal	None
Foulweald Shaman	24	25	Humanoid	Normal	None
Foulweald Totemic	23	24	Humanoid	Normal	None
Foulweald Ursa	24	25	Humanoid	Normal	None
Gelthanis	32	32	Demon	Normal	None
Ghostpaw Alpha	27	28	Beast	Normal	None
Ghostpaw Howler	23	24	Beast	Normal	None
Ghostpaw Runner	19	20	Beast	Normal	None
Giant Ashenvale Bear	29	30	Beast	Normal	None
Horde Grunt	29	30	Humanoid	Normal	None
Horde Peon	26	27	Humanoid	Normal	None
Horde Scout	26	28	Humanoid	Normal	None
Horde Shaman	28	29	Humanoid	Normal	None
Lady Vespia	22	22	Humanoid	Rare Spawn	None
Laughing Sister	24	25	Humanoid	Normal	None
Legion Hound	29	30	Demon	Normal	None
Lesser Felguard	23	24	Demon	Normal	None
Mannoroc Lasher	29	30	Demon	Normal	None
Mavoris Cloudsbreak	32	32	Undead	Normal	Charm, Fear and Sleep
Mist Howler	22	22	Beast	Rare Spawn	None
Mugglefin	23	23	Humanoid	Rare Spawn	None
Mystlash Flayer	20	21	Unknown	Normal	None
Mystlash Hydra	19	20	Unknown	Normal	None
Oakpaw	27	27	Humanoid	Normal	None
Prince Raze	32	32	Demon	Normal	None
Ran Bloodtooth	30	30	Humanoid	Normal	None
Rorgish Jowl	25	25	Humanoid	Rare Spawn	None
Rotting Slime	20	22	Unknown	Normal	None
Ruuzel	22	22	Humanoid	Normal	None
Saltspittle Muckdweller	20	21	Humanoid	Normal	None
Saltspittle Puddlejumper	19	20	Humanoid	Normal	None
Saltspittle Warrior	19	20	Humanoid	Normal	None
Severed Druid	28	29	Undead	Normal	Charm, Fear and Sleep
Severed Sleeper	28	29	Undead	Normal	Charm, Fear and Sleep
Shadethicket Bark Ripper	26	27	Elemental	Normal	None
Shadethicket Moss Eater	21	23	Elemental	Normal	None
Shadethicket Oracle	30	30	Elemental	Normal	None
Shadethicket Raincaller	22	23	Elemental	Normal	None
Shadethicket Stone Mover	25	26	Elemental	Normal	None
Shadowhorn Stag	22	23	Beast	Normal	None
Taneel Darkwood	32	32	Undead	Normal	None
Terrowulf Fleshripper	28	29	Humanoid	Normal	None
Terrowulf Packlord	31	32	Humanoid	Rare Spawn	None
Thistlefur Avenger	23	24	Humanoid	Normal	None
Thistlefur Den Watcher	23	24	Humanoid	Normal	None
Thistlefur Pathfinder	23	24	Humanoid	Normal	None
Thistlefur Shaman	23	24	Humanoid	Normal	None
Thistlefur Totemic	23	24	Humanoid	Normal	None
Thistlefur Ursa	23	24	Humanoid	Normal	None
Ursol'lok	31	31	Beast	Rare Spawn	None
Uthil Mooncall	32	32	Undead	Normal	Charm, Fear and Sleep
Warsong Shredder	27	28	Mechanical	Normal	Special - Piloted Mechanical
Wild Buck	18	19	Beast	Normal	None
Wildthorn Lurker	28	29	Beast	Normal	None
Wildthorn Stalker	20	21	Beast	Normal	None
Wildthorn Venomspitter	24	25	Beast	Normal	None
Wrathtail Myrmidon	20	21	Humanoid	Normal	None
Wrathtail Priestess	20	21	Humanoid	Normal	None
Wrathtail Razortail	19	20	Humanoid	Normal	None
Wrathtail Sea Witch	19	20	Humanoid	Normal	None
Wrathtail Sorceress	18	19	Humanoid	Normal	None
Wrathtail Wave Rider	18	19	Humanoid	Normal	None
Xavian Felsworn	28	29	Demon	Normal	None
Xavian Hellcaller	29	30	Demon	Normal	None

AZSHARA

NAME	MIN	MAX	TYPE	CLASSIFICATION	IMMUNITIES
Antilos	50	50	Beast	Rare Spawn	None
Arkkoran Clacker	53	54	Humanoid	Normal	None
Arkkoran Oracle	54	55	Humanoid	Normal	None
Azshara Sentinel	44	44	Humanoid	Normal	None
Azurgos	65	65	Dragon	Elite	None
Blood Elf Defender	51	51	Humanoid	Normal	None
Blood Elf Surveyor	51	52	Humanoid	Normal	None
Blue Dragonspawn	50	51	Dragon	Normal	None
Caravan Master Tset	53	53	Humanoid	Normal	None
Cliff Breaker	54	55	Giant	Elite	None
Cliff Walker	52	53	Giant	Elite	None
Coralshell Lurker	53	54	Beast	Normal	None
Coralshell Tortoise	50	52	Beast	Normal	None
Draconic Magelord	53	54	Dragon	Normal	None
Draconic Mageweaver	51	52	Dragon	Normal	None
Forest Ooze	52	53	Unknown	Normal	None
Gatekeeper Rageroar	49	50	Humanoid	Rare Spawn	None
General Fangferror	50	51	Humanoid	Rare Spawn	None
Great Wavethrasher	53	54	Unknown	Normal	None
Haldarr Satyr	45	46	Demon	Normal	None
Hetaera	55	55	Unknown	Elite	None
Highborne Apparition	45	46	Undead	Normal	Charm, Fear, Sleep and Bleed
Lady Sesspira	51	51	Humanoid	Rare Spawn	None
Legashi Satyr	51	52	Demon	Normal	None
Lingering Highborne	48	50	Undead	Normal	Charm, Fear, Sleep and Bleed
Magister Hawkhelm	51	52	Humanoid	Rare Spawn	None
Makrinni Scrabbler	52	53	Humanoid	Normal	None
Master Feardred	51	52	Demon	Rare Spawn	None
Mistwing Ravager	52	53	Beast	Normal	None
Monnos the Elder	53	54	Giant	Rare Spawn Elite	None
Mosshoof Courser	52	53	Beast	Normal	None
Mosshoof Runner	45	47	Beast	Normal	None
Mosshoof Stag	49	50	Beast	Normal	None
Servant of Arkkoroc	53	54	Giant	Elite	None
Spitelash Battlemaster	53	54	Humanoid	Normal	None
Spitelash Myrmidon	50	51	Humanoid	Normal	None
Spitelash Serpent Guard	48	49	Humanoid	Normal	None
Spitelash Siren	51	52	Humanoid	Normal	None
Spitelash Sorceress	49	50	Humanoid	Normal	None
Spitelash Warrior	46	47	Humanoid	Normal	None
Storm Bay Warrior	51	52	Humanoid	Normal	None
The Evalcharr	48	48	Beast	Rare Spawn	None
Thunderhead Hippogryph	46	48	Beast	Normal	None
Thunderhead Patriarch	52	54	Beast	Normal	None
Thunderhead Skystormer	50	52	Beast	Normal	None
Thunderhead Stagwing	48	50	Beast	Normal	None
Timbermaw Den Watcher	49	50	Humanoid	Normal	None
Timbermaw Pathfinder	46	47	Humanoid	Normal	None
Timbermaw Shaman	50	51	Humanoid	Normal	None
Timbermaw Ursa	51	52	Humanoid	Normal	None
Timbermaw Warrior	47	48	Humanoid	Normal	None
Timberweb Recluse	47	48	Beast	Normal	None
Varo'then's Ghost	48	48	Undead	Rare Spawn	Charm, Fear, Sleep and Bleed
Warlord Krellian	55	55	Humanoid	Normal	None
Wavethrasher	52	53	Unknown	Normal	None

BADLANDS

NAME	MIN	MAX	TYPE	CLASSIFICATION	IMMUNITIES
Ambassador Infernus	42	42	Elemental	Elite	Special - Elemental Fire
Blacklash	50	50	Dragon	Normal	Special - Fire Dragon
Boss Tho'grun	41	42	Humanoid	Normal	None
Buzzard	37	39	Beast	Normal	None
Crag Coyote	35	36	Beast	Normal	None
Dustbelcher Brute	39	40	Humanoid	Normal	None
Dustbelcher Lord	44	45	Humanoid	Normal	None
Dustbelcher Mauler	41	42	Humanoid	Normal	None
Dustbelcher Mystic	36	37	Humanoid	Normal	None
Dustbelcher Ogre	38	39	Humanoid	Normal	None
Dustbelcher Ogre Mage	43	44	Humanoid	Normal	None
Dustbelcher Shaman	42	43	Humanoid	Normal	None
Dustbelcher Warrior	35	37	Humanoid	Normal	None
Dustbelcher Wyrmhunter	40	41	Humanoid	Normal	None
Elder Crag Coyote	39	40	Beast	Normal	None
Enraged Rock Elemental	42	43	Elemental	Normal	Special - Elemental Earth
Fam'retor Guardian	45	45	Elemental	Normal	Special - Elemental Earth
Feral Crag Coyote	37	38	Beast	Normal	None
Giant Buzzard	39	41	Beast	Normal	None
Greater Rock Elemental	42	44	Elemental	Normal	Special - Elemental Earth
Hematus	50	50	Dragon	Elite	Special - Fire Dragon
Lesser Rock Elemental	37	39	Elemental	Normal	Special - Elemental Earth
Murdaloc	42	42	Humanoid	Normal	None
Rabid Crag Coyote	42	43	Beast	Normal	None
Ridge Huntress	38	39	Beast	Normal	None
Ridge Stalker	36	37	Beast	Normal	None
Ridge Stalker Patriarch	40	41	Beast	Normal	None
Rock Elemental	39	40	Elemental	Normal	Special - Elemental Earth
Scalding Whelp	41	43	Dragon	Normal	None
Scorched Guardian	43	45	Dragon	Elite	Fire Magic
Shadowforge Chanter	38	39	Humanoid	Normal	None
Shadowforge Darkweaver	36	37	Humanoid	Normal	None
Shadowforge Tunneler	35	36	Humanoid	Normal	None
Shadowforge Warrior	38	39	Humanoid	Normal	None
Starving Buzzard	35	37	Beast	Normal	None
Stone Golem	38	39	Elemental	Normal	Special - Golem
Stonevault Basher	39	40	Humanoid	Elite	None
Stonevault Bonesnapper	39	40	Humanoid	Normal	None
Stonevault Shaman	40	41	Humanoid	Normal	None
Wayward Buzzard	35	37	Beast	Normal	None
Zaricotl	55	55	Beast	Rare Spawn Elite	None

BLASTED LANDS

NAME	MIN	MAX	TYPE	CLASSIFICATION	IMMUNITIES
Akubar the Seer	54	54	Humanoid	Rare Spawn	None
Archmage Allistarj	58	58	Demon	Elite	Special
Black Slayer	46	48	Beast	Normal	None
Clack the Reaver	53	53	Beast	Rare Spawn	None
Deatheye	49	49	Beast	Rare Spawn	None
Dreadlord	63	63	Demon	Elite	Special
Dreadmaul Brute	46	47	Humanoid	Normal	None
Dreadmaul Mauler	53	54	Humanoid	Normal	None
Dreadmaul Ogre	45	46	Humanoid	Normal	None
Dreadmaul Ogre Mage	46	47	Humanoid	Normal	None
Dreadscorn	57	57	Humanoid	Rare Spawn	None
Felguard Elite	60	60	Demon	Elite	Special
Felguard Sentry	54	55	Demon	Normal	None
Felhound	54	55	Demon	Normal	None
Grol the Destroyer	58	58	Demon	Elite	Special
Grunter	50	50	Beast	Rare Spawn	None
Helboar	52	53	Demon	Normal	None
Kirith the Damned	55	55	Demon	Elite	None
Lady Sevine	59	59	Demon	Elite	Special
Magronos the Unyeilding	56	56	Humanoid	Rare Spawn	None
Manahound	60	60	Demon	Elite	Special
Mojo the Twisted	48	48	Humanoid	Rare Spawn	None
Nethergarde Analyst	49	51	Humanoid	Normal	None
Nethergarde Cleric	49	51	Humanoid	Normal	None
Nethergarde Elite	55	55	Humanoid	Elite	None
Nethergarde Engineer	47	48	Humanoid	Normal	None
Nethergarde Miner	47	48	Humanoid	Normal	None
Nethergarde Officer	50	51	Humanoid	Normal	None
Nethergarde Soldier	49	50	Humanoid	Normal	None
Portal Seeker	51	53	Humanoid	Normal	None
Ravage	51	51	Beast	Rare Spawn	None
Redstone Basilisk	47	48	Beast	Normal	None
Scorpok Stinger	50	51	Beast	Normal	None
Shadowsworn Cultist	51	52	Humanoid	Normal	None
Shadowsworn Dreadweaver	54	55	Humanoid	Normal	None
Shadowsworn Thug	52	53	Humanoid	Normal	None
Snickerfang Hyena	49	50	Beast	Normal	None
Spiteflayer	52	52	Beast	Rare Spawn	None
Teremus the Devourer	60	60	Dragon	Rare Spawn	Special

BURNING STEPPES

NAME	MIN	MAX	TYPE	CLASSIFICATION	IMMUNITIES
Black Broodling	51	52	Dragon	Normal	None
Black Dragonspawn	52	53	Dragon	Elite	None
Black Drake	50	52	Dragon	Elite	Special - Fire Dragon
Blackrock Battlemaster	57	58	Humanoid	Normal	None
Blackrock Raider	59	59	Humanoid	Normal	None
Blackrock Slayer	56	57	Humanoid	Normal	None
Blackrock Soldier	55	56	Humanoid	Normal	None
Blackrock Sorcerer	55	56	Humanoid	Normal	None
Blackrock Warlock	56	57	Humanoid	Normal	None
Blackrock Worg	54	55	Beast	Normal	None
Deathmaw	53	53	Beast	Rare Spawn	None
Firegut Captain	55	55	Humanoid	Rare Spawn	None
Firegut Ogre	50	51	Humanoid	Normal	None
Firegut Ogre Mage	51	52	Humanoid	Normal	None
Flamekin Rager	54	56	Demon	Normal	None
Flamekin Spitter	51	53	Demon	Normal	None
Flamekin Sprite	51	53	Demon	Normal	None
Flamekin Torcher	54	56	Demon	Normal	None
Flamescale Broodling	55	56	Dragon	Normal	None
Flamescale Dragonspawn	56	57	Dragon	Elite	None
Frenzied Black Drake	54	54	Dragon	Elite	Special - Fire Dragon
Gorgon'och	54	54	Humanoid	Rare Spawn	None
Gor'tesh	54	54	Humanoid	Normal	None
Gruklash	59	59	Humanoid	Rare Spawn	None
Hahk'Zor	54	54	Humanoid	Rare Spawn	None
Hematos	60	60	Dragon	Rare Spawn Elite	Special - Fire Dragon
Krom'Grul	54	54	Humanoid	Normal	None
Malfunctioning Reaver	56	56	Elemental	Rare Spawn	None
Scalding Broodling	53	54	Dragon	Normal	None
Scalding Drake	53	55	Dragon	Elite	Special - Fire Dragon
Searscale Drake	56	58	Dragon	Elite	Special - Fire Dragon
Slavering Ember Worg	53	54	Beast	Normal	None
Terrorspark	55	55	Demon	Rare Spawn	None
Thauris Balgarr	57	57	Humanoid	Rare Spawn	None
Thaurisan Spy	53	54	Humanoid	Normal	None
Volchan	60	60	Giant	Rare Spawn Elite	None
War Reaver	53	55	Elemental	Normal	None
Yuka Screwspigot	53	53	Humanoid	Normal	None

DARKSHORE

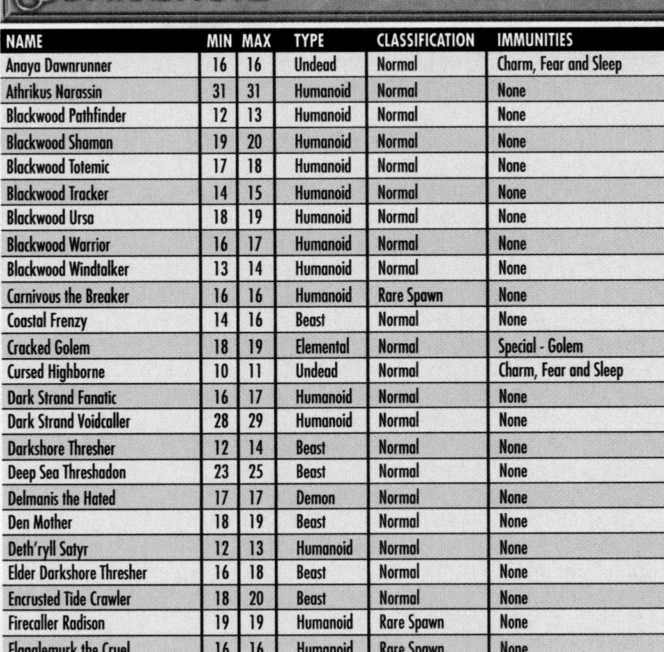

NAME	MIN	MAX	TYPE	CLASSIFICATION	IMMUNITIES
Anaya Dawnrunner	16	16	Undead	Normal	Charm, Fear and Sleep
Athrikus Narassin	31	31	Humanoid	Normal	None
Blackwood Pathfinder	12	13	Humanoid	Normal	None
Blackwood Shaman	19	20	Humanoid	Normal	None
Blackwood Totemic	17	18	Humanoid	Normal	None
Blackwood Tracker	14	15	Humanoid	Normal	None
Blackwood Ursa	18	19	Humanoid	Normal	None
Blackwood Warrior	16	17	Humanoid	Normal	None
Blackwood Windtalker	13	14	Humanoid	Normal	None
Carnivous the Breaker	16	16	Humanoid	Rare Spawn	None
Coastal Frenzy	14	16	Beast	Normal	None
Cracked Golem	18	19	Elemental	Normal	Special - Golem
Cursed Highborne	10	11	Undead	Normal	Charm, Fear and Sleep
Dark Strand Fanatic	16	17	Humanoid	Normal	None
Dark Strand Voidcaller	28	29	Humanoid	Normal	None
Darkshore Thresher	12	14	Beast	Normal	None
Deep Sea Threshadon	23	25	Beast	Normal	None
Delmanis the Hated	17	17	Demon	Normal	None
Den Mother	18	19	Beast	Normal	None
Deth'ryll Satyr	12	13	Humanoid	Normal	None
Elder Darkshore Thresher	16	18	Beast	Normal	None
Encrusted Tide Crawler	18	20	Beast	Normal	None
Firecaller Radison	19	19	Humanoid	Rare Spawn	None
Flagglemurk the Cruel	16	16	Humanoid	Rare Spawn	None
Foreststrider	14	16	Beast	Normal	None
Foreststrider Fledgling	11	13	Beast	Normal	None
Giant Foreststrider	17	19	Beast	Normal	None
Gravelflint Bonesnapper	19	20	Humanoid	Normal	None
Gravelflint Geomancer	20	21	Humanoid	Normal	None
Gravelflint Scout	18	19	Humanoid	Normal	None
Greymist Coastrunner	12	13	Humanoid	Normal	None
Greymist Hunter	16	17	Humanoid	Normal	None
Greymist Netter	14	15	Humanoid	Normal	None
Greymist Oracle	18	19	Humanoid	Normal	None
Greymist Raider	11	12	Humanoid	Normal	None
Greymist Seer	13	14	Humanoid	Normal	None
Greymist Tidehunter	19	20	Humanoid	Normal	None
Greymist Warrior	15	16	Humanoid	Normal	None
Grizzled Thistle Bear	16	17	Beast	Normal	None
Lady Moongazer	17	17	Undead	Rare Spawn	None
Lady Vespira	22	22	Humanoid	Rare Spawn	None
Licillin	14	14	Demon	Rare Spawn	None
Lord Sinslayer	15	16	Humanoid	Rare Spawn	None
Marosh The Devious	16	16	Humanoid	Normal	None
Moonkin	12	13	Beast	Normal	None
Moonkin Oracle	13	14	Beast	Normal	None
Moonstalker	14	15	Beast	Normal	None
Moonstalker Runt	10	11	Beast	Normal	None

DARKSHORE

NAME	MIN	MAX	TYPE	CLASSIFICATION	IMMUNITIES
Moonstalker Sire	17	18	Beast	Normal	None
Murkdeep	19	19	Humanoid	Normal	None
Pygmy Tide Crawler	9	10	Beast	Normal	None
Rabid Thistle Bear	13	14	Beast	Normal	None
Raging Moonkin	12	14	Beast	Normal	None
Raging Reef Crawler	20	21	Beast	Normal	None
Reef Crawler	15	17	Beast	Normal	None
Shade of Elura	11	11	Undead	Normal	None
Shadowclaw	13	13	Beast	Rare Spawn	None
Stormscale Myrmidon	18	19	Humanoid	Normal	None
Stormscale Siren	16	17	Humanoid	Normal	None
Stormscale Sorceress	19	20	Humanoid	Normal	None
Stormscale Warrior	20	21	Humanoid	Normal	None
Stormscale Wave Rider	15	16	Humanoid	Normal	None
Strider Clutchmother	20	20	Beast	Rare Spawn	None
Thistle Bear	11	12	Beast	Normal	None
Thistle Cub	9	10	Beast	Normal	None
Tide Crawler	12	14	Beast	Normal	None
Twilight Thug	17	18	Humanoid	Normal	None
Vile Sprite	10	11	Humanoid	Normal	None
Wailing Highborne	12	13	Undead	Normal	Charm, Fear, Sleep and Bleed
Wild Grell	11	12	Humanoid	Normal	None
Writhing Highborne	11	12	Undead	Normal	Charm, Fear, Sleep and Bleed
Xabraxxis	19	19	Demon	Normal	None
Young Moonkin	11	12	Beast	Normal	None
Young Reef Crawler	10	11	Beast	Normal	None

DESOLACE

NAME	MIN	MAX	TYPE	CLASSIFICATION	IMMUNITIES
Aged Kodo	34	35	Beast	Normal	None
Bonepaw Hyena	33	35	Beast	Normal	None
Burning Blade Adept	31	32	Humanoid	Normal	Fear
Burning Blade Augur	30	31	Humanoid	Normal	Fear
Burning Blade Felsworn	31	32	Humanoid	Normal	Fear
Burning Blade Reaver	30	31	Humanoid	Normal	Fear
Burning Blade Shadowmage	32	33	Humanoid	Normal	Fear
Burning Blade Summoner	38	39	Humanoid	Normal	Fear
Carrion Horror	35	37	Beast	Normal	None
Deepstrider Giant	38	39	Giant	Elite	None
Doomwarder	37	38	Demon	Normal	None
Doomwarder Captain	38	39	Demon	Normal	None
Dread Ripper	39	40	Beast	Normal	None
Dread Swoop	32	33	Beast	Normal	None
Drysnap Crawler	33	34	Humanoid	Normal	None
Dying Kodo	35	36	Beast	Normal	None
Elder Thunder Lizard	37	38	Beast	Normal	None
Galthogran the Callous	40	40	Humanoid	Normal	None
Gelkis Earthcaller	34	35	Humanoid	Normal	None
Gelkis Marauder	35	36	Humanoid	Normal	None
Gelkis Mauler	35	36	Humanoid	Normal	None
Gelkis Scout	32	33	Humanoid	Normal	None
Gritjaw Basilisk	31	32	Beast	Normal	None
Hatefury Betrayer	32	33	Demon	Normal	None
Hatefury Rogue	31	32	Demon	Normal	None
Hulking Gritjaw Basilisk	35	36	Beast	Normal	None
Khan Dez'hepah	35	35	Humanoid	Normal	None
Khan Hratha	42	42	Humanoid	Elite	None
Khan Jehn	37	37	Humanoid	Normal	None
Khan Shaka	37	37	Humanoid	Normal	None
Kodo Spirit	60	60	Beast	Normal	None
Kolkar Battle Lord	32	33	Humanoid	Normal	None
Kolkar Centaur	30	31	Humanoid	Normal	None
Kolkar Destroyer	32	33	Humanoid	Normal	None
Kolkar Windchaser	31	32	Humanoid	Normal	None
Lesser Infernal	36	37	Demon	Normal	None
Ley Hunter	39	40	Demon	Normal	None
Mage Hunter	38	39	Demon	Normal	None
Magram Bonepaw	37	38	Beast	Normal	None
Magram Marauder	35	36	Humanoid	Normal	None
Magram Necromancer	39	40	Humanoid	Normal	None
Magram Pack Runner	34	35	Humanoid	Normal	None
Magram Wrangler	33	34	Humanoid	Normal	None
Mana Eater	37	38	Demon	Normal	None
Maraudine Khan Advisor	38	39	Humanoid	Elite	None
Maraudine Khan Guard	39	40	Humanoid	Elite	None
Maraudine Marauder	39	40	Humanoid	Elite	None
Maraudine Scout	37	38	Humanoid	Elite	None
Maraudine Windchaser	38	39	Humanoid	Elite	None
Nether Maiden	37	38	Demon	Normal	None
Nether Sister	38	39	Demon	Normal	None
Nether Sorceress	39	40	Demon	Normal	None
Rabid Bonepaw	36	38	Beast	Normal	None
Scorpashi Lasher	34	35	Beast	Normal	None
Scorpashi Snapper	30	31	Beast	Normal	None
Slitherblade Razortail	35	36	Humanoid	Normal	None
Slitherblade Sorceress	32	33	Humanoid	Normal	None
Slitherblade Tidehunter	36	37	Humanoid	Normal	None
Starving Bonepaw	30	32	Beast	Normal	None
Undead Ravager	37	38	Undead	Normal	Charm, Fear, Sleep and Bleed
Warug's Bodyguard	35	36	Humanoid	Normal	None

DUN MOROGH

NAME	MIN	MAX	TYPE	CLASSIFICATION	IMMUNITIES
Bjarn	12	12	Beast	Rare Spawn	None
Burly Rockjaw Trogg	2	2	Humanoid	Normal	None
Captain Beld	11	11	Humanoid	Normal	None
Crag Boar	5	6	Beast	Normal	None
Dark Iron Spy	9	10	Humanoid	Normal	None
Edan the Howler	9	9	Humanoid	Rare Spawn	None
Elder Crag Boar	7	8	Beast	Normal	None
Frostmane Headhunter	8	9	Humanoid	Normal	None
Frostmane Hideskinner	9	10	Humanoid	Normal	None
Frostmane Novice	3	4	Humanoid	Normal	None
Frostmane Seer	8	9	Humanoid	Normal	None
Frostmane Shadowcaster	9	10	Humanoid	Normal	None
Frostmane Snowstrider	8	9	Humanoid	Normal	None
Frostmane Troll	7	8	Humanoid	Normal	None
Frostmane Troll Whelp	3	4	Humanoid	Normal	None
Gibblewilt	11	11	Humanoid	Rare Spawn	None
Great Father Arctikus	11	11	Humanoid	Rare Spawn	None
Grik'nir the Cold	5	5	Humanoid	Normal	None
Hammerspine	12	12	Humanoid	Rare Spawn	None
Ice Claw Bear	7	8	Beast	Normal	None
Juvenile Snow Leopard	5	6	Beast	Normal	None
Large Crag Boar	6	7	Beast	Normal	None
Leper Gnome	8	10	Humanoid	Normal	None
Mangeclaw	11	11	Beast	Normal	None
Old Icebeard	11	11	Humanoid	Normal	None
Ragged Timber Wolf	2	2	Beast	Normal	None
Ragged Young Wolf	1	1	Beast	Normal	None
Rockjaw Ambusher	9	10	Humanoid	Normal	None
Rockjaw Backbreaker	11	12	Humanoid	Normal	None
Rockjaw Bonesnapper	9	10	Humanoid	Normal	None
Rockjaw Raider	3	4	Humanoid	Normal	None
Rockjaw Skullthumper	8	9	Humanoid	Normal	None
Rockjaw Trogg	1	2	Humanoid	Normal	None
Scarred Crag Boar	9	10	Beast	Normal	None
Small Crag Boar	3	3	Beast	Normal	None
Snow Leopard	7	8	Beast	Normal	None
Snow Tracker Wolf	6	7	Beast	Normal	None
Starving Winter Wolf	8	9	Beast	Normal	None
Timber	10	10	Beast	Rare Spawn	None
Vagash	11	11	Humanoid	Normal	None
Vejrek	11	11	Humanoid	Normal	None
Wendigo	6	7	Humanoid	Normal	None
Winter Wolf	7	8	Beast	Normal	None
Young Black Bear	5	6	Beast	Normal	None
Young Wendigo	5	6	Humanoid	Normal	None

DUROTAR

NAME	MIN	MAX	TYPE	CLASSIFICATION	IMMUNITIES
Armored Scorpid	7	8	Beast	Normal	None
Bloodtalon Scythemaw	8	10	Beast	Normal	None
Bloodtalon Taillasher	6	8	Beast	Normal	None
Burning Blade Apprentice	10	11	Humanoid	Normal	Fear
Burning Blade Cultist	10	11	Humanoid	Normal	Fear
Burning Blade Fanatic	9	10	Humanoid	Normal	Fear
Burning Blade Neophyte	9	10	Humanoid	Normal	Fear
Burning Blade Thug	8	9	Humanoid	Normal	Fear
Captain Flat Tusk	11	11	Humanoid	Rare Spawn Elite	None
Clattering Scorpid	5	6	Beast	Normal	None
Corrupted Bloodtalon Scythemaw	10	11	Beast	Normal	None
Corrupted Dreadmaw Crocolisk	11	12	Beast	Normal	None
Corrupted Mottled Boar	10	11	Beast	Normal	None
Corrupted Scorpid	10	11	Beast	Normal	None
Corrupted Surf Crawler	10	11	Beast	Normal	None
Death Flayer	11	11	Beast	Rare Spawn	None
Dire Mottled Boar	6	7	Beast	Normal	None
Dreadmaw Crocolisk	9	11	Beast	Normal	None
Durotar Tiger	7	8	Beast	Normal	None
Dustwind Harpy	7	8	Humanoid	Normal	None
Dustwind Pillager	7	8	Humanoid	Normal	None
Dustwind Savage	9	10	Humanoid	Normal	None
Dustwind Storm Witch	10	11	Humanoid	Normal	None
Elder Mottled Boar	8	9	Beast	Normal	None
Encrusted Surf Crawler	9	10	Beast	Normal	None
Felstalker	3	4	Demon	Normal	None
Felweaver Scornn	11	11	Humanoid	Rare Spawn Elite	None
Fizzle Darkstorm	12	12	Humanoid	Normal	None
Gazz'uz	14	14	Humanoid	Normal	None
Geolord Mottle	9	9	Humanoid	Rare Spawn	None
Hexed Troll	8	9	Humanoid	Normal	None
Kolkar Drudge	6	7	Humanoid	Normal	None
Kolkar Outrunner	7	8	Humanoid	Normal	None
Kul Tiras Marine	6	7	Humanoid	Normal	None
Kul Tiras Sailor	5	6	Humanoid	Normal	None
Lieutenant Benedict	8	8	Humanoid	Normal	None
Lightning Hide	10	11	Beast	Normal	None
Makrura Clacker	6	7	Humanoid	Normal	None
Makrura Snapclaw	8	9	Humanoid	Normal	None
Minor Manifestation of Fire	12	12	Elemental	Normal	Special - Elemental Fire
Mottled Boar	1	2	Beast	Normal	None
Pygmy Surf Crawler	5	6	Beast	Normal	None
Razormane Dustrunner	8	9	Humanoid	Normal	None
Razormane Quilboar	6	7	Humanoid	Normal	None
Sarkoth	4	4	Beast	Normal	None
Scorpid Worker	3	3	Beast	Normal	None
Surf Crawler	7	8	Beast	Normal	None
Thunder Lizard	9	10	Beast	Normal	None
Venomtail Scorpid	9	10	Beast	Normal	None
Vile Familiar	3	4	Humanoid	Normal	None
Voodoo Troll	8	9	Humanoid	Normal	None
Warlord Kolkanis	9	9	Humanoid	Rare Spawn	None
Watch Commander Zalaphil	9	9	Humanoid	Rare Spawn	None
Zalazane	10	10	Humanoid	Normal	None

DUSKWOOD

NAME	MIN	MAX	TYPE	CLASSIFICATION	IMMUNITIES
Black Ravager	24	25	Beast	Normal	None
Black Ravager Mastiff	25	26	Beast	Normal	None
Black Widow Hatchling	24	25	Beast	Normal	None
Bone Chewer	26	27	Undead	Normal	Charm, Fear and Sleep
Brain Eater	28	29	Undead	Normal	Charm, Fear and Sleep
Carrion Recluse	25	26	Beast	Normal	None
Commander Felstrom	32	32	Undead	Rare Spawn	Charm, Fear, Sleep and Bleed
Defias Agent	24	25	Humanoid	Normal	None
Defias Enchanter	26	27	Humanoid	Normal	None
Defias Night Blade	25	26	Humanoid	Normal	None
Defias Night Runner	24	25	Humanoid	Normal	None
Eliza	31	31	Undead	Elite	Charm, Fear and Sleep
Fenros	32	32	Humanoid	Rare Spawn	None
Fetid Corpse	29	30	Undead	Normal	Charm, Fear and Sleep
Flesh Eater	24	25	Undead	Normal	Charm, Fear and Sleep
Grave Robber	24	25	Humanoid	Normal	None
Green Recluse	21	22	Beast	Normal	None
Gutspill	32	32	Humanoid	Normal	None
Insane Ghoul	26	26	Undead	Normal	Charm, Fear and Sleep
Lord Malathrom	31	31	Undead	Rare Spawn	Charm, Fear and Sleep
Lupos	23	23	Beast	Rare Spawn	None
Morbent Fel	35	35	Humanoid	Elite	None
Mor'Ladim	35	35	Undead	Elite	Charm, Fear, Sleep and Bleed
Naraxis	27	27	Beast	Rare Spawn	None
Nefaru	34	34	Humanoid	Rare Spawn	None
Nightbane Dark Runner	28	29	Humanoid	Normal	None
Nightbane Shadow Weaver	27	28	Humanoid	Normal	None
Nightbane Tainted One	30	31	Humanoid	Normal	None
Nightbane Vile Fang	29	30	Humanoid	Normal	None
Nightbane Worgen	26	27	Humanoid	Normal	None
Plague Spreader	27	28	Undead	Normal	Charm, Fear and Sleep
Pygmy Venom Web Spider	18	19	Beast	Normal	None
Rabid Dire Wolf	20	21	Beast	Normal	None
Rotted One	25	26	Undead	Normal	Charm, Fear and Sleep
Skeletal Fiend	24	25	Undead	Normal	Charm, Fear, Sleep and Bleed
Skeletal Healer	26	27	Undead	Normal	Charm, Fear, Sleep and Bleed
Skeletal Horror	23	24	Undead	Normal	Charm, Fear, Sleep and Bleed
Skeletal Mage	22	23	Undead	Normal	Charm, Fear, Sleep and Bleed
Skeletal Raider	27	28	Undead	Normal	Charm, Fear, Sleep and Bleed
Skeletal Warder	28	29	Undead	Normal	Charm, Fear, Sleep and Bleed
Skeletal Warrior	21	22	Undead	Normal	Charm, Fear, Sleep and Bleed
Splinter Fist Fire Weaver	26	27	Humanoid	Normal	None
Splinter Fist Firemonger	28	29	Humanoid	Normal	None
Splinter Fist Ogre	25	26	Humanoid	Normal	None
Splinter Fist Taskmaster	27	28	Humanoid	Normal	None
Splinter Fist Warrior	29	30	Humanoid	Normal	None
Stalvan Mistmantle	35	35	Undead	Normal	None
Starving Dire Wolf	19	20	Beast	Normal	None
Stitches	35	35	Undead	Normal	Charm, Fear and Sleep
Unseen	49	51	Undead	Normal	Charm, Fear and Sleep
Venom Web Spider	19	20	Beast	Normal	None
Watcher Bukouris	37	37	Humanoid	Normal	None
Watcher Hartin	38	38	Humanoid	Normal	None
Watcher Jan	39	39	Humanoid	Normal	None
Watcher Keefer	40	40	Humanoid	Normal	None
Watcher Keller	39	39	Humanoid	Normal	None
Watcher Mocarski	38	38	Humanoid	Normal	None
Watcher Royce	37	37	Humanoid	Normal	None
Watcher Wollpert	37	37	Humanoid	Normal	None
Young Black Ravager	23	24	Beast	Normal	None
Zzarc' Vul	33	33	Humanoid	Normal	None

DUSTWALLOW MARSH

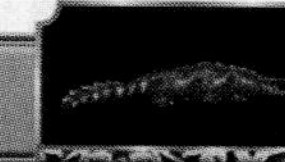

NAME	MIN	MAX	TYPE	CLASSIFICATION	IMMUNITIES
Balos Jacken	38	38	Humanoid	Normal	None
Bloodfen Lashtail	40	41	Beast	Normal	None
Bloodfen Screecher	36	37	Beast	Normal	None
Centaur Outrunner	38	38	Humanoid	Normal	None
Corrosive Swamp Ooze	38	40	Unknown	Normal	None
Dagun the Ravenous	43	43	Humanoid	Elite	None
Darkfang Lurker	36	37	Beast	Normal	None
Darkfang Spider	35	36	Beast	Normal	None
Darkfang Venomspitter	37	38	Beast	Normal	None
Darkmist Lurker	37	38	Beast	Normal	None
Darkmist Spider	35	36	Beast	Normal	None
Darkmist Widow	40	40	Beast	Rare Spawn	None
Deadmire	45	45	Beast	Normal	None
Drywallow Crocolisk	35	36	Beast	Normal	None
Drywallow Daggermaw	40	41	Beast	Elite	None
Drywallow Snapper	37	38	Beast	Normal	None
Drywallow Vicejaw	36	37	Beast	Normal	None
Firemane Ash Tail	42	43	Dragon	Elite	None
Firemane Scalebane	43	44	Dragon	Elite	None
Firemane Scout	41	42	Dragon	Elite	None
Giant Darkfang Spider	40	41	Beast	Normal	None
Mirefin Coastrunner	36	37	Humanoid	Normal	None
Mirefin Muckdweller	36	37	Humanoid	Normal	None
Mirefin Murloc	35	36	Humanoid	Normal	None
Mirefin Oracle	37	38	Humanoid	Normal	None
Muckshell Clacker	39	40	Humanoid	Normal	None
Muckshell Pincer	41	42	Humanoid	Normal	None
Muckshell Scrabbler	42	43	Humanoid	Normal	None
Mudrock Tortoise	36	37	Beast	Normal	None
Murk Thresher	41	43	Beast	Normal	None
Searing Hatchling	41	42	Dragon	Normal	None
Sentry Point Captain	34	35	Humanoid	Normal	None
Sentry Point Guard	32	33	Humanoid	Normal	None
Strashaz Hydra	59	61	Beast	Elite	None
Strashaz Myrmidon	60	61	Humanoid	Elite	None
Strashaz Serpent Guard	59	61	Humanoid	Elite	None
Strashaz Warrior	59	60	Humanoid	Elite	None
Theramore Deserter	37	37	Humanoid	Normal	None
Theramore Infiltrator	35	36	Humanoid	Normal	None
Theramore Sentry	35	36	Humanoid	Normal	None
Withervine Bark Ripper	36	37	Elemental	Normal	None
Withervine Creeper	35	36	Elemental	Normal	None
Withervine Mire Beast	37	38	Elemental	Normal	None

EASTERN PLAGUELANDS

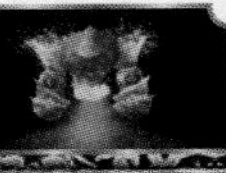

NAME	MIN	MAX	TYPE	CLASSIFICATION	IMMUNITIES
Blighted Horror	56	57	Elemental	Normal	Special - Elemental Water
Blighted Surge	54	55	Elemental	Normal	Special - Elemental Water
Blighthound	58	59	Beast	Elite	Special
Bloodletter	57	58	Undead	Elite	Charm, Fear and Sleep
Borelgore	61	61	Beast	Elite	None
Carrion Grub	54	55	Unknown	Normal	None
Crusader Lord Valdalmar	58	58	Humanoid	Elite	None
Crypt Fiend	53	54	Undead	Normal	Charm, Fear and Sleep
Crypt Robber	54	55	Humanoid	Normal	None
Crypt Slayer	58	59	Undead	Normal	Charm, Fear and Sleep
Crypt Walker	55	56	Undead	Normal	Charm, Fear and Sleep
Dark Adept	58	59	Humanoid	Normal	None
Dark Caster	56	57	Undead	Normal	Charm, Fear, Sleep and Bleed
Deathspeaker Selendre	56	56	Humanoid	Rare Spawn	None
Diseased Flayer	58	59	Undead	Normal	Charm, Fear and Sleep
Duggan Wildhammer	55	55	Humanoid	Rare Spawn	None
Duskwing	60	60	Beast	Elite	None
Eyeless Watcher	57	58	Undead	Normal	Charm, Fear, Sleep and Bleed
Frenzied Plaguehound	57	58	Demon	Normal	None
Gangled Golem	58	59	Undead	Normal	Charm, Fear and Sleep
Gish the Unmoving	56	56	Undead	Rare Spawn	Charm, Fear and Sleep
Hed'mush the Rotting	57	57	Undead	Rare Spawn	None
High General Abbendis	59	59	Humanoid	Rare Spawn	None
Horgus the Ravager	60	60	Undead	Elite	Special
Lord Darkscythe	57	57	Undead	Rare Spawn	Charm, Fear, Sleep and Bleed
Marauding Corpse	56	57	Undead	Normal	Charm, Fear and Sleep
Mercutio Filthgorger	57	57	Humanoid	Normal	None
Mossflayer Berserker	53	55	Undead	Normal	Charm, Fear and Sleep
Mossflayer Scout	57	58	Humanoid	Normal	None
Mossflayer Shadowhunter	58	59	Humanoid	Normal	None
Mossflayer Zombie	53	54	Undead	Normal	Charm, Fear and Sleep
Plaguehound Runt	53	54	Demon	Normal	None
Putrid Gargoyle	54	56	Undead	Normal	Charm, Fear and Sleep
Putrid Shrieker	56	58	Undead	Normal	Charm, Fear and Sleep
Ranger Lord Hawkspear	60	60	Humanoid	Rare Spawn	None
Redpath the Corrupted	60	60	Undead	Elite	None
Rotting Sludge	54	55	Unknown	Normal	None
Scarlet Archmage	55	57	Humanoid	Elite	None
Scarlet Cleric	54	55	Humanoid	Elite	None
Scarlet Praetorian	56	57	Humanoid	Elite	None
Scarlet Warder	53	54	Humanoid	Elite	None
Scourge Guard	57	58	Undead	Normal	Charm, Fear, Sleep and Bleed
Scourge Soldier	53	54	Undead	Normal	Charm, Fear, Sleep and Bleed
Scourge Warder	55	56	Undead	Normal	Charm, Fear, Sleep and Bleed
Servant of Horgus	57	58	Undead	Elite	Charm, Fear and Sleep
Spectral Betrayer	57	58	Undead	Normal	Charm, Fear, Sleep and Bleed
Stitched Horror	57	58	Undead	Normal	Charm, Fear and Sleep
Tirion Fordring	61	61	Humanoid	Normal	None
Unseen Servant	55	56	Undead	Normal	Charm, Fear, Sleep and Bleed
Warlord Thresh'jin	58	58	Humanoid	Rare Spawn	None
Woodsman	58	59	Humanoid	Normal	None
Zul'Brin Warpbranch	59	59	Humanoid	Rare Spawn	None

ELWYNN FOREST

NAME	MIN	MAX	TYPE	CLASSIFICATION	IMMUNITIES
Defias Bandit	8	9	Humanoid	Normal	None
Defias Bodyguard	10	10	Humanoid	Normal	None
Defias Cutpurse	5	6	Humanoid	Normal	None
Defias Dockworker	8	9	Humanoid	Normal	None
Defias Rogue Wizard	9	10	Humanoid	Normal	None
Defias Thug	3	4	Humanoid	Normal	None
Erlan Drudgemoor	8	8	Humanoid	Normal	None
Fedfennel	12	12	Humanoid	Rare Spawn	None
Forest Spider	5	6	Beast	Normal	None
Garrick Padfoot	5	5	Humanoid	Normal	None
Goldtooth	8	8	Humanoid	Normal	None
Gray Forest Wolf	7	8	Beast	Normal	None
Gruff Swiftbite	12	12	Humanoid	Rare Spawn	None
Hogger	11	11	Humanoid	Elite	None
Kobold Geomancer	7	8	Humanoid	Normal	None
Kobold Laborer	3	4	Humanoid	Normal	None
Kobold Miner	6	7	Humanoid	Normal	None
Kobold Tunneler	5	6	Humanoid	Normal	None
Kobold Vermin	1	2	Humanoid	Normal	None
Kobold Worker	3	3	Humanoid	Normal	None
Longsnout	10	11	Beast	Normal	None
Mangy Wolf	5	6	Beast	Normal	None
Mine Spider	8	9	Beast	Normal	None
Morgaine the Sly	10	10	Humanoid	Rare Spawn	None
Morgan the Collector	10	10	Humanoid	Normal	None
Mother Fang	10	10	Beast	Rare Spawn	None
Murloc	6	7	Humanoid	Normal	None
Murloc Forager	9	10	Humanoid	Normal	None
Murloc Lurker	9	10	Humanoid	Normal	None
Murloc Streamrunner	6	7	Humanoid	Normal	None
Narg the Taskmaster	10	10	Humanoid	Rare Spawn	None
Porcine Entourage	7	7	Beast	Normal	None
Princess	9	9	Beast	Normal	None
Prowler	9	10	Beast	Normal	None
Riverpaw Outrunner	9	10	Humanoid	Normal	None
Riverpaw Runt	8	9	Humanoid	Normal	None
Rockhide Boar	7	8	Beast	Normal	None
Stonetusk Boar	5	6	Beast	Normal	None
Surena Caledon	9	9	Humanoid	Normal	None
Thuros Lightfingers	11	11	Humanoid	Rare Spawn	None
Timber Wolf	2	2	Beast	Normal	None
Young Forest Bear	8	9	Beast	Normal	None
Young Wolf	1	1	Beast	Normal	None

FELWOOD

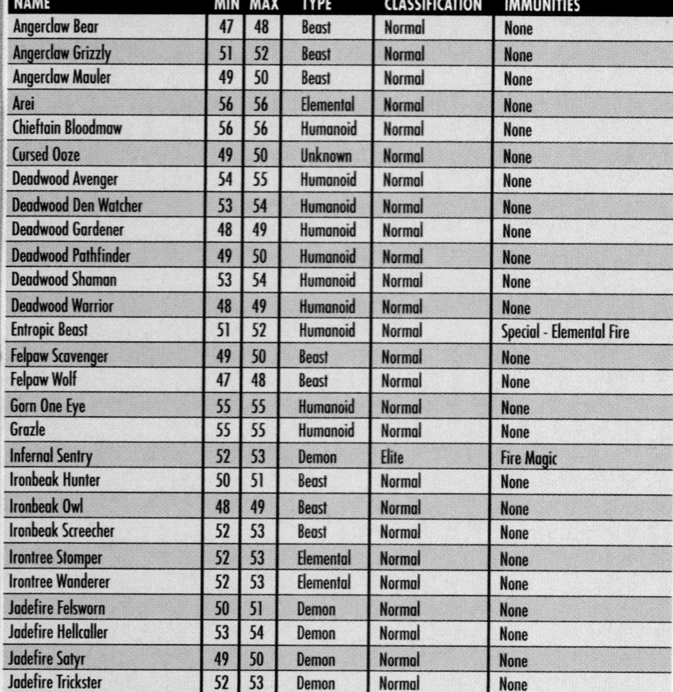

NAME	MIN	MAX	TYPE	CLASSIFICATION	IMMUNITIES
Angerclaw Bear	47	48	Beast	Normal	None
Angerclaw Grizzly	51	52	Beast	Normal	None
Angerclaw Mauler	49	50	Beast	Normal	None
Arei	56	56	Elemental	Normal	None
Chieftain Bloodmaw	56	56	Humanoid	Normal	None
Cursed Ooze	49	50	Unknown	Normal	None
Deadwood Avenger	54	55	Humanoid	Normal	None
Deadwood Den Watcher	53	54	Humanoid	Normal	None
Deadwood Gardener	48	49	Humanoid	Normal	None
Deadwood Pathfinder	49	50	Humanoid	Normal	None
Deadwood Shaman	53	54	Humanoid	Normal	None
Deadwood Warrior	48	49	Humanoid	Normal	None
Entropic Beast	51	52	Humanoid	Normal	Special - Elemental Fire
Felpaw Scavenger	49	50	Beast	Normal	None
Felpaw Wolf	47	48	Beast	Normal	None
Gorn One Eye	55	55	Humanoid	Normal	None
Grazle	55	55	Humanoid	Normal	None
Infernal Sentry	52	53	Demon	Elite	Fire Magic
Ironbeak Hunter	50	51	Beast	Normal	None
Ironbeak Owl	48	49	Beast	Normal	None
Ironbeak Screecher	52	53	Beast	Normal	None
Irontree Stomper	52	53	Elemental	Normal	None
Irontree Wanderer	52	53	Elemental	Normal	None
Jadefire Felsworn	50	51	Demon	Normal	None
Jadefire Hellcaller	53	54	Demon	Normal	None
Jadefire Satyr	49	50	Demon	Normal	None
Jadefire Trickster	52	53	Demon	Normal	None
Jaedenar Adept	51	52	Humanoid	Normal	None

NAME	MIN	MAX	TYPE	CLASSIFICATION	IMMUNITIES
Jaedenar Cultist	51	52	Humanoid	Normal	None
Jaedenar Darkweaver	53	54	Humanoid	Normal	None
Jaedenar Guardian	50	51	Humanoid	Normal	None
Jaedenar Hound	50	51	Demon	Normal	None
Jaedenar Hunter	52	53	Demon	Normal	None
Jaedenar Legionnaire	55	55	Humanoid	Normal	None
Kernda	55	55	Humanoid	Normal	None
Lord Banehollow	59	59	Humanoid	Elite	None
Meilosh	55	55	Humanoid	Normal	None
Moora	52	52	Humanoid	Normal	None
Overlord Ror	51	51	Humanoid	Normal	None
Prince Xavalis	55	55	Demon	Normal	None
Rakaiah	56	56	Humanoid	Normal	None
Salfa	55	55	Humanoid	Normal	None
Salia	54	54	Humanoid	Normal	None
Shadow Lord Fel'dan	57	57	Humanoid	Normal	None
Tainted Ooze	51	52	Unknown	Normal	None
Timbermaw Warder	53	54	Humanoid	Normal	None
Timbermaw Woodbender	52	53	Humanoid	Normal	None
Toxic Horror	53	54	Elemental	Normal	Poison
Vile Ooze	53	53	Unknown	Normal	None
Warpwood Moss Flayer	52	53	Elemental	Normal	None
Warpwood Thunder Caller	56	56	Elemental	Rare Spawn Elite	None
Winna's Kitten	1	1	Beast	Normal	None
Withered Protector	55	56	Elemental	Normal	None
Xavaric	55	55	Demon	Normal	None
Xavathras	54	54	Demon	Normal	None

FERALAS

NAME	MIN	MAX	TYPE	CLASSIFICATION	IMMUNITIES
Antilus the Soarer	48	48	Humanoid	Rare Spawn	None
Arash-ethis	49	49	Beast	Rare Spawn	None
Bloodroar the Stalker	48	48	Humanoid	Rare Spawn	None
Captured Sprite Darter	42	43	Dragon	Normal	None
Coast Crawl Deepseer	43	44	Humanoid	Normal	None
Cursed Sycamore	45	45	Elemental	Normal	None
Diamond Head	45	45	Humanoid	Rare Spawn	None
Edana Hatetalon	50	50	Humanoid	Elite	None
Elder Rage Scar	48	49	Humanoid	Normal	None
Enraged Feral Scar	44	45	Humanoid	Normal	None
Feral Scar Yeti	43	44	Humanoid	Normal	None
Frayfeather Hippogryph	43	44	Beast	Normal	None
Frayfeather Patriarch	46	47	Beast	Normal	None
Frayfeather Skystormer	45	46	Beast	Normal	None
Frayfeather Stagwing	44	45	Beast	Normal	None
Gnarl Leafbrother	44	44	Elemental	Rare Spawn	Nature Magic
Gordok Brute	60	60	Humanoid	Elite	None
Gordunni Brute	42	43	Humanoid	Normal	None
Gordunni Mauler	43	44	Humanoid	Normal	None
Gordunni Ogre	40	41	Humanoid	Normal	None
Gordunni Shaman	44	45	Humanoid	Normal	None
Gordunni Warlord	46	47	Humanoid	Normal	None
Grimtotem Raider	42	43	Humanoid	Normal	None
Grimtotem Shaman	43	44	Humanoid	Normal	None
Grizzled Ironfur Bear	44	45	Beast	Normal	None
Groddoc Ape	42	43	Beast	Normal	None
Hatecrest Myrmidon	43	44	Humanoid	Normal	None
Hatecrest Sorceress	43	44	Humanoid	Normal	None
Hatecrest Warrior	42	43	Humanoid	Normal	None
Hulking Feral Scar	45	46	Humanoid	Normal	None
Jademir Dragonspawn	60	60	Dragon	Elite	None

NAME	MIN	MAX	TYPE	CLASSIFICATION	IMMUNITIES
Lady Szallah	46	46	Humanoid	Rare Spawn	None
Land Walker	48	49	Giant	Elite	None
Longtooth Howler	43	44	Beast	Normal	None
Longtooth Runner	40	41	Beast	Normal	None
Lord Shalzaru	47	47	Humanoid	Normal	None
Lurking Feral Scar	46	46	Humanoid	Normal	None
Northspring Harpy	48	49	Humanoid	Normal	None
Northspring Slayer	49	50	Humanoid	Normal	None
Old Grizzlegut	43	43	Beast	Rare Spawn	None
Qirot	47	47	Unknown	Rare Spawn	None
Rabid Longtooth	47	48	Beast	Normal	None
Rage Scar Yeti	46	47	Humanoid	Normal	None
Rogue Vale Screecher	44	46	Beast	Normal	None
Scillia Daggerquil	52	52	Humanoid	Rare Spawn Elite	None
Sea Elemental	48	49	Elemental	Normal	Special - Elemental Water
Sea Spray	47	48	Elemental	Normal	Special - Elemental Water
Shore Strider	48	49	Giant	Elite	None
Snarler	42	42	Beast	Rare Spawn	None
Sprite Darter	43	45	Dragon	Normal	None
Sprite Dragon	47	50	Dragon	Normal	None
Vale Screecher	41	43	Beast	Normal	None
Wandering Forest Walker	44	46	Elemental	Elite	None
Woodpaw Alpha	43	44	Humanoid	Normal	None
Woodpaw Brute	41	42	Humanoid	Normal	None
Woodpaw Mongrel	40	41	Humanoid	Normal	None
Woodpaw Mystic	42	43	Humanoid	Normal	None
Woodpaw Reaver	42	43	Humanoid	Normal	None
Zukk'ash Stinger	45	46	Unknown	Normal	None
Zukk'ash Tunneler	45	46	Unknown	Normal	None
Zukk'ash Wasp	44	45	Unknown	Normal	None

HILLSBRAD FOOTHILLS

NAME	MIN	MAX	TYPE	CLASSIFICATION	IMMUNITIES
Arados the Damned	35	35	Undead	Normal	None
Blacksmith Verringtan	26	26	Humanoid	Normal	None
Captain Ironhill	32	32	Humanoid	Elite	None
Citizen Wilkes	25	25	Humanoid	Normal	None
Clerk Horrace Whitesteed	26	26	Humanoid	Normal	None
Condemned Acolyte	30	31	Undead	Normal	None
Condemned Cleric	32	33	Undead	Normal	None
Condemned Monk	31	32	Undead	Normal	None
Cursed Justicar	32	33	Undead	Normal	None
Cursed Paladin	30	31	Undead	Normal	None
Daggerspine Screamer	29	30	Humanoid	Normal	None
Daggerspine Shorehunter	30	31	Humanoid	Normal	None
Daggerspine Shorestalker	28	29	Humanoid	Normal	None
Daggerspine Siren	31	32	Humanoid	Normal	None
Dun Garok Mountaineer	28	29	Humanoid	Normal	None
Dun Garok Priest	29	30	Humanoid	Normal	None
Dun Garok Rifleman	29	30	Humanoid	Normal	None
Dun Garok Soldier	28	29	Humanoid	Normal	None
Elder Gray Bear	25	26	Beast	Normal	None
Elder Moss Creeper	26	27	Beast	Normal	None
Farmer Getz	24	24	Humanoid	Normal	None
Farmer Kalaba	25	25	Humanoid	Normal	None
Farmer Kent	25	25	Humanoid	Normal	None
Farmer Ray	23	23	Humanoid	Normal	None
Feral Mountain Lion	27	28	Beast	Normal	None
Foreman Bonds	30	30	Humanoid	Normal	None
Forest Moss Creeper	20	21	Beast	Normal	None
Giant Moss Creeper	24	25	Beast	Normal	None
Granistad	40	40	Beast	Normal	None
Gray Bear	21	22	Beast	Normal	None
Hillsbrad Apprentice Blacksmith	24	25	Humanoid	Normal	None
Hillsbrad Councilman	25	26	Humanoid	Normal	None
Hillsbrad Farmer	23	24	Humanoid	Normal	None
Hillsbrad Farmhand	22	23	Humanoid	Normal	None
Hillsbrad Footman	25	26	Humanoid	Normal	None
Hillsbrad Foreman	27	28	Humanoid	Normal	None
Hillsbrad Miner	26	27	Humanoid	Normal	None
Hillsbrad Peasant	24	25	Humanoid	Normal	None
Hillsbrad Sentry	27	28	Humanoid	Normal	None
Hillsbrad Tailor	24	25	Humanoid	Normal	None
Jailor Eston	24	24	Humanoid	Normal	None
Jailor Marlgen	24	24	Humanoid	Normal	None
Judge Thelgram	34	34	Undead	Normal	None
Kurdros	40	40	Beast	Normal	None
Magistrate Burnside	30	30	Humanoid	Normal	None
Miner Hackett	29	29	Humanoid	Normal	None
Mudsnout Gnoll	26	27	Humanoid	Normal	None
Mudsnout Shaman	27	28	Humanoid	Normal	None
Shadowy Assassin	37	38	Humanoid	Normal	None
Southshore Crier	32	32	Humanoid	Normal	None
Stanley	24	24	Beast	Normal	None
Starving Mountain Lion	23	24	Beast	Normal	None
Syndicate Rogue	21	22	Humanoid	Normal	None
Syndicate Shadow Mage	21	22	Humanoid	Normal	None
Syndicate Watchman	20	21	Humanoid	Normal	None
Torn Fin Coastrunner	29	30	Humanoid	Normal	None
Torn Fin Muckdweller	28	29	Humanoid	Normal	None
Torn Fin Oracle	30	31	Humanoid	Normal	None
Torn Fin Tidehunter	31	32	Humanoid	Normal	None
Vicious Gray Bear	22	23	Beast	Normal	None
Wild Gryphon	40	40	Beast	Normal	None
Writhing Mage	31	32	Undead	Normal	None

HINTERLANDS

NAME	MIN	MAX	TYPE	CLASSIFICATION	IMMUNITIES
Cerulean Dragonspawn	48	49	Dragon	Normal	None
Emerald Ooze	46	47	Unknown	Elite	None
Gammerita	48	48	Beast	Elite	None
Green Sludge	46	47	Unknown	Normal	None
Grimungous	50	50	Giant	Rare Spawn Elite	None
Highvale Marksman	45	46	Humanoid	Normal	None
Highvale Outrunner	43	44	Humanoid	Normal	None
Highvale Ranger	46	47	Humanoid	Normal	None
Highvale Scout	44	45	Humanoid	Normal	None
Hitah'ya the Keeper	52	52	Humanoid	Normal	None
Ironback	51	51	Beast	Rare Spawn	None
Jade Ooze	47	48	Unknown	Normal	None
Jade Sludge	47	48	Unknown	Elite	Special
Jalinde Summerdrake	49	49	Humanoid	Rare Spawn	None
Mangy Silvermane	41	42	Beast	Normal	None
Marauding Owlbeast	46	46	Beast	Normal	None
Mith'rethis the Enchanter	52	52	Humanoid	Rare Spawn Elite	None
Morta'gya the Keeper	50	50	Humanoid	Normal	None
Old Cliff Jumper	42	42	Beast	Rare Spawn	None
Primitive Owlbeast	44	45	Beast	Normal	None
Qiaga the Keeper	52	52	Humanoid	Normal	None
Razorbeak Gryphon	43	45	Beast	Normal	None
Razorbeak Skylord	46	48	Beast	Normal	None
Razortalon	44	44	Beast	Rare Spawn	None
Retherokk the Berserker	48	48	Humanoid	Rare Spawn	None
Saltwater Snapjaw	49	50	Beast	Normal	None
Savage Owlbeast	46	47	Beast	Normal	None
Shadra	55	55	Beast	Normal	None
Silvermane Howler	45	46	Beast	Normal	None
Silvermane Stalker	47	48	Beast	Normal	None
Silvermane Wolf	43	44	Beast	Normal	None
The Reak	49	49	Unknown	Rare Spawn	None
Trained Razorbeak	40	42	Beast	Normal	None
Vicious Owlbeast	42	43	Beast	Normal	None
Vile Priestess Hexx	53	53	Humanoid	Elite	None
Vilebranch Aman'zasi Guard	50	51	Humanoid	Elite	None
Vilebranch Ambusher	47	47	Humanoid	Normal	None
Vilebranch Axe Thrower	45	46	Humanoid	Normal	None
Vilebranch Berserker	47	48	Humanoid	Elite	None
Vilebranch Blood Drinker	49	50	Humanoid	Elite	None
Vilebranch Headhunter	46	47	Humanoid	Elite	None
Vilebranch Hideskinner	48	49	Humanoid	Elite	None
Vilebranch Raiding Wolf	50	51	Beast	Elite	None
Vilebranch Scalper	46	47	Humanoid	Normal	None
Vilebranch Shadow Hunter	48	49	Humanoid	Elite	None
Vilebranch Shadowcaster	47	48	Humanoid	Elite	None
Vilebranch Soothsayer	46	47	Humanoid	Normal	None
Vilebranch Soul Eater	49	50	Humanoid	Elite	None
Vilebranch Warrior	45	46	Humanoid	Elite	None
Vilebranch Witch Doctor	46	47	Humanoid	Normal	None
Vilebranch Wolf Pup	46	47	Beast	Normal	None
Wildhammer Sentry	55	55	Humanoid	Normal	None
Witherbark Broodguard	44	45	Beast	Normal	None
Witherbark Caller	45	46	Humanoid	Normal	None
Witherbark Hideskinner	42	43	Humanoid	Normal	None
Witherbark Sadist	44	45	Humanoid	Normal	None
Witherbark Scalper	40	41	Humanoid	Normal	None
Witherbark Venomblood	43	43	Humanoid	Normal	None
Witherbark Zealot	41	42	Humanoid	Normal	None
Witherheart the Stalker	45	45	Humanoid	Rare Spawn	None
Zul'arek Hatefowler	43	43	Humanoid	Rare Spawn	None

LOCH MODAN

NAME	MIN	MAX	TYPE	CLASSIFICATION	IMMUNITIES
Black Bear Patriarch	16	17	Beast	Normal	None
Boss Galgosh	22	22	Humanoid	Rare Spawn	None
Brawler	16	16	Humanoid	Normal	None
Chok'sul	22	22	Humanoid	Normal	None
Cliff Lurker	13	14	Beast	Normal	None
Dark Iron Ambusher	10	10	Humanoid	Normal	None
Dark Iron Insurgent	18	19	Humanoid	Normal	None
Dark Iron Raider	14	14	Humanoid	Normal	None
Dark Iron Sapper	17	17	Humanoid	Normal	None
Elder Black Bear	11	12	Beast	Normal	None
Elder Mountain Boar	16	17	Beast	Normal	None
Forest Lurker	10	11	Beast	Normal	None
Gnasher	16	16	Humanoid	Normal	None
Gradok	19	21	Humanoid	Elite	None
Grawmug	17	17	Humanoid	Normal	None
Grizlak	15	15	Humanoid	Rare Spawn	None
Grizzled Black Bear	13	14	Beast	Normal	None
Haren Swifthoof	19	21	Humanoid	Elite	None
Large Loch Crocolisk	22	22	Beast	Rare Spawn	None
Loch Crocolisk	14	15	Beast	Normal	None
Loch Frenzy	12	13	Beast	Normal	None
Magosh	21	21	Humanoid	Rare Spawn	None
Mangy Mountain Boar	14	15	Beast	Normal	None
Mo'grosh Brute	19	20	Humanoid	Normal	None
Mo'grosh Mystic	19	20	Humanoid	Normal	None
Mo'grosh Ogre	18	19	Humanoid	Normal	None
Mountain Boar	10	11	Beast	Normal	None
Mountain Buzzard	15	16	Beast	Normal	None
Ol' Sooty	20	20	Beast	Elite	None
Stonesplinter Bonesnapper	15	16	Humanoid	Normal	None
Stonesplinter Digger	18	19	Humanoid	Normal	None
Stonesplinter Skullthumper	13	14	Humanoid	Normal	None
Stonesplinter Trogg	11	12	Humanoid	Normal	None
Thragomm	19	21	Humanoid	Elite	None
Tunnel Rat Digger	12	13	Humanoid	Normal	None
Tunnel Rat Forager	11	12	Humanoid	Normal	None
Tunnel Rat Kobold	11	12	Humanoid	Normal	None
Tunnel Rat Surveyor	14	14	Humanoid	Normal	None
Tunnel Rat Vermin	10	11	Humanoid	Normal	None
Wood Lurker	17	18	Beast	Normal	None
Young Threshadon	19	20	Beast	Normal	None

MULGORE

NAME	MIN	MAX	TYPE	CLASSIFICATION	IMMUNITIES
Adult Plainstrider	6	7	Beast	Normal	None
Arra'chea	11	11	Beast	Normal	None
Bael'dun Appraiser	8	9	Humanoid	Normal	None
Bael'dun Digger	7	8	Humanoid	Normal	None
Battleboar	3	4	Beast	Normal	None
Bristleback Battleboar	4	5	Beast	Normal	None
Bristleback Interloper	9	10	Humanoid	Normal	None
Bristleback Quilboar	3	4	Humanoid	Normal	None
Bristleback Shaman	3	4	Humanoid	Normal	None
Chief Sharptusk Thornmantle	5	5	Humanoid	Normal	None
Elder Plainstrider	8	9	Beast	Normal	None
Enforcer Emilgund	11	11	Humanoid	Rare Spawn	None
Galak Centaur	8	9	Humanoid	Normal	None
Kodo Bull	10	11	Beast	Normal	None
Kodo Calf	7	8	Beast	Normal	None
Kodo Matriarch	11	12	Beast	Normal	None
Mazzranache	9	9	Beast	Rare Spawn	None
Mountain Cougar	3	3	Beast	Normal	None
Palemane Poacher	7	8	Humanoid	Normal	None
Palemane Skinner	6	7	Humanoid	Normal	None
Palemane Tanner	5	6	Humanoid	Normal	None
Plainstrider	1	2	Beast	Normal	None
Prairie Stalker	7	8	Beast	Normal	None
Prairie Wolf	5	6	Beast	Normal	None
Prairie Wolf Alpha	9	10	Beast	Normal	None
Sister Hatelash	11	11	Humanoid	Rare Spawn Elite	None
Snagglespear	9	9	Humanoid	Rare Spawn	None
Squealer" Thornmantle"	5	5	Humanoid	Normal	None
Supervisor Fizsprocket	12	12	Humanoid	Normal	None
Swoop	7	9	Beast	Normal	None
Taloned Swoop	8	10	Beast	Normal	None
The Rake	10	10	Beast	Rare Spawn	None
Venture Co. Hireling	5	6	Humanoid	Normal	None
Venture Co. Laborer	6	7	Humanoid	Normal	None
Venture Co. Supervisor	9	10	Humanoid	Normal	None
Venture Co. Taskmaster	7	8	Humanoid	Normal	None
Venture Co. Worker	8	9	Humanoid	Normal	None
Windfury Harpy	7	8	Humanoid	Normal	None
Windfury Matriarch	10	11	Humanoid	Normal	None
Windfury Sorceress	9	10	Humanoid	Normal	None
Windfury Wind Witch	8	9	Humanoid	Normal	None
Wiry Swoop	5	7	Beast	Normal	None

REDRIDGE MOUNTAINS

NAME	MIN	MAX	TYPE	CLASSIFICATION	IMMUNITIES
Ardo Dirtpaw	24	24	Humanoid	Normal	None
Bellygrub	24	24	Beast	Normal	None
Black Dragon Whelp	17	18	Dragon	Normal	None
Blackrock Assassin	18	18	Humanoid	Normal	None
Blackrock Champion	24	25	Humanoid	Normal	None
Blackrock Gladiator	24	25	Humanoid	Elite	None
Blackrock Grunt	19	20	Humanoid	Normal	None
Blackrock Hunter	23	24	Humanoid	Elite	None
Blackrock Outrunner	20	21	Humanoid	Normal	None
Blackrock Renegade	21	22	Humanoid	Normal	None
Blackrock Scout	20	21	Humanoid	Elite	None
Blackrock Sentry	21	22	Humanoid	Elite	None
Blackrock Shadowcaster	22	23	Humanoid	Elite	None
Blackrock Summoner	22	23	Humanoid	Normal	None
Blackrock Tracker	23	24	Humanoid	Normal	None
Chatter	23	23	Beast	Rare Spawn	None
Dire Condor	18	19	Beast	Normal	None
Gath'Ilzogg	26	26	Humanoid	Elite	None
Great Goretusk	16	17	Beast	Normal	None
Greater Tarantula	19	20	Beast	Normal	None
Grurk	18	18	Humanoid	Normal	None
Il'thurk	17	17	Humanoid	Normal	None
Kazon	27	27	Humanoid	Rare Spawn	None
Lieutenant Fangore	26	26	Humanoid	Normal	Shadow Magic
Lumurk	17	17	Humanoid	Normal	None
Morganth	27	27	Humanoid	Normal	None
Murloc Flesheater	18	19	Humanoid	Normal	None
Murloc Minor Tidecaller	17	18	Humanoid	Normal	None
Murloc Nightcrawler	21	22	Humanoid	Normal	None
Murloc Scout	19	20	Humanoid	Normal	None
Murloc Shorestriker	16	17	Humanoid	Normal	None
Murloc Tidecaller	19	20	Humanoid	Normal	None
Rabid Shadowhide Gnoll	21	22	Humanoid	Normal	None
Redridge Alpha	21	22	Humanoid	Normal	None
Redridge Basher	19	20	Humanoid	Normal	None
Redridge Brute	17	18	Humanoid	Normal	None
Redridge Drudger	20	21	Humanoid	Normal	None
Redridge Mongrel	15	16	Humanoid	Normal	None
Redridge Mystic	18	19	Humanoid	Normal	None
Redridge Poacher	16	17	Humanoid	Normal	None
Redridge Thrasher	14	15	Humanoid	Normal	None
Rohh the Silent	26	26	Humanoid	Rare Spawn	None
Servant of Ilgalar	24	25	Demon	Normal	None
Shadowhide Assassin	23	24	Humanoid	Normal	None
Shadowhide Brute	23	24	Humanoid	Normal	None
Shadowhide Darkweaver	25	26	Humanoid	Normal	None
Shadowhide Gnoll	22	23	Humanoid	Normal	None
Shadowhide Slayer	25	26	Humanoid	Normal	None
Shadowhide Warrior	24	25	Humanoid	Normal	None
Singe	24	24	Dragon	Elite	None
Tarantula	15	16	Beast	Normal	None
Tharil'zun	24	24	Humanoid	Elite	None
Yowler	25	25	Humanoid	Normal	None

SEARING GORGE

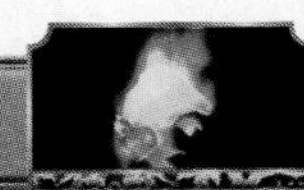

NAME	MIN	MAX	TYPE	CLASSIFICATION	IMMUNITIES
Blazing Elemental	45	47	Elemental	Normal	Special - Elemental Fire
Clunk	48	48	Mechanical	Elite	None
Dark Iron Geologist	43	44	Humanoid	Normal	None
Dark Iron Lookout	47	48	Humanoid	Normal	None
Dark Iron Marksman	55	55	Humanoid	Normal	None
Dark Iron Sentry	50	50	Humanoid	Elite	None
Dark Iron Slaver	45	46	Humanoid	Normal	None
Dark Iron Steamsmith	46	47	Humanoid	Normal	None
Dark Iron Taskmaster	47	48	Humanoid	Normal	None
Faulty War Golem	46	46	Elemental	Rare Spawn	Special - Golem
Glassweb Spider	43	45	Beast	Normal	None
Greater Lava Spider	47	49	Beast	Normal	None
Heavy War Golem	47	49	Elemental	Normal	Special - Golem
Highlord Mastrogonde	51	51	Humanoid	Rare Spawn Elite	None
Incendosaur	47	49	Beast	Normal	None
Inferno Elemental	47	49	Elemental	Normal	Special - Elemental Fire
Magma Elemental	46	48	Elemental	Normal	Special - Elemental Earth
Margol the Rager	48	48	Beast	Elite	Nature Magic
Muck Splash	47	49	Elemental	Normal	Special - Elemental Water
Obsidion	52	52	Elemental	Elite	Special - Statue
Rekk'tilac	48	48	Beast	Rare Spawn	None
Scald	49	49	Elemental	Rare Spawn	Special - Elemental Fire
Searing Lava Spider	45	47	Beast	Normal	None
Shadowsilk Poacher	47	50	Humanoid	Normal	None
Shleipnarr	47	47	Demon	Rare Spawn	None
Slave Master Blackheart	50	50	Humanoid	Rare Spawn	None
Slave Worker	45	47	Humanoid	Normal	None
Smoldar	50	50	Elemental	Rare Spawn	Special - Elemental Earth
Tempered War Golem	45	47	Elemental	Normal	Special - Golem
Twilight Dark Shaman	47	48	Humanoid	Elite	None
Twilight Fire Guard	48	49	Humanoid	Elite	None
Twilight Idolater	49	51	Humanoid	Elite	None

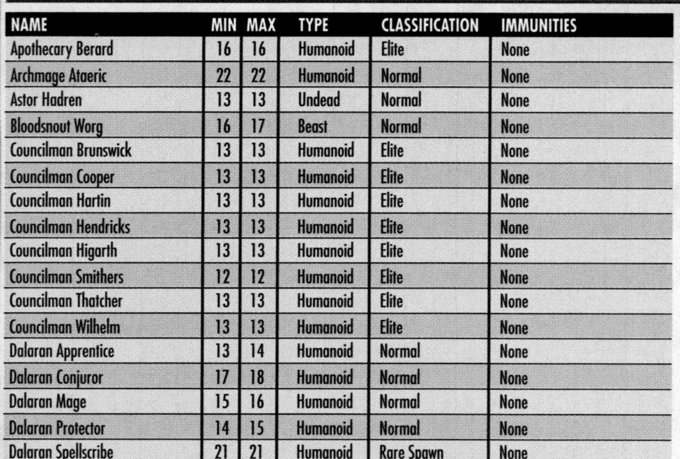

SILVERPINE FOREST

NAME	MIN	MAX	TYPE	CLASSIFICATION	IMMUNITIES
Apothecary Berard	16	16	Humanoid	Elite	None
Archmage Ataeric	22	22	Humanoid	Normal	None
Astor Hadren	13	13	Undead	Normal	None
Bloodsnout Worg	16	17	Beast	Normal	None
Councilman Brunswick	13	13	Humanoid	Elite	None
Councilman Cooper	13	13	Humanoid	Elite	None
Councilman Hartin	13	13	Humanoid	Elite	None
Councilman Hendricks	13	13	Humanoid	Elite	None
Councilman Higarth	13	13	Humanoid	Elite	None
Councilman Smithers	12	12	Humanoid	Elite	None
Councilman Thatcher	13	13	Humanoid	Elite	None
Councilman Wilhelm	13	13	Humanoid	Elite	None
Dalaran Apprentice	13	14	Humanoid	Normal	None
Dalaran Conjuror	17	18	Humanoid	Normal	None
Dalaran Mage	15	16	Humanoid	Normal	None
Dalaran Protector	14	15	Humanoid	Normal	None
Dalaran Spellscribe	21	21	Humanoid	Rare Spawn	None
Dalaran Warder	16	17	Humanoid	Normal	None
Dalaran Watcher	18	19	Humanoid	Normal	None
Dalaran Wizard	19	20	Humanoid	Normal	None
Dalin Forgewright	20	20	Humanoid	Normal	None
Dalin Forgewright Projection	20	20	Humanoid	Normal	None
Elder Lake Creeper	18	19	Elemental	Normal	None
Elder Lake Skulker	16	17	Elemental	Normal	None
Ferocious Grizzled Bear	11	12	Beast	Normal	None
Giant Grizzled Bear	12	13	Beast	Normal	None
Grimson the Pale	15	15	Humanoid	Normal	None
Haggard Refugee	18	19	Humanoid	Normal	None
Hand of Ravenclaw	15	16	Undead	Normal	Charm, Fear, Sleep and Bleed
Ivar the Foul	13	13	Undead	Normal	Charm, Fear and Sleep
Lake Creeper	17	18	Elemental	Normal	None
Lake Frenzy	15	16	Unknown	Normal	None
Lake Skulker	15	16	Elemental	Normal	None
Lord Mayor Morrison	15	15	Humanoid	Elite	None
Mist Creeper	13	14	Beast	Normal	None
Moonrage Bloodhowler	15	16	Humanoid	Normal	None
Moonrage Darkrunner	11	12	Humanoid	Normal	None
Moonrage Darksoul	13	14	Humanoid	Normal	None
Moonrage Glutton	12	13	Humanoid	Normal	None
Moonrage Whitescalp	10	11	Humanoid	Normal	None

STONETALON MOUNTAINS

NAME	MIN	MAX	TYPE	CLASSIFICATION	IMMUNITIES
Antlered Courser	22	23	Beast	Normal	None
Besseleth	22	22	Beast	Normal	None
Blackened Basilisk	23	24	Beast	Normal	None
Bloodfury Harpy	23	24	Humanoid	Normal	None
Bloodfury Roguefeather	25	26	Humanoid	Normal	None
Brother Ravenoak	29	29	Humanoid	Rare Spawn Elite	None
Cenarion Botanist	23	24	Humanoid	Normal	None
Cenarion Caretaker	25	26	Humanoid	Elite	None
Cenarion Druid	26	27	Humanoid	Elite	None
Charred Ancient	25	26	Elemental	Normal	None
Charred Stone Spirit	22	23	Elemental	Normal	Special - Elemental Earth
Chimaera Matriarch	28	28	Beast	Normal	None
Cliff Stormer	15	17	Beast	Normal	None
Daughter of Cenarius	23	25	Humanoid	Normal	None
Deepmoss Creeper	16	17	Beast	Normal	None
Deepmoss Venomspitter	17	18	Beast	Normal	None
Deepmoss Webspinner	19	20	Beast	Normal	None
Enraged Stone Spirit	24	25	Elemental	Normal	Special - Elemental Earth
Fey Dragon	24	25	Dragon	Normal	None
Fledgling Chimaera	25	27	Beast	Normal	None
Foreman Rigger	24	24	Humanoid	Rare Spawn Elite	None
Furious Stone Spirit	26	27	Elemental	Normal	Special - Elemental Earth
Gatekeeper Kordurus	25	25	Humanoid	Elite	None
Gerenzo Wrenchwhistle	27	27	Humanoid	Normal	None
Grimtotem Brute	15	16	Humanoid	Normal	None
Grimtotem Ruffian	14	15	Humanoid	Normal	None
Mirkfallon Dryad	25	26	Humanoid	Elite	None
Mirkfallon Keeper	26	27	Humanoid	Elite	None
Nal'taszar	30	30	Dragon	Rare Spawn Elite	None
Pridewing Consort	22	23	Beast	Normal	None
Pridewing Skyhunter	23	24	Beast	Normal	None
Pridewing Wyvern	21	22	Beast	Normal	None
Raging Cliff Stormer	18	19	Beast	Normal	None
Rynthariel the Keymaster	29	29	Humanoid	Elite	None
Sap Beast	22	23	Unknown	Normal	None
Sentinel Amarassan	27	27	Humanoid	Rare Spawn Elite	None
Sister Riven	28	28	Humanoid	Rare Spawn Elite	None
Son of Cenarius	24	25	Humanoid	Normal	None
Sorrow Wing	27	27	Beast	Rare Spawn Elite	None
Taskmaster Whipfang	21	21	Humanoid	Rare Spawn Elite	None
Twilight Runner	23	24	Beast	Normal	None
Venture Co. Builder	20	21	Humanoid	Normal	None
Venture Co. Logger	18	19	Humanoid	Normal	None
Venture Co. Machine Smith	21	22	Humanoid	Normal	None
Venture Co. Operator	19	20	Humanoid	Normal	None
Windshear Digger	21	22	Humanoid	Normal	None
Windshear Geomancer	20	21	Humanoid	Normal	None
Windshear Overlord	21	22	Humanoid	Normal	None
Windshear Stonecutter	22	23	Humanoid	Normal	None
Windshear Tunnel Rat	19	20	Humanoid	Normal	None
Windshear Vermin	20	21	Humanoid	Normal	None
XT:4	23	23	Mechanical	Normal	Special - Piloted Mechanical
XT:9	23	23	Mechanical	Normal	Special - Piloted Mechanical
Young Chimaera	23	25	Beast	Normal	None
Young Pridewing	19	20	Beast	Normal	None

STORMWIND

NAME	MIN	MAX	TYPE	CLASSIFICATION	IMMUNITIES
Bazil Thredd	29	29	Humanoid	Elite	None
Dextren Ward	26	26	Humanoid	Elite	None
Hamhock	28	28	Humanoid	Elite	None
Kam Deepfury	27	27	Humanoid	Elite	None
Marzon the Silent Blade	30	30	Humanoid	Normal	None
Sewer Beast	50	50	Beast	Rare Spawn	None
Summoned Voidwalker	10	10	Demon	Normal	None
Targorr the Dread	24	24	Humanoid	Elite	None

STRANGLETHORN VALE

NAME	MIN	MAX	TYPE	CLASSIFICATION	IMMUNITIES
Ana'thek the Cruel	45	45	Humanoid	Normal	None
Bhag'thera	40	40	Beast	Normal	None
Bloodsail Deckhand	43	44	Humanoid	Normal	None
Bloodsail Elder Magus	44	45	Humanoid	Normal	None
Bloodsail Raider	40	41	Humanoid	Normal	None
Bloodsail Sea Dog	44	45	Humanoid	Normal	None
Bloodsail Swashbuckler	42	43	Humanoid	Normal	None
Bloodscalp Axe Thrower	33	34	Humanoid	Normal	None
Bloodscalp Beastmaster	34	35	Humanoid	Normal	None
Bloodscalp Berserker	36	37	Humanoid	Normal	None
Bloodscalp Headhunter	36	37	Humanoid	Normal	None
Bloodscalp Hunter	34	35	Humanoid	Normal	None
Bloodscalp Mystic	34	35	Humanoid	Normal	None
Bloodscalp Scavenger	33	34	Humanoid	Normal	None
Bloodscalp Scout	34	35	Humanoid	Normal	None
Bloodscalp Warrior	33	34	Humanoid	Normal	None
Bloodscalp Witch Doctor	37	37	Humanoid	Normal	None
Brutus	43	43	Elemental	Normal	None
Captain Keelhaul	47	47	Humanoid	Normal	None
Captain Stillwater	46	46	Humanoid	Normal	None
Chucky Ten Thumbs""	43	44	Undead	Normal	Charm, Fear and Sleep
Cold Eye Basilisk	39	40	Beast	Normal	None
Colonel Kurzen	40	40	Humanoid	Elite	None
Crystal Spine Basilisk	34	35	Beast	Normal	None
Elder Mistvale Gorilla	40	41	Beast	Normal	None
Elder Shadowmaw Panther	42	43	Beast	Normal	None
Elder Stranglethorn Tiger	34	35	Beast	Normal	None
Enraged Silverback Gorilla	41	42	Beast	Normal	None
Fleet Master Firallon	48	48	Humanoid	Normal	None
Foreman Cozzle	38	38	Humanoid	Normal	None
Gan'zulah	41	41	Humanoid	Normal	None
Garr Salthoof	43	43	Humanoid	Normal	None
Gazban	40	40	Humanoid	Normal	None
Gorlash	47	47	Giant	Elite	None
Gurubashi Warrior	54	55	Humanoid	Elite	None
High Priestess Hai'watna	57	57	Humanoid	Elite	None
Ironjaw Basilisk	43	44	Beast	Normal	None
Ironpatch	43	43	Humanoid	Normal	None
Jaguero Stalker	50	50	Beast	Normal	None
Jon-Jon the Crow	43	44	Undead	Normal	Charm, Fear and Sleep
Jungle Stalker	40	41	Beast	Normal	None
Jungle Thunderer	37	38	Beast	Normal	None
King Bangalash	46	46	Beast	Normal	None
King Mukla	55	55	Beast	Elite	None
Konda	43	43	Beast	Normal	None
Kurzen Commando	34	35	Humanoid	Normal	None
Kurzen Elite	36	37	Humanoid	Normal	None
Kurzen Headshrinker	34	35	Humanoid	Normal	None
Kurzen Jungle Fighter	32	33	Humanoid	Normal	None
Kurzen Medicine Man	32	33	Humanoid	Normal	None
Kurzen Shadow Hunter	38	38	Humanoid	Normal	None
Kurzen Subchief	38	38	Humanoid	Normal	None
Kurzen War Tiger	32	33	Beast	Normal	None
Kurzen Witch Doctor	36	37	Humanoid	Normal	None
Kurzen Wrangler	34	34	Humanoid	Normal	None
Kurzen's Agent	32	33	Humanoid	Normal	None
Lashtail Raptor	35	36	Beast	Normal	None
Lesser Water Elemental	36	37	Elemental	Normal	Special - Elemental Water
Lord Sakrasis	47	47	Humanoid	Rare Spawn Elite	None

NAME	MIN	MAX	TYPE	CLASSIFICATION	IMMUNITIES
Mai'Zoth	47	47	Humanoid	Elite	None
Maury Club Foot" Wilkins"	43	44	Undead	Normal	Charm, Fear and Sleep
Mistvale Gorilla	32	33	Beast	Normal	None
Mogh the Undying	44	44	Humanoid	Elite	None
Mokk the Savage	44	44	Beast	Normal	None
Mok'rash	50	50	Giant	Elite	None
Mosh'Ogg Brute	36	37	Humanoid	Normal	None
Mosh'Ogg Butcher	44	44	Humanoid	Elite	None
Mosh'Ogg Lord	45	45	Humanoid	Elite	None
Mosh'Ogg Mauler	43	44	Humanoid	Elite	None
Mosh'Ogg Warmonger	41	42	Humanoid	Elite	None
Mosh'Ogg Witch Doctor	36	37	Humanoid	Normal	None
Murkgill Warrior	35	36	Humanoid	Normal	None
Naga Explorer	43	44	Humanoid	Normal	None
Negolash	52	52	Giant	Elite	None
Nezzliok the Dire	40	40	Humanoid	Normal	None
Panther	32	33	Beast	Normal	None
Private Merle	31	31	Humanoid	Normal	None
River Crocolisk	30	31	Beast	Normal	None
Saltscale Forager	35	36	Humanoid	Elite	None
Saltscale Warrior	35	36	Humanoid	Elite	None
Saltwater Crocolisk	35	36	Beast	Normal	None
Scale Belly	45	45	Beast	Rare Spawn	None
Sharptooth Frenzy	31	32	Beast	Normal	None
Silverback Patriarch	42	43	Beast	Normal	None
Sin'Dall	37	37	Beast	Normal	None
Skullsplitter Axe Thrower	39	40	Humanoid	Normal	None
Skullsplitter Beastmaster	41	42	Humanoid	Normal	None
Skullsplitter Berserker	43	44	Humanoid	Normal	None
Skullsplitter Hunter	41	42	Humanoid	Normal	None
Skullsplitter Mystic	39	40	Humanoid	Normal	None
Skullsplitter Scout	41	42	Humanoid	Normal	None
Skullsplitter Spiritchaser	44	44	Humanoid	Normal	None
Skullsplitter Warrior	39	40	Humanoid	Normal	None
Skymane Gorilla	50	50	Beast	Normal	None
Snapjaw Crocolisk	35	36	Beast	Normal	None
Southern Sand Crawler	40	41	Beast	Normal	None
Stone Maw Basilisk	31	32	Beast	Normal	None
Stranglethorn Raptor	33	34	Beast	Normal	None
Stranglethorn Tiger	32	33	Beast	Normal	None
Stranglethorn Tigress	37	38	Beast	Normal	None
Tethis	43	43	Beast	Normal	None
Thrashtail Basilisk	41	42	Beast	Normal	None
Venture Co. Geologist	35	36	Humanoid	Normal	None
Venture Co. Lumberjack	34	35	Humanoid	Normal	None
Venture Co. Mechanic	34	35	Humanoid	Normal	None
Venture Co. Miner	34	35	Humanoid	Normal	None
Venture Co. Shredder	37	37	Mechanical	Normal	Special - Piloted Mechanical
Venture Co. Strip Miner	40	41	Humanoid	Normal	None
Venture Co. Surveyor	41	42	Humanoid	Normal	None
Venture Co. Tinkerer	40	41	Humanoid	Normal	None
Venture Co. Workboss	36	36	Humanoid	Normal	None
Young Jungle Stalker	36	37	Beast	Normal	None
Young Lashtail Raptor	33	34	Beast	Normal	None
Young Panther	30	31	Beast	Normal	None
Young Stranglethorn Raptor	30	31	Beast	Normal	None
Young Stranglethorn Tiger	30	31	Beast	Normal	None
Zanzil the Outcast	46	46	Humanoid	Normal	None
Zanzil Zombie	43	44	Undead	Normal	Charm, Fear and Sleep

SWAMP OF SORROWS

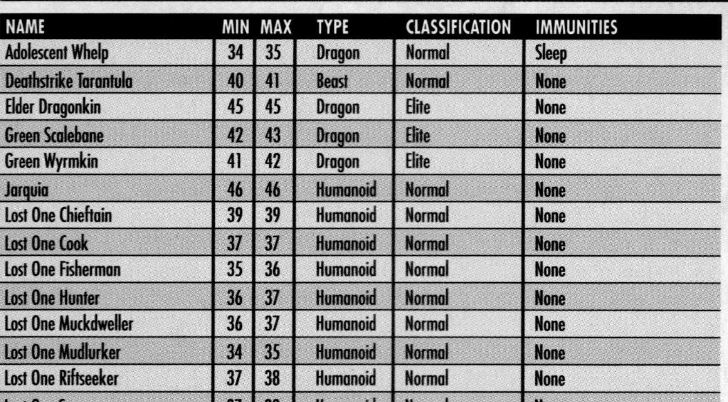

NAME	MIN	MAX	TYPE	CLASSIFICATION	IMMUNITIES
Adolescent Whelp	34	35	Dragon	Normal	Sleep
Deathstrike Tarantula	40	41	Beast	Normal	None
Elder Dragonkin	45	45	Dragon	Elite	None
Green Scalebane	42	43	Dragon	Elite	None
Green Wyrmkin	41	42	Dragon	Elite	None
Jarquia	46	46	Humanoid	Normal	None
Lost One Chieftain	39	39	Humanoid	Normal	None
Lost One Cook	37	37	Humanoid	Normal	None
Lost One Fisherman	35	36	Humanoid	Normal	None
Lost One Hunter	36	37	Humanoid	Normal	None
Lost One Muckdweller	36	37	Humanoid	Normal	None
Lost One Mudlurker	34	35	Humanoid	Normal	None
Lost One Riftseeker	37	38	Humanoid	Normal	None
Lost One Seer	37	38	Humanoid	Normal	None
Marsh Flesheater	43	44	Humanoid	Normal	None

NAME	MIN	MAX	TYPE	CLASSIFICATION	IMMUNITIES
Marsh Inkspewer	42	43	Humanoid	Normal	None
Marsh Murloc	41	42	Humanoid	Normal	None
Marsh Oracle	44	45	Humanoid	Normal	None
Monstrous Crawler	43	44	Beast	Normal	None
Sawtooth Crocolisk	38	39	Beast	Normal	None
Sawtooth Snapper	41	42	Beast	Normal	None
Shadow Panther	39	40	Beast	Normal	None
Silt Crawler	40	41	Beast	Normal	None
Sorrow Spinner	36	37	Beast	Normal	None
Swamp Jaguar	36	37	Beast	Normal	None
Swampwalker	38	39	Elemental	Normal	None
Swampwalker Elder	39	40	Elemental	Normal	None
Tangled Horror	40	41	Elemental	Normal	None
Young Sawtooth Crocolisk	35	36	Beast	Normal	None

TANARIS

NAME	MIN	MAX	TYPE	CLASSIFICATION	IMMUNITIES
Andre Firebeard	45	45	Humanoid	Normal	None
Aquementas	54	54	Elemental	Normal	Frost
Blisterpaw Hyena	44	45	Beast	Normal	None
Caliph Scorpidsting	46	46	Humanoid	Normal	None
Centipaar Tunneler	47	48	Unknown	Normal	None
Centipaar Wasp	47	48	Unknown	Normal	None
Chronalis	54	54	Dragon	Elite	Special - Bronze Dragon
Coast Strider	48	49	Giant	Elite	None
Cyclok the Mad	48	48	Humanoid	Rare Spawn	None
Deep Dweller	49	50	Giant	Elite	None
Dune Smasher	48	49	Giant	Elite	None
Dunemaul Brute	47	48	Humanoid	Normal	None
Dunemaul Ogre	45	46	Humanoid	Normal	None
Fire Roc	43	45	Beast	Normal	None
Giant Surf Glider	48	50	Beast	Elite	None
Glasshide Basilisk	42	43	Beast	Normal	None
Glasshide Gazer	45	46	Beast	Normal	None
Gnarled Thistleshrub	48	49	Elemental	Normal	None
Gor'marok the Ravager	49	49	Humanoid	Normal	None
Greater Firebird	46	46	Beast	Rare Spawn	None
Haarka the Ravenous	50	50	Unknown	Rare Spawn	None
Hazzali Wasp	47	48	Unknown	Normal	None
Hazzali Worker	47	48	Unknown	Normal	None
Jin'Zallah the Sandbringer	46	46	Humanoid	Rare Spawn Elite	None
Kregg Keelhaul	47	47	Humanoid	Rare Spawn	None
Land Rager	45	47	Elemental	Normal	Special - Elemental Earth
Murderous Blisterpaw	43	43	Beast	Rare Spawn	None

NAME	MIN	MAX	TYPE	CLASSIFICATION	IMMUNITIES
Occulus	50	50	Dragon	Elite	Special - Bronze Dragon
Omgorn the Lost	50	50	Humanoid	Rare Spawn	None
Rabid Blisterpaw	47	48	Beast	Normal	None
Roc	41	43	Beast	Normal	None
Sandfury Hideskinner	42	43	Humanoid	Elite	None
Scorpid Duneburrower	46	47	Beast	Normal	None
Scorpid Dunestalker	46	47	Beast	Normal	None
Scorpid Hunter	40	41	Beast	Normal	None
Scorpid Tail Lasher	43	44	Beast	Normal	None
Searing Roc	47	49	Beast	Normal	None
Soriid the Devourer	50	50	Unknown	Rare Spawn	None
Southsea Dock Worker	44	45	Humanoid	Normal	None
Southsea Freebooter	44	45	Humanoid	Normal	None
Southsea Pirate	44	45	Humanoid	Normal	None
Southsea Swashbuckler	44	45	Humanoid	Normal	None
Starving Blisterpaw	41	42	Beast	Normal	None
Surf Glider	48	50	Beast	Normal	None
Thistleshrub Dew Collector	47	48	Elemental	Normal	None
Thistleshrub Rootshaper	49	50	Elemental	Normal	None
Tick	52	52	Dragon	Elite	Special - Bronze Dragon
Warleader Krazzilak	45	45	Humanoid	Rare Spawn Elite	None
Wastewander Assassin	44	45	Humanoid	Normal	None
Wastewander Rogue	43	44	Humanoid	Normal	None
Wastewander Scufflaw	45	45	Humanoid	Normal	None
Wastewander Shadow Mage	42	43	Humanoid	Normal	None
Wastewander Thief	40	41	Humanoid	Normal	None

TELDRASSIL

NAME	MIN	MAX	TYPE	CLASSIFICATION	IMMUNITIES
Agal	8	8	Humanoid	Normal	None
Blackmoss the Fetid	13	13	Elemental	Rare Spawn	None
Bloodfeather Fury	9	10	Humanoid	Normal	None
Bloodfeather Harpy	8	9	Humanoid	Normal	None
Dark Sprite	6	7	Demon	Normal	None
Elder Nightsaber	8	9	Beast	Normal	None
Elder Timberling	10	11	Elemental	Normal	None
Feral Nightsaber	10	11	Beast	Normal	None
Ferocitas the Dream Eater	8	8	Humanoid	Normal	None
Githyiss the Vile	5	5	Beast	Normal	None
Gnarlpine Ambusher	6	7	Humanoid	Normal	None
Gnarlpine Augur	8	9	Humanoid	Normal	None
Gnarlpine Avenger	9	10	Humanoid	Normal	None
Gnarlpine Defender	7	8	Humanoid	Normal	None
Gnarlpine Instigator	8	8	Humanoid	Normal	None
Gnarlpine Mystic	6	7	Humanoid	Normal	None
Gnarlpine Shaman	7	8	Humanoid	Normal	None
Gnarlpine Ursa	5	6	Humanoid	Normal	None
Gnarlpine Warrior	6	7	Humanoid	Normal	None
Greenpaw	10	10	Humanoid	Normal	None
Grell	2	3	Demon	Normal	None
Grellkin	3	4	Demon	Normal	None
Lady Sathrah	12	12	Beast	Normal	None
Lord Melenas	8	8	Demon	Normal	None
Mangy Nightsaber	2	3	Beast	Normal	None
Minion of Sethir	8	10	Humanoid	Normal	None
Nightsaber	5	6	Beast	Normal	None
Nightsaber Stalker	7	8	Beast	Normal	None
Oakenscowl	9	9	Elemental	Elite	None
Rageclaw	10	10	Humanoid	Normal	None
Rascal Sprite	5	6	Demon	Normal	None
Sethir the Ancient	13	13	Humanoid	Normal	None
Spirit of Sathrah	12	12	Beast	Normal	None
Strigid Hunter	8	9	Beast	Normal	None
Strigid Owl	5	6	Beast	Normal	None
Strigid Screecher	7	8	Beast	Normal	None
Thistle Boar	2	3	Beast	Normal	None
Timberling	5	6	Elemental	Normal	None
Timberling Bark Ripper	7	8	Elemental	Normal	None
Timberling Mire Beast	9	10	Elemental	Normal	None
Timberling Trampler	8	9	Elemental	Normal	None
Ursal the Mauler	12	12	Humanoid	Normal	None
Vorlus Vilehoof	10	10	Demon	Normal	None
Webwood Lurker	5	6	Beast	Normal	None
Webwood Silkspinner	8	9	Beast	Normal	None
Webwood Spider	3	4	Beast	Normal	None
Webwood Venomfang	7	8	Beast	Normal	None
Young Nightsaber	1	2	Beast	Normal	None
Young Thistle Boar	1	2	Beast	Normal	None

THE BARRENS

NAME	MIN	MAX	TYPE	CLASSIFICATION	IMMUNITIES
Affray Challenger	26	27	Humanoid	Normal	None
Azzere the Skyblade	25	25	Beast	Rare Spawn	None
Bael'dun Excavator	21	22	Humanoid	Normal	None
Bael'dun Foreman	22	23	Humanoid	Normal	None
Bael'dun Officer	26	26	Humanoid	Normal	None
Bael'dun Rifleman	24	25	Humanoid	Normal	None
Bael'dun Soldier	23	24	Humanoid	Normal	None
Barak Kodobane	16	16	Humanoid	Normal	None
Baron Longshore	16	16	Humanoid	Normal	None
Barrens Giraffe	15	16	Beast	Normal	None
Barrens Kodo	19	20	Beast	Normal	None
Big Will	33	33	Humanoid	Normal	None
Boss Copperplug	19	19	Humanoid	Normal	None
Bristleback Geomancer	19	20	Humanoid	Normal	None
Bristleback Hunter	18	19	Humanoid	Normal	None
Bristleback Thornweaver	17	18	Humanoid	Normal	None
Bristleback Water Seeker	16	17	Humanoid	Normal	None
Brokespear	17	17	Humanoid	Rare Spawn	None
Burning Blade Acolyte	11	12	Humanoid	Normal	Fear
Burning Blade Bruiser	10	11	Humanoid	Normal	Fear
Cannoneer Smythe	19	19	Humanoid	Normal	None
Cannoneer Whessan	19	19	Humanoid	Normal	None
Captain Fairmount	20	20	Humanoid	Normal	None
Captain Gerogg Hammertoe	27	27	Humanoid	Rare Spawn Elite	None
Dig Rat	1	1	Critter	Normal	None
Digger Flameforge	24	24	Humanoid	Rare Spawn	None
Dishu	13	13	Beast	Rare Spawn	None
Echeyakee	16	16	Beast	Normal	None
Elder Mystic Razorsnout	15	15	Humanoid	Rare Spawn Elite	None
Engineer Whirleygig	19	19	Humanoid	Rare Spawn	None
Fleeting Plainstrider	12	13	Beast	Normal	None
Foreman Grills	19	19	Humanoid	Rare Spawn	None
Foreman Silixiz	25	25	Humanoid	Normal	None
General Twinbraid	30	30	Humanoid	Normal	None
Geopriest Gukk'rok	19	19	Humanoid	Rare Spawn	None
Gesharahan	20	20	Beast	Rare Spawn Elite	None
Grand Foreman Puzik Gallywix	26	26	Humanoid	Elite	None
Greater Plainstrider	11	12	Beast	Normal	None
Greater Thunderhawk	23	24	Beast	Normal	None
Hagg Taurenbane	26	26	Humanoid	Rare Spawn Elite	Special
Hecklefang Hyena	15	16	Beast	Normal	None
Hecklefang Snarler	18	19	Beast	Normal	None
Heggin Stonewhisker	24	24	Humanoid	Rare Spawn	None
Hezrul Bloodmark	19	19	Humanoid	Normal	None
Humar the Pridelord	23	23	Beast	Rare Spawn Elite	None
Isha Awak	27	27	Beast	Normal	None
Ishamuhale	19	19	Beast	Normal	None
Kolkar Bloodcharger	14	15	Humanoid	Normal	None
Kolkar Invader	16	17	Humanoid	Normal	None
Kolkar Marauder	15	16	Humanoid	Normal	None
Kolkar Pack Runner	14	15	Humanoid	Normal	None
Kolkar Packhound	13	13	Beast	Normal	None
Kolkar Stormer	13	14	Humanoid	Normal	None
Kolkar Stormseer	15	16	Humanoid	Normal	None
Kolkar Wrangler	12	13	Humanoid	Normal	None
Kreenig Snarlsnout	15	15	Humanoid	Normal	None
Kuz	21	21	Humanoid	Normal	None
Lakota'mani	22	22	Beast	Normal	None
Lok Orcbane	25	25	Humanoid	Normal	None
Lord Cyrik Blackforge	23	23	Humanoid	Normal	None
Lost Barrens Kodo	14	15	Beast	Normal	None
Malgin Barleybrew	25	25	Humanoid	Rare Spawn	None
Muck Frenzy	14	15	Beast	Normal	None
Mutated Venture Co. Drone	25	25	Undead	Normal	None
Nak	23	23	Humanoid	Normal	None
Oasis Snapjaw	15	16	Beast	Normal	None
Ornery Plainstrider	16	17	Beast	Normal	None
Overseer Glibby	16	16	Humanoid	Normal	None
Owatanka	24	24	Beast	Normal	None
Prospector Khazgorm	26	26	Humanoid	Normal	None
Rathorian	15	15	Demon	Rare Spawn	None
Razorfen Servitor	23	24	Humanoid	Elite	None
Razormane Defender	12	13	Humanoid	Normal	None
Razormane Geomancer	12	13	Humanoid	Normal	None
Razormane Hunter	11	12	Humanoid	Normal	None
Razormane Mystic	13	14	Humanoid	Normal	None
Razormane Pathfinder	20	21	Humanoid	Normal	None
Razormane Seer	23	24	Humanoid	Normal	None
Razormane Stalker	22	23	Humanoid	Normal	None
Razormane Warfrenzy	24	25	Humanoid	Normal	None
Razormane Water Seeker	10	11	Humanoid	Normal	None
Rocklance	17	17	Humanoid	Rare Spawn Elite	None
Savannah Highmane	12	13	Beast	Normal	None
Savannah Huntress	11	12	Beast	Normal	None
Savannah Matriarch	17	18	Beast	Normal	None
Savannah Patriarch	15	16	Beast	Normal	None
Savannah Prowler	14	15	Beast	Normal	None

THE BARRENS

NAME	MIN	MAX	TYPE	CLASSIFICATION	IMMUNITIES
Serena Bloodfeather	20	20	Humanoid	Normal	None
Silithid Creeper	20	21	Unknown	Normal	None
Silithid Grub	20	20	Beast	Normal	None
Silithid Harvester	24	24	Unknown	Rare Spawn	None
Silithid Swarmer	21	22	Unknown	Normal	None
Sister Rathtalon	19	19	Humanoid	Rare Spawn Elite	None
Slimeshell Makrura	18	19	Humanoid	Normal	None
Sludge Beast	19	19	Unknown	Rare Spawn	None
Snort the Heckler	17	17	Beast	Rare Spawn	None
Southsea Brigand	12	13	Humanoid	Normal	None
Southsea Cannoneer	13	14	Humanoid	Normal	None
Southsea Cutthroat	14	15	Humanoid	Normal	None
Southsea Privateer	14	15	Humanoid	Normal	None
Stonearm	15	15	Humanoid	Rare Spawn	None
Stormhide	22	23	Beast	Normal	None
Stormsnout	18	19	Beast	Normal	None
Summoned Felhunter	30	30	Demon	Normal	None
Sunscale Lashtail	11	13	Beast	Normal	None
Sunscale Screecher	13	15	Beast	Normal	None
Sunscale Scytheclaw	16	18	Beast	Normal	None
Supervisor Lugwizzle	18	18	Humanoid	Normal	None
Swiftmane	21	21	Beast	Rare Spawn Elite	None
Swinegart Spearhide	22	22	Humanoid	Rare Spawn Elite	None
Takk the Leaper	19	19	Beast	Rare Spawn Elite	None
Tazan	13	13	Humanoid	Normal	None
Theramore Marine	15	16	Humanoid	Normal	None
Theramore Preserver	16	17	Humanoid	Normal	None
Thunderhawk Cloudscraper	20	22	Beast	Normal	None
Thunderhawk Hatchling	18	20	Beast	Normal	None
Thunderhead	20	21	Beast	Normal	None
Thunderstomp	24	24	Beast	Rare Spawn	None
Tinkerer Sniggles	16	16	Humanoid	Normal	None
Venture Co. Drudger	14	15	Humanoid	Normal	None
Venture Co. Enforcer	16	17	Humanoid	Normal	None
Venture Co. Lookout	24	26	Humanoid	Normal	None
Venture Co. Mercenary	15	16	Humanoid	Normal	None
Venture Co. Overseer	17	18	Humanoid	Normal	None
Venture Co. Patroller	24	25	Humanoid	Normal	None
Venture Co. Peon	13	14	Humanoid	Normal	None
Verog the Dervish	18	18	Humanoid	Normal	None
Wandering Barrens Giraffe	18	19	Beast	Normal	None
Warlord Krom'zar	20	20	Humanoid	Normal	None
Washte Pawne	25	25	Beast	Normal	None
Witchwing Ambusher	17	18	Humanoid	Normal	None
Witchwing Harpy	14	15	Humanoid	Normal	None
Witchwing Roguefeather	15	16	Humanoid	Normal	None
Witchwing Slayer	16	17	Humanoid	Normal	None
Witchwing Windcaller	17	18	Humanoid	Normal	None
Zhevra Charger	17	18	Beast	Normal	None
Zhevra Courser	20	21	Beast	Normal	None
Zhevra Runner	13	14	Beast	Normal	None

THOUSAND NEEDLES

NAME	MIN	MAX	TYPE	CLASSIFICATION	IMMUNITIES
Achellios the Banished	31	31	Humanoid	Rare Spawn	None
Arnak Grimtotem	29	29	Humanoid	Normal	None
Boiling Elemental	27	28	Elemental	Normal	Special - Elemental Water
Cloud Serpent	25	26	Beast	Normal	None
Crag Stalker	25	26	Beast	Normal	None
Elder Cloud Serpent	27	29	Beast	Normal	None
Galak Flame Guard	30	30	Humanoid	Normal	None
Galak Marauder	26	27	Humanoid	Normal	None
Galak Messenger	26	26	Humanoid	Normal	None
Galak Pack Runner	25	26	Humanoid	Normal	None
Galak Packhound	24	24	Beast	Normal	None
Galak Scout	24	25	Humanoid	Normal	None
Gravelsnout Digger	28	29	Humanoid	Normal	None
Gravelsnout Forager	27	28	Humanoid	Normal	None
Gravelsnout Kobold	26	27	Humanoid	Normal	None
Gravelsnout Vermin	25	26	Humanoid	Normal	None
Grenka Bloodscreech	31	31	Humanoid	Normal	None
Grimtotem Bandit	25	26	Humanoid	Normal	None
Grimtotem Geomancer	25	27	Humanoid	Normal	None
Grimtotem Reaver	28	28	Humanoid	Normal	None
Heartrazor	32	32	Beast	Rare Spawn Elite	None
Highperch Wyvern	28	29	Beast	Normal	None
Ironeye the Invincible	37	37	Beast	Rare Spawn Elite	None
Needles Cougar	27	28	Beast	Normal	None
Pesterhide Hyena	26	27	Beast	Normal	None
Pesterhide Snarler	28	29	Beast	Normal	None
Rok'Alim the Pounder	30	30	Elemental	Elite	Special - Elemental Earth
Salt Flats Scavenger	30	32	Beast	Normal	None
Salt Flats Vulture	32	34	Beast	Normal	None
Saltstone Basilisk	30	31	Beast	Normal	None
Saltstone Crystalhide	32	33	Beast	Normal	None
Saltstone Gazer	34	35	Beast	Normal	None
Scorpid Reaver	31	32	Beast	Normal	None
Screeching Harpy	28	29	Humanoid	Normal	None
Screeching Roguefeather	29	30	Humanoid	Normal	None
Silithid Hive Drone	33	34	Unknown	Normal	None
Silithid Invader	34	35	Unknown	Normal	None
Silithid Ravager	36	36	Unknown	Rare Spawn	None
Silithid Searcher	32	33	Unknown	Normal	None
Sparkleshell Snapper	34	35	Beast	Normal	None
Sparkleshell Tortoise	30	31	Beast	Normal	None
Steelsnap	30	30	Beast	Normal	None
Thundering Boulderkin	28	29	Elemental	Normal	Special - Elemental Earth
Venomous Cloud Serpent	26	28	Beast	Normal	None
Vile Sting	35	35	Beast	Rare Spawn Elite	None

TIRISFAL GLADES

NAME	MIN	MAX	TYPE	CLASSIFICATION	IMMUNITIES
Bayne	10	10	Demon	Rare Spawn	None
Bleeding Horror	9	10	Undead	Normal	Charm, Fear and Sleep
Captain Dargol	13	13	Undead	Normal	Charm, Fear, Sleep and Bleed
Captain Melrache	12	12	Humanoid	Normal	None
Captain Perrine	9	9	Humanoid	Normal	None
Captain Vachon	11	11	Humanoid	Normal	None
Cracked Skull Soldier	8	9	Undead	Normal	Charm, Fear, Sleep and Bleed
Cursed Darkhound	7	8	Demon	Normal	None
Daniel Ulfman	2	3	Undead	Normal	Charm, Fear and Sleep
Darkeye Bonecaster	7	8	Undead	Normal	Charm, Fear, Sleep and Bleed
Decrepit Darkhound	5	6	Demon	Normal	None
Deeb	12	12	Humanoid	Rare Spawn	None
Devlin Agamand	9	9	Undead	Normal	Charm, Fear, Sleep and Bleed
Duskbat	1	2	Beast	Normal	None
Farmer Solliden	8	8	Humanoid	Rare Spawn	None
Fellicent's Shade	12	12	Undead	Rare Spawn	None
Greater Duskbat	6	7	Beast	Normal	None
Gregor Agamand	10	10	Undead	Normal	Charm, Fear and Sleep
Gunther's Minion	7	8	Undead	Normal	Charm, Fear, Sleep and Bleed
Hungering Dead	7	8	Undead	Normal	Charm, Fear and Sleep
Karrel Grayves	2	3	Undead	Normal	Charm, Fear and Sleep
Lillith Nefara	12	12	Undead	Normal	Charm, Fear, Sleep and Bleed
Lost Soul	6	7	Undead	Rare Spawn	Charm, Fear and Sleep
Maggot Eye	10	10	Undead	Normal	Charm, Fear and Sleep
Mangy Duskbat	3	4	Beast	Normal	None
Meven Korgal	5	5	Humanoid	Normal	None
Mindless Zombie	1	1	Undead	Normal	Charm, Fear and Sleep
Muad	10	10	Humanoid	Rare Spawn	None
Night Web Matriarch	5	5	Beast	Normal	None
Night Web Spider	3	4	Beast	Normal	None

TIRISFAL GLADES

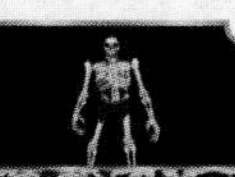

NAME	MIN	MAX	TYPE	CLASSIFICATION	IMMUNITIES
Nissa Agamand	10	10	Undead	Normal	Charm, Fear and Sleep
Ragged Scavenger	2	3	Beast	Normal	None
Rattlecage Skeleton	2	3	Undead	Normal	Charm, Fear, Sleep and Bleed
Rattlecage Soldier	6	7	Undead	Normal	Charm, Fear, Sleep and Bleed
Ravaged Corpse	6	7	Undead	Normal	Charm, Fear and Sleep
Ravenous Darkhound	9	10	Demon	Normal	None
Ressan the Needler	11	11	Beast	Rare Spawn	None
Rot Hide Gnoll	6	7	Undead	Normal	Charm, Fear and Sleep
Rot Hide Graverobber	6	7	Undead	Normal	Charm, Fear and Sleep
Rot Hide Mongrel	7	8	Undead	Normal	Charm, Fear and Sleep
Rotting Ancestor	10	11	Undead	Normal	Charm, Fear and Sleep
Rotting Dead	5	6	Undead	Normal	Charm, Fear and Sleep
Samuel Fipps	2	3	Undead	Normal	Charm, Fear and Sleep
Scarlet Bodyguard	10	11	Humanoid	Normal	None
Scarlet Convert	3	3	Humanoid	Normal	None
Scarlet Friar	9	10	Humanoid	Normal	None
Scarlet Initiate	3	4	Humanoid	Normal	None
Scarlet Missionary	7	8	Humanoid	Normal	None
Scarlet Neophyte	10	11	Humanoid	Normal	None
Scarlet Vanguard	10	11	Humanoid	Normal	None
Scarlet Warrior	6	7	Humanoid	Normal	None
Scarlet Zealot	8	9	Humanoid	Normal	None
Shambling Horror	8	9	Undead	Normal	Charm, Fear and Sleep
Sri'skulk	13	13	Beast	Rare Spawn	None
Stephen Bhartec	2	3	Undead	Normal	Charm, Fear, Sleep and Bleed
Thurman Agamand	10	10	Undead	Normal	Charm, Fear and Sleep
Tirisfal Farmer	6	7	Humanoid	Normal	None
Tirisfal Farmhand	5	6	Humanoid	Normal	None
Tormented Spirit	8	9	Undead	Rare Spawn	Charm, Fear and Sleep
Ulag the Cleaver	11	11	Undead	Normal	None
Vampiric Duskbat	8	9	Beast	Normal	None
Vicious Night Web Spider	9	10	Beast	Normal	None
Vile Fin Minor Oracle	8	9	Humanoid	Normal	None
Vile Fin Muckdweller	9	10	Humanoid	Normal	None
Vile Fin Puddlejumper	7	8	Humanoid	Normal	None
Wailing Ancestor	9	10	Undead	Normal	Charm, Fear and Sleep
Wandering Spirit	10	11	Undead	Normal	Charm, Fear and Sleep
Wretched Zombie	1	2	Undead	Normal	Charm, Fear and Sleep
Young Night Web Spider	2	3	Beast	Normal	None
Young Scavenger	1	1	Beast	Normal	None

UN'GORO CRATER

NAME	MIN	MAX	TYPE	CLASSIFICATION	IMMUNITIES
A-Me 01	48	48	Mechanical	Normal	None
Blazerunner	56	56	Elemental	Elite	Special - Elemental Fire
Bloodpetal Flayer	51	52	Unknown	Normal	None
Bloodpetal Lasher	48	49	Unknown	Normal	None
Bloodpetal Pest	40	40	Unknown	Normal	None
Bloodpetal Trapper	52	53	Unknown	Normal	None
Clutchmother Zavas	54	54	Beast	Rare Spawn	None
Devilsaur	53	54	Beast	Elite	None
Diemetradon	51	52	Beast	Normal	None
Elder Diemetradon	54	55	Beast	Normal	None
Fledgling Pterrordax	48	50	Beast	Normal	None
Frenzied Pterrordax	52	54	Beast	Normal	None
Glutinous Ooze	52	54	Unknown	Normal	None
Gorishi Hive Guard	54	54	Unknown	Normal	None
Gorishi Hive Queen	56	56	Unknown	Normal	None
Gorishi Reaver	51	53	Unknown	Normal	None
Gorishi Wasp	51	52	Unknown	Normal	None
Gruff	57	57	Beast	Rare Spawn Elite	None
King Mosh	60	60	Beast	Rare Spawn Elite	Special
Lar'korwi	56	56	Beast	Normal	None
Lar'korwi Mate	49	50	Beast	Normal	None
Muculent Ooze	48	50	Unknown	Normal	Disease
Primal Ooze	50	52	Unknown	Normal	None
Pterrordax	50	52	Beast	Normal	None
Ravasaur	48	49	Beast	Normal	None
Ravasaur Hunter	49	50	Beast	Normal	None
Ravasaur Matriarch	50	50	Beast	Rare Spawn	None
Ravasaur Runner	49	50	Beast	Normal	None
Scorching Elemental	53	54	Elemental	Normal	Special - Elemental Fire
Stegodon	52	53	Beast	Elite	None
Stone Guardian	60	61	Elemental	Elite	Special - Golem
Tar Creeper	51	52	Elemental	Normal	None
Tar Lurker	52	54	Elemental	Normal	None
U'cha	55	55	Beast	Normal	None
Uhk'loc	52	53	Beast	Rare Spawn	None
Un'Goro Gorilla	50	51	Beast	Normal	None
Venomhide Ravasaur	50	51	Beast	Normal	Poison
Young Diemetradon	49	50	Beast	Normal	None

WESTERN PLAGUELANDS

NAME	MIN	MAX	TYPE	CLASSIFICATION	IMMUNITIES
Araj the Summoner	61	61	Undead	Elite	Special
Blighted Zombie	52	53	Undead	Normal	Charm, Fear and Sleep
Blood Wraith	55	56	Undead	Normal	Charm, Fear and Sleep
Carrion Lurker	52	53	Beast	Normal	None
Carrion Vulture	50	52	Beast	Normal	None
Cauldron Lord Bilemaw	53	53	Undead	Normal	Charm, Fear and Sleep
Cauldron Lord Malvinious	55	55	Undead	Normal	None
Cauldron Lord Razarch	56	56	Undead	Normal	None
Cauldron Lord Soulwrath	58	58	Undead	Normal	Charm, Fear and Sleep
Devouring Ooze	55	56	Unknown	Normal	None
Dreadwhisper	58	58	Undead	Rare Spawn	Charm, Fear and Sleep
Farmer Dalson	56	56	Undead	Normal	Charm, Fear and Sleep
Fetid Zombie	54	56	Undead	Normal	Charm, Fear and Sleep
Flesh Golem	56	57	Undead	Elite	Charm, Fear and Sleep
Foreman Jerris	62	62	Humanoid	Rare Spawn Elite	None
Foreman Marcrid	58	58	Humanoid	Rare Spawn	None
Foulmane	52	52	Undead	Rare Spawn	Charm, Fear and Sleep
Freezing Ghoul	55	56	Undead	Normal	Charm, Fear and Sleep
Grand Inquisitor Isillien	64	64	Humanoid	Elite	None
Haunting Vision	57	58	Undead	Normal	Charm, Fear, Sleep and Bleed
High Priest Thel'danis	65	65	Humanoid	Normal	None
High Protector Lorik	61	61	Humanoid	Elite	None
High Protector Tarsen	59	59	Humanoid	Normal	None
Highlord Taelan Fordring	65	65	Humanoid	Elite	None
Hungering Wraith	56	58	Undead	Normal	Charm, Fear and Sleep
Jabbering Ghoul	54	54	Undead	Normal	Charm, Fear and Sleep
Lord Maldazzar	56	56	Humanoid	Rare Spawn	None
Plague Lurker	54	55	Beast	Normal	None
Putridius	58	58	Undead	Rare Spawn Elite	Charm, Fear and Sleep
Redpath Militia	56	57	Undead	Normal	None
Rotting Behemoth	55	56	Elemental	Normal	None
Rotting Cadaver	53	54	Undead	Normal	Charm, Fear and Sleep
Rotting Ghoul	54	55	Undead	Normal	Charm, Fear and Sleep
Scarlet Avenger	56	57	Humanoid	Normal	None
Scarlet Cavalier	57	58	Humanoid	Elite	None
Scarlet Executioner	60	60	Humanoid	Rare Spawn Elite	None
Scarlet High Clerist	63	63	Humanoid	Rare Spawn Elite	None
Scarlet Hunter	52	53	Humanoid	Normal	None
Scarlet Interrogator	61	61	Humanoid	Rare Spawn Elite	None
Scarlet Invoker	53	54	Humanoid	Normal	None
Scarlet Judge	60	60	Humanoid	Rare Spawn	None
Scarlet Knight	54	55	Humanoid	Normal	None
Scarlet Lumberjack	54	56	Humanoid	Normal	None
Scarlet Magus	56	57	Humanoid	Elite	None
Scarlet Medic	52	54	Humanoid	Normal	None
Scarlet Paladin	55	56	Humanoid	Elite	None
Scarlet Priest	55	57	Humanoid	Elite	None
Scarlet Sentinel	55	56	Humanoid	Elite	None
Scarlet Smith	58	59	Humanoid	Rare Spawn	None

WESTERN PLAGUELANDS

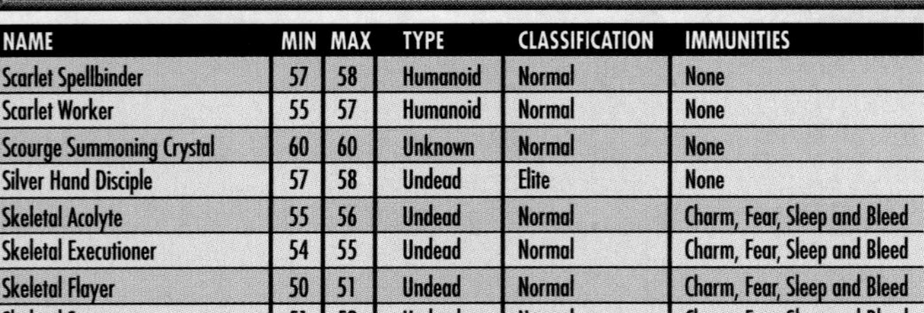

NAME	MIN	MAX	TYPE	CLASSIFICATION	IMMUNITIES
Scarlet Spellbinder	57	58	Humanoid	Normal	None
Scarlet Worker	55	57	Humanoid	Normal	None
Scourge Summoning Crystal	60	60	Unknown	Normal	None
Silver Hand Disciple	57	58	Undead	Elite	None
Skeletal Acolyte	55	56	Undead	Normal	Charm, Fear, Sleep and Bleed
Skeletal Executioner	54	55	Undead	Normal	Charm, Fear, Sleep and Bleed
Skeletal Flayer	50	51	Undead	Normal	Charm, Fear, Sleep and Bleed
Skeletal Sorcerer	51	52	Undead	Normal	Charm, Fear, Sleep and Bleed
Skeletal Terror	52	54	Undead	Normal	Charm, Fear, Sleep and Bleed
Skeletal Warlord	56	57	Undead	Elite	Charm, Fear, Sleep and Bleed
Slavering Ghoul	50	52	Undead	Normal	Charm, Fear and Sleep
Soulless Ghoul	54	55	Undead	Normal	Charm, Fear and Sleep
Spectral Attendant	60	60	Undead	Normal	Charm, Fear, Sleep and Bleed
Spectral Corpse	57	58	Undead	Normal	None
Spectral Defender	57	58	Undead	Normal	None
The Husk	62	62	Elemental	Rare Spawn	None
Venom Mist Lurker	50	51	Beast	Normal	None
Vile Slime	54	55	Unknown	Normal	None
Wailing Death	56	57	Undead	Normal	Charm, Fear, Sleep and Bleed
Wandering Skeleton	55	55	Undead	Normal	Charm, Fear and Sleep

WESTFALL

NAME	MIN	MAX	TYPE	CLASSIFICATION	IMMUNITIES
Benny Blaanco	15	15	Humanoid	Normal	None
Brack	19	19	Humanoid	Rare Spawn	None
Coyote	10	11	Beast	Normal	None
Coyote Packleader	11	12	Beast	Normal	None
Defias Drone	22	22	Undead	Normal	None
Defias Footpad	10	11	Humanoid	Normal	None
Defias Highwayman	17	18	Humanoid	Normal	None
Defias Knuckleduster	16	17	Humanoid	Normal	None
Defias Looter	13	14	Humanoid	Normal	None
Defias Pathstalker	15	16	Humanoid	Normal	None
Defias Pillager	14	15	Humanoid	Normal	None
Defias Raider	17	18	Humanoid	Normal	None
Defias Smuggler	11	12	Humanoid	Normal	None
Defias Tower Patroller	24	24	Humanoid	Normal	None
Defias Tower Sentry	24	25	Humanoid	Normal	None
Defias Trapper	12	13	Humanoid	Normal	None
Dust Devil	18	19	Elemental	Normal	Special - Elemental Air
Fleshripper	13	14	Beast	Normal	None
Foe Reaper 4000	20	20	Mechanical	Rare Spawn	Special - Mechanical
Ghoul	14	15	Undead	Normal	Charm, Fear and Sleep
Goretusk	14	15	Beast	Normal	None
Greater Fleshripper	16	17	Beast	Normal	None
Harvest Golem	11	12	Mechanical	Normal	Special - Mechanical
Harvest Reaper	17	18	Mechanical	Normal	Special - Mechanical
Harvest Watcher	14	15	Mechanical	Normal	Special - Mechanical
Klaven Mortwake	26	26	Humanoid	Elite	None
Kobold Digger	12	13	Humanoid	Normal	None
Leprithus	19	19	Undead	Rare Spawn	Charm, Fear and Sleep
Malformed Defias Drone	24	24	Humanoid	Normal	None
Master Digger	15	15	Humanoid	Rare Spawn	None
Murloc Coastrunner	12	13	Humanoid	Normal	None
Murloc Hunter	16	17	Humanoid	Normal	None
Murloc Minor Oracle	13	14	Humanoid	Normal	None
Murloc Netter	14	15	Humanoid	Normal	None
Murloc Oracle	17	18	Humanoid	Normal	None
Murloc Raider	11	12	Humanoid	Normal	None
Murloc Tidehunter	18	19	Humanoid	Normal	None
Murloc Warrior	15	16	Humanoid	Normal	None
Old Murk-Eye	20	20	Humanoid	Normal	None
Riverpaw Bandit	16	17	Humanoid	Normal	None
Riverpaw Brute	15	16	Humanoid	Normal	None
Riverpaw Gnoll	11	12	Humanoid	Normal	None
Riverpaw Herbalist	14	15	Humanoid	Normal	None
Riverpaw Miner	14	15	Humanoid	Normal	None
Riverpaw Mongrel	13	14	Humanoid	Normal	None
Riverpaw Mystic	18	19	Humanoid	Normal	None
Riverpaw Overseer	19	20	Humanoid	Normal	None
Riverpaw Scout	12	13	Humanoid	Normal	None
Riverpaw Shaman	12	13	Humanoid	Normal	None
Riverpaw Taskmaster	17	18	Humanoid	Normal	None
Rusty Harvest Golem	9	10	Mechanical	Normal	Special - Mechanical
Sand Crawler	13	14	Beast	Normal	None
Sea Crawler	15	16	Beast	Normal	None
Sergeant Brashclaw	18	18	Humanoid	Rare Spawn	None
Shore Crawler	17	18	Beast	Normal	None
Slark	15	15	Humanoid	Rare Spawn	None
Venture Co. Drone	22	22	Undead	Normal	None
Vultros	26	26	Beast	Rare Spawn	None
Young Fleshripper	10	11	Beast	Normal	None
Young Goretusk	12	13	Beast	Normal	None

WETLANDS

NAME	MIN	MAX	TYPE	CLASSIFICATION	IMMUNITIES
Balgaras the Foul	34	34	Humanoid	Elite	Shadow Magic
Black Ooze	23	24	Unknown	Normal	None
Black Slime	20	21	Unknown	Normal	None
Bluegill Forager	22	23	Humanoid	Normal	None
Bluegill Muckdweller	23	24	Humanoid	Normal	None
Bluegill Murloc	20	21	Humanoid	Normal	None
Bluegill Oracle	25	26	Humanoid	Normal	None
Bluegill Puddlejumper	21	22	Humanoid	Normal	None
Bluegill Raider	28	29	Humanoid	Normal	None
Bluegill Warrior	24	25	Humanoid	Normal	None
Captain Halyndor	30	30	Undead	Normal	Charm, Fear and Sleep
Cave Stalker	21	22	Beast	Normal	None
Chieftain Nek'rosh	32	32	Humanoid	Normal	Fire Magic
Comar Villard	22	22	Humanoid	Normal	None
Crimson Ooze	24	25	Unknown	Normal	None
Crimson Whelp	25	26	Dragon	Normal	None
Cursed Marine	27	28	Undead	Normal	Charm, Fear, Sleep and Bleed
Cursed Sailor	26	27	Undead	Normal	Charm, Fear and Sleep
Dark Iron Demolitionist	30	31	Humanoid	Elite	None
Dark Iron Dwarf	27	28	Humanoid	Elite	None
Dark Iron Rifleman	27	28	Humanoid	Elite	None
Dark Iron Saboteur	28	29	Humanoid	Elite	None
Dark Iron Tunneler	29	30	Humanoid	Elite	None
Dragonmaw Battlemaster	30	30	Humanoid	Normal	None
Dragonmaw Bonewarder	27	28	Humanoid	Normal	None
Dragonmaw Centurion	28	29	Humanoid	Normal	None
Dragonmaw Grunt	20	21	Humanoid	Normal	None
Dragonmaw Raider	26	27	Humanoid	Normal	None
Dragonmaw Scout	19	20	Humanoid	Normal	None
Dragonmaw Shadowwarder	28	29	Humanoid	Normal	None
Dragonmaw Swamprunner	27	28	Humanoid	Normal	None
Elder Razormaw	29	29	Beast	Normal	None
Fen Creeper	24	25	Elemental	Normal	None
Fen Dweller	20	21	Elemental	Normal	None
Fen Lord	25	26	Elemental	Normal	None
First Mate Snellig	29	29	Undead	Normal	Charm, Fear and Sleep
Flamescale Drake	39	39	Dragon	Elite	None
Flamesnorting Whelp	26	27	Dragon	Normal	None
Garneg Charskull	29	29	Humanoid	Rare Spawn	Fire Magic
Giant Wetlands Crocolisk	25	26	Beast	Normal	None
Gobbler	22	22	Humanoid	Normal	None
Hargin Mundar	20	20	Humanoid	Normal	None
Highland Lashtail	24	25	Beast	Normal	None
Highland Raptor	23	24	Beast	Normal	None

WETLANDS

NAME	MIN	MAX	TYPE	CLASSIFICATION	IMMUNITIES
Highland Razormaw	27	28	Beast	Normal	None
Highland Scytheclaw	25	26	Beast	Normal	None
Leech Stalker	21	22	Beast	Normal	None
Leech Widow	24	24	Beast	Rare Spawn	None
Lost Whelp	24	25	Dragon	Normal	Shadow Magic
Ma'ruk Wyrmscale	23	23	Humanoid	Rare Spawn	None
Monstrous Ooze	25	26	Unknown	Normal	None
Mosshide Alpha	27	27	Humanoid	Normal	None
Mosshide Brute	24	25	Humanoid	Normal	None
Mosshide Fenrunner	22	23	Humanoid	Normal	None
Mosshide Gnoll	20	21	Humanoid	Normal	None
Mosshide Mistweaver	22	23	Humanoid	Normal	None
Mosshide Mongrel	21	22	Humanoid	Normal	None
Mosshide Mystic	25	26	Humanoid	Normal	None
Mosshide Trapper	23	24	Humanoid	Normal	None
Mottled Raptor	22	23	Beast	Normal	None
Mottled Razormaw	26	27	Beast	Normal	None
Mottled Screecher	24	25	Beast	Normal	None
Mottled Scytheclaw	25	26	Beast	Normal	None
Murphy West	20	20	Humanoid	Normal	None
Razormaw Matriarch	31	31	Beast	Rare Spawn	None
Red Dragonspawn	47	48	Dragon	Normal	Fire Magic
Red Scalebane	49	50	Dragon	Normal	None
Red Whelp	23	24	Dragon	Normal	None
Sarltooth	29	29	Beast	Normal	None
Scalebane Lieutenant	51	52	Dragon	Normal	None
Scalebane Royal Guard	53	54	Dragon	Normal	None
Thomas Booker	20	20	Humanoid	Normal	None
Timothy Clark	20	20	Humanoid	Normal	None
Wetlands Crocolisk	23	24	Beast	Normal	None
Wyrmkin Firebrand	52	53	Dragon	Normal	None
Young Wetlands Crocolisk	21	22	Beast	Normal	None

WINTERSPRING

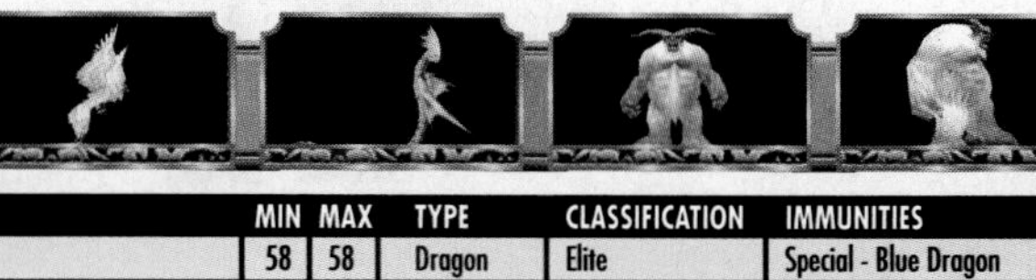

NAME	MIN	MAX	TYPE	CLASSIFICATION	IMMUNITIES
Anguished Highborne	55	56	Undead	Normal	Charm, Fear, Sleep and Bleed
Azurous	59	59	Dragon	Rare Spawn Elite	Special - Blue Dragon
Brumeran	58	58	Beast	Elite	None
Chillwind Chimaera	55	57	Beast	Normal	None
Chillwind Ravager	57	59	Beast	Normal	None
Cobalt Broodling	55	56	Dragon	Normal	None
Cobalt Mageweaver	57	58	Dragon	Elite	None
Cobalt Whelp	54	55	Dragon	Normal	None
Crazed Owlbeast	56	57	Humanoid	Normal	None
Elder Shardtooth	57	58	Beast	Normal	None
Fledgling Chillwind	53	55	Beast	Normal	None
Frostmaul Giant	59	60	Giant	Elite	Frost
Frostsaber	56	57	Beast	Normal	None
Frostsaber Cub	55	56	Beast	Normal	None
Frostsaber Huntress	58	59	Beast	Normal	None
Frostsaber Stalker	59	60	Beast	Normal	None
General Colbatann	56	57	Dragon	Rare Spawn Elite	None
Grizzle Snowpaw	59	59	Humanoid	Rare Spawn	None
Hederine Slayer	59	60	Demon	Elite	None
High Chief Winterfall	59	59	Humanoid	Elite	None
Ice Thistle Matriarch	56	57	Humanoid	Normal	None
Ice Thistle Yeti	55	56	Humanoid	Normal	None
Kashoch the Reaver	60	60	Giant	Rare Spawn Elite	Frost
Lady Hederine	61	61	Demon	Rare Spawn Elite	None
Manaclaw	58	58	Dragon	Elite	Special - Blue Dragon
Mezzir the Howler	55	55	Humanoid	Rare Spawn	None
Moontouched Owlbeast	57	58	Humanoid	Normal	None
Rabid Shardtooth	59	60	Beast	Normal	None
Ragged Owlbeast	53	55	Humanoid	Normal	None
Raging Owlbeast	54	56	Humanoid	Normal	None
Rak'shiri	57	57	Beast	Rare Spawn	None
Rogue Ice Thistle	53	55	Humanoid	Normal	None
Scryer	59	59	Dragon	Elite	Special - Blue Dragon
Shardtooth Bear	53	54	Beast	Normal	None
Shardtooth Mauler	55	56	Beast	Normal	None
Shy-Rotam	60	60	Beast	Elite	None
Sian-Rotam	60	60	Beast	Elite	None
Spellmaw	56	56	Dragon	Elite	Special - Blue Dragon
Suffering Highborne	54	55	Undead	Normal	Charm, Fear, Sleep and Bleed
Ursius	56	56	Beast	Elite	None
Winterfall Den Watcher	55	56	Humanoid	Normal	None
Winterfall Pathfinder	53	54	Humanoid	Normal	None
Winterfall Runner	57	57	Humanoid	Normal	None
Winterfall Shaman	56	57	Humanoid	Normal	None
Winterfall Totemic	54	55	Humanoid	Normal	None
Winterfall Ursa	57	58	Humanoid	Normal	None
Winterspring Owl	54	56	Beast	Normal	None
Winterspring Screecher	57	59	Beast	Normal	None

PET SHOP

"How much is that Zergling in the window?" Non-combative pets are available to everyone in Azeroth. After specific level milestones, pets can be purchased and brought out by any character. Pets appear near your character and follow you around while you explore, talk to friends, etc. These little creatures are safe from harm, because they don't enter combat. Especially rare, high-level pets can add some passive bonuses to your character and are the envy of all!

PLAYFUL COMPANIONS

PET NAME	COST	LEVEL	RARITY
Ancona Chicken	1	35	Common
PURCHASE/DROP LOCATION			
Purchased (Magus Tirth) Thousand Needles Raceway			

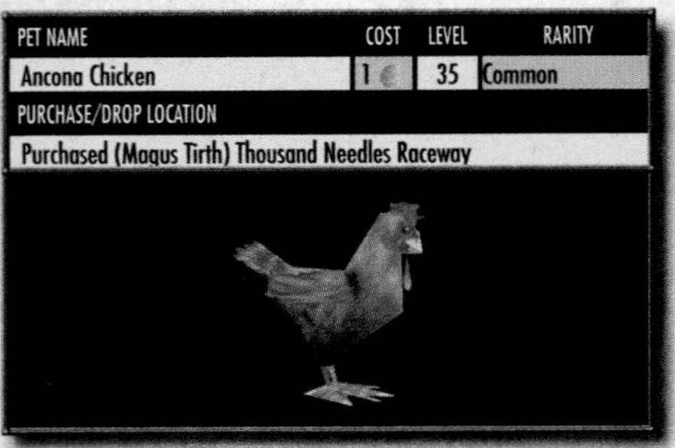

PET NAME	COST	LEVEL	RARITY
Black Kingsnake	50	30	Common
PURCHASE/DROP LOCATION			
Purchased (Xan'tish) Orgrimmar			

PET NAME	COST	LEVEL	RARITY
Bombay	40	20	Common
PURCHASE/DROP LOCATION			
Purchased (Donni Anthania) Elwynn Forest			

PET NAME	COST	LEVEL	RARITY
Brown Snake	50	30	Common
PURCHASE/DROP LOCATION			
Purchased (Xan'tish) Orgrimmar			

PET NAME	COST	LEVEL	RARITY
Cockatiel	40	20	Common
PURCHASE/DROP LOCATION			
Purchased (Narkk) Booty Bay			

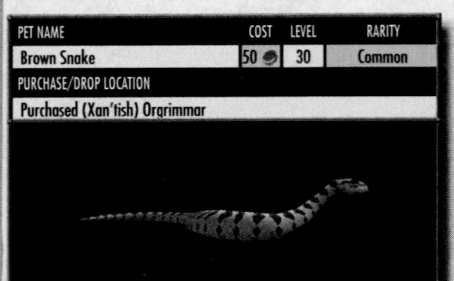

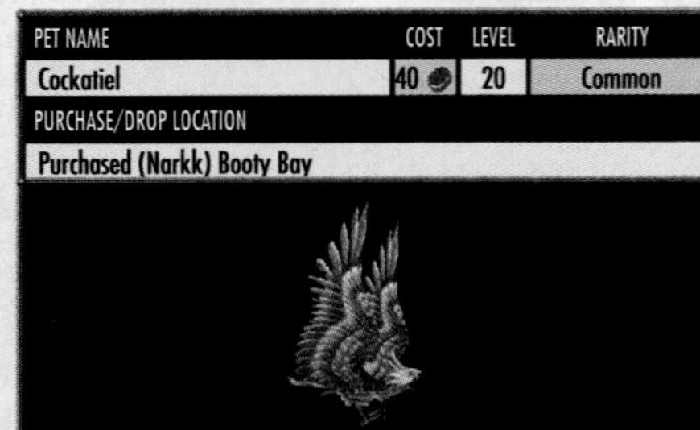

PET NAME	COST	LEVEL	RARITY
Cockroach	50	30	Common
PURCHASE/DROP LOCATION			
Purchased (Jeremiah Payson) Undercity			

PET NAME	COST	LEVEL	RARITY
Cornish Rex	40	20	Common
PURCHASE/DROP LOCATION			
Purchased (Donni Anthania) Elwynn Forest			

PET NAME	COST	LEVEL	RARITY
Crimson Snake	50	30	Common
PURCHASE/DROP LOCATION			
Purchased (Xan'tish) Orgrimmar			

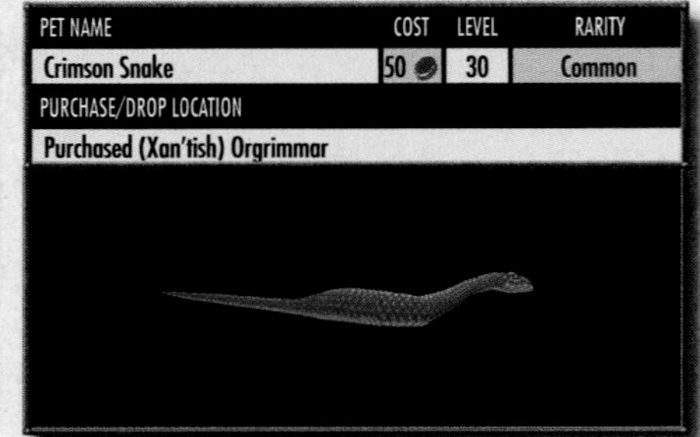

PET NAME	COST	LEVEL	RARITY
Great Horned Owl	50	30	Common
PURCHASE/DROP LOCATION			
Purchased (Shylenai) Darnassus			

PET NAME	COST	LEVEL	RARITY
Green Wing Macaw	40	20	Uncommon
PURCHASE/DROP LOCATION			
Dropped (Defias Pirate) Deadmines Elite			

PET NAME	COST	LEVEL	RARITY
Hawk Owl	50	30	Common
PURCHASE/DROP LOCATION			
Purchased (Shylenai) Darnassus			

PET NAME	COST	LEVEL	RARITY
Hyacinth Macaw	40	20	Rare
PURCHASE/DROP LOCATION			
Dropped (Bloodsail Opponents) Stranglethorn Vale			

PET NAME	COST	LEVEL	RARITY
Maine Coon	60	20	Rare
PURCHASE/DROP LOCATION			
Dropped (Dalaran Opponents) Alterac Mountains			

PET NAME	COST	LEVEL	RARITY
Mechanical Chicken	40	40	Common
PURCHASE/DROP LOCATION			
Quest (An OOX of Your Own) Booty Bay			

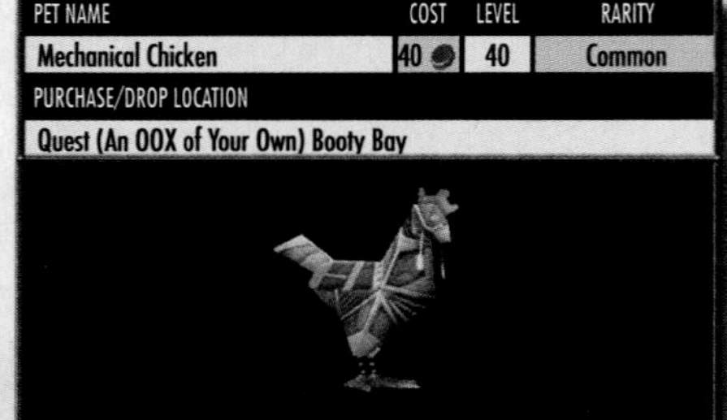

PET NAME	COST	LEVEL	RARITY
Mechanical Squirrel	4	15	Common
PURCHASE/DROP LOCATION			
Engineering Product			

PET NAME	COST	LEVEL	RARITY
Mini Diablo	N/A	20	Special
PURCHASE/DROP LOCATION			
Collector's Edition Gift			

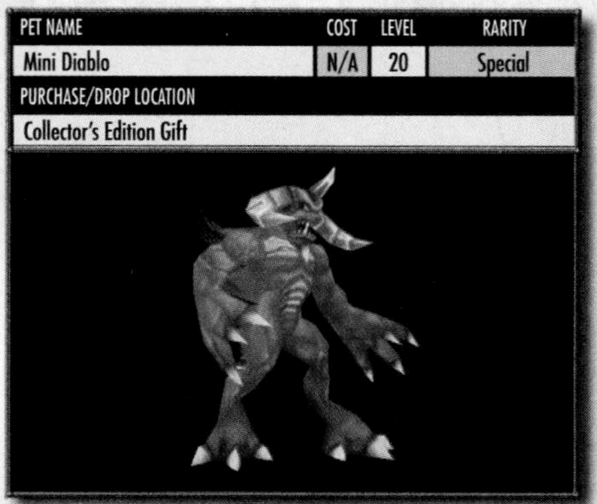

PET NAME	COST	LEVEL	RARITY
Orange Tabby	40	20	Common
PURCHASE/DROP LOCATION			
Purchased (Donni Anthania) Elwynn Forest			

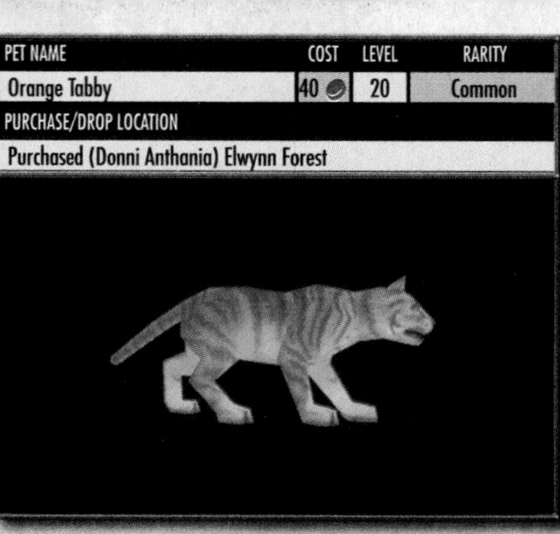

PET NAME	COST	LEVEL	RARITY
Panda Cub	N/A	20	Special
PURCHASE/DROP LOCATION			
Collector's Edition Gift			

PET NAME	COST	LEVEL	RARITY
Pet Bombling	1	30	Uncommon
PURCHASE/DROP LOCATION			
Engineering Product (Goblin Engineering)			

PET NAME	COST	LEVEL	RARITY
Prairie Dog	50	30	Common
PURCHASE/DROP LOCATION			
Purchased (Halpa) Thunder Bluff			

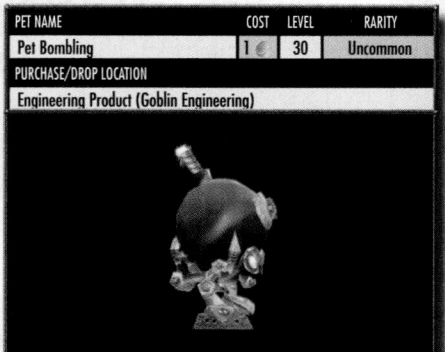

PET NAME	COST	LEVEL	RARITY
Senegal	40	20	Common
PURCHASE/DROP LOCATION			
Purchased (Narkk) Booty Bay			

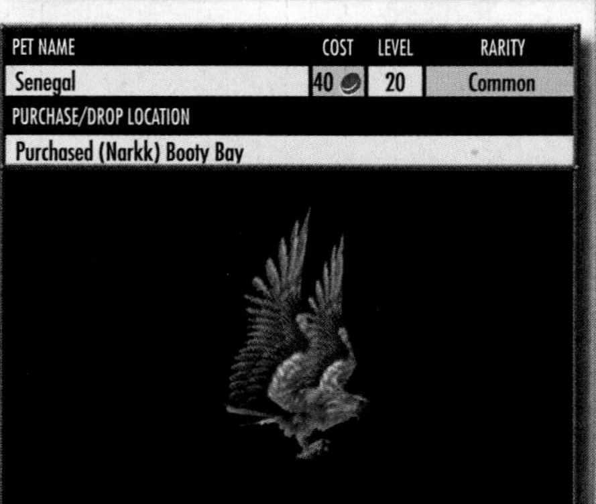

PET NAME	COST	LEVEL	RARITY
Siamese	60	20	Uncommon
PURCHASE/DROP LOCATION			
Dropped (Cookie) Murloc Boss Deadmines			

PET NAME	COST	LEVEL	RARITY
Silver Tabby	40	20	Common
PURCHASE/DROP LOCATION			
Purchased (Donni Anthania) Elwynn Forest			

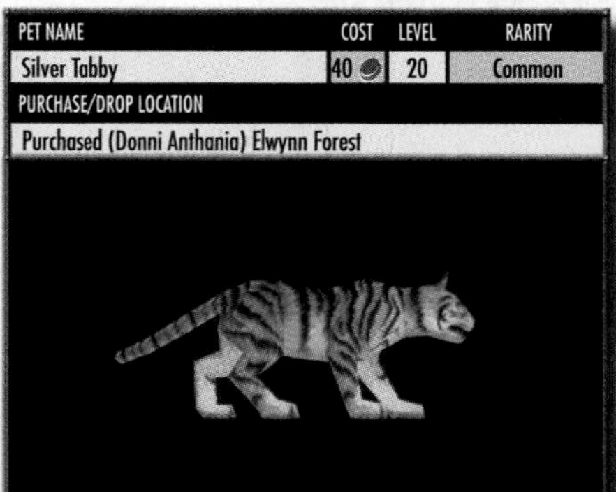

PET NAME	COST	LEVEL	RARITY
Snowshoe Rabbit	20	20	Common
PURCHASE/DROP LOCATION			
Purchased (Yarlyn Amberstill) Dun Morogh			

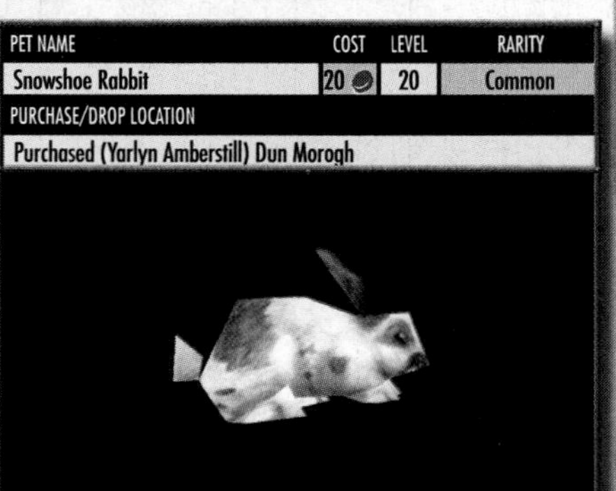

PET NAME	COST	LEVEL	RARITY
Sprite Darter	20	47	Rare
PURCHASE/DROP LOCATION			
Quest (Becoming a Parent) Given in Hinterlands by Agnar Beastamer			

PET NAME	COST	LEVEL	RARITY
Tiny Black Whelpling	1	30	Rare
PURCHASE/DROP LOCATION			
Dropped (Scalding Whelp, Searing Whelp) Badlands			

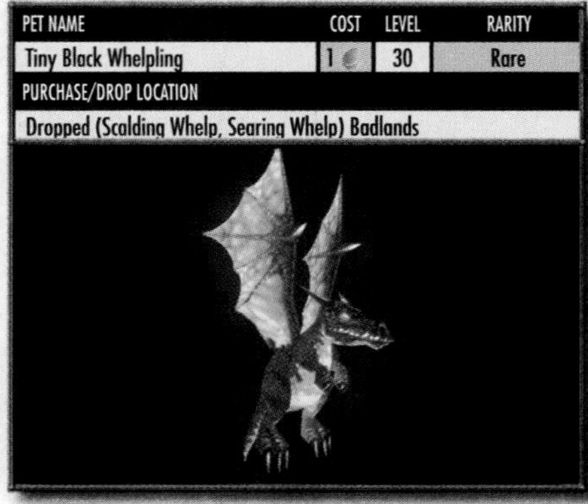

PET NAME	COST	LEVEL	RARITY
Tiny Crimson Whelpling	1	30	Rare
PURCHASE/DROP LOCATION			
Dropped (Red Whelp, Crimson Whelp, Flamesnorting Whelp) Wetlands			

PET NAME	COST	LEVEL	RARITY
Tiny Emerald Whelpling	1	30	Rare
PURCHASE/DROP LOCATION			
Dropped (Dreaming Whelp) Swamp of Sorrows			

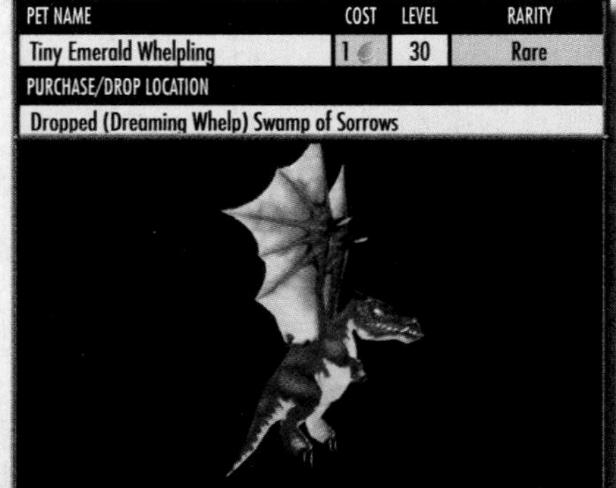

PET NAME	COST	LEVEL	RARITY
White Kitten	60	20	Uncommon
PURCHASE/DROP LOCATION			
Purchased (Lil Timmy) Stormwind City			

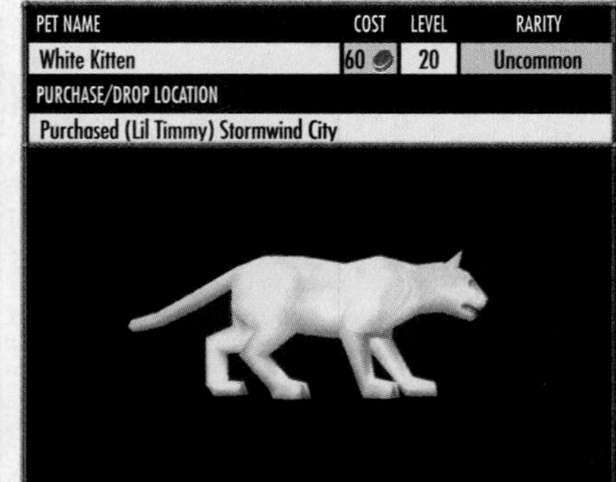

PET NAME	COST	LEVEL	RARITY
Zergling	N/A	20	Special
PURCHASE/DROP LOCATION			
Collector's Edition Gift			

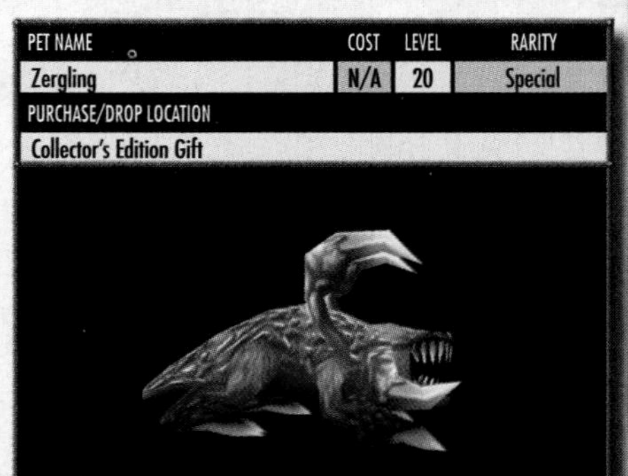

WORLD OF WARCRAFT™
OFFICIAL STRATEGY GUIDE

AUTHOR
Michael Lummis
"Kemp"

AUTHOR
Danielle Vanderlip
"Sachant"

BradyGAMES® Publishing

An Imprint of Pearson Education
800 East 96th Street, Third Floor
Indianapolis, Indiana 46240

ISBN: 0-7440-0405-5

Library of Congress Catalog No.: 2004114056

Printing Code: The rightmost double-digit number is the year of the book's printing; the rightmost single-digit number is the number of the book's printing. For example, 04-1 shows that the first printing of the book occurred in 2004.

09 08 07 06 20 19 18 17 16 15 14 13

Manufactured in the United States of America.

BRADYGAMES STAFF

PUBLISHER
David Waybright
"Bencer"

EDITOR-IN-CHIEF
H. Leigh Davis
"Glinka"

LICENSING MANAGER
Mike Degler

CREATIVE DIRECTOR
Robin Lasek

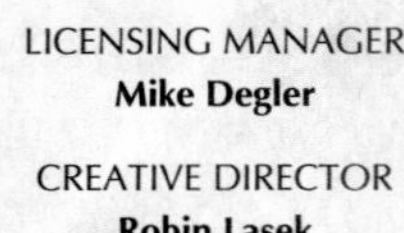

DIRECTOR OF MARKETING
Steve Escalante
"Mexikhan"

MARKETING MANAGER
Janet Eshenour

ASSISTANT MARKETING MANAGER
Susie Nieman

TEAM COORDINATOR
Stacey Beheler

CREDITS

SR. DEVELOPMENT EDITOR
Christian Sumner
"Balthazaar & Goldsnatcher"

SCREENSHOT EDITOR
Michael Owen
"Devon"

LEAD BOOK DESIGNER
Dan Caparo
"Orapac & Night Falcon"

BOOK DESIGNER
Brent Gann

PRODUCTION DESIGNER
Bob Klunder

ADDITIONAL BRADY *WORLD OF WARCRAFT* JUNKIES:

Christopher Hausermann
"Olin"

Doug Wilkins
"Papa"

Ken Schmidt
"Oot"

COMICS

Penny Arcade

www.penny-arcade.com

BRADYGAMES ACKNOWLEDGEMENTS

First and foremost, BradyGames would like to extend their sincere gratitude to everyone at Blizzard who helped out on this project, especially Elaine Di Iorio, Denise Lopez, and Kaéo Milker. Thanks to the contributing testers for being dedicated and incredibly hardcore. Finally, to Penny Arcade (Jerry, Mike, and Robert): your loyal Brady fans thank you for joining us on this guide.

THE "CORE"

Christopher Burton, Edwin Kern, Kathleen Pleet, & Misael "Chito" Villegas

Undead Lords: Buliwyk, Donar, Exyle, Mirtai, Naergoth, Orcsoul, Rayven, Sinsear, Tivoli, & Zophar

TESTERS

Smallz, Moktor, Dave "Kernal" Kern, Johannes "Hadjinim" Grahmann, ElfyDirk, & Vinadir. Everyone from Blade of the Immortals, especially Draeke & Mazzarin.

Undead Lords: Barbar, Brega, Cybsled, Dementia, Gau, Ghoul, Grayvemark, Indalamar, Indaree, Kamillia, Lobo, Madness, Malotesta, Mierin, Mortgar, Ralg, Savante, Scy, Stavros, Terror, Tourach, Vicious Rumor, Xagar, Xymox & Zavein

XIAN'S ACKNOWLEDGEMENTS

I began a little tradition a while back in my first MMORPG strategy guide and it's time to pick that torch back up. I had my first acknowledgements section in that guide and I'm including another here, in a guide that has been my life for months. I'm very pleased to say that it was not wasted time.

As a fan of games myself, Blizzard's products, and the company itself, always held a special, undeniable allure. When I was assigned this project, I couldn't (and still can't) put my excitement into words. Amazingly, that excitement only grew with the development of this guide and the game it supports. It's incredible.

As an editor, it's extremely rare for me to let my voice be heard except vicariously through the writings of authors. However, so many people helped out on this guide and this project received so much attention and support, that it would be foolish not to take a second to acknowledge them.

Players of the beta may recognize the guild tags, "Scholars of Ydarb," "Horde of Ydarb," and/or "Vigilant Ydarb." Yes, that's us. Editors, designers, and managers were playing *World of Warcraft* until the wee hours of the morning and rushing into work only to discuss their first experience in an instance dungeon, or their first PvP kill. That, my friends, is one factor that makes this guide great. BradyGames fosters enthusiasm and passion for the games (not to mention knowledge) for which we publish guides.

Without exception, everyone from Blizzard who was associated with this project was amazing. It's inspiring to realize that they're willing to transfer the drive that pushes them to make games like *World of Warcraft* into a licensed product. They work at Blizzard and they care about this guide—that's exciting!

Testers from other guilds agreed to forego their own guild tags and join Ydarb to assist on the project. They're the hardcore element that the guide couldn't do without. I've met quite a few, but regret to say that there are still many I have yet to meet. I hope to remedy that situation on a battleground in Azeroth; regardless of whether they're friend or foe, it's sure to be a day worth remembering.

Before I forget, there's a "little" thing called Penny Arcade and I wanted to thank the guys for the comics they provided and, more importantly, for jumping in on a project that they, too, were excited about. Your fans are going to love the comics; I should know since I'm one of them.

Finally, imagine two, sparkling diamonds. Then, imagine pounding them until you actually get a drop of moisture, something that couldn't even be detected, from them—and then started pounding again. Now imagine you're the diamond. Thanks to Michael and Danielle for their incredible work on this guide; I'll stop pounding now.

MICHAEL "KEMP" LUMMIS' ACKNOWLEDGEMENTS

My deepest thanks to Kathleen Pleet and Edwin Kern for Love, Friendship, Support, and Maps. Hail to kin Chris Burton for his economic wisdom. My gratitude and best wishes to Eric, "Sinsear" by his guild, for rallying our troops so often! To Naergoth and Tivoli, I salute your skills and performance. To Danielle, my fellow author, I wish long rest, good health, and much deserved family time after a long and successful fight. To Christian Sumner, editor and friend, I am deeply in debt for dedication beyond normal sanity. Dan Caparo, our primary designer for the guide, has my thanks and admiration for making beauty where once was lifeless text (and no less thanks to the other designers who jumped in on this mammoth). Hail to the folks on Beta 1 and the PvP Server, where we cut our teeth. And of course, our hat goes off to Blizzard for a brilliant game made and decisive support given. And, of course, praise Elune and the Earthmother.

DANIELLE "SACHANT" VANDERLIP'S ACKNOWLEDGEMENTS

There are many people that I would like to thank not only for their support, but also for their aid in this project. First and foremost, I'd like to thank my family for putting up with the many nights of pizza, Chinese food and takeout. I'm sure someday I will be able to dig my way to the kitchen and get some laundry done once more provided I don't play *World of Warcraft* too obsessively from here on out...

About my co-author Michael Lummis, what can I say but I've been fortunate to work with one of the best. He was always there to talk to and give his support and inspiration. He is a true professional and a talented author to work with. His tireless work and effort can be seen throughout the guide and his talent shines.

Once again, I have found myself fortunate to work with my editor Christian Sumner. He is a demanding and always fair taskmaster and it is always a privilege to work with him. His dedication and support on these projects is inviolate. He keeps us focused and driven and never lets us do less than our best. I would like to thank my guild, the Undead Lords, and various friends (even the ones that play Paladins) within the World of Warcraft for their constant help and support in working on this book. They provided both in game and out of game support.

This has been an amazing book to work on and the staff at Brady has once again made us look good. I would be remiss if I didn't make note of the amazing support they have given us as well as their willingness to listen to our ideas and suggestions on making this guide the best that it could be. The layout and design team, as always, have done a beautiful job and each time I look at what they have created, I am thankful to be a part of such a talented team. I couldn't have been more fortunate to work on such a great project!

Welcome To The Next Level Of MMORPG Strategy Guides!

Updating your guide is as easy as signing up, logging in, and hitting "Print!"

BUY THE 2-SIDED BINDER

Go to www.bradygames.com/wow to get an exclusive *World of Warcraft* binder to use with your strategy guide! With its unique double-sided printing, you have the choice of making it a Horde or an Alliance binder!

EXCLUSIVE ONLINE UPDATES

These updates are available only to those who purchase a BradyGames *World of Warcraft* Binder. Downloadable topics include:

- **Instance Dungeon Walkthroughs**
- **Content Updates**
- **Character Templates**
- **Maps and Icons**

ISBN 0-7440-0520-5

ACCOUNT CREATION

1. Go to **www.bradygames.com** to become a BradyGames member. Be sure to select the ***World of Warcraft*** newsletter.
2. Once you're a BradyGames member, go to **www.bradygames.com/wow**. A sign up form is on this page.
3. Enter your ISBN into the field provided.

THAT'S IT!

Once you've Once you've registered with BradyGames and entered your key code, the exclusive updates are all yours.

The BradyGames website will be updated with new information and downloadable PDFs to print out and place in your Binder.

JUST WANT UPDATES?

You still have an opportunity to gain access to free content provided by BradyGames. You immediately have a source for news and general content updates without having to purchase a Binder.

UPDATES

MMORPGs change, and it's inevitable that the accuracy of the information within this guide will change as well. At BradyGames, we realize this is a constant occurrence with this type of game, and we've incorporated our online updates to help solve this issue. In addition, we've purposely withheld certain information so as not to ruin any of the huge surprises that Blizzard has planned for the game. However, as time passes, this too will be placed on our site. This guide is accurate as of the initial launch of Open Beta.